CHALLENGE OF ASIAN DEVELOPING COUNTRIES

CHALLENGE OF ASIAN DEVELOPING COUNTRIES

Issues and Analyses

Edited by
Shinichi ICHIMURA

Asian Productivity Organization

The publication is based on economic studies commissioned by the Asian Productivity Organization (APO) to members of the Advisory Group drawn from various universities, institutes, and international and regional organizations. Views and opinions expressed in these studies are those of the contributing authors and do not necessarily reflect the official views of the organizations to which they belong or of the APO.

The publication also does not use the official country names and hence the countries of the People's Republic of China (PRC), the Republic of China (ROC) and the Republic of Korea (ROK) have been referred to as China, the ROC (Taiwan) and Korea, respectively.

Designed and Produced by
Nordica International Ltd.
Hong Kong for
Asian Productivity Organization
4-14, Akasaka 8-chome
Minato-ku, Tokyo 107, Japan

© Asian Productivity Organization, 1988

ISBN: 92-833-1095-0 (Casebound)
92-833-1096-9 (Limpbound)

Printed in Hong Kong

Introduction

This is the report of the research study on Development Strategies and Productivity Issues in Asia commissioned by the Asian Productivity Organization (APO) to an Advisory Group of which I was the Chairman and Professor Shinichi Ichimura of Kyoto University, the Vice-Chairman.

The overall objectives of the research study were to analyze the factors that influence productivity at macro-level expressible in terms of per capita GNP, to identify the major issues in the development process, and to suggest the policy measures for the improvement of productivity at macro-level in Asian countries in the coming decade. The research study was undertaken with the joint effort of a group of economists who exchanged views and discussed together the assigned problems at the two workshops held in Tokyo in January 1985 and January 1986 and one at Colombo, Sri Lanka in July 1985. The final draft report of each author was edited by Professor Ichimura with the assistance of Dr. William James of the Resource Systems Institute of the East-West Center, Hawaii, U.S.A.

The APO is an intergovernmental, regional organization located in Tokyo, and its members comprise seventeen Asian countries now. It was established in 1961 for the purpose of increasing productivity in the Asia and Pacific region through mutual cooperation. All its activities, whether they be research, surveys, symposia, seminars, training courses, observational study missions, fellowships or technical services, are basically related to human resource development in the field of industry, agriculture and service sectors.

The main exercises by the APO to improve productivity hitherto have been in the area of selected industries and related to the activities of individual industries and specific sectors. In the light of the changing socio-economic circumstances in Asian countries, however, there has been increasing recognition of the need for viewing productivity as a reflection of total development process of industrial complex. The interdependent relations among industries have become very important not only within a national economy but also beyond the national barriers. Against such a background the APO decided to launch this study and try to grasp the fundamental factors influencing the future trends in industrial productivities in the context of overall macro-level increase in per capita GNP. It is hoped that this study would give some suggestions for finding the broad and realistic directions for increasing productivity in the Asia and Pacific Region. It is also hoped that other countries, developed and developing, will find this report equally relevant in grasping productivity issues in the years to come.

To realize its objectives, the research study separated the issues involved into two parts: part one related to key issues and part two pertained to country problems. For both the issues the authors were asked to deal not only with past trends but also with future prospects and policy recommendations whenever they found themselves capable of boldly doing so. Thus, two categories of papers have emerged in this final report: key issue papers and country papers. Under key issues, eight papers were developed, entitled, The Pattern and Prospects of Asian Economic Development; Human Resources and Macro-Comparative Productivity Trends; Economic Conditions of East and Southeast Asian Development; Agricultural Development in Asia; Performance, Issues and Policy Options; Role of Trade Policies: Competition and Cooperation; Industrial Restructuring and Technology Transfer; Foreign Capital, Balance of Payments and External Debt; and Income Distribution: A Brief Comparative Review. Each paper has been authored by one or two economists. These papers form chapters 1 through 8 of this publication. Under part two, five main country studies were carried out on Northeast Asia covering Korea, the ROC (Taiwan), and Hong Kong; ASEAN; China; India; and other four South Asian countries. Studies on Burma, Vietnam and Iran were also undertaken. These studies are given as chapters 9 to 17.

The subject areas covered in the country studies as well as in key issue papers were left to the authors' choice who, nevertheless, generally dealt the suggested topics of development strategies, agricultural development, small- and medium-size enterprises, infrastructure and productivity in the tertiary sector, human resource development, efficiency of government and other institutions, importance of regulations and their implementation, socio-political considerations, and future prospects and policy recommendations.

As the Chairman of the Advisory Group, I wish to place on record my indebtedness to all members of the Group for their active involvement in the research and for their thorough reports on various issues. Special thanks are due to Prof. Shinichi Ichimura for his untiring effort and commitment from the conceptual stage to the final editorial stage of this study.

Taroichi Yoshida

Tokyo, January 1988.

Contents

Appendix: Members of Advisory Group and Consultants

Contents

Editor's Summary

Asia in this study includes all Asian countries from Japan in the northeast to Iran in the west and to Indonesia in the south, but it does not cover the Oceanic and Pacific countries. In this sense it is different from both the United Nations' ESCAP region and the popular grouping of the Pacific-basin countries. The study does not exclude the Socialist countries like Vietnam, Burma and the Islamic Republic of Iran. They are analyzed as much as the available data and information permit. Japan is considered only to the extent that she is essential to the analysis of problems of developing countries in Asia. For the productivity and other issues facing Japan are of very different nature, and she is the only country in Asia whose per capita income is above $10,000 at the exchange rate of mid-1986. This is almost equivalent to the United States' per capita income in 1986. The rest of Asian countries are developing countries, and their per capita incomes seem to permit more or less the following classification into three regional groups.

1. Northeast Asia (Korea, ROC (Taiwan) and Hong Kong) plus Singapore:
It consists of the countries whose per capita GNP is between $2,000 and $7,000. They are usually identified as Asian NICs (newly industrializing countries) and correspond to "Upper Middle Income Economies" in the World Bank definition.

2. Southeast Asian countries minus Singapore — ASEAN-5:
It consists of the Philippines, Thailand, Malaysia, Brunei and Indonesia whose per capita GNPs are between $400 and $2,000. Except for Brunei and Malaysia, they correspond to "Lower Middle Income Economies." Brunei's per capita GNP is above $20,000 and its economy depends solely on the oil sector. Its high income level can hardly be taken as an index of economic development. Very little is known about the non-oil industries of Brunei, so that the following discussions on this group of countries often exclude Brunei. In that sense reference is often made to ASEAN-4. Malaysia belongs to Upper Middle Income Economy. Since, however, its economy has many common features to ASEAN countries, it is included in ASEAN-5 here.

3. South Asia and China
All of them are below $400 in per capita GNP, and they correspond to "Low Income Economies." It should be remembered that this group includes two giant economies: India and China, because the issues and strategies for development of such giant economies are very different from those in middle sized economies.

Some may argue against the use of per capita GNP as a basic index to use for the analysis of the factors influencing productivity at macro-level in Asian countries. A typical case in point is the oil-producing economy like Brunei, because it does not necessarily reflect the productive capacity of the nation whose majority population are engaged in much less productive non-oil industries. Indonesia and Malaysia have the same problems. One should not deny that the productivities in the manufacturing industries and agriculture must be distinguished from the sheer high income accruing to the nation from oil and other resources explorations. For the productivities of such resource-extracting industries, particularly those of non-renewable resource-extracting industries, require careful considerations. Ordinary definition of depreciation or depletion cannot be applied to the non-renewable resources or capital stocks, so that the term "productivity" must be used with great care for those industries.

Since, however, there is no better alternative, we must satisfy ourselves by using it as much as other economic text books do. Nevertheless, we are more keenly aware of the weakness of the definition, because most developing economies depend very heavily on the productivities of primary industries and resource explorations rather than the manufacturing and service industries. What eventually determines the achievement of the national economy is, however, always the productive capacity of the population engaged in all kinds of industrial activities sooner or later. If these additional considerations are properly kept in mind, per capita GNP is still the best single index of economic performance of national economy.

We will try to analyze the economic development of Asian countries, largely classifying them according to the above-mentioned three groups in the following chapters. In *Part I: Key Issues in Asian Economic Development,* the eight main issues are taken up as the major issues confronted by Asian developing countries in the 1970s and the early 1980s.

Chapter 1: The Pattern And Prospects of Asian Economic Development (Shinichi Ichimura) classifies the Asian countries according to their conditions of resource endowment and development pattern more or less the same way as explained in the paragraphs above. Then, it explains the factors to explain the differences in per capita income and the characteristics of development strategies in the 1970s and the early 1980s. After giving an overall assessment of Asian economic development, it analyzes their different ways of meeting the challenge of oil crises and growing successfully out of them. It summarizes their economic growth in terms of ten main factors: (1) the high rate of capital accumulation, (2) the high saving ratio, (3) successful transfer of technology in agriculture and manufacturing industries, (4) highly qualified human resources with declining fertility rate, (5) virtuous circles of export-led growth in the open economies, (6) the locomotive roles of the United States and Japan, (7) relatively sound fiscal and monetary policies, (8) tolerable distribution of income, (9) fairly reliable public and private institutions and (10) infrequency of social unrest and political instability. At the end it presents the future prospects of their respective economic growth up to the Year 2000.

Chapter 2: Human Resources and Macro-Comparative Productivity Trends (Harry Oshima) begins with a review of economists' views on the role of human factors in economic development including the modern discussions on human capital and relates them to development theories in recent literature. It relates the differentiation of productivity trends in three major regions in Asia to the different historic backgrounds in culture and human factors, paying attention to the roles played by mass media and general social conditions. In particular it emphasizes the importance of full employment in improving the quality of human resources through the training on the job.

Chapter 3: Economic Conditions in East and Southeast Asia and Development Perspective (Kiyoshi Kojima and Tsuneo Nakauchi) gives a review of the overall performance of Asian countries particularly emphasizing the role of export growth and industrial restructuring in East and Southeast Asian countries. Then it proceeds to the analysis of the important roles of foreign direct investment particularly by the United States and Japan. It gives cruxes of the well-known Kojima thesis on Foreign Direct Investment comparing the US' FDI and Japanese FDI. Asian countries were lucky to have both types of FDI competing each other in their efficiencies.

Chapter 4: Agricultural Development in Asia: Performance, Issues and Policy Options (Vijay S. Vyas and William E. James) gives a review of excellent performance of Asian agriculture which was really the base of economic development in almost all the Asian countries. Then it analyzes the significant difference in distribution of such gains between traditional small holders or peasants and large public or private estates in major food crops and cash crops. The authors go into the detailed discussions on the government policies on price and non-price interventions in agriculture including the most important recent issue of technological innovations called "green revolution." It also points out the emerging issues of agriculture in the future such as the large capital requirements, diversification and persistent trends to protectionism in agricultural policies all over the world.

Chapter 5: Role of Trade Policies: Competition and Cooperation (Seiji Naya) focuses its analysis on the crucial relations between industrialization and trade strategies in Asian developing countries. Tracing back these relations among three major Asian regions, it appraises the export-led industrialization in Asian NICs which successfully competed in the world markets and quick adaptability of their industrial production and export diversification to the changing world demand. It presents somewhat cautious appraisal about ASEAN-4 and South Asian countries. As for intra-regional trade among NICs and ASEAN-4 countries, it points out the predominant role of Hong Kong and Singapore and reserves simple optimism about its expansion but expects the high potentials, even advocating to fight against all kinds of protectionist policies in themselves.

Chapter 6: Industrial Restructuring and Technology Transfer (Ippei Yamazawa and Toshio Watanabe) analyzes the changing pattern of Asia-Pacific trade over time and points out the shifting comparative advantages among Asian countries both in the commodity composition and the country destination. The commodity composition was analyzed in terms of labor-intensive manufactures (L), capital-intensive manufactures (C) and machinery (M). It points out for example that the composition of Korean exports is already in 1985 decreasing in L and increasing in C and M, whereas the Philippines' composition of exports remains almost unchanged from 1970 to 1983. It further analyzes the changing comparative advantage among Asian countries by means of Ballassa's index of revealed comparative advantage. It points out by defining an intensity index of trade that while the comparative advantages have changed among Asian countries, complementarity in trading relations has also increased. By this chapter the reader will be able to understand quantitatively the multiple stages of catching-up among Asian developing countries.

Chapter 7: Foreign Capital, Balance of Payments and External Debt in Developing Asia (Evelyn M. Go and Jungsoo Lee) reviews the pattern of foreign capital inflow into Asian developing countries and finds their positive role in foreign trade and investment. It critically reviews the linkage between the foreign loans and domestic investment with fair amount of leakage to consumption in some countries. It examines the government policies affecting the optimality of borrowing in Asian countries and points out the dangers involved in servicing the heavy debts in many Asian countries.

Chapter 8: Income Distribution: A Brief Comparative Review (Harry Oshima) gives a review of changing income distribution in three major regions in Asia and explains the reasons why it has remained within the tolerable range and did not result in extreme inequality, as observable in some other developing countries. It gives emphasis on the pattern of agricultural development, population growth and government regulations on domestic migration as well as employment situations in manufacturing industries in the determination of income distribution.

In *Part II: National and Regional Problems in Asian Development,* the development experiences in three major regions are comparatively surveyed.

Chapter 9: Development Strategies and Productivity Issues in Korea, ROC (Taiwan), and Hong Kong: A Comparative Study (Wan-Soon Kim and Hojin Kang in cooperation with Paul K.C. Liu and Yung-wing Sung) not only gives a review of outstanding performance of three of four dragons in Asia but identifies major problems of the so-called export-led growth in Asian NICs. It makes some further analysis of productivity changes in selected industries mainly in Korea but with frequent references to the experiences in the ROC (Taiwan) and Hong Kong. These three countries and areas are mutually compared with regard to export-led industrialization, industrial restructuring, government's role and monetary policies. Anticipating the days of approaching to the stage of industrialized countries in the future, it makes some suggestions for the future directions of these truly developing economies.

Chapter 10: ASEAN Countries: Economic Performance and Tasks Ahead (Jun Nishikawa) gives first a review of the impressive development of ASEAN-6 countries in the 1970s and touches upon the regional cooperation. Then it analyzes the characteristics of each country's performance with the emphasis on the issues related to the international economic relations and the role played by multinational corporations in each economy. It expresses serious concerns with some issues in all countries. For example, Indonesia faces the problem of mobilizing domestic resources. Malaysia may confront the difficulty in moving from import-substitution to export promotion in industrialization. The Philippines may not be able to overcome the regional gaps deeply seated in land ownership and industrial organization in the economy. Singapore may have to find appropriate new lines of manufacturing industries with ever increasing wages and standard of living on the islands. Thailand may be able to hope to shift from agricultural and low middle income status to semi-industrial and middle income status soon, if she succeeds in investing productively the foreign loans in light manufacturing industries and promote the export.

Chapter 11: Economic Reforms and the Open Door Policy in China (Reiitsu Kojima) gives first a survey of the dramatic happenings in the Chinese economy from high saving type economy to consumption oriented economy, and then appraises the most recent economic reform which seems to have released the cumulated people's energy to growth and led to overheated economy. It further tries to investigate the bottlenecks for the Chinese economy to continue the unusual growth performance in recent years and point out the following four factors: insufficient energy resources and transportation facilities, shortage of housing, and difficulty of overcoming pollution in China. It presents also some studies of Chinese foreign trade figures. After all, China cannot rely upon foreign capital as much as Asian

NICs or ASEAN countries did because of its gigantic scale and cannot possibly open the economy as much as they did. Besides, political instability in the future cannot be excluded. Hence, the shortage of capital and potential political instability will prevent us from holding too optimistic view on the future of Chinese economy.

Chapter 12: Special Economic Zones in China (Tien-tung Hsueh and Tun-oy Woo) serves as an appendix to the preceding chapter and deals with the special problems related to the rapidly industrializing coastal zones in China. These special zones are indeed a new challenge to Asian NICs and ASEAN-4, because they have enormous advantage of unlimited supply of labor and industriousness of selected workers under the new modernization policies of Chinese government. Only the institutional rigidities and limitations are still very great. The chapter discusses the various issues in these rapidly changing special zones.

Chapter 13: Productivity Issues and Development Strategies in India (V.R. Panchamukhi and K.M. Raipuria) tries to assess the productivity increases in different industries in India and also appraise the development strategies as reflected in the performance of those industries and their productivities. It goes into the controversial policy questions of expanded public sector and government intervention in private enterprises and pricing. It points out that the recent emphasis of "liberalization" for greater efficiency and competitiveness still remains very limited in the effects. Relying on the documents of the Seventh Five Year Plan, it presents the future prospects of the Indian economy.

Chapter 14: Growth and Resource Mobilization in four South Asian Countries (Godfrey Gunatilleke) was prepared with the cooperation of Reza H. Syed from Pakistan, Maurice Wanigaratne from Sri Lanka, Atiqur Rahman from Bangladesh and Durgeshman Singh from Nepal. It compares these four South Asian countries in their economic performance. All of them have characteristically experienced the radical ups and downs due to both economic and non-economic factors. It gives a good review of economic development of each economy and points out the various difficulties being experienced particularly in recent years. As the result the increase in labor productivity in manufacturing industries are slowing down in most countries. Fortunately, even in the poor countries like Bangladesh and Nepal there are some signs of better growth performance in recent years. This seems to be due to the external economic cooperation and the appropriate government policies. The author ends with the hope on the South Asian Association for Regional Cooperation which can promote the complementary development efforts among these nations.

There are three special papers on relatively under-studied economies: Burma, Vietnam and Iran. Chapter 15: Economic Development and Issues in Burma (Kazushi Hashimoto) gives a concise survey of the Burmese economy and its problems on the bases of official data and his personal observations in Rangoon. Chapter 16: Indo-China Economy (Tetsusaburo Kimura) gives a summary of his years long research on these three countries — Vietnam, Laos and Kampuchea with so little information. Together with Chapter 17: Economic Development and Issues in Iran (A.A. Zaker-Shahrak), we are fortunate in having them offer the precious information on their recent economic conditions to the reader on these diplomatically famous but economically unknown countries.

PART I:

KEY ISSUES OF ASIAN ECONOMIC

DEVELOPMENT

1. The Pattern and Prospects of Asian Economic Development

Shinichi Ichimura

PATTERN AND PROCESS

Asian Development Performance

The economic performance of Asian countries in the 1970s and the early 1980s surprised everyone in the world. Asia was once known as the place of Oriental despotism and widespread irreducible poverty. *The Asian Drama* was conceived as a tragedy of stagnation by the best known authority, Dr. Gunnar Myrdal even as late as in 1968. This pessimism has gradually yielded, however, to optimism in the 1960s, since most Asian underdeveloped countries began to follow suit to the fast growth of Japanese economy that quadrupled its GNP in a decade of the 1960s. Even so the most authoritative study known as the Hla Myint report — undertaken by Asian Development Bank study group just before 1970 — predicted modestly a 5.5 percent growth rate for East and Southeast Asian countries in the 1970s. This projected growth was superseded by the actual performance of 7.4 percent. The East and Southeast Asian countries achieved faster growth than any other region in the world whether industrialized or underdeveloped, including oil-rich Middle Eastern countries in the 1970s. Since the late 1970s, South Asian countries have also joined in this rapid development performance.

Four Groups of Asian Countries

An examination of the economic development of Asian countries in the 1960s to the early 1980s suggests, as Figure 1 demonstrates, that their growth performance may be classified into four groups. As Table 1 and Table 2 shows that they correspond approximately to the income levels of Asian developing countries.
1. Resource-poor Northeast Asian countries: Korea, ROC (Taiwan), Hong Kong and Singapore — the so-called Asian NICs;
2. Resource-rich Southeast Asian countries: the Philippines, Thailand, Malaysia,

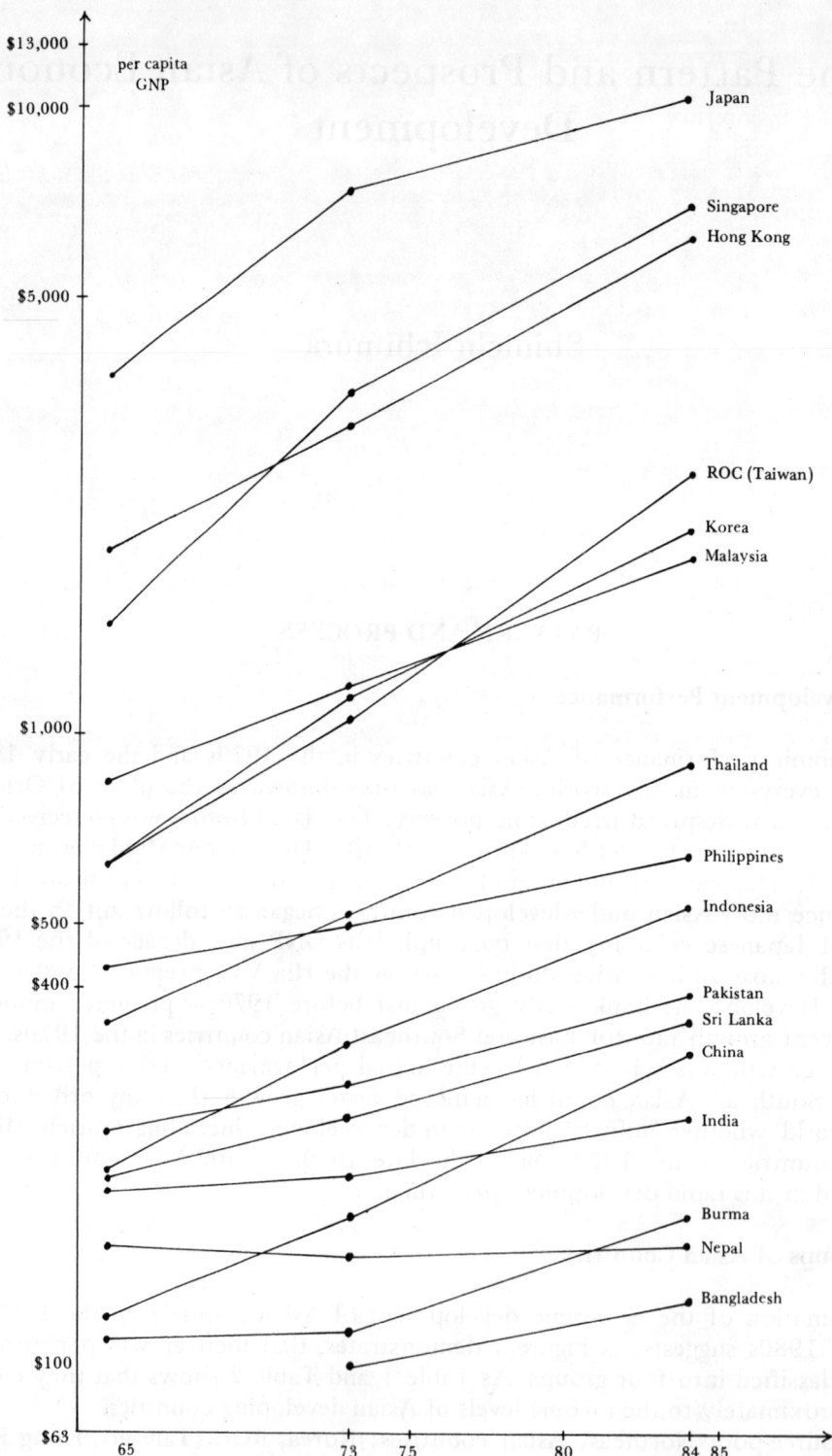

Figure 1. Performance of Asian Development for 1965-1985

Brunei and Indonesia — ASEAN minus Singapore;
3. Primarily agrarian South Asian countries: Burma, Bangladesh, Nepal, Pakistan and Sri Lanka;
4. Giant Economies: China and India.

It is interesting to notice that the pattern of growth, development mechanism and choice of economic policies seem to differ among these four groups. It seems more appropriate to classify such patterns and processes into the following three.

Table 1. Grouping of Asian Developing Economies

	Population in mid-1984 (million)	GNP per capita in 1984 ($)	GNP in 1984 (billion $)
Industrial Market Economy			
Japan	120.0	10,630	1,275.6
Asian NICs			
Singapore	2.5	7,260	18.2
Hong Kong	5.4	6,330	34.2
ROC (Taiwan)	18.6	2,612	48.6
Korea	40.1	2,110	84.6
ASEAN-4			
Malaysia	15.3	1,980	30.3
Thailand	50.0	860	43.0
Philippines	53.4	660	35.2
Indonesia	158.9	540	85.8
Giant Economies			
China	1,029.2	310	319.1
India	749.2	260	194.8
South Asia			
Pakistan	92.4	380	35.1
Sri Lanka	15.9	360	5.7
Burma	36.1	180	6.5
Nepal	16.1	160	2.6
Bangladesh	98.1	130	12.8
Socialist Economies			
Vietnam	60.1	..	..
Kampuchea, Dem.	..	..	..
Lao, P.D.R.	3.5	..	..
Korea, D.P.R.	19.9	..	..

Sources: World Bank, *World Development Report,* 1985 and 1986 and official statistical sources of various countries.

Table 2. Basic Indicators of Asian Economic Development, 1960—1984

(Unit: %)

	Growth Rates in the 1960s		GDP growth rate		Industry growth rate	
	GNP	Popul.	65-73	74-84	65-73	74-84
Industrial Market Economy						
Japan	10.4	1.0	9.8	4.3	13.5	5.9
Asian NICs						
Singapore	7.6	2.4	13.0	8.2	17.6	8.6
Hong Kong	8.0	2.3	7.9	9.1	8.4	8.0
ROC (Taiwan)	9.2	2.5				
Korea	6.4	2.1	10.0	7.2	7.1	4.7
ASEAN-4						
Malaysia	6.2	3.1	6.7	7.3	..	8.7
Thailand	6.2	3.1	7.8	6.8	9.0	8.7
Philippines	5.9	3.0	5.4	4.8	7.4	5.3
Indonesia	3.0	2.0	8.1	6.8	13.4	8.3
Giant Economies						
China	..	..	7.8	6.6	12.1	8.7
India	..	..	3.9	4.1	3.7	4.1
South Asia						
Pakistan	2.5	2.5	5.4	5.6	6.6	7.6
Sri Lanka	..	..	4.2	5.2	7.3	4.8
Burma	..	..	2.9	6.0	3.6	7.7
Nepal	1.8	1.8	1.7	3.1	..	..
Bangladesh	3.3	2.5	..	5.0	−6.1	7.6
Socialist Economies						
Vietnam, North	6.0	2.8	..	..	..	..
(South)	3.6	2.6	..	..	..	..
Kampuchea, Dem.	2.5	2.5	2.7	..	..	..
Lao, P.D.R.	4.5	2.5	..	..	..	..
Korea, D.P.R.	6.0	2.5	..	..	..	..

Sources: World Bank, *World Development Report,* 1985 and 1986 and official statistical sources of various countries.

Three Patterns of Growth Dynamics

The first pattern holds to resource-poor Northeast Asian countries or Asian NICs, and the second holds to the resource-rich ASEAN-minus Singapore or, due to the shortage of data for Brunei, simply ASEAN-4. The third holds to large countries like China and India. The economies of South Asian countries excluding India is primarily agrarian and may be characterized as those somewhere between the first and the second; as it were, resource-poor ASEAN-type. The dynamic mechanism of industrial development differs among these three types as follows:

1. Resource-poor country type of industrialization
They must first develop labor-intensive light industries like textiles, footwears, then try to increase productivity and export the products. Earning foreign exchange this way, they import capital equipment to invest in infrastructure and export industries. Further they expand exports and move up the market to higher stages of industries. After achieving some industrialization, the government tries to support agricultural development. This is typically the industrialization pattern in Korea and the ROC (Taiwan).

2. Resource-rich country type of industrialization
The first step in this pattern is resource exploration (oil and other mining resources) or development of agricultural and other primary industries (plantation, fishery and forestry). Then they export these natural resources, primary products or processed raw materials. With the foreign exchange earnings thus obtained, they import capital goods, which they invest in infrastructure and resource exploration, agro-industry, resource-related industries or, if government desires, light industries. In these countries a significant amount of investment in human capital was required because of the serious shortage of skilled workers, engineers, bureaucrats and businessmen. Only after some preparatory stage of development it became possible to make a gradual shift to higher degree of industrialization.

3. Large country type of economic development
They are rich in natural and human resources and very large in the scale of the national economies. This makes it possible for them to undertake development strategies at several fronts at the same time, without relying much on external trade or foreign investment for a considerable period. The most natural first step is resource exploration and agricultural development. With little external help, domestic savings must have been squeezed. Even with out-of-date technology they invest in infrastructure and some labor-intensive light industries under strict protection of consumption goods industries. What they can export is limited to some natural resources, primary products and light industrial products. While restricting imports to minimum essentials for industrialization, they try to slowly and simultaneously develop capital goods industry by themselves. This self-reliance policies tend to necessitate the retardation of technological progress and after a while makes it impossible to keep pace with the surrounding industrializing countries of smaller scales. As the result they are forced to open up their economies.

These patterns of industrialization may be awarded with the titles of virtuous circles of development rather than the vicious circle of poverty and stagnation. This decribes the core of the success story of Asian development. The process of industrial development for each type of development may be summarized by listing each step of development strategies as follows.

1. Resource-poor country type of industrialization
    1) Development of light industries,
    2) Export of light industrial products,
    3) Foreign exchange earnings,

4) Import of capital goods,
5) Domestic investment in infrastructure and export industries,
6) Export expansion – foreign exchange earnings,
7) Import of capital goods and intermediate products,
8) Development of intermediate stage of heavy-chemical industries.

2. Resource-rich country type of industrialization

1) Resource exploration or development of agriculture and other primary industries,
2) Export of natural resources, primary products or processed raw materials,
3) Foreign exchange earnings,
4) Import of capital goods,
5) Domestic investment in infrastructure, resource exploration, agro-industry, resource-related industries or light industry,
6) Investment in human resources,
7) Gradual shift to higher degree of industrialization,

3. Large country type of economic development

1) Resources exploration and agricultural development,
2) Forced domestic savings and less reliance on foreign loans,
3) Gradual development of light industries of consumption goods,
4) Export of natural resources and primary products and light industrial products,
5) Import of minimum essentials for industrialization,
6) Slow and simultaneous development of capital goods industry with the restriction on the import of capital goods.

In order, however, for this virtuous circle to be successfully complete, there seem to be at least three requirements on each of the domestic economic policies and the international environment.

On the domestic policies: (1) the national economies must be fundamentally open to international trade, foreign direct investment and international loans – trade and investment policies of Asian governments have been largely adequate in this sense; (2) the government policies must be directed to increase growth particularly by promoting exports – all East Asian countries and most South Asian countries and China in recent years, more or less, have adopted such policies; (3) The rate of foreign exchange should not be over-valued – the policies not satisfied by some countries.

In the international environment, at the same time: (1) the importing countries' markets must be open for their exports, (2) the supply of capital equipments, financial loans, technology and management know-how must be offered from industrial countries; (3) law and order of fair competition and peaceful political environment must prevail.

These conditions have been satisfied for almost all Asian countries most of the time. Thus, they have been very successful in achieving such export-led growth and increasing the share of manufactures in their exports as shown by Tables 3 and 4.

There are some differences in the relative importance in the conditions related to these domestic and international requirements among three types of virtuous circles.

For the first type, the most crucial condition is to succeed in industrializing in labor-intensive industries and realize the productivity increase so as to make them

Table 3. Growth of Sectoral Production in Asian Countries

(Unit: %)

	GDP		Agriculture		Industry		Service	
	65-73	73-83	65-73	73-83	65-73	73-83	65-73	73-83
Industrial Market Economy								
Japan	9.8	4.3	2.1	−1.6	13.5	5.5	8.3	3.8
Asian NICs								
Singapore	13.0	8.2	5.7	1.5	17.6	8.5	11.5	8.1
Hong Kong	7.9	9.3	−0.6	1.1	8.4	8.2	8.1	9.8
ROC (Taiwan)*	9.0	10.3	0.8	2.5	12.0	13.5	8.1	9.1
Korea	10.0	7.3	2.9	1.5	18.4	11.2	11.3	6.9
ASEAN-4								
Malaysia	6.7	7.3	—	4.4	—	8.7	—	8.2
Thailand	7.8	6.9	5.2	3.8	9.0	9.0	9.1	7.6
Philippines	5.4	5.4	4.1	4.3	7.4	6.4	4.8	5.2
Indonesia	8.1	7.0	4.8	3.7	13.4	8.6	9.6	9.0
Giant Economies								
China	7.4	6.0	1.9	3.5	9.1	8.4	—	4.5
India	3.9	4.0	3.7	2.2	3.7	4.3	4.2	6.1
South Asia								
Pakistan	5.4	5.6	4.7	3.4	6.6	7.2	5.4	6.3
Sri Lanka	4.2	5.2	2.7	4.1	7.3	4.8	3.8	6.0
Burma	2.9	6.0	2.8	6.6	3.6	7.7	2.8	5.1
Nepal	1.7	3.0	1.5	1.0	—	—	2.1	0.9
Bangladesh	—	5.2	0.4	3.2	−6.1	8.1	1.5	7.4
Socialist Economies								
Vietnam	—	—	—	—	—	—	—	—
Kampuchea, Dem.	−2.7	—	—	—	—	—	—	—
Lao, P.D.R.	—	—	—	—	—	—	—	—
Korea, D.P.R.	—	—	—	—	—	—	—	—

Sources: World Bank, *World Development Report,* 1985 and 1986 and official statistical sources of various countries.

    * The periods for the ROC (Taiwan) are 1971-75 and 75-80.

the export industries. At the same time the terms of trade after adjustment to the rate of foreign exchange must remain unfavorable to promote export. Otherwise, the resource-poor countries cannot compete with the old industrialized countries and take off. Government support in various forms of subsidies usually played a crucial role in the early stage of industrialization. In fact in many Asian countries, however, protection and subsidies were often extended too much and dragged on too long.

Among Asian NICs, Korea seems to have proceeded to light industrialization and moved further in her early stage of development to capital goods industry or even technology-intensive industries, whereas the ROC (Taiwan) at about the same level of per capital income as Korea seems to be satisfied with her more balanced structure of light industries, intermediate goods and capital goods industries. Only in recent years she is beginning to start some capital goods or technology-intensive industries.

In small economies like Singapore and Hong Kong there is no other choice but to keep the economy open. Amazingly, Hong Kong has succeeded in export-led industrialization with no government help, relying completely on free market mechanism in trade and capital transactions. Singapore is a more government-led economy but with no tariffs or restrictions on capital transactions. Both may be regarded as show-cases of successful free enterprise system.

For the second type, the favorable terms of trade are critical, because the export earnings depends not only on the development of new export industries but also to a great extent on the export prices of primary commodities exports and imported capital goods. As is well-known, the prices of primary products fluctuate very much. The oil bonanza greatly contributed to raising the growth rate of Malaysia, Indonesia and Brunei. Thailand, the Philippines and Malaysia also benefited from an increase in the prices of agricultural and forest products in the early 1970s. The same price hike did not occur, however, after the second oil shock. That was the reason why they had to rely heavily on the borrowings from abroad to keep the pace of rapid growth in the late 1970s and the early 1980s.

For the large economies, however, the balanced growth of agriculture, resource development and some manufacturing industries is the more normal pattern of development. Import-substitution policy can go a longer way for them. Nevertheless, those conditions mentioned for Types 1 and 2 are important for large countries as well. For despite the fact that they can develop the economies by inward-looking policies for a considerable period, they must open the economies before the vested interests of established enterprises become insurmountable in order to avoid being locked into isolation from the progressing world. Failure to open up soon enough has made it necessary for China to undertake radical changes in her economic policies and endorse entrenched interests, and this also appears to be the motive for the policies of privatization and deregulation of the Rajiv Gandhi government of India in recent years. To a lesser extent the same observations may be made about Pakistan in South Asia and also Indonesia in Southeast Asia.

Multi-Stage Process of Catching-Up

Asian scenes look like a multi-stage catch-up process in which all four groups have been moving up the market as if they are trying to catch up with one after another. Asian NICs try to catch up with Japan, ASEAN-4 try to catch up with the NICs, South Asian countries try to catch up with ASEAN-4, while India and China suddenly appear from below the ASEAN level and challenge them in many industrial products, because some industrialized districts are far more advanced than in the rest of the economies and can easily compete with ASEAN-4, if not with Asian NICs. This multi-stage process of catching up is a unique picture of developing Asian countries, and it requires a constant restructuring of industries among Asian countries at their respective development stages. Such structural shift has been taking place in the 1970s, as is shown in Figure 2 by Watanabe-Kajiware.[1]

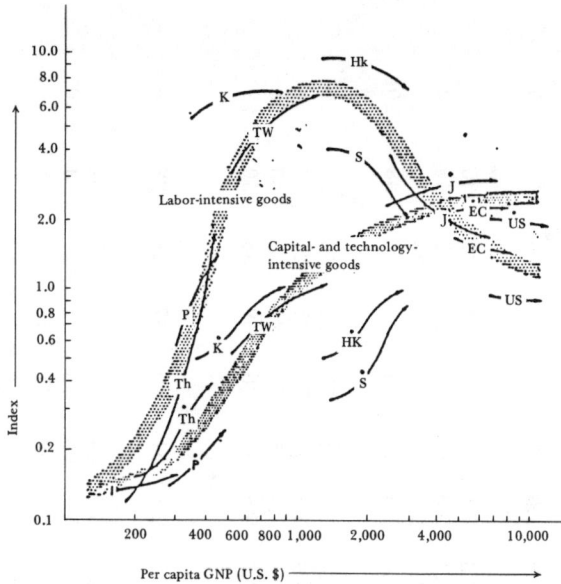

Source: Watanabe and Kajiwara, "Pacific Manufactured Trade and Japan's Options," *The Developing Economies,* Vol. 21, No. 4, December 1983.

Notes: 1. RCA Index is Revealed Comparative Advantage Index calculated by
$$(1/n) = \Sigma i \left[(Ehi/EH)/(Wi/W) \right],$$
where Ehi/Eh stands for the ratio of the export of product i to the total exports of the country, and Wi/W is the same ratio for the world.
2. I for Indonesia, Th for Thailand, P for Philippines, K for Korea, Tw for ROC (Taiwan), H for Hong Kong, S for Singapore, J for Japan, EC for European Economic Community, and US for the United States.

* stands for capital-intensive goods and otherwise labor intensive goods industries.

Figure 2. Multiple Stages of Industrial Development in Asia
— as revealed by RCA indices for manufacturers, 1970-77 —

The NICs are already losing the comparative advantage in labor-intensive industries, and instead ASEAN countries are developing the comparative advantages in those industries. Korea and the ROC (Taiwan) are beginning to show advantages in capital and technology-intensive industries earlier than Singapore and Hong Kong owing to the scale effects and deliberate government policies. Development strategies must be guided by careful observation of international competition and an appropriate choice of industries at each stage of development. It goes without saying that the increasing productivities of export industries are most crucial to the success of export-led growth in Asian countries.

The same pattern of shifting comparative advantage and the corresponding change of industrial development among Asian countries can be observed in the following Table 4.

---

[1] Toshio Watanabe and Kajiwara, "Pacific Manufactured Trade and Japan's Options, " *The Developing Economies,* Vol. 21, No. 4, December, 1983.

Table 4. Industrialization and Changing Composition of Exports and Imports

	Value added of Manufacturing Industry (mill. $ in '75)		Annual growth rate	Gr. Rate of Exports		Gr. Rate of Imports		Share of Prim. Ex.		Share of Mach. Im.		Share of Other Manuf.	
	1970	82	82	65-73	73-83	65-73	73-83	65	82	65	82	65	82
Industrial Market Economy													
Japan	118,403	252,581	6.5	14.7	7.4	14.9	1.3	9	3	9	6	11	15
Asian NICs													
Singapore	827	2,431	9.4	11.0	7.1	9.8	7.1	63	43	14	28	30	26
Hong Kong	1,914	3,679	5.6	11.7	10.3	10.5	12.0	13	8	13	22	46	52
ROC (Taiwan)	1,242	4,325	10.9	26.0	10.2	19.1	5.2	–	11	–	28	–	27
Korea	2,368	11,492	14.1	31.7	14.8	22.4	7.5	40	8	13	23	38	20
ASEAN-4													
Malaysia	1,022	3,287	10.3	8.0	4.9	4.4	7.3	94	77	22	40	32	29
Thailand	1,675	4,837	9.2	6.9	9.0	4.4	3.3	95	71	31	24	49	33
Philippines	2,659	5,510	6.1	4.2	7.5	3.1	1.3	95	50	33	22	30	38
Indonesia	1,517	6,072	12.3	11.1	1.4	13.9	9.8	96	96	39	38	50	29
Giant Economies													
China													
India	10,232	16,210	4.0	2.3	4.9	-5.7	2.8	51	40	37	18	22	28
South Asia													
Pakistan	1,492	2,967	6.0	3.7	8.1	-2.9	5.7	64	40	38	23	34	26
Sri Lanka	556	748	2.5	-4.7	2.6	-3.2	4.7	99	73	12	24	34	30
Burma	287	486	4.5	-4.8	4.9	-6.7	-0.6	99	11	18	–	58	–
Nepal	–	–	–	–	–	–	–	–	72	–	18	–	50
Bangladesh	647	1,294	5.9	-6.5	1.7	-8.2	4.1	–	38	–	22	–	32
Socialist Economies													
Vietnam	–	–	–	–	–	–	–	–	–	–	–	–	–
Kampuchea, Dem.	–	–	–	–	–	–	–	99	–	26	–	58	–
Lao, P.D.R.	–	–	–	–	–	–	–	94	–	19	–	34	–
Korea, D.P.R.	–	–	–	–	–	–	–	–	–	–	–	–	–

Sources: World Bank, *World Development Report*, 1985 and 1986 and official statistical sources of various countries.

Note: All figures are in percentage unless otherwise stated.

TEN FACTORS FOR FAST ASIAN DEVELOPMENT

The reasons why Asian countries grew so fast in the 1960s to the early 1980s and why they could maintain the fast pace of growth in the 1970s by adapting themselves so well to the two oil crises are inter-related. For the governments capable of choosing the appropriate policies for development could find the ways and means of adjustment to oil crises, and it was easier for them with the expanding pie than under austerity. It was really surprising that not only oil-producing countries but also resource-poor Asian NICs kept the 1960s momentum of rapid growth still in the 1970s and also remained resilient to the world recession in the early 1980s. In these responses of Asian developing countries as well as in the process of growth four groups seem to show the distinctive patterns. The ten factors that could explain their fast growth and responses to external shocks may be summarized as follows:

1. The high rate of capital accumulation.
2. The high saving ratio.
3. Successful transfer to technology in agricultural development (Green Revolution) and industrialization.
4. Highly qualified human resources with declining fertility rate.
5. Virtuous circles of export-led growth in the open economies.
6. The locomotive roles of the United States and Japan.
7. Relatively sound fiscal and monetary policies.
8. Tolerable distribution of income.
9. Fairly reliable public and private institutions.
10. Infrequency of social unrest and political instability.

The High Rate of Capital Accumulation

The ratio of capital formation to GNP has increased from somewhat below 20 percent in the 1960s to nearly 30 percent or even higher in the early 1980s in NICs and ASEAN. In South Asia, investment rates increased toward the end of the 1970s. Table 5 demonstrates this fact together with the second factor of high and rising saving ratios.

This steady increase in the rate of capital accumulation is a characteristic observable in Japan's process of rapid growth for the past one hundred years. The prewar Japanese rate of capital accumulation never exceeded 15 percent. In postwar years, however, the same ratio began to increase from 14.6 percent in 1953, rose as high as 32 percent in 1965 and remained arounds 28 to 30 percent in the early 1980s.

The actual figures in Asian countries can be seen in Table 5. It is surprising that all of them (except for Pakistan and Sri Lanka) have ratios above 20 percent; some exceeding even 30 percent.

Thus, a large proportion of annual domestic product was invested in constructing infrastructure and building up industrial productive capacity of private and public enterprises in various industrial sectors. Since most Asian LDCs were in the early stage of development, the proportion of investment in overhead capital had to be fairly large, except for the insular city-states like Singapore and Hong Kong. The proportion of investment in productive capital equipment in the private sector, therefore, remained relatively small at the beginning.

But in the case of the NICs, the proportion soon became significant and began

Table 5. Rates of Capital Accumulation and Saving: 1965-83

(Unit: %)

	Rate of Capital Accumulation			Saving Ratio			Resource Gap		
	65-72	73-78	79-83	65-72	73-78	79-83	65-72	73-78	79-83
Industrial Market Economy									
Japan	31.9	35.9	32.0	30.8	33.6	36.8	-0.9	-2.3	4.8
Asian NICs									
Singapore*	36.7	34.9	40.4	23.6	32.8	35.6	-8.1	-2.1	-4.7
Hong Kong	21.4	24.2	35.9	25.0	25.3	31.4	3.6	1.1	-4.5
ROC (Taiwan)*	26.2	30.6	32.4	23.1	29.3	37.0	-3.1	1.3	4.6
Korea	24.1	29.0	30.0	14.9	24.9	23.7	-9.2	-4.1	-6.3
ASEAN-4									
Malaysia	19.6	25.7	33.4	20.8	27.2	26.3	1.2	1.5	-7.1
Thailand	23.8	25.4	25.3	21.3	23.6	20.5	-2.5	-1.8	-4.8
Philippines	20.9	28.6	29.6	17.1	23.9	23.3	-3.8	-4.7	-6.3
Indonesia	12.6	20.6	23.0	6.9	18.8	20.1	-5.7	-1.8	-2.9
Giant Economies									
China*	–	–	33.6	–	–	33.2	–	–	-0.4
India	18.3	21.7	24.6	13.4	19.2	21.0	-4.9	-2.5	-3.6
South Asia									
Pakistan	16.3	15.9	15.8	10.2	10.0	12.1	-6.1	-5.9	-3.7
Sri Lanka	16.1	16.2	29.9	11.3	11.9	10.9	-4.8	-4.3	-19.0
Burma*	11.8	10.0	21.5	9.2	8.9	17.7	-2.6	-1.1	-3.7
Nepal	–	9.3	18.3	–	4.8	11.1	–	-4.5	-7.2
Bangladesh*	–	5.5	13.2	–	-0.6	2.8	–	-6.1	-10.4
Socialist Economies									
Vietnam	–	–	–	–	–	–	–	–	–
Kampuchea, Dem.	–	–	–	–	–	–	–	–	–
Lao, P.D.R.	–	–	–	–	–	–	–	–	–
Korea, D.P.R.	–	–	–	–	–	–	–	–	–
Argentina	20.4	24.6	20.5	20.3	26.2	17.9	-0.1	1.6	-2.6
Brazil	25.6	28.1	22.5	24.0	24.0	17.6	-0.8	-4.1	-4.9
Chile	15.3	15.3	17.2	13.0	11.9	7.0	-2.3	-3.4	-10.2
Colombia	19.0	18.8	20.0	15.4	19.1	17.2	-3.6	-0.3	-2.8
Ecuador	18.6	26.4	24.2	11.3	20.4	20.5	-7.3	-6.0	-3.7
Mexico	21.3	23.4	26.1	19.2	20.2	24.2	-2.1	-3.2	-1.9
Peru	16.7	16.0	17.0	15.2	11.4	13.5	-1.5	-6.6	-3.5
Venezuela	29.1	35.4	26.2	29.8	36.1	29.3	0.7	0.7	3.1

Sources: World Bank, *World Development Report*, 1985 and 1986 and official statistical sources of various countries.

* Figures for the ROC (Taiwan) and Singapore are those in 1970 and 1982; those for Bangladesh, Burma and China are for 1970, 75 or 80.

to result in rapid industrial development. In ASEAN countries a significant portion of capital formation was undertaken in the rural areas to promote agricultural development. This was one of the reasons for successful agricultural development.

The High Saving Ratio

The rates of saving in Asian countries are also very high, as was shown in Table 5. The saving ratio has quickly gone up from about 16 percent in the late 1960s over 20 percent in the early 1980s. In the ROC (Taiwan) and Singapore the saving rates are even above the Japanese gross saving ratio of about 30 percent, although in these two countries special policies of government have played an important role to bring up the saving ratios. In Singapore forced savings through a device called the Central Provident Fund is responsible, whereas in the ROC (Taiwan) it is government savings that is particularly high. Apart from this, however, the household saving rates are also very significant in most East Asian countries. This steady increase of the rates of capital accumulation and saving with rising per capita income over the past three decades is indeed the most fundamental characteristic of the Asian economies.

One should not take this fact as something which automatically or easily accompanies economic growth in any country. For instance, in the case of Latin American countries both ratios did not increase with the rise of per capita income. In particular, the saving ratios are stable at around 20 percent, and in some countries they are coming down. In Asia only the Philippines seems to show some resemblance to Latin America. Indeed, in many other aspects too, the Philippines is, as it were, a Latin American country in Asia.

Except for Singapore and the ROC (Taiwan), households saving rates in East and Southeast Asian countries seem to reach a ceiling slightly below 30 percent though their per capita income is well below the Japanese standard. Their inherent propensities to save may be slightly lower than the Japanese. This is why they had to borrow from abroad so much to sustain the rate of capital accumulation and growth in the recent past. The resource gaps are shown also in Table 5. It is remarkable that in these ratios three groups are distinctively different according to their per capita income levels.

Successful Transfer of Technology in Agricultural Development (Green Revolution) and Industrialization

Even if the rate of capital accumulation is high, rapid growth may not result unless capital is efficiently utilized. The so-called "Incremental Capital-Output ratio" (ICOR) is an over-all index of efficiency in the use of capital. It can be calculated from the rates of capital accumulation in Table 1 divided by the growth rates given by Table 5, as shown in Table 6.

One has to be careful of interpreting the values of these coefficients particularly in the 74-84 period, because this covers the recession years when heavy foreign debt forced some countries to adopt tight fiscal and monetary policies so that the degree of capital utilization was not very high. This makes the above-mentioned ICOR estimates very high, but these do not necessarily reflect the technical requirements of marginal capital per unit of incremental GDP. Nevertheless, the ratios over the decade will show an indication of the changes in the efficiency of capital usage in

Table 6. International Comparison of Incremental Capital-Output Ratio: 1965-83

(Unit %)

	1965-73			1974-83		
	Growth Rate	Rate of Accumul.	ICOR	Growth Rate	Rate of Accumul.	ICOR
Industrial Market Economy						
Japan	9.8	30.0	3.1	4.3	22.7	5.2
Asian NICs						
Singapore	13.0	36.7	2.8	8.2	37.6	4.6
Hong Kong						
ROC (Taiwan)	10.1	26.2	2.6	8.5	31.5	3.7
Korea	10.0	24.1	2.4	7.3	29.5	4.0
ASEAN-4						
Malaysia	6.7	19.6	2.9	7.3	29.1	4.0
Thailand	7.8	23.8	3.1	6.9	25.4	3.7
Philippines	5.4	20.9	3.9	5.4	29.1	5.4
Indonesia	8.1	12.6	1.6	7.0	21.8	3.1
Giant Economies						
China						
India	3.9	18.3	4.7	4.0	23.2	5.8
South Asia						
Pakistan	5.4	16.3	3.0	5.6	15.9	2.8
Sri Lanka	4.2	16.1	3.8	5.2	23.1	4.4
Burma	–	–	–	5.5	15.8	2.8
Nepal	–	–	–	3.7	13.8	3.7
Bangladesh	–	–	–	5.2	9.4	1.8
Socialist Economies						
Vietnam	–	–	–	–	–	–
Kampuchea, Dem.	–	–	–	–	–	–
Lao, P.D.R.	–	–	–	–	–	–
Korea, D.P.R.	–	–	–	–	–	–
Argentine	4.3	20.4	4.7	0.4	22.6	56.4
Brazil	9.8	25.8	2.6	4.8	25.3	5.3
Chile	3.4	15.3	4.5	2.9	16.3	5.6
Colombia	6.4	19.0	3.0	3.9	19.4	5.0
Mexico	7.9	21.3	2.7	5.6	24.7	4.4
Peru	3.5	16.7	4.8	1.8	17.5	9.7
Venezuela	5.1	29.1	5.7	2.5	25.8	10.3

Sources: World Bank, *World Development Report,* 1985 and 1986; official statistical sources of various countries; and Asian Development Bank, *Key Indicators of Developing Member Countries of ADB.*

various countries.

It is well known that as per capita income goes up, the ICOR usually increases. Table 6 shows that this is true with all Asian countries. But the increases have been relatively mild. The ROC (Taiwan) has kept an impressively low ratio. The Indonesian ICOR, though relatively low, must be considered relatively high for the country with its low per capita income. Korea has a high ICOR with its per capita income slightly lower than the ROC (Taiwan's) mainly because she has adopted deliberate policies to emphasize heavy chemical industries. Malaysia and Singapore have high ICOR's corresponding to their high and rising per capita incomes. The Philippines with an income level similar to Thailand has an ICOR as high as Japan's.

From these observations one may get the impression that even in East Asian countries capital may be excessively utilized, and the ideal value should have been something like the ROC (Taiwan's). India has an extremely high ICOR despite its low income level, implying her inefficient use of capital. It is clear that compared with South Asia or Latin America, East and Southeast Asian countries' usage of capital has been much more efficient. ICOR values in Latin America are particularly high. Even if we consider the conditions of debt-ridden recession, still their ICOR's are too high, because even under the hypothetical growth rate for 74-83 remaining the same as that for 65-73, the ICOR's for Argentina, Peru and Venezuela will be 5.3, 5.0 and 5.1 respectively. They are just about the same values as in the Philippines.

As for the sectoral break-downs of the increase of productivity, the most remarkable progress is noticeable in agriculture. It is very well-known that the so-called Green Revolution introduced high-yielding varieties of rice, wheat and corn. Rice is the most important crop in the Asian region. New technology offered new opportunities to increase productivity to Asian countries where the use of land was already very intensive and the potential for extensive expansion of production was very limited. The Green Revolution seems to have spread first in East and Southeast Asia and then to South Asia, as Table 7 shows.

Introduction of high-yielding varieties of rice required additional investments in fertilizer and irrigation. Such complementary investments were made possible by the conscious efforts of the governments to expand agricultural investment in order to attain self-sufficiency in food supply. Food self-sufficiency became a national goal of the governments. Meeting this goal has been a major accomplishment of the new independent-minded nations of Asia.

In the manufacturing sector, a calculation was made to measure the degree of contribution of technical progress to productivity increase by means of the Cobb-Douglas production function applied to these countries. It was found then:[2]

The marginal productivity of capital is higher in East and Southeast Asia than in Latin America, but in the period of 65-73 Asian countries were not doing any better on the average than Latin American countries.

The marginal productivity of capital has declined sharply in East and Southeast Asia after the first oil crisis. The only exception is the ROC (Taiwan). (This is also reflected in the rising ICOR reported in Table 6.)

The marginal productivity of capital in Latin America after the oil shocks is hard to measure due to the decline of growth, but the calculation based on limited information seems to show that it has sharply declined also in Latin America. We

---

[2] See an excellent survey of macro-production functions in Asian countries by Yukio Ikemoto, "Technical Progress and Level of Technology: 1970-80," *Developing Economies*, December, 1986.

may conjecture that in 1983 it was lower in Latin America than in East and Southeast Asia.

The marginal productivity of labor has very significantly increased in East and Southeast Asia, but nevertheless it does not match the growth rate in per capita GNP. This is due to the fact that the per capita income can increase not only owing to labor productivity but also because of increased input of labor and capital. The input of labor can increase more rapidly than population if the productive age group increases or the labor participation rate goes up. Both of these facts were observed in almost all Asian countries.

Table 7. Average Growth Rate of Cereal Yields

(Unit: %)

	1967-73	73-80	80-84
Industrial Market Economy			
Japan	0.4	−2.6	2.1
Asian NICs			
Singapore	0	0	0
Hong Kong	0	0	0
ROC (Taiwan)	0.6	1.4	−0.8
Korea	2.4	1.9	2.0
ASEAN-4			
Malaysia	3.2	2.5	−0.9
Thailand	1.1	1.5	1.9
Philippines	3.3	4.0	2.1
Indonesia	..	4.7	5.4
Giant Economies			
China	3.9	2.4	6.2
India	4.3	2.9	5.1
South Asia			
Pakistan	7.0	2.9	5.1
Sri Lanka	3.4	1.6	4.5
Burma	2.6	6.8	6.3
Nepal	−0.4	0.9	4.9
Bangladesh	1.9	3.4	1.4
Socialist Economies			
Vietnam	−	0.7	7.5
Kampuchea, Dem.	−	−	−
Lao, P.D.R.	−	−	−
Korea, D.P.R.	−	−	−

Sources: World Bank, *World Development Report,* 1985 and 1986 and official statistical sources of various countries. Asian Development Bank, *Key Indicators of Developing Member Countries of ADB.*

Highly Qualified Human Resources with Declining Fertility Rate

There is no doubt that all East and Southeast Asian countries have emphasized education and thereby improvement in the quality of workers, engineers, salaried men, executives, government officials and intellectuals. In South Asia, Sri Lanka and Burma seem to have done the same with less resources available. But other South Asian countries did less to invest in human resources. Table 8 next page implies that the majority of the Asian people are now able to absorb knowledge by reading.

Moreover, the majority of workers now have secondary education, and there are enough number of middle managers and engineers so that the transfer of technology from industrialized countries to Asian countries can be made much more easily.

The health of workers has also improved very much. As the last column of Table 8 shows, the majority of workers are now able to take more than the required minimum daily amount of calories so that they can work as hard as they are willing to. In these social development indicators three groups show distinctive characteristics.

Another important feature which has contributed to the improvement of the quality of labor in Asia is that the demographic transition has been successfully progressing in almost every country, Japan leading the way. Table 9 demonstrates that there exists a high correlation between the increase of per capita income and the decline of the fertility rate. This is typically realized in East Asia. The pattern in South Asia is not so clear as in East Asia, but it seems that they are following more or less the same pattern as well.

This will increase the opportunities for Asian workers and executives to receive better education and training and thereby improve the quality of work and management. Such conditions are probably lacking in some LDC's in other parts of the world.

Virtuous Circles of Export-led Growth in Open Economies

All East and Southeast Asian countries have fundamentally adopted the open economy policies and have tried to promote exports and reduce trade barriers as much as possible. Recently China also adopted open door policies, and India has begun to liberalize her international trade and foreign investment policies. The virtuous circles of this Asian pattern of growth have already been discussed in the earlier part of the chapter. The trade dynamism which supported the rapid growth of NICs lies within this paradigm. There are some differences, however, in the manner of pursuing the same mechanism among the NICs, ASEAN and South Asia. Such differences can be observed in Table 4.

Japan and Asian NICs clearly show the growth rates of exports far exceeding the growth rates of value added in manufacturing industry, but this export-led growth does not seem to be obvious in the ASEAN and South Asian countries. In those countries primary goods like agricultural, fishery, forestry, petroleum, natural gas and mining products are still their major export goods. Asian NICs are advancing their stage of industrialization, and this is reflected in the increasing importance of machinery import and declining significance of other manufacturing imports.

ASEAN member countries other than Singapore grew mainly by exporting the

Table 8. Basic Indicators of Social Development

	Literacy Rate (%)		Newspaper circul. per 1,000		Primary School Enrol. (%)		Secondary School Enrol. (%)		Higher Education Enrol. (%)		Daily Calorie per capita, 1982	
	70	80	70	80	65	82	65	82	65	82	Total Calorie	% of requir.
Industrial Market Economy												
Japan	99	99	520	569	100	100	82	92	13	30	2,891	124
Asian NICs												
Singapore	72	84	200	255	105	108	45	66	10	11	2,954	128
Hong Kong	77	90	498	309	103	105	45	66	10	11	2,774	121
ROC (Taiwan)	85	90	–	–	98	100	–	–	–	–	–	–
Korea	88	93	136	173	101	100	35	89	6	24	2,936	125
ASEAN-4												
Malaysia	58	60	75	174	90	92	28	49	2	5	2,688	120
Thailand	79	86	20	42	78	96	14	29	2	22	2,296	103
Philippines	83	75	14	21	113	106	41	64	19	27	2,393	106
Indonesia	57	62	–	28	72	120	7	16	–	2	2,393	111
Giant Economies												
China	43	69	–	33	–	110	–	35	–	1	2,562	109
India	33	36	16	20	74	79	27	30	5	9	2,047	93
South Asia												
Pakistan	21	24	–	14	40	44	4	20	–	1	2,277	99
Sri Lanka	78	85	20	27	93	103	35	54	2	4	2,393	107
Burma	66	–	9	10	71	84	15	20	1	4	2,483	115
Nepal	13	19	2	7	20	73	5	21	1	3	2,018	86
Bangladesh	–	26	–	6	49	60	13	15	1	4	1,923	83
Socialist Economies												
Vietnam	–	–	–	–	–	113	–	48	–	3	2,017	93
Kampuchea, D.	–	–	–	–	77	–	9	–	1	(.)	1,792	81
Lao, P.D.R.	–	–	–	–	40	97	2	18	(.)	(.)	1,992	90
Korea, D.P.R.	–	–	–	–	–	–	–	–	–	–	3,051	130

Sources: World Bank, *World Development Report*, 1985 and 1986 and official statistical sources of various countries; Asian Development Bank, *Key Indicators of Developing Member Countries of ADB*.

Table 9. Correlation Between Income Level and Fertility Rate

	GDP per capita 1983 (US$)	Fertility Rate 1983 (%)	Predicted Fertility Rate 2,000 (%)
Industrial Market Economy			
Japan	10,120	1.7	1.9
Asian NICs			
Singapore	6,620	1.7	1.9
Hong Kong	6,000	1.8	2.0
ROC (Taiwan)	2,612	1.3	—
Korea	2,010	2.7	2.1
ASEAN-4			
Malaysia	1,870	3.7	2.4
Thailand	820	3.4	2.2
Philippines	760	4.2	2.7
Indonesia	560	4.3	2.8
Giant Economies			
China	300	2.3	2.0
India	260	4.8	2.9
South Asia			
Pakistan	390	5.8	4.2
Sri Lanka	330	3.4	2.3
Burma	168	5.5	3.6
Nepal	160	6.3	5.4
Bangladesh	130	6.0	3.7
Socialist Economies			
Vietnam	—	4.9	3.1
Kampuchea, Dem.	—	—	—
Lao, P.D.R.	—	6.4	5.5
Korea, D.P.R.	—	4.0	2.6

Sources: World Bank, *World Development Report,* 1985 and 1986 and official statistical sources of various countries.

primary commodities, as we discussed before. But the fact that even they are successfully industrailizing is demonstated by the declining weights of primary goods in total exports and manufactured goods imports. This points to the simultaneous development of import-substituting and export-oriented industries in these countries in 1974-83. As Table 10 shows, the percentage shares of manufacture exports in ASEAN and South Asia greatly increased from 1965 to 1982.

Industrialization in South Asia has also progressed successfully mainly in the form of import substitution. It may be noted that the percentage of manufacture exports in the case of China in 1982 is as high as 55 percent, so that rapid industrialization has started in China as well.

Table 10. Percentage Share of Manufactures Exports in 1965 & 82

	1965	1982	(Textiles)
Industrial Market Economy			
Japan	91	96	(4)
Asian NICs			
Singapore	34	58	(4)
Hong Kong	86	92	(34)
ROC (Taiwan)	43	68	(30)
Korea	59	92	(21)
ASEAN-4			
Malaysia	6	23	(3)
Thailand	4	29	(10)
Philippines	6	49	(7)
Indonesia	.0	4	(1)
Giant Economies			
China	—	55	(15)
India	4	60	(24)
South Asia			
Pakistan	36	60	(46)
Sri Lanka	1	27	(17)
Burma	.0	—	—
Nepal	—	—	—
Bangladesh	—	62	(47)
Socialist Economies			
Vietnam	—	—	—
Kampuchea, Dem.	.0	—	—
Lao, P.D.R.	.0	6	(.0)
Korea, D.P.R.	—	—	—

Sources: World Bank, *World Development Report,* 1985 and 1986 and official statistical sources of various countries.

The Locomotive Role of the US and Japan in Trade and Investment

The importance of the US role as the major market of Asian exports of manufactures and the sources of funds and technology can hardly be exaggerated. The US occupied about 10 to 34 percent of Asian countries exports in 1975, and Japan's shares were just about the same as is shown in Table 11. The US was the market mainly for Asian NICs, whereas Japan was the market for ASEAN-4.

These percentages have not changed very much since then. Japan's shares are more important for the imports than exports, and more so than the US is for the exports. The US is offering primarily the market, whereas Japan is supplying primarily the capital goods. In exports as well as imports, the US and Japan, taken

Table 11. The Share of the US and Japan in Asian Exports
and Imports, in 1975 and 1984

(Unit %)

	Exports to				Imports from			
	US		Japan		US		Japan	
	75	84	75	84	75	84	75	84
Industrial Market Economy								
Japan (the U.S.)*	24.8	35.6	8.7	10.8)	16.9	19.6	(13.9	19.0)
Asian NICs								
Singapore	15.4	20.0	8.7	9.4	15.7	14.6	16.9	18.4
Hong Kong	26.4	33.2	6.4	4.4	11.8	10.9	20.9	23.6
ROC (Taiwan)	34.3	48.8	13.1	10.5	27.8	23.0	30.4	29.3
Korea	30.2	36.0	25.4	15.8	25.9	22.5	33.5	24.9
ASEAN-4								
Malaysia	16.1	13.5	14.4	22.8	10.7	6.1	20.1	26.3
Thailand	11.1	17.2	27.6	13.0	14.8	13.5	32.4	26.9
Philippines	29.2	38.0	37.8	19.4	22.1	27.4	27.2	13.6
Indonesia	26.3	20.6	44.0	47.3	17.4	18.4	30.9	23.8
Giant Economies								
China	2.7	9.3	24.1	20.8	5.1	14.8	37.9	31.0
India	10.9	33.6	10.3	13.9	22.3	14.5	8.3	10.8
South Asia								
Pakistan	4.4	10.3	6.8	9.2	12.6	10.9	13.1	14.8
Sri Lanka	5.6	19.5	4.6	4.3	6.4	8.9	8.5	16.7
Burma	.0	4.0	1.6	1.0	11.7	3.3	29.7	37.3
Nepal	0	0	57.1	3.6	0	0	21.0	17.1
Bangladesh	16.3	13.9	.0	8.7	25.9	9.5	5.4	9.7
Socialist Economies								
Vietnam	0	0	.0	.0	0	0	.0	.0
Kampuchea, Dem.	0	0	.0	.0	0	0	.0	.0
Lao, P.D.R.	—	—	—	—	—	—	—	—
Korea, D.P.R.	—	—	—	—	—	—	—	—

Sources: World Bank, *World Development Report,* 1985 and 1986 and official statistical sources of
various countries; Asian Development Bank, *Key Indicators of Member Developing
Countries of ADB.*

* The figures in parantheses are those for the US occupying the trade with Japan in the
total of US exports or imports.

together, are playing the role of locomotives to pull the industrial freight trains of Asian countries.

In addition, the US and Japan are the major direct investors in the region and also extended the largest amount of loans. Without them the pattern of economic development in this region would have been very different. The roles played by direct investment of both countries and their implications for Asian development are discussed more in detail later. Needless to say, this imposes heavy responsibility for Asian development on these two industrialzed countries and requires close cooperation between the two countries and the Asian developing countries.

Relatively Sound Fiscal and Monetary Policies

The fiscal policies in East and Southeast Asian countries have not been always sound in the sense of keeping the budget balanced all the time. As Table 12 shows, the revenue and expenditure of each country's central government left a considerable amount of deficit. If, however, these budgets are compared with those of Latin American countries, then the soundness of fiscal policies in Asia cannot be doubted. In South Asia, however, the fiscal deficits are as serious as in some Latin American countries.

On the expenditure side, as Table 13 shows, despite the heavy burden of defense expenditure, Asian governments have spent the higher proportions of their budgets for education and economic services, whereas Latin American governments have, despite the relatively negligible defense expenditure, spent the largest amounts for social welfare and personnel expenditures. A pattern similar to them is found in Indonesia and the Philippines, so that these two countries are clearly different in the fiscal policies or their implementation from the countries like Singapore, Korea, the ROC (Taiwan), and Thailand. Malaysia is somewhere in between and seems now to be in an unstable budgetary position.

The monetary policies were also relatively sound in most Asian countries, but this will not be discussed here.[3]

Tolerable Distribution of Income

It seems safe to say that income distribution in Asian countries is relatively egalitarian in comparison with the income distribution in almost all LDC's in the rest of the world. This does not mean that Asian income distribution does not pose any problem. If Japan's income distribution is taken as a standard, then the indices of income distribution in most Asian countries do not give the impression of egalitarian societies. Since, however, Japan has a very homogeneous population, she can hardly be an appropriate international standard for income distribution. But compared with Latin American countries, Asian developing countries are much more egalitarian, as Table 14 shows.

This table gives the percentage of income of the richest 10 percent and 20 percent of the population, and the poorest 20 percent based on household and expenditure surveys of various countries. The study years are different from one country to another, but they can give a rough picture of income distribution in different regions.

---

[3] As for the issues related to monetary policies, there is a comprehensive report: Augustine H.H. Tan and Basar Kapur (ed.), *Pacific Growth and Financial Interdependence*, Australia: Allen & Unwin, 1983.

Table 12. Government Budget, 1971-82

(Unit: %)

	Gov. Expend./GDP			Gov. Tax Revenue/GDP			Budget Balance/ GDP	
	71-75	76-80	82	71-75	76-80	82	72	82
Industrial Market Economy								
Japan	22.3	27.7	29.8	20.1	20.8	23.9	−1.7	−5.9
Asian NICs								
Singapore	24.4	29.6	22.6	25.8	17.4	28.5	1.3	2.7
Hong Kong	15.3	16.7	20.4	9.8	10.8	12.4	..	−8.4
ROC (Taiwan)	19.4	22.9	28.2	15.6	17.8	25.6	..	2.6
Korea	18.6	18.9	19.5	12.7	16.0	19.1	−3.9	−3.2
ASEAN-4								
Malaysia	27.6	33.9	41.0	18.7	22.1	29.2	−9.8	−15.9
Thailand	15.4	16.9	19.9	12.1	12.7	13.9	−4.3	−5.9
Philippines	13.1	14.2	12.2	10.2	11.4	11.2	−0.2	−4.3
Indonesia	18.7	24.6	23.5	14.8	19.8	22.2	−2.6	−2.1
Giant Economies								
China	—	—	27.1	—	—	26.4	—	−0.7
India	13.3	16.1	15.1	7.8	7.9	13.6	—	−1.6
South Asia								
Pakistan	22.3	24.1	16.1	9.4	10.8	14.6	—	−4.5
Sri Lanka	25.9	35.9	34.4	16.2	24.7	17.2	—	−14.4
Burma	15.8	13.7	17.1	9.3	12.6	38.2	—	0.7
Nepal	9.9	13.9	17.2	5.2	6.7	8.7	−1.2	−5.2
Bangladesh	11.8	16.1	15.9	5.3	6.6	7.7	—	−8.2
Socialist Economies								
Vietnam	—	—	—	—	—	—	—	—
Kampuchea, Dem.	—	—	—	—	—	—	—	—
Lao, P.D.R.	—	—	—	—	—	—	—	—
Korea, D.P.R.	—	—	—	—	—	—	—	—

Sources: World Bank, *World Development Report,* 1985 and 1986 and official statistical sources of various countries.

The income share of the richest 10 percent in Asia is in the 30 percent range, whereas that in Latin America is between 40 and 50 percent. Only Argentina is as low as East Asian countries. The income share of the poorest 20 percent in Asian countries ranges from 3.5 to 6.6 percent, whereas in Latin America it varies from only 1.9 to 2.9 percent, except for Argentina. Among Asian countries, however, inequality in the Philippines and Malaysia stands out. The Philippines has a land-ownership pattern similar to Latin American countries, and its industrial organization is also of the Latin American type. Malaysia has three distinctively different ethnic groups

Table 13. Major Components of Central Government's Expenditure, 1972 and 1982

(Unit: %)

	Defense 72	Defense 82	Education 72	Education 82	Health 72	Health 82	Welfare 72	Welfare 82	Economic Services 72	Economic Services 82	Other 72	Other 82
Industrial Market Economy												
Japan**	6.4	5.5	11.1	10.3	..	..	18.2	22.0	..	..	..	..
Asian NICs												
Singapore	35.3	22.9	15.7	19.0	7.8	6.4	3.9	8.2	9.9	14.2	27.3	29.1
Hong Kong	3.0	4.3	16.2	14.2	8.6	6.9	12.5	12.7	36.4	10.5	23.3	51.4
ROC (Taiwan)	.*	.*	7.5	4.4	0	1.1	14.8	11.9	10.3	17.6	67.4	65.0
Korea	25.8	31.3	15.9	19.5	1.2	1.4	5.8	10.5	25.6	13.3	18.1	19.5
ASEAN-4												
Malaysia	10.5	15.1	23.4	15.9	6.8	4.4	4.4	10.5	14.2	29.0	32.7	25.2
Thailand	20.2	20.6	19.9	20.7	3.7	5.0	7.0	4.9	25.7	22.2	23.5	26.5
Philippines	10.9	13.6	16.3	10.0	3.2	5.3	4.3	4.2	17.6	53.7	47.7	7.2
Indonesia		13.9		8.4		2.5		1.1		31.3		42.8
Giant Economies												
China												
India		20.2		1.9		2.2		4.3		24.3		47.1
South Asia												
Pakistan	—	33.5	—	2.2	—	1.1	—	6.8	—	31.0	—	25.3
Sri Lanka	—	1.4	—	7.4	—	3.3	—	2.8	—	13.1	—	62.0
Burma	—	19.0	—	11.2	—	7.0	—	9.3	—	35.2	—	18.4
Nepal	7.2	5.4	7.2	9.9	4.7	4.5	0.7	4.3	57.2	53.1	23.0	22.7
Bangladesh	—	6.4	—	7.4	—	4.8	—	4.5	—	56.3	—	0.6
Socialist Economies												
Vietnam	—	—	—	—	—	—	—	—	—	—	—	—
Kampuchea, Dem.	—	—	—	—	—	—	—	—	—	—	—	—
Lao, P.D.R.	—	—	—	—	—	—	—	—	—	—	—	—
Korea, D.P.R.	—	—	—	—	—	—	—	—	—	—	—	—

Sources: World Bank, *World Development Report*, 1985 and 1986 and official statistical sources of various countries; Asian Development Bank, *Key Indicators of Member Developing Countries of ADB*.

* As for the defense expenditure in the ROC (Taiwan), it is included in the expenditure of the Department of Foreign Affairs, so that it is not separable. Here it is included in Others.

** Classification of Japanese government expenditure according to the categories presented here are not readily available.

in the population — approximately 55 percent Malays, 35 percent Chinese and 10 percent Indians and others — and inequality reflects the income differentials among them.

If we define an index of inequality as the average income of the richest 10 percent divided by the average income of the poorest 20 percent, that index shown in the last column of Table 14 indicates an enormous difference in relative inequality between

Table 14. International Comparison of Income Inequality

(Unit %)

	Year Studied	Lower 20%	Upper 20%	Upper 10%	Degree of Inequality
Industrial Market Economy					
Japan	79	8.7	37.5	22.4	5.1
Asian NICs					
Singapore	75	5.4	48.9	28.7	10.6
Hong Kong	80	5.4	47.0	31.3	11.6
ROC (Taiwan)	79	8.6	37.5	22.0	4.4
Korea	76	5.7	45.3	27.5	9.6
ASEAN-4					
Malaysia	73	3.5	56.1	39.8	22.7
Thailand	76	5.6	49.8	34.1	12.2
Philippines	71	5.2	54.0	38.5	14.8
Indonesia	76	6.6	49.4	34.0	10.3
Giant Economies					
China	—	—	—	—	—
India	76	7.0	49.4	33.6	9.6
South Asia					
Pakistan	—	—	—	—	—
Sri Lanka	70	7.5	43.4	28.2	7.5
Burma	—	—	—	—	—
Nepal	77	4.6	59.2	46.5	20.2
Bangladesh	77	6.2	46.9	32.0	10.3
Socialist Economies					
Vietnam	—	—	—	—	—
Kampuchea, Dem.	—	—	—	—	—
Lao, P.D.R.	—	—	—	—	—
Korea, D.P.R.	—	—	—	—	—
Argentine	70	4.4	51.4	34.6	15.8
Brazil	72	2.0	66.6	50.9	50.9
Mexico	77	2.9	57.7	40.6	28.0
Peru	72	1.9	61.0	42.9	45.2

Sources: World Bank, *World Development Report,* 1985 and 1986 and official statistical sources of various countries.

Asia and Latin America. The data presented here are very preliminary and seem to have a considerable underestimation of income inequality in the Philippines, Indonesia and Hong Kong. But we shall not go into the examination of those cases here.[4] Nevertheless, one cannot escape from the conclusion that Asian societies are much more egalitarian than Latin American societies.

This relative equality was brought about primarily by successful development of agriculture and labor-intensive industries in Asian economies which included a wide range of small and medium size farmers, proprietors and enterprises.

Fairly Reliable Public and Private Institutions

Many scholars including Simon Kuznets who investigated the modernization of late-coming nations pointed out that Modern Economic Growth requires not only the necessary economic conditions but also at least the following two conditions:[5]

1. establishing and managing a modern social and institutional framework;
2. learning appropriate ways of thinking to be compatible with modern technology and society.

These problems are often analyzed in terms of social development and political development. Needless to say, it takes a longer time to achieve them than to achieve economic development. In most Asian countries, political basis of such institutions was typically the cooperation of the military and technocratic bureaucrats. Within such an institutional framework, the private enterprise system has steadily prospered, co-existing with numerous state enterprises often created by nationalization of colonial enterprises and plantations.

Governments in Asia, though mostly authoritarian, have been fairly efficiently administered. Most of their technocrats were educated in western universities, and many military officers were also trained in the western military academies. While they were abroad, they must have learnt about working of Western democratic institutions as well as the way of running them. These elite intellectuals did not object to maintaining the market economies for development strategies.

The only serious problem remaining is the "succession problem". No country in Asia, except for Japan, seems to have succeeded yet in establishing the rules of transferring political power peacefully from one political leader to another. Even in this difficult task of achieving political maturity in peaceful transfer of political leadership, Asian countries seem to be beginning to show their painful experiments in a number of countries. Anyhow in the past, except for the intermittent occurance of political instability mainly arising from succession of leadership, Asian politics has been relatively less turbulent most of the time in comparison with the rest of the Third World.

Under the circumstances not only the government offices have successfully run the administration and solved adequately the difficult problems of policy-making and its implementation, but also many private enterprises have been established one after another and managed well to sustain rapid growth of a new nation's

---

[4] For instance, there are later studies in Indonesia based on the household survey: *Level and Development of Income Distribution, 1978, 1982 and 1984,* Central Bureau of Statistics, Jakarta, Indonesia, 1986 to be included in *Indonesian Economic Development,* edited by Shinichi Ichimura, Japanese International Cooperation Agency, 1987. This study supports approximately the figures indicated by the World Development Report, but indicates the income distribution in 1978 was less egalitarian than that in Table 14.

[5] See Simon Kuznets, *Modern Economic Growth*, New Haven: Yale University Press, 1966.

economy appraised above. All that is a remarkable achievement in the course of postwar forty years.

Infrequency of Social Unrest and Political Instability

The tolerable inequality of income mentioned above must have contributed to the relative scarcity of social unrest or political disturbances in Asian countries throughout the postwar years. They too, however, experienced a number of coup d'etats and student uprising which caused serious political consequences and occasionally even toppled the governments. But frequency of such serious events in Asia has been much less than in other regions.

To understand the reasons why Asian developing countries experienced less frequently social unrest and political instability, the following formulae offered by political scientists are useful. This is a simplified version of the formula developed by political scientists to analyze the relations between economic grievances and socio-political instability.[6]

Economic Discontent   = Material Want/Consumption
Social Frustration   = Economic Discontent/Income Distribution
Social Unrest   = Social Frustration/Social Mobility
Political Instability   = Social Unrest/Political Participation

In terms of these formulae, Asian scenes in the recent few decades can be explained as follows. Asian countries could overcome the social frustration thanks to rapid growth and somewhat egalitarian distribution of income. The majority of population could feel that they were benefiting from economic development and suffering equally from whatever hardships they might have. Rapid economic growth and equal opportunities to education gave a large section of the population the chance to rise in the social hierarchy — high social mobility, so that not many of those with social frustration did cause social unrest. Moreover, the fairly democratic political systems in Asian countries — all the countries have one form of electoral parliament or another — and the chances offered to the leading intellectuals and the high-ranking military officers in the high ranks of technocratic or administrative positions in bureaucracy gave them a sense of political participation. This must have contributed to the political stability in most Asian countries. Needless to say, these conditions are not always and sufficiently satisfied. To that extent some countries at some stage faced serious political instability and may face it again in the future.

INVESTMENT IN ASIA

The US and Japanese Direct Investment in Asia

As argued above, the US and Japan have played very significant roles not only in offering the markets and supplying capital goods, external loans, technology and management know-how. Many corporations in the new industries developed in Asia are affiliated predominantly with the US or Japan. The economic development of Asian countries would have been very different without their participation in the

---

[6] See, for instance, Samuel P. Huntington, *Political Order in Changing Societies*, New Haven: Yale University Press, 1968.

development process.

It is remarkable, however, that this foreign influence has not created any significant antagonism against foreign corporations or multinational corporations the way it did in Latin America. This probably implies that the subsidiaries or joint-ventures of American or Japanese parent companies have been successful in maintaining cooperative business relations with local entrepreneurs and governments in Asia who must naturally have had nationalistic inclinations along with their own business and bureaucratic interests. The behavior of those joint-ventures or subsidiaries must have been adequate enough to satisfy the requirements imposed by the local governments in their regulations and restrictions on foreign direct investment but also satisfied the essential needs of the recipient countries' economies at different stages of industrialization. It was Professor Kiyoshi Kojima[7] who discussed the details of their contributions, comparing US direct investment with Japanese direct investment. Kojima's arguments are summarized below.

The US' Overseas Investment in Asia

Cumulative US investment in Asia is known to the present writer only up to year-end 1977 and is shown in Table 15. From this table alone, a few characteristics of US direct investment are already noticable.

1. The businesses which invest abroad most extensively are: banking and insurance, oil, commercial and chemical companies. Multinational corporations dominate in these industries and figure prominently in the US direct investment all over the world.

2. As far as the relative importance of these top industries are concerned, there does not seem to be any difference in any part of the world. The US investment pattern in Latin America and Asia are remarkably similar.

3. As for the investment in manufacturing industries, the order of importance seems to differ somewhat from one region to another. This difference is, however, not so much even for different countries in the same region, as Table 16 shows.

   It gives the detailed industrial break-downs in Asian countries, which shows that the industrial composition of the US investment in Asia does not differ from one country to another. It is most prominent in exploration of natural resources, particularly minerals and petroleum. Banking and insurance is second largest followed by commerce. There are some manufacturing industries in which US multinationals have competitive strength. But they often face protectionistic restrictions in foreign countries. To overcome barriers and get around the protection of domestic market in LDCs, these MNCs invest in the processing plants for their products abroad. In other cases, lower labor costs are the main factor encouraging US firms to invest abroad.

4. The US corporations definitely prefer retaining a high ownership share in joint-ventures, whereas Japanese corporations accept, if required by the recipient countries' regulations or government policies, to hold only 49 percent of equity. This is an interesting contrast between Japanese and US direct investment in Asia.

---

[7] Kiyoshi Kojima, *Nippon-no Kaigai Chokusetsu Toshi*, (Japanese Overseas Direct Investment), Tokyo: Bunshindo, 1985.

Table 15. US Overseas Direct Investment Up to 1977-End

		World bill. $	Latin bill. $	Amer-rank	Asia bill. $	Rank
1	Bank, Ins.	415.6	114.0	1	25.7	1
2	Petroleum	114.8	8.0	2	6.1	2
3	Commerce	56.1	5.4	4	1.7	4
4	Chemical	38.8	7.5	3	2.5	3
5	Other Ind.	33.8	3.6	7	1.1	6
6	Transp. Mach.	32.1	4.4	5	.49	7
7	Machinery	28.4	2.5	10	.43	9
8	Metal & Prod.	21.4	3.4	8	.44	8
9	Mining	18.3	3.7	6	.22	12
10	Electr. prod.	17.1	2.4	11	1.3	5
11	Food	14.2	2.8	9	.42	10
12	Paper	7.9	1.4	12	.08	17
13	Rubber	6.3	1.2	13	.25	11
14	Music Instr.	5.6	.42	16	.03	20
15	Tex. apparel	3.4	.77	14	n.a.	15
16	Stone, Cement	3.4	.71	15	.22	13
17	Other Manuf.	2.9	.38	17	.11	16
18	Tobacco	2.8	n.a.	18	.06	18
19	Glass	2.7	.34	19	.04	19
20	Wood Prod.	1.7	n.a.	20	.13	14
21	Plastics	1.3	.28	21	.01	21
22	Print. & Publ.	1.1	.09	22	n.a.	22

Source: Dept. of Commerce, *US Direct Investment Abroad,* 1977, April, 1981.

Japan's Direct Investment in Asia

Japanese overseas investment in Asia seems to have played a more important function than that of the US in promoting the industrialization of Asian developing countries in the late 1960s through the early 1980s. Japanese overseas investments followed her reparation payments, but their amount did not become significant until the early 1970s. By that time US direct investment was well under way all over the world. The magnitude of Japan's direct investment became significant after she quadrupled her GNP in the 1960s and completed her reconstruction and started here re-emergence as an industrial country. Japan's foreign investment growth can be seen in Table 17. What Japanese direct investment has accumulated can be seen from Table 18.

This table indicates that Japanese direct investment in Asia consists of many cases of small scale investments, except for Indonesia, where Japanese direct investment includes a few exceptionally large scale ventures like the ASAHAN hydro-

Table 16. The US' Cumulated Amount of Direct Investment in Asian Countries at 1977-End

(Unit: US$ billion)

	Hong Kong		Singap.		Phil.		Indonesia		Korea		ROC (Taiwan)		Thail.	
1 Bank & Ins.	8,640	1	8,610	1	3,385	1	545	2	752	3	1,582	1	484	1
2 Petroleum	569	3	577	2	n.a.	2	2,327	1	945	1	45	7	241	2
3 Commerce	838	2	250	5	207	5	28	5	72	4	94	5	111	3
4 Misc. Man.	n.a.	4	n.a.	4	265	3	n.a.	4	22	9	n.a.	4	102	4
5. Chemical	128	7	12	10	180	8	87	3	865	2	351	2	46	5
6 Other Ind.	343	5	110	8	n.a.	6	n.a.	6	33	6	6	10	n.a.	6
7 Transp. Mach.	1	10	n.a.	7	n.a.	7	3	9	n.a.	7	77	6	1	11
8 Machinery	38	8	168	6	2	12	1	12	n.a.	8	n.a.	8	0	12
9 Metal Pr.	21	9	69	9	98	9	15	7	1	11	2	11	29	8
10 Mining	0	11	0	12	n.a.	10	n.a.	11	0	12	0	12	13	10
11 Electr.	175	6	263	3	n.a.	11	n.a.	11	67	5	315	3	25	9
12 Food	n.a.	12	11	11	238	4	11	8	18	10	40	9	37	7
Total	10,909		10,121		5,480		3,619		3,021		2,574		1,205	

Source: The same as Table 15.

Table 17. Japanese Overseas Direct Investment from 1951 to 1981

(Unit: US$ million)

Annual Average	World		Asia		N. America	
	cases	$	cases	$	cases	$
1951-62	62	44	17	7	16	9
63-67	201	173	79	41	48	51
68-71	589	736	265	167	154	180
72-73	1,970	2,655	845	690	547	577
74-77	1,515	2,893	521	979	465	715
78-81	2,230	5,632	658	1,690	854	1,655

Source: Ministry of Finance, Government of Japan.

Table 18. Japan's Cumulated Overseas Direct Investment
in Different Regions and Countries, 1951-1982

	Cases	Amount bill. $	% Share
USA	9,995	13.970	26.3
North America	10,594	15.225	28.7
Latin America	3,427	8.852	16.7
Hong Kong	2,002	1.825	3.4
Singapore	1,373	1.383	2.6
Korea	1,105	1.383	2.5
ROC (Taiwan)	1,225	.479	0.9
Indonesia	1,148	7.268	13.7
Malaysia	720	.764	1.4
Philippines	583	.721	1.4
Thailand	853	.521	1.0
Brunei	19	.100	0.2
Others	316	.180	0.3
ASIA	9,344	14.552	27.4
Mid & Near East	274	2.479	4.7
Europe	3,023	6.146	11.6
Africa	923	2.507	4.7
Oceania	1,478	3.370	6.3

Source: *Kaigai Todokeide Jisseki* (Overseas Direct Investment Applications) Ministry of Finance, June 1983.

electric power station project and some oil and gas exploration projects. In other countries, however, many investments from Japan were those by medium size enterprises which tried to locate their factories in nearby countries partly to capture a share of the local markets, partly to hire cheaper workers, and partly to overcome the restrictions imposed on Japanese exports in the US and the domestic markets of the developing countries. An important point is that whatever the motivations behind Japanese direct investment may have been, these investments were almost exactly the kind of investments that these developing countries needed for their industrialization.

As Japan was quickly moving up the market, she had to restructure various manufacturing industries. This offered fewer opportunities to capable and experienced engineers and managers inside Japan. But they possessed precisely the kind of human capital and technical know-how needed in the Asian newly industrializing countries. The sooner the countries grabbed these talents, the better off those countries became. In this game of catching-up the most advantageous countries were the ROC (Taiwan) and Korea, which had many Japanese-speaking people. Besides, there were many personal and business connections between Japanese businessmen and local businessmen. Executives or top managers in Japanese medium and small enterprises who could not speak any foreign languages could easily go to invest in Korea and the ROC (Taiwan). This was particularly so in the ROC (Taiwan), because antagonistic sentiment toward Japanese was much less there than in Korea and Southeast Asia. The early start and fast increase of Japanese direct investment in the ROC (Taiwan) and, to a lesser extent, Korea can be explained by these psychological factors.

It seems, however, that cultural advantages and long time business ties alone do not fully explain the pattern of Japanese overseas direct investment in Asia. The other important motives seem to be as follows.

1. Natural resource development: Japan lacks many natural resources and therefore invests to develop and secure the supplies in foreign countries. Mining and forestry are the areas in which Japanese direct investment is motivated for this purpose. Japanese direct overseas investment is important in Australia and some resource-rich Asian countries like Indonesia, Malaysia and the Philippines (copper).

2. Domestic market oriented: Most of Japanese direct investment in both North America and Asia have been motivated by the need to capture some countries' markets restricted to Japanese exports. The data show that the domestic sales of the products of Japanese subsidiaries and joint-ventures occupy 71 to 94 percent of the total sales in North America and 75 to 90 percent in Asia. Japanese joint-ventures in the fields of non-ferrous metals, petroleum products, fertilizers and wood products, utilizing the materials available in the countries, not only supplied the products to the domestic markets but also exported the rest of their production abroad including to Japan. This is a very good contribution to the development of Asian LDCs.

3. External market orientation: There are some industries in which Japan made direct investment but whose products are not exported to Japan so much but primarily to the US market. Typical industries are electronics, general machinery and precision machinery. Most of these corporations sell about half of their products (52 to 66 percent) to the domestic markets, only a small fraction (4 to 16 percent) to Japan, and the rest (29 to 35 percent) to third

countries. These industries often import the materials and intermediate products from Japan. This is one of the causes of trade imbalances Japan has been criticized for by Asian countries. But the net trade balance of these industries has often been favorable, and they have contributed to the development of each Asian country.

4. Accord with an appropriate international division of labor: The predominant part of manufacturing industries developed by Japanese direct investment in Asia were either those mentioned under 3 or in this category: textiles, apparels and miscellaneous goods. Investment in these industries was motivated typically by the comparative advantages in cost by relocating the plants abroad. At the beginning they imported most of the materials from Japan and exported to the same markets as those to which Japan used to export. But by and by they obtained the materials from the domestic markets or neighboring Asian countries according to cost-minimizing principles and began to export the products to Japan, while still buying the capital equipments mainly from Japan. Thus, the industries and the countries chosen by Japanese overseas investors were by and large consistent with shifting comparative advantage among Asian countries with a different industrial composition in successive development stages. In this way, Japan herself had a great advantage in being surrounded by a group of rapidly developing countries who were ready to succeed the various industries at preceding development stages. This picture can be seen by observing the industrial composition of Japan's direct investment in Asian countries in 1973 and 1983, as is shown in Table 19.

POLICY RESPONSES TO OIL SHOCKS

The adaptation of Asian developing countries to the oil shocks in the 1970s was very impressive in comparison with the less-adaptive responses of LDCs in other regions and proved their resilience to external shocks. At the same time, however, some weak points of their institutions and behaviors were also revealed. There are enough variations in their responses to the oil price hikes in 1973 to 74 and 78 to 79 among Asian countries. These issues will be discussed in this section.

The Effects of Terms of Trade Changes

The impact of oil shocks on the balance of payments differed very much from one country to another, depending on its energy situation. To estimate the effect of an oil price hike on the Balance of Trade, the actual BOT of each country from 74 to 82 is compared with the one recalculated with the pre-oil-shock export and import prices and the same volumes of exports and imports. Needless to say, the effect is positive for oil-exporting countries like Indonesia and Malaysia and negative for oil-importing countries like the rest of Asian developing countries. The difference between the actual BOT and the hypothetical BOT with no oil price hike is shown as the "terms of trade effect" in Table 20. Subtracting this effect from the actual balance of trade, the difference is regarded as the "volume of trade effect" and presented in the same table.

The table shows that the terms of trade effects over the period of two oil shocks are greater than the volume of trade effects for most countries. This demonstrates

Table 19. Industrial Composition of Japan's Overseas Direct Investment in Asia in 1973 and 1983 (March)

(Unit: US$ million)

	India 73	India 83	H.K. 73	H.K. 83	Singapo. 73	Singapo. 83	Korea 73	Korea 83	Malay. 73	Malay. 83	Philip. 73	Philip. 83	Thail. 73	Thail. 83	ROC (T) 73	ROC (T) 83
Mining	1	1	12	14	17	17	12	16	1	2	1	1	8	15	10	14
Other Serv.	5	5	1	1	6	2	8	1	8	7	5	5	6	8	7	10
Commerce	12	13	3	2	11	7	15	14	13	10	10	15	3	3	13	9
Bank & Ins.	3	11	4	3	8	11	11	13	17	14	11	9	13	12	14	17
Textile	2	3	2	4	9	13	1	3	9	3	4	7	1	1	2	5
Wood, Pulp	9	8	11	11	7	14	14	15	2	6	15	12	15	14	12	12
Real Estate	17	16	6	6	10	8	6	8	10	15	8	14	11	16	6	7
Metal	3	2	8	13	12	9	3	5	4	5	3	2	4	7	9	6
Electronics	13	12	7	8	3	5	2	4	3	4	7	13	10	13	1	1
Transp. Mach.	18	9	17	17	1	6	9	10	14	12	14	3	9	5	16	8
Chemical	11	7	14	15	5	1	5	2	7	1	13	4	5	6	4	4
Machinery	14	16	13	9	4	3	7	7	16	13	17	16	14	9	5	2
Other Manuf.	8	4	5	5	2	4	4	6	5	8	12	8	7	2	3	3
Food	10	14	10	12	13	10	10	11	6	11	9	10	2	4	8	11
Agricul.	4	6	15	7	15	15	17	12	12	9	2	2	12	11	17	16
Fishery	6	10	16	16	16	16	16	17	11	17	16	17	17	17	15	15
Constr.	15	15	9	10	14	12	13	9	15	16	6	11	16	10	11	13
Total (mill. $) 1973	437		100		90		207		76		88		129		108	
1983	7,268		1,825		1,383		1,312		721		721		521		479	
83/73	15.4		18.3		15.4		6.3		9.6		8.2		4.0		4.4	
Gr. rate	36.0		38.5		36.0		22.6		28.6		26.6		16.7		18.1	

Sources: *Zaisei Kinyu Tokei Geppo* (Monthly Bulletin of Fiscal and Monetary Statistics), Sept., 73 and Dec., 83. 73 and Dec., 83.

Table 20. Balance of Trade and Terms of Trade Effect, 1974-82

(Unit: US$ million)

	BOT	Term of Trade Eff.	Volume of Trade Eff.
Industrial Market Economy			
Japan			
Asian NICs			
Singapore	−3,881	−2,458	−1,422
Hong Kong	−1,645	−998	−647
ROC (Taiwan)	760	−1,034	−1,794
Korea	−2,890	−3,053	163
ASEAN-4			
Malaysia	1,117	499	618
Thailand	−1,539	−2,158	619
Philippines	−1,884	−1,900	16
Indonesia	5,806	6,470	−644
Giant Economies			
China			
India	−3,143	−2,772	−371
South Asia			
Pakistan	−1,601	−1,472	−129
Sri Lanka	−391	−404	13
Burma	−141	−81	−60
Nepal	—	—	—
Bangladesh	—	—	—
Socialist Economies			
Vietnam	—	—	—
Kampuchea, Dem.	—	—	—
Lao, P.D.R.	—	—	—
Korea, D.P.R.	—	—	—

Sources: Seiji Naya et al: "External Shocks and Policy Responses: The Asian Experience," *Asian Development Review,* Vol. 2, No. 1, 1984.

the seriousness of oil shocks to Asian developing countries. The only impressive exception is the ROC (Taiwan), whose positive volume of trade effect outweighed the negative terms of trade effect. Korea too showed some positive volume of trade effect, but her negative terms of trade effect was so large that her balance of trade remained unfavorable. Singapore suffered more seriously from terms of trade effects than Hong Kong, but both could not overcome the effects by the volume of trade effects. Indonesia gained two oil bonanza, but her volume of trade effect suffered from Dutch disease and was negative. On the other hand, in the case of Malaysia both terms of trade effect and volume of trade effect were positive. Thailand and the Philippines managed to offset the negative terms of trade effect only partially by the positive volume of trade effects. Thailand did slightly better than the Philippines in this respect.

The Effects of Energy Conservation Policies

The above-mentioned effects are the outcome not only of the natural responses of the national economies but also the deliberate policies of the government concerned to cope with the situation of highly expensive energy. At any rate the balance of payments must be adjusted sooner or later. There are four ways of adjustment available: (1) promotion of exports, (2) reducing the propensity to import, (3) slowing down the growth rate, and (4) borrowing foreign loans.

In order to see how these four policies were combined in the choice of adaptation policies by Asian countries, the tentative estimation of the effects of oil shocks on the balance of payments and their decomposition into these four parts were attempted by some economists at Asian Development Bank. The methods used are similar to those of Bela Balassa's work. The economic policies and the effort of Asian developing countries are evaluated in comparison with the trend which would have prevailed, were it not for the oil crises. It would seem that interpretation of their findings had to be made carefully. The main parts are reproduced here with some modifications as Table 21. Interpretation of this table must be carefully made.

Export Promotion
It is the most fundamental and positive approach to pay the higher bill for import of energy. Policies must be directed to diversify the export commodities, trading partners, or expanding the market share of the country in the world trade. These are exactly the policies pursued so successfully by Asian NICs.

It must be observed, however, that oil-importing ASEAN countries: Thailand and the Philippines also did fairly well in promoting their exports, but the Philippines did less than Thailand. Oil-producing countries naturally did well in exporting oil, but this has the undesirable effects on the non-oil exports due to the terms of trade turning too favorably for them — the so-called "Dutch disease". It is impressive that Malaysia succeeded in expanding her exports so much. She fortunately had such important non-oil primary commodities as rubber, tin, timber, palm oil etc. whose demands increased, but the export of basic manufactures increased as well. Indonesia, however, had to spend a considerable portion of oil price bonanza for fighting against inflation and erosion of incomes of small holders, peasants and poor city dwellers in order to keep the prices of rice and kerosene from going up.

The only country showing a negative export promotion is Burma. As a matter of fact the same thing has happened to all South Asian countries except for India. This is only partly a reflection of the sagging world demand. The problem there lies on the supply side, stagnating productivity causing the higher cost of production. Hence, they are losing the edge of comparative advantage against progressing Southeast Asian countries even in their traditional markets of Europe.

Table 21. Oil Shocks and Policy Responses

	Effect on BOP (mill. $)	Terms of Trade (%)	Exp. Vol. (%)	Exp. Promot. (%)	Imp. Substi. (%)	Slow GDP Eff. (%)	Total (%)	Net External Finance (%)
Industrial Market Economy								
Japan								
Asian NICs								
Singapore	−2,506	−98	−2	67	−47	18	43	57
Hong Kong	−2,800	−36	−64	85	−2	14	97	3
ROC (Taiwan)	−2,360	−44	−56	133	14	14	163	−63
Korea	−3,668	−83	−17	105	17	5	126	−26
ASEAN-4								
Malaysia	697	72	28	40	−25	4	19	−119
Thailand	−2,394	−90	−10	26	9	3	37	63
Philippines	−2,532	−75	−25	18	2	−3	17	83
Indonesia	7,741	84	16	2	−1	1	2	−102
Giant Economies								
China								
India								
South Asia								
Pakistan								
Sri Lanka								
Burma	−51	−159	59	−154	−1	111	−44	144
Nepal								
Bangladesh								

Sources: For the details of this calculation, see William E. James, "External Shocks, Energy Policy and Macroeconomic Performance of Asian Developing Countries: A Policy Analysis," Asian Development Bank Economic Staff Paper, No. 17, July 1983, Manila: Asian Development Bank.

For example an interpretation of export promotion should be: Korean exports achieved 1.05 times as much as the amount needed to recover the balance of payments loss above the trend value of BOP.

Reducing Propensity to Import

The second way of adaptation is to reduce the propensity to import by substituting domestic products for imports or economizing the materials or energy for consumption and production. Here too the adaptation of Korea and the ROC (Taiwan) is very impressive. But Singapore and Hong Kong could not do very much but to import more due to the small industrial base of their economies. Thailand did better than the Philippines, but both tried hard to succeed in achieving import substitution to some extent.

Among oil producing countries Indonesia did nothing special, but Malaysia substantially increased the import propensity. This is a consequence of its effort of building up socio-economic infrastructure and rapid industrialization in recent years, because the most significant increase took place in the import of basic manufactures and machine and transport equipments.

Slowing Down The Growth of GDP

This is commonly called "belt-tightening". Indeed this is what Japan did after the first oil shock. Japan reduced the growth rate virtually to zero for two consecutive years and thereby saved the import of oil. Her thorough-going policies impressed the neighboring countries and more or less directed their policies. The situations in Japan and her policies are discussed in the last part of this section.

More or less all the countries did the same to some extent. Among Asian NICs Korea after the first oil shock was an exception. The Korean government tried hard to maintain the high growth rate simply holding up the export-drive but could not do so any longer after the second oil shock. They too had to adapt themselves to this "belt-tightening" policies.

Burma's case may appear to be anomalous because the significant reduction of growth rate may be inconsistent with strong growth records for 74 to 82. It would seem that the high growth was largely due to the rapid improvement of agricultural production for the past decade. Burmese government's policies to adjust to oil crises have been primarily to slow down the growth of non-agricultural sectors. Thailand tried this policy in a modest way, but the Philippines did not try to tighten the belt.

Net External Finance

If the effects of all these three policies were not enough to cover all of the Balance of Payments deficit, then the necessary amount required by the external shock amount — shown in the first column in Table 21 — must be financed by external finance. The last column of Table 21 shows this last way of adaptation taken by Asian countries.

Korea and the ROC (Taiwan) succeeded in saving the large amount of foreign loans which would have been necessary even in moving along the trend in 65-73. This was done primarily by their high domestic savings and increased exports. The ROC (Taiwan's) saving is more impressive than Korea's. Singapore relied heavily upon external finance. Hong Kong did much less. But more dependent on foreign finance were the Philippines and Thailand. Weakness of policy adjustment in the case of the Philippines is very clear by now. Indonesia and Malaysia were net creditors in comparison with the trend, but in reality they are heavily relying on the international aid and credit.

Thus, the policy responses to oil crises and recessions among Asian developing countries may be summarized. Asian NICs improved their competitive position by vigorously promoting export and penetrating into the world competitive markets, while having recourse to external finance. Oil-importing Asian LDCs managed fairly well to promote the exports and achieve some import substitution but had to rely heavily on external finance. Thailand showed somewhat better adjustment than the Philippines. Oil exporters like Malaysia and Indonesia adequately expended their oil dollars to achieve the satisfactory rates of economic growth but did not make policy adjustment like oil importing Asian developing countries such as Korea and the ROC (Taiwan).

Bullish Growth Push and Heavy Reliance on Foreign Loans

Under the circumstances Asian developing countries tried not only to overcome the balance of payment difficulties by increasing exports and saving non-oil imports but also to maintain the high rate of growth by stimulating the domestic demands for capital formation especially after the second oil shocks. Table 22 shows such efforts of Asian countries.

Despite the two oil shocks they increased the proportions of capital formation in GDP and matched them with the increased rates of domestic saving. Except for the ROC (Taiwan), they all invested more than they saved, so that the resource gaps were fulfilled by inflow of foreign capital. The public external debt of Asian developing countries rose at the annual rate of 16 percent between 72 and 81, which is less than the corresponding figure for LDC's in other regions. The main sources of foreign loans were, however, private borrowings from commercial banks. Immediately after the first oil shock, foreign loans were made available on easy terms due to the unexpected availability of oil dollars in the world. Since Asian countries could bear the reasonable interest and amortization cost with little difficulty, they could easily obtain external finance for their energy programs, industrial projects or investment in infrastructure. After the second oil shocks, international financial market conditions became tighter. The governments of Asian countries, however, did not change their perception of international financial market conditions until they were hard hit by the prolonged recession in 82 and 83, the worst since the 1930s. Only then the full impact of steep decline of primary commodity prices, decreased demand for manufactured exports and protectionist measures in industrialized countries had to be encountered by Asian countries at the same time. These factors together contributed to the reduction of foreign exchange earnings of some Asian developing countries, and their debt problems became very acute. The Philippines was the most noticable case, but the debt situations of Korea, Thailand, Indonesia and Malaysia were not completely free from worry. Table 23 shows a worrisome picture of the debt situation in Asia at the end of 1982.

The internal policies of most Asian countries were not stringent enough to avoid the debt crisis. Even those attaining the high growth rates with credit-worthiness faced the difficulty in restructuring the debt composition from short-term loans to long-term loans.

Industrial Restructuring and Austere Fiscal-Monetary Policies

Restructuring industries is very important to take advantage of export potentials whenever and wherever possible in the world markets. The governments of Asian countries, particularly Asian NICs tried to help export industries succeed in expanding the exports in the industrialized economies. For this purpose as well as to satisfy the consumers' want, austere measures in fiscal and monetary policies are desirable to keep inflation from occurring. For these purposes such policies as

Table 22. Capital Formation and Resource Gap

(Unit: %)

	Invest./GNP		Saving Ratio		Resource Gap	
	64-73	74-82	64-73	74-82	64-73	74-82
Industrial Market Economy						
Japan						
Asian NICs						
Singapore*	30.9	40.9	18.8	30.0	12.1	10.9
Hong Kong	–	26.7	–	25.5	–	1.2
ROC (Taiwan)	24.7	30.3	25.0	35.5	−0.3	−5.2
Korea	22.6	27.4	14.5	22.4	8.1	5.0
ASEAN-4						
Malaysia	18.5	28.7	19.2	26.8	0.3	1.9
Thailand	23.4	26.2	21.6	22.9	1.8	3.3
Philippines	21.0	29.9	17.4	24.0	3.6	5.9
Indonesia*	12.2	21.2	6.4	22.9	5.8	−1.7
Giant Economies						
China						
India						
South Asia						
Pakistan						
Sri Lanka						
Burma	12.3	19.2	6.2	11.7	6.1	7.5
Nepal						
Bangladesh						
Socialist Economies						
Vietnam						
Kampuchea, Dem.						
Lao, P.D.R.						
Korea, D.P.R.						

Sources: The same as Table 3.

* Figures are the annual average over the period, except for those of Singapore and Indonesia in the first period taken for 65-73.

Table 23. External Debt and Debt Service Ratios

	Debt incl. short-term at 82-end (US$ billion)	Debt excl. short-term (US$ billion)	Debt-Service ratio est. for 83 (%)	Ibid excl. short-term debt (%)
Industrial Market Economy				
Japan	—		—	—
Asian NICs				
Singapore*	—	1.4	—	1.7
Hong Kong	—	0.3	—	0.2
ROC (Taiwan)*	9.3	6.0	19	6
Korea	36.0	20.1	49	17
ASEAN-4				
Malaysia	10.4	7.6	15	7
Thailand	11.0	6.2	50	19
Philippines **	23.6	8.8	79	33
Indonesia	25.4	18.4	28	14
Giant Economies				
China	—	—	—	—
India	—	19.6	—	—
South Asia				
Pakistan	—	9.2	—	9.3
Sri Lanka	—	1.8	—	10.1
Burma	—	—	—	27.5
Nepal	—	—	—	—
Bangladesh	—	—	—	—
Socialist Economies				
Vietnam	—	—	—	—
Kampuchea, Dem.	—	—	—	—
Lao, P.D.R.	—	—	—	—
Korea, D.P.R.	—	—	—	—

Sources: Morgan Guranty, *World Financial Review,* 1983; World Bank, *World Debt Tables,* 1983, 1984.

Notes: * Debt service ratios for Singapore and the ROC (Taiwan) are for 1982.

** The Philippine figure of external debt available in early 83 was 16.6, but later it was discovered by IMF's close examination that there was approximately 7 billion US$ more debt. But debt service ratios are not corrected accordingly here.

budgetary discipline, pruning of luxurious imports, tight monetary policies and flexible exchange rate policy to adjust it at least to the purchasing-party rate vis a vis trading partners' rates were successfully implemented in most Asian countries. These policies were often against the vested interests of some social groups. Nevertheless, Asian countries maintained the stability policies and kept inflation down to the single digit level. Low inflation rate and avoidance of over-valued exchange rate characterize Asian economies in comparison with Latin American economies. The only exception in Asia on this score is the Philippines.

Korea cut the rate of inflation very sharply after 1980, regaining the momentum of high growth rate. The ROC (Taiwan) never experienced inflation to speak of and realized the trade surplus. The ROC (Taiwan) is the only country among LDC's to follow Japan in the midst of all the screams of debt crisis and unemployment all over the world. Singapore also maintained simultaneously price stability and high growth for many years. Only Hong Kong was not so successful in controlling inflation but managed to keep its competitive edge in international trade and resumed the high rate of growth in the early 1980s.

ASEAN-4 were not as successful as Asian NICs in transforming their industries to compete in the world markets, but some progress is observable. Malaysia achieved high growth with stable prices. Indonesia maintained a fairly high rate of growth but with creeping inflation so that she had to appeal to sudden and bold devaluation of Rupiah. Thailand and the Philippines struggled to contain inflation and reduce the trade deficit. Thailand succeeded in developing some new export industries.

Since many of those export industries could develop themselves only with significant protection, ASEAN countries were not necessarily as successful as Asian NICs in fostering new export industries and increase new export items in the world market. As was argued earlier, ICOR of ASEAN-4 do not show as efficient use of capital as those in Asian NICs. ICOR calculated over the period of 64 to 82 are:

Singapore	3.8	Malaysia	3.4	Burma	2.7
Hong Kong	2.6	Indonesia	3.2	India	5.3
ROC (Taiwan)	3.3	Philippines	4.0	Pakistan	2.9
Korea	3.2	Thailand	3.5	Sri Lanka	4.1

It must be pointed out that these ICORs show a sharp upward trend in most countries in Asia. This may be a warning implying that the industrial structure chosen by Asian economies may be too capital-intensive at the present stage of economic development, because such industrial development was realized with very heavy reliance on external borrowings.

Japanese Adaptation to Oil Shocks

The Japanese government's responses to two oil shocks were not the same from the first to the second. The first oil price hike was literally a "shock" and indeed received by most Japanese as "crisis" to the Japanese economy. It hit Japan right after the Nixon Shock which consisted of three shocking events: Yen revaluation, soya bean embargo and US-China rapprochement with no consultation with Japan. It appeared to typical government officials and most intellectuals as a signal of the changing world situations. It reminded many senior citizens of the war-time experiences of shortage of food and materials. Therefore, there was no difficulty in obtaining the consensus immediately to tighten the belt by postponing almost all the public works and reduce the domestic demand for energy where possible and restraint the consumption of energy at home and offices. For instance, the government offices stopped half of the elevators in their offices and urged the private businesses to do the same. They were urged to do everything possible to conserve the energy in every sphere of economic activities. The Ministry of Construction quickly published a book of building designs with energy-conserving devices. The result was the recession immediately following the oil crisis in Middle East. But how swiftly the switch took place can be seen in Table 24.

The increasing trend in oil import in the recent past was immediately reversed. Conservation of energy was so successful that GNP could increase with less amount of oil import, which is shown in Table 25.

The Japanese government's policies at the time of the second oil shock were different. For the government realized during the period of adjustment after the first oil shock that she could import petroleum if she had paid the price. So long as she was able to pay the necessary cost, there was no need to curtail the level of domestic production with necessary oil import. Thus, the government did not reduce the public expenditure this time but continued only the energy conservation policies such as substituting non-oil energy like nuclear energy for petroleum. Direction of government policies was to guide Japanese industries in the medium run toward less material-using, more sophisticated and processing technology types of composition. As a result a significant change in Japanese industrial composition has taken place since then, which is shown in Table 26.

This change must be caused by the new types of investment decisions. A study of the motivations behind the investment decision is shown as Figure 3, which shows the importance of investment for energy-saving purposes. This determined switch of industrial composition is one of the main reasons why Japanese economy has emerged so successfully competitive in the world market after the second oil crisis.

FUTURE PROSPECTS

A 1985 Switch in Asian Economic Development

The impressive development of Asian countries demonstrated in the 1970s and the early 1980s seems, however, around 1984 and 85 to have started showing a sign of growth recession not just in the short -run but for a considerable period to come, perhaps a decade or so. This is particularly noticeable in East Asian NIC's and ASEAN countries.

In 1984, the Philippine economy showed an annual rate of decline of 5.5 percent. The Philippine economy may be thought of as a special case in Asia, mainly due to the deterioration of political stability. It was followed, however, in 1985 when the Singapore economy, which had been growing every year by more than 10 percent, declined by 1.5 percent for the first time since its independence twenty years before. Many other countries slowed down, and the rates of growth, if not negative, are also expected to continue significant decreases in 1986 and thereafter.

This rather sudden change in growth performance is demonstrated in Table 27 which gives the predicted growth rates of real GDP of most Asian countries. Those predictions excluding the last column are the ones presented by representative

Table 24. Main Economic Indicators of Adjustment During the First and the Second Oil Crises

	Annual Rate of increase in real quarterly GNP (%)	Annual Rate of increase in Manufacturing prod. (%)	Producers' inventory sales ratio of finished products (75 = 100)	Annual Rate of increase in wholesale prices (%)	Annual Rate of increase in consumer prices (%)	Monthly average current a/c balance (mill. $)
1st Oil Crises						
Oct-Dec, 73	5.3	2.2	63.5	24.0	16.5	−307
Jan-Mar, 74	−2.9	−0.2	77.7	35.4	24.3	−869
Apr-Jun,	−1.0	−4.4	90.9	35.4	24.0	−613
Jul-Sep,	−0.3	−3.9	95.4	32.5	24.8	−253
Oct-Dec,	−0.9	−5.0	107.6	23.4	24.5	106
Jan-Mar, 75	1.5	−6.7	105.8	7.3	15.6	21
Apr-Jun,	2.5	1.5	98.8	3.4	13.4	37
Jul-Sep,	2.0	2.0	95.8	0.8	10.2	−175
Oct-Dec,	3.5	0.5	91.2	0.7	8.5	−39
2nd Oil Crises						
Jan-Mar, 79	5.6	2.0	79.0	−0.8	2.7	32
Apr-Jun,	5.8	2.2	75.9	3.6	3.2	−244
Jul-Sep,	5.6	2.0	78.1	10.5	3.5	−1,292
Oct-Dec,	5.4	2.7	78.0	16.1	4.9	−1,384
Jan-Mar, 80	5.3	3.8	82.3	21.2	7.5	−1,658
Apr-Jun,	4.4	0.3	87.2	22.0	8.3	−1,370
Jul-Sep,	4.1	−2.0	90.6	17.1	8.4	−616
Oct-Dec,	3.3	1.5	89.4	11.5	7.8	−75
Jan-Mar, 81	3.5	1.6	92.4	4.1	6.7	−241

Source: *Economic Survey of Japan*, 1983.

Table 25. Japanese Economic Growth and Petroleum Import

	Real (80-Yen tril.)	GNP growth rate (%)	Growth Rate of Oil Con. (%)	Oil Import (.1 bill. kilo. 1.)	Mineral Fuel Import (bill. $)	Oil Import / real GNP
1968	127.7	(12.8)	—	1.40	2.675	1.10
69	143.0	(12.0)	20.5	1.67	3.044	1.17
70	153.9	(7.6)	21.7	1.97	3.905	1.28
71	161.7	(5.0)	9.9	2.22	4.751	1.37
72	176.6	(9.2)	6.8	2.49	5.715	1.41
73	184.6	(4.5)	15.9	2.89	8.327	1.56
74	183.8	(−0.4)	−2.7	2.78	24.895	1.51
75	190.9	(3.9)	−6.5	2.63	25.641	1.38
76	199.6	(4.6)	5.0	2.68	28.287	1.34
77	210.2	(5.3)	4.6	2.78	31.149	1.32
78	221.2	(5.2)	0.8	2.71	31.336	1.23
79	232.9	(5.3)	0.3	2.81	45.286	1.21
80	242.1	(4.0)	−10.2	2.54	69.991	1.05
81	250.2	(3.3)	−2.5	2.27	72.563	0.91
82	258.2	(3.2)	−2.5	2.12	65.618	0.82
83	267.8	(3.7)	1.0	2.07	58.925	0.77
84	281.3	(5.1)	4.8	2.13	60.337	0.76
85	293.3	(4.3)	—	1.96	55.790	0.67

Sources: *Economic Survey of Japan,* 1982, 85; Bank of Japan, *Economic Statistics Annual,* 1986; Bank of Japan, *Comparative Economic and Financial Statistics: Japan and Other Major Countries,* 1987.

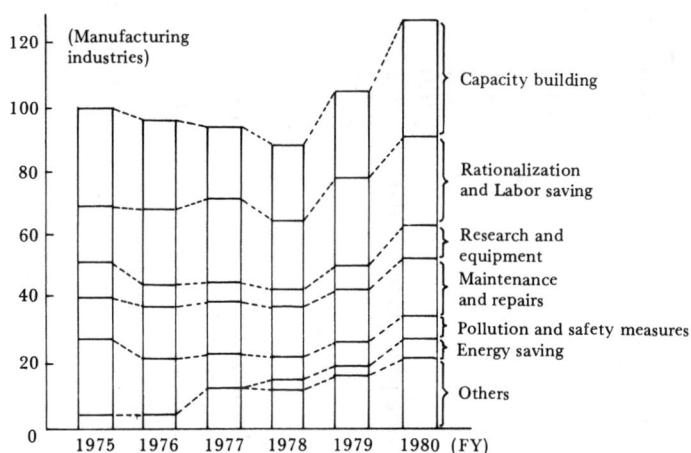

Notes: 1. Prepared from the MOF "Quarterly Report on Financial Statements of Incorporated Businesses" and the Japan Development Bank's "Survey of Investment Plan."
2. The index was prepared with the amount of plant and equipment investment in 1975 as 100. The deflator is based on estimates made by the 1st Domestic Research Division of the Economic Planning Agency. (Economic White Paper).

Figure 3. Motivation of Investment in Plant and Equipment

Table 26. Shift of Industrial Structure from Material-Type to Processing-Type

(Unit: %)

	1973	1974	1975	1976	1977	1978	1979	1980	1981 July-Sept.
Mining & Manufacturing	100.0	100.0	100.0	100.0	100.0	100.0	100.0	100.0	100.0
Mining	0.7	0.7	0.7	0.7	0.6	0.6	0.6	0.5	0.5
Manufacturing	99.3	99.3	99.3	99.4	99.3	99.4	99.5	99.5	99.5
Material-type	39.4	38.9	39.2	38.9	38.1	37.7	37.1	34.8	32.6
Steel	6.7	6.9	6.6	6.5	6.2	5.9	6.1	5.8	5.3
Non-ferrous metals	2.1	2.0	2.0	2.1	2.1	2.1	2.1	2.0	1.9
Ceramics	6.2	6.0	5.8	5.7	5.7	5.7	5.6	5.3	4.9
Chemicals	9.0	9.3	9.5	9.6	9.7	10.2	10.3	9.7	9.5
" (excluding pharmaceuticals)	7.2	7.1	7.1	7.0	6.9	7.0	7.1	6.4	6.0
Oil coal	2.7	2.7	2.9	2.7	2.7	2.5	2.4	2.1	1.9
Pulp. paper	3.6	3.5	3.5	3.6	3.5	3.4	3.4	3.2	2.9
Textiles	9.1	8.5	9.0	8.8	8.3	7.9	7.3	6.8	6.4
Processing-type	37.4	38.5	37.2	38.1	39.1	39.8	41.4	45.5	49.0
General machinery	14.1	14.4	12.9	12.7	13.0	13.2	13.9	14.4	14.2
Electric machinery	11.5	11.6	11.0	12.7	13.0	14.0	14.7	16.5	19.7
Transport machinery	10.4	11.0	11.8	10.9	10.8	10.3	9.9	10.9	11.0
Precision machinery	1.3	1.5	1.6	1.8	2.2	2.4	3.0	3.8	4.1
Others	22.6	21.9	22.8	22.4	22.2	21.9	21.0	19.2	18.0
Metal products	5.8	5.5	5.1	5.3	5.5	5.6	5.2	4.7	4.2
Lumber	3.1	2.9	2.9	2.8	2.7	2.6	2.4	2.1	1.8
Foods	7.6	7.9	9.0	8.2	8.2	7.9	7.5	6.9	6.7
Others	6.2	5.7	5.8	6.0	5.9	5.9	5.9	5.6	5.3

Sources: *Trade Statistics*, Ministry of International Trade and Industry, *Present Situation of Japanese Economy*, Economic Planning Agency, Government of Japan.

Table 27. Short-Term Forecast of Asian Economic Development

	GDP 84 (bill. US$)	Real GDP Growth Rate 84	85	86	86* (%)
Industrial Market Economy					
Japan	1,233.0	5.8	5.8	3.8	2.5
Australia	174.0	5.4	3.9	2.0	2.0
New Zealand	24.1		0.9	1.0	−1.9
Asian NICs					
Singapore	18.4	8.2	−1.6	0.3	0.0
Hong Kong	31.8	9.8	0.8	2.7	2.0
ROC (Taiwan)	57.5	10.4	4.1	6.8	4.8
Korea	83.2	7.7	5.0	4.7	4.7
ASEAN-4					
Malaysia	32.6	7.3	4.7	4.7	4.3
Thailand	42.0	6.0	4.0	4.7	3.9
Philippines	32.5	−5.6	−3.6	0.8	1.0
Indonesia	83.5	5.2	2.4	3.2	0.3
Giant Economies					
China	269.0	10.8	10.1	7.3	3.5
India	191.0	4.6	3.8	4.6	4.0
South Asia					
Pakistan	27.2	—	6.4	6.1	6.1
Sri Lanka	5.0				
Burma		5.6	6.2		
Nepal	2.2	7.4	2.8		
Bangladesh	11.2	4.2	3.1		
Socialist Economies					
Vietnam	—	—	—	—	—
Kampuchea, Dem.					
Lao, P.D.R.		10.9	8.2		
Korea, D.P.R.					

Sources: Project Link, ADB, ESCAP, Ichimura, EPA (Japan) and national plans of various governments.

Note: 84 and 85 figures are real and 86 figures are forecast. 86* is the revised prediction with devalued $ and reduced oil price.

econometric model-builders at the United Nations meetings in Bangkok and New York in late 1985, prior to the sharp decline in the exchange rate of the US dollar and oil prices. Oil prices were assumed about $20 per barrel and the US dollar was assumed to be much stronger than was the case in early 1986. The last column (86*) shows, however, the revised predictions after knowing the conditions in early 1986. The contrast of the two columns shows the effects of the changes in oil price and the rate of foreign exchange on the growth rates of various countries.

Thus, 1985 seems to mark a turning point of Asian economic development. The growth rates of all the countries show rather sharp decline in 1985, continuing into 1986. This change of pace is partly due to the fall of oil and other primary products' prices in the case of Indonesia, Malaysia, Singapore, Thailand, Philippines and China, and partly due to the difficulties in the export expansion in the case of the NICs. But more fundamentally it is due to the ways of adjustment to the second oil shock in most Asian countries discussed in the previous section.

In 1985, the decline of the US$ vis a vis the Japanese Yen and other major currencies also began, and it helped most Asian countries increase their exports, because their currencies' exchange rates were almost fixed to the US dollar. But it was not enough to offset the negative effects imposed by the other causes mentioned above, and even some newly industrializing countries could not sufficiently overcome the protectionist restrictions of imports in industrialized countries.

The Medium-Term Prospects of Asian Economic Development and Their Implications

There is, however, some possibility that those unfavorable conditions observable in 1985 and 1986 may not persist into the rest of the 1980s. Oil and other primary commodities' prices may go up, and the exports of NICs may continue to maintain an adequate pace of increase. Table 28 is a preliminary prediction primarily based on our study, it shows medium-term projections up to 1990. These projections depend heavily on two variables; namely, the oil price and the exchange rate of the US dollar with major currencies. In this study, it was assumed that Japanese Yen will be about US$ = Y175(86), 164(87), 159(88), 154(89), and 149(90). It is clear now — in late 1986 — the Dollar-Yen rate is as low as around 155, so that the prediction must be readjusted. The oil price index was assumed to change as −6.0 percent (85), −35 percent (86), +0.1 percent (87), +5.2 percent (88), +5.6 percent (89) and +4.6 percent (90). Needless to say, there is much uncertainty with these variables. Nevertheless, we take these projections as the baseline scenario of Asian development in the 1980s and give some tentative discussion of the underlying factors for slower growth and the corresponding development strategies for Asian countries.

The first observation in this medium term projection is that a partial recovery in the growth rates of some countries in East Asia and the continued high growth pressed throughout the 1980s. An observation of the growth performance among the countries indicates that the development differentials between most Asian countries (the South-South income gap) become widened. It would seem, however, that exceptionally prosperous two commercial centers in Asia, Hong Kong and Singapore, can no longer maintain their quick pace of growth and will slow down to match the development of other East and Southeast Asian countries.

Second, no significant improvement of growth seems likely to occur in Indonesia and the Philippines in the rest of the 1980s, although they will recover somewhat in the 1980s. These are the two countries whose industrialization was very much behind the rest of East and Southeast Asia. In view of the high rate of increase in population, their per capita incomes are likely to remain as low as they are now. Thus, the pattern of industrial growth in Asia seems to be diversified from developing NICs to somewhat stagnant ASEAN countries. The pattern of industrial growth

Table 28. The Perspectives of Asian Economic Development 1985-1990

	GDP average growth rate (%)	CPI infl. (%)	Trade bal. bill. $	Debt outstanding 85	90
Industrial Market Economy					
Japan	3.7	2.1	61.8		
Australia	2.8	7.1*	−1.9		
New Zealand	0.7	10.9*	−1.2		
Asian NICs					
Singapore	2.2	2.7*	−6.1	3.6	5.4
Hong Kong	3.0	4.3	1.2		
ROC (Taiwan)	5.9	2.9	5.3	7.1	8.6
Korea	6.1	3.9	−0.02	46.7	49.7
ASEAN-4					
Malaysia	4.2	6.3	3.4	15.6	18.5
Thailand	4.4	2.7	−1.5	15.9	23.3
Philippines	0.8	16.2	−0.4	26.5	30.3
Indonesia	1.8	4.0	5.9	34.3	46.8
Giant Economies					
China	5.0	16.9	−4.4		
India	4.4	7.8*	−7.4	21.7	28.0
South Asia					
Pakistan	6.3	3.5*	−3.6	12.9	15.9
Sri Lanka	3.0	8.0			
Burma					
Nepal	2.0	5.0			
Bangladesh	3.8	4.5			
Socialist Economies					
Vietnam					
Kampuchea, Dem.					
Lao, P.D.R.					
Korea, D.P.R.					

Sources: Project Link, ADB, ESCAP, Ichimura, EPA (Japan) and national plans of various governments.

Note: Those with * are GDP deflators.

depicted in Figure 1 cannot take place as smoothly as the figure seems to imply. Some countries will remain less industrialized and predominantly in the primary industry at least for another decade.

Third, the sectoral composition in manufacturing indutries will, therefore, become more widely differentiated from one country to another so that the trade of manufactures among Asian LDC's will develop further. Intra-regional South-South trade will become more and more important both in vertical and horizontal directions. It may become almost like the pattern in the European Community toward the end of this century, because many countries in Asia will have reached the 1960s level of incomes of European nations at the turn of the century.

Fourth, development strategies and industrial policy in each Asian country must, therefore, be guided by the proper recognition of a country's place in the whole configuration of Asian industrial development. The guiding principle in directing the industrial composition must be the market mechanism and comparative advantage in free trade. Excessive planning or administrative guidance on the part of the governments have proved to be unsuccessful in most Asian countries, and the change in policy direction in this regard is very noticeable in most Asian countries. International direct investment and finance must remain fundamentally liberalized. Yet it seems very important to recognize that an appropriate combination of successive protection of some infant industries and elimination of such protections with no delay after an appropriate period in each stage of industrialization is essential to the success in moving up the market in Asia. The countries that go up the ladder more quickly will be more successful. In this sense rivalry will be very keen among Asian nations.

Fifth, in this connection it must be recognized that the challenge of China and India will become very serious, in particular competition between China and other East and Southeast Asian countries (except for Korea and the ROC-Taiwan) and between India and other South Asian countries. These two giant countries are coming up from below in terms of per capita income or wages and also have the advantage of economies of scale. Unless the other countries' governments succeed in advancing their industries to respond to the challenge of Chinese and Indian industries, they may not be able to expand their labor-intensive manufactured exports due to the serious competition with the two giant economies.

Sixth, the external debt situation in Asia is not likely to improve by 1990. The Philippines case is so serious that unless some international supervisory body on her economic policies is organized, the economy will not be able to grow out of the debt trap. The debt situation is also very serious in Korea, Indonesia, Thailand and Malaysia. So long as these countries maintain the appropriate rate of increase in exports, their credit-worthiness will remain high. This may be the case with the ROC (Taiwan) and Korea. At any rate, however, it is clear that all Asian countries must manage their debt much more carefully than they have done so far. This requirement of debt management and increasing difficulty in export expansion might lead the governments of many Asian countries to slow down imports and economic growth in order to overcome their debt-servicing difficulties. This may imply that the projections in Table 28 may turn out to be even somewhat optimistic. On the other hand, they may be able to mobilize greater domestic savings. Saving rates have tapered off in recent years to below 25 percent of GNP in these countries. The behavior patterns in consumption and investment are critical in determining the relative advantage of each national economy.

Lastly, increasing productivity in leading industries in each country depends also on the absorptive capacity of workers, engineers and business officials as well as the managerial ability of top executives and administrative capabilities of bureaucrats in the government. Among the Asian nations there seem to be significant differences in the ability and willingness to learn. The transfer of technology and business know-how is determined by these capabilities much more than many people seem to realize. This will be increasingly important as the level of economic development becomes higher and the required technology becomes more sophisticated. All the Asian countries must pay closer attention to human and organizational problems in the future.

The Long-Term Scenarios of Asian Development in the Changing World

The changes taking place in the world economy in the latter half of the 1980s would seem likely to persist well beyond 1990. Some of those changes may be listed here.

1. Deterioration of the prices of primary commodities including petroleum relative to the prices of manufacturing industries' products
This is mainly due to the break-down of OPEC cartel and the excess supply of many agricultural commodities caused by the high prices in the 1970s and the efforts of many countries' governments to attain the self-sufficiency and exports.

2. Slower growth of industrialized countries
The USA and Canada, EC and Japan have reached the high levels of industrialization so that the domestic demands do not increase very much. Many of their trading partners in the developing world are suffering from the shortage of capital so that the demands from outside are not sufficient either.

3. Changes in the types of technological innovations
Technology seems to be progressing firstly toward less material-intensive and less energy-intensive technology, which works less favorably for resource-rich countries, and secondly toward more knowledge-intensive and more technology-intensive technology, which makes industrial production more favorable for industrialized countries and less dependent on the employment of unskilled labor or even semi-skilled labor.

4. Steady but slower expansion of the world trade markets
The world trade has expanded significantly in the 1970s, the primary cause being an increase of the merchandise imports to GDP ratio in the US from 4.8 percent in 72 to 8.2 percent in 82 and the imports expansion of OPEC's. This would not continue or has reversed the trend after the recent fall in oil price.

5. Increasing importance of financial capital transactions as well as relatively declining but still significant role of foreign direct investment in the international economic relations
The former is now more determinate than international trade in influencing the international exchange rates and accordingly the international distribution of trade

benefits among the countries. The direct foreign investment is losing its relative importance in promoting the industrialization in most LDC's in the world in recent years, but their functions are still extremely important in resolving the North-South problems with high efficiency in resource allocation and transferring the technology of industrialized countries to LDC's with little politicization of the economic conflicts among the nations.

6. Emergence of two giant economies — China and India — into the open market economies

It is a big question mark how these two countries will behave in the international markets. Their capital requirements are very large. The recent participation of China in the World Bank, IMF and ADB makes the increase of the funds in these financial institutions almost necessities. India is also changing the funding policies and now seem to be willing to borrow from commercial banks at the market rates of interest.

All the scenarios about the future prospects of Asian development must take into account these factors. There are a number of scenarios about the Asian economies up to the year 2000 prepared by experts or government agencies in several Asian countries. Most of them pay attention to the factors listed above. Tables 29 and 30 give the summary versions of those scenarios of Asian economic development up to the Year 2000.

These predictions were based on the official indicative plans of the respective governments, so that for some countries they are slightly on the optimistic sides. But the final calculations presented here are the modified versions of those figures on the bases of a number of macro-model simulations.

The basic assumptions underlying the predictions are the following:
1. No major political changes occur in the international affairs, so that neither any substantial reduction nor increase in the military expenditure in the US, USSR or any other OECD countries become necessary for the rest of this century.
2. It is assumed that OECD countries maintain the fairly steady growth rates (USA 3 percent, Japan 4 percent and EC 2.5 percent, and their exports and imports will increase annually about 5 percent. It was 9.3 percent in the 1960s and 4.5 percent in the 1970s in real terms, so that it implies a slight deceleration in trade expansion.
3. The United States' propensity to import and exports to GDP ratio will remain more or less about the present levels despite the radical changes in the dollar/yen exchange rate.
4. Japanese export to import ratio for non-durable consumption goods and labor-intensive intermediate commodities will decrease, but the same ratio for capital or high-tech goods will go up and gradually taper off in the mid-1990s. The import of manufactured goods will steadily increase corresponding to the falling dollar/yen exchange rate and bring down the export to import ratio of manufactured goods.
5. The US and Japan are both likely to increase the export of business services, banking and other financial services mutually as well as the developing countries.
6. The fiscal deficit of the US government budget will decrease year after year, but the speed will be slow. The international balance of payments will not be balanced until the mid-1990s.

Table 29. GDP and Its Growth Rate in Asian Countries

	Growth rate % 85-90	GDP 90	share in PB	Growth rate % 90-2000	GDP 2000	Share in PB
		(US$ billion)				
Industrial Market Economy						
Japan	4	1,473	21.2	3-4	2,078	22.9
Australia	1	212	3.1	2-3	271	3.0
New Zealand	1	29	0.4	2-3	37	0.4
USA	3	4,011	57.7	1-3	4,889	53.8
Canada	3	374	5.4	2-3	479	5.3
Asian NICs						
Singapore	2	21	0.3	2-4	28	0.3
Hong Kong	3	38	0.5	2-4	51	0.6
ROC (Taiwan)	7	86	1.2	4-6	140	1.5
Korea	7	125	1.8	4-6	204	2.2
ASEAN-4						
Malaysia	4	41	0.6	4-5	64	0.7
Thailand	4	53	0.8	3-4	75	0.8
Philippines	1	34	0.5	3-4	48	0.5
Indonesia	2	94	1.4	3-4	133	1.5
Giant Economies						
China	5	360	5.2	4-6	586	6.5
India	4	242	3.5	3-5	358	3.9
South Asia						
Pakistan	6	39	0.6	4-5	61	0.7
Sri Lanka	2	5	0.07	2-3	6.4	0.07
Burma	3	8	0.1	2-4	10	0.1
Nepal	2	2.5	0.04	1-2	2.9	0.03
Bangladesh	4	14	0.2	2-4	19	0.2
Socialist Economies						
Vietnam						
Kampuchea, Dem.						
Lao, P.D.R.						
Korea, D.P.R.						

Source: The same as Table 28.

Note: PB denotes Pacific Basin countries.

Table 30. Perspective Income Levels in Asian Countries

	1985 GNP pc (US$)	Growth %	1990 GNP pc	Growth %	2000 GNP pc
Industrial Market Economy					
Japan	11,310	3.1	13,175	3.1	17,879
Australia	11,930	−0.3	11,752	1.4	13,505
New Zealand	8,140	0.5	8,346	1.8	9,976
USA	14,760	2.0	16,296	1.3	18,543
Canada	11,490	1.8	12,562	1.6	14,723
Asian NICs					
Singapore	7,180	0.6	7,398	2.0	9,018
Hong Kong	6,110	1.6	6,615	1.8	7,907
ROC (Taiwan)	3,160	5.5	4,130	3.7	5,939
Korea	2,330	5.4	3,031	3.6	4,317
ASEAN-4					
Malaysia	2,110	2.2	2,353	2.4	2,983
Thailand	880	2.0	972	2.0	1,185
Philippines	740	−1.2	697	1.8	833
Indonesia	640	−0.2	634	1.7	750
Giant Economies					
China	400	4.6	501	4.0	742
India	265	2.0	293	2.3	368
South Asia					
Pakistan	386	3.1	450	2.0	549
Sri Lanka	361	0.2	365	0.7	391
Burma	182	1.0	191	1.0	211
Nepal	160	−0.5	156	−1.0	141
Bangladesh	132	1.5	142	0.6	151
Socialist Economies					
Vietnam					
Kampuchea, Dem.					
Lao, P.D.R.					
Korea, D.P.R.					

Note: The growth rates of GDP are taken from Table 28, and the rates of growth in population are taken from the *World Bank Development Report*, 1986.

7. The Japanse fiscal deficit will also remain large for the rest of the 1980s but gradually decrease. The current account balance of trade will gradually decline but not so easily narrowed to 20 to 30 billion dollars until the mid-1990s.

IMPORTANT CONSIDERATIONS

Under the above assumptions the scenarios of the Asian countries and some Pacific-basin countries were given in Table 28. They are based mainly on the examination of the supply of capital to increase productive capacity and the estimated rates of return to investment activities. Some important considerations of the economic conditions surrounding Asian countries are discussed here.

Availability of capital

Foreign capital available to Asian NICs will become more limited due to the gradual decrease of their exports to GDP ratios. This condition will not be so serious for ASEAN countries, because their exports to GDP ratios in Thailand and the Philippines are not very large yet, and Indonesia and Maylaysia have oil, rubber, tin and other primary commodities whose exports do not seem to encounter any particularly difficulties. The critical problems are the prices of those primary commodities, but the oil prices are likely to gradually go up for the rest of the 1980s and the 1990s.

The capital funds available in the financial market will not increase in the rest of the 1980s as much as in the 1970s due to the demands from the US and other OECD countries. The uncertainty associated with the investment in LDCs will make it more risk-taking for the part of lending banks and financial institutions to lend to LDCs including Asian developing countries. In the 1990s, however, most of Asian developing countries will be able to overcome the debt problems if they do not pursue too ambitious development strategies. They may be able to obtain the adequate finance at the reduced rate of interest in the sound financial market. The scenarios given in Table 28 imply that Asian NICs will borrow in the rest of the 1980s less than so far but will borrow positively in the 1990s again and thereby try to maintain the high rates of growth. ASEAN countries, however, may have to borrow more in the rest of the 1980s because of the unfavorable terms of trade in recent years and will probably be able to reduce the indebtedness only in the 1990s, when the terms of trade are expected somewhat to improve.

Investment Opportunities in Asia

Asian NICs will have reached the high levels of income so that wages and salaries will be higher. The rate of return to investment must, therefore, be higher than before to attract steady flow of investment from abroad as well as within. Whether such investment opportunities increase or decrease depends on many factors; among others, the productivities of relevant industries are the most crucial one. The various factors discussed earlier which made Asian development so successful must be maintained particularly in the newly emerging industries as well as the overall social capability of the nation.

In view of these conditions, investment to GDP ratio seems likely to decline slightly in Asian NICs in the 1980s and 1990s, whereas the same ratio remains about the same in ASEAN countries and may have to increase further in the 1990s mainly due to the requirements of new industries that they must start building up. At the same time, the ICORs in these countries are likely to increase, particularly in ASEAN and China so that the rates of growth in these countries are not likely as high as in the 1970s or the early 1980s, as Table 28 showed.

Moreover, as we discussed earlier, the debt burdens are very heavy in most of Asian countries. In early 1986, the estimated debt amounts are 45 billion dollars for Korea, 15 billion dollars for Thailand, 19 billion dollars for Malaysia, and 33 billion dollars for Indonesia. Repayment of the debt has begun to absorb the resources which could have been invested domestically for productive purposes. Singapore, for instance, has exhausted the investment opportunities for housing and business infrastructure. The industrial wages and salaries may have been too high in comparison with the labor productivities in the corresponding industries.

A Scenario of the Challenge of Chinese Economy in the 1990s

The official target of Chinese modernization plan is to make the industrial and agricultural production in the year 2000 four times as much as in 1980. This requires the annual rate of increase of 7.2 percent over two decades. The announced pace of development is 4-5 percent from 80 to 85, 7 percent from 85 to 90 and 8-9 percent from 90 to 2000. To expect such an acceleration of growth rate may be unrealistic. As a matter of fact, the short-term effects of reshuffling the various economic activities in different sectors due to liberalization and deregulations may push up the growth rate for a while, but soon such effects will be exhausted. Shortage of infrastructure and capital cannot be overcome in a decade or so. In the 1990s, the growth rate may be slower than the early 1980s.

In perceiving the future of Chinese economy we have to differentiate three regions or zones: the coastal special zones chosen for industrialization, including Hong Kong after 1997, the main parts of inner mainland, and the peripheral regions inhabited mainly by minorities. The pattern of development will be very different among these three zones. The coastal special zone may develop very rapidly and become very competitive with ASEAN countries or even some industries in NICs. For instance, the Shanghai Special Area alone has the population over 12 million and per capita income about 1,000 dollars in 1983. These special zones have an advantage of having the enormous reservoir of surplus labor in the background with low wages. A number of industries rapidly developing in Shanghai will become very competitive with those in other Asian countries.

The amount of capital funds and the technology transfer associated with direct investment required to accelerate the growth of Chinese economy and Indian economy will be enormous. Unless China is offered an access to capital, technology and market as much as other Asian market economies have had in the 1960s to the early 1970s, she will not be able to achieve a similar high growth rate. This will require an enormous amount of capital and other material and human resources transferred to China from the industrialized countries, especially from Japan and the US. The order of magnitude involved is so large that it is inconceivable for China to attain the growth rate of Asian NICs in the next decade or so.

The Future Scenarios of Asian Development and Development Strategies

Table 29 showed that the relative importance of Asian developing countries steadily increases from 72 percent scale of the Japanese economy in 1984 to 86 percent in 2000. In twenty years from now the Asian economy excluding Japan will almost match the Japanese economy in the total scale. Moreover, the international trade occupies much larger proportion of their GDP's. At the moment, the export of East and Southeast Asian countries alone correspond to 2/3 of Japanese exports and 1/2 of the US' exports. The trade expansion will become very significant not only to the major trading partners, the US and Japan, but also among Asian countries themselves. This increasing share of Asian economies in the world trade may have a far-reaching effect in the balance of economic and political power in the next century. Under such circumstances the role of Japan will gradually shift from just as that of pace-maker cum care-taker to the additional role of a coordinator of competing Asian countries' conflicts with the industrialized countries and among themselves.

Table 30 has indicated that the levels of income are widening among Asian countries. NIC's and China are quickly moving up the markets but ASEAN and South Asian countries are slower in the pace of development. Every country must figure out how to restructure the industries in view of the shifting comparative advantages of their own industries. The domestic industrial policies as well as trade policies must be chosen while observing carefully these changes in industrial composition all the time. The scope of observation should not be limited to Asian countries but must be global. The industrial restructuring discussed by Yamazawa-Watanabe in Chapter 6 gives essential clues to guide the various industries. It is important to keep in mind that the business linkage of transnational corporations through overseas investment and loans often offer an important part of industrial strategies in most countries. It is a recent phenomenon in some South Asian countries like India that deregulation and more liberal promotion of private enterprises are regarded more appropriate for industrial development strategies rather than trusting State enterprises mostly run by bureaucrats.

Protectionism has become rather strong in major industrialized countries like the US and other OECD countries. But it must be pointed out that it is strong also, often unneccessarily, in many developing countries. Restrictions are likely to be imposed upon the exports from Japan and other industrialized countries but also on those from LDCs, as their exports become increasingly important in proportion. For the same reason, preferential treatment can no longer be expected to last. As the results of all these conditions, the export growth will be slower. According to the latest estimate of simple elasticity, 5 percent decline of exports reduces the GDP growth rate by 2 percent; in other words, the elasticity is 0.4. Approximately, this is what we expect to happen in the rest of the 1980s and the 1990s in exports and GDP growth rate to Asian countries on the whole.

The transfer of technology to NICs will become more and more expensive, if not refused, as the required levels of technology go up, because the development of such recent technology must have been more costly than the old techniques, and the industrialized countries may worry about the "boomerang effect" of technology transfer. At the same time, the industrialized countries seem to be trying to apply the new technological advances like robots to old industries like textiles and apparels. Such extremely labor-saving devices may revive the old industries in some OECD countries and make them more competitive with the same industries in developing countries where production lines depend on unskilled or simi-skilled labor with cheap wages. Development strategies in developing countries must pay attention to such recent development of new technology, because as technology becomes more sophisticated, the quality requirements for intermediate and final products become more important than just the prices. The problems are neither just wages or salaries nor even the unit labor cost but the unit labor cost with quality consideration. This means that cheap labor does not automatically give a comparative advantage to less developed countries. It will be much more important for the governments to accelerate the efforts for improving the quality of human resources at all levels.

The heavy debt of every country has reached such a level that each country must comply with the strict conditions to be imposed by the IMF and other financial institutions and foreign governments throughout the rest of the 1980s and the 1990s. This would imply that the government budget to domestic capital formation should be restricted more severely than so far, and the government subsidies to the State enterprises and selected private corporations will have to be curtailed very much. All this means the slower rate of industrial growth. Therefore, the development strategies in most Asian countries must place more and more emphasis on the activities in the private sector.

Slower growth is expected, but the need to promote exports and save the imports is all the more strong. This tends to encourage the protectionist trade policies in Asian developing countries. The governments must fight against this trap and try. Instead they could try not to set their foreign exchange rate overvalued against the currencies of major trading partners.

Slower growth requires that more attention be paid to socio-political factors; in particular, more egalitarian distribution of income, wealth and employment opportunities. This means usually that increasing social cost must be borne by the better-off classes of people who may not be willing to give up the vested interests, when the resources become more limited to the economy as a whole. Unless they succeed in achieving to reduce the social tensions in the rest of the 1980s and the 1990s, political instability may be unavoidable.

One should not forget also some political issues still hanging on the Asian scenes; the Hong Kong issue in 1997, the war in Indochina, the Iran-Iraq war and the war in Afganistan. They are all in Asia.

Finally, it must be pointed out that as the national economies develop themselves, institutional reforms of one sort or another will become necessary. Privatization of public enterprises is one of those cases; the need to improve the functioning of bureaucracy is another; and new regulations or deregulations are just one of many remaining changes required. In other words, along with economic development, social and political developments are needed. Often the hindrances to economic development are not the inappropriateness of economic policies but the inadequate officials who handle the problems or inadequate personnel policies to build up an appropriate human hierarchy of capable officials particularly in public organizations with power.

In order to recognize all these needs and implement the necessary changes of policies and institutions, new and bold ways of thinking and devices must be initiated by an elite group of leading persons and accepted by the following middle levels of intellectuals and officials. They must find the original ways and means appropriate to their own societies. How far and how fast they succeed in achieving all these will determine the future course of their development in the 1990s, because they are the first group of developing countries in the world to catch up with the West and Japan.

2. Human Resources and Macro-Comparative Productivity Trends

Harry Oshima

INTRODUCTION

Human resources are now accorded an important place in the growth of productivity in the modern economy, but this was not always so. In this section, we sketch out briefly the historical background of the growing attention paid to human resources before discussing what they are and their interrelations with other factors in the process of productivity growth, and then outline the role of human resources in development strategies as viewed by development economists.

The earliest economists listed the factors of production to be land, labor and capital. With the emergence of modern economic growth, land began to stand for all nature-endowed resources like minerals and fuels as the rise of modern industry made them increasingly valuable in the productive activities of the first industrial revolution (e.g., iron ore and coal). Since the new technologies of the early industrial revolution began to make feasible economies of scale and extensive external economies, capital rose to the fore as it was needed for large scale production and for physical infrastructure which generated externalities throughout the 19th century in Europe, and superseded land as countries outside of Europe became major sources of food and raw materials that could be cheaply transported by the steam-powered railroads and ships.

It was in the 20th century, with the spread of the second industrial revolution that technology began to emerge as a factor to be reckoned with. The acceleration in the pace of technological progess rendered existing equipment obsolete, augmented the fertility of existing lands with new crops, high-yielding varieties, and chemical inputs, besides generating new sources of industrial materials. Above all, the new technologies based increasingly on science succeeded in mechanizing

---

*   This chapter is an extended version of two previous papers in the *Philippine Review of Economics and Business*, December 1978, entitled "Role of Manpower in Postwar Asian Differential Growth," and in the *Philippine Economic Journal*, Nos. 3 and 4, 1980 entitled "Manpower Quality in the Differential Growth Between East and Southeast Asia."

most operations in industry and many in agriculture and services. In so doing, they wiped out the need for most of the unskilled laboring classes which the first industrial revolution created to comprise the industrial proletariat of Marxian economics. It was the dwindling importance of the class of unskilled workers "with nothing to lose but, their chains" which nullified the predictions of Marx who died half a century before the coming of the second industrial revolution.

The new products from the emerging technologies opened up many new industries, and multiplied many times the number of enterprises as the decades of the 20th century wore on. The upshot was that by the middle of this century, the knowledge and skills needed by workers who replaced the proletariat of the 19th century were so extensive that the more comprehensive concept, human resources, began to replace the more quantitative concept, labor, as a factor of production. The early censuses' one digit classification of industries and occupations had to be expanded to 3, then to 4 and even to 5 in some cases in order to classify the multitudinous trades. Instead of a few pages, the cross-classified industry/occupation tables required a volume to list all the different types of workers in the labor force. Skills and knowledge rather than muscle power emerged as the main contribution of human beings to the production process, and as machines replaced unskilled laborers, quality rather than quantity came to be critical, with major implications on the demand for education and children fertility, and on population growth. England, which gave birth to the first industrial revolution, with its almost unlimited supply of surplus labor thrown out from the enclosed and consolidated capitalistic farms, lost its industrial leadership to the United States with its limited labor supply, working with more machinery and equipment than British workers by the early decades of the present century.[1]

Then, in the post-World War II decades, Japan began to make rapid headway and by the end of the 1970s began to catch-up with the technology of the West, and in the 1980s began to challenge the supremacy of the undisputed leaders of the industrial world in a number of industries. Japan's successes could hardly be attributed to material resources, having to import most of its oil, coal, iron, copper, paper pulp, lumber, goods, and other natural resource-based products; nor to capital resources, substantial parts of which were wasted away in military campaigns abroad or destroyed by Allied bombs. Hence, one must attribute Japan's rapid growth to its human resources not so much to their quantitative aspects as in dualist theories, but rather their qualitative aspects, as Western entrepreneurs and managers coming into head-on competition with Japanese firms are beginning to realize.[2] Beyond Japan, the importance of human resources is being shown by Asia's NICs (Hong Kong, ROC-Taiwan, Korea and Singapore), countries with even less natural and capital resources than Japan. Their ability to penetrate Western markets

---

[1] For details of the impact of restrictions on migration, wages and the substitution of electric-and gas-powered machinery on farm and factories in the 1920s, see my note in the *Journal of Economic History*, March 1984, entitled "The Growth of U. S. Factor Productivity: The Significance of New Technologies in the Early Decades of the Twentieth Century"; *Philippine Review of Economics and Business*, March 1983, "Problems of Heavy Industrialization in Asia"; and *Population and Development Review*, October 1983, "The Industrial and Demographic Transitions" for population dynamics.

[2] Japanese enterprises moving into the U. S. and European countries are beginning to demonstrate that their competitive strength comes not so much from the lower wages they pay in Japan but to their ability to motivate employees in the Western countries. See *Asian Wall Street Journal*, April 3, 1985, and various issues of *Euro-Asia Business Journal*. I have touched on this issue in *Economic Development and Cultural Change*, October 1982, "Reinterpreting Japan's Postwar Economic Growth".

better than other countries in Asia and elsewhere with lower wages indicates that qualitative aspects of human resources may be, as in Japan, the sources of their successes. (See below.) The emergence of human resources to the forefront in the growth of economies in the second half of the present century may be linked to the progress of technologies, increasingly toward skill and knowledge-intensive directions, compelling manpower to become more highly qualified in many directions.

A Conceptual Simplification

To simplify conceptually, we can think of land and capital as representing material resources, with capital, inclusive of its quality, particularly the technology associated (embodied and disembodied) with it, as all man-made material resources, and land as all nature-endowed material resources, inclusive of climate, location, land fertility, and so on. Labor, then, represents all human resources, that is, the total population both as consumers and as producers, their size, sex, age, location, labor force status in all its manifestations — industrial attachments, employment status, income classes, occupation, skills, and work culture. By the closing decades of the present century, the two industrial revolutions would have created several hundreds of thousands of different types of man-made material resources, especially with respect to machinery and equipment which manpower must learn to operate, work, and live with effectively, if the modern economy is to produce optimally.

Moreover, in the operation and organization of this vast array of technologies, man cannot work individually and alone but in groups of varying sizes and complexities as this is not a Robinson Crusoe economy. Hence, human resources, in managing material resources, must work in an organized fashion under patterned or set ways of doing and thinking, in a word, institutions. As the number and complexity of institutions multiplied, their role in the functioning of the economy increased, and they could not be left out in the growth process as the early economists did. Manpower, through the social sciences and humanities, had to be trained to learn about institutions, in order to operate them properly.

In the inter-relations of human resources with material resources and institutions, human resources are strategic in the interactions as it is manpower which manipulates material resources through institutions. There is no *deus ex machina* in the secular growth of the modern economy. And the niggardliness of nature and the occasional misbehavior of heaven can be offset by the diligence and ingenuity of manpower, except in the extreme hostility to man of the Alaskan cold or the burning sun of Africa.

To avoid confusion, we think of secular growth in the standard fashion found in the recent literature, as sustained growth of real GDP per capita, usually unidirectional and accompanied by structural changes, and the growth of productivity per worker.[3] Trends as short as a decade are distorted by what occured before (shortages and spillovers) and by long swings, short cycles, and episodic events. This is particularly the case with the turbulent decade of the 1970s, disturbed by two oil shocks and business cycles. Growth rates were pushed above the trends by the

---

[3] The literature referred to is the numerous volumes of the late Simon Kuznets, and of Moses Abramovitz on the U.S., R.C.O. Matthews and Associates on the U.K., E. Malinvaud and Associates on France, various volumes on productivity trends, written or edited by John Kendrick. Edward Denison takes too short a period for his growth accounting exercise and gets into difficulties with his projections, as in the case of U.S. and Japan.

large flow of foreign credit, and pulled below by excessive supplies from the overexpanded productive capacities in the industrialized countries. It will be misleading and hazardous to project trends into the 1980s and 1990s based only on data the 1970s.[4] This is true especially with human resources development which takes one to two decades for schooling and one to two more decades for experience and learning by doing for manpower to grow into positions of decision-making and commanding heights in a world of complex technologies and institutions. One is reminded of a number of studies on rates of return to higher education made in the earlier decades which showed high return, and on the basis of which governments expanded educational facilities in the tertiary levels. But these returns turn out to be misleading since in the 1950s and 1960s the newly independent countries of Asia were establishing the comprehensive infrastructure needed for a modern society including the bureaucracies and public utilities, and were planning for the rapid rise of modern industries. By the 1970s and 1980s, with the (more or less) completion of the basic core of public utilities and administration, and the slow growth of sophisticated modern industrialization in several countries, the existence of higher levels of educated unemployment is increasingly becoming a problem in the countries of Southeast and South Asia. It is already a serious problem for the Philippines, Thailand, India, and Sri Lanka, and emerging even for high-growth economies such as Korea, Malaysia and the ROC (Taiwan) and low-growing ones such as Nepal and Bangladesh.

Strategies Derived from Development Theories

In the strategies derived from development theories, the conception of the role played by human resources is different from the above. The most influential theory was that of Ragnar Nurkse in his Problem of Capital Formation in Underdeveloped Countries, published in 1953.[5] Low productivity was attributed to the weak inducement to invest due mainly to small market size. He seized on what he thought was the existence of a large pool of surplus labor in agriculture which should be shifted to the production of public works, roads, factories, and machines. This strategy was bolstered by Arthur Lewis in 1958 who thought that shifting the unlimited supply of workers from agriculture to other sectors at constant wages could accelerate growth, and by a more elaborate and extended theory by Ranis and Fei in 1961. Thus, the stage was set for the UN to come out with an industrialization decade for the 1960s, although several countries in Asia had earlier begun to move into industrialization. Like their forerunners, the classical economic theories, these strategies dealt with unskilled workers in the rural areas whom they were going to use to accelerate development.[6]

There was another genre of theories which were also influential in the 1950s, and these came out in favor of heavy industries as the type of industries to develop first. The seminal theorist was G.A. Feldman of the Soviet Union whose theories

---

[4] Thus, the projections for the NICs and ASEAN made in the early 1980s heavily relying on 1970s data, such as the Wharton and IDE projections, had to be revised substantially downward in 1985. Their performance in the 1970s may turn out to be far above the normal secular trend, propelled as they were by abnormally large foreign borrowings for construction. This will be discussed in detail later.

[5] See Amfai and Eva Exsioni (ed.), *Social Change,* New York: Barie Books, 1964.

[6] This section is a quick summary of a paper published in the *Singapore Economic Review,* Octocber 1984, and a paper on heavy industry in the *Philippine Review of Economics and Business,* March 1983.

influenced Mao in 1952 to get China on the heavy industry road, (Mao was also influenced in the late 1950s by Nurkse's view of the large amount of rural surplus labor in starting the disastrous "Great Leap Forward"). It was argued that in the early stages of development, growth is constrained by insufficient savings and foreign exchange earnings so that it is best to build first the heavy, capital-intensive industries upstream which can then produce the basic industrial raw materials and machinery, (such as steel, lighter metals, chemicals, petrochemicals, paper and pulp, cement, fertilizer, machinery, and so on), required for the downstream smaller and lighter industries and agriculture. Unlike the Lewis theory, this theory required ample supply of a top echelon of a wide array of scientists, engineers, and other technicians, besides large numbers of highly skilled workers. Thus, tackling head-on the sinews of modern industries such as the integrated complex of iron and steel making, of petrochemicals, and of heavy machinery, manpower of the highest quality became of critical importance in the successful establishment and operations of these complex industries, and later on even more advanced manpower for R and D efforts to keep the industries up to date with technological progress. The use of low skilled workers was limited so that the problem of surplus labor was skirted.

A somewhat similar theory by Nehru's head planner, Mahalonobis, brought the heavy industry strategy to India in the mid-1950s. It was based on Nehru's observation that the manpower problem can be solved as India is blessed with the third largest number of scientists, next to the U.S. and U.S.S.R., and presumably with a better chance of success than China which adopted the heavy industry strategy half a decade earlier. A. Hirschman in the 1960s by a somewhat different route came up with a heavy industry strategy which was influential for the Latin American countries.[7]

All these theories and their strategies were written long before the insights from the experience of the NICs in the 1960s and the 1970s could be distilled. These writers, trying to be helpful to the newly independent nations in Asia, could not wait until the 1970s. Lewis, a leading historian, was mainly looking at the early 19th century experience in Europe, Nurkse in the 1950s watched the surplus workers in Egypt, and Feldman was writing in the 1920s in the USSR. Hence, today on the basis of hindsight it is not difficult to see the limitations of the above theories and the associated strategies.

Monsoon Economy

It may be that these theorists from the West, with limited experience living in Asia, failed to grasp the nature of the monsoon economy so different from the West. Briefly put, the economy that evolved over the past three millennia in Asia reflected an adjustment of human resources to the pronounced seasonality of the monsoon winds which deposited huge amounts of rain suitable for a type of agriculture quite different from Western wheat agriculture. The rice grown in the paddies of the river valleys of Asia required a vast workforce, as the traditional technologies (such as transplanting, reaping with a small knife, and double-cropping) required many times the labor per hectare for wheat growing where seeds were broadcast for single crops and reaped with scythes.[8] But this most labor-intensive of grain culture

---

[7] P. C. Mahalanobis "Science and National Planning", Sankhya, *The Indian Journal of Statistics*, Sept. 1958, Parts 1 and 2, Calcutta; A.O. Hirschman, ed., *Latin American Issues: Essays and Comments*, N.Y., 1961.

[8] The monsoon rain schedule of coming and going called for quick plowing, planting, and harvesting, unlike the more leisurely pace of work along the Nile which watered the paddies all year round.

known to mankind was feasible in most parts of Asia mainly during one-half of the year when the rains came. In the other half when the rains went away, work was difficult to find in the densely populated lands of the "teeming millions" and, when found, was of low remuneration. Thus, the poverty of Asia as evolved over the centuries was due to the vast population needed for the rainy season, and its redundancy in the dry half of the year. And all the while, the mercantile, agricultural and industrial revolutions from the 15th century on lifted living standards far above the feudal levels of the previous centuries in the West.[9]

Under the circumstances, Asia, emerging from the grip of colonial powers in the early postwar years, should have adopted a strategy to overcome further the obstacles imposed by the monsoons. Policies should have focussed on the development of agriculture — to raise yields per hectare with modern varieties and inputs, to wipe out underemployment with irrigation and cropping during the dry months, and, after rice self-sufficiency was attained, to diversify into non-rice agriculture (fruits, pulses, vegetables, animal husbandry, fishery, and forestry) and with off-farm employment in agro-industry.[10] The aim in the beginning of the postwar decades should have been to achieve year-round, full employment in agriculture as soon as possible, raise annual farm incomes and purchasing power before shifting the focus to industrialization.

Ragnar Nurkse was looking at Egyptian rice agriculture which was not watered by the monsoons but by the waters of the Nile. The 19th century European wheat agriculture combined with animal husbandry during the winter months did not have to contend with a seasonally underemployed workforce. The reorganization of peasant agriculture into larger scale capitalistic farming in England could successfully transfer unwanted workers to industrialization at constant wages in the early period of the industrial revolution, as in the Lewis strategy. But the workers in the monsoon paddies were needed for the busy seasons in the early postwar years in Asia and could not be transferred without reducing farm production. And the high level manpower needed to achieve successfully heavy industrialization was not found in India or China. The large number of scientists that Nehru counted in the high schools and colleges of India did not have the experience for the complex specialized technical operations and R and D of postwar heavy industries.

But there was one writer who was aware of the impositions of the monsoons. This was Gunnar Myrdal whose views in his *Asian Drama* put human resource development at the center of his strategy. But his approach was too one-sidedly focused on manpower and institutions without sufficient regard for their inter-relations with technology and material resources. He dismissed seasonality with arguments about more crop diversification and less festivals and ceremonial holidays in the dry months, contending that Western farmers in the wintry north found plenty to do during the snow-bound months: repairing tools, and engaging in craftwork, concluded that it was the lack of diligence of Asian peasants which was at the root of the poverty of Asia.[11]

---

[9] This and the following sections are discussed in detail in my volume *Economic Growth in Monsoon Asia: A Comparative Survey*, 1987, University of Tokyo Press. A short version is found in "The Transition to an Industrial Economy in East Asia", ADB. Paper No. 20, October 1983.

[10] On multiple-cropping, see special issue of *Philippine Economic Journal*, Nos. 1 and 2, 1975; on off-farm employment, see forthcoming volume edited by R.T. Shand, Australian National University, and on labor-absorption, see special issue of *Philippine Economic Journal*, Nos. 1 and 2, 1976.

[11] Pages 1077-1079, Vol. 2 of his *Asian Drama*. Excluding East Asia, these volumes included Indo China, Burma, the rest of Southeast Asia, but with main emphasis on India.

But crop-diversification requires vast expenditures for irrigation, drainage, and other infrastructures whose costs will be too much if capital-intensive industries with their vast demand for physical infrastructure must be put in place, even for giant nations such as India and China. And Asians cannot be faulted for using their idle time in festivals and holidays during the slack dry season when they have little to do but must work hard dawn to dusk when the rains come. With few tools to work with, the repair work can be finished in no time, while craftwork is the specialization of a few families, which in the case of India, is monopolized by special castes.

Myrdal's views about monsoon agriculture leads him to conclude that what is needed in Asia is the conversion of the peasant farms into capitalistic farms which, as in Europe, can instill sufficient discipline to raise diligence to levels which can transform poverty into the wealth of Asia. Despairing of the political feasibility of comprehensive land reform as in East Asia or of consolidation into large-scale communes as in China, he espouses capitalistic farming as the solution to landlord/ tenant peasant farming in South Asia.[12] Nearly two decades have gone by since the *Asian Drama,* and nowhere in Asia, not even in Japan, the ROC (Taiwan) and Korea where rice farming has developed to the highest levels, can one find capitalistic rice-growing where most of the work is done by hired laborers. A few attempts in Indonesia and elsewhere have been dismal failures while the giant rice communes of China have been dismantled and turned over to the family for cultivation.[13]

Asia's peasant agriculture apparently operates most efficiently on a peasant basis with small machines which are scale-neutral, although Japan and the ROC (Taiwan) may now be ready for larger-scale machines in larger estates, with the displaced workers finding jobs in the relatively large non-agricultural sector. Both countries, however, are converting to a larger-scale basis slowly, and on a group-farming basis, not capitalistically. China learned that to get high yields in their communes, there is a need to put up Western type, large-scale infrastructure for irrigation and drainage but the cost of this will be prohibitive, and the vast numbers displaced by large-scale mechanization cannot possibly be absorbed in the relatively small non-agriculture sector.

Setting aside the industrialization and the one-sided human resource strategies, we favor an approach which will aim for full employment as soon as possible at the outset of development. Under this strategy, annual productivity grows at first with fuller utilization of labor in the rural areas throughout the year, as jobs increase during the slack months with multiple-cropping, especially diversified agriculture, and off-farm work when the various products must be cleaned, graded, cooked, canned, packed, etc. in the agricultural processing industries. With increasing farm incomes and purchasing power, the nascent import-substituting industries such as textiles begin to expand, acquiring scale-economies and extrnalities from the construction of supporting urban infrastructure. This, accompanied by greater activities in the service industries, induced by a larger volume of commodity

---

[12] See Chapter 26 of *Asian Drama.*

[13] It has been argued in my volume, op. cit., that the strong ethics for which Asians are known for all over the world originate in the rigid and rigorous schedules imposed by the regular coming and going of the monsoon rains. The crop must be quickly put in and elaborately cared for, requiring the labor of women and children, unlike in the West where the rains leisurely come and go. Nor is discipline wanting in Asia where group work with close cooperation and reponsible behavior is necessary for the exacting demands of paddy rice, unlike the individualism of wheat agriculture.

production, brings about full employment. From this point on, productivity growth takes the form mainly of increasing substitution of equipment and mechanized technologies for unskilled labor as their wage rates rise in a tightening labor market and with the disappearance of the labor surplus.[14] Thereafter, generally speaking, the shift is from lower-stream. Labor-intensive industries upward, and toward greater capital-and skill-intensities as the main source of labor productivity growth.

Progress is rapid and stable since the meager stock of capital and human resources available at the beginning of development have time to increase as the economy moves to the middle stage and then to the later stage of the agro-industrial transition.[15] Time is the very essence of this process not only in the construction of long gestation dams, irrigation/drainage, roads, public utilities, schools, etc. but in the education of the younger generation, their graduation into the labor force, and the process of learning through experience in the workplace, all of which take at least two to three decades.

To short-cut this process may be destabilizing, requiring governments (themselves at the outset with meager and inexperienced human resources) to undertake functions far beyond the competence of bureaucracies such as nationalizing and operating large and complex industries, intervening in markets through heavy-handed regulations, licensing, rationing and so on, matters more efficiently carried out by market institutions.

The approach is in consonance with the improvements in the distribution of incomes as year-round employment and mechanization spread to the smaller farms while the use of more equipment and machines in factories by the unskilled laborers raise the incomes of the lowest income groups. The spread of mechanization compels parents of peasant and working class families to save and send their children to education beyond the primary and into secondary schools, as the demand for unskilled labor falls relative to skill work. I have argued elsewhere that these are the basic forces which lead to substantial fertility declines and the completion of the demographic transition.[16] The upshot is the slowing down of population and labor force growth, which then induces entrepreneurs to hasten the substitution of technologies for labor.

In the foregoing, the main elements of human resources in the development process brought into the interplay of material and human resources are namely, labor force, population, employment, migration, education, skill formation, entre-

---

[14] In rice culture, at first power cultivators and threshers are introduced to speed up operations, and later mechanized transplanters and reapers to replace peak season labor. In industry, the main industries are food-processing, clothing, footwear, woodworking such as furniture, and metal works such as kitchen utensils and house hardware, all of them producing labor-intensive wage goods. Not only the core machinery such as powered spindles and looms are installed, but rising wages induce even small entrepreneurs to purchase small machines and electrically-operated tools and equipment in the auxiliary operations.

[15] Stylistically viewed, this transition starts with about 3/4 of the labor force in agriculture, which falls to about 1/2 around the mid-stage and then to about 1/4 at the completion, about which time the industrial labor force rises to exceed the agricultural labor force. In the second transition, the industrial society is transformed into a predominant service society such as in the main OECD countries including Japan. Though somewhat arbitrary, these transitions are convenient frames to track the movement of economies in modern economic growth.

[16] See for details, my "Industrial and Demographic Tansition," *Population and Development Review*, December 1983; also "The Growth of U.S. Factor Productivity: the Significance of New Technologies in the Early Decades of the 20th Century," *Journal of Economic History*, March 1984.

preneurship, and the distribution of income.[17] In the next section, we discuss how countries coming closer to the foregoing strategy tended to perform better than those which did not.

DIFFERENTIATION IN PRODUCTIVITY GROWTH AND HUMAN RESOURCE DEVELOPMENT

The differential growth rates shown in Table 1 have produced something unprecedented in the history of Asia. The postwar decades started with fairly even per capita incomes throughout the regions of Asia — no more than a difference of about three times between East Asia and South Asia. In three decades, the differences have multiplied to 20 or more between the two regions while Japan's per capita income climbed 70 times higher than that of Nepal by 1980. Since the gaps were slight at the beginning of the postwar era, the huge gap at the end was the result of the differentials in the growth rate of GDP per capita. Nor can statistical limitations account for such large gaps, even though the national accounting statistics of South Asia are much less reliable than those of Southeast Asia, and the latter much less reliable than those of East Asia. Even if the levels of South Asia in 1980 are doubled, the gap is still wide.

The widening is related to the differential growth rates of GDP, not to population growth. Table 1 shows that population growth rates were higher in East Asia than in South Asia (where mortality is high). Neither do the other components of human resources (Table 2) show differentials as large as per capita product in 1980. Adult literacy levels, life expectancy and calorie consumption were less than double in East over South Asia, in 1980, with average years of schooling completed by the labor force about four times. Though this type of comparative analysis is useful it can be misleading as it is static. In dealing with rapid growth, we deal with a highly dynamic process.

Rates of return to education have been computed by a number of scholars, and brought together by George Psacharopoulos.[18] He recomputes these studies into earnings of labor as a percent of the direct cost of eduction. Strangely, the social returns turn out to be lowest in Asia for all levels of eduction (primary, secondary, and higher), compared to other less developed areas, Latin America, Africa and middle eastern countries. But the rate of return analysis is also static, and as Theodore Schultz notes, "growth is beset with disequilibrial". The process of growth is a movement from one disequilibrium level to the next, with time too short for equilibrating forces to work themselves out, as Abramovitz observes.[19]

As noted earlier, the returns to higher education were high at the time of independence when higher levels of manpower were needed to staff the newly established bureaucracy, public utilities, etc., for infrastructures necessary to begin

---

[17] Health comes in implicitly with improved nutrition due to rice self-sufficiency and diversified cropping, and falling family size. Besides improved nutrition, life expectancy rises with more income for health care services and less strenuous work with machinery. Not to be ignored as we shall see are ethnicity and international migration of human resources.

[18] "The Contributions of Education to Economic Growth," in John Kendrick, ed. *International Comparisons of Productivity and Causes of the Slowdown*, Cambridge, Mass: 1984; also *World Development Report* 1980, Chapter 5, IBRD, Washington, D.C., 1980.

[19] *ibid.*, p. 359. M. Abramovitz in *American Economic Review*, March 1981, entitled "Welfare Quandary and Productivity Concerns."

Table 1.   Average Growth Rates, 1950 to 1980: Population, Employment, GDP in Asia in Percent, and Levels

	Population	Employment	GDP	GDP per capita	GDP per worker	Levels of per capita dollar GNP 1980	Agri. Pop. per hectare of agri. land 1979
East Asia	2.4%	3.5%	8.4%	6.1%	4.8%	4,446	5.1
Japan	1.1	1.6	8.0	6.9	6.3	9,890	2.7
Korea	2.1	3.5	7.7	5.7	4.2	1,520	6.7
ROC (Taiwan)	2.7	4.0	8.7	5.7	4.7	2,150	5.8
Hong Kong	3.2	4.9	9.5	6.0	4.7	4,240	–
Singapore	2.9	3.6	8.1	6.2	4.0	4,430	–
Southeast Asia	2.6	3.4	6.1	3.5	2.9	853	2.7
Malaysia	2.6	3.0	6.0	3.2	3.0	1,620	1.7
Thailand	2.8	3.6	7.1	4.2	3.5	670	2.0
Indonesia	2.1	3.1	5.2	3.3	3.0	430	4.6
Philippines	2.8	3.9	6.0	3.1	2.0	690	2.3
South Asia	2.2	2.3	3.7	1.5	1.8	190	3.8
India	2.1	2.7	3.6	1.8	0.9	240	2.6
Bangladsh	2.5	–	3.8	0.7	–	130	7.9
Burma	2.2	–	4.5	2.2	–	170	1.8
Sri Lanka	2.2	1.8	4.2	2.0	2.6	270	3.6
Nepal	1.8	–	2.5	0.7	–	140	3.2

Sources: Employment data are computed from various issues of *ILO Yearbook of Labour Statistics*. Unless otherwise indicated, product and population data for the 1950s and 1960s were taken from *IBRD World Tables 1980* and those for the 1970s from *IBRD World Development Report 1982*. Taiwan's data for the 1970s computed from various issues of *National Income of ROC* and *Statistical Yearbook of ROC*.

Note: Regional averages are simple, unweighted averages.

Table 2. Indicators of Human Resource Development (Ca. 1980)

	Adult literacy rate	Life expectancy at birth (years)	Total fertility rate	Daily per capita calorie	TDI of quintiles	% of male agri. labor force in total labor force	Female working rate	Average years of school completed
East Asia	87	71	2.4	2,879	.49	14	36	8.5
Japan	99	76	1.8	2,912	.41	6	39	11.5
China	59	64	2.9	2,539	.50	41	35	—
ROC (Taiwan)	90	72	2.5	2,812	.40	13	35	8.5
Hong Kong	90	74	2.2	2,898	.57	2	35	8.0
Singapore	83	72	1.8	3,158	.52	2	34	6.0
Korea	93	65	3.0	2,957	.55	19	37	8.5
Southeast Asia	71	61	4.3	2,381	.67	34	39	5.8
Malaysia	60	64	4.2	2,625	.73	24	36	6.6
Thailand	86	63	4.0	2,308	.62	36	47	5.8
Philippines	75	64	4.6	2,275	.68	37	37	7.1
Indonesia	62	53	4.5	2,315	.66	38	36	3.7
South Asia	46	52	5.2	2,046	.60	56	22	2.1
India	36	52	4.9	1,880	.60	55	17	0.7
Sri Lanka	85	66	3.6	2,238	.50	39	28	4.6
Burma	66	54	5.3	2,174	—	—	—	—
Nepal	19	44	6.1	1,977	.78	57	35	1.0
Bangladesh	26	46	6.0	1,960	.51	71	6	2.0

Sources: *IBRD World Development Report,* 1982, 1983, and 1984 editions except column 6 which is computed from *ILO Yearbook of Labour Statistics 1982,* for early years see previous report. Years of school completed of labour force computed from the 1980 Census. 1971 Census of Population for India and Sri Lanka.

Notes: TDI derived as the sum of differences between shares of income and household of each quintile with signs ignored. To give an idea of relationship between TDI and gini coefficient, the latter is generally about three-fourth of the former. Female workers as percent to total labor force.

modern economic growth. The changing needs of the economy at the different stages of the transition relative to the supply of educated manpower are crucial in returns to particular types of education.

Most important, since the training received in a lifetime is far more than years of schooling, the differences even within Asia in child rearing practices in the home, in the quality of schooling, patterns of training in the workplace, in the variety of mass media, and other forms of nonformal and informal learning are enormous as between a Confucian society, and a Catholic/Spanish society, or a Muslim society, or a Hindu caste community or a Theravada Buddhist or Marxist society. Elsewhere I have argued that the secret of the formidable productive power of the Japanese economy resides in a highly motivated manpower propelled by incentives which are not the same as in Western communities.[20]

For example, in the Japanese home a pre-school child is exhorted to excel in work and learning, to be alert at all times, demonstrate ingenuity in problem-solving, and to keep busy at all times with useful activities. He is kept in schools longer hours throughout the year than other children, and loaded with home work for the evening. Learning is continued into the workplace after graduation where training on and off the job is more extensive than for workers elsewhere. When he goes home in the evening the television beams a long menu of educational programs, not seen in other countries. The ideal goal is a lifetime of learning, seeking life's fulfillment in excelling at work and not so much in leisure and pleasure. In such a community, the social milieu is one of hustle and bustle, giving rise to a working environment of vigor and vitality. Such a macro atmosphere is itself a major contributor to productivity, and a worker on the shop floor toiling in such surroundings cannot help but be more productive than in other situations.[21]

Much of the foregoing influences on human resource development are not easily quantifiable and even if, for some, proxies can be obtained, they may not be fully satisfactory.[22] Nevertheless, rates of return and output elasticities with respect to schooling from regression results do give us a notion of the importance of schooling in economic growth, even though they do not tell us how important it is when account is taken of the non-quantifiable aspects. And there may be no way in which we can ever know how important it is. Rates of return, taken as "ball park" estimates, do no harm. But it is unsatisfactory to leave the matter at that. Perhaps a comparative historical analysis within a framework of economic growth as outlined in the previous section may give us insights which despite their approximate nature (as rough as rates of return) may be helpful for policy perspectives. Moreover, these quantifiable and non-quantifiable influences vary in their role in the different stages of different strategies of development. In the next section, we turn to a brief comparative, historical investigation.

---

[20] "Reinterpreting Postwar Japanese Growth," *Economic Development and Cultural Change*, October 1982.

[21] It is interesting to note the concern in Japan for continued vitality of manpower in the long-range plan toward the Year 2000 as it moves toward a mature and aged society. See *Japan in the Year 2000*, Economic Planning Agency, Tokyo: 1981. For notes on the sources of differentials in manpower quality, see my "Manpower Quality in the Differential Growth of East and Southeast Asia," *Philippine Economic Journal*, Nos. 3 and 4, 1980.

[22] See J.R. Behrman and N. Birdsall, The Quality of Schooling: Quantity Alone is Misleading, "World Bank Reprint Series, No. 311 reprinted from the *American Economic Review*, Dec. 1983. Even the authors' measurement of quality using public resource allocated to schooling may not be enough if the appropriateness of the curriculum, the quality of the teachers, the motivations of students and their quality, and so on are not taken into account.

ROLE OF HUMAN RESOURCES IN POSTWAR ASIAN GROWTH

It may be noted in Tables 1 and 2 that the growth rate of employment in East Asia is 3.5 percent (compared to 2.3 percent per year in South Asia), 1950 to 1980, higher than East Asia's growth rate of labor force of about 2.5 percent. This suggests that full employment was attained in East Asia. Moreover, the female employment rate is also substantially higher in East Asia than South Asia, with income inequalities significantly lower. Accordingly, the countries which were able to reach full employment succeeded in putting to use as large a proportion of the workforce as early as possible, and thereby achieved high rates of GDP per capita. This gave them an earlier start in the adoption of modern technologies, especially mechanized ones, thereby opening up opportunities for developing higher skills through the use of more sophisticated technologies. Rising wages, instead of constant wages in the countries with much surplus labor, motivated wokers to put forward their best efforts; similarly for entrepreneurs who found their returns rising.[23]

And the high growth of GDP per capita enabled governments and households to receive incomes to spend more on food, education, housing, and health services. (See Table 3.)

East Asian Experience

The generalization above is largely derived from the experience of East Asian countries, Japan and the NICs, whose economies by the 1970s were fully employed, Japan and Hong Kong by the end of the 1950s, the ROC (Taiwan) and Singapore by the end of the 1960s, and Korea in the latter 1970s. The key to the achievement was agricultural development in the earlier decades for Japan, the ROC (Taiwan) and Korea, assisted by labor-intensive industrial exports. For the city-states, it was the influx of a sizeable number of experienced textile entrepreneurs and their skilled technicians from Shanghai to Hong Kong in the late 1940s, and in Singapore of foreign multinationals in the latter 1960s. Both city-states were helped by modern and efficient financial, commercial, and public sectors inherited from the pre-war British days. Without their help in financing and marketing, the Hong Kong enterprises would not have succeeded so well. The efficiencies of the service sector in the city-states are demonstrated by their ability to become shopping centers in East and Southeast Asia, its entrepreneurs' ability to buy cheaply the manufactured products from all over the world and sell to millions of tourists who come to shop every year. But as the experience of city-states is not very relevant for Southeast and South Asia, we dwell on the experience of the other East Asian countries, although it should be kept in mind that the role of the tertiary sector is always important for all countries as it generates externalities in the form of efficient financing, marketing, warehousing, technical, professional and various public services. The last should be singled out because red-tape, corruption and inefficiencies, poor roads, transport, health, communication, sanitary, water, power, and educational service, monopolistic nationalized industries, onerous market interventions and regulations can be major obstacles to competition and entrepreneurship, and raise the cost of household activities, cost of living for workers, as they have in the Philippines and other countries. Besides this historical legacy, superb harbors and location strategic to foreign commerce and travel, these city-states were inhabited

---

[23] For data on wages, see my note on dualistic theories in the *Malayan Economic Review*, October 1981.

Table 3. Projected Growth Rate of Population and Labor Force, 1980-2000

Country	Population	Total Fertility Births		Labor Force	Life Expectancy at birth (1995-2000)
		1983	2000		
East Asia	1.1%/year	2.0	2.0	1.4%/year	74.2 years
Japan	0.5	1.7	1.9	0.7	77.6
China	1.2	2.3	2.0	1.8	71.0
Hong Kong	1.3	1.8	2.0	1.3	76.0
Singapore	1.0	1.7	1.9	1.1	74.4
Korea	1.4	2.7	2.1	1.9	71.9
Southeast Asia	1.9	3.9	2.5	2.4	66.8
Malaysia	2.0	3.7	2.4	2.7	70.7
Thailand	1.7	3.4	2.2	2.1	66.8
Philippines	2.1	4.2	2.7	2.5	70.1
Indonesia	1.9	4.3	2.8	2.4	59.7
South Asia	2.2	5.2	3.6	2.4	59.6
India	1.8	4.8	2.9	2.1	58.6
Sir Lanka	1.8	3.4	2.3	2.2	72.0
Burma	2.3	5.3	3.6	2.2	61.9
Nepal	2.6	6.3	5.4	2.5	51.9
Bangladesh	2.3	6.0	3.7	2.9	53.4

Sources: *World Development Report 1985*, IBRD, Tables 19, 20, 21. These projects are based on updated computer printouts of the *UN World Population Prospects as Assessed in 1982*, from the most recent issues of the *UN Population and Vital Statistics Report* and *International Migration: Levels & Trends* and from the World Bank, the Population Council, the US Bureau of the Census, Demographic Statistics (Eurostat 1984), and national censuses. The estimates of the sectoral distribution of the labor force are from International Labor Organization (ILO), Labor Force Estimates and Projections, 1950-2000 and from the World Bank, Life expectancy at birth from *UN World Population Prospects as Assessed in 1982*, Table A-15.

Note: Unweighted simple averages.

by a supply of skilled labor with a strong culture of work with extensive education at the beginning of the postwar era.[24]

Japan in the late 1940s and the 1950s pursued a policy of agricultural development which through extensive institutional changes such as land reform and participation enhanced the work motivation of peasants, agricultural and home service extension agents, experiment station staffs, and rural school teachers, and so on, to improve productivity. These institutional changes enabled wide-spread participation in decision-making and implementation in various rural organizations such as cooperatives, reducing substantially the power of the large landowners. Fortunately, with educational attainment averaging 7 years of schooling in 1950, (by far the highest in Asia and as high as in the West), and almost complete literacy combined with the decades of experience with the major rudiments of scientific agriculture in the prewar period, the peasantry was able to progress rapidly when the institutional reforms opened up new opportunities. Yields per hectare in rice rose sharply with rising labor productivity during the 1950s; then there was a quick shift to diversified crops, fruits, vegetables, animal husbandry, aquaculture, forestry, which in turn generated off-farm employment during the drier months. Multiple-cropping reached its peak in the latter 1950s, and rice self-sufficiency was reached in the early 1960s. Farm family incomes rose substantially with plenty of work for all members and for all months. With the expansion of the rural domestic market and exports, urban industries began to attract young rural workers with higher wages and migration accelerated. From the latter 1950s, farm mechanization began to spread, replacing the migrants to the cities. For the first time in monsoon padi agriculture, there was the clear beginning of the long-term, absolute decline of the labor force in the agricultural sector, which was undergoing the first modern agricultural revolution in monsoon farming.[25] It is important to note that the rapidity of changes in the Japanese countryside during the late 1940s and 1950s, sustained into the subsequent decades, would not have been possible without the transformation of institutions which raised the quality of rural manpower at all levels and made possible the quick dissemination of new technologies.

This improvement in the quality of human resources able to organize and operate modern mechanical, biological and chemical technologies meant that a smaller quantity of human resources was needed on the Japanese farms. This was one but not the only reason, why birth rates in some areas began to fall sharply.

With full employment attained, growth in the 1960s accelerated with rapid substitution of mechanized and other technologies for labor, in industries, and then in services during the latter 1970s. These were the decades when the capital- and knowledge-intensive industries, particularly the heavy industries were expanded and modernized with the latest technologies from the West. Since these technologies could be easily imported from the West, it was again the human factor that was strategic to the progess of the capital-and knowledge-intensive industries — in the selection, adaptation, dissemination, and efficient operation of the new industrial technologies. For this, entrepreneurship and management had to be improved,

---

[24] In Hong Kong 70 percent and Singapore 50 percent were literate in 1960 compared to 28 percent for India. *UNESCO Statistical Yearbook 1976.*

[25] For data cited above, see my "Significance of Off-Farm Employment and Incomes in Post-war East Asian Growth", Asian Development Bank, Paper No. 21. Slight tendencies for the farm labor force to decline in the prewar 1930s (from 14.5 million in 1930 to 14.2 million in 1940) may be attributable to the growth of the economy which absorbed men from agriculture to the armed forces and military industries.

and the workers motivated to produce diligently. Despite high levels of protection in the capital-intensive industries, domestic competition was sharp, enabling them to grow out of infancy into international competition in the 1970s. A form of industrial democracy was introduced which called for wide-spread participation in decision-making, for long-term and permanent hiring practices, seniority wage-payments and profit-sharing bonuses, extensive in-service training, and so on. Although private enterprises were not permitted to act as freely as in the West, the bureaucracy consulted frequently with them, and decisions were made with participation and mutual consent so that cumbersome regulations were avoided. In all this, the small and medium enterprises were not left out.

As in agriculture, the efficiency of Japanese industry was partly due to the high levels of schooling of its manpower, averaging about 10 years in the early 1950s, and the industrial experience from several pre-war decades.[26] But perhaps more important is the ability of the Japanese industry to grow so quickly and into highly sophisticated industrial sectors without encountering severe skilled-labor shortages was what the ILO terms as its "continuous" in-service training programs, and the day-to-day, intimate working of upper and lower echelons of the workforce on the factory floor. The practice of supervisors, managers, and production workers wearing the same uniforms, eating in the same cafeteria, and other egalitarian ways facilitated communications, contacts, transmissions of know-how and skills, and quick problem-solving which cannot be done well only by the front office. These day to day routines turned out to be good ways of improving manpower at all levels, besides serving to motivate manpower and making the workday less boring. In these and other ways, not least the democratization of other institutions, a vibrant social milieu and a vigorous economic environment were maintained.

In short, considering the direction in which modern industrial technology is moving, from simple and few types (as in 19th century textile factories) to complex and diversified machines and equipment interconnected in serialized groupings (as in the assembly lines in auto assembly), the lesson of Japan's experience may be that manpower cannot be adequately trained by schooling alone.[27] A decade or so of schooling can facilitate the absorption of in service training and on-the-job, day-to-day learning which must be the main source of rapidly changing skills in the workplace during the four long decades of work-life after schooling. And the transmission of the accumulated skills and know-how in the workplace may be most effective in an egalitarian surrounding than in the caste divisions of occupations in Hinduism or in the detailed work specifications of modern labor union contracts.

The ROC (Taiwan's) experience resembled that of Japan, even more so than that of Korea. Full employment was reached about a decade later than in Japan with policies to develop agriculture in the 1950s and 1960s and labor-intensive, import-substitution industrialization in the 1950s and their export-promotion in the 1960s, with Korea trailing behind the ROC (Taiwan) by about half a decade, in part retarded by the Korean War in the early 1950s. The ROC (Taiwan's) agricultural development was like that of Japan, with the multiple-cropping rate reaching nearly two by the latter 1960s, and diversification into fruits and vegetables, substantial portions

---

[26] For the quality and extensiveness of pre-war education in Japan, see Toshio Toyoda, "Role of Education in Japan's Industrialization," *Look Japan*, May 10, 1983. He points out that already in the mid-19th century Japanese educational levels were comparable to those of the advanced countries in the West.

[27] The technologies of the microelectronic revolution are making many old skills obsolete and accelerating the demand for some of the conventional and new skills, with implications for re-training programs.

of which were exported, and whose processing provided off-farm employment to the rural population.[28] Farm family incomes rose faster than the labor force and, with full employment, mechanization began to accelerate in the 1970s. In both Korea and the ROC (Taiwan), there was acceleration of GDP per capita after full employment, as mechanization substituted for labor.

The ability of both countries to take off quickly into postwar growth was aided by their experience in the colonial period. Japan, unlike other colonial powers, had to develop rice production in these countries in order to feed its population for its militarization and industrialization drive. For this, the rudiments of modern agriculture had to be introduced into the colonies, especially to raise rice yields, and the ROC (Taiwan) and Korea started the postwar decades with yields substantially higher than in Southeast Asia.

For the "Japonification" of society and the modernization of the economy, the colonial governments sought to educate a good portion of the population. By the mid-1940s more than one-half of the children of primary school ages were attending public schools, greater than in the colonies of the Dutch, British, and French.[29] The education provided in school was of good quality, better than the Buddhist temple education in the pre-colonial period, or in the Theravada temples of Sri Lanka, Burma, Thailand and Cambodia. The ROC (Taiwan) and Korea started the postwar era with literacy levels higher than those of any other country in Asia (with the exception of Japan) with three-fourths able to read and write. The emphasis in the Japanese schools on Confucian morals and work education was important in contributing to a strong work ethic and a bureaucracy dedicated to national development.

There were two advantages in human resource development that the ROC (Taiwan) and Korea had at the beginning of the postwar decades. Already in the prewar decades, their economies were growing at rates as high as in Japan.[30] Once freed from Japanese domination, both countries were able to develop their economies, beginning with agriculture which attained the highest growth rates found in Asia in the 1950s, 5.5 percent for Korea and 4.8 percent for the ROC (Taiwan). In the 1960s, agricultural output grew by more than 4 percent, second only to Thailand and Malaysia with over 5.5 percent. (Korea's high rate in the late 1950s was partly due to the low level of agricultural production reached in early 1950s due to the Korean War.) Not without a background of experience in the colonial period, their entrepreneurs borrowed technologies and institutions freely from abroad. They were helped by large amounts of financial assistance from the United States, mainly to defray the costs of maintaining large forces against threatening Communist armies. And when import-substitution industrialization saturated domestic markets and began to lose momentum, both countries turned to export-promotion in the 1960s, opening their economies to foreign enterprises, learning from them through joint-ventures, technical tie-ups, and from mass distributors like Sears who taught them to produce for large orders. From the 1950s and 1960s, these economies emerged with a highly productive peasantry and a large shelf of

[28] The multiple-cropping rate is the ratio of harvested area to arable land. See Special Issue on Multiple-Cropping in Asia, *Philippine Economic Journal*, Nos. 1 and 2, 1975.

[29] See Samuel Ho, *Economic Development of Taiwan*, 1860-1970, pp. 99-102, Yale: 1978; N.F. Mc Ginn and Associates, *Education and Development in Korea*, pp. 80-85, Harvard, 1980.

[30] See recent estimates of national product statistics for prewar decades by T. Mizoguchi, *The Economic Growth of Taiwan and Korea*, Tokyo, 1975.

efficient labor-intensive industries largely managed by their own entrepreneurs, ready to move into more capital-and knowledge-intensive industries from the latter 1970s.

As in the case of Japan, with rapidly rising levels of education of the labour force and high levels of school enrollment for the young, Taiwanese and Korean families began to substitute quality for quantity in child rearing, completing the demographic transition in the 1970s with low levels of total fertility. And as in Japan, land reform, agricultural development, and labor-intensive industrialization kept income disparities low in the 1960s, though inequality increased in the latter 1970s for Korea.[31]

Southeast Asian Experience

Southeast Asia has done better in the postwar decades than South Asia partly because of the fuller utilization of its labor force, with lower rates of open unemployment, underemployment, higher female participation rates and educational attainments. As in East Asia, this is related to the greater efforts to develop agriculture in Southeast Asia. Southeast Asian growth rates of agriculture for the entire three decades are about double those of South Asia and, the growth of per worker agricultural product about triple. Of the countries which have accomplished most in Southeast Asia, Malaysia and Thailand have the highest agricultural growth rates. West Malaysia in the first half of the 1980s has approached full employment. The high level of efficiency reached by its plantations (which were not excessively regulated by the government nor nationalized but were left to their own devices), and the development of irrigation and multiple cropping in Muda and elsewhere in Malaysia have been major forces in the full utilization of its labor force. Malaysia's levels of per capita income (and life expectancies) in 1982 were nearly as high as those of Korea. Industrialization was labor-intensive, much of it related in one way or another with foreign enterprises, and left free to develop.

The greatest disappointment is the Philippines which started out strong in the early 1950s with levels of literacy, schooling, and per capita incomes, almost as high as in the ROC (Taiwan) and Korea. But unlike the latter, the Philippines chose to put their available resources not in agriculture but in capital-intensive industrialization, and ended the postwar period with low growth rates, large amounts of unemployed labor, and unequal income distribution. In the early 1980s, growth came to a stop when the authoritarian regime squandered vast amounts of foreign borrowings.[32] Protection has encouraged inefficiencies in many groups of entrepreneurs despite their sophisticated training. High levels of human resource development are no assurance to successes in development. Perhaps the failures of the Philippines may be traceable to the inappropriate institutions accumulated over the long periods of foreign occupation, which bred ways of thinking quite the opposite of Confucianism among the oligarchic elites. When economies are badly led and managed, high levels of human resources may go to waste. The Philippines faces a bleak future, saddled not only with huge foreign debts, but more

---

[31] Data and other details of this section are found in *Economic Development and Cultural Change*, July 1986, paper entitled "The Transition from an Agricultural to an Industrial Economy in East Asia."

[32] For details see "An Analysis of the Philippine Economic Crisis," a report of a group of faculty members of the School of Economics, University of the Philippines, edited by E. De Dios, University of the Philippines Press, Diliman, Quezon City: 1985.

crucially, with institutions that have degenerated from years of avaricious authoritarianism, sapping the vitality of a once lively society. And it remains to be seen how much the new government can accomplish despite its good intentions.

In contrast with the Philippines, Thailand started out in the early 1950s with the smallest amount of modernized manpower among the ASEAN-4, partly because it was never occupied by Western countries, even though the British exerted considerable influence in Bangkok. Its high literacy rate in 1960, like that of Burma and Sri Lanka, was the product of traditional education conducted by the Theravada Buddhist priests in the village temples, but this was confined to the reading of Buddhist scripts. Bangkok in the early 1950s was an ancient Asian city lined with Klongs (canals) and few modern, concrete roads and buildings. Despite the backwardness, its peasantry was much freer and more independent than the Filipino peasantry, and in the postwar decades was able to expand its production rapidly, with much of the rice and diversified produce exported for foreign exchange to modernize the country.[33] On the strength largely of peasant production, Thailand achieved the most rapid growth among the ASEAN-4, and starting with nearly one-half the per capita income of the Philippines, it was able to surpasss the latter in the early 1980s. In no sense a democratic government free of mismanagement and corruption, the Thai leadership did not lose sight of national goals unlike the authoritarian regime in the Philippines.

Indonesia started late. Exports of natural resources, mainly oil, gas, timber, which financed a fairly successful agricultural development program contributed to its good performance in the 1970s. As a legacy of Dutch negligence, Indonesia started out the postwar decades with four-fifths of its population illiterate as in India, so that despite valiant efforts, its labor force in 1980 attained educational level averaging only 3.7 years. Dutch efforts to preserve traditional ways of living, despite good intentions, have left the Indonesian entrepreneur with old ways of thinking which look down upon competitive enterprising as a sign of greediness. But without rivalry the skills of entrepreneurship are slow to evolve, and without vigorous enterpreneuring, the labor force is also slow to develop. And like other military authoritarianism, the closed nature of its governance does not permit a full view of its doings, some of which may turn out to be distressing, as in the case of the Philippines.

South Asian and Chinese Experience

Sri Lanka was exceptional among Asian countries (indeed among all LDC) in that it put more faith in human investment than in material investment — in free education all the way to the university, free health services, subsidized food, housing, and transport, and other welfare, for all its people. It achieved the highest literacy rates, (which were the highest to begin with in 1950), longest life expectancy rates, lowest income inequality, and lowest total fertility rates in South and Southeast Asia, excepting Singapore. But its growth rates of GDP per capita were lower than those of the Philippines and Sri Lanka's per capita income levels were in 1980 less than one-half those of the Philippines, with larger amounts of unemployed

---

[33] An illustration would be the Philippines which started the postwar decades with the largest sugar industry in Asia whose sugar production was overtaken by Thai production. Perhaps the sugar entrepreneurs of the Philippines were spoiled by the easy access to the U.S. market through assured quotas. They lost the vitality which their ancestors possessed in the latter 19th century and early 20th century.

labor, particularly among the educated. Sri Lanka was spending on welfare as though it was a developed country rich with material capital, hoping to grow up through human resource development under socialistic slogans. Its experience points to the need for balance in the allocation of resources for human and material development, a balance which must change with the stages of development. Much of the investment in developing human resource may go to waste if the appropriate material resources do not exist for human beings to work on and with. Rather than providing "handouts" governments must concern themselves with putting human resources to work to produce and earn scarce food, housing, and transport.

China's welfare program also tried to provide a minimum level of welfare within a socialist context (with a much stronger emphasis on socialism than in Sri Lanka). Besides free education and subsidized food, pensions and so on, China's experience was unique even for Asia in that it had an extreme egalitarian manpower policy symbolized in the "iron rice bowl" to motivate manpower to work hard and diligently. The experiences of welfarist Sri Lanka and socialist China show that the culture of work cannot be developed to high levels of vitality if it is spoiled with too many handouts, entitlements, and guarantees. The lesson to be learned is that human resources, unlike other resources, require some degree of self-reliance, independence, rivalry, and risk-taking to meet the challenges of raising productivity in the workplaces, homes, schools, and markets.

The giants of Asia, however, began with vast investments in material resources, even though in 1950 education levels of the labor force were low. In the 1951 Indian census, 83 percent were found to be without education (compared with Sri Lanka's 40 percent). There is no comparable information for China, but in 1950 the number of students enrolled in primary and secondary schools as a percent of total population was as low as in India. Since the size of the educational system depends on the existing stock of educated manpower, this may be taken to be indicative of the low level of educational attainment in China.

India and China gamble by concentrating their resources in heavy industries in the 1950s, following Soviet growth strategy. China's efforts were more concentrated in the military-related industries than in India, which attempted to establish a wider range of basic and heavy industries. Since the heavy industry required large and varied amounts of top level manpower with experience for R and D work, this strategy soon bogged down. There was insufficient top manpower to operate efficiently complexes (i.e., groups of industries)such as iron and steel, other metal complexes, petrochemicals, heavy machinery, and so on, and to keep up with the R and D of industrialized countries. These industries soon became obsolete despite heavy spending for rehabilitation. The slow growth of the overall economy was due to the "cascading" effect of poor quality and high cost equipment and industrial materials from the heavy industries to downstream light industries, and due to insufficient resources left over for agriculture after paying for the costs of establishing and maintaining the heavy industries. The mass markets for the heavy industries were slow to emerge, and were spread thinly over their vast countries, which in turn called for massive development of transport and other infrastructure nation-wide to service the heavy industries, reducing investments in irrigation and rural roads for the modernization of agriculture.

The need for higher level heavy industrial manpower may be related to India's concentration of funds for education on the upper levels. In 1981, 8 percent of the population, 20-24 years old, were enrolled in higher education, compared to 3 percent for Sri Lanka, Indonesia, Pakistan, and 1 percent for China leaving a large pool of educated unemployed, and with too little education in the lower levels of manpower needed to modernize the rural areas and improve the lot of the vast millions living in dire poverty and abject ignorance.

Caste is a special factor in Indian human resource development (and also in Nepal and Sri Lanka). The partitioning of the workforce into a large number of occupational groupings reduces substantially the easy flow of communication, contacts, information, and the transmission of skills in the workplace and society. This creates difficulties in management not only in modern enterprises but also on the farms and in craft shops where the extension agents may find obstacles to communication and instruction, retarding the day-to-day, on-the-job training and learning process, particularly for the "untouchables". And, in general, the caste differentiations, which multiply cultural and social differences by a larger factor than in non caste societies, make way for additional sources of suspicions, misunderstandings, and conflicts, instead of promoting the cooperative, participatory, and egalitarian institutions needed for the operation of modern technology with its inter-connected and integrative tendencies within each factory or plant. This may be the reason for the proliferation of managements schools in India (but of more limited demand in Japan despite the sophisticated levels of organization).

Thus, the capital-intensive strategy has left India not only with the slow growth of material resources but also of human resources. There will be much to do in the future, all of which could have been done in the earlier decades — to raise educational attainments, food consumption beyond the meager 2,000 calorie intake, life expectancy levels and female participation rate and, at the same time, reduce unemployment and underemployment, total fertility, and population growth. China's growth performance was no better but its successes in improving human resources were greater. (See Table 2.) Hence, once the constraints of socialist institutions such as rigid planning, the "iron rice bowl" and so on were lessened, it was able to quickly speed up growth.

Nepal and Bangladesh have problems similar to those of India, but compounded by the more severe scarcity of natural resources. Bangladesh's density as measured by the agricultural population per hectare of agricultural land is nearly three times that of India. It is not as bad in Nepal but its hilly lands are much less fertile. (See Table 1.) Their problems, like those of India, are the large pool of unemployed and underemployed labor, especially in the dry months, the low level of educational attainment of the workforce, and poor health. The share of arable land under irrigation, off-farm incomes and the fertility of rice lands are the lowest among countries in Asia while total fertility (birth) rates are the highest. Under these circumstances food becomes the next urgent problem. Household income and expenditure surveys for India, Nepal and Bangladesh show that the share of food expenditures in family incomes (Engel coefficient) begin to fall only from the middle deciles unlike other Asian countries where they fall from the lowest decile. The rising portion of the Engel curve may be interpreted to mean that families in the lower deciles are not eating enough so that when their incomes rise, more income must be spent for food, not less.[34]

---

[34] Data underlying the paragraph are from the *FAO Production Yearbook,* and income surveys of various countries.

The low levels of literacy and educational attainments of the labor force in India, Nepal and Bangladesh may be traced to Hinduism in India and Nepal, and Islam in Bangladesh. Unlike Buddhism in Sri Lanka, Burma, Thailand, and in East Asia, only members of highest caste, mainly Brahmans, were educated under Hinduism and Islam taught the young to memorize rather than to read the Koran.[35] To make up for these unfavorable historical legacies a major effect to raise primary and secondary enrollment was made in the postwar decades but the accumulation of educational stock is a slow, generational process.

The total fertility rates in Nepal and Bangladesh of over 6, highest in Asia, may be linked to the low levels of educational attainment of the labor force, averaging only one year of schooling in both countries in the late 1970s, and low levels of school enrollment in the past. With the quality of the population increasing slowly, farm families must continue to keep the quantity of children large as it is the only means to raise family incomes under conditions of declining quantity of agricultural land per family. In Nepal, fertility rates in the 1970s do not appear to be falling.[36] In either case, hand labor must be substituted for insufficient or inadequate land, more hands are needed because of the short work-life span of the labor force (with life expectancies lowest in Asia), and food consumption is insufficient for vigorous, prolonged work. These two countries with the lowest per capita incomes appear to be caught in a cruel dilemma: manpower must be increased to make up or substitute for extemely scarce material resources and short life but the greater the manpower the lower the per capita resources, and hence per capita income; with low incomes it is difficult to invest sufficiently to improve the quality of human and material resources.

Natural resources are by no means as scarce in Burma as in South Asian countries. Indeed it is blessed with land as plentiful as in Malaysia and the monsoons bring more water. The Theravada priests left a valuable legacy of education which enabled Burma to start the postwar era with a literacy rate higher than in Malaysia. Geographically it belongs to Southeast Asia but its postwar progress is more like that of South Asia. Unlike Southeast Asia, it isolated itself from the world, closed its society, and moved into a socialized economy with a military autocracy unable to work out ways of developing the economy. In the meantime, Thailand replaced Burma as the major rice basket of Asia, despite poorer soils and insufficient rain.

To conclude, this quick review of postwar experience shows that there is a variety of interactions between material and human welfare, varying from stage to stage under different patterns of strategies. Human resource development is a necessary but by no means a sufficient condition for an economic development as the experience of Sri Lanka and the Philippines shows. The strategy selected at the beginning of growth is crucial in the optimal and balanced use of resources. The strategy most appropriate to resource endowments appears to have been selected by the NICs, Thailand and Malaysia. The question arises: how was it that some countries did better than others in the selection of strategies? This is not an easy question and not enough economic history research has been done to get definitive answers. Off-hand, it looks as though the colonial policies of the past had much

---

[35] See T. Toyoda, "Difficulties in Educational Development in Asia", a draft paper, Institute of Developing Economics, Tokyo, 1984.

[36] See mimeographed studies of the Central Bureau of Statistics "Population Division from the 1971 and 1981 Population Censuses." Fertility is said to be rising, although part of the increase is attributed to improved data reporting in 1981 over 1971.

to do in contributing to the strategy perceptions of the indigenous elites and the peasantry right after independence. The harsh treatment of the elites and peasantry in South Asia by the colonial powers contributed to socialist tendencies. The elites avenged the former rulers and their cronies by the nationalization of their properties, and distributing the rice lands to the peasantry. The harsher the treatment, the more complete the nationalization and asset redistribution, as seen in Burma, Sri Lanka, and Vietnam. In the Philippines, the Spanish rulers with little interest in agriculture permitted the rise of an indigenous elite who exploited the peasantry and continued to strengthen its power under U.S. occupation and in the postwar decades. Treated better in Thailand, Malaysia, Indonesia, Korea, and the ROC (Taiwan), both the elites and the peasantry responded in ways more conducive to the development of productivity.[37] Of course, the long traditions prior to colonial occupation also influenced the direction that post-independence policies took, e.g., caste in India, Islam in Bangladesh, Theravada Buddhism in Sri Lanka and Burma, and Confucianism in East Asia.

The review also tends to cast doubt on the accuracy of estimates of rates of returns to education in growth accounting and output elasticities with respect to education in regressions. These returns and outputs are far more than the function of the quantified variables found in the accounting and regression models. More difficult to quantify are the effects of patterns of child rearing in the home, of curricula, skills and diligence of teachers, and motivation of students in the schools, kinds of training and experience in the workshop, mass media programs, and the sum total of the social milieu and economic environment. No technique we know of can capture the influence of these in productivity growth, compelling us to resort to qualitative and historical assessments. With the insights from history and clues from measurable returns and output, we now move to our final objective, namely, the assessment of the future and the identification of emerging problems whose solutions or amelioration must be provided for, if productivity is to propel the growth of per capita incomes to heights permitting better living in the years to come. And the speculative nature of the insights and clues calls for further research in the years ahead, so that some of the research issues should be specified.

FUTURE PROSPECTS, PROBLEMS AND POLICY PERSPECTIVES

A broad consensus is emerging that the postwar era has come to an end and a new one has begun — one whose global prospects are not likely to be as favorable as in the past. The high growth decades of the past have been part of the upswing of a long wave in the industrialized countries, fueled by the pent-up demand from the depressed 1930s and militarized 1940s when consumer demand for durables and housing, business, and public demand for capital goods were exceptionally low. The pent-up demand had not only been met in the recent decades but production capacities appear to have over-shot the aggregate purchasing power indigenous to the normal secular growth and productive levels.[38] The present downswing in the OECD countries has been accompanied by a changeover in basic technologies to

---

[37] For details of these generalizations, see my forthcoming volume.

[38] Details are in my "Perspectives on the Prospects for Southeast Asia Growth in the 1980s," *Journal of Philippine Development,* Second Semester, 1980, NEDA; this paper summarizes the arguments of M. Abramovitz in his lectures on the industrialized countries at the School of Economics in 1977.

electronic-guided technologies, prolonging the downswing with large pools of unemployment. And it is difficult to see at this stage how soon the adjustments will be completed so that the industrialized countries can resume once again high and stable growth. If so, we need to begin discussing the implications of the global slowdown for the Asian countries.[39]

I have noted elsewhere that the high growth of East and Southeast Asia was in large part the direct and indirect product of the high growth of the industrialized countries in the 1950s and 1960s. With the Western slowdown in the 1970s, Asian growth should have come down to levels more consonant with the slower pace of the global economy, perhaps to one-half the levels in the OECD countries. That the growth of the NICs and ASEAN did not fall, was mainly due to the substantial inflow of foreign borrowing of petrol-dollars. These were invested in an enormous construction boom in the 1970s through 1982. (Contributing to Japan's slowdown in the 1970s was the slowdown in construction expenditures.) In 1983 and 1984, the cyclical expansion of the U.S. economy sustained the high growth of NIC/ASEAN exports. But when the export boom subsided in 1985, large foreign debt servicing burdened the budgets of most of the NICs and ASEAN countries, rendering impossible the resumption of the construction boom or other forms of pump-priming to sustain high growth levels. Since foreign debts will take some years to liquidate, and the OECD countries do not appear to be returning to high levels of growth and importation, high growth is likely to be difficult to achieve in the NIC and ASEAN region.[40]

With these presumptions on the exogenous forces shaping the growth of GDP in Asia in the coming years, it is difficult to be up-beat about the role of manpower in future productive power. We shall see in the next section that this is not only because of the tight budget situation left by the excessive foreign borrowing. The approach will be topical, starting with population trends, going on to more qualitative dimensions of human resources, and concluding with the larger, over-all policy concerns.

Projections of Popular Trends

Population trends projected into the coming decades are firmer than other dimensions. In Table 4 are the most widely used projections, based on the work of the UN Population Division. With the completion of the demographic transition, rapid population growth is of little concern for East Asia, except possibly for China. In fact, one detects in the public statements the emergence of pro-natal views in the fully employed countries as they are worried about labor shortages with slow labor force growth.[41] But this tendency may change in the light of the appearance of unemployment in 1985, even in Singapore and Malaysia, and the realization that the decades of high growth have come to an end. If the NICs were to slowdown to

---

[39] The projections to the year 2000 made for Japan's long range plans assume the growth of GDP to be 4 percent for Japan and 2 percent for other OECD countries, far less than the 9 percent and 5 percent for the decade of the 1960s. See *Japan in the Year 2000,* op. cit.

[40] Details are found in my "Construction Boom in the 1970's: The end of High Growth in the NIC's & ASEAN?" *Developing Economies,* October 1986.

[41] See *Japan in the Year 2000, op. cit.,* where the hope is expressed that birth rates pick up in the 1990s. The Prime Minister of Singapore is concerned with the low birth rates of the educated women, and the Prime Minister of Malaysia has come out flatly for a pro-natal program.

Table 4. Average Years of School Completed of Employed Persons in Occupation

Occupation	Japan		ROC (Taiwan)		Korea		Hong Kong		Singapore*	
	1960	1979	1970	1980	1970	1980	1971	1981	1970	1980
Professional	13.5	14.3	12.4	13.4	13.7	14.5	13.9	13.6	9.8	10.9
Administrative	12.3	13.0	10.4	11.3	12.6	13.9	8.6	12.5	9.3	10.5
Clerical workers	12.0	12.6	10.9	11.9	12.7	12.7		11.2	7.2	7.6
Sales workers	10.0	11.9	6.4	8.4	8.3	9.6	8.8	7.7	6.2	4.6
Service workers	9.6	10.4	8.2	7.4	7.9	9.1	5.5	6.4	6.1	3.9
Agricultural workers	8.5	9.8	4.3	5.5	4.4	5.3	2.4	3.7	6.0	2.9
Production workers	9.2	10.6	6.1	7.7	8.2	9.6	6.0	7.1	6.1	4.5
Others	9.4	10.7	3.5	10.9	11.9	10.9	6.6	8.7	7.5	7.8
Total	9.7	11.5	6.5	8.5	6.8	8.5	6.8	8.0	6.7	6.0

Sources: Respective national census of population and labor force survey.

*The fall in 1980 in this and the next table for Singapore is puzzling and we need to look into this in the future.

Table 4 (Continued)

Occupation	West Malaysia		Thailand		Philippines		Indonesia	
	1967-1968	1980	1971	1981	1970	1980	1971	1980
Professional	10.4	11.3	6.6	5.1	13.3	16.2	9.3	10.7
Administrative	8.2	11.0	8.8	8.6	9.3	14.1	8.3	10.5
Clerical workers	9.3	10.4	10.5	9.6	11.9	13.3	7.4	9.3
Sales workers	5.4	6.7	5.2	6.0	6.6	8.5	3.1	3.7
Service workers	5.0	6.9	7.0	7.0	5.9	7.0	2.7	3.8
Agricultural workers	3.8	4.2	5.1	5.4	3.9	4.8	2.2	2.7
Production workers	5.4	6.7	5.6	6.0	6.0	7.7	3.5	4.2
Others	5.9	6.9	6.1	5.6	7.6	8.7	3.7	8.3
Total	5.0	6.6	5.3	5.8	5.6	7.1	2.9	3.7

Sources: Respective national census of population and labor force survey.

GDP growth rates of about 4 percent, instead of 8 percent, the spread of electronic technologies will require a smaller but better trained manpower than a larger, less trained one. Countries with too much surplus labor are already hesitating to introduce computerized machinery because of the adverse impact on employment.

As for Southeast and South Asia, 2 percent population growth and fertility levels for the rest of the century are too high. (Table 2) With labor force projected to grow at 2.4 percent per year, full employment may be difficult to reach if GDP growth is to be only 4 percent. This rate implies a growth of GDP per capita less than the growth of the labor force, or 1.5 percent.

For South Asia there are more compelling reasons to quickly bring down the high fertility. Average per capita available supply of calories of 2000 or so is too low for health or for vigorous work as it signifies per capita supply lower by 10 percent or more for most peasants and laborers in the lower income groups and a lower actual intake figure of another 10 percent or so. In the Philippines, the intake figure from consumption surveys is 30 percent lower than the available supply estimated from production data and food balance sheets. The slow rise in the index of food production per capita in India and declines in Nepal and Bangladesh are indicative of the inability to produce food as fast as the production of human beings, entailing the use of valuable foreign exchange earnings for food imports that predominantly agricultural economies should be exporting.

There is an urgent need for present policies to focus on the reduction of mortality, the increase in health and educational facilities and raise life expectancies and work-life span. Otherwise the prerequisites of bringing down fertility substantially among the peasants and workers are not established. These classes need the extra hands from high birth rates in order to cope with early deaths. Policies to forcibly reduce births are not the answer. Besides more spending on human resource development, more should be spent on agricultural development, especially to assist the small peasants to improve their food consumption, and to provide more employment during the slack months for both the small peasants and landless workers. This calls for diversifying agricultural production and agro-industrialization, but this means that more must be spent on irrigation, rural roads, rural electrification, and schools. After three decades, if the public enterprises are not self-sustaining and self-reliant, they may never be. And so they should be speedily sold to private enterprises to reduce the drain on the national budget.

It has been observed that the decline in fertility has slowed down in several countries and saturation in the use of contraception has been approached. It may be that the easy period of initial declines is over, and to keep up the pace of the decline, lower income groups among the peasant and working classes must be reached. But this will be more difficult, as modernization has not affected these groups in most of South Asia and parts of Southeast Asia.[42]

Female Participation Rates

Female participation rates are exceptionally low in South Asia except in Nepal. Part of the reason is traditional and cultural, particularly in Bangladesh where Moslem women are not encouraged to be seen working in the fields. But they do

---

[42] I have pursued this thesis in *Population and Development Review,* op. cit. The Philippine Population Institute has reported that the crude birth rate was unchanged in 1983, and the use of contraceptive devices has dropped.

spend much time hard-threshing rice in homes and away from the fields. More research may be needed. The low participation may also be due to still backward technology for rice and other types of farming. The use of modern, labor-intensive farming methods like those used in East Asia during the early 1950s, may yield output greater than the added labor absorbed. But greater labor-intensity will mean costly fertilizer and water inputs. Also South Asia uses more children in the field in place of wives as the young are not sent to schools as in East and Southeast Asia. Women are needed for old ways of time—consuming work in the house, especially in cloth and garment making. Handlooms and spindles have been replaced in East and Southeast Asia with machines in the factories. But factory production will require rural electrification and roads which cannot be constructed if the big industries annually require rehabilitation, and more and more power, roads, and railways.

Employment Creation and Labor Absorption

Employment creation and labor absorption also are no longer an issue in East Asian countries, except in China. The large increase of population from the north in Korea and from China in the ROC (Taiwan) immediately after the war was put to work as the economy grew faster than the labor force in the latter 1950s and throughout the 1960s and into the 1970s. This is not the case elsewhere, except in West Malaysia which became fully employed in the first half of the 1980s. The unemployment figures of most countries are difficult to make out. They do not at first glance appear alarming, although this is not the view of the labor economists in these countries. The fact of the matter is that the full extent of unemployment (in the sense of idleness throughout the year) is difficult to measure because of the pronounced seasonality of the monsoons, the nature of paddy technology and associated activities, infrequencies of labor force surveys, difficulties of defining the labor force and the fuzzy nature of unemployment in the rural areas where subsistence farming prevails.[43] Under subsistence production, there is at one time or another something one can do around the farm or nearby in the communal lands to scratch out bits here and there for one's own consumption, unlike in specialized, commercialized agriculture.

When underemployment at different times of the year is put together in monsoon Asia, not only in the dry months but also between the peak periods after the crops are planted and before the harvesting, estimates of idleness range from 20 to 30 percent in South Asia and 10 to 20 percent in Southeast Asia. All this is consistent with per capita, per day caloric intake below levels of 2,000. When East Asian countries attained full employment, these levels rose beyond 2,200. It is also in the countries with much idleness that the exodus of their skilled workers to foreign countries is large — the Philippines, Sri Lanka, India, Bangladesh and Nepal. The question arises whether the drain of skilled workers abroad will slow down productivity growth more than the contribution of the foreign exchange earned. This will depend on the use of the foreign earnings that often seem to cover imports of

---

[43] For a discussion of these issues, see Labor Absorption in East and Southeast Asia, special issue of *Philippine Economic Journal*, Nos. 1 and 2, 1976, which also contains the data and information on underemployment for Southeast Asian countries. Also Special Issue on internal migration, ibid., Nos.1 and 2, 1977, edited by E. Pernia, and Special Issue on education, ibid., No. 3, 1979, edited by E. Tan. All three issues are papers from the Council for Asian Manpower Studies' conferences.

luxuries. The high level of idleness is basically structural, the product of seasonality and the uneven pattern of labor demand in monsoon paddy agriculture, and certain to continue into the future, unless infrastructure and institutions are put in place to overcome the basis of idleness. Full employment in the rural sector was achieved in Japan in the 1950s and the ROC (Taiwan) in the 1960s only after sufficient irrigation, roads and other infrastructure were built. With rice self-sufficiency, there was a shift to diversified agriculture in the drier months which in turn increased off-farm employment in the agro-industries to process the harvested crops. [44]

In sum, macro productivity can be increased substantially in South Asian countries (and to a lesser but significant extent in Southeast Asia) with fuller utilization of the existing work force — through more work for the adults, higher female participation, greater vigor in work, and longer work-life span. The extensive use of child labor in countries like India should be discouraged, and their substitution by adult labor should release children for schooling, thereby lowering fertility by raising the opportunity cost of female time, and the cost of raising children, and improving the quality of the future workforce. A major reason for the slow growth of South Asian economies in the past decades may be the absence of policies to use human resources sufficiently.[45] In the next section, we turn from the quantitative to the qualitative aspects of human resources.

Role of Education

Education has not been neglected in East Asia where Confucian teachings have extolled it not only as a source of skills but also of enlightenment. East Asian countries, and Malaysia and Thailand (where the competitive pressures from the East Asian population are strong) have consistently spent about one-fifth of their budgets for education in the 1970s but elsewhere the levels are closer to one-tenth.[46] As a result of past enrollment, years of schooling attained by the labor force may be too low for Indonesia and South Asia to move speedily into higher levels of industrialization and into the modernization of agriculture. The farmers in the ROC (Taiwan), Korea, and Thailand in 1970 averaged 4 years of schooling compared to Indonesian farmers with less than 3 years in 1980. (See Table 4) Even though science-based machines used in modern agriculture are far less than in industry, some familarity with biology, botany, chemistry, etc., is necessary to make the proper use of science-based high yielding varieties and the chemical fertilizers and insecticides required, together with the good use of water. Reading ability beyond levels taught in primary schooling is valuable in decision-making in management and marketing.[47] For production workers in industry, attainments are lower for

---

[44] For data and details, beside ibid., see my "Seasonality and Underemployment in Monsoon Asia," *Philippine Economic Journal*, lst Semester 1971, and "Food Consumption and Economic Development," Economic Development and Cultural Change, Oct. 1967. Also "Multiple-Cropping in Asian Development," special issue of the *Philippine Economic Journal*, Nos. 1 and 2, 1975.

[45] In the Economic Development and Cultural Change paper on food consumption, the contention is made that in a fully employed economy, there is a significant economy in the use of food supplies. If per capita consumption of food is at a level associated with per capita calorie consumption of 2,000, about 1,000 is consumed for the basic metabolic requirements, (i.e., the amount needed for biologic functioning when the body is at complete rest); but roughly the same amount is needed even when the workforce is fully employed and the calorie intake rises to 2,300. Now, 1,300 calories go into the energy for work.

[46] *UNESCO Statistical Yearbook 1984.*

[47] See M. Lockheed, D.T. Jamison, and L.J. Lau, "Farm Education and Farm Efficiency," *Economic Development and Cultural Change*, October 1980. For India, census figures for agriculture in 1971 show average years of schooling to be 1.3 for cultivators and only 0.5 for agricultural laborers.

Indonesia than for other countries in Southeast Asia. For countries in South Asia, except Sri Lanka, the data are not available but must be even lower than for Indonesia, considering the lower average attainments in Table 2.

The exception is the Philippines with high levels of enrollment and attainment but low levels of government support for education. This means that the quality of education suffers. Pre-college education is 10 years compared to the usual 12 years, and teachers are poorly paid and motivated, and teaching materials and equipment obsolete and insufficient. It may be that fewer years of schooling but higher quality may be just as good while enabling parents to keep teenagers at workplace longer before they marry and establish new households. But after decades of rapid expansion, more attention on the quality of education may be needed in other countries as well, even though quality has not been deteriorating as rapidly as in the Philippines.[48]

Insufficient spending for schooling by the State contributes not only to poor quality but also to the maldistribution of educational opportunities which in turn will have an adverse impact on income distribution. It is the children of the lowest income groups who will be mainly deprived. If only about one-half or less of the age groups from 6 to 12 can be enrolled as was the case in South Asia (except Sri Lanka) in 1960, the earning power of those without education in the later years will be less than the others. This reinforces the maldistribution of finance going to large and small farms and firms in the capital-intensive strategies pursued in several of the South Asian and, to a lesser extent, the Southeast Asian countries. The dual maldistribution accompanied by the slow growth of GDP in turn translate into excess capacities in capital-intensive enterprises and the unemployment of educated manpower which comprise costly social waste. Since human and material capital formation are invested for long periods, the situation is likely to carry over into the rest of this decade, although a comprehensive restructuring and new strategies may shorten the period of over-capacities.

The process of accumulating educational stock is a slow one, on the average one year or less per decade for each occupation or industry. Plans for changes in the future must start early since the demand patterns for types of education needed by the labor force vary for different stages in the transition from an agricultural to an industrial economy. Tables 4 and 5 tend to show that in the early stages, the big demand is for education for white-collar workers, particularly for professional and administrative staff needed for the public services, with the exception of Thailand which probably met the needs in the 1950s and 1960s. Then toward the latter stage of the transition, the demand for education for blue-collar workers increasingly comes to the fore relative to white-collar education, as industry and agriculture become modernized with more sophisticated technologies, and this probably continues into the industrial stage. After that the predominantly service economy may once again push white-collar education to the fore. The nature of the skills between and within white and blue-collar occupations will vary because the industrial structure will be different.

ASEAN countries which aspire to complete the transition to an industrial economy will have to shift their emphasis from education for white to blue collar

---

[48] J. S. Furnival shows that the Philippines was far ahead of other countries in Southeast and South Asia in the prewar decades, with the budget allocating 20 percent to education in 1938, *Educational Progress in Southeast Asia,* p. 112, NY, 1943. American commitment to education in the Philippines was just as strong as the Japanese in the ROC (Taiwan) and Korea, although the quality may not have been as good.

Table 5. Average Years of School Completed of Employed Persons in Industry

Industry	Japan		ROC (Taiwan)		Korea		Hong Kong		Singapore	
	1960	1979	1979	1980	1970	1980	1971	1981	1970	1980
Agriculture	8.5	9.9	4.4	5.6	4.4	5.3	2.6	3.5	6.1	3.3
Mining	9.4	9.7	4.9	6.2	7.4	8.4	5.8	7.6	7.2	4.6
Construction	9.3	10.5	5.9	8.7	8.1	9.3	6.9	7.3	6.2	4.4
Manufacturing	9.9	10.8	7.1	11.3	8.9	10.3	6.3	7.5	6.4	5.7
Trade	10.0	21.6	6.4	7.5	8.4	9.7	8.0	7.8	6.4	5.2
Finance	12.2	11.6	11.2	8.7	12.1	12.2		11.6	7.8	8.1
Transport	10.4	12.8	7.6	9.2	10.3	10.9	7.0	8.2	6.4	5.7
Utilities	11.1	11.4	10.2	12.3	11.6	12.3	8.4	9.6	6.8	6.4
Personal services	11.1	12.1	9.3	10.6	10.4	11.9	7.9	9.2	7.3	
Public services	11.7	12.5								
Others			7.7				7.3	7.8	6.0	7.2
Total	9.7	11.5	6.5	8.5	6.8	8.5	6.8	8.0	6.7	6.0

Sources: Respective national census of population and labour force survey.

Table 5 (Continued)

Industry	West Malaysia		Thailand		Philippines		Indonesia	
	1967-1968	1980	1971	1981	1961	1965	1971	1980
Agriculture	3.5	4.4	5.1	5.4	3.7	3.8	2.2	2.7
Mining	5.3	5.8	5.3	5.8	3.4	5.7	5.8	4.4
Construction	5.6	6.4	6.0	6.1	5.7	5.7	4.0	4.4
Manufacturing	5.5	7.4	5.7	6.1	5.4	5.5	3.0	3.9
Trade	6.0	6.9	5.7	6.4	5.9	6.1	3.2	3.7
Finance		10.4					9.1	8.7
Transport	6.2	6.9	6.8	7.0	6.3	6.9	4.6	5.3
Utilities	6.6	8.5	9.9	8.5	7.2	6.6	7.2	8.0
Personal services	7.0	8.9	6.7	6.3	5.4	6.0	5.9	
Public services					10.0	10.4		6.6
Others	6.1	7.5	6.2	5.2	5.1	6.0	3.7	5.9
Total	5.0	6.6	5.3	5.8	4.6	5.0	2.9	3.7

Sources: Respective national census of population and labor force survey.

occupations while the South Asian countries cannot neglect blue collar education for agriculture.

I have elsewhere raised the issue whether public schools in South and Southeast Asia have been influenced unduly by Western systems — in the emphasis on higher education, in the short duration children are kept in school during the year, and above all in the curriculum.[49] The situation in the West is quite different with a large middle class clamoring for higher education, short hours to accommodate manifold activities outside the schools, the teaching of morals and work education left out for the churches to undertake, and the lesser need for vocational and technical education under conditions of slower growth, large number of private commercial and technical schools, and large pools from the long past of high level experienced and skilled workmen on the plant floor. Japan from the early decades of this century with the acceleration of modern industrialization found the need to expand rapidly technical-vocational education to meet the demand for the new and diverse skills to operate the new technologies. From the beginning, Japanese education has been strong on technical education.[50]

Thus, newly independent countries trying speedily to modernize are compelled in education, as well as in other endeavors, to accomplish more than in the Western countries. Besides skill formation, education has to lay the ground work to modernize social values, develop national unity, consensus and familiarity with new institutions and new ways of living and working, with students who come from traditional homes. Schools must have longer time in the year than in the West, and teachers must be paid adequately to do the job. Part of the job must be shared with the mass media, especially radio, and in the workplace, as noted below.

Learning and Training in the Workplace

Learning and training in the workplace can be the major source of skill formation and work education for the young workers getting into the workforce, as the experience of Japan shows. This requires a system of industrial and labor-management relations different from the West, whose practices originated in the simpler technologies of the 19th century when skill requirements were fewer and simpler. The apprentice system of traditional societies is too slow to suit the requirements of rapid skill formation for modern productivity growth. The workplace can be the best source if a system can be devised which can motivate the more skilled workers to transmit their experience to the less skilled. But this requires management to aim to maximize long-run profits, rather than quick profits, and incorporate industrial relations which motivate workers to learn and share, and involve them in problem-solving on the plant floor. Top-down, autocratic methods from the West are less conducive than more participatory ones in establishing the proper atmosphere for optimal learning experience. Management must also be prepared to invest in on-and-off-the job training to develop new skills and for retraining. The practices must not ignore strongly held cultural values if they are to succeed. And just as the West today is experimenting with new methods, so do Asian countries need to

---

[49] The U.S. system in the Philippines, the Dutch in Indonesia, the French in Indo-China, and the British elsewhere.

[50] See T. Toyoda in a series of articles in *Look Japan* on "The Role of Education in Japan's Development," May 10, 1983.

try out new approaches suited to their own endowments and historical legacies. Needless to say, these complex institutions cannot be devised by management alone in the front offices or by academics in their ivory tower but must emerge from the workplace with inputs from all relevant parties. Since the systems cannot be the same for large and small firms, attention must be paid for practices suitable for the latter which are responsible for the bulk of the output in most Asian countries.

Contribution of Mass Media

The contribution of mass media can be substantial, if they are not viewed solely as sources of entertainment and leisure. Particularly after schooling, mass media can be the major sources of life-long learning, promoting skill formation, extending and enriching the knowledge acquired in schools in the social and physical sciences, history, humanities and about the larger world, and contributing to social and political consensus. For the media to attract audiences to its educational programs, the schools, and the homes must prepare the young to cherish the pursuit of life-long education not only for skill development to improve "the life of business" but even more for "the business of life" through enlightenment. If the educational function of mass media can be integrated with schooling, skill formation can be shared with the schools, and modifications of social values can be promoted in the homes, then the burdens of schooling can be lightened through a carefully coordinated integration of the major sources of human resource development. Although few countries in Asia are thinking about or working toward such ambitious goals, the exigencies of the future may call for such steps to be taken.

Distribution of Family Incomes

For the distribution of family incomes in nearly all countries of Asia for which we have information has shown no improvement in the late 1970s, and in some countries there has been deterioration.[51] If so, the increases in unemployment and consumer prices in the first half of the 1980s, may worsen the position of the lower income groups even more, and the slowdown in GDP growth in the rest of the 1980s may hold no prospects for improvements. Even if the shares of the lower income groups in the totality of family incomes remain constant, the slow over-all growth of incomes will mean slower absolute growth of lower incomes than experienced in the 1960s and 1970s. The fall in the size of families may be slower than the rise in the size of absolute family incomes, so that the size of poverty groups may not diminish.

East Asia has made good progress toward the elimination of poverty, particularly after full employment when more earners in the lower income families found good jobs. Southeast Asia has made slower progress, except in the Philippines in the 1980s, where idleness has reached alarming levels and steep price rises have forced many families to subsist on 1 or 2 meals daily, — and all these following the

---

[51] Recent data, available in the 1970s for the Philippines, Korea, Thailand, Malaysia and Sri Lanka, show lower shares for the lowest deciles, and higher shares for the highest groups. Data are based on a volume on postwar trends in Asian income distribution, presently under preparation. The generality of this outcome about the late 1970s in Asia is difficult to make out, and it may be linked to the peculiar nature of the pattern of development noted previously. But it remains to be studied in the future with the availability of detailed data.

late 1970s which saw no increase in the average calorie/protein intake per capita as reported in the national nutrition surveys, 1978 and 1982. It is difficult to see how poverty can be alleviated in South Asia with so much idleness and a fast growing population. Even for the welfare state of Sri Lanka disparities have been rising.

Problems of Developing Entrepreneurs

The problem of developing entrepreneurs has been the concern of Malaysia and Indonesia in Southeast Asia and perhaps in other places where the supply of entrepreneurs is extremely scarce. Policies to develop them in schools may not be too successful. I know of no schools for entrepreneurs in the U. S. although there are many for management. But this is a slightly different bird, and rather costly. And public crutches such as subsidies, guaranteed loans and markets protection from both foreign and domestic competition, and the like generally do more harm than good as postwar examples amply attest and the recent Philippine disaster with crony entrepreneurs also attests. But the subject is a complex one and there are only a few studies in Asia to go by. The difficulty is with the methodology to study the multi-dimensional trait, many of the factors involved not easily specified quantifiable. Perhaps educational methods are not sufficient to produce entrepreneurs; techniques of management may be helpful but to learn how and when to take risks, to attract capital, to use it efficiently, manage the workers, to innovate, and toil long, at varying mix require much learning from exposure and trial and error. The unique subjective, psychological, innovative, venturing attributes required of good entrepreneurs are difficult to teach in classrooms. And the supply side interacts with the demand for entrepreneurs under intangible, macro conditions.

One noteworthy study of Korean entrepreneurship concluded with the identification of Confucian virtues as the major ingredient in successful entrepreneurship.[52] Schooling was not unimportant especially in learning the basic techniques of managing business, but the most important common denominator showing up in the dozen or so of interviews of successful entrepreneurs in smaller enterprises was the learning experience obtained from working in the family business or working in other firms. This may be a basic necessary condition but the sufficient ones are difficult to pinpoint — the venturing spirit, the ability to take a calculated risk, the determination to succeed, and so on. None of these suffices if the operations have not been learned in formal training or in actual practice. This learning is different from that of a person aiming to be a good employee. Instead of excelling in one portion of the entire operation, the would-be entrepreneur must master all the skills of the entire operation if he is to venture out on his own.

There may be something to the Confucian hypothesis. After independence, the ROC (Taiwan) and Korea had no trouble generating plenty of entrepreneurs who eventually succeeded in exporting. They had no entrepreneurial experience in the colonial period nor training in schools but they learned quickly while working for others whether foreign or local, or as partners in joint-ventures, from licensing and technical tie-ups, and most important from the hundreds of buyers from abroad. The big department and other stores of the U. S. (Sears, Penney, Ward, etc.) and Europe sent their buyers with designers and engineers to teach the Japanese and

---

[52] L. P. Jones and Il. Sakong, *Government, Business, and Entrepreneurship in Economic Development: the Korean Case,* Harvard: 1980.

Hong Kong entrepreneurs to produce radios, T.V., shoes and garments, toys, house-wares, etc., which they purchased in large quantities for sale in their stores. When in the 1950s full employment raised wages in Japan and Hong Kong, they began to teach entrepreneurs in the ROC (Taiwan) and Korea in the 1960s. (They skipped nearby Philippines deterred by the many barriers to free trade).[53]

It takes determined diligence to learn from others, dedication to long hours of labor and few hours of leisure, unmindful of arduous manual work, and willingness to face competition and risks — all in furthering the fortunes of the family and ancestors. Confucian traditions are much more in line with these attributes than are Islamic, Hindu, Catholic and other teachings.

Important, too, was the demand side. The comprehensive land reform and rural development raised incomes. Domestic purchasing power for labor-intensive wage goods accelerated making it easier for new entrepreneurs to sell profitably, accumulate capital, expand production scale and then sell abroad, with more scale-economies. The forces on both the supply and demand sides interacted and inter-penetrated to generate a work environment of exuberance and vigor. But the whole subject of entrepreneurship needs more researching in Asian countries, starting with case studies of successful entrepreneurs, which one finds plentiful only in Japan. The revival of the importance of small enterprises with the emergence of electronic technologies makes the topic a worthwhile area of serious study.

Conclusions

In concluding by way of a summary, we explore what broad policy changes that the end of the high growth decades and the beginning of worsening income distributions may portend for the future.

For countries in Asia which have yet to exploit fully the quantitative sources of productivity growth, top priority should be given to achieve full employment. It is difficult to imagine anything more wasteful than large pools of idle manpower. East Asia has shown one way for approaching full utilization — via a strategy of agricultural development including rising rice yields, multiple-diversified cropping, off-farm employment, supplemented with labor-intensive industrialization. This is appropriate for the meager pool of modernized manpower in the beginning of growth since the demand of labor-intensive agriculturalization and light industriali-zation for educated manpower is minimal. Moreover, with the retardation of export growth the time is ripe for a more domestically-led strategy with faster development of manpower quality and rural infrastructure. This is urgent for South Asia, especially India with the world's largest poverty groups in the rural sector, but Indonesia and the Philippines can benefit from more rural development.

For countries operating at full employment levels, more technology-intensive and capital-intensive strategies with plans to reduce their agricultural sector are desirable. It is imperative that they do so and open their economies for the importation of labor-intensive diversified food products and light industrial products from countries striving to generate more jobs.

Once full employment is approached, the qualitative aspects of human resources can be more readily exploited for productivity growth. Real wages should rise

---

[53] On the role of department stores, mail order houses, and supermarkets of United States and Europe in establishing the foundations of the consumer electronic industry in East Asia in the 1950s and 1960s, see Gene Gregory, "Asia's Electronic Revolution," *Euro-Asia Business Review*, No. 1, 1982.

consonant with productivity increases, compelling entrepreneurs to adopt technologies to substitute for labor, and motivating workers to improve their efficiency. If wages rise more than productivity, profits will not be available in new technologies, while constant wages will fail to motivate workers.

Full employment, rising wages and profits, increasing food consumption and more health services and better distribution of incomes should contribute to a more energetic work force better motivated to learn and improve skills. Throughout, we have emphasized the strategic role played by the macro atmosphere in productive growth which for want of a better term was variously called the social milieu, or the surrounding environment. This topic needs to be researched to know more clearly what it is and how it is that a lethargic, lackadaisical milieu is transformed into one of vigor and vitality, and how it influences sectoral productivity. Pending such studies, we may assume that the milieu is the sum total of the bits of influences emanating from some of the sources of manpower development discussed above: the home, the schools, the workshops, and the mass media, under varying levels of employment utilization. In turn, this sum total is an entity which reacts on the sector sources to influence their productivity. But there may be more than sector sources that go to make up the macro environment.

The competitive spirit of the market and the vigor of the market forces and institutions in the market are critical ingredients. Let the market degenerate with heavy-handed intervention, overprotected market forces and monopolistic and monopsonistic organizations and vitality will be endangered. After being nurtured for decades in the postwar era the market and the market forces must be permitted to play a bigger role everywhere.

Political authoritarianism for long periods can blunt the initiative of the populace, especially if it is based on intensive military rule at the various levels of government. An increasingly educated labor force needs to participate much more not only in the market place but in the governance of the nation. This labor force is no longer the illiterate, tradition-bound citizenry of the early postwar years. It cannot be pushed around and ordered to do this or that as with the older generation. It will demand more participation in decision-making in economic and political affairs in the decade to come. If not, it will sap the exuberance of the young and drive others to rebel.

Community organizations can help to improve the vitality of the environment. This is particulary the case with religious institutions which pervade countries in South and Southeast Asia. The doctrines of certain religions rooted in ancient conditions may have to be modified and the archaic elements replaced. Excessive concerns for the life hereafter breed fatalism and asceticism, debilitating the drive to improve the well-being of mankind in the present and the striving for a better future of descendants. Over the decades, Buddhism in East Asia, has achieved a better balance between the weltanschauung of life here and hereafter with Confucian ethics intervening as guideposts in the relation of man to man.

As we turn our eyes to the future, the vision of a Pacific Century looms in the distant horizon, as the vitality and vigor of northwestern Europe weakens and as the progress of Eastern Europe is obstructed with obsolete Communist institutions. But not all nations of Asia may make it to the Pacific Century. The message of this chapter is that only those who can sustain a high level of vitality and vigor of their manpower, and the dynamism of institutions staffed with good human resources can hope to move into the Pacific Century.

3. Economic Conditions in East and Southeast Asia and Development Perspective

Kiyoshi Kojima and Tsuneo Nakauchi

INTRODUCTION

In the 1960s and 1970s we have observed remarkable economic development in the East Asia (the ROC-Taiwan, Korea, and Hong Kong) and in the five original ASEAN (Association of Southeast Asian Nations) countries (Singapore, Malaysia, Thailand, the Philippines, and Indonesia). We will refer to these countries as the East Asian NICs (newly industrializing countries) and the ASEAN group. These countries have attracted the world's attention as a focal point of economic development.

The world economic environment during the 1970s, however, was not particularly favorable to developing countries in general, or to the NICs and ASEAN inter alia. A number of "external shocks" posed serious challenges to the outward-looking countries in East and Southeast Asia. Among these shocks were the following events:

1. In December, 1971, foreign exchange rates were adjusted under the Smithsonian Agreement. This agreement amounted to a devaluation of the dollar and an appreciation of the yen, the mark, and the franc. In fact, this was a de facto collapse of the Bretton Woods regime. In 1973, general floating was instituted and the flexible exchange rate system which followed has allowed several major readjustments of exchange rates. This change reflected the end of American dominance in the world economy and signalled the re-emergence of Japan and western Europe. The United States experienced widening current account deficits and these placed downward pressure on the value of the dollar during the 1970s.

   The "floating system" has tended to make trade relationships between the developing and developed countries unstable and also has tended to inhibit direct foreign investment in \ the developing countries.[1] On top of this America's

---

[1] See, for example, Rokuro Tsuchiya, *Floating Exchange Rate* (in Japanese), Chuo University Press, Tokyo, 1980.

external deficit and budgetary problems have led to a slowdown of economic assistance programs. Trade friction has increased not only between the U.S. and Japan, but also between the U.S. and the Asian NICs and ASEAN countries that have rapidly increased exports to the U.S. Trade friction has also become serious with respect to relations between the European Community (EC), Japan, and the faster growing Asian economies.

2. The two oil crises of 1973 and 1979 and subsequent world recession created balance of payments and macroeconomic problems that were especially severe for oil-importing countries. The growth rate of the Japanese economy, which had been above 10 percent, was cut in half in the period after 1974. Asian NICs and ASEAN countries recovered from the first oil shock, but since 1980 they too have had much lower growth rates.

The causes of the success the NICs and ASEAN had in sustaining economic growth in the 1970s have to be studied. Analysis of these causes is the first task of this chapter. In the 1980s a number of developing countries, including oil-exporters like Mexico had substantial problems servicing their debts. The Philippines can be said to have the same kind of problem. A number of other Asian countries — Korea, Indonesia, Thailand, and Malaysia also have large external debts, but the problem of debt servicing does not seem insurmountable in these cases. Furthermore, the upturn in the world economy that began in 1984 will help these countries solve this problem. However, in our view, this fact does not justify the continuation in the NICs and ASEAN of previous economic development strategies based on export promotion policies. One must then ask what the new strategies and policies should consist of. To explore this question is the second task of this chapter.

In evaluating future strategies it is necessary to take into account the new role China has taken on since the adoption of policies promoting modernization and opening up of the economy. China's "open-door" policy has contributed to the economic development and to trade expansion in the region.

ECONOMIC GROWTH RATES

Southeast Asia's Economy in the 1970s,[2] the Hla Myint Report commissioned by the Asian Development Bank and published in 1971 surveyed the developing countries of Asia. One of the authors of the paper attempted with the help of Dr. Saburo Okita and Dr. Peter Drysdale to predict the foreign trade of 1980 using 1967 as a base year for nine Southeast Asian countries (Burma, Cambodia, Indonesia, Laos, Malaysia, the Philippines, Singapore, Thailand, and Vietnam). The actual performance during the 1970s greatly surpassed the predictions but the degree of difference differed depending upon the countries. Burma and the ASEAN-five countries did exceptionally well, but the three Indochina nations were unable to expand foreign trade. The main purpose of this section is to compare the actual figures for the 1970s with the predictions and to examine the reasons for the differences observed.

After a close examination of past performance, the ADB report casted the following predictions-cum-targets:

---

[2] Asian Development Bank, *Southeast Asia's Economy in the 1970s,* Longman, Part 4, 1971.

1. The nine Southeast Asian countries were to double their GNP in the 1970s (an annual growth rate of 7.2 percent).[3]
2. The total import bill might reach US$16 billion (cif) in 1980.[4]
3. The ADB report proposed the goal of increasing exports (fob) from the Southeast Asian countries to US$15.2 billion in 1980 an annual growth rate of 11.7 percent.[5]
4. Even if the target was reached, a trade deficit would still be incurred and should be financed by foreign aid, direct foreign investment, and other capital inflows.

The ADB report did not envision the 'oil crises' or the "industrial revolution" in the region. Trade-oriented industrial growth was the most important distinguishing factor of the economic development path followed by the successful Southeast Asian countries in the 1970s.

As compared to the ADB report's prediction, actual figures of Southeast Asian countries' GNPs for the 1970s period are shown in Table 1. Though the NICs — the ROC (Taiwan) and Hong Kong — were not explicitly included in the ADB study, for comparative purposes their performance will be assessed against the general targets set by the ADB report. A further refinement is to include Singapore (an ASEAN member) in the NICs as it has more common characteristics with them than the larger ASEAN economies.

The Asian NICs include, then, the ROC (Taiwan), Korea, Hong Kong and Singapore. Their annual average real GNP growth rates during the 1970s ranged

Table 1. Annual Growth Rates of GNP, Per Capita GNP and Population
1970-1979

	GNP Growth Rate (%)*	Per Capita GNP Growth Rate (%)*	1979 US$	Population Growth Rate (%)	1979 Million
NICs					
ROC (Taiwan)	9.86	7.79	1,800	1.98	17.31
Korea	9.80	7.98	1,490	1.99	37.53
Hong Kong	9.54	7.03	3,960	2.35	4.88
Singapore	8.97	7.32	3,730	1.57	2.38
ASEAN-4					
Malaysia	7.18	4.35	1,360	2.75	13.28
Thailand	6.75	4.45	600	2.51	45.46
Philippines	6.57	3.66	630	2.80	47.10
Indonesia	7.04	5.08	380	2.32**	139.38

Source: ADB, *Key Indicators*.

 * Real GNP figures in domestic currencies.
 ** From IMF, *International Financial Statistics, 1983 Yearbook*.

[3] *Ibid.* p. 263.
[4] *Ibid.* p. 315.
[5] *Ibid.* p. 316.

from a high of 9.86 percent (the ROC-Taiwan) to a low of 8.97 percent (Singapore). All of these countries thus surpassed the target of doubling GNP during the 1970s by a significant margin. The NICs did so well that only Hong Kong with an average annual per capita growth rate of 7.03 percent did not double the per capita GNP. (The term income level is also used to refer to per capita GNP in this chapter.)

The NICs share some important characteristics, though they vary in size and population. Korea is by far the largest and most populous of the NICs, followed by the ROC (Taiwan), Hong Kong, and Singapore. Each of the NICs has a high population density and an acute shortage of domestic natural resources. This fact has forced all of them to adopt export-led economic development strategies based on labor intensive, processing type of industrialization. A distinguishing characteristic is then the dominance of industries which rely on the import of raw materials and intermediate goods and on the export of finished products. This pattern of growth has, in some cases, been relentlessly promoted by the governments involved and during the 1970s resulted in high growth rates.

Another significant element is the role of foreign investment in export industries; the ROC (Taiwan) and Korea made especially strong efforts to promote foreign investment in their export sectors. In all cases, however, foreign firms appear to have made substantial contributions to the national economic effort. In addition, the entrepot services supplied by Hong Kong and Singapore in the form of banking, shipping and foreign trade related industries have also made considerable contributions to growth in these economies.

The second group consists of the four resource-based ASEAN countries, Malaysia with a relatively small population, Thailand and the Philippines with medium populations, and Indonesia with the largest population.

Real GNP growth rates in this group ranged from a high of 7.18 percent in Malaysia to a low of 6.57 percent in the Philippines. Thus while these countries did not grow as fast as the NICs, they almost doubled their GNPs during the 1970s.

The ASEAN-4 countries had relatively high population growth rates.[6] Accordingly, the growth rate of per capita GNP was rather low in the group ranging from a high of 5.08 percent in Indonesia to a low of 3.66 percent in the Philippines. The level of per capita GNP was also rather low in 1979; Indonesia's per capita GNP of US$380 was less than one tenth that of Hong Kong's US$3,960. In view of this fact, a vigorous effort is required to control population growth as well as to promote economic activity in the 1980s.

It is important to note that ASEAN-4 countries are more favorably endowed with natural resources than the NICs. These resources include those used to produce various tropical cash crops, forest products, tin, copper, petroleum, natural gas, and other mineral ores. The development and export of these resources have greatly contributed to the economic growth of these four countries in the 1970s. The abundance of natural resources and reliance on them has often tended to retard the progress of industrialization.[7] Furthermore, the pace of industrialization has tended to be much slower in this group than in the NICs and only a limited number of industries have reached the exporting stage. In short, though the industrial sectors of these countries have yet to become export oriented, their contribution to their

---

[6] See Chapter 2 of this book.

[7] See, for example, Corden, M. and P. Neary, "Booming Sector and Deindustrialization in Small Open Economy," *Economic Journal*, December, 1982, and Sweden van Wijinbergen, "The Dutch Disease: A Disease After All?" *Economic Journal*, March, 1984.

respective economies has been substantial and can be expected to increase in the future.

In summary, the four NICs have experienced real GNP growth rates of 9-10 percent in the 1970s and have managed to double per capita income levels as well. The four ASEAN countries almost managed to double real GNP during the 1970s but with high population growth rates, per capita income levels have grown at annual rates of only 3.7 — 5.1 percent.

The differences in growth rates of the NICs and ASEAN-4 may be ascribed to differences in initial condition and in the speed of industrialization. The gap between the per capita income levels of the NICs and ASEAN-4 increased as population growth was higher in the latter countries in the 1970s. Nevertheless, the economic growth of these 8 Asian nations in the 1970s was impressive by any standard. Trade expansion played a major role in their achievement of high growth.

EXPANSION OF TRADE

The four larger ASEAN countries almost attained the target of doubling GNP in the 1970s and the NICs surpassed it. According to the ADB report the attainment of this goal was to require a four-fold increase in exports. The actual increase in trade, however, vastly surpassed the ADB projections. For all five ASEAN countries exports actually increased seven-fold and for the three East Asian NICs[8] the actual increase was eleven-fold for the decade.

A trade matrix is made for 1967 and 1979 from which Tables 2 and 3 are calculated. Table 2 gives the export figures for the five ASEAN countries and Table 3 shows similar information for the three East Asian NICs. These two tables reveal some interesting trends.

Exports and Growth in the 1970s

ASEAN's exports to the world have increased 11.2 times during the 1967 — 1979 period according to Table 2. This is equivalent to an annual growth rate of 22.5 percent implying a seven-fold increase over ten years. This rate of increase is over three times larger than the 7.3 percent increase predicted by the ADB report. Correspondingly, Table 3 shows that the East Asian NICs exports to the world increased 18.6 times implying an annual growth rate of 27.2 percent or an eleven-fold increase in ten years. Thus, the actual growth rate was 3.7 times the predicted one.

Furthermore, if we compare trade growth rates with GNP growth rates, the dramatic growth of trade in the region is highlighted. The GNP of ASEAN countries increased approximately six times at current prices while exports increased by 11 times between 1967 and 1979 and the GNP of the East Asian NICs increased by 11 times while exports increased about 19 times. This increase in trade at almost twice the rate of GNP is indeed remarkable and it leads one to seek an answer to the question: What has brought about such a rapid expansion of trade in the region?

Accordingly, as shown in Table 4, the dependency on external trade of the Asian developing countries increased markedly in the 1967-1979 period. It is quite high in

---

8 Singapore was treated as one of NICs in the previous section but now it is changed to belong to ASEAN for it is the center of ASEAN trade.

Table 2. Exports of the Five ASEAN Countries

(Unit: US$ million)

Trading Partner	(1-2) Value of Exports		1979/ 1967	(4-5) Annual Growth Rate		(6-7) Export Shares (%)		(8-9) Value of Imports		(10-11) Export/Import Ratios (%)	
	1967 (1)	1979 (2)	(3)	1967-1979 (4)	ADB Pro-jection (5)	1967 (6)	1979 (7)	1967 (8)	1979 (9)	1967 (10)	1979 (11)
1. Japan	916	13,485	14.7	24.8	14.3	20.1	26.5	1,107	9,628	82.7	140.1
2. USA	812	9,026	11.1	22.3	4.4	17.9	17.7	761	6,494	106.7	139.0
3. Australia and New Zealand	148	1,381	9.3	20.3	1.4	3.2	2.7	214	1,669	69.2	82.7
4. Western Europe	774	7,948	10.3	21.8	0	17.0	15.6	1,050	7,061	73.7	112.6
5. East Asia (ROC-Taiwan, Korea, Hong Kong)	206	2,681	12.2	23.4	10.9	4.5	5.2	299	3,652	68.9	73.4
6. ASEAN	981	8,893	9.1	20.2	0	21.6	17.5	981	8,893	100.0	100.0
7. Others	700	7,383	10.6	22.0		15.4	14.5	492	8,899	142.3	83.0
8. Total (World)	4,537	50,797	11.2	22.5	7.3	100.0	100.0	4,904	46,296	92.5	109.7

Source: UN, ESCAP, *Foreign Trade Statistics of Asia and the Pacific*, Bangkok, 1967-1979.

Table 3. Exports of the East Asian NICs (ROC-Taiwan, Korea, Hong Kong)

(Unit: US$ million)

Trading Partner	(1-2) Value of Exports		1979/ 1967	Annual Growth Rate (%)	(5-6) Export Shares (%)		(7-8) Value of Imports		(9-10) Export/Import Ratios (%)	
	1967 (1)	1979 (2)	(3)	(4)	1967 (5)	1979 (6)	1967 (7)	1979 (8)	1967 (9)	1979 (10)
1. Japan	287	6,636	23.1	30.0	11.5	14.3	1,084	14,284	26.5	46.5
2. USA	765	14,217	18.6	27.2	30.7	30.7	837	8,997	91.4	158.0
3. Australia and New Zealand	66	1,122	17.1	26.8	2.6	2.4	83	948	79.5	118.4
4. Western Europe	493	9,535	19.4	28.3	19.8	20.5	546	6,549	90.3	145.6
5. East Asian NICs	120	2,377	19.7	27.9	4.8	5.1	120	2,377	100.0	100.0
6. ASEAN	299	3,652	12.2	23.4	12.0	7.8	206	2,681	145.1	136.2
7. Others	456	8,926	19.6	27.8	18.3	19.3	382	12,144	119.4	73.5
8. Total (World)	2,486	46,285	18.6	27.2	100.0	100.0	3,258	47,980	76.3	96.5

Source: Same as Table 2.

several countries, for example, imports were close to half of GDP in the ROC (Taiwan) and Malaysia, and 19-32 percent of GDP in Thailand, Indonesia, Korea, and the Philippines. The very large import/GDP ratios of Hong Kong and Singapore reflect their entrepot status. Such high rates of trade dependency inevitably increase the vulnerability of the economies in question to world economic fluctuations.[9]

In the NICs, rapid industrialization has indeed been the engine of growth. In turn rapid industrialization has depended on export promotion. However, imports of raw materials, intermediate goods, and capital goods inevitably increase during the process of industrialization. This then results in the increase of exports at a rate faster than which domestic value added increases. This phenomenon typically occurs in the international division of the production process. This process results in production activity in the host country involving only one part of the production process (e.g. assembly or the production of parts alone) and often occurs under joint ventures with foreign firms or in subsidiaries wholly owned by trans-national corporations (TNCs).

In other words, this type of production process leads to a divergence between the growth rate of exports and the growth rate of domestic value added because dependence on imported intermediate and capital goods rises quickly.

Table 4. Import Dependency Ratio (Value of Import/GDP and Export/GDP, at current prices, %)

		Import/GDP		Export/GDP	
		1967	1979	1967	1979
1.	ROC (Taiwan)	22.3	45.8	17.7	49.8
2.	Korea	21.4	31.5	6.9	23.3
3.	Hong Kong		96.3*		84.6*
4.	Singapore	131.0	109.5	93.2	151.3
5.	Malaysia	34.0	38.1	38.0	53.7
6.	Thailand	20.5	26.3	13.1	19.5
7.	Philippines	15.9	22.1	11.0	15.3
8.	Indonesia	18.0	18.6	18.4	40.2
9.	Japan	9.4	11.1	8.4	10.3
10.	United States	3.6	9.4	4.0	7.7
11.	Australia	14.8	15.0	13.1	15.4
12.	United Kingdom	15.8	23.9	18.3	28.1
13.	West Germany	14.2	21.0	17.6	22.6

Source: ROC (Taiwan): Executive Yuan, Republic of China, *Taiwan Statistical Data Book* 1983.
　　　　Hong Kong: Asian Development Bank, *Key Indicators of Developing Member Countries of ADB.*
　　　　All others: IMF, *International Financial Statistics, 1985 Yearbook.*

Note: * 1980.

---

[9] Such vulnerability is fully analyzed in the Korea, Taiwanese and Hong Kong cases by the Kim and Kang in Chapter 9 of this book.

It seems to us that we should re-examine the export oriented industrialization strategy which results in the drastic increase of exports and relatively smaller increases in GNP and per capita incomes. Indeed it seems that the Asian NICs and possibly Malaysia have reached the limits of exports as a share of GDP and that a new pattern of economic development is called for.[10] We wonder whether export-oriented industrialization has gone too far in the East Asian NICs and Singapore. This point seems particularly important in view of the difficulties they may encounter in the attempt to promote further export market development. In other ASEAN countries industrial exports need to be promoted, but these countries need to avoid attempting to overly subsidise manufactured exports and rely more on market forces to determine the structure of their industrial sectors.

Trade with Japan

The Asian developing countries have expanded trade with Japan at a particularly rapid rate. Looking at Table 2 we can see that ASEAN expanded their exports to Japan at an annual rate of 24.8 percent, an increase of 14.7 times. This compares to the ADB prediction of a 14.3 percent annual increase. As a result Japan's share of ASEAN's exports has risen from 20.1 percent to 26.5 percent. Also the ratio of ASEAN's exports to Japan to ASEAN's imports from Japan has increased from 0.83 (indicating a deficit) to 1.40 (indicating a surplus). Furthermore, Japan has been the largest and fastest growing market for ASEAN exports. The latter fact is largely due to the relatively high growth rate in Japan as compared to the USA and Europe. However, this growth rate has decreased somewhat since the first oil shock in 1973. Another significant cause of the rapid expansion of ASEAN's exports to Japan was Japan's emphasis on heavy and chemical industries which resulted in increased need for ASEAN's raw materials (Indonesia's oil, Malaysia's rubber, Thailand's Tin, the Philippines' copper, etc.).

Turning to Table 3 we can see that, while Japan is not the largest market for East Asian NIC exports, here again exports to Japan grew most rapidly during this period. The increase was 23.1 times implying an annual growth rate of 30.0 percent. As a result Japan's share of the region's total exports rose from 11.5 percent to 14.3 percent. The ratio of exports to Japan to imports from Japan was 0.265 in 1967 and 0.465 in 1979. The region still has a substantial trade deficit with Japan. The deficit as a percentage of trade narrowed during this period, though in dollar amounts it increased substantially. Japan exports manufactured goods including capital equipment, consumer durables, and intermediate goods to the region. Japanese companies with investments in the region export parts which are then assembled and the final products then exported to Japan and the USA. This is how the international division of labor in the region's manufacturing industry has evolved. Furthermore, this process has contributed substantially to the increase of exports to the United States from the region.

It should also be pointed out that Japan's trade has also grown more rapidly than GNP and, correspondingly, trade dependency has increased during this period. This is reflected in the increase of Japan's import to GDP ratio from 9.4 percent in 1967

---

[10] Arthur Lewis stresses in his paper, "The Slowing Down of the Engine of Growth", *American Economic Journal,* March, 1980, that the engine of growth in developing countries must turn a fuel other than trade expansion with developed countries as such expansion has slowed since the mid-1970s. See also James Riedal "Trade as the Engine of Growth in Developing Countries, Revisited," *Economic Journal,* March, 1984.

to 11.1 percent in 1979. This is the other side of the coin showing the pulling effect Japan's increasing import demand on ASEAN and East Asian exports. As mentioned above there are several important factors to note in this respect, the most important of which are Japan's high growth rate and emphasis on heavy and chemical industries. Liberalization of imports, promotion of natural resource imports through direct investments, and promotion of labor-intensive assembly and processing activities in manufacturing through direct investments and other policy measures are also important factors to consider.[11]

What about the future? There are two important points to consider in this respect. First of all, Japan's growth rate has been cut to only about 5 percent since the first oil shock. This lower growth rate will affect trade with the East Asian NICs and ASEAN countries in the future. Although Japan is not likely to increase protectionism, further trade liberalization is not likely to be very significant either. Secondly, the Japanese shifted emphasis from the heavy and chemical industries to knowledge and capital intensive industries after the first oil shock. The effect of this change on the East Asian and ASEAN countries and those countries' responses are important factors to consider.

Trade with USA and other OECD Countries

For the Asian developing countries trade with advanced countries outside the Asian region such as the US, Europe, and Australia/New Zealand will continue to remain important. According to Table 2, ASEAN exports grew at annual rates of 22.3 percent to the USA, 21.8 percent to Europe, and 20.3 percent to Australia/ New Zealand during the 1967-1979 period. The share of the non-Asian countries increased from 58.2 percent in 1967 to 62.5 percent in 1979, an increase slightly smaller than the increase in Japan's share. Similarly, Table 3 shows that East Asian NIC exports grew at annual rates of 27.2 percent to the USA, 28.3 percent to Europe, and 26.8 percent to Australia/New Zealand. Japan's offshore production and exports from the East Asian NICs have contributed to such growth. As a result the share of non-Asian countries increased from 64.6 percent in 1967 to 67.9 percent in 1979, an increased slightly larger than the increase in Japan's share.

Thus, the relative importance of the USA, Western Europe, and Australia/New Zealand as a market for the NICs and ASEAN has remained high although the shares of some of these markets has been declining. However, as is well known, in most of these countries there is a trend toward increased protection of manufacturing industries associated to a large degree with the emergence of substantial unemployment problems. Despite our hope that the recovery begun in late 1983 will reverse this trend, it does not appear reasonable for the Asian developing countries to expect exports to these regions to grow as rapidly as they have in the past. Therefore, restructuring of previous trade patterns and trends seems warranted. This topic is of grave importance to the NICs and ASEAN countries.

---

[11] An increase of Japan's (country i) import from country j (for example, Indonesia) depends on many factors such as the growth rate of GNP in country i, the change in i's industrial and/or import structure, and the relative competitiveness of goods from j. In empirical work constant market share analysis is quite informative but it alone is not sufficient. Supplementary use of import functions estimated for country i becomes necessary. An excellent piece of empirical work in this area is Mitsuo Ezaki, "Various Factors of Southeast Asia's Export Growth — An Economic Analysis from the Demand Side", (in Japanese), *Tonan Ajia Kenkyu*, (Southeast Asian Studies), Kyoto University, December, 1981. See also Naya's chapter in this book.

Trade among Asian Developing Countries

In the 1970s, there is already a noticeable trend toward diversification of trade partners in the trade patterns of the NICs and ASEAN. The most important element is the increase of trade between the Asian developing countries themselves. In the future this trend is likely to lead to a lessening of trade dependence on non-Asian developed countries.

The trend toward increased intra-regional trade is particularly clear within the East Asian NICs. Intra-regional trade between these three countries has grown at an annual rate of 27.9 percent during the 1967-1979 period. Correspondingly, the share of intra-regional trade grew from 4.8 percent to 5.1 percent. Exports to ASEAN also increased at a substantial rate of 23.4 percent annually but the share of such exports decreased from 12.0 percent to 7.8 percent.

On the other hand, ASEAN exports to the East Asian NICs grew more rapidly than ASEAN's intra-regional trade. ASEAN's exports to East Asia grew at an annual rate of 23.4 percent and East Asia's share increased from 4.5 percent to 5.2 percent during the 1967-1979 period. The increase in trade between East Asia and ASEAN has been based on a vertical relationship in which East Asia exports manufactured products and ASEAN exports primary products. According to Table 2, intra-ASEAN trade decreased from 21.6 percent in 1967 to 17.5 percent in 1979.

There are several ways the Asian developing countries can seek to reduce dependence on non-Asian developed countries and still facilitate trade expansion.[12] First of all, the trade between East Asia and ASEAN could be expanded and diversified. Secondly, trade with China could be expanded. Finally trade links with South Asia and the Middle East could be encouraged.

The International Division of Labor

The basic problem in this respect has to do with the international division of labor between four groups, (1) Japan, (2) North America, Western Europe, and Oceania, (3) East Asia, and (4) ASEAN. One must consider how the division of labor between these regions should evolve in the next decade or two. There are a number of possibilities in this respect but we would like to highlight one of them below.

A suggestion often heard is that a "horizontal division of labor" or "horizontal trade" offers the most hope for successful evolution of the international division of labor.[13] Horizontal trade, or intra-manufacturing trade, in principle, would involve exchange of a wide range of manufactured products. However, so far no concrete proposals have been made for the evolution of the division of labor between the four regions identified above using this principle. The major difficulty lies in deciding which countries should produce which products. Furthermore, we do not believe that this "horizontal division of labor" has been an operating principle in the world yet, even among advanced industrial countries.

Rather, when considering trade between ASEAN and Japan or between ASEAN and East Asia, we think it is more feasible to utilize more traditional vertical trading relationships. ASEAN would supply traditional primary products (foods, agricul-

---

[12] Further investigation is presented in Chapters 5, 6 and 10.

[13] See Toshio Watanabe, "The Market Structure of Asia and Japan's Response," (in Japanese), *Ajia Keizai*, October-November, 1983. See also Chapter 6.

tural and forestry based raw materials, minerals, and fuels) and semi-processed intermediate goods (iron and steel semi-finished goods, copper products, aluminum, basic chemicals, and petroleum products) to Japan and East Asia and the latter partners would in turn provide machinery, durables, and capital goods. This sort of vertical inter-industry trade should be expanded and provide benefits to all involved.

In particular, the four larger ASEAN countries seem to be in a position to benefit from expansion of semi-processed intermediate good exports. Furthermore, with the rise in income levels in these countries, domestic demand for such goods should become substantial as well. Japan has found it profitable to curtail the production of such goods at home, encourage offshore production, and then eventually import from these offshore producers. East Asian NICs are still in the process of import substitution in such industries but they will find it profitable to import from ASEAN to fill gaps between domestic demand and supply.

Another trend of significance is for multinational firms to promote the intra-firm division of labor thereby affecting the international division of labor. In most cases, parts, knocked-down appliances, and semi-finished goods are brought to the host country, then processed or assembled and the final goods are then re-exported. This international division of the production process is expanding at present and will continue to do so especially among firms operating in Japan, the USA, East Asia, and ASEAN. This pattern can be referred to as vertical intra-manufacturing sector trade. This type of intra-manufacturing trade has usually involved MNCs that shift unskilled labor-intensive aspects of the production process to labor abundant LDCs. The developing countries provide little more than labor and domestic value-added content of exports or, in the case of many durables, import substitutes remain low. Asian developing countries are attempting to raise domestic content of exports and import substitutes, but often lack the technology and skills to do so effectively. This is an example of one of the many issues involved in the discussion of the "international division of labor" that needs to be closely re-examined. We will touch upon this topic again below.

CHANGES IN THE STRUCTURE OF INDUSTRY AND TRADE

The Asian developing countries have experienced rapid changes in their industrial structures largely due to the expansion of the export sector in the 1960s and 1970s. As a result the industrial and trade structures of the NICs have come to resemble those of developed countries. Now the period of export-led structural change is coming to a close and it is necessary to focus on problems such as promotion of productivity growth in each sector of the economy and rectification of sectoral income discrepancies. A new strategy based on efficiency oriented development of the national economy needs to be pursued.

Table 5 presents some statistics on the changing economic structure of the NICs and ASEAN assembled from different sources. A major problem is the fact that the period of observation differs somewhat between data sets. More detailed country data is available in the country studies. Nonetheless, Table 5 presents information that allows the isolation of some important characteristics of the region.

Table 5. Changes in Industrial Structure & Trade Structure of the Asian Developing Countries

	ROC (Taiwan)	Hong Kong	Korea	Singapore	Malaysia	Thailand	Philippines	Indonesia	Japan[+]
Annual Growth Rates 1970-1979 (%)									
(1) GDP	8.0*	9.4	10.3	8.4	7.9	7.7	6.2	7.6	5.2
(2) Industry	12.9*	4.3	16.5	8.6	9.9	10.4	8.4	11.3	5.5
(Manufacturing)	(13.2)*	(6.1)	(17.8)	(9.3)	(12.4)	(11.4)	(6.7)	(12.5)	(6.4)
Shares of GDP (%)									
(3) Agriculture 1960	28	4	37	4	37	40	26	54	13
Agriculture 1979	10**	2***	20	2	24	26	24	30	5
(4) Industry 1960	29	34	20	18	18	19	28	14	45
(Manufacturing)	(22)	(25)	(14)	(12)	(9)	(13)	(20)	(8)	(34)
Industry 1979	48**	31***	39	36	33	28	35	33	42
(Manufacturing)	(38)**	(25)***	(27)	(28)	(16)	(19)	(24)	(9)	(30)
(5) Services 1960	43	62	43	78	45	41	46	32	42
Services 1979	42**	67***	41	62	43	46	41	37	53
Shares of Employment									
(6) Agriculture 1960	56	8	66	8	63	84	61	75	33
Agriculture 1979	37**	3	36	2	51	77	47	59	13
(7) Industry 1960	11	52	9	23	12	4	15	8	30
Industry 1979	37**	57	30	38	16	9	17	12	38
(8) Services 1960	33	40	25	69	25	12	24	17	37
Services 1979	26*	40	34	60	33	14	36	29	49
(9) Per Capita Manufacturing Production (1975 US Dollars)									
1970	180	–	182	1,628	311	210	193	50	2,867
1979	935	1,920	621	3,084	–	–	–	92	4,556
(10) Structure of Exports (Industrial Exports/Total Exports)									
1969	67.0	92.5	76.9	23.6	24.3	16.5	8.1	21.6	93.6
1979	87.6	96.2	89.2	47.2	57.8	32.3	23.6	5.3	96.1
(11) Growth of Exports									
1979 Exports/ 1969 Exports	15.3	5.1	24.2	9.2	6.7	7.4	5.6	19.5	6.4
Average Annual Growth Rate 1969-1979	31.7	17.8	37.7	25.1	21.2	22.0	18.9	35.1	20.3

Sources: (1) − (8): World Bank, *World Development Report, 1980, 1981.*

    (9): World Bank, *World Development Report, 1982, 1983* and (for ROC-Taiwan) Executive Yuan, *Taiwan Statistical Data Book of the Rep. of China 1982* as cited in John Wong, "ASEAN Economies: Growth and Structural Adjustment," *The Studies of Business and Industry,* March, 1984.

    (10) − (11): Ippei Yamazawa et al., "Trade and Industrial Adjustment in the Asian-Pacific Countries" (in Japanese), Tables 2A and 2B, *Ajia Keizai* Oct.-Nov., 1983.

Note: (1), (2) and (9) are in constant prices, whereas (11) is in current prices.
     * = 1970-1978
     ** = 1978
    *** = 1977
    (+) For reference.

Industrialization

The first and second rows in Table 5 indicate that, except for Hong Kong, the growth rate of industry has been higher than that of GDP. In these rows industry includes mining as well as manufacturing (a fact of much significance when considering a country such as Indonesia). Using this definition of industry it can be said that "industrialization" has been a leading element of structural change during the 1960s and 1970s.

Row (10) reinforces this perception by showing that the proportion of exports accounted for by industrial goods has increased in all countries except Indonesia. Here industrial goods are defined as those falling in SITC classes five through eight. As such petroleum and crude mineral ores are not included and as a result the figure for Indonesia fell from 21.6 percent in 1969 to 5.3 percent in 1979.

As is shown in row (11), the annual growth rate of exports has been very high in every country. Given the rising share of industrial exports in total it is possible to infer that the industrialization which occurred was export-oriented. Export-oriented industrialization was a leading source of growth during this period.

If we assume that sectoral shares of GDP reflect industrial structure, then several points of interest emerge from rows (3) − (5). Here it can be seen that the share of agriculture has declined and the share of industry (including mining) has increased rapidly. Indeed by end of the 1970s the industrial structures of countries such as Korea, the ROC (Taiwan), Hong Kong, and Singapore resembled those of developed countries. If we focus on the size of the manufacturing sector alone (excluding mining) we see a big difference in the cases of Indonesia and Malaysia because of the presence of large mining sectors. However, using the broad sectoral definitions in Table 5, it can be said that, in general, the Asian developing countries have industrialized to a significant degree already. Indeed in the NICs it appears as though there may not be much room for further increase in the share of the industrial sector in GDP. Services shares still appear to be low in the ROC (Taiwan) and Korea. In Singapore, the share of services in GDP fell sharply. Thus, the services sector may require higher priority. Therefore, we cannot help but feel the need for shifting policy priorities. Export-led industrialization should be reconsidered in favor of a new approach.

Structure of Employment

Let us now turn to the sectoral distribution of the labor force. According to rows (6) − (8), most of the work force in the four larger ASEAN economies was still in the agricultural sector in 1979; that sector absorbed 47 percent − 77 percent of all labor in these countries. However, the industrial sector's share of the total labor force is quite small. Labor's employment share is only 1/3 to 2/5 of the industrial sector's share of value added. In Korea, this ratio is 3/4. From these statistics we may conclude that there still remains a sizeable difference between labor productivity (and income levels) in the agricultural sector and that in the industrial sector in the four larger ASEAN countries. These statistics may also reflect the fact that the pattern of industrialization has been fairly capital intensive in the ASEAN-4 countries.

Another observation is that, as is shown in row (9), there are considerable differences in per capita gross production both among the Asian developing countries and between them and Japan. These differences correspond to differences in per capita incomes between these countries. Indeed, despite the fact that industrial structures in these countries are becoming more similar over time, differences in productivity between countries are still vast.

There is a need to restructure industry within each country and to improve productivity. In the resource based ASEAN economies small and medium scale enterprises (SMSEs) need to be modernized. Large-scale, capital-intensive industrial enterprises should not be promoted excessively. There is an urgent need to improve labor absorption in the industrial sector of the larger ASEAN countries, there is also a need to raise productivity in the agricultural sector and reduce the income discrepancy between the industrial and agricultural sectors. In order to achieve this latter goal it is essential that population growth be controlled and orderly migration of the labor force from the agricultural sector to the industrial and services sectors be promoted. In addition, agro-industries should be promoted according to comparative advantage. The agricultural development of the larger ASEAN countries and the ROC (Taiwan) and Korea depends partly on their ability to secure abundant and economical supplies of fertilizer and farm machinery.[14] Village electrification for the purpose of raising rural productivity and developing rural industry is also needed.

Wages in the industrial and service sectors should not be artificially raised above equilibrium levels. The failure of ASEAN-4 countries to sustain adequate rates of employment in large part resulted distortion in relative factor prices. Wages in large-scale industrial firms were raised prematurely and capital investment was excessively subsidized. Unless productivity and wage levels in the agricultural sector are increased, sustained increases in real wages will not be possible for the majority of workers in other sectors. As long as there is an excess supply of labor firms in general and, in particular, foreign firms, will plan employment based on the general wage level although they may offer higher wages to workers with special skills. Related to this point is the need for education or human resource development.[15] Improving the talents, skills, and general health level of the population is important.

These are the most important aspects of efficiency oriented development of the national economy. This strategy relies mainly on free market forces to achieve efficient resource allocation and structural change. Government has an important role to play in macroeconomic management, human resource development and in adopting policies that provide balanced incentives to the various sectors. The public sector must also provide infrastructure to help improve transportation, communication, energy distribution, marketing, and banking systems.

CAPITAL FORMATION AND DIRECT FOREIGN INVESTMENT

The Complementary Nature of Domestic and Foreign Capital

The economic growth of a country is strongly conditioned by its ability to increase its productive capacity, i.e. the rate of domestic capital formation. However, in order to promote growth and rapid structural change, many developing countries find it necessary to promote an inflow of foreign capital to supplement inadequate

---

[14] See Vyas and James's chapter 4.
[15] See Oshima's chapter 8.

domestic resources. Aid, direct foreign investment (abbreviated DFI), and other capital transfers have been effective, even crucial, means of promoting economic growth where such transfers have worked to complement domestically generated economic activity. This is true despite the fact that the amount of such capital transfers has generally been small.

Furthermore, in the case of DFI, transfer of managerial assets and technologies have been particularly significant elements and, as such, the contribution of DFI to growth and structural change cannot be measured by the size of the investment alone. DFI has stimulated significant rises in productivity and has been particularly helpful in promoting the development of export industries. In this section, we will review the complementary role international capital has played in the region. However, as emphasized above, new development strategies seem to be called for in the region and thus it is important to emphasize that we are now facing a turning point with respect to the role of foreign capital in the region. In particular we must consider the complementary role of foreign capital in the promotion of a new division of labor in the East and Southeast Asian region.

In this connection it is informative to look at the data in columns (1) – (6) in Table 6 (for comparative purposes, India, Pakistan and Sri Lanka have been included). This information is considered in connection with Harrod's growth formula: $gc = s$; where g is the growth rate of real GDP, c is the incremental capital-output ratio, and s is the corresponding marginal saving ratio. If g and c are considered fixed then s becomes the required saving rate to maintain that growth rate. Thus, utilizing the actual growth rates in columns (1) and (2) and the actual incremental capital-output ratios in columns (3) and (4), we can derive the required saving rates given in columns (7) and (8). Comparison of actual rates in columns (5) and (6) with the required ones then yield the "deficit" saving rates given in columns (9) and (10). Where this figure is negative foreign inflows must fill the "savings gap."

In some countries (such as Pakistan and Sri Lanka), actual saving rates were below 10 percent, levels below that thought to be required for a "takeoff into sustained development."[16] In most of the NICs and ASEAN countries (Thailand and the Philippines are the exceptions), saving rates in the second period (1977-1982) were substantially higher than rates in the first period (1966-1975). Indeed saving rates in this second period had reached a rather high level; 31 percent in Korea and the ROC (Taiwan). This is higher than saving rates of many developed countries. The rate in Singapore reached a phenomenal 48 percent. Saving rates in Hong Kong and the four larger ASEAN countries were 22 percent – 26 percent and were high enough to facilitate rapid economic growth.

Since actual saving rates were higher in the second period than in the first it might be expected that the ratio of foreign capital inflows to GNP (a ratio assumed to be equal to the savings deficit) decreased. However, with the exceptions of Singapore (and India) the savings deficit and foreign capital inflow ratios have increased. Two things, rapid increases of economic growth rates and/or increases in the incremental capital-output ratios, could have caused this phenomenon.

A sharp rise in external debt of many Asian countries occurred. When interest rates rose and exports were slowed by recession, debt serving problems resulted. Table 6 indicates that the growth rate decreased in all countries except Hong Kong,

---

[16] See W. Arthur Lewis "Economic Development with Unlimited Supplies of Labor", *The Manchester School*, May, 1954, pp. 139-191; also see Go and Lee's chapter 7.

Table 6. Capital Formation of the NICs and ASEAN

	(1-2) Growth Rates of Real GDP (%) (= g)		(3-4) Incremental Capital-Output Ratios (= c)		(5-6) Actual Saving Ratios (%) (= s')		(7-8) Required Saving Ratios (%) (= s) $(1)\times(3)$ / $(2)\times(4)$		(9-10) Deficit Saving Ratios (%) (= s' − s) $(5)-(7)$ / $(6)-(8)$	
	(1) 1966-1975	(2) 1976-1982	(3) 1966-1975	(4) 1976-1982	(5) 1966-1975	(6) 1976-1982	(7) 1966-1975	(8) 1975-1982	(9) 1966-1975	(10) 1976-1982
NICs	9.5	9.2	2.9	3.8	27.1	31.9	27.6	35.0	−0.5	−3.1
ROC (Taiwan)	9.3	8.6	3.0	3.8	29.1	31.9	27.9	32.7	1.2	−0.8
Korea	10.0	9.1	2.7	4.3	24.6	31.2	27.0	39.1	−2.4	−7.9
Hong Kong	7.4	10.9	2.8	2.5	24.3	24.6	20.7	27.3	3.6	−6.6
Singapore	11.2	8.6	3.2	4.3	33.8	48.2	35.8	37.0	−2.0	11.2
4 Larger ASEAN Countries	7.0	7.1	2.8	3.7	22.1	22.7	19.6	26.3	2.5	−3.6
Malaysia	6.6	7.7	3.2	3.7	24.6	26.0	21.1	28.5	3.5	−2.5
Thailand	7.7	6.9	3.3	3.7	24.2	21.8	25.4	25.5	−1.2	−0.1
Philippines	5.6	5.4	3.3	4.7	26.5	21.8	18.5	25.4	8.0	−3.6
Indonesia	7.5	7.9	2.2	3.3	18.0	22.6	16.5	26.1	1.5	−3.5
(For Reference)										
South Asia	4.0	4.1	4.1	4.3	18.6	20.0	16.4	17.6	2.2	2.4
India	3.8	3.8	4.4	4.7	20.2	21.8	16.7	17.9	3.5	3.9
Pakistan	5.3	5.9	2.6	2.2	9.0	5.5	13.8	13.0	−4.8	−7.5
Sri Lanka	5.8	5.5	2.5	3.4	8.5	10.7	14.5	18.7	−6.0	−8.0

Source: Seiji Naya, "External Shocks, Policy Responses and External Debt of Asian Developing Countries", presented to the 14th Pacific Trade and Development Conference, June 18-21, 1984, at Singapore.

Malaysia, and Indonesia. Therefore, most of the increase in the saving deficit was brought about by sharp increases in the capital-output ratios. This ratio has become larger in seven countries although it declined to 2.5 in Hong Kong. The highest ratio in the region is the Philippines' 4.7 (equal to India's). This is far higher than ratios in developed countries. What accounts for these high incremental capital-output ratios?[17]

Several factors can be identified. The growth of the capital intensive, heavy industrial sector is an important cause. It is significant that the low ratio observed in Hong Kong corresponds to the relatively small size of this sector in that economy. Another factor is the shift of manufacturing production in multinational corporations promoting specialization in the production process away from the labor-intensive textile industry into the more capital-intensive machinery industry. Other significant factors are the increase in very capital intensive and large sized resource development investments and the rise in the price of oil. Many of these factors are a result of misguided industrial promotion policies. Excessive emphasis on a strategy of heavy industrial development can thus be viewed as a cause of the phenomenon of rising capital/output ratios. Furthermore, non-optimal policies have also resulted in inefficient utilization of investment funds. The impact of slow growth in world trade in the 1980s also contributed as many export sectors operated at less than full capacity. Bottlenecks in transport and energy and public enterprise inefficiency likewise caused under-use of industrial capacity in import-substitution industries. Given the slower growth of world trade in the 1980s, it is important to reconsider the strategy of export-oriented industrialization.

The Amount of Foreign Capital Inflow

In view of these problems, it is then important to ask whether the region received sufficient foreign capital. In examining this question both quantitative and qualitative issues must be considered.

Table 7 shows the net capital inflow from the OECD's DAC (Development Assistance Committee) member countries to the East and Southeast Asian countries. Capital inflows are divided into ODA (Official Development Assistance) and "other" (mainly private) inflows. Doubts exist about data accuracy and coverage is not as complete as desired but, nonetheless, the data is useful to show some trends.

The ratio of ODA to total foreign capital inflows for all the countries except Hong Kong decreased between 1969 — 1971 and 1979 — 1981. Among the NICs, the ROC (Taiwan), Hong Kong, and Singapore are no longer in need of much economic aid and, correspondingly ODA to these countries is very limited. In other countries, the share of ODA in the total ranged from 15 percent in Korea to 39 percent in Indonesia.

On the other hand, the share of "other" funds increased rapidly. The vast majority of these funds are from private sources and the growth of their share indicates the rapid increases in DFI, export credits, and short term loans (provided mainly by commercial banks) to finance balance of payments deficits in the region. The latter items have attracted much attention in the early 1980s because of the high levels of interest rates and the problems some countries have had servicing foreign debts.

---

[17] Concerning the incremental capital-output ratio, see Go and Lee's chapter 7.

Table 7. Foreign Capital Flow into East Asian Countries

(Unit: US$ million)

	ODA			ODA/Total (%)		"Other" (Primarily Private) Flows			(9) Annual Growth Rates (%)	Total			(13) Annual Growth Rates (%)	Ratio of Total Flow to GNP (%)	
	(1) 1969-71 Average	(2) 1979-81 Average	(3) (2)/(1) Average	(4) 1969-71 Average	(5) 1979-81 Average	(6) 1969-71 Average	(7) 1979-81 Average	(8) (7)/(6) Average		(10) 1969-71 Average	(11) 1979-81 Average	(12) (11)/(10) Average		(14) 1969-71 Average	(15) 1979-81 Average
ROC (Taiwan)	13.1	3.8	0.290	7.03	0.73	173.2	513.9	2.967	11.46	186.3	517.7	2.779	10.77	3.28	1.31
Korea	312.6	201.1	0.643	57.12	15.37	234.7	1,107.7	4.720	16.81	547.3	1,308.8	2.391	9.11	6.69	2.20
Hong Kong	1.9	10.8	5.667	0.83	0.90	227.3	1,188.5	5.229	17.67	229.2	1,199.3	5.233	18.27	7.13	5.40
Singapore	25.1	13.8	0.912	30.87	1.64	56.2	840.2	14.950	31.10	18.3	854.0	10.504	27.19	4.19	7.72
Malaysia	33.2	134.0	4.036	40.49	16.74	48.8	666.7	13.662	29.47	82.0	800.7	9.764	25.28	2.20	3.62
Thailand	68.4	405.9	5.934	75.16	33.63	91.0	801.1	8.803	24.03	159.4	1,207.0	7.572	22.53	2.43	3.83
Philippines	66.5	314.6	4.731	29.45	28.08	159.3	805.6	5.057	17.66	225.8	1,120.2	4.961	17.32	2.94	3.32
Indonesia	461.0	881.9	1.931	88.42	39.17	60.4	1,369.6	22.675	36.31	521.4	2,251.5	4.318	15.77	5.93	3.36

Source: OECD, Geographical Distribution of Financial Flows to Developing Countries, 1969-1975, 1978-1981, 1979-1982.

In the ROC (Taiwan), total inflows grew at a rate of 10.8 percent annually and "other" inflows grew at a rate of 11.5 percent annually in the period under consideration. In Korea, these rates were 9.1 percent and 16.8 percent, respectively. In the case of Hong Kong both rates were 18 percent. It is the only East Asian country where capital inflows grew as fast as exports.[18]

In ASEAN, total inflows grew at rates between 15.8 percent (Indonesia) and 27.2 percent (Singapore). These rates are about equal to the growth rate of exports. The growth rates of "other" inflows were higher in all cases and substantially higher in the case of Indonesia.

It appears that the growth of foreign capital inflows was fast enough to avoid any severe capital shortages. Where deficient, domestic savings were complemented by an inflow of foreign capital. Foreign capital inflows also helped relax foreign exchange constraints and, thus, played an important role in the rapid growth and structural change experienced by the economies in the region. Without these inflows economic growth and structural change would not have occurred at such a rapid pace. In this sense, these inflows were crucial, though the actual amount of capital involved was a rather small share of total investment. However, it is important to note that some countries that relied excessively on foreign loans eventually faces substantial debt service problems.

Direct Foreign Investment

Direct Foreign Investment (DFI) is different from other capital inflows in that finance (foreign exchange) is not the only item involved. DFI is associated with the transfer of physical capital, technology, and managerial skill. These unique characteristics allow DFI to be a catalyst to the creation of new industries in the host country, as well as to improvements in overall productivity, and export growth. As a result, DFI's impacts on growth and structural change can be significant. This catalytic function is the most important contribution DFI can make to a host economy.

On the one hand, promotion of economic cooperation between Pacific Basin countries or formation of a Pacific Economic Community[19] can be expected to result in the realization of static benefits associated with economic integration. Abolishing tariffs and other trade barriers are important in this respect. However, on the other hand, even more important are the dynamic benefits resulting from development of comparatively advantageous industries in each country in the region and the subsequent expansion of trade that could then be facilitated. The role of DFI is particularly crucial in this process.

DFI data are not easily obtained and do not always easily allow international comparisons to be made. However, using existing data, some interesting patterns emerge. More than 50 percent of DFI in the NICs and ASEAN countries is accounted for by the United States and Japan (Table 8). At the end of 1980, the total cumulative investment of the United States worldwide was US$213.5 billion. The corresponding figure for Japan was US$36.5 billion, about one-sixth that of the

---

[18] Go and Lee's chapter 7 discusses in detail the growth and change in external flows.

[19] See Kiyoshi Kojima, How to Strengthen Economic Cooperation in the Asia — Pacific Region?" ed., *Pacific Economic Cooperation: The Next Phase.* Hadi Soesastro and Han Sung-joo, Centre for Strategic and International Studies, Jakarta, October, 1983.

Table 8. Outstanding Direct Investment, 1980

(Unit: US$ million)

Investment in	Investment by	
	United States	Japan
Japan	6,274	—
United States	—	8,878
Korea	587	1,137
ROC (Taiwan)	510	370
Hong Kong	1,969	1,095
Indonesia	1,334	4,424
Malaysia	618	650
Philippines	1,244	615
Singapore	1,196	936
Thailand	360	396
Subtotal: East Asia	3,066	2,602
ASEAN	4,752	7,021
World Total:	213,460	36,497

Source: *Pacific Economic Community Statistics*, Pacific Basin Economic Council/Japan National Committee, May 1982, pp. 169, 171.

Note: These figures are based on investing country sources. Host country figures are often quite different.

United States. However, American investment in East Asia and ASEAN totaled US$7.8 billion while Japanese investment in the region totaled US$9.6 billion (1.2 times the amount of American investment).

Furthermore, there are some differences between the investment patterns of the United States and Japan in the region. We now turn to a country by country investigation of these differences.[20]

American DFI

Table 9 ranks American investment by sector according to the sector's share of total investment in a given country for all countries in the region. The table refers to the cumulative stock of actual American investment (calculations are based on a survey conducted by the United States Department of Commerce at the end of calendar 1977). Furthermore, for host countries or areas receiving relatively large amounts of American investment, the category "Other Manufacturing" is divided into eleven more narrowly defined categories. However, such detailed figures were not published for the countries that receive relatively little American investment. Finally, it should be noted that figures are not available in some cases due to the

[20] See Kiyoshi Kojima, "Japanese and American Direct Investment in Asia: A Comparative Analysis," *Hitotsubashi Journal of Economics*, June, 1985.

Commerce Department's policy of not revealing investments made by individual firms. Thus, categories marked by a "D" indicate that the figure was suppressed to avoid disclosure of an individual firm's investment.

From Table 9 it can be seen that the pattern of American investment is very similar in the developed countries and Asia. Although not shown in the table, this is still the case when the category "Other Manufacturing" is further disaggregated. Furthermore, American investment patterns in each Asian country are very similar to each other and to the patterns in the World, Asia, and Japan. This observation provides a rationale for assuming that sectors marked with a "D" are of the same relative importance in the country in question as they are in the world. Using this assumption, the major differences between patterns of investment in Japan, Asia, and East and Southeast Asian countries and the pattern of investment in the world is indicated using a "+" or a "−". A "+" means that the sector in question is at least four ranks higher than in the world pattern and a "−" means that it is at least four ranks lower. The relative lack of these marks in the table leads to the conclusion that the pattern of American investment is uniform irrespective of the host country or region concerned. Investment patterns between the world and each region or country mentioned above were correlated. The resulting Pearson rank correlation coefficients were all positive and statistically significant.

The most important investment category is finance followed by oil and oil refining, commerce, chemicals, transport equipment (automobiles), non-electric machinery, metals, mining, electronics, and food and beverages. In Asia, the share of electronics is exceptionally high. This type of investment is based on the availability of cheap labor and reflects the tendency toward the "international division of the production process" discussed above.

It is notable that the important categories in this investment pattern are those dominated by multinational firms. Direct foreign investment is then a means by which multinationals maximize profits through internalization of the production process and marketing. In short, American DFI can be classified as the "multinational corporation type" of DFI in which there is no identifiable national economic strategy at work. As a result, microeconomic considerations of the firms involved then determine the macroeconomic impacts of such DFI.

Japanese DFI

How about the pattern of Japan's DFI? Table 10 provides information for Japanese DFI similar to that given in Table 9 for American DFI. Columns A provide figures covering the cumulative total of approved investments through the end of fiscal 1972 (March, 1973) and columns B give the same information through the end of fiscal 1982 (March, 1983). These approval figures are different than the American ones in that they include investments approved but not implemented and investments that have been withdrawn. However, these figures are still useful in analyzing the pattern of Japanese DFI. Finally, it should be noted that a "+" and a "−" are interpreted in Table 10 as in Table 9.

Japanese DFI totalled US$53.1 billion by the end of March, 1983 with US$14.55 billion (27.4 percent of the total) invested in Asia. Total investment grew at an annual rate of 23.5 percent between March, 1973 and March, 1983 while investment in Asia grew at an annual rate of 26.3 percent in the same period. Thus, the share of investment in Asia increased during this period, although recently

Table 9. Sectoral Rankings of American DFI (end of 1977)

	World	Developed Countries	Japan	Asia***	ROC (Taiwan)	Korea	Hong Kong	Singapore	Malaysia	Thailand	Philippines	Indonesia
Banking and Insurance	1	1	1	1	1	3	1	1	1	1	1	2
Oil	2	2	2	2	7−	1	3	2	2	2	2^D	1
Commerce	3	3	3	4	5	4	2	5	5	3	5	5
Other Manufacturing*	4	4	6	7	4^D	9−	4^D	4^D	4^D	4	3	4^D
Chemicals	5	5	5	3	2	2	7	10−	7	5	8	3
Other Industries**	6	8	11−	6	10−	6	5	8	6^D	6^D	6^D	6^D
Transportation Equipment	7	6	4	8	6	7^D	10	7^D	12−	11−	7^D	9
Non-Electric Machinery	8	7	7	10	8	8^D	8	6	8^D	12−	12−	12−
Metals	9	9	9	9	11	11	9	9	11	8	9	7
Mining	10	11	12	12	12	12	11	12	10^D	10	10	10^D
Electronics and Electrical Machinery	11	10	10	5+	3+	5+	6+	3+	3+	9	11^D	11^D
Foodstuffs	12	12	8+	11	9	10	12^D	11	9	7+	4+	8+
Total (US$ Million)	829,617	572,403	55,681	41,538	2,574	3,021	10,909	10,121	1,399	1,205	5,480	3,619

Source: U.S. Department of Commerce, (April 1981) *U.S. Direct Investment Abroad, 1977.*

* Total of Labor Intensive Industries: Paper; Rubber; Musical Instruments; Textiles; Cement; Tobacco; Glass; Furniture; Plastics; Printing; Others.
** Agriculture, Forestry and Fisheries; Constructions; Other Services.
*** Excluding Japan, Australia, New Zealand and the South Pacific.
+ Indicates items four ranks or more higher than the world ranking.
− Indicates items four ranks or more lower than the world ranking.
D Indicates items of same ranking as the world ranking.

Table 10. Sectoral Ranking of Japanese DFI (Columns A: end of March, 1973, Columns B: end of March, 1983)

	World		Asia		ROC (Taiwan)		Korea		Hong Kong		Singapore		Malaysia		Thailand		Philippines		Indonesia	
	A	B	A	B	A	B	A	B	A	B	A	B	A	B	A	B	A	B	A	B
Mining	1	1	1	1	10	14⁻	12	16⁻	12	14	17	17	1	2	8	15⁻	1	1	1	1
Other Services	2	2	6	2	7	10	8	1⁺	1	1	6	2⁺	8	7	6	8	5	5	5	5
Commerce	3	3	10	6⁺	13	9⁺	15	14	3	2	11	7⁺	13	10	3	3	10	15⁻	12	13
Finance & Insurance	4	4	5	10⁻	14	17	11	13	4	3	8	11	17	14	13	12	11	9	3	11⁻
Textiles	5	9⁻	2	4	2	5	1	3	2	4	9	13⁻	9	3⁺	1	1	4	7	2	3
Timber & Pulp	6	13⁻	13	15	12	12	14	15	11	11	7	14⁻	2	6⁻	15	14	15	12	9	8
Subsidiaries & Real Estates	7	8	15	13	6	7	6	8	6	6	10	8	10	15⁻	11	16⁻	8	14⁻	17	17
Steel & Non-Ferrous Metals	8	5	7	3⁺	9	6	3	5	8	13⁻	12	9	4	5	4	7	3	2	7	2⁺
Electrical Machinery	9	7	3	7⁻	1	1	2	4	7	8	3	5	3	4	10	13	7	13⁻	13	12
Transportation Equipment	10	9	12	11	16	8⁺	9	10	17	17	1	6⁻	14	12	9	5⁺	14	3⁺	16	9⁺
Chemicals	11	6⁺	9	5⁺	4	4	5	2	14	15	5	1⁺	7	1⁺	5	6	13	4⁺	11	7⁺
Machinery	12	11	14	9⁺	5	2	7	7	13	9⁺	4	3	16	13	14	9⁺	17	16	14	16⁻
Other Manufacturing Industries	13	12	4	8⁻	3	3	4	6	5	5	2	4	5	8	7	2⁺	12	8⁺	8	4⁺
Foodstuffs	14	14	11	14	8	11	10	11	10	12	13	10	6	11⁻	2	4	9	10	10	14⁻
Agriculture & Forestry	15	15	8	12⁻	17	16	17	12⁺	15	7⁺	15	15	12	9	12	11	2	6⁻	4	6
Fisheries	16	17	16	17	15	15	16	17	16	16	16	16	11	17⁻	17	17	16	17	6	10
Construction	17	16	17	16	11	13	13	9⁺	9	10	14	12	15	16	16	10⁺	6	11⁻	15	15
Total	A 6,773	B 53,131	1,390	14,552	108	479	207	1,312	99.6	1,825	90	1,383	75.5	721	129	521	88	721	473	7,268
(US$ millions)																				
B/A	7.84		10.47		4.44		6.34		18.32		15.38		9.55		4.04		8.19		15.37	
Annual Growth Rate (%)	22.63		26.20		16.05		20.10		33.80		31.40		25.57		14.95		23.25		31.40	

Source: Ministry of Finance, *Zaisei Kinyu Tokei Geppo*, Sept., 1973 and Dec., 1983.

+ Indicates items four ranks or more higher than the world ranking.
− Indicates items four ranks or more lower than the world ranking.

investment in the USA increased more rapidly than that in Asia.

In contrast to the American patterns observed above, a marked difference in Japanese investment patterns between countries is observed in Table 10. This dissimilarity is illustrated by the lack of significant Pearson rank correlation coefficients for pairs of Asian countries. Particularly important in this respect is the Japanese practice of considering the impact of its DFI on the pattern of comparative advantage. Japan makes a noticeable effort to develop an investment strategy which promotes the development of industries which have or are gaining comparative advantages in the host country concerned.

As we have shown, the DFI pattern of the US can be characterized as of the "multinational corporation" or "microeconomic type". In contrast, the pattern of Japanese DFI can be characterized as of the "trade oriented"or "macroeconomic type." This type of DFI is consistent with the market mechanism in that it promotes economic development and harmonious evolution of the international trade and comparative advantage. American corporations have invested mainly in the financial sector and in large-scale industries like oil, petrochemicals, and automobiles. In contrast, Japanese companies have invested in a wider range of manufacturing industries that are indispensable to the development of host country economies. In this respect it is significant that much Japanese investment has been made by small-and medium-size firms in industries producing standarized products. Futhermore, new forms of DFI like production sharing, joint ventures, and non-equity arrangements are adopted to a greater degree by Japanese firms than by American firms. There are, however, some common characteristics of American and Japanese DFI. That is the involvement of both Japanese and American firms in the offshore production of electrical machinery and electronic goods and parts.

As a whole, Japanese and American investments in different industries have complemented each other in the East and Southeast Asian countries. DFI has helped to promote the restructuring of industries, expansion of trade, and overall economic development as well.

DFI Between Asian Developing Countries

Over the years there has been a gradual increase of direct foreign investment among the Asian developing countries themselves. Some information on this investment is given in Table 11, from a 1980 JETRO survey based on host country foreign investment statistics. Although these statistics are incomplete some interesting patterns can be observed.

By 1980, mutual investment among the NICs and ASEAN countries amounted to US$2.4 billion. This figure is 42.3 percent of the amount of investment from Japan which was calculated at US$5.68 billion. (This latter figure is surprisingly low in view of the fact that the Japanese figures given in Table 8 put Japanese investment in the region at US$9.62 billion). A few points about Table 11 should be made.

Data dealing with DFI by other NICs or ASEAN countries in the ROC (Taiwan) and Singapore were unavailable; thus zeros appear in the relevant columns. Investments from Hong Kong and Singapore account for most of the DFI within the region. Such investments are directed mainly to Indonesia, Malaysia, and the Philippines. Investments by ethnic Chinese in finance and commerce are most important in this respect.

All the countries except Thailand have invested in Indonesia. This indicates the

Table 11. DFI Between Asian Developing Countries (End of 1980)

(US$ million)

From: \ To:	ROC (Taiwan)	Korea	Hong Kong	East Asia Total	Singapore	Malaysia	Thailand	Philippines	Indonesia	ASEAN Total	Asian Developing Countries Total
ROC (Taiwan)	—	0.6	5.6	6.2	0	0	31.5	4.2	128.6	164.3	170.5
Korea	0	—	0	0	0	0	0	6.0	84.8	90.8	90.8
Hong Kong	0	12.5	—	12.5	0	119.0	17.2	84.2	1,062.3	1,282.7	1,295.2
East Asia Total	0	13.1	5.6	18.7	0	119.0	48.7	94.4	1,275.7	1,537.8	1,556.5
Singapore	0	0	16.0	16.0	—	277.1	3.2	12.7	145.1	438.1	454.1
Malaysia	0	0	0	0	0	—	7.8	0	60.4	68.2	68.2
Thailand	0	0	13.4	13.4	0	0	—	0	0	0	13.4
Philippines	0	0	16.8	16.8	0	0	0.9	—	292.6	293.5	310.3
Indonesia	0	0	0	0	0	0	0	0	—	0	0
ASEAN Total	0	0	46.2	46.2	0	277.1	11.9	12.7	498.1	799.8	846.0
WPDC Total	0	13.1	51.8	64.9	0	396.1	60.6	107.1	1,773.8	2,337.6	2,402.5

Source: JETRO Survey: CSIS, Issues for Pacific Economic Cooperation, A Report of the Third Pacific Economic Cooperation Conference, Bali, November 1983, Jakarta, March 1984, p. 89.

desire of these countries to promote economic ties and good relations with this huge neighbor. Investments between the four NICs are unexpectedly small. This indicates that these countries prefer to promote investments from developed countries.

Future DFI in East and Southeast Asia

There are some problems regarding future inflows of direct investment into the region that should be addressed.

The possible resurgence of economic nationalism in the countries of East and Southeast Asia must be considered in selecting strategies for direct foreign investment. Neither the enclave type of DFI characteristics of the colonial era, nor the "final-touch" assembly type operation of modern multi-national corporations are suited to the needs of these countries.

Therefore, it is necessary to develop intermediate goods industries like steel, aluminum, copper, and chemicals in the countries with suitable resource bases. As industrialization in these countries proceeds, a huge demand for such goods will be created. Furthermore, it is efficient for Japan to import intermediate goods from offshore locations and so another source of demand will be created. International joint venture projects in which Japan provides capital, management know-how, and a market to absorb the final products, the United States provides technology, Australia provides raw materials (when necessary), and host countries in Asia provide electricity and labor, should be pursued in these industries.

NICs and ASEAN countries have a strong desire to establish high technology industries such as electronics and automobile manufacturing. However, inexpensive labor which once provided a strong motive for offshore production in these industries is becoming less attractive to developed country firms because of factory automation and robotization. Furthermore, when DFI is part of the subcontracting process, the host countries get only limited value added from wage income. This is usually true irrespective of the type of industry involved. Typically, the wage level in these ventures is linked to the agricultural wage and may be quite low.

In the larger ASEAN countries there is no reason to emphasize high technology industries. Instead it would be more rational for these countries to focus on promotting investment and production processes which absorb the largest amounts of labor. This point is especially relevant for the larger ASEAN countries (the Philippines, Malaysia, Thailand and Indonesia). These countries are still in the early stages of industrialization in which it is more efficient to promote traditional manufacturing activity rather than the development of high technology industries.

Production of clothes, foodstuffs, and materials for housing construction are very important in developing and deepening the national economy. These activities should be promoted by modernizing and expanding the small and medium sized business sector. In this case, transfer of technology (and management know-how) from Japan and the United States and/or direct investment by firms from NICs in the four larger ASEAN countries could be useful.

It is necessary for the four larger ASEAN countries to develop and organize various elements of business infrastructure.[21] Banking, trading companies, com-

---

[21] See Kiyoshi Kojima, "Development Oriented Direct Foreign Investment and the Role of the Asian Development Bank," Manila: *Economics Office Report Series, No. 4,* April, ADB, 1982.

munication facilities, shipping facilities, roads, electricity, and warehouses are the elements of business infrastructure. It is particularly desirable for the ASEAN countries to cooperate in the development of this infrastructure. Improvements in business infrastructure will attract greater DFI and enhance competitive abilities of domestic enterprises.

Generally speaking, the NICs and ASEAN countries have already gained the momentum necessary to induce greater DFI and expand trade in a fashion consistent with the workings of the market mechanism. It is possible for these countries to successfully cope with a dynamic restructuring of the industries in line with comparative advantage. This process could be further expedited by the removal of excessive restrictions on DFI as well as trade regulations and barriers. Deregulation is important to promote needed direct investment inflows, that have stagnated in recent years. In this context the aforementioned development and efficient organization of business infrastructure would be particularly helpful in improving the efficiency of the market mechanism.

SUMMARY, POLICY ISSUES, AND LONG TERM PROSPECTS

Growth rates of the East and Southeast Asian nations fluctuated in the 1980 — 1984 period, with a marked slowdown since 1981. Largely as a result of slow economic growth in the developed countries, the international environment has become increasingly unfavorable to Asian developing economies in the 1980s. Thus, it seems unlikely that the export oriented growth patterns observed in the 1970s will be repeated in the 1980s. In view of this change, we attempt to summarize the major points of the foregoing analysis, emphasizing the policy issues most likely to be relevant for the next ten years. As a rather substantial revision of previous policies is argued for, further research is essential to the formulation of appropriate policies and some recommendations are made in this respect as well. Finally, we conclude with a couple of remarks on the prospects for long term growth in the region.

The actual performance of the Southeast Asian economies in the 1970s was spectacular. This performance surpassed the ADB predictions made in 1969-1970. The NICs succeeded in doubling per capita GNP and more than doubling GNP. The four larger ASEAN countries almost succeeded in doubling GNP but income levels grew at a much slower rate due to the rapid increase in population. In the early 1980s we would have suggested establishing a similar target of doubling GNP, but this now appears unrealistic.

The high rate of growth in the East and Southeast Asian region in the 1970s was due primarily to export oriented industrialization. The impact of foreign capital inflows, ODA, DFI (including technology transfers), and other (mainly private) foreign inflows, was also significant and favorable. The result was substantial change in industrial and trade structures. The changes in the export sectors foreshadowed economy-wide structural changes. This is illustrated by the fact that exports grew almost twice as fast as GNP (whereas the ADB had predicted a much lower growth rate of exports).

However, as noted above, it has been impossible to expand exports as rapidly in the 1980s. In the 1970s large, developed country markets (Japan, the USA, and other non-regional developed economies) absorbed most of the growth in Asian countries' exports. Unfortunately, the prospects for exports to these markets are not all that bright in the 1980s and actual performance in the first half of the 1980s reflects this. Slower growth and protectionist trends in the developed countries caused by substantial structural problems are the major cause of slowed Asian export growth. As a result it is possible that export growth rates in the 1980s may be only half as large as they were in the 1970s. Consequently the process of export-led economic development will inevitably be slowed.

Given this outlook, one wonders whether an export-led development strategy is the best of all possible strategies. Here some very important questions arise. What is the purpose of export expansion? If the purpose is to increase GNP and thus living standards one must then ask another question. Is intensification of export efforts the most efficient way to increase GNP or is there a more efficient alternative? In view of the increasing difficulty the NICs and ASEAN countries are having in expanding exports to the developed countries it seems most reasonable to expect a more efficient alternative to exist.

However, this position should not be interpreted as a support of protection in the developed countries; on the contrary, it is our belief that increased pressure to open such markets is warranted. Yet, one must be realistic about the prospects for increased trade when formulating policies and setting targets.

In addition, it must also be realized that some Asian countries, most notably, the ROC (Taiwan), Hong Kong and Singapore, have no realistic alternative to export-led industrialization. Yet, even in these economies, excessive export orientation is not desirable because it will result in unnecessary dependence on developed economies. This, in turn, will result in an unnecessarily large sacrifice of policy independence.

Thus, on balance there is an increasing need for the NICs and ASEAN to reduce emphasis on export-led development strategies that result in making economic growth ever more dependent on the world economy and to increase emphasis on measures that promote the development of the domestic economy. This is an important general point. In other words, in order to sustain economic growth at adequate rates some policy shifts are inevitable. The concept of "efficiency-oriented development of the domestic economy" is compatible with outward-looking, market-oriented policies. A more detailed outline of the kinds of policy shifts we envision is given below. However, there is a lot of additional research which needs to be done if implementation of policies based on this approach is to be successful.

Striking an appropriate balance among the various sectors of the economy is a difficult task for economic policymakers. Large differences in productivity and income levels exist between regions within the country, urban versus rural areas, industry versus agriculture and even within specific sectors and industries themselves. It is not possible to quickly overcome such imbalances and inequalities. Deliberate interventionist policies to overcome imbalances may not accomplish much in reducing inequality, but are likely to have negative effects on overall income growth.

A balanced incentive system that does not introduce unwarranted distortions in prices and profits can be useful in gradually reducing sectoral inequalities. Trade, macroeconomic and sectoral pricing policies should neither be tilted excessively toward export promotion nor import substitution. Rather than viewing export promotion and import substitution as targets, in a good development strategy they are best viewed as results of efficiency oriented development. This type of development not only promotes an appropriate balance between the external and domestic sectors of an economy, but also an appropriate balance between and within agriculture, mining, manufacturing, and the service sectors.

The role of agriculture is particularly important in times of world recession in the ASEAN-4 countries, and to a lesser extent in Korea and the ROC (Taiwan). Countries with a relatively large agricultural sector that were not overly dependent on exports were able to maintain relatively steady rates of economic growth (South Asian countries in the 1980s for example). In this sense the agricultural sector can act as a buffer cushioning the domestic economy in times of world recession.

It is crucial to insure that agriculture grows steadily in the larger ASEAN countries. Agriculture and agro-business should be encouraged by measures to encourage the efficient production and increased utilization of fertilizer and farm machinery.

Turning to the mining sector, resource rich ASEAN countries should increase the production of intermediate goods. The prospect for increased demand for many resource intensive, intermediate goods is promising, both at home and abroad. By increasing dependence on intermediate goods production and reducing dependence on unprocessed mineral production it may be possible in several of these economies to reduce vulnerability to world price fluctuations.

Efficient development of energy from domestic sources such as hydro-power and geothermal power should be promoted where possible. Electrification of rural areas will aid the process of rural industrialization. Electrification by increasing air conditioning enables office and factory workers to work more intensively. This is helping the countries in the southern part of the region to overcome a substantial climatic disadvantage.[22] Increased utilization of refrigerators and freezers (in warehouses, ships, railroad cars, and as household appliances) facilitates increased production and demand for marine and dairy products, and other perishables. Growth of rural off-farm employment, particularly for young women would eventually help reduce population growth. Much of the expansion of rural employment will occur in small and medium sized enterprises producing labor-intensive consumer goods. Increased farm incomes will create demand for these goods and this is essential to creating a balanced manufacturing sector.

Savings and rural banking facilities need to be expanded so that house-hold saving can be encouraged. An expanding financial sector can increase efficiency of investment and encourage greater savings.[23] Trading companies and transportation, communication, and warehouse facilities need to be developed and expanded to facilitate business transactions and minimize the cost of those transactions. These points illustrate the important role of the service sector, especially in finance and trading activities.

It must be realized that human resource development is a pre-condition for overall economic development.[24] Education, training, and improvements in health and nutrition are pre-requisites for the increased supply of skilled workers and managers. Ensuring the development of human resources may be the most urgent task facing the governments in the larger ASEAN countries.

Turning to long term issues, the prospects for harmonious evolution of the

---

[22] See Kiyoshi Kojima, "ASEAN and Pacific Economic Cooperation," UMBC (United Malayan Banking Corporation) *Economic Review*, 1984.

[23] See Asian Development Bank, *Domestic Resource Mobilization through Financial Development*, February, 1984.

[24] See Oshima's chapter 2.

international division of labor between East and Southeast Asia and China[25] appears promising, based on recent expansion of trade between these countries. More research is needed to promote trade between these countries. Furthermore, the question of economic integration and cooperation should be looked at anew. An original aim of ASEAN was to investigate this possibility within the context of ASEAN. The potential for expanding the area of integration and cooperation to include the East Asian NICs and China is interesting in that a more beneficial division of labor might be obtained. The increase of DFI within this region is significant and we hope that this trend will continue and assist the harmonious evolution in international economic relations in the region.

The region including China appears to have a promising future for two additional reasons. First of all, population control programs are being implemented and correspondingly population growth rates are being reduced. This factor is a very important element in promoting the orderly migration of labor from the agricultural to the industrial and service sectors. The stage has thus been set for balanced increases of productivity in all sectors. Second, it should be pointed out that the rich natural resource endowments of the four larger ASEAN countries complement the resource poor NICs and, to some extent, China. Thus, the region can hope to become a dynamic industrial center in the twenty first century and also still be a source of supply of primary products well into that century.

---

[25] See R. Kojima's chapter 11.

4. Agricultural Development in Asia: Performance, Issues and Policy Options

Vijay S. Vyas and William E. James

INTRODUCTION

Agricultural development in most of Asia has proceeded more rapidly than expected since the early 1970s and, with some qualifications, can be considered a major success story. In the middle of the 1980s, India has apparently achieved self-sufficiency in food grains. Indonesia, formerly the largest rice importer in the world, had surplus rice production in 1984 and 1985. Asian less-developed countries, with one or two exceptions, have taken giant steps on the road to feeding themselves. Only a decade ago, there were few, if any, experts predicting such dramatic progress in Asian agriculture.[1]

In this chapter we begin with a review of performance of agriculture in 12 Asian developing countries after the introduction of high-yielding cereal varieties in the mid-1960s. Our focus is on developments in the 1970s and early 1980s. After reviewing their performance, the policies and other factors determining agricultural growth are assessed. Then the future requirements for sustained agricultural development, domestic and international, are discussed. We conclude with a summary of key policy issues and indicate strategic measures needed to assure continued success.

For analytical purposes we subdivide the 12 developing Asian countries into the following three subgroups: South Asia, Southeast Asia and Northeast Asia. South Asia includes six low-income, agrarian countries: Bangladesh, Burma, India, Nepal, Pakistan and Sri Lanka. Southeast Asia includes four middle-income countries: Indonesia, Malaysia, the Philippines and Thailand. Northeast Asia includes two newly-industrializing countries: Korea and the ROC (Taiwan). Hong Kong, Brunei,

---

[1] Asian Development Bank, *Rural Asia: Challenge and Opportunity: Report on the Second Asian Agricultural Survey* (New York; Praeger Publishers, 1977) predicted mounting foodgrain deficits unless remedial policies were undertaken in most of Asia. The prevalence of poverty, underemployment and maldistribution of wealth and income meant most households in many Asian LDCs lacked purchasing power to obtain an adequate diet.

and Singapore have tiny agricultural sectors and are thus excluded. Vietnam, Cambodia, Laos, Afghanistan, North Korea, and Mongolia are not included for lack of adequate data. The absence of China is a major gap but recent agricultural performance there is covered in the China country chapter.

REVIEW OF PERFORMANCE

During the 1970s, agricultural GDP in constant prices, grew at an average rate of over three and one-half percent in the Asian developing countries (Table 1). In eight Asian countries agriculture, including crops, animal husbandry, fisheries and forestry, grew at rates of three percent per annum or better. In Bangladesh and India growth was slightly under three percent; in ROC (Taiwan) it averaged two percent. Cereal and food production, the major subsectors, grew even faster and exceeded population growth in all countries, save Nepal (Table 2).

The growth record of Asian agriculture in the 1970s is in marked contrast to the stagnation that has occurred in many developing countries in other parts of the world. The Asian countries' performance was not a result of particularly favorable internal or external conditions. In fact, serious domestic constraints on growth had to be overcome even as external shocks added to difficulties.

The main features of agriculture in Asia are the high density of rural population,

Table 1. Real Growth of Agricultural GDP

Country	1971-1981	1980-1984
NICs		
ROC (Taiwan)	2.0	0.2
Korea	4.7	2.7
ASEAN-4		
Indonesia	3.7	4.6
Malaysia	4.7	3.4
Philippines	4.9	2.1
Thailand	6.0	3.4
South Asia		
Bangladesh	2.9	2.5
Burma	3.4	6.9
India	2.9	2.8
Nepal	1.2	3.1
Pakistan	3.2	2.3
Sri Lanka	3.8	2.1

Source: ADB, *Key Indicators of DMCs of ADB,* April 1985 and Supplement October 1985.
IBRD, *World Development Report* 1986, Appendix, Table A6, p. 156.

Table 2. Growth Rates of Food and Cereals Production and Population

Country	Average Annual Growth Rates				
	Food Production		Cereals Production		Population
	1971-81	1981-84	1971-81	1981-84	1971-1984
NICs					
ROC (Taiwan)	–	–	–	–	1.9
Korea	3.8	0.2	2.0	4.3	1.6
ASEAN-4					
Indonesia	4.8	4.5	5.2	5.5	2.3
Malaysia	5.4	4.1	3.2	−3.5	2.8
Philippines	4.2	2.0	4.3	1.6	2.7
Thailand	5.1	3.7	4.0	3.8	2.4
South Asia					
Bangladesh	2.0	2.6	2.6	1.2	2.2
Burma	3.2	6.9	5.6	3.2	2.3
India	2.8	4.8	2.8	5.3	2.2
Nepal	1.5	5.0	1.3	4.7	2.2
Pakistan	3.2	3.2	3.9	1.4	3.1
Sri Lanka	5.0	−1.0	4.1	2.0	1.7

Sources: ADB, *Key Indicators of DMCs of ADB*, April 1985 and earlier editions.
　　　　FAO, *FAO Production Yearbook*, 1984 and earlier editions.

the prevalence of small-scale farms, the scarcity of additional land for conversion to agricultural uses, and the monsoon rainfall pattern on which most cultivation depends. Agricultural land per person averaged only one-fifth of a hectare in Asia in 1980. The ratio of rural population to arable land in Asia is twice as great as in Africa and three times that of Latin America.[2]

In the mid-1960s, a number of Asian countries began placing greater emphasis on agricultural development in their economic plans and policies. The availability of new technology in the form of fertilizer-responsive high-yielding varieties of rice and wheat coupled with problems of rapidly growing population and widespread rural poverty prompted the shift in policy-orientation toward agriculture. The focus of agricultural strategies in food deficit countries (all except Nepal, Burma, ROC (Taiwan) and Thailand) was to increase production of major cereals with the eventual goal of attaining self-sufficiency. Rice, being the single most important agricultural activity in Asia was singled out for special attention. Major efforts were made to spur adoption of new varieties, to promote use of new inputs, chemical fertilizer in particular, and to expand irrigation to bolster yields and permit multiple-cropping.

---

[2]　Oshima, Harry, "The Transition to an Industrial Economy in Monsoon Asia," Asian Development Bank Economic Staff Paper No. 20, October 1983. See Appendix 2, p. 86.

In the mid-1970s, self-sufficiency appeared to be further out of reach than in the mid-1960s in countries like Indonesia, India, Bangladesh, and Sri Lanka. Drought and pest attacks led to harvest failures between 1972 and 1975 in many parts of Asia. Per capita food supplies were no larger than in the 1960s and in some cases were lower. A somber mood prevailed as cereal imports in Asia reached record levels in 1972 and 1973 and foodgrain prices skyrocketed.

The Asian Development Bank's Second Asian Agricultural Survey[3] presented a grim picture. Rural poverty was spreading in many parts of Asia, landlessness was on the rise, agricultural real wages were falling, and because larger farmers were apparently the main beneficiaries of the new technology and government credit programs, rural income distribution was also worsening. The ADB report warned that the rates of adoption of high-yielding seed varieties and chemical fertilizers were slowing down and that new initiatives would be necessary to increase their momentum. Sudden upsurges in fuel and fertilizer prices in 1973-74 made promotion of crop intensification more difficult as well. The 1970s closed with a second sharp rise in petroleum prices followed by a deep and long world recession that reduced demand for agricultural exports and led to increased agricultural protectionism in the more developed countries.

The impressive growth of agricultural production in Asian developing countries in the face of major difficulties must in large part be attributed to the policies adopted. Asian policymakers, as well as international development agencies had learned from mistaken neglect of agriculture in the 1950s and early 1960s. The progress and achievements made in individual countries and subregions within Asia have varied. In addition, certain subsectors have done especially well, others have lagged. The differences in performance are hardly surprising in a region as large and diverse as Asia.

Initial Conditions for Growth

The initial conditions in the three subgroups at the beginning of the 1970s were distinctly different. The quality of agricultural performance of the Asian developing countries in the 1970s and early 1980s reflects to some degree differences in the initial physical and social conditions in each country. Some of the most important factors in determining subsequent growth performance are: (1) the country's capacity to save and invest; (2) the supply of arable land in relation to its population; (3) the distribution of landholdings among agricultural producers; (4) the quality of land and the availability of an adequate and timely supply of water and other inputs; (5) the composition of its agricultural production; and (6) the ability and willingness of farmers to adopt improved methods of production. The following indicators are proxies for these six factors: (1) per capita GNP; (2) cropped land per capita; (3) the Gini coefficient of distribution of land; (4) the ratio of irrigated land to total arable land; (5) the share of agricultural exports to agricultural GDP; and (6) the literacy rate among the rural population[4] (Table 3).

In addition to these factors one must take stock of the relative importance of agriculture in GDP and employment (Table 4). The list of factors is by no means

---

[3] *Op. cit.* This may be contrasted with the relatively optimistic scenario presented by the ADB's First *Asian Agricultural Survey,* University of Tokyo Press, 1969.

[4] For details see Vijay S. Vyas, "Asian Agriculture: Achievements and Challenges," *Asian Development Review,* Vol. 1, No. 2, 1983, p. 33.

Table 3. Selected Data Relevant to Agricultural Growth[a]

Country	GNP Per Capita ($)	Cropped Land Per Capita (ha)	Concentration in Landholding[b]	Ratio of Irrigated to Arable Land (%)	Ratio of Agricultural Exports to Agricultural GDP (%)	Literacy Rate (%)
ASEAN-4						
Indonesia	80	0.15	0.49	34.6	14.7	62
Malaysia	400	0.53	—	27.5	67.8	60
Philippines	240	0.19	0.46	12.1	22.8	88
Thailand	210	0.38	0.42	16.9	39.2	84
South Asia						
Bangladesh	70	0.13	0.39	11.8	3.0	26
Burma	80	0.37	0.41	8.6	8.7	67
India	110	0.30	0.58	19.4	3.4	36
Nepal	90	0.17	0.52	5.9	3.5	24
Pakistan	130	0.29	0.47	67.9	13.8	24
Sri Lanka	100	0.16	—	49.1	60.6	86

Sources: ADB, *Key Indicators of DMCs of ADB*, April 1983.
FAO, *FAO Production Yearbook*, 1981.
(In Vyas, V.S., "Asian Agriculture: Achievements and Challenges," *Asian Development Review*, Vol. 1, No. 2, 1983).

— = not available.
a Data pertains to 1970 or thereabout.
b Concentration ratio as measured by the Gini coefficient of distribution for holdings calculated from FAO Printout of Census of Agricultural Holdings.

Table 4. Comparative Shares of Agricultural Sectors and the Growth
in Output Per Worker, 1970-1983

Country	Share of GDP (%) 1970	1983	Share of Employment (%) 1970	1983	Average Annual Growth of Agricultural Output Per Worker 1970-1983
NICs					
ROC (Taiwan)	17.7	7.2	35.4	18.6	3.4[i]
Korea	28.9	15.8	50.4	29.7	3.9
ASEAN-4					
Indonesia	43.6[a]	29.9	66.3	54.7[f]	3.1[j]
Malaysia	29.1[b]	22.0	55.5	37.0	4.5
Philippines	28.8	24.8	53.8	52.1	0.7
Thailand	30.3[c]	23.7	79.9	69.1	1.5
South Asia					
Bangladesh	57.9[b]	49.4	85.9	66.7	1.1
Burma	38.3	37.8	66.7	66.1	2.9
India	47.4[d]	37.3[e]	69.3	58.9	0.4
Nepal	67.5	59.0	93.9	92.6[g]	--
Pakistan	37.0[d]	28.8	58.8	52.7	0.9
Sri Lanka	32.9	26.8	55.1	45.5[h]	2.2[k]

Sources: ADB, *Key Indicators of DMCs of ADB,* April 1985 and Supplement October 1985.
FAO, *FAO Production Yearbook,* 1984 and earlier editions.
World Bank, *World Development Report,* 1985.

[a]1971.   [b]1973.   [c]1972.   [d]GDP data are at factor cost.
[e]1982 GDP data at factor cost.   [f]1982.   [g]1980.   [h]1981.
[i]1971-1983.   [j]1976-1982.   [k]1971-1981.

exhaustive, nor are the indicators without deficiencies, but they give a general indication of conditions in the early 1970s.

The countries of Southeast Asia, in general, had the strongest ability to increase agricultural production in the 1970s. The Southeast Asian countries save Indonesia had per capita incomes of over $200 in 1970. Malaysia and Thailand had abundant land resources, though population densities were greater in Indonesia and the Philippines.[5] Land holdings were less concentrated in Thailand or Malaysia than

---

[5] Population is very unevenly distributed in Indonesia. About two-thirds of the population is concentrated on Java, Bali and Madura. The outer islands are very thinly populated. Population densities in 1980 were 680 people per square kilometer on the densely populated islands compared to a national average of 77. Uneven distribution of population is not as pronounced in the Philippines. See William James, "An Economic Analysis of Public Land Settlement Alternatives in the Philippines," Ph.D. dissertation, University of Hawaii, 1979.

in the Philippines or Indonesia. Irrigation development was relatively greater in Indonesia and Malaysia. There were high agricultural export to agricultural GDP ratios in the Southeast Asian countries and literacy rates were high, particularly in Thailand and the Philippines.

For the two Northeast Asian NICs, conditions differed in the early 1970s. The ROC (Taiwan) had already experienced two decades (1950-1970) of high agricultural growth. It was shifting its emphasis strongly to promotion of manufacturing exports by the late 1960s. It already had reached self-sufficiency in rice. Korea lagged behind the ROC (Taiwan) in agricultural development until the mid-1960s when it adopted policy reforms encouraging agricultural production. Korea and the ROC (Taiwan) were constrained by their limited agricultural land and water resources. But both had highly literate farm populations, egalitarian distribution of land holdings, and high income levels. Korea was late in promoting high-yielding rice varieties compared to the ROC (Taiwan). It also was slower in making the structural transformation from agriculture to industry and services. Both countries were, in the 1970s, experiencing rapid declines in the share of agriculture in GDP. Absolute declines in farm population were occurring in the ROC (Taiwan) by the late 1960s and in Korea by the mid-1970s.[6]

South Asian countries were less prepared to meet the challenges of the 1970s than were those of the NICs and Southeast Asia. They had lower levels of income, averaging under $100. Except for Burma, cultivated land per capita was under a third of a hectare, land holdings tended to be more concentrated, the ratio of irrigated land to total arable land was low (except in Pakistan and Sri Lanka), agricultural exports were low and literacy rates were under 40 percent in four of the six countries.

The relationship between the initial conditions and subsequent growth performance are complex. The countries that had the most favorable starting positions indicated by higher income levels, more land per capita, low concentration of holdings, more irrigated land in proportion to total, a high ratio of exports to total agricultural output and a high literacy rate tended to grow faster than the others. But in some cases countries with disadvantaged starting positions (Indonesia, Burma, Sri Lanka) achieved high growth despite initial handicaps. Strong growth performance can be attributed to policy changes that corrected or compensated for initial deficiencies.

Agricultural Growth and Development Performance

In the 1970s, the Southeast Asian countries had the strongest agricultural growth performances, ranging from 3.7 percent in Indonesia to 6.0 percent in Thailand (annual averages, in constant prices) (Table 1). The exceptional agricultural growth of these four ASEAN countries was led by food production. Food output grew much faster than population in each country (Table 2). Cereals output grew faster than population, and per capita food supplies increased steadily. Cereal production growth (and rice in particular) was a strong contributing factor in the high growth of the Philippines, Indonesia, and Thailand. In Malaysia, non-cereal crops contributed to growth. Exports of forestry and fishery products also made strong contributions to high growth in the ASEAN-4 countries.[7]

---

[6] See Oshima, *op. cit.,* pp. 89-90.
[7] Asian Development Bank, *Agriculture in Asia,* ADB Staff Working Paper, September 1984, pp. 48-67 and 93.

In the 1980s, agricultural growth rates declined in all but Indonesia – with the Philippines growth rate falling to less than half the average of the 1970s (Table 1). Lower agricultural export growth was a major cause of reduced overall agricultural growth as the ASEAN-4 were hit hard by the long recession of 1980-83 and the even longer stagnation of agricultural commodity prices. Indonesia compensated for lower export growth by very high growth in cereals (rice) production in the first half of the 1980s. This main subsector grew at better than 5 percent a year between 1980 and 1984. Indonesia entered the latter half of the 1980s with burgeoning surpluses of rice.[8]

In South Asia in each country, except Nepal, food and cereals production outpaced population growth in the 1970s. After worsening in the first half of the 1970s food and cereals supplies improved steadily thereafter. Farm exports did not contribute as strongly to growth in most of South Asia during the 1970s as in Southeast Asia.

Agricultural growth performance in the 1980s was mixed in South Asia. In Pakistan and Sri Lanka production growth slipped from over 3 percent in the 1970s to slightly over 2 percent between 1980-84. In Bangladesh it was only slightly lower between 1980-84 than the previous decade and for India it was about the same. The continued growth in rice and wheat production in India, resulted in surplus production by the mid-1980s. In Burma and Nepal agricultural growth actually improved sharply in the 1980s over the 1970s. For South Asia as a whole, its agricultural growth in the 1980s has held up quite a bit better than other Asian countries that are more dependent on external demand for agricultural commodities. Declines in prices and volumes of agricultural exports were a cause of slower growth for Pakistan, Bangladesh, and Sri Lanka and could create problems for grain exports of Burma and Nepal as well.

In Korea and the ROC (Taiwan), agricultural growth rates diverged sharply in the 1970s. Korea's high growth rate reflects its catching-up with the ROC (Taiwan) in cereals and diversified agriculture, livestock and fisheries. Yields of cereals improved sharply in Korea in the 1970s as newer HYVs were rapidly adopted. The ROC (Taiwan), which was by the late 1970s facing problems of high-cost rice surpluses, sought to de-emphasize foodgrain production and shift resources to higher-valued crops and livestock or out of agriculture altogether. The 1980s saw declines in agricultural growth in the both the ROC (Taiwan) and Korea. Weak markets for exports and internal constraints on improving productivity of crop production were the causes. With rising rural wages, Korea and the ROC (Taiwan) were losing their comparative advantage in agricultural production. The protection of agriculture and rice, in particular, has increased land values and made it difficult to consolidate farmland into economic-sized units. This has prevented development of modern mechanized farm operations.

In comparing agricultural growth performance it is important to recognize the different stages of development and resource endowment of the Asian countries and subgroups. The NICs have to a great extent made a transition from an agrarian-based economy to a modern manufacturing and service economy. The NICs are

---

[8] Indonesia first had surplus production of rice in 1984. Even larger harvests in 1985 led to serious problems of grain storage. See *Far Eastern Economic Review,* "Problems of Plenty," 7 November 1985, pp. 82-83 for a discussion of Indonesia's rice situation. By year-end 1985 it was conservatively estimated that 3.3 million tons were in government storage. Whether or not there will be longer-term self-sufficiency in rice remains uncertain.

relatively poorly endowed with natural resources. The ASEAN-4 have abundant agricultural resources and have much further to go in structural change. Manufacturing employs a much smaller portion of the labor force in ASEAN than in the NICs. Agriculture still must absorb much of the increments in the fast-growing work force. In some areas of Southeast Asia, the numbers of landless rural laborers have been increasing. These landless workers are employed in agriculture only on a seasonal basis. Many of these workers seek employment in the off-season in non-farm enterprises. The informal services sector acts as the residual employer of this group, often in low productivity activities with subsistence-level wages.

The South Asian countries are overwhelmingly agricultural economies — even though India and Pakistan have relatively large industrial sectors, two-thirds or more of the population remains in rural communities and depends mainly on agriculture for income and employment.

These differences were primarily caused by differing rates of growth in agricultural labor productivity (Table 4). The pace of occupational diversification was faster in countries where growth in agricultural labor productivity was faster. In Korea and the ROC (Taiwan) between 1970-1983 agricultural output per worker rose by nearly 4 percent a year. Similar growth was experienced in Malaysia. In Thailand, the Philippines and Indonesia output per worker in agriculture grew between 1 to 3 percent a year. In South Asia, output per agricultural worker, save in Burma and Sri Lanka, grew by 1 percent or less annually. In Nepal it actually declined.

Unlike the growth in labor productivity, which was pronounced only in a few countries, the successes of Asian agriculture in terms of output growth was more pervasive and in the 1970s had a number of favorable consequences for the overall economic development performance of these countries. The expansion of food and cereals production in traditional food deficit countries, particularly Indonesia, Sri Lanka, markedly reduced their dependence on food imports. Grain exporters like Thailand, Burma, and Pakistan were able to increase earnings. Real food prices rose sharply during the 1972-74 food crisis. Harvest shortfalls in major importing countries led to aggressive competition for cereal imports and forced import prices upwards throughout Asia. Governments often have subsidized food consumption in Asia — and this has proven to be very costly. But since the mid-1970s improved domestic production and expanded supplies of cereals for export have helped keep food prices stable. In the mid-1980s real foodgrains prices have fallen and this has benefited low income households. Productivity improvements in agriculture reduced the need for costly food subsidies.

There was also increased production of agricultural raw materials and export crops like cotton, jute, rubber, palm oil, sugar, spices, pineapple and assorted tree crops in most of Asia in the 1970s. The expanding supply of grains and exportable crops encouraged processing industries and allowed greater attention to be focused on other subsectors — animal husbandry, fisheries, and forestry.

Exports of agricultural products grew faster than imports in much of Asia. Between 1973 and 1980, agricultural exports increased rapidly in all countries save in Nepal and Bangladesh. Agricultural trade surpluses of increasing size were generated in all the ASEAN-4 countries and in Sri Lanka, Pakistan, Burma, and India between 1973 and 1980 (Table 5). The positive contribution of agriculture to the balance of payments was a major factor in helping the countries adjust to the

Table 5. Agricultural Sector Net Exports, 1973-1984

(Unit: US$ million)

Country	1973	1974	1975	1976	1977	1978	1979	1980	1981	1982	1983	1984
NICs												
Korea	(555)	(983)	(792)	(824)	(553)	(1,156)	(2,146)	(2,589)	(3,277)	(2,339)	(2,645)	(2,136)
ASEAN-4												
Indonesia	756	1,132	671	1,216	1,703	1,627	2,974	3,111	1,121	939	1,626	1,562
Malaysia	1,360	1,383	1,499	2,298	2,622	2,837	4,773	4,443	3,434	3,376	4,174	3,114
Philippines	954	1,435	1,091	1,099	1,458	1,342	1,705	1,893	1,719	1,215	1,161	1,146
Thailand	842	1,520	1,337	1,831	1,681	2,120	2,599	2,874	3,537	3,705	3,052	3,653
South Asia												
Bangladesh	(356)	(377)	(429)	(313)	(4)	(243)	(97)	(380)	(240)	(304)	(195)	(222)
Burma	90	124	108	153	152	133	242	311	350	299	330	169
India	255	285	(19)	198	641	683	1,134	1,055	1,150	1,234	760	580
Nepal	64	31	39	58	43	53	48	7	25	5	31	26
Pakistan	12	(53)	(106)	1	(17)	(84)	9	218	469	5	(2)	(336)
Sri Lanka	120	85	61	232	331	376	330	212	265	297	277	708

Source: FAO, *FAO Trade Yearbook*, 1984 and earlier editions.

Notes: Agricultural sector includes forestry and fishery products.
Agricultural trade deficits are shown within parentheses.

external shocks of the 1970s.[9] In India, Sri Lanka, Pakistan, and the Philippines, the export surplus expanded and at the same time grain importation was lessening.

Rising farm incomes in rural communities helped stimulate domestic demand for labor-intensive manufactured goods and services. Construction of improved housing in rural areas also created greater demand for domestically produced construction materials and added to employment.[10] Higher tax revenues and savings by rural households contributed to higher domestic saving rates in most Asian countries.[11]

Agricultural growth is a major determinant of the overall economic growth rate in Asian countries — in South and Southeast Asia in particular. The ASEAN-4 countries economic growth in the 1970s was much higher than that of South Asia. The average agricultural growth rate of about 5 percent in the ASEAN-4 was associated with average real economic growth of about 7 percent in the 1970s. The South Asian countries agricultural growth of 3 percent was associated with overall economic growth averaging under 5 percent in the 1970s.

In the 1980s, real economic growth rates of these two subregions have converged. Agricultural growth rates have fallen to just above 3.3 percent in the ASEAN-4 and have increased slightly to an average of 3.3 percent in South Asia. The period since the late 1970s has been one of sustained growth in a number of South Asian countries — Sri Lanka, Burma, Pakistan, India. Agriculture has been a major factor in allowing these countries to continue growing at real rates of 5 percent or better since the late 1970s.

Pressure of Population on Land

The growth contributions of agricultural subsectors changed during the 1970s in Asia. A major influence on differences in growth of various subsectors has been the increasing scarcity of cultivable land (and rising concern with environmental issues). The scope for opening new land for agriculture (mainly through conversion of forest land) has been very limited since the late 1960s, outside of Thailand, Malaysia, and Indonesia.[12]

From 1966 to 1982 the area of cultivable land increased by less than four percent in South Asia.[13] The farm population over the same years increased by over 21 percent. In the ASEAN-4 countries the farm area grew slightly faster than the farm population. If Thailand is treated separately, for the remaining countries farm population increased by 16 percent; farm land by only 12 percent. Even in Thailand, by 1980 population densities in rural areas began to rise as the land frontier was reached. In Korea and the ROC (Taiwan) farm population declines were matched by conversion of farm land to non-agricultural uses. There the farm land per capita

---

[9] See William James, "Asian Agriculture in Transition: Key Policy Issues," ADB Economic Staff Paper No. 19, September 1983.

[10] In densely populated Java this was a major reason for rising rural real wages in the late 1970s and early 1980s. See W. Collier, "Acceleration of Rural Development on Java," *Bulletin of Indonesian Economic Studies*, Vol. 18, No. 3, November 1982, pp. 82-101.

[11] Asian Development Bank, *Domestic Resource Mobilization through Financial Development*, Vol. II, Economics Office, Manila, February 1984. Also: W. James, S. Naya, and G. Meier, *Asian Development: Economic Success and Policy Lessons*, forthcoming, see chapter IV.

[12] See W. James, "Asian Agriculture and Economic Development," ADB Economic Staff Paper No. 5, March 1982, pp. 9-15.

[13] *Agriculture in Asia, op. cit.*, pp. 38-48.

ratio remained about a twentieth of a hectare. Throughout rural Asia, the ratio of farm population to farm land continued to rise; the ratio of total population to farm land rose even more.

Increasingly population pressure on land in Asia had led to a particular pattern of growth of production. Intensification of land use through improving yields per hectare has increasingly been the means to increase overall production. Irrigation investment allows better water control and permits raising more than one crop per year on the same parcel of land (multiple-cropping). Improved cropping systems; greater use of variable inputs (especially fertilizer); improved management; selective use of mechanical equipment (irrigation pumps, rice threshing machines, small tractors to prepare land for planting); continued scientific research to improve technologies; and more and better support services for farmers have helped to boost yields of crops. From 1973-1982 about 75 percent of increased production of cereals in Asia have been accounted for by improved yields and multiple cropping; only 25 percent from expanding the area of agricultural land through clearing forest and land settlement.

The increasing pressure on land has also affected the relative strength and growth in subsectors like livestock, forestry, and fisheries production. Activities requiring large land inputs have diminished in importance and experienced slower gains in production (pasture-based cattle production and dairying is one example). Forestry has also declined, as forest land has increasingly been reduced in favor of agricultural uses. Activities requiring less land showed strong gains (poultry and hog-raising; fisheries production). There were, of course, differences between countries and subgroups. We will review in the following paragraphs growth in various subsectors.

Growth in Subsectors

Cereals and Staple Food Crops.
Production of cereals, pulses, and other staple crops are by far the most important agricultural activity in Asia. Cereals account for about 60 to 70 percent of crop land in most of the Asian developing countries. Rice is the most important crop in area, numbers of producers, and contribution to total agricultural production in Asia. Wheat and corn are the two other major cereals. Wheat is grown mainly in the semi-arid South Asian countries, India and Pakistan account for over 90 percent of production. Corn is grown in all the Asian countries, and is often the preferred food staple in upland areas. In most Asian countries these three cereals account for the greatest shares of food production and consumption. Rice and wheat account for about 85 percent of all food production in the Asian developing countries (rice alone accounts for two-thirds).[14] Cereals accounted for three-fourths of all calories and six-tenths of protein consumed in Korea between 1978-80; in Bangladesh cereals supplied 84 percent of calories and three-fourths of protein.[15]

Since the mid-1960s cereals production increases have mainly been based on improved yields and double-cropping in irrigated areas rather than on area expansion — Thailand is an exception. Yields grew at a fast rate in most of the Asian countries between the mid-1960s and mid-1970s — again, with the exception of Thailand (and Nepal). The oil shocks of 1973 and 1979 led to higher fertilizer prices and

---

[14] *Ibid.*, pp. 48-49.
[15] *Ibid.*, p. 7.

were expected to have negative impacts on agricultural performance. Despite the higher costs for fertilizer, yields continued to improve in most Asian countries after 1973, and again after 1979, though growth rates of yields varied (Table 6).

The drive to attain greater cereals production in Asia focused on the most important crop — rice. Rice self-sufficiency has been a major objective in deficit countries of Asia. Rice production (dry paddy) increased from under 140 million tons in 1973 to 190 million tons in 1982. Production reached 206 million tons in 1984, resulting in an overall rice surplus. Rice imports have been reduced substantially in Bangladesh, India, Sri Lanka, Indonesia and Korea. Rice exports of Burma, Pakistan and Thailand increased in the early 1980s. Thailand's rice exports exceeded those of the U.S. in 1984 and 1985. The rice surplus situation in Asia in the mid-1980s caused prices of internationally traded rice to fall sharply to levels far below those of a decade earlier.

The impressive gains in rice production reflect long-term increases in production capacity, better yields, and favorable weather conditions in recent years. Average rice yields vary greatly in Asia. In the ROC (Taiwan) and Korea yields per hectare average 4 to 5 tons; in Southeast Asia they average 2.5 tons; and in South Asia only 2 tons. The lower yields in South and Southeast Asia are because of lower intensity of input use (particularly chemical fertilizers); less efficient irrigation systems; less developed support services and marketing infrastructures; institutional problems; lower levels of farmers' education; and lesser price incentives.

Yield differentials of the magnitude found between the Northeast Asian countries and the other subregions are indicative of qualitative differences in the level of development. Modernization of farming has gone much farther in the ROC (Taiwan), Korea (and Japan) than elsewhere in Asia. There are no other Asian countries that

Table 6. Average Annual Growth Rates of Cereals Yields

Country	1967-1973	1973-1980	1980-1984
NICs			
Korea	2.4	1.9	2.0
ASEAN-4			
Indonesia	—	4.7	5.4
Malaysia	3.2	2.5	−0.9
Philippines	3.3	4.0	2.1
Thailand	1.1	1.5	1.9
South Asia			
Bangladesh	1.9	3.4	1.4
Burma	2.6	6.8	6.3
India	4.3	2.9	5.1
Nepal	−0.4	0.9	4.9
Pakistan	7.0	2.9	0.5
Sri Lanka	3.4	1.6	4.5

Source: FAO, *FAO Production Yearbook,* 1984 and earlier editions.

have reached the stage of structural transformation where the size of the agricultural labor force has started to decline absolutely. There is substantial scope for improving productivity in terms of yields. In Java rice yields exceed three and one-half tons per hectare and this has enabled Indonesia to attain full rice self-sufficiency. Whether similar gains can be made elsewhere depends on improvement of all the factors listed above. (The role of policies in tackling these problems are considered in the later part of this chapter.)

Wheat is the second most important crop in Asia in terms of production and area, though it is grown mainly in South Asia. Wheat production between 1973 and 1982 rose by nearly 60 percent in the five main producing countries (India, Pakistan, Bangladesh, Nepal, and Korea) — an annual rate of increase of over six percent. The introduction of wheat HYVs combined with the larger area planted because of irrigation and substitution of wheat for other crops helped to increase output.

Domestic wheat prices in India were maintained at or above import prices — in contrast to domestic rice prices which were held below import prices.[16] In Pakistan domestic wheat procurement prices were increased to more economic levels in the mid- to late 1970s, and the area planted to wheat HYVs increased sharply.[17]

Net imports of wheat fell dramatically in the late 1970s from peak levels in the mid-1970s. Imports of wheat have risen over time in most of East and Southeast Asia and in Sri Lanka where wheat cannot be economically grown. The income elasticity of demand for wheat and wheat flour is high in these countries. There is increased preference for consumption of wheat products — particularly in urban areas. Hence, it is unlikely bumper rice harvests will lead to much, if any, decline in wheat imports. Wheat prices on the international market are lower and more stable than those of rice. About one-quarter of wheat production is internationally traded compared to only 5 to 10 percent of rice.[18] The "thinness" on rice markets contributes directly to the price volatility of trade rice.

Maize is the third most important food crop. Maize is produced as a source of food and of feed for poultry and other livestock. Output growth has been less spectacular in maize than in rice or wheat — about 30 percent increase between 1973 and 1982. Indonesia, Thailand, and the Philippines had the most significant gains in output as both yields and area were increased. Thailand has become a substantial net exporter of feed corn.

Maize production has expanded only slowly in most of South Asia. The technological basis for more rapid increases in production is increasing with the introduction of new disease-resistant high-yielding seeds. Production and yields of maize, as well as other secondary food crops — cassava, sweet potatoes, soybeans, potatoes, peanuts — have not done as well as rice or wheat. These crops have been somewhat neglected in agricultural research and extension work. With the more favorable supply situation of rice and wheat it would be timely to shift resources to promote production of secondary food crops and higher value crops as well. Achievement of productivity improvements in these crops may be more difficult than for irrigated rice. It is unlikely a single "technology package" approach will work because of the more varied conditions under which these crops are produced.

---

[16] See S. Roy, "Pricing, Planning, and Politics," Occasional Paper, pp. 48-49.

[17] Asian Development Bank, *Strategies for Economic Growth and Development in Pakistan*, July 1985, pp. 201-212.

[18] Amar Siamwalla and Stephen Haykin, "The World Rice Market: Structure, Conduct, and Performance," International Food Policy Research Institute, Research Report No. 39, June 1983.

Cash Crops

The cash crop sector is second in size to staple foods in most Asian developing countries. The export of crops like sugar, coconut, rubber, palm oil, cotton, jute, coffee, tea, and a host of other tropical products provides a major share of foreign exchange earnings in most of South and Southeast Asia. Many of these crops are processed or used as raw materials by industry and their supply expansion is important in its own right for industrial growth.

The ASEAN-4 countries experienced rapid gains in production of cash crops during the 1970s (Table 7.1). In large part, this sector's fast growth accounts for much of the agricultural growth differential between these countries and the South Asian group. The NICs, with a fairly small area devoted to non-food crops and lacking the comparative advantage of the labor-abundant, resource-rich ASEAN-4 countries, had only minor gains in production.

Thailand and Malaysia had very substantial growth in a large number of non-cereal cash crops. During the 1970s, they were able to rapidly expand exports of a range of crops. Indonesia, with its main focus on rice self-sufficiency, began to increase investment in its "estate crops" subsector in the mid-1970s. The expansion of rubber, palm oil, coconut, and some other crops on the outer islands made Indonesia a major producer — but rapid expansion in domestic demand and pricing policies that discouraged exports limited foreign exchange earnings in some crops. The Philippines had rapid gains in a number of newer cash crops — but its two major agricultural exports, sugar and coconut, exhibited slow growth in the 1970s (Table 7.1).

Table 7.1 Annual Production Growth Rates of Export Crops, 1970-1984

(Unit: %)

Crop	ASEAN-4			
	Indonesia	Malaysia	Philippines	Thailand
Banana	0.2[a]	0.9	9.1	3.9
Cassava	1.8	4.1	11.1	13.1
Cocoa	21.3	16.5	3.3	—
Coffee	3.0	5.1	8.3	3.0[c]
Pineapple	5.8[b]	−4.3	11.5	15.3
Palm Oil	9.8	13.5	—	—
Rubber	1.4	27.8	8.7	4.5
Sugar	5.2	8.4	1.8	11.2
Tobacco	2.9	10.4	−1.1	2.5
Tea	2.5	2.1	—	—
Coconut	5.2	3.1	1.2	0.7

Source: FAO, *FAO Production Yearbook*, 1984 and earlier editions.

Note: Used average values of 1970-1972 and 1982-1984 in computing for compounded annual growth rates.

[a]1973-1984.   [b]1977-1984.   [c]1980-1984.

The commodity boom of the early 1970s lifted prices of cash crops and enabled Thailand and the Philippines to have their only current account surpluses of the decade. In the 1970s, prices of cash crops showed their usual cyclical pattern – so that gains during periods of high world growth helped to offset losses during recessions. But in the 1980s, prices of most cash crops became severely depressed. Countries that were able to improve productivity and lower costs (Malaysia and Thailand) had far better growth performance than countries like the Philippines where productivity of major cash crops slumped.

Area expansion played a major role in increased cash crop production in Thailand, Malaysia and Indonesia. New plantings of improved varieties of rubber, coconut, and palm oil and increased inputs also led to higher yields, particularly in Malaysia and Thailand. Malaysian growers substituted more profitable palm oil for rubber, and achieved high productivity and export earnings as a result. Rubber has been a "declining industry" in Malaysia and rubber smallholders remain one of the poorest groups.[19] The ASEAN-4 countries have emerged as the leading exporters of diversified tree and field crops in Asia. To sustain momentum, further increases in yields, particularly of smallholders, will be needed.

Indonesia, like Malaysia, embarked on ambitious area expansion programs for major tree crops and, palm oil, in particular. The emphasis of improving yields and quality through expansion of state-managed plantations and nucleus estate schemes for rubber, coconut, and palm oil has been successful but costs have been high. The large smallholder sectors in rubber and coconut have not participated to a significant degree in productivity gains. Rubber and coconut smallholders account for larger shares of area and production than do modern estates in Indonesia. Increased efforts to provide technical assistance and credit for improved planting materials and increased input use are difficult because of sharp declines in petroleum-based government revenues in the mid-1980s. In order to diversify Indonesia's economy and exports away from petroleum – cash crops are exceedingly important. There are opportunities for efficiently increasing production of a number of exportables (cocoa, pineapple, banana, spices, horticultural products) and a few import-replacing crops (cotton). But Indonesian authorities have often chosen to seek to replace imports with domestic production even at high cost. Sugar is an example; domestic supply and demand have been balanced at a domestic price three times the international price. High cost sugar has displaced other crops (cassava, corn, and other secondary crops) not enjoying such protection.

As new tree crop areas planted in past years begin to produce, Indonesia's supply of cash crops for export will increase. The strong competition for external markets will require Indonesian producers to improve quality and take measures to keep costs down.

The Philippines relied on traditional cash crops for sustaining export earnings in the face of oil shocks and recessions during the 1970s. The government imposed export levies on these crops and increased its control over marketing and processing of sugar and coconut. The coconut sector is dominated by smallholders, many of whom have little alternative source of income or employment. In the sugar sector, large-scale estates figure more prominently in production, though there are also numerous smaller production units. There is some geographical concentration of

---

[19] Colin Barlowe, "The Rubber Smallholder Economy," *Bulletin of Indonesian Economic Studies*, Vol. 18, No. 2, July 1982.

sugar estate production on Negros island where sugar workers have almost no alternative employment opportunities. Coconut production is more widely dispersed. The government policies were, in principle, to encourage replanting of higher-yielding coconut varieties and also raise sugar yields, while smoothing out fluctuations in earnings and keeping domestic prices of refined sugar and coconut oil stable. In practice, the government policies created disincentives to producers and stifled productivity-enhancing investments.[20] The export levies kept domestic consumer prices down for a time — but revenues garnered during years of favorable external market demand were not plowed back into production. When external markets were weak, government-created agencies were unable to provide relief to hard-pressed planters. The collapse of sugar production and exports in the 1980s and the stagnation in coconut exports demonstrated the negative effects of excessive government regulation.

The cash crops that were of lesser importance and that were not excessively regulated showed strong gains in production (Table 7.1). They were not large enough, however, to offset declines in production and exports of the two major crops. Recovery and rehabilitation of the export crop sector will be a pressing priority for the government in the remainder of the 1980s.

The South Asian countries cash crop sectors performed rather poorly in the 1970s and early 1980s (Table 7.2). The heavy emphasis on raising production of cereals to meet "self-sufficiency" objectives by governments led to the neglect of the cash crop sector in most countries. Plantations producing tea, sugar, rubber, natural fibers, and coconut have been extensively regulated with regard to labor practices, marketing and pricing. Sri Lanka nationalized tea plantations (and most other plantations as well) and productivity has stagnated or declined. Lax management, underbudgeting for research on and investment in new varieties, and greater concern for political than economic gains from control of the plantation sector have contributed to slow growth.

The range of crops grown in India, Burma and Sri Lanka is diverse (Table 7.2). Yet major exports from the cash crop sector are still largely confined to tea, rubber, jute, and small amounts of coconut. Sri Lanka's expanded production of secondary food crops, fruits, and vegetables is beginning to be reflected in higher export earnings. Together with minor export crops (coffee, pepper, cloves, cocoa, etc.) these crops accounted for 5 percent of total exports in 1984.[21] Other South Asian countries have even narrower non-cereal crop export bases — Bangladesh exports mainly jute and tea; Pakistan, cotton; Nepal, jute and ghee. There is export potential for a variety of fruit and vegetable products to the Middle East and for import replacement of edible oils.

From the standpoint of income distribution and poverty amelioration, improvement of cash crop smallholder productivity in South and Southeast Asia is of particular importance. At present, smallholders are reluctant to adopt the costly approaches used by modern estates. These usually require replanting, large amounts of working capital, and intensive management and supervision. With higher investment comes higher risk of losses if prices decline. Smallholders' reluctance to adopt such technologies results from their own calculation of benefits and costs, as well

---

[20] Ramon Clarete and James Roumasset, "An Analysis of the Economic Policies Affecting the Philippine Coconut Industry," Philippine Institute of Development Studies, Working Paper 83-80, Manila, 1983.

[21] N. Gunasinghe, "Open Economic Policy and Peasant Production," *Upunathi*, Vol. 1, No. 1, January 1986, pp. 37-105.

Table 7.2 Annual Production Growth Rates of Export Crops, 1970-1984

(Unit: %)

Crop	South Asia					
	Bangladesh	Burma	India	Nepal	Pakistan	Sri Lanka
Banana	0.7	2.3[a]	2.3	—	6.4	—
Cassava	—	13.3	0.1	—	—	4.3
Coffee	—	0.0	2.6	—	—	5.1
Pineapple	2.9	—	14.7	—	—	0.7
Rubber	—	1.5	4.1	—	—	−0.5
Sugar	6.9	−4.6	5.2	5.1	6.7	8.2
Tobacco	1.9	0.8	2.7	−2.0	−2.9	4.2
Tea	5.4	—	2.3	—	—	−0.5
Jute	−1.6	−0.3	2.7	−2.9	—	—
Coconut	0.8	2.1	−0.5	—	—	−0.7

Source: FAO, *FAO Production Yearbook,* 1984 and earlier editions.

Note: Used average values of 1970-1972 and 1982-1984 in computing for compounded annual growth rates.

[a]1970-1975.

as constraints in access to credit, their levels of knowledge, skills, and management capacity. The performances of rural financial institutions, research and extension services are of great importance to lessening these constraints.

The preoccupation with cereal self-sufficiency has understandably diverted resources from cash crop production. In future, it may be more efficient to shift some emphasis to raising productivity of this sector than to focus exclusively on grains. A policy of balanced incentives for production for domestic and external markets coupled with improvements in institutional and technological support would encourage growth and help increase smallholder incomes. Crop diversification strategies are discussed later under a sub-heading Agricultural Trade.

Livestock and Dairying

The livestock and dairy sector has been a relatively lagging area of agricultural development in Asia. Within Asia there were in 1980 approximately 28 livestock units per 100 people compared to 83 in western Europe.[22] Food output per livestock unit is quite low in Asia at the equivalent of only 150 kilograms a year of meat, milk, and eggs compared to over 600 kilograms in the United States.[23] The comparision is of limited relevance. Asia's farmers regard their livestock (cattle and buffalo in particular) as a source of draft power and manure for farming, and as a means of wealth accumulation.

Demand for livestock and dairy products has been rising faster than supply in

---
[22] Food and Agriculture Organization statistics cited in *Agriculture in Asia, op. cit.,* p. 63.
[23] *Ibid.*

a good number of Asian developing countries, but particularly those in the NICs and ASEAN-4 where per capita income has been rising rapidly. Technical and manpower bottlenecks, constraints in providing fodder and feed, and acute scarcity of land have hampered growth of livestock and dairy production in Asian LDCs. There are exceptions — growth rates of dairy and meat production have been high in Korea, the ROC (Taiwan), and Pakistan. Also poultry production and (in non-Muslim areas) pig raising have grown rapidly in the ASEAN countries.

Increased numbers and quality of cattle and cattle products have been constrained in densely-populated areas throughout Asia because of scarcity of pasture land and fodder. In addition problems of disease, weakness of technical and veterinary services, and capital market imperfections have been limiting factors in the sector. These seem to be more serious in the case of large ruminants (cattle, buffalo, oxen) than smaller species.

Cattle and other draft animals will continue to be important for small- to medium-sized peasant farmers. Better measures to prevent disease and to improve quality of draft animals are needed. Technical services and extension work to assist farmers in health measures and means to improve fodder and use of manure for improved crop yields have led to some gains but more is possible. Throughout most of South and Southeast Asia improvements of quality — not just numbers — of livestock are needed.

Poultry, small ruminants, and (in non-Muslim areas) hog raising, can provide strong sources of additional income to smallholders and land-poor rural households. Integration of village and backyard poultry production with commercial enterprise has been successful in Thailand. Private firms supply inputs, technical advice, and marketing services on credit for smallholders who raise chickens, and share in profits. Dairying has successfully involved smallholders organized in cooperatives in India. Effective organization and marketing with adequate support in technical areas (like quality control) are elements in successful involvement of smallholders.

The promotion of commercial livestock production should not be excessive. Demand for feed can lead to higher grain imports (as in Korea and the ROC-Taiwan) or cause, in low income and foodgrain deficit areas, shifts in domestic grain from food to feed uses that may bid up staple food prices to impoverished households.

Manpower bottlenecks and problems in breeding, disease control, and management remain to be solved. Livestock production may pose environmental problems — pollution of water supplies and pressures on land for grazing and fuelwood for preparation of feed present potential problems. In general, small-scale livestock production that requires less land and fewer non-labor inputs is likely to be more suited to the South and Southeast Asian LDCs, than large-scale capital- or land-intensive types.

Fisheries

Asian developing countries increased their share of the world's total fish catch from 12 percent in 1965 to 14 percent in the early 1970s and almost 20 percent by the early 1980s.[24] The volume of production by Asian fisheries more than doubled between 1965 and 1982. Marine fisheries account for 80 percent of total production with inland fisheries and aquaculture accounting for the remainder. Expanded

---

[24] Food and Agriculture Organization data cited in *Agriculture in Asia*, p. 64.

marine production has contributed strongly to agricultural GDP growth, employment and foreign exchange earnings in the majority of Asian developing countries. Exports of fish products to Japan and the U.S. grew sharply. Fish are the major source of animal protein in the diets of Asian peoples, and rapid expansion of supply has been necessary to meet domestic demand.

India and Korea have the largest fisheries sectors but Thailand, Indonesia, the Philippines, and the ROC (Taiwan) also annually produced nearly two million tons of fish by the early 1980s. Korea and India are the largest exporters. Between 1973 and 1982, fisheries product export growth was exceptional in each of the above countries. Thailand, the Philippines and Indonesia are major exporters of fishery products. The Philippines developed into a net fishery exporter only in the late 1970s. In all of the ASEAN countries overfishing and pollution of coastal waters adjacent to urban centers and densely-populated rural areas have reduced the fish catch of artisanal fishermen. Small fishing villages in these areas have suffered declines in income as a result.

Fisheries production has been adequate to meet domestic demand with some surplus for export (usually higher-value demersal species like shrimp) in most South Asian countries — except landlocked Nepal. Bangladesh is a large inland fish producer — second only to India. Bangladesh has rapidly expanded exports of fresh and frozen shrimp products.

Future fisheries production growth has been enhanced by the extension of exclusive economic zones to 200 mile limits. Marine production capacity is great in the vast Indo-Pacific oceanic region. Current production is below maximum sustainable yield for countries like Indonesia, Malaysia, Bangladesh, Pakistan, India, Burma, and Sri Lanka.

There is also good potential for development of aquaculture and brackishwater ponds in coastal areas in large parts of Asia — particularly Indonesia and Eastern Malaysia. Rapid growth in fisheries production contributes to improved nutrition as well as income, employment and foreign exchange. Environmental problems and inappropriate fishing practices could constrain fishery production growth in future, however. Continued growth in demand for marine products in the OECD countries will be another important factor in growth of this sector.

Forestry

The forestry sector has long provided substantial export earnings and government revenue to the countries of Southeast Asia. Forestry's contribution to agricultural GDP growth has been declining rather sharply in the 1980s. Forests covered about one-third of the land area of the Asian developing countries — over 300 million hectares in 1981. But it is estimated that 11 million hectares are deforested annually (1985) and that the rate of deforestation is accelerating.[25]

There are great disparities in the distribution of forestry resources among Asian countries. Southeast Asia — particularly Indonesia and Malaysia — have large tropical forests and there are two-thirds of a hectare of forest per person. In contrast, South Asian countries have only one-tenth of a hectare of forest per person. The ratio is four-tenths of a hectare per capita in the ROC (Taiwan) and Korea. Even in Southeast Asia the disappearance of natural forests or their degradation is reaching alarm-

---

[25] *Far Eastern Economic Review*, "Southeast Asia's Forests: Lost for the Trees," April 10, 1986, p. 89.

ing proportions. Thailand, a major former exporter now is a net importer of tropical hardwood. The Philippines is expected to become a net importer by the end of the 1980s. Malaysia and Indonesia with their relatively rich forest resources are having difficulty supplying wood processing industries with logs. Forestry plantations based on fast-growing hardwood species are one alternative that is increasingly pursued though such projects face uncertainty regarding economic returns. Corruption, illegal logging, shifting cultivation and mounting population pressures are making it more and more difficult to preserve remaining natural forests.

Past policies of allowing loggers to exploit forests rather freely and relying on natural regeneration of forests have clearly failed. Hunger for land, demand for fuelwood, administrative difficulties, and lack of knowledge, have also contributed to forest degradation. Vast areas of Southeast Asia are now covered by tenacious but worthless *alang-alang* grass — the result of logging followed by improper cultivation of the fragile soils. Reclamation of such land is possible through planting of fast-growing tree species but the costs are high and the eventual economic benefits are uncertain.

The degradation of forests in watershed areas has contributed to severe environmental problems. Soil erosion, flooding and drought have common causes in deforestation. In turn, erosion has led to siltation of irrigation reservoirs and canals, reducing the net benefit from expensive investments by limiting crop production particularly during the dry season. Erosion has also damaged breeding grounds for fish and other valuable marine and freshwater species.

In South Asia, forests have been critically depleted and even fuelwood is becoming increasingly scarce. About four-fifths of all tree cutting in South Asia results from fuelwood demand — mainly for rural household uses. In South Asia, roughly two-thirds of energy requirements are met by fuelwood. The rate of depletion of forests is far above the rate of natural regeneration of trees in South Asia.

The need for new and effective approaches to forestry management is urgent. Development of community forestry programs, replanting schemes, and increased protection of remaining forests are all required. The severe environmental externalities caused by deforestation justify strong conservation measures. Research to improve the quality of fast-growing species so they become commercially viable is vital. There will be few takers in expensive forestry plantation projects unless economic returns are improved. The eventual ability to arrest the decline of the forestry sector depends on improved capabilities of governments and effective incentives to investment in reforestation.

AGRICULTURAL GROWTH: PRICE AND NON-PRICE INTERVENTIONS

A major reason for the improved agricultural performance in Asia has been the active role of government in promoting development of the sector. The role of improved incentives in encouraging greater production was substantial, yet policies in areas other than price were even more important. Advances in technology and organization, investments in infrastructure, and institutional improvements all contributed. In practice, it is difficult to neatly separate government policies into those affecting prices and those affecting non-price variables. This becomes clear in discussing institutional reforms in the areas of credit, and labor. It is also true in policies dealing with agricultural mechanization. With this in mind, we may proceed to discuss agricultural policies.

Agricultural Pricing Policies

In the 1970s, Asian governments increased incentives to farmers in order to stimulate agricultural production. Whereas in the 1950s and 1960s governments often acted to hold down agricultural prices, in the 1970s parity between farm and non-farm output prices was maintained in most Asian developing countries.[26] In few cases can it be said that agricultural pricing was left completely to competitive market forces. More often than not, governments intervened in markets in order to try to stabilize prices or to achieve discrete changes in relative prices of different crops or of input prices relative to output prices at the farmgate.

The responsiveness of agricultural supply to price incentives has generally been shown to be positive. Though price elasticities of supply of individual crops can be quite high, aggregate supply elasticity is probably low. Exceptions are in countries where agricultural output has been heavily taxed and state control has been pervasive for long periods, then, a shift to (higher) market prices may result in (temporary) rapid growth of aggregate supply.

In Asia, countries have pursued different types of price interventions in order to meet the objectives of providing sufficient incentives to farmers, at the same time, maintaining stable prices to consumers of food staples. Over time, individual countries have also shifted pricing interventions in response to changing circumstances and needs. International or border prices of traded inputs and outputs are a reference point for measuring distortions in domestic farmgate prices. In Asia, as elsewhere, there appears to be a positive income elasticity of protectionism for agricultural outputs.[27]

The burden of price policy interventions on government budgets limits the low-income countries' ability to protect farming interests through devices like price support schemes. The availability of foreign assistance to finance imports of grain and other staples may also encourage governments in low-income countries to hold food prices down. Procurement of cereals and edible oils by state marketing authorities at low farmgate prices is also a common practice. The higher income NICs, the ROC (Taiwan) and Korea, in the 1970s protected farmers with price support programs, import restrictions and other measures.

Low-income Asian countries tended to offset artifically low output prices by subsidizing inputs. India (and Indonesia during the 1970s) are examples — farmgate rice prices were long held substantially below international prices but subsidies on fertilizer, seed, pesticides and irrigation water acted as offsets. In other countries, like the Philippines, output prices were kept down and, at the same time, input prices for fertilizer were artificially increased in order to protect domestic fertilizer producers. Though subsidies were given to irrigation water, machinery and credit, they did not completely offset price disincentives. Moreover, subsidies were distributed unevenly — larger farmers and landowners benefited disproportionately — small farmers and landless rural laborers were harmed. Similarly in large countries like India and Indonesia, some regions benefited more than the others.

The budgetary burdens imposed by government price interventions are severe, particularly for low-income countries and those with heavy external debts. Reducing subsidies on food and farm inputs could substantially improve the budgetary

---

[26] Vyas, *op. cit.*, pp. 36-38.

[27] Chung H. Lee and James Roumasset, "Food Policy and Rice Trade in the Pacific Basin Region," International Workshop on Food and Development, Mexico City, June 1982.

position of the government in countries like Pakistan, Bangladesh and India. The ability of governments to reduce subsidies is often constrained by political factors.

The ROC (Taiwan) and Korea artificially increased farmgate prices, particularly of rice. Rice price supports and cheap fertilizer led to a problem of high cost surplus rice production in the ROC (Taiwan). The rice surpluses could only be exported at a substantial financial loss, and the alternative of storing burgeoning surpluses of rice was even more costly. Indonesia maintained input subsidies and gradually raised farmgate paddy prices. By the mid-1980s, domestic rice supply exceeded demand and large surpluses accumulated. Some rice was exported at a loss, but most had to be stored under poor conditions resulting in substantial spoilage. The Indonesian government's Bureau of Logistics could not support floor prices and at the same time pay the costs of storage without risking bankruptcy. Hence, pressures have built for a more market-based approach to pricing.

In general, governments have succeeded in keeping domestic rice and cereal prices more stable than international prices — though at the cost of maintaining excess storage. During the 1970s, wide price fluctuations and uncertain availability of supply characterized the international rice and grains markets. The instability in world markets provided a major part of the rationale for widespread intervention in domestic markets by governments. In the 1980s, the large surpluses of rice have dampened prices. Large capacities exist for generating additional production of rice and other cereal grains in the MIDCs (more developed countries) and in Asia. Sharply reduced fertilizer prices resulting from excess production capacity and the glut of petrochemical products will make it cheaper to increase input use as well. The real price of food grains is declining and is likely to continue to do so. Therefore, worries about price shocks to importing countries are less serious than in the 1970s.

Maintaining a balance between output and input prices at the farmgate that provides adequate incentives without leading to large distortions in resource allocation or heavy government budget deficits is a worthy policy objective. Governments should rely as much as possible on market forces — in periods of short domestic supply, in the absence of greater imports, market forces will result in bidding up prices and encouraging greater domestic production. During excess domestic production, governments are hard-pressed to support artificially high floor prices and unless quality is sufficiently high for export, can usually only absorb a small fraction of the surplus into storage. Farmers will usually be forced to sell at lower prices, but this will encourage greater consumption and help offset the problem of surplus production.

Improved institutional arrangements to provide competitive supply of inputs and ensure competition in procuring grain from farmers is a cost-effective approach to achieve policy objectives of farm incentives and domestic price stability. Credit availability from lending institutions is also of importance in allowing farmers to make efficient use of fertilizer and other inputs. Subsidies on interest rates are unnecessary and, in any case, usually disproportionately benefit large farms just like price supports on output.

The paddy-fertilizer price ratio at the farmgate is an important determinant of fertilizer use. And fertilizer application is strongly correlated with yields. But it would be a mistake to rely too much on price manipulation to attain target rates of output growth and higher yields. Other factors, particularly irrigation, research and extension work, farmer education, transport, and conditions in labor, credit and land markets are more important in determining supply and long-term production growth. These complementary factors enable fertilizer-responsive grain varieties to perform up to their potential in terms of per hectare yields.

Agricultural Trade

In contrast to the booming commodity markets of the 1970s, the 1980s decade began with a long and devastating recession that had significant adverse effects on all primary goods exporters in Asia including oil-exporting Southeast Asian countries (Indonesia and Malaysia). By the mid-1980s, continued softness in oil and commodity markets indicated that a downward secular price trend in commodities rather than a mere cyclical decline was occurring. External debt servicing problems were aggravated throughout South and Southeast Asia by worsening terms of trade — though oil-importing countries did gain a measure of benefit from plunging oil prices. Korea and the ROC (Taiwan) were more positively affected by the decline in oil prices than other Asian countries (other than Japan).

The prolonged 1980s recession sharply reduced agricultural export earnings of Asian developing countries. Agricultural export earnings were lower in 1982 than in 1979. Agricultural exports fell again in the mid 1980s. Growth of agricultural exports in the first half of the 1980s was significantly below the trend in the previous decades (Table 8). Prices of agricultural commodities declined by nearly one-third between 1982 and 1985 according to the International Monetary Fund (IMF).[28] With agricultural products accounting for between 32 and 96 percent of total merchandise exports (Table 9) in South and Southeast Asia (excepting Indonesia), the overall effect on economic growth has been quite serious.

The uncertainties in markets for Asian agricultural exports have been added to by increased agricultural protectionism in the more developed countries. In addition subsidized exports of surplus sugar, rice, feed, dairy products, and other agricultural goods by European and North American producers have increased competition for shrinking markets. Reducing protection of domestic agriculture in the European Community and Japan would substantially benefit Asian agricultural exporters but strong farm lobbies make such reform politically difficult to enact.

The various schemes established by the United Nations, Lome convention and IMF to help stabilize commodity export earnings have been of some help to Asian producers but are generally too small to offset the type of sharp downturns the 1980s have brought. It is improbable that such schemes will be expanded much if at all.

To some extent, structural change in Asia has lessened the weight of primary goods in total exports in South and Southeast Asia. Manufactured exports have grown more rapidly than primary goods exports. In the ROC (Taiwan) and Korea, by the 1980s, export composition was more than 90 percent manufactured goods. In Southeast Asia, agricultural products accounted for over two-thirds of total exports, on average. Agricultural products were almost half of total exports in South Asia (and even higher if lightly-processed agricultural raw materials are included). The shift in export composition to manufactures will require a long period of time and may also be slowed by various protectionist barriers put up in the OECD as well as Eastern European countries. Therefore, for the foreseeable future Asian primary producers will continue to rely on agriculture for a substantial share of their foreign

---

[28] International Monetary Fund, *World Economic Outlook,* Washington, D.C., April 1986.

Table 8. Agricultural Export Growth Rates[a]

Country	1971-1980	1980-1984
NICs		
Korea	23.3	−7.7
ASEAN-4		
Indonesia	24.3	−13.5
Malaysia	21.3	−5.9
Philippines	13.2	−5.4
Thailand	24.5	3.9
South Asia		
Bangladesh	6.0	3.3
Burma	12.9	−14.2
India	15.1	0.2
Nepal	−3.1	6.6
Pakistan	18.0	−7.9
Sri Lanka	9.1	8.6

Source: FAO, *FAO Trade Yearbook*, 1984 and earlier editions.

[a]Average annual growth rates calculated from current US$ values.

Table 9. Agricultural Exports as a Percentage Share
of Total Merchandise Exports, 1983

Country	%
NICs	
Korea	6
ASEAN-4	
Indonesia	17
Malaysia	42
Philippines	33
Thailand	62
South Asia	
Bangladesh	33
Burma	96
India	32
Pakistan	32
Sri Lanka	61

Source: FAO, *FAO Trade Yearbook*, 1984.

exchange earnings.

The ability of South and Southeast Asian countries to improve productivity in the agricultural sector – particularly cash crops – will be crucial to future trade performance. Windfalls from booming commodity prices seem less likely in the 1980s than before. Efforts to improve cultural practices, upgrade the mix of crops, raise quality and reduce costs through better management and technology are needed. Investment will be required for replanting aged, low-yielding perenials and to allow experimentation with new varieties. In order to encourage innovation, higher levels of input use, and better management, incentives must be appropriate. In this regard, adoption of a balanced system of protection that provides a more or less neutral framework for production for domestic or external markets could help. In several Asian countries, there is disincentive to agricultural exports. Effective protection rates for agricultural exports are frequently below average. In some cases, like the Philippines, negative effective protection rates on the order of 20 percent or more faced producers of copra, sugar, and forestry products.[29] Reducing punitive export levies, realistic pricing of foreign exchange, and lessening tariffs and their dispersion would greatly encourage expansion of agricultural exports.[30] In turn, improved efficiency in agriculture would improve overall economic performance.

Non-Price Interventions

Agricultural Technology
In the 1970s, a shift in emphasis in three new directions occurred in agricultural research in the Asian developing countries. First has been the development of grain varieties that perform better than the original HYVs because they are more disease-resistant, require shorter growing seasons, and are photosensitive providing greater flexibility in planting dates. Some of these varieties are more inured to water-stress (drought or excess water). The international research centers had developed complementary links to national and local research centers in Asia. This greatly facilitated adaptation of new HYVs and improved cropping systems into local environments. Improved palatability of high-yielding rice also encouraged wider adoption by Asian farmers in the 1970s.

A second new direction has been the extension of genetic research to crops other than wheat and rice. The development of improved varieties of important secondary food crops – maize, cassava, pulses, tubers, and legumes – is extremely important to farm and low-income households in unirrigated and upland areas of Asia. These foods are substitutes for grains and can be important in enhancing food security in the case of reduced grain harvests. They are also important potential sources of livestock feed and foreign exchange earnings or savings.

A third new research direction has been work aimed at raising productivity of the cash crop sector. This research has involved development of new varieties of traditional export crops (coconut, tea, rubber). It has also sought to promote adoption of entirely new cash crops (palm oil, cocoa, horticultural products).

Agricultural research has also been expanding into other new areas – aquaculture, dairying, and fast-growing hardwood species for tree plantations are a few examples.

---

[29] Clarete and Roumasset, *op. cit.*

[30] R.M. Bautista, "Domestic Price Distortions and Agricultural Income in Developing Countries," International Food Policy Research Institute, mimeo, 1986.

Despite initiatives in several directions, international and national agricultural research has focused principally on raising productivity in rice and wheat and that too in areas that are relatively prosperous and favorably endowed in terms of capital, infrastructure, land and water resources. Investments by Asian countries in agricultural research have been concentrated on lowland irrigated rice and on staying abreast of processing techniques for major export crops (e.g., sugar, rubber). Yet much of agricultural land is in rainfed and upland areas where yields are low and poverty is widespread. The increasing population pressures in upland areas have led to encroachment by cultivators onto steeper terrain. This has been associated with deforestation and degradation of watershed areas with serious environmental, economic, and social consequences. Research that focuses on developing sustainable patterns of agro-forestry and intercropping in upland areas is of increasing importance and has been recognized as such by many governments.

Budgetary resources for development of appropriate land-saving, adaptable technologies have been very limited. Typically Asian LDCs allocate a far smaller share of agricultural GDP for research than do MDCs. Tackling the problems of upland and other bypassed areas will be more difficult than research on lowland irrigated rice. Heterogeneity and environmental and social diversity are much greater in rainfed and upland rural areas. There can be no simple "expansion" of the "green revolution" to the uplands and limited resource farmers. In most such areas cropping patterns are more complex than in rice bowl areas. There are some places where specialization in one or few crops with promising yields could be a feasible development strategy — but these are exceptions. A more location-specific research approach that carefully examines cropping patterns, social, and environmental conditions is needed. Special attention to impact assessment of new technologies on limited resource farmers will be essential if poverty reduction is to accompany maximization of economic benefits.[31]

Technologies aimed at improving fishery and livestock production and yields will also need to take into account potential social impact on traditional fishermen and smallholders. Extension work and educational outreach will be necessary to support appropriate farming systems involving components of cropping, livestock, and fishpond production together or separately. These efforts will scarcely be feasible unless local and provincial facilities are upgraded and training of well-rounded knowledgeable field staff is increased. The complexities and diversity of conditions will make it more difficult to apply the "technology-package" approach that worked for lowland irrigated rice intensification programs. Realization of this reality is not sufficiently advanced at the national or international level. Until it becomes so, the rate of costly mistakes remains high.

Institutions

The institutional setting of Asian agriculture is extremely diverse and rural institutions often have been viewed as requiring reform before effective agricultural development programs could be implemented. In the 1960s and 1970s there was concern that, in much of rural Asia, the institutional structure was lagging behind the need for change and, therefore, limiting the benefits of technological breakthroughs and investments in public goods like irrigation systems. Highly inequitable

---

[31] Bruce Koppel, "Technology Adoption Among Limited Resource Rice Farmers in Asia," *Agricultural Administration,* 20 (1985), pp. 201-223.

distribution of land ownership, weak organization of farmers and poorly developed capital markets were serious obstacles to rapid diffusion of new HYV-type technology and widespread gains in production.

The rapid agricultural and rural development that transpired in Japan and the ROC (Taiwan) in the 1950s and 1960s and in Korea in the 1960s and 1970s was, in large measure, due to institutional reforms that provided relatively equitable distribution of land. Effective political and economic reorganization efforts were made in rural areas in response to crises and under strong external pressures (the American occupation of Japan after the second world war; the retreat of nationalist forces to the ROC (Taiwan) in 1948; the Korean war). The application of science to farming, establishment of effective farmer organizations, investment in irrigation and marketing infrastructure, accompanied land reform. Research stations and extension services worked closely with farmers' cooperatives to diffuse technology. The direct involvement of farmers in planning, constructing, operating and maintaining irrigation works contributed to efficient use of water and land. No less important was the improvement of the public education systems in the ROC (Taiwan) and Korea.

Economic reforms that established effective incentives to save and invest, that provided incentives to farmers, and that accelerated growth of demand for labor in non-agricultural rural activities, all helped raise rural incomes. Macroeconomic policies created an atmosphere conducive to rapid rural development. Increased incomes led to greater savings and capital formation; better technology and higher levels of input use led to higher yields of crops; greater opportunities for off-farm enterprises led to more employment. Among the results were greatly reduced incidences of rural poverty, reduced fertility and population growth rates, rising rural real wages, and low inequality in income distribution.

Institutional reform in South Asian and the ASEAN-4 countries has been focused in the areas of land tenure and credit markets. Labor legislation has also been enacted, particularly with regard to large-scale plantation agriculture. Minimum wages have been established for farm work but these are poorly enforced except, perhaps, in the plantation sector.

The imposition of minimum wages and other work rules and conditions in plantation agriculture has mixed results. It may benefit employed workers, but also acts as a deterrent to growth of employment. Lay-offs and adoption of labor-saving machinery have occurred in some parts of Indonesia and the Philippines. When economic downturns occur unemployment has become a severe problem in rural areas where plantation production of cash crops is the dominant economic activity (as in the sugar areas of the Philippines). Labor legislation has been ineffective in protecting the interests of the majority of rural workers, except perhaps in Malaysia where agricultural labor is becoming relatively scarce.

Credit Policies

In the early 1970s, financial institutions provided but a small share of credit in most Asian developing countries (Table 10). The adoption of the new rice technology required substantial cash outlays for inputs like fertilizer, pesticides, and power to operate irrigation pumps and other machinery. The limited access of small farmers to credit from banking institutions was believed to be a major constraint on intensification of agriculture.

Table 10. Percentage Distribution of Agricultural Credit by Source

		Institutional Loans (IL)		Noninstitutional Loans (NL)
		% of Farmers with IL	IL as % of Agri. Credit	NL as % of Agricultural Credit
NICs				
Korea	1974	40	34	66
	1979	n.a.	65	35
ROC	1974	95	65	35
(Taiwan)	1977	n.a.	59	41
ASEAN-4				
Indonesia	1979	n.a.	5	95
Malaysia	1974	2	n.a.	n.a.
	1979	n.a.	18	82
Philippines	1974	28	42	58
	1978	n.a.	61	39
Thailand	1974	7	8	92
	1981	n.a.	64	36
South Asia				
Bangladesh	1974	15	14	86
	1981	n.a.	15	85
India	1974	20	30	70
	1974-75	n.a.	33	67
Nepal	1974	n.a.	25	75
	1976-77	n.a.	43	57
Pakistan	1956	n.a.	29	71
	1970-71	5	40	60
Sri Lanka	1974	14	20	80
	1978-79	n.a.	22	78

Sources: World Bank, *Bank Policy on Agricultural Credit,* 1974, Annex Tables 2 and 3. All estimates of types of lenders are based on sample surveys except in India where a national
credit survey was available. Estimates of farmers getting institutional loans are usually
nationwide, but some are from sample surveys; in a few cases they represent potential
rather than actual borrowers in a given year. Asian Productivity Organization, *Farm
Credit Situation in Asia,* 1984, p. 19, ILO, "Group-based Savings and Credit for the
Rural Poor," 1983, p. 106. Arun Kumar Bandyopadhyay, *Economics of Agricultural
Credit,* 1984, p. 121. R.J.G. Wells, *The Informal Rural Credit Market in Malaysia,* 1980,
p. 20.

n.a. = not available.

Governments, often with foreign assistance, sought to expand rural financial facilities, with some positive results. Institutional sources provided a larger share of farm credit for working capital and for equipment, land improvements and buildings. The expansion of the financial institutions and loan programs encouraged the spread of new technology in most Asian countries.

The interest rates charged by formal institutional lenders were far lower than those of traditional money lenders. However, a high proportion of institutional credit went to large-scale farmers who often used the funds to acquire labor-saving equipment. The problems of lending to small farmers — their lack of collateral, the high costs of administering many small loans — became evident. Attempts by governments to provide credit to small-scale farmers by setting up specialized financial institutions or by earmarking a certain percentage of advances for them from existing institutions generally met with very limited success. Some of these lending agencies paid too little attention to tailoring loan operations to the needs of small farmers. Excessive paperwork, delays in disbursement of funds, and other problems made it difficult to attract participation of many small farmers. In effect, non-interest borrowers' costs were so high that the specialized institutions were hard-pressed to compete with informal lenders in rural areas.

Farm lending programs placed undue emphasis on reaching loan disbursement targets with adverse consequences. First, in some cases, as repayments were not carefully monitored and enforcement mechanisms were lax, financial institutions soon faced severe difficulties caused by loan arrears and outright defaults. Second, by neglecting saving deposits and given the poor record of loan recovery, many of these institutions became increasingly dependent on injections of government funds. In the worst cases (e.g., the Philippines), specialized financial institutions and rural banks ceased to be viable with the consequence that credit programs collapsed or contracted, rather than expanding with the requirements of agricultural growth.

In the ROC (Taiwan) and Korea rural bank facilities were successfully expanded to serve the financial needs of small-scale farmers. The success of land-reform made it far easier to erect a viable rural banking system there. From their inception rural banks placed strong emphasis on mobilization of savings with good results. By the early 1970s, in Korea, the major source of funds for on-lending to small-scale farmers was from savings deposits within the rural financial system.

Land Reforms

Two types of legislation have been enacted in the Asian developing countries to ensure more equitable relationships in land tenure, namely legislation imposing a ceiling on landholdings and legislation protecting the rights of tenants. The first type of reform set ceilings on individual ownership of agricultural land, but often exempted land not under specific crops and thereby provided a major loophole to large landowners. Laws of the second type typically set the shares of output to be received by landlords and tenants, prohibited various types of intermediary tenure, and provided deterrents to eviction of tenants. In some cases land reform laws allowed land to be gradually acquired by the tiller.

It is difficult to generalize briefly on the overall effectiveness of land reform, but there appear to have been certain common results. In localities where tenants were unorganized and weak and landowners controlled local political institutions and military or police forces, there were large-scale evictions of tenants. However, in areas where the social gap between landlords and tenants was not very wide and tenants had recourse to legal action, they benefited from reforms. Tenancy legislation designed to abolish landlordism often gave rise to clandestine subleasing arrangements. In some cases investment in agricultural improvement was adversely affected by legislation because of the uncertainty created over conditions of land ownership and property rights.

Laws setting ceilings on the amount of agricultural land that could be owned had inconsequential results. In almost all countries, estimates of idle or surplus land were exaggerated. Furthermore, there was a large gap between the identified and the declared surplus land, between the declared surplus land and the land actually acquired, and between the acquired land and that actually distributed. It is difficult to identify (except the ROC (Taiwan) and Korea) any country where even 5 percent of the land was transferred to small tenants, submarginal farmers, or landless rural workers. The major positive result of this type of legislation may have been to have helped stop trends toward growing inequality in land ownership, but other factors were also important. Technological developments favoring more intensive farming helped remove some of the incentive to acquire larger holdings. Demographic change (lower rates of population growth and outmigration to urban areas) may also have lessened pressures on land.

There is a voluminous literature on the implementation of land reform in Asian developing countries.[32] The studies show that the scope for redistributive land reform is more limited than originally envisaged and suggest that abolition of tenancy, at this stage, could harm rather than help tenants. Past experience shows that land reform legislation cannot have the desired results unless the intended beneficiaries are organized and assert their rights. Land reform, in the absence of consideration of linkages between land, credit and labor markets is ineffective. More importantly, a focus on land redistribution meant that other pressing problems were neglected, e.g., the fragmentation of smallholdings, the exclusion of small farmers from sources of credit and inputs, and above all, provision of gainful employment to landless rural workers. These problems warrant as much attention as land reform itself.

Irrigation and Infrastructure

The 1970s witnessed a dramatic expansion of rural infrastructure in most of Asia. Irrigation, farm-to-market roads, rural electrification, government and private warehouses, transport, communications all increased significantly. Irrigation has been a high priority because of its importance in improving crop yields and intensification of land use in the dry season.

Since the 1960s the rate at which unirrigated land was incorporated into irrigation schemes exceeded the rate of expansion of farmland through land opening and settlement. The proportion of rice and other cropland under irrigation increased impressively. Irrigation greatly facilitated rapid adoption of HYVs and encouraged higher levels of input use. The practices of multiple-cropping increased particularly in densely populated areas of Java (Indonesia), Bangladesh, and Central Luzon (the Philippines).

---

[32] See, e.g., R. Berry and W. Cline, *Agrarian Structure and Productivity in Developing Countries*, Baltimore; Johns Hopkins University Press, 1979; P. Dorner, *Land Reform and Economic Development*, New York; Penguin, 1972.

The improvement of irrigation systems has been a major element in rapid agricultural growth in Asia. By the late 1970s and early 1980s it was recognized, however, that much of the easily irrigated land had been covered and that unit costs of extending irrigation to new areas were high and rising. Between 1978 and 1983, costs per hectare for new irrigation schemes had roughly doubled according to an Asian Development Bank (ADB) study.[33]

A major problem with some large-scale irrigation schemes has been the failure to create suitable organizational and institutional arrangements for equitable distribution of water and for proper maintenance. As a result, often less than two-thirds of the planned command areas are effectively irrigated. Further, available evidence on multiple-cropping indicates it has not been rising in proportion to the expansion of irrigation. Irrigation investment has increasingly been focused on improving existing systems, both through rehabilitation of the systems themselves, and through greater attention to participation by farmers. Investment in groundwater irrigation schemes and small-scale village self-help projects have also increased.

Nevertheless, there will also be some need to expand the area covered by large-scale irrigation, particularly in South Asia, though costs will be higher and technical difficulties will be experienced.

Aside from irrigation, other support facilities have been built up. Among the most important are those that reduce post-harvest wastage. Losses from pests and spoilage remain a serious problem in South and Southeast Asia. An FAO study (1982) estimated that annual losses of cereals amounted to 260,000 tons. The value of annual losses of pulses and cereals in the Asian LDCs (excluding the People's Republic of China) was estimated by FAO at $4.6 billion.[34] Improved transport, storage, and marketing facilities are needed to lessen losses from spoilage and pests. But in developing additional capacity for efficient post-harvest storage, balance between the private sector and government needs to be attained. Expansion of government facilities has sometimes merely substituted for private facilities, with little net addition. There is also concern that government operations often tend to be less efficient than those of private grain and food merchants, though some government capacity is necessary so that exposed and low-income groups can be served in times of stress from crop shortfalls and rising prices of staples. The budgetary costs of replacing most private traders can be onerous, hence a mixed system is to be preferred when scarce financial resources are considered.

Mechanization

The use of mechanical power to till the soil, plant and harvest the crop and prepare it for marketing has greatly increased in the 1970s in Asia, despite the increase in fuel prices. The number of tractors in operation rose from about 322,000 in 1973 to over 1,201,000 in 1982. The amount of arable land per tractor fell from about 700 hectares to only about 200. Surprisingly, tractorization was more advanced in South Asia in the early 1970s than in Southeast Asia. However, this picture was partly reversed by the 1980s. In East Asia, mechanical power has increasingly substituted for costly labor and there is one tractor for every 5 hecatres of farm

---

[33] Asian Development Bank, "Asian Agriculture: Review of Past Performance and Future Needs," ADB Staff Working Paper, Manila, May 1983.

[34] FAO, *Agriculture Towards 2000: Regional Implications with Special Reference to the Third Development Decade*, Rome, 1979.

land. India, Pakistan and Sri Lanka have greater tractor-use on a per hectare basis than Indonesia and even the Philippines. Sri Lanka's tractor density greatly exceeds even that of Malaysia.

On a *priori* grounds it has been argued that mechanization in countries with rapidly expanding rural populations is undesirable since it is likely to displace labor. The argument was based on the fact that well-to-do farmers have been encouraged to purchase tractors through inducements such as concessionary credit, duty-free importation and overvalued domestic currency. Some evidence of labor displacing use of tractors has been uncovered in parts of India, Pakistan and Indonesia.

Part of the problem is that land holdings in some areas are rather concentrated. Mechanization of operations is sometimes undertaken in order to reduce the costs of hiring and supervising a large number of field workers. For large farm operators machines cause fewer troubles than laborers. With subsidies on tractor purchases and use (e.g., through cheapened diesel fuel) large farmers may be given additional incentive to substitute mechanical power for hired labor. Mechanization, in such cases may be premature and could add to problems of rural underemployment and income disparities. In the ROC (Taiwan) and Korea where land reforms and trade and incomes policies allowed agriculture to develop in a labor-using manner, widespread tractorization (and then usually small-hand tractors) occurred only after sustained increases in real agricultural wages.

Mechanization is not always labor displacing, even when adopted in low-income countries. In most of Asia, rural labor is no longer in continuous surplus (except, perhaps in Bangladesh and poorer parts of Java, Nepal, India, Pakistan, Sri Lanka and the Philippines). Rising rural wages have encouraged increased use of mechanical equipment in East Asia, Malaysia and the Pubjab of India. However, it is also true that where, by reducing the interval between harvesting one crop and planting the next, that mechanization can facilitate multiple-cropping and thereby enhance labor-absorption.

EMERGING ISSUES

The foregoing review has shown that the developing countries of Asia have recorded a creditable performance in the agricultural sector. This was done in the face of severe internal handicaps and an international economic environment which was not very supportive. The results were achieved by initiating suitable policies or correcting the wrong ones in technology transfer, resource allocation, agricultural prices and credit. However, there are still quite a few unresolved problems. And new issues are emerging on the horizon. As the following discussion will indicate agricultural development in the future will pose increasingly difficult problems.

Promotion of agricultural growth in the future will require larger investments in fixed and working capital than in the past. Partly, this is because of the capital intensive nature of the technology which is, and will continue to remain, the main source of growth; partly, it is because of the increasing demands for investment in infrastructure as agricultural development covers less endowed regions. Some estimates of capital requirements to sustain the tempo of growth will be instructive. According to the Food and Agricultural Organization of the United Nations (FAO) to attain the desirable level of growth in agriculture by the year 2000, in South Asia alone an annual gross investment of about $21.5 billion will be needed in 1990, investment requirements will rise to $28.0 billion in the year 2000. The FAO estimates for Southeast Asia are $7.1 billion in 1990 and $10.3 billion in the year 2000.[35] The bulk of this investment will be needed for creating additional irrigation facilities or renovating the existing ones, for farm machinery, fuel and maintenance and for fertilizers and other chemical inputs. By all accounts, future agricultural development will be expensive in terms of capital investment.

In most of the Asian developing countries, the high capital requirements are not matched by equally vigorous efforts to mobilize savings. The rates of national savings in several countries are low even when account is taken of their low per capita income. This is due to an inelastic fiscal system which does not permit an effective cost-recovery, and underdeveloped financial markets which inhibit mobilization of private savings. The need for savings mobilization and financial intermediation has only recently been properly appreciated. In the past, in countries where state policy resulted in the spread of formal credit institutions in the rural areas, such institutions were often used to serve as outlets for dispensing subsidised credit rather than instruments for deposit mobilization.

Slackness in domestic resources mobilization is one obvious handicap, an equally important problem is that of high and, in many cases, rising incremental capital output ratio (ICOR) in agriculture, as in the other sectors. The high ICOR is not necessarily a reflection of "capital deepening", but may reflect inefficiencies in investment allocation, biases in favor of capital-intensive techniques, and under-utilization of capacity because of institutional and management shortcomings. Effective policies to improve the institutional environment so that existing capacities of rural infrastructure — roads, irrigation systems and marketing networks — can be used more fully are needed. Policies should reinforce domestic resource mobilization, financial intermediation and, above all, more efficient use of scarce capital.

The trend towards a higher ICOR could also be partially offset by development of more efficient machinery like the newer energy-saving tubewells and small multi-purpose tractors that have been developed in Japan and other East Asian countries. New, efficient machines and technologies may eventually reduce the capital-output ratio in agriculture.

In terms of future growth paths, two groups of Asian developing countries can be distinguished: (1) those that have reached or exceeded "self-sufficiency" in major foodgrains; and (2) those that are food deficit. In some respects the problems faced by the first group of countries are more difficult than those faced by the second group of countries. This is because by now we have acquired some insights in the production technology, in supportive policies and in investment priorities necessary for augmenting agricultural output. The countries concerned have to adapt the experience of more successful countries to suit their social, economic and physical environment and proceed in more or less the same directions. As against that, the group of countries which have started accumulating food surpluses have to cope with the tougher problems associated with diversification, within agriculture and to non-agricultural activities. The technical and infrastructural underpining for a diversified agriculture would be different from those for augmenting production of cereals like rice and wheat. The markets for these commodities, particularly for rice, is shrinking. On the other hand, an upsurge in demand can be expected for maize, millet, sorghum and oilseeds. The prospects of breakthrough in yields of

---

[35] *Ibid.*

these crops are still uncertain. Along with technological and infrastructure hurdles, the orientation of economic policies to provide suitable incentives for shifting resources from rice and wheat to other crops, to fruits and vegetables or to fishery, forestry or animal husbandry products is another area where our knowledge is not adequate.

Asian developing economies have, by and large, shown enough resilience to cope with the production related problems. The prospects for the future are no doubt difficult, but they do not warrant undue pessimism. Agricultural production growth will be favorably affected by the sharp declines in crude oil prices as farm input costs will also fall. The recent surpluses of agricultural commodities will work their way through the system and agricultural commodity prices should begin to recover in the latter 1980s. New technologies for agriculture that are less capital intensive and make better use of indigenous resources are being developed and these could lower costs of production significantly.

The real difficulties are faced in sharing the results of growth. The past experience has shown that when the growth in agricultural production is extraordinarily high, say, 5 to 7 percent per annum (e.g. in parts of India, Pakistan, Thailand or Indonesia), the benefits do percolate to a wide spectrum of society. But in a normal growth situation, i.e. with growth of agricultural output between 3 to 4 percent per year, a large section of people get bypassed. If the goal of the development strategies is to usher in a participatory type of growth, this situation needs to be corrected. Unfortunately, our understanding of the conditions for participatory growth is not deep enough. Alternatives such as redistribution of assets, particularly land, have not been politically feasible in most of the countries. The target-group oriented investment efforts (in health, nutrition, education and skills) have met with only marginally superior results.

The problem of participatory growth acquires importance as it is being increasingly realized that not only the pace of agricultural growth but also its pattern determines its contribution to the overall economic development. Agricultural growth that is reasonably broad based ("unimodal") also promotes faster growth in other sectors, as rural incomes are shared by a large section of producers, including small and marginal producers, whose demand is more likely to be for goods and services with larger labor content and larger share of local resources.[36] In other words, such a pattern of growth ensures stronger linkages between agriculture and non-agriculture sectors. The reverse will be the case if agricultural output is contributed mainly by large, affluent farmers. The demand signals they would give will be for more capital and skill intensive goods and services. There is a need, therefore, to design public policies to facilitate contribution of a large section of agricultural producers and workers in the production process.

Positive linkages between agriculture and industry need to be fully exploited in order to generate off-farm employment, improved rural income distribution and stronger overall economic growth. The process of structural transformation in rural Asia can be accelerated if appropriate unimodal strategies are implemented. Rising off-farm incomes and employment are central to transformation and modernization of rural society.

Import substitution in agriculture should not be excessively promoted any more

---

[36] Bruce Johnson and Peter Kilby, *Agriculture and Structural Transformation*, New York; Oxford University Press, 1975.

than in industry. Agriculture and industry linkages should be developed in accord with the resources available to each country in the context of dynamic comparative advantage.

Finally, as more countries reach comfortable levels of staple food production in Asia, different patterns of trade will emerge. The market for staple cereals such as rice and wheat will shrink while markets for feedgrain, some of the export crops, animal husbandry, fishery and forestry products will expand. Numerous possibilities for technology transfer, joint ventures and expanded trade among the developing countries of Asia will emerge, which even a few years back did not exist. However, the policy framework and the organizational efforts needed to benefit from these possibilities are not yet fully appreciated.

Agricultural development strategies suited for the changing environment in Asia require an inward look to make agricultural growth more broad based, to mobilize investible resources and to deploy these resources more efficiently; the changing circumstances also suggest an outward orientation to capitalize on emerging opportunities for collaboration and trade, principally among the Asian developing countries but also with their major trading partners in the more developed world.

5. Role of Trade Policies: Competition and Cooperation

Seiji Naya

INTRODUCTION

Countries in East and Southeast Asia have been generally open to international trade and investment, and as a result, have become increasingly integrated into the world market. They have relied on trade for growth to a greater extent than most other countries, as can be seen by their high trade-to-income ratios. On the other hand, South Asian countries have placed less emphasis on trade, though several of these countries have become more open to trade in the 1980s.

Although resource endowments, political and social conditions, and historical affiliations determine to a large degree the framework of development patterns, domestic policy choices have a preponderant influence on the course and pace of industrial growth and trade. The outward-looking policies of several East and Southeast Asian developing countries helped to bring about more efficient allocation of resources. The positive efficiency and growth effects of outward-looking policies are examples of indirect gains to the economy resulting from a development policy choice.

Yet, export-led development strategies are more effective when world demand is rising. Several East and Southeast Asian developing countries were able to expand exports and maintain high rates of real economic growth throughout the 1970s despite a slowdown in the growth of world output and trade after the first oil shock in 1973 (Tables 1 and 2). The situation worsened in the 1980s, however. Table 2 shows large fluctuations and relatively slower rate of growth in world trade (Table 3).

Real economic growth rates were also generally lower for the Asian developing countries in the 1980s. The four resource-rich Southeast Asian countries, in particular, had trouble regaining the 6 and 7 percent rates of real economic growth of the 1970s (Table 1). The lower growth rates of these resource-rich countries can be partly attributed to the prolonged, low prices of primary commodities, such as rice, rubber, tin, and palm oil. Because these commodities are major export

169

items of these countries, their export revenues declined. Oil price declines, on the other hand, benefited Thailand and the Philippines, but hurt oil-exporting Indonesia and Malaysia. Lower export revenues combined with high debt-servicing requirements forced these countries to reduce imports and further decelerate their growth.

The newly industrializing countries (NICs) of East Asia also saw their outstanding rates of growth decline in the 1980s, though the appreciation of the yen in 1985 increased the competitiveness of their goods vis-a-vis Japanese goods and along with cheaper oil helped restore high growth rates for Korea and the ROC (Taiwan). Protectionist sentiments in developed countries, particularly in the United States, however, have increased with the influx of imports from these countries.

Table 1. Average Annual Rates of Growth of Real GDP and GNP Per Capita

| | Average Annual Rates of Growth (%) | | | |
| | Real GDP | | | GNP Per Capita |
	1960-70	1970-80	1980-85	1965-84
NICs				
Hong Kong	10.0	9.0	6.7	6.2
Korea	8.8	8.6	5.3	6.6
Singapore	9.6[a]	9.6	6.8	7.8
ROC (Taiwan)	9.3	9.8	6.3	7.0
ASEAN-4				
Indonesia	3.9	7.9	5.5[b]	4.9
Malaysia	6.5	7.8	6.5	4.5
Philippines	4.8	6.0	0.8	2.6
Thailand	8.1	6.9	5.4	4.2
South Asia				
Bangladesh	—	5.9[c]	3.5	0.6
Burma	2.6	4.0	6.3	2.3
India	3.9[a]	3.5	5.3[b]	1.6
Nepal	1.6	2.1	3.2	0.2
Pakistan	4.3	4.0	6.9	2.5
Sri Lanka	5.8	5.7	5.2	2.9
World	5.0[a]	3.7	2.3	

Sources: International Monetary Fund, *International Financial Statistics,* Yearbook 1986, and November 1986.
World Bank, *World Development Report,* 1986 and 1984.
Asian Development Bank, *Key Indicators of Developing Member Countries of ADB,* July 1986.
Republic of China, Council for Economic Planning and Development, *Taiwan Statistical Data Book,* 1985.

[a] 1961-70.
[b] Preliminary estimates.
[c] 1974-80.

(Unit: %)

Table 2. Real Growth of World Trade, 1968-1985[a]
(Annual Change in Volume)

	Average 1968-77[b]	1978	1979	1980	1981	1982	1983	1984	1985
World Trade[c]	7.9	5.4	6.6	1.3	0.5	-2.3	2.8	8.6	3.1
Exports									
Industrial Countries	8.0	6.0	7.3	4.0	3.6	-2.1	2.7	9.6	4.3
Developing Countries	5.7	4.2	5.0	-4.1	-5.9	-8.2	3.1	6.7	0.7
Africa	3.5	3.7	7.9	-0.6	-15.8	-7.5	3.1	4.8	3.7
Asia	10.9	10.8	9.5	9.0	8.2	0.8	10.8	13.8	3.8
Europe	7.5	6.7	2.7	4.8	11.2	1.1	7.2	14.2	4.9
Middle East	7.2	-3.3	0.4	-15.2	-17.6	-19.7	-9.2	-5.4	-5.4
Western Hemisphere	1.1	10.0	7.6	1.2	6.1	-2.5	8.5	8.6	-1.7
Imports									
Industrial Countries	8.0	4.8	8.8	-1.7	-2.2	-0.6	4.6	12.5	4.8
Developing Countries	9.2	7.1	4.7	8.5	6.7	-4.1	-2.7	1.7	-1.1
Africa	7.6	4.2	-3.8	8.7	10.9	-8.3	-10.3	0.2	-7.0
Asia	7.8	16.3	13.3	10.2	3.4	-0.3	8.1	5.5	5.6
Europe	7.6	0.8	5.4	0.5	2.2	-7.8	2.3	8.0	4.8
Middle East	17.1	3.1	-3.7	9.4	16.0	5.9	-2.9	-7.0	-14.0
Western Hemisphere	7.0	5.6	7.9	9.8	2.5	-17.7	-22.3	3.0	0.6

Source: International Monetary Fund, *World Economic Outlook*, October 1986.

   [a] Excluding China prior to 1978.
   [b] Compound annual rates of change.
   [c] Averages based on data for the two groups of countries shown separately below and on partly estimated data for the U.S.S.R. and other non-member countries of Eastern Europe and, for years prior to 1978, China.

Table 3. Growth of Exports[a]

(Unit: %)

	1960-70	1970-80	1980-85	1981	1982	1983	1984	1985	1985 (F.O.B.; US$ billion)
NICs									
Hong Kong	14.5	22.8	12.9	10.5	-3.8	4.6	29.0	6.9	30.184
Korea	40.9	37.1	12.2	21.4	2.8	11.9	19.6	1.1	29.566
Singapore	3.5	27.6	8.9	8.2	-0.9	5.0	10.3	-5.2	22.812
ROC (Taiwan)	23.4	31.7	11.8	14.1	-1.8	13.2	21.2	0.9	30.723
ASEAN-4									
Indonesia	2.2	38.3	4.3	1.6	0.2	-5.1	3.6	-15.1	18.590
Malaysia	4.8	22.9	6.3	-9.1	2.2	17.2	16.9	-6.3	15.442
Philippines	7.3	20.9	0.9	-1.5	-12.2	-1.6	7.9	-12.7	4.607
Thailand	6.8	23.7	5.6	8.1	-1.2	-8.3	16.4	-4.0	7.120
South Asia									
Bangladesh	—	15.1[b]	7.8	4.4	-2.8	-5.9	28.6	7.3	0.999
Burma	-5.0	14.6	-2.8	1.1	-17.4	-4.1	0.3	-20.1	0.303
India	4.3	15.4	0.7	-3.4	12.8	-2.2	3.2	-16.2	7.915
Nepal[c]	2.7	5.8	13.3	75.0	-37.1	6.8	36.2	25.8	0.161
Pakistan	3.5	21.0	6.5	10.1	-16.9	28.4	-16.9	7.1	2.739
Sri Lanka	-0.5	12.0	6.2	2.4	-5.2	3.1	38.0	-9.1	1.333
World	9.5	20.8	2.9	-1.7	-7.3	-2.9	5.8	1.1	1,782.900
Industrialized Countries	10.5	18.9	3.3	-1.7	-5.2	-1.4	6.6	3.6	1,258.500
U.S.	8.6	18.0	3.2	5.9	-9.2	-5.5	8.7	-2.2	213.144
Japan	17.1	21.6	10.2	16.1	-8.7	6.2	15.5	4.4	177.164
Developing Countries	6.5	26.4	1.8	-2.2	-11.7	-6.9	3.4	-4.8	493.761

Sources: IMF, *International Financial Statistics*, Yearbook 1986, October 1986.
Republic of China Council for Economic Planning and Development, *Taiwan Statistical Data Book*, 1985.
Department of Statistics, Ministry of Finance. *Monthly Statistics of Exports and Imports*, The Republic of China (Taiwan District), February 20, 1986.

Note: a   Average annual rates of growth based on current prices.
         b   1973-80.
         c   1964-70.

In addition, one of the most successful countries in the region, Singapore, had a negative real economic growth rate in 1985 for the first time in nearly 20 years. For Singapore, a combination of several special factors have come into play; the high wage policy has eroded its competitiveness and the poor economic performance of ASEAN-4 countries has hurt Singapore's entrepot trade. Key Singaporean industries, including petroleum refining, shipbuilding, and electronics have been negatively affected.

The slowdown in these countries has contributed to a resurgence of export pessimism, i.e., a growing concern that a slow growth environment combined with possible increased protectionism by developed countries would all but preclude developing countries in Asia and elsewhere from continuing the export success experienced in the 1970s. The worsened conditions and increased uncertainties in the 1980s make the outlook for the future less bright. Has the world trade environment become such that an export-led development path is no longer possible?

The purpose of this chapter is to examine the nature of the adjustment undertaken by the Asian developing countries in the 1970s and early 1980s. The first section will present the variations and changes in industrial and trade policies followed by these countries and will examine the changing industrial structures of the economies as manifested in their actual patterns of trade. Empirical testing of determinants of their export performance in Japan and the United States will be done in subsequent section. The last section will discuss trade within the developing countries in the region and prospects for the expansion of intra-Asian trade. This should provide some insight into the prospects for trade in the Asia-Pacific region and options for developing countries in this region for further expansion of their exports in the 1980s.

For our present purposes, it is convenient to distinguish between the NICs (Hong Kong, Singapore, Korea and the ROC-Taiwan), and the four resource-rich Association of Southeast Asian Nations or ASEAN-4 (Indonesia, Malaysia, the Philippines, and Thailand), and South Asian countries (Bangladesh, Burma, India, Nepal, Sri Lanka, and Pakistan).[1] The classification is natural since the NICs made the transition to export-led growth based on labor-intensive manufactured goods by the late 1960s, and have very high trade-income ratios (see Table 4). The resource-rich ASEAN countries (ASEAN-4), on the other hand, have only begun to increase their non-traditional, labor-intensive manufactured export share in the 1970s and in general, face lower trade-income ratios than those of the NICs. But, it should be noted that these ratios were still much higher than the trade-income ratios of the U.S. or even Japan. The South Asian countries, with the exception of Sri Lanka, are characterized by a lower dependence on the foreign sector. On average, their manufactures comprise a fairly large part of total exports, but they have not yet begun to expand into non-traditional exports. Textiles are overwhelmingly the largest manufactured export in South Asia. Moreover, they rely heavily on exports of agricultural and food products.

---

[1] The usefulness of the classification scheme is somewhat complicated by Singapore, which is included as one of the NICs despite its membership in ASEAN. Structurally, Singapore is very similar to the other NICs with its small agricultural sector, its openness to trade, its high per capita income and its vibrant industrial sector. However, Singapore's share of manufactures in total exports is only about half as large as those of the other NICs, though this is much higher than those of the ASEAN countries. In addition, Burma is geographically located and traditionally included in Southeast Asia, but its economic policies and performance are closer to those of South Asian countries. Therefore, it is grouped with South Asian countries.

Table 4. Asian Lesss Developed Countries, U.S, and Japan:
Ratios of Exports and Imports of Goods and Services to GNP

	Exports		Imports	
	1970-71	1983-84	1970-71	1983-84
NICs				
Hong Kong[a]	68.9	83.5	80.5	87.2
Korea	14.7	37.9	24.7	38.1
Singapore[b]	80.3	135.4	127.8	164.2
ROC (Taiwan)	32.6	55.6	31.3	45.0
ASEAN-4				
Indonesia	13.9	29.0	16.5	27.6
Malaysia	44.3	58.4	42.5	60.5
Philippines	19.0	21.0	19.6	24.2
Thailand	17.0	24.1	21.0	27.9
South Asia				
Bangladesh	4.9[c]	5.2	8.2[c]	10.8
Burma	5.9	6.8	8.4	10.4
India	4.3	6.9[d]	4.8	9.8[d]
Nepal[b]	5.0	4.5	9.0	19.1
Pakistan	7.9	10.9	14.7	21.0
Sri Lanka	27.2	28.6	29.9	38.9
United States	5.3	7.5	5.6	9.9
Japan	11.8	16.5	10.0	14.0

Sources: ADB, *Key Indicators of DMCs of ADB,* April 1984 and Supplement October 1985.
IMF, *International Financial Statistics,* Yearbook 1985 and May 1986,
World Bank, World Tables, 1983.

[a]Value of merchandise goods as percent of GDP.
[b]Value of merchandise goods only.
[c]1973-74.
[d]1981-82.

INDUSTRIALIZATION AND TRADE STRATEGIES

The Asian developing countries have been expanding the manufacturing sector of their economies. With the exception of Hong Kong and Singapore, this has meant transforming basically agrarian economies into more industrialized ones. The timing and policies used varies by country, but similarities can be found within the three subgroups. Since the 1960s, exports have been an important source of growth for the developing Asian countries, especially the NICs and ASEAN-4 countries. For these eight countries, exports increased at a rate of over 25 percent per annum in the 1970s — manufactured exports grew even more rapidly.[2] This growing import-

---

[2] United Nations, *Handbook of International Trade and Development Statistics,* 1985 Supplement.

ance of manufactured exports was accompanied by significant changes in the product composition and destination of exports. As shown in Table 5, there has been a large increase in the number of commodities exported (SITC 3 digit) and also a decrease in the concentration index (a measure of commodity diversification). Interestingly, the diversification indicators of Asian countries more closely resemble those of developed than developing countries.

The next section discusses trade and industrialization policies and corresponding changes in the export composition of the three country groups. To simplify the analysis, commodities are classified into eleven major export products (or product groups) which comprise 80 to 98 percent of total export values.

Newly Industrializing Countries

The Asian NICs as a group were the most dynamic exporters among all developing countries in the 1970s. Manufactured exports, accounting for 70 percent of total exports in 1970, became even more important as they maintained an annual average rate of growth of nearly 30 percent between 1970 and 1979.[3]

A prominent feature of industrial development in the NICs is the emphasis on market-oriented, outward-looking policies. Hong Kong was from the outset a virtually free-trade economy. Singapore became a free-trade economy after a brief period of import substitution in the first half of the 1960s. Korea and the ROC (Taiwan) made more gradual transitions to trade liberalization.

During the 1950s, both Korea and the ROC (Taiwan) made use of multiple exchange rates and import controls that were designed to protect the domestic market. However, both countries quickly recognized that due to their narrow domestic market, import substitution was a self-limiting process. The countries realized that once domestic markets of non-durable consumer goods were exhausted, industrial growth would inevitably slow down and adjust to the expansion of domestic demand. Industrial growth could be maintained if the expansion could be carried over to foreign markets or if import substitution moved into the second stage with production of intermediate and capital goods.

In addition, under import substitution policies, exports often received negative protection. That is, exporters were faced with tariffs on inputs and received no subsidies, making the effective rate of protection on the export products negative.[4] Thus, after completing the first phase of import substitution in the 1950s, the policies were changed to eventually provide relatively equal opportunities for expansion of all economic activities in Korea and the ROC (Taiwan). The negative protection on exports resulting from import barriers was balanced by a subsidy scheme (mainly tax and credit preferences and exemptions from tariffs) so that exports remained as profitable as domestic sales. This also prevented home country exporters from being disadvantaged vis-a-vis foreign competitors. Moreover, the stable price ratio among sectors, especially in the ROC (Taiwan), encouraged agricultural investment and technological improvements in agricultural production that, in turn, led to an increasing supply of agricultural inputs into industrial and food production and prevented excessive outmigration of labor from rural areas.[5]

---

[3] Ibid.

[4] On the theory and formulation of the effective rate of protection see Balassa, B and Associates, *The Structure of Protection in Developing Countries*, Chapter 1 and also Corden, M., *Trade Policy and Economic Welfare*.

[5] See Ranis in *New Direction in Asia's Development Strategies*.

Table 5. Export Concentration Indices (Rankings in parentheses)

	Number of Commodities Exported[a]		Concentration Index[b]	
	1970	1982	1970	1982
NICs				
Hong Kong	108 (5)	125 (7)	0.342 (7)	0.325 (10)
Korea	122 (4)	151 (4)	0.271 (4)	0.185 (2)
Singapore	159 (1)	174 (1)	0.295 (5)	0.252 (5)
ASEAN-4				
Indonesia	48 (9)	114 (8)	0.368 (9)	0.654 (13)
Malaysia	131 (3)	155 (3)	0.371 (8)	0.308 (8)
Philippines	78 (8)	129 (6)	0.324 (6)	0.261 (6)
Thailand	92 (6)	138 (5)	0.262 (2)	0.195 (3)
South Asia				
Bangladesh	—	40 (11)	—	0.326 (11)
Burma	17 (11)	39 (12)	0.499 (10)	0.313 (9)
India	141 (2)	166 (2)	0.139 (1)	0.133 (1)
Nepal	6 (12)	35 (13)	0.597 (12)	0.262 (7)
Pakistan	91 (7)	110 (9)	0.264 (3)	0.212 (4)
Sri Lanka	33 (10)	79 (10)	0.584 (11)	0.348 (12)
Simple Averages[c]				
Asian Dev. Countries	86	118	0.360	0.287
Developing Countries	42	58	0.545	0.512
Developed Countries	154	161	0.168	0.184

Source: United Nations, *Handbook of International Trade and Development Statistics*, 1984 and 1985 Supplement.

[a] Number of products exported at the three-digit SITC level; this figure includes only those products which are greater than $50,000 in 1970 or $100,000 in 1982 or more than 0.3 percent of the country's total exports.

[b] Hirschmann index normalized to make values ranging from 0 to 1 (maximum concentration), according to the following formula:

$$H_j = \frac{\sqrt{\sum_{i=1}^{182} (\frac{x_1}{x})^2} - \sqrt{1/182}}{1 - \sqrt{1/182}}$$

where j = country index;
x_i = value of exports of commodity i;
$$x = \sum_{i=1}^{182} x_i$$

and 182 = number of products at the three-digit SITC level.

[c] Average taken of countries with data available for both years. This includes 12 Asian developing countries, 120 developing countries, and 25 developed countries.

At the same time, outputs and inputs of domestic sales were generally valued at world market prices; i.e., domestic value added was not allowed to exceed international value added. This protection structure left little room for excess profits and/ or inefficiencies, thus facilitating spill-over of protection from domestic to export markets.

The overall industrialization strategy also supported an output mix which made intensive use of the existing factor endowment. Production of labor-intensive manufactures for export was encouraged by government policies (except in Hong Kong). In 1970, exports of Hong Kong, Korea, and the ROC (Taiwan) were largely concentrated in simple manufactures; textiles, clothing and miscellaneous manufactures together accounted for approximately 60, 50, and 40 percent of total exports, respectively in the three countries (Table 6a). In Singapore, primary commodities accounted for nearly 80 percent of total exports, reflecting Singapore's traditional role in entrepot trade. A large share of primary commodities are exported through Singapore from neighboring ASEAN-4 countries.

The requirement to produce at world market prices tended to discourage excessively capital-intensive activities, despite some incentives in favor of capital accumulation. Emphasis on labor-intensive exports led to increases in the importance of the manufacturing sector in terms of both total output and labor force. Labor absorption by the rapidly growing manufacturing industry was exceptional. On average, manufactures in 1970 accounted for more than 25 percent of GDP in the NICs and its share of employment was 22 percent. In the 1980s, manufacturing activities made up more than 30 percent of GDP and employment (Tables 7 and 8). The increased demand for labor and the subsequent rise in wage rates helped to spread the benefits of growth widely and encouraged directly productive activities and attitudes.

The slowdown in world trade, the increase in protectionism in the industrialized countries after the first oil shock, and the rising unit labor costs (which reduced the international competitiveness of the traditional exports) forced the NICs to readjust their industrialization strategy. These changes in external and internal economic conditions, however, did not significantly affect the export performance of the NICs until the late 1970s. But by this time, the governments had already started implementing new policies aimed at diversifying industrial exports. These policies were based on the assumption that the negative effects of the new protectionism in developed countries and the loss of competitiveness due to increasing domestic wages could best be avoided by shifting the emphasis of industrial production toward technology-intensive and heavy industrial activities. This strategy also reflected the concern about the deterioration of the balance-of-payments due to the increasing oil bill. The rise in petroleum product imports from 7 to almost 25 percent of total imports between 1970 and 1981 drained foreign exchange reserves. Therefore, it was thought that domestic production of some raw materials and machinery hitherto imported would help save foreign exchange.

The impact of this strategy is clearly reflected in the changing composition of exports and imports in these countries. Exports of the NICs have become broader-based since 1970, making these countries less vulnerable to price and demand fluctuations for individual products. They increased the already large number of commodities exported in 1970, though Hong Kong was less successful than Korea and Singapore. Export shares of clothing, textiles, and miscellaneous manufactures have declined, while the shares of more skill- and capital-intensive products, such as

Table 6a. Exports by Principal Commodity: 1970, 1978, 1983
(As percent of total commodities)

		Raw Mat.	Mineral Fuels	Agr. & Food	Chemicals	Res. Based Mfg.	Textiles	Non-Elec. Mach.	Elec. Mach.	Clothing	Trans. Equip.	Misc. Mfg.	Manuf. Goods	Total	Total (US$ mn)
NICs															
Hong Kong	1970	3.7	0.3	3.7	4.0	5.6	10.9	1.5	9.2	27.8	0.7	24.6	92.2	100.0	2,514
	1978	3.7	0.4	3.2	3.6	4.4	8.7	4.4	10.9	30.0	0.7	16.2	92.3	100.0	11,499
	1983	5.0	0.5	3.9	3.7	2.7	9.3	6.4	14.8	24.2	1.6	14.6	90.4	100.0	21,960
Korea	1970	15.3	1.0	9.6	1.4	12.5	10.2	1.0	5.3	25.6	1.1	14.0	75.1	100.0	835
	1978	7.7	0.3	8.3	2.6	8.7	12.2	1.7	10.8	20.3	8.9	7.0	83.8	100.0	12,695
	1982	11.9	1.4	5.5	3.1	5.6	10.3	2.2	10.4	17.3	15.4	5.7	82.3	100.0	21,853
Singapore	1970	53.9	23.2	16.4	2.7	3.0	3.5	4.0	4.0	2.0	3.0	1.9	26.7	100.0	1,554
	1978	46.4	28.3	9.1	3.8	2.7	2.6	5.7	15.5	2.9	3.7	2.0	43.0	100.0	10,134
	1983	38.0	28.1	6.2	4.2	2.3	1.8	9.8	16.9	2.2	5.0	2.3	48.1	100.0	21,833
ROC (Taiwan)[a]	1970	9.6	1.8	20.3	2.3	9.2	13.3	3.3	11.9	14.3	0.8	10.4	70.0	100.0	1,481
	1978	6.3	2.1	10.2	1.9	8.1	9.2	4.7	15.3	13.8	3.3	13.4	83.4	100.0	12,686
	1985	6.0	1.8	5.6	2.5	6.1	8.2	8.8	15.3	11.4	3.8	15.7	88.3	100.0	30,726
ASEAN-4															
Indonesia	1970	79.0	32.8	19.6	0.5	0.0	0.0	0.3	0.0	0.0	0.0	0.0	1.1	100.0	1,055
	1978	87.3	68.6	10.8	0.5	0.2	0.1	0.0	0.3	0.1	0.0	0.0	1.7	100.0	11,643
	1983	86.3	76.4	5.9	0.6	3.5	0.6	0.0	0.6	0.7	0.0	0.0	6.5	100.0	21,146
Malaysia	1970	77.3	7.4	13.5	1.1	2.7	0.4	0.9	0.4	0.5	0.8	0.4	8.2	100.0	1,764
	1978	63.2	14.0	17.4	0.6	2.6	1.3	0.5	9.0	1.2	0.6	0.5	18.8	100.0	7,388
	1982	61.0	28.7	15.7	0.8	1.8	1.3	1.4	13.2	1.4	0.6	0.6	22.9	100.0	12,031
Philippines	1970	49.5	1.6	44.0	0.5	4.4	0.5	0.0	0.0	0.0	0.0	0.4	6.3	100.0	1,060
	1978	24.6	0.3	42.9	1.8	5.0	1.3	0.0	0.9	4.7	0.6	2.4	20.0	100.0	3,425
	1982	18.4	0.7	32.7	1.9	3.5	1.1	0.3	2.3	6.1	0.4	2.8	22.6	100.0	5,021
Thailand	1970	39.0	0.7	50.5	0.4	2.0	1.2	0.0	0.0	0.1	0.0	0.3	5.2	100.0	710
	1978	23.5	0.1	51.3	0.5	4.3	6.4	0.0	2.7	3.6	0.0	2.3	22.0	100.0	4,085
	1983	16.1	0.4	51.7	0.9	6.3	4.9	0.3	4.7	6.4	0.1	2.4	30.3	100.0	6,368
South Asia															
Bangladesh	1970	–	–	–	–	–	–	–	–	–	–	–	–	–	0
	1978	23.7	1.2	13.5	0.4	10.7	49.6	0.0	0.1	0.0	0.3	0.2	61.5	100.0	553
	1983	19.2	3.7	19.0	1.3	9.5	44.9	1.0	0.6	2.6	0.6	0.3	61.0	100.0	789
Burma	1970	32.7	1.3	65.7	0.1	1.4	0.0	0.0	0.0	0.0	0.0	0.0	1.5	100.0	108
	1977	32.9	1.0	64.2	0.5	2.3	0.0	0.0	0.0	0.0	0.0	0.0	2.9	100.0	193
	1983	–	–	–	–	–	–	–	–	–	–	–	–	–	
India	1970	24.7	0.8	29.5	2.3	8.5	22.7	1.9	1.1	1.8	2.3	1.7	45.4	100.0	2,026
	1978	15.3	0.4	28.4	2.7	18.1	13.0	3.2	1.8	6.6	2.5	2.8	55.8	100.0	6,190
	1981	14.1	0.4	28.1	4.2	14.2	15.2	3.4	1.5	7.8	3.2	2.9	57.5	100.0	7,529
Nepal	1970	–	–	–	–	–	–	–	–	–	–	–	–	–	0
	1978	42.3	0.0	34.3	0.3	0.8	15.3	0.0	0.0	0.9	0.0	5.7	23.3	100.0	73
	1981	35.8	0.0	12.2	0.5	14.7	17.3	0.0	0.0	2.1	0.0	16.8	51.9	100.0	75
Pakistan	1970	30.9	1.2	10.2	0.8	4.8	44.3	1.1	0.0	0.7	2.8	2.0	58.8	100.0	723
	1978	15.7	3.1	25.8	1.0	5.9	39.9	1.6	0.3	3.7	0.4	2.5	57.9	100.0	1,475
	1983	16.1	1.9	21.0	1.0	4.3	42.7	1.0	0.0	7.4	0.0	2.7	61.6	100.0	3,075
Sri Lanka	1970	25.7	0.0	71.7	0.4	0.0	0.0	0.0	0.0	0.4	0.0	0.0	1.5	100.0	335
	1978	28.6	5.9	63.6	1.7	0.6	0.2	0.1	0.0	3.6	0.1	0.9	7.6	100.0	846
	1983	25.4	10.9	46.5	0.6	4.6	0.6	0.3	0.0	18.9	0.4	0.9	28.0	100.0	1,066

Sources: United Nations, *Yearbook of International Trade Statistics,* 1972-73, 1981, 1982, and 1983 issues.
   The Republic of China, Department of Statistics, Ministry of Finance, *Monthly Statistics of Exports and Imports,* (Taiwan District), February 20, 1986.

[a] Taiwan's electrical machinery for 1970 includes office machines and automatic data processing equipment.

Table 6b. Imports by Principal Commodity: 1970, 1978, 1983
(As percent of total commodities)

		Raw Mat.	Mineral Fuels	Agr. & Food	Chemi-cals	Res. Based Mfg.	Tex-tiles	Non-Elec. Mach.	Elec. Mach.	Cloth-ing	Trans. Equip.	Misc. Mfg.	Manuf. Goods	Total	Total (US$ mn)
NICs															
Hong Kong	1970	14.6	2.9	19.7	8.2	10.6	17.1	5.5	8.6	1.6	2.4	4.7	65.6	100.0	2,905
	1978	15.4	5.0	15.0	7.3	12.5	13.8	7.5	9.4	2.1	2.8	3.8	69.1	100.0	13,455
	1983	14.8	6.6	12.6	7.4	8.0	13.7	6.8	12.9	4.8	2.7	4.9	72.2	100.0	24,027
Korea	1970	32.5	6.9	17.2	8.3	1.0	6.4	15.4	6.7	0.0	7.6	1.1	50.2	100.0	1,983
	1978	40.3	16.4	7.8	8.6	2.3	2.7	18.3	7.9	0.0	7.2	0.9	51.8	100.0	14,972
	1982	49.0	31.4	7.8	8.5	2.4	2.1	11.2	7.8	0.0	5.8	0.9	42.8	100.0	24,251
Singapore	1970	29.5	13.5	16.4	5.2	3.9	10.8	11.2	6.5	0.9	5.1	3.3	52.0	100.0	2,461
	1978	36.7	23.9	10.0	5.4	3.7	4.7	10.3	12.1	0.9	6.6	2.6	52.1	100.0	13,049
	1983	39.6	31.3	7.8	5.0	3.9	3.4	11.1	12.8	1.0	6.4	2.1	51.5	100.0	28,158
ROC (Taiwan)[a]	1970	28.7	4.5	14.6	10.1	1.2	4.7	14.2	10.2	0.0	10.6	1.5	56.4	100.0	1,524
	1978	39.0	17.2	10.5	10.8	2.0	1.8	12.1	10.8	0.1	7.2	1.4	50.3	100.0	11,028
	1985	38.7	21.5	9.6	11.9	2.4	2.0	11.2	11.1	0.0	5.6	3.7	51.5	100.0	20,101
ASEAN-4															
Indonesia	1970	13.5	1.6	14.7	12.8	6.6	11.8	16.8	5.9	0.0	11.6	1.8	71.5	100.0	892
	1978	22.0	8.8	17.6	11.4	3.4	2.8	16.1	8.7	0.0	11.8	1.1	60.0	100.0	6,655
	1983	36.6	25.4	7.7	11.7	2.6	0.9	20.6	5.4	0.0	8.8	0.6	55.3	100.0	16,352
Malaysia	1970	24.0	11.9	22.1	7.4	4.6	4.8	11.6	4.4	1.1	11.0	2.2	51.8	100.0	1,489
	1978	22.6	10.8	16.2	8.9	3.7	3.1	13.7	12.8	0.4	9.9	2.0	60.0	100.0	5,897
	1982	26.1	15.2	11.5	7.4	3.5	2.3	14.3	16.6	0.3	8.9	1.9	61.4	100.0	12,400
Philippines	1970	30.7	12.0	11.2	11.5	4.3	2.1	20.0	5.4	0.0	10.0	1.1	57.7	100.0	1,210
	1978	34.2	21.2	7.9	11.2	2.7	1.8	15.1	4.2	0.0	8.1	1.0	48.1	100.0	5,143
	1982	36.2	26.5	10.1	10.1	2.3	1.9	12.7	4.9	0.0	3.9	0.9	40.7	100.0	8,263
Thailand	1970	22.9	8.7	5.2	12.9	4.2	6.4	17.0	8.1	0.4	10.4	2.4	67.8	100.0	1,293
	1978	36.9	21.1	4.2	13.6	3.1	2.2	14.9	6.4	0.0	8.9	1.3	54.5	100.0	5,356
	1983	38.2	24.3	4.1	12.9	3.6	2.5	·14.1	8.4	0.0	6.3	1.2	53.5	100.0	10,287
South Asia															
Bangladesh	1970	—	—	—	—	—	—	—	—	—	—	—	—	—	0
	1978	33.4	14.6	20.6	12.3	5.0	5.8	9.7	3.5	0.0	4.9	1.0	45.6	100.0	1,333
	1983	26.4	10.7	20.0	14.7	6.2	4.9	13.0	4.3	0.0	5.5	1.1	53.4	100.0	1,502
Burma	1970	12.8	3.0	7.0	6.8	7.4	22.5	16.8	3.4	0.0	6.3	2.3	71.6	100.0	169
	1977	13.6	2.5	9.1	10.5	7.3	11.0	20.9	5.1	0.0	14.0	2.2	76.8	100.0	299
	1983	—	—	—	—	—	—	—	—	—	—	—	—	—	0
India	1970	34.9	7.7	20.9	11.2	3.6	0.5	16.2	4.3	0.0	3.0	0.4	41.4	100.0	2,094
	1978	42.8	26.1	13.8	11.7	9.9	0.7	11.4	2.5	0.0	4.3	0.4	43.2	100.0	7,562
	1981	60.0	43.6	8.5	9.4	6.3	0.6	9.0	1.9	0.0	1.8	0.3	31.5	100.0	14,457
Nepal	1970	—	—	—	—	—	—	—	—	—	—	—	—	—	0
	1978	18.2	17.5	5.4	10.1	2.7	21.0	11.1	3.9	0.0	13.1	5.5	73.2	100.0	135
	1981	27.0	19.1	9.5	11.7	2.0	16.7	7.2	5.2	1.0	7.7	4.4	62.9	100.0	296
Pakistan	1970	22.0	6.5	20.7	16.1	3.0	0.8	17.7	5.7	0.0	7.9	1.0	57.1	100.0	1,171
	1978	31.2	18.9	19.0	14.4	3.2	3.8	12.6	4.7	0.0	7.1	1.0	49.6	100.0	3,161
	1983	38.8	28.3	13.8	11.0	3.5	2.9	13.2	4.5	0.0	8.6	0.9	47.3	100.0	5,341
Sri Lanka	1970	14.0	7.9	44.1	8.9	4.1	7.7	8.7	2.8	0.0	4.9	0.9	41.4	100.0	410
	1978	23.5	16.5	29.7	7.8	3.6	6.1	10.7	4.0	0.0	9.1	1.2	45.9	100.0	942
	1983	29.3	23.9	17.1	6.7	4.5	8.2	1.2	7.5	0.0	7.5	2.1	53.3	100.0	1,788

Sources: The Republic of China, Department of Statistics, Ministry of Finance, *Monthly Statistics of Exports and Imports*, (Taiwan District), February 20, 1986.
United Nations, *Yearbook of International Trade Statistics*, 1972-73, 1981, 1982 and 1983 issues.

[a] Taiwan's electrical machinery for 1970 includes office machines and automatic data processing equipment.

Table 7. Structure of GDP in the Asia-Pacific Developing Countries, Japan, and the U.S.

(Percent of GDP at current prices)

Group/Country	1970				1978				1985			
	Agri.	Manuf.	Other Ind.[a]	Serv.	Agri.	Manuf.	Other Ind.[a]	Serv.	Agri.	Manuf.	Other Ind.[a]	Serv.
NICs												
Hong Kong[b]	2.0	30.9	6.3	60.8	1.1	24.3	7.9	66.6	0.5	24.6	7.6	67.2
Korea	26.9	20.9	8.6	43.6	20.2	27.8	10.4	41.6	13.8	28.1	12.7	45.4
Singapore	2.3	20.4	9.7	67.5	1.5	26.0	8.5	63.9	0.8	24.0	13.9	61.3
ROC (Taiwan)[c]	15.6	33.5	7.8	43.2	9.5	41.9	9.7	38.9	6.0	40.7	9.0	44.3
ASEAN-4												
Indonesia[b]	47.2	9.3	8.6	34.9	29.5	10.6	25.1	34.7	24.9	12.0	24.2	38.8
Malaysia[d]	29.6	14.3	12.4	43.7	25.2	18.3	11.1	45.4	19.5	20.5	16.6	43.3
Philippines	27.6	22.6	7.1	42.7	26.7	24.6	9.9	38.8	26.5	24.7	8.0	40.8
Thailand	28.3	16.0	9.3	46.4	27.5	19.0	8.6	44.9	17.4	19.8	10.0	52.8
South Asia												
Bangladesh[a]	57.9	6.4	3.7	32.0	54.7	9.1	4.4	31.7	48.4	8.7	5.9	37.1
Burma	38.3	10.4	4.0	47.4	44.2	10.0	2.6	43.2	47.8	9.9	3.4	38.9
India[b]	47.4	14.2	7.5	30.9	38.6	16.9	8.5	36.0	33.3	16.3	10.2	40.2
Nepal	67.5	9.0	2.4	21.0	63.0	4.3	7.6	25.0	56.6	4.3	10.8	28.3
Pakistan[e]	36.0	16.0	6.1	41.9	31.1	16.6	7.7	44.6	24.7	19.7	8.2	47.4
Sri Lanka	35.9	9.9	8.4	45.8	27.2	22.6	7.3	43.0	23.6	16.9	10.3	49.8
Japan[b]	6.1	35.9	10.7	47.3	4.6	29.6	12.1	53.7	3.2	29.8	11.1	56.0
U.S.[f]	2.7	25.7	9.2	62.4	2.9	24.4	9.9	63.0	2.0	21.1	10.6	66.3

Sources: Asian Development Bank, *Key Indicators of Developing Member Countries of ADB*, April, 1984, April, 1985, July, 1986. OECD, *National Accounts Statistics*, 1963-1980, and 1972-1984.

a   Includes construction, utilities, and mining.
b   1984.
c   Data reported is the sector's percentage of net domestic product (NDP) instead of GDP.
d   In constant 1970 or 1978 prices. Data reported is for 1971.
e   1973.
f   1983.

Table 8. Structure of Employment (Percent of total employed)

Group/Country	1970 Agri.	Ind.	Manuf.	Mining	Other	1978 Agri.	Ind.	Manuf.	Mining	Other	1985 Agri.	Ind.	Manuf.	Mining	Other
NICs															
Hong Kong[a]	1.9	n.a.	35.4	n.a.	62.7	1.4	n.a.	43.3	n.a.	55.8	1.6	n.a.	36.2	n.a.	62.2
Korea	50.4	n.a.	13.2	1.1	35.2	38.4	n.a.	22.4	0.8	38.4	24.9	n.a.	23.4	1.0	50.6
Singapore	3.4	n.a.	22.0	0.3	74.3	1.9	n.a.	28.8	0.1	69.1	0.7	n.a.	25.9	0.2	73.2
ROC (Taiwan)[b]	35.4	n.a.	20.4	1.6	42.7	24.9	n.a.	30.5	0.8	43.7	17.4	n.a.	33.5	0.5	48.6
ASEAN-4															
Indonesia[c]	61.6	n.a.	8.4	n.a.	30.1	60.9	n.a.	7.4	n.a.	31.6	54.7	n.a.	10.4	0.7	34.2
Malaysia	53.2	n.a.	9.0	2.6	35.2	43.3	n.a.	14.6	1.8	40.3	35.5	n.a.	15.7	1.1	47.6
Philippines	53.8	n.a.	11.9	n.a.	34.3	52.8	n.a.	11.5	n.a.	35.7	49.3	n.a.	9.7	0.6	40.4
Thailand	72.2	n.a.	7.7	0.7	19.4	73.7	n.a.	6.8	0.1	19.4	69.1	n.a.	7.3	0.2	23.4
South Asia															
Bangladesh[d]	73.9	n.a.	6.8	n.a.	19.3	70.3	n.a.	7.7	n.a.	22.0	64.0	n.a.	8.5	n.a.	27.6
Burma	66.7	n.a.	6.8	n.a.	26.4	67.2	n.a.	7.5	0.5	24.7	65.8	n.a.	8.5	0.6	25.0
India[e]	74.0	11.0	n.a.	n.a.	15.0	70.3	12.7	n.a.	n.a.	17.0	71.0	13.0	n.a.	n.a.	16.0
Nepal	n.a.	n.a.	n.a.	n.a.	n.a.	n.a.	n.a.	n.a.	n.a.	n.a.	n.a.	n.a.	n.a.	n.a.	n.a.
Pakistan[f]	57.3	n.a.	12.5	n.a.	30.2	54.8	n.a.	13.6	n.a.	31.6	52.7	n.a.	13.4	n.a.	33.8
Sri Lanka[d]	50.1	n.a.	9.3	0.4	40.2	n.a.	n.a.	n.a.	n.a.	n.a.	45.5	n.a.	0.8	9.9	43.7
Industrialized Countries															
Japan	20.0	34.0	n.a.	n.a.	46.0	13.3	38.1	n.a.	n.a.	48.6	12.0	39.0	n.a.	n.a.	49.0
United States	3.7	34.4	n.a.	n.a.	61.9	2.3	32.5	n.a.	n.a.	65.2	2.0	32.0	n.a.	n.a.	66.0

Sources: Asian Development Bank, *Key Indicators of Developing Member Countries of ADB*, April 1982, April 1984, April 1985, and July 1986 issues.

Republic of China, Council of Economic Planning and Development, *Taiwan Statistical Data Book*, 1985.

World Bank, *World Tables*, Third Edition, Volume II, Social Indicators.

a   1971, 1979, and 1985.
b   1970, 1978, and 1984.
c   1976, 1978, and 1982.
d   1973, 1978, and 1985.
e   Only India's data was obtained from World Bank. Data refers to percent of labor force, not percent of employed.
f   1971 and 1981.

electrical and non-electrical machinery and equipment, have increased dramatically. This is indicative of their increasing competitiveness in more sophisticated products (Table 6a). On the other hand, imports of transportation equipment, especially automobiles, and chemicals dropped as a percentage of total imports (Table 6b). Non-electrical and electrical machinery imports continued to expand due to high rates of economic growth.

Some differences in the strategies pursued by the NICs should be noted. Korea embarked on an industrialization policy emphasizing the development of heavy industry by providing credit at artificially low interest rates, strengthening direct government intervention through state-owned companies, and by introducing import controls in addition to tariff protection for selected goods.[6] The effect of this strategy can be clearly seen in the changing structure of Korean exports. In Korea, more than in the other NICs, heavy industries such as transport equipment (ships and automobiles), and iron and steel have become important. For example, Korean exports of iron and steel in 1983 accounted for nearly 9 percent of total exports as compared to less than 2 percent in 1970.[7] This emphasis on heavy industries encouraged private investment to reach an unprecedented level in 1979. But in 1980, a year of social and political unrest that was compounded by a poor harvest and rising prices of food and other necessities, a downturn occurred. This crisis led the new Korean government to undertake a critical reassessment of the heavy-industry strategy.

Meanwhile, the ROC (Taiwan) and Singapore opted for a different structural adjustment path aimed at sustaining export-led growth through expanded production of standardized, technology-intensive, product cycle goods and selected heavy engineering goods. Instead of direct intervention in capital markets and foreign trade, the ROC (Taiwan) focused on facilitating the inflow of advanced technology and by establishing a science-based industrial park. The Singapore government, on the other hand, chose to intervene in the labor market through wage increases that were meant to induce a shift from unskilled to skilled labor-intensive activities. It was believed that higher labor productivity would allow higher wages without granting specific advantages to capital-intensive industries. Singapore's growth slowdown in the mid-1980s, however, is causing the government to take a hard look at its strategies and policies in the science-based, skill-intensive sectors.

In terms of direction of trade, the United States is the largest purchaser of NICs' exports but the EEC and other developing countries have also become increasingly important purchasers of their traditional manufactures as well as of electrical and non-electrical machinery exports. The NICs, however, were not able to make any inroads into the Japanese market with their more sophisticated export products. About one-half of Japan's imports from the NICs consisted of raw materials, while the other half consisted almost entirely of traditional labor-intensive or resource-based products.[8] The larger share of the NICs' exports going to the U.S. compared to Japan reflects the wider access NICs have to the U.S. market and the difficulty of penetrating Japan's market for manufactured consumer goods, especially dur-

---

[6]   Balassa, B., and M. Sharpston, *Export Subsidies By Developing Countries: Issues of Policy.*

[7]   UN. op. cit.

[8]   See Naya S. "The Role of Trade Policies in the Industralization of Rapidly Growing Asian Developing Countries," in *Explaining the Success of Industrialization in East Asia,* (Forthcoming, 1987).

ables. With the recent appreciation of the yen, however, the NICs should improve their performance in the Japanese market.

The share of exports to developing countries in the Pacific region, on the other hand, remained virtually unchanged. There were, however, several significant shifts in the product composition of exports to these countries. Exports of raw materials continued to account for about a quarter of the trade among NICs, and also represented a significant portion of NICs exports to ASEAN countries.[9] Semi-processed items such as textile yarn and fabrics also continued to be intensively traded among NICs but trade in clothing has virtually disappeared. The NICs have all established their own internationally competitive clothing industries and have also begun investing in the ASEAN-4 countries in these industries. It is not surprising that exports of traditional products from NICs to the ASEAN-4 have declined in relative terms since the ASEAN-4 have become competitive exporters of these products. Exports of electrical machinery to other NICs and to the ASEAN-4 have expanded while the share of non-electrical machinery exports was halved in the 1970s. One may speculate that the NICs used the ASEAN-4 as test markets for more sophisticated products such as non-electrical machinery until they were able to complete successfully in the markets of the industrialized countries.

ASEAN-4

The ASEAN-4 countries, like most developing countries, adopted import-substituting strategies to push ahead with their industrialization efforts. This strategy involved selective protection of domestic producers against foreign competition and explicitly attempted to foster the development of domestic industries at a faster rate than that which would occur naturally. Domestic output prices were raised over world market prices by using tariffs on imports of manufactured goods which stimulated high-cost import substitution and by imposing taxes on the primary sector to subsidize this process.

Because protection allowed domestic industries to produce goods with a higher value-added and higher profits than under free trade, productive resources were induced to move into the protected industries. Consequently, these policies often discouraged export-oriented industrial production and even non-industrial activities via reduced availability of productive factors, i.e., higher factor costs and higher prices of inputs. At the same time, overvalued exchange rates sustained by import protection further discouraged exports.

Though the pattern of government intervention was similar among the ASEAN-4 countries, the degree and timing of protection varied somewhat between the countries. The Philippines began its import substitution process early (in the 1950s) and provided substantial protection to its domestic producers of consumer goods. Malaysia also followed the usual pattern of import-substitution in the 1960s and early 1970s, but the government did not discriminate seriously against other traded goods nor overvalue its domestic currency. Although its tariff rates diverged widely, the overall simple average tariff rate on manufactures was low. Thailand, like Malaysia, did not favor wide-spread import substitution, although its tariffs were higher than those of Malaysia. Indonesia, on the other hand, could be characterized as having the most inward-looking industrial orientation despite the dismantling of

---

[9] *Ibid.*

some controls by the present government in the 1970s.

In addition to import protection, strong incentives in all ASEAN-4 countries favored the use of physical capital. Indeed, the use of capital was subsidized to a great degree while the use of labor was somewhat discouraged, giving rise to an obviously distorted set of incentives in these labor-abundant economies. This is reflected in the relatively poor absorption of labor in the manufacturing sector of these countries.

Import-substitution policies do not lead to a reduction in total imports.[10] On the contrary, the more inward-looking industrialization is, the greater the requirement for imported capital and technology. The increased import dependence that accompanies import-substituting industrialization caused severe balance-of-payments problems for the oil-importers during the 1970s, when their import bills were additionally burdened by rising oil prices. Until then, their rich natural resource endowments allowed them to keep their trade deficits within reasonable limits by using agricultural and raw materials export earnings to finance imports of capital and technology necessary for continued import-substituting industrialization.

Therefore, in an effort to adjust to the increases in the oil-import bill, the Philippines and Thailand attempted to promote manufactured exports in the second half of the 1970s. Malaysia and, to a lesser extent, Indonesia also attempted to diversify exports. The ASEAN-4 countries sought greater balance to the incentive systems to encourage exports of manufactures. Export controls were relaxed and export taxes abolished. Duty-free importation allowances for necessary inputs were granted to exporters, special rebates on income and turnover taxes were introduced, and new (mostly short-term) export credit facilities were opened.

Some countries even made cautious attempts to reduce the overvaluation of their currencies, but due to the fact that their domestic inflation rates remained above those of their major trading partners, real exchange rates soon returned to their former levels.[11] With the drop in oil prices in the early 1980s, current account deficits rose in Indonesia, making it apparent that Indonesia would have to expand non-oil exports for it to attain acceptable economic growth without an unacceptable level of foreign debt into the 1990s. As a result, a second major devaluation coupled with reforms in customs, taxation, and pricing policies occurred in 1984 and in 1986, the Indonesian rupiah was further devalued by 30 percent against the U. S. dollar. Even Thailand, a country that avoided devaluation in the 1970s, took a bold step in substantially devaluing the baht in 1984.

The adoption of more export-oriented policies corresponded with increases in the number of ASEAN-4's export commodities. However, this was primarily due to diversification of primary commodity exports, especially for Thailand. Thailand's low concentration index reflects the diversification of its export crop sector away from rice and rubber into tapioca, maize, pineapples, sugar, palm oil, and marine products. Thus, despite the push for diversification toward manufactured exports, exports of primary commodities continue to account for the bulk of ASEAN-4

---

[10] This point is stressed by I. Little, T. Scitovsky and M. Scott, *Industry and Trade in Some Developing Countries.*

[11] Bautista, Power and Associates, *Industrial Promotion Policies in the Philippines.* pp. 29-30 and 79 ff. Rana also found that real effective exchange rates appreciated in the Philippines, Thailand and Indonesia between 1967 and 1979, indicating a loss of competitiveness in export markets. (Rana. P., "The Impact of the Current Exchange Rate System on Trade and Inflation of Selected Developing Member Countries," ADB Staff Paper No. 18.)

countries' total exports, ranging from 93 percent of total exports in Indonesia to 51 percent in the Philippines (Table 6a). The share of raw material exports is especially high in Indonesia reflecting the large volume and relatively high unit price of petroleum exports for Indonesia in the 1970s. Both indexes in Table 5 reflect the high degree of concentration of Indonesia's exports. This was less evident in Malaysia which only became a net oil exporter since 1975.

Nonetheless, the overwhelming importance of primary commodities for ASEAN-4 trade decreased while manufactured exports rose. The share of manufactures in total exports rose to about 20 percent in Malaysia, the Philippines, and Thailand by 1978, and to more than 30 percent in Thailand in 1983. The least developed ASEAN-4 country, Indonesia, achieved a similarly high rate of manufactured export growth as the other countries in this group, but given the low base in 1970, the share of manufactured in total exports was still low (6.5 percent) in 1983. It should be noted that Indonesia's low manufactures-to-total-exports ratio was also due to the huge rise in oil export earnings that resulted from the oil price hikes of the 1970s.

Manufactured exports also became more diversified, but this process was less marked than in the NICs. In 1970, when the industrial base was still very small in Malaysia, the Philippines,, and Thailand, a large percentage of manufactured exports consisted of resource-based manufactures. The production of these goods is based on locally available materials such as leather, rubber, wood or cork, as well as on traditional skills and relatively high labor inputs. New products, however, such as the "classical trio" of textiles, miscellaneous manufactures, and clothing, became prominent by 1978. In the Philippines and Thailand, the share of clothing increased from 0 percent of total exports in 1970 to more than 6 percent of total exports in 1982 and 1983. Malaysia also increased exports of clothing and significantly increased exports of electrical machinery, largely to the United States. In Indonesia, on the other hand, the export of resource-based manufactures was nil in 1970, but accounted for 3.5 percent of total exports in 1983. Since 1980, Indonesia has phased out exports of unprocessed timber and has become the leading supplier of plywood in the world market.

The United States, the EEC, and other developing countries emerged as important markets for the manufactured exports of these ASEAN-4 countries. The United States, in fact, replaced Japan as the largest market for Thailand. Still, Japan was the main customer of ASEAN-4's primary commodities, and the total exports for Indonesia and Malaysia.

The import structure of the ASEAN-4 countries also reflects these structural changes (Table 6b). Shares of the classical trio decreased. On the other hand, the growing importance of the manufacturing sector made large imports of manufactured inputs necessary, and the percentage of chemicals and machinery grew.

Thus, the change to more export-oriented policies contributed to significant changes in the import and export structures of these countries. However, the new policies favoring manufactured exports were adopted without simultaneously reducing protection and other preferences for import substitution. Discrimination against exports was only partly mitigated by the new measures, and that the incentive structure favoring capital-intensive industrial activities remained basically unchallenged. Table 9 shows that average nominal rates of protection of the ASEAN-4 countries are still higher than those of the NICs (except for Korea), though lower than the South Asian countries.

The inability of overly capital-intensive import-substituting industries to provide sufficient employment opportunities has been well documented. The growth of manufactures in GDP has not been matched by growth in manufacturing employment. In the ASEAN-4 countries, the share of manufactures in GDP rose, on average, but industrial employment generally remained low. For example, although the manufacturing sector accounted for about 20 percent of GDP in Indonesia, the Philippines, and Thailand in 1985, employment in that sector remained at less than 10 percent. Malaysia was more successful, with the manufacturing sector comprising 21 percent of GDP and nearly 16 percent of employment in 1985. Unless this pattern is changed, however, serious social problems will result, as labor-force growth is extremely high.

South Asian Countries

The South Asian countries have lagged behind the other Asian developing countries in terms of economic and export growth in the 1960s and 1970s. The rate of growth of total and manufactured exports of the South Asian countries was below the world average, though they also had increased in the average share of manufactured exports in total exports in the 1970s.

The poor growth rates of industry in India, Sri Lanka, and Pakistan cannot be attributed to the difficulties usually associated with the initial phase of industrialization, since these countries had already built up a sizeable industrial sector by 1960. For example, in 1960, the industrial sector comprised 16 percent of Pakistan's GDP and 20 percent of GDP in India and Sri Lanka. This is similar to the shares of the industrial sector in Malaysia, Thailand, and Singapore which were about 18 and 19 percent.

Rather, the slow growth in the above three countries, as well as in Bangladesh and Burma, appears to be the outcome of a number of mutually reinforcing economic policies which were aimed at industrial self-sufficiency under close government supervision. In the five South Asian countries, policies were geared to establishing a diversified national industrial sector with particular emphasis on basic industries (e.g., chemical products, steel, and cement) until the late 1970s (for Pakistan the 1960s). This involved a high degree of direct government involvement in industrial production coupled with a tight net of regulations affecting nearly every step of production and distribution.

Adjustment of the industrial structure has been impeded by government policies favoring large-scale, physical capital- and technology-intensive goods industries, and by artificially high wage costs and extensive employment guarantees to employees of public enterprises. Thus, the industrialization strategy followed by all of the South Asian countries has placed heavy demand on scarce factors such as skilled labor and financial capital. These policies largely disregarded the countries' factor endowments and existing bottlenecks to industrial development such as insufficient infrastructure. The result has predictably been low growth of output and industrial employment. In 1970, the share of industry in both GDP and employment was generally lower for the South Asian countries than those of the ASEAN-4 countries (Tables 7 and 8).

The inward-orientation of these countries' industrial policies has constrained their ability to diversify exports, which, because of limitations in terms of natural resource endowment and the low level of labor skills, were already concentrated

Table 9. Average Ad Valorem Rate on Total and Specific Commodity Groups

Country	All Commodities	Food, Live Animals (SITC 0)	Beverage, Tobacco (SITC 1)	Crude Materials (SITC 2)	Mineral Fuels (SITC 3)	Animal, Veg. Oil, Fats (SITC 4)	Chemicals (SITC 5)	Basic Manuf. (SITC 6)	Machines, Trans. Equip. (SITC 7)	Misc. Manuf. Goods (SITC 8)
NICs										
Korea[a]	32.9	35.6	94.0	14.3	8.6	27.8	23.8	30.9	21.4	39.7
Singapore	0.5	0.2	0.0	0.0	2.2	0.0	0.0	0.0	0.4	1.7
ASEAN-4										
Indonesia	30.9	44.0	49.2	18.1	6.3	28.1	18.9	36.8	26.7	49.8
Malaysia	10.4	5.3	33.3	3.2	1.5	1.5	10.1	11.2	12.9	14.2
Philippines	29.9	37.6	45.7	20.7	17.4	28.4	21.2	33.3	22.5	42.3
Thailand	25.9	26.1	30.0	14.1	8.9	37.5	15.4	29.6	20.4	50.9
South Asia										
Bangladesh	74.7	64.7	159.7	42.2	33.9	47.6	54.8	87.2	64.9	118.2
India[a]	71.5	81.5	100.0	59.6	44.5	62.8	65.8	81.3	59.7	88.3
Pakistan	80.6	81.0	176.9	45.9	42.6	62.2	64.0	94.4	55.2	103.2
Sri Lanka	41.2	48.2	93.0	35.2	14.4	53.5	23.2	37.1	23.8	42.3

Source: United Nations Conference on Trade and Development, *Trade Information System* (Computer Tape, 1984).

[a] Special preference rates granted to imports from Bangladesh and Lao People's Democratic Republic under in Bangkok Agreement are not reflected in the data.

in a few industries. In Burma and Sri Lanka, primary commodities made up more than 97 percent of total exports in 1970. In the same year, raw materials, agricultural products and textiles made up more than 75 and 85 percent of total exports in India and Pakistan, respectively.

In recent years, however, all of the governments of the South Asian countries have announced more or less drastic policy changes, and some measures have already been put into effect. More liberal market-oriented policies have been adopted in order to boost exports so that higher growth can be sustained.

Sri Lanka, in particular, is undergoing a significant structural change toward the production of traditional light consumer goods. Its government has taken major steps to rationalize the incentive system and to abolish discrimination against private investors. The results have been encouraging both with respect to industrial investment and output growth. Balance-of-payments problems arising from swiftly expanding imports, however, has forced the government to review its ambitious plans. Granting more freedom to the private sector has similarly yielded an upswing in industrial output growth in Pakistan, while India has streamlined incentives for production of exports. Meanwhile, Bangladesh has undertaken a return to private ownership of jute mills and other enterprises that were poorly managed by the public sector.

Changes in the export and import structure reflect some of these policy changes. Import shares of chemicals declined significantly in Sri Lanka, India, and Pakistan, while import shares of textiles declined in all of South Asia, except Sri Lanka. Export shares of raw materials and agricultural goods, on the other hand, declined significantly for most of South Asia and exports of manufactured goods, especially clothing, increased dramatically. These examples indicate that national policies can enchance industrial development, despite foreign exchange constraints and deficiencies in infrastructure that the South Asian countries face.

Sri Lanka, unlike the other South Asian countries, has trade-income ratios comparable to those of the ASEAN-4 countries. Despite a large increase in the number of commodities exported, its exports remain highly concentrated. Sri Lanka's export composition is similar to that of the ASEAN-4 countries with its large dependence on exports of primary commodities. Primary commodity exports comprised over 70 percent of total exports in 1983, down from more than 97 percent in 1970. In particular, tea alone accounted for one third of Sri Lanka's total exports in 1983, while rubber and refined petroleum products together accounted for more than another one fifth. The increases in the share of manufactured exports is primarily due to increases in clothing exports from 1 percent of total exports in 1970 to nearly 19 percent in 1983, or 67 percent of manufactured exports.

The trade structure of Nepal in 1981 had a similar emphasis on primary product exports, in particular jute and animal hides. The bulk of its manufactured exports consisted of jute manufactures and textiles. Thus, Nepal, like Burma and Sri Lanka, maintained what could be called a traditional developing country export pattern in that they relied mainly on primary products with manufactured exports concentrated in textiles and clothing.

India and Pakistan, on the other hand, already had large manufactures-to-total-exports ratios in 1970. Since then, both countries have decreased the share of raw material exports, while exports of agricultural and food products have increased. For Pakistan, the dramatic improvement in agricultural production raised the

Table 10. Direction of Exports and Imports

Direction of Exports (as percent of total exports in f.o.b. values)

SOURCE	1970 NICs	ASEAN4	S.ASIA	US	JAPAN	EEC	1978 NICs	ASEAN4	S.ASIA	US	JAPAN	EEC	1985 NICs	ASEAN4	S.ASIA	US	JAPAN	EEC
NICs	7.3	10.2	0.7	31.2	11.5	15.1	7.8	8.7	1.9	29.6	12.6	14.8	8.4	7.0	2.2	34.7	10.0	10.3
Hong Kong	5.7	4.7	0.8	35.7	7.1	21.3	7.2	6.8	1.0	30.4	7.7	21.8	5.6	3.6	1.0	30.8	4.2	12.3
Korea	6.3	1.2	0.1	47.1	28.1	7.6	5.2	2.5	1.8	32.0	20.7	14.7	7.6	2.7	2.8	36.2	15.5	10.4
Singapore[a]	4.9	27.8	1.7	10.7	7.3	15.1	9.2	22.3	5.2	15.4	9.3	12.1	8.6	22.2	5.6	20.8	9.4	10.4
ROC(Taiwan)[b]	13.5	5.8	0.0	38.1	14.6	9.3	10.2	5.7	0.1	39.5	12.5	11.3	12.0	3.1	0.3	48.1	11.3	8.3
ASEAN-4	19.0	3.9	0.6	19.6	29.9	13.1	16.5	3.2	1.7	22.4	29.5	14.9	18.9	4.5	2.1	20.2	32.1	11.9
Indonesia	17.5	5.6	0.0	13.0	40.8	5.9	15.7	2.0	0.5	25.4	39.2	7.5	12.8	1.9	0.6	22.7	49.1	6.6
Malaysia	27.0	3.3	0.9	13.0	18.3	19.3	22.3	2.4	4.4	18.6	21.7	18.4	29.5	6.2	4.1	12.8	24.6	14.4
Philippines	6.8	0.3	0.1	41.5	40.1	7.3	8.0	4.0	0.2	33.8	24.2	18.6	13.1	6.0	0.6	35.9	19.0	14.0
Thailand	20.0	8.0	1.3	13.5	25.5	18.3	15.7	7.3	1.2	11.0	20.3	26.4	15.7	6.3	2.8	19.6	13.3	18.9
South Asia	4.0	1.7	5.2	12.0	10.7	21.4	5.7	2.7	5.6	12.3	9.6	25.8	6.3	2.0	3.9	21.1	10.8	21.9
Bangladesh	—	—	—	—	—	—	1.8	0.3	12.3	15.4	4.7	17.0	3.9	0.9	8.2	18.1	7.2	17.4
Burma	15.1	12.3	24.5	0.0	7.5	20.8	24.7	15.3	17.5	0.9	11.5	18.2	18.9	11.7	5.3	2.7	6.4	11.5
India	2.5	1.6	5.1	13.5	13.9	18.7	4.1	2.5	4.2	13.6	9.5	26.4	5.7	1.4	2.2	22.9	11.1	20.9
Nepal	0.0	0.0	61.9	9.5	4.8	19.0	4.6	2.5	31.5	8.6	13.4	26.1	1.7	0.0	33.2	35.1	0.7	24.6
Pakistan	7.9	1.1	1.9	11.7	5.9	23.9	10.5	2.8	4.5	6.6	10.2	22.6	5.9	2.6	5.4	10.0	11.3	22.2
Sri Lanka	0.9	0.0	3.3	7.2	3.3	32.8	3.5	0.5	6.3	6.8	5.6	19.4	4.4	1.1	3.8	22.3	5.1	19.4
Industrialized Countries																		
Japan	13.7	7.2	1.6	31.1	—	9.6	15.1	6.5	1.7	25.8	—	12.3	12.8	4.2	1.8	37.6	—	11.9
U.S.	4.2	2.0	2.1	—	10.8	26.1	5.8	2.2	1.2	—	9.0	22.8	7.8	2.1	1.4	—	10.5	23.0

Direction of Imports (as percent of total imports in c.i.f. values)

IMPORTING COUNTRY	1970						1978						1985					
	NICs	ASEAN4	S.ASIA	US	JAPAN	EEC	NICs	ASEAN4	S.ASIA	US	JAPAN	EEC	NICs	ASEAN4	S.ASIA	US	JAPAN	EEC
NICs	5.1	11.6	1.5	17.8	29.3	13.8	6.3	9.7	0.9	15.8	27.7	10.7	8.1	8.7	0.9	16.3	22.2	10.1
Hong Kong	8.1	3.8	2.2	13.1	23.8	18.2	15.0	3.7	2.1	11.9	22.8	14.2	17.9	2.8	1.0	9.5	23.1	11.6
Korea	3.3	6.1	0.3	29.5	41.0	10.5	1.8	4.9	0.3	20.3	39.9	9.3	3.3	6.6	1.1	21.5	25.3	9.5
Singapore[a]	4.6	28.1	2.2	10.6	18.9	15.2	5.5	24.0	1.1	11.5	17.4	10.6	6.9	20.7	1.4	14.5	16.3	10.8
ROC(Taiwan)[b]	3.1	6.8	0.4	23.9	42.9	8.1	3.4	6.0	0.2	21.6	33.4	9.4	3.9	5.7	0.1	23.6	27.6	9.5
ASEAN-4	7.5	4.0	1.6	17.3	28.4	20.8	11.8	3.8	1.6	15.1	27.9	16.2	16.1	6.1	0.9	15.4	23.8	15.9
Indonesia	11.5	1.9	3.1	17.9	29.4	21.6	15.2	3.0	3.1	12.5	30.1	18.7	12.3	1.3	0.4	14.4	28.1	21.7
Malaysia	10.9	8.6	2.6	8.6	17.5	23.3	12.9	5.8	1.7	13.9	23.1	18.1	21.5	6.5	1.2	15.3	23.0	14.4
Philippines	3.0	2.3	0.2	29.4	30.6	15.4	7.8	4.5	0.3	21.1	27.5	12.6	15.2	11.9	0.3	25.1	14.0	8.5
Thailand	5.0	2.2	0.8	14.9	37.4	22.6	10.2	1.9	0.8	13.7	30.7	14.5	13.2	7.1	1.2	11.2	26.0	16.4
South Asia	0.8	0.7	4.3	25.3	7.8	22.4	3.6	3.9	3.9	13.9	10.8	29.5	8.3	4.6	2.1	11.5	13.0	26.0
Bangladesh	-	-	-	-	-	-	4.2	2.3	5.1	12.8	13.1	15.9	14.0	6.4	4.3	9.4	13.3	13.3
Burma	6.6	0.7	15.1	5.9	26.3	25.7	8.6	2.3	5.4	12.9	30.5	24.4	13.2	4.5	2.0	1.8	31.6	24.7
India	0.2	0.6	1.4	29.3	4.6	17.9	2.3	4.2	0.7	11.9	7.7	29.5	7.3	3.3	0.7	10.2	10.0	27.4
Nepal	1.9	0.0	73.6	1.9	9.4	11.3	12.4	0.9	48.1	6.5	22.6	7.6	14.2	2.0	32.2	2.8	23.7	14.0
Pakistan	0.9	0.6	0.7	28.4	10.9	29.8	3.7	3.4	4.3	15.0	9.7	25.0	3.4	5.8	1.6	14.0	12.6	19.8
Sri Lanka	1.8	2.1	16.2	5.7	8.5	26.7	4.8	1.0	13.5	8.0	10.6	25.7	9.7	3.3	6.4	7.1	15.4	15.5
Industrialized Countries																		
Japan	3.5	9.4	2.5	29.5	-	8.2	7.2	11.4	1.4	18.7	-	7.7	7.9	12.9	1.4	20.0	-	7.2
U.S.	4.9	2.6	1.0	-	14.7	23.1	7.8	3.9	0.7	-	14.2	16.8	11.2	3.1	0.9	-	20.0	19.8

Sources: International Monetary Fund, *Direction of Trade Statistics Yearbook,* 1970-76, 1985, and 1986 issues.
Department of Statistics, Ministry of Finance, *Monthly Statistics of Exports and Imports,* The Republic of China (Taiwan District), February 20, 1986.

a Singapore does not record trade with Indonesia. Singapore's trade with Indonesia is derived from Indonesian data. To account for costs of freight and insurance, Indonesian exports are multiplied by 1.1 and shown as estimates of Singapore's imports from Indonesia. Indonesian imports are divided by 1.1 and shown as estimates of Singapore's exports to Indonesia.

b All countries' trade with Taiwan are derived from Taiwan's own records. Taiwan's exports are multiplied by 1.1 to account for costs of freight and insurance, and shown as imports from Taiwan. Taiwan's imports data are divided by 1.1 and shown as estimates of various countries' exports to Taiwan.

importance of agricultural and food exports, especially rice exports to other developing countries in the Middle East and Africa, which more than offset the decrease in raw materials. This was not the case for India, where primary commodities still accounted for approximately 40 percent of total exports in 1980. In India, the share of manufactures, in particular, clothing and resource-based manufactures, increased significantly. Of the South Asian countries, only India has achieved much in the way of export diversification. In fact, it has done better than most Asian developing countries in both indexes of diversification (Table 5). Moreover, India has good prospects for expansion in areas such as machinery, certain types of transport equipment and some engineering and consumer goods.

The South Asian countries as a whole are less dependent on the Asia-Pacific region as markets for their exports than are the NICs and ASEAN-4 countries; the EEC is their most important market (Table 10). Although the EEC's share of primary commodity exports has decreased, the EEC has maintained its position as the largest importer of primary commodities from these countries with the exception of raw materials from India and agricultural and food products from Bangladesh where Japan imports the largest share. The EEC is also the largest importer of manufactures for India and Pakistan and is also an important market for Sri Lankan manufactures.

The U. S. and other developed countries drastically reduced their share of primary commodity imports from the South Asian countries, but the United States continues to provide an important market for manufactures. In particular, the United States is the largest market for Sri Lanka, increasing its share from a little more than 10 percent of manufactured exports in 1970 to more than 40 percent in 1981. Japan, however, remained a very small importer in terms of manufactures (4.1 percent in 1981). The industrialized countries provided the largest markets for the traditional manufactured exports, but the slight increase in the shares of the more skill-intensive commodity, non-electrical machinery, was due to purchases by other developing countries. Other developing countries purchased nearly 50 percent of the South Asian exports of non-electrical machinery, implying that they have some advantage in these markets. It may also indicate that South Asian exports in this commodity group are not yet able to compete in the markets of industrialized countries.

MEASURING EXPORT PERFORMANCE

We have already pointed out structural differences in the trade patterns of the Asia developing countries with Japan and the United States. Japanese imports from these countries are comprised largely of primary products. Even the NICs have not been able to penetrate the Japanese market with their manufactured exports. In addition, export growth to Japan has generally been slower than to the United States. From 1972-1973 to 1982-1983, exports from the three groups of Asian developing countries to Japan fell as a percentage of their total exports, whereas exports to the United States increased.

In both the U. S. and Japanese markets, the NICs and ASEAN-4 countries have done comparatively well. Hence, the share of total U. S. and Japanese imports from ASEAN-4 countries rose from 9 to 13 percent in Japan and from 2.6 to more than 3 percent in the U. S. from 1970 to 1985, while the share of imports from the

NICs more than doubled in Japan (3.5 to 7.9) and almost tripled in the U. S. (4.9 to 11.2). In other words, both Japan and the U. S. are increasing imports relatively faster in the NICs and ASEAN-4 countries than other countries. The South Asian countries, on the other hand, were able to maintain their share of the U. S. market but saw a decline in their share of Japan's imports from 2.5 percent in 1970 to 1.4 percent in 1975. It is useful to infer the broad factors that have been responsible for changing the shares of the Asian developing countries' exports to two major trading partners.[12] Exports are affected by three factors:

1. the rate of growth of the total importing country market;
2. the degree of concentration of exports in those products which are growing rapidly or slowly in total imports of the recipient country; and
3. the ability of the exporting country to expand exports of individual commodities more rapidly than competing exporters.

The first factor is defined as the average growth effect (W) measured by the growth rate of total imports. The second factor is defined as the (commodity) compositional effect (C) as it is related to the commodity make-up while the third is defined as the share effect (S) as it measures the commodity share of exports.

In examining the export growth of the Asian developing countries (A) to the United States, it is useful to compare this growth with the average growth of the U. S. imports (W) as the difference indicates how the export growth of the country (or region) has deviated from the average trend. This difference is referred to as export performance (A-W). This same procedure is also applied to exports to Japan.

In explaining export performance, it is reasonable to suppose that the commodity compositional effect is affected more by external (or U.S. and Japan) than internal conditions, and vice versa for the share effect.[13] That is, the external factors (e.g. import demand and policies of developed countries) favoring (or not favoring) the particular export structure is regarded as a major determinant of the compositional effect. On the other hand, the share effect reflects the competitive position and whether, and to what extent, the Asian developing countries have kept up with external demand. This would also indicate the scope for the exporting countries to encourage or discourage (directly and indirectly) their exports through appropriate policies.

---

[12] The analytical device is known as the constant-market share model. For a good theoretical evaluation of this model, see J.D. Richardson, "Constant Market Shares Analysis of Export Growth," *Journal of International Economics*, I:1971, pp. 227-39. The algebraic formula used is:

$$dx \equiv s^0 dM + (\Sigma s_k^0 \, dM_k - s^0 \, dM) + (\Sigma ds_k M_k^0 + \Sigma ds_k dM_k)$$

where x, M, and s refer to ASEAN-4 exports to the U.S., total imports of U.S., and x/M, respectively. Although the constant market share model is usually discussed in terms of the share, it is useful to express it in terms of the growth rate as follows:

$$dx \equiv gx^0 + (\Sigma g_k x_k^0 - gx^0) + [(dx - \Sigma r_k x_k') + (\Sigma r_k x_k' - \Sigma g_k x_k^0)]$$

where g and r are the growth rate of imports with M^0 and M' as the base, respectively. The three right hand terms in each equation correspond to W, C and S discussed in the text, though all of these terms in the text are expressed as a proportion of x^0 or the growth rate of exports.

[13] This interpretation is only a matter of degree and, for example, the commodity share of a given item can be altered as a result of such factors as a change in the country import quota rather than as a change in the competitive position of this export. Also, the commodity structure of exports can be altered by internal conditions and measures.

In computing the export performance, import data of the U.S. and Japan are used, i.e., U. S. imports from Indonesia are treated as the latter's exports to the former. The eleven export classifications used in Table 6(a) are also used here. The growth rates presented are simple average growth rates of imports from 1972-1973 to 1982-1983. The numerical results of one (simple) application of this methodology are presented in Table 11.

Several noteworthy points are indicated by the results. First, as mentioned previously, the Asian developing countries have done considerably better in the American than in the Japanese market, though export performance (A-W) of individual countries varies substantially in both the U.S. and Japan. But it is not surprising to find that the performance of Philippine exports is negative in both markets.

Second, export expansion of the NICs (except for Singapore), and South Asian countries (except for Burma in the U. S. and Bangladesh in Japan) has been pulled down by their poor commodity composition in both Japan and the United States. The external demand factor was not very favorable for these countries in this period. For the resource-rich ASEAN countries (except for Philippines in the U.S.) and Singapore, the compositional effect was generally positive. This is not surprising, since in Japan, imports of raw materials, particularly petroleum and petroleum products, are relatively more important than agricultural and food products and manufactured imports.

It should be noted, however, that with the drop in commodity prices in the 1980s, the situation is likely to have changed substantially. The compositional effect is now likely to be positive for the NICs (except Singapore) and South Asian countries, and negative for the resource-exporting ASEAN-4 countries and Singapore. But the compositional effect is not simply a matter of specializing in primary or manufactured goods. For example, imports of manufactures increased overall in the United States. Yet export expansion of Korea was slightly reduced by an unfavorable compositional effect despite its overwhelming make-up of manufactured exports.

Finally, there is a close association between export performance and the share effect. That is, the countries that do well in their exports are those with positive share effect. In fact, in many instances, countries have been able to more than offset their unfavorable commodity make-up with favorable share or competitive effects to yield rapid export expansion and favorable export performance (e.g. Thailand exports to the U.S. and Hong Kong and Korean exports to the U.S. and Japan).

In our discussion, the positive (negative) share effect has been interpreted as an indication of an improved (worsened) competitive position in a given country's exports in relation to those of others. It is, however, difficult to pinpoint what the competitiveness is comprised of or what it means. Obviously, price is an important variable, but other factors such as the quality and uniqueness of the good, distance (transport cost), the speed of delivery, after-sales service, and commercial and financial ties and arrangements can be important determinants of the competitiveness.

Although the above analysis indicates that the NICs and ASEAN-4 countries have improved their competitive position *vis-a-vis* the rest of the world in the Japanese and particularly the U. S. markets, the increasing trend toward protectionism would hurt them through the worsening of the average growth and compositional effects. With exports looming so large in the economic performance of these countries,

Table 11. Export Performance of Asian Developing Countries from 1972-73 to 1982-83 (Simple average)

	Exports to U.S.							Exports to Japan						
	Export Growth Rate (A)	Average Growth (W)	Commodity Composition Effect (C)	Share Effect (S)	Export Performance (A−W)	Average Total Exports ($US mil) 1972-73	1982-83	Export Growth Rate (A)	Average Growth (W)	Commodity Composition Effect (C)	Share Effect (S)	Export Performance (A−W)	Average Total Exports ($US mil) 1972-73	1982-83
Hong Kong	37.1	32.0	0.5	4.7	5.1	1,349.6	6,359.9	22.6	31.8	−4.5	−4.6	−9.2	197.7	646.2
Korea	71.3	32.0	−0.0	39.4	39.3	840.7	6,832.6	30.6	31.8	−5.3	4.1	−1.2	815.3	3,309.4
Singapore	61.7	32.0	9.5	20.1	29.7	365.6	2,621.3	85.7	31.8	3.9	50.0	53.9	172.1	1,646.8
NICs	51.9	32.0	1.6	18.3	19.9	2,555.9	15,813.9	37.3	31.8	−3.9	9.3	5.5	1,185.4	5,602.4
Indonesia	119.9	32.0	6.9	81.0	87.9	391.4	5,082.7	55.7	31.8	6.1	17.8	23.9	1,707.0	11,218.7
Malaysia	46.2	32.0	8.5	5.7	14.2	370.4	2,082.0	124.2	31.8	4.4	88.0	92.4	228.8	3,070.1
Philippines	25.4	32.0	−12.3	5.8	−6.6	580.6	2,057.5	12.4	31.8	4.1	−23.5	−19.4	644.6	1,441.4
Thailand	67.7	32.0	3.4	32.4	35.7	128.1	995.8	21.9	31.8	3.5	−13.5	−9.9	323.1	1,029.7
ASEAN	59.5	32.0	−0.6	28.1	27.5	1,470.5	10,218.0	47.7	31.8	5.2	10.7	15.9	2,903.5	16,759.8
Bangladesh	7.5	32.0	−28.3	3.8	−24.5	56.5	98.7	55.4	31.8	0.6	23.0	23.6	9.2	60.5
Burma	121.4	32.0	1.6	87.8	89.4	1.1	14.8	2.5	31.8	−6.8	−22.5	−29.3	38.2	47.9
India	34.7	32.0	−19.1	21.8	2.7	431.8	1,928.0	12.9	31.8	−0.1	−18.8	−18.9	492.2	1,126.5
Nepal	14.6	32.0	−23.1	5.5	−17.4	1.8	4.3	−4.4	31.8	−9.0	−45.2	−36.2	2.0	1.2
Pakistan	35.6	32.0	−15.4	19.1	3.6	39.8	181.7	9.2	31.8	−8.9	−13.7	−22.6	130.1	249.6
Sri Lanka	60.4	32.0	−10.5	39.1	28.5	28.4	200.2	13.5	31.8	−8.5	−9.7	−18.2	29.7	50.3
South Asia	33.4	32.0	−19.3	20.7	1.4	559.4	2,427.6	12.2	31.8	−2.4	−17.2	−19.6	701.4	2,079.9
Asia and Pacific	54.5	32.0	−0.6	23.1	22.5	6,151.8	39,678.6	39.6	31.8	1.0	6.7	7.8	5,848.4	28,986.5
World Developing	51.1	32.0	0.2	18.9	19.1	17,189.8	105,117.3	47.0	31.8	3.0	12.2	15.2	12,769.0	72,809.7
Latin Am. Developing	40.1	32.0	−0.1	8.2	8.1	8,293.8	41,559.1	27.5	31.8	−0.6	−3.8	−4.3	1,679.8	6,294.4

Source: United Nations, *Commodity Trade Statistics*, various years.

it is important to ascertain whether exports are expected to rise substantially in the future, given the somewhat restrictive trade policy environment in many advanced countries. These countries will have to promote greater trade within the region. Cultivating markets in developing countries is difficult, but will be extremely important for future trade.

INTRA-REGIONAL TRADE

Merchandise trade among the Asian developing countries (intra-regional trade) has not been very large, though it is substantially larger than intra-regional trade among other developing countries. In most cases, it has fluctuated annually with no discernable increasing or decreasing trend. It should be remembered, however, that although the share of intra-regional trade has not increased in some countries like Korea, the large growth in total trade implies that the volume of intra-regional trade has increased significantly. In other countries like Nepal, the high intra-regional trade ratios are somewhat misleading. In Nepal, trade is small and is largely the result of trade with one large partner, India. For example, in 1985, more than 80 percent of Nepal's intra-regional exports went to India, while approximately thirty percent of the country's total imports were from India. The share of imports from the NICs and ASEAN-4 has increased in the 1980s. For Hong Kong, its role in Chinese trade explains the seemingly large increase in intra-regional trade. Excluding China, Hong Kong's intra-regional trade accounted for 10 percent of exports and 22 percent of imports in 1985.

Intra-regional trade is generally high and growing in the ASEAN-4 countries, but even it has not increased as much as one might expect. Despite ASEAN's trade cooperation efforts, trade among members of ASEAN (intra-ASEAN trade) and therefore, ASEAN-4's intra-regional trade centers primarily on Singapore.

In general, it is believed that the effect of ASEAN preferential trading arrangements (PTA), which were enacted in 1977, on intra-ASEAN trade has been small, but that the potential for trade expansion is large.[14] The number of tariff concessions exchanged by the ASEAN countries increased from 71 items when the PTA was begun, to nearly 20,000 items as of 1985. After 1980, the deficiency of the cumbersome product-by-product approach to PTA was recognized and some across-the-board tariff reductions were included. A 20 to 25 percent margin of preference was now automatically given to items with import values of under US$10 million in 1982. In 1984, the ASEAN foreign ministers approved the application of 20 to 25 percent tariff cut on all items with import value beyond US$10 million, effectively doing away with the ceiling. But, it must be noted that there are an extensive number of goods that are exempt from the across-the-board reductions, and thus, the benefits of the tariff reductions may not be substantial. Although it is still too early to judge the effect of ASEAN PTA on intra-ASEAN trade expansion, it appears that the previously noted declining trend of intra-ASEAN trade had reversed by the late 1970s, with the share of such trade increasing from about 14 percent of the total in 1974 to 23 percent by 1983. Since then, however, the share of intra-ASEAN trade declined to 17 percent in 1985.

---

[14] See Naya, *ASEAN Trade Development and Cooperation: Preferential Trading Arrangements and Trade Liberalization.*

There are a number of economic reasons for the relative stagnation of intra-regional trade: (1) Most Asian countries specialize in primary products and generally lack complementarity in their economic structures. The resultant trade and production patterns have not provided a favorable basis for integration. (2) Many of the Asian countries have responded to the large export markets in developed countries. (3) The push for import substitution has resulted in certain policies which are biased against regional trade. For example, high priority is given to imports of capital and intermediate goods which are mostly supplied by developed countries. On the other hand, imports of consumer, light industrial, and agricultural goods in which regional countries may have a comparative advantage are generally restricted. (4) Aid and loans from developed countries are often tied to imports from donor countries. For these reasons, it is not surprising that intra-regional trade has been small.

Yet, in recent years, it has become more important to emphasize South-South trade, especially trade among developing Asian countries. There are several reasons for this. First, the increasing trend toward protectionism in developed countries may to some extent close these markets to developing countries' exports. Second, the developed countries are not growing as rapidly, thus limiting the expansion of the market for ASEAN developing country's exports. Finally, as the Asian developing countries proceed with economic development, industrial complementarity will emerge. This has already occurred to some degree. While the comparative advantage of the NICs has shifted toward the production of skill- and technology-intensive goods, the ASEAN-4 and South Asian countries have concentrated on resource- and labor-intensive goods. The scope for increases in Asian intra-regional trade is large.

CONCLUSION

The outward-looking, market-oriented approach taken by most of these countries has made Asia the most dynamic region in terms of economic growth. Moreover, in the Asia-Pacific region intra-regional trade has been expanding, especially among the NICs, ASEAN-4, Japan, and the United States. Among these relatively open economies, there is kinetic interaction due to their complementarity not only in terms of natural resource endowment, but also as a result of the different stages of development of these countries.

The NICs have, to some degree, replaced Japanese exports of labor-intensive and standarized consumer goods in the U. S. market. In spite of this competition between the NICs and Japan in some final goods markets, there is a great deal of complementarity between them in the market for intermediate goods. The increased technological sophistication of the NICs exports was facilitated by imports of Japanese capital goods and intermediate inputs. In turn, the exports of these same goods to the NICs helped sustain Japan's economic expansion in recent years.

As the comparative advantage of the NICs shifted to more skill- and technology-intensive products, such as electrical and non-electrical machinery, as a result of higher labor costs and an increased maturity of the industrial sector, the ASEAN-4 and South Asian countries have the opportunity to take the place of the NICs in exporting these products. The ASEAN-4 countries have begun this process and have efficiently used their abundant labor supply for exports of unskilled-labor- and raw material-intensive products. Such a pattern of specialization among developing Asian countries can also help to increase trade with industrialized countries which are shifting to production and export of technology-intensive goods.

Even if external demand for commodities picks up, the impact on total export revenues for the ASEAN-4 countries is likely to be modest and will continue to be subject to sudden supply or demand disruptions. Recent experience has shown that, in the face of declining world prices for commodities in 1981 and 1982, efforts to cope with this price instability through international commodity agreements have proved ineffective. Despite the mobilization of a variety of stabilization instruments, including export quotas, buffer stocks, and even production cutbacks, these schemes have been unsuccessful in reversing price declines or improving export volumes.

The ASEAN-4 countries will, therefore, have to continue their efforts to diversify and expand manufactured exports, if export revenues are to be stabilized and increased. This is not to suggest, however, that the ASEAN-4 countries should follow the development strategy of the NICs. With their large domestic markets and natural resource wealth, trade dependency ratios are much lower in the ASEAN-4 countries. The ASEAN-4 countries should emphasize processing of primary products along with labor-intensive manufactures to exploit their comparative advantage. The resource wealth of these countries should provide a considerable range of opportunities in processing and resource-based manufacturing.

The South Asian countries have recently altered their industrial strategies, adopting a more outward-looking approach to development. These policies have proven to be successful, but there remains scope for further improvement. Continued liberalization of trade policies are necessary for the increased growth performance of these countries. The South Asian countries would profit by redirecting their trade to the Asia-Pacific region. Both developing and developed countries in the region have had the highest growth rates in the past decade, making this region the most vibrant. The South Asian countries with their high ratio of manufactures to total exports combined with their low wages would be able to take advantage of the dynamism in the region through exports of unskilled labor-intensive commodities.

This chapter has argued that there is a link between outward-looking development strategies and rapid economic growth. This is not only because rapid growth in trade has allowed direct contraints to growth to be overcome, but also because of the beneficient, if indirect, effects participation in world trade has on domestic resource allocation and of increasing domestic efficiency. The better performance of the NICs with respect to economic growth, employment, and income distribution can, to a large extent, be related to a combination of more thorough and timely adoption of outward-looking, market-oriented policies. But, this is not meant to suggest that export promotion policies are necessarily desirable, or that import substitution policies are undesirable per se. The economic benefits accruing to society from either strategy will depend on the extent to which the chosen industrialization strategy supports a trade pattern which is in line with the country's factor endowment. It is, therefore, important that the Asian developing countries provide balanced incentives for growth in both the export and domestic industries.

At the same time, world trade expansion and trade policies of industrial nations will have a significant effect on the export and economic growth of Asia. Commercial policies of advanced industrial countries have substantial impact on the ability of developing nations to expand exports of manufactured goods. Whether or not trade restrictions or liberalizations are aimed directly at developing nations matters less than the general direction toward which the policy is headed. Unquestionably, trade policy is becoming more protectionist in the majority of industrial nations.

An UNCTAD study has found that the brunt of these protectionist policies, both in terms of tariff and non-tariff barriers, falls on labor-intensive exports of developing countries, especially textiles and footwear.[15] The data on nominal tariffs and domestic price differentials due to non-tariff barriers indicate that in the mid-1970s, the highest protection was accorded to those industries where developing countries have a comparative advantage, e.g., processed agricultural goods, apparel and clothing, and paper and paper products. In addition, trade barriers tend to escalate with processing and, thus, are biased against the importation of manufactured goods.

But even more dangerous for Asian developing countries than direct protectionist legislation could be the indirect fallout from trade frictions between industrial nations. The handling of the U. S. — Japan trade conflict has serious implications for the Asian developing countries. Failure to achieve market-opening by Japan, coupled with impossibly large U. S. trade deficits, could lead to wide-ranging U. S. restrictions. Measures such as a large (20 percent) surcharge on imports by the U. S. could have serious direct and indirect adverse effects on Asia. The cost of a protectionist approach to settling trade imbalances between the U. S., the EEC, and Japan is substantially higher to developing Asia than the market-opening approach that has so far been favored by the rhetoric of American and Japanese political leaders.

The increasing trend toward protectionism and the slower growth in developed countries may to some extent close or limit trade to these previously large markets. It is thus imperative that developing Asian countries promote greater trade within the region, but cultivating markets in developing countries is difficult. The Asian developing countries tend to specialize in primary products or labor-intensive manufactures and generally lack complementarity in their economic structures. Additionally with the push for import substitution, priority is given to imports of capital and intermediate goods which are mostly supplied by developed countries, while imports of light consumer goods in which developing countries may have comparative advantage are restricted. As the Asian developing countries proceed with economic development, however, industrial complementarity will increase. The comparative advantage of the NICs will continue to shift toward the production of skill-and-technology-intensive goods. The ASEAN-4 and South Asian countries will tend to concentrate on resource- and labor-intensive goods. The rapid growth in the region indicates that the scope for increase of intra-regional trade is large.

The coexistence of highly advanced countries and rapidly developing countries in the region will enhance trade, but, both the developed and developing countries will have to face painful adjustments in their industrial structures. If trade expands, adjustment will be far easier than if it continues to stagnate.

---

[15] UNCTAD, *Trade and Development Report,* 1984.

REFERENCES

Ahmad, M., "Strategy for Industrialization and Equity: An Approach for South Asian Countries", ESCAP Doc. No. DP/STR/SAG (2) 19, Bangkok: Economic and Social Commission for Asia and the Pacific, 1979.

Asian Development Bank, *Key Indicators of Developing Member Countries of ADB*, Vol. 17, Manila, July 1986.

——, *Key Indicators of Developing Member Countries of ADB*, Vol. 16, Manila, April 1985.

——, *Key Indicators of Developing Member Countries of ADB*, Vol. 15, Manila, April 1984.

——, *Key Indicators of Developing Member Countries of ADB*, Vol. 14, Manila, April 1983.

Balassa, B., ed., *Development Strategies in Semi-Industrial Countries*, Baltimore, Md: Johns Hopkins University Press, 1982.

——, "Prospects for Trade in Manufactured Goods between Industrial and Developing Countries, 1978-1990", *Journal of Policy Modeling*, (3), 1980, pp. 437-455.

——, "The 'New Protectionism' and the International Economy", *Journal of World Trade Law*, 12(5), 1978, pp. 409-36.

Balassa, B. and Associates, *The Structure of Protection in Developing Countries*, Baltimore, Md: Johns Hopkins University Press, 1971.

Balassa, B., and M. Sharpston, *Export Subsidies by Developing Countries: Issues of Policy*, Geneva: Graduate Institute of International Studies, 1977.

Bautista, R.M., J.H. Power, and Associates, *Industrial Promotion Policies in the Philippines*, Manila: Philippine Institute for Development Studies, 1979.

Chee Peng Lim, *From Import Substitution to Export Promotion: A Study of Malaysia's Industrial Policy*, Faculty of Economics and Administration, University of Malaysia, Kuala Lumpur (mimeo), 1980.

Chia Siow Yue, "Singapore's Trade and Development Strategy and ASEAN Economic Cooperation, with Special Reference to the ASEAN Common Approach to Foreign Economic Relations", *ASEAN in a Changing Pacific and World Economy*, ed., Ross Garnaut, Canberra: Australian National University Press, 1980.

Chong Hyun Nam, *Trade and Industrial Policies on the Structure of Protection in Korea*, Korea Development Institute, Seoul (mimeo), 1980.

Corden, M., *Trade Policy and Economic Welfare*, London: Oxford University Press, 1974.

Economic and Social Commission for Asia and the Pacific (ESCAP), *Problems and Prospects of the Economic Development of Bangladesh in the 1980s*, Development Planning Division Discussion Papers No. 14, Bangkok, 1981;

——, *Policies, Programmes and Perspectives for the Development of the ESCAP Region: Regional Development Strategy for the 1980s*, E/ESCAP/L. 45, Bangkok, 1980.

Findlay, R., "Trade and Development: Theory and Asian Experience", *Asian Development Review*, 2(2) : pp. 23-42, 1984.

Galenson, W., ed., *Foreign Trade and Investment: Economic Development in the Newly Industrializing Asian Countries*, Madison, WI: University of Wisconsin Press, 1985.

——, *Economic Growth and Structural Change in Taiwan,* New York: Cornell University Press: Ithaca, 1979.

Helleiner, G.K. "Intrafirm Trade and the Developing Countries: An Assessment of the Data", *Journal of Development Economics,* 6(3): 1979, pp. 391-406.

Hiemenz, U., *Industrial Growth and Employment in Developing Asian Countries: Issues and Perspectives for the Coming Decade,* Asian Development Bank, Economic Staff Paper No. 7, Manila, 1982.

Ho, S.P.S. "Decentralized Industrialization and Rural Development: Evidence from Taiwan", *Economic Development and Cultural Change,* 28(1): 1979, pp. 77-96.

Hughes, H., and J. Waelbroeck, "Can Developing-Country Exports Keep Growing in the 1980s?" *The World Economy,* 4: 1981, pp. 127-147.

International Monetary Fund (IMF), *Direction of Trade Statistics Yearbook,* Washington, D.C. 1986, 1985, 1970-76.

——, *International Financial Statistics, Yearbook 1986,* Washington, D.C., 1986.

——, *World Economic Outlook,* Washington, D.C., 1986.

Lewis, W. Arthur, "The Slowing Down of the Engine of Growth", *American Economic Review,* 70(4): 1980, pp. 555-564.

Little, I., T. Scitovsky, and M. Scott, *Industry and Trade in Some Developing Countries,* London: 1970, Oxford University Press.

Liu, T., and Y. Ho. "Export-Oriented Growth and Industrial Diversification in Hong Kong", Hong Kong Series Occasional Paper No. 7, Economic Research Centre, Hong Kong: The Chinese University of Hong Kong, 1980.

McCawley, P., "Employment in Manufacturing, 1970-77: A Reply", *Bulletin of Indonesian Economic Studies,* 15(3): 1979a, pp. 132-44.

——, *Industrialization in Indonesia: Developments and Prospects,* Development Studies Centre Occasional Paper No. 13, Camberra: Australian National University, 1979b.

——, and M. Tait, "New Data on Employment in Manufacturing, 1970-1976", *Bulletin of Indonesian Economic Studies,* 15(1): 1979, pp. 125-136.

Morawetz, D., "Employment Implications of Industrialization in Developing Countries: A Survey", *The Economic Journal,* 84: 1974, pp. 491,542.

Naya, S., "The Role of Trade Policies in the Industrialization of Rapidly Growing Asian Developing Countries", in *Explaining the Success of Industrialization in East Asia,* ed. Helen Hughes Dyndey: Australian National University, Forthcoming, 1987.

——, *ASEAN Trade Development and Cooperation: Preferential Trading Arrangements and Trade Liberalization,* ESCAP and UNDP Project RAS/77/015/A/40, (mimeo), 1980.

——, and U. Hiemenz, "Changing Trade Patterns and Policy Issue: The Prospects for East and Southeast Asian Developing Countries", Asian Development Bank Economics Office Report Series, No. 23, Manila, 1984.

——, et al., (1983). "North-South Issue Paper on Industrial Restructuring", A paper presented at the International Economic Association and the Federation of ASEAN-4 Economic Association Conference on Economic Interdependence: Perspective from Developing Countries, Manila, Philippines, 1983.

Organisation for Economic Co-operation and Development (OECD), *National Accounts Statistics,* Paris, 1986.

——, *National Accounts Statistics,* 1963-1980, Paris, 1982.

Oshima, H.T., "Perspectives and Prospects for Southeast Asian Growth in the 1980s and Research Issues", Manila, Philippines (mimeo), 1980.

Power, John H., "The Structure of Protection in West Malaysia", in *The Structure of Protection in Developing Countries,* B. Balassa, ed., Baltimore, Md: Johns Hopkins University Press, 1971.

Rana, P., "The Impact of the Current Exchange Rate System on Trade and Inflation of Selected Developing Member Countries", Asian Development Bank Staff Paper No. 18, Manila, 1983.

Ranis, G., "Prospective Southeast Asian Strategies in a Changing International Environment", *New Directions in Asia's Development Strategies,* Institute of Developing Economies, Tokyo, 1980.

——, "Equity with Growth in Taiwan: How 'Special' is the 'Special Case'?" *World Development,* 6(3): 1978, pp. 397-409.

——, J.C. Fei, and S.W.Y. Kuo, *Growth with Equity: The Case of Taiwan,* New York: Oxford University Press, 1979.

Rao, D.C., "Economic Growth and Equity in the Republic of Korea", *World Development,* 6(3): 1978, pp. 383-96.

Republic of China (Taiwan), Council of Economic Planning and Development, *Taiwan Statistical Data Book,* 1985, Taipei, 1985.

——, Ministry of Finance, *Monthly Statistics of Exports and Imports,* Taipei, 1982.

Rhee, H.Y., "Nominal and Effective Protection Structures in the Pacific Rim", (unpublished mimeo), 1984.

Richardson, J.D., "Constant-Market-Shares Analysis of Export Growth", *Journal of International Economics* 1:1971, pp. 227-39.

Swee-Hock, Saw, *ASEAN Economies in Transition,* Singapore: Singapore Universtiy Press, 1980.

Thai University Research Association, "Industrial Development in Thailand and Industrial Development Policies, 1982-1986", *Report of the Research Project on Industrial Development Plan of Thailand, 1982-1986,* Bangkok: Thai University Research Association, 1980.

Tan, A.H.H. and Ow Chin Hock, "Singapore", *The Structure of Protection in Developing Countries,* ed., B. Balassa, Baltimore, Md: Johns Hopkins University Press, 1982.

United Nations (UN), *Commodity Trade Statistics,* Washington, D.C. Various years.

——, *Handbook of International Trade and Development Statistics,* 1985 Supplement and 1984 Supplement, Washington, D.C. 1986, 1985.

——, *Yearbook of International Trade Statistics,* Washington, D.C. 1983, 1982, 1981, 1972-73.

——, *Yearbook of National Accounts Statistics,* Vol. I and II, New York: United Nations, 1980.

United Nations Conference on Trade and Development (UNCTAD), *Trade and Development Report, 1984,* Report by the Secretariat of the United Nations Conference on Trade and Development, New York, 1984.

——, *Trade Information System,* Computer Tape, New York, 1984.

de Vries, B., "Transition Toward More Rapid and Labor-Intensive Development: The Case of the Philippines", World Bank Staff Working Paper No. 424, Washington, D.C., 1980.

Westphal, L.E., "The Republic of Korea's Experience with Export-Led Industrial Development", *World Development*, 6(3): 1978, pp. 362-82.

Westphal, L.E., and K.S. Kim, *Industrial Policy and Development in Korea*, World Bank Staff Working Paper No. 263, Washington, D.C., 1977.

Wong, J., *ASEAN Economies in Perspective*, Philadelphia: Institute for the Study of Human Issues, 1979.

World Bank, *World Development Report 1985*, Washington, D.C.: Oxford University Press, 1984.

——, *World Tables, Vol. II: Social Indicators*, Washington, D.C., 1983.

6. Industrial Restructuring and Technology Transfer

Ippei Yamazawa and Toshio Watanabe

INTRODUCTION

In the 1970s, the developing countries of the Asia-Pacific region had among the highest growth rates of exports and imports in the world. The dynamic force of industrial growth of the NICs (Newly Industrializing Countries) and ASEAN (Association of Southeast Asian Nations) was a factor in trade expansion. The Asian developing countries traded less intensively with each other than with Japan, the United States, Western European Countries and other developed countries. The NICs exported labor-intensive manufactures and the ASEAN countries mainly exported primary commodities to developed countries, from which they imported intermediate inputs and investment goods. Increased manufactured exports especially from the NICs led to competition with labor-intensive industries of developed countries. Still the relationship that resulted between Asian developing countries and their more developed trading partners was mainly complementary.

Further, industrialization in the NICs and ASEAN countries, however, had led to increased competition with the developed nations and with each other. The NICs have started to supply a part of their domestic needs for intermediate inputs and investment goods and even to export them and the four ASEAN countries have begun to demonstrate increased competitiveness in labor-intensive manufactures. Developed countries still supply intermediate inputs and investment goods to the NICs and ASEAN, thus maintaining the complementary relationship with them. It can also be said that both competitive and complementary relationships are growing not only between developed countries, on the one hand, and the NICs and ASEAN, on the other, but also between the latter two country groups. This increased competitive and complementary trend among market economies of the Asia-Pacific region can be expected to continue in the future.

The spread of industrialization to the developing Asian countries occurred only after World War II. In the 19th and early 20th century, the industrial revolution was spread from England to Western Europe and North America, and then to

Russia and Japan. It was accompanied by the transfer of capital and technology from early starters like England to later starters like the United States. Modern industrial capacity was transplanted to late starting countries and, taking advantage of their lower costs of labor or raw material, late-comers became new supply sources to the world market. The spread of industrialization included both early and late starters in the restructuring of industrial production and trade.

Industrialization was spread to East and Southeast Asia after World War II. They have succeeded in introducing new industries and exporting their products to the world market. Industrialization after World War II is distinguished from earlier episodes by two characteristics. One is the more rapid restructuring of production and trade. This provided a dynamic source of growth to the world economy but at the same time it has caused trade policy problems between trade partners. Coexistence of competition and complementarity described in the opening paragraphs is an aspect of this rapid industrial restructuring.

The second feature is the more active role played by multinational corporations (MNCs). The MNCs provide not only production technology but also management and marketing knowhow that are required for the successful transfer of new industries. In the post-WW II period, the technical gap between developed and developing countries is wider than that of the 19th century. Correct understanding of the MNCs' strategy is indispensable for the present study of industrial restructuring and technology transfer among the Asia-Pacific countries.

The following section describes the changing patterns of trade and production of the Asia-Pacific countries and the process of rapid industrialization. The comparative advantage structure of individual countries in terms of indexes of revealed comparative advantage (RCA) has been analyzed and the direction of their changes in the NICs and ASEAN examined under the heading "Changes in Comparative Advantage Structure". Changes in the industrial and trade structure of individual countries are interrelated. Our indexes of complementarity enable us to combine individual country changes within the global trade matrix. The section under heading Direct Investment Technical Transfer and Productivity Improvement analyzes the mechanism underlying the rapid spread of industrialization to the NICs and then to ASEAN, focusing on the catching-up product-cycle and the role played by MNCs in it. Productivity improvement is a pre-requisite for successful catching-up. The last section overviews the unbalanced state of mutual exchange of manufactures among the Asia-Pacific countries, reviews the effects of technical transfer from Japan to the NICs and ASEAN, and presents a simulation of the restructuring of trade and production of intermediate inputs. The last section concludes with policy implications for harmonious industrial restructuring.[1]

---

[1] In this study the trade relationship among East and Southeast Asian countries are focused on in the context of the spread of industrialization to the region. They are grouped into Japan, Asian NICs (ANICs) (Korea, ROC-Taiwan, Hong Kong and Singapore), and other four ASEAN (Thailand, Philippines, Indonesia, and Malaysia) according to their stages of industrialization but the last two groups are sometimes regrouped into East Asia (Korea, ROC-Taiwan and Hong Kong) and ASEAN (Singapore plus other four) according to their geographical proximity, that is, two groupings depending on the intermediate position of Singapore. Brunei, the sixth ASEAN member since 1984, is excluded from our comparison because of its lack of industrial performance. China and India are fully entitled for being included in our analysis, but they are referred to occasionally when comparable data are available.

CHANGING PATTERN OF THE ASIA-PACIFIC TRADE

The composition and direction of international trade flows and the location of industries changed drastically in the Asia-Pacific countries over the past thirty years. A remarkable record of industrial growth was made by the Asian NICs and the ASEAN countries. The NICs achieved high economic growth rates of 8-10 percent through the 1960s and 1970s. In the 1960s ASEAN countries, except Indonesia, grew at 5-8 percent. In the 1970s, all ASEAN countries achieved growth rates of 6-9 percent. Industrialization has been the main engine of rapid growth in the NICs. In the ASEAN countries, the industrial sector grew at an average rate of 10-13 percent during the 1970s. However, the ASEAN economies remained highly dependent on primary production, with the exception of Singapore.

Competition and Complementarity

The impact of their rapid industrialization is reflected in changing trade patterns. Table 1 shows changes in trade flows of industrial goods among major trading countries and country groups from 1970 and 1980. East Asian NICs represent Korea, the ROC (Taiwan) and Hong Kong, while Singapore is in ASEAN, because of her geographical location. World exports of industrial goods increased 5.65 times (annual average growth rate of 17.3 percent) during the decade. Exports from East Asian NICs and the ASEAN countries increased twice or three times as much as the world average and their imports of industrial goods also increased much more than the world average. In contrast, industrial goods trade of developed countries (except Japan's exports) grew at a slower rate than the world average.

Nevertheless, a substantial portion of industrial goods trade of East Asian NICs and ASEAN was recorded with their developed country partners. Eighty to ninety-five percent of industrial goods imports of the East Asian NICs and ASEAN came from the developed countries and 53-70 percent of industrial goods exports of the East Asian NICs and ASEAN went to the developed countries (Table 2). Intra-regional trade of East Asia and ASEAN increased at high rates in the 1970s (total trade expanded by as much as 9-26 times). Trade between countries in East Asian NICs and ASEAN accounted for 14-28 percent of industrial goods exports and 12-24 percent of industrial goods imports. But a careful check of the world trade matrix shows that entrepot trade of Hong Kong and Singapore dominates the intra-East Asian NICs and intra-ASEAN trade.

It is also to be noted that (1) East Asian NICs and ASEAN exports to Japan, United States, and Western Europe expanded more than twice as much as the industrial goods imports of the latter countries, and (2) the latter's exports of industrial goods to East Asian NICs and ASEAN expanded more than their export total. This is especially the case with the United States, the exports of which to East Asian NICs and ASEAN grew at twice as much as her total exports. This implies that East Asian NICs and ASEAN countries shares increased rapidly in the developed country markets, while exports to East Asian NICs and ASEAN supported the growth of industrial exports from the developed countries. The rapid expansion of industrial goods trade between fast growing countries of East Asian NICs and ASEAN, on the one hand, and stagnant developed countries, on the other, has tended to increase both competition and complementarity. Trade conflict of various types has emerged between the two groups as a result.

Table 1. Trade Matrix of Manufactured Goods in the Asia-Pacific Region

(Unit: Yen million)

		East Asian NICs	ASEAN	Japan	U.S.A.	Western Europe	World Total
East Asian NICs	1970	198	184	317	1,776	767	4,075
	1980	2,757	4,225	4,150	16,041	109,929	51,343
		(13.9)	(23.0)	(13.1)	(9.0)	(14.2)	(12.6)
ASEAN	1970	45	428	113	304	166	1,089
	1980	1,152	3,700	1,648	3,909	3,803	17,546
		(25.6)	(8.6)	(14.6)	(12.9)	(22.9)	(16.1)
Japan	1970	1,927	1,705		5,760	2,637	18,116
	1980	14,140	12,383		30,884	20,660	124,379
		(7.3)	(7.3)		(5.4)	(7.8)	(6.9)
U.S.A.	1970	695	743	1,751		1,091	29,370
	1980	6,538	7,146	8,975		9,365	144,897
		(9.4)	(9.6)	(5.1)		(8.6)	(4.9)
Western Europe	1970	866	1,227	1,464	9,314		101,121
	1980	6,005	7,742	6,764	35,858		612,253
		(6.9)	(6.3)	(4.6)	(3.9)		(6.1)
World Total	1970	3,692	4,311	4,876	26,145	91,650	202,287
	1980	33,595	33,189	26,812	124,245	520,333	1,143,858
		(9.1)	(7.7)	(5.5)	(4.8)	(5.7)	(5.7)

Source: AIDXT, *Institute of Developing Economies*, Tokyo, Japan.

Note: Western Europe includes all European members in OECD.
1980/1970 magnification in parentheses.

Table 2. Export and Import Composition by Partner Countries

(A) Export composition

(Unit: %)

		East Asian NICs	ASEAN	Japan	U.S.A.	Western Europe	World Total
East Asian	1970	4.9	4.5	7.8	43.6	18.8	100.0
NICs	1980	5.4	8.2	8.1	31.2	21.3	100.0
ASEAN	1970	4.1	39.3	10.4	27.9	15.2	100.0
	1980	6.6	21.1	9.4	22.3	21.7	100.0

(B) Import composition

		East Asian Three	ASEAN	Japan	U.S.A.	Western Europe	World Total
East Asian	1970	5.4	1.2	52.2	18.8	23.5	100.0
NICs	1980	8.2	3.4	42.1	19.5	17.9	100.0
ASEAN	1970	4.3	9.9	39.5	17.2	28.5	100.0
	1980	12.7	11.1	37.3	21.5	23.3	100.0

Source and Footnotes: The same as Table 1.

Changes in Trade and Industrial Structure

The structure of trade and industrial production of the Asia-Pacific countries provides an overview of the dynamic changes in the NICs and ASEAN countries. Similarities are observed in both the structure and its changes among some countries and groups enabling us to make some generalizations.

Japan's export structure was characterized by a predominant share of chemicals, steel, and machinery, and was similar to those of the European Community and the United States. However, Japan had a much smaller share of primary product exports and the composition of her exports changed significantly (especially in the expansion of machinery exports) in comparison to other developed countries. In contrast, Japan's imports were dominated by primary products, with much larger shares than in the European Community and the United States. Throughout the 1970s, the share of mineral fuels expanded and that of labor-intensive other manufactures remained unchanged and, therefore, increased relative to the rest of the industrial imports.

The NICs had small shares of primary product exports, similar to Japan, but larger shares of labor-intensive manufactures. Between 1970 and 1980, the labor-intensive manufactures had decreased shares while electric machinery, precision instruments, and others had increased shares. Singapore's export structure was unique in her predominant share of petroleum and refinery products but her exports of electric machinery also expanded between 1970 and 1980. The NICs' import structure was characterized by the large share of primary products, on the one hand, and chemicals, metal products, and machinery, on the other. The latter's share decreased during the 1970s but it still was more than a third of all imports in 1980.

The four ASEAN countries (other than Singapore) had export structures dominated by primary products in raw and processed forms. But it should not be overlooked that the share of primary products decreased while that of industrial goods (especially electric machinery and clothing) increased throughout the 1970s. The ASEAN-4's imports were mainly composed of chemicals, steel, and machinery. India's structure was in between that of the East Asian NICs and ASEAN. Her exports were composed of primary products and labor-intensive industrial products and her imports were similar to those of the ASEAN-4.

Trade structures of the NICs, ASEAN and Japan all changed between 1970 and 1980; in other developed countries trade structures were more static. Generally speaking, for non-oil producing countries, individual country's specialization was revealed more in its changing export structure; changes in import structures were less characteristic.

Changes in industrial structure (excluding primary production) for selected countries are consistent with changes in trade structures. Industrial production is divided into three broad groups reflecting factor intensity in their production, labor intensive manufactures (L), capital intensive manufactures (C) and machinery (T), to facilitate the following analyses.

Japan's industrial structure was fairly equally distributed in the three broad groups, with L's share remaining at about a quarter. Japan's industrial restructuring was less apparent than changes in her trade structure, except for the increase in petroleum products. Korea had a greater share of L and a smaller share of T than Japan and C's share was much greater than indicated by export structure. Korea underwent an apparent industrial restructuring with declining L and increasing T and C. It is shown that in the ROC (Taiwan), T's share was almost equal to Japan's. The ROC (Taiwan) would be closer to Korea both in industrial structure and changes overtime, if miscellaneous products were separated from T and if petroleum products were ignored.

In the Philippines, L had a much greater share and T the smallest share, but there was little change in her industrial structure between 1970 and 1980. In Indonesia, with a small share of industrial production, L dominated. But Indonesia's increasing shares of T and C and decreasing L were similar to the NICs. India has an industrial structure closer to Korea and the ROC (Taiwan).

CHANGES IN COMPARATIVE ADVANTAGE STRUCTURE

The drastic changes in the composition of Asia-Pacific trade were caused by changes in comparative advantage of individual countries and by rapid economic growth, both of which resulted from the spread of industrialization in the developing countries of the region.

The comparative advantage of a country is determined principally by factor endowment (availability of cheap inputs) and the stage of industrialization (level of technology) it has reached. In the process of industrialization, the structure of a country's comparative advantage shifts from simple labor-intensive products to sophisticated capital- and technology-intensive ones as was observed in Japan and the Asian NICs. The ASEAN-4 countries and China will be no exception to this trend if they promote industrialization.

Indexes of Revealed Comparative Advantage

Comparative advantage is traditionally measured through the comparison of costs between trading partners but reliable cost data are seldom available. Alternatively, we assume a country's comparative advantage is reflected or revealed in her exports to the world market. This leads us to the index of revealed comparative advantage (RCA) of exports, RCAX, defined by Balassa as the country's commodity composition of exports vis a vis that of total world trade. Similarly, we can define the index of comparative disadvantage as the country's import composition vis a vis the world total. This is the revealed comparative advantage of imports (RCAM).

$$\text{RCAX}_i = \frac{X_i^h}{X_i} \Big/ \frac{W^h}{W}, \quad \text{RCAM}_j = \frac{M_j^h}{M_j} \Big/ \frac{W^h}{W}$$

where

X_i, (X_i^h) . . . the i-th country's export of all commodities (commodity group h)

M_j, (M_j^h) . . . the j-th country's import of all commodities (commodity group h)

W, (W^h) . . . . the world total trade of commodities (commodity group h)

Table 3 depicts both RCAX and RCAM for some selected countries. They are measured for 24 industry groups but they are illustrated for five broad industry groups. They are (A) agro-based products, (M) minerals and mineral products, (L) labor-intensive manufactures, (T) machinery and (C) capital-intensive industries.[2]

---

[2] The broad classification of L, C and T is for manufacturing industries and has already been used in the previous analysis, while A and M are for primary industries. Their precise definition is given in the footnote to Table 3.

Since the weighted average of all 24 groups is unity, the departure of RCAs of individual groups from unity shows the structure of comparative advantage and disadvantage.

Changing Comparative Advantage

Japan has comparative advantage in groups L to C, and comparative disadvantage in A and M. The RCA of L and C decreased whereas that of T increased during the 1970s. For Japan, the structure of RCAX is symmetrical with that of RCAM, although the change is larger for RCAX than for RCAM.[3]

Developed countries show a common strength (i.e. above-unity RCAXs) in machinery and capital-intensive industrial goods (commodity groups T and C). Both Japan and the EC are weak in resource goods (A and M) while the U.S., Canada, and Australia-New Zealand are strong in A and/or M. Korea and the ROC (Taiwan) continue to show the highest RCAXs in labor-intensive industrial goods (L) and both countries increased their RCAXs in the T and C groups, as their patterns of trade became closer to that of Japan during the 1970s. The ASEAN countries are still strong in the resource-goods groups (A and M) but have shown increasing strength in the L group also.

The RCAX structure of China and India is in between that of the NICs and ASEAN with strong advantage in the L and A groups, reflecting their development stage and resource endowments. The RCAM structure of India is symmetrical to her RCAX, while this symmetry is ambiguous in the case of China.

The RCA index of imports reveals the pattern of comparative disadvantage for individual countries. It is dissimilar to that of RCAX except in the cases of entrepot traders, Singapore and Hong Kong. But the divergence of RCAMs from unity is much less than that of RCXs, reflecting, in part, the greater modification of imports than exports by government intervention.

Changes in comparative advantage structures of the NICs and ASEAN are inter-related with those of Japan and other developed countries through international input-output relationships. The increases in the RCAX of labor-intensive commodities (L) in the NICs and ASEAN are related to the decrease of Japan's RCAX of L and the increase of her RCAX of T and C. The NICs, and to a lesser degree the ASEAN countries, overtook Japan in export of consumer goods but they cannot yet domestically supply a large part of their intermediate and investment goods demand. Thus, they had to import them from Japan and other developed countries.

Direction of Changes in RCA Structure

Changes in RCA structures of Japan, the NICs and ASEAN depicted in Table 3 imply the direction of changes in RCA structures through different stages of industrial development.

In Japan, the RCAX of the L group declined to near unity, while those of the T and C groups exceeded L and rose to 1.5-2.0. In the NICs, L's RCAXs reached near peaks and that of Korea started to decrease, while those of T and C increased but

---

[3] The sub-group mix of each broad industry group differs between pairs of countries, and similar figures of a RCA index for a broad commodity group do not necessarily indicate severe competition between the pairs of countries.

Table 3. Changing Pattern of Comparative Advantage of the Asia-Pacific Countries

		(A)	(M)	(L)	(T)	(C)
Japan						
RCAX	1970	0.228	0.096	1.672	1.435	1.355
	1980	0.120	0.066	1.033	2.161	1.232
RCAM	1970	1.739	2.475	0.380	0.401	0.452
	1980	1.461	2.076	0.538	0.251	0.414
U.S.A.						
RCAX	1970	1.046	0.533	0.656	1.457	0.891
	1980	1.608	0.307	0.831	1.484	0.998
RCAM	1970	0.963	0.917	1.410	0.964	0.916
	1980	0.676	1.311	1.197	0.940	0.756
EC9						
RCAX	1970	0.603	0.477	1.220	1.244	1.281
	1980	0.804	0.411	1.391	1.239	1.431
RCAM	1970	1.206	1.217	1.024	0.758	1.017
	1980	1.107	0.973	1.313	0.816	1.094
Canada						
RCAX	1970	0.908	1.572	0.271	1.065	0.983
	1980	1.310	1.002	0.426	0.933	1.207
RCAM	1970	0.562	0.563	0.879	1.694	0.805
	1980	0.657	0.598	0.959	1.714	0.810
ANZ						
RCAX	1970	3.213	1.304	0.257	0.222	0.453
	1980	3.654	0.827	0.727	0.261	0.674
RCAM	1970	0.438	0.540	1.228	1.374	1.181
	1980	0.492	0.637	1.465	1.327	0.771
Korea						
RCAX	1970	0.635	0.397	5.336	0.253	0.271
	1980	0.612	0.046	4.579	0.751	1.169
RCAM	1970	1.594	0.750	0.606	0.967	0.935
	1980	1.460	1.245	0.444	0.840	0.863
ROC (Taiwan)						
RCAX	1970	1.179	0.117	3.861	0.557	0.476
	1980	0.722	0.067	16.877	0.897	0.610
RCAM	1970	1.397	0.501	0.535	1.213	1.041
	1980	1.211	1.093	0.431	1.034	0.984
Hong Kong						
RCAX	1970	0.262	0.101	5.157	0.457	0.639
	1980	0.331	0.086	5.163	1.020	0.582
RCAM	1970	1.343	0.298	1.978	0.698	1.123
	1980	1.142	0.259	2.472	1.030	1.195
Singapore						
RCAX	1970	2.420	1.494	0.994	0.419	0.389
	1980	1.348	0.965	1.185	1.092	0.582
RCAM	1970	1.390	0.896	1.403	0.825	0.771
	1980	1.024	1.060	0.922	1.108	0.787

Table 3. (Continued)

		(A)	(M)	(L)	(T)	(C)
Malaysia						
RCAX	1970	3.431	1.781	0.303	0.055	0.104
	1980	3.430	1.354	0.554	0.418	0.095
RCAM	1970	1.223	1.065	0.776	0.945	0.986
	1980	0.966	0.668	0.589	1.415	1.139
Thailand						
RCAX	1970	4.097	0.884	0.574	0.024	0.124
	1980	4.281	0.487	1.681	0.221	0.292
RCAM	1970	0.418	0.739	0.730	1.040	1.356
	1980	0.553	1.191	0.490	1.078	1.200
Philippines						
RCAX	1970	3.831	1.346	0.432	0.003	0.103
	1980	3.114	0.745	1.123	0.434	0.211
RCAM	1970	0.742	0.915	0.303	1.191	1.445
	1980	0.637	1.097	1.398	0.879	1.092
Indonesia						
RCAX	1970	2.988	2.610	0.039	0.011	0.030
	1980	1.636	2.604	0.122	0.017	0.035
RCAM	1970	0.868	0.223	1.187	1.155	1.403
	1980	1.097	0.650	0.404	1.216	1.476
China						
RCAX	1970	2.077	0.252	3.338	0.109	0.563
	1980	1.393	0.922	3.536	0.227	0.648
RCAM	1970	1.118	0.752	1.081	0.539	1.725
	1980	2.074	0.189	1.643	0.647	1.675
India						
RCAX	1970	1.917	0.754	2.561	0.185	0.661
	1980	2.569	0.240	3.352	0.257	0.911
RCAM	1970	1.595	1.047	0.287	0.813	1.168
	1980	0.775	1.393	0.135	0.615	1.631

Note:

Sectors	Industries	Corresponding SITC Code Numbers
01	Crude foodstuff	0 − ⑥
02	Agricultural materials	2 + 4 − ③ − 251
03	Mineral materials	27 + 28
04	Mineral fuels	3 − 332
05	Processed food	
06	Beverage and tobacco	1
07	Textiles	65
08	Clothing	84
09	Leather and footwear	61, 851
10	Furniture and wood products	63, 82
11	Pulp, paper and paper products	251, 54, 892
12	Chemicals	5 − 58
13	Petroleum products	332
14	Rubber and plastic products	62, 58
15	Glass, and non-metal products	66
16	Iron and steel	67
17	Non-ferrous metals	68
18	Metal products	69
19	Industrial materials	71
20	Electric machinery	72
21	Motor vehicles	732
22	Other transport equipments	73 − 732
23	Precision instruments	86
24	Miscellaneous manufactures	

Broad industry groups	Industries
A: Agricultural products	1, 2, 5
M: Minerals	3, 4, 13, 17
L: Labor-intensive Manufactures	7, 8, 9, 10, 14, 24
T: Machinery	19, 20, 21, 22, 23
C: Capital-intensive manufactures	6, 11, 12, 14, 16, 18

still stayed around 0.5. In the ASEAN-4, RCAXs of L group were still increasing and those of Thailand and Philippines exceeded unity, while RCAXs of T and C stayed at low levels. To sum up, in the process of industrialization, the RCAX of L group increases first followed, and then replaced, by those of T and C.

Figure 1 illustrates the dynamic changes in RCA structures through industrialization. Along the horizontal axis are plotted per capita incomes of individual countries as a proxy measure of their industrialization stage, and along the vertical axis average levels of RCAX of L and T and C together of individual countries. Arrows indicate changes from 1970 to 1980. Life cycle curves are drawn for both L and T and C by linking RCAXs at different income levels. The L-curve reaches its peak around the $1,500 income level and turns down afterward, while the T & C-curve continues to rise up to the $10,000 level. Although inspired by cross-country plotting of actual RCAXs over different income levels, the two curves illustrate our image of future changes in the RCAX structures of the NICs and ASEAN countries.

Complementarity in the Asia-Pacific Trade

Similar structures of RCAXs between two countries do not necessarily mean a lack of complementarity and absence of trade opportunities between the two. Under a horizontal division of labor (i.e. exchange of commodities within individual industries), the RCAX and RCAM structures of a country become similar and still strong complementarity and large trade volume could result from closer correspondence of the exporter's RCAX to the importer's RCAM. The degree of similarity between an exporting country's RCAX and an importing country's RCAM measures the degree of complementarity and the possibility of trade expansion between them.

The index of trade complementarity of an exporting country i with an importing country j is defined as the covariance of $RCAX_i$ and $RCAM_j$ minus unity.

$$C_{ij} = \sum_{h=1}^{24} w^h (RCAX_i{}^h - 1)(RCAM_j{}^h - 1) - 1$$

$$= \sum_{h=1}^{24} w^h\, RCAX_i{}^h \cdot RCAM_j{}^h$$

It coincides with the hypothetical trade intensity between two countries when trade is solely determined by comparative advantage and disadvantage.[4] Actual trade intensity (I_{ij}) departs from complementarity (C_{ij}) because of economic distances, preferential arrangements and other factors between two countries.

Table 4 shows the C_{ij}'s for pairs of 15 countries/country groups in 1970 and 1980.

C_{ij}'s vary between pairs, either above, below, or around unity and they either increase, decrease or remain unchanged (including changes less than ±0.10) from 1970 to 1980. C_{ij} structures are summarized as follows for Japan, NICs, and ASEAN-4.

Japan had high C_{ij}'s with the resource-rich ASEAN-4 and Australia/New Zealand (ANZ) and above unity C_{ij} with other countries (or groups) except Korea, EC, U.S., and India in both exports and imports. Japan's C_{ij}'s increased during the 1970s with most of her trading partners. The ASEAN-4 also had a symmetrical C_{ij} pattern; above-unity C_{ij}'s in export and import trade with Japan, NICs, and EC, and below-

---

[4]   For details of the derivation of trade intensity (I_{ij}) and complementarity (C_{ij}), refer to Ippei Yamazawa, "Intensity Analysis of World Trade Flow," *Hitotsubashi Journal of Economics*, February, 1972.

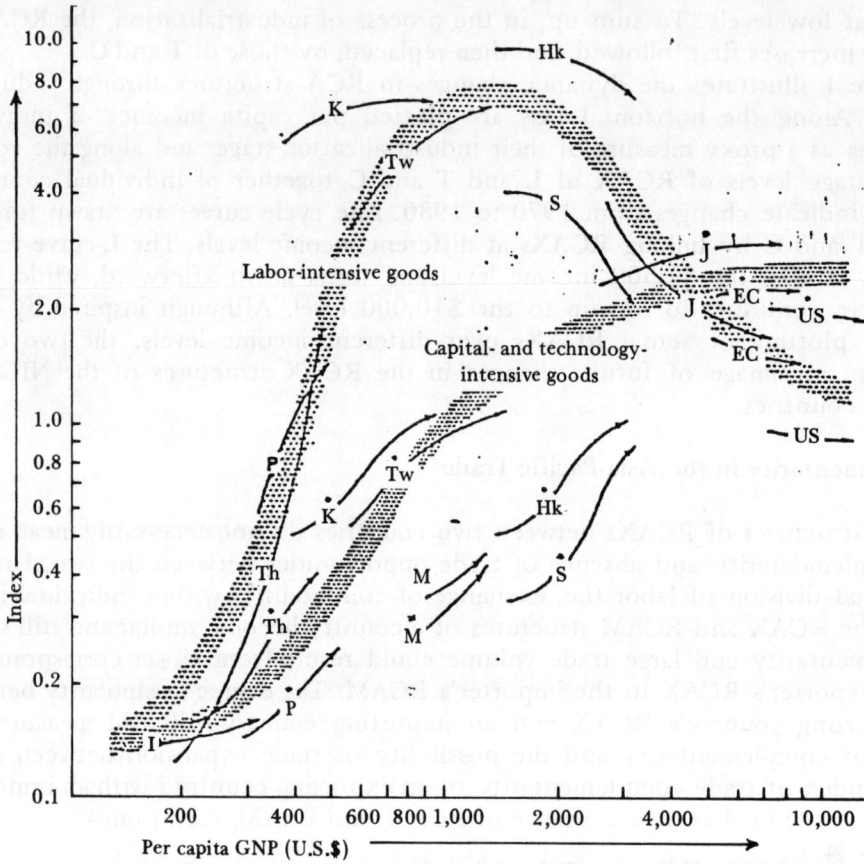

Notes: Along the horizontal axis are plotted per capita incomes as proxy measures of industrialization stage and along the vertical axis averages of RCAXs of L and T & C of individual countries. Arrows indicate changes from 1970 to 1980. Life cycle curves are drawn for both L and T & C by linking RCAXs over different income levels.

I stands for Indonesia, Th for Thailand, P for the Philippines, M for Malaysia, K for Korea, Tw for ROC (Taiwan), H for Hong Kong, S for Singapore, J for Japan, EC for European Economic Community, and US for the United States. The symbols with asterisks are for capital- and technology-intensive goods and without asterisks for labor-intensive goods.

Since RCAXs of industrial products of individual countries are affected by their natural resource endowments, it is not strictly correct to link individual country RCAXs. Besides, the RCAs of Fig. 1 are calculated from different data and are not strictly consistent with the RCAs of Table 3.

Figure 1. Direction of Changes in RCAX Structure

Table 4. Index of Trade Complementarity Among Asia-Pacific Countries

1970

from (i) \ to (j)	JPN	KOR	ROC	HKG	SGP	MAL	THL	PHL	INE	IND	USA	CAN	ANZ	EEC	CHN
1. JPN	0.325	0.785	1.005	1.278	1.040	1.343	1.028	1.073	1.240	0.804	1.017	1.417	1.242	0.934	1.060
2. KOR	0.529	0.743	0.828	1.875	1.030	1.000	0.836	0.990	0.819	0.656	0.979	0.896	1.160	1.138	1.172
3. ROC	0.563	0.666	0.784	1.932	1.094	1.066	0.759	1.278	0.745	0.456	1.138	1.030	1.292	1.195	1.208
4. HKG	0.587	0.646	0.779	2.112	1.064	0.941	0.735	1.329	0.637	0.495	1.203	1.065	1.303	1.221	1.073
5. SGP	0.883	1.061	1.199	1.389	1.282	1.339	1.282	0.937	1.056	1.139	0.902	0.770	1.208	1.034	0.939
6. MAL	1.805	1.781	1.676	0.939	1.460	0.815	0.975	0.719	0.693	1.281	0.921	0.669	0.672	1.073	0.960
7. THL	1.127	1.133	1.021	1.370	0.906	1.007	0.628	0.893	1.068	0.746	0.876	0.784	0.733	1.142	2.039
8. PHL	1.427	1.346	1.184	1.024	0.918	1.009	0.683	0.671	0.807	0.878	0.749	0.851	0.713	1.032	1.439
9. INE	2.151	1.549	1.308	0.365	1.257	0.588	1.047	1.036	0.646	1.300	1.218	0.604	0.538	0.968	0.490
10. IND	0.897	0.970	0.773	1.754	0.822	0.873	0.615	0.780	0.883	0.741	0.880	0.885	0.982	1.164	1.488
11. USA	0.785	1.117	1.138	1.089	1.062	1.130	0.986	1.104	1.145	0.923	0.866	1.172	1.121	1.003	1.421
12. CAN	1.115	1.046	0.984	0.758	0.836	0.965	0.884	0.905	0.977	0.984	1.027	1.159	0.995	1.046	1.001
13. ANZ	1.400	1.190	1.111	1.062	0.942	0.971	0.786	1.018	0.908	0.984	0.893	0.866	0.792	1.143	1.443
14. EEC	0.618	0.810	0.913	1.244	0.939	1.121	0.997	1.061	1.106	0.939	0.939	1.121	1.169	1.030	1.179
15. CHN	1.188	1.018	0.959	1.574	1.118	0.818	0.831	1.502	0.791	0.789	1.159	0.902	1.056	1.149	1.367

1980

from (i) \ to (j)	JPN	KOR	ROC	HKG	SGP	MAL	THL	PHL	INE	IND	USA	CAN	ANZ	EEC	CHN
1. JPN	0.452	0.962	1.152	1.239	1.032	0.928	1.017	1.067	1.308	0.815	1.012	1.146	1.224	0.905	1.209
2. KOR	0.768	0.691	0.634	1.573	1.158	0.827	0.684	0.447	0.910	0.435	1.316	0.794	0.913	1.081	0.703
3. ROC	0.635	0.902	0.839	1.641	1.206	0.937	0.761	0.668	1.172	0.669	1.190	0.863	0.962	1.070	0.742
4. HKG	0.486	0.582	0.623	1.603	1.105	0.776	0.635	0.458	0.838	0.507	1.337	0.876	1.027	1.033	0.920
5. SGP	1.506	1.146	1.349	1.263	1.781	0.957	0.896	0.685	0.746	1.075	1.015	0.716	0.709	1.028	0.724
6. MAL	2.259	1.378	1.739	0.925	1.444	0.670	0.592	0.648	0.365	1.461	0.825	0.513	0.576	1.224	1.160
7. THL	1.671	1.391	1.214	1.220	1.211	1.064	0.419	0.636	0.787	1.562	1.004	0.581	0.513	1.206	1.370
8. PHL	2.626	1.667	1.548	0.984	1.297	1.027	0.467	0.506	0.506	1.452	0.901	0.561	0.537	1.199	1.007
9. INE	2.729	1.529	1.476	0.726	1.380	1.052	0.591	0.847	0.295	1.342	0.768	0.565	0.500	1.236	0.777
10. IND	1.303	1.337	1.022	1.752	1.286	1.129	0.801	0.633	1.323	1.035	1.031	0.786	0.935	1.100	1.065
11. USA	0.948	1.118	1.196	0.903	0.943	0.970	0.915	1.040	1.017	1.068	0.928	1.100	1.105	0.952	1.013
12. CAN	1.274	0.945	0.838	0.664	0.748	1.054	0.837	0.955	0.876	0.950	1.151	1.162	0.965	1.037	0.889
13. ANZ	1.761	1.132	1.076	1.052	1.072	1.129	0.664	0.894	0.785	1.152	1.005	0.688	0.627	1.188	0.904
14. EEC	0.641	0.923	0.978	1.128	0.997	0.985	1.048	1.066	1.197	0.908	1.036	1.135	1.121	0.956	1.000
15. CHN	1.014	1.117	0.969	1.826	1.403	1.069	0.747	0.651	1.218	0.926	1.132	0.773	0.969	1.097	1.177

Note: $C_{ij} = \sum_{h=1}^{24} w^h (RCAX_i^h)(RCAM_j^h)$

unity C_{ij}'s with ANZ, Canada, and within the ASEAN-4. The C_{ij}'s increased in the trade with Japan, the NICs, and EC, and decreased in the case of ANZ and Canada and especially in the intra-ASEAN-4 trade. On the other hand, the change in the NICs' C_{ij}'s in both export trade with U.S., EC, Canada and ANZ, and import trade with U.S., ANZ, Japan and ASEAN, reflected the concentration of exports in labor-intensive manufactures and that of imports in resource products and capital- and technology-intensive manufactures. During the 1970s, the NICs restructuring toward capital- and technology-intensive manufactures decreased C_{ij}'s with major export markets, while the NICs continued import reliance on Japan and ASEAN increased C_{ij}'s with both of them.

Table 5 shows impacts of C_{ij}'s on the trade flow between the 15 countries/country groups. The trade flow is regressed on economic distance and GDP of both exporters and importers as well as on the complementarity indexes. A stable relationship was obtained with statistically significant coefficients of proper signs for all variables. Economic distance has a negative impact. Coefficients for GDP of exporter's and importer's are almost the same (positive) and since the two coefficients sum up to over unity, the trade flow expanded more than in proportion to GDP. C_{ij}'s have positive coefficients but below-unity C_{ij}'s tend to decrease the trade flow. The coefficient for C_{ij}'s was halved during the 1970s, lessening the effect of complementarity.

What will happen to the Asia-Pacific trade flow, if the past trend continues? Rapid growth of the NICs and ASEAN increased further their exports and imports, enlarging their shares in world trade. ASEAN's C_{ij}'s will possibly tend to turn downward as they continue industrialization, but the negative impact of the NICs and ASEAN decreasing C_{ij}'s will not be serious because of the reduced coefficients.

DIRECT INVESTMENT, TECHNOLOGY TRANSFER AND PRODUCTIVITY IMPROVEMENT

What is the mechanism underlying the spread of industrialization in developing countries? Processes of transplanting new industries in developing countries vary

Table 5. Determinants of the Asia-Pacific Trade Flows

Explanatory variables	1970			1980		
	Estimate	Standard error	t-value	Estimate	Standard error	t-value
Intercept	3.03	1.25	2.43	5.03	0.88	5.70
Distance	−0.59	0.18	−3.25	−0.77	0.11	−6.91
Export's GDP	0.66	0.08	8.52	0.62	0.05	11.43
Import's GDP	0.69	0.08	7.67	0.62	0.05	11.43
Complementarity	2.22	0.49	5.00	1.12	0.25	5.00
$\bar{R}^2$	0.422			0.563		

Notes: Explained variable is the export volume from i to j. Estimated by cross country (15 countries/country groups) log-line or least square (LLS).

between industries and between countries. Who introduces a new industry, indigenous entrepreneurs or foreign companies or a combination of the two? Where does the demand for the new product come from? How difficult is it to assimilate the technology? Does the factor intensity of production fit with the factor endowment of the country? The answers vary according to the type of industry and technology in question.

Catching-up Product Cycle (CPC) Development

Japan started industrialization in the late 19th century, introducing modern industries from Europe and North America. The development of a new industry followed the typical Catching-up Product Cycle (CPC); import of new product followed first by import substituting production and later by exporting. The introduction of new products creates its own domestic demand. Through import, domestic demand for the new product is expanded. When it increases to a certain size, domestic production starts up, partly to substitute for imports and partly to meet the growing demand. Domestic production of the new good is made possible through economies of scale, productivity improvements,and cost reductions that come about with the expansion of output. Exporting is an extension of the substitution of domestic products for foreign products in the foreign markets. Japan's major manufacturing industries were created through CPC development and many have remained in the export stage.

What characterizes Japan's CPC development? First, Japan's domestic market was of adequate size and had good growth prospects. Second, Japanese entrepreneurs directed the development of new industries. Japan received foreign direct investment in electric appliances, chemicals and some others before World War II, but foreign partners only contributed machines and technology. They did not have command of management. Third, Japanese aimed to transplant the whole industry, not just one or few production stages. And fourth, the role of government was limited before World War II. Import restrictions were confined to tariffs of moderate rate and state support was limited to a few strategic industries (iron and steel and shipbuilding) and industrial infrastructure (communication, transportation and utilities).

Technology Transfer through Product Cycle (PC)

Some elements in the industrialization of the NICs and ASEAN are similar to Japan's experience. Except for Hong Kong and Singapore, they have domestic markets of sufficient size for many industries. Although varying in their resource endowments, all adopted an industrialization strategy based on abundant labor endowments. Indigenous entrepreneurship exists including that of overseas Chinese, and entrepreneurs are assisted by government (more strongly than in Japan).

However, the industrialization of the NICs and ASEAN is distinguished from that of Japan's by the active role of the MNCs. R. Vernon[5] formulated in his Product Cycle (PC) Theory how American-based MNCs transferred new technology to developing countries once the technology had been standardized. The MNCs took advantage of cheaper labor costs to supply the American market. Vernon's theory

---

[5]   Vernon R. "International Investment and International Trade in the Product Cycle", *Quarterly Journal of Economics*, May, 1964.

explains the transfer of an assembly-operation or simple processing of a new product of an industry with a constant flow of new product innovation. But the theory does not explain the transfer of the whole industry generating the innovation flow itself. The transplanting of modern industry to the NICs and ASEAN is better explained by a combination of the CPC and PC theories.

MNCs have been most active in the electric and electronic industries. Table 6 gives an overview of changes in Asian countries' shares in the American import market for TV sets, radio receivers, and electronic parts. In the first two, Japan's predominant shares were replaced quickly by Korea and Hong Kong, but Singapore and Malaysia were also catching up. Changes in market shares were more rapid in electronic parts where Japan and Hong Kong were quickly replaced by Korea and Singapore, which in turn are being caught by other ASEAN countries. And the transfer of electronic assembly technology has been directed by American MNCs.

Local entrepreneurs prevail more in textile production. Japanese textile firms invested in each of the NICs and ASEAN countries in the 1960s but local firms joined the industry later, and in both Korea and the ROC (Taiwan) local firms have dominated the textile industry in recent years. Furthermore, local firms gradually upgraded their production from fabric to yarn and to textile material and transplanted all the stages of textile production. Textile technology has been more or

Table 6. Changing Shares of Asian Countries in American Market of
Selected Electronic Appliances

(Unit: %)

Commodities and years		Singa-pore	Malay-sia	Japan	Korea	Hong Kong	Philip-pines	Thai-land	Indo-nesia	Total
TV set	1969	0	0	84.8	0	0.5	0	0	0	85.3
	1971	0	0	77.8	0.5	0.1	0	0	0	78.4
	1973	0	0	50.9	3.1	0	0	0	0	54.0
	1975	0	0	59.7	4.4	0	0	0	0	62.8
	1977	0.3	0	60.8	6.5	0	0	0	0	67.6
	1980	1.0	0	41.5	17.0	0	0	0	0	59.5
Radio receiver	1969	0	0.1	68.2	1.2	12.8	0	0	0	82.3
	1971	2.1	0	65.5	0.8	14.3	0	0	0	82.7
	1973	4.2	0	55.6	2.7	15.7	0	0	0	78.2
	1975	5.9	0.6	43.5	4.5	16.8	0	0	0	71.3
	1977	3.7	1.9	47.3	6.7	15.8	0.2	0	0	75.6
	1980	3.0	0.1	38.0	9.5	8.0	1.0	0	0	59.6
Electronic parts	1969	4.3	0.1	18.9	9.0	16.2	0	0	0	48.5
	1971	16.9	0.1	12.7	12.0	12.5	0	0	0	54.2
	1973	21.7	5.4	9.2	12.2	10.8	0.6	0	0	59.9
	1975	17.6	17.8	8.7	11.5	7.8	2.9	0.1	0.1	66.6
	1977	18.5	19.1	9.8	15.0	5.7	4.7	1.6	1.0	75.4
	1980	15.0	27.0	8.0	14.0	3.5	7.2	3.8	2.1	80.6

Source: United Nations, *World Trade Annual*, various issues, New York, U.S.A.

less standardized and its transplantation fits the CPC type, but not the PC type, development.

Meanwhile, clothing production in the NICs and ASEAN is often conducted under subcontracting with big retailers in developed countries. A significant proportion of clothing imports to developed countries is handled by these MNCs.

On the other hand, the MNCs have seldom invested in the iron and steel industry in developing countries. Integrated steel production has started in Korea, the ROC (Taiwan), Malaysia and Indonesia and both Philippines and Thailand plan to establish this industry. But they are undertaken by local firms, frequently state enterprises (except Mala-yawata in Malaysia). In iron and steel, they have followed a typical CPC development although only Korea has reached the export stage.

Catching-up in Double Track

The PC development directed by the MNCs does not rely upon domestic market but is oriented to exporting through the MNCs' marketing channels. Electronic parts and clothing production (mentioned above) belong to this category. However, to the extent that local firms participated in domestic production, the domestic market becomes important and its development follows CPC with sequential increases of import, production, and export. A similar CPC development was also followed by the MNCs that were oriented for domestic market. However, the domestic market is limited and easily saturated in the NICs, so there emerges a strong need for early exportation.

CPC does not proceed in all industries simultaneously. The CPC of final products proceeds first and is then followed by the CPC of intermediate and capital goods. Domestic demand for the latter does not exist at first. As the import substituting production of final products takes place, demand is created for intermediate inputs. They are imported at first but as domestic demand reaches a certain amount, domestic production starts. That is, the CPC of final products induces the CPC of intermediate and capital goods. In Figure 2 the production curve of the final product (DP_f) is connected with the domestic demand curve of intermediate input (DD_i), reflecting the backward linkage effect from the former to the latter.

The inducement of another CPC development through the backward linkage effect was observed in Japan as the CPC of cotton textiles induced that of synthetic dye stuff and textile machinery. Uniquely, in today's NICs, the two CPC's proceed with only a short time interval. This may be referred to as "catching-up in double-track".

The quick linkage effect as well as the quick achievement of exportation by the NICs and ASEAN countries shows that the catching-up process has been compressed in comparison with that of their predecessors (Japan, USA, and ANZ). The compressed development is not free of disadvantages. One disadvantage is an intensified need for inputs of all kinds, and especially of intermediate inputs at the same time, resulting in accute balance of trade deficits. The present balance of payments deficit of Korea reflects this structural element and the ASEAN countries will not be free from it if they follow "catching-up in double-track".

Technology Levels of NICs and ASEAN

The successful CPC is not simply an expansion of the volume of domestic pro-less standardized and mass-production fits the CPC type, but not the PC type of development.

Meanwhile, clothing production in the NICs and ASEAN is often concentrated under subcontractions with big retailers in developed country's. A significant proportion of clothing imports to developed counties is handled by these MNCs.

On the other hand, the MNCs have seldom invested in the iron and steel industry in developing countries. Integrated steel production has started in Korea, the ROC (Taiwan), Malaysia and Indonesia, and both Philippines and Thailand plan to establish this industry. But they are undertaken by local firms, frequently state enterprises (except Malaywawong in Malaysia), therefore, and steel, they have followed a typical CPC development although only Korea has reached the export stage.

Catching-up in Double Track

The PC development directed by the MNCs does not rely upon domestic market but is geared to exports through the MNCs marketing channels. Electronic parts and leading products are typical examples above, but in to PC development. However, to the essential local firms participation in domestic production, the domestic market requires imports and its development follows CPC with sequential increases of import, production, and export. A similar CPC development was also followed by the PC, that were oriented but domestic market. However, the domestic market is limited but easily saturated in the NICs, so there emerges a strong need for early exportation.

CPC does not proceed in all industries simultaneously. The CPC of final product proceeds first and is then followed by the CPC of intermediate and capital goods. Domestic demand for the latter may be expressed by the residual, capital substituting production of final product. The residual need is covered by intermediate input. These are represented at the upper portion, reaching at peak, before local domestic production rises, that is, the CPC of final product starts. The CPC of intermediate and capital goods. In Figure 2 the production dual curve of the final product (DPf) is connected with the domestic demand curve of intermediate input (DDi) through the backward linkage of the firm the former to the latter.

The intermediate and another CPC development through the backward linkage which was observed in Japan, is the CPC of cotton textile demanded that of synthetic fibre stuff and textile machinery. Uniquely, it underwrites that the two CPCs proceed with only a short time interval. This may be referred to as "catching-up in double-track".

The same likeage effect is not clear in the intermediate goods exports of the NICs and ASEAN countries now that the import/output prices has risen to almost in comparison with that of major producing areas (Japan, USA, and ANA). The corresponded development is not to be disadvantages. One disadvantage is the frustated mass import of all kinds of, especially of intermediate inputs, so do also not suffer an adverse balance of trade. The other is balance of payments deficit. Korea reflects this signature. Korea and the ASEAN countries will not be free from till they follow "catching-up in double track".

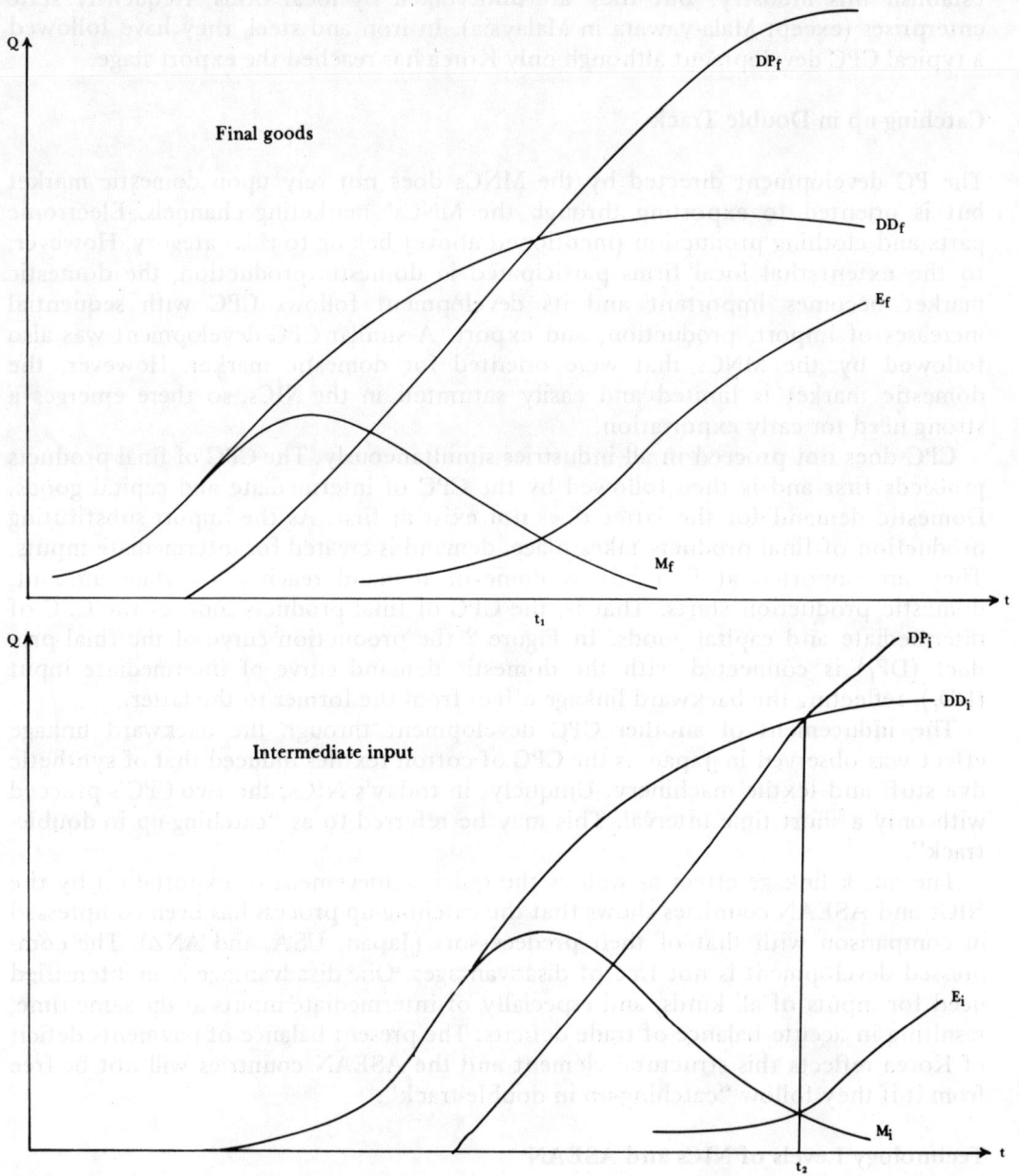

Figure 2. Catching-up in Double Track

duction, but is accompanied by productivity improvement. Without productivity improvement, import substitution is possible under strict restrictions but export expansion cannot last long even under heavy promotion. The ASEAN-4 have started the export of their industrial products, but it is still to be seen whether they can achieve as rapid growth as their predecessors, the NICs.

Upgrading of the level of technology is an essential element of productivity improvement. How are technology levels of the NICs and ASEAN evaluated by experts and what is their future prospects for catching-up with Japan? Table 7 provides an answer to this question. It summarizes the interview survey as to the present level of Asian machinery industry conducted by the Japan Economic Journal in the late 1970s. Sixty five representative Japanese machine producers were asked their evaluation of technology levels of their affiliate factories located in individual Asian countries. The evaluation is made by four grades; (1) the country will take longer than 10 years to catch up with Japan; (2) will take 5-10 years; (3) will take less than 5 years; and (4) has already reached the Japanese level.

It shows that the NICs, especially Korea and the ROC (Taiwan), have already achieved high technology levels in comparison with the ASEAN-4 and Japan. The technical gap between Japan and the NICs was narrowed substantially in many household electric and electronic appliances. In such products as batteries and radio receivers with technology that had long been standardized, the ASEAN-4 have almost reached the Japanese level. As a matter of fact, these products as well as some textile products have already started to be imported into the Japanese market. We may conclude from this table that the technical gap between the NICs and ASEAN has already become less than it was generally conceived to be and that it will not be long before the ASEAN-4 catch up with the NICs in some lines of production technology.

RESTRUCTURING OF TRADE AND PRODUCTION

The spread of industrialization to the NICs and ASEAN has inevitably been accompanied by the restructuring of trade and production and has caused some trade disputes with their trading partners in the developed countries. The restructuring also occurred in the 19th century, but in the period since World War II the process has been intensified by the activity of the MNCs. How can the restructuring process be adjusted to become more harmonious?

Tendency Toward Intra-Industry Trade

The spread of industrialization has changed the vertical trade between primary products and manufactures to horizontal trade — a mutual exchange of manufactured goods. This mutual exchange consists of the trade between labor-intensive and capital- and technology-intensive manufactures and is still far from "intra-industry trade," but the merits of this mutual exchange should not be overlooked. Under horizontal trade of manufactures, the mutual spread of effective demand is secured and big imbalances of trade cannot be continued for long. How far along has Asia-Pacific trade gone in approaching horizontal trade? We will explore two possibilities. One is the trend of export/import ratios of manufactures for the NICs and ASEAN and the other is the possibility of Japanese increasing imports of

Table 7. Technological Levels of Asian NICs and ASEAN Countries

Products	Thailand	Indonesia	Philippines	Malaysia	Singapore	Hong Kong	ROC (Taiwan)	Korea
Atomic energy devices	1	1	1	1	1	1	1	2
Washing machines	1	1	1	1	2	3	4	4
Refrigerators	2	1	2	2	3	3	3	4
Lighting fixtures	2	2	2	2	2	3	4	4
Communications apparatus	1	1	1	1	1	1	2	2
Transistor radios	3	3	3	3	3	4	4	4
TV sets	2	2	2	2	3	3	4	4
Computers	1	1	1	1	1	1	1	1
Electric instruments	1	1	1	1	2	2	2	2
Resistors and condensers	1	1	1	1	2	2	3	3
Semi-conductors	1	1	1	1	2	3	3	3
Batteries	3	3	3	3		4	3	4
Automobiles	1	1	1	1	1	1	1	3
Buses and vans	1	1	2	1	1	1	2	3
Automobile parts	1	1	2	-1	1	1	2	3
Motorbicycles	1	1	1	1				3
Bicycles							3	3
Rolling stocks	1	1	1	1		1	3	3
Ships	1	1	1	1	3	1	3	3
Airplanes							1	1
Cameras	2	2	2	2	2	2	3	3
Boilers	1	1	1	1	1	1	1	2
Power shovels	1	1	1	1	1	1	2	2
Valves	2	2	2	2	2	1	3	3
Tanks	1	1	2	2	2	3	3	3
Bearings								1
Pumps	2	2	2	2	2	2	2	3
Effluent treatment devices	1	1	2	2	3	3	3	3
Agricultural machines	2	2	2	2	2	1	3	3
Lathes	1	1	1	1	1	1	2	2
Textile machines	1	1	1	1	1	1	2	3
Household sewing machines	1	1	1	1	1	1	2	2
Desk and pocket calculators				2	3	3	3	3
Electronic cash registers	1	1	1	1	1	2	2	3
Watt-hour meter							3	3
Wrist watches	1	1	1	1	2	3	2	2
Lighters					2			
Generators	1	1	1	1	1	1	2	3
Motor engines	1	1	1	1	2	4	3	3
Transformers	1	1	1	1	2	1	3	3

Source: Nihon Keizai Shimbun, ed., *Japan's Rivals of Tomorrow: Growing Machinery Industries in Asia.* Nihon Keizai Shimbun Press, 1978.

Notes: 1. Figures in the table signify as follows: (1) The country will take longer than 10 years to catch up with Japan; (2) will take 5-10 years; (3) will take less than 5 years; and (4) has already reached the level of Japan.

2. Sample Japanese firms are asked to evaluate local enterprises and joint companies with foreign capital. When answers vary, the most frequent one is adopted.

intermediate inputs.

Figure 3 illustrates the projection by EPA for future pattern of export/import ratios of Japan, Asian NICs and ASEAN for industrial products classified by end uses. It is of course based on an assumption; export/import ratio reaches a turning point at per capita income level of 70 percent of world average, between middle and high income stage, after which the ratio declines for non-durable consumer goods (ND) and labor-intensive intermediate goods (LI), remains constant for durable consumer goods (D) and capital intensive intermediate goods (CI) and continues to grow slowly for capital goods (C). The tendency is based on the past experience of major countries and reflects shift in comparative advantage from labor-intensive to capital and technology-intensive ones analyzed in the earlier section.

Figure 3 provides a future structure of manufactured goods trade in Asia-Pacific, on the assumption that this tendency will continue toward the next century. Japan's per capita GNP will continue the present 4 percent growth toward the year 2000 and the export/import ratio will decline further for ND and LI, while that for D and CI remain constant and that for C increase further. Asian NICs will continue rapid growth and soon reach the turning point. Export/import ratio will turn downward while that for other three will continue near the year 2000. Their trade balance will turn to the surplus in due course. On the other hand, ASEAN-4 will reach the turning point after 2000. Export/import ratio of all categories will continue to increase. Therefore, intra-Asia-Pacific trade will be characterized by the decline of Japanese share in major categories replaced by Asian NICs and ASEAN countries, a further approach to intra-industry trade of manufactures.

Another possibility toward horizontal trade will be found in Japan's adjustment of her industrial structure. Japan has succeeded in transplanting major manufacturing industries in full-scale and maintained low dependence on imports of intermediate inputs. Table 8 shows import dependence of intermediate inputs in major subsectors as defined in the Input-Output table. Except for over 20 percent for non-ferrous metal and 12-13 percent for chemicals, import dependence is less than 10 percent and the average is as low as 5 percent. The similar figure for Germany is 20 percent and there is room for increased dependence. The two right-hand columns show the simulation of doubling the import dependence ratio with unchanged final demand. Total import increases by 4,600 billion yen or 23 billion dollars at 200 yen per U.S. dollar rate, but the number of employment decreases by 550 thousand through both direct and indirect effect of the decreased production of intermediate input. The impact of this restructuring seems to justify further study on this issue.

CONCLUSION: POLICY IMPLICATIONS

The spread of industrialization to the NICs and ASEAN provides a growth source in the world economy but the rapid restructuring of trade and production has caused trade frictions in the Asia-Pacific. It is important to understand the structural element of this phenomenon and to implement correct policy measures. A desirable direction of restructuring is horizontal trade of manufactures. The restructuring of Japanese trade and industry is of vital importance in that direction. Japan should not fear a boomerang effect and take positive steps toward technical transfer to her Asian neighbors. Both the NICs and ASEAN should understand that further productivity improvement is crucial for their continued growth. Trade liberalization and flexible implementation of policies toward MNCs are recommended at both official and private levels.

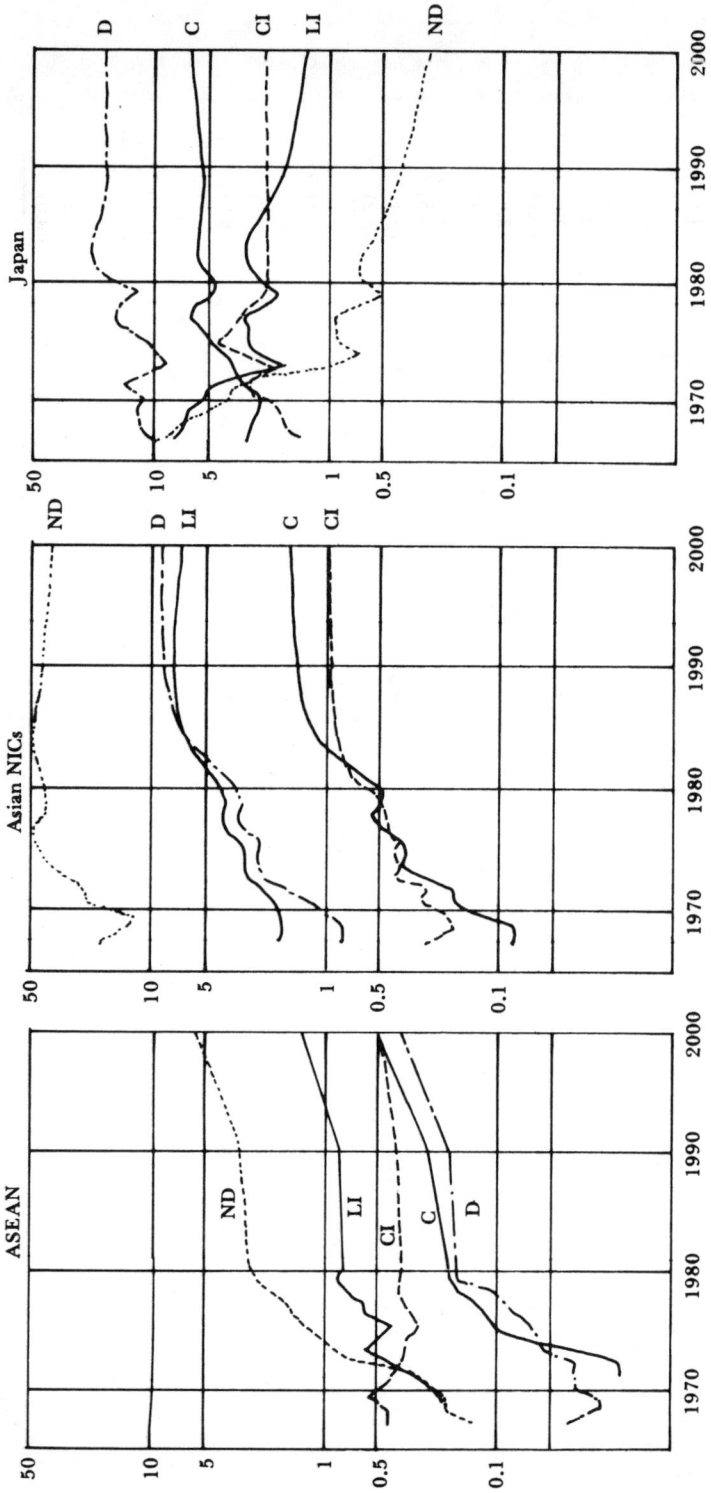

Source: Economic Planning Agency (1985).
Notes: a. Scale is logarithmic.
 b. ND = non-durable consumer goods
 D = durable consumer goods
 LI = labor-intensive intermediate goods
 CI = capital-intensive intermediate goods
 C = capital goods

Figure 3. Outlook for Export/Import Ratios of Manufactured Products

Table 8. Restructuring of Japan's Intermediate Input Production and Its Impact on Import and Employment

	Share in all intmd. input imports (%)	Intmd. input imports/all imports (%)	Intmd. input imports/dom. intmd. input (%)	Increase in imports (billion yen)	Reduction of employment (thousand persons)
Manufacturing total	100.0	17.7	5.2	4,566.8 (100.0)	319.9 (58.6)
Yarn	0.6	6.9	8.9	131.7 (2.9)	18.2 (3.3)
Fabrics	2.9	84.5	6.1	138.3 (3.0)	23.3 (4.3)
Wood Products	1.0	3.3	6.1	291.0 (6.4)	29.2 (5.3)
Basic chemicals	3.0	53.5	12.3	408.3 (8.9)	16.0 (2.9)
Petro-chemicals	1.5	12.9	3.3	145.9 (3.2)	3.9 (0.7)
Final chemical goods	6.3	70.7	13.8	288.2 (6.3)	15.8 (2.9)
Pig iron & crude steel	6.8	24.7	6.2	223.5 (4.9)	4.6 (0.8)
Non-ferrous metal	1.9	9.7	21.3	1,284.8 (28.1)	12.1 (2.2)
Non-ferrous metal products	16.7	95.3	28.4	149.9 (3.3)	6.5 (1.2)
General machinery	6.6	77.2	2.6	255.3 (5.6)	26.9 (4.9)
Light electric machinery	15.0	88.1	7.9	405.5 (8.9)	38.0 (7.0)
Agriculture	—		—	0 (—)	62.2 (1.4)
Services	—		—	0 (—)	123.5 (22.5)
Total				4,566.8 (100.0)	564.4 (100.0)

Source: MITI. Calculated from 1980 Input-Output Table.

7. Foreign Capital, Balance of Payments and External Debt in Developing Asia

Evelyn M. Go and Jungsoo Lee

INTRODUCTION

The importance of capital accumulation is perhaps one of the least disputed tenets of economic growth theory which transcends even ideological barriers. Although foreign capital augments the total availability of resources to a country, the role of foreign capital in economic development has provoked continuous debate.

In the wake of a decade of unprecedentedly large LDC payment deficits and external debt burdens, the role of foreign capital has been thrust to the forefront of development issues. A confluence of adverse external developments in the 1970s and early 1980s enlarged the balance of payments gaps of developing countries, which were bridged to a large extent by commercial borrowings due in large part to an elastic supply of funds in international capital markets. This experience has imparted to many developing countries, including several in Asia, a legacy of debt that endangers creditworthiness and has led to disruption in financial flows. Such disruptions, even when they are not necessarily associated with explicit episodes of rescheduling, nevertheless impede financial flows and have adverse implications on growth as sudden contractions in external finance are likely to entail reductions in imports, transfer of technology and investment.

The prospect of modest growth in output and trade of developing countries in the 1980s does not preclude the possibility of further debt difficulties over the medium term. Moreover, during the coming decade it is expected that the capital flows, especially concessional flows, from developed to developing countries will grow more slowly than they did in the 1960s and 1970s. This implies that external debt problems and the shortage of foreign capital inflow may emerge as critical constraints to the economic development of developing countries. Major concerns about external finance are, thus, addressed to the debt service burden as an impediment to further finance and prospective growth and the related question of how external finance affects development. Particularly, the heavy debt burdens have drawn attention to longer term productivity of investment financed through

227

external capital inflow which underlies solvency of debtors. Furthermore, the unfavorable outlook for the external finance calls for a reconsideration of the role of foreign capital.

The diversity of development experience indicates that foreign capital is neither necessary nor sufficient for economic development; growth attainable is only partly constrained by an inadequacy of investible resources but more often by weak institutions and poor policy which contributes to inefficient use of both domestic and external resources. That foreign aid manifested limited association with growth in various empirical studies may be explained by the overriding importance of the economic policy environment or system.[1] Case studies of selected countries suggest varying degrees of success with foreign aid with notable successes cited in the Korea and the ROC (Taiwan). From this more complex view of the development process, in which the role of capital has been downgraded, interest has shifted to how external finance can overcome bottlenecks or constraints to contribute to development. Investment remains the vehicle linking external finance and growth. Although some consumption smoothing and cushion for adjustment might be valuable services provided by external finance, at now higher real resource costs the criterion of productivity assumes greater significance. Unless external finance is utilized to put into place productive capacity, the burden of servicing may well impinge on future consumption and savings.

We address the issues of foreign capital inflow and external debt problems in relation to the economic development of Asian developing countries (ADCs). For this purpose, we first review the role and pattern of external finance in Asia by country group and examine the empirical evidence for a sample of major ADCs. We consider the external debt situation which has evolved from past financing and examine its relationship with balance of payments disturbances of the past decade. Finally, we summarize major conclusions of the study and draw together the major policy lessons regarding external finance and external debt.

FOREIGN CAPITAL FLOWS TO ASIAN DEVELOPING COUNTRIES

In this section we review the pattern of external finance of ADCs, beginning with the financing of investment by domestic and foreign sources. We then examine the composition and trends in external finance disaggregated into its major component parts before turning to the relationship between gross flows, net flows and net transfers. This paves the way for an examination of linkages between investment and various components of external finance. For planning purposes, investment and external resource requirements are conventionally projected from a growth model which assumes a constant capital-output ratio and negligible consumption leakages. Recognizing that in fact external capital is neither homogeneous nor perfectly substitutable but often tends to be rather specific in its actual application and return servicing obligations, a disaggregation of external flows would form a useful basis for exploring the impact of external finance on investment which is the main channel for its contribution to productivity and economic development.

We disaggregate country groups into low income countries (LICs), middle income countries (MICs) and newly industrialized countries (NICs) which roughly corres-

---

[1]   Gorgens, "Developing Aid — An Obstacle to Economic Growth in Developing Countries," *German Economic Review*, Vol. 14, 1976.

pond to both differences in levels of living and geography (South Asia, Southeast Asia and East Asia, respectively). MICs can be further subdivided between oil exporters (OXs) and non-oil exporters which will be indicated in certain presentations which follow. Limited information on Indochina (Cambodia, Lao PDR and Viet Nam) will be added where available.

Data are derived from a variety of sources as indicated (see Appendix A) but principally from World Bank, *World Tables,* IMF, *Balance of Payments Yearbook* and OECD, *Geographical Distribution of Financial Flows.*

Financing of Investment

Table 1 summarizes the domestic (savings) and foreign (savings) components of the financing of gross domestic capital formation in fourteen ADCs during 1968-1982, all in nominal terms. Averages are given for each country and country groups for investment rate (GDI/GNP), domestic saving rate (GNS/GNP), and foreign saving rate (FS/GNP). Despite variations among individual countries, the pattern manifests highest investment rates in NICs, averaging 29.9 percent, followed by MICs at 23.9 percent and LICs at 15.6 percent which generally conforms with stage of development as proxied by recent per capita income levels.[2] On the basis of variations in investment rates alone, growth in output would differ among country groups and generate growing per capita income gaps in the future.

Gross national savings is computed as a residual by subtracting foreign savings from recorded gross investment data in the national accounts.[3] Two alternative concepts of foreign savings are contained in Table 1, one which includes transfers from abroad as foreign savings (FS) and one which excludes transfers from abroad from foreign savings (FS') and so implicitly regards them as part of national savings.[4] Under both sets of estimates, workers remittances have been transferred to GNS and are not counted as part of foreign savings.

While the apportionment of domestic and foreign savings is sensitive to the definition of foreign savings,[5] even when workers remittances are excluded from foreign savings altogether, it is clear that the choice makes a more material difference to LICs where foreign saving rate is raised by 2 percentage points from 2.7 to 4.7 percent when all transfers are considered part of foreign savings. The discrepancy is smaller for MICs and NICs. Although NICs have high average foreign savings

---

[2]   These data are taken from WB *World Tables,* where workers remittances have been deleted from private transfers and transferred to net factor income and so are reflected under GNS rather than foreign savings. Thus private transfers here differ and are generally smaller (because of reclassification of remittances) in *World Tables* than the data presented in IMF *Balance of Payments Yearbook.*

[3]   GNS = GDI − [(M − X) − NFY], where (M − X) is net imports of goods and non-factor services or resource gap and NFY is net factor income from abroad. For further discussion of methods and problems in the measurement of savings, see Iwasaki, "Methods of Estimating Savings and Their Implication", in *Domestic Resource Mobilization Through Financial Development,* Vol. II, ADB, 1984.

[4]   We present both sets because, conceptually, only capital transfers ought to be regarded as part of foreign savings which finances investment, data on transfers (private and official) available from balance of payments do not segregate capital from current transfers. As a result, without further information on composition of transfers we are left with choice of treating all transfers as current (capital) transfers and so exclude (include) them entirely from (in) foreign savings. Undoubtedly, the truth lies somewhere in between the two estimates as, for example, transfers for emergency food relief, etc. are typically intended for consumption purposes and so represent current transfers while others are channeled to capital formation.

[5]   For example, Fry suggests that foreign transfers be treated as part of national savings. See Fry, "Econometric Analyses of National Saving Rates" in *Ibid,* p. 51. Others regard foreign transfers as part of foreign savings. See Krueger, *The Developmental Role of the Foreign Sector and Aid,* 1979, pp. 206-207.

Table 1. Financing of Investment: Domestic and Foreign Saving Rates* (Average, 1968-1982)

(Unit: %)

	GDI/GNP	GNS^1/GNP	FS^2/GNP	GNS'^{3}/GNP	FS'^{4}/GNP
LICs					
Bangladesh	11.1	3.4	7.7	7.7[a]	3.9[a]
Burma	15.3	12.4	2.9	13.1	2.2
India	20.5	19.2	1.3	19.6[b]	0.5[b]
Nepal	10.3	7.5	2.8	14.8[c]	−0.9[c]
Pakistan	15.7	10.3	5.4	11.5	4.1
Sri Lanka	20.4	12.2	8.1	14.3	6.1
Average	15.6	10.8	4.7	13.5	2.7
(1968-73)	13.2	10.1	3.1	12.2	1.9
(1974-82)	17.1	11.3	5.8	14.1	3.1
MICs					
Non-Oil					
Philippines	26.3	22.1	4.2	23.5	2.7
Thailand	25.3	20.9	4.4	21.6	3.7
(1968-73)	22.8	20.3	2.5	21.7	1.1
(1974-82)	27.8	22.3	5.5	23.2	4.7
OXs					
Indonesia	18.6	16.0	2.6	16.3	2.4
Malaysia	25.2	24.8	0.4	24.4	0.8
(1968-73)	17.8	16.0	2.6	16.3	1.8
(1974-82)	24.7	23.4	1.3	23.3	1.5
All MICs Ave.	23.9	21.0	2.9	21.5	2.4
NICs					
ROC (Taiwan)	29.2	30.4	−1.2	30.3[d]	−0.8[d]
Korea	28.0	20.8	7.3	22.1	5.9
Hong Kong	23.1	25.6	−2.5	—	—
Singapore	39.2	27.2	12.1	26.7	12.6
Average	29.9	26.0	3.9	26.4	5.9
(1968-73)	26.4	22.3	4.1	22.6	6.5
(1974-82)	32.2	28.4	3.8	28.9	5.5

Source: WB, *World Tables*.

* In current prices.
1 Excluding net current transfers from abroad.
2 Including net current transfers from abroad.
3 Including net current transfers from abroad.
4 Excluding net current transfers from abroad.

a 1973-1982.
b 1968-1981.
c 1976-1982.
d 1968-1981.

rates, the ROC (Taiwan) and Hong Kong actually had negative foreign saving rates.[6]

If investment rates and their financing are segregated into two periods, 1968-1973 and 1974-1982, then we observe the following: The increase in investment rates between the two periods was highest for oil exporters (6.9 percentage point increase) followed by NICs (5.8 percentage points), Non-oil MICs (5.0 percentage points) and LICs (3.9 percentage points). The increase in foreign saving rates (where transfers are wholly included in foreign savings) was largest for Non-oil MICs (3.0 percentage points) followed by LICs (2.7 percentage points) while NICs (−.3 percentage points) and OXs (−1.3 percentage points) showed on the average declines in foreign saving rates. Thus OXs and NICs were able to finance increased investment through their own saving mobilization, abetted by oil price bonanza in the case of the OXs. The other oil importers of Asia utilized foreign finance to a greater extent to raise investment rates. Although the increase in foreign saving rates was larger for MICs than LICs between the two periods, as a proportion of the change in investment rate, more than two-thirds of LICs' increment was financed by foreign savings as compared to more than one-half share for MICs suggesting improvement in domestic saving effort was greater in non-oil MICs than in LICs.

The range of domestic saving (GNS/GNP) rates during the period as a whole varied widely among ADCs — from 3.4 percent in Bangladesh to 30.4 percent in the ROC (Taiwan). Similarly foreign saving rates ranged from −2.5 percent in Hong Kong to 12.1 percent in Singapore.

The scatter of foreign saving rates (FS/GNP) against domestic saving rates (GNS/GNP) reveals no systematic relationship between the two with high foreign saving rates found in such diverse countries as Bangladesh, Sri Lanka, Pakistan and Singapore. It is more probable, however, that a large share of the transfers in poorer South Asian countries do indeed constitute current or consumption transfers. The two MIC oil exporters appear to have relatively low foreign saving (FS/GNP) rates, unlike their oil-importing MIC counterparts. Two NICs, the ROC (Taiwan) and Hong Kong, have negative foreign saving (FS/GNP) rates due to net outward transfers.

The bulk of the empirical work using cross section data on single equation models of saving functions has found a negative relationship between national saving rate as the dependent variable and foreign saving rate as an independent variable.[7] In a recent econometric analysis of saving functions in a number of Asian countries using time series data, the coefficient of the foreign saving rate was significantly negative in three (Bangladesh, Nepal and Thailand) of the four countries investigated.[8] In the fourth country Korea, the coefficient was also negative though not significant at conventional levels of significance. In each case, except in Bangladesh the coefficient was less than one, suggesting that national savings was only partially displaced by foreign savings which therefore augmented both consumption and investment. However, statistical problems and specification errors suggest caution in the interpretation of this finding.[9]

In the absence of an apparent relationship in the scatter of average investment

---

[6]   The absence of transfers data on Hong Kong prevents us from calculating FS' for Hong Kong.

[7]   See Weisskopf, "The Impact of Foreign Capital Inflow on Domestic Savings in Underdeveloped Countries" in *Journal of International Economics,* Vol. 2, 1972, Singh, *Development Economics,* 1975. On direction of causality, see Iwasaki, "Cause and Effect in The World Sugar Market. Some Emperical Findings 1951-82", ADB, *Economic Office Report Series,* No. 29.

[8]   Fry, op. cit.

[9]   See Rana, "Sources of Balance of Payment Problems in 1970: The Asian Experience" (Draft) 1984.

rates against average foreign saving rates during the period, a linear regression of investment rates on the foreign saving rate was conducted with pooled time series data using three-year averages for the two alternative definitions of foreign savings, FS and FS'. Dummy variables were introduced to allow intercepts to vary among countries and also to differentiate pre (1968-73) from post oil shock (1974-82) periods.

Both specifications of foreign saving rates were significantly different from one at .01 level of significance although R^2 was slightly higher when FS was the explanatory variable. The case was reversed with regards to the coefficient of the foreign saving rate (t values given in the parentheses below coefficients).[10] F tests on country and period dummies were significant and indicated that the investment rate was higher by approximately 4.3 percentage points in the post shock years, lending some support to the hypothesis of an autonomous increase in the investment rate in the latter period.[11] The coefficient on the foreign saving rate variable indicates that a one percentage point increase in the foreign saving rate contributed to about one-half of one percentage point increase in the investment rate, both variables measured in current price terms. The range of empirical observations for the Asian countries in the sample does not rule out the possibility of an important asymmetry, i.e. that an infusion of foreign savings may improve the investment rate while a reduction might not reduce the investment, as this has been the experience of countries making a transition from aid dependence to self-sustained growth.[12]

Composition and Trends in External Finance

We describe the composition and trends in external finance by examining data on type and source of foreign finance.[13] Then we examine the role of borrowings from international capital markets which altered the terms of foreign capital inflows for those creditworthy countries which raised substantial borrowings at commercial terms, thereby contributing to a growing divergence between gross flows and net transfers.

From the balance of payments accounts of Asian countries for which data are given in IMF sources, we have developed Table 2 which disaggregates external finance into its major components, inclusive of private and official (unrequited)

---

[10] The equations (country dummies not reported).

$$I/GNP = .5027 \ FS/GNP + 4.1560D \qquad R^2 = .9160$$
$$\qquad (4.20) \qquad\qquad (5.65)$$
$$I/GNP = .5512 \ FS'/GNP + 4.3258D \qquad R^2 = .9112$$
$$\qquad (4.21) \qquad\qquad (5.64)$$

Where: FS' — foreign savings excluding transfers
FS — foreign savings including transfers
D — (= 0 for 1968-73)
(= 1 for 1974-82)

[11] Sachs "The Current Account and Macro Economic Adjustments in 1970s," in *Brooking Papers on Economic Activity*, 1, 1981.

[12] See Singh op. cit., p. 182.

[13] These are two separate and distinct time series which are not directly reconcilable. Since they are broadly overlapping OECD data may be viewed roughly as subset of balance of payments data, but has limited coverage of private, particularly Eurocurrency flows.

Table 2. Disaggregated External Financing Flows to Asian Countries, 1968-1983
(Average Annual in Constant 1980 Prices)

(Unit: US$ million)

	Private Transfers* (1)	Official Transfers* (2)	Direct Investment (3)	Long-Term Borrowings+ (4)	Short-Term Borrowings° (5)	Others# (6)	Investment Outflows (7)	Net Flows (8)	Net Transfers (9)
LICs									
Bangladesh	232.96	674.00	0.33	535.99	1.33	73.94	−75.04	1,518.55	1,443.51
Burma	4.32	46.01	—	159.82	33.42	17.57	−36.43	261.13	224.70
India^a	973.66	687.15	−7.48	1,220.11	−268.06	102.25	−745.73	2,707.63	1,961.90
Pakistan	1,497.34	259.09	45.19	875.52	107.89	157.24	−293.69	2,942.27	2,648.58
Sri Lanka	63.33	92.96	16.67	196.72	29.82	40.34	−71.83	439.84	368.01
Nepal	33.71	74.35	—	45.93	13.09	−8.66	−2.70	158.41	155.71
Total	2,805.31	1,833.55	54.71	3,034.10	−82.52	382.68	−1,225.42	8,027.84	6,802.42
MICs									
Indonesia	—	95.94	275.11	1,941.83	−641.43	38.96	−2,038.99	1,710.40	−328.59
Malaysia	−135.29	25.06	664.71	612.15	−449.84	69.74	−1,119.79	786.54	−333.25
Philippines	221.29	212.54	111.29	873.62	528.56	132.37	−829.65	2,079.68	1,250.03
Thailand	267.22	107.53	181.74	743.19	354.46	143.63	−526.59	1,797.77	1,271.18
Total	353.23	441.07	1,232.86	4,170.79	−208.25	384.70	−4,515.02	6,374.39	1,859.37
NICs									
ROC (Taiwan)	−22.20	−6.95	117.79	507.86	−467.95	54.09	−596.27	182.64	−413.63
Korea	381.45	139.97	77.12	1,993.08	779.03	180.24	−1,394.41	3,550.87	2,156.46
Singapore	−57.92	4.57	943.45	110.84	923.57	159.05	−678.99	2,083.56	1,404.57
Total	301.33	137.59	1,138.36	2,611.78	1,234.65	393.37	−2,669.67	5,817.08	3,147.40
Grand Total	3,459.87	2,412.20	2,425.93	9,816.67	943.88	1,160.74	−8,410.11	20,219.30	11,809.19

Source: IMF, *IFS* and *Balance of Payments Yearbook*.

a 1968 to 1981.
* Including subsidy account grants
+ Including trust fund loans.
# Reserve-related plus counterparts items.
° Including errors and omissions

Deflator: Export unit values of industrial countries (1980 = 100)

(8) = (1) to (6)
(9) = (8) − (7)

transfers.[14] The summation of all components gives net flows. Also provided in Table 2 are investment outflows representing interest and dividends on debt and equity (but not amortization of debt or withdrawal of investment which are capital account items) as given in current account as debit items. We have deflated the data by the export unit value index of industrialized countries (IMF, IFS) in order to facilitate intercountry comparisons of period averages. Table 3 presents a similarly deflated decomposition of external finance by source. Official sources in this OECD series can be broken down into three groups: DAC bilaterals, traditional multilaterals (excluding OPEC), and OPEC/Arab bilaterals and multilaterials.[15] Average annual ODA flows are given as memo item for each country and country group.[16] For the Indochinese country group for which aid flows from Socialist countries have been significant, some estimates on flows from Centrally Planned Economies (CPE) are supplied as they are not encompassed by the official flows referred to above.

For the 13 ADCs listed in Table 2, the totals indicate that long-term borrowings were the leading form of financing followed by private transfers, direct investment, and official transfers. Short-term borrowings and others were relatively smaller in size for the group as a whole.

In Tables 2 and 4, long-term borrowings cover the entire gamut of debt financing — from private and official sources, at concessional and at commercial terms so long as maturities exceed one year. Short-term borrowings cover both contractual borrowings of one year or less (mostly trade credits) and accommodating finance (monetary capital) as well as errors and omissions. Others represent a composite of residual items including IMF credits other than minor items covered under grants or long-term borrowing, plus various valuation adjustments, monetization of gold and SDR allocations. While net flows are the sum of the disaggregated components, net transfers deduct investment outflows.

Despite differences in composition of external finance among LICs, MICs and NICs, long-term borrowings were the leading type of financing for all groups with just a few individual country exceptions. Pronounced differences among country groups were also found in the size of direct investment inflows and short-term borrowings. While short- and long-term borrowings are debt creating flows, private and official transfers and direct investment do not affect indebtedness. Indochina is excluded from Table 2 due to non-availability of data but is covered in Table 3 and partially covered in Table 4.

---

[14] The measurements of current account deficit is affected by the treatment of transfers as current or capital account item. Conventionally, IMF includes private transfers in current account while official transfers are regarded as a financing item (see IMF World Economic Outlook). Since we cannot segregate capital from current portion of transfers, either private or official, partitioning remains arbitrary (see preceding section).

[15] DAC Bilaterals: Australia, Austria, Belgium, Canada, Denmark, Finland, France, Federal Republic of Germany, Italy, Japan, the Netherlands, New Zealand, Norway, Sweden, Switzerland, U.K. and U.S. Multilaterals: World Bank, IFC, IDA, IADB, AfDB, AfDF, ADB, CarDB, IFAD and various UN agencies. OPEC/ Arab Bilaterals or Multilaterals: OPEC-member countries and Arab Fund for Economic and Social Development, The Special Account of OAPEC, OPEC Fund for International Development, Islamic Development Bank and Islamic Solidarity Fund. However, about 35 per cent of OPEC bilateral is not allocable by recipient country. For further details and exact country and institution coverage, see OECD, *Geographical Distribution of Financial Flows,* Introduction.

[16] ODA refers to Official Development Assistance which comprise foreign capital flows from official sources which have promotion of economic development and welfare of developing countries as its principal objective and contains a grant element of at least 25 per cent. Remainder of official flows or OOF are transaction whose main objectives is other than development or if development whose terms fall below the 25 per cent minimum grant element to qualify as ODA. See OECD, *Ibid.,* Annex.

Table 3. OECD Financial Flows to Asian Countries, 1969-1983
(Average Annual in 1980 Prices)

(Unit: US$ million)

	Official	Bilateral	Multilateral	OPEC Arab	Private	Memo: ODA	Memo: CPE
LICs							
Bangladesh	1,055.3	681.7	309.6	96.2	6.6	1,138.3	
Burma	205.4	150.0	57.3	4.6	41.7	205.1	
India	2,142.6	1,177.7	895.7	177.6	72.5	2,154.4	
Nepal	113.9	67.4	43.6	4.9	0.02	113.6	
Pakistan	1,010.2	597.7	274.4	312.3	47.9	1,039.5	
Sri Lanka	289.1	208.1	73.2	25.4	4.1	283.5	
Total	4,816.5	2,882.6	1,653.8	621.0	172.8	4,934.4	
MICs							
Indonesia	1,408.7	1,043.2	354.7	16.8	1,127.5	1,092.7	
Malaysia	238.8	127.5	105.0	11.8	377.6	126.1	
Philippines	612.3	347.7	262.0	9.9	395.9	321.1	
Thailand	487.5	247.0	226.9	25.9	230.5	277.6	
Total	2,747.3	1,765.4	948.6	64.4	2,131.5	1,817.5	
NICs							
ROC (Taiwan)	197.0	147.5	40.8	18.4	219.1	1.9	
Korea	1,054.6	677.3	367.1	20.7	579.0	460.4	
Hong Kong	93.7	86.6	6.9	3.2	683.1	6.1	
Singapore	85.2	56.9	28.2	0.2	394.2	36.7	
Total	1,430.5	968.3	443.0	42.5	1,875.4	505.1	
INDOCHINA							
Cambodia	135.1	99.0	36.1	1.0	-1.4	161.4	
Lao, PDR	103.3	90.0	12.7	1.9	0.5	103.4	
Viet Nam	720.9	667.0	50.9	13.5	26.1	723.5	
Total	959.3	856.0	99.7	16.4	25.2	988.3	
Grand Total	9,953.6	6,472.3	3,145.1	744.3	4,204.9	8,245.3	1,176.4 [a]

Source: OECD, *Geographical Distribution of Financial Flows* and ADB *Key Indicators*.

[a] 1969 to 1982.

Table 4. Annual Growth Rates* of Selected Components of Foreign Inflows to Asian Country Groups by Type and by Source

	LICs	MICs	NICs	OXs	Indochina
By Type:[a] (1968-83)					
Private Transfers	29	30	22	c	na
Official Transfers	18	8	ns	ns	na
Direct Investment	18	15	19	18	na
Long Term Borrowings	10	28	21	29	na
Short Term Borrowings	10	25	17	ns	na
Investment Outflows	ns	27	37	27	na
Total Net Flow	15	23	18	16	na
Total Net Transfers	18	22	10	17	na
By Source:[b] (1969-83)					
Total Net	13	20	11	14	−13
Private	ns	20	16	20	ns
Official	12	19	5	10	−13
DAC Bilateral	7	12	ns	6	20
Multilateral	23	30	14	26	20
OPEC-Arab	ns	ns	ns	36[d]	−27[e]
Memo: Official from Centrally					
Planned Economies	na	na	na	na	3[f]

[a] IMF, *Balance of Payment Yearbook.*
[b] OECD, *Geographical Distribution of Financial Flows.*
[c] Outflows for Malaysia; zeros for Indonesia.
[d] 1973 to 1983.
[e] 1975 to 1983.
[f] 1972 to 1982.

* All exponential growth rates shown significant at 10 per cent or higher L/S.

ns — not significant
na — no data available

Growth Trends

To summarize trends over time for each country group, it is convenient to fit an exponential curve to obtain compound growth rates for most categories of flows which were contained in Tables 2 and 3. Differences in compound exponential growth rates among various categories of external finance contributed to shifts in composition of flows over time. These growth rates are given in Table 4 for each group of countries, where oil-exporting MICs (OXs) are segregated from oil-importing MICs and partial data are given for Indochinese countries. In the upper portion of Table 4 disaggregated component categories are given together with aggregate concepts of net flows and net transfers. Exponential growth rates for OECD external finance by source are given in lower half of Table 4. In order to translate external finance flows into real terms, it may be noted that during the period 1968 to 1983, prices (export unit value index for industrialized countries) was growing at a compound rate of 8 percent.

Credit from Commercial Sources

The role assumed by international capital market borrowings, particularly in the form of syndicated bank credits, was an outstanding feature of the external financial flows during the past decade. While an elastic supply of this source facilitated financing of large current account deficits for a number of countries, mobilization of these credits altered the average terms of external finance and therefore the burden of debt service. In Asia, as in other regions, flows from international capital markets were concentrated in those middle and higher income developing countries, whose relative economic performance rendered them creditworthy. A breakdown of gross borrowings by Asian developing country groups is given in Table 5 to indicate the concentration of capital market borrowings by MICs and NICs in East and Southeast Asia.

Although syndicated bank loans predominated throughout, bond issues acquired increased importance over time. Portfolio investment (equities and bonds) as distinguished from direct investment is subsumed under long-term borrowings in Table 2.[17] For 13 ADCs covered, portfolio investment for the period 1971-82 was reported in seven countries (Sri Lanka, Philippines, Thailand, Indonesia, Malaysia, Korea, Singapore) and amounted to $5,494.0 million or 22.8 percent of direct investment ($23,965.2 million). Certainly Eurocurrency bond issues have become a significant feature of borrowings by ADCs during the past decade — though clearly of varying significance for individual countries as shown in Table 6. However, even a low income country, India, was able to issue bonds as early as 1971, though bond issues have been relatively small for LICs with only two countries reporting Eurocurrency bond placements.

As a result of differences in access and availaments of commercial borrowings and unequal access to concessional (aid) flows, average terms of external debts varied among countries but reflected a gradual tendency to harden for MICs and NICs while for LICs this tightening trend is less pronounced and only slightly discernible after 1978.

The changes in terms of new commitments (on external public debt) are summarized in Table 7 for LICs (South Asia) and NICs and MICs (East and Southeast Asia) where grant element is a convenient index summarizing terms (where 100 percent is a pure grant) which encompass interest, maturity and grace period.[18] In the last column we provide the grant element of all loans (comprising external public debt) plus grants which is referred to as the overall grant element. Since this grant element index is higher than the grant elements of both official and private loans to LICs throughout the period 1970-1982 (except for 1974), we can infer that this subregion was benefitting from sizeable grant inflows (or official transfers) unlike MICs and NICs where the overall grant element remained in between the grant element of official and private creditors in all years. In fact, despite the fact that average terms on loans from private sources were actually harder in some years for LICs than for MICs and NICs based on grant element, overall grant element was still substantially raised by receipts of grants and scarcely diluted by credits from

---

[17] Based on the assumption that bulk of portfolio investment reported represents bonds rather than equities — which is substantiated for those Asian countries which sufficient detail is available in Balance of Payments (i.e., Malaysia, Thailand, Korea, Sri Lanka).

[18] Calculated as face value of loan less the present value of repayments (discounted at 10 per cent) expressed as a proportion of the face value. See OECD, *Development Cooperation*.

Table 5. Gross Borrowings[a] in International Capital Markets by Selected Asian Countries

(Unit: US$ million)

	Total	Euro-currency Credits	Bonds	% Distribution			
				LICs	MICs	NICs	Indochina
1971	78.2	40.0	38.2	1.5	—	98.5	—
1972	520.4	394.6	125.8	—	67.1	32.9	—
1973	696.9	533.3	163.6	1.8	51.3	41.1	—
1974	2,078.4	1,956.1	122.3	—	66.8	32.5	—
1975	3,396.9	3,317.9	79.0	0.2	67.1	30.9	1.1
1976	3,597.1	2,970.4	626.7	—	57.3	42.7	—
1977	3,175.4	2,623.5	551.9	3.6	40.3	51.9	2.3
1978	7,191.4	6,561.7	629.7	0.9	65.4	33.7	—
1979	8,602.9	7,937.0	665.9	2.9	41.0	55.2	—
1980	9,106.9	8,845.6	261.3	3.3	47.9	47.4	—
1981	12,816.6	12,298.0	518.6	12.2	36.2	49.7	—
1982	13,050.7	11,098.8	1,951.9	7.2	45.2	44.4	—
1983	11,033.5	8,750.1	2,283.4	9.7	43.2	46.3	—
1984	11,164.6	8,150.9	3,013.7	9.5	40.4	48.0	—

Sources: OECD, *Financial Statistical Monthly*, various issues.

[a] Publicized only, but believed to encompass vast majority of such borrowings.

LICs: Burma, India, Pakistan, Sri Lanka, Nepal, Bangladesh
MICs: Indonesia, Malaysia, Philippines, Thailand.
NICs: ROC (Taiwan), Hong Kong, Korea, Singapore.
Indochina: Viet Nam.

private sources which must have been relatively small to have had such limited influence on the overall grant element.

Since virtually all borrowings of LICs were undertaken by public agencies or guaranteed by government while private direct investment inflows were relatively small, the overall grant element gives a good approximation of changing terms on total inflows received by LICs.[19] However, the overall grant element is not very representative of total debt and grant flows to MICs and NICs and because they fail to consider both direct investment and sizeable borrowings without guarantee from capital market which were undertaken by borrowers in this subregion.

Although terms have been changing at the margin on increments to debt (net commitment) as depicted in Table 7, average terms of debt outstanding change rather slowly when debts are contracted at fixed terms. However, floating interest rates became a more prevalent feature of commercial borrowings during the past decade with the result that a growing proportion of outstanding debt from private sources and not just increments to debt was subject to variable interest rates.

[19] Against this growth in debt, there was growing external asset position (reflecting for most part reserve accumulation), such that South Asia had a positive net asset position during most of the period.

Table 6. Gross Borrowing in International Capital Markets
Via Bond Issues of Asian Developing Countries

(Unit: US$ million)

	1971-75	1976-80	1981-84
LICs			
India	3.7	0	824.3
Sri Lanka	0	0	11.3
MICs			
Indonesia	17.5	212.7	875.3
Malaysia	42.0	345.3	2,842.6
Philippines	67.2	955.7	98.5
Thailand	0	290.9	698.0
NICs			
ROC (Taiwan)	20.0	74.8	265.0
Hong Kong	166.1	128.3	433.9
Korea	30.9	293.1	2,067.1
Singapore	103.0	379.7	250.6

Sources: OECD, *Financial Statistics Monthly,* various issues.

Gross Flows, Net Flows and Net Transfers

Gross flows, net flows and net transfers are graphed in Figure 1 for 13 ADCs classified into (LICs), (MICs) and (NICs) with (OXs) given separately. Gross flows represent total net flows taken from balance of payments to which amortization payments are added. The deduction of interest and profit remittances from net flows gives net transfers.[20]

Grants and concessional aid flows reduce the gap between net flows and net transfers because of their respective zero and low interest charges. Similarly, longer maturities and grace periods which characterize concessional aid flows, ease the burden of annual amortizations which are reflected in the differential between gross and net flows. Increased mobilization of borrowings from commercial sources, especially by NICs and MICs during the 1970s translated into growing current account outflows to service debt (and equity) which is reflected in the growing divergence between net flows and net transfers in recent years.

Since debt service is payable in convertible foreign exchange while the original inflows are sometimes distorted and overvalued by tying, there may be significant

---

[20] Gross flows, net flows and net transfers are calculated from balance of payments data on net flows, investment outflows and repayments on loans (see preceding section) augmented by the *World Debt Tables.* Thus withdrawal of investment as occurred with nationalization of oil in Indonesia during the 1970s is neglected in this computation of gross flows. Net transfers are derived by deduction of investment outflows (debits only) representing interest and profit payments on current account. For details on individual countries, see Appendix 2.

Table 7. Terms on New Commitments on External Public Debt
by Asian Country Groups

LICs (South Asia)[a]   (Unit: %)

	Official Creditor		Private Creditor		Overall Grant Element (on Loans and Grants)
	Interest	Grant Element	Interest	Grant Element	
1971	2.3	60.3	6.6	12.5	65
1972	1.8	66.2	5.2	22.1	68
1973	2.2	61.2	5.3	26.1	64
1974	2.4	58.2	8.3	4.7	60
1975	2.3	61.6	7.7	10.7	67
1976	3.1	54.6	7.9	6.1	60
1977	2.4	63.0	7.5	10.8	67
1978	1.7	69.7	8.3	8.0	74
1979	2.0	64.3	11.0	−2.2	69
1980	1.9	64.8	13.0	−15.8	58
1981	3.1	58.0	12.4	−11.3	60
1982	4.1	50.9	12.7	−12.6	50
1983	3.3	57.2	9.0	3.2	60

NICs and MICs (East and Southeast Asia)[b]

	Official Creditor		Private Creditor		Overall Grant Element (on Loans and Grants)
	Interest	Grant Element	Interest	Grant Element	
1971	4.7	40.2	7.6	9.6	39
1972	4.4	41.9	8.0	7.4	36
1973	3.9	48.3	9.8	0.8	34
1974	5.3	33.7	9.1	4.7	19
1975	6.9	21.8	8.9	3.8	16
1976	7.2	19.0	8.3	6.6	15
1977	6.6	23.2	8.1	7.7	19
1978	6.0	28.3	9.5	1.8	15
1979	5.6	31.2	10.2	−1.8	16
1980	6.5	24.6	13.4	−16.4	7
1981	7.9	14.6	12.5	−12.1	1
1982	9.0	7.6	11.5	−8.3	0

Source: World Bank, *Annual Reports* and *World Debt Tables*.

   [a] South Asia: Bangladesh, Burma, India, Maldives, Nepal, Pakistan, Sri Lanka.
   [b] East Asia and Pacific: Fiji, Hong Kong, Indonesia, Korea, Malaysia, Papua New Guinea, Philippines, Singapore, Solomon Islands, Thailand, Western Samoa.

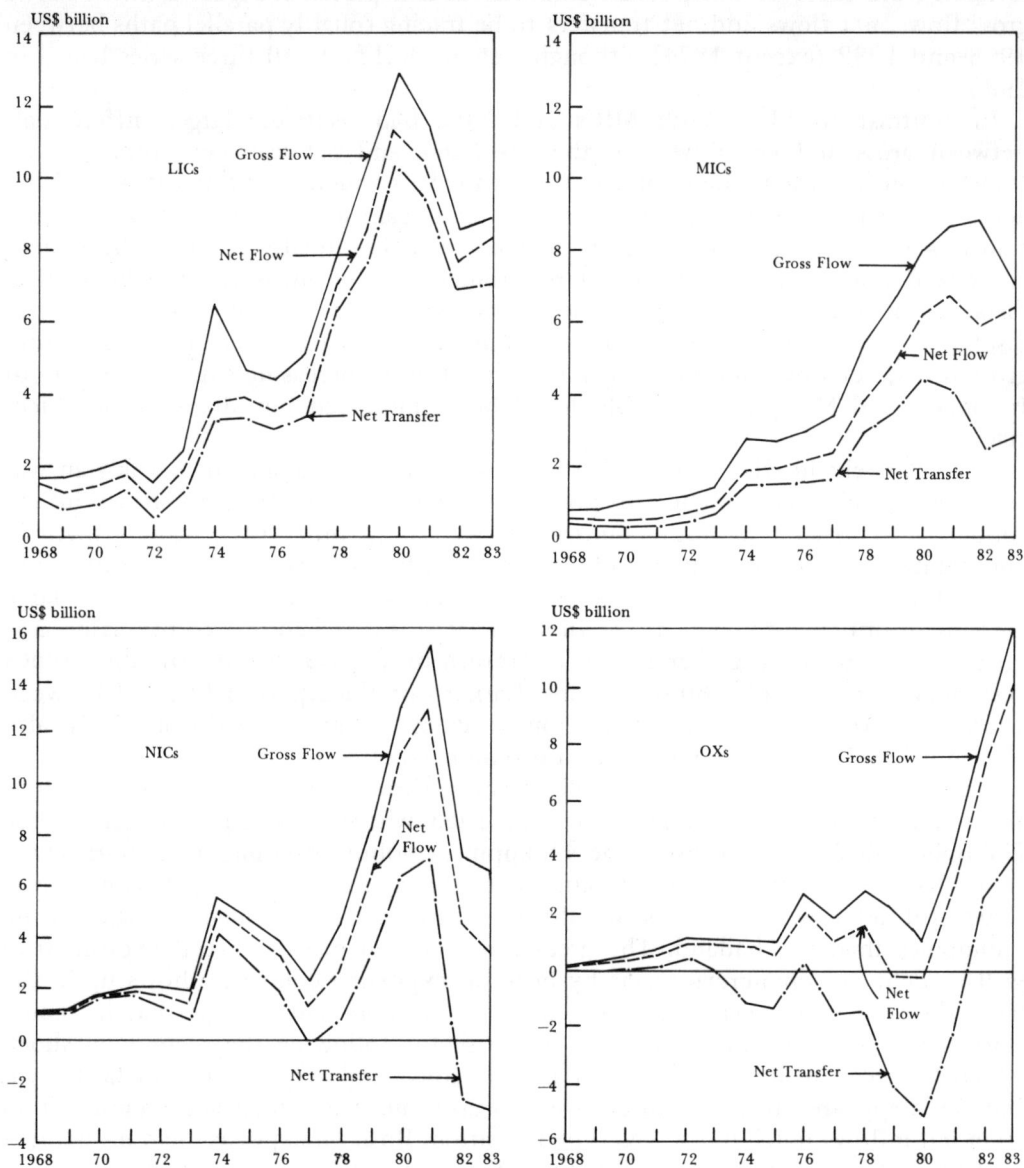

Sources: IMF, *Balance of Payments Yearbook;* World Bank, *World Debt Tables* and Tape.

    LICs: Bangladesh, Burma, India, Pakistan, Sri Lanka, Nepal.
    MICs: Philippines. Thailand.
    NICs: ROC (Taiwan), Singapore, Korea.
    OXs: Indonesia, Malaysia.

Figure 1. Gross Flow, Net Flow and Net Transfer
to Asian Country Groups, 1963-1983 (At Current Prices)

overstatement of gross and net flows, as well as net transfers while debt service and profit remittances are not subject to similar distortions.[21] The experience of LICs differed from those of other Asian countries as is depicted in Figure 1 which shows gross flows, net flows and net transfers to be tracing roughly parallel paths between 1968 and 1982 (except 1974) although a sharp decline in all three series began in 1980.

In contrast to LICs, both MICs and NICs had relatively larger differentials between gross and net flows, on the one hand, and between net flows and net transfers on the other; these differentials tended to widen over time. In fact, NICs actually had negative net transfers in 1977 and again in 1982 and 1983 while net transfers of MICs remained positive throughout. The relatively heavy burden of amortization and interest and profit remittances can be measured by the vertical distances between gross flows and net transfers. OXs are presented separately and display distinctly different experience from other groups in recent years in that gross flows, net flows and net transfers have all been increasing since 1980 as both Indonesia and Malaysia were able to mobilize increased net flows as oil prices stagnated.

The relatively heavier debt service burden of India as compared to Pakistan was reflected in relatively smaller proportion of net transfers to gross flows in the former.[22] In general in both countries as well as in other LICs, slow growth in amortization and investment (largely interest) outflows kept profiles of gross flows, net flows and net transfers in relatively close alignment over time. The very large amount of principal repayments of India in 1974 is matched by exceptionally large grant inflows which together reflect the return by the US to India of rupee funds accumulated out of PL 480 operations. Earlier installments of debt relief between 1968-73 as well as debt relief operations in Pakistan between 1971 and 1978 also altered debt service profile but without pronounced effects.

Non-oil MICs, Thailand and the Philippines, show similar patterns of growth in flows and transfers over time, except in 1983 where flows and transfers in the Philippines declined. However, the Philippines mobilized commercial borrowings somewhat earlier and in larger amounts with the result that the gap between gross flows and net flows as well as net flows and net transfers widened earlier in the Philippines than in Thailand. The greater reliance on private direct investment as well as debt at commercial terms by both oil exporting countries shows up in the large divergence between net flows and net transfers and this gap has increased since 1973. Prior to the slowdown in oil sector following the second oil shock which led to sharp increases in gross and net flows and net transfers, Malaysia and Indonesia appeared to be moving toward negative net transfer suggesting graduation from aid inflows much like a NIC type transition. Both oil exporters had investment outflows which were substantially larger than principal repayments and reflected preponderance of direct investment outflows over interest outflows.

While the large gap between net flows and net transfers largely reflected interest on long-term borrowings in Korea, Singapore's investment outflows reflected a relatively smaller proportion of interest vis-a-vis dividend payments. Consequently,

---

[21] See N. Islam "The External Debt Problem of the Developing Countries with Special Reference to the Least Developed" in *A World Divided*, 1976. Alternatively tied loans have effective interest costs which exceed nominal rates. See C. Frank, Jr. "Debt and Terms of Aid", Overseas Development Council, (Monograph), 1970.

[22] The discussion in this and the next two paras are based on data on individual country patterns contained in Appendix 2.

the burden of loan repayments were smaller in Singapore in contrast to heavy amortizations paid by Korea. Despite increases in external financing coinciding with the first and second oil shocks, oil importer ROC (Taiwan) did not mobilize borrowings at commercial terms to a significant extent to respond to oil shocks and kept gross, net flows and net transfers in rather close alignment, like LICs, although creditworthiness was presumably not a constraining factor here. Before the occurrence of a second oil shock the ROC (Taiwan) appeared to be moving toward termination of debtor status with growing negative transfers between 1976 and 1978. Although this trend was reversed in the next three years, a sharp reduction to a negative position was resumed in 1982 and 1983.

The size of net transfers is determined by the terms of repayments on debt (and equity) as well as by the growth of debt. As long as growth of debt exceeds the average rate of interest paid on it, net transfers will remain positive.[23] It can thus be concluded that interest rates in excess of 10 percent which have become prevalent on commercial credits imply quite high required growth rates of net borrowing to prevent transfers from becoming negative. But continuous high growth in gross borrowing is only sustainable under certain favorable economic circumstances. The variability in average interest rates enhanced by the mechanism of floating rate debt necessitates concomitant variability in gross or net borrowing if a positive transfer is to be maintained.[24] Accordingly, if amortization and interest payments are fixed contractual obligations, a sudden downturn in gross borrowing can impose financial strain as debt service obligations continue regardless of a country's capacity to raise new funds. Alternatively, if average terms on external finance are hardening as they can rather quickly when substantial amounts of debt outstanding are subject to variable interest rates, a constant net transfer requires accelerating gross flows.

So long as a country has a positive resource gap, negative transfers are premature and imply that external resources are no longer augmenting investment and growth and in fact are imposing adverse balance of payments effects.[25] There is nothing inherently unhealthy about a negative net transfer which is, after all, inevitable for a country terminating its status as a debtor country as NICs appear to be doing. Moreover, countries have occasionally made advance repayments when external conditions permitted, thus voluntarily depressing net flows.

To improve net transfers (setting aside the important but conceptually distinct possibility of improving internal allocation of resources in a developing country) requires easing terms of new borrowings or easing terms on existing debt (prior borrowings). Since donors have only agreed to retroactive adjustment/cancellations of terms on existing debts to a rather limited extent and then generally only for the least developed,[26] a major means for improving net transfers then rests with

[23] This principle was established mathematically by E. Domar, "The Effect of Foreign Investment on Balance of Payments," in *Essays in the Theory of Economic Growth,* 1957.

[24] If we infer that required rate of return on new direct investment must exceed interest cost on borrowing at the margin, private direct investment must grow faster than borrowings to ensure positive transfer. Private Direct Investment then has the effect of raising the required growth of net external finance above that based on debt alone. However, if profits fail to materialize, remittance of profits may be suspended while debt service would not be. It is this flexibility rather than implied cost which makes equity finance now more attractive (as well as possibility that shortfalls in realized profit on equity investment now reduce outflows though this must be empirically validated).

[25] Thus, for example, a country (like the Philippines) which is unable to generate adequate new loans (because of lack of creditworthiness) but must still service interest component of debt service even during a debt moratorium, may actually experience negative transfers.

[26] See OECD, *DAC Review,* for examples.

changing the blend of new borrowings in favor of those with higher grant elements, namely ODA or other official flows, to bring down average costs. Although heavier gross borrowings even at commercial terms can temporarily increase the level of net transfers, they impose a future debt service burden and cannot contribute to lasting relief or improvements in net transfers (unless interest costs and maturities are expected to soften).

It is also possible to improve net flows and net transfers via debt relief which may or may not be accompanied by fresh inflows. Debt relief encompasses cancellation, refinancing and rescheduling. Cancellation has not taken place as part of official multilateral debt relief operations (thru Paris Club) or, where commercial bank debt bulks large, via commercial bank reschedulings. Refinancing has been seldom used. The most common form of debt relief has involved rescheduling which usually applies to principal due over 1 to 2 year period.[27] Rescheduling usually involves stretching out maturities and in recent experience interest rates applied close to market rates.[28] Moreover the spread above LIBOR on commercial bank debt is usually larger on rescheduled debt and post-moratorium new finance than on pre-moratorium borrowings.[29]

Linkages Between External Finance and Investment

In this section we examine, with the assistance of regression analysis, alternative aggregate and disaggregated concepts of external finance to evaluate investment propensities with respect to each individual component of external finance including investment outflows which reduce the amount of external finance available for investment purposes. This investigation has its roots in a long standing controversy as to whether foreign savings substitute for domestic savings, which was the finding of various empirical studies.[30] A second concern is whether mobilization of external finance has contributed to deterioration in incremental capital output ratio which is a proxy for marginal productivity of capital. The efficacy of foreign capital inflows can be undermined by consumption leakages on the one hand and deterioration in the incremental capital output ratio on the other. The linkages between growth and foreign capital are explored using two single equation models, estimated by ordinary least squares with dummy variables, and variance components methods on pooled time series data to estimate average behavior across a sample of 13 ADCs.[31]

In theory, financial resources are fungible and substitutable; in practice, they may be considerably less so. Therefore, a critical question is to what extent external financing for investment releases resources for consumption. If external finance augments resources available to a country in the current period, it can increase both consumption and investment possibilities. Moreover, we would expect debt and equity service requirements to be negatively related to investment because they represent withdrawal of resources available for domestic use. If consumption leak-

---

[27] This para is largely based on C. Hardy, *Rescheduling Developing Countries 1956-81: Lessons and Recommendations*, 1982, pp. 24-25.

[28] *Ibid.*, pp. 24-25.

[29] William Cline, "International Debt and the Stability of the World Economy," in *Policy Analyses in International Economies, No. 4*, 1983, pp. 82-87.

[30] See, for example, Weisskopf, op. cit. and Meier, *Leading Issues in Economic Development*. 1976.

[31] See Appendix 3.

ages can be minimized, this strengthens chances that foreign investment can add to productive capacity. Foreign capital should have little influence on investment if, in fact, it largely substitutes for domestic savings. On the other hand, if propensities to invest differ systematically according to the source of finance, this would have important implications for borrowing and aid strategies.[32] If certain forms of finance have higher investment propensities and indeed are channeled into distinctive investment applications, external borrowing and debt management may be improved.

An implicit proposition in many critiques of foreign aid is that aid is unlikely to be productive precisely because it is subsidized.[33] Much of bilateral and multilateral flows is project-type aid and so contributes directly to investment. By the same token, project loans financed at commercial terms should be associated with more demanding standards of financial profitability and investment augmentation. To the extent that official loans are used to finance specific kinds of projects, say infrastructure investment, to which private capital is too short-sighted to engage and/or whose benefits may be difficult to appropriate but which have high social (though not necessarily private) profitability, there may be systematic differences between public and private sector investment in their productivity aspects. However, here disparities between social and private incentives may arise from the system of protection. Opportunity costs diverge from market prices due to market failure and various interventions in product and factor markets.

Private direct investment while associated with most stringent expected returns may in fact be the least fungible form of external capital. Presumably, it flows in response to very specific investment opportunities and in that respect is not easily substitutable (but whether it augments or displaces other domestic investment and enterprise remains an open question). However, from a debt or equity service viewpoint, its firm linkage to investment instills some confidence that it will generate its own repayment. However, investment itself is influenced by the policy setting particularly factor market distortions, exchange rates and structure of protection. Thus, we look at the relationship first between real investment and foreign sources of finance, and second between real investment and component of foreign finance which may be important for its productivity implications.

To investigate whether different types of finance have different implications for investment (investment propensities) we use the following partial equilibrium framework to describe investment behavior:

$$I = f(GNP, F)$$

where investment (I) is specified in real terms and foreign capital (F) is decomposible into $F_1 \ldots F_n$ components (see Table 2), and GNP is proxy for all other excluded explanatory variables.[34]

By estimating a single equation model of the investment function without taking explicit consideration of the fact that GNP is also simultaneously a function of investment, we are simply examining the first round impact of external finance on investment and ignoring possible secondary effects which arise because increments

---

[32] This kind of reasoning apparently underlies preference of some economists for project over program aid because of its closer linkages to investment applications. Cf, Harberger. But for opposing views see Ohlin, *op. cit.*, p. 222 and N. Islam, *op. cit.*, p. 239.

[33] See, for example, Bauer in Meier, op. cit.

[34] If GNP is endogenous, then single equation may not yield consistent and unbiased estimates though in small samples the former property may not matter.

to income also eventually add to investment. An alternative specification is tested using lagged investment as an additional explanatory variable. In both models, both GNP and F are expected to be positively correlated with real investment.

The results of least squares regressions using dummy variables on data transformed to remove heteroscedasticity are given in Table 8. For each of the six equations the estimated coefficients are presented with t-statistics given below in parentheses to test the null hypothesis that the coefficient on F is different from 1. The adjusted R^2 and F statistics are significant in all cases. Country dummies are omitted from the table, but were significant in all equations.

The disaggregated external finance variables regardless of their decomposition, are expected to have a positive sign, while investment outflows are expected to have a negative sign because they reduce resources available to the country for investment. If there are no leakages to consumption, the coefficients of the components of external finance would be unity. Similarly the coefficients would be −1 if payments are financed wholly out of investment. Although "other" flows were significantly different from zero in all of the models, no analytical significance is attached to this residual category of external finance. A dummy variable DUM was also included in all models to detect whether an upward shift in investment occurred in the post oil shock period and was found to be significant in most specifications but only marginally so in equations (4) and (5) in Table 8. Such a finding is consistent with the hypothesis that balance of payments shocks may have been due to domestic factors such as increments in investment rather than external disturbances.[35]

The inclusion of lagged investment in a model with a partial adjustment or distributed lag specification (equation 6 in Table 8) appears to reduce the coefficients of external financing components sufficiently so that all become significantly different from one. However, the long-run coefficient of GNPR obtained by setting I_{-1} equal to I_0 are substantially closer to those models without a lagged investment variable. The following discussion therefore focusses on equations (1) to (5) in Table 8.[36]

Equation (1) which represents the simplest disaggregation of foreign capital into two components, the variables representing aggregate net flows (FLOW)[37] and investment outflows (IOUT) had the expected signs. However, while the marginal propensity to invest out of foreign flows was significantly less than 1, the coefficient of outflows was not found to be significantly different from −1. Nevertheless the marginal propensity to invest out of foreign inflows is higher than the marginal propensity to invest out of GNP. In equation (2) net flows are further decomposed into four constituent parts, all (unrequited) transfers (TRN), private direct investment (PDI), all borrowings (BORR) and other flows (OTHER), along with investment outflows (IOUT) as before. Here the coefficient is lowest for unrequited transfers (.004), higher for borrowings (.239) and highest for private direct investment (.762). Further decomposition of unrequited transfers (TRN) into private (PTRN) and official (OTRN), and all borrowings (BORR) into short-term borrowings (STBOR) and long-term borrowings (LTBOR), are contained in equations (3) and (4), respectively.

[35] As suggested by Sachs, op. cit.

[36] The long-run coefficients of GNP, PDI and Borrowings are close to those estimated by Equations (1) to (5) without a lagged investment regressor, while coefficient on TRN was significantly different from unity but higher than in Equations (1) to (5), and that of IOUT was significantly smaller than −1.

[37] Net of amortization but not interest and dividends.

Table 8. LSDV Regression Results: Real Investment on Selected Explanatory Variables (1968-81)*

Equation	GNPR	FLOW	IOUT	TRN	PDI	BORR	OTHER	LGI	PTRN	OTRN	STBOR	LTBOR	D	$\bar{R}^2$	F
(1)	.117 (7.1)	.217 (9,65)	-1.388 ns										.015 (1.82)	.9188	31.88
(2)	.115 (6.78)		-1.278 ns	.004 (3.61)	.762 ns	.239 (8.64)	-.002 (1.78)						.0187 (2.05)	.9236	26.73
(3)	.116 (6.98)		-1.183 ns		.724 ns	.253 (8.51)	.041 (1.75)		-.339 (3.88)	1.037 ns			.021 (2.31)	.9281	26.47
(4)	.113 (6.85)		-1.051 ns	.0499 (3.52)	.914 ns		-.024 (1.88)				.140 (8.46)	.773 ns	.011 ns	.9294	27.0
(5)	.114 (6.97)		-1.007 ns		.861 ns		.014 (1.83)		-.232 (3.55)	.873 ns	.166 (8.10)	.709 ns	.013 ns	.9322	26.20
(6)	.0744 (4.60)		-.041 (3.11)	.127 (3.86)	.387 (1.70)	.126 (11.50)	.005 (2.19)	.496 (4.74)					.018 (2.47)	.9294	39.51

t — statistic in parentheses, if significant at .10 or less country dummies not presented.

GNPR — real GNP	PDI — private direct investment	PTRN — private transfers
FLOW — net flows	BORR — all borrowings	OTRN — official transfers
IOUT — Investment outflows	OTHER — "other" flows	LTBOR — long term borrowings
TRN — all transfers	LGI — lagged Investment	STBOR — short term borrowings
		DUM — post shock dummy variable
		LSDV — lease squares with dummy variable

Memo: Long run coefficients of Equation (6)

.48   -.081   .250   .768   .250   .121
(9.22) (2.02) (3.31) ns (9.87) (1.94)

* See Appendix C for details on data.

Only private direct investment (PDI) and investment outflows (IOUT) were not significantly different from hypothesized value of 1 and —1, respectively. The high coefficient on PDI is in consonance with the hypothesis that direct investment is not fungible. That is, foreign capital inflows stimulate domestic investment which would not have occurred otherwise and therefore can have a coefficient significantly larger than 1. The coefficient of combined borrowings variable is however significantly smaller than 1 in equations (2) and (3). A further disaggregation however showed that this was not due to long-term borrowings, which did not differ significantly from 1, while the coefficient of short-term borrowings was much smaller. A similar disaggregation of unrequited transfers into its private and official components showed that the low (significantly less than one) coefficient on transfers was entirely attributable to private transfers as official transfers had coefficients not significantly different from unity. The coefficients of private transfers while significantly less than one were not significantly different from zero. The inclusion of workers' remittances as a component of private transfers which has been a rapidly growing source of foreign finance for many countries in Asia may explain its consumption augmenting effect. By contrast the coefficient of official transfers suggests that they are not channeled to consumption but are found instead to be substantially investment augmenting.[38]

The second linkage between productivity and foreign capital focuses on aggregate gross incremental capital-output ratio as a proxy for capital productivity. Here we examined the hypothesis that foreign capital inflows contribute to overall capital efficiency by regressing incremental capital-output ratios on an aggregate external finance variable, the foreign saving rate. A priori, either a negative or positive relationship would be plausible.

Our findings from regression analysis is on the average, for countries in the sample, ICORs were negatively associated with foreign capital inflows as a share of GNP and positively associated with investment rate.[39] Subject to the usual

---

[38] By dividing the sample into two groups, LICs and non-LICs, it was intended to examine differences in investment propensities between country groups as LICs were known to have had limited inflows of commercial bank borrowings and private direct investment as compared to MICs (including OXs) and NICs. The F-test on equality of coefficients between two groups could not be rejected. However, the large apparent differences in coefficients between two groups may be attributable to multicollinearity between regressors, especially since those countries which had high official transfers tended to be those with low private direct investment and low borrowings. Multicollinearity is further suggested by significant F-ratio but insignificant t-statistics on external finance variables in aggregate flow model (see equation 1) runon pooled data for LICs.

[39] By including the investment rate as another explanatory variable to represent differences in per capita income levels or capital deepening which accompanies structural change in the course of development, we have the following model:

ICOR = h(F/GNP, I/GNP)

where $ICOR_{t-1} = (I_{t-1})/(GNP_t - GNP_{t-1})$

Three models were tried: (i) ordinary least squares, (ii) least squares with dummy variables, and (iii) variance component estimates with best results given by the second model using semi-log specification and is reproduced below.

$$\ln ICOR_t = -1.40(F/GNP)_t + 6.63(I/GNP)_t \ldots (7)$$
$$(2.01) \qquad (4.30)$$

$R^2 = .5382$
$F = 3.75$

The best linear specification was given by the variance components estimate:

$$ICOR_t = -.1097 - 4.96(F/GNP)_t + 19.36(I/GNP)_t$$
$$(1.32) \qquad (2.58)$$

$R^2 = .1206$
$F = 3.91$

The signs are the same as equation (7) but the t-value of the foreign capital coefficient is significant only at 20 percent.

caveats on the limitations of ICORs, we conclude that when the investment rate is held constant a one percentage point increase in foreign capital to GNP ratio is associated with a decrease in the log of ICOR by 1.4 percentage points.[40]

Our results contrast with those of an earlier study which used a linear specification of a similar model on a pooled time series regression using a sample of 22 developing countries for 1950s and 1960s. This study established a significant positive relationship between ICOR and foreign saving rate, while the coefficient of investment rate was negative, which are just opposite of our findings on Asian countries in a later period.[41]

Subject to the limitations of the single equation models in which econometric work was conducted, our examination of linkages between external finance and investment yields some interesting implications for both donor and recipient countries. Each component of external finance has a different first round implication for investment, ranging from private direct investment inflow, long-term borrowings and official transfers which have largest investment augmenting contribution. However, investment outflows representing debt and equity service have a fully diminishing effect on investment. Short-term borrowings have significantly lower investment propensities while private transfers did not contribute positively to investment at all. This last statistical result, however, may be associated with the different treatment of workers remittances among countries which deserves further investigation. These remittances might more appropriately be separated from other private transfers, as they may represent current income inflows which finance consumption of the workers' families.

High investment propensities would not be a sufficient argument for reconstituting external capital inflows (to the extent that there is substitutability which is most doubtful for direct investment and other components in the short-run). If there is inefficiency or waste in application of investment, then more investment spending does not necessarily contribute to growth. On this matter the regression of ICOR on the foreign saving rate suggests that capital efficiency or quality is not adversely effected by larger foreign savings inflows (in relation to GNP) when variation in investment rate is taken into consideration.[42]

BALANCE OF PAYMENTS AND EXTERNAL DEBT SITUATIONS

Foreign capital inflow contributes to economic development through higher investment and technology transfer. Empirical analysis reported in the previous section supports this hypothesis by finding out that foreign capital generally played a positive role in increasing investment in ADCs. Foreign capital inflows, on the other hand, may bring about the accumulation of external debts and make the recipient countries more vulnerable to fluctuations in world economy. This section looks into the external debt aspect of foreign capital inflows.

---

[40] There are well known difficulties in estimating and interpreting aggregate ICORs. One difficulty is choice of lag. Another is that marginal product is a ceteris paribus concept where ICOR measured empirically allows other inputs to vary. Only when there is no substitutability between capital and labor or where labor is in surplus so its marginal product is zero, is the reciprocal of ICOR equal to the marginal product of capital. Finally, valuation of output is subject to policy distortions in the domestic prices of a country.

[41] See Voivodas, "Exports, Foreign Capital Inflow and Economic Growth," in *Journal of International Economics*, Vol. 3, 1973. Foreign savings appears to have been defined as net imports of goods and country dummies were included. His use of gross (without deduction of amortization interest and dividends) rather than net transfers may have also contributed to the difference in results.

[42] Nevertheless, critical interest rate analysis in the following section, Table 17, points to a secular erosion in debt service capacity which is largely attributed to increases in ICORs for a number of countries between 1966-75 adn 1976-82.

The rapid growth of external debts of developing countries and the unprecedented number and amount of debt reschedulings have brought serious concern about the stability of present international financial system as well as the sustainability of foreign capital inflows to developing countries.[43] External debts are not only an issue for the debtor developing countries but also a serious problem for the international financial system as a whole.

The origin of the debt crisis in early 1980s is debatable, but it is generally agreed that both domestic and external factors were responsible for the crisis. The increase in oil prices during the first and second oil shock periods compelled the oil-importing developing countries to borrow heavily to meet their increasing current account deficits. At the same time, international banks, with ample deposits, responded quickly to the credit demand of developing countries. The low, and sometimes negative, real interest rates prevailing in the 1970s provided a strong incentive for developing countries to increase their borrowings from international commercial banks.

The external debt problem of developing countries aggravated in 1980-82 due to the prolonged global recession and high real interest rates. Particularly, the global recession had an adverse effect on the price and volume of developing countries' exports, the increase of which is essential for the repayment of their debt. Furthermore, abnormally high real interest rates and increasing dependence of developing countries on commercial bank financing with variable interest rates contributed to the rapid increase in interest payments.

The external debt situation of developing countries, however, improved significantly in 1983-84. The build-up in the total outstanding external debt (nominal) of developing countries decelerated from an annual rate of 11 percent in 1980-82, to 8 percent in 1983, and to about 5 percent in both 1984 and 1985. The deceleration was the result of the tightening of external financial conditions, and of the greater relative importance of non-debt-creating flows in financing current account deficits.[44] Although this recent improvement has led to some easing of external debt problems of developing countries, it should be remembered that a slowdown in world economic recovery and/or an increase in protectionism in industrial countries may easily trigger another round of external debt crisis.

Compared with the debt-servicing difficulties experienced by some African and Latin American countries, the situation of ADCs except in the case of the Philippines, was much less serious. It should, however, be noted that Korea, Indonesia, India, the Philippines, Thailand and Malaysia are heavily indebted and the possibility of debt difficulties in these countries cannot be precluded. Moreover, during the coming decade it is expected that the capital flows, especially concessional flows, from developed to developing countries will grow more slowly than they did in the 1960s and 1970s. This implies that external debt problems and the lower levels of foreign capital inflows may emerge as critical constraints to the economic development plans of many developing countries, at least as they have been previously envisioned.

---

[43] International financial institutions such as IMF, World Bank, OECD and BIS endeavored to deal with debt problems of developing countries by providing relevant data, analyzing debt situations, making projections for the years to come and making suggestions for the resolution of global as well as individual country debt problems. Analysts in the governments of developed and developing countries, research institutes, international banks and academic circles also expressed their serious concern on this issue. Research works on this issue are too abundant to be summarized here.

[44] See IMF, *World Economic Outlook,* April 1986, p. 70.

With this background, this section first reviews the developments in the balance of payments of ADCs. Then the external debt situation of these countries will be discussed with a view to assessing the severity of external debt problems as a constraint to economic growth.

Developments in the Balance of Payments

During the last 15 years most of ADCs experienced current account deficits (see Table 9). Only the ROC (Taiwan) recorded current account surplus over the period. In amount Korea had the biggest cumulative current account deficit ($27 billion) followed by Thailand ($16.6 billion) and the Philippines ($16.4 billion). For these countries, trade deficits were the main reason for current account deficits.

Some countries such as India, Pakistan and Bangladesh had huge trade deficits but their deficits were largely covered by private and official transfers. Among ADCs Singapore had the biggest trade deficit ($46.2 billion) during the last 15 years but it was mainly covered by the surplus in the invisible trade account. It is interesting to note that the huge trade surpluses of the oil-exporting Indonesia and Malaysia did not imply current account surpluses because of their much bigger invisible trade deficits.

Changes in the balance of trade deficits (or surpluses) are caused by changes in the prices of exports and imports as well as by changes in their volume. The former is called the terms of trade (TOT) effect,[45] the latter the volume effect. The TOT of ADCs have generally deteriorated during the last decade except in oil-exporting Indonesia and Malaysia. Among NICs, Korea and the ROC (Taiwan) experienced significant deterioration in their TOT. The non-oil MICs, the Philippines and Thailand were hard hit by the rapid increase in their import prices. On the other hand, two OXs experienced improvement in their TOT. Most LICs were seriously affected by TOT deterioration due mainly to a rapid increase in their import prices.[46]

Partly due to the deterioration in their TOT and partly due to the increase in their domestic investment[47] non-oil ADCs generally experienced balance of trade deficit during the period 1974-1982 (see Table 10). Among non-oil ADCs, only the ROC (Taiwan) could achieve a favorable balance of trade during the period. The performance of this country is particularly impressive since its volume effect outweighed its big negative TOT effect. Korea also achieved a positive volume effect, but it was not enough to offset its huge negative TOT effect. Two OXs, Indonesia and Malaysia, had a positive TOT effect due to the oil price hike enabling them to achieve a favorable balance of trade. Malaysia has gained in both TOT and volume effects, while Indonesia's TOT effect was partly offsetted by its negative volume effect.

The annual TOT effect can be added up to produce the cumulative TOT effects. The cumulative TOT effect of Korea during 1974-82 reached $24.7 billion. The other ADCs whose cumulative TOT effect exceeded $10 billion include Singapore

---

[45] The calculation of the terms of trade effect reported here does not consider the dynamic effect of terms of trade changes on exports and imports.

[46] See earlier section for the definitions of NICs, MICs, OXs, and LICs.

[47] See section 'Financing of Investment' and Table 1 for the changes in investment rates in ADCs. According to Sachs, op. cit, different investment activities among countries are at least as important as oil price changes in explaining current account deficit. This section, however, does not examine the effects of investment on current account deficit.

Table 9. Cumulative Balance of Payments of Asian Developing Countries (1970-1984)

(Unit: US$ million)

| | Current Account Balance | Breakdown of Current Account Balance | | | Sources of Finance[1] | | |
		Trade Balance	Balance in Other Goods and Services	Net Trans-fers	Direct Invest-ment	Long-Term Borrowing	Short-Term Borrowing
NICs							
Korea	−27,168	−27,362	−5,019	5,213	637	23,999	7,281
Singapore	−12,204	−46,202	34,881	−883	12,952	609	7,711
ROC (Taiwan)	+16,735	26,479	−10,042	298	1,205	5,983	−10,066
MICs							
Non-oil							
Philippines	−16,408	−16,272	−4,811	4,674	724	9,850	4,448
Thailand	−16,609	−15,308	−6,677	5,374	2,088	10,359	5,004
OXs							
Indonesia	−14,872	43,060	−58,968	1,034	2,362	24,354	−8,670
Malaysia	−10,576	14,326	−24,446	−555	9,157	10,261	−6,086
LICs							
Bangladesh[2]	−5,286	−12,148	−2,509	9,371	0	4,861	10
Burma[3]	−2,508	−2,542	−497	530	0	2,092	190
India[4]	−3,339	−19,099	−3,377	19,133	−29	7,342	−1,853
Nepal[5]	−411	−1,830	546	873	0	379	100
Pakistan[3]	−9,375	−21,813	−5,209	17,646	442	5,904	1,382
Sri Lanka	−2,673	−3,669	−1,560	2,556	276	2,387	72

Source: IMF, *International Financial Statistics*, Yearbook.

1 These three items do not exactly add up to current account balance, since other items are left out.
2 1973-84.
3 1970-83.
4 1970-82.
5 1976-84.

Table 10. Balance of Trade, Terms of Trade Effect and Volume Effect
(1974-1982; Annual Averages)

(Unit: US$ million)

	Balance of Trade	Terms of Trade Effect	Volume Effect
NICs			
Hong Kong	−1,518	−1,027	−491
Korea	−2,384	−2,751	367
Singapore	−3,512	−2,000	−1,512
ROC (Taiwan)	1,089	−1,043	2,132
MICs			
Indonesia	3,891	5,647	−1,756
Malaysia	1,087	1,047	40
Philippines	−1,362	−1,575	213
Thailand	−1,001	−1,234	233
LICs			
Bangladesh	−910	−272	−638
Burma	−222	−155	--67
India	−1,135	−1,719	584
Pakistan	−1,977	−1,381	−596
Sri Lanka	−303	−330	27

Sources: IMF, *International Financial Statistics* (Tape and 1983 Yearbook).

($18.0 billion), the Philippines ($14.1 billion), India ($12.0 billion), Pakistan ($12.4 billion) and Thailand ($11.1 billion). Elsewhere it has been demonstrated that in most ADCs cumulative TOT effect during the last decade was larger than the increase in their long-term debt during the same period.[48]

The burden of a current account deficit to each country might be assessed better by the ratio of its current account deficit to its exports of goods and services or GDP than by the deficit's absolute amount. Ratios of current account deficits to goods and services exports were particularly high in most LICs because of their low exports. On average the ratio for LICs exceeded 30 per cent (see Table 11). The ratios for non-oil MICs as well as those of OXs were not relatively high in the 1970s, but they increased significantly in recent years. Among NICs, Korea had a relatively high ratio during 1970-1982, but the ratio has decreased substantially since 1982.

During 1970-1982, the ratio of current account deficits to GDP was high in Singapore, Korea, Pakistan and Bangladesh. However, the ratio of Korea has decreased in recent years. On the other hand, those of non-oil MICs have increased indicating worsening balance of payment situation. In the case of OXs, this ratio seems to have increased in recent years because of the fall in oil prices. Singapore is the country which had by far the highest ratio among ADCs during last 15 years

---

[48] See Jungsoo Lee, *ADB Economic Office Report Series No. 25*, 1985.

Table 11. Current Account Balance as Percentage of Exports and GDP
(Annual Averages)

(Unit: %)

	Current Account Balance as percentage of Exports		Current Account Balance as percentage of GDP	
	1970-1982	1983-1984	1970-1982	1983-1984
NICs	−9.1	3.2	−5.8	0.9
Korea	−20.9	−4.7	−5.4	−1.9
Singapore	−10.5	−3.2	−14.0	−6.0[4]
ROC (Taiwan)	4.1	17.6	2.0	10.5
MICs	−11.8	−22.1	−2.7	−7.1
Indonesia	−9.7	−20.6	−1.6	−8.1[4]
Malaysia	−4.5	−14.9	−2.2	−8.4
Philippines	−15.7	−24.7	−3.2	−5.8
Thailand	−17.2	−28.1	−3.8	−6.0
LICs	−32.2	−34.1	−3.1	−5.5
Bangladesh	−72.6[1]	−21.6	−4.7	−2.0
Burma	−48.2	−77.6[2]	−3.5	−5.6[4]
India	−3.1	..	−0.1	−
Nepal	−8.7[3]	−43.2	−1.1	−6.3[4]
Pakistan	−44.1	−11.9	−5.1	−9.2
Sri Lanka	−16.5	−16.4	−4.3	−4.6

Source: IMF, *International Financial Statistics*, Yearbook, 1985.

[1] 1973-1982.
[2] 1983.
[3] 1976-1982.
[4] 1983.
[5] Figures for country groups are simple averages of individual country ratios.

on the average, but since its deficit has largely been financed by foreign direct investment, servicing external debts has not been a problem.[49]

The current account deficit can be financed by foreign direct investment, long-term borrowing, short-term borrowing and/or drawing down of international reserves. Among ADCs, Singapore relied most heavily on foreign direct investment, while the Republic of Korea, Indonesia, the Philippines, Thailand and most LICs depended mainly on long-term borrowings (see Table 9). Foreign direct investment was negligible in LICs. Malaysia depended almost equally on foreign direct investment and long-term borrowings to finance its current account deficit.

The accumulation of external debt is closely related to the developments in current accounts and their financing. By definition, the countries that relied heavily

---

[49] However, as the inflows of Asian dollars into Singapore increase, the external debt situation of Singapore could become serious in the future.

on the long-term or short-term borrowings incurred large amounts of external debt, while the countries that financed their current account deficit by foreign direct investment generally accumulated less debt. Singapore belongs to the latter group, Korea, Thailand, the Philippines, Indonesia and most LICs belong to the former group.

External Debt Situations

Reflecting their sustained current account deficits, public long-term debt of ADCs increased rapidly at an average annual rate of 15.8 percent during 1970-1983, reaching $119 billion at the end of 1983 (see Table 12). This implies a real annual growth of 9 percent during the same period.[50] There were, however, marked differences in growth rates between the country groups. The public debt of LICs grew at an annual rate of about 10 percent, of non-oil MICs by about 26 percent, and of the NICs and OXs by about 21 percent.

The total public debt of ADCs increased less rapidly than the total public debt of all developing countries: consequently, the debt share of ADCs in total developing country debt fell from about 35 percent in 1971 to 24 percent in 1983. This was mainly due to the sharp decline in the share of the LICs in the total debt; however, the shares of both the NICs and OXs increased slightly and that of non-oil MICs increased significantly (see Table 13).

So far our review of external debt situation was based on the World Bank data. Recently, OECD published new series of external debt data which are more comprehensive than those reported elsewhere.[51] In particular, those data include short-term debt which to date has not been adequately covered by other sources. According to these data external debt outstanding of ADCs reached $210 billion as at the end of 1984. It is surprising to note that the size of external debt in OECD data is approximately twice as big as public long-term debt.

OECD data also show that the main source of external finance of ADCs was international banks, which had a 42 percent share of the total debt outstanding of ADCs as at the end of 1984. On the other hand, the share of multilateral institutions was 16 percent and that of Official Development Assistance (ODA) was 14 percent. The reliance on international banks was particularly high in NICs and MICs, while the reliance on ODA and multilateral institutions was high in LICs (see Table 14). Over time, a significant feature of the growth in the total external public debt of ADCs was the increase in the proportion owed to private creditors. Changes also occurred in the composition of official creditors. The percentage of debt incurred under bilateral arrangements decreased and that due to multilateral agencies increased significantly.

Partly as a result of above changes in the composition of the sources of their external finance and partly of increase in international interest rates, the terms and conditions of new loans (new commitments) of ADCs generally became increasingly

---

[50] US GNP deflator was used in this calculation.

[51] The new OECD series includes not only individual country total disbursed outstanding long-term and short-term debt, but also service payments (i.e. amortization and interest payments) on long-term debt and, beginning 1982, interest payments on short-term debt. Thus, compared to other sources, the new series gives a more complete assessment of a country's total external indebtedness and of its debt service burden. On the other hand, the series consists of two parts which are not directly comparable; and old series with data for 1975 and 1979-1982, and a new series with data from 1982-1984. (See OECD *External Debt of Developing Countries*, 1984 and 1985 issues).

Table 12. Debt Outstanding (Disbursed) of Asian Developing Countries

(Unit: US$ billion)

Country Groups	Public Debt		Private Non-Guaranteed Debt		Total		Annual Ave. Growth Rate of Public Debt (%)
	1970	1983	1970	1983	1970	1983	(1971-1983)
NICs	2.6	29.1	0.1	2.9	2.7	32.0	20.6
MICs	3.7	50.0	1.3	5.9	5.0	55.8	22.1
Non-oil	0.9	17.4	1.3	5.9	2.2	23.4	25.7
OXs	2.8	32.4	..	..	2.8	32.4	20.6
LICs	11.4	39.7	..	0.2	11.4	39.9	10.1
Total	17.7	118.7	1.5	9.0	19.2	127.7	15.8

Source: World Bank, *Data Tape on World Debt and World Debt Tables*, (1983-84 edition).

Table 13. Regional Composition of External Public Debt Oustanding of Developing Countries

(Unit: %)

Region	1971	1983
Asian Developing Countries	35.0	23.7
NICs	(5.2)	(5.8)
MICs		
Non-oil	(1.7)	(3.5)
OXs	(6.3)	(6.4)
LICs	(21.8)	(7.9)
Latin America and the Caribbean	28.7	43.4
North Africa and Middle East	13.2	10.0
European and Mediterranean	13.0	11.7
Africa, South of the Sahara	9.9	11.1
South Pacific	0.2	0.2
Total	100.0	100.0

Source: World Bank, *Data Tape on World Debt and World Debt Tables*. (1983-84 edition).

Table 14. External Debt Structure as at the End of 1984
(Per Cent of Total Debt)

	NICs	MICs	LICs	ADC Total	Total Developing Countries
Long-term	59.6	73.9	82.3	71.7	74.4
ODA	4.1	11.0	29.4	13.7	6.8
Official other than ODA	20.1	14.1	5.9	13.9	15.2
Banks	25.5	28.8	5.9	21.7	33.0
Multilateral	7.2	12.8	33.4	16.5	10.2
Others	2.7	7.2	7.8	6.0	9.2
Short-term	37.9	23.6	6.9	23.7	22.1
Banks	35.6	17.6	5.4	20.0	19.7
Export Credit	2.3	6.0	1.5	3.7	2.4
IMF Credit	2.4	2.5	10.8	4.7	3.5
Total	100.0	100.0	100.0	100.0	100.0

Source: OECD. *Statistics on External Indebtedness.* Paris 1985.

onerous in the 1970s, with marked differences among the country groups. The terms and conditions of new loans to the LICs, most of which were on concessional terms, changed far less than those of new loans to countries in the other two groups.

As a result of the worsening terms of borrowing, the debt-service payments of ADCs increased at a much faster rate than their external debt. The debt-service payments of public long-term debt by the NICs and the MICs increased at average annual rates of 25 percent and 28 percent respectively during 1972-1983, exceeding the increase rate of their debt outstanding during the same period.[52] On the other hand, the debt-service payments of the LICs increased at a much slower rate (See Table 15).

With regard to the trend of external debt situation of ADCs, the following two features stand out.[53] First, the trend of debt indicators show that the situation of ADCs were relatively comfortable compared with the averages of total developing countries. ADCs are believed to have performed better than other developing countries in managing their debts due mainly to their good export performances and better utilization of borrowed foreign capital. Second, the indicators of ADCs aggravated rapidly since 1980 and have not shown signs of improvement. The deterioration was most severe in non-oil MICs, while the situations of LICs, having started from particularly onerous positions in early 1970s, still remain at an uncomfortable level. To have more correct assessment of the debt situation in ADCs we

---

[52] This is based on World Bank data. OECD data show similar trend. OECD data, however, provide a broader picture of debt service payment, since they include private non-guaranteed debt and interest payment of short-term debt. The size of OECD debt service payment is twice as much as that of World Bank data.

[53] See Jungsoo Lee, *ADB Economic Staff Paper* No. 16, 1983b.

Table 15. Debt Service Payments

(Unit: US$ million)

		NICs	MICs	LICs	ADC Total
W O D R A L T D A[1]	1971	281	283	747	1,311
	1980	3,052	3,153	1,922	8,127
	1983	4,183	5,710	2,623	12,516
B A N K	Annual Average Growth Rate (1972-1983) (%)	25.2	28.5	11.0	20.7
O D E A C T D A[2]	1975	1,364	1,650	1,857	4,871
	1980	5,078	4,792	3,762	13,632
	1983	8,028	8,599	3,181	19,808
	Annual Average Growth Rate (1976-1983) (%)	24.8	22.9	7.0	19.2
Memo: Total Debt-Service[3] (1983)		10,341	10,683	3,539	24,563

Sources: World Bank, *Data Tape on World Debt and World Debt Tables* (1984-85 edition) and OECD, *External Debt of Developing Countries in 1984*, Paris 1985.

[1] Long-term public debt only.
[2] Long-term debt (private and public) only.
[3] Debt service payment of long-term debt plus interest service payment of short-term debt.

now turn to the individual country data.

Table 16 shows the OECD data on the external debt outstanding of individual ADCs up to 1984. As at the end of 1984, the most heavily indebted ADC in absolute terms is Korea ($46.0 billion), followed by Indonesia ($33.2 billion), India ($30.5 billion), Philippines ($23.8 billion), Malaysia ($16.8 billion), Thailand ($16.7 billion), and Pakistan ($12.4 billion). The table also shows that the external debt of China increased rapidly in recent years to reach $12.4 billion at the end of 1984. External debt situations of the above high-debt ADCs will be reviewed individually in the following paragraphs (See Appendix 4 for the external debt data of individual countries).

Korea is the largest debtor among ADCs and its debt in per capita terms is the highest among them. The debt situation of Korea assessed by various debt indicators

Table 16. External Debt Outstanding of Asian Developing Countries

(Unit: US$ billion)

	Old Series[1]			New Series[2]		
	1975	1980	1982	1982	1983	1984
NICs	8.8	26.7	34.1	59.5	64.4	64.9
Hong Kong	0.4	2.5	3.8	5.5	63.1	6.2
Korea	5.8	17.6	22.0	40.7	43.3	46.0
Singapore	0.7	1.7	2.0	3.4	3.6	3.1
ROC (Taiwan)	1.9	4.9	6.2	9.9	1.2	9.6
MICs	14.5	34.6	48.1	74.3	85.2	90.4
Indonesia	8.7	16.7	20.4	27.9	32.0	33.2
Malaysia	1.8	3.9	8.2	11.7	16.8	16.8
Philippines	2.7	8.7	11.9	22.6	22.6	23.8
Thailand	1.3	5.2	7.6	12.2	14.5	16.7
LICs	20.4	34.1	38.7	46.8	52.5	55.2
Bangladesh	1.6	3.6	4.4	4.8	5.2	5.7
Burma	0.3	1.5	2.0	2.5	2.9	2.7
India	12.5	18.2	20.5	24.9	28.3	30.5
Nepal	—	0.2	0.3	0.4	0.4	0.5
Pakistan	5.4	9.2	9.6	11.5	12.5	12.4
Sri Lanka	0.6	1.4	2.0	2.8	3.2	3.4
(Memo)						
China	..	..	..	7.2	9.7	12.4
Total Asian Developing Countries	43.7	95.4	120.9	180.6	202.2	210.4
Total Developing Countries	173.0	449.0	555.0	813.0	879.0	921.4

Source: OECD, *External Debt of Developing Countries in 1984*, Paris 1985.

[1] Long-term debt only.
[2] Long-term and short-term debt.
.. not available.

is relatively uncomfortable. Debt-service ratio[54] is over 20 percent; interest-service ratio[55] is over 10 percent; the ratio of debt outstanding to GNP is close to 60 percent; and the ratio of external debt outstanding to exports of goods and services is over 130 percent. Furthermore, the ratio of short-term debt is relatively high and

[54] The ratio of debt service payments (amortization of long-term debt put interest payments of long-term and short-term debt) to the exports of goods and services.
[55] The ratio of interest-service payments to the exports of goods and services.

increasing and the ratio of concessional debt to long-term debt has decreased significantly during the last decade. Debt indicators of Korea, however, seem to indicate improvement in recent years in which exports earings continued to outgrow debt outstanding and debt-service obligations.

The debt-service ratio of Indonesia had been increasing in recent years. The additional debt service payments from the increase in total debt in 1983-84 and a continuing sluggish export performance due to decline in oil revenues could aggravate Indonesia's debt service burden in the next few years. Interest-service ratio which rose to 10 percent in 1983 is expected to increase further on account of the debt accumulation and the rapid decrease in concessional debt relative to total long-term debt.

A decade ago, India was the largest debtor country among ADCs. The country's external debt situation improved significantly in the late 1970s due mainly to its prudent policy toward extenal resources: its interest-cost (interest payments/total debt) of 2 percent and total debt/GNP ratio of 15 percent remain among the lowest of the developing countries. Its debt-servicing capacity, in the next few years at least, appears good on account of its low debt-service ratio and interest-service ratio. The country has relied mostly on long-term debt which comprises over 90 percent of its total external obligations. In recent years, however, there has been a rapid increase in borrowings from international banks, which is partly responsible for the reduction in the concessional debt/long-term debt ratio.

The Philippines is the only ADC which experienced debt rescheduling in recent years. Although its external debt stabilized since 1983 when, as a consequence of a unilateral declaration of a moratorium on debt service payments, it could not increase its borrowing, especially from international banks, its debt servicing difficulties are far from over. Its external debt as of the end of 1984 stood at $23.8 billion. In addition to this, there was a big amount (over $5 billion) of cross-border deposits by non-resident non-banks with Philippine banks. Although this latter amount is generally not considered as external debt, its size is to be reckoned with as a potentially unstable and destablizing factor under conditions of politico-economic uncertainty.

Based on various indicators, the Philippines' external debt situation is not comfortable at all: in the short- to medium-term, the country will continue to be saddled by high debt service ratio (in the neighborhood of 40 percent) and interest-service ratio (25 percent). In the longer term, the indicators are not reassuring either: the 1984 outstanding debt was almost three times annual export earnings and almost three-fourths of GNP; over 30 percent of it was short-term, and almost 90 percent of the long-term borrowing was at non-concessional terms.

Although Malaysia's debt in per capita terms is one of the highest among the ADCs, its external debt situation is relatively comfortable compared to other highly indebted DMCs such as Korea and the Philippines. Its debt service ratio in 1983 was just under 10 percent and its interest-service ratio was still under 7 percent. However, the rapid increased in its debt from 1983 was a matter of concern, as this increase would soon cause the above ratios to rise rapidly, particularly since the new borrowings were mostly commercial bank loans obtained at non-concessional terms.

Thailand also borrowed heavily in 1983-84. Its external debt increased much faster than its exports or GNP, causing the ratio of external debt to exports or GNP to rise. The country's short- to medium-term liquidity indicators reached very high levels; in 1983 the debt service ratio stood at 27 percent and the interest-service ratio was 13 percent. Moreover, the debt structure has been aggravated. The concessional debt/long-term debt ratio decreased rapidly to under 10 percent in 1984, while the short-term debt/total debt ratio stood at 25 percent.

Pakistan had its external debt rescheduled in 1972-74 and in 1981. The debt indicators show that the situation has been deteriorating with the debt service ratio increasing to an alarming 29 percent in 1983. Moreover, outstanding debt was over three times annual exports. The problem was not a rapid increase in either outstanding debt or service payments, but sluggish exports which increased at an annual rate of only 5.6 percent in 1981-84.

External debt data of China are available only since 1980. The data show that external debt increased rapidly in recent years recording 35 percent increase in 1983 and 29 percent in 1984. Despite the rapid increase in external debt, debt situation assessed from various debt indicators is relatively comfortable: (1) the ratio of debt outstanding to GNP is less than 10 percent; (2) the ratio of debt outstanding to exports is less than 50 percent; and (3) debt-service ratio is less than 10 percent. The situation may, however, aggravate in the long-term due to the rapid increase in external debt in recent years.

Long-Run Debt-Servicing Capacities

The previous section examined the external debt situations of ADCs by using some external debt indicators. In this section, external debt situations of ADCs are reviewed with reference to the management of their domestic economies. The so-called critical interest rate[56] (CIR) is used for this purpose. The CIR combines three basic domestic economic indicators — namely, GDP growth rate, marginal saving rate and incremental capital output ratio (ICOR) — into a single indicator which can be used for the assessment of long-run debt-servicing capacity of a country. The CIR indicates the level of interest rate on the external debt of a country at which the country's external debt will grow at the same rate as its GDP. In other words, the CIR is the maximum interest rate that can be paid on external debt without increasing the ratio of debt outstanding to GDP. If the average interest rate exceeds the CIR for a long period of time, the ratio of debt outstanding to GDP will continue to increase leading to an unbearable level. Thus, a comparison of the CIR with actual average interest rates on external debt provides a measure of the long-run debt-servicing capacity of a borrowing country.

The benefit of using the CIR in the analysis is that it can be used to identify the factors which affect a country's debt-servicing capacity. The formula for determining CIR indicates that a country's long-run debt-servicing capacity is determined by the above-mentioned three indicators of domestic economy.[57] It shows basically

---

[56] This is the concept developed in the pioneering book by D. Avramovic and Associates *Economic Growth and External Debt,* 1964. See in particular p. 172 for the rationale given to this name.

[57] Algebraically, J.P. Hayes shows:

$$\text{CIR} = \frac{r(S' - So)}{k.r - So}$$

where CIR = critical interest rate

So = initial savings rate (average savings rate which was in existence before capital was introduced)

k = incremental capital output ratio

r = the rate of growth of GDP

S' = marginal savings rate

(See D. Avramovic and Associates (1964), p. 171).

that the efficiency with which capital is used and the extent to which domestic savings are mobilized are major determinants of the long-run debt-servicing capacity of a country. Thus, the CIR can be viewed as relating a country's external debt problem to the management of its domestic economy.[58]

The CIRs for 11 ADCs were calculated for the period 1966-1982. The period was divided into two sub-periods: 1966-1975 and 1976-1982. The first sub-period includes the first oil shock, while the second sub-period includes the second oil shock. A comparison of the CIRs for the two periods shows the direction of change in the long-run debt-servicing capacities of ADCs.

The critical interest rate analysis shows that the long-run debt-servicing capacities of ADCs have generally deteriorated (see Table 17). The CIRs of these countries declined mainly because of the increased inefficiency of their invested capital represented by the increased ICOR.[59] In contrast to the declining critical interest rate, the average interest rates on foreign loans have risen sharply. The debt-servicing capacities were therefore adversely affected by both domestic and external conditions.

During the 1966-1975, the CIR of the NICs was 9.6 percent per annum in real terms and declined slightly to 9.2 percent during 1976-1982. Although marginal domestic saving rates in three countries significantly improved, the ICORs of these countries increased rapidly due mainly to the industrialization policies pursued in these countries. The NICs, especially the ROC (Taiwan) and Korea, have in recent years pursued policies designed to alter their industrial structures, placing greater emphasis on skill-intensive and capital-intensive manufactures. The long-gestation periods involved in heavy industries seem to have contributed significantly to the increase in their ICORs. Furthermore, prolonged world recession and growing trade protectionism exacerbated the problem by causing a slowdown in the growth of their exports which, in turn, contributed to the increase in the ICOR by causing low capacity utilization.

The CIR for non-oil MICs is lower than that for the NICs. The CIR also declined, from 8 percent in 1966-1975 to about 5 percent in 1976-1982. The main contributory factor for the decline was the increase in the ICOR and the declining marginal saving rate. The fall in CIR of OXs is not as significant as that of non-oil MICs. Although the ICORs of OXs increased somewhat, the increase in marginal saving rate prevented the CIR from falling rapidly.

Compared with the NICs and the MICs, CIR for LICs was low, about 4 percent in 1976-1983. The major reasons for the low CIR seem to be the high ICOR, which may be due to India's past industrial policy of favoring capital-intensive industries and the low marginal saving rate in Pakistan and Sri Lanka.

It should also be noted that the single major factor that distinguished the relative performance of each country group among the ADCs was the marginal saving rate. The relatively better performance of the NICs was mainly due to their high and

---

[58] Refer to J. Lee, "Relative External Debt Situation of Asian Developing Countries: An application of Ranking Method", *ADB, Economics Office Report Series* No. 19, 1983. (1983a) for the discussion on the strengths and weaknesses of CIR as an indicator of repayment capacity.

[59] ICOR may not be a good indicator of measuring capital efficiency since it disregards the effect of other factor. An improved approach in the measurement of efficiency is the total factor productivity (TFP). TFPs of ADCs during the period 1970-1983 have been estimated using Cobb-Douglas production function specification. The growth in TFP of ADCs during 1970-1983 was negligible or negative except in Malaysia and Singapore.

Table 17. Critical Interest Rates[1] of Asian Developing Countries

	Growth Rate of Real GDP (%)		Incremental Capital-Output Ratio		Marginal Saving Rate (%)		Critical Interest Rate (%)	
	1966-75	1976-82	1966-75	1976-82	1966-75	1976-82	1966-75	1976-82
NICs	9.5	9.3	2.9	3.7	28.0	34.0	9.6	9.2
Hong Kong	7.4	10.9	2.8	2.5	24.3	24.6	9.1	9.6
Korea	10.0	9.1	2.7	4.3	24.6	31.2	8.9	7.0
Singapore	11.2	8.6	3.2	4.3	33.8	48.2	10.5	11.6
ROC (Taiwan)	9.3	8.6	3.0	3.8	29.1	31.9	9.8	8.4
Non-oil MICs	6.6	6.1	3.3	4.2	25.4	21.8	8.0	5.1
Philippines	5.6	5.4	3.3	4.7	26.5	21.8	8.9	4.5
Thailand	7.7	6.9	3.3	3.7	24.2	21.8	7.2	5.7
OXs	7.0	7.8	2.7	3.5	21.3	24.3	8.2	6.8
Indonesia	7.5	7.9	2.2	3.3	18.0	22.6	8.5	6.6
Malaysia	6.6	7.7	3.2	3.7	24.6	26.0	8.0	6.9
South Asia	5.0	5.1	3.2	3.4	12.6	12.7	3.1	4.0
India[2]	3.8	3.8	4.4	4.7	20.2	21.8	4.9	5.0
Pakistan	5.3	5.9	2.6	2.2	9.0	5.5	2.4	4.2
Sri Lanka	5.8	5.5	2.5	3.4	8.5	10.7	2.1	2.8

Source: ADB. *Key Indicators of DMCs of ADB*. Various issues.

[1] The critical interest rate is calculated using the following formula:
$$CIR = r(S_1 - S_0)/(k \cdot r - S_0);$$
where CIR = critical interest rate, r = the rate of growth of real GDP, S_1 = marginal saving rate, S_0 = initial saving rate (assumed to be 5 percent), and k = incremental capital-output ratio.
[2] The data cover only up to 1981.

increasing marginal domestic saving rate over the period examined. This emphasizes the importance of domestic resource mobilization in meeting the external debt problems.

Prospects

The outlook for the developing countries to achieve sustained economic growth and manageable external debt situations in the coming decade will depend very much upon the external economic conditions and the management of domestic policies. Included in the list of important external factors are the sustainability of economic recovery in industrial countries, movements of real interest rates in the international capital market and the protectionism against developing countries exports. The *World Development Report* (1984) of the World Bank provided a ten-year prospect for the world economy in 1985-1995. Two scenarios — Low case and High case — were assumed.[60] In the Low case, GDP in developing countries is expected to grow at an average rate of 4.7 percent a year in 1985-95, which is much lower than their performance in earlier years. But, in the high case, the prospects for developing countries would improve. Their GDP would grow at about 5.5 percent a year, almost as fast it achieved in the 1960s and 1970s. Prospects differ greatly depending upon countries. The main cause of different prospects is the variance in the trade outlook for each country. Exports of primary commodities would be growing more slowly than the exports of manufactures in either case. Among the Asian developing countries, the countries such as Korea, Malaysia and Singapore would fare better than other developing regions and low income countries of Asia.

World Development Report (1985) of the World Bank, on the other hand, pays greater attention to the next five years, in which period about two-thirds of the debt of the developing countries will have to be rolled over or amortized. Two scenarios — a Low and a High — have been prepared.[61] High scenario indicates 3.5 percent GDP growth rate in industrial countries, while low scenario shows 2.7 percent. Accordingly, GDP growth of developing countries is to be sustained at a healthy 5.5 percent a year in the High simulation, but would be only 4.1 percent a year in the Low simulation. Under both the High and Low simulations, the more flexible east Asian economies would continue to grow faster than Latin American countries. The Low simulation would be a setback for low-income Asia, but if the High simulation prevails, they would grow at 5.8 percent a year.

The outlook by IMF recapitulates the importance of sound policies in industrial as well as in developing countries. The analysis shows that better policies in industrial countries could result in an improvement in the international environment that would add more than 1.5 percentage points p.a. to the rate of growth attained by developing countries. Even in the absence of such policies in industrial countries, better policies in developing countries could add almost 1 percentage point p.a. to their growth performance.[62]

The financial implications of the two scenarios assumed in *World Development Report* show profound differences. In the High simulation, total net financial flows would increase at an average annual rate of 3.8 percent in real terms, while they would decline by 1.7 percent a year in the same period in the Low simulation. Despite the increase in external finance in the High simulation, the main debt indicators would improve over the period. For developing countries as a group, debt outstanding as a percentage of exports declines from 135 percent in 1984 to 98 percent in 1990, and their debt-service ratio falls from 20 to 16 percent. How-

---

[60] The Low case indicates what might happen if the industrial countries were to do nothing to improve their performance of the past ten years. The High case, by contrast, offers industrial economies a path of sustained and steady expansion. (see *World Development Report* 1984, p. 34).

[61] The Low simulation makes three basic assumptions: no progress in reducing budgetary deficits and in improving the monetary-fiscal balance so that real interest rates remain high; a failure to tackle labor market rigidities so that unemployment stays high and real labor costs continue to increase; and a substantial increase in protection. By contrast, the High simulation assumes reduced fiscal deficits compared with the Low simulation, thus permitting improvements in the monetary-fsical balance and a resultant lowering of real interest rates; reductions in labor market rigidities such that unemployment declines and the increase in real labor costs slow down; and an increasing success in adjustment that results in a steady decline in protection (see *World Development Report* 1985, p. 10).

[62] See IMF, *World Economic Outlook*, 1985, p. 6.

ever, in the Low simulation, the outstanding debt of all developing countries would fall only slightly from the high present level of about 135 percent of exports, and the debt-service would rise to 28 percent in 1990, from 20 percent in 1984. The report also shows that Asian countries will generally perform better than Latin American countries.

The report notes that the prospects for the next ten years do not exclude the possibility of further debt servicing difficulty for many developing countries. If industrial economies grow at 2.7 percent a year for the next five years, as in the low simulation, and this growth is accompanied by high real interest rates and increased protectionism, several groups of developing countries could find themselves with heavier debt-servicing burdens at the end of this decade.[63] It should also be noted that both high and low scenario do not allow for any exogenous shocks to the world economy that could result from a severe disruption of energy supplies and that both simulations assume substantial policy reforms and adjustment efforts on the part of developing countries. Therefore, the external debt situation could be even worse than the low scenario if developing countries do not continue policy reforms or if a severe disruption in the energy supplies occurs.

Finally, in relation to the prospects for foreign capital flow, we believe that foreign capital will continue to flow into ADCs and play an important role in their economic development. It is also believed that, in most of ADCs, external debt situation will not develop into an unmanageable level as the effects of the recent adjustment policies of ADCs gradually materialize. However, the size of capital funds available in the world financial market may not increase very much in the coming decade. This implies that ADCs are to adjust their economies further to meet the reduced foreign capital inflows in the coming years if they intend to have a sustained economic growth and maintain manageable external debt situation.

CONCLUSIONS

This chapter analyzed various aspects of foreign capital inflows, balance of payments and external debt problems of ADCs. First it reviewed the pattern and trends of foreign capital inflows into ADCs and examined the linkages between investment and various components of external finance. Empirical analysis shows that foreign capital plays a positive role in increasing investment in ADCs. Particularly, private direct investment, long-term borrowings and official transfers have significant investment augmenting contributions. Empirical analysis also suggests that capital efficiency is not adversely effected by larger foreign saving inflows. Both of these findings support the positive role of foreign capital in the economic development of ADCs.

The chapter continued to examine the balance of payments and external debt situations of ADCs. The debt situations of 14 ADCs have been reviewed by analyzing the developments in their external current accounts and various external debt indicators. ADCs are believed to have performed relatively better than other developing countries in managing their debts due mainly to their good export

---

[63] There are some studies which found that OECD growth rate of above 3 per cent is crucial to ease the external debt problems of developing countries and to help achieve sustained growth in developing countries (see W. Cline, op. cit.).

performances and better utilization of borrowed foreign capital. The trends of debt indicators show that the external debt burdens of ADCs are less onerous than those of other developing countries. However, debt indicators also show that the external debt situations of ADCs worsened during the last decade. The deterioration was most severe in Non-oil MICs, while the situations of the LICs, having started from particularly onerous positions in early 1970s, still remain at an uncomfortable level. The analysis of critical interest rate also indicates that the long-run debt-servicing capacities of ADCs have deteriorated because of the increased inefficiency in their invested capital and/or declining domestic saving rate.

In view of the deteriorated external debt situations of ADCs during the last decade, recent difficulties experienced by ADCs in expanding their exports and various uncertainties that will be confronted by developing countries in the coming years, the prospect for external debt situation of ADCs is not particularly promising. This, in turn, forebodes that debt-service burden might emerge as a constraint to economic development of these countries by reducing the availability of foreign exchange.

When external resources are in elastic supply as commercial loans have been during much of the past decade, optimal borrowing and indebtedness becomes a more important discretionary policy variable. According to two-gap theory, a temporary increase in investible resources leads to higher production/income level which enables an increase in savings (by way of a rising marginal propensity to save in the savings function) and thus the achievement of self-sustained growth. But in this formulation of external finance requirements, the question of repaying borrowed resources is generally circumvented by assuming all external inflows to be grant aid or equivalently, by regarding the inflows as net inward transfers.

The chief impediments to attaining the growth scenario posited by the two-gap model are two: leakages of external finance into consumption rather than investment, and wasteful or inefficient use of borrowed resources. The introduction of debt servicing or reverse flows obligations adds an additional complication — the real returns on investment must exceed the costs of borrowings in order to yield a net positive contribution to income and savings after debt service. Since debt service payments are foreign exchange costs, real returns must be calculated at shadow prices or world prices; policy distortions can lead to inappropriate investment decisions. Reverse service obligations also impose stiffer requirements on minimizing consumption leakages and securing high rates of return on investment. So long as the marginal rate of return on investment is at least equal to the marginal cost of funds, debt servicing should present no serious difficulty for a country provided that fiscal capacity and export capacity permit repayment to be effected. However, these capacities can present serious stumbling blocks and have been advanced in justification of aid on soft terms particularly for low income countries.[64] Nevertheless, countries must not lose sight of the relationship between export performance and external borrowings.[65]

The critical interest rate is a macroeconomic concept for evaluation of debt (equity) service capacity in terms of affordability at the national level as distinct

---

[64] Paul Streeten "Why Concessionary Aid?" in *International Journal of Development Banking*, Vol. 2, 1982.

[65] Cline has stressed that "debt sustainability", a concept he attributes to Simonsen, can be interpreted as necessitating rate of growth of exports in excess of nominal interest rate on foreign debt. See Cline, op. cit.

from the project level.[66] This affordability is defined in terms of the growth rate of output, the marginal saving rate and the incremental capital output ratio. However, this does not consider a possible transfer problem. A concept of "borrowing capacity" has also been defined with focuses explicitly on exports. Borrowing capacity is the "highest level of borrowing relative to exports that can be maintained indefinitely with debt service kept below stated limits.[67] The principal implication of this additional criterion is the need to take cognizance of export growth to avoid exceeding debt service capacity.

Domestic policy distortions can complicate the assessment of optimal borrowing. Since domestic resource costs diverge from world prices when domestic policy distortions are present, it is possible that what appears worthwhile from domestic price calculations is not so from a social viewpoint. The major domestic policies that would affect capital inflows and indebtedness appear to be of (1) domestic interest rate policy which influences both domestic investment and savings and also bears on external borrowings decisions, (2) public sector resource mobilization policy which affects external financing (since governments typically find foreign financing easier than raising tax revenues), and (3) exchange rate and trade policies which influence both trade performance (relative price of tradeables and non-tradeables) as well as capital flows (domestic currency price of foreign exchange). Low interest rates and overvalued exchange rates induce excessive use of foreign borrowing. Much as domestic price distortions impair allocative efficiency, they can also obscure an appropriate borrowing strategy, as when domestic resource costs of saving foreign exchange via import substitution implies an exceedingly high shadow foreign exchange rate.

It is, thus, important to eliminate domestic price distortions if a debtor country is to achieve optimal borrowing, efficient resource allocations and adequate domestic saving. While there are common areas which require policy reforms, specific recommendations and priorities would require more detailed analysis of individual countries.

External debt problems cannot, however, be resolved by developing countries alone. There are critical roles that need to be played by the industrial countries. In particular, since the high real interest rates pose serious threat to the resolution of the current debt problems, a lowering of interest rates is an important task that remains in hands of industrial countries. Since the large budget deficits in industrial countries are the main cause of abnormally high real interest rates, it is incumbent on these countries to trim their budget deficits. Such a development would also foster increased private investment which is needed to sustain growth of industrial countries. This implies that domestic adjustment policies are required not only in developing countries but also in developed countries.

Another important task for industrial countries to alleviate external finance constraints is the dismantling of protectionist barriers which have been fortified by prolonged recession in recent years. If access to markets is restricted, developing countries will find it more difficult to achieve improved foreign exchange earnings from trade. Interdependence in the process of industrial transition suggests too that trade protection policies in industrial countries holds back industrial restructuring in developing countries.

---

[66] Hayes in Avramovic, op. cit. Also see section entitled, "Foreign Capital Flows to Asian Developing Countries."
[67] See Dhonte, *Clockwork Debt.*

The lowering of real interest rates and trade barriers will be realized only when industrial countries achieve sustained and non-inflationary economic growth. Following the 1980-82 recession, economic activity in industrial countries recovered in 1983-84 reaching 5 percent in 1984. However, this promising trend did not last long. OECD real GNP growth rate in 1985 is unlikely to be much above 2.5 percent, little more than half the 1984 result.[68] It is worried that the recent slowdown in industrial countries' economic growth may reinforce protectionist trend in industrial countries.

The uncertainties facing developing countries makes the choice of development strategy very difficult. An all-out export oriented strategy may be risky in the face of increasing protectionism in industrial countries. The strategy of borrowing abroad to increase investment and promote economic growth is also risky if the markets for exports are difficult to expand. These imply that the past success story of the Asian NICs may not be directly applicable to the future unless the external environments turn more favorable to developing countries. It is, thus, important for developing countries to maintain flexibility in the management of their domestic policies to make it easier to make necessaryadjustments to external pressures without much delay. This policy direction does not deny the importance of export-oriented strategy. It rather implies that domestic prices should not be distorted too much in the name of supporting export industries.

Finally, it is essential for industrial countries to provide orderly external finance to support the adjustment process. Here, the international financial institutions have a vital role to play and for this purpose the resources of multilateral and regional development banks and the IMF must be strengthened. This will enable these institutions not only to provide larger resource flows but to be more effective catalysts and co-financiers in mobilizing external finance from other sources. Moreover, their contribution to policy dialog and reform may have more lasting benefits on judicious lending and borrowing decision. It is particularly important to foster cooperation with the international commercial banks which have become and must continue to be major creditor to many developing countries. Such cooperation is critical to the resolution of debt problems and to the provision of net new finance which developing countries will require in the years ahead.

---

[68] Morgan Guaranty Trust Company of New York, *World Financial Market; September/October 1985*, p. 4.

APPENDIX 1

The Data

There are four principal sources of data on external finance provided by IMF, OECD, BIS and WB. This paper employs IMF and OECD data, although the latter series supplements its own monitoring with a memo item on "bank sector loans" which is actually derived from BIS.

The financing categories given in IMF Balance of Payments series include all capital account items plus official transfers taken from the current account.[1] We have followed this IMF practice in treating official transfers but add private transfers as a financing item.

A brief description of these balance-of-payments items follows:

1. Transfers refers to real or financial flows for which no offsetting payment (quid pro quo) is made. They are classified as private or official according to whether transaction involves an official transactor. Thus, net official transfers include grants received by government (net of grants extended by a government) as well as grants from official sources, including international organizations.

2. Private Direct Investment refers to capital flows — real or financial — in which foreigners have a controlling interest. While in concept controlling interest requires at least 50 percent ownership, in practice difference countries observe different definitions. Since multinational firms may also make loans between their companies in different countries which do not necessarily engender a definitive repayment obligation, intercompany lending can also be a form of private direct investment. Since these transactions often go unreported in the balance of payments, coverage of intrafirm transactions among multinational firms, like the reporting of reinvested earnings, are believed to be relatively incomplete in the balance-of-payments records.

3. Portfolio Investment covers net sales of securities, including equities, and bonds, excluding transactions in which controlling interest is with foreigners (in which case it should be reflected under direct investment).

4. Short-Term Borrowing is less well measured than long-term borrowings with an original maturity of one year or more and normally includes errors and omissions in the balanace-of-payments accounts which are attributed to un-recorded short-term capital movements. For the most part, short-term capital flows are associated with trade financing, although it is recognized that short-term credits can be used to cover medium- and long-term financing.[2] If short-term credit is continuously rolled over as many revolving credits are, the short-term credit has in effect an indefinite maturity.

Although balance-of-payments records provide comprehensive information on the functional categories of worldwide external financing, we turn to OECD data on financial flows (net disbursements) to developing countries to expand the picture of external financing with respect to source and concessionality. These are

---

[1] While segregating current transfers (which do not contribute to savings) from capital transfers (which is finance investment) would be desirable here, conventional balance-of-payments account does not do this.

[2] In a study of external debt, AMEX Bank considered normal trade financing to equal six months of imports. Cf, The AMEX Bank Review, Bank and LDCs, Special Paper No. 10, 1984.

probably the most reliable data on financial flows available and have been systematically collected from DAC member countries.[3] Conceptually, the financial flows in the balance-of-payments records cover all financial inflows net of outflows with errors and omissions, a balancing item, conventionally regarded as part of short-term capital movements. The OECD data, however, are confined to a subset of financial flows from DAC countries, thus excluding, for example, export credits extended by other developing countries or socialist countries. Furthermore, the OECD series includes only those flows with maturities of one year or more which are economically motivated (development aid, trade-related credits or commercial loans). The principal exclusions are those flows representing loans and grants for military purposes, IMF credits other than Trust Fund loans, grants by private voluntary agencies and all credits with maturities of less than one year.[4] Finally, balance-of-payments records are on an accrual basis as compared to the disbursements data of OECD, which may be recorded at several stages not necessarily corresponding to actual cash disbursement.[5]

Because OECD data are derived from reports made by donor country/institution rather than recipient country, the disbursements data net out repayments and debt cancellations (which appear as grant inflow and negative loan entry) but do not net out, in the balance-of-payments sense of net, either private direct investment outflows or lending/transfer outflows from a developing country. Both series on direct investment omit intracompany transfers which are a form of investment of growing importance. Similarly, the capital subscriptions (outflows) to various multilateral agencies by developing countries themselves are not netted out as they would be in the balance-of-payments data.

OECD data provide considerable detail on official flows, most especially from the DAC countries which provide the majority of these financial flows. Over the years the data coverage on private flows has been improved although some problems remain. The most serious limitation of these data concerns their inadequate (although recently improved) coverage of private sector flows, namely Eurocurrency bank loans, which makes it difficult to quantify the magnitude of growing commercial bank lending.[6] While significant amounts of bank funds may have originated from OPEC countries, the bulk of these were probably channeled through establish-

---

[3] DAC countries: Australia, Austria, Belgium, Canada, Denmark, Finland, France, Federal Republic of Germany, Italy, Japan, Netherlands, New Zealand, Norway, Sweden, Switzerland, United Kingdom and United States.

[4] However, balance-of-payments records also have their own data problems, highlighted by finding a growing asymmetry in global aggregations which in concept should sum to zero. See, IMF, *World Economic Outlook* (1982 and 1983).

[5] OECD, *Geographical Distribution of Financial Flows to Developing Countries*, 1982, p. 252. This convention is also under review according to OECD, *Development Cooperation*, 1983, p. 168.

[6] This is because "loans by banks resident in each DAC member country are included indistinguishably in the total "total receipt net" data. However, portfolio investment figure for most countries diverges sharply from bank sector loans given as a memorandum item. Bank sector loans given as memo item in DAC-OECD source since 1977 includes both direct loans by banks resident in DAC countries (whether headquarters are in that country or not) and loans from offshore centers in DAC countries or developing countries. Apparently, the sources of these bank loans may originate outside of DAC countries so they need not strictly represent DAC country sources. At the same time, except U.S. banks which report on a consolidated basis inclusive of their foreign affiliates, lending by affiliates of DAC country parent banks resident in developing countries is excluded from total net flows but is included in bank sector loans. Bank loans from non-DAC parents or affiliates such as OPEC banks in non-DAC countries are omitted from both total net flows and bank sector loan coverage in DAC-OECD data until 1981 and 1982 when Bank sector loan data include claims on non-OECD banks to the extent of their participation in international syndicated loans.

ed international banks of OECD member countries especially in the earlier years.[7] Thus, "bank sector" loan figures derived from BIS system are not strictly comparable in geographical origin to portfolio investment and export credits flows which are confined to DAC countries or to official flows (available for DAC countries, OPEC and multilateral agencies).

Compared to the $121.2 billion of aggregate (ex post) financing measured by the cumulative NEFG for the 12 NODMCs, total flows reports in OECD-DAC flows (see Table 10) amounted to $75 billion. If flows explicitly excluded by OECD series are deducted (i.e., short-term borrowing, reserve-related credits, SDR allocation, subsidy account grants), then OECD flows amount to about 84 percent of the adjusted NEFG of the 12 NODMCs reflected in Table 5 as compared to 62 percent of unadjusted NEFG.

---

[7] It was estimated that 80 percent of lending by OPEC-Arab commercial banks went to oil exporters and Arab countries and only 10 percent to oil-importing developing countries in 1977-78; by 1980-81, the share of oil-importing developing countries had risen to 20-30 percent. IBRD, *World Development Report 1981*, p. 62.

APPENDIX 2

Gross Flows, Net Flows, Net Transfers of Asian Countries
(At Current Prices)

(Unit: US$ million)

	1968	1969	1970	1971	1972	1973	1974	1975	1976	1977	1978	1979	1980	1981	1982	1983
LICs																
Bangladesh																
Gross Flows	—	—	—	—	—	481.7	717.6	1,014.5	663.3	661.2	1,093.9	1,835.7	1,831.5	1,864.3	1,924.4	2,085.6
Net Flows	—	—	—	—	—	475.5	713.5	1,006.9	650.6	626.4	1,046.3	1,441.6	1,744.7	1,822.3	1,852.9	2,005.8
Net Transfers	—	—	—	—	—	471.1	702.3	986.1	610.3	567.8	985.0	1,375.7	1,675.1	1,726.1	1,704.6	1,858.1
Burma																
Gross Flows	98.0	32.4	58.9	49.5	55.1	145.3	132.4	67.8	65.1	116.4	262.6	575.3	546.2	458.8	480.7	505.8
Net Flows	88.9	21.4	46.5	36.1	44.2	122.8	111.4	49.0	36.1	95.0	232.3	522.3	484.9	369.1	412.5	419.7
Net Transfers	84.3	14.8	39.7	27.1	37.5	109.7	96.7	35.2	18.1	76.6	209.0	484.7	424.0	299.5	348.4	352.8
India																
Gross Flows	860.0	937.0	1,000.0	1,384.8	792.4	1,123.4	4,055.2	1,694.1	1,740.5	1,959.7	3,669.2	3,852.5	5,413.4	4,216.3	—	—
Net Flows	860.0	628.0	706.8	1,087.0	408.0	730.0	1,642.7	1,291.0	1,318.0	1,408.6	3,133.3	3,162.6	4,601.2	3,543.7	—	—
Net Transfers	549.0	297.0	345.0	737.0	58.0	339.0	1,338.7	905.0	972.0	995.6	2,699.3	2,687.6	4,107.6	3,045.7	—	—
Nepal																
Gross Flows	—	—	—	—	—	—	—	—	61.3	63.7	90.8	108.5	173.3	169.7	233.9	230.5
Net Flows	—	—	—	—	—	—	—	—	60.1	62.1	89.1	106.8	171.2	167.3	231.6	225.9
Net Transfers	—	—	—	—	—	—	—	—	58.5	61.3	87.9	104.0	168.3	164.1	229.3	221.9
Pakistan																
Gross Flows	615.8	579.0	693.0	646.2	573.0	553.1	1,257.6	1,584.5	1,570.6	1,889.8	2,372.0	3,098.4	4,107.7	3,926.2	4,658.9	5,052.0
Net Flows	524.0	491.0	583.0	567.0	481.8	450.6	1,148.1	1,423.1	1,417.0	1,700.7	2,184.2	2,681.1	3,757.6	3,696.2	4,236.1	4,496.4
Net Transfers	453.0	391.0	469.0	494.0	384.8	369.6	1,070.1	1,312.1	1,319.0	1,575.7	2,051.2	2,370.1	3,399.6	3,319.2	3,705.1	3,918.1
Sri Lanka																
Gross Flows	78.1	133.7	95.6	71.0	93.9	89.8	240.5	273.6	209.8	258.8	308.5	597.1	794.2	1,007.2	1,184.8	959.8
Net Flows	60.4	120.8	76.7	54.8	73.1	52.9	182.2	175.3	127.6	188.7	240.1	536.8	673.8	914.9	1,046.4	879.1
Net Transfers	49.4	100.6	51.3	32.2	52.3	33.0	160.1	150.0	103.6	161.8	205.0	482.0	600.9	797.7	913.0	697.4
MICs																
OX																
Indonesia																
Gross Flows	303.0	457.0	480.0	536.3	876.1	819.0	239.4	603.8	2,404.4	1,721.5	2,459.6	1,335.7	127.3	1,371.4	5,384.1	8,489.5
Net Flows	251.0	418.0	414.0	437.0	773.0	751.0	136.0	231.0	1,841.0	882.0	1,433.0	275.0	−867.0	243.0	4,236.0	7,192.0
Net Transfers	173.0	311.0	281.0	265.0	426.0	122.0	−1,193.0	−1,154.0	629.0	−803.0	−585.0	−2,190.0	−4,194.0	−2,885.0	1,307.0	2,933.0

APPENDIX 2 (Continued)

	1968	1969	1970	1971	1972	1973	1974	1975	1976	1977	1978	1979	1980	1981	1982	1983
Malaysia																
Gross Flows	-37.0	-149.0	-18.0	161.0	252.5	209.4	752.7	360.8	296.1	128.7	290.6	-263.6	891.7	2,671.8	3,109.7	3,335.7
Net Flows	-47.0	-160.0	-31.0	149.0	234.0	188.0	707.0	317.0	250.0	47.0	183.0	-394.0	729.0	2,469.0	2,964.0	3,050.0
Net Transfers	-165.0	-341.0	-224.0	-57.0	26.0	-186.0	131.0	-137.0	-287.0	-675.0	-820.0	-1,854.0	-1,021.0	849.0	1,157.0	896.0
Non-OX																
Philippines																
Gross Flows	337.4	371.0	564.0	566.8	615.0	740.2	1,573.1	1,703.7	1,913.7	1,703.9	3,349.8	3,424.2	4,402.5	3,920.6	4,986.0	2,756.5
Net Flows	296.0	265.0	293.0	277.0	387.0	435.0	1,050.0	1,348.0	1,498.0	1,126.0	2,357.0	2,441.0	3,826.0	3,133.0	3,999.0	2,155.0
Net Transfers	184.0	180.0	153.0	160.0	239.0	256.0	825.0	1,053.0	1,118.0	666.0	1,771.0	1,712.0	2,781.0	1,588.0	1,883.0	-79.0
Thailand																
Gross Flows	379.0	394.0	398.0	425.5	510.9	715.9	1,117.1	880.6	978.0	1,634.8	2,189.4	3,148.8	3,684.6	4,766.3	3,855.6	4,573.6
Net Flows	260.0	242.0	217.0	232.0	323.0	487.0	885.0	605.6	687.0	1,309.0	1,626.0	2,424.0	2,487.2	3,698.0	1,939.0	4,155.0
Net Transfers	222.0	191.0	157.0	165.0	249.0	397.0	742.0	419.0	491.0	1,088.0	1,225.0	1,772.0	1,675.2	2,485.0	609.0	2,895.0
NICs																
ROC (Taiwan)																
Gross Flows	120.1	3.7	243.3	-42.3	166.2	-323.9	1,354.3	789.5	370.9	-785.4	-1,208.1	92.2	2,538.8	5,072.7	-157.0	-266.2
Net Flows	95.3	-37.3	182.3	-124.5	12.0	-525.9	1,192.3	582.5	145.9	-1,072.4	-1,637.1	-417.8	1,962.8	4,445.7	-1,015.0	-1,017.0
Net Transfers	65.3	-77.3	117.3	-207.5	-80.0	-653.9	1,003.3	298.5	-181.1	-1,458.4	-2,150.1	-1,151.8	977.8	3,027.7	-2,448.0	-2,198.0
Korea																
Gross Flows	751.7	1,028.0	965.0	1,016.4	1,080.7	1,117.2	2,538.0	2,927.8	2,506.2	2,258.3	3,452.2	6,617.4	7,992.1	7,399.1	5,100.9	4,343.2
Net Flows	700.0	955.0	858.0	880.0	869.0	843.0	2,200.0	2,617.0	2,064.0	1,601.0	2,368.0	5,359.0	6,684.0	5,819.0	3,308.0	2,344.0
Net Transfers	682.0	913.0	783.0	762.0	708.0	630.0	1,877.0	2,168.0	1,547.0	869.0	1,344.0	3,846.0	4,024.0	2,119.0	-527.0	-1,080.0
Singapore																
Gross Flows	339.9	279.0	760.0	1,164.0	835.2	1,125.9	1,537.2	869.5	944.8	802.5	2,286.2	1,599.0	2,425.0	2,767.8	2,232.6	2,371.9
Net Flows	337.0	273.0	750.0	1,150.0	808.0	1,108.0	1,518.0	844.0	917.0	771.0	2,027.0	1,484.0	2,291.0	2,677.0	2,131.0	2,094.0
Net Transfers	322.0	254.0	721.0	1,120.0	680.0	839.0	1,163.0	558.0	583.0	397.0	1,543.0	682.0	1,273.0	1,373.0	566.0	389.0

Source: IMF, *Balance of Payments Yearbook* and World Bank, *World Debt Tables*.

Net Flows = Private and official transfers plus direct investment plus borrowing plus others (see Table 2).
Gross Flows = Net Flows plus principal repayments.
Net Transfers = Net flows minus investment outflows.

APPENDIX 3

Notes on Data Used in Section entitled "Linkages Between External Finance and Investment". (Page 244)

Investment data (1968 to 1981) taken from the World Bank's *World Tables* were deflated by the investment deflator (1980 = 100) [Deflator = (data in current prices)/data in constant prices)].

All variables were further deflated by real GNP to remove heteroscedasticity, the presence of which was suggested by a plot of residuals on the original investment function (i.e. I/GNP was regressed on 1/GNP, F/GNP, etc.).

In computing incremental capital-output ratios (ICORs), external financing data in constant prices and local currency were used. The following three-year averages were used for all countries: 1968-70, 1971-73, 1974-76, 1977-79, and 1980-82.

External finance data was taken from IMF, *Balance of Payments Yearbook,* various issues. The functional classifications are the same except that errors and omissions are added to short-terms borrowings as given there. "Others" is a residual category encompassing IMF credits (with minor exceptions), plus valuation adjustments, monetization of gold, and SDR allocations.

F, the net transfers variable (net of amortization and interest and dividends), was computed as the sum of official and private unrequited transfers, direct investment, long-term and short-term borrowings and "others" all on a net basis, less investment outflows deflated by the export unit value index of industrialized countries. Real GNP was used as the denominator. The variance components model and the data transformations used were those suggested in Fuller, W. and Battese, G., "Estimation of Linear Models with Cross-Error Structure," *Journal of Econometrics,* Vol. 2, 1974.

F defined as net transfers (net of amortization and interest and dividends) was computed as the sum of official and private unrequited transfers, direct investment, long-term and short-term borrowings and "others" all on a net bases less investment outflows deflated by export unit value index (above). Real GNP was used as denominator.

APPENDIX 4

External Debt Situation in Individual Countries

Indonesia

	Old Series					New Series		
	1975	1979	1980	1981	1982	1982	1983	1984
A. Total Debt								
Outstanding ($ Mn)[a]	...	...	...	...	...	27,888	32,007	33,152
1. Long Term	8,702	15,117	16,671	17,561	20,398	21,686	25,205	26,512
of which: Concessional	4,772	7,037	7,841	7,974	8,156	8,062	8,440	7,411
(Memo: Other identified liabilities)	...	...	...	...	...	—	—	—
B. Total Debt Service ($ Mn)	...	...	...	...	...	3,592	3,582	...
1. Amortization, long term	686]	2,391]	2,081]	2,478]	2,832]	1,590	1,610	...
2. Interest, long term	}	}	}	}	}	1,279	1,365	...
3. Interest, short term	...	...	...	...	...	724	607	...
C. Economic Aggregates								
1. Population (Mn)	132.0	144.7	148.0	151.3	154.7	154.7	158.1	161.6
2. GNP ($ Mn)	29,125	49,018	69,275	82,471	87,199	87,199	77,046	78,878
3. Exports of Goods & Services ($ Mn)	7,025	15,552	22,241	24,878	21,274	19,906	19,906	19,906
Ratios								
A/C1 ($)	...	...	...	...	...	180	202	205
A/C2 (%)	...	...	...	...	...	32.0	41.5	42.0
A/C3 (%)	...	...	...	...	...	140	161	150
B/C3 (%)	...	...	...	...	...	18.0	18.0	...
(B2 + B3)/C3 (%)	...	...	...	...	...	10.1	9.9	...
Concessional debt/long term debt (%)	54.8	46.6	47.0	45.4	40.0	37.2	33.5	28.0
Short term/Total debt	...	...	...	...	...	22.2	19.9	20.0

Sources: For debt data: OECD, *External Debt of Developing Countries 1984* and *Statistics on External Indebtedness: The Debt and Other External Liabilities of Developing CMEA and Certain Other Countries and Territories at End-December 1983 and End-December 1984.* Paris, 1985.

For economic aggregates: ADB, *Key Indicators,* April and October Supplement 1985; IMF, *International Financial Statistics,* January 1986; and World Bank, *World Debt Tables,* 1984-1985 Edition.

a Includes Use of IMF credit.

APPENDIX 4 (Continued)

India

	Old Series					New Series		
	1975	1979	1980	1981	1982	1982	1983	1984
A. Total Debt Outstanding ($Mn)[a]	...	...	...	...	...	24,873	28,307	30,532
1. Long Term	12,471	16,545	18,183	18,874	20,537	20,767	23,099	28,042
of which: Concessional	11,356	15,149	16,332	16,428	17,117	17,103	18,097	17,293
(Memo: Other identified liabilities)	—	—	—	—	—	—	—	—
B. Total Debt Service ($Mn)	..	..	..	..	..	1,571	1,763	..
1. Amortization, long term	861]	1,195]	1,394]	1,380]	1,649]	778	928	...
2. Interest, long term	]	]	]	]	]	599	659	...
3. Interest, short term	...	...	...	...	...	194	177	...
C. Economic Aggregates								
1. Population (Mn)	603.5	660.3	675.2	690.3	705.8	705.8	721.6	738.0
2. GNP ($Mn)	88,145	132,070	162,521	171,694	173,876	173,876	187,616	191,880
3. Exports of Goods & Services ($Mn)	6,079	10,428	12,332	12,206	12,768	12,768	13,540	3,453
Ratios								
A/C1 ($)	...	...	...	...	...	35	39	41
A/C2 (%)	...	...	...	...	...	14.3	15.1	15.9
A/C3 (%)	...	...	...	...	...	195	209	884
B/C3 (%)	...	...	...	...	...	12.3	6.9	...
(B2 + B3)/C3 (%)	...	...	...	...	...	6.2	6.2	...
Concessional debt/long term debt (%)	91.1	91.6	89.8	87.0	83.3	82.4	78.3	61.7
Short term/Total debt	...	...	...	...	...	7.3	5.3	8.2

[a] Includes use of IMF credit.

APPENDIX 4 (Continued)

Korea

	Old Series					New Series		
	1975	1979	1980	1981	1982	1982	1983	1984
A. Total Debt Outstanding ($Mn)[a]	...	...	...	...	...	40,708	43,332	45,964
1. Long Term	5,762	15,484	17,579	20,036	21,985	25,261	27,188	27,185
of which: Concessional	1,851	2,694	2,970	3,132	3,006	2,921	2,959	2,840
(Memo: Other identified liabilities)	...	...	...	...	...	252	438	556
B. Total Debt Service ($Mn)	...	...	...	...	...	6,414	6,485	...
1. Amortization, long term	687]	2,920]	3,310]	3,917]	4,519]	2,311	2,781	...
2. Interest, long term	]	]	]	]	]	2,417	2,170	...
3. Interest, short term						1,687	1,534	...
C. Economic Aggregates								
1. Population (Mn)	35.3	37.5	38.1	38.7	39.3	39.3	40.0	40.6
2. GNP ($Mn)	20,234	64,564	61,250	67,214	70,832	70,832	75,318	81,119
3. Exports of Goods & Services ($Mn)	5,883	19,530	22,577	27,269	28,356	28,356	30,383	33,651
Ratios								
A/C1 ($)	...	...	...	...	...	1,036	1,083	1,132
A/C2 (%)	...	...	...	...	...	57.5	57.5	56.7
A/C3 (%)	...	...	...	...	...	144	143	137
B/C3 (%)	...	...	...	...	...	22.6	21.3	...
(B2 + B3)/C3 (%)	...	...	...	...	...	14.5	12.2	...
Concessional debt/long term debt (%)	32.1	17.4	16.9	15.6	13.7	11.6	10.9	10.4
Short term/Total debt	...	...	...	...	...	34.9	34.1	37.4

[a] Includes Use of IMF credit, but excludes "other identified liabilities" amounting to $252 Mn (1982), $438 Mn (1983) and $556 Mn (1984), which comprise deposits by non-residents with banks in the borrowing country.

APPENDIX 4 (Continued)

Malaysia

	Old Series					New Series		
	1975	1979	1980	1981	1982	1982	1983	1984
A. Total Debt Outstanding ($Mn)[a]	...	...	...	...	...	11,681	16,759	16,811
1. Long Term	1,775	3,511	3,924	5,494	8,208	8,604	11,743	13,971
of which: Concessional	380	588	730	711	729	739	848	886
(Memo: Other identified liabilities)	...	...	...	...	...	155	1,197	213
B. Total Debt Service ($Mn)	...	...	...	...	...	1,151	1,620	...
1. Amortization, long term	214]	620]	506]	8-0]	1,059]	245	530	...
2. Interest, long term	]	]	]	]	]	572	693	...
3. Interest, short term	...	...	...	...	...	333	396	...
C. Economic Aggregates								
1. Population (Mn)	11.9	13.3	13.8	14.1	14.5	14.5	14.9	15.3
2. GNP ($Mn)	8,998	19,690	23,024	23,480	24,964	24,964	27,614	30,637
3. Exports of Goods & Services ($Mn)	4,393	12,418	14,836	13,879	14,298	14,298	16,256	19,134
Ratios								
A/C1 ($)	...	...	...	...	...	806	1,125	1,099
A/C2 (%)	...	...	...	...	...	46.8	60.7	54.9
A/C3 (%)	...	...	...	...	...	82	103	88
B/C3 (%)	...	...	...	...	...	8.1	10.0	...
(B2 + B3)/C3 (%)	...	...	...	...	...	6.3	6.7	...
Concessional debt/long term debt (%)	21.4	16.7	18.6	12.9	8.9	8.6	7.2	6.3
Short term/Total debt	...	...	...	...	...	24.0	28.0	16.7

[a] Includes Use of IMF credit, but excludes "other identified liabilities" amounting to $155 Mn (1982), $1,197 Mn (1983) and $213 Mn (1984), which comprise deposits by non-residents with banks in the borrowing country.

APPENDIX 4 (Continued)

Pakistan

	Old Series					New Series		
	1975	1979	1980	1981	1982	1982	1983	1984
A. Total Debt Outstanding ($Mn)[a]	...	...	...	...	...	11,452	12,490	12,398
1. Long Term	5,400	8,348	9,204	9,194	9,576	9,691	10,414	10,699
of which: Concessional	4,728	7,196	7,794	7,847	8,134	8,132	8,557	6,661
(Memo: Other identified liabilities)	—	—	—	—	—	—	—	—
B. Total Debt Service ($Mn)	...	...	...	...	...	846	1,096	...
1. Amortization, long term	280]	553]	701]	679]	836]	472	697	...
2. Interest, long term						303	331	...
3. Interest, short term	...	...	...	...	...	71	68	...
C. Economic Aggregates								
1. Population (Mn)	70.9	79.8	82.6	85.1	87.8	87.8	90.5	93.3
2. GNP ($Mn)	11,456	21,376	25,816	30,919	29,391	329,391	30,891	32,636
3. Exports of Goods & Services ($Mn)	1,351	2,530	3,300	3,485	3,267	3,267	3,805	...
Ratios								
A/C1 ($)	...	...	...	...	...	130	138	133
A/C2 (%)	...	...	...	...	...	39.0	40.4	38.0
A/C3 (%)	...	...	...	...	...	351	328	...
B/C3 (%)	...	...	...	...	...	25.9	28.8	...
(B2 + B3)/C3 (%)	...	...	...	...	...	11.4	10.5	...
Concessional debt/long term debt (%)	87.6	86.2	84.7	85.3	84.9	83.9	82.2	62.3
Short term/Total debt	...	...	...	...	...	5.2	5.6	3.6

[a] Includes Use of IMF credit.

APPENDIX 4 (Continued)

Philippines

	Old Series					New Series		
	1975	1979	1980	1981	1982	1982	1983	1984
A. Total Debt Outstanding ($Mn)[a]	...	...	...	...	...	22,566	21,990	23,771
1. Long Term	2,690	7,506	8,721	10,193	11,885	13,956	14,118	15,238
of which: Concessional	479	1,021	1,277	1,415	1,498	1,483	1,626	1,656
(Memo: Other identified liabilities)	...	...	...	...	...	5,202	5,277	5,216
B. Total Debt Service ($Mn)								
1. Amortization, long term	424]	1,320]	1,220]	1,692]	1,834]	1,191	1,121	...
2. Interest, long term	]	]	]	]	]	1,126	1,292	...
3. Interest, short term	...	...	...	...	...	925	778	...
C. Economic Aggregates								
1. Population (Mn)	42.1	47.0	48.3	49.5	50.8	50.8	52.1	53.4
2. GNP ($Mn)	15,766	29,950	35,290	38,432	39,274	39,274	34,141	32,170
3. Exports of Goods & Services ($Mn)	3,170	6,255	7,997	8,583	8,005	8,005	8,132	8,017
Ratios								
A/C1 ($)	...	...	...	...	...	444	422	445
A/C2 (%)	...	...	...	...	...	57.5	64.4	73.9
A/C3 (%)	...	...	...	...	...	282	270	297
B/C3 (%)	...	...	...	...	...	40.5	39.2	...
(B2 + B3)/C3 (%)	...	...	...	...	...	25.6	25.5	...
Concessional debt/long term debt (%)	17.8	13.6	14.6	13.9	12.6	10.6	11.5	10.9
Short term/Total debt	...	...	...	...	...	34.5	31.5	32.7

[a] Includes Use of IMF credit, but excludes "other identified liabilities' amounting to $5,202 Mn (1982), $5,277 Mn (1983) and $5,216 Mn (1984), which comprise deposits by non-residents with banks in the borrowing country.

APPENDIX 4 (Continued)

Thailand

	Old Series					New Series		
	1975	1979	1980	1981	1982	1982	1983	1984
A. Total Debt Outstanding ($Mn)[a]	...	...	...	...	...	12,161	14,476	16,674
1. Long Term	1,324	4,047	5,239	6,611	7,632	8,996	10,337	12,511
of which: Concessional	313	824	1,130	1,245	1,374	1,335	1,556	1,590
(Memo: Other identified liabilities)	...	...	...	...	...	161	253	298
B. Total Debt Service ($Mn)								
1. Amortization, long term	326]	945]	985]	1,238]	1,592]	966	1,175	...
2. Interest, long term	]	]	]	]	]	790	813	...
3. Interest, short term	...	...	...	...	...	293	301	...
C. Economic Aggregates								
1. Population (Mn)	41.4	45.5	46.5	47.5	48.5	48.5	49.5	50.4
2. GNP ($Mn)	14,652	26,762	32,840	35,032	35,642	35,642	39,083	40,628
3. Exports of Goods & Services ($Mn)	2,971	6,662	8,574	9,254	8,781	9,415	9,227	10,415
Ratios								
A/C1 ($)	...	...	...	...	...	251	292	331
A/C2 (%)	...	...	...	...	...	34.1	37.0	41.0
A/C3 (%)	...	...	...	...	...	129	157	160
B/C3 (%)	...	...	...	...	...	21.8	24.8	...
(B2 + B3)/C3 (%)	...	...	...	...	...	11.5	12.1	...
Concessional debt/long term debt (%)	23.6	20.4	21.6	18.8	18.0	14.8	15.1	12.7
Short term/Total debt	...	...	...	...	...	20.3	22.3	25.0

[a] Includes Use of IMF credit, but excludes "other identified liabilities" amounting to $191 Mn (1982), $253 Mn (1983) and $298 Mn (1984), which comprise deposits by non-residents with banks in the borrowing country.

APPENDIX 4 (Continued)

China

	Old Series					New Series		
	1975	1979	1980	1981	1982	1982	1983	1984
A. Total Debt								
Outstanding ($ Mn)[a]	..	..	..	..	..	7,174[a]	9,668	12,434
1. Long Term	..	..	4,198	3,509	3,891	4,954	6,601	6,078
of which: Concessional	..	..	11	32	658	775	1,286	..
(Memo: Other identified liabilities)	..	..	..	..	..	496	—	..
B. Total Debt Service ($ Mn)	..	..	1,456	2,333	1,454	1,679	1,652	..
1. Amortization, long term	..	..	..	..	..	1,099	1,056	..
2. Interest, long term	..	..	..	..	..	425	342	..
3. Interest, short term	..	..	..	..	..	155	254	..
C. Economic Aggregates								
1. Population (Mn)	132.0	975.4	987.1	1,000.7	1,015.4	1,015.4	1,025.0	..
2. GNP ($ Mn)	134584	215434	244261	227633	224412	224412	236524	236422
3. Exports of Goods & Services ($ Mn)	..	..	..	..	24729	24729	24735	..
Ratios								
A/C1 ($)	..	..	..	..	..	7.1	9.4	..
A/C2 (%)	..	..	..	..	..	3.2	4.1	5.3
A/C3 (%)	..	..	..	..	..	29.0	39.1	..
B/C3 (%)	..	..	—	—	5.9	6.8	6.7	..
(B2 + B3)/C3 (%)	..	..	..	..	..	2.3	2.4	..
Concessional debt/long term debt (%)	..	..	0.3	0.9	16.9	15.6	19.5	..
Short term/Total debt	..	..	..	..	..	24.0	31.7	..

a Includes Use of IMF credit.

REFERENCES

American Express International Banking Corporation. *International Debt, Banks and the LDCs,* London, 1984.

Aerskoug Kaj. *External Public Borrowing: Its Role in Economic Development,* New Yor: Praeger, 1969.

Asian Development Bank. *Key Indicators of the DMCs of ADB,* various issues.

Avramovic D., and Associates, *Economic Growth and External Debt,* 1964.

Cline William, "International Debt and the Stability of the World Economy." *Policy Analyses in International Economies,* No. 4, Washington, D.C.: Institute for International Economies, 1983.

Dhonte Pierre, *Clockwork Debt,* Lexington, Massachusetts: D.C.: Heatn and Company, 1979.

Domar Evsey, "The Effect of Foreign Investment on the Balance of Payments," *Essays in the Theory of Economic Growth.* New York: Oxford University Press, 1957.

Frank Charles, Jr., "Debt and Terms of Aid, Overseas Development Council," Monograph, 1970.

Fry Maxwell, "Econometric Analyses of National Saving Rates," *Domestic Resource Mobilization Through Financial Development,* Vol. II. Asian Development Bank, 1984.

Go Evelyn M., "Notes on External Debt," *ADB Economic Office Report,* Series No. 6, 1982.

———, "Patterns of External Financing of DMCs," *ADB Economic Staff Paper,* No. 26, May 1985.

Gorgens, E., "Developing Aid — An Obstacle to Economic Growth in Developing Countries", *German Economic Review,* Vol. 14, 1976.

Harberger, Arnold, "Issues Concerning Capital Assistance to Less-Developed Countries," *Economic Development and Cultural Change,* Vol. 10, July 1972.

Hardy Chandra, *Rescheduling Developing Country Debts 1956-1981: Lessons and Recommendations,* Washington, D.C.: Overseas Developmnt Council, 1982.

Hughes Helen, "Capital Needs of Developing Countries in the Eighties," Paper presented at the Seventieth IEA World Congress, Madrid, 1983.

———, "Debt and Development: The Role of Foreign Capital in Economic Development," *World Development,* Vol. 7, 1979.

IMF, *Balance of Payments Yearbook,* various issues.

———, *International Financial Statistics,* various issues.

———, *External Indebtedness of Developing Countries,* Occasional Paper No. 5, May 1981.

———, *World Economic Outlook,* 1985.

Nurul, Islam, "The External Debt Problem of the Developing Countries with Special Reference to the Least Developed," *A World Divided,* edited by G.K. Helleiner, London: Cambridge University Press, 1976.

Iwasaki Y., "Methods of Estimating Saving and Their Implications," *Domestic Resource Mobilization Through Financial Development,* Vol. II, Asian Development Bank, 1984.

Krueger Anne, *The Developmental Role of the Foreign Sector and Aid,* Cambridge, Mass.: Harvard University Press, 1979.

Lee Jungsoo, "Long-Run Debt Servicing Capacity of Selected Asian Developing Countries: An Application of Critical Interest Rate Approach," *ADB Economic Staff Paper*, No. 16, 1983b.

———, "External Debt Servicing Capacity of Asian Developing Countries," *Asian Development Review*, Vol. I, No. 2, Manila, 1983c.

———, "A Study on the External Debt Indicators Applying Logit Analysis," *ADB, Economics Office Report Series*, No. 25, 1984a.

———, "The Effect of Terms of Trade Changes on the Balance of Payments and Real National Income of Asian Developing Countries," *ADB, Economics Office Report Series*, No. 28, 1985.

McDonald D.C., "Debt Capacity of Developing Country Borrowing: A Survey of Literature," *IMF Staff Paper*, December 1982.

Meier G., *Leading Issues in Economic Development*, New York: Oxford University Press, 1976.

Naya S., D.H. Kim, and W. James, "External Shocks and Policy Responses: The Asian Experience." *Asian Development Review*, Vol. 2, No. 1, Manila, 1984.

Newlyn W., et. al., *The Financing of Economic Development*, Oxford: Clarendon Press, 1977.

Ohlin Goran, "Debts Development and Default," *A World Divided*, ed. G.K. Helleiner, London: Cambridge University Press, 1976.

OECD, *Development Cooperation*, Paris: OECD, various issues.

———, *External Debt of Developing Countries: 1982 Survey* (1983) *and Survey* (1984).

———, *Geographical Distribution of Financial Flows*, Paris: OECD, various issues.

———, *External Debt of Developing Countries in 1984*, Paris, 1985.

———, *Statistics on External Indebtedness: The Debt and Other External Liabilities of Developing CMEA and Certain Other Countries and Territories at End-December 1983 and End-December 1984*, Paris, 1985.

Rana P. Sources of Balance of Payments Problem in the 1970s: The Asian Experience (Draft), 1984.

Sachs J.P. "The Current Account and Macroeconomic Adjustment in the 1970s," *Brookings Papers on Economic Activity*, 1, 1981.

Singh S.K., *Development Economics*. Lexington, Mass.: D.C. Heath and Co., 1975.

Streeten Paul, "Why Concessionary Aid?", *International Journal of Development Banking*, Vol. 2, January 1984.

Voivodas C.S., "Exports, Foreign Capital Inflow and Economic Growth," *Journal of International Economics*, Vol. 3, 1973.

Weisskopf Thomas, "The Impact of Foreign Capital Inflow on Domestic Savings in Underdeveloped Countries," *Journal of International Economics*, Vol. 2, (1972).

World Bank, *"World Debt Tables,"* 1982-83 Edition (1983) and 1983-84 Edition (1984).

———, *World Development Report 1984*, Washington, D.C. 1984.

8. Income Distribution: A Brief Comparative Review

Harry Oshima

Central to the incentives to work and save is the distribution of the rewards from participation in productive activities. If participants are not properly paid, the propensity to work as well as productivity will be adversely affected. If savings are not adequately compensated, the propensity to save may fall. If incomes are too low in the lower income groups and too high in the upper income groups, the aggregate demand for basic needs will not be met while demand for luxuries, especially imports, will be large, distorting production patterns and structures, and imposing strains on the balance of payments.

Distribution affects production but production affects distribution even more. If a strategy of capital-intensive instead of labor-intensive production in the early stages of development is followed, capital and other resources will be concentrated in a few, large industries to the neglect of the numerous smaller industries and also agriculture and incomes paid to the participants in the large, capital-intensive industries, will be larger than those in the latter. Moreover, with population and labor force growing rapidly, many will not be able to find jobs, hence unemployment will keep wages of the unskilled from rising. With these and other interrelations between production and distribution, the latter cannot be neglected in the discussion of the growth of production and productivity. In this chapter, we review the record of income distribution of various Asian countries[1] and look into some of the varied experience underlying the trends in order to get perspectives on the prospects and policies for the coming decade.[2]

---

[1]   See appendix for bibliography of recent surveys and other studies on income distribution.

[2]   This paper is a condensed presentation of Chapter 10 of my volume: *Economic Growth of Monsoon Asia: A Comparative Survey,* University of Tokyo Press, 1987. See also my papers, "Income Inequality and Economic Growth: The Postwar Asian Experience," *Malayan Economic Review,* October 1970, "Trends in Growth and Distribution of Income in Selected Asian Countries," *Philippine Economic Journal,* No. 3, 1977; "Perspectives on Trends in Asian Household Income Distribution," *Economics and Finance in Indonesia,* March 1982; *Income Distribution, Employment and Economic Development in Southeast and East Asia,* Vols. 1 and 2, 1975, and *Income Distribution by Sectors and Overtime in East and Southeast Asia,* 1978, published by the Council for Asian Manpower Studies, Manila and Tokyo.

FAMILY INCOME DISTRIBUTION

One of the problems in distributive studies is the limited supply of data and their reliability. Because of the costs, most countries in Asia do not conduct household income surveys frequently enough so the trends overtime can be properly worked out, while the quality of the data collected raises a number of issues which are discussed elsewhere — the most serious being the understatement of the highest incomes and the lowest incomes. Under these circumstances, only broad and large changes in Table 1 can be taken seriously for analysis. Our approach, therefore, is to use simple measures which do not presume unwarranted precision in the data. We divide families in five broad, equal groups, or quintiles (Q), with the highest quintile (or 20 percent) of families containing the highest incomes and the lowest quintile containing families with the lowest incomes. These broad groupings and their share of total incomes are convenient because the ratio of the income shares of the lowest Q to the highest Q (both whose incomes are understated) can be taken as a quick and easily understood measure of inequality.

When the differences in the income shares of other Q's need to be taken into account to derive an over-all inequality measure, all we need to do is to sum up (ignoring pluses or minuses) the differences in the share of income and the share of families (20 percent) in each quintile, (as in the last column of Table 1). Each income share of the quintiles is much easier to analyze than segments of the Lorenze curve which are cumulation. It is difficult to identify the households comprising the segments of the Lorenze curve whose simplicity on the diagram is deceptive since the diagram is not a two dimensional area or surface but actually three or a solid. Besides length and width, there is depth as the Lorenze curve rises from zero to 100 percent upward with cumulation of incomes and families. In the case of the lognormal as a measure of inequality, the assumption of lognormality is not satisfied for the agricultural sector.

The sum of the differences between the income shares and family shares for each Q, quintile inequality index in Table 1, is zero if the income share in each Q is 20 percent. Overtime if the shares of the higher Qs rise and the shares of the lower Qs fall, the quintile inequality index increases. In the analysis, the economy is divided into two major sectors, agriculture and nonagriculture, and the impact of the growth of these two sectors on income inequalities is assessed, with the impact of agricultural growth affecting mainly the lower quintile shares and that of non-agriculture affecting mainly the upper shares.

In Table 1 are shown the income shares of quintiles for various countries in the world for the late 1970s. East Asian countries have the highest ratios of the lowest Q to the highest Q and the lowest quintile inequality index (QII) in the table, with Japan and the ROC (Taiwan) having the highest ratio of QI/Q5 and the lowest QII. Southeast Asia shows the lowest ratios and highest index in Asia, second only to Latin America in the world. In large part, it is the comprehensive land reform in East Asia and the lack of such reforms in Southeast Asia and Latin America which underlie these differences in inequality. For low-income South Asia, the indices are surprisingly high, partly due to the absence of comprehensive land reform, particularly so for Nepal. Also important is the extent of unemployment and under-employment, which is lowest for East Asia and highest in South Asia. East Asian inequalities were already low in the 1950s after the land reforms (and this was true for China in the late 1970s). In the next section, a quick look into the differentials

Table 1. Quintile Share of Household Income
(Q$_1$ = lowest quintile; QII = quintile inequality index)

	Q$_1$	Q$_2$	Q$_3$	Q$_4$	Q$_5$	Q$_1$/Q$_5$	QII
East Asia	7.2	12.2	16.4	22.5	41.6	0.18	.30
Japan (1979)	8.7	13.2	17.5	23.1	36.8	0.24	.25
ROC (Taiwan) (1976)	8.9	13.6	17.5	22.7	37.3	0.24	.25
Korea (1976)	5.7	11.2	15.4	22.4	45.3	0.13	.35
Hong Kong (1980)	5.4	10.8	15.2	21.6	47.0	0.11	.36
Southeast Asia	5.2	8.5	12.9	21.0	52.3	0.10	.42
Malaysia (1973)	3.5	7.7	12.4	20.3	56.1	0.06	.46
Philippines (1971)	5.2	9.0	12.8	19.0	54.0	0.10	.43
Thailand (1975/76)	5.6	9.6	13.9	21.1	49.8	0.11	.39
Indonesia (1976)	6.6	7.8	12.6	23.6	49.4	0.13	.41
South Asia	6.1	9.7	14.0	20.1	50.1	0.12	.39
India (1975/76)	7.0	9.2	13.9	20.5	49.4	0.14	.37
Sri Lanka (1978/79)	5.7	10.3	14.3	19.8	49.9	0.11	.37
Nepal (1976/77)	4.6	8.0	11.7	16.5	59.2	0.08	.49
Bangladesh (1973/74)	6.9	11.3	16.1	23.5	42.2	0.16	.32
Western DC's	6.2	11.1	16.0	22.9	43.8	0.15	.34
Italy (1977)	6.2	11.3	15.9	22.7	43.9	0.14	.33
U.K. (1979)	7.0	11.5	17.0	24.8	39.7	0.18	.31
France (1975)	5.3	11.1	16.0	21.8	45.8	0.12	.35
W. Germany (1978)	7.9	12.5	17.0	23.1	39.5	0.20	.28
U.S. (1978)	4.6	8.9	14.1	22.1	50.3	0.09	.41
Latin America	3.1	7.3	12.1	20.4	57.2	0.06	.48
Brazil (1972)	2.0	5.0	9.4	17.0	66.6	0.03	.58
Mexico (1977)	2.9	7.0	12.0	20.4	57.7	0.05	.48
Argentina (1970)	4.4	9.7	14.1	21.5	50.3	0.09	.40
Venezuela (1970)	3.0	7.3	12.9	22.8	54.0	0.06	.46
Miscellaneous	5.0	9.8	15.4	21.0	48.9	0.11	.38
Yugoslavia (1978)	6.6	12.1	18.7	23.9	38.7	0.17	.28
Turkey (1973)	3.5	8.0	12.5	19.5	56.5	0.06	.46
Sudan (1967/68)	4.0	8.9	16.6	20.7	49.8	0.08	.38
Tanzania (1969)	5.8	10.2	13.9	19.7	50.4	0.12	.38

Source: Based on data from *IBRD World Development Report 1984.*

in equalities shown in Table 1 in each region of Asia in the latter 1970s is undertaken.[3] The analysis will refer to the patterns of growth discussed in Chapter 2 entitled, "Human Resources in Macro-Comparative Productivity Trends" and others in this volume, since the links between growth and distribution of income and between growth and distribution of population are many and intimate.

Income Disparities in East Asia

The inequalities in Hong Kong are higher than in the other East Asian countries, and this is also true for Singapore. The reason is that the city-states have much smaller agricultural sector and larger service sector and the incomes tend to be dispersed more widely in the latter than in the former. The firms in the service sector are more heterogeneous than the peasant farms in monsoon agriculture — in size, activities, and incomes. There is a large traditional service sector producing low incomes, (domestic services, small stalls and stores, peddling, and like), alongside a large, modernizing sector of corporations, department stores, professional offices, and government agencies, employing highly educated labor. And compared to manufacturing firms, firms in services use proportionately smaller number of unskilled and semi-skilled workers relative to skilled workers, managers, and entrepreneurs, so that the pyramid of incomes paid out as in the usual frequency curves is relatively flat and not as peaked as in agriculture and industry. This produces "within-sector" disparities greater in services than in industry and agriculture.[4]

What accounts for low income disparities is not only the comprehensive land reform that Japan, the ROC (Taiwan), and Korea completed in the postwar era, but also the high degree of success achieved in raising yields, multiple-cropping, and diversification in agriculture following the land reform.[5] These contributed to the initiation of labor-intensive industrialization which in turn created jobs in off-farm activities for farm families, enabling them to raise incomes beyond what was earned in agriculture and thereby keep up with the rise in urban incomes, and reducing "between sector" disparities.

In monsoon peasant farming, the size of land cultivated is the smallest in the world, and even with persistent rises in yields and multiple-cropping, farm incomes tend to fall behind rapidly-growing urban incomes if earnings from off-farm work during the dry season do not rise. Urban incomes tend to rise faster than rural incomes in the past because Western technologies are more readily applicable to the industries in the urban section than in monsoon paddy agriculture. Korean disparities were greater than the other East Asian countries because of the shortcomings of the rural development program after land reform and the slow growth of off-farm incomes. This was also true of China which because of the ban on private business was unable to create enough off-farm incomes for members of farm families

---

[3] Table from my University of Tokyo Press volume, *op. cit.* for the data underlying the discussion of the various sectors of each country for East and Southeast Asia, India and Sri Lanka, see the frequency distribution curves in Charts 1 to 16 found in *Income Distribution, Employment and Economic Development, op. cit.* pp. 26-47, 1975.

[4] For data see my University of Tokyo Press volume, *op. cit.*

[5] As noted in ibid., even without Land reform, the distribution of land in monsoon Asia cannot be dispersed over a wide range because of the labor-intensity of paddy cultivation and the great population densities, except for countries where the perennial crop plantations dominate agricultural production, as in Malaysia and Sri Lanka.

to supplement their farm incomes.[6]

Land reform and agricultural development were favorable to the establishment of labor-intensive industries and services in the urban sector, as the higher incomes of peasants were spent on processed foods, clothing, and other wage goods. The expanding domestic markets enabled labor-intensive industries to gain experience and achieve scale-economies, enabling them to export abroad, and import machinery for further increase in their efficiencies and growth rates. The high growth rates of the over-all economy soon outpaced the growth of labor supply and full employment levels of operations were reached later in Korea than in the ROC (Taiwan) and Japan. With full employment, real wages of unskilled workers began to rise as fast or faster than skilled workers, inducing urban businesses to accelerate mechanization and the use of labor-saving technologies. These contributed to rising incomes of lower-income families in the urban sector. Full employment also enabled housewives to get jobs in industries after their children were old enough to enroll in primary schools. And when the children were old enough to go to secondary schools, the higher incomes enabled urban families to pay for the costs of secondary education and forego earnings of teenagers as they went to school instead of work. With rapid technological progress, parents perceived the need to educate their children beyond primary schooling. Housewives had to go out to work for further schooling of the children and this made it difficult to have more children; birth rates began to fall among lower income families in both the urban and rural sectors. By the latter 1970s, the new workers coming into the labor market began to grow slowly as a result of falling birth rates in the 1960s, inducing further the use of modern technologies. These circumstances raised the incomes of industrial workers and thereby improved the income distribution.[7]

China's income inequality was as low as Japan and the ROC (Taiwan). For a vast country with many regional diversities, the low inequality was notable, and can only be explained by socialist institutions such as a ban on private enterprise and entrepreneurial incomes, and also on many forms of property income, assured employment, extensive employment of housewives, egalitarian educational opportunities, and so on. And compared with the small communist countries in Europe, as shown in Table 1, it is relatively low. This may be due to the decade of campaign and deliberate policies, mainly taxes and subsidies, to transfer more resources from the urban to the rural sectors,[8] to equalize wages and salaries between intellectual and manual labor, and between skilled and unskilled labor under the Cultural Revolution in the latter 1960s and early 1970s. This is reflected in the lowest "within disparities" in the urban sector that one can find in distribution statistics (a Gini of 0.19). What pushes up the quintile inequality index beyond that of the ROC (Taiwan) and Japan is the Maoist policy of developing industry at the expense of agriculture which left farm incomes far below the others, insuffi-

---

[6] See "Levels and Trends of Farm Families' Nonagricultural Incomes," *Philippine Review of Economics and Business,* Sept./Dec. 1985, for data on off-farm family incomes, which were nearly four times of on-farm incomes in Japan, two times in the ROC (Taiwan), one-third in Korea, and one-tenth in China in the late 1970s. With rural private enterprise, China's off-farm incomes have doubled to nearly 20 percent in the early 1980s.

[7] For details and data, see my "The Industrial and Demographic Transitions in East Asia," *Population and Development Review,* Dec. 1983.

[8] See Shigeru Ishikawa, "Pattern and Processes of Intersectoral Resources Flow: Comparison of Cases in Asia," paper presented at Economic Growth Center, Yale University, April, 1986.

cient resources for the even development of agriculture in the different regions of the country, and the ban on rural private business which limited off-farm jobs in the dry season. The new strategies in the 1980s by the Deng group are likely to lower the quintile inequalities by raising farm family incomes, and to increase within disparities in the rural and urban sectors by differentiating wages, salaries, and profits. All these are much more in consonance with a structure of incentives favorable to labor productivity and growth. Maoist experience demonstrates that both too much "between sector" and too little "within sector" inequalities contribute to unfavorable incentives to produce.

Income Disparities in the ASEAN-4

The high inequalities in the Philippines, Thailand, Malaysia, and Indonesia are partly the product of historical circumstances as there has not been any substantial changes in land distribution among peasants as was the case in East Asia. Moreover, the plantation sector from the prewar period has remained large and growing except in Thailand which has the lowest inequalities. The high inequalities in Indonesia are due to the greater diversities in the different regions of this far-flung archipelago with extreme differences in farm size, population densities, rainfall, and so on. Ethnic and cultural diversities are also much greater in the ASEAN countries than in East Asia.

It was not only the absence of comprehensive land reform but also the rural development programs which were less comprehensive and persistent over the period than in East Asia. The best programs were in Malaysia but even here the rain-fed rice farms fared poorly, compared to the irrigated rice farms and those who received land for perennial crops. Institutions such as cooperatives did not perform as well as in East Asia in spreading the benefits of the programs. Multiple-cropping and diversified agriculture were unevenly developed since irrigation facilities were much less developed than in East Asia. As a consequence, off-farm incomes of farm families were far less than in Japan and the ROC (Taiwan). Thus, the limited size of the rural development program meant that the main beneficiaries were the larger farmers, many of whom could borrow and mechanize.

Population growth in the ASEAN-4 was greater than in East Asia. The new workers coming into the rural labor market in the 1970s increased in the Philippines and Java, but the shortage of land to accommodate them enlarged the size of the landless and near-landless classes, which comprise the lowest income groups in the rural areas. In Thailand, the population moved out to the forests and hacked out new farms. But in the Northeast where most of them went, much of the land was marginal with insufficient water such that yields were low and second crops were difficult to grow, producing extensive underemployment. In Malaysia, the areas which were furnished with irrigation succeeded in raising yields and in cultivating a second crop of rice. Their incomes rose much faster than the large number of rainfed farms which can only grow one crop of rice.

Those unable to find work in the rural sector came to the cities, but many who could not find jobs in the factories and offices, drifted into odd jobs in the informal sector, particularly in the services, with intermittent and irregular work, unlike in East Asia. This drift to the informal sectors paying the lowest wage was particularly large in the Philippines and Java, where the industrial expansion was the slowest and capital-intensity of the industries was the highest.

Those who were fortunate to get jobs in the new factories and modern services were the better educated ones and were paid far better, in part because these were highly protected industries. Together with the modern bureaucracy in the rapidly expanding public sector, the educated labor force and the urban rich and well-to-do made up a new urban class in the higher income quintiles in Metro-Manila or Greater Jakarta. Unlike in urban East Asia, however, not enough jobs were created and too many were coming into the labor market there, so that real wages in the 1970s grew only very slowly in Indonesia and even fell in the Philippines. Thus, the rapid growth in the ASEAN-4 left a dualistic structure in which the modern sector paying high incomes was super-imposed on the traditional sector not yet wiped out by a longer period of high growth as was the case in East Asia.

One puzzling aspect is the high inequality index of Malaysia. The highest in ASEAN in the late 1970s when the labor market tightened and unemployment declined. It may be due to the heterogeneity of Malaysian agriculture which is an amalgam of very large and modern plantation sector efficiently operated but paying low wages due to unmechanized work, a fairly prosperous multiple-cropping farms with mechanized equipment, small holders producing rubber and other commercial crops, the rain-fed rice farms with only one-crop and still cultivating in traditional ways, especially in Sarawak, tenant farms, and the small fishermen in the coastal areas losing out to the large trawlers. Malaysia has the most diverse agricultural sector, with the largest share of farm land devoted to perennial crops and not to monsoon rice and diversified crops.

Even more puzzling is the inequality index in the nonagricultural sector, by far the highest in Asia. More data may be needed to get an understanding of this. One conjecture is that the dualism in the urban sector was sharpest in Malaysia. Malaysia was separated from Singapore only in 1965 and previously Singapore was its main business center where large financial, marketing, shipping, and the head offices of the plantations were found. With separation, there started a series of structural changes and many large companies shifted their management centers north to the cities of Malaysia. These were superimposed on the existing small sector catering to the smaller urban units. Malaysia may be exceptional in having a number of these large units. In fact, the exporting plantation sector was the largest in Asia and grew most rapidly in the 1960s and 1970s. This meant that the factories processing rubber, palm oil and other commerical crops expanded rapidly and required modern marketing, shipping and financial services in the cities. In the public sector, the emerging Malay elites began to demand their share of the boom and set out to establish the largest public enterprise sector in the ASEAN-4, and their own companies in banking, industries, and other private activities.

Finally, ethnic and cultural heterogeneities in the Malaysian cities are more pronounced than in other areas with four large groups: the Westerners and Chinese dominant in the higher quintiles and the Malay and Indian groups in the lower quintiles.

A special feature of the Philippine rural scene is the dominant position of the landlords who grew into a powerful oligarchy under the Spanish colonialists who were not interested in plantations, unlike the British and the Dutch. The other side of the coin was the prevalence of a large class of tenants and landless workers, probably the largest in Asia relative to the total agricultural population. Another feature is the long term decline of real wages since the mid-1960s, accompanied by a slow rise in the per capita intake of calories and protein from scattered nutrition surveys, not withstanding official data from food balance sheets of rapidly rising per capita supplies. (The data since 1971 are puzzling, the 1975 and 1979 surveys show much greater inequalities, to about 0.6 Gini but the 1985 preliminary data point to a Gini of about 0.46. This may be due to the possibility that the 1971 and 1975 surveys understated the samples for the highest and lowest income groups.)

An unusual feature of Indonesian income distribution as shown in its 1976 survey is the higher quintile inequality index in the rural than in the urban areas. In monsoon Asia, rural areas show lower inequalities in nearly all countries. It may be the diversities found in the different islands of the archipelago with relatively large farms and plantations in sparsely settled Sumatra, Kalimantan, and Sulawesi, tiny farms in Java and Bali, and non-monsoon agriculture further south. Java has the largest dispartities mainly because of the large size of the landless and near-landless tenant peasants, with most of the latter operating farms with less than one-fifth hectare, and without work in the drier months. Moreover, because the government put so much into the establishment of large industries, the growth of small industries, the main source of off-arm employment, was slow; accordingly off-farm incomes were insufficient for the landless and the tenants with much time on hand during the dry season. All this meant that real wages were probably not rising in the 1960s and into the early 1970s.

The lowest inequality among the ASEAN-4, that of Thailand is due in large part to the policy of permitting peasants to move out of their old farms and carve out new farms out of nearby forests. As population pressure mounted, parents left their farms to be tilled by their son and his family, a tradition rooted in the prewar decades. In the urban areas, Thai industrialization was the most labor intensive in the region, and this together with the agro-processing of diversified agriculture were the sources of off-farm incomes whose share was the largest among the ASEAN-4. Recent surveys show inequalities to be falling from the mid-1970s, but they continue to be higher than East Asia due to the greater inequalities in land ownership with tenancy in the Central Region.

Income Disparities in South Asia

It is difficult to say much about South Asia where distributive data are even scarcer than Southeast Asia, except in Sri Lanka and Bangladesh. Since countries like India, Bangladesh, Nepal and Burma are still in the early stage of the agro-industrial transition, with a large share of the labor force in agriculture and very low levels of per capita incomes, one would expect their inequalities to be low although that of Nepal is the highest in Asia. In Southeast Asia where growth accelerated from low levels in the 1950s, there was a superimposition of modern economic activities over the traditional, causing a sharpening of dualism and hence increasing disparities, as noted above. One reason that disparities are higher than expected is the large amounts of unemployed and underemployed workers with the labor force increasing faster than per capita incomes and the slow growth of the agricultural sector. Another is that these countries (India, Bangladesh, Burma and Sri Lanka) adopted a socialistic industrialization policy of creating a large number of government-owned industries where incomes paid were high.

For the larger countries, India and Bangladesh, the over-all inequalities are not high by Southeast Asian standards as can be seen in Table 1. In these low income countries, the overwhelmingly large rural population subsisting around the poverty levels are crammed into the lowest three quintiles (or 60 percent of the families) where the variations in family incomes are slight between the quintiles. In lower quintiles the families do not have enough to eat, so that the share of food expenditures in total spending is large, from 70 to 80 percent, and the cross section data show that when incomes rise the food share does not fall. This probably accounts for the relatively low quintile inequality index in the poorest countries in Asia compared to Southeast Asia.[9]

It is difficult to account for the very high income inequalities in Nepal shown by the 1967-1977 survey. It is frequently reported that much remains in Nepal of the feudalistic land system with large land owners using tenants and serfs as cultivators, a system which existed in Thailand in most of the 19th century but was terminated by the end of the century and which has been long abolished by the colonial powers in the other Asian countries during the prewar century. With 95 percent of the labor force in agriculture, the pattern of land ownership and tenure is likely to dominate the nation-wide distribution of income. On the basis of the table below, one can conjecture that the lowest 3 quintiles will be mainly made up of landless rural

Share of Farm Families by Holdings and by their Annual Average Family Income, 1976/1977

Families, Holding	Share of Families	Average Income in 1,000 Rupees
No Land (Landless)	10.4%	4.9
Marginal Unirrigated	20.3%	4.9
Marginal Irrigated	5.5%	3.5
Small Unirrigated	23.7%	4.9
Small Irrigated	7.6%	5.7
Medium Unirrigated	14.4%	5.9
Medium Irrigated	5.5%	8.6
Large Unirrigated	9.4%	6.6
Large Irrigated	3.4%	10.2
Total	100.0%	5.6

Source: From Table A-4 and Table 8.1, *A Survey of Emoloyment, Income Distribution and Consumption Patterns in Nepal*, National Planning Commission, Kathmandu, 1983.

---

[9] S. R. Osman and A. Rahman find that inequalities have been rising in Bangladesh in the 1970s over the 1960s primarily due to the large increase in the labor force in the rural areas, and stagnation of rice yields. Under Muslim inheritance law, the farm must be subdivided to all the young, and this has reduced the size of farm in the small holdings to levels below subsistence since yields have not risen to offset the smaller plots. This forces them into indebtedness and eventual sale of land to the larger farms. Thus without the population pressures the inequality index would have been much lower. See their *Study of Income Distribution in Bangladesh*, Institute of Development Studies, Dacca: 1981.

families, marginal irrigated, marginal and small unirrigated farm families, the next quintile of small irrigated and medium unirrigated, the highest of medium irrigated and the large farm families, and the high income families in business and in the upper echelon of the bureaucracies, Nepal's highest quintile's income share of 59 percent is the highest in Asia. It is said that the upper classes in Nepal, as inheritance from the feudal past, posses estates as large as thousands of hectares. Higher education in the past decades was available only to the students from these families, the higher levels of government, professions, and management of large businesses are probably manned by those coming from these families.

Along with Malaysia, the two lowest quintiles have the smallest share of income in Asia. The explanation for this may be the complex diversities among the farming population where the range and types of land tenure and tenancy arrangements among the innumerable castes and ethnic groups in the heterogenous terrain of Nepal (mountain, hill, and lowlands) countribute to a wide variation of incomes among the families, despite the small size of the nation's area and population. Two-thirds or so of the farmers are tenants, many of whom are obligated to render free labor to the owners, and are heavily indebted to moneylenders. Rents have been rising as population pressure sharpens the competition of tenants to rent land, and small farmers are forced to sell their land as they fall deeper into debt with larger families to feed, as in Bangladesh and elsewhere in the 1970s. Compounding all this is the long period of the dry weather (8 months in many areas) in which off-farm jobs must be sought but difficult to find in an economy whose growth of per capita GDP (1965-1973) has been been only 0.1 percent.

Some of the disparities in incomes may not be real as prices vary considerably. The rugged terrain in the mountains and hills prevent or limits the exchange of goods from one village to another, obstructing the tendencies of prices to equalize across the country. Also, as in most countries but not in urban China, family size is positively associated with income with the smallest families among the landless (4.6 members) and marginal farms (5.2) and the largest families among the medium (6.8) and large (8.3) farms.[10]

There appears to be no nation-wide family income survey in Burma, a socialist country of low income levels and GDP growth. But the abolition of tenant rents, and low ceilings on land ownership (which imply that the number of landless families may be small) point to low income disparities in the rural areas. Also, the nationalization of much of the nonagricultural sector has substantially reduced proprietors' incomes and property incomes which are mainly received in the upper quintiles. Under a welfare program, the distribution of education and health services among different quintiles is more egalitarian than in other countries. All this suggests that Burma's income disparities are not likely to be great and may turn out to be low, assuming that underemployment during the dry monsoon season is not too extensive.

This is suggested by the data of Sri Lanka, an extensive welfare state with a large number of nationalized industries, some amount of land reform, slow growth, and the lowest income inequality in South Asia. But its income inequality is substantial-

---

[10] Ibid., 33. Much of the information for the above generalization on Nepal was based on George L. Harris et al, *Area Handbook for Nepal, Bhutan, and Sikkim,* Chapters 5, 7, 17, etc., second Edition, Washington, DC: 1973. On the positive association between family size and total income and the negative association between per capita income and family size, see my "Low Income and Poverty in Monsoon Asia: A Comparative Survey" forthcoming in the *Philippine Review of Economics & Business.*

ly higher than the ROC (Taiwan), and this may be attributed to the limited coverage of land reform, a great deal of unemployment and underemployment, slow growth of industrialization, and insufficient off-farm incomes accruing to farm families compared to the ROC (Taiwan) — all of these more than offsetting the fact that the ROC (Taiwan) was not a welfare state.

PROSPECTS FOR THE 1980s

From the late 1970s and into the 1980s income inequality has been rising in many of the countries of Asia. Generally speaking, this may be attributable to the faster growth of the labor force relative to the growth of GDP per capita, producing in the rural areas diminishing size of farm land operated by the smaller farmers, and increasing amounts of underemployment among landless workers in the rural areas, and of unemployment in the urban sector. The population explosion of the 1960s is being transformed into a labor force explosion in the 1980s while the sluggish growth of OECD countries has contributed to the slow down of exports of most of Asia.

Accordingly, rapid growth of GDP relative to the labor force in the context of land scarce Asia is a major factor in income distribution. The problem with welfare/ socialist policies is that their direct, favorable impact on distribution is offset by the indirect effect of retarding GDP growth and hence the creation of employment. This was the case in Sri Lanka as reported in the 1978-79 survey which showed that the slow growth of the plantation sector caused underemployment to rise among its workers, substantially raising income inequalities in 1973.[11] The experience of Burma, Sri Lanka, and Maoist China suggest that there is a trade-off between growth and equity in a welfare/socialist development strategy.

Capital-intensive industrialization through government protection and subsidization also slows down GDP growth because of inefficiencies and by reducing resources which could have gone into labor-intensive industries and agricultural development, as the experience of the Philippines, Korea, and Malaysia indicates. Growth of GDP and employment is slowed down even more in the case of China, India and South Asian countries where governments invested and operated a large number of industries. Singapore's attempt to speed up capital-intensity through efforts by the government to push up wages by 20 percent was detrimental to the labor-intensive industries and small firms and contributed to slow growth and unemployment in the mid-1980s. Thus, postwar experience in Asia indicates that intervention and regulation into industrial development may not be favorable to improved income distribution. Government resources are better used in human resource development including family planning, and agricultural development particularly in physical infrastructure such as for irrigation.

In the latter 1980s, with slower growth of GDP in all countries and rapid growth in the labor force in South and Southeast Asia to be expected, the size of farms of peasant families may become smaller and underemployment and unemployment more extensive. These will tend to worsen the distribution of incomes. To counter this, ASEAN and South Asian countries should not put their main resources in capital-intensive industries but in labor-intensive ones, and especially into

---

[11] Report on Consumer Finances and Socio-Economic Survey, 1978/79, Sri Lanka, Part I, pp. 74, 105-108, Central Bank of Ceylon, Colombo: 1983.

agriculture. As rice self-sufficiency is attained in ASEAN countries, diversified agriculture (fruits, vegetables, livestock, fishery and forestry product) should be promoted to create jobs in the dry seasons and in the agro-processing of diversified products. Japan and the NICs should open up their markets for these products instead of increasing protection of their agricultural sector. South Asia has a long way to go even in rice production. If farm family incomes are not raised in South Asia and ASEAN the market for labor-intensive industrial products will not be sufficient to create jobs in the urban sector. As was pointed out above, external changes like the oil shocks and world recessions can have strong effects on income distribution, particularly in countries where external trade is a significant share of GNP.

A new factor has recently been injected into the prospects for the future. The yen has appreciated to high levels and if sustained into the 1990's may have major implications. It is said that there will be an exodus of smaller firms from Japan to other Asian countries, with the industrialization of the NIC's accelerating. If so, the strong yen may prove in the long run to be favorable for both growth and equity, especially in the NIC's and ASEAN. The ASEAN-4 may be able to offset the decline in plantation product price with the export of labor-intensive diversified farm products not only to Japan but to the ROC (Taiwan) and Korea whose agriculture will shrink even faster than hitherto expected beyond the rise of the yen. This calls for more attention to be paid to agriculture's development instead of capital-intensive, second stage, import substitution industrialization.

REFERENCES

Adleman, I. and S. Robinson. *Income Distribution Policy in Developing Countries: A Case Study of Korea.* Oxford, 1978.

Choo, Hakchung. "Estimation of Size Distribution of Income and Its Sources of Change in Korea, 1982." *Korean Social Science Journal,* Vol. 12, 1985, pp. 90-105.

Creedy, John. *Dynamics of Income Distribution.* N.Y., 1985.

Gupta, Anand P. "Poverty and Unemployment in India: Is there light at the End of the Tunnel?" A study prepared for the International Labor Organisation within the framework of the World Employment Programme, Geneva, 1981.

Hong Kong, Census and Statistics Department. *Report of the Household Expenditure Survey,* 1970-80 and the *New Consumer Price Index System.*

ILO, *Household Income and Expenditure Statistics,* No. 3, 1968-1976, Geneva, 1979.

Indonesia, Central Bureau of Statistics. *Income Distribution in Indonesia.* 1976.

Jain, Shail. "Size Distribution of Income, A Compilation of Data." Washington D.C.: World Bank, 1975.

Kaksani, N.C. *Income Inequality and Poverty: Methods of Estimation and Policy Application.* Oxford, 1980.

Korea, Republic of, National Bureau of Statistics. *Annual Report on the Family Income and Expenditure Survey* 1984.

Lecaillon, Jacquer et al. *Income Distribution of Income and Economic Development, An Analytical Survey.* Geneva: International Labor Organisation, 1984.

Meesook, O.A. *Income Consumption and Poverty in Thailand,* 1963/1964 to 1975/1976. Washington D.C.: International Bank for Reconstruction and Development, 1979.

Nepal, National Planning Commission, *A Survey of Employment Income Distribution and Consumption Patterns in Nepal,* 1983.

Osman, S.R. and A. Rahman, "Study of Income Distribution in Bangladesh," Dacca: Institute of Development Studies, 1981.

Philippines, National Census and Statistics Office, "Family Income and Expenditure Survey 1985," (preliminary).

Snodgrass, Donald. *Inequality and Economic Development in Malaysia.* Oxford, 1980.

Sri Lanka, Central Bank of Ceylon. *Report on Consumer Finances and Socio-Economic Survey* 1978-79.

Taiwan, Directorate-General of Budget. *Accounting and Statistics: Report on the Survey of Personal Income Distribution in Taiwan Area,* 1983.

Tan Tat Wai. *Income Distribution and Determination in West Malaysia.* Oxford, 1982.

Thailand, National Statistical Office. *Report on Socio-Economic Survey* 1975-76 Whole Kingdom.

United Nations, Statistical Office. *A Survey of National Sources of Income Distribution Statistics,* No. 72, 1982.

_____ , *National Accounts Statistics: Compendium of Income Distribution,* No. 79, 1985, N.Y.

PART II:

NATIONAL AND REGIONAL PROBLEMS IN ASIAN

DEVELOPMENT

9. Development Strategies and Productivity Issues in Korea, ROC (Taiwan), and Hong Kong: A Comparative Study

Wan-Soon Kim and Hojin Kang

INTRODUCTION

For more than two decades (1962-1982) Korea has demonstrated remarkable economic performance, while continuing to maintain a heavy defense burden. Gross National Product (GNP) grew at an average annual rate of 8.4 percent in real terms over the period and per capita real GNP more than tripled. As a result of this rapid growth, Korea has been acclaimed as one of the outstanding newly industrializing countries (NICs).

It is generally argued that such sustained high output growth was due largely to the shift in Korea's development strategy that took place in the early sixties. Korea's rapid industrialization was made possible by the shift in development strategy from import substitution to export promotion in the early sixties and by the successful implementation of the export-oriented policies thereafter. The ROC (Taiwan), Hong Kong, and Singapore are also some of the outward-looking developing countries that have succeeded in promoting manufactured exports.
factured exports.

However, it is to be noted that this rapid growth of the Korean economy has not been without some negative aspects. Compared with other newly industrializing countries such as the ROC (Taiwan), the Korean economy suffered from a high rate of inflation during most of the period. Despite the rapid increase in exports, the balance of payments deficit has continued to be a serious constraint on the steady growth of the economy. Sectoral imbalances and industrial concentration are other important problems that have been unsolved during Korea's rapid export-led industrialization. Although the authorities are making an all-out effort to elevate to the ranks of the developed nations, the specter of protectionism casts a shadow over Korea's prospects for meeting its growth potential and its debt-servicing obligations.

---

* In writing this chapter, material and data on Hong Kong and the ROC (Taiwan) have been drawn from the reports of the two consultants, Dr. Yung-Wing Sung and Dr. Paul K.C. Liu, associated with this research study.

PRODUCTIVITY CHANGES IN MAJOR SECTORS

Trends in Overall Economy

Korea achieved one of the highest growth rates in the world during the period, 1962-1982. As shown in Table 1, over this period of two decades, the Korean economy grew at an average annual rate of 8.4 percent, and per capita GNP (in 1975 constant U.S. dollars) rose from $239 to $815, an average annual growth rate of 6.3 percent.

Overall growth was accompanied by favorable changes in the structure of economy. The share of production and employment in various sectors of the economy changed appreciably. The manufacturing sector expanded at an average annual rate of 15.9 percent, increasing its share in the economy from 9 percent in 1962 to 34 percent in 1982. Korea's commodity exports, the engine of output expansion, increased from less than US$55 million in 1962 to US$21.9 billion in 1982, an average annual growth rate of 34.9 percent. Relative to GNP, gross commodity exports rose dramatically from about 2 to 32 percent. In 1982, manufactured products made up nearly 94 percent of the total commodity exports.

The ROC (Taiwan) and Hong Kong also achieved similarly high economic growth rates during the period, 1961-1983. In a comparable basis, Table 2 shows that over this period of two decades GDP grew at an average annual rate of 8.8 percent for the ROC (Taiwan) and 8.7 percent for Hong Kong. As was the case in Korea, export expansion was the prime mover of high output growth. For the ROC (Taiwan), total exports recorded an average annual growth rate of 17 percent, surpassing the overall economic growth rate. In the case of Hong Kong, the growth rate of exports was 10.5 percent, a somewhat less impressive number compared with those of Korea and the ROC (Taiwan). However, when we consider the fact that Hong Kong has already started exporting manufactures in the fifties and that Hong Kong is a manufacturing city state and a major entrepot, there is no doubt that export growth was the dynamic force leading economic growth in Hong Kong.

Changes in the Output Share of Agriculture, Manufacturing and Service Sectors

The long-range growth pattern is usually characterized by an uneven growth of various sectors, particularly by a relatively higher growth of the industrial sector compared with the other sectors in the economy. Evidence for this can be seen in the rapid industrialization of the advanced countries during the eighteenth and nineteenth centuries.

The high economic growth rates of both Korea and the ROC (Taiwan) over the last two decades were accompanied by their rapid industrialization. Table 3 shows that the expansion of the manufacturing sector in Korea, faster than the growth of the overall economy, raised its output share in GNP from about 9 percent in 1962 to 34 percent in 1982. In comparison, the primary sector grew at an average annual rate of only 4 percent during the same period. As a result, its share in GNP declined from about 45 percent to 19 percent. The share of the services sector in GNP remained almost unchanged at about 47 percent between 1962 and 1982, so it grew at a rate almost equal to that of the overall economy.

Similarly, rapid industrialization changed the economic structure of the ROC

Table 1. Korea: Major Indicators of Economic Performance, 1962-82

	1962	1972	1982	Annual Average Growth Rate (%)		
				1962-1972	1972-1982	1962-1982
1. Population (in million)	26.5	33.5	39.3	2.4	1.6	2.0
2. GNP (in 1975 constant billion Won)	3,071	7,336	15,509	9.1	7.7	8.4
Per Capita GNP (in 1975 constant Won)	115,887	219,881	394,631	6.6	6.0	6.3
(in 1975 constant US$)	239	454	815	6.6	6.0	6.3
3. Exports and Imports						
Commodity exports (million US$)	55	1,624	21,853	40.3	29.7	34.9
Commodity imports (million US$)	422	2,522	24,251	19.6	25.4	22.5
Share of manufactured exports (%)	27.0	87.7	93.7			
Ratio of exports to GNP (%)	2.0	16.4	31.8			
Ratio of imports to GNP (%)	15.6	23.7	36.5			
4. Investment and Savings Ratio (to GNP)						
Gross investment (%)	12.8	22.2	27.0			
Domestic savings (%)	3.2	16.5	22.4			
Foreign savings (%)	10.7	5.1	4.5			

Source: Bank of Korea, *Economic Statistics Yearbook*, various years; and *National Income Accounts*, 1984.

Table 2. Economic Performance of Hong Kong, the ROC (Taiwan) and Korea

					(Real Average Annual Growth Rate in %)		
	1961-65	1966-70	1971-75	1976-80	1981-83	1961-83
Hong Kong						
GDP	11.80	6.44	6.57	12.32	5.40	8.74
Per capita GDP	8.34	4.42	4.36	9.29	3.55	6.18
Total exports	9.3	14.36	4.64	16.67	8.46	10.49
ROC (Taiwan)						
GDP	8.40	9.79	8.84	10.25	5.31	8.79
Per capita GDP	5.05	6.54	6.78	8.12	3.54	6.21
Exports	20.60	22.02	15.37	16.31	7.15	16.99
Korea						
GDP	6.52	10.37	9.52	7.58	7.12	8.31
Per capita GDP	3.60	8.23	6.93	5.89	5.53	6.07
Exports	23.88	48.76	23.68	17.47	7.08	21.14

Sources: Hong Kong:
Census & Statistics Dept., *Estimates of Gross Domestic Product*, various issues.

—, *Hong Kong Statistics 1947-1967*, 1969.

Hong Kong Government, *Economic Prospects*, various issues.
Hsia, Ho & Lim, *The Structure and Growth of the Hong Kong Economy* (Wiesbanden, 1975).
Edward K.Y. Chen, *Hyper-growth in Asian Economies* (Macmillan, 1979).

ROC (Taiwan):
Executive Yuan, *Statistics Yearbook for Republic of China*, various issues.

—, *Industry of Free China*, various issues.

United Nations, *Statistical Yearbook for Asia and Pacific*, various issues.

Korea:
Same as Table 1.

Table 3. Korea: Growth and Change in the Industrial Structure, 1962-82

(Unit: %)

	Changes in Output Share by Major Sector			Annual Average Growth Rate		
	1962	1972	1982	1962-72	73 82	62 82
GNP	100.0	100.0	100.0	9.1	7.7	8.4
Primary Industry	45.3	29.2	19.2	4.5	3.3	3.9
Manufacturing	9.1	20.9	34.2	18.6	13.2	15.9
Social Overhead & Service	45.6	49.6	46.6	10.1	7.0	8.6

Source: Same as Table 1.

Table 4. ROC (Taiwan): Gross Domestic Product by Industrial Origin, 1951-80

(Unit: %)

	Share in GDP			
	1951	1960	1970	1980
1. Primary	32.5	28.7	15.5	7.7
2. Secondary	23.9	29.6	41.3	52.2
3. Tertiary	43.6	41.7	43.2	40.1

Sources: S.C. Tsiang and Rong-I Wu, "Foreign Trade and Investment as Boosters for Take-off: The Experiences of the Four Asian Newly Industrializing Countries", W. Galenson ed. *Foreign Trade and Investment – Economic Growth in the Newly Industrializing Asian Countries,* (Madison, Wisconsin: The University of Wisconsin Press, 1985), p. 313.

Table 5. Hong Kong: Gross Domestic Product by Industrial Origin, 1960-1982

(Unit: %)

	Share in GDP				
1960/61[1]	1960/61[1]	1970	1976	1980	1982
1. Primary	3.6	2.2	1.4	1.1	0.9
2. Secondary	32.4	37.1	35.3	31.9	30.5
Mfg.	24.7	30.9	28.2	23.9	21.8
3. Tertiary	63.9	60.7	63.3	67.0	68.6

Sources: Census & Statistics Department, *Estimates of Gross Domestic Products,* various issues. Hong Kong Government, *Report on the National Income Survey of Hong Kong,* 1969. Hsia, Ho & Lim, *The Structure and Growth of the Hong Kong Economy,* 1975.

Note: 1   1960/61 Fiscal Year.

(Taiwan) noticeably over the period 1952-1979. Table 4 shows that the share of agriculture in gross domestic product (GDP) dropped from about 33 percent in 1951 to only 8 percent in 1980, while the share of industrial sector rose from 24 percent to 52 percent.

The high growth of the industrial sector in the ROC (Taiwan) in the sixties was caused primarily by the unprecedented rate of output growth of the three manufacturing industries: food processing, textiles, and electrical machinery. These three industries contributed more than a third of the total manufacturing expansion during the period of light manufacturing expansion (up until 1970).[1]

Table 5 shows the industrial origin of GDP for Hong Kong. The primary sector in Hong Kong is insignificant. The share of the industrial sector expanded in the sixties, because of the expansion of manufacturing export about 80% of manufacturing output is exported directly or indirectly. In the seventies, however, the relative share of the industrial sector declined, largely due to weaker export performance than in the sixties leading to the relative decline of manufacturing, and the rapid expansion of financial and other services.

The share of the tertiary sector in GDP declined in the sixties, largely a result of the relative expansion of the manufacturing, but increased since 1970, partly a result of the relative decline of manufacturing in the early seventies, but also partly due to the dramatic expansion of the service sector, reflecting the development of Hong Kong as a financial center.

Growth and Productivity Changes in the Manufacturing Sector

Table 6 shows that between 1963 and 1982 Korea's labor productivity in manufacturing, as measured by value added per employee, grew at an annual average rate of 6.4 percent. Further, Table 7 indicates labor productivity by major industrial sectors over the same period. A couple of points should be noted from Table 7. First, there has not been much difference in the growth rate of productivity among sectors since 1970. Between 1960 and 1982, the productivity of the primary sector relative to that of the manufacturing sector declined only slightly from about 37 percent to 34 percent, whereas that of social overhead and other service sector rose rapidly in the sixties but did not increase relative to other sectors between 1970 and 1982. Second, the manufacturing sector has continued to be the highest productivity sector. Its rapid expansion absorbed surplus labor from relatively low productivity sectors, thereby improving productivity of the overall economy.

Paul K.C. Liu[2] observes similar differences in productivity growth among sectors in the ROC (Taiwan). The manufacturing sector has shown the most rapid productivity growth and become the highest productivity sector since the seventies. Liu argues that the difference in growth rates undoubtedly reflect: first, sectoral efficiency in removal of limitations of natural resources; and second, capacity for absorbing labor force, human investment and technology. Since the cultivated land is limited, the law of diminishing returns has been manifested in the trend of agricultural production: its average annual growth rates dropped from 3.7 percent in 1953-62 to 2.8 percent in 1963-72 and then 0.7 percent in 1973-82.

---

[1] Shirley Kuo, G. Ranis, and J. Fei *The Taiwan Success Story* (Boulder, Colorado: Westview Press), 1981, p. 10.

[2] Consultant from the ROC (Taiwan) associated with this research study.

Table 6. Korea: Manufacturing Labor Productivity and Real Wages, 1963-82

(Unit: %)

Year	Value added per employee[1]		Average real wages[2]	
	1975 constant Won (1,000)	Annual increase (%)	1975 constant Won (1,000)	Annual increase (%)
1963	425.4	—	16,224	—
1964	447.7	5.2	15,276	−5.8
1965	445.2	−0.6	15,862	3.8
1966	483.9	8.7	16,780	5.8
1967	480.1	−0.8	18,496	10.2
1968	532.9	11.0	21,053	13.8
1969	615.4	15.5	25,672	21.9
1970	708.0	15.0	29,416	14.6
1971	808.4	14.2	31,259	6.3
1972	852.0	5.4	32,374	3.6
1973	896.6	5.2	34,891	7.8
1974	915.5	2.1	38,143	9.3
1975	940.6	2.7	38,378	0.6
1976	949.5	0.9	44,788	16.7
1977	1,039.6	9.5	54,377	21.4
1978	1,164.2	12.0	63,854	17.4
1979	1,233.3	5.9	69,566	8.9
1980	1,282.9	4.0	66,403	−4.5
1981	1,421.8	10.8	64,392	−3.0
1982	1,392.4	−2.1	68,888	7.0
Annual average increase (%):				
1963-72		8.0		8.0
1972-82		5.0		7.8
1963-82		6.4		7.9

Source: Bank of Korea, *Economic Statistics Yearbook*, various issues.

Notes: 1 The gross domestic product of manufacturing at 1975 constant factor cost, divided by the number of employees in that sector.
     2 Monthly earnings of regular employees in manufacturing.

Common to resource-poor industrializing countries, the ROC (Taiwan) has long been highly dependent on foreign sources for most of minerals, energy, and basic industrial raw materials to foster her industrial development. These imported raw materials were largely obtained through net earnings from trading the processed goods in the competitive international market place. In spite of such natural resources limitations, the industrial sector of the ROC (Taiwan) has been capable of removing physical constraints and absorbing surplus labor and has been one of the most important determinants in the sustained increase of labor productivity.

As in the case of Korea, the service sector in the ROC (Taiwan) is characterized

Table 7. Korea: Sectoral Productivity Measured by
Value Added per Employee (Manufacturing = 100)

(Unit: %)

	1963	1970	1982
Primary	36.6	34.1	34.3
Manufacturing	100.0	100.0	100.0
Social Overhead & Service	77.8	93.7	93.0

Source: Same as Table 1.

Table 8. ROC (Taiwan): Gross Domestic Product per worker and
Average Annual Growth Rate by Industries, 1951-1983

	GDP per worker (NT$ at 1976 Prices)			
	Agriculture	Manufacturing	Services	Total
1951-55	17,915	30,398	49,787	29,485
1956-60	21,864	43,904	59,556	37,785
1961-65	31,307	79,242	88,096	58,304
1966-70	40,232	121,372	103,889	80,627
1971-75	44,887	154,840	128,756	107,808
1976-80	56,209	187,628	158,306	141,826
1981-83	65,315	217,403	177,446	166,096

	Average Annual Growth Rate (%)			
1951-55	—	—	—	—
1956-60	4.41	8.89	3.92	5.63
1961-65	8.64	16.10	9.58	10.86
1966-70	5.70	10.64	3.59	7.66
1971-75	2.31	5.51	4.79	6.74
1976-80	5.04	4.24	4.59	6.31
1981-83	5.40	5.29	4.03	5.70

Sources: Directorate General of Budget, Accounting and Statistics, *National Income of Republic of China* Taiwan Provincial Labor Force Survey and Research Institute, *Quarterly Report on the Labor Force Survey in Taiwan, Republic of China.*

by dualism. The rise in productivity was not only closely linked with the production activities of the remaining sectors but also depended on the speed of structural transformation from traditional to modern organizations. Services needed by the export industries were largely concentrated on the modern sectors of transportation, communication, storage, insurance and financial institutions which had a relatively high growth of labor productivity.

Table 9 shows the distribution of employment by sector and the relative labor productivities of different industries of Hong Kong. Manufacturing employs over 40 percent of all workers, and its labor productivity is low, reflecting the fact that Hong Kong specializes in labor-intensive manufactures. In contrast, the relative productivity of the service sector exceeds the nationwide average.

Sources of Economic Growth

Both demand and supply factors have been responsible for Korea's rapid growth during this period. To begin with, it was a lowering of the growth rate of population. This is beneficial to overall labor productivity because it eventually reduces the denominator. Like the ROC (Taiwan) and Hong Kong, Korea is a densely populated nation. Therefore, rapid growth of population is certainly a heavy economic burden. The Korean government's effective family planning program helped lower the population growth rate from 3 percent during 1955-1962 to 2 percent during 1963-1982 and to about 1.58 percent in 1983.

From 1963 to 1982, Korea's national income grew at an annual average rate of 7.6 percent, in spite of the worldwide energy crisis and the consequent recessions in the world economy. According to an analysis of the sources of economic growth a la Denison, some 64 percent of the 7.6 percent income growth — or 4.9 percentage points — was attributable to increases in factor inputs such as labor and capital. The remaining 2.7 percentage points (about 36 percent) resulted from rises in productivity per unit of factor input or total factor productivity.

Table 9. Hong Kong: Share in Employment and Relative Productivity
of Different Industries, 1961-81

	Share in Employment (%)				Relative Productivity			
	1961	1971	1976	1981	1961	1971	1976	1981
1. Primary	8.09	4.27	2.60	2.01	0.44	0.44	0.54	0.45
2. Secondary	48.97	53.54	51.20	49.76	0.66	0.65	0.69	0.64
Mfg.	43.02	47.73	44.98	41.22	0.57	0.59	0.63	0.55
3. Tertiary	42.94	42.19	46.20	48.23	1.49	1.50	1.37	1.40

Sources: Census and Statistics Department, *Population Census-Basic Tables,* various issues.

Note: Relative productivity figures are derived by dividing the output share for an industry by its corresponding employment share (in terms of man-hours). An industry with a relative productivity measure greater than 1.00 has an above average productivity level.

Table 10 shows in detail the contributions to growth by factor inputs. It can be seen that increase in labor inputs except education accounted for 2.92 percentage points (38 percent). Increases in capital inputs accounted for 1.58 percentage points or 21 percent of national income growth. But it can be easily seen that compared with the growth of labor input, that of capital input was much faster during the 1972-1982 period, due to heavy industrialization with subsidized capital. In sum, an increase in total factor input contributed 4.89 percentage points, or 64 percent of national income growth, while the remaining 2.72 percentage points (36 percent) are accounted for by an increase in output per unit of input. Of the elements that accounted for the increase in total factor productivity, about 0.7 percentage points was contributed by the resource reallocation associated with the relative decline of labor employed in agriculture and other low-productivity sectors. While technological progress[3] accounted for a little more than 1 percentage point (14 percent), economies of scale resulting from the rapid growth and the changing patterns of consumption expenditure contributed about 1.5 percentage points (nearly 20 percent) to overall economic growth.

Compared with similar estimates for the ROC (Taiwan) in Table 11, the size of the contribution of factor input to growth in Korea appears high. In the case of the ROC (Taiwan) over the period, 1962-1982, increases in capital and labor inputs only contributed about 20 percent of gross output. But it is important to note that when the increase in total factor input including material and energy inputs was taken into account, total factor input accounted for more than 80 percent.

Though in both Korea and the ROC (Taiwan) the size of the contribution of total factor input to overall growth was unusually high, the more efficient use of

Table 10. Korea: Sources of Growth of Actual National Income 1963-82

(Unit: percent change in annual rates)

	1963-72	1972-82	1963-82
National Income (growth rate)	8.22	7.05	7.61
Factor Input	4.19	5.58	4.89
Labor	2.74	3.04	2.92
Capital	1.14	2.10	1.58
Output per unit of Input	4.03	1.47	2.72
Resource Reallocation	0.63	0.68	0.66
Economies of Scale	1.52	1.46	1.49
Technological Progress	1.89	0.30	1.09
Increased Workers's Education	0.31	0.44	0.39
Others	−0.01	−0.97	−0.52

Source: Kwang-suk Kim and Joon-kyung Park, *Sources of Economic Growth* (Seoul: Korea Development Institute, 1985), Table 4-6.

---

[3] Contributions of technological progress are residuals obtained by subtracting the effects of all other determinants from the growth in output per unit of input.

Table 11. ROC (Taiwan): Output, Input, and Productivity Trends, 1962-82

(Unit: percent change in annual rates)

	1962-66	1967-71	1972-76	1977-82	1962-82
Gross Output	10.7	15.0	10.3	7.9	10.8
Total Factor Input	7.1	12.8	9.1	6.3	8.7
Total Factor Productivity	3.6	2.2	1.2	1.5	2.1
Scale Economies	1.2	1.9	1.2	0.8	1.3
Technical Change	2.4	0.3	−0.1	0.8	0.8
Net Output	9.5	10.5	8.7	7.7	9.1
Primary Factor Input	3.8	6.3	6.3	4.5	5.2
Primary Factor Productivity	5.7	4.2	2.5	3.2	3.9

Source: Tze-Tseng Huang. "Measurement of Total Factor Productivity in the Republic of China,"
in Tzong-shian Yu ed. *Raising Productivity-Experience of the Republic of China*. (Tokyo:
Asian Productivity Organization, 1985), p. 40.

factor inputs assumed a predominant role for the economy of Hong Kong. As
shown in Table 12, over the entire period, 1961-1984, an increase in total factor
productivity explained more than 58 percent of output growth, although the
contribution share slowed down sharply to about 27 percent in the most recent
period, 1981-1984. Relatively fast growth of total factor productivity in Hong
Kong, particularly in the period 1966-1981 was attributable to the rising level of
education, the youthfulness of the labor force, the high rate of investment, and the
shift from manufacturing, a sector of relatively low productivity, into finance and
tourism, sectors of high productivity.

Second, the decomposition of the growth of total factor productivity of both
Korea and the ROC (Taiwan) indicates that technical retardation was responsible
for almost all the decline in productivity. In Korea, technical progress made the
second largest contribution to growth during period, 1963-1972, but made the
lowest contribution during the latter period, 1972-1982. This is reflected in the
increased incremental capital-output ratio (ICOR). ICOR for the whole economy
showed a sharp rise from 2.5 during 1963-1972 to 4.7 during 1973-1982. This trend
in technical retardation was equally observable in the ROC (Taiwan) up to 1976
but reversed itself slightly in the 1977-1982 period.

Technical innovation is critical to the rise in labor productivity and hence to
sustain the rate of growth. In Korea, the ROC (Taiwan), and Hong Kong since the
pattern of industrial exports is expected to shift toward higher value-added,
technology-intensive products, and since the development of new technologies
and technological innovation would release the resource constraints on economic
growth, investment in human capital should be a central component of their
development policies in the future.

If we analyze the sources of Korea's economic growth, as measured from the
demand side, the expansion of both domestic and export demand was the major
source of the overall growth, accounting for about 70 percent over the corresponding period.

What is, however, interesting is the comparison in Table 13 of the relative contributions to growth by the demand factors. It shows a distinctive shift in the sources of growth starting in 1964. While domestic demand expansion and import substitution explained most of the growth and structural change prior to 1963, export expansion cmcrgcd as a major source of growth from 1964, replacing import substitution. Import substitution accounted for 34 percent of the overall economic growth during the period from 1955 to 1963, but contributed only 10 percent between 1963 and 1973. In comparison, the contribution made by export expansion rose from about 9 percent to 40 percent over the corresponding period, outweighing even domestic expansion. This coincides with the shift in Korea's strategy for industrialization from import substitution toward export promotion in the 1960s.

Compared with Korea, export expansion was much more a decisive factor in the ROC (Taiwan's) economic growth since the 1960's. Table 14 shows the result of a similar decomposition of the sources of demand for the ROC (Taiwan) during the period of 1956-1976. As a source of output expansion, export expansion has become increasingly important. In the early period, 1956-61, the contribution of export expansion to output growth was 22.5 percent. It increased rapidly to 35.0 percent in 1961-66, 45.9 percent in 1966-71, and 67.7 percent in 1971-76. Entering into the 1960s, it is evident that export expansion was a decisive factor in the rapid growth of the ROC (Taiwan); furthermore, in the 1970s, its importance outweighed even domestic expansion. Import substitution was a trivial factor, although it registered a slight contribution in the 1950s.

OUTWARD-LOOKING DEVELOPMENT STRATEGY

Foreign-Sector Industrial Policies

The military revolution in 1961 opened a new page in Korea's political and economic history. Economic growth and modernization became an ideology, under the auspices of which the military government launched large-scale industrial development programs. Because of its poor natural resource endowment and small domestic market, Korea's policy makers chose an outward-looking development strategy, turning away from then on-going inward-looking development strategies based on import substitution. Therefore, in 1962 when the government launched its First Five-Year Plan (1962-1966), it emphasized trade in labor-intensive manufacturing exports in which Korea had comparative advantage, and mobilized foreign savings for needed capital formation since domestic savings were quite meager.

One important characteristic of this policy innovation was export promotion to solve balance of payments problems in financing various investment projects. Korea, being one of the most densely populated countries in the world, possessed a strong potential for production of labor-intensive export manufactures, and this latent potential could be effectively exploited by positive government policies. Export promotion policies gathered momentum as time passed. As a result, the period after 1962 is identified as the export-led growth phase in Korea's economic development.

In support of export expansion, a number of important government measures were subsequently implemented. A unified exchange rate system replaced the

Table 12. Hong Kong: Growth Rates of Total Factor Productivity, 1961-1984

(Unit: %)

Economy	Growth Rate	Capital Input	Labor Input*	Total Factor Productivity
1961-66	10.9 (100)	4.0 (37)	3.1 (28)	3.8 (35)
1966-71	6.7 (100)	0.4 (7)	0.2 (3)	6.1 (90)
1971-76	8.4 (100)	1.2 (14)	1.3 (16)	5.9 (70)
1976-81	10.8 (100)	2.5 (23)	1.7 (16)	6.6 (61)
1981-84	5.1 (100)	2.8 (56)	0.9 (18)	1.4 (27)
1961-84	8.7 (100)	2.1 (25)	1.5 (17)	5.0 (58)
Manufacturing				
1961-66	8.3 (100)	5.0 (60)	1.0 (12)	2.4 (28)
1966-71	7.0 (100)	1.0 (14)	2.6 (38)	3.4 (48)
1971-76	5.4 (100)	0.5 (10)	0.9 (17)	3.9 (73)
1976-81	10.4 (100)	3.7 (36)	1.4 (14)	5.3 (51)
1981-84	9.7 (100)	1.1 (12)	0.7 (8)	7.8 (81)
1961-84	8.0 (100)	2.4 (29)	1.4 (17)	4.3 (53)

Sources: *Census & Statistics Dept., Industrial Production,* 1971, 1973, 1976, 1978, 1979, 1980, 1981.
—————, *Estimates of Gross Domestic Product,* various issues.
—————, *Monthly Digest of Statistics,* various issues.

Values in parentheses are shares of respective factors in percentage.
* The change in hours worked is adjusted.

Table 13. Korea: Demand Related Sources of Growth, 1955-1973

(Unit: %)

	Domestic Demand Expansion	Export Expansion	Import Substitution	Others
1955-1963	25.6	8.7	33.7	32.0
1963-1973	34.4	40.1	9.9	15.6
1955-1973	33.7	38.9	11.0	16.4

Source: Kwang-suk Kim and Michael Roemer, *Growth and Structural Transformation* (Cambridge, Mass: Harvard University Press, 1979), p. 114.

Table 14. ROC (Taiwan): Demand Related Sources of Growth, 1956-76

(Unit: %)

	Domestic Demand Expansion	Export Expansion	Import Substitution	Others
1956-61	61.6	22.5	7.7	8.2
1961-66	63.2	35.0	0.5	1.3
1966-71	51.4	45.9	5.7	−3.0
1971-76	34.7	67.7	−2.4	0.0

Sources: Shirley Kuo, *et al. The Taiwan Success Story* (Boulder, Coloradio: Westview Press, 1981), p. 110.

existing multiple exchange rate system and the Korean Won was occasionally devalued. Earlier, in the late 1950s, similar measures were adopted in the ROC (Taiwan), and these were considered to be most important for the export expansion of the country, because they assured the exporters of making a sound economic calculation and realizing reasonable earnings from exchange rate uncertainties.

Corporate and income taxes on export earnings were also reduced by 50 percent and the business activity tax was exempted for exporters. In addition, the government made available short-term export financing at the preferential interest rate and allowed tariff rebates on materials imported for export production. These measures enabled Korea exporters to conduct their business as if they were operating under a free trade regime.

But the most important incentive offered to exporters was that they could cope with the chunk of their financing requirements by borrowing from the bank at the preferential interest rate. In 1965, the preferential interest rate on export financing was 6.5 percent when the ordinary commercial lending rate was 26 percent. An almost unlimited supply of short-term credits to exporters at such a preferential interest rate was an enormous incentive for exporters in an economy where credits were tightly controlled by the government and access to the banking institutions was very selective.

In the ROC (Taiwan), the trade and payments regime went through several changes in the postwar period. In 1949, a monetary reform was effected and attention was directed to trade policy in the early fifties. In 1952 a program of import substitution was initiated, based on existing economic conditions and circumstances. As circumstances changed in the latter half of the fifties when the ROC (Taiwan) completed the relatively easy task of replacing imports of nondurable consumer goods with domestic production, it was faced with a problem that is now well recognized as inherent in an import-substitution strategy. Policy could respond to these circumstances either by broadening and deepening import substitution to include consumer durables and some capital equipment, or by reversing its thrust and beginning to promote exports. Taiwan chose a strategy of export promotion.[4]

Ranis gives three major reasons why the ROC (Taiwan) chose export promotion, equally relevant for Korea as well. Of greatest importance was the relatively small size of the domestic market which continues to condemn any strategy of import substitution to low-volume, high-cost output. Next, the ROC (Taiwan) faced continuing pressure of surplus labor, which could be absorbed through expansion of production of labor-intensive consumer goods. Finally, a strategy of broadening and deepening import substitution would have required production of capital- and skill-intensive products which would have involved steeply rising costs for Taiwan.[5]

The transition from import substitution to export promotion was rather smooth. Between 1954 and 1958 there were signs that a new strategy was evolving, although much hesitancy remained. In 1954, tax rebates were begun on the import content of exports, and in 1956, import privileges were awarded to enterprises in response to their success in exporting. The export promotion strategy became more clearly dominant in 1960-61 as part of the third Four-Year Economic Plan (1961-64), which contained both financial reform and some liberalization of trade controls. Another step toward an export-oriented development strategy was taken in 1965, when export-processing zones were authorized and one was established in Kaohsiung. This outward-oriented strategy has been sustained to the present.[6]

Historically, Hong Kong evolved economically as an entrepot. In 1950, the entrepot function was interrupted due to the U.N. embargo on trade with the China and the population of Hong Kong was expanding massively due to the inflow of refugees from the mainland. Thus, the only alternative for Hong Kong was to become a producer of industrial goods rather than just a trader of such products. Given the size of Hong Kong and the limitations of its agricultural lands, they have to import raw materials and export to pay for them, that is, import substitution was not an option open to them. An outward-oriented growth came out of sheer necessity.[7]

But the question still remained with respect to a type of policy that would best support an outward-oriented strategy. Under colonial rule and as an entrepot, Hong Kong has developed a well-established tradition of free trade. Given the uncertainties of the fifties, free trade embedded in a more general laissez-faire regime became the obvious choice because no one knew what else to do. Industrialization in Hong Kong was thus created not by design but by the dictates of the market and social necessity.[8]

Role of Foreign Capital

Another measure taken by the Korean government was to encourage the inflow of foreign savings to make up for the insufficiency of domestic savings and foreign exchange. In 1966, the government enacted a comprehensive Foreign Capital

---

[4] Shirley Kuo and John Fei, "Causes and Roles of Export Expansion in the Republic of China," *Foreign Trade and Investment — Economic Growth in the Newly Industrializing Asian Countries,* ed. W. Galenson (Madison, Wis.: The University of Wisconsin Press, 1985), pp. 48-53.

[5] Laurence B. Krause, "Introduction," *Foreign Trade and Investment,* ed. W. Galenson (Madison, Wis.: The University of Wisconsin, 1985), pp. 6-7.

[6] *Ibid.*

[7] *Ibid.*

[8] *Ibid.,* p. 10.

Promotion Act whereby the government underwrote the risk borne by foreign investors. As shown in Table 15, the rapid growth and structural changes that took place in Korea were made possible to a great extent by a rapid rise in capital formation, a significant portion of which was accounted for by foreign savings. Between 1962 and 1971, foreign savings accounted for more than 40 percent of total savings. Since then the share of foreign savings in financing gross investment was down considerably and accounted for about 10 percent in 1983.

Korea's outward-looking development strategy brought a rapid growth in exports. The annual growth rate of exports between 1962-1972 was more than 40 percent in real terms. (see Table 1) By the early 1970s, Korea emerged as a dominant exporter in a number of labor-intensive commodities such as footwear, plywood, textiles, and clothing.

Aid from the U.S. was particularly important for the ROC (Taiwan) from 1951 through 1962, when it constituted over 90 percent of all foreign capital commitments and between 35 percent and 45 percent of gross domestic capital formation in each year. The U.S. aid declined rapidly in the early sixties, and foreign direct

Table 15. Korea: Trends in the Ratios of Gross Investment and
Foreign Savings to GNP, 1962-1982

(Unit: %)

	Gross Investment (A)	Foreign Savings (B)	B/A (%)
1962	12.8	10.7	83.3
1963	18.1	10.4	57.5
1964	14.0	6.9	48.8
1965	15.0	6.4	42.6
1966	21.6	8.4	39.1
1967	21.9	8.8	40.2
1968	25.9	11.2	43.1
1969	28.8	10.6	36.8
1970	26.8	9.3	34.7
1971	25.1	10.5	41.8
1972	22.2	5.1	23.0
1973	25.7	3.7	14.4
1974	31.7	12.1	38.2
1975	30.0	10.1	33.7
1976	25.6	2.3	9.0
1977	27.7	0.6	2.2
1978	31.2	3.1	9.9
1979	35.6	7.1	19.9
1980	31.3	9.4	30.0
1981	29.1	7.7	26.5
1982	27.0	4.5	16.7
1983	27.8	2.9	10.4

Source: Bank of Korea. *National Income Accounts*, 1984.

investment then began to increase. In overall, however, foreign capital was no longer a major share of gross domestic investment. The economy of the ROC (Taiwan) has not only graduated from an aid to a self-sustaining growth situation but been continuously moving toward a capital exporting situation since 1970.

With respect to the role of foreign direct investment (FDI), there is a crucial difference between the ROC (Taiwan) and Korea. Ranis and Schive conclude that FDI has been of considerable quantitative importance to the ROC (Taiwan), especially during the late sixties, and that it assumed growing importance in the years that followed. From 1951 to 1960, during the import-substitution phase of ROC (Taiwan's) development, FDI represented only 1.8 percent of total investment and 3.9 percent of private investment. During 1961-70, the primary export-substitution stage, FDI increased to 3.2 percent of total investment and 5.1 percent of private investment. FDI in the ROC (Taiwan) has been a major channel of continuing technology transfer.[9]

Ranis and Schive find a significant impact of FDI on the exports of the ROC (Taiwan), because of the relatively superior marketing ability of the foreign firms. On average, FDI firms export almost 46 percent of their sales, while domestic enterprises in manufacturing are less vented for outside, exporting about 34 percent of sales. Also, they find that FDI firms use more foreign technologies than domestic firms, since FDI firms have more knowledge of and greater access to foreign technologies.[10]

As pointed out already, foreign capital in all its forms has made an important contribution to the Korea economy, but the contribution of FDI alone has not been of great importance. As analyzed by Bohn Young Koo, FDI has been approved by the Korean government since 1962. But it was effectively discouraged because government screened FDI if it harmed domestically owned firms. As a result, there was no great response until the FDI guidelines were liberalized in 1980. In the meantime, specific projects were not open to foreign investors, and joint ventures were encouraged rather than wholly-owned firms.[11]

In sum, for almost all of the postwar period, state policy has been quite restrictive with respect to foreign investors. FDI in Korea was valued at only US$1 billion at the end of 1980. FDI as a share of gross domestic capital formation never reached 3 percent in any year except 1973, when it was 4.7 percent. In most years it was 1 percent or less. Thus, FDI made at most a modest contribution to the Korean economy. Koo concludes that FDI contributed about 1 percent per year to Korea's growth in the late seventies. It is quite negligible compared with the role of FDI in the ROC (Taiwan), which contributed between 6.4 percent and 8.3 percent to GNP between 1974 and 1979.[12]

Much about the role of foreign capital in Hong Kong is not known. Indeed, even the term "foreign" is ambiguous, given the role of British firms that have been resident in the colony for over a hundred years, and the existence of "Overseas Chinese" owners who have recently taken up residence in Hong Kong. However, the inflow of capital combined with earnings from banking, shipping, and tourism

[9] G. Ranis and C. Shive, "Direct Foreign Investment in Taiwan's Development," *Foreign Trade and Investment,* ed. W. Galenson (Madison, Wis.: The University of Wisconsin, 1985), pp. 94-95.

[10] *Ibid.,* pp. 105-111.

[11] Bohn Young Koo, "The Role of Direct Foreign Investment in Korea's Recent Economic Growth," *Foreign Trade and Investment,* ed. W. Galenson (Madison, Wis.: The University of Wisconsin, 1985), pp. 177-179.

[12] *Ibid.,* pp. 190-204.

must have played a significant role in financing the persistent merchandise trade deficit Hong Kong has had in recent years. There are a couple of features that distinguish Hong Kong from the other LDCs at the initial stage of industrialization. The first is the complete absence of foreign aid. There was no capital inflow at the government level for the purpose of capital formation. The second is Hong Kong's policy toward foreign direct investment to permit it freely. Overseas investors are not discriminated against, but neither are they attracted to Hong Kong by consessions or tax holidays.[13]

Overseas investment in Hong Kong's manufacturing sectors was insignificant in the initial stage of Hong Kong's industrialization. It was not until the mid-sixties after Hong Kong had already established its manufacturing industries that overseas investors started to move into that sector at an accelerated rate. They were drawn to Hong Kong by its favorable investment climate such as nondiscriminatory policies, free foreign exchange, low tax rates, good labor relations, and excellent supporting facilities.[14]

Quantitatively overseas investments accounted for 1 percent of, Hong Kong's manufacturing establishments, approximately 10 percent of their employment, and some 16 percent of their output in 1978.[15]

Qualitatively, as overseas investment poured in, it brought new industries and technology, in addition to supplementing old ones, broadening the industrial base of Hong Kong. Some of Hong Kong's new industries such as electronics and watches and clocks were first brought in by overseas investors. In an environment where overseas and local firms work competitively side by side, imitation by local entrepreneurs was almost immediate. In just a few years, numerous local firms sprang up and eventually took over the bulk of the business. The overseas firms served as a catalyst to Hong Kong's further industrialization.[16]

Government Intervention and Factor Price Distortion

There were at least two factors which worked in favor of Korea's competitive advantage during this period. For one, Korea was fortunate to be endowed with a well educated population. For centuries the Korean people have placed a high value on education. This heritage of respect for learning has made Korea one of the most literate countries in the developing world. By the early 1960s, the literacy rate in Korea was already reaching 80 percent. This large pool of literate well-educated people provided an ample supply of capable and efficient workers for labor-intensive manufacturing industries. In addition, the international economic environment was quite favorable for execution of the outward-looking development strategy in the 1960s. During the period, world trade volume was expanding nearly at 8 percent per annum, and major industrial nations were abiding by the GATT rules and regulations.

Propelled by the expansion in exports, real GNP grew at an annual rate of 8.7 percent between 1961-71, and some manufacturing industries expanded very rapidly. While the primary sector including mining accounted for 72 percent of total

[13] Tzong-biau Lin and Victor Mok, "Trade, Foreign Investment, and Development in Hong Kong," *Foreign Trade and Investment*, ed. W. Galenson (Madison, Wis.: The University of Wisconsin, 1985), pp. 237-239.
[14] *Ibid.*, p. 246.
[15] *Ibid.*, p. 251.
[16] *Ibid.*, p. 251-252.

exports in 1962, the manufacturing sector accounted for 86 percent of total exports in 1971. Among the items of exports, footwear, plywood, textiles and clothing accounted for over 60 percent of total exports in 1971.

The other side of expanding industrial exports was, however, imports of basic raw materials needed for exports. Between 1962 and 1972, the imported raw materials increased nearly 5-fold from US$0.2 billion to US$1.1 billion.

Although exports contributed substantially to Korea's industrialization, some of the policy measures taken to promote rapid export promotion might have caused distortions in factor use. A study by Professor Won Tack Hong, which estimates changes in the factor intensities of exports and imports, shows that exports were becoming as capital intensive as import substitutes in the 1970s. Government policies such as massive credit subsidization and underpricing of imported capital must have affected the prices of factors of production, thus changing the factor proportions. A sharp rise in the wage/rental ratio in Korea since 1966 substantiates this viewpoint.

The increase in the capital intensity of exports may have been caused by several other factors such as shortage of skilled and semi-skilled workers, and choice of wrong industries as strategic export industries. However, Hong argues that there were much more significant changes in factor intensity of Korea's exports due to factor substitution in the production process. Some of the sectoral capital-labor substitutions as well as shifts in export composition, may be attributed to the increase in per capita capital stock in Korea and the associated rise in the wage-rental ratio. However, a substantial portion of the factor substitutions may have to be attributed to the subsidy on capital.[17]

Table 16 indicates that aggregate capital intensity of exports (capital valued at 1970 dollars divided by the number of workers employed for export production) rose from 0.6 to 1.5 between 1960 and 1970. Korea's exports might have been less capital intensive if there had been no subsidy on capital use, but it is questionable whether Korea could have expanded its exports so rapidly if it had insisted upon using less capital-intensive production techniques in order to maximize employment. This is because capital and labor might not be good substitutes for each other in terms of product quality and there might have been limited foreign demand for extremely labor-intensive goods. One might also argue that once a developing country becomes successful in exporting large amounts of simple labor-intensive goods, the developed countries, as we see today, would erect sufficiently high trade barriers against these exports so that the developing country has no other choice but to expand capital-intensive exports.

Shown in Table 17, the government's interventions to distort factor prices appear to have been much less in the case of the ROC (Taiwan). Calculating factor intensity of competitive imports and exports based on input-output tables, Dr. Shirley Kuo shows that the total capital intensity of competitive imports was higher than that of exports. This result supports the Heckscher-Ohlin theorem. As exports were more labor-intensive than imports it appears that the development of the ROC (Taiwan) was in accord with its comparative advantage.[18]

---

[17] Wontack Hong, *Trade and Employment Growth in Korea* (Seoul: Korea Development Institute, 1979), p. 215.

[18] Shirley Kuo and John Fei, "Causes and Roles of Export Expansion in the Republic of China" *Foreign Trade and Investment,* ed. W. Galenson (Madison, Wisconsin: The University of Wisconsin, 1985), p. 66.

Table 16. Korea: Changing Factor Intensity of External Trade, 1960-73

	Aggregate Capital Intensity of Exports	Aggregate Capital Intensity of Imports
1960	0.59	1.16
1963	0.85	1.00
1966	0.93	1.78
1968	1.12	1.51
1970	1.48	1.62
1973	2.20	2.20

Source: Won Tack Hong, *Factor Supply and Factor Intensity of Trade in Korea* (Seoul, Korea Development Institute, 1976), pp. 82-83.

Notes: 1. The capital intensity of exports is obtained by capital valued at 1970 dollars divided by the number of workers employed for export production.
2. The capital intensity of imports is obtained by the same method for competitive imports or import replacement.

Table 17. ROC (Taiwan): Total Factor Intensity of Exports and
Competitive Imports

(Unit: %)

Year	Competitive Import	Exports	Export to Developed Countries	Export to Developing Countries
1961	88.3	84.8	82.8	87.8
1966	98.9	88.5	80.2	100.7
1971	113.6	98.3	92.8	110.1

Source: Shirley Kuo and John Fei, "Causes and Roles of Export Expansion in the Republic of China" in W. Galenson, ed. *Foreign Trade and Investment* (Madison, Wisconsin: The University of Wisconsin, 1985), p. 66.

Note: Factor intensity is measured by capital/labor ratio including direct and indirect effects; NT$1,000/person.

Since 1969, however, the real wage started increasing at a more rapid pace, relative to the price of capital. Accordingly, the ROC (Taiwan) economy should be evolving from labor-intensive production methods toward more and more capital-intensive techniques.

Treating skill and technology embodied in labor as the third factor of production, that is, human capital as opposed to labor and physical capital, Lee shows that in both Korea and the ROC (Taiwan), comparative advantage in trade was moving towards more human capital-intensive products. However, as compared with the ROC (Taiwan), Korean firms chose relatively more physical capital-intensive lines than human-capital intensive ones, due to the distorted incentive for capital use.[19] As a result, Korean exporters concentrated on expanding the existing capacities of mostly standardized labor-intensive goods by an increasingly capital-intensive method and neglected developing high quality products requiring new skills.[20] To that extent, a transformation into skill- and capital-intensive products lines was more costly and painful for Korea than for the ROC (Taiwan).

In the case of Hong Kong, an outward looking policy was not a strategy but a way of life under the general umbrella of a laissez-faire policy. The government generally refrained from intervening in economic affairs. Export promotion was directed toward providing favorable background conditions, and the market was relied upon to work out the details. Thus, the comparison of the labor and capital requirements of exports and imports shows that imports of Hong Kong were more capital intensive than its exports, as hypothesized by the Heckscher-Ohlin theory. Over a period of 10 years, there was little change in the labor/capital ratio of its exports, while that of imports has substantially declined. As Table 18 shows, the pattern hypothesized by the Heckscher-Ohlin theory had become more definite in the process of Hong Kong's economic development.

Table 18. Hong Kong: Total Labor/Capital Requirement Ratios
of External Trade

Year	L/K Ratio of Exports (1)	L/K Ratios of Imports (2)	(1)/(2)
1964	2.69	2.23	1.21
1970	2.92	2.31	1.26
1974	2.86	1.74	1.64

Source: Tzong-biau Lin and Victor Mok, "Trade, Foreign Investment, and Development in Hong Kong, in W. Galenson ed. *Foreign Trade and Investment* (Madison, Wisconsin: The University of Wisconsin, 1985), p. 231.

INDUSTRIAL RESTRUCTURING AND PROMOTION OF HEAVY AND CHEMICAL INDUSTRIES

Shift in Comparative Advantage and Industrial Restructuring

After a decade of successful promotion of labor-intensive manufactures for export, the Korean authorities have come to the view that Korea was about to lose its comparative advantage in simple labor-intensive products in the early 1970s. It

[19] Young Sun Lee, *Changing Export Patterns in Korea, Taiwan, and Japan* Working Paper, No. 9 (Seoul, Korea: KIET, June 1980) pp. 29-32.
[20] Young-Chul Park, "Industrial Restructuring in Korea." Seoul, December 1982. (mimeo.).

was believed that the high growth objective could not be achieved with the same industrial development strategy that had been pursued during the 1960s. Major shifts in production and exports in favor of the expansion of heavy and chemical industries were required since Korea was bound to lose its static comparative advantage in labor-intensive exports in the world markets. This was because of the rapid increase in Korean wages and strong competition from other LDCs embarking upon export-led industrial growth. This new Korean strategy was made public in 1973.

There were also other developments which prompted this shift in strategy. After the oil crisis in 1973, Korean exports have suffered from a variety of protectionist measures such as import quotas, non-tariff barriers, and forced voluntary export curbs imposed by the advanced countries which had provided the largest export markets for Korea. It was argued that unless new exports were developed, Korea could not expect to capture an increasing share of the world market and hence would not be able to absorb the large expected addition to the labor force. Since trade barriers have been erected mostly against labor-intensive manufactures, Korean planners have attempted to avoid these obstacles by developing new skill- and capital-intensive exports. Or, in some cases, Korean manufacturers made foreign direct investment to avoid high tariff on imports by setting up factories in the tariff raising countries, such as the U.S.A.

Pattern of Industrialization

As a result of changing industrial development strategy, various incentives given to export in general were gradually reduced while a preferential tax and credit system was increasingly intensified particularly for the heavy and chemical industries. A series of preferential tax and credit system were devised in order to induce investment into the heavy and chemical industry. The Korean government established a National Investment Fund (NIF) in 1974 to help the entrepreneurs' long-term investment in these industries with the loans at a preferential interest rates. In addition, the government made large investments either in the form of related infrastructure construction or subscriptions to major corporations.

The government also provided various fiscal incentives for the promotion of heavy and chemical industries such as tax holidays, investment credits, and accelerated depreciation allowance. There was also a change in tariff system in favor of domestic producers of intermediate and capital goods.

As the result of these incentives, there was a rush of investment in the heavy and chemical industry in the latter half of the 1970s. Due mainly to the massive investment in heavy and chemical industry, fixed investment as a proportion of GNP rose to 35 percent during the 1977-79 period, up from an annual average of 25 percent in the first part of the 1970s. This has greatly affected the pattern of industrial growth in Korea.

While the Korean government took an interventionistic approach to changing economic environment, the ROC (Taiwan) did not show any noteworthy changes in its economic policy in the 1970s. A dominantly observable phenomenon of this period was the emergence of an export surplus, which was due to the country's economic maturity as well as due to deliberate government policies that encouraged exports. Nevertheless, changing comparative advantage has noticeably affected the pattern of industrialization in the ROC (Taiwan) as well.[21]

Up to 1971, the rapid growth of the industrial sector was primarily propelled by the rapid growth of those labor-absorbing industries. As shown in Table 19, food processing, textiles and footwear, and electrical machinery industries contributed more than a third of the total manufacturing expansion up until 1970. The three accounted for 35.5 percent of the manufacturing expansion in 1954-61, 37.6 percent in 1961-66, and 49.0 percent in 1966-71, respectively.

It can be seen from Table 19 that food processing expanded first, followed by textiles and footwear and then electrical machinery. The growth of food processing was very rapid during the earlier period 1954-61; but in the two subsequent periods, its relative share declined significantly. The textile industry replaced food processing in manufacturing expansion. The strategies of import substitution in the 1950s and of export expansion in the 1960s were crucial in the rapid expansion of textile products. In the latter part of the 1960s, the most rapid expansion was accounted for by the electrical machinery industry.

Then, with the change from a labor surplus to labor scarce economy, the industrial pattern of the ROC (Taiwan) also changed. The share of the three traditional industries in manufacturing expansion started to decline. During 1971-79, the expansion of these three industries accounted for a smaller share — 28.1 percent — of manufacturing expansion. In turn, a relatively large increase was observed for more capital- and skill-intensive industries, such as petrochemicals, metals, and machinery. It is obvious that with the rise in the wage/rental ratio the center of gravity shifted from agriculture to industry and, within industry, it shifted from labor-intensive light manufacturing to more capital- and skill-intensive manufacturing.[22]

Table 19. ROC (Taiwan): Relative Share of Expansion of Food Processing, Textiles and Footwear, and Electrical Machinery Industries in Manufacturing Expansion, 1954-79

(Unit: %)

Industry	1954-61	61-66	66-71	71-79
1. Food processing	25.4	14.6	8.9	3.8
2. Textiles and footwear	7.3	14.2	27.3	11.5
3. Electrical machinery	2.8	8.8	12.8	12.8
The three labor-absorbing industries (1 + 2 + 3)	35.5	37.6	49.0	28.1
4. All other subindustries	64.5	62.4	51.0	71.9
Total manufacturing	100.0	100.0	100.0	100.0

Source: Taken from Shirley Kuo *et al. The Taiwan Success Story* (Boulder, Colorado: Westview Press, 1981), p. 10.
Directorate-General of Budget, Accounting and Statistics, Executive Yuan, *National Income of the Republic of China*, various years.

[21] Shirley Kuo, *et al. The Taiwan Success Story*, pp. 8-12.
[22] *Ibid.*

While Hong Kong's exports remained labor-intensive, a subtle change did take place as the economy developed. The labor force became fully utilized and real wages began to rise rapidly. It is at this point in the development of the ROC (Taiwan) and Korea that exports became more capital-intensive. A different kind of structural adjustment was made in Hong Kong, however. Certain export industries, such as textile and footwear, suffered a relative decline because Hong Kong without cheap labor could not sustain its comparative advantage in them. Other labor-intensive industries did expand, including clothing, toys and plastic goods, electrical goods and horological instruments. In these industries it was possible to introduce higher technology without greater capital intensity and to substitute higher quality and more skilled labor, which were found in relatively greater abundance in Hong Kong, for unskilled labor. Furthermore, these industries didn't require economies of scale, thus the highly skilled, small enterpreneurs who are abundant in Hong Kong were able to pursue them. However, as the possibilities of utilizing skilled labor to overcome wage increase are being exhausted, the thrust of industrial expansion has passed to other industries. The importance of the manufacturing sector, in terms of output contribution, has begun to level off since the 1970s.[23]

Growth and Productivity Change in Selected Key Industries

Manufacturing production had grown at a high rate with rapid structural change toward heavy and chemical industry. As shown in Table 20, according to the manufacturing census data, the output of manufacturing sector grew at 24 percent per annum between 1967 and 1979. An extremely rapid growth rate was observable in such heavy industries as machinery and equipment including electric apparatus, basic metals, and chemicals followed by rubber products, metal products, leather products, wearing apparel and other manufacturing industries. All of them are either heavy and chemical industries and/or export-oriented industries. The traditional domestic market oriented industries such as beverage, food, wood products and the like showed lower output growth rates.

Thus, the production and employment structure of manufacturing sector moved in favor of heavy and chemical industries. The share of heavy and chemical industries in total manufacturing production went up from 37.7 percent in 1967 to 56.7 percent in 1979, and the employment share rose also from 39.4 percent to 49.7 percent. The share in total manufactured exports rose to 50 percent in 1979 from less than 20 percent in 1972. To make this possible, an increasing share of preferential bank credit estimated to be 60 percent was given to these industries.

The sectoral imbalance in the allocation of capital for the heavy and chemical industries aggravated inflationary pressure and brought about distortions in resource allocation. Between 1972-1979, the average annual rate of inflation measured in wholesale prices was nearly 18 percent as compared with about 12 percent between 1962-1971. Those sectors squeezed out by the modernization and capacity expansion drive, such as agriculture, small- and medium-sized firms, and the commodity distribution system found difficult to ensure a smooth supply of daily necessities and other essential commodities, which became a major source of inflation and productivity lag.

In retrospect, Korea shifted too quickly into heavy, capital-intensive industrial-

---

[23] L.B. Krause, "Introduction," *Foreign Trade and Investment,* p. 20.

Table 20. Korea: Output Growth in Manufacturing Industry, 1967-1979

(Unit: %)

Industry	Output Growth	Total Factor Productivity Growth
1. Wearing Apprarel	25.3	6.6
2. Clay & Stone Products	18.7	5.5
3. Other Manufacturing Industries	25.6	7.4
4. Furniture and Fixtures	24.0	11.6
5. Leather and its Products	26.3	4.9
6. Scientific & Measuring Equipments	44.0	14.5
7. Plastic Products	47.5	16.3
8. Rubber Products	37.2	8.1
9. Electrical Machinery & Apparatus	47.6	15.0
10. Metal Products	28.2	7.6
11. Printing and Publishing	15.9	4.4
12. Other Chemicals	25.7	8.4
12. Food	20.1	2.8
14. Wood and its Prodcuts	15.6	−0.1
15. Machinery	29.1	5.9
16. Glass and its Products	25.5	4.8
17. Petroleum and Coal Products	12.5	3.8
18. Textiles	25.0	7.9
19. Paper and its Products	12.5	3.8
20. Transport Equipment	30.5	7.2
21. Non-ferrous Metals	27.4	4.9
22. Tobacco	14.5	2.3
23. Beverages	15.5	−2.3
24. Non-metallic Mineral Products	18.5	4.8
25. Industrial Chemicals	31.4	15.1
26. Basic Metals	30.7	−2.3
27. Petroleum Refining	2.3	−18.1
Manufacturing Total	24.0	5.0

Source: Chuk Kyo Kim, "Industrial Growth and Productivity Trends in Korea" *Essays in Memory of Sang Chul Suh*, 1985, p. 46.

ization in 1973-1975 when its primary sector still retained some 48 percent of the labor force. Despite the existence of much surplus labor in agriculture, the government's speedy drive for heavy industrialization caused severe labor shortages especially in the skilled categories and wages rose very sharply. In the end, both high inflation and rising wages outstripped productivity gains by wide margins, and Korea's external competitiveness was gradually eroded. Further, the erosion of competitiveness, compounded by a slower growth of external markets and greater protectionism abroad, led to a steady reduction in the rate of growth of exports and overall output.

Professor Harry Oshima holds the short-sighted government policy of rushing into heavy industrialization responsible for such an outcome. In the mid-1970's, Professor Oshima argues, neither had Korean agriculture shed its labor surplus, nor had light industry expanded and developed experience in more sophisticated, high-technology operations and industries. Further, the educational system had not yet reached levels of higher manpower training capabilities.[24] This may partly answer the question as to the drop in the contribution of technical progress to productivity growth in the 1977-1982 period.

PROBLEMS AND ISSUES

Vulnerability and Instability of International Trade

The KDI Report on Korean Society in the Year 2000 suggests that Korea should continue to follow the outward-looking development strategy that has proved to be so successful over the past twenty years. It is debatable, however, whether such export-led industrial development is going to be as viable as it has been in view of the problems it has created and of an adverse trade environment that has come into being especially after 1980. For future economic growth, therefore, it is important to take a close look at some of the problems and issues that have been generated in the wake of Korea's pursuit of export-led industrialization.

Reliance on export growth has made the Korean economy excessively vulnerable to the vagaries of international markets, which are entirely beyond its control. In particular, the Korean case is more serious than others, because its exports depend largely on the markets of the developed countries while it imports essential raw materials and energy almost entirely from abroad. On the eve of the first oil crisis, Korea imported 55 percent of its primary energy supply. It has no hope of increasing domestic energy production. Therefore, Korea would be dealt a severe blow if foreign markets are abruptly closed or if key raw materials or energy cannot be imported. With heavy accumulated debt Korea does not seem to have any effective policy instruments nor good bargaining position to insulate the economy from secular and cyclical changes in trading partners economic conditions and policies.[25]

---

[24] Harry T. Oshima, "A Lewis Dualistic Theory and Its Relevance for Postwar Asian Growth," *Malayan Economic Review*, vol. 20, No. 2. (October 1981), p. 21.

[25] Yung-Chul Park, *Prospects of the Korean Economy as a Trading Nation*. Paper Presented to Conference on Korea in the Year Two Thousand, May 30 — June 1, 1985, Prepared by ARC, Korea University, Seoul, Korea, p. 12.

Balance of Payments and Foreign Debt

Despite the rapid growth in exports since 1962, Korea has experienced chronic balance of payments difficulties. As shown in Tables 21 and 22, during the period, 1970-1983, Korea had the biggest cumulative current account deficit, amounting to US$25.8 billion. In comparison, the ROC (Taiwan) recorded cumulative current account surplus, US$8.9 billion, over the same period. In the case of Hong Kong, detailed balance of payments data are scanty. According to the estimates made by Lin and Mok, Hong Kong's invisible trade surplus was more than enough to cover its deficit in the goods account from 1971 to 1977. In the early eighties, there was a small trade deficit.[26]

Essentially, balance of payments difficulties stem from the loss of export competitiveness. According to Professor Shinohara, who measures a country's export strength by computing real exchange rates by dividing an index of exchange rates by an index of relative price changes vis-a-vis those in the U.S., the Korean Won was overvalued during most of the period since 1962. In the case of the ROC (Taiwan), the domestic currency was more often undervalued over the same period. Furthermore, even during periods of overvaluation, their extent was much briefer than in Korea. As a result, Korea's export competitiveness was reduced, growth in domestic savings was suppressed, and there was an increase in capital imports. In turn, Korea's net foreign indebtedness bulged. In comparison, in the case of the ROC (Taiwan), inflation was not a problem except for the two violent but brief period of imported inflation in 1973-1974 and 1979-1980. Thus, during the 1960s there was continual growth with relatively little import of capital, and the domestic savings ratio was much higher than in Korea.[27]

Deteriorating developments in the balance of payments and their financing are reflected in the accumulation of external debt. Relying largely on long-term borrowings to finance the current account deficit, Korea has incurred large amounts of external debt. At the end of 1983, the accumulation of external debt reached as much as US$40.2 billion, 54 percent of GNP and 132 percent of exports of goods and services. In the same year, debt service payments totalled US$4.8 billion. (At the end of 1982, the net external debt outstanding in respect of the ROC (Taiwan) was only US$9.3 billion.)[28]

In this connection, a matter of some concern is the observed increase in the incremental capital output ratio (ICOR) in Korea. While its marginal savings rate improved significantly and did not differ much from that of the ROC (Taiwan), the incremental capital output ratio rose sharply from 2.7 in 1966-1975 to 4.3 in 1976-1982. The long gestation periods in heavy industries seem to have contributed significantly to the increase in the ICOR. Also, prolonged world recession and growing trade protectionism brought forth a slowdown in the growth of exports, which, in turn, raised the ICOR by causing low capacity utilization.[29] This evidence

---

[26] Lin, Tzong-biau and Victor Mok. "Trade, Foreign Investment, and Development in Hong Kong."

[27] M. Shinohara, "Trends and Dynamics of East and Southeast Asian Economies," *Asian Development Review*, Vol. 3. No. 1, 1985, pp. 58-61.

[28] Bijan B. Aghevli and Jorge Marguez-Rutarte, *A Case of Successful Adjustment: Korea's Experience During 1980-84*, IMF Occasional Paper (August 1985), p. 21.

[29] See Chapter 7 by Jungsoo Lee and Evelyn M. Go.

Table 21. Korea: Major Items in Balance of Payments

(Unit: US$ million)

Year	Current Account Balance	Trade Balance	Balance on = + Service, etc.	Net Direct Investment	Net Long-Term Capital	Basic Balance	Overall Balance of Payments
1970	−622.5	−922.2	299.5	n.a.	n.a.	−173.7	−56.5
1971	−847.5	−1,040.6	198.4	n.a.	n.a.	−319.7	−172.0
1972	−371.2	−574.5	202.7	n.a.	n.a.	133.9	147.7
1973	−308.8	−566.0	257.2	n.a.	n.a.	357.5	460.3
1974	−2,022.7	−1,936.8	−85.9	124.1	822.3	−1,076.3	−1,093.8
1975	−1,886.9	−1,671.4	−215.5	61.6	1,116.7	−708.6	−150.6
1976	−313.6	−590.5	276.9	85.5	1,285.7	1,057.6	1,173.6
1977	12.3	−476.6	488.9	104.4	1,208.3	1,325.0	1,314.7
1978	−1,085.2	−1,780.8	695.6	100.5	2,065.8	1,081.1	−401.9
1979	−4,151.1	−4,396.5	244.4	126.0	2,536.9	−1,488.2	−973.3
1980	−5,320.7	−4,384.1	−692.5	96.2	1,760.3	−3,464.2	−1,889.6
1981	−4,646.0	−3,628.3	−1,710.2	105.4	2,736.5	−1,804.1	−2,297.0
1982	−2,649.6	−2,594.4	−55.2	100.6	1,129.7	−1,419.3	−2,711.2
1983	−1,606.0	−1,763.5	157.5	101.4	1,169.0	−335.6	−384.4

Source: Bank of Korea, *Monthly Bulletin*, various issues.

Table 22. ROC (Taiwan): Major Items in Balance of Payments

(Unit: US$ million)

Year	Current Account Balance	=	Trade Balance	+	Balance on Service, etc.	Net Direct Investment	Net Long-Term Capital	Basic Balance	Overall Balance of Payments
1970	1		106		−105	61	62	124	135
1971	173		292		−119	52	37	262	254
1972	513		647		−134	24	45	582	607
1973	566		734		−168	61	137	764	610
1974	−1,113		−830		−283	83	304	−726	−597
1975	−589		−255		−334	34	497	−58	−149
1976	292		688		−396	68	531	891	981
1977	920		1,177		−257	44	305	1,269	1,132
1978	1,669		2,234		−565	110	243	2,022	1,951
1979	241		1,408		−1,167	122	361	724	96
1980	−965		147		−1,112	119	1,087	241	−127
1981	497		1,970		−1,473	101	738	1,336	1,299
1982	2,248		3,646		−1,398	71	1,197	3,516	2,589
1983	4,452		5,951		−1,499	130	913	5,495	4,862

Source: Shirley Kuo. "Price Stabilization Policy in Taiwan, 1946-1983," in Tzong-Shian Yu ed. *Raising Productivity*, (Tokyo: Asian Productivity Organization, 1985), p. 179.

Economic Research Department, The Central Bank of China, *Financial Statistics Monthly, Taiwan District, the Republic of China*, January 1977, May 1981.

of the detoriorating efficiency of invested capital is a warning sign regarding Korea's long-run foreign debt servicing capacity.

In Korea, foreign direct investment amounted to a negligible US$637 million as a source of financing for its current account deficit in 1970-1984. In comparison, even in a capital-exporting country like the ROC (Taiwan), private foreign investment (commitment basis) constituted about 3 to 10 percent of the sources of funds for gross fixed capital formation.[30]

One of the important lessons one may draw from the ROC (Taiwan) experience is that direct foreign investment has played a crucial role in raising the nation's productivity by filling savings and foreign exchange gaps. At the same time, it has proved an effective vehicle for transfer of technology, compared with technical licensing agreements. Direct investment has also been helpful in avoiding serious mistakes in investment decisions because foreign investors are often better informed of marketing conditions abroad.

Efficiency of Resource Mobilization

Self-sustaining growth requires the average propensity to save in the economy to be greater than the incremental capital/output ratio (K/Y) times the rate of population growth. For the ROC (Taiwan), the average savings ratio began to exceed the K/Y ratio times by the population growth rate in 1963; Hong Kong followed in 1963; and Korea came along in 1966-67. Such achievements by the three Asian NICs suggest that programs to raise the propensity to save, including monetary and taxation policies that provide incentives to save and to invest in productive enterprises, are highly desirable.

Household Savings

At least since the early 1960's Korea has invested a greater share of GNP than the ROC (Taiwan). However, the ROC (Taiwan) appears to have saved a higher fraction of GNP than Korea, as shown in Table 23. Throughout the period, 1970-1984, except for 1974, 1975 and 1980, the ROC (Taiwan) saved enough to run a positive current account balance and moved toward a capital exporting situation, which was not achieved by Korea over the same period (except for 1977).

Naturally, we are then bound to raise a question of whether Korea has been as efficient as generally thought in mobilizing domestic resources for economic development. During the past two decades, the Korean economy depended substantially on foreign resources, whereas, the performance of household savings has been relatively low and often erratic. Household savings relative to GNP varied over the period, ranging from a low of 4.1 percent in 1975 to a high of 10.9 percent in 1978.

The ROC (Taiwan's) performance of relatively high personal savings presents interesting material for comparative analysis. The rapid increase in the household savings in the ROC (Taiwan) could be largely attributable to the land reform carried out in the early 1950's and the setting of high real interest rates.

Because of the ROC (Taiwan)'s subtropical climate, and as a result of the land reform which improved farmers' work incentives and motivations due to its broadly based and participatory nature, agricultural output grew at an annual rate of about

---

[30] S.C. Tsiang and Rong-I Wu, "Foreign Trade and Investment as Boosters for Take-off," pp. 320-325.

Table 23. Comparison of Savings Ratios, Korea,
ROC (Taiwan), Hong Kong, and Japan

	Per Capita GNP	Domestic Savings Ratio	Household Savings Ratio
Korea (1984)	US$1,999	27.3	9.3
ROC (Taiwan) (1979)	US$1,866	34.6	13.5
Hong Kong (1974)	US$2,007	23.5	n.a.
Japan (1970)	US$1,947	40.2	11.5

Source: Korea Development Institute, *Quarterly Economic Outlook* IV No 1 (1985), p. 61.

3.7 percent in 1952-1960 and 5.3 percent in 1960-1970. This increase in agricultural production made it possible for the ROC (Taiwan) not only to meet the domestic food requirements of the population, but also leave considerable surplus for household savings and exports. Liu observes that land reform completed in the early 1950's allow only the tillers and tenants to invest on improvements on owned land. Land markets in fact have not functioned or even unexisted for any potential investors. This forestalls land speculations on the one hand and forces the flows of savings to nonagricultural sectors. A built-in mechanism in land reform that the payment to landlord was made in form of stocks of industrial companies, helped move the surplus of resources into industrial sector.[31] Of the total flow of resources and funds out of the agricultural sector, net personal savings deposited and invested in nonagriculture through financial institutions was about 16 percent in 1956-1960 and rapidly increased to 65 percent in 1961-1969.[32]

In comparison, Korea's agricultural sector was relatively stagnant, and there was little vendable surplus from agriculture to pay for needed industrial goods imports. Consequently, Korea was forced at an early stage to become a net importer of food. In the 1970s, however, increased production of grains, vegetables and fruits could have saved a large part of the $5 billion of food imports.[33] In short, instead of playing the historical role of providing agricultural surplus to the industrial sector, agriculture became a burden on the export-oriented manufacturing sector.[34]

In financial terms, McKinnon attributed Korea's poor personal savings to price inflation resulting from inappropriate provision of preferential export credits. As the result, the real rate of return on bank deposits was lowered, and individual savers were lured into relatively lucrative markets for land, apartments, jewelry, and the like. A comparison of real rates of return in Korea and the ROC (Taiwan) on holding one-year time deposits shows that Korea maintained a higher real return than the ROC (Taiwan) since the monetary reform in 1965. But the gap was

[31] Based on the report of the consultant from the ROC (Taiwan) associated with this research study.

[32] T.H. Lee and Kuo-shu Liang, *"Process and Pattern of Economic Development in Taiwan,"* Economic Essays Vol. IV (Taipei: National Taiwan University, November 1973), p. 101.

[33] Harry T. Oshima, *The Transition to an Industrial Economy in Monsoon Asia* (ADB Economic Staff Paper, No. 20, October 1983), p. 35.

[34] Wan-Soon Kim, "Transformation of the Korean Economy: Its Causes and Consequences," *Korea and Japan,* eds. Hahn and Yamamoto (Seoul: Korea University, Asiatic Research Center, 1978), pp. 73-75.

narrowed and by 1972 it turned in favor of the ROC (Taiwan). During the period, 1973-1978, real interest rates in Korea were close to zero, and there was little room for expansion of bank intermediation.[35]

After Korea experienced a severe economic setback in 1980, a negative growth rate of 5.2 percent for the first time in more than 20 years and an inflation rate of 39 percent in terms of wholesale prices, the economy soon recovered with prices dropping very sharply. Now, the Korean government argues that because of its successful anti-inflationary measures, a positive real rate of interest could be attainable at relatively low nominal interest rates. Obviously, the government uses the current rate of inflation in its computation of the real interest rate, but fails to consider whether or not the yield on monetary savings is at least comparable to the rate of return on holdings of goods or other tangible assets. Adjusted by the GNP deflator, average interest rates were positive 3.4 percent, in 1981, 3.8 percent in 1982, 5.1 percent in 1983, and 5.7 percent in 1984. The rise in Seoul's house and land prices were, however, more than 30 percent and 50 percent, respectively, in 1983. The currently used price indices underweigh the rapidly rising urban housing costs and cannot represent the opportunity cost of holding financial assets. A high positive interest rate is called for, not only because it functions as an unambiguous, direct inducement to save, but also because it helps channel idle funds into organized institutional savings.

The monetary experience of Hong Kong is different from both Korea and the ROC (Taiwan) because of its status as an open entrepot, which does not permit fully independent monetary policies, and because of its ability to rely upon inflows of foreign capital in addition to domestic savings. In Hong Kong, interest rates are relatively lower due to the openness of the economy and the greater accessibility to international capital markets. Consequently, Hong Kong has not needed to subscribe to such a policy as a government-enforced low interest rate. Nor could Hong Kong arbitrarily raise interest rates to stimulate saving and encourage capital inflows.[36]

The percentage of gross domestic capital formation was about 21 percent in 1961 when the ratio of gross domestic savings was only 5 percent. But when the domestic savings propensity picked up strength, say, 24 percent in 1974, Hong Kong largely replaced the inflows of foreign capital and turned the country from a heavy capital importer into a net capital exporter in the late sixties and the seventies. Consequently, the percentage of gross capital formation in Hong Kong seldom increased much above 25 percent of the GDP.[37]

Government Savings
Korea is a classical case in which tax policy has been geared almost exclusively to growth. One of the major considerations in the rapid growth of tax revenues since 1964 has been the desire to increase the government's contribution to domestic savings. In Korea, public sector enterprises are not an important source of public savings; the realization of public savings depends largely on the efforts of the central government.

[35] Ronald I. McKinnon, "Saving Propensities and the Korean Monetary Reform in Retrospect", *Money and Finance in Economic Growth and Development: Essays in Honor of Edward S. Shaw*, ed. Ronald I. McKinnon (New York: Marcel Dekker, Inc., 1976), pp. 83-90.
[36] S.C. Tsiang and Rong-I Wu, "Foreign Trade and Investment as Boosters for Take-off," pp. 317-318.
[37] *Ibid.*, pp. 319-320.

Table 24. Korea: Revenue and Expenditure Items as a Proportion of GNP

(Period Averages)

	1960-80[1] (1)	60-70[1] (1)	70-80	70-75	75-80
I. Total Revenue	16.9	17.3	16.4	14.9	17.9
Current Revenue	13.6	11.3	16.1	14.3	17.8
A. Tax Revenue	12.2	10.1	14.5	13.0	16.0
Non-Tax Revenue	1.4	1.2	1.6	1.3	1.8
B. Direct Taxes	4.1	3.6	4.7	4.7	4.8
Tax on income & prof.[2]	—	—	4.2	3.9	4.3
Indirect Taxes	6.4	3.6	9.2	7.7	10.8
Dom. tax on goods & serv.[2]	—	—	7.1	6.3	7.9
Tax on int'l trade[2]	—	—	2.3	1.7	2.8
II. Total Expenditure					
A. Current	12.3	11.1	13.3	12.3	14.3
Capital	4.9	6.6	3.5	4.1	3.0
B. Current exp. by econ. class					
Exp. on goods & serv.	6.6	6.7	6.5	5.2	6.7
Interest payments	0.7	0.2	1.1	1.2	1.7
Subsidies & other current transfers	4.9	4.3	5.6	5.5	5.6
C. Total exp. by functional class	17.0	17.3	16.9	16.4	17.3
Gen. public serv.	2.1	2.0	2.1	2.3	1.9
Defense	4.8	4.3	5.1	4.4	5.8
Education	2.6	2.5	2.7	2.6	2.8
Health	0.2	0.2	0.2	0.2	0.2
Soc. security & welfare	0.9	0.9	0.9	0.9	0.9
Housing & comm. amenities	0.5	0.9	0.3	0.4	0.2
Other comm. & soc. serv.	0.2	0.2	0.2	0.2	0.1
Econ. service	4.3	5.3	3.6	3.9	3.4
Other purposes	1.5	1.2	1.8	1.6	2.0
Current acct. deficit/surplus	2.7	2.7	2.9	2.3	3.4

Source: IMF, *Government Finance Statistics Yearbook*, various issues.

Notes: 1. Earliest data available is 1961 for expenditures.
          2. Earliest date available is 1971.

Table 25. Korea: Composition of Revenue and Expenditure by Major Items

(Period Averages)

	1960-80[1]	60-70[1]	70-80	70-75	75-80
I. Total Revenue					
A. Tax Revenue	7.35	59.5	88.2	87.4	89.5
Non-Tax Revenue	8.3	6.9	9.4	9.0	9.6
B. Direct Taxes	33.5	'34.4	33.0	35.6	29.8
Tax on income & prof.[2]	–	–	29.1	30.6	27.1
Indirect Taxes	49.8	35.5	63.1	59.1	67.6
Dom. tax on goods & serv.[2]	–	–	48.9	48.8	49.3
Tax on int'l trade[2]	–	–	15.7	13.2	17.6
II. Total Expenditure					
A. Current	72.2	63.5	79.4	75.8	82.8
Capital	27.8	36.5	20.6	24.2	17.2
B. Current exp. by econ. class					
Exp. on goods & serv.	56.7	60.5	52.8	51.4	54.6
Interest payments	3.0	1.3	4.5	3.1	5.8
Subsidies & other current transfers	40.3	38.2	42.7	45.5	39.7
C. Total exp. by functional class					
Gen. public serv.	12.2	11.7	12.5	14.3	11.1
Defense	28.3	25.1	30.4	26.9	33.6
Education	15.3	14.5	16.1	15.9	15.9
Health	1.1	1.0	1.2	1.2	1.3
Soc. security & welfare	5.2	5.1	5.3	5.3	5.2
Housing & comm. amenities	2.8	4.6	1.5	2.1	0.9
Other comm. & soc. serv.	1.1	1.2	1.0	1.1	0.8
Econ. service	25.4	30.3	21.1	23.3	19.5
Other purposes	8.7	6.7	10.9	9.9	11.6

Source: IMF, *Government Finance Statistics Yearbook*, various issues.

Notes: 1. Earliest data available is 1961 for expenditures.
        2. Earliest data available is 1971.

As stated, financial resource constraints are the principal factors that could limit self-sustaining growth of developing countries, and a good public saving performance could ease the financial squeeze. Tax revenue and expenditure trends, to the extent that they determine public savings, are presented in Tables 24 and 25.

A phenomenally rapid growth of tax revenue had been taking place in Korea since the mid-1960s. This substantial growth in the nation's tax collections could be traced to two broad developments — legislative or discretionary decisions and economic growth. The modernization of the tax system and the improvement in administrative enforcement process especially since 1966 were mainly responsible for the sharp increases in tax revenues. Economic growth, on the other hand, resulted in an expansion of the tax base — the natural or automatic increase that takes place as the economy grows.

Although the overall tax ratio increased from 11.1 percent to 17.2 percent between 1960 and 1980, there was a wide variation in the ratio up to 1973. This meant that the relation between tax receipts and GNP had been quite unstable from year to year. The decline in the tax/GNP ratios since 1962 largely reflected unusual increases in price and the structural defect of the tax system. The sharp increase in government expenditures in 1962 triggered the inflation that impaired tax collection in 1963 and 1964. Between 1963 and 1964, the growth in tax revenues failed to keep up with the increase in GNP.

The most rapid growth in total tax revenue was recorded in 1966. The sharp decline in the tax/GNP ratio in 1973 is attributable to major tax reforms that reduced the personal income and corporate tax rates. On the whole, since 1966, the rate of economic growth slowed down steadily as increases in tax revenue through administrative improvement reached their limits.

The government projects a growth in total expenditure by the central government from about 18 percent of GDP in 1976 to 24 percent in 1991 and a growth in tax revenue from about 16 percent to 23 percent of GDP. As total tax revenues in 1976 were less than 16 percent of GDP, the above expenditure objectives imply that the mobilization of additional tax revenue will be an important preoccupation of the government throughout the 1980s.

The period, 1950-70, is marked by a gradual shift from a commodity-oriented indirect taxation to modern income taxes. As real income rose in the process of economic development, the proportion of tax revenue derived from income and profit taxes also increased. Since the mid 1960s, the government had made significant efforts to correct the shortcomings of the previous tax system. Revisions of the tax laws and their administration have taken place in various ways almost every year since 1961. With this big fiscal push, the budget deficit as a proportion of total current expenditures began to decline gradually, and the overall budget was in balance by 1964. 1966 marked the beginning of a new era in tax administration in Korea, which saw the establishment of the Office of National Tax Administration. The 1967 tax reform, the largest scale of reform since 1961, partially introduced global system in addition to the existing system.

Since 1971, the relative importance of income taxes has declined somewhat. The direct tax ratio declined from about 39.7 percent in 1971 to 27.4 percent by 1980; the ratio for all indirect taxes increased from 59.6 percent to about 70.2 percent. The decline in the relative importance of income taxes partly reflects the structural changes in the tax system.

The major objective of the 1975 tax reform was to consolidate various taxes at schedular rates on factor incomes by introducing a progressive tax on a more "global" income measure. At the same time, it aimed at providing tax relief to low income earners. The size of the basic exemption was also increased several times since 1971. A series of tax reforms during the early 1970s granted tax exemptions and allowances to the corporate sector, averaging nearly 20 percent of corporate income tax revenue during the period, 1971-78. These changes in tax structure contributed significantly to the slowing down of the growth in revenue yields from income taxes.

In 1977, the value added tax and special consumption tax were introduced to meet more effectively the rising need for financial resources, to strengthen the incentive schemes for exports and investments, and to maintain the neutrality of indirect taxes. These replaced eight existing indirect taxes at the rate of 10 percent of the value added of a product or service, whether domestically produced or imported. The value added tax and special consumption tax together have been instrumental in broadening the indirect tax base.

Besides the introduction of the value-added tax, Korea has removed many of the differential or schedular characteristics of the personal income tax in order to achieve a more global income tax system. But the important question for the long-run overall tax structure is whether Korea's tax system is well adapted to the current and expected future changes in the Korean economy. The authorities can afford to make the tax system easier for both the public and the administrators to understand. The built-in revenue elasticity of the tax system does not seem to be more than unity, adequate to finance the existing plans of the government to commit more of the expenditures to social development. If the tax system were to achieve equity and better resource allocation, or achieving comprehensive tax base is quite vital.

With respect to public expenditure, the growth of Korea's central government spending has not been steady and sometimes erratic. The expenditure share of GNP ranged from 11 to 22 percent over the 1960-80 period. A look at the movement of the share of government expenditure in GNP shows a rapidly rising trend up to 1962, a drastic decline in 1963 and 1964, a more or less rising trend up to 1980, with a sharp decline in 1973.

Between 1960 and 1962, there was a sharp rise in the expenditure to GNP ratio associated with the revolution and the expansionary policy of the military government. There was a drastic decline in 1963 and 1964 because of the deflationary policy. In 1964, the expenditure/GNP ratio reached its lowest level (13.2 percent) since 1953. The sharp decline in 1973 resulted from the exceptionally high growth of GNP combined with a tight fiscal policy. The rise in 1974 and 1975 was due to rising subsidies and expenditures on defense.

Between 1975 and 1980, based on the IMF data, the current expenditure to GNP ratio was in the range of about 14.3 percent (subsidies and transfers 5.6 percent); capital expenditure to GNP ratio 3 percent; and total general government expenditures about 17.3 percent.

The claim of defense spending on the national budget has been on the rise since 1974 after a steady long-term decline. The defense surtax, introduced in 1975, in order to finance modernization of the national defense force, raised its share in GNP. The shares of economic, social and general public services in GNP have declined gradually since 1960, but the decline in spending for economic services relative to GNP has been sharpest of the three since 1970. It reflects a shifting of expenditure priorities.

A breakdown of social service expenditures shows a relatively rising share by the education function since 1960, whereas the housing expenditure component showed a steady decline. The shares of social security and health in GNP were held approximately constant. Within the social services category, the education component accounted for 2.8 percent of GNP in the 1975-80 period. Within the economic services, expenditure for the primary sector has been the largest item, followed by expenditure for transportation and communication and manufacturing and construction programs.

Between 1975 and 1980, defense expenditure was the largest item in the central government budget, followed by social services, economic services, and general public services, respectively.

The share of subsidies and transfers since 1974 has been increasing and reached 3.2 percent Capital expenditure, on the other hand, increased within the 1964-68 period, decreased in 1969-74 and started to increase until 1976, but started to decline since then. The emphasis on subsidies and transfers starting in 1974 indicates that there has been a relative shift in expenditure priorities from economic to social services. From an examination of the expenditure trends since 1960, the picture that emerges is the growing share of defense spending relative to GNP.

The shift of the fiscal sector from a deficit to a positive savings position resulted in the stabilization of price and growth in domestic savings. This was partly due to sharp increases in the revenue since 1964. Deficit financing was a major factor contributing to inflation during the 1950s and the early 1960s. In 1957, for instance, the government incurred a budget deficit which amounted to 30 percent of total current expenditures. The fiscal deficit was financed by borrowings mainly from the banking system. Government borrowing from the central bank was the major source of inflation in the early 1960s. During 1961 and 1962, the government overdraft with the central bank constituted roughly 30 percent of the increase in the money supply. Contributions from counterpart funds generated by foreign aid played a significant role in financing government budgetary expenditures during the 1950s and the 1960s. In 1958, counterpart funds accounted for about 52 percent of the total central government revenue. But, despite contributions from counterpart funds, the government still incurred budget deficits.

In the 1950s and the early 1960s, public savings were negative, as shown in Table 26. Since 1964 there was an almost uniterrupted improvement through 1970, when the public savings to gross domestic capital formation ratio reached 25.2 percent. Most of the increase was concentrated in the period 1965-68, when the ratio jumped from 11.4 percent to 23.6 percent. After 1970 public savings showed a declining trend, resulting in a minimum of 8.0 percent in 1974. Thereafter, the ratio moved up reaching 22.8 percent by 1982.

The sharp rise in public savings after 1964 was made possible by the rapid increase of government tax revenue, a tight control over government current expenditures, and improved performance of government enterprise. From the tax revenue side, although the government introduced major tax reforms in 1962, a major breakthrough in the tax effort came only in 1965-69, such that the tax ratio went up from 8.6 percent to 14.6 percent of GNP. This breakthrough was the result of a dramatic improvement in tax administration, which probably was the most important single factor explaining the rapid rise in the tax ratio in the 1960s.

Between 1971 and 1974, public savings suffered a severe setback. The main cause of the deterioration was a fall in the tax to GNP ratio; it fell from 14.8 percent in 1970 to 12.5 percent in 1973. The drop in the public savings ratio in 1974, despite a recovery of the tax to GNP ratio, was due to the sharp rise in subsidies in foodgrains and fertilizers (almost 7 times those in 1973), and expenditures on defense. The drop in the tax ratio in 1972 and 1973 was due to a relative decline in revenue from the income and corporation taxes, selective excises and customs duties, resulting from a slow-down of economic activity and increased tax incentives. In short, the deterioration of public savings during 1971-74 found its roots principally in

Table 26. Korea: Savings Ratios and Composition of Savings, 1953-82

	Percentage of GNP	Percentage of Gross Domestic Capital Formation			
		S_f	Sg + Sp	Sg	Sp
1953	8.8	42.7	57.3	−15.6	72.9
1954	6.6	44.6	55.4	−22.8	78.2
1955	5.2	57.6	42.4	−19.1	61.5
1956	−1.9	121.8	−21.8	−32.7	10.9
1957	5.5	64.0	36.0	−19.9	55.9
1958	4.9	62.4	37.6	−24.4	62.0
1959	4.2	62.1	37.9	−24.5	62.4
1960	0.8	78.8	7.5	−18.8	26.3
1961	2.9	65.3	21.6	−13.8	35.4
1962	3.2	83.4	25.5	−12.0	37.5
1963	8.7	57.5	48.0	−2.0	50.0
1964	8.7	48.8	62.3	3.3	59.0
1965	7.4	42.6	49.1	11.4	37.7
1966	11.8	39.1	54.9	12.8	42.1
1967	11.4	40.2	51.9	18.7	33.2
1968	15.1	43.1	58.3	23.6	34.7
1969	18.8	36.9	65.3	20.5	44.8
1970	15.7	36.0	62.1	25.2	36.9
1971	14.6	41.6	58.0	20.8	37.2
1972	16.5	22.9	74.4	15.5	58.9
1973	22.8	14.4	88.7	15.7	73.0
1974	19.9	38.4	62.8	8.0	54.8
1975	19.1	33.8	63.6	12.4	51.2
1976	23.9	9.0	93.1	22.7	70.4
1977	27.5	2.0	99.1	18.9	80.2
1978	28.5	10.0	91.3	20.4	70.9
1979	28.1	19.9	78.8	19.4	59.4
1980	21.9	30.0	69.9	18.6	51.3
1981	21.7	26.3	74.3	21.4	52.9
1982	22.4	16.6	82.9	22.8	60.1

Source: Bank of Korea, *National Income Accounts*, 1984.

Note: S_f: foreign savings; Sg: general government savings; Sp: private sector savings.

weaknesses in the tax effort and rising subsidies for foodgrains and fertilizer. And the recovery of the public savings picture from 1975 onwards reflects the reversal of the two trends above.

Since the early 1970s, the savings ratio in the ROC (Taiwan) has exceeded the level of 30 percent, contributed to by high government savings. Table 27 shows that as in the case of Korea, the government savings in the ROC (Taiwan) were negative in the early stage of development. The deficit was fortunately made up by U.S. aid from 1951 to 1965. Relatively large injections of foreign resources into an economically undeveloped and near destitute country would be helpful to propel the economy into self-sustained growth if and only if proper strategy of development is adopted. In the case of the ROC (Taiwan), instead of using aid for relief, social welfare or other urgent governmental needs, the U.S. aid had been administrated by semi-autonomous institutions outside of government budget to concentrate upon economic development purposes. Of all U.S. capital assistance (US$384.2 million) plus local currency generated by payments for U.S. aid imports (US$664.4 million) during the period, 1951-63, 40.7 percent went to infrastructure; 21.8 percent to agriculture; 20.0 percent to human resources; and 17.5 percent to industry. Within each aid-granted sector, projects were selected with special emphasis on maximizing the rate of social return by creating a favorable climate for private enterprise. Incorporated with planned economic reforms toward competitive markets, the U.S. aid had assisted in solving the then salient problems of monetary and price stability, infrastructure building, human resource development and agricultural and industrial growth in chronological order. The success of the foreign aid program enabled the government gradually to have a budget surplus after the termination of the U.S. aid in 1965. As a share of gross domestic capital formation, the general government savings ratio rose sharply from 7.8 percent in 1965 to 30.8 percent in 1978.

Total government real current revenues increased 13-fold from 1952 to 1983 while total consumption expenditure increased 10-fold only. Even within the consumption expenditures category, administration and defense gave way to development expenditures, particularly spending on education and research which increased about 45-fold. Capital expenditures were also devoted largely to capital formation for economic infrastructure, but investment in education and research grew at a much faster pace in recent years.

On the revenue side, as shown in Table 28, the share of current revenue was predominant and became increasingly important in recent years. Indirect tax remained the main source of government current revenues. Its share in total taxes, however, increased from 69 percent in 1952 to a peak of 77 percent in 1967 and thereafter steadily decreased to 60 percent in 1983. Among indirect taxes only the share of import tariffs fluctuated within a limit of 20 to 35 percent as a consequence of an accelerated rate of increase in imports accompanying a reduction in tariffs. The revenue from direct taxes increased steadily from 23 percent in 1968, the year that launched the overall tax system reform, to nearly 40 percent in 1983. The total tax burden of the economy varied at around 16 to 22 percent of GDP during 1952-83.

It has been well acknowledged that the ROC (Taiwan) government relied upon agricultural taxes, explicitly or implicitly, in mobilization of resources for development. In addition to the progressive land taxes paid in kind, the low agricultural pricing policy and rice-fertilizer barter system also imposed a hidden tax burden on farmers before these hidden taxes were abolished in 1971. It is estimated that the total hidden rice tax in 1952-71 amounted to 1.5 times the explicit agricultural land tax.

It is true that the agricultural sector played an important role in mobilizing resources in earlier periods of the economic development of the ROC (Taiwan); nevertheless, with a continuous decrease in its share from 35 to 20 percent of the total indirect tax revenues for period 1952-1961 and 20 to 6 percent for period 1962-71, the tax burden on the agricultural sector remained moderately low. This

Table 27. ROC (Taiwan): Savings Ratios and Composition of Savings, 1952-82

Year	Gross Savings (% of GNP) Percentage of GNP	Composition of Savings (% of Gross Domestic Capital Formation)				
		S_f	Total	Capital Consumption	Sg	Sp
1952	9.2	40.0	60.0	31.3	−0.9	29.6
1953	8.9	36.9	63.1	33.0	1.0	29.1
1954	7.7	52.2	47.8	31.2	−2.9	19.5
1955	9.0	32.5	67.5	37.6	2.7	27.2
1956	9.2	42.8	57.2	33.2	−0.1	24.1
1957	10.6	33.2	66.8	36.9	3.4	26.5
1958	9.9	40.9	59.1	35.1	3.5	20.5
1959	10.3	45.6	54.4	33.3	2.1	19.0
1960	12.7	37.5	62.5	32.0	5.0	25.5
1961	12.8	36.6	63.9	31.3	1.3	31.3
1962	12.4	30.8	69.2	35.3	1.1	32.8
1963	17.1	7.0	93.0	34.0	8.7	50.3
1964	19.6	−4.2	104.2	34.7	16.9	53.6
1965	19.6	14.0	86.0	27.6	15.3	43.1
1966	21.5	−1.0	101.0	29.3	16.1	55.6
1967	22.5	9.2	90.8	25.8	16.8	48.2
1968	22.1	12.4	87.6	25.6	24.9	37.1
1969	23.8	3.4	96.6	27.1	32.1	37.4
1970	25.5	0.9	99.1	26.4	23.6	49.1
1971	28.8	−9.2	109.2	26.4	23.1	59.7
1972	32.1	−24.4	124.4	27.8	32.1	64.5
1973	34.6	−18.2	118.2	24.2	25.7	68.3
1974	31.7	19.8	80.2	17.0	25.7	37.5
1975	26.9	12.7	87.3	22.9	29.9	34.5
1976	32.5	−4.7	104.7	23.9	34.4	46.5
1977	33.0	−15.4	115.4	27.3	34.2	53.9
1978	35.2	−22.6	122.6	27.8	38.6	56.2
1979	34.6	−2.8	102.8	23.4	34.9	44.5
1980	32.7	4.4	95.6	21.7	29.1	44.8
1981	31.4	−5.9	105.9	26.8	34.4	44.8
1982	30.6	−23.4	123.4	33.7	35.8	54.8

Source: *Taiwan Statistical Data Book*, 1983, Council for Economic Planning and Development, Executive Yuan, Republic of China.

S_f: foreign savings; Sg: net government savings; Sp: net private sector savings; Total = Sg + Sp + Savings of Public Corporation + Capital Consumption.

Table 28. ROC (Taiwan): Structure of Tax Revenue, 1952-83

	Total Taxes as % of GDP	as % of Total Tax		Indirect Taxes as % of GDP		
		Direct Taxes	Indirect Taxes	Agri.	Industry	Services
1952	17.6	30.9	69.1	8.4	15.6	9.5
1953	17.4	29.7	70.3	9.9	12.5	11.6
1954	21.1	26.4	73.6	7.9	14.9	12.0
1955	21.7	28.1	71.8	10.3	16.7	12.1
1956	21.5	24.9	75.1	8.6	15.8	13.4
1957	22.1	24.3	75.7	9.0	13.8	15.1
1958	21.1	24.0	76.1	8.4	13.8	15.2
1959	19.6	26.7	73.4	8.1	13.0	14.5
1960	18.0	28.2	71.7	8.6	12.6	13.2
1961	17.5	24.2	75.8	8.8	11.4	12.7
1962	16.7	22.6	77.4	7.7	14.1	13.7
1963	16.1	21.3	78.7	7.8	14.1	12.4
1964	15.6	22.5	77.5	6.8	13.1	12.8
1965	16.7	22.2	77.8	6.8	15.1	11.5
1966	16.9	21.9	78.1	6.5	15.3	12.7
1967	16.5	21.4	78.6	7.2	16.6	10.3
1968	17.6	23.1	76.8	7.2	19.3	9.7
1969	20.3	25.9	74.1	5.3	20.1	12.1
1970	19.4	25.0	74.9	5.3	19.2	10.0
1971	18.2	26.4	73.5	5.4	19.4	7.6
1972	17.8	27.9	72.1	3.4	17.8	8.5
1973	17.4	27.7	72.3	3.2	19.1	8.5
1974	19.0	28.1	71.9	3.5	19.3	8.2
1975	19.5	29.6	70.4	3.8	18.8	8.9
1976	20.3	30.8	69.2	3.9	18.2	8.6
1977	19.9	32.1	67.9	2.9	18.0	8.4
1978	20.3	31.9	68.1	1.5	19.1	8.6
1979	22.4	33.1	66.9	1.2	20.2	9.1
1980	21.2	34.2	65.8	1.3	19.3	7.8
1981	21.3	37.0	63.0	1.1	16.4	7.9
1982	21.0	39.6	60.4	0.9	14.8	7.8
1983	19.6	39.6	60.4	1.0	16.0	7.7

Sources: Council for Economic Planning & Development, Executive Yuan, ROC, *Taiwan Statistical Data Book*, 1983.
Shirley W.Y. Kuo, "The Taiwan Economy in Transition," Department of Statistics, Ministry of Finance, *Yearbook of Financial Statistics of the ROC, FY 1983*.
Bureau of Accounting & Statistics Taiwan Provincial Government, *Statistical Abstract of Taiwan Province, 1946-67*.

was partly due to the fact that the government policy was intended to encourage private savings and investment, but largely due to the fact that the land reform in the early fifties brought the fastest increase in agricultural productivity, a rise of 2.3 time within a decade. The abolition of the rice-fertilizer barter system in 1971 and reduction in agricultural taxes in recent years signals a change in importance in government resource mobilization as sustained economic growth proceeds.

In summary, in many developing countries, large government budget deficits result from rapidly rising military expenditures, overambitious industrial investment programs, or expanding social expenditures, all combined with a weak tax system. This does not hold true for the three East Asian countries, particularly for the ROC (Taiwan). As we have seen, the supply of foreign savings started to fall drastically since 1963 for the ROC (Taiwan). For the first time in 1964, the government current surplus net of foreign transfers as a percent of government expenditures registered positive 6.5 percent. During the years 1971-1973, there even appeared a net surplus on current account. The decline in the supply of foreign savings has been more than compensated for by the rapidly increasing share of private savings and to some extent, of government savings.

Government savings contributed about 30 percent to the high savings rate of the ROC (Taiwan) in the 1970s. The high government savings ratio was the major financial source of public investment. Furthermore, the policy of keeping relatively high interest rates (in real terms) as a stimulus to private savings and enforcing economy in the use of financial resources has not been accompanied by too rapid a rise in government debt. Government budget deficits, except in the early 1950s, were not serious obstacles to an anti-inflation policy.

Industrial Concentration and Efficiency of Invested Capital

The outward-looking strategy may have been one of the important factors that contributed to an increasing business concentration in a few urban centers, thereby preventing the growth of off-farm income and the employment of farm families.[38]

For the reasons elaborated already, Korea encouraged import substitution of intermediate and capital goods during the seventies, in connection with the government-promoted development of heavy and chemical industries. Given the limited domestic market, these industries could easily induce one or a few corporations to a dominant position either as a monopoly or oligopoly. When small open economies like Korea try to establish a presence in world markets for heavy industrial and chemical products, the government tends to channel underpriced financial resources to a handful of business groups selected for export promotion to reap economies of scale. Such an interventionistic allocation inevitably resulted in relatively great industrial concentration in Korea.

It is estimated that the largest 30 industrial groups accounted for 16 percent of GNP in 1983. A year earlier, the proportion was about 15 percent. On the other hand, no significant progress was made in the area of import liberalization during this period, particularly for items mainly produced by the monopoly and oligopoly firms. Thus, the increased business concentration in Korea probably reduced competition in production and marketing, thereby reducing industrial efficiency, and stifled Korea's "up-market" move in export of high quality, skilled-labor-intensive

---

[38] Oshima, *The Transition*, p. 35.

products. This reduction in industrial efficiency and product diversification lag should answer partly the earlier question of the sharp decline in total factor productivity in general and in the contribution of technical progress to productivity growth in particular during the 1977-82 period.

Small- and Medium-Scale Firms vs. Large-Scale Establishments

Unequal efficiency of resource use between small-scale and large-scale enterprises may account for part of the decline in industrial efficiency in Korea. A study by Dr. C.K. Kim made an assessment of the economic efficiency of the resource mis-allocation caused by the government promotion of heavy industries. It shows that small- and medium-sized industries have been more efficient in terms of productivity growth than have the large scale industries.

In order to verify this point he studied Korea's industrial growth and productivity trends during the 1967-1979 period. Between 1967 and 1979, the output growth was in general higher as the size of the firm increased. Thus, the relative position of small- and medium-sized firms with less than 500 employees in total manufacturing sector continued to decline in terms of their shares in number of establishment, employees and output during this period. On the other hand, the relative position of large scale firms with 500 or more employees increased in all aspects: between 1967 and 1979, their output and employment shares increased from 39 percent to 58 percent and from 27 percent to 45 percent, respectively.

This is in sharp contrast to the ROC (Taiwan) in which the relative position of small- and medium-sized firms was stronger than that of the firms with more than 500 employees in terms of output, employment and number of establishment.

Whether the industrial structure in favor of large-scale enterprises is desirable or not is not an important question; what is at issue is whether it is accompanied by an increase in efficiency or not. In other words, if the productivity increase of large-scale enterprises is higher than that of small- and medium-sized industries, the structural change in favor of large-scale enterprises is not undesirables in terms of resource allocation.

As shown in Table 29, the productivity growth of the Korean manufacturing sector as a whole averaged 5 percent per annum between 1967 and 1979. As output growth averaged 24 percent over the same period, productivity increases accounted for only 20 percent of output growth. With respect to the manufacturing sector of the ROC (Taiwan), its productivity growth was more or less the same – 4.8 percent, while output growth averaged 17.7 percent during the same period, 1967-1979. As a result, the productivity increase in the ROC (Taiwan) accounted for nearly 30 percent of output growth, higher than that of the Korean manufacturing sector.

The study finds that the relatively low contribution of factor productivity of the Korean manufacturing sector to output growth was to a considerable extent due to the low or negative productivity growth in capital intensive industries with high capital-labor ratios, like oil refining, basic metals, wood and wood products, and beverages. Also, the study finds that the large-scale firms recorded lower factor productivity growth than small- and medium-sized firms. This is illustrated in Table 30. While firms with less than 200 employees generate a higher productivity growth of 7 or 8 percent and nearly 60 percent of total output increase, the firms with more than 500 employees averaged productivity growth of 4 percent, with about 14 percent of the total increase in output. This seems to reveal that the lower

Table 29. Korea and ROC (Taiwan): Growth Rates of Output,
Input and Productivity in Manufacturing, 1967-79

(Unit: %)

	Korea				ROC (Taiwan)			
	Output (1)	Labor Input (2)	Capital Input (3)	Total Factor (4)	Out. (1)	Lab. (2)	Cap. (3)	Tot. (4)
1. Food, Beverage & Tobacco	16.4	6.5	18.8	0.0	10.3	-2.6	7.0	5.3
2. Textile, Wearing Apparel & Leather	25.2	9.9	19.5	7.4	21.6	6.2	15.7	9.8
3. Wood & Wood Products including Furniture	17.4	7.6	16.9	2.1	6.6	4.8	4.3	2.1
4. Paper and Paper Products, Printing & Publishing	18.5	7.8	15.1	4.9	14.3	3.9	10.8	6.0
5. Chemicals, Petrol, Coal, Rubber, Plastic	23.5	11.2	17.7	6.3	19.0	7.0	19.1	2.1
6. Non-Metallic Mineral (Ex. Petrol, Coal)	19.6	6.7	16.2	5.6	11.4	2.6	13.0	0.9
7. Basic Metal	30.2	10.8	36.9	-1.5	16.8	6.8	23.0	-0.9
8. Fabricated Metal Machinery & Equipment	34.7	15.3	26.5	9.3	25.8	11.6	19.5	7.9
9. Others	25.6	9.7	19.0	7.4	28.1	13.2	13.8	13.0
Manufacturing Total	24.0	10.4	20.9	5.0	17.7	6.3	15.5	4.8

Source: Chuk Kyo Kim, "Industrial Growth and Productivity Trends in Korea," p. 56.

factor productivity growth of the total manufacturing sector in Korea has stemmed largely from the lower factor productivity growth of large-scale firms. Therefore, there has been inefficiency in resource allocation within the manufacturing sector.

In the case of the ROC (Taiwan), Table 30 shows the firms with more than 500 employees had the least productivity growth, while firms with 100 to 499 employees the largest productivity growth. But this difference was relatively small and altogether they exhibit more or less similar productivity growth and economic efficiency between 1966 and 1976.

In summary, first, compared with the ROC (Taiwan), Korea's output growth depended less heavily on total factor productivity growth and more heavily on factor input increase. Second, in Korea, the rate of factor productivity increase in small- and medium-sized firms was higher than that of larger enterprises because of a successful adoption of new technologies by the former. Third, and more importantly, the medium-sized firms played a leading role in the growth process of the ROC (Taiwan)'s industrialization, while larger establishments assumed a similar role in Korea. This difference in the pattern of industrial growth seems to be closely related to a difference in the government's incentive measures in two countries. While the ROC (Taiwan) has applied general tax incentives for industrial promotion, Korea adopted interventionistic credit policies which favored well-established large-scale enterprises over small- and medium-sized firms.

A comparative review of industrial growth in both Korea and the ROC (Taiwan) has several policy implications. First, Korea ought to increase efficiency of larger establishments, namely those in the heavy and chemical industries. Secondly, small- and medium-sized firms which contribute substantially to employment creation and generation of income, particularly for low-income groups, should have equal access to the formal credit market by providing interest spreads that make lending to small-scale establishments more attractive to commercial and state banks. Finally, except in cases of obvious market failure, one may cast doubt over the "strategic industry" approach because of the dubious ability of government to pick "winning" industries and firms. Even if government should somehow make the right choice of winning industries or firms, heavy government subsidies protect these industries from the strong market test, and these industries are prone to rely more on debt financing, to take the risk of overexpansion, and to lose incentive to be more efficient. In short, selective credit policies and factor price distortions easily lead to misallocation of capital and hamper financial saving and efficient investment. It is instructive to learn that the investment efficiency of Hong Kong, which rejects a "picking the winner" approach, is higher than Singapore, the ROC (Taiwan) and Korea.

Labor Absorption, Employment and Income Distribution

Finally, a serious matter is income distribution which seems to have deteriorated since the latter half of the 1970s, a fact that is associated with the rising in industrial concentration. Compared with some other developing countries, Korea has been praised for its relatively fair income distribution despite rapid growth. There are several reasons for this. A land reform carried out in 1949 and the Korean War removed several institutional barriers to social mobility. In the 1960s, the outward-looking growth strategy had favorable effects on income distribution in Korea. The

Table 30. Growth Rates of Output and Total Factor Productivity
by Size of Firm for Manufacturing in Korea & ROC (Taiwan)

(Unit: %)

Korea: 1967-1979 Size of Firm (workers)	Output	Labor Prod.	Capital Prod.	Total Factor Productivity
5 — 9	11.1	12.8	4.9	7.8
10 — 19	13.9	11.5	5.2	7.6
20 — 49	20.1	11.5	6.0	8.0
50 — 99	21.7	11.7	4.5	6.8
100 — 199	25.8	12.5	4.1	7.5
200 — 499	22.1	8.6	0.7	2.4
500 or More	27.6	11.0	2.3	4.0
Total	24.0	12.3	2.6	5.0

ROC (Taiwan): 1966-1976 Size of Firm (workers)	Output	Labor Prod.	Capital Prod.	Total Factor Productivity
5 — 9	17.8	8.9	−0.7	3.2
10 — 19	19.9	9.9	0.5	4.9
20 — 49	21.5	9.4	0.5	4.3
50 — 99	25.1	8.7	0.7	4.4
100 — 499	26.1	8.9	4.5	6.3
500 or More	19.5	6.7	0.7	3.0
Total	21.4	8.0	1.5	4.0

Source: Chuk Kyo Kim, "Industrial Growth and Productivity Trends in Korea," p. 57.

rapid labor absorption through export expansion of labor-intensive manufactured goods contributed substantially to the rise in relative incomes of lower-income families. But in the course of the 1970s, Korea's income distribution showed signs of deterioration. According to the KDI estimates, the income share held by the lowest 40 percent of income groups declined from 19.3 percent in 1965 to 16.1 percent in 1980. There are two important factors behind the deterioration. First, major investment projects undertaken in the latter half of 1970s were of the capital-intensive type which usually do not provide extensive employment opportunities. Second, the real purchasing power of "have-nots" was more severely affected by the high rate of inflation than that of "haves" because the price of basic necessities rose faster than those of other commodities.

Korea's current efforts to improve income distribution are based on the expansion of employment opportunities through growth with price stability. Since 1982, the rate of inflation has declined very sharply. A combination of declining import prices, a balanced budget, and tight control over money supply may have kept the inflation within bounds. However, the expansion of employment opportunities through growth has proven to be more difficult to accomplish. Table 31 reveals that the Korean economy no longer generates employment opportunities as widely as in the last two decades. During the period, 1963-1979, the growth of labor supply and employment exceeded that of total population. During the 1979-1984 period, however, both the growth of labor supply and employment dropped sharply to 1.1 percent, falling short of the population growth rate. This trend, if it continues, has very serious implications for Korea's future economic growth. From the efficiency viewpoint, it may mean that since the whole population is to be supported by a declining labor force, either the economy is not efficienctly mobilizing its human resources, or the growth rate of per capita GNP would slow down unless rapid capital accumulation and technological advancement compensate for the loss in labor inputs. On the other hand, if the marked drop in the labor force participation rate is only a temporary phenomenon, its reversal will give rise to an increase in unemployment, the consequences of which would adversely affect income distribution. Higher policy priority should be given to generating new employment opportunities and putting more people to work.

CONCLUSION AND PROSPECTS – A COMPARATIVE REVIEW

Frequent references have been made to the experience of both the ROC (Taiwan) and Hong Kong in order to recognize particularities in Korea's industrial development and policies. This concluding section presents a comparative review of the three economies, Korea, the ROC (Taiwan), and Hong Kong by pointing out directly their important similarities and differences in a number of major areas. Their future directions are also considered.

Export-led Industrialization

Korea, the ROC (Taiwan), and Hong Kong, three of the Asian NICs, are small, resource scarce economies with a very limited endowment of arable land and natural resources. Therefore, development efforts had to focus on the expansion of non-agricultural sectors right from the beginning and production for export was unavoidable in order to be able to pay for necessary raw materials imports. In short, export-led industrialization was the only realistic alternative to breakthrough the natural resources constraint on their economies.

Their implementation of export-oriented industrialization since the fifties for both Hong Kong and the ROC (Taiwan) and the sixties for Korea is believed to have generated significant productivity gains through the positive effects of intensifying competition upon domestic entrepreneurs, increasing technology transfers, and encouraging the exploitation of internal scale economies, and the dynamic external economies that arise only in export production activities.

Korea, the ROC (Taiwan), and Hong Kong have been the fastest growing countries in the world. They reached sustained average annual rates of real output growth of more than 8 percent (Table 32). This impressive growth performance has resulted from an enhanced process of industrial development geared toward the manufacture of exportable products, turning away from the policy of import substitution. A number of empirical evidence indicate higher output growth trends to be associated with better export performance, although the latter's relative contribution to growth has declined after the first oil shock and consequent world-wide recessions.[39]

In all three of the countries, a low and stable relative wage rate was perhaps the most important single factor determining the rapid industrialization process based on labor-intensive manufactured exports. However, after pursuing an export promotion strategy for more than a decade, and with the sharp rise in the wage/rental ratio beginning in the late 1960s, both Korea and the ROC (Taiwan) have attempted to move up to a technology- and capital-intensive type of export promotion. In the case of Hong Kong, however, since the shortage of land is relatively more acute than the other two, the scope for developing capital-intensive industries is quite limited; hence, skill-intensive industries with short gestation periods are the prime choices for its further industrial development.

The openness of the three economies is striking. All three lack substantial natural resources such as oil. Their economies are therefore quite vulnerable to interruptions in the supply, or increases in the cost, of imported raw materials. Also because the three depend largely on the markets of the industrialized countries for their exports of manufactured goods, they are subject to the vagaries of foreign markets. In 1983, as a share of GNP, exports ranged from 69 percent in Hong Kong, and 50 percent in the ROC (Taiwan) to 32 percent in Korea. Therefore, diversification is necessary to dampen export fluctuations and supply disruptions.

Structural Changes

Although Korea, the ROC (Taiwan) and Hong Kong have pursued export-led development strategies, their economies differ in size, per capita GNP, and industrial structure.

Of the three, Hong Kong, a major entrepot, is more advanced economically than the ROC (Taiwan) and Korea, measured by differences in GNP per capita and in the share of agriculture in real GDP. Hong Kong's GNP per capita stood at US$5,802 in 1982, which was 2.3 times as large as Taiwan's (US$2,554) and 3.2 times that of Korea (US$1,800). In both the ROC (Taiwan) and Hong Kong, agriculture's shares of GDP (1982) are relatively small; a virtually indistinguishable 0,7 percent for Hong Kong and 7.7 percent for the ROC (Taiwan). In contrast, Korea's agricultural sector accounted for 17.3 percent of real GDP in 1982.

In terms of the share of manufacturing output in real GDP, the ROC (Taiwan) ranked the first with the share of 42.4 in 1982, followed by Korea with 32.8 percent, and Hong Kong with 21.8 percent. The comparatively smaller share of Hong Kong's manufacturing output in real GDP was due to the sharp expansion of the service sector. For Hong Kong, having emerged as an important financial center, the growth in financial, real estate, insurance, and other business services has been the major factor accounting for the relative expansion of the service sector, both in terms of output (69 percent) and employment (57 percent) shares.

---

[39] B. Balassa, "Exports and Economic Growth: Further Evidence," *Journal of Development Economics*, 15, 1978, pp. 181-189; W. Tyler, "Growth and Export Expansion in Developing Countries; Some Empirical Evidence," *Journal of Development Economics*, 9, No. 2 (August 1981), pp. 121-130; and P.B. Rana, *Exports and Economic Growth in the Asian Region* (ADB Economic Staff Paper No. 25, (February 1985), pp. 1-25.

Table 31. Korea: Population, Labor Force, and Employment, 1963-1984

	Total Population (million)	Population above 14 yrs. (million)	Labor Force (million)	Employed (million)	Unemployed Rate (%)	Labor Force Participation Rate (%)
1963	27.26	15.09	8.34	7.66	8.2	55.3
1973	34.10	20.44	11.60	11.14	4.0	56.8
1979	37.53	24.68	14.21	13.66	3.8	57.6
1984	40.58	27.79	14.98	14.42	3.8	53.9
Annual Average Rate of Increase						
1963-73	2.5	3.5	3.9	4.5	—	—
1973-79	1.7	3.5	3.8	3.8	—	—
1979-84	1.6	2.5	1.1	1.1	—	—

Source: Bank of Korea, *Economic Statistics Yearbook*, various years.

Table 32. Exports and Economic Growth of Korea, ROC (Taiwan), and Hong Kong, 1961-1983

(Unit: %)

	Average Growth Rate of Real GNP			Average Growth Rate of Exports		
	Korea	ROC (Taiwan)	Hong Kong[1]	Korea	ROC (Taiwan)	Hong Kong
1961-1965	6.5	9.5	11.8	23.9	20.6	9.3
1966-1970	10.4	9.8	6.4	48.8	22.0	14.4
1971-1975	8.6	8.9	6.6	23.7	15.4	4.6
1976-1980	7.6	10.4	12.3	17.5	16.3	16.7
1981-1983	7.2	5.3	5.4	7.1	7.2	8.5

Source: Asian Development Bank, *Key Indicators*, 1984, and various country sources.

1. GDP basis.

Labor Productivity, Unit Labor Costs and Export Competitiveness

Table 33 compares the growth of labor productivity in the manufacturing sector of the trio. Over the 1966-1982 period, the record of Korea was better than the other two. From 1980 to 1982, however, Hong Kong's performance was the fastest, followed by the ROC (Taiwan).

In comparing Korea's falling labor productivity in manufacturing with that of the ROC (Taiwan) in 1980-1982, an analysis by the Bank of Korea attributes the deceleration in recent years to lagging technological innovation. Despite a significant increase in capital per worker, (8.2 percent in 1974-79 and 8.1 percent in 1980-1982) the growth of labor productivity was sluggish because of the decline in capital productivity.[40] Sung holds the view that more selective credit policies to promote heavy and chemical industries — much more extensive in Korea than in the ROC (Taiwan) — have led to misallocation of capital and hampered saving and investment.[41]

Because the exports of Korea, the ROC (Taiwan) and Hong Kong are largely of labor-intensive manufactured products, labor costs constitute a large share of total costs of final goods. Therefore, unit labor costs derived by dividing nominal wage rate by real average labor productivity, may be useful in indicating to some extent export competitiveness.

In Korea and the ROC (Taiwan), labor productivity in manufacturing has risen at a rate slower than the nominal wage rate since the early 1970s. This has generated an increase in unit labor costs for both countries. Between 1981 and 1982, however, unit labor costs rose at an annual rate of 13.3 percent in Korea, a faster rate compared with that of 7.4 percent in the ROC (Taiwan). But much of the increase in Korea was nullified by a depreciation of the Korean Won. After the exchange rate was adjusted in Korea, unit labor costs in U.S. dollars rose at a similar rate as in the ROC (Taiwan) — about 3 percent for each.[42]

In more detail, Table 34 gives the rates of increase of unit labor costs in U.S. dollars in 1975-1982 for Korea, the ROC (Taiwan) and Hong Kong. During the period, 1976-1979, Korea's export competitiveness deteriorated sharply. Unit labor costs, expressed in U.S. dollars, increased by some 78 percent in Korea, while increases were 33 percent in the ROC (Taiwan) and 29 percent in Hong Kong. Although in 1980-1982, Korea's unit labor costs in domestic currency rose much faster than in the ROC (Taiwan) and Hong Kong, unit labor costs in U.S. dollars did not rise because of the depreciation of the Korean Won. As shown in Table 33, between 1979 and 1982, unit labor costs in U.S, dollars even fell slightly and recovered part of the loss in relative export competitiveness that took place in 1976-1979. Korea's export performance during the 1979-1982 period was relatively better than the other two. Further analysis is needed to ascertain a precise relationship between unit labor costs and export competitiveness, and of the many factors that influence exports.

---

[40] Bank of Korea, "Trends in Korea's Labor Productivity in Manufacturing Sector," *Monthly Bulletin* (December 1984), pp. 11-13, (Korean).

[41] Views of the consultant from Hong Kong.

[42] Bank of Korea, "Export Competitiveness of Korean Industry," *Monthly Bulletin* (June 1985), p. 4. (Korean).

Table 33. Comparisons of Growth Rate of Labor Productivity in the Manufacturing Sector of Korea, ROC (Taiwan) and Hong Kong

(Unit: %)

Korea		Hong Kong		ROC (Taiwan)		ROC (Taiwan)[1]	
1966-73	9.5	1966-71	3.3	1966-70	10.6		
1974-79	5.8	1971-81	4.4	1971-80	4.9	1974-79	8.7
1980-82	3.2	1981-84	8.7	1981-83	5.3	1980-82	5.4
1966-82	7.1	1966-84	5.3	1966-83	6.4		

Sources: For Korea, Bank of Korea, "Trends in Korea's Labor Productivity in the Manufacturing Sector," *Monthly Bulletin* (in Korean), December 1984, p. 12. Labor Productivity is measured by value added per worker.
Figures of Hong Kong and ROC (Taiwan) based on reports of consultants associated with this study.
Labor productivity of in the ROC (Taiwan) is measured by GDP per worker. (1) Based on Korean data.

Table 34. Rates of Increase of Unit Labor Costs in U.S. Dollars in Korea, ROC (Taiwan) and Hong Kong

	Unit Labor Costs (in US$)			Merchandise Exports (in US$)		
	Korea	ROC (Taiwan)	Hong Kong	Korea	ROC (Taiwan)	Hong Kong
1975	100.0	100.0	100.0	5,081	5,302	6,010
1976	133.4	109.3	109.1	7,715	8,156	8,526
1979	237.4	145.0	140.4	15,055	16,103	15,147
1982	235.1	183.2	146.3	21,853	22,100	20,984
1976-79	78.0%	32.7%	28.7%	95.1%	97.4%	77.7%
1979-82	-0.9%	26.3%	4.2%	45.2%	37.2%	38.5%

Sources: 1) Sang-woo Nam, "Korea's Stabilization Efforts Since the Late 1970s" (unpublished mimeo, February 1984), Table 14, p. 77; and ADB, *Key Indicators*, 1984.

The Role of Government

The role of government in economic activities could be beneficial or detrimental to industrial development, depending on what it does. Even in advanced Hong Kong, which may have been ruled by positive non-interventionism, the Industrial Development Board was established to plan, to monitor and to advise the government on various programmes in industrial development. Though our Hong Kong consultant, Sung is highly critical of government intervention, he strongly supports the role of government in promoting education, and research and development.

Both Korea and the ROC (Taiwan) are examples of highly successful government fiscal efforts. Through tighter control on wasteful spending, including the elimination of unnecessary subsidies and weeding out of low-priority non-developmental expenditures, the two have generated substantial government savings, leaving wider scope for private investment.

A crucial difference between Korea and the ROC (Taiwan) is revealed, however, in the extent of their intervention in financial markets. Although both Korea and the ROC (Taiwan) subsidized interest rates for loans offered to priority borrowers, the use of preferential credit was much wider in Korea than in the ROC (Taiwan). For example, in Korea in 1979, about 50 percent of bank loans were "policy" loans to preferred borrowers, extended at the government direction, to promote capital-intensive investments and export expansion.[43]

In the ROC (Taiwan), in comparison, the share of subsidized loans amounted to a mere 7 percent.[44] Financial repression has been, therefore, quite low in the ROC (Taiwan). This was mainly because the gap between real interest rates in the banking system and those in the private money market has narrowed down, stemming from the increase in national income and in household savings, and from a stable financial environment and stable prices.[45]

It is difficult to deny the financial assistance extended by both Korean and the ROC (Taiwan) governments to infant industries was responsible for their sustained and rapid growth. As a general rule, however, intervention by the government should not be a substitute for the market mechanism, except in cases of obvious market failures. Relatively speaking, government intervention in financial markets in Korea was much more pervasive and prolonged, and brought about misallocation of scarce resources and resulted in chronic inflation.

Industrial Adjustment and Restructuring

After pursuing an export promotion strategy based on labor-intensive products for more than a decade, both Korea and the ROC (Taiwan) have begun in the early 1970s to move up to technology-intensive lines in heavy and chemical industries as the new export sector in the future. In Korea, however, a number of factors have hampered smooth structural changes consistent with expected shifts in Korea's factor endowment and comparative advantage.

---

[43] Wan-Soon Kim, *Financial Development and Household Savings: Issues in Domestic Resource Mobilization in Asian Developing Countries* (ADB Economic Staff Paper, No. 10, July 1982), p. 44.

[44] Korea Economic Research Institute. *The Industrial Policies in Taiwan*. (Seoul, Korea, December 1984), p. 68. (Korean).

[45] Findings of our consultant from Hong Kong.

Faced with the limits of further growth in labor-intensive exports, due to a rising wage/rental ratio and other factors indicated earlier, Korea decided to shift quickly to heavy industrialization. In retrospect, the hasty push toward heavy industrialization appears to have led only to need for painful structural adjustment. Instead of undertaking investment in research and development for new technology, training workers for new skills, and in acquiring marketing expertise, the biased incentive system led to the adoption of a higher capital-intensity in the production of those already successful export products initially intensive in labor. As a result, firms were induced to stay on with the existing export products longer than they otherwise would.[46] Furthermore, prolonged world recessions and growing trade protectionism slowed down the growth of exports which, in turn, contributed to the decline in capital productivity by causing capacity under-utilization. Korea realized its mistakes in the early 1980s belatedly. It had neither the capital resources nor the technological experience for undertaking heavy industries, hence, the bulging external debt was the price Korea had to pay for short-sighted government policy.

Compared with Korea, the adjustment efforts have been met with less formidable obstacles in the ROC (Taiwan). As Liu our consultant from the ROC (Taiwan) points out, in the choice of technology and industries, the ROC (Taiwan) has been on the track of the normal pattern of industrialization, that is, a shift from labor-intensive to high technology lines, shown by the changing revealed comparative advantage indices. There were also other factors, conducive to a smooth transition. To begin with, although the ROC (Taiwan) central government is as authoritarian as Korea's, decisions in economic matters seem to have been made on a much broader basis. In comparison, major mistakes were made in Korea in large part because basic strategies and policies have been selected by a small group of power elites.[47] Secondly, a larger share of foreign direct investment in the ROC (Taiwan) and Hong Kong could have facilitated technology transfer and lessened the marketing problems of industrial exports. It is also reasonable to agree that greater participation of foreign investors in the development of the ROC (Taiwan)'s industries could have checked any tendency to excessive investment. Thirdly, as was discussed already, the productivity growth of small- and medium-scale firms in the manufacturing sectors has been essential for continuing and relatively balanced industrial development of the ROC. Also, the small-size of firms may partly explain the relative industrial strength of both the ROC (Taiwan) and Hong Kong in times of global trade protectionism and recessions, due to their flexibility and adaptability to changing circumstances.

Our Hong Kong consultant, Sung, argues, however, that when the size of firms remains small, this implies an inability on the part of firms to grow, reap scale economies, and accumulate skills. Thus, he contends that Hong Kong may succeed in fashionable electronics consumer products of short life cycles. This could be also true in the case of the ROC (Taiwan). If the size of the firm is an important factor for raising industrial efficiency and export competitiveness in high technology industries requiring vast facility investment, Korea (which also has larger internal markets) may have better prospects of succeeding in industries like semiconductor and computers compared with the other two.

---

[46] Y.C. Park, "Industrial Restructuring in Korea."

[47] Oshima, *The Transition,* pp. 40-41.

Finally, one cannot ignore the fact that the opening up of China has significant implications for the economic management of the three countries. China has rich human and natural resources and has a fairly big potential for foreign trade. Nevertheless, given the potential for political conflict one can only entertain a number of possible scenarios as to the economic impact of political uncertainties. Despite the current rumors and possible development of the so-called South Korea-China economic interaction, it may be too early for Korean policymakers to consider integrating the "China factor" into their industrial and trade policies. Similarly, it is quite difficult to say precisely how the on-going issue of the ROC (Taiwan)-China relations would affect business climate and long-term investments in the ROC (Taiwan).

With respect to the "China factor" for Hong Kong's industrial policy, Sung's analysis begins with an economic picture of Hong Kong in which there will be long-term political stability. Sung argues that the Chinese modernization drive would have mixed effects. On the one hand, it may strengthen the status of Hong Kong as entrepot, financial center, channel of information, and source of direct investment and expertise. On the other hand, the opening up of China could be competitive to Hong Kong's industrial development, instead of being complementary. Further, if Hong Kong manufacturers take advantage of cheap labor in China and supply the Chinese market with standardized technology, labor-intensive consumer products, Sung sees this would retard the process of Hong Kong's industrial transformation into high-technology sectors.[48]

Korea, the ROC (Taiwan) and Hong Kong have been the fastest growing countries in the world. Undoubtedly, the achievements of the East Asian NICs have benefited greatly from the work ethic of its people with their strong sense for hard work. Vitally important also was the American economic assistance given to Korea and the ROC (Taiwan) in their initial efforts to overcome major economic dislocations. Without U.S. aid, their recovery and further economic development would have undoubtedly taken a much longer period.

As their industrialization strategies shift from labor-intensive to technology- and capital-intensive lines, they have to make a difficult transition to differentiated products in the areas where design, marketing and quality control are crucial. Equally important, they should be prepared to pay for technology transfers or they will have to carry out their own indigenous research and development to a far greater extent than ever before. As Japan's experience suggests, in introducing and spreading new technologies, it should be clear that policies to develop absorptive capability are of crucial importance. Foremost, human resources must be developed through education and training, research and development activities encouraged, and an efficient network established to acquire information about foreign technologies, and make them available to small-scale enterprises.

In 1986, the Korean economy has resumed showing an exemplarly performance, as real GNP grew 12.5 percent, while consumer prices rose only 2.3 percent and wholesale prices declined more than 2 percent. Since the latter part of 1985, the balance of payments difficulties, as we have seen constraining the Korean economy in the past, has been considerably eased. In 1986, blessed with "three lows" — low oil prices, low world interest rates and a lower value of the U.S. dollar against other major currencies, Korea recorded a trade surplus of 4.2 billion U.S. dollars and a current account surplus of 4.6 billion U.S. dollars. As a result, gross external debt

[48] Consultant from Hong Kong.

peaked at 46.8 billion U.S. dollars in 1985 fell to 35.5 billion U.S. dollars at the end of 1987. Looking ahead, unless some major unforeseen international disturbances occur, Korea and Asian NICs appear to be ready to graduate into ranks of the advanced industrial countries in the near future.

REFERENCES

Aghevli, Bijan B. and Jorge Marquez-Ruarte. *A Case of Successful Adjustment: Korea's Experience During 1980-1984.* IMF Occasional Paper 39, August 1985.

Balassa, B. "Export and Economic Growth: Further Evidence," *Journal of Development Economics,* 15, 1978.

Bank of Korea. *Economic Statistics Yearbook,* various years.

Bank of Korea. "Export Competitiveness of Korea Industry," *Monthly Bulletin,* June 1985. (Korean).

Bank of Korea. *National Income Accounts,* 1984.

Bank of Korea. "Trends in Korea's Labor Productivity in Manufacturing Sector," *Monthly Bulletin,* December, 1984. (Korean)

Galenson, Walter, ed. *Foreign Trade and Investment,* Madison, Wisconsin: The University of Wisconsin Press, 1985.

Hiemenz, Ulrich and Mathias Bruch. *Small- and Medium-Scale Manufacturing Establishingments in Asian Countries: Perspectives and Policy Issues.* Asian Developemnt Bank Economics of Staff Paper No. 14, March 1983.

Hong, Wontack. *Factor Supply and Factor Intensity of Trade in Korea.* Seoul, Korea: Korea Development Institute, 1976.

Huang, Tze-tseng. "Measurement of Total Factor Productivity in the R.O.C." *Raising Productivity-Experience of the Republic of China,* ed. Tzong-Shian Yu. Tokyo: Asian Productivity Organization. 1985.

Kim, Chuk Kyo. "Industrial Growth and Productivity Trends in Korea" *Essays in Memory of Sang Chul Suh,* ed. S.K. Kwack et al. Seoul, Korea: The Essays in Memory of Sang Chul Shu Editorial Committee, 1985. (Korean).

Kim, Kwang-suk. and Joon-kyung Park. *Sources of Economic Growth: 1963-1982.* Seoul, Korea: Korea Development Institute, 1985.

Kim, Kwang-suk and Michael Roemer. *Growth and Structural Transformation.* Cambridge, Mass.: Harvard University Press, 1979.

Kim, Wan-Soon. *The August 3, 1972, Emergency Decree for Economic Stability and Growth: Causes and Consquences.* Honolulu, Hawaii: East-West Center, December 1984.

Kim, Wan-Soon. *"Financial Development and Household Savings: Issues in Domestic Resource Mobilization in Asian Developing Countries."* ADB Economic Staff Paper, No. 10, July 1982.

Kim, Wan-Soon. "Transformation of the Korean Economy: Its Cause and Consequences," Korea and Japan, ed. Hahn and Yamamoto, Seoul: Korea University, Asiatic Research Center, 1978.

Koo, Bohn Young. "The Role of Direct Investment in Korea's Recent Economic Growth," *Foreign Trade and Investment,* ed. Walter Galenson. Madison, Wisconsin: The University of Wisconsin Press, 1985, pp. 176-216.

Korea Development Institute. *Quarterly Economic Outlook,* Vol. 4, No. 1, 1985.

Korea Economic Research Institute. *The Industrial Policies in Taiwan,* Seoul, Korea, December 1984.

Krause, Lawrence B. "Introduction" in W. Galenson ed. *Foreign Trade and Investment.* Madison, Wisconsin: The University of Wisconsin Press, 1985, pp. 3-41.

Kuo, Shirley W.Y. "Price Stabilization Policies in Taiwan, 1946-1983." *Raising Productivity-Experience of the Republic of China,* ed. Tzong-Shian Yu. Tokyo: Asian Productivity Organization, 1985.

Kuo, Shirley and John Fei. "Census and Roles of Export Expansion in the Republic of China," *Foreign Trade and Investment,* ed. Walter Galenson. Madison, Wisconsin: The University of Wisconsin Press, pp. 45-84.

Kuo, Shirley, Gustav Ranis, and John Fei. *The Taiwan Success Story.* Boulder, Coloradio: Westview Press, 1981.

Lee, T.H. and Kuo-shu Liang. *Process and Pattern of Economic Development in Taiwan.* Economic Essays Vol. IV, Taipei: National Taiwan University, November, 1973.

Lee, Young Sun. "Changing Export Patterns in Korea, Taiwan and Japan," KIET (Korean Institute of Industrial Economics & Technology), Working Paper, No. 9, Seoul, KIET, June 1980.

Lin, Tzong-biau and Victor Mok. "Trade, Foreign Investment, and Development in Hong Kong," *Foreign Trade and Investment.* ed. Walter Galenson. Madison, Wisconsin: The University of Wisconsin Press, 1985. pp. 219-256.

McKinnon, Ronald I. "Saving Propensities and the Korean Monetary Reform in Retrospect," *Money and Finance in Economic Growth and Development: Essays in Honor of Edward S. Shaw,* ed. R.I. McKinnon. New York: Marcel Dekker, Inc., 1976.

Oshima, Harry T. "A Lewis' Dualistic Theory and Its Relevance for Postwar Asian Growth," *Malayan Economic Review,* Vol. 20, No. 2, October 1981.

Oshima, Harry T. "The Transition to an Industrial Economy in Monsoon Asia." ADB Economic Staff Paper, No. 20, Manila: ADB, October 1983.

Park, Yung-Chul. "Industrial Restructuring in Korea." Unpublished Mimeo, December 1982.

Park, Yung-Chul. "Prospects of the Korean Economy as a Trading Nation." Paper Presented to Conference on Korea in the Year Two Thousand, May 30-June 1, Seoul, Korea: Asiatic Research Center, Korea University, 1985.

Rana, P.B. "Exports and Economic Growth in the Asian Region." ADB Economic Staff Paper, No. 25, Manila: ADB, February 1985.

Ranis, Gustav. "Industrial Development." *Economic Growth and Structural Change in Taiwan.* Walter Galenson, Ithaca, N.Y.: Cornell University Press, 1979.

Ranis, Gustav and Chi Schive. "Direct Foreign Investment in Taiwan's Development," *Foreign Trade and Investment.* ed. Walter Galenson. Madison, Wisconsin: The University of Wisconsin Press, 1985, pp. 85-137.

Shinohara, M. "Trends and Dynamics of East and Southeast Asian Economics," *Asian Development Review,* 1985, Vol. 3, No. 1.

Tsiang, S.C. and Rong-I Wu. "Foreign Trade and Investment as Boosters for Take-off: The Experiences of the Four Asian Newly Industrializing Countries," *Foreign Trade and Investment,* ed. Walter Galenson. Madison, Wisconsin: The University of Wisconsin Press, 1985, pp. 301-332.

Tyler, W. "Growth and Export Expansion in Developing Countries: Some Empirical Evidence," *Journal of Development Economics,* 9, No. 2, August 1981.

10. ASEAN Countries: Economic Performance and Tasks Ahead

Jun Nishikawa

OVERALL REVIEW OF THE REGION

High Economic Growth in The 1970s

The six ASEAN countries — Brunei, Indonesia, Malaysia, the Philippines, Singapore and Thailand — together have a population of 287 million as of 1985 (Table 1). This population surpasses that of the U.S.A. and the U.S.S.R. ASEAN countries total GNP of US$211 billion in 1985 surpasses GNP of Oceania or Africa (south of the Sahara except South Africa). In terms of per capita GNP, however, the average figure of $735 for this group hides some facts: in Singapore, the GNP per capita has reached $7,420 — Japan's mid-1970s level — and in Indonesia it is only $530. Malaysia has a per capita GNP of $1,220, but this is also deceptive. The figure includes oil production from eastern Malaysia and tells little about the unequal distribution of wealth among the ethnic groups. The Philippines and Thailand have an average income of about $600 for their inhabitants. The average Brunei income reached $25,466 in 1980, largely surpassing the other states because of its large oil and natural gas production relative to its small population. However, this is a rather exceptional case and, in talking about ASEAN countries, we will mostly exclude this small, rich state.

ASEAN countries all experienced very high economic growth based on industrialization. Already by the 1960s, the GDP growth rate, except economically-troubled Indonesia before 1967, attained 5-9 percent, and in the 1970s, all registered a growth rate of 6-8 percent in an epoch of worldwide economic turmoil (Table 2). High economic growth resulted in the 1960s, partly because of the demand stimulus from the war in Vietnam, as was the case with Japan at the time of the Korean War, and the establishment of labor-intensive industries. In the 1970s, these countries advanced in industrialization by exporting products to the world market; this export-oriented industrialization was facilitated mainly by three factors: (1) the propagation of the "green revolution", (2) a high price for fuels and raw materials, and (3) the progress of transnational enterprises in this region, which exported labor-intensive products to the world market, in particular, North America and Japan.

The high economic growth brought about important changes in the socio-economy of the region. In 1960, agricultural income share in the GDP was 50 percent in Indonesia, 36 percent in Malaysia, 26 percent in the Philippines and 40 percent in Thailand. The manufacture share was around 12-20 percent in the total GDP of these countries. However, in 1985, the agriculture share decreased to only 21-27 percent in ASEAN countries and that of the manufacturing sector increased to 19-20 percent in Malaysia and Thailand, 25 percent in the Philippines and 24 percent in Singapore. Including construction and mining, industrial production accounted for 30-36 percent in 1981 (Table 3).

Rapid industrialization accompanied modernization in rural areas, as witnessed by the diffusion of new high-yielding varieties, in particular those of rice and maize, the increase in agricultural inputs and the use of agricultural machinery, the exten-

Table 1. ASEAN Countries: Economic Features

	Population* (Mid-1985) (million)	Percentage Share (%)	GDP** (1985) (US$ million)	Percentage Share (%)
ASEAN	287.0	100	210,904	100
Brunei**	0.2	—	4,864	2.3
Indonesia	162.2	56.5	86,470	41.0
Malaysia	15.6	5.4	31,270	14.8
Philippines	54.7	19.1	32,590	15.5
Singapore	2.6	0.9	17,470	8.3
Thailand	51.7	18.0	38,240	18.1

	Per Capita** GNP (1985) (US$)	Gross** capital formation (1985) (%)	Gross** domestic saving (1985) (%)	Resource balance
ASEAN	—	—	—	—
Brunei***	25,466	n.a.	n.a.	n.a.
Indonesia	530	30	32	2
Malaysia	2,000	28	33	5
Philippines	580	16	13	−3
Singapore	7,420	43	42	−1
Thailand	800	23	21	−2

Sources: * UN, Statistical Office, Dept. of International Economic and Social Affairs;
           ** The World Bank, *World Development Report 1987*, Table 5;
          *** The figures for Brunei are those of 1980; *Brunei Statistical Yearbook*.

Table 2. ASEAN Countries: Growth Rate of Production

(Unit: %)

	GDP		Agriculture		Industry	
	1965-80	1980-85	1965-80	1980-85	1965-80	1980-85
Indonesia	7.9	3.5	4.3	3.1	11.9	1.0
Malaysia	7.3	5.5	–	3.0	–	6.7
Philippines	5.9	-0.5	4.6	1.7	8.0	-2.8
Singapore	10.2	6.5	3.1	-1.8	12.2	5.9
Thailand	7.4	5.1	4.9	3.4	9.5	5.1

	Services	
	1965-80	1980-85
Indonesia	7.3	6.3
Malaysia	–	5.9
Philippines	5.2	0.1
Singapore	9.7	6.9
Thailand	8.0	6.0

Source: The World Bank, *World Development Report 1987*, Table 2.

Table 3. ASEAN Countries: Industrial Structure

(Unit: %)

		Agriculture	Industry/Mining (manufacturing)		Services
Brunei	1960	n.a.	n.a.	(n.a.)	n.a.
	1980	0.5	84	(0.5)	15
Indonesia	1960	50	25	(n.a.)	25
	1985	24	36	(14)	41
Malaysia	1960	36	18	(9)	46
	1985	21	35	(19)	44
Philippines	1960	26	28	(20)	46
	1985	27	32	(25)	41
Singapore	1960	4	18	(12)	78
	1985	1	37	(24)	62
Thailand	1960	40	19	(13)	41
	1985	17	30	(20)	53

Sources: The World Bank, *World Development Report 1987*, Table 3; *Brunei Statistical Yearbook.*

sion of the irrigation system, land reforms in certain countries, etc. However, problems of regional and social inequalities emerged in the ASEAN countries.

There are roughly three dimensions to the social problems of ASEAN countries which have accompanied development. The first is the gap between the city and countryside. The second is the gap between modern sectors and traditional sectors. The third is the gap between advantaged and disadvantaged sectors, this gap being often associated with the ethnic problem. The polarization of the three dimensions above occurs commonly, though not in uniform fashion, in market-oriented high-growth-rate economies.

These gaps related to an exodus of rural people and subsequent proliferation of urban squatter areas, labor conflicts, racial animosity, and increasing internal threat to law and order, all resulting in substantial social costs.[1] They brought a certain change of orientation in development plans and policies in ASEAN countries.

Shift in Emphasis in Development Plans and Policies

Since the 1950s, ASEAN countries have made efforts to transform the primary commodity-based economy. There were two main pillars of this transformation: (1) resource development and agricultural diversification and (2) the strategy for industrialization.

Each ASEAN country has made strong efforts to develop its agricultural, mineral, energy and marine resources. Examples are spectacular growth of palm oil pro-

---

[1] Chen et al., *Studies in ASEAN Sociology*, pp. 321-431; Nishikawa, *ASEAN and the United Nations System*, pp. 43-50.

duction in Malaysia in the 1970s; natural gas production in Indonesia and Malaysia; minerals and fisheries production in the Philippines; and development of a wide variety of tropical agricultural exports including new exports like cassava and maize in Thailand.

However, it was the strategy in industrialization which has dominated the concerns of policy-makers in many Southeast Asian states. The strategy was not uniform. It varied according to development stages and countries. During the last half of the 1950s and the 1960s, the import-substitution industrialization policy was the main thrust in development plans and policies of the region.

Import-substitution industrialization has the following characteristics: (1) the substitution of actual imports of manufactured goods by domestic production, (2) the protection of domestic manufacturing industries, and (3) the attraction of foreign enterprises by offering various favorable measures such as the exoneration from or reduction of taxes for a certain period, the provision of an industrial site and utilities and other concessions.

Industrialization progressed rapidly due to import-substitution industrialization but several serious problems appeared by the end of the 1960s[2] First, trade imbalances did not disappear but widened. The import-substitution policy was promoted after the first Indochinese war because of the deteriorating terms of trade for primary products. However, the import-substitution industrialization consisted mainly of the establishment of knock-down type factories, the products of which were destined for the domestic market. Therefore, as industrialization progressed, the imports increased and contributed to the widening trade deficits. Second, since the main outlet for import-substituting industries was the domestic market, in which a limited number of middle-class people consumed the products of these industries (textiles, automobiles, electrical products), the size of the market was limited and the costs of production remained high. They could continue to exist only by a high-tariff policy of the government. Third, since the import-substitution industries mainly took the form of joint-ventures or 100 percent subsidiaries of foreign enterprises which imported the materials from abroad, the spill-over effects or technology-transfers in the domestic economy were very limited. These problems seriously hampered the further growth of Southeast Asian economies based on the import-substitution industrialization strategy.

In the beginning of the 1970s, the Asian Development Bank launched the idea of export-oriented industrialization.[3] This strategy was conceived at the time of the rapid progression of the green revolution in Asian countries. Taking advantage of the increase of agricultural productivity, the strategy professed as the base of industrialization to use surplus agricultural products which would be destined for export. This apparently would rectify the perverse effects of the import-substitution strategy, increasing exports as well as using domestic resources. The strategy had merit in drawing the attention of the people to the necessity of an export-oriented policy. Why did not the export-oriented industrialization policy succeed as well in the Southeast Asian countries as in the Asian NICs? There are several reasons. First, just after this idea was launched in the ADB report on "Southeast Asian Economy in the 1970s", a severe drought hit the region in 1973-74 and producing enough surplus agricultural products for export became difficult. Second, processing of

2   Wong, *ASEAN Economics in Perspective*, pp. 53-54.
3   Myint, *Overall Report, Southeast Asian Economy in the 1970s.*

agricultural products for export was made difficult by trade barriers in developed countries; and this discouraged development of processing industries based on exports. Third, sharp fluctuations in world demand and supply made reliance on primary exports an increasingly risky development strategy.

However, the importance of an export-promotion strategy was recognized by all the countries of the region and export-oriented policies were included, more or less, in the development plans and policies of the region. All five countries of ASEAN tried to invite TNCs which would use local labor to process or furnish products which were to be reexported to the developed market: electronics and apparel were examples of such products. Together with the resource exports, this policy contributed greatly to the high growth of the region.

Around 1980, the policy turned. On the one hand, social problems, which arose from high economic growth became apparent, as was already pointed out. Malaysia already launched the New Economic Policy (NEP) in 1970, aiming at rectifying the income and employment gaps between bumiputras (native Malays) and other races as well as eradicating rural poverty (the majority of rural inhabitants being bumiputras). This policy became the basic tone for three successive economic development plans up to now. Thailand has adopted the Fourth and Fifth Development Plans (1977-81; 1982-86), of which the main pillars aim at correcting regional gaps; the Philippines, after a period of serious economic decline and political turmoil, is attempting to restructure its society through the new Medium-Term Development Plan 1987-92, with emphasis on employment and rural uplift.

On the other hand, several international as well as domestic circumstances contributed to re-orienting the industrialization policy of the Southeast Asian nations. First, the world depression as well as the rapid automation or robotization in the developed countries hindered the continuing growth of ASEAN and East Asian countries rooted in export-led industrialization. Second, through the 1970s, the idea of NIEO was promoted in the international scene and contributed to the confirmation of the sovereignty of producing countries over their natural resources. Therefore, the use and processing of these resources in the local market was put on the agenda of development policy. Third, in the domestic field, through the two periods of import-substitution and export-led industrialization policies, the employment problem became serious as modernization progressed in the rural areas. Employment creation was not enough to meet the increasing need. According to these changing circumstances, resource-based industrialization became important in the majority of ASEAN countries where natural resource endowment is relatively rich: Indonesia opened a large-scale Asahan Aluminum plant (225,000 tons/year) as well as an Aceh fertilizer plant (urea, 570,000 t/year; ammonium, 1,000 t/day) — the concepts of both were to use local resources; the Philippines established phosphate fertilizer plants — joint-ventures with Nauru — which produce 3,200 t/day and a copper processing plant with a capacity of 138,000 t/year in Leyte island; Malaysia is establishing heavy and petrochemical industries; Thailand is examining the development of big heavy and chemical complexes in the East Coast of Gulf of Siam.

At the same time, the promotion of private and native industries became an important item in development plans and policies. This promotion was necessitated by the concern to alleviate their dependence on TNCs, to effectively use private dynamism and to decrease the weight of public expenditure.

In the 1980s, therefore, the combination of various development strategies —

import-substitution, export-substitution and resource-based — and the promotion of private enterprises have become the conspicuous aspects of the development plans and policies for the majority of ASEAN countires. Together with this, the concern for social justice, the eradication of poverty and unemployment and the reduction of regional gaps constitute the pillars for the new stage of development strategy.

Creation of Domestic Economic Circuit and Foreign Resources

The high economic growth in ASEAN countries was led, on the one hand, by the will and leadership toward national unity and modernization of the governments. On the other hand, it was largely facilitated by the huge inflow of external resources in the region. In the latter half of the 1970s, an average of US$3.5 billion of net financial flows per year was injected from external sources into ASEAN economies. In 1981 alone, the total flow of resources amounted to $7,979 million, 80 percent of which came from private sources, largely surpassing the resource gap of the region (Table 4), though the total flow, in particular the private flow has since decreased in the first half of the 1980s, leading to relative stagnation of the region in this period.

Of the sources stemming from private flows, private direct investment is the most connected to industrialization. Table 5 shows the foreign direct investment accumulated by the end of 1985 in ASEAN countries. The reading shows that the total figure amounts to $32,887 million, of which Japan accounts for 24 percent, the U.S.A. 16 percent and EEC 11 percent. These figures concern the foreign investment registered under the current laws on foreign capital or investment promotion instituted mainly in the 1960s: thus, they underestimate the investment made by the U.S.A. in the Philippines and by the U.K. in Malaysia. The investment made by other ASEAN countries or Hong Kong and the ROC (Taiwan) is also a considerable amount, relating mainly to investment by overseas or ethnic Chinese capital.[4]

Of the total share of Japanese investment in Asia, 39 percent has been made in the manufacturing sector; in the resource development sector, it accounts for 34.5 percent and, in commerce and other service sectors, 26.5 percent (up to March 1986). In the case of American investment, the above sectors received one-third each of the total investment. From these figures, it is clear that ASEAN countries have encouraged foreign investment in the industrial sector, though other sectors, such as petroleum and mineral development, have also received substantial investments.

The foreign capital was mostly connected with the establishment of big enterprises. The TNC subsidiaries were established mainly in the framework of development strategies and policies adopted by ASEAN countries and were given pioneer and other preferential measures of investment.[5]

In Singapore, which has typically encouraged TNC investment in every field, the foreign capital-dominated industries, comprising 41 percent of the total establishments, invested 63 percent of the capital expenditure, generated 64 percent of the value added and accounted for 84 percent of the manufacturing exports. It is clear that these foreign capital-dominated industries contributed to the capital formation as well as export-led growth.

---

[4] Wu and Wu, *Economic Development in Southeast Asia*, pp. 29-37.
[5] Siddayao, ed., *ASEAN and the Multinational Corporations*, pp. 4-5.

Table 4. ASEAN Countries: Flow of Resources from the OECD Countries

(Unit: US$ million)

	Total Flows				ODA			
	1970	1975	1981	1983	1970	1975	1981	1983
Brunei	85.8	–2.8	–30.3	4.2	–	0.1	0.2	0.4
Indonesia	701.2	2,403.0	4,008.1	2,437.2	493.0	600.2	799.5	852.3
Malaysia	79.0	243.6	866.7	1,617.9	24.1	92.2	117.2	217.7
Philippines	128.3	261.2	688.7	818.9	128.4	152.7	331.0	529.7
Singapore	81.1	99.4	1,285.1	184.8	39.4	26.5	18.4	–30.9
Thailand	58.9	104.2	1,160.5	729.1	94.2	73.7	315.9	479.2
ASEAN	1,134.3	3,108.6	7,978.8	5,792.2	779.1	945.4	1,582.2	2,048.5

	Private Flows*			
	1970	1975	1981	1983
Brunei	85.8	–3.0	–30.5	3.8
Indonesia	117.2	1,802.8	3,286.2	1,548.9
Malaysia	45.4	151.4	738.8	1,400.2
Philippines	172.4	108.4	375.2	289.2
Singapore	53.0	72.9	1,271.5	215.7
Thailand	73.3	30.4	779.4	249.9
ASEAN	546.1	2,162.9	6,420.6	3,743.7

Sources: OCED-Development Assistance Committee, *Development Co-operation*, various issues; UNCTAD, *Handbook of International Trade and Development Statistics Supplement 1985* (E/F. 85.II.D.2), Table 5.6.

* Including public funds in support of private export credits and private investment.

Table 5. ASEAN Countries: Origin of Foreign Direct Investment (End of 1985)

(Unit: US$ million)

	Total	USA	(%)	Japan	(%)	EEC	(%)
Indonesia	15,266	1,143	7.5	4,980	32.6	2,089	14.5
Malaysia[1]	1,854	152	8.2	411	22.2	393[3]	21.2
Philippines[2]	2,839	1,509	53.2	468	16.5	213[3]	7.5
Singapore	5,587	1,673	30.0	1,318	23.6	1,708	30.6
Thailand	7,381	751	10.2	1,792	24.3	1,219	16.5
ASEAN	32,887	5,228	15.9	7,969	24.2	3,622	11.0

	Other ASEAN	(%)	Hong Kong/ ROC (Taiwan)	(%)
Indonesia	974[3]	6.4	2,065	13.5
Malaysia	533[4]	28.7	148[5]	8.0
Philippines	n.a.		196	6.9
Singapore	n.a.		n.a.	
Thailand	468	6.4	786	10.6
ASEAN	n.a.		n.a.	

Sources: Indonesia: BKPM; Malaysia: Industrial Development Agency; Philippines: Board of Investment; Singapore: Economic Development Bureau; Thailand: Board of Investment.

Note: These figures are accumulated total disbursed, excluding those of Indonesia and Malaysia which are approval basis. Indonesian figures exclude oil and finance. Singaporean figures relate to manufacturing only. The Total includes investment from plural countries and tax-havens.

[1] End 1984.
[2] June 1985.
[3] Estimates
[4] Singapore only
[5] Hong Kong only

However, as the industrial development reaches a certain stage, there is a problem in linking local small and middle-scale enterprises with the TNC-dominated large enterprises. The linkage creates spill-over effects and promotes technology transfer in the domestic economy. As well, small and middle-scale enterprises have their own right of existence. For example, they create more employment per capital invested or value added than larger enterprises. Take the example of Indonesia (Table 6). According to the industrial census made in 1979, the number of large/middle establishments was 7,960 and small establishments 113,024. These establishments engaged 870,000 and 827,000 workers respectively. The former produced 1.9 million rupiahs of value added per worker/year and the latter only 26,500 rupiahs. As for the employment costs per worker, the former paid 369,823 rupiahs and the latter 84,722 rupiahs. This shows that, although added value is smaller in smaller establishments, the employment costs are far smaller in small establishments, allowing easier entry by the local small capital into the market. From the point of view of employment creation, therefore, the role of small and cottage enterprises may be considered important.

At the same time, the small and medium enterprises could use more local resources than the larger ones as the former are rather separated from foreign channels and largely produce for the local market.

It is also important to consider the debt problem which has been putting considerable burden on certain ASEAN countries. The Philippine economy has been troubled for several years with a debt amortization and conditionality problem. In Thailand, Indonesia and Malaysia too, the weight of debt is being felt as of the middle of the 1980s (Table 7). The increase of exports, the decrease of imports and the active use of local resources as well as productivity increase should constitute an authentic reply to the debt problem, the effects of which are increasingly being perceived in the ASEAN region.

Thus, the problem of combining large enterprises, which have led ASEAN growth up to now, and small and medium enterprises of domestic origin which would use more local resources becomes important for the future development of ASEAN economies.[6]

Progress of Regional Cooperation

The idea of regional cooperation among Southeast Asian nations is not a new one. Already in the 1960s, there were two attempts at creating regional cooperation schemes. In 1961, Malaya, the Philippines and Thailand created the Association of Southeast Asia (ASA), which was paralyzed shortly after due to the conflict between the Philippines and Malaysia concerning the Sabah territorial problem. On the other hand, in 1963 the idea of forming MAPHILINDO was proposed by Malaya, the Philippines and Indonesia, but it never functioned due to Indonesia's dissent on the formation of Malaysia. At that time, contradictions among Southeast nations were so strong that no proposed regional body was viable. In 1967, however, five regional countries — Indonesia, Malaysia, the Philippines, Singapore and Thailand — established the Association of South-East Asian Nations (ASEAN) by the Bangkok Declaration signed by the foreign ministers of the five countries.[7]

---

[6] Asian Development Bank, *Small—and Medium—Scale Manufacturing Establishments in ASEAN Countries.*
[7] Asian Productivity Organization, *Development Strategies for the 1980s.*

Table 6. Indonesia: Number of Establishments, Persons Engaged, Employment Costs of Large/Medium, Small and Household Manufacturing Establishments (1979)

	Number of Establish- ments	Persons Engaged = TK	Employment Costs = W (million Rp)	Value Added = VA (million Rp)
Large/Medium	7,960	870,019	321,753	1,660,459
Small	113,024	827,035	70,068	187,323
Household	1,538,786	2,794,833	37,973	291,442

	$\dfrac{W}{TK}$ (Rp)	$\dfrac{VA}{TK}$ (Rp)
Large/Medium	369,823	1,908,532
Small	84,722	226,499
Household	13,587	104,279

Source: Biro Pusat Statistik, *Statistik Indonesia 1983*, Table VI. 1.2a/2b.

Note: Large/Medium: Engaging 20 or more persons
       Small: Engaging 5-19 persons
       Household: Engaging under 4 persons

Table 7. ASEAN Countries: External Public Debt (Middle- and Long-term) (1985)

	Total Debt (US$ million)	Total Debt Service (US$ million)	Debt Service Ratio ($)
Indonesia	26,625	1,036	20.1
Malaysia	13,834	33	22.3
Philippines	13,561	1,290	15.8
Singapore	1,791	n.a.	2.4
Thailand	9,898	1,094	14.7

Source: The World Bank, *World Debt Tables* 1986-87.

The history of ASEAN can be divided into several periods: the first is from 1967, the year of inception, to 1970; the second is from 1971, when the first special meeting of the Ministers for Foreign Affairs adopted the Kuala Lumpur Declaration which advocated the establishment of a Zone of Peace, Freedom and Neutrality (ZOPFAN) in Southeast Asia, to 1975; the third started with the first meeting of the Heads of Governments in February 1976, and continues today.[8]

---

[8]   Nishikawa, *op. cit.*, pp. 4-24.

In the first period, the basic structure of ASEAN was defined. In the second period, political cooperation among member countries was strengthened and economic cooperation schemes were groped for. But it was in the third period that regional economic cooperation advanced considerably.[9]

There are four main schemes of economic cooperation, which were adopted by member nations.

First, the ASEAN Preferential Trading Arrangements (PTA), which establish trade preferences among member states in order to expand intra-regional trade. As of June 1987, about 18,341 items were listed on the preferential list. As well, a 20-25 percent across-the-board tariff cut was implemented on the items with an import value of less than US$500,000.

Second, the ASEAN Industrial Project (AIP), which intended to establish large-scale industrial plants which would meet "regional requirements for essential commodities" and give preferential tariffs to its products. This scheme took the form of a joint-venture project of five countries, the host country assuming 60 percent of the capital share and the other four countries the remaining 40 percent. At the end of 1984, Indonesia established a urea factory with a 570,000 tons/year capacity in Aceh, Sumatra, and Malaysia constructed a similar urea plant in Bintulu, Sarawak. However, Singapore differed from the others in its interests and virtually withdrew from these projects, participating with a nominal 1 percent. Therefore, of the capital share for these two projects, the host country possesses 60 percent, the other three 13 percent each, and Singapore, 1 percent. Thailand has adopted a project on rock salt soda and the Philippines proposed successively a pulp plant and a copper smelting plant, but so far neither has materialized. Also, it should be pointed out that the product of the two urea factories in Indonesia and Malaysia is destined for the extra-regional market and not the regional market, as initially conceived.

Third, the ASEAN Industrial Complementation (AIC), which allocates certain products of an industry to participating countries. These products are given tariff preferences. The other participating countries cannot set up new production facilities or expand existing ones for a period of 2 (existing product) to 4 (new product) years. The AIC started with two packages (existing products and new products) in the automotive industry in 1981. However, since the automotive industry is highly vertically-integrated rather than horizontally-integrated through transnational corporations, the implementation of this scheme has been difficult.

Fourth, the ASEAN Industrial Joint Ventures (AIJV), which encourages joint ventures of more than two countries in the region, giving trade preferences to the products of joint venture enterprises. The ASEAN Finance Corporation, based in Singapore, supports such projects.

It is too early to evaluate the full extent of the effects of these cooperation schemes. However, intra-regional trade as well as various other approaches increased considerably among member nations. The intra-regional trade among ASEAN countries decreased from 17.8 percent in 1968 to 12.7 percent in 1976 (one of the reasons for this decrease being the world-wide inflation after the oil shock); however, in 1980, it increased again to 18.6 percent.[10] Also, the simplification of

---

[9] Garnaut, ed., *ASEAN in a Changing Pacific and World Economy*, pp. 54-56; Mokhzani et al. (ed.), *ASEAN Economic Cooperation and the New International Economic Order*; Ariff et al., *ASEAN Cooperation in Industrial Projects*.

[10] Nishikawa, *op. cit.*, Table 2.4.

the visa procedure among member states constitutes one of the reasons for the intensification of the people's movement across the border.

However, during the 1970s, new problems arose: the income gap between member nations increased. In 1970 — putting 100 as a GNP per capita for Singapore — Malaysia was 36.4, the Philippines 20.7 and Thailand 19.6. In 1985, Malaysia's GNP per capita decreased to 27.0, the Philippines' to 7.8 and Thailand's to 10.8 (Table 8). Singapore also dominates intra-regional trade, i.e., the number of Singapore's exports to Indonesia is 22 times larger than that of Malaysia to Indonesia.

This reflects the different degrees of industrialization and the divergent interests according to this fact.[11] It explains why in recent years the progress of regional cooperation has slacked.

In any case, the will of member nations to promote step by step regional cooperation (not to mention regional integration) being strong, ASEAN cooperation will constitute one of the pillars for supporting the economic and social development of each country. First, when industrialization progresses, the regional market will provide a relatively reliable outlet for developing industries. Second, since the business of the East Asian NICs has been dependent on the developed market and this fact has affected to a certain extent the stable progress of the economy of the NICs, the development of the regional market would constitute indispensable support for an industrializing economy. Third, since the level of technology is more or less the same except in Singapore, member nation industries can exchange products suited to each other's needs. In this connection, it is desirable that the ASEAN countries cooperate in productivity issues too. Fourth, cooperation among member countries will strengthen ASEAN bargaining power vis-a-vis third nations, especially the developed countries and Indochinese countries.[12]

Therefore, we can reasonaly expect positive effects of regional cooperation on the development of the socio-economy of Southeast Asian nations.

Table 8. ASEAN Countries: Per Capita GNP and Income GAP (1970-85)

(Unit: US$), Figure in parenthesis shows the income gap when GNP/capita of Singapore is 100.

	1970		1975		1985	
Indonesia	77	(8.4)	225	(9.0)	530	(7.1)
Malaysia	333	(36.4)	781	(31.2)	2,000	(27.0)
Philippines	190	(20.7)	374	(14.9)	580	(7.8)
Singapore	916	(100.0)	2,507	(100.0)	7,420	(100.0)
Thailand	180	(19.6)	348	(13.9)	800	(10.8)

Source: United Nations, *Yearbook of National Accounts Statistics* 1978 and The World Bank, *World Development Report* 1987.

---

[11] Concerning the particular position of Singapore in ASEAN, see Lim, *Economic Development in Southeast Asia*, 1981.

[12] Mokhzani et al., *ASEAN Economic Cooperation and the New International Economic Order*; Garcia, *New Horizons of Regionalism in Asia and the Pacific*.

INDONESIA

Oil and Oil-related Economy

In 1973, Indonesia had a per capita national income of US$115. In 1982, it rose to US$550. This five-fold increase in the decade was largely due to the increase of oil prices (oil accounts for three-quarters of the total exports), as well as the inflow of foreign resources that was brought in by an active development policy and industrialization.

Indonesia actually produces 1.5-1.6 million barrels/day of crude oil (580-590 million b/year or 75-80 million tons/year). Through international sources, its proved reserves are estimated to be around 10,000 million barrels. Therefore, the years for exploitation at the current rate are estimated to be about 17, well under the OPEC average. In recent years, newly-discovered oil fields reveal rather minor reserves, however, and the one in Minas, Sumatra remains the largest field, producing 57 percent of the total oil production (off-shore oil constitutes 35 percent) in 1982.

That is why the shift from an oil economy to non-oil economy is the major concern in development plans.

From Third Repelita to Fourth Repelita

Since the launching of the First Repelita (Five-Year Plan: 1969/70 – 1973/74), the growth rate has been constantly high in this large population country where two-thirds of the population was in the primary industry sector in 1970. This was largely due to the increase in oil production and in oil prices following 1973 as mentioned earlier. However, the growth rates of industry, construction and other infrastructures have also been high and have pulled overall growth rates.

The First Repelita emphasized self-sufficiency in food as well as development of infrastructure and light industry. It contributed to the alleviation of the chronic inflation inherited from the Soekarno era. The Second Repelita continued the main goals of the First Repelita, however, import-substitution industrialization such as for fertilizers, cement, textiles received attention and factory decentralization was also promoted.

In the Third Repelita, launched in 1979, the social problems which accompanied high economic growth in the decade were taken into account and the "equitable distribution" of the fruits of development was given priority. During this plan, self-sufficiency in food production was almost realized. The plan also emphasized promotion of exports of the non-oil sector together with the activation of the private sector. The production of electronic goods, textiles and transport machines increased considerably. The plan also stressed the importance of the development of labor-intensive middle and small industries as well as promotion of indigenous entrepreneurs in the economy.

The Fourth Repelita is in effect from 1984/85. It is based on the long-term national development guidelines formulated in the Guidelines of State Policy in 1983. The main goal of Repelita IV is "to raise the standards of living, intellectual abilities and general welfare of the people and to lay strong foundations for subsequent stages of the nation's development". The priorities in this plan were continuously given to food self-sufficiency and machinery industries. The plan also pays attention to social development. It is based, as was the case in the Repelita III, on the need for realizing the Development Trilogy, namely, equity, economic growth and national stability with an equitable distribution of resources.[13]

Industrialization and Employment

Indonesia has a market of 160 million and imports many industrial goods. Therefore, import-substitution has been the main concern in all the successive development plans. In the Repelita IV, during which it became clear that no further oil price increase could be expected, emphasis was laid on non-oil exports, and projects for export-processing zones were started. In the 1980s, the projects for basic industries which use natural resources locally produced were actively promoted. The Asahan Aluminium Complex, which has a 225,000 t/year capacity, or the Aceh fertilizer and Iscandar Muda Urea Plants (both having a urea production capacity of 570,000 t/year) are examples of resource-based industrialization.

However, due to an oil price decrease and a debt problem, several major projects of this type, including the Bintan Alumina Project and the Aromatic and Olefin Centers, were put off or reduced in 1983.

In the Repelita IV, there are four types of industry which should be developed. First, the industries which produce basic necessities for mass consumption, including food-processing, textiles, electric appliances. Second, metal and machinery industries which will be substitutes for actual imports. Third, basic chemicals which use oil and gas locally produced. Fourth, small-scale and handicraft industries, the main objective of which is to create employment.

In the early 1980s, the Indonesia population increased by 2.4 percent a year. At this pace, the population will double within 30 years. During the Repelita IV, 9.3 million people will enter the labor market, which needs an employment rate of 1.86 million a year. The industrial sector is expected to create employment for 1.2 million, of which one-third, 325,000 is expected to be employed in the small-scale and handicraft sector.

Trends in Agriculture

Indonesian agriculture has several characteristics. First, in this huge country 78 percent of the population live in the rural area. Second, in Jawa in particular, the rural area is densely inhabited and the majority of the rural households exploit a very tiny amount of land. In 1980, 37 percent of rural households cultivated over 0.5 hectare (ha) and 64 percent under 0.5 ha. Rural underemployment is a chronic problem. Third, there is a coexistence of big estates producing rubber, palm-oil, tea or sugar (2,230 thousand ha) and a number of small-scale farms producing mainly rice, maize, cassavas and other food products (1.4 million ha). Fourth, though an agricultural country, Indonesia used to import rice until very recently, so that food self-sufficiency constituted one of the major concerns in development plans.

In 1982, Indonesia produced 23 million tons of rice on 9 million ha of rice-fields. The rice productivity of 2.6 t/ha is quite high for a developing country. During the period of 1981 to 83, rice import dropped to less than 1/3 of the import level in the 1970s which was almost 2 million tons. In fact, in the decade starting in 1970, agricultural production increased at a pace of 4 percent per annum. Though it

---

[13] Bappenas, *Repelita IV*, p. 7.

dropped to 3.5 percent per annum during the Repelita III, the Repelita IV forecasts that the average annual growth rate of agriculture will be 3.0 percent and that of rice 4.1 percent by 1988. These rates should meet the needs of the growing population.

The increase of rice production was partly due to expansion of cultivated area for rice but mainly due to productivity increase (1.8 ton/ha in 1973). The latter was realized by the adoption of an intensive farming method using HYV, fertilizers and other inputs, together with the enlargement of the irrigation system. The modernized method was launched in the early 1970s by BIMAS/INMAS projects which enjoyed the participation of a number of farmers.

The government has allocated a considerable percentage of resources to rural development (13-14 percent in Development Plans, which is double the allocation to the industrial sector). The Plans have also encouraged the immigration of rural people from densely-populated Jawa to the Outer Islands (2.5 million during the Repelita III and a projected 0.8-1 million during the Repelita IV).

There are several problems that the Indonesian agriculture is facing. First, in order to continue raising productivity, the irrigation system should be improved. However, this is costly and the small-scale exploitation would limit productivity increase from this source to a modest amount. Second, rural income is estimated to be half of the national average and underemployed people abound. There are estimated to be around 4 million landless households comprising about 35 percent of the rural population. The raise employment and income levels, therefore modern sector employment and immigration are not enough and the development of rural industries is needed. The importance of household/cottage industry in the creation of employment is clear. Third, the diversification of agriculture as well as the processing of agricultural products will be necessary in order to raise rural incomes.

Table 9. Indonesia: Growth Targets and Achievements in Development Plans

	GDP (Target rate) (%)	GDP (Realized rate) (%)	Industrial Production (Realized rate) (%)
First Five-Year Plan (1969/70-73/74)	5	7.7	13.0
Second Five-Year Plan (1974/75-78/79)	7.5	6.9	13.7
Third Five-Year Plan (1979/80-83/84)	6.5	5.7-6.0*	9.6
Fourth Five-Year Plan (1984/85-88/89)	5.0	—	9.5**

Source: Each Development Plan.
     * estimate given by JETRO, Jakarta.
    ** target rate.

Domestic and Foreign Resources

Through successive Development Plans, the fixed capital formation/GDP rates have been constantly raised. In 1970/79, the investment ratio was 21 percent, which reached 23 percent by 1983/84. The Repelita IV has forecast an increase to 29.4 percent by 1988/89.

The high investment rate was largely sustained by oil revenue and foreign resources.

In the Repelita II, 30 percent of the development budget was financed by foreign resources and in the Repelita III it was nearly 40 percent. In the Repelita IV, 30 percent of the budget was expected to be financed by foreign resources in 1983. Dependence on foreign resources should decrease through the Repelita, however, and, from 1983 to 1988, they should account for 19 percent on the average (Table 10).

Foreign resources financed 16-20 percent of the government budget in recent years (1983-84). This created a debt problem. The total public debt amounted to US$22 billion at the end of 1983 and the debt service ratio was 13.6 percent in 1984. In the 1984 budget, the government expects to spend 27 percent as debt service, which is closer to the total of salaries, wages, pensions and other payments for public employees (32 percent). Through the Repelita IV, $9 billion should be paid abroad as debt service. Since debt service is expected to increase further in the 1990s, this constitutes a huge burden, for the government budget as well as the economy. Therefore, the government has tried to decrease the weight of foreign resources.

In order to increase domestic savings and resources, however, two measures will be needed. First, private saving should be encouraged: in fact, in the Repelita IV, the share of private savings is expected to increase from 8.4 percent in 1983 to 15.5 percent in 1988. This would require the control of inflation together with the reform of a highly-oligopolistic economic structure.[14] Second, public saving should also be increased. However, the increase of oil revenue being difficult, the government may try to reform inefficient public enterprises that often run deficits. Here, the productivity campaign would be useful.

Table 10. Indonesia: Financial Resource for the Repelita IV

	1983 billion Rp	%	1988 billion Rp	%	1983-88 billion Rp	%
Domestic saving	11,671	70	34,060	85	117,464	81
government	5,589		13,048		48,354	
private sector	6,081		21,012		69,111	
Foreign resource	5,007	30	5,966	15	27,760	19
Total	16,678	100	40,021	100	145,225	100

Source: *Repelita IV.*

[14] Japan External Trade Organization, *Indonesia ni okeru minzoku-kei kigyo no taito to kajin-shibon.*

Social Problems

Major social problems in Indonesia are three-fold. First, the income gap between the urban area and the countryside.[15] This gap is the main reason for the huge inflow of people from the rural areas to the urban centers, in particular Great Jakarta. Second, the income gap between pribumis (indigenous Indonesians) and non-pribumis. Modern industrial and commercial sectors are often controlled by non-pribumis.[16] Third, the problem of absolute poverty of the unemployed and underemployed both in the urban and rural areas. The lower social strata are increasingly exposed to the charm of numerous consumption goods, which increases the sense of relative poverty in addition to absolute poverty.[17]

Therefore, the concern for social equity becomes more and more important in Development Plans.[18]

MALAYSIA

Role of the Primary Products Sector in Capital Formation

Malaysia is considered one of the second generation NICs or "quasi-NICs". Its GDP growth rate was 8.8 percent per annum from 1970 to 1982. Its per capita GDP reached US$1,860 in 1982 more than double that of 1970 in constant prices.

The high economic growth was led by fast industrialization. The annual growth rate of the manufacturing industry was 10.6 percent p.a. from 1970 to 82. However, agricultural production, in particular export-oriented primary products, was also stimulated in this period. As we see in Table 11, natural rubber production increased from 1.27 million tons in 1970 to around 1.6 million tons p.a. in the first half of the 1980s. Palm-oil production increased nine-fold and sawlogs nearly doubled from 1970 to 84. The growth rate of agricultural production was quite high in this period. Besides, petroleum production and, recently, natural gas production have increased rapidly. Crude oil is exploited off-shore of Sabah, Sarawak and, more recently, Terengganu, where significant reserves were found. Crude oil production increased from 18,000 barrels/day in 1970 to 440,000 b/d in 1984. The production and export of liquefied natural gas, which began in Bentulu, Sarawak in 1983, amounted to 3 million tons in 1984; it earned $1,845 million which corresponded to 21 percent of crude oil export earning.[19]

The development of agricultural and mineral production and exports constituted important sources for capital formation in Malaysia. In fact, in Malaysian exports, two-thirds consisted of commodities and 30 percent manufactures in 1983.[20]

The development of commodity exports contributed also to the maintenance of the surplus in the Malaysian trade account in the 1970s; however, in the first half of the 1980s, the recession in the commodity market (in particular, tin and rubber), together with the fall in petroleum price, brought some instability to the Malaysian trade balance. Added to this was the recession in the electronics industry most of

[15] Arief, *Indonesia: Growth, Income Disparity and Mass Poverty.*

[16] Palmer, *The Indonesian Economy since 1965*, pp. 166-170.

[17] Arief, *Consumption Pattern in Indonesia.*

[18] Moertropo, *The Acceleration and Modernization of 25 Years Development*, pp. 8-21.

[19] Malaysian Government, *Mid-Term Review of the Fourth Malaysia Plan 1981-1985.*

[20] Bank Negara Malaysia, *Annual Report 1983*, Table 62.

Table 11. Malaysia: Major Primary Products

	Natural Rubber (1,000 tons)	Palm-oil (1,000 tons)	Sawlogs (1,000 m^3)	Tin (1,000 tons)	Crude oil (1,000 b/d)
1970	1,269	431	17,698	73.8	18
1980	1,680	2,300	24,300	65.0	317
1984	1,562	3,700	32,000	39.0	440

Source: Ministry of Finance, *Economic Report.*

the production of which were exported. This caused an unemployment problem in manufacturing industry. Thus, we see export-led growth in Malaysia can be hampered by the international business situation.

Trends in Economic Development Plans

Since its separation from Singapore, Malaysia has adopted four successive plans (1966-70, 1971-75, 1976-80, and 1981-85).

During the first plan, economic growth was the primary objective and investment effort went mainly to infrastructure and agricultural development. However, the social imbalances originating from the growth-oriented policy led to interracial conflict, and the well-known May 13th incident in 1969 led Dr. Mahathir to write "The Malay Dilemma" which proclaimed the Malayan will for economic and social progress.[21]

In 1971, the government launched the New Economic Policy (NEP), with the main targets of eradicating poverty and restructuring society. It intended to combine economic growth with social equity in order to ensure national unity. The NEP aimed first at reducing the huge income and asset gaps between the Malay population (55 percent in the peninsular part), whose mean income was 35 percent below the national average, and the Chinese (34 percent) and Indian (10 percent) population, whose mean income was far above the average. The programs for rural and land development were implemented, and the specific programs for small farmers, estate workers and fishermen were adopted. The incidence of poverty (households with income under the poverty line) was estimated to be 40 percent in 1970 in peninsular Malaysia, but it decreased to 30 in 1983.[22]

On the other hand, the restructuring of the society corresponds with the reduction of income disparity among ethnic groups and to the enlarged accessibility of education, jobs and professional activities to disadvantaged native groups. It will ensure them of owning and managing business enterprises and acquiring a fair share in the growth of national wealth. The creation of an active Bumiputera commercial and industrial community (which would hold at least 30 percent of the ownership and control by 1990) was forecast. In the 1970s and 80s, there was

[21] Mahathir, *The Malay Dilemma.*

[22] Malaysian Government, *Mid-Term Review,* op. cit., p. 75.

steady progress in the restructuring of society by an active governmental public policy, though the income imbalances continued to remain wide; in 1979, the Malay mean income was $492 against the Chinese $938, Indian $756 and $1,904 of others.[23]

The characteristics of the Fourth Plan (1981-85), implemented in the difficult period of world recession, were as follows:

First, a high investment growth rate of 11 percent p.a. and high economic growth of 7.6 percent (in real terms) were forecast. However, the recession and fall of commodity and oil prices directly hit the Malaysian economy. The growth rate will be under the target. Malaysian economy is particularly sensitive to the external business situation, as exports and imports account for 43-48 percent of GDP.

Second, manpower development and employment creation were emphasized. The actual population increase was 2.6 percent as of the first half of the 1980s. With this rate, the population will double in thirty years. In particular, urban population will grow at an average rate of 4.1 percent p.a., while the urban Malays will at 5.7 percent p.a. The fourth plan envisaged the reduction of the 5.3 percent unemployment rate in 1980 to 4.9 percent in 1985, creating 860,000 new jobs during 1981-85, which would increase employment from 5 to about 6 million. However, due to recession in this period, the number of unemployed was estimated to have increased. On the other hand, in spite of the existence of a surplus labor force, our survey conducted in August 1984 revealed that there was some tightness in the supply of skilled labor. The labor shortage problem in the estate work and manufacturing firms employing young female workers was also reported. Therefore, manpower training and formation will become more and more important.

Third, concerning the objectives of the NEP, as we already examined, there was steady progress in its two main objectives: eradication of poverty and restructuring of society. However, in the first half of the 1980s, some stagnation and even setbacks were observed in these objectives. Additionally, the new problem of gaps within the ethnic Malay community emerged.[24] Therefore, the objectives of the NEP will continue to be important in Malaysian development plans. Fourth, the improvement of the quality of life (social services) was stressed. This consisted of development of education, housing, utilities and health and social welfare. Though there were important achievements in these fields, the government was obliged to drastically reduce development expenditure from 1982 ($11.5 billion) to 1985 ($6.5 billion).[25] On the one hand, the revenue was largely under the forecast due to recession. On other hand, costs and debt service increased considerably. Debt service increased from 11 percent in 1980 to 19 percent in 1983 in the government expenditure. In fact, due to ambitious industrialization and other development programs, the Malaysian public external debt increased from US$867 million in 1974 to US$10,665 million in 1983 while the debt service ratio went from 2.5 percent to 5.8 percent in the same period.[26]

Because of the fiscal constraints which appeared in recent years, on the one hand, and a new environment favorable for business created through high economic growth on the other, the government deliberately adopted a new orientation in executing the plan.

[23] *Ibid.*, Tables 3-8.

[24] Snodgrass, *Inequality and Economic Development in Malaysia*, p. 84.

[25] Malaysia, Ministry of Finance, *Economic Report 1983/84*, p. 71.

[26] World Bank, *Debt Tables 1984/85*, pp. 136-137.

This is the development of the private sector and the privatization of the economy. However, the promotion of the private sector should be made under the guidance of and in association with the government. This is the idea of "Malaysia Incorporated." The government decided to form a co-operative framework with the private sector and promote privatization in economic development. For this purpose, the promotion of productivity and efficiency would have important social value. The development of human resources will be equally emphasized.

The Problems of Industrialization

In the 1970s, the industrial growth rate was 11.3 percent per annum; industry which includes the mineral sector led overall economic growth. The contribution of the industrial sector reached 30 percent (manufacturing sector 18 percent) in the total GDP in 1983. As of 1980, 76 industrial estates was created all over the country. However, reflecting the general business situation, the rate dropped to around 4 percent p.a. (compared with the plan target of 11 percent) in the first half of the 1980s.

In the decade following the formation of Malaysia, we saw considerable progress in the development of import-substitution industries, such as textiles, transport equipment, cement and related products, basic metal industries and food products.[27] However, after the first oil shock, two new orientations in industrialization emerged. One was the fast progress of export-oriented manufacturing industries. Another was large-scale industrialization using local resources.

The growth of export-oriented industries, consisting mainly of electrical and electronics products (accounting for half of manufactured goods exports in the first half of the 1980s), textiles and clothing (12 percent), food products (8 percent) and wood products, in recent decades has been remarkable. In fact, it was export-oriented industries which largely led industrial growth in the 1970s and 1980s. In order to stimulate these industries, eight Free Trade Zones were established by the end of 1980. The Fourth Plan forecast the export growth rate at 24 percent p.a. in 1981-85; however, since they are heavily dependent on the world business situation, this target could not be achieved during this period. At the same time, the high import-content of electric and electronics industries (together with the import-substitution industries) did not contribute considerably to ameliorating the trade imbalance at the time commodity prices went down and a protectionist trend arose in the international market.[28]

Since the oil price increase of 1973-74, Malaysia has actively pursued resource-based large-scale industrialization. This was the case for chemical textiles (Penang), ammonium (1,000 t/d), urea (1,500 t/d) (Bintulu, Sarawak), liquefied natural gas (Bintulu), petroleum products and gas (Terengganu). In Terengganu, using local oil and mineral resources, the construction of a large industrial complex has been planned. The development of resource-based industries is also associated with the governmental policy of industrial dispersal.

Resource-based industrialization should be an authentic path of industrialization for Malaysia. However, there are several problems with this type of industrialization. First is the debt problem. In executing an ambitious large-scale industrialization

---

[27] Rao, *Malaysia Development Pattern and Policy*, pp. 92-138.
[28] Lim & Chee, ed. *The Malaysian Economy at the Crossroads*, pp. 11-62.

program, the government relied on foreign aid which has brought about debt and debt service. Second, the link between resource-based industry and domestic downstream small- and medium-scale industries has not yet been developed to any large extent. For example, many domestic apparel and plastic firms still import their materials from Singapore and other countries. Third, besides the large-scale chemical sector, smaller-scale processing industries using primary products (rubber, wood and other agricultural products) are yet to be developed.

Therefore, in recent years, the government has proposed an integrated industrial strategy. First, in establishing heavy and chemical industries based on domestic resources, the government would stimulate the downstream machinery industry. The machinery industry, in turn, would create spin-off effects for the growth of small and medium-scale industries. This is the case for the first Malaysian national car firm that the government established in a joint-venture with a Japanese company in 1984, of which over 50 percent of parts are already localized and local components will increase progressively during the twenty-year contract. This is an example of the so-called "selective second-round import-substitution development" that the government will stimulate in future years. This type of industry would be a first sure step in reducing the dependency on foreign countries for the supply of machinery and intermediate goods.

The other aspect of an integrated strategy consists of industrial diversification, diversification of the export markets, the development of small-scale enterprises and R & D development. All of these would contribute to the further diversification of Malaysian industrial structure. In particular, the development of domestic and local markets will be encouraged by these measures for diversification and development of small-scale industries. Taking an example of bicycle industry, Fong Chan Onn showed how an industry which has an intermediate degree of factor-intensity

Table 12. Malaysia: Incidence of Poverty by Rural-Urban Strata (1980, 84)

| | 1980 | | |
	Total Households (1,000)	Total Poor Households (1,000)	Incidence of Poverty (%)
Rural	1,450	542	37.4
Urban	744	94	12.6

| | 1984 | | |
	Total Households (1,000)	Total Poor Households (1,000)	Incidence of Poverty (%)
Rural	1,490	620	41.6
Urban	881	98	11.1

Source: *Mid-term Review of the Fourth Malaysia Plan 1981-85,* Table 3-2.

could widen the domestic market.[29] The adoption of an integrated industrial strategy shows already how the stages in industrialization have progressed in this country.

Agriculture and Rural Development

The agricultural production has registered a growth of 4.3 percent p.a. (in real terms) in the 1970s and 4.0 percent in 1981-83. Its share in the GDP declined from 31 percent in 1970 to 22 percent in 1983.

Before independence, the Malay peninsular economy had a monocultural production of mainly rubber with a little acreage in palm-oil. However, in two decades, its agriculture has been considerably diversified. Now, together with the increase in rubber and palm-oil production, sawlogs, padi, pineapple, pepper, cocoa and livestock production have been encouraged.

The government actively promoted land-development programs. From 1970-83, drainage, irrigation and agricultural development projects covered 850,000 ha and were expected to benefit nearly half a million families. These schemes contributed to the increase in rice production. Malaysia produced 1,364,000 tons of rice in 1983, of which 57 percent was derived from newly-developed areas. This production covered 77 percent of the total rice demand of the country. The rest was imported from Thailand, Burma and Pakistan.

The replanting and rehabilitation of commercial plants were also promoted. A number of agencies undertook rehabilitation and replanting operations for rubber, coconut, palm-oil, padi, pepper, pineapple and coffee. This was to increase productivity as well as to help smallholders.

In livestock production, there was a marked growth in the poultry and pig-rearing industries. In recent years, the government has been encouraging cattle-raising, beef and milk being largely imported.

Fisheries are rapidly developing. In 1983, Malaysia produced 730,000 tons of fish. The government has constructed fishing harbour complexes and auxiliary facilities at a number of places throughout the country.

The problems of Malaysian agriculture are, however, as follows:

First, there is still a coexistence of a highly-productive and well-organized estate sector and a non-organized small-farm sector. The increase of productivity in the latter would be an important policy target in the years to come.

Second, in recent agricultural development based on individual commodities, a competition of resources such as land and labor has arisen. In some areas and sectors, the labor shortage problem has become serious.[30] The government proposes, therefore, an integrated agricultural policy.

Third, rural poverty still exists and indeed seems to have increased in recent years. In the urban area, the incidence of poverty is estimated to have decreased from 1980 to 1984, but in the rural area it is estimated to have increased from 37.4 percent to 41.6 percent in the same period.

Therefore, the problem of the dissolution of rural poverty as well as the supply of welfare to rural people poses one of the major targets in the formulation of the development plan.

[29] Fong Chan Onn, "Appropriate Technology: An Empirical Study of Bicycle Manufacturing in Malaysia", in Lim (ed.), *Further Readings on Malaysian Economic Development*, pp. 181-195.
[30] Malaysian Government, *Mid-Term Review*, pp. 243-244.

Population and Manpower Policy

Malaysia has a population of about 15.6 million as of 1985. In the first half of the 1980s, the growth rate was 2.5 percent p.a.

The population density of Malaysia still being low, i.e., 41/km² (compared with the ASEAN average of 87/km²), the government has adopted a policy of encouraging a population increase. The population of 70 million in 2100 is believed to be the optimum for this country.

Urbanization is rapidly progressing, the urban population growth rate being 4.5 percent in 1981-85, compared with the rural growth of 1.1 percent. The problem of the creation of urban employment, on the one hand, and rural development, on the other, should be one of the major policy attentions in the near future.[31]

Malays and Indians live for the most part in the rural area (70 percent and 58 percent respectively), and Chinese in the urban area (60 percent). Since it is mainly Malays who are classed in a poverty bracket and two-thirds of the rural population are Malays, the continuing execution of the NEP policy will be called for.

The prospects of increasing population would necessitate further development of education and training facilities. On the industrial plan, the formation of high and middle-level manpower together with skilled and semi-skilled manpower will be developed. As we pointed out earlier, in the time of employment slack, labor tightness for trained manpower has continued. At the same time, since the industrialization in heavy and chemical industries and high-technology industries goes on, the skill upgrading of workers will be needed.

The government has been encouraging the creation of new social values, strong and firm leadership together with a clean and efficient administration, as industrialization and modernization make progress.[32] In this new orientation, increasing productivity and efficiency can be considered one of the major growth sources.

PHILIPPINES

Trends in the Overall Economy

During 1970-80, the Philippines' real GDP grew at a rate above 6 percent. Its growth rate dropped by one half during 1980-82 and even plunged to negative rates in 1984-85. Like Thailand, the growth during 1970-80 was attributable to the rapid expansion in the industry and construction sector. The industrial sector grew at an average annual rate of 8 percent and its share in GDP rose from 27 percent in 1970 to 36 percent in 1980. While the rate of industrial expansion was slightly slower than in Thailand, the Philippines' agricultural sector grew faster than Thailand's during this period. The service sector grew, on the other hand, at a pace of 6 percent per annum.

In agriculture, there was noticeable crop diversification — increasing importance of banana and coconut and decreasing importance of rice and sugar cane.

In industry, food (beverage and tobacco included), textiles, chemicals, petroleum products, wood and wood products, iron and steel, transport equipment, machinery,

---

[31] Lim, ed., *op. cit.*, pp. 111-124.

[32] Malaysian Government, *Mid-Term Review*, pp. 25-31.

non-ferrous metal products and paper are the major manufactured items. The growth of cement production was remarkable in this period; it increased its share in the manufacturing sector from 12.4 percent in 1970 to 22 percent in 1982. This corresponds with the high growth of construction (at a 12.3 percent average): its share in the service sector rose from 7.3 percent in 1970 to 17.4 percent in 1982.

Exports and imports grew rapidly during 1970-80 but fell after 1980. Imports grew most rapidly due to an oil price increase in the first half of the 1970s but slowed down in the second half and finally halted after 1980 due to the severe balance of payments crisis.

Traditionally, ten commodities (copra, sugar, bananas, logs and lumber, desiccated coconut, coconut oil, pineapple, gold, abaca and copper concentrates) accounted for a major part of the Philippine export economy (though bananas and gold are relatively recent items). They still occupied 76 percent of the total exports in 1970. However, in the 1970s and 80s, the share of non-traditional products, both manu-factured and unmanufactured, increased considerably: in order of importance, they are electrical and electronic products, garments, food products and beverages, handicrafts, metalliferous ores and metal scrap, chemicals and iron ore agglomerates. Electrical and electronic products (including semi-conductors) accounted for some 60 percent of the total manufacturing exports in 1984. In 1985, the situation had drastically changed: the share of the ten traditional items declined to only 24 percent and that of others (the majority of which are non-traditional items) was 76 percent.

As for imports, in 1970-84, the share of fuel oil increased more than two-fold while the shares for machines, transport equipment and basic manufactured goods dropped by one-third. The Philippine economy was revealed to be vulnerable to the oil price increase. Among the total imports, in 1985, consumer goods accounted for 30 percent, capital goods 15 percent and raw materials and intermediate goods 55 percent (of which half was fuel). Both import-substitution and export-oriented industries have developed on the basis of imports of raw materials and intermediate goods from abroad. The crisis and consequent resort to import controls of 1984-85, therefore, hit these industries, reducing raw materials and intermediate goods, as well as capital goods to be used in domestic industry. The resource-based industries are still limited to copper concentrates, food products, wood products and some others.

After the commodity boom was over, the oil price hike started to reveal its true effects on the current account. The current account deficits rose from about 39 percent of exports in 1975 to 67 percent in 1982. This was financed mainly by creation of external debt. Long-term public external debt alone rose from about US$2.3 billion in 1974 to about US$12 billion in 1982. The problem of servicing such a huge debt burden, however, seemed to be ignored.

The increasing trade deficits were due to worsening terms of trade as well as the increasing propensity to import. The terms of trade deteriorated from 1.00 to 0.60 during 1972-81. This was mainly due to the two oil crises and successive world-wide recession that hit Philippine exports. The increase in import/GNP ratio probably resulted from overvalued currency, a higher rate of inflation relative to other countries, and increase in demand for import inputs in newly-established export industries.[33]

---

[33] De Dios, ed., *An Analysis of the Philippine Economic Crisis*, pp. 52-56.

During 1970-82, the investment-saving gap widened from 0.9 percent of GNP to 7.4 percent. The widening gap was due to savings growing slower than investment in the early 1970s, then falling sooner and sharper. On the other hand, it was due as well to declining export incomes: recession in the commodity market together with the protectionist trend in developed countries seriously affected the Philippine economy.

On the other hand, aggressive government spending was largely responsible for the widened resource gap. Government construction expenditure increased five fold in the second half of 1970s from 2 billion pesos annually during 1971-75 to 10.5 billion annually during 1976-80, sharing more than 40 percent of total expenditure in the country. Private sector investment was also largely into construction. Private construction increased from 4 billion pesos per year in the first half of 1970s to 14 billion pesos per year in the second half. A large part of private construction was also financed by government money through loans from government financial institutions. This increased government deficits from the 0.8 billion pesos annual average in the first half of 1970s to a 2.2 billion pesos annual average in the second half. And since domestic resource gap was widening, public external borrowing was increased from $2.6 billion to $15.5 billion between 1975-84.[34]

With increasing foreign indebtness and an increasing interest burden more borrowing was made for repaying interest while there was large current account deficits. Large government spending also generated inflation and consequently caused overvaluation of the peso. Increasing demand for foreign exchange for imports and debt-servicing was met by short-term loans which constitute about 43 percent of total public external debt on the average during 1981-83. As short-term loans were no longer available after a crisis of confidence and the government seized the foreign banks following the ex-Senator Benigno Aquino assassination international reserves fell sharply in 1983. This necessitated adoption of strict foreign exchange controls.

Income distribution was reported to have worsened. The income share of the poorest 50 percent of total households declined from 17.6 percent of total income in 1971 to 15.7 percent in 1979, while that of the richest 10 percent increased from 37.1 percent to 41.9 percent.[35] There was also evidence that the income gap within the agricultural sector as well as the non-agricultural sector had widened. More disturbing was the discovery that the real wage was falling from 100 in 1972 to 90 in 1980 for wage earners and that even the legal minimum wage was lower than the poverty threshold.[36] According to the new *Medium-Term Development Plan 1987-1992,* 59.3 percent of the population fell under the poverty line in 1985; a 10 percent increase from 49.3 percent in 1971.[37]

Economic Recession and Productivity

After the Aquino assassination in August 1983, the political instability led to a huge outflow of capital abroad. This coincided with the period in which the Philippine

---

[34] *Ibid.*, pp. 11-12; World Bank, *Debt Tables 1984/85.*

[35] *Philippine Yearbook 1983*, H. Oshima, "Changes in Philippines Income Distribution in 1970s" (unpublished paper).

[36] *Understanding Poverty in the Philippines,* unpublished paper presented to the School of Economics, University of the Philippines, 3 April 1984, Annex X. According to the "Central Bank Statistical Bulletin", the wage index for unskilled workers dropped from 100 in 1972 to 53.4 in 1980.

[37] National Economic and Development Authority (NEDA), *Medium-Term Development Plan 1987-1992,* 1987, Table 1.9.

terms of trade worsened and its exports stagnated due to the recession in the developed market. The period 1984-86 is characterized as a period in which the economic crisis accelerated.

The Philippine government faced first the problem of meeting its debt service payments and was obliged to accept IMF conditionalities in December 1984 in exchange for a standby credit of SDR 615 million. The IMF conditionalities, which consisted mainly of: (1) floating of the peso, (2) reduction of the financial deficit, (3) tightening of liquidity, (4) balance in the trade account (reduction of imports) and (5) freeze of the real wage, have their own rationality. Though the economic adjustment program included tax and tariff reforms which were necessary in correcting imbalances in the Philippine economy, these belt-tightening and hasty liberalization policies contributed to the subsequent depression. The Philippine economy experienced a minus 5 percent growth rate in 1984 and a minus 4.5 percent rate in 1985. The Five-Year Development Plan 1983-87 was rapidly abandoned, as political instability increased.

Second, the Philippines is a country where industrialization had started on an import-substitution basis already in the 1950s and many factories still operated with their old machinery and equipment.[38] In the 1970s, the government promoted an export-oriented, labor-intensive industrialization, though inefficient import-substitution industries operated behind the protective custom tariff barriers. It was necessary to reinvest in the latter and to renovate the old industrial base in order to develop it into an internationally competitive one. In this way, the export-oriented sector could have been developed, sharing the same industrial basis which had been formed. However, this did not happen.

Third, the Marcos administration made big efforts in developing new entrepreneurship, allocating to the "cronies" and the Marcos family highly-lucrative coconut, sugar, construction, automobile and other sectors and undermining the power of traditional big business groups. This was to consolidate the President's power base. However, many of them were not necessarily efficient entrepreneurs and this "crony capitalism" resulted in a deficit of many state and state-sponsored enterprises. The number of government-owned or -controlled corporations was 65 in total, which increased to 212 in 1981 (a three-fold increase in twelve years) and 303 in 1984 (a fifty-per-cent increase in three years). The majority of them were in deficit.[39] This became one of the reasons for the increasing government deficit and the acceleration of inflation.

Fourth, the active population engaged in the tertiary sector increased from 32 percent in 1972 to 36 percent in 1985, absorbing the population which has increased by 2.8 percent per annum during this period. The productivity of the tertiary sector declined by 20 percent in the same period, which means there has been an inefficient over-employment in this sector. In fact, the unemployment rate was estimated to be 12.5 percent in 1985; however, if we take into account underemployment both in the urban and rural areas, the urban underemployment is seen to be estimated at 22.0 percent and that in the rural area at 42.4 percent (see Table 13): in average, one to three of the active population is underemployed (working less than 40 hours a week). In the Philippines, not only a more efficient economy but also greater employment creation is needed. 1984-85 were particular crisis years,

---

[38] Bautista and Power, *Industrial Promotion Policies in the Philippines*, pp. 33-45.

[39] NEDA, *Medium-Term Philippine Development Plan 1987-1992*, op. cit., pp. 391-393.

Table 13. Philippines: Active Population by Industrial Sectors, 1986 and 1992

(Unit: %)

	1986	1992
Agriculture	49.6	45.5
Industry	14.5	17.8
Manufacturing	9.8	12.0
Construction	3.8	4.9
Electricity, Gas and Water	0.3	0.3
Mining and Quarrying	0.6	0.6
Services	35.9	36.7
Unemployment rate	11.8	4.9
Male	11.6	4.3
Female	12.2	5.8
Underemployment rate	35.2	23.7
Urban	22.0	12.7
Rural	42.4	31.2

Source: National Economic and Development Authority, *Medium-Term Development Plan 1987-1992*, Table 1.7.

since we witnessed the jump in unemployment, heavy inflation (50.3 percent in 1984 and 23.1 percent in 1985) and the decline in overseas migration due to the recession in the Middle East. However, we may say it was at the same time the culmination of bad economic management which benefited mainly a few privileged people.

The people's dissatisfaction was behind the political change which took place in February 1986.

Development Strategy of the New Government

The new Corazon Aquino Government, which took office supported by the "people's power", made the following promises:
— the establishment of a democratic and clean government
— the abolition of monopolistic policies by a certain privileged circle ("cronies")
— renegotiation regarding conditionalities imposed by IMF and the World Bank
— a guarantee for human and workers' basic rights
— an independent and nuclear-free diplomacy

The new regime intends to reconstruct the national economy, which was once hit by a hasty liberalization policy, and consolidate its social basis by reforming monopolistic practices which were prevalent under the preceding regime.

These objectives were consolidated in the Constitution of the Philippine Republic, adopted by the people's referendum in February 1987. The Constitution pursues democracy, a guarantee of human and civil rights, regional autonomy to the Muslim Mindanao and the Cordierra and social justice including land reform.

Thus, the Comprehensive Agrarian Reform Program,[40] published by the government at the same time, was officially endorsed by the nation. The Comprehensive Agrarian Reform Program consists of four factors:

1. Concerning rice and corn fields, which were the objectives of the land reform under the Marcos administration, the first phase was finished (sharecropping turned into lease-holding) for 538,758 farmers; however, the actual transfer of land, which is the objective of the second phase, was considerably delayed and, before the Aquino government started, only 3.2% of 440,239 farmer-tenants who received certificates of land-transfer acquired emancipation patents which are actually titles.[41] In the new Program, 557,000 ha are estimated to be distributed and, when accomplished, 1.3 million ha shall be reformed, in total, by this program.

2. The lands provided voluntarily or abandoned by the landowners; the lands owned by the Marcos family and cronies; the lands mortgaged and seized by the banks. These lands amount to approximately 940,000 ha.

3. The lands owned by big landowners, which were previously excluded from the Marcos reform. These lands include sugar, banana and coconut plantations and total some 3,850,000 ha. However, the "appropriate limit" of holding should be decided later by the National Assembly.

4. Public lands which will generate some 5 million ha for farm and home lots under the land classification and land capability surveys. These include logged-over areas, unnecessary civilian and military reservations and idle or cancelled pasture leases.

The land will be reformed first, until 1990, for land holdings over 50 ha; second, until 1992, for land holdings over 24 ha; the third and last phase, until 1997, will be for land holdings over 7 ha.

Under the Marcos reform, the entitled tenants could receive up to 3 ha of irrigated land or 5 ha of unirrigated land. The new comprehensive land reform should include landless farmers or agricultural workers (who were excluded from the Marcos reform) as beneficiaries of the reform: the total number of beneficiaries are estimated to be around 2.6 million. However, the concrete size of holdings and beneficiaries, in particular for Program 3. are still to be fixed in the new Assembly. In any event, the land reform stipulated in the Constitution from the point of view of social justice should enlarge the domestic market and its execution is crucial for the enlargement of the social basis of the new government as well as the execution of a new development plan.

The Aquino Government adopted the *Medium-Term Development Plan 1987-1992.* Its major objectives are: (1) alleviation of poverty, (2) generation of more productive employment, (3) promotion of equity and social justice, and (4) the attainment of sustainable economic growth. It inherits the concerns of economic adjustment which prevailed during the crisis period of the Marcos administration; however, it intends to resolve them in the framework of sustainable economic growth.

From 1987 to 1992, the GNP is estimated to grow at the rate of 6.8 percent p.a. (per capita GNP 4.4 percent). The leading sector will be the industrial (mainly

---

[40] Ministry of Agrarian Reform, *The Comprehensive Agrarian Reform Program,* June 1987.

[41] NEDA, *Medium-Term Philippine Development Plan 1987-1992,* op. cit., p. 96. As of June 1986, only 3.2% of 440,239 farmer-tenants, beneficiaries of the operation, acquired land transfer titles.

manufacturing and construction) sector, the share of which will rise from an actual 31.3 percent to 34.7 percent (Table 14). In order to assure the high growth of the industrial sector (8.8 percent on average during 1987-92), the gross domestic investment should rise from an actual 15.0 percent of the GDP to 26.7 percent in 1992. At the same time, the gross national savings should rise from an actual 16.0 percent to 23.6 percent in 1992 and the remaining investment-saving gap should be financed by foreign savings, which should correspond to 2.7 percent (in 1986, minus 1.0 percent) of the GNP during the period 1987-92 (Table 15).

This will increase the share of the work force in the industrial sector from 14.5 percent in 1986 to 17.8 percent in 1992 and the services sector from 35.9 percent to 36.7 percent; the share of agricultural population is estimated to decrease from 49.6 percent in 1986 to 45.5 percent in 1992. And it is expected that the actual unemployment rate of 11.8 percent will be reduced to 4.9 percent in 1992, while the underemployment rate of 35.2 percent will fall to 23.7 percent in 1992 (Table 13).

Besides the eradication of poverty, the Plan states it is necessary to rectify the actual regional gaps which had been widening during the Marcos period. In fact, three higher income regions (Metro Manila, South Tagalog, Central Luzon) account for 54.7 percent of the GDP in 1984 (they accounted for 51.9 percent in 1975) and four less-developed regions (Northern Mindanao, Eastern Visayas, Ilokos and Southern Mindanao) account for only 17.3 percent of the GDP in 1984 (they accounted for 19.1 percent in 1975). Therefore, the Plan proposes, in the short-term, a Community Employment and Development Program to mobilize regional resources and realize regional development and, in the medium-term, an employment-oriented rural and regional development program.

Table 14. Philippines: Distribution of GDP by Industrial Sectors,
1986 (Estimates) and 1992 (Forecasts)

(Unit: billion pesos, at
constant 1972 prices)

	1986 (estimates) billion pesos (%)		1992 (forecasts) billion pesos (%)		Annual average growth rate (%)
GDP	90.9	(100.0)	135.3	(100.0)	6.9
Agriculture	26.8	(29.5)	35.9	(26.6)	5.0
Industry	28.4	(31.3)	47.1	(34.7)	8.8
Manufacturing	21.7	(23.9)	33.7	(24.5)	7.6
Construction	3.6	(4.0)	9.0	(6.6)	16.5
Electricity, Gas and Water	1.3	(1.4)	2.1	(1.6)	8.4
Mining and quarrying	1.8	(2.0)	2.3	(1.7)	4.2
Services	35.7	(39.3)	52.2	(38.7)	6.6

Source: Same as Table 13: Tables 3 and 4.

Table 15. Philippines: Investment and Saving Forecast According
to the Medium-Term Plan, 1986-1992

(Unit: %)

	1986 (estimates)	1987	1992	Annual average 1987-92
Gross Domestic Investment	15.0	18.7	26.7	23.3
Gross National Savings	16.0	17.4	23.6	20.6
Foreign Savings	−1.0	1.3	3.1	2.7

Source: Same as Table 13: Table 6.

The Aquino Government also will emphasize de-nationalization of state-owned corporations and enterprises which proliferated under the Marcos administration; its aim is to reduce governmental deficits and to reactivate private initiative.

Until 1992, the major issues of development will be: (1) the reconstruction and adjustment of the economy (reducing budgetary and trade deficits), (2) increase of productive investment and creation of employment, and (3) correction of regional imbalances. These goals will be attained through sustainable economic growth. In order to realize these goals, therefore, both mobilization of domestic resources and foreign assistance will play an important role. In the context of this perspective, the agrarian reform, which will increase domestic savings and reduce unproductive rural unemployment and underemployment, is considered crucial.

At the same time, in the industrial sector, the efforts of productivity increase will be important, as this sector is expected to increase its exports. In this sector, the renovation of age-old equipment in the local small- and medium-enterprises is also due. Therefore, the productivity issues will be faced on several levels: small farming areas and the cooperative sector in the rural area, small- and medium-scale industries in the urban area and the non-traditional export-oriented industries, including mines and plantations, all over the country. It is most important to establish an economic link between these sectors.

SINGAPORE

High Growth and Upgrading of the Industrial Structure

Before its independence Singapore was an entrepot port in the Malay peninsula. At the time of its separation from Malaysia in 1965, three-quarters of its national income was derived from services and industrial production accounted for only 20 percent.

Since independence, Singapore has basically followed the path of modernization paved from colonial times but this time with industrialization.[42] During the 1960s

---

[42] Goh Ken Swee, *The Economics of Modernization,* pp. 1-18.

and 1970s, Singapore energetically pursued industrialization. Industrial production grew 12.5 percent p.a. in the decade from 1960 and 9 percent in the 1970s and led the high 8.5-8.8 percent economic growth rate during these twenty years. In 1984, the share of the industrial sector accounted for 32 percent (of which manufacturing was 20 percent) and the service sector 66 percent.

In 1984, the per capita GNP in Singapore reached US$7,100; but, if we deduct from the total GNP the share for resident foreigners and resident foreign companies, the indigenous per capita GNP was US$5,791 (*Singapore Economic Survey 1984*). This distinction is important since, in 1981, the United States set the upper limit for the application of GSP: GSP shall be applied to imports from countries which have a national income per capita below US$8,500. Singapore is now ranked among Newly-Industrializing Countries or Upper-Middle Income countries, together with Hong Kong, the ROC (Taiwan) and Korea.

However, in the 1980s, as the wage level has increased and as industrialization progresses in neighboring countries, Singapore has faced competition with a second generation of NICs, in particular, to other ASEAN countries. TNC investment, which has contributed much to the industrial growth of this country, has slowed down. In the U.S. market, in textile and electronic fields in particular, the share of ASEAN (except Singapore) labor-intensive goods has increased.

At the same time, a rising protectionist trend in developed countries and a depression in semi-conductor industries gave a shock to the Singapore economy, which was one of the reasons why her growth rate dropped under zero in 1985, for the first time since the separation from Malaysia.

Facing the new international and domestic circumstances, in 1981 Singapore launched a National Economic Plan for the 1980s, which consisted of the realization of a high economic growth rate of 8-10 percent p.a. By 1990, she is expected to realize the income level of US$9,000, which corresponds to that of Japan in 1983. After this plan, Singapore deliberately moved to a high-wage policy, restraining the entry of non-skilled foreign workers and giving incentives to domestic workers in upgrading their skill level. A low-wage level stagnates productivity, leading to a loss of international competition. Foreign capital goes out, resulting in unemployment. Therefore, Singapore deliberately opted for an economy in which high wage and high skill would increase productivity through the adoption of a capital-intensive production method and international competition. The productivity increase is now considered a key factor for a high economic growth path.

Industry, Finance and Trade

Major industrial production in Singapore consists of: petroleum and petroleum-related products, electric and electronic goods, general machinery, food/beverage and tobacco, transport machinery, metal products and apparel/footwear (Table 16). These seven industries produce two-thirds of the total manufacturing production.

In the ten-year development plan, together with manufacturing industries, commerce, tourism, transport, communication, knowledge-intensive industries such as computers, finance, medical service and consultancy service were chosen as strategic industries. These high-technology and information-handling professional services will contribute to the increase of Singapore's weight in ASEAN and the Pacific region. First, these knowledge-intensive industries would provide the basis

Table 16. Singapore: Major Industrial Production (1983)

(Unit S$ million)

	Production	Value Added
Petroleum and petroleum-related products	12,369	1,422
Electric and electronic goods	7,786	2,210
General machinery	1,852	888
Food, beverage and tobacco	2,322	541
Transport machinery	1,591	805
Metal products	1,630	553
Apparel/footwear	1,228	433
Total manufacturing industries	35,409	9,231

Source: Singapore: *Yearbook of Statistics, 1983/84.*

for more investment from TNCs which have been developing similar activities in the region. Second, the development of the high-science and technology activities would be favorable in upgrading the structure of its manufacturing industries.[43] Thirdly, the needs for Singapore's services by neighboring industrializing countries would increase in the future.

Actually, as seen in Table 16, the local value-added in the Singapore industry remains a minor part of total production (only 26 percent in 1983). Therefore, the strategy consists of increasing the value-added. Unlike a simple knock-down industry, the development of parts production, industrial service, investment abroad for materials/parts production and the enlargement of upstream/downstream production will be emphasized.

In 1984, 36 percent of its exports consisted of re-exports (Table 17). It seems that the role of entrepot and the distribution of resources have again become important as the industrialization of Southeast Asian progresses. In fact, the majority of intraregional trade among ASEAN countries passes through Singapore.[44] Singapore is likely to develop further as a regional commerce and trade center. Singapore's position would become more important, since it has begun investment in neighboring ASEAN countries.

Both in exports and imports, about half of the trade partners are developed countries while the other half are developing countries. But to developed countries (USA, Japan, EC, Australia), Singapore mainly exports labor-intensive goods. To developing countries of the region, the share of re-exports is still important. However, this trade structure will gradually be modified and Singapore's role in promoting horizontal trade in the Southeast Asian region will become increasingly vital.

Concerning the external account, its balance has always been in deficit; however, a huge inflow of foreign resources to Singapore as the Asian dollar center has sustained the value of the Singapore dollar. The total amounts of assets/liabilities

---

[43] Saw and Bhathal, ed., *Singapore Towards the Year 2000*, pp. 87-93.
[44] Lim, Chong-Yah, *Economic Development in Southeast Asia*, passim.

grew from US$390 million in 1970 to US$128,058 million in 1984 (Table 18) in Singapore's financial market.

By the end of 1983, there were 122 commercial banks, which accounted for about half of the total assets/liabilities for Singapore's financial institutions. Besides this, finance companies and merchant banks have been developing operations in recent years.[45]

There are two problems with financial operations in Singapore. First, local loans account for a rather small percentage in bank operations (a quarter of the total assets in 1984). Second, the debt problem with developing countries seems to hinder the financial operation of banks based in Singapore.

However, since political stability, business efficiency and the development of the communication/information infrastructure are assets in Singapore, it may develop, together with Hong Kong, as a regional financial center. The ASEAN Financial Corporation, which is based in Singapore and has developed a financing operation in promoting joint-ventures among ASEAN countries, is an example of this type of regional financing. In the future, Singapore's financial institutions may develop their operations in South Asia and in the Pacific area, too.

Human Resources and Productivity Movement

Singapore is a small city-state in which approximately 2.5 million live as of 1983, of which Chinese account for 77 percent, Malays 15 percent, Indians 6.4 percent and others 1.6 percent. The population growth rate, which was around 3 percent in the beginning of the 1960s, dropped around 1970 to 1.7 percent and in the 1980s to 1.2 percent.[46] This contributed to the rise of the general living standard as income and productivity levels increased.

The actual average literacy rate was 84 percent in 1980, however, for the younger generation (age 15-29), 95-97 percent are literate. Primary education for six to eight years is free and begins at the age of six.

The People's Action Party (PAP), which has established its control over Singapore politics since independence, succeeded in giving Singaporeans a strong sense of national identity. The suppression of Nanyang University in 1980 should be understood in this context. Since the middle of the 1970s, on the vernacular school education level, Chinese, Malay and Tamil language students have decreased considerably and the gap between English language students and other language students has widened.[47] This added to the strengthening of national homogeneity.

The industrial environment in Singapore has been excellent for private enterprises. In 1974, 1,091 trade disputes and 10 industrial stoppages, with 5,380-man days lost, were recorded. However, after 1978, trade disputes decreased to an average of 350 p.a. and no industrial stoppage was recorded. Drysdale attributes this atmosphere to a consultation system among the government, the National Trade Union Congress (which organized 205,155 employees in 1983 — the total number of workers amounts to 1,170,000) and employers at the forum of a National Wages Council.[48]

---

[45] *Singapore Economic Survey 1984,* Table 48.
[46] *Singapore Statistics 1960-82,* Table 2.5.
[47] Drysdale, *Singapore, Struggle for Success,* pp. 426-427.
[48] *Ibid.,* p. 411.

Table 17. Singapore: External Trade (1984)

(Unit: S$ million)

	Imports	%	Exports	%
Developed Countries	30,409	49	25,715	50
Japan	11,218		4,807	
USA	8,923		10,292	
EC	6,140		4,980	
Oceania	1,785		2,916	
Developing Countries	30,342	50	23,990	47
Southeast Asia*	11,593		12,181	
Malaysia	9,180		8,324	
Northeast Asia	6,958		5,392	
China	2,881		519	
South Asia	612		2,994	
West Asia	11,179		3,423	
Saudi Arabia	5,688		1,364	
Socialist Countries	383	0.6	1,635	3
Total	61,134	100	Total* 51,340	100

Domestic Exports 33,063
Re-exports 18,277

Source: *Economic Survey of Singapore 1984.*

* Excluding Indonesia.

Table 18. Singapore: Asian Currency Units, 1970 and 1984

(Unit: US$ million)

	1970	1984
Assets	389.8	128,057.5
Loans to No-bank Customers	13.9	33,768.7
Interbank Funds	370.2	85,329.0
Other assets	5.7	8,959.8
Liabilities	389.8	128,057.5
Deposits of No-bank Customers	243.7	21,525.9
Interbank Funds	141.0	100,186.6
Other Liabilities	5.1	6,345.0

Source: *Economic Survey of Singapore 1984.* Table 5.6.

Actually, as increased productivity is considered the key factor in assuring the further development of Singapore, as we pointed out earlier, the government has strengthened the productivity movement, establishing the National Productivity Council and its executive body, the National Productivity Board (NPB).

The National Economic Plan for the 1980s expects a productivity increase of 6-8 percent during the decade. In 1981, the overall productivity increase was 5.5 percent; in 1982, 1.1 percent; and in 1983, 5.2 percent.[49]

In transport and communications, financial and business services, construction and manufacturing industries, the productivity increase was relatively high.

The NPB launched a campaign in 1983 to strengthen the "productivity will", which intended to promote positive work attitudes among employees. An estimated 200,000 people participated in the movement. The training enrollment reached 12,400 in 1983 (a 42 percent increase compared to 1982). The number of quality control circles jumped from 2,682 in 1982 to 8,179 in 1983. In 1979, the Skills Development Fund was created in order to promote training programs among employers.

However, a study of total factor productivity in Singapore made by Tsao suggested that the rapid growth of Singapore's economy in the 1970s was not necessarily associated with a corresponding growth in total factor productivity.[50] On the other hand, an APO study conducted in 1977-80 revealed that in Singapore most firms had not involved workers deeply in decisions which affected plant productivity.[51] There are still productivity problems both at macro- and micro-levels. In this regard, the productivity movement which will involve education, training, QCC, or seminars on labor-management relations will be further promoted.

The productivity movement will continue to play an important role in increasing the supply of skilled and trained people in a full-employment economy.

Singapore, NICs and the ASEAN Economy

Today, Singapore's national income per capita far surpasses that of the ASEAN average. Between Singapore and Malaysia, the income gap is four to one; Singapore and Thailand, nine to one; and Singapore and Philippines/Indonesia, thirteen/fourteen to one. Singapore is often called a "Little Japan". This small country serves as a vital link in the regional trade chain; however, some conflicts of interest exist between Singapore and its ASEAN neighbors.

An example of this was ASEAN's disapproval when Singapore wanted to establish a diesel engine factory as an ASEAN joint-industrial project. Singapore was obliged to turn it into a national project. As the engine is considered a key precision part in a growing car industry, other countries wanted to have their own plant. The progressive industrialization in ASEAN countries will deprive Singapore of its traditional market.

The conflicts also became apparent when Singapore participated nominally in ASEAN fertilizer plants in Indonesia and Malaysia. As Singapore had already proceeded to establish a petroleum refinery and a petrochemical plant, it was not enthusiastic about big-scale projects in the petrochemical industry of neighboring

---

[49] *Singapore Economic Survey 1984*, Table 31.
[50] Tsao, Yuan, "Growth Without Productivity: Singapore Manufacturing in the 1970s".
[51] Pang, Eng Fong, *Factors which hinder or help Productivity Improvement*, pp. 46-47.

countries. Resource-based industrialization, which has progressed in Southeast Asia, would diminish demand for intermediate products that Singapore exports to the region.

Singapore, being a small country surrounded by far bigger countries of the region, has been very attentive to security issues. That is why it gave up the "global city" slogan it once seemed to follow and decided to make progress as an ASEAN country. That is also why, in spite of the fact that it is a country dominated by people of Chinese origin, Singapore decided to establish diplomatic relations with China, after the other four did so.

On the other hand, Singapore has strong economic and financial ties with Hong Kong and the ROC (Taiwan). Financial resources move among these three economies: Singapore also has business ties with Korea. In this regard, Singapore may serve as an intermediary between the NICs and ASEAN countries.

Today, the NICs, in particular Korea and ROC (Taiwan), are moving toward the formation of a domestic economy circuit by developing heavy and chemical industries. Hong Kong will develop its links with the hinterland economy of China. Singapore has developed a petrochemical plant; however, due to the lack of space, the development of basic industries might be difficult. Therefore, the Singapore economy has several choices. One is to become an investor in the ASEAN region: it may be a bridge between developed countries and ASEAN countries. Second is to develop knowledge-intensive and high-technology industries and to upgrade its economic structure, a direction in which Singapore has been making efforts in the 1980s. Third is to again promote its entrepot and consultant function, however, this time for the development of horizontal trade among Asian countries, including the NICs. Fourth is to develop as a regional communication and co-ordination center which would connect the ASEAN region with emerging Pacific cooperation schemes as well as other cooperation schemes such as the South Asian Association of Regional Cooperation or the cooperation between Islamic countries or, in the long-run, with a modernized developing China. Of all the possible choices, which do not exclude each other, the development of human resources will be crucial.

THAILAND

Thailand has apparently survived the world-wide economic depression and crises of the 1970s and 80s better than many other developing countries. The country managed to sustain the annual average GDP growth rate at 6.8 percent from 1973 to 84, as compared with the developing countries' average of 4.8 percent.[52] Among ASEAN countries, Thailand's per capita GDP of about $900 in 1985 is ranked between those of Malaysia and the Philippines. Thailand shares the same characteristics of the other two countries: it is a rapidly-industrializing country, though most of its exports are still primary products. Unlike Malaysia, Thailand does not possess the huge reserve of oil resources which has helped in elevating Malaysia's per capita GDP. However, due to a recently-discovered reserve of natural gas, it proceeded with an ambitious heavy and chemical industrialization program. Though Thailand's external debt problem is becoming serious, the sophisticated economic policies of the government have succeeded in containing the varied expressions of criticisms and dissatisfaction, including abortive attempts at coup d'etat, by some

---

[52] *Agricultural Statistics of Thailand Crop Year 1983/84,* Tables 35 and 38.

sectors of the population. Such expressions led to the fall of the Philippine Government in February 1986.

We will briefly see here the past performance of this middle-ranked industrializing/ developing country and identify the principal problems that it is facing both in agricultural and industrial fields. Then we will examine the major issues of development and productivity for the years to come.

Trends in the Overall Economy

Thailand's economic growth, measured in terms of GDP at constant price, has been fluctuating between the low rate of 4.1 percent and the high rate of 10.1 percent, with an average of 6.4 percent during 1970-85. The first oil shock temporarily slowed down the growth of the Thai economy to the rate of 5.4 percent in 1974. Riding high with the commodity boom, the growth rate rose to the peak of 10.1 percent in 1978. After the second oil shock in 1978-79, however, Thailand could only manage to grow at the rate of about 6 percent at best and, since 1982, the growth rate has fallen to the 4-5 percent level.

The GDP growth has been largely attributable to the rapid growth in the industrial sector, especially the manufacturing sector which, with the annual average of growth of about 9 percent, has been the fastest growing sector, and of which the contribution to GDP rose from about 13 percent in the 1960s to about 20 percent in the early 1980s. The service sector has also been a major force — growing at the annual average rate of 7 percent and increasing its share in the GDP from just above 40 percent in the 1960s to about 50 percent in the1980s. On the other hand, agriculture has also contributed considerably to the expansion of economy, though its growth rate has been comparatively lower than that of the industrial sector. Its growth rate dropped from a 5.6 percent annual average during the 1960s to 4.4 percent during the 1970s and further down to 2.8 percent in the early 1980s. Its share in the GDP declined from 40 percent during the 1960s to only about 22 percent in the mid-1980s.

Through a quarter century of the implementation of the Plan, which began in 1961, the productive force in Thailand has widened considerably. Per capita GNP increased from US$103 in 1961 to $860 in 1984: an increase of more than eight times. The agriculture has been quite diversified and developed. The industrialization based on an import-substitution policy led the overall growth.

The fifth five-year plan (1982-86) forecasts the average GDP growth rate of 6.9 percent, which is far from being reached. In fact, the fifth plan's target for agricultural expansion was at an average of 4.5 percent per annum, but its performance for the first three years was only 2 percent. The target for industrial development was 7.5 percent per annum and its real growth rate was at an average of 6.1 percent for the first three years.

Dry weather conditions in 1982-83 and the world-wide recession for primary products from 1983-86 were major reasons for the failure of agriculture. The recession, over-evaluation of bahts and protectionist trend of developed countries are all responsible for the low performance of the industrial sector. The fifth plan had forecast that, for the first time, the share of the industrial sector would surpass that of the agricultural sector during the plan period. However, this objective was not realized and was transposed to the late 1980s.

Closer analysis shows there were two major causes inherent in Thai economy that hindered the expected results of the Plan: the closely-interrelated problems of the investment-saving gap and the external debt.

First, let us see the evolution of the investment-saving gap. In 1961, the ratio of domestic fixed capital formation was 14 percent and it increased at the end of the fourth five-year plan (1977-81) to 24 percent. The fifth five-year plan forecast 31 percent, but through the first half of the 1980s it stagnated around 23-24 percent. The domestic saving ratio was lagging behind the investment ratio by some 4-5 percent, particularly after the mid-1970s. The fifth plan forecast an increase to 27 percent by 1986, but it also stagnated at around 20 percent.[53]

The investment-saving gap has been financed mainly by two sources: the governmental finance deficit and external resources.

The government, in fact, has audaciously led the capital formation in this country. During the fourth plan period, governmental saving was only 1.5 percent of 23 percent of the planned saving figure, but the government invested over a third of the total fixed capital formation (8 percent out of 22.0 percent in 1982-84). Through trying to increase tax revenues, borrowing money from the domestic financial market and using inflationary means such as issuing bonds to the Central Bank, the government has assumed the role of industrialization leader.

However, the financial deficit increased at the same time, particularly after the oil crisis, and became 27.5 percent of the total governmental expenditure in 1976. Throughout the fourth plan, the budget deficit was around 19 percent, which corresponds to 3.1 percent of the total GDP.

This governmental deficit put constraints on further public-led expansion of economy. In fact, besides the inflation problem, debt amortization increased from 12.5 percent in 1981 to 21.5 percent of governmental expenditure, crowding out the increase of expenditure for productive purposes and giving further accumulation of deficit.

On the other hand, external resources have played an important part in Thai industrialization. First external, finance accounted for 25 percent in the first 6-year plan (1961-66), 20 percent in the second (1967-71) and 15-16 percent in the third (1972-76) and fourth (1977-81) 5-year plans. (See Table 19) The fifth 5-year plan expected to have 19 percent of its finance from external sources, which seemingly was not reached. Of these external finances, some 90 percent have been loans. Second, the deficit in the trade balance largely filled up the investment-saving gap. In fact, Thailand's current account was surplus in the mid-1960s. It turned to a deficit of US$248 million in 1970 which, during the fourth plan, increased eight times, reaching to around $2 billion. In 1983, the trade deficit reached $2,827 million.

The governmental budget deficit, together with the deficit in the current account, became the origin of the rapidly-accumulating external debt. In fact, the public external long-term debt was $313 million in 1970. It was still $604 million in 1975 but, after 1976, it rapidly increased and became $8,538 million in 1984. The plans had fixed the debt-service ratio at under 9 percent of the total export revenue (excluding the debt related to defense, 7 percent), which seems a sound figure. However, in 1984, the debt service ratio surpassed this target and, together with the debt-service of the private sector, was 13 percent of export revenue, jumping

---

[53] *Investment Promotion in Export-Oriented Industries and Agro-Industries and Decentralization,* vol. I, pp. 27-30.

Table 19. Financing of Thai Development Plans (1961-1986)

(Unit: million bahts)

	First 6-year Plan (1961-66) Plan	First 6-year Plan (1961-66) Achievement	Second 5-year Plan (1967-71) Plan	Second 5-year Plan (1967-71) Achievement
Domestic resource	22,019	20,980	41,920	37,881
government finance	9,411	8,540	10,000	
government bond	5,045	5,900	15,000	
central bank	3,712	3,100	7,000	
public enterprises	4,945	4,540	6,345	
others	1,094	1,100	3,575	
External resources	10,639	7,240	15,600	9,247
loan	7,187	4,840	10,600	5,465
grant	3,452	2,400	5,000	3,762
Total	32,658	28,220	57,520	47,128

	Third 5-year Plan (1972-76) Plan	Third 5-year Plan (1972-76) Achievement	Fourth 5-year Plan (1977-81) Plan	Fourth 5-year Plan (1977-81) Achievement	Fifth 5-year Plan (1982-86) Plan	Fifth 5-year Plan (1982-86) (%)
Domestic resource	83,545	78,197	220,150	264,898	649,340	81
government finance	27,265	26,209	106,860	111,831	437,820	55
government bond	42,235	34,551	78,270	80,730	85,660	11
central bank						
public enterprises	13,845	17,437	35,020	72,237	125,860	15
others						
External resources	16,930	14,351	32,300	45,330	150,000	19
loan	11,930	11,684	29,800	35,420	135,360	17
grant	5,000	2,667	2,500	9,910	14,640	2
Total	100,275	92,548	252,450	311,228	799,340	100

Source: National Economic and Social Development Board, *Successive Plans.*

from 7 percent in 1981.[54] This burden of debt in the Thai international balance of payment, together with a governmental finance deficit (and, consequently, an accumulating public debt) gave birth to a tightening policy in governmental finance, together with a development plan.

Why didn't the domestic saving ratio increase as expected in the 1980s? There are several reasons. One is that Thailand has been launching an ambitious industrialization policy which could only be financed through external funds and technology. Another reason relates to the fall of prices for primary commodities, including rice and other principal export items of Thailand, which took place after 1983. For example, the export price for rice fell from $500/tons in 1981 to $200/tons in 1985.[55] This largely handicapped the increase in export income and income in the rural sector. The protectionist trend in the market of developed countries to which the Thai industry is increasing its outlet also put pressure on the increase of the export income. However, a delay in structural reform in the domestic market where income gaps are widening between economic sectors, regions and income groups is another reason, to which we will refer later.

Dr. Snoh Unakul, Director-General of the National Economic and Social Development Board (NESDB), declared in 1983 that the "growth plus Four" should be the major objective of the fifth 5-year Plan.[56] "Four" refers to stability, diversification, decentralization and cooperation: the stability of the baht and containment of inflation, the diversified development of the industrial structure, decentralization of industries which concentrate heavily in Bangkok and cooperation of various sectors of the population, especially public and private sectors. These major objectives should continue to be those of coming Plans, in spite of international circumstances which hinder a high growth-oriented policy in ASEAN countries.

Agricultural and Industrial Development

As of the middle of the 1980s, 70 percent of the labor force in Thailand is still engaged in the primary industry sector.

From the 1950s to the 1980s, the Thai agriculture considerably developed and diversified. In this period, for the traditional crop of this country (rice), the planted land increased twofold, from 5.5 million hectares to 9.6 million ha.[57] Its productivity was 277 kg per rai (2 1/2 rai = 1 acre) in the first crop and 538 kg per rai in the second crop in the first half of the 1980s. Rice still accounts for 15 percent of Thai exports as of 1984 and remains the largest item as a single export product.

In the 1970s, Thailand diversified its agriculture considerably. From 1950-51 to 1982-83, the planted land area for maize increased 48 times, reaching 1.7 million ha. In the same period, cassava increased 91 times, reaching 1.2 million ha; rubber five times/1.6 million ha; sugar cane 11 times/583,000 ha.[58] Together with rice and marine products, these six items accounted for 51 percent of the total exports in 1984. The increase of these commercial crops responded positively to the market prices.[59] However, some problems arose in the development of agriculture and

---

[54] World Bank Country Study, *Thailand: Managing Public Resources for Structural Adjustment*, Table 8.5, p. 214.

[55] Go and Lee in Chapter 7.

[56] See Chapter 7 by World Bank Country Study, *op. cit.*, Table 2.16, p. 33.

[57] *Ibid.*, pp. 64-77.

[58] *Ibid.*, pp. 93-101.

[59] Go and Lee, *op. cit.*, Table 15.

related industries (livestock, forestry and fishing).

The Thai Government has supported the rice price since 1966. The Public Ware-house Organization and the Marketing Organization for Farmers are in charge of buying rice, maize and other agricultural products and exporting them. However, since these organizations are facing a huge deficit, the government adopted a liberalization policy in the 1980s with the result that the guidance price for rice fixed by the government has been virtually stagnating. Cassava is mainly transformed in pellet form (tapioca) and exported to the European Community as animal feed. However, the EC decided to hold down imports of animal feed and, in 1982, a new agreement between the EC and Thailand fixed the ceiling for tapioca imports at 5 million tons a year for 1982-86. Besides these quantitative limitations, the price fall hit rice, sugar and rubber, together with another important export item of mineral products: tin.

From 1961 to 1982, there was a decrease in the number of water buffalo and cattle, which reflected the modernization and mechanization in agriculture. How-ever, there was a considerable increase in chicken and duck raising. This was mainly due to the broiler chicken industry. 25.2 million chickens were raised in 1961. In 1982, the number reached 65.2 million. Export of frozen broiler, mainly to Japan, increased from 4,254 tons in 1977 to 22,926 tons in 1983, which caused a tariff reduction problem for boneless chicken between Japan and Thailand.[60] On the other hand, duck, which is consumed mainly in the domestic market, increased from 7.2 million in 1961 to 13.7 million in 1982.

Fast development of commercial crops induced a rapid depletion of forest resources. In 1961, over 50 percent of the Kingdom was covered by forests. In 1973, this was reduced to 43 percent and, in 1982, only 30.5 percent.[61] The major cause of this depletion was: first, the burning of forests in order to ensure land for com-mercial crops such as cassava and maize; second, the demand for firewood due to an increasing population; third, the production of lumber, which increased from $1,283,000^{m3}$ in 1961 to the peak $3,340,000^{m3}$ in 1977 (in the 1980s, lumber production stagnated around $1,700,000\text{-}1,800,000^{m3}$); fourth, a lack of refore-station investment.

With the depletion of forest resources becoming the origin of flood and drought, conservation and reforestation efforts are vitally needed. The importing of forest products from neighboring countries has been rapidly increasing in the 1980s.

Thailand is one of the principal fishing countries in the world, producing the peak 2.2 million tons in 1977. However, the depletion problem in forestry has taken place as well in the fishing industry in recent years. One cause of this is the indis-criminant fishing, using the trawling system. Another concern was the declaration of a 200-sea-mile economic zone by neighboring countries. In the 1980s, the total amount of fishing rests at around 2 million tons. In recent years, there was some increase in prawns and cuttle-fish, mainly exported to Japan (189,000 tons and 117,000 tons each in 1982).

Let us see next the industrialization aspect. The Thai manufacturing industry has been developing since around 1960, based on an import-substitution policy. In order of sales, food processing (28 percent of total manufacturing production in 1983), textile (20 percent), transport machines (10 percent), petroleum refining

---

[60] Direk, "Saving Behavior and the National Income Account", Table 1.
[61] World Bank Country Study, *op. cit.*, Table 2.11, p. 25.

and related products (8 percent), and non-ferrous metal products (7 percent) are major industries.

There are some industries which expanded to the overseas market: this is the case for textiles and garments, canned fruits, plastic products, machinery parts, sport shoes and electrical and electronic appliances.

As well, in recent years, export-oriented industries such as integrated circuits, miniature ball bearings, frozen and canned seafood, toys, artificial flowers and jewelry have been actively promoted.

In 1977, the newly-established military government instituted a new act of investment promotion that strengthened the power of the Board of Investment and assured promoted business firms of considerable advantages. In 1983, some 105 industries, including agricultural processing, mining, metals, chemicals, machinery and shipbuilding were designated as promoted activities. This largely encourages export-oriented as well as decentralized activities.

In the 1980s, some 24-25 percent of approved investment under the investment promotion law was foreign capital, of which Japan ranked first. Foreign capital is particularly strong in textiles, food processing, electric and electronic products, automobile, chemical and petrochemical products: almost all products which led Thai industrialization. Among Thai capital, at the same time, big business groups, having the connection of overseas Chinese, often have close ties with foreign technology and marketing skills.[62]

The share of industrial products in total exports rose from 22 percent in 1972-74 to 37 percent in 1983. However, it did not reach 42 percent, the objective of the fifth plan. Some problems arose in the industrial sector. First, the protectionist trend in the developed countries imposes the serious problem of hampering growth in export-oriented sectors. That is why the Thai Government published a *White Paper on the Adjustment of Thai-Japan Economic Relations* in June 1985 and urged Japan to gradually enlarge imports from Thailand and to promote the transfer to Thailand industries as well as technology no longer possessing comparative advantages in Japan. Second, large-scale foreign firms operating mainly in Bangkok widened gaps between the metropole and other areas as well as big business and middle-and-small business. The latter gap is seen particularly in the case of the construction sector where big projects have been mainly executed by big business, including foreign enterprises, thus widening the gap between them and local middle-and-small firms.[63] Third, as the industrial structure advances from simple import-substitution to export-oriented sectors and from the latter to the more complex stage of the formation of a domestic circuit of economy, the limitations in management capabilities and the limitation in government finance began to be major constraints in the further upgrading and development of the economy.[64]

In fact, in the 1980s, the government proceeded to large-scale heavy and chemical industrialization project in the Eastern seaboard region in order to cope with constraints posed in the past development strategies as well as to respond to the imperatives of decentralization. This project consists of two parts: one is the Mab Ta Pud area, where an important reserve of natural gas exists.[65] A gas separation

---

[62] Medhi and Tinakorn, "Poverty and Income Distribution in Thailand 1975-1981", pp. 51-53.

[63] Kurosawa and Kobayashi, *op. cit.*, Table 6.7.

[64] Wattanasiritham Paiboon, "Review of Existing Savings Institutions and Method Used in Mobilization of Small Savings in Thailand", in Vichitvong Na Pombhejara, ed., *Readings in Thailand's Political Economy*, pp. 15-16.

[65] Yuthavong Yongyuth et al., "The Role of Science and Technology in National Development".

plant, where 350 MM ft^3/a day of methane gas is separated into 350,000 tons of ethane and 82,000 tons of propane, was constructed in 1985. Using the downstream products of natural gas, petrochemical, fertilizer, soda ash and steel factories will be constructed, though there are problems concerning outlets for some of the planned products. In the Lemchaban area, an industrial site and export-processing zone are proposed for light and labor-intensive factories. Total costs for these two industrial areas are estimated to be around 100 billion bahts ($3.6 billion), half of which will be financed by external resources. However, discussion continues concerning the aggravation of the debt problem which might arise from this ambitious plan.

Though some projects have already started in the Eastern seaboard area, and though there is an uncontestable necessity for promoting this decentralized resource-based industrialization program, the Thai Government seems to be reducing to some extent these ambitious large-scale development projects.

Orientation of Development Plans

The Thai development plan was the first in Asia that advocated the necessity of incorporating "social development" already in the late 1960s. In fact, the second plan was named the "National Economic and Social Development Plan (1966-1971)". Since then, the Thai plan has mainly pursued three objectives: higher economic growth, equitable distribution of development among various social strata, and national security.

Certainly, a high economic growth was achieved in this quarter of the century and modernization in production as well as consumption has penetrated many aspects of Thai life. In general, the bottom line of people's life was elevated considerably. The number of absolute poor (annual income under 2,000 bahts in 1972 fixed prices) was estimated to be around 57 percent of the total population in 1962, but, in 1976, its proportion was estimated to be around 31 percent. However, as of around 1980, 34 percent of the rural population still live under the poverty line.[66]

In this sense, economic growth in order to dissolve absolute poverty and assure national cohesion should constitute the major objective of the plan in the years to come.

There are also several problems that we should take into account when we consider orientation and execution of the plan.

First is the role of government in conducting the general orientation of economic development. The Thai plan is, like the plans of other developing countries, an indicative plan and not a coercive plan, like those in socialist countries. It fixes major targets of development and elaborates working programs according to them. However, the controlling power of the government is limited in its own resources and investment, which amount to a third of the total fixed capital formation of the past two decades. The government, on the other hand, is responsible for drawing external resources in order to finance the investment-saving gap as well as the deficit in the current account, which amounts to 3-4 percent of the GDP in recent years. In short, the Thai nation has conducted a life which exceeds its own resources, thanks to the government's efforts and external resources.

---

[66] The Brunei Darussalam State Chamber of Commerce Review, *Independence Year Issue* 1984, p. 11.

In the private sector, some big business groups, traditionally concentrated in commercial and financial sectors, have developed their business in accordance with general orientation of governmental guidance. However, since constraints such as fiscal deficit and managerial limits appeared in the expansion of governmental activities, and since further governmental activity may crowd out resources which could be used productively by the private sector, it is time to develop an active cooperation network between public and private sectors. In this situation, co-operation should not be limited to that between governmental leaders and big business, but should be developed on every level of government and private sectors, including medium and small enterprises and cooperatives. The public-private co-operation needs at the same time a thorough re-organization of its administration, including decentralization of power as well as an active policy of regional development.

Second, though the absolute poverty problem diminished thanks to economic growth and the modernization policy, the problem of gaps between rich and poor, i.e., the problem of relative poverty, seem to have become serious.

In 1978, the per capita income of the agricultural population was, in average, 4,199 bahts, while for the non-agricultural population it was 23,728 bahts, the gap being 1:5.7. However, in 1982, the former was 5,337 bahts and the latter 39,350 bahts, which widened the gap to 1:7.4. (See Table 20). If we compare only the per capita income of the Northeastern area (agricultural and non-agricultural population totaled), where half of the population lives, with that of Bangkok, the former is only 13.9 percent of the latter (7,146 bahts against 51,441 bahts), as of 1983.[67]

Therefore, it is the government's task to correct the income gaps which are widening and which are subject to political disturbance. If the domestic purchasing power is further strengthened thanks to the active redistribution policy of the fruits of economic growth, it could become one of the strong factors in increasing the domestic saving ratio, thus narrowing the investment-saving gap.

Third, by the same token, regional gaps should be corrected. Decentralization should not be limited to large-scale industrialization projects. It should be related also to the town (tanbon)/village (mu bahn) level. In the urban slum area, citizens' self-help projects could be promoted. The vitality of the private sectors could be

Table 20. Thailand: Per Capita Income of Agricultural and
Non-Agricultural Population

	Agricultural Population Average/Northeast/North/Central/South					Non-agricultural Population
1978	4,199	2,285	4,399	6,697	5,695	23,728
1980	5,445	3,221	5,444	8,355	7,499	32,346
1982	5,337	2,831	5,579	8,755	6,894	39,350

Source: NESDB, Office of Agricultural Economics.

---

[67] D.S. Ranjit Singh, *Brunei 1839-1983: The Problems of Political Survival*, p. 222.

coordinated by the government/semi-public agency. The grass-root network of citizens needs the formation of local leaders. On every level of socio-economic activities, the development of human resources will be vital.

Finally, until now, a non-controlled economic growth was accompanied by deterioration of environment: depletion of forest and fishery resources, degradation of life quality in the urban area, etc. The coordination of development and environmental conservation is important in order to assure further economic growth in this country.

In all these huge efforts, the role of government is crucial. Until now, NESDB has acted mainly as the operational office of investment promotion; but, in the future, it could be transformed into a policy planning and coordinating agency equipped with necessary resources and a coordination capacity.

BRUNEI

Natural Resources

Brunei is a small country with a population of about 200,000, of which 65% are Malaysan, 20 percent Chinese, 8 percent other indigenous and 7 percent foreigners.[68] 84 percent of its GDP is derived from crude oil and natural gas. In 1980, there were 576 oil wells, producing 11,172,000 tons. Natural gas production was 9,208 million m^3. The proved reserves for oil and natural gas are quite high and the possible years with the current rate of production are estimated to be around 70. These hydrocarbon fuels brought in US$3 billion a year in recent years and the per capita national income reached US$25,466 in 1980.

Almost all oil and gas in exported. Gas is liquefied in the LNP plant and 5 million tons are exported to Japan. Brunei had official foreign exchange reserves of US$14 billion in 1980.

Brunei and the ASEAN Economy

In 1984, Brunei, at the same time of its independence, joined ASEAN. This might be related to Brunei security concerns.[69]

In 1983, the labor force was 31,000, of which 40 percent worked for the government and 8 percent were employed by Brunei Shell.

With the oil-boom, labor shortages have persisted. The government employs foreigners for high-skilled professional functions. Many Philippines and Malaysians are engaged, in general, in unskilled work.

The government adopted the Bumiputra policy and education and training for Bumiputras are being encouraged. Among the youth, the literacy rate is 95 percent, however, there are no universities in Brunei. Therefore, the majority of students go to the United Kingdom on government scholarship.

Brunei should prepare its post-oil economy. It may develop in the future following Singapore's style of development. First, it may become a regional finance center, contributing to the development of the region. Brunei should prepare to establish

---

[68] *The Brunei Darussalam State Chamber of Commerce Review,* Independence Issue, p. 11.
[69] D.S. Ranjit Singh, *Brunei 1839-1983: The Problems of Political Survival,* p. 222.

its own bank (actually there is no national bank). Second, it may produce high-skilled and knowledge-intensive people and act as a high-tech center (tropical medicine, agriculture and forestry, aquaculture, biotechnology, fine chemistry, etc.) of the region.

REFERENCES

Agricultural Statistics of Thailand Crop Year 1983/84. Center for Agricultural Statistics, Office of Agricultural Economics, Ministry of Agriculture and Co-operatives (Agricultural Statistics No. 213).

Asian Productivity Organization Symposium, *Productivity Measurement: An Asian Analysis, Country Exercises, 1979.*

Arief, S. *Indonesia: Growth, Income Disparity and Mass Poverty,* Jakarta: SAA, n.d.

Arief, S. *Consumption Pattern in Indonesia,* Jakarta: SAA, 1980.

Ariff, Mohamed, Fong Chan Onn and R. Thillainathan (ed.), *ASEAN Cooperation in Industrial Projects,* Kuala Lumpur: The Malaysia Economic Association, 1977.

Asian Productivity Organization, *Development Strategies for the 1980s,* Tokyo, 1981.

Bank Negara Malaysia, *Annual Report 1983,* Kuala Lumpur, 1984.

BAPPENAS (National Development Planning Agency), *Repelita IV — The Fourth Five-Year Development Plan of Indonesia 1984/85 — 1988/89,* 1984.

Bautista, Romeo M. and John H. Power, *Industrial Promotion Policies in the Philippines,* Philippine Institute for Development Studies, 1979.

Bruch Mathias and Ulrich Hiemerz. Asian Development Bank, *Small- and Medium-Scale Manufacturing Establishments in ASEAN Countries: Perspectives and Policy Issues,* Manila, 1983.

The Brunei Darussalam State, Chamber of Commerce Review, *Independence Year Issue 1984,* Brunei, 1984.

Brunei Statistical Yearbook. 1980, Brunei.

Chen Peter S.J. and Hans-Dieter Evers, *Studies in ASEAN Sociology,* Singapore: Chopmen Enterprises, 1978.

De Dios, Emmanuel S. (ed.), *An Analysis of the Philippine Economic Crisis,* A Workshop Report, June 1984, University of the Philippines Press, 1984.

Drysdale John, *Singapore, Struggle for Success,* Singapore: Times Book International, 1984.

Garcia, Adriano R., *New Horizons of Regionalism in Asia and the Pacific,* Manila: Phoenix Press, 1985.

Garnaut Ross (ed.), *ASEAN in a Changing Pacific and World Economy,* Canberra: Australian National University Press, 1980.

Goh Keng Swee, *The Economics of Modernization,* Singapore: Asia Pacific Press, 1972.

Investment Promotion in Export-Oriented Industries and Agro-Industries and Decentralization, 3 vols., a report prepared for the Board of Investment (Thailand) by the Industrial Management Co., Ltd., November 1985.

Japan External Trade Organization, *Indonesia ni okeru minzoku-kei kigyo no taito to kajin-shihon* (The rise of indigenous capital in Indonesia and ethnic Chinese capital), Tokyo: JETRO, 1975.

Juanjai Ajanant, Supote Chunanuntatham and Sorrayuth Meenaphant, *Trade and*

Industrialization of Thailand, prepared for International Development Research Center, Canada, March 1984.

Krongkaew Medhi and Pranee Tinakorn, "Poverty and Income Distribution in Thailand 1975-1981", paper presented at the Seminar on Thailand's Poverty Review at Thammasat University, 15 July 1985.

Lim, Chong-Yah, *Economic Development in Southeast Asia,* Singapore: Federal Publications 1981.

Lim David (ed.), *Further Readings on Malaysian Economic Development,* Kuala Lumpur, Oxford University Press, 1983.

Lim Lin Lean & Chee Peng Lim, *The Malaysian Economy at the Crossroads: Policy Adjustment or Structural Transformation,* Kuala Lumpur: Malaysian Economic Association, 1984.

Mahathir bin Mohamad, *The Malay Dilemma,* Kuala Lumpur: Federal Publication, first edition 1970; new edition 1984.

Malaysia, Ministry of Finance, *Economic Report 1983/84,* Kuala Lumpur, 1984.

Malaysian Government, *Fourth Malaysia Plan 1981-1985,* Kuala Lumpur, 1981.

Malaysian Government, *Mid-Term Review of the Fourth Malaysian Plan 1981-1985,* Kuala Lumpur, 1984.

Moertopo Ali, *The Acceleration and Modernization of 25 Years Development,* Jakarta: Centre for Strategic and International Studies, 1973.

Mokhzani B.A.R., Khong Kim Hoong and R.J.G. Wells (ed.), *ASEAN Economic Cooperation and the New International Economic Order,* Kuala Lumpur, Malaysian Economic Association, 1980.

Myint Hla, *Overall Report, Southeast Asian Economy in the 1970s,* Asian Development Bank, 1971.

National Economic and Social Development Board (Thailand), *The Fifth National Economic and Social Development Plan (1982-86),* Bangkok.

————, *Summary Direction of the Sixth National Economic and Social Development Plan,* October, 1985.

————, *Gross Regional and Provincial Product 1983,* Bangkok.

National Economic and Development Authority (Philippines), *Medium-Term Development Plan 1987-1992,* Manila, 1986.

Nishikawa Jun, *ASEAN and the United Nations System,* New York: United Nations, 1983.

Oshima, H. "Changes in Philippines Income Distribution in the 1970s", (unpublished paper).

Palmer Ingrid, *The Indonesian Economy since 1965,* London: F. Cass, 1978.

Pang Eng Fong, *Factors which Hinder or help Productivity Improvement,* Tokyo: Asian Productivity Organization, 1980.

Philippine Yearbook, 1983, 1984, 1987.

Rao V.V. Bhanoji, *Malaysia Development Pattern and Policy,* Singapore: Singapore University Press, 1980.

Saw Swee-Hock and R.S. Bhathal (ed.), *Singapore Towards the Year 2000,* Singapore: Singapore University Press, 1981.

Siddayao Corazon M. (ed.), *ASEAN and the Multinational Corporations,* Summary and Proceedings of a Round Table Discussion, organized by the Institute of Southeast Asian Studies, Singapore and the Center for Strategic and International Studies, Jakarta 12-13 March 1977, 1978.

Singapore, Department of Statistics, *Report on the Census of Industrial Production 1982,* Singapore.

Singapore, Ministry of Trade and Industry, *Economic Survey of Singapore 1984,* *1985.*

Singapore, Department of Statistics, *Economic & Social Statistics, Singapore 1960-* *1982,* Singapore 1983.

Singh D.S. Ranjit, *Brunei 1839-1983: The Problems of Political Survival,* Singapore: Oxford University Press, 1984.

Snodgrass Donald R., *Inequality and Economic Development in Malaysia,* Kuala Lumpur, Oxford University Press, 1980.

Tsao Yuan, "Growth Without Productivity: Singapore Manufacturing in the 1970s", mimeo. 1984.

Understanding Poverty in the Philippines, unpublished paper presented to the School of Economics, University of the Philippines, 3 April 1984.

Vichitvong Na Pombhejara (ed.), *Readings in Thailand's Political Economy,* Bangkok Printing Enterprise Co., Ltd., 1978.

Wong John, *ASEAN Economics in Perspective,* London, MacMillan, 1979.

World Bank, *Debt Tables 1984/85, 1986/87,* Washington, D.C., 1985, 1987.

World Bank, *World Development Report,* each edition.

Yuan-Li Wu and Chung-hsi Wu, *Economic Development in Southeast Asia. The Chinese Dimension,* Stanford: Hoover Institution Press, 1980.

11. Economic Reforms and the Open Door Policy in China

Reiitsu Kojima

INTRODUCTION

Over the period from 1950 to the present, the Chinese economy has passed through two major periods. The first was from 1950 to 1978, or what may be called the Mao Zedong era. The second was from 1979 to the present, or what may be called the Deng Xiaoping era.

During the first period, the Chinese economy was an investment oriented economy, with the system being set up to realize a high savings rate and policies taken to maintain that system. Under this economic system, China realized a high savings rate and succeeded in ensuring employment for its people and in providing their basic consumption needs. China in fact enjoyed "surplus" (more than full) employment and solved the food problem, the basic consumption item. It freed the people from starvation and provided them with medical care, primary school educations, and other basic minimum human public consumption needs. The overful employment, however, was a problem because of stagnating labor productivity and personal consumption.

During the second period, that of Deng Xiaoping, policies were set to improve labour productivity and personal consumption in addition to sustaining past successes. For this reason, China began the reform of the various social systems established during the Mao Zedong era for realizing a high savings rate. These were the economic reforms which began in 1979. The economic reforms gave birth to various new problems. Whether China can overcome these and simultaneously realize both improved labor productivity and personal consumption will be the key to whether the economic reforms of the Deng Xiaoping era succeed.

The bold decision of the Chinese government to embark upon an economic open door policy was a tactic designed to simultaneously achieve two goals. The open door policy was meant to create an infusion of the advanced technology and capital needed for improving labor productivity. It was also a means to overcome the shortage of domestic investment funds arising from the rise in personal consumption.

The open-door policy was a dramatic change from the past era in which 'self-reliance' had always been emphasized.

The creation of foreign debt inevitably forced the Chinese to take measures to promote exports. The importance of China in the international economy is thus expected to gradually rise in the future. The analysis that follows has been undertaken from these viewpoints.

STRUCTURAL CHANGES IN THE ECONOMY
– FROM SAVINGS TO CONSUMPTION

General Rise in Personal Consumption

In the period from the establishment of the People's Republic of China (PRC) in 1949 to 1956, the government based its economic policies on changing the capitalist and feudalist economy to a socialist economy. This is commonly referred to by the Chinese as their "socialist conversion". Looking at this from the viewpoint of savings in economic development, China successfully created a new savings pattern reversing the old pattern of economic waste under the small ruling class. Details of the changes instituted are given below.

Elimination of Wasteful Classes
The Chinese eliminated the bureaucratic comprador ruling class and landlord class and placed the resources previously controlled by them under the management of the people's government. The former was eliminated in 1950. The landlord class was eliminated by 1952 through the land reforms that began in 1947. The assets owned by capitalists of minority groups were placed under the management of the people's government by 1956.

Creation of Savings Pattern Using Tax System and Scissor Prices to Cause Capital to Accumulate in Government
The agricultural surplus which the landlord class had previously acquired in the form of rents and high interest rate loans after land reform changed into income of the farmers. In the early 1950s, peasant incomes rose rapidly. The Chinese Communist Party (CCP), however, was forced to create a savings pattern enabling the central government to collect part of that surplus so as to obtain the funds required for economic construction. It did this through scissor prices and agricultural commodity taxes. "Scissor prices" refer to the relatively unfavorable terms of trade dealt to the farmers in the economic exchange between agriculture and industry. This price structure had been prevalent throughout China's modern history. Having received the bulk of its support through the agricultural revolution, the Chinese Communist Party took a policy of gradually increasing government purchase prices of farm goods and keeping down sales prices of industrial goods in the countryside, giving the farmers a better margin in the distribution process. The unfavorable position of the peasants in the economic exchange between agriculture and industry, however, continued for a long time. The government obtained inexpensive agricultural products, processed them at state-run enterprises, and sold the resulting light industrial goods at high prices to the consumers (most of whom were farmers) so as to acquire the funds required for construction. This pattern of savings continued

until the large scale increases in the government purchase prices of agricultural products in 1979.

The economic system for ensuring this pattern of savings was established through the collectivization of the peasants. The collectives took away the rights to agricultural products held by the individual peasants so as to ensure government control over the bulk of the farm output.

Creation of Pattern of Labor Accumulation Among Peasants

In the first five-year plan, from 1953 to 1957, China obtained loans from the Soviet Union. The amount of those loans, however, was just about 2.5 percent of state finances. This was far from sufficient to meet the needs of rising consumption and massive construction. To make up for the shortage, the government decided to mobilize the peasants for water conservation, road construction, creation of arable land, forestry, and other work. In other words, it converted construction force labor into fixed capital. This is known as "labor accumulation."

The systems that made this feasible were the collectives and the people's communes. The peasants were deprived of the right to manage their own work by themselves. The production teams, production brigades, and people's communes each controlled the labor of the peasants. In the period from the collectivization of 1956 to the arrest of the so-called "Gang of Four" in 1976, the amount of rural construction achieved through brute force "human wave tactics" reached astronomical proportions.

This was the basic mechanism of savings created during the Mao Zedong era. It is due to the successful creation of this mechanism of savings that the government was able to secure the funds for development of modern weapons, support the North in the Vietnam War, assist the African nations, and the like, even during the 1960's when it was isolated internationally.

This is not to say, however that the Mao Zedong era was characterized by sheer strengthening of savings. Despite the burgeoning population, the Chinese were able to ensure fundamental consumption needs and minimum social benefits for all but a few years after the "Great Leap Forward". China established a social security system known as the "five guarantees". Though imperfect, it covered not only employees of the state-run enterprises and government, but also vast numbers of peasants. The "five guarantees" referred to food subsidies for rural families which had lost their working members, medical services, primary school education, funerals, and other minimum social needs. The bottom line social guarantee of meeting food requirements led to the increases in population after 1962.

On the other hand, this was at the sacrifice of the improvement of per capita personal consumption. There were no rapid improvements in this area. The sharp increase in population worked as a negative factor on the improvement of per capita personal consumption. Figure 1 shows the trends in social consumption funds for public use, social consumption funds for personal use, per capita public consumption, and per capita personal consumption. Statistics in the figures are current prices converted to an index using 1965 as the base year. It will be seen that the rate of increase of public consumption from around 1969 and 1970 rose at far greater speed than the rate of increase of personal consumption. A look at the wage system of China shows that in the Yenan days, the Communists basically provided wages in kind. That system began to be changed from 1950 through the introduction of the Soviet wage system. The Soviet model wage system spread throughout almost the entire state-run sector by 1956. During the establishment of the people's communes in 1958, however, the Yenan system of supply was revived. The public dining hall system instituted in the rural areas, in particular, was a typical example of this. Up until 1978, history continually repeated itself, with public consumption expanding when the leftists seized power and personal consumption expanding when the rightists seized it. As shown by (d) in Figure 1, the increase in per capita personal consumption was the lowest during the Cultural Revolution, even in its later stages.

Figure 2 shows the trends in per capita personal consumption as divided into the urban and rural sectors. Figures here are given in real terms. This figure shows a considerable real rise even in personal consumption though it was suppressed from 1966 to the middle of the Cultural Revolution. Next, starting around 1970, real per capita consumption among urban residents rose rapidly. In the countryside, it did not begin to rise rapidly until after 1978.

From the two figures, it may be seen that in the latter stages of the Cultural Revolution, there was a considerable improvement in overall consumption. In particular, there was a large increase in egalitarian public consumption expenditure, and, in personal consumption, a great improvement in the consumption of urban residents. In other words, egalitarianism and the overall frugalism began to gradually wane in the early 1970's. This may have laid the groundwork for the later repudiation of the Cultural Revolution.

Below is an analysis of the rise in consumption in individual sectors.

Grain Consumption

Figure 3 shows the trend in per capita consumption of grain. The figure shows not the actual amount of per capita consumption, but the apparent consumption. When the Chinese speak of "grain", they refer not only to the usual cereal grain, but also to some potatoes and soybeans. Cereal grains are entered into statistics in the unpolished state. In accordance with this concept, the amount of grain consumption in Japan was calculated to show the changes in the per capita consumption in the two countries.

Here, the author would like to discuss the level of per capita consumption and the social phenomenon of grain consumption from his own observations. When the per capita consumption reaches the level of 300 kg, if good distribution can be obtained, the great majority of the people will have enough staple food to fill their stomachs. Below 250 kg, starvation occurs occasionally. In China, this corresponded to the period from 1959 to 1961. During that period, roughly 5 million people died early deaths each year. When the level of 350 kg is passed, consumption of alcohol and animal protein begins to rapidly increase. Cereal grain is processed through fermentation and passed through the bellies of domestic animals before being consumed. When the 400 kg line is passed, the absolute amount of direct consumption of grain declines and the indirect consumption of cereal grain through alcohol and meat increases much more. At the same time, obesity due to overeating increases. To correct this, weight reducing industries begin to be established. When the 450 kg stage is passed, in societies with relatively equal distribution of income, the majority of people are satiatied with their grain intake. Japan reached this state in the 1980s.

In the 1950s, Japan and China enjoyed a roughly parallel growth in per capita grain consumption. Due to the failure of the Great Leap Forward, however, con-

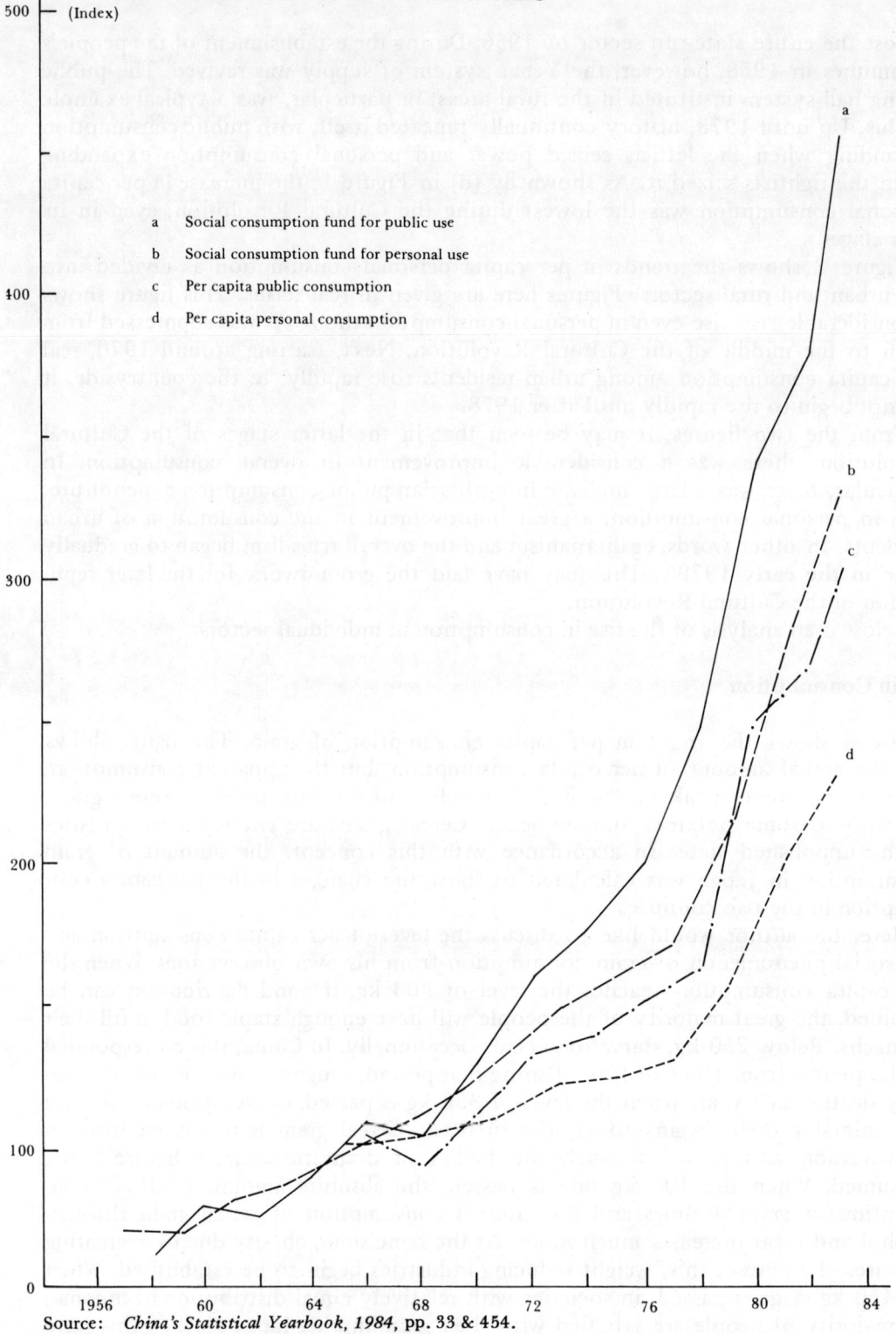

500 — (Index)

a   Social consumption fund for public use
b   Social consumption fund for personal use
c   Per capita public consumption
d   Per capita personal consumption

Source: *China's Statistical Yearbook, 1984,* pp. 33 & 454.

Figure 1. Expansion of Public Consumption

(in real terms, 1952 = 100)

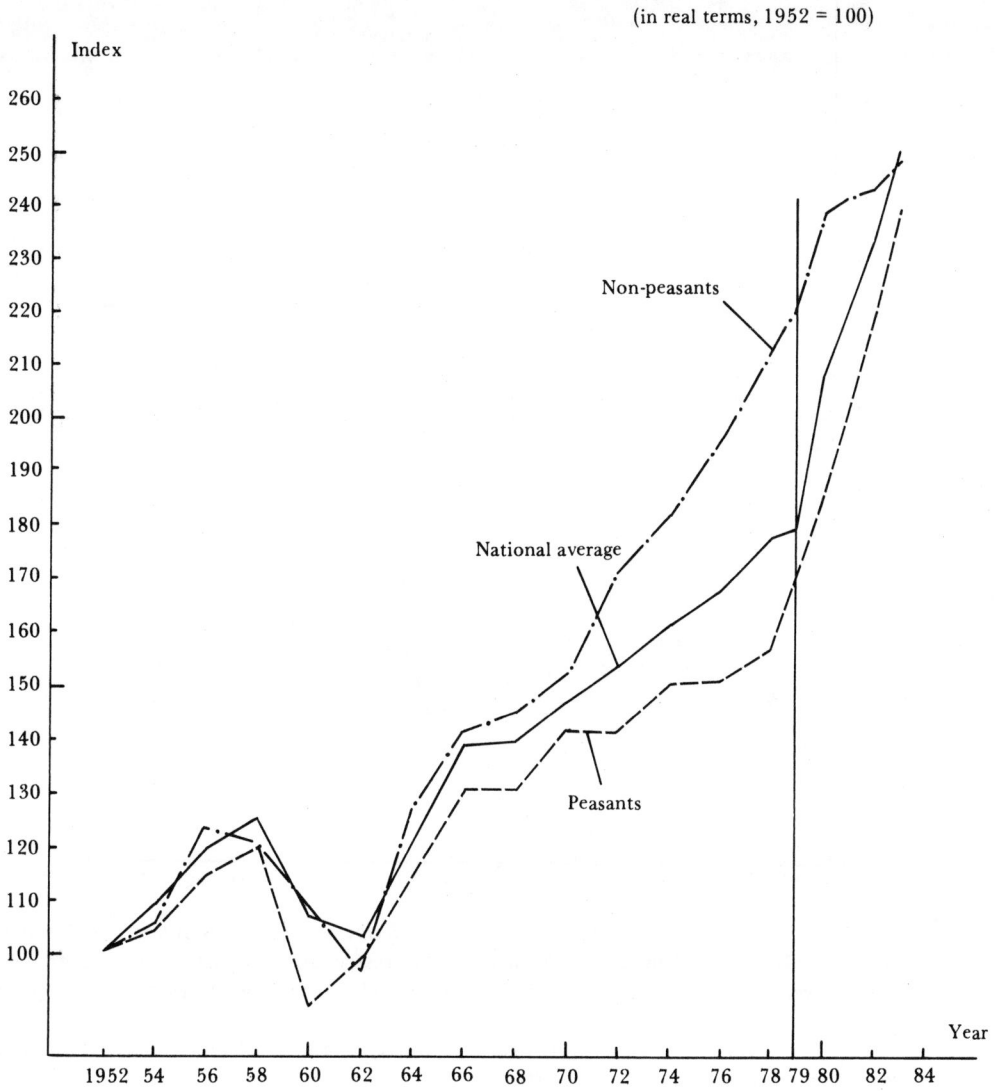

Source: *Ibid.*, p. 454.

Figure 2. Real Increase in People's Personal Expenditure
(Excluding Public Consumption)

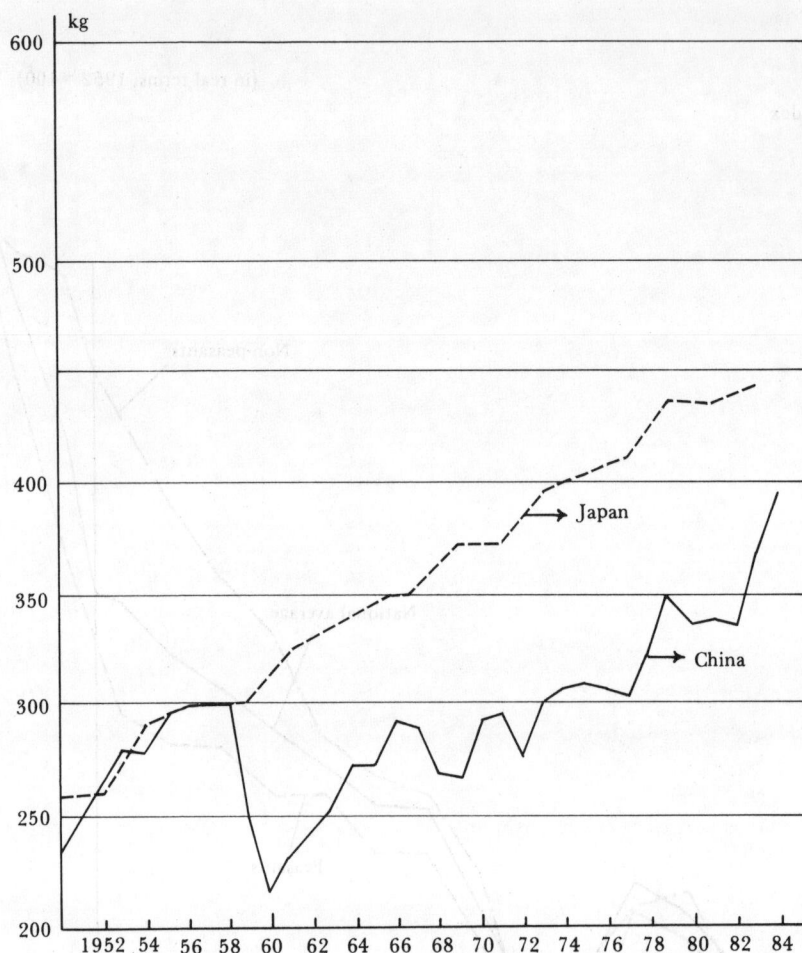

Sources: Japan, until 1975, *Shokuryo-Juyo ni kansuru Kisotokei* [Basic Statistics on Food De-
mand], edited by Ministry of Agriculture, Forestry and Fishing, 1976. After 1976,
Norintokeibyo [Agricultural Statistical Yearbook], edited by Ministry of Agriculture,
Forestry and fishing.
China: Until 1982, *China's Statistical Yearbook,* 1983, 1983/84, calculated from the
government annual economic reports.

Note 1: *Consumption Stages*
    250 kg line — below the line, frequent observance of death by starvation
    300 kg line — 'full stomach' state of staple food
    350 kg line — Start of sharp increase in meat and alcohol consumption
    400 kg line — Increase in number of alcoholics and rise of new activities such as jogging to
                reduce weight.
    450 kg line — Grain becomes side dish. Many over weight persons observed.

Note 2: *Concepts*
    1) Grain concept: gain + potatoes + soybeans
                  potatoes are converted to gain by 5 to 1.
    2) Unpolished
    3) Apparent consumption

Figure 3. Per Capita 'Food' and Consumption Stages

sumption in China fell drastically from 1959 to 1961 and it was not until the early 1970's that the 300 kg level was reached again. The Cultural Revolution ended in 1976, but the population had already enjoyed the "full stomach" state of staple food for several years. While China had completely freed itself from starvation, the Cultural Revolution faction had still been taking policies calling for severe frugality in daily life. The Vietnam War ended in May 1975 and it was unquestionably this which was behind the sudden relaxation in the strained domestic Chinese economy. The strength of the Cultural Revolution faction declined due to this situation. The people were enjoying their fill of staple foods and therefore sought a new level of consumption. The Cultural Revolution faction could not formulate policies meeting those demands.

Clothing Consumption

The same trend can be observed in the consumption of clothing. First, Figure 4 shows the per capita consumption of clothing in terms of yarn in China in the past years. In the six to seven year period from 1959 to the early 1960s, visitors to China reported they observed many people wearing patched up clothes even in Beijing and Shanghai. This phenomenon was caused by the great decline in production of cotton and the drive to export textiles in order to acquire the foreign exchange to repay the loans to the Soviet Union. The per capita consumption at the time was about 0.3 to 1.3 kg. When the per capita consumption passes the level of 2.5 kg, patched up clothing disappears from the cities. From the figure, it may be seen that clothing consumption was rapidly improved starting from around 1970.

When the per capita consumption passes the 7.5 kg level, people start wanting diverse designs and colorful patterns. Starting in the 1980s, Beijing, Shanghai, and other major cities reached this level. The people took off their ubiquitous navy blue people's uniforms and began to seek designs to countries with large textiles consumption. The national average was still 3.3 kg in 1982, but in 1983 the old rationing system for cotton cloth had already been abolished.

Figure 5 shows the relationship between national income and textile consumption. Textile consumption in China is low, so a comparison was made using materials on textile consumption in other countries in the 1960s. In the figure, the figures for China are only those for 1971 and 1981. The figures for the other countries are for 1961 and 1971. The lines for per capita consumption can be seen to level off once the 7.5 kg level is passed. In other words, once that level is passed, the elasticity of income to textile consumption falls under unity. Below this level, the elasticity of income is above one and, it may be seen, increases in income lead to rapid increases in textile consumption. China is just at that stage. This indicates that until its per capita national income reaches US$1,000, its textile supply will have to be rapidly increased. The CCP National Party Congress of September 1982 decided upon a target of increasing per capita national income to US$850 (1980 prices) by the year 2000. This means that China will probably have to increase its production of clothing by 10 percent or more annually upto 2000 or 2010.

Durable Consumer Goods

Figure 6 shows the rate of diffusion of durable consumer goods. Starting in the 1970s inexpensive durable consumer goods such as wristwatches and radios began to spread. With the onset of the Deng Xiaoping era, sewing machines and television

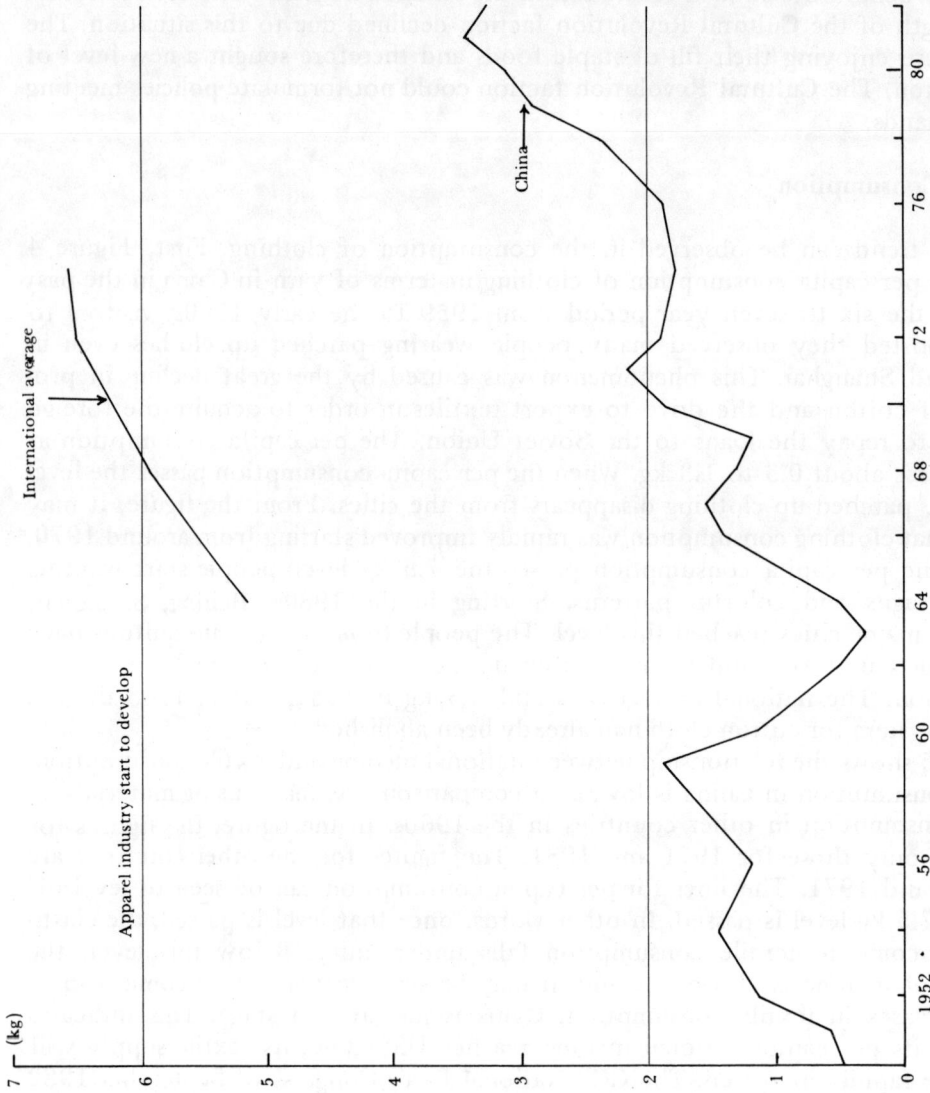

Source: Calculated from *China's Statistical Yearbooks* and others.

Note: Clothing is converted into yarn.

Figure 4. Per Capita Apparent Consumption in Terms of Yarn

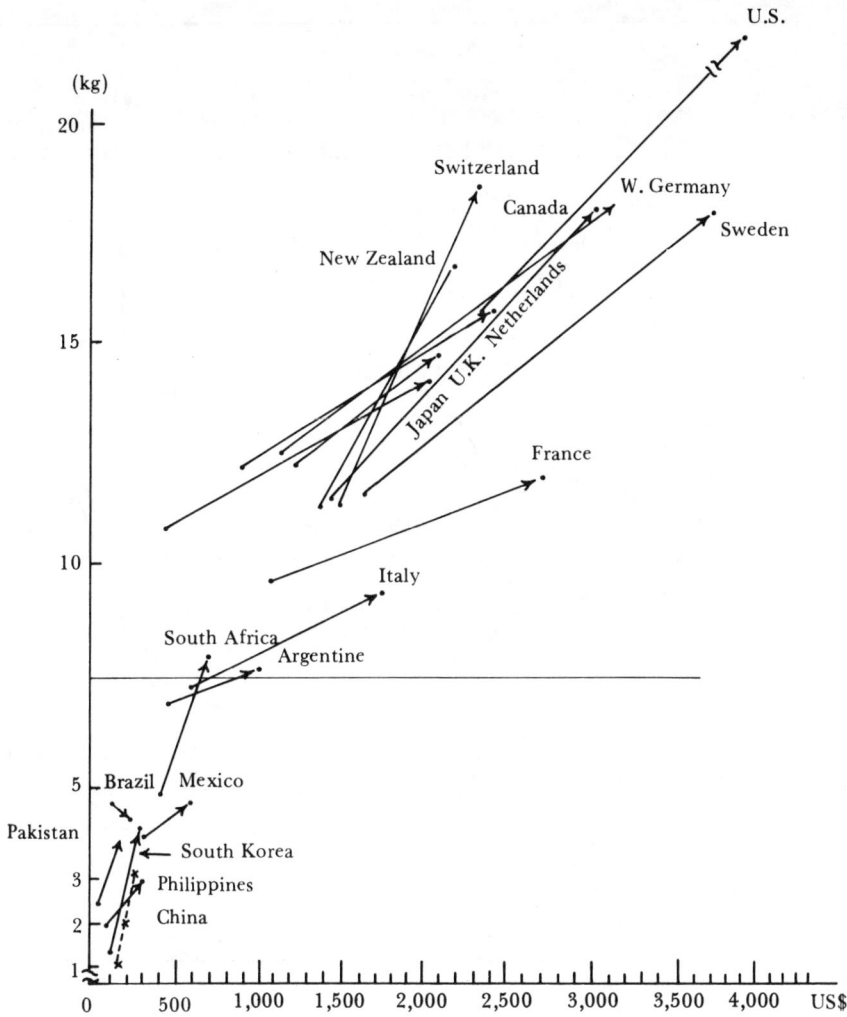

Source: R. Kojima, 'Industry', in *Long- and Middle-Term Projection of China's Economy*, edited
by S. Ishikawa, R. Kojima & S. Sekiguchi, p. 91.

Figure 5. International Comparison of Per Capita Textile Consumption

sets began to rapidly spread. Taking television sets as an example, the method of
diffusion resembles that in Japan around 1959 and 1960. In general, durable consumer goods rapidly spread when their price falls to the equivalent of about two
months of a worker's salary. This was the experience in Japan in the 1950s and
1960s. In China too, though there have been no verification studies, it would seem
that this is generally a rule of thumb. In Japan, mass production lines for television
sets were established around 1960, allowing the relative price of television sets to
be lowered. Further, there were two major events in the process of diffusion. One
was the marriage of the Crown Prince in 1959. The rate of diffusion rose 30 percent

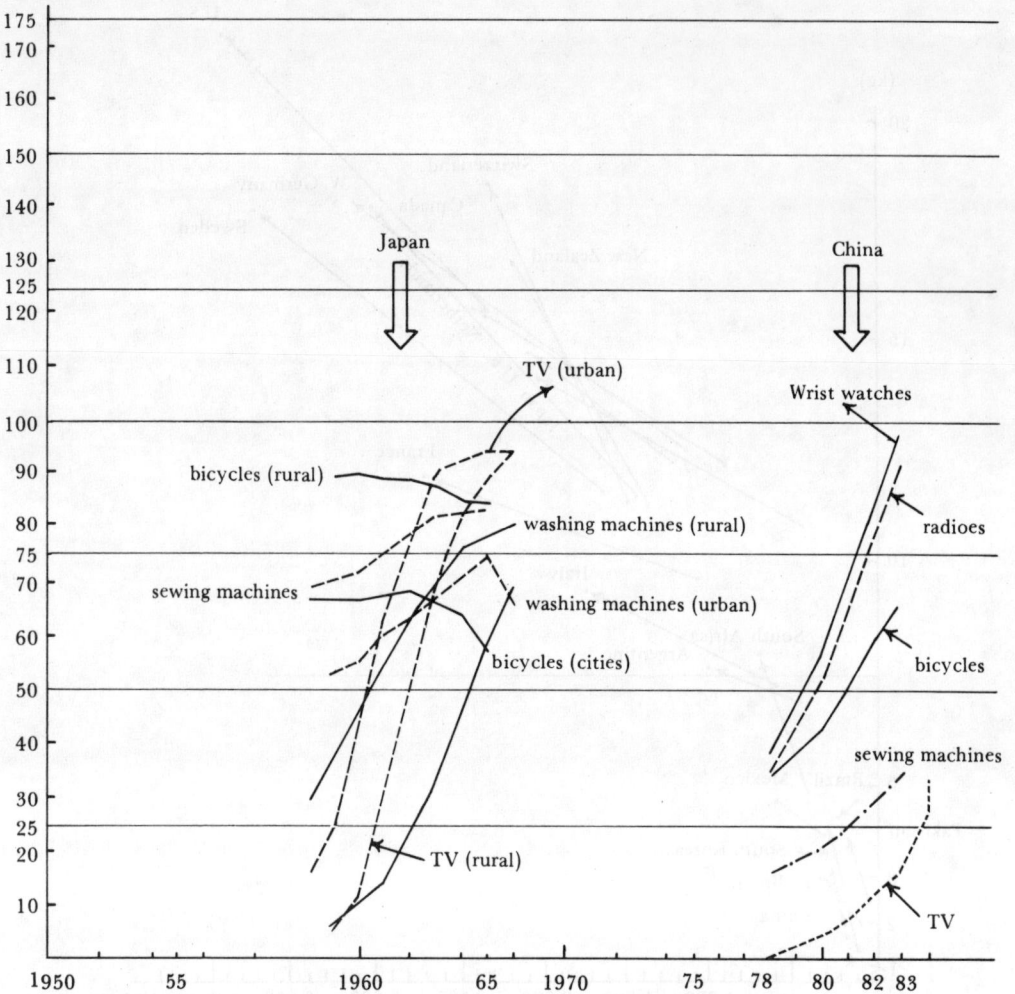

Sources: Japan, *Shobido-ko-chosa* [Consumption Survey, Annual Report], Economic Planning Agency.

China, *China's Statistical Yearbook*, 1984 and others.

Figure 6. Diffusion Rate of Consumers' Durables

in a year's period among urban households as they wished to watch the ceremony on television. The other event was the sponsoring of the Olympics in Tokyo in 1964. At this time, urban households began changing over from black and white televisions to color televisions.

In 1988, the Olympics will be held in Seoul. The fervor among the Chinese people to buy televisions is expected to become much stronger as they will wish to watch the event. Therefore, television sets may be expected to spread most rapidly in the coming few years. However, one-third of the countryside still does not have electricity. This corresponds to about 60 million households. The remaining 120 million households in the rural region may be expected to have television by the beginning of the 1990s.

The diffusion of television sets is accompanied simultaneously with the diffusion of other electrical appliances. Considering this, the coming 10 years should be a period of rapid diffusion of medium level durable consumer goods.

Public Consumption — Increase in Educational Expenses

Public consumption includes public consumption facilities in the cities, social security, medical and health care, and the like. Here, the subject of educational expenses is considered. Since no data concerning educational expenses as a whole could be obtained, it was decided to look at it through the trends in the number of students in school.

Figure 7 shows indexes of the number of students registered in primary schools, junior secondary schools, and senior secondary schools using 1957 as 100. The number of registered students in primary schools (A) was highest in 1975, being 2.35 times that of 1957. No sharp increase is recognized since the rate of school attendance had already reached 80 percent[1] by 1965. After 1976, the number declined due to the decline in births starting 1973. After 1982, the people's communes were dismantled and a return made to individual farming. Under this system, the number of farmers who make their children quit school to help with farm work has increased and the rate of school attendance has also been declining.

In the figure, a point which should be noted is the rapid increase in the number of students undergoing junior secondary school education during the Cultural Revolution, from 1966 to 1976. What caused this rapid increase? It was the spirit of egalitarianism which reigned during the Cultural Revolution and the construction of junior secondary schools and senior secondary schools by the people's communes. The CCP allocated only limited funds for this, so school construction was promoted as a task of the people's communes. This policy resulted in suppression of personal consumption by the farmers. However, the proportion of public consumption in the national income increased.

Line D indicates the trend in the number of students in universities. It is true that this dropped sharply during the Cultural Revolution. It has been said that education was destroyed during the Cultural Revolution. However, as can be seen from the figure, primary, junior secondary, and senior secondary school education actually progressed. The only thing destroyed was university education. Starting with the Deng Xiaoping era, the number of students in junior and senior secondary schools began to drop rapidly.

Viewed overall, up until the late 1970s, the percent of educational expenses in the national income can be estimated to have increased.

Housing Construction

Housing construction constitutes the greatest expense sector in all items of consumption. Trends in those expenses may be seen in Figures 8 and 9. Figure 8

---

[1]   Zhang, Jian.*"Renzhen Yanjiu Shiho Guomingjingji Fazhan Xuyao de Jiaoyujihua he Jiaoyutizhi" [To study seriously educational plan and system to fit for national economic development], *Renmin Jiaoyu* [People's education], 1980, No. 8, p. 16.

  *   *China's Economic Annual 1981* (Chinese edition), Economic Management Magazine Co., p. VI-26.

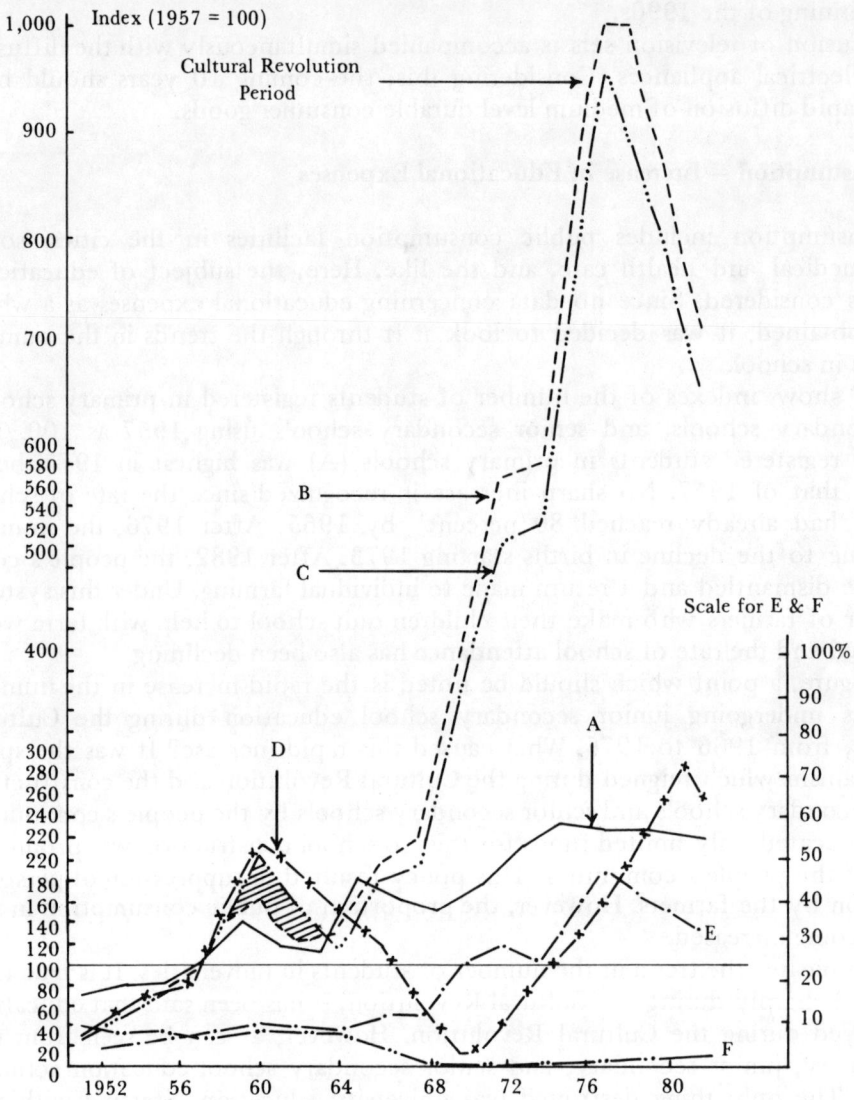

Source: *China's Statistical Yearbook, 1983*, p. 511.

Note: Number of pupils of primary schools.
        Number of students in senior secondary high school.
        Ordinary high school students plus vocational school students.
        University & college students.
        B over A (right scale).
        D over B (right scale).

Figure 7. Development in Education during Cultural Revolution Period —
Number of Students According to School Students (1957 = 100)

Figure 8. Housing Construction in Cities (1957 = 100)

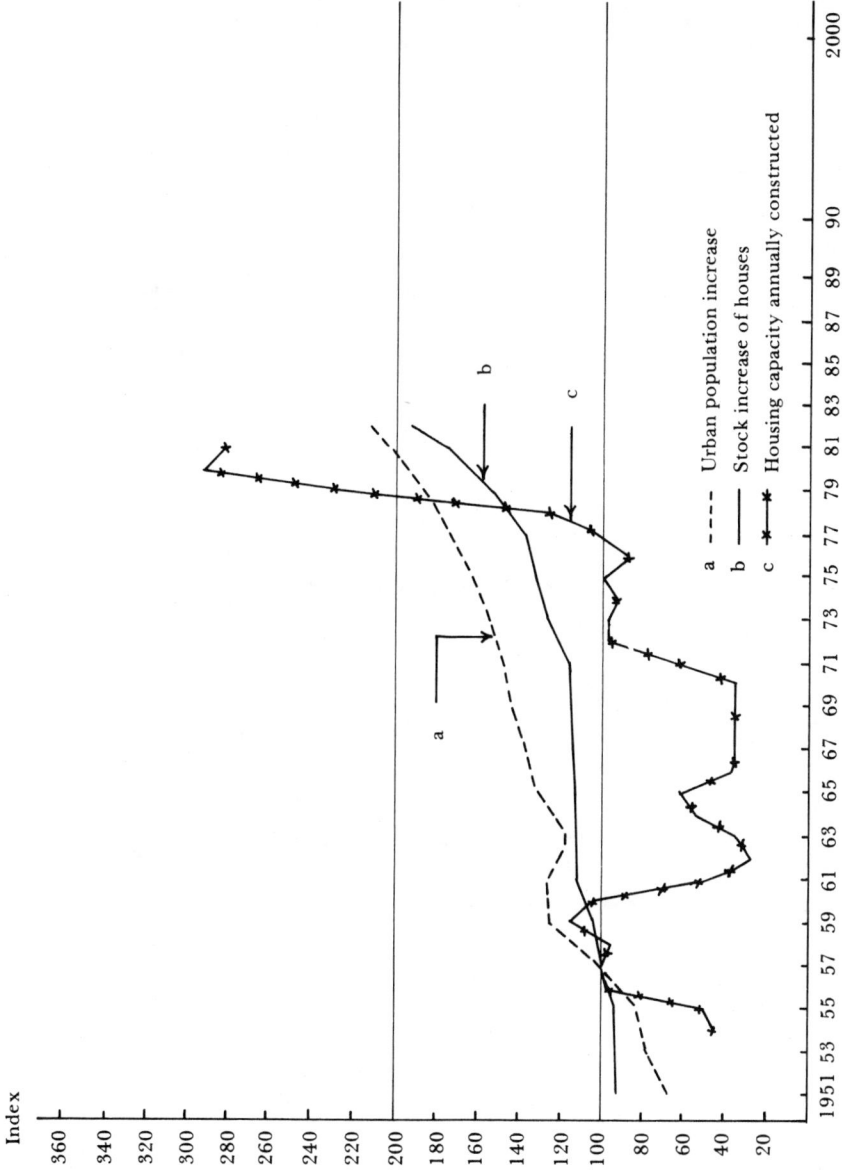

Source: R. Kojima; 'Industry' in *Long- and Middle-Term Projection of China's Economy*, edited by S. Ishikawa, R. Kojima & S. Sekiguchi, p. 78.

a - - - - Urban population increase
b ——— Stock increase of houses
c ✱—✱ Housing capacity annually constructed

Index

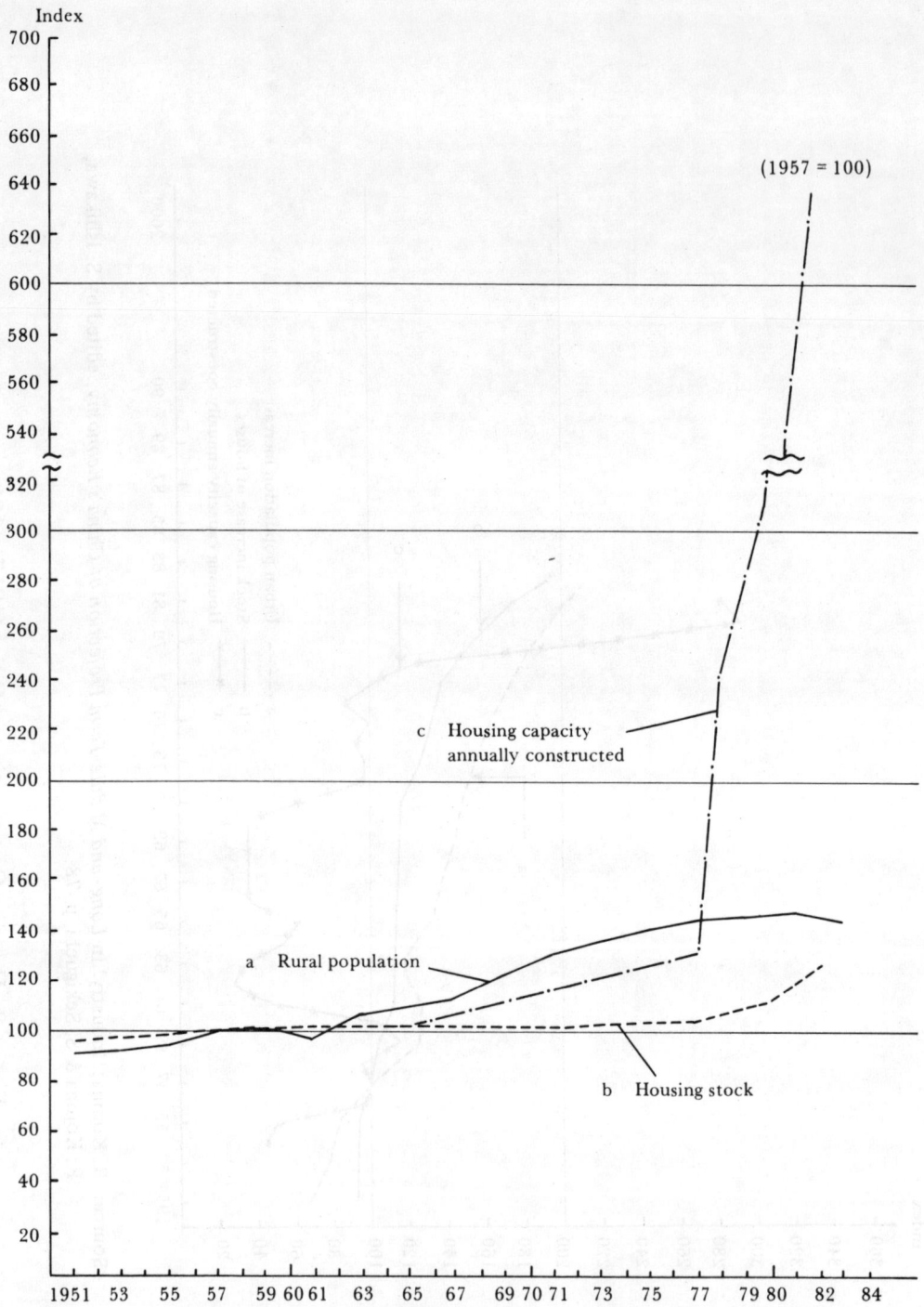

Sources: *China's Statistical Yearbook,* 1984 and other various sources.

Figure 9. Housing Construction in Countryside

shows the state of housing in the cities and Figure 9 that in the countryside. In both figures, the trends in urban and rural population are shown by (a) with 1957 as 100. Line (b) shows the stock of housing and (c) the flow. In both figures, it may be seen that (a) and (b) have gradually been growing apart since 1957. In other words, the per capita housing area has been deteriorating. For example, in the cities, the per capita housing area in 1950 was 4.5 m².² In 1978, it fell to 3.6 m².³ This resulted from the drastic cutbacks on housing construction investment in the 1960s and 1970s. During that period, China allocated its domestic resources to the development of modern weapons, support to the North Vietnamese, and assistance to Africa. In both the cities and countryside, as shown by (c), new housing construction began to increase rapidly from 1978. In the rural regions, the large increases in the government purchase price of agricultural products in 1979 created a rise in income, enabling massive new housing construction. In the cities, government organizations and state-run enterprises began giving priority to housing construction. Figure 10 shows the trends in the share of housing investment in China's capital construction investment. In China, capital investment is divided into productive investment and nonproductive investment. Housing investment belongs to nonproductive investment. From the figure, it will be seen that the share of housing investment was low from 1958 to 1978, accounting for just 3 to 8 percent of total capital investment. In 1981 and 1982, this share leaped to 25 percent.

As seen above, with the exception of housing investment, real consumption has been rising, even with the Cultural Revolution. In particular, the rise in public consumption has been striking. Seen overall, starting in the 1970s, the Chinese people have been guaranteed their basic human consumption requirements. Having reached that stage, they are now seeking a better quality of life. The Cultural Revolution faction failed to establish policies satisfying this newly blooming desire of the people. The Deng Xiaoping administration may be said to have made its appearance to solve this problem.

ECONOMIC REFORMS AND OVERHEATED INVESTMENT

The purpose of the recent economic reforms has been to change the economic system of the Mao Zedong era, that enabled high savings, to a new system enabling satisfaction of rising consumer demand. The reforms began with the countryside and, even in 1985, have been leading to reforms of the overall national economy.

Dismantling of People's Communes

Up until 1949, the revolution in China was led by the revolution in the countryside. The economic construction policies after the establishment of the PRC continued to be considerably influenced by trends in the rural areas. The rapid "leftward shift" in 1956 to 1958 was caused by the acceleration of rural collectivization. The "rightward shift" after 1979 began with the institutional reforms in the people's communes.

The December 1978 session of the Central Committee of the CCP made two

---

² Si, Xing. "Zhenyang shi Zhuzhai Wenti Jiejue de Kuaixie" [How to quickly solve housing problems], *Hongqi* [Red flag], 1980, No. 2, p. 8.
³ Xue Xin's article, *Guangmingribao,* Oct. 17, 1981, p. 3.

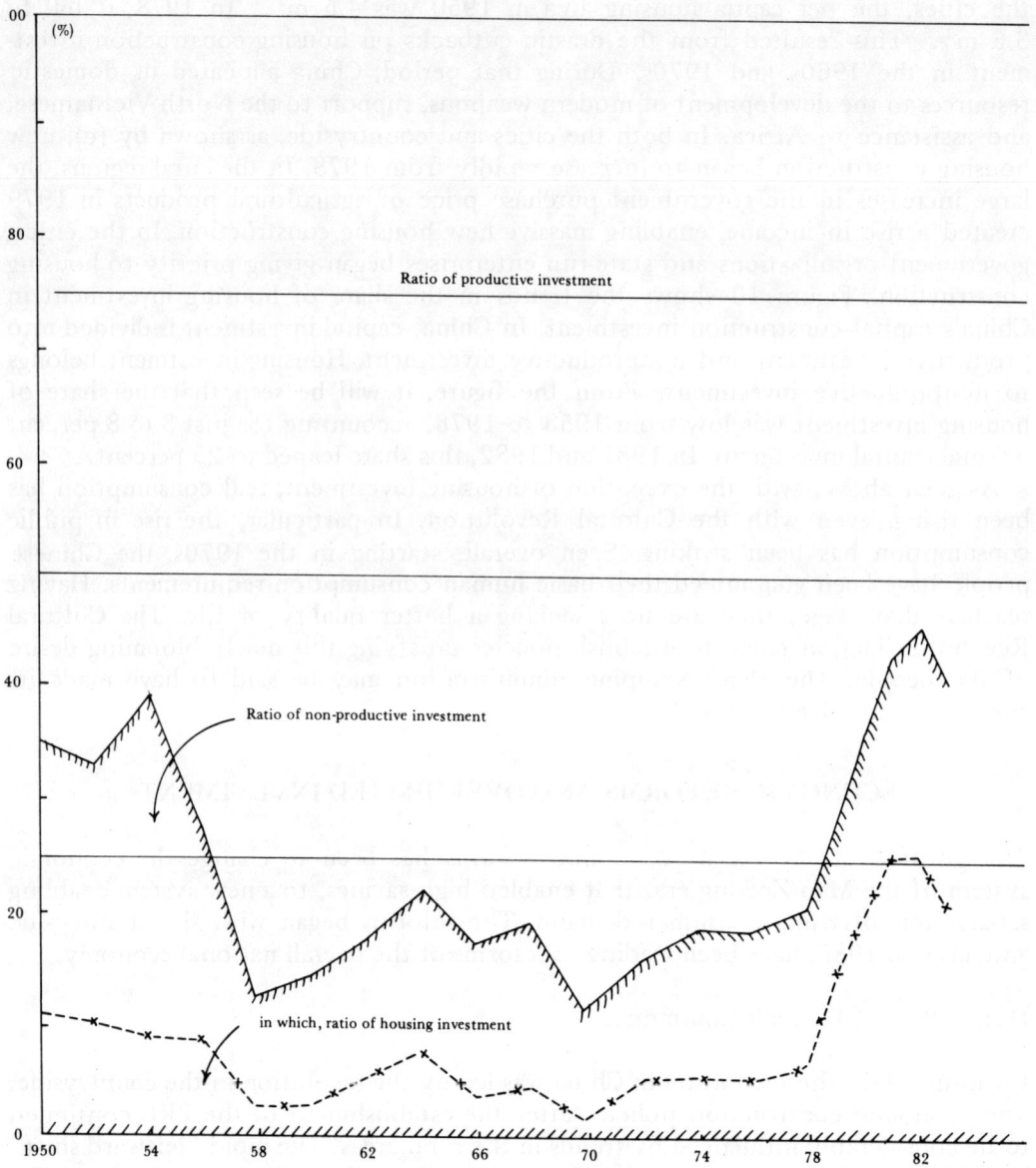

Sources: 1. *China's Statistical Yearbook, 1983,* p. 339 (Chinese edition).
2. 1983 figure, *ibid.* 1984, p. 318.

Figure 10. Investment Structure and Housing Investment

decisions. One was to raise the government purchase price of agricultural products from 1979 and the other was to give greater respect to the autonomy of production teams, the smallest production units of those times.

Figure 11 shows the indexes of government purchase prices of agricultural products with 1950 as 100. In the 1950s, these prices rose gradually every year. In 1961, China faced an agricultural crisis and raised prices drastically. In subsequent years, however, until 1978, government purchase prices were generally kept down. In 1979, however, they were raised by an average 25 percent all at once. At the same time, the government tacked on a 50 percent premium on all products sold to it after the obligatory amount was supplied. This double pricing system prompted farmers to sell at the premium prices and ended up considerably raising the overall price of agricultural products procured by the government. This led to a massive fiscal deficit.

Figure 12 shows the process of destruction of the people's communes. The people's communes were divided into three levels in their internal organization: the management committees of the people's communes, the production brigades, and the production teams. Of these, the production teams were the smallest units. They engaged in the agricultural production and were the basic accounting units. The higher units, the management committees and the production brigades engaged in water conservation projects, construction of schools, forestry, and other major projects and procured funds, labor, materials, and the like from the production teams. A December 1978 decision banned higher units from procuring various production requirements from the production teams and stressed the strengthening of the authority of the production teams.

The Central Committee of the CCP did not take much initiative in dismantling the people's communes. In the process of strengthening the authority of the production teams, individual farms appeared in Anhui province in 1980. The movement to dismantle the communes spread like a prairie fire and led to the rapid transition to individual farms from late 1981 to 1982. The Central Committee of the CCP was forced to extend belated recognition of these. This was with the first document of the Central Committee of the CCP of January 1985. There, the CCP set a term of no less than 15 years for leasing of land from village governments to farmers. There was no upper limit set. In the case of opening up wasteland, rental of land for 30 to 50 years is now possible. Further, while the village governments own forest land, it was prescribed that persons planting trees could pass them on to their descendants.

The reforms in the agricultural system went a step further in 1985. During the era of the people's communes, agricultural production targets were all set by the county governments. The production teams did not have the authority to freely select the types of agricultural products to plant. The government held a firm grasp over the direct production process. With the dissolution of the people's communes, the government was no longer able to control production through issuing orders. Instead, it took the method of controlling it from the distribution stage, allocating compulsory amounts of agricultural products to be supplied from each farm. In other words, it used an indirect method. However, starting from 1983, China entered an era of surplus agricultural production. 1984 was a year of a bumper harvest. This ended up increasing the fiscal burden on the government even more. For this reason, the government abolished the compulsory supply system in 1985 and established a limited purchasing system. For example, it set an upper limit on

Index

400

300

Purchase price index of
agricultural products (a)

250

200

150

Retail price index of
industrial goods (b)

100

50

(b)
(a)

0
1950   1960   1970   1980

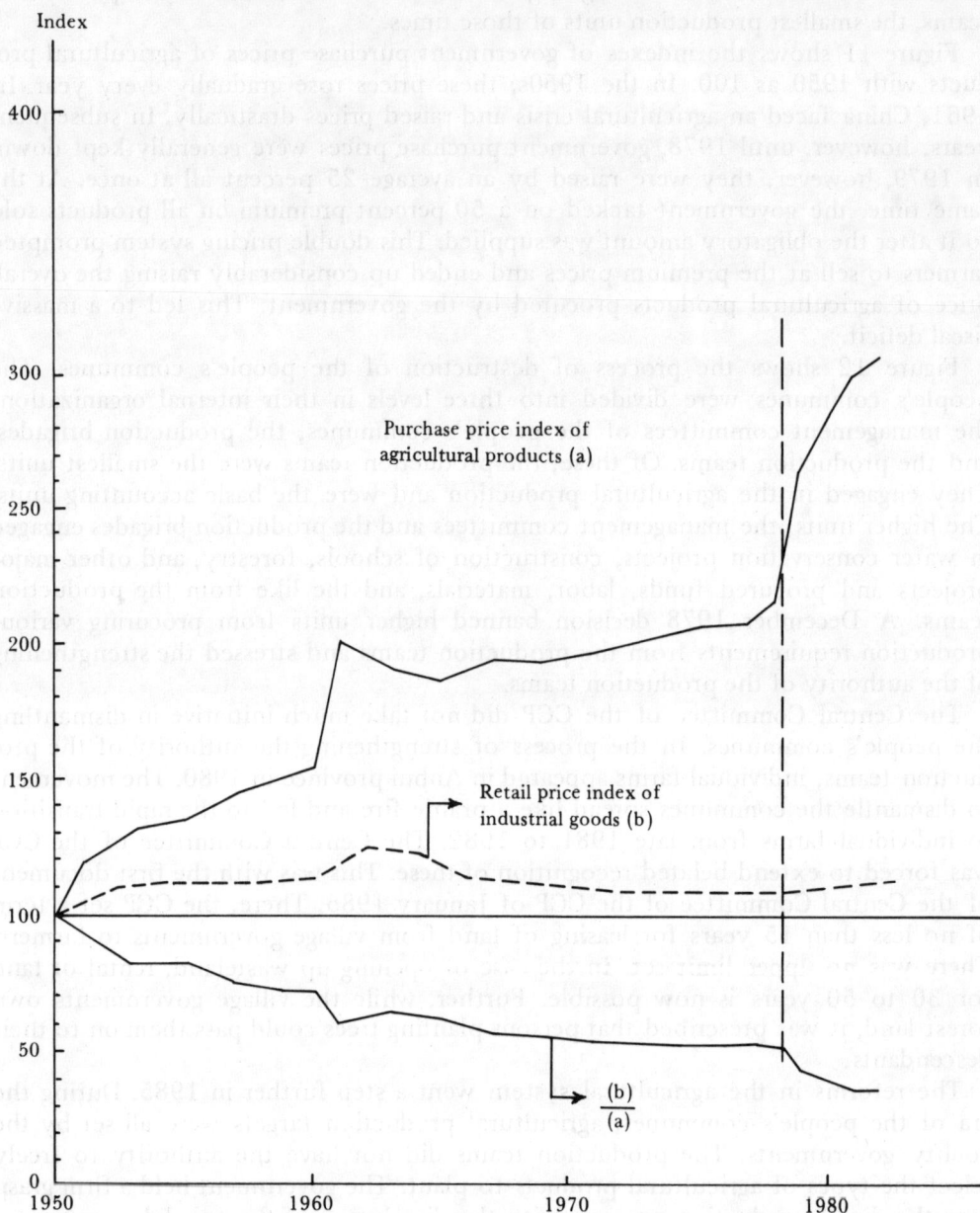

Source: *China's Statistical Yearbook*, 1983, p. 455.

Figure 11. Government Purchase Prices of Agricultural Products
and Retail Prices of Industrial Goods in Countryside

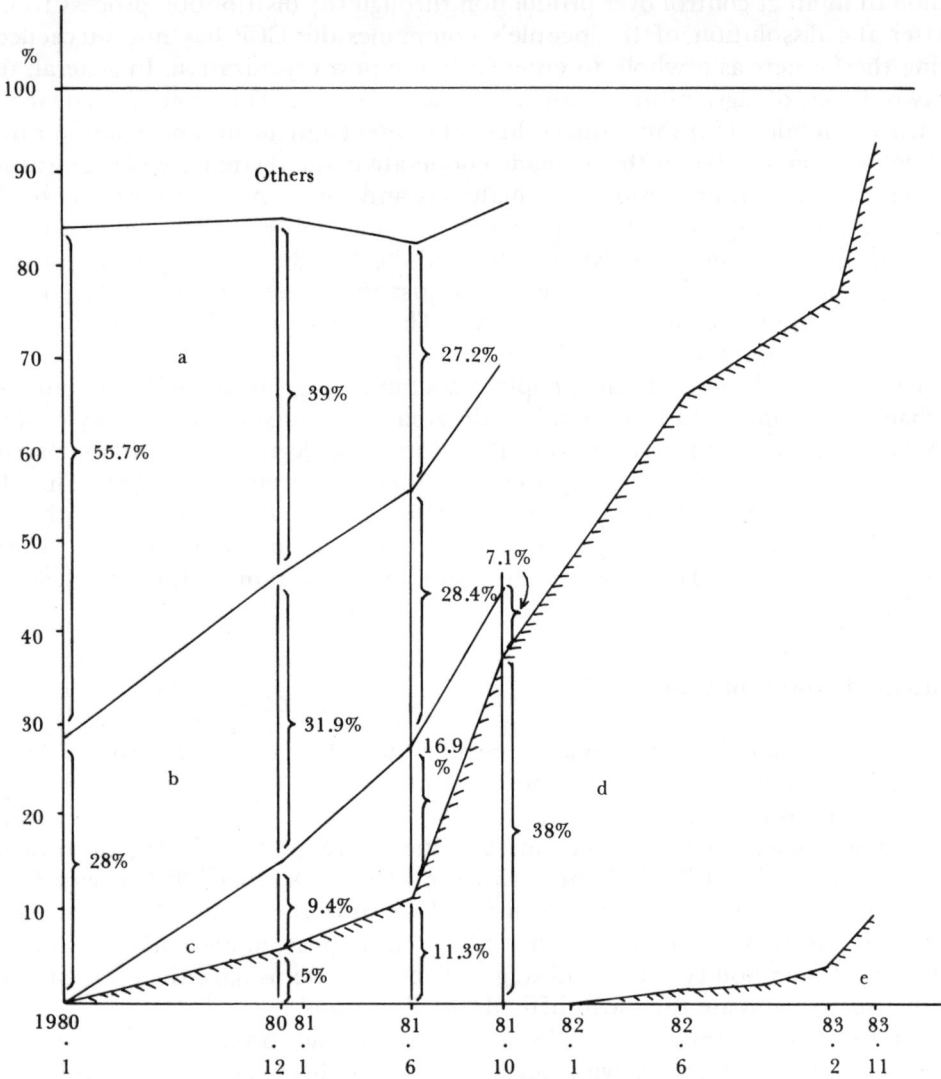

Source: *Chugoku no Keizai Kaikaku to Kaiho Seisaku* [Economic reform and open door policy in China] (in Japanese), Tokyo; Institute of Developing Economies, July 1986, p. 12.

Note: a   — People's communes
        b c — Transitional forms
        d   — Individual farming system
        e   — Private specialized households. So called 'wanyuanhu' (10 thousand yuan income households) come out from this group. At present 100 — 500 thousand yuan income households have appeared.

Figure 12. Dissolution of People's Communes

purchases of grain of 80 million tons. It allowed the farmers to sell any amount over that to anyone they wished. In other words, the government abolished the method of indirect control over production through the distribution process too.

After the dissolution of the people's communes, the CCP has not succeeded in getting the farmers as a whole to enter into any new organization. In general, there are two types of agricultural cooperative associations. The first is that seen in socialist economies, i.e., the model where the direct agricultural production process is made cooperative. When this is made cooperative, the related pre-planting aspects of supply of agricultural production materials and the post-harvest aspects of shipment and processing of the produce are also inevitably made cooperative. The second is that seen in capitalist societies, where the direct production process is left in the hands of individual farmers and just the related input supply and post-harvest operations are made cooperative. The Japanese agricultural cooperative associations are typical examples of the latter type.

Since the dissolution of the people's communes, great numbers of individual merchants have appeared in China, but they have not organized into any powerful cooperative associations as in Japan. Therefore, the degree of economic freedom of the farmers in China may be greater than their counterparts in Japan. This alone has resulted in greater freedom in the rural economy. For this reason, the rural economy is undergoing very rapid growth. At the same time, however, it is suffering from severe problems. These will be discussed in the section entitled, "Bottlenecks in Four Sectors."

Economic Reforms in Cities

The reforms of the economic management system begin in 1979, roughly at the same time as the reforms of the people's communes. The dismantling of the people's communes, however, proceeded too rapidly. Compared with that, the reforms of the economic management system in the cities were gradual. In the third plenary session of the National Party Congress of the CCP of October 1984, it was decided to deemphasize rural economic reforms and to shift the focus of reforms to the cities. The results of urban reforms had not been so great, in particular, with respect to reform of commodity prices and wages. These two items have the greatest impact on other sectors and are the most difficult of all reforms.

In matters of reform of a socialist system, China has predecessors in the Soviet Union and Eastern Europe, who began to reform their economies in the 1960s. These reforms took two directions. One left the economy under the control of the administrative authorities, but transferred power from the central government to local governments. The reforms of the Soviet Union and East Germany were of that type. The other basically expanded use of the market mechanism. This was the type adopted by Yugoslavia and Hungary. Up until 1978, China had repeatedly experimented with reforms of the former type. Since 1979, however, it seems to have gone over to the latter type. Therefore, the focus is being placed on expanded use of the market mechanism.

The biggest aim of the reforms of the economic management system is the reform of the extremely centralized administrative control methods and the creation, from the enterprises, of relatively independent economic entities. This can be rephrased to mean the creation of a system for evaluating enterprises by improvements in productivity and production performance and a system for the evaluation of workers, either in groups or as individuals, by their performance within the enterprises. Previous state-run enterprises were supplied with the funds, materials, and labor required for construction from the government treasury. For example, the government used to provide 100 percent of the equipment investment and 70 percent of the working capital from the treasury on a grant basis. The only funds which the enterprises could procure on their own judgement were 30 percent of the working capital. The distribution of profits was made in accordance with set provisions through payment of profit to higher authorities and through taxes, with almost the entire amount going to the government. The only amount the enterprises could use freely was the portion they were able to retain due to having exceeded their targets. China has implemented the following reforms to this basic system.

Change of Medium and Small Scale State-Run Enterprises into Collectively Owned Enterprises

In the past, the state-run enterprises were placed under the direct management of the government. As against this, the collectively owned enterprises were placed under indirect control. While the government would not use its funds to resolve problems of collectively owned enterprises, those enterprises only had to pay certain prescribed taxes. The collectively owned enterprises also enjoyed less direct control from the government than the state-run enterprises in areas such as appointments or dismissals of enterprise managers, orders for obligatory production, etc. In other words, they had far more self-management rights. In the economic reforms of the past six years, China has been changing its state-run medium and small scale enterprises into such collectively owned enterprises.

Financial Reforms

China's financial institutions have traditionally only functioned as entry clerks for state finances. This system has been changed and the banks have been given the function of checking up on the economic activities of the state-run enterprises. When fiscal funds are turned over to the enterprises, they are now passed through the banks with interest charged. The aim of this is to improve the turnover of funds, so that the performance of the enterprises would also be improved. Further, for working capital, China has switched over completely to bank loans. Also, the Chinese have significantly increased bank autonomy, allowing banks to make loans to enterprises for equipment investment and technical renovation funds of a non-massive size.

Expansion of Funds Retained By Enterprises

A basic reform for building up enterprises, not as appendages of the administrative government but as independent economic entities is the expansion of funds retained by the enterprises. In the past, enterprises were only allowed to retain a portion of their profits from surplus production and a very small portion of their depreciation expenses as enterprise funds. They are now able to retain part of the target production profits themselves, 50 percent of the depreciation expenses, and 40 percent of the profits from surplus production. Aside from this, they can keep items prescribed by the state, such as technical renovation funds. The amount of funds available to be used by the enterprises has been increased considerably.

Expansion of Management Powers of Enterprises Managers
In the past, the party committees inside the enterprises held the absolute authority
in matters of management. The position of enterprises, as were appendages of the
administrative government was due in fact to the power of the party committees.
To correct this situation, it has been decided that the party committees may decide
the general direction of the enterprises, but specific matters of enterprise management should be left to the enterprise managers. Further, the enterprise managers
have been given increased authority over personnel matters.

Reduction of Production Items Under Direct State Control
This is one of the measures taken to expand use of the market mechanism. In 1985,
the 123 *command type* production items which had previously been controlled by
the State Planning Commission were reduced to 60. Along with this, the items
under the control of the ministries and provincial governments were also reduced
sharply. Before 1979, capital goods were under the direct control of the *State
Commodites Bureau* and did not pass through the market. Starting from 1980,
China has created a market for some capital goods. In 1985, the 250 capital goods
under the direct control of the *State Commodities Bureau* were cut to 65.[4]

Further, enterprises previously were not allowed to sell their own products on
their own. They may now sell on the market up to 2 percent of their target production and their entire surplus production — even for capital goods. At that time,
the price is allowed to be set anywhere in a range of 20 percent above or below the
official price.[5]

China is implementing numerous other reforms aside from the above. Next, let
us study what kind of situation these reforms and the dissolution of the people's
communes are creating.

Impact of Reforms in Economic System on National Economy

Since the dissolution of the people's communes, the CCP has not yet succeeded
in creating any sort of organization for steering the now independent peasants in
any particular direction. In the urban economy, enterprises with sufficient funds
are also beginning to engage in economic activities other than those intended by
the government. Here, we look at the kind of phenomena occurring in the running
of the macroeconomy.

Stagnation of Fiscal Revenue and Massive Fiscal Deficits
Figure 13 shows the indexes of fiscal revenue and expenditure with 1957 as 100.
One glance will clearly show that China has suffered from massive fiscal deficits
since the economic reforms were begun in 1979. Fiscal revenues stagnated in the
five years from 1979. Fiscal deficits continued for the seven years from 1978. This
situation had never occurred before in the history of the PRC. Even during the
latter half of the Great Leap Forward, when economic conditions were at their
worst, China only suffered from a deficit for three years. According to recent

[4] *People's Daily*, April 13, 1985, p. 2.
[5] Guo, Wuyuan. "Guanyu Jinyibu Kuoda Guoyinggongyeqiye Zizhuquan de Zanxingguiding" [State council, the provision on enlargement of state-run industrial firm's decision-making], *Xinhuayuebao*, 1984, No. 5, p. 129.

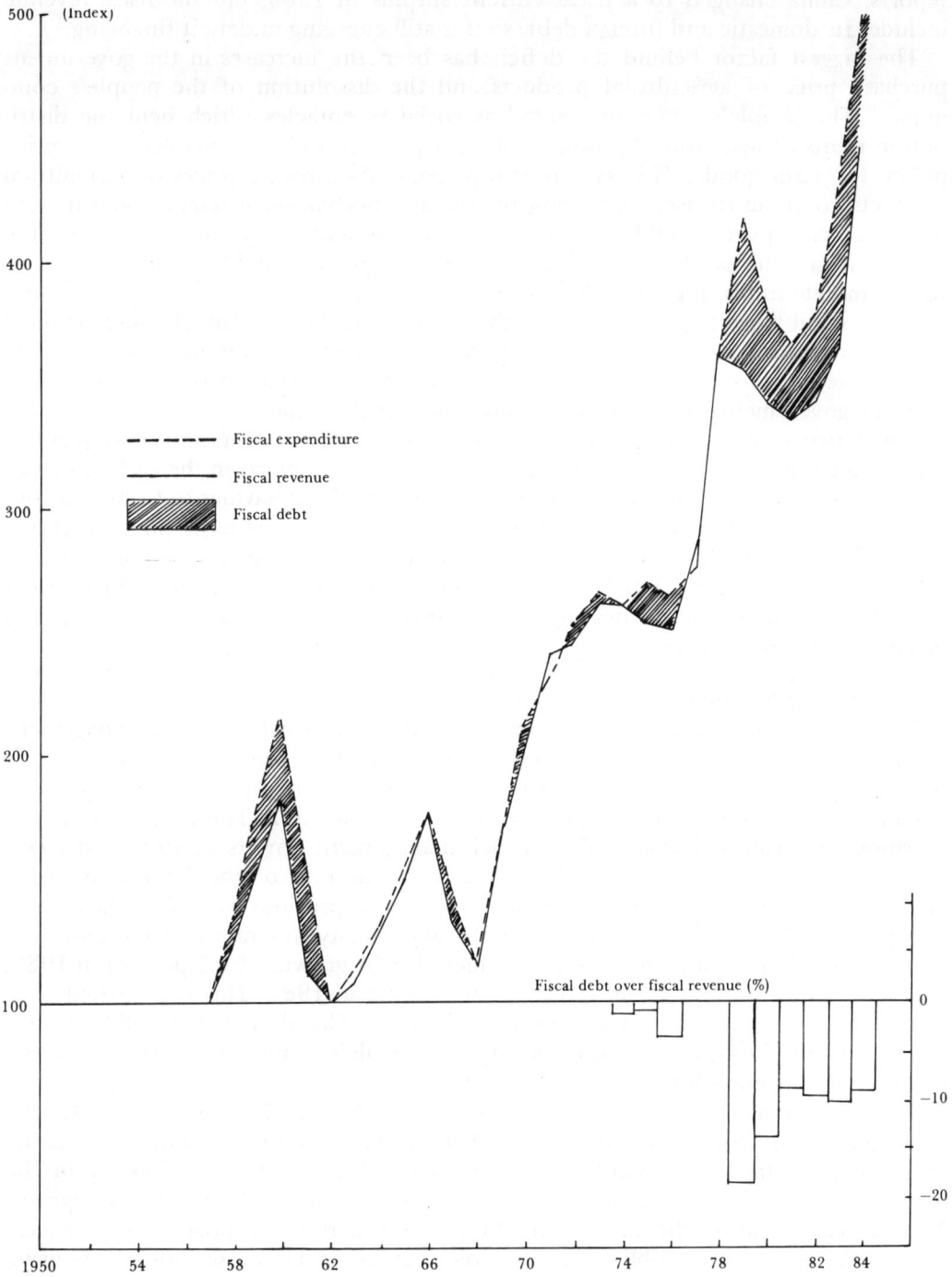

Source: *China's Statistical Yearbook, 1983,* p. 445.

Figure 13. Budget Revenue and Expenditure

reports, China changed to a fiscal current surplus in 1985, but the fiscal revenue includes its domestic and foreign debt, so it is still engaging in deficit financing.

The biggest factor behind the deficit has been the increases in the government purchase price of agricultural products and the dissolution of the people's communes. The people's communes acted as social receptacles which held the distribution rights of agricultural products of each peasant and thus enabled a low price policy for farm goods. This system is now gone. As a result, prices of agricultural products continue to rise, destroying the savings mechanism wherein state-run light industrial enterprises could acquire inexpensive agricultural products, process the same, and sell the products at a high price to the people, enabling the government to accumulate funds. Figure 13 shows this fiscal situation.

The second biggest factor has been the increase in the amount of funds retained by the enterprises, as explained above. In the past, most of those funds were entered as fiscal revenue. They have now come under the management of the enterprises, with the government having lost direct control over the same.

These two changes have resulted in increases in consumption and investment in the national income. This situation has already been discussed in the earlier section under heading Structural Changes in the Economy — From Savings to Consumption.

Up until 1978, China considered self-reliance as one of its basic policies. It had denounced the method of relying on foreign debt for economic construction. However, starting from 1979, it had no choice but to embark upon investment using foreign loans. The greatest reasons for this were the two changes in the savings mechanism discussed here.

Overheating of Economy
The dissolution of the people's communes and the expansion of self-management among the enterprises created an overheated state of the economy. Figure 14 shows the economic performance of China using macroeconomic indicators. The people's communes had almost all disappeared by the end of 1982. The enterprises began to enjoy full scale expansion of their self-management powers in 1983 and 1984. In this figure, the line graph indicates the growth rate of the Chinese national income (net domestic material product) over each previous year. The high rates in 1977 and 1978 were in reaction to the abnormally low rate in 1976 and were thus abnormal. The Chinese economy achieved high growth of 8.5 percent in 1982, 9 percent in 1983, and no less than 12.6 percent in 1984. This high growth rate owed much to favorable agricultural production. The dark bar graphs indicate total agricultural output. This includes the old people's commune enterprises, which enjoyed striking growth rates.

Total industrial output grew 11.5 percent in 1983 and 14 percent in 1984. This abnormal overheating from the second half of 1984 continued and failed to be suppressed by the government in the first half of 1985. The overheating in the industrial sector arose from the urban state-run enterprises and the rural enterprises. The reason for the overheating among the urban state-run enterprises was the excess investment and excess public consumption engaged in by those enterprises using their abundant funds in disregard of the central government's wishes. Figures since 1984 have not be obtained, but the trends in the amount of investment by investment entities up until 1983 are shown in Figure 15. China's investment statistics are divided into budget investment and extra-budget investment. The former is the investment performed using state finances, and the latter is the investment perform-

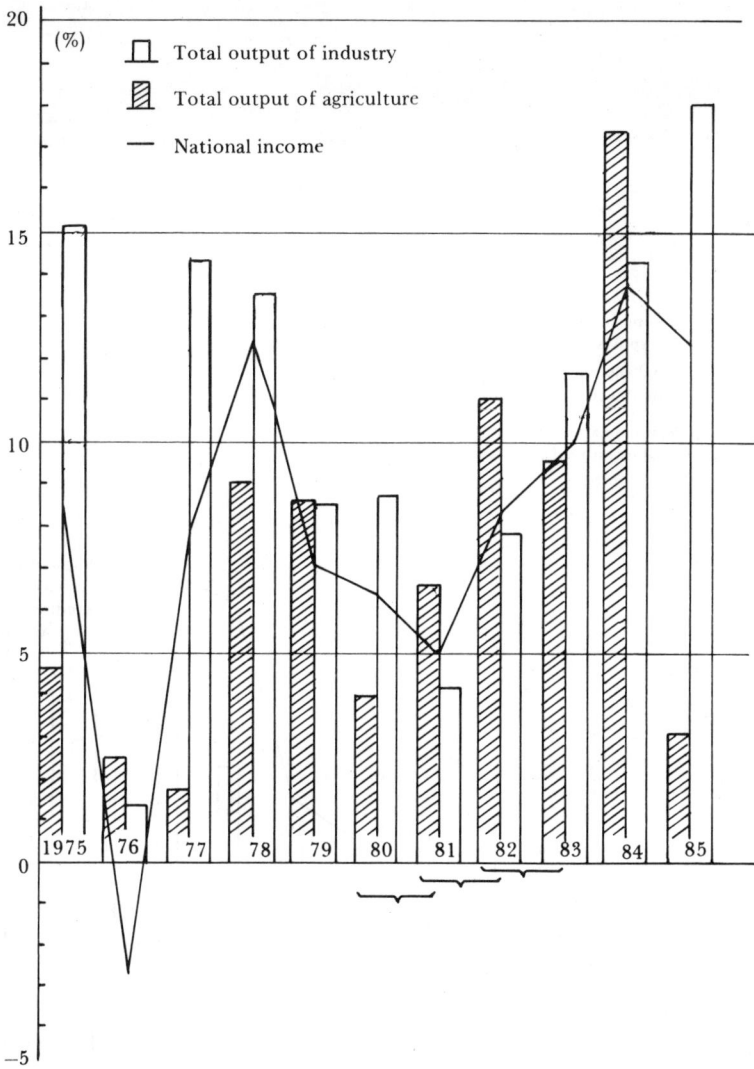

Sources: 1. 1975-88 *China's Statistical Yearbook, 1984,* pp. 26, 30.
      2. 1984   Jingjiribao (Economic Daily), April 12, 13, 1985.
      3. 1985   Jan.-April, Jingjiribao May 18, 1985.

Notes: 1976: Economic turmoil caused by straggle against 'Four-Man-Gang'.
      1978: Huaguo-fenge leap forward.
      1979: The start of economic reform.
  1980-1981: A potential danger of inflation.
  1981-1982: Dissolution of people's communes.
  1982-1983: The start of the 2nd economic reform.
  1983-   : A kind of creeping inflation.
      1984: An agricultural over production.
  1984/1985: A speedy economic growth.

Figure 14. Growth Rate of National Economy

(Index)

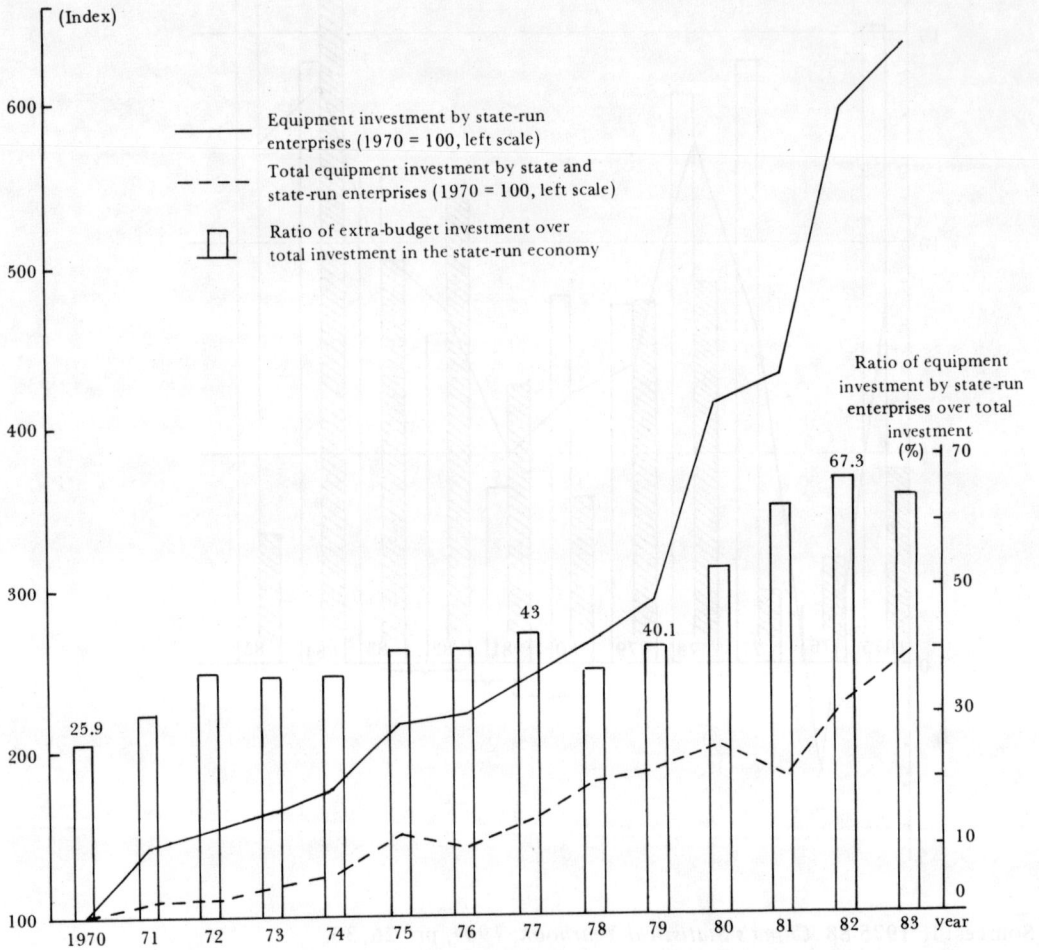

Source: *China's Statistical Yearbook, 1984*, p. 301

Figure 15. Expansion of Investment by Enterprises

ed using the extra-budget funds of the local governments, enterprise funds, and bank loans. The latter, as is well known, have grown rapidly since 1980. In 1982, over two-thirds of the equipment investment in the state-run economy sector was accounted for by this extra-budget investment.

In running the Chinese economy, the biggest problem now is that the government has abandoned the policy instruments for controlling extra-budget investments and has not yet created any new ones. For example, it has not created policy instruments like the adjustment of the official discount rate used by the central banks of the developed nations. Further, while banks can now loan funds for equipment investment upon the request of enterprises, those enterprises are often government enterprises and the government level concerned may exercise control over the banks, including personnel matters. Therefore, the credit banks cannot refuse loans to such enterprises. This is a factor behind the overextension of loans. Consequently, the current Chinese state-run economy has by its very nature created the overheating.

While detailed discussion is not possible due to space limitations, the same trend is true for small rural enterprises.

This economic overheating is exacerbating the bottlenecks in the economy. As a result, it is increasing the reliance on foreign debt for investment funds.

Acceleration of Urbanization

The dissolution of the people's communes and the overheating of the urban economy have promoted the migration of the rural population to the cities. This migration is massive in size and for that reason necessitates massive public investment in the cities to enable them to absorb the impact. Figure 16 shows the growth rate of national economy and absolute figures for the urbanization of the population.

The CCP has placed restrictions on the migration of peasants to the cities as a consistent policy since the founding of the PRC. This policy went to extremes in the 1960s, when urban populations were packed off to the countryside. Despite this, as seen in Figure 16, the influx of population to the cities from 1964 to 1977 has far exceeded the outflow. In 1977, the government announced the revival of selective university entrance examinations. About 20 million young people who had been sent out into the countryside during the Cultural Revolution also returned to the cities. This was a direct reason for the sudden deterioration of housing situation in the cities. This point will be discussed again in the next section.

The government continued to severely suppress the influx of peasants into the cities even after this, but people kept entering the cities through various means. After the people's communes disappeared in 1982, the influx of population to the cities began to reach astronomical proportions. In 1983, no less than 30 million and nearly 90 million people in 1984 joined the urban population. Of course, half of this figure seems to have been an artificial increase due to a classification change wherein some existing rural regions were incorporated into urban administrative regions. Still, even an influx of 15 or 45 million people respectively must have a giant impact on the urban economy.

Why did the disappearance of the people's communes lead to this migration of population? The people's communes prevented people from flowing to the cities. Under the system of people's communes, it was possible to move goods but there was no substantial movement of money or people. The disappearance of this system meant the elimination of a social brake preventing the movement of people and funds. Further, as already discussed, two-thirds of the countryside has enjoyed

(ten thousand)

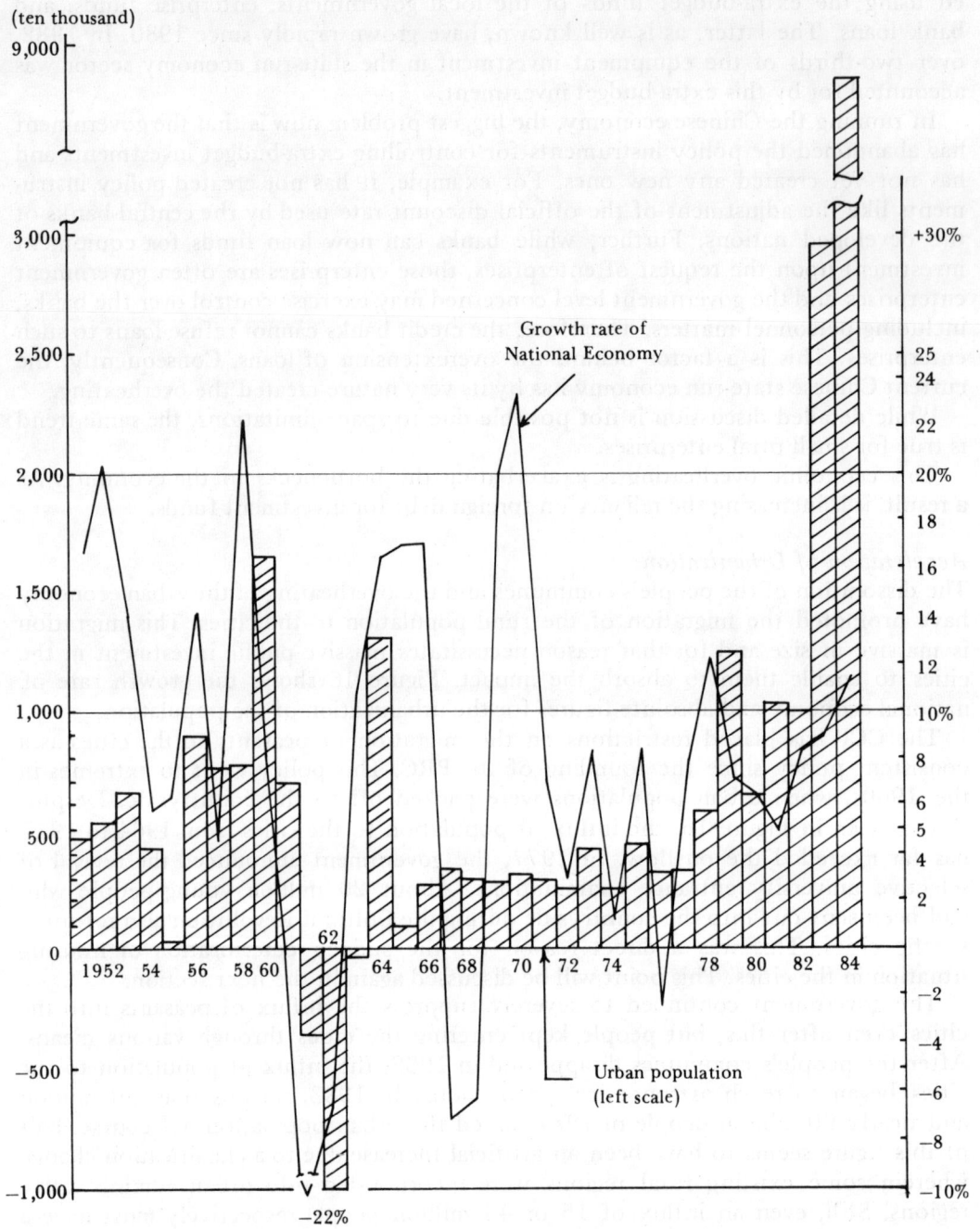

Sources: 1950-83: Calculation from *China's Statistical Yearbook, 1984*, p. 81
1984: *Ibid.* 1985, p. 185

Note: The concept of city is samd as Chinese Government definition.

Figure 16. Growth Rate and Migration to Cities

higher income under the new policies of fund movement allowed to rural enterprises. Any number of people can jointly invest, allowing individuals to quit
farming and start new enterprises. Thus, the elimination of past prohibitions has
enabled the farmers to go beyond their towns and villages and engage in non-
agricultural enterprises. This trend has been striking.

The large number of workers engaged in housing construction in the large cities
are comprised of the hundreds of thousands and millions of farmers arriving for
work from the countryside. This urbanization, which began to increase conspicuously in 1983, was beyond the control of the government. In October 1984, the
government finally issued a notification that peasants could transfer their residences
and live in the urban regions if those regions were small cities or towns.[6] At the
present time, peasants may go to the large and medium size cities and county
capitals for work, but are not allowed to reside there permanently. However, it is
projected that a large percentage of such emigrant workers will end up residing in
the cities permanently.

This will necessitate massive urban redevelopment and housing construction.

In the above, a study was made of the impact of the dissolution of the people's
communes and the reforms in the urban economy on the Chinese economy. It is
clear from the way the economy is now working that a massive demand for capital
is being created and a number of bottlenecks are being worsened.

Therefore, in the next section, the four main bottlenecks of the economy will
be taken up and estimates made on the funds required for alleviating these.

BOTTLENECKS IN FOUR SECTORS

The increase in consumption has prompted the economic reforms which in turn
created the overheating of the economy. As a result of the overheated economy, the
problems in the weakest economic sectors have begun to act as severe bottlenecks.

Insufficient Energy and Transportation

The shortage of energy began to act as a bottleneck in the Chinese economy around
1976. In that year, China was short 20 million tons of coal and 10 million tons of
oil needed for the normal operation of its factories.[7] Shortages of energy in 1977
and 1978 adversely affected no less than one-quarter of all Chinese enterprises.
Of the total 175 million rural households throughout the country, 40 percent
suffered from insufficient fuel and thus could not even cook three meals a day.[8]
The shortage of electricity is particularly severe in the coastal provinces where the
economies are the most developed. The shortage of electricity reportedly keep the
provinces from using 20 percent of their production capacities.[9] The energy short-

---

[6] Guo, Wuyuan. "Guanyu Nongmin Jinru Jizhen Luohu Wenti" [State council, on the provisional issue for
    farmer's settlement in market towns], *People's Daily,* Oct. 22, 1984.

[7] Xia, Meng. "Nengyuan yu Tiaozheng" [Energy and adjustment], in *F3 Industrial Economy,* Publication
    Resource Room of People's University, Reprint, 1981, No. 17, p. 61.

[8] Sun, Shangqing. "Nengyuan Jiegou" [Energy structure], in *Zhongguo Jingjijiegou Wenti Yanjiu* [Studies
    on structural problems of Chinese economy], Vol. 1, ed. Hong Ma and Shangqing Sun, 1981, p. 277.

[9] Li, Peng. "Jingjiyao Zhenxing Dianli bixu Xianxing" [Energy must go ahead economic development],
    Hongqi, 1983, No. 13, p. 18.

age, which became prominent in the middle 1970s, has not been improved even by 1985 — rather, it has continued to worsen.

Figure 17 shows a comparison between trends in energy production and trends in total industrial output. The rate of increase in production of energy since the middle of the 1960s began below that of total output in the heavy industries and, beginning in the 1970s, fell far behind. A comparison with the growth rate of total industrial output, including that in the light industries, shows the growth rate of energy beginning to fall below that of the former in 1982. One of the economic reforms begun in 1979 was the reform of the economic structure. Here, China attempted to slow down construction in the high energy consuming heavy industries and to lay emphasis on the light industries. However, so far as Figure 17 shows, the more such measures were taken, the greater the gap between the industrial growth rate and the energy rate became.

While the energy shortage was becoming so severe, the 12th National Party Congress of the CCP of September 1982 decided upon a grandiose policy of quadrupling the 1980 level of total industrial and agricultural output by 2000. However, it called for only doubling production of energy, in standard coal conversion, and covering the remaining half of the requirements through improvements in heat efficiency. In 1980, China produced 640 million tons of energy in standard coal conversion through fossil fuels and hydroelectric energy, not including organic energy.[10] Its production of organic energy is estimated at around 270 million tons in standard coal conversion,[11] giving a total of around 900 million tons. China set the target of doubling just its fossil fuel and hydroelectric energy. If we assume no increase in production of organic energy, then China would have to have a massive energy supply of 1,550 million tons in standard coal conversion.

In actuality, however, the author estimates that it will probably need far greater energy production than that. The reasons for this are given below.

Already High Heat Efficiency in China
Estimating the elasticity of energy consumption to the GNP, one gets, for Japan,[12] 1.22 from 1955 to 1960, 1.15 from 1960 to 1965, and 1.15 from 1965 to 1972. In Asia as a whole, the elasticity was 1.49 for 1961 to 1969. As opposed to this, China had an elasticity of 1.42 from 1952 to 1982, but a low 1.1 from 1965 to 1980 and 1.03[13] from 1970 to 1980. To reduce this even further would probably require massive investment in improved facilities. Therefore, the realistic chances for success of a policy for significantly increasing the heat efficiency are slim.

Changes in Energy Structure in Rural Regions
CCP projections on energy demand until the year 2000 do not seem to take into consideration changes in the energy structure in the countryside. The rural energy structure in 1977 was 77 percent organic energy, 11.4 percent coal, 3.9 percent

---

[10] Kojima, Reeitsu. "Kogyo" [Industry], in *Chugoku no chuchoki tenbo* [Long- and middle-term projection], ed. S. Ishikawa, R. Kojima, and S. Sekiguchi, Nicchu Keizai Kyokai, 1984, p. 67.

[11] Shi, Wen. "Shin enerugishigen to saisei enerugi no riyo" [New energy resources and utilization of reproduced energy], *Peking Review* (Japanese edition), 1982, No. 16, p. 26.

[12] Japan, Ministry of Industry and Commerce. "Sangyo kozo no choki bijon" [Long-term projection of industrial structure], 1974, p. 267.

[13] Calculated from *China's Statistical Yearbook, 1983*, p. 149, p. 215, p. 249. Energy elasticity to industrial and agricultural gross total output.

(1957 = 100)

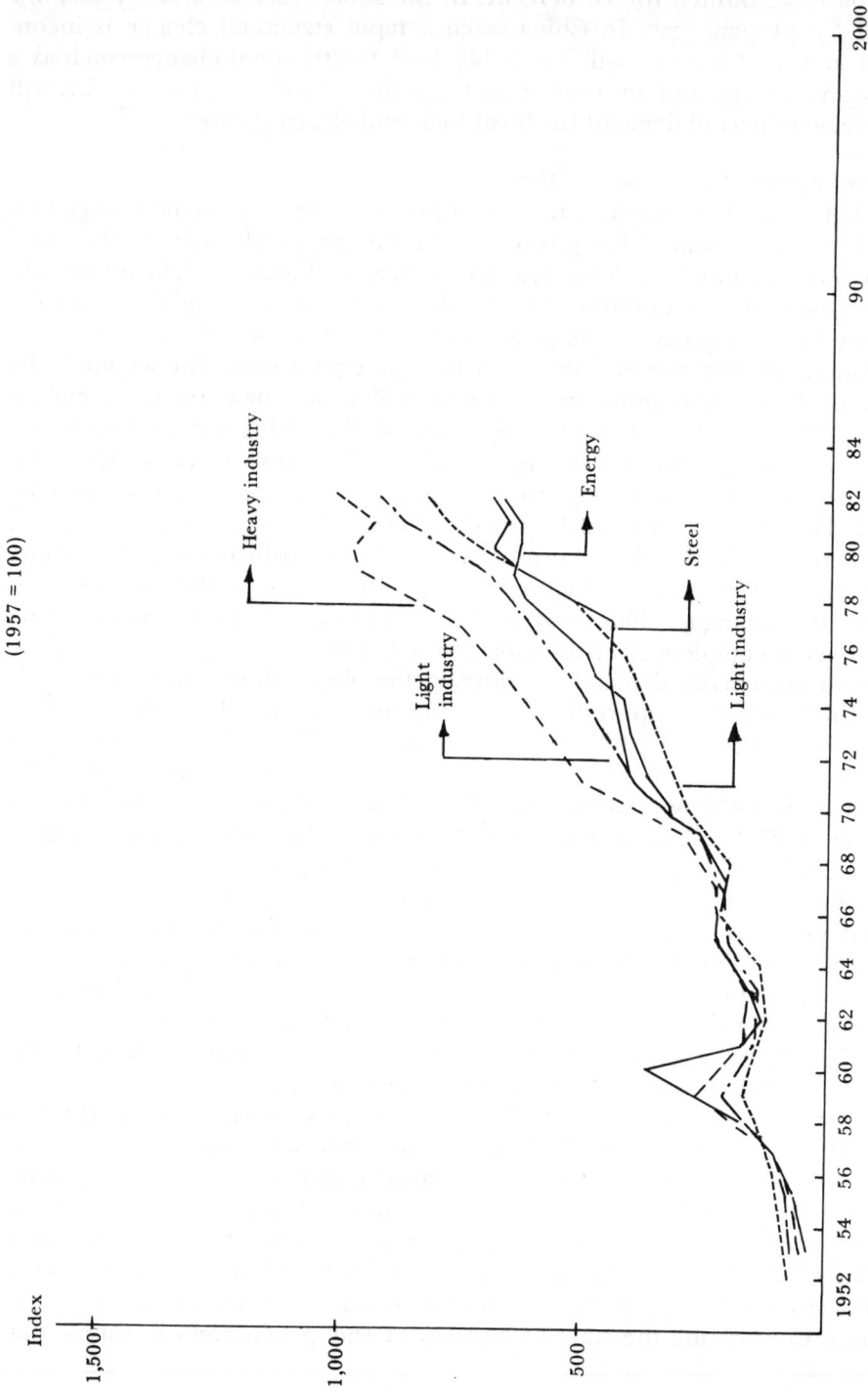

Figure 17. The Growth Rates of Total Industrial Output Value, Energy & Steel

Source: Reiitsu Kojima: 'Industry in Long- and Middle-Term Projection of China's Economy, edited by S. Ishikawa, R. Kojima & S. Sekiguchi, p. 54.

electricity, 3.4 percent oil, 0.4 percent methane gas, and 3.7 percent other.[14] Japan underwent an energy revolution in the late 1950s. In the countryside, organic energy previously accounted for 70 percent. In the short space of a few years, this was replaced by propane gas. In China, such a rapid structural change is inconceivable, but increased income will inevitably lead to structural changes such as a decline in organic energy and an increase in fossil fuel and electric power. This will create an increase in overall demand for fossil fuels and electric power.

Increase in Energy for Private Use in Cities

Due to the following three reasons, there will probably be an extremely large rate of increase in energy demand for private use in the cities. The first is the rapid urbanization going on in China. This was already seen in Figure 16. The industrialization of the towns and small cities after the dissolution of the people's communes is promoting greater mobility in the population. Probably, for the time being, the urban population will increase at a rate of 3 to 4 percent a year. The second is the construction of high-rise housing in the cities will create new types of energy demand. The housing constructed since the start of the 1980s has, in the case of the large cities, been apartment buildings of 12 to 13 storeys or more. With this type of high-rise housing, firewood, briquets, coal, and the like can no longer be used for fuel. Demand for secondarily processed high efficiency city gas, propane, etc. should increase. The third is the progress in the electrification of the home. The state of progress was seen in Figure 6. After television sets, the most popular items are electric washing machines and electric refrigerators. Along with this, China is on its way toward complete electrification of the home.

Estimating future energy demand considering the above three factors, it is calculated that China will need approximately 1,300 million tons of energy by 1990, including organic energy, and 2,600 million tons in 2000. Calculating the amount of investment necessary from the amount of standard coal conversion energy obtained by investment of 100 million renminbi in the fossil fuel and electric sectors, one can obtain a figure of 21.1 billion renminbi (in 1980 prices) for 1990 and 42.3 billion renminbi for 2000. By way of comparison, fiscal revenue in the state budget in 1980 was 108.5 billion renminbi and total equipment investment in the state-run economy that year was 74.6 billion renminbi. This shows how massive an amount of investment would be needed just to meet energy development targets alone.

Making the energy problem even more serious is the bottleneck in transportation. In 1980, the Chinese energy structure was based on coal. Coal accounted for roughly 55 percent of all its energy. This structure will not fundamentally change by the year 2000. In other words, the economy will rely on solid fuel.

The distribution of coal production areas is remarkably unbalanced. Of the 670 million tons of coal produced in 1982, Shanxi province accounted for a full one-quarter, or 145 million tons. In 1981, due to insufficient transportation capacity, there were 18 million tons of coal stacked in the open in Shanxi,[15] some of which naturally combusted. In the Mao Zedong era, emphasis was placed on inland power plant locations. The inland regions enjoy greater energy production than the coastal provinces. In the Deng Xiaoping era, the coastal provinces are being built up as key industrial bases. Considering the state of reserves of energy resources in China, this

---

[14] Kojima. *Ibid.* p. 57.

[15] Koshizawa, Akira. "Kotsu unyu" [Transportation], in *Chugoku no chuchoki tenbo, . . .* , p. 179.

new industrial siting policy will work to increase the burden of transporting energy unless she imports by sea from abroad.

This is a factor aggravating the shortage in investment funds.

Insufficient Intermediate Goods

In the initial stage of industrialization under import substitution, there is a time when an absolute shortage occurs in intermediate goods. Import substitution policy of final and capital goods often results in a rise of dependence on imports of intermediate goods. This applies to China today. China has made use of an import substitution policy for all manufactured goods since the start of its national construction. In particular, the orientation toward import substitution for machinery and equipment remains a consistently strong policy even today. However, this policy has created an increase in dependence on imports of intermediate goods.

The CCP inherited a colonial economy. A look at the characteristics of that economy from the viewpoint of advancement of the degree of processing reveals the following ordering: from raw materials and the fuel sector to the materials production sector to the materials processing sector. However, several years after beginning national construction, efforts to advance the degree of processing in the key industries ran ahead. The raw materials and fuel sector stagnated so that the materials processing sector itself suffered from a low operating rate due to shortage of the raw materials and this state of affairs has continued up until today. The most typical example of this is the relation between the coal, iron ore, and steel-making sector and machinery sector; and between the cotton production sector, yarn sector, and cloth and sewing sector. The yarn sector had been suffered from the shortage of cotton supply, though China imported a considerably large amount of cotton. Starting in the 1980s, with the exception of cotton production, this structure has not changed.

Here, the four major materials of iron and steel, lumber and wood materials, plastics, and cement are selected from among the intermediate goods. First, a look at the shortage of materials in 1980 shows the following.[16] The rate of satisfaction of demand was 35 percent in capital construction and 40 percent in technical renovation for finished steel, 40 percent and 45 percent for cement, 30 to 40 percent and 31 percent for lumber. This is for the state-run economy. The shortage is clear.

Figure 18 illustrates the trends in the savings rate and the trends in import dependence. A constant correlation can be seen between the two, but they began to move differently after 1982. Despite the fall in the savings rate, the import dependence on finished steel and plastic rose sharply. This resulted from the institutional reforms, which gave the local governments and enterprises greater autonomy and thus enabled them to hold more funds on their own, leading to an increase in inventories.

Looking at long-term trends, it is projected that China will change over to imports even for cement, the only material of the four which it can now export. As for lumber, China will end up the world's largest importer. To improve the degree of

---

[16] Xu, Yi. "Dangqian Caizheng Jingjizhong Cunzai de Wenti he Women de Duice" [Some issues in present budget and economy, and our policy], in *Flo Guomin Jingji Jihua yu Guanli* [National economic planning and management], ed. Publication Resource Room of People's University, 1981, No. 5, p. 104.

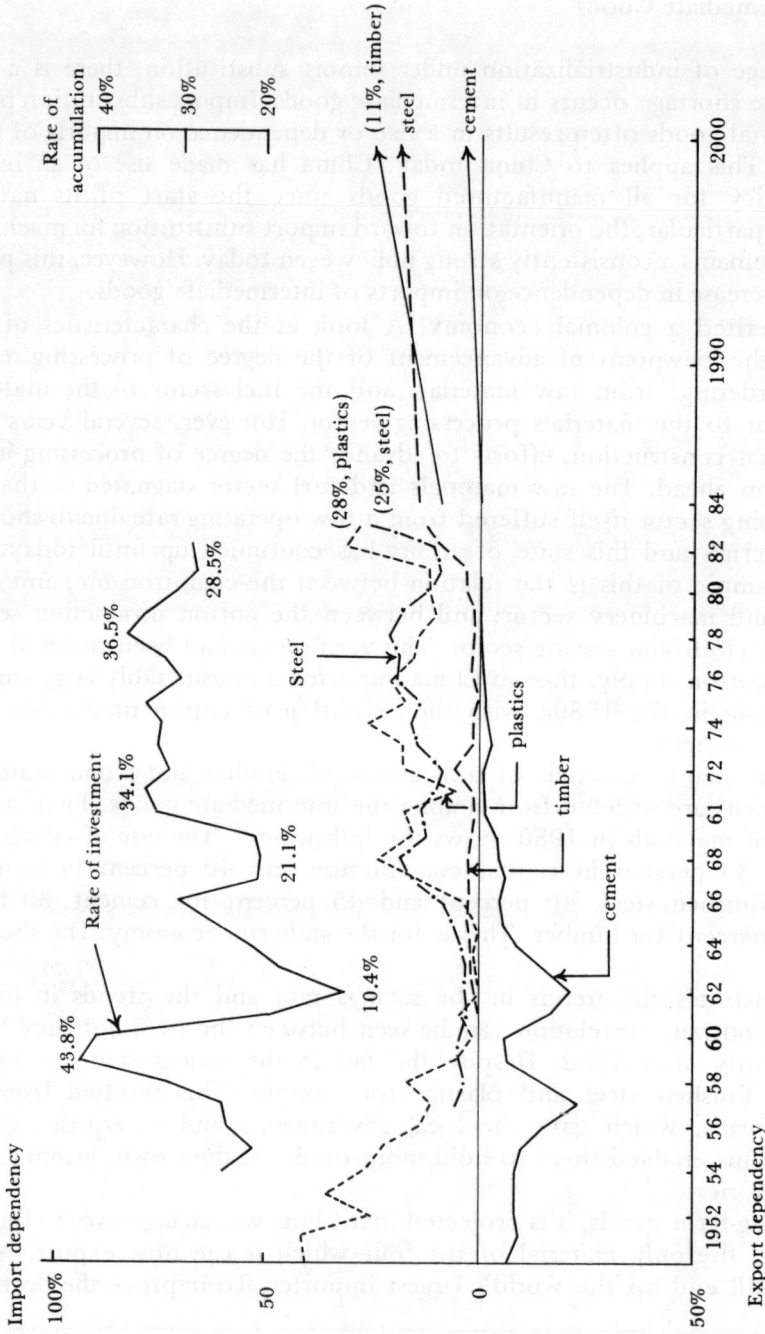

Figure 18. The Import Dependency in Some Basic Materials

Source: R. Kojima, 'Industry', in *Long- and Middle-Term Projection of China's Economy*, edited by S. Ishikawa, R. Kojima & S. Sekiguchi, p. 73.

self-reliance in plastic and finished steel, China will have to make massive investments just as in the energy sector. If import of these three materials continues
along the present trends, China will be forced to adopt policies stimulating exports
so as to earn sufficient foreign exchange to pay.

The Housing Shortage

Housing construction accounts for a large proportion of demands for materials and
for investment funds. In this regard, we would like to touch upon future housing
demand.

As was already stated, China has allocated a large portion of its national income
to housing construction since 1978. Have there been any signs of improvement due
to this? At the present time, it is like trying to put out a fire with a water pistol.
The shortage in housing has become more severe; there has been no improvement.
One of the officials in charge of housing, Lin Zhiqun, spoke of the seriousness of
the problem,[17] stating that the number of families with poor housing in the cities
totaled 6.26 million in 1977, 6.89 million in 1978, and 7.90 million in 1980.

Two reasons are given for the increasing seriousness of the shortage despite the
increase of housing construction in urban areas. One was the abysmal lack of
housing construction in the 1960s and 1970s, which led to a "hidden rise of slums."
The more surveys are made, the more families with poor housing turn up. Another
reason, as seen in Figure 16, was the massive influx of population into the cities
from the countryside after the dissolution of the people's communes. Half of the
inflow of people of the cities shown for 1983 and 1984 in Figure 16 may have been
due to a redefinition of the city boundaries. Still, even if this is true, there was a
substantial increase in urbanization. If the current level of housing construction in
the cities is not further raised, there is the risk of a prolification of squatters.

Based on several assumptions, an attempt is made herein to estimate the housing
construction required for the years 1990 and 2000. (See Table 1) It is estimated
that construction of 1.16 to 1.46 billion m² will be necessary for 1990 and 1.5 to
1.9 billion m² for 2000. How will China be able to procure the funds and materials
for housing construction of such enormous size?

Increasing Pollution

There are various types of pollution, but here the problem of water pollution will
be taken up. In China's industrial zones, water shortages began to hinder factory
operations starting in the 1970s. For example, this happened in Tianjin city starting
1970, in Qingdao city starting 1976, in Shanghai city starting 1979, and in Dalian
starting from 1981. China's terrain can be roughly divided into two types: the dry
regions in the North and West and the monsoon regions of Central and South China.
The amount of rainfall in the North is from about one-half to one-third that of the
South. The annual rainfall in Beijing is 700 to 800 mm, compared with 1,800 mm
in Tokyo. The further to the Northwest one goes, the less rainfall there is. Taiyuan
and Lanzhou receive about 500 mm. Shanghai began a water conservation campaign

---

[17] Lin, Zhiqun. "Woguo Zhuzhaijianshe Cunzai de Zhuyao Wenti ji Jigaige de Jianyi" [Main issues in our housing construction and some proposal to reform], in *Jianzhu Xuebao* [Journal of construction], 1982, no. 1,
p. 41.

Table 1. Projection for Housing Construction

(Unit: million m²)

	Cities	Urban houses constructed over total urban construction	Countryside	Total
1957	28.16	41.5%	110	
1965	12.28	36.7	110	
1966-69	Annually 10.8	26.8		
1977	28.28			
1978	37.5	37.1	260	297.52
1979	62.56	41.6	300	362.56
1980	82.3	52.1	340	422.3
1981	79	56.8	600	679
1982	90.2	62.8	700	790.2
1980 ⟩ 1985			Annual plan 600-800	Annual plan 710-915
1985	Plan 60 Annual rate +70% 115		1,000-1,300	
1985 ⟩ 1990	—			
1990	Annual rate +70% 162		1,000-1,300	1,162-1,462
2000	300		1,200-1,600	1,500-1,900

Source: For detail, see R. Kojima's article in Japanese, in *Long- and Middle-Term Projection of China's Economy*, edited by S. Ishikawa, R. Kojima & Sekiguchi. p. 91.

Note: Figures till 1982 are actual.

in 1979, and yet that city is located in a seasonal region with large amounts of rain. The industrial water problem is thus not directly related to the amount of rainfall. The problem is that the water intake capacity can no longer keep up with demand for water for industrial and private use. This is a typical example of social capital not being able to keep up with economic activity. An actual example will be given here.

Shanghai[18] now discharges 5 million tons of wastewater a day. Of this, only a very small portion is reportedly treated before being discharged. As a result, it is said that "the untreated waste is exhausted directly in large amounts into the Huangpu river and the Suzhou river, considerably polluting those water sources. As a result, the water quality has deteriorated and bad smells have been caused.

[18] Qiu, Kenmao. "Wushui Chuli yu Nengyuan Liyong" [Waste water disposal and energy utilization], *Chengxiangjianshe* [Journal of city and country construction], 1982, No. 2, p. 21.

The problem of treatment of the wastewater of the cities is an urgent one requiring immediate resolution."

Take the example of the drop in the underground water table. In Shijiazhuang city[19] of Hebei province, a drop in the underground water table began to be observed in 1965 around the region of the No. 1 Dye Factory. By 1982, this had spread to a wide range of 200 km^2. "The average annual drop in the underground water table from 1953 to 1980 was 70 cm or so. In 1981 to 1982, the water table dropped as much as 2 meters a year. Compared with the initial period after the establishment of the PRC, the water table has sunken from 5 to 25 metres", it has been said. The problem of a dropping underground water table may be seen in all the major cities around the country, with the exception of South China. The situation is particularly serious in the North and West. There, the surface water freezes in the water and cannot be used, so these regions depend on underground sources for almost all their industrial water and private use water.

There have been increasingly numerous reports of pollution of underground water due to overuse of chemical fertilizers.[20] A survey of 41 cities in 1978 showed that the underground water of nine cities was polluted with nitrates, with the level of pollution serious in seven. By 1981, the pollution had reportedly spread to 11 cities. If 100 kg of nitrogenous fertilizers is estimated to be used for 1 mu (6.6 acres), then 6.5 kg makes its way to the underground water and the content of the same in 1 liter of underground water becomes 10 mg. This pollution is reaching all parts of the country, both North and South. There are some scientists who warn that if the situation continues unchecked it will no longer be possible to use underground water for drinking purposes.

The time has come when China must treat wastewater in some way to stop the deterioration of water quality. Table 2 shows the actual state of treatment and the estimated amount of wastewater up until 2000. The rate of treatment in 1979 was a mere 2 percent on a national average. Even in the capital Beijing, the rate was just 8 percent. Projections on the amount of wastewater in the year 2000 indicate a 4.6 fold increase, greater than the 4 fold increase targeted for total industrial and agricultural output.

How much investment is needed for wastewater treatment? To just treat the wastewater at the low 1982 level, a reported 25 billion renminbi worth of capital construction and another 4 billion renminbi of management and operating expenses would be necessary.[21] By way of comparison, the total capital investment in the state-run sector in 1982 was 84.5 billion renminbi, so the above figure corresponds to one-third of that amount. The treatment talked about also does not include the cost for treatment of underground water polluted by chemical fertilizers. Further, it does not include the costs for obtaining water supply. The amount of water supply required will reach 230 million tons a day by the year 2000. The amount of investment required to secure this is estimated at 46 billion renminbi.[22] This is

19 Shi, Mensi. "Fadong Junzhong Jieshui" [To mobilize mass for water saving], *Chengxiangjianshe*, 1983, No. 11, p. 9.
20 Ma, Meisheng. "Xiao suan yan shi Dixia shui de Zhongyao Wujanyuan" [Nitric acid is the main polluting element of underground water], *Chengxiangjianshe*, 1982, No. 5, p. 28.
21 Cheng, Hua. "Shilun Woguo Shuiwuran Fangzhi de Jibenduice" [On the basic policy to overcome our water pollution], *Chengxiangjianshe*, 1982, No. 12, p. 22.
22 Pinglunyuan [The observer]. "Yao Jixu hen Zhua Jieyue Yongshui" [Water should be saved continuously], *Chengxiangjianshe*, 1983, No. 8, p. 17,

Table 2. Quantity of Waste Fluid

	Daily Discharge (thousand ton)	Annual Discharge (billion ton)	Rate of Cleaning Disposal
1970	40,000	14.6	
1978	50,000	18.3	
1979	78,000	28.5	1) National 2%
			2) Beijing 8%
1980	85,750	31.3	
1985	125,000	45.6	
1990	183,000	66.8	
1995	267,000	97.7	
2000	391,000	142.8	

Sources: 1) Hiu Shiwei's article, in *Gongyuan Liangqian Nian de Zhongguo* (China in 2000),
edited by the 2000 study group, p. 67.
2) Li Shihao's article, ibid. p. 191.

Others: Li Shiao's article, ibid. p. 195.

higher than the estimated amount of investment required for energy in the year 2000. The basis on which the Chinese came up with this estimate of 46 billion renminbi for the amount of investment required is unclear, so the accuracy of the estimate cannot be evaluated. However, the urge of the people for improved consumption has been great and, after purchasing of color televisions, people buy electric washing machines. Further, the high-rise apartment houses all use flush toilets. If modernization of daily life is to proceed even greater water consumption per capita will be necessary. This is epitomized by the above two phenomena. Therefore, the amount of investment required for water supplies may rise above the official estimate.

Another problem that has been increasing in severity is air pollution. In 1983, it was estimated[23] that China discharged 14 million tons of soot and 15 million tons of sulfur dioxide into the atmosphere as a result of fuel combustion for industrial and civilian use. As estimated earlier, by the year 2000, China will be burning 1.4 to 1.5 billion tons of coal alone, in standard coal conversion. The problem of acid rain has already partially arisen. The cost for treating this would be additional to the estimated 46 billion reminbi needed for waste water treatment.

Pollution prevention became a major issue in the advanced countries in the 1970s. There is some data on how much some countries spent for pollution prevention during that time with respect to their GNP's.[24] Japan spent 1.3 percent, West Germany 1.85 percent, the U.S. 1.8 percent, and France 1.1 percent. If China were to try to clean up its pollution to the same extent as these countries, what percent of its GNP would it have to spend? To answer this, it is first of all necessary to start with the recognition that the natural ability of the environment to clean

---

[23] Calculated from burned oil and coal.

[24] Imura, Hidefumi. "Kankyo hozen hiyo no doko" [National expense for main training environment], *Kankyo kenkyu* [Journal of environment studies], 1983, No. 42, p. 89.

itself is extremely weak in China.

Figure 19 shows the sea level of the key inland industrial cities and their distance from the river mouths. Chongqing is 230 meters above sea level and 2,500 km from the mouth of the Changjiang. This indicates that once water is polluted in Chongqing, it will pollute everything downstream. Further, the river gradient is extremely gentle. Obviously, compared with Japan, the natural ability of the environment to clean itself up is poor. Japan, first of all, enjoys abundant rainfall: 1,500 to 2,200 mm a year. Second, the terrain is sharply graded and the flow of water fast. Third, it has 34,000 km of coastline, with the tide continually washing away its pollution. Fourth, seasonal winds are always blowing. Fifth, 80 percent of Japan's factories are less than 50 m above sea level and situated within 50 km from river mouths. In China, all these factors are by far worse than in Japan. And yet even Japan, blessed with this excellent natural ability of the environment to clean itself, suffered from serious pollution during the high growth period of the 1960s and 1970s. Furthermore, the spread of pollution has just been slowed down. Even this unsatisfactory degree of treatment cost 1.3 percent of Japan's GNP. Even if China were to spend 2 percent or more of its GNP, it would not be able to clean up its environment to the same degree as Japan's. Expenditure of close to 3 percent might be needed.

Our review of the four major bottlenecks in the economy indicates a massive amount of investment funds will be needed to break through each of them.

FOREIGN TRADE AND OPEN DOOR POLICY

National Economy and Foreign Trade

First, let us examine the main characteristics of China's foreign trade from its history.

1. The size of foreign trade in the Chinese national economy is rather small by international standards. However, starting from the late 1970s, the ratio of trade to national income has continued to grow. This growth trend increased conspicuously in 1979 when the economic reforms were launched. This is shown in Figure 20. Line (a) shows the total value of imports and exports and (b) the Chinese national income. Both are indexed in nominal terms with 1957 = 100. A major reason for the sudden increase in total imports and exports in 1973 and 1974 was the rise in prices due to the first oil crisis. Consideration must be given to the price factors of the second oil crisis in 1979 and 1980, but a look at the individual items shows there was a sharp increase in trade growth far above the rate of increase in the national income.

As a result, the ratio of foreign trade in the GNP has been rising rapidly. China does not announce GNP statistics of the type used in capitalist countries, so the Chinese style national income is used as the denominator. Looking at this, we get a minimum trade to income of 6.2 percent in 1971. This rose to 18.20 percent by 1981. In general, this ratio is low in large continental countries like the U.S., the USSR, and India. In 1981, it was 17.3 percent in the U.S., 12 percent in the USSR, and 14 percent in India. The ratio for West Germany was 49.6 percent, for the United Kingdom 41 percent, and for Japan 25.8 percent.[25] China is expected to increase the ratio in the future. As a result,

---

[25] Kojima, Sueo. "Taigai boeki" [Foreign trade], in *Chugoku no chuchoki tenbo*, . . . , p. 251.

Above the sea level

m
1,500
1,000
500
400
300
200
100
50
0

Tianjin Nanjing

Shinyang

Laoyang

Beijing

(80% of Japanese industrial goods may be produced in this range)

Wuhan

Jilin

Baotou

Lanzhou (1,554 m)

Chongqing (230m)

Distance from river mouths

500   1,000   1,500   2,000   2,500

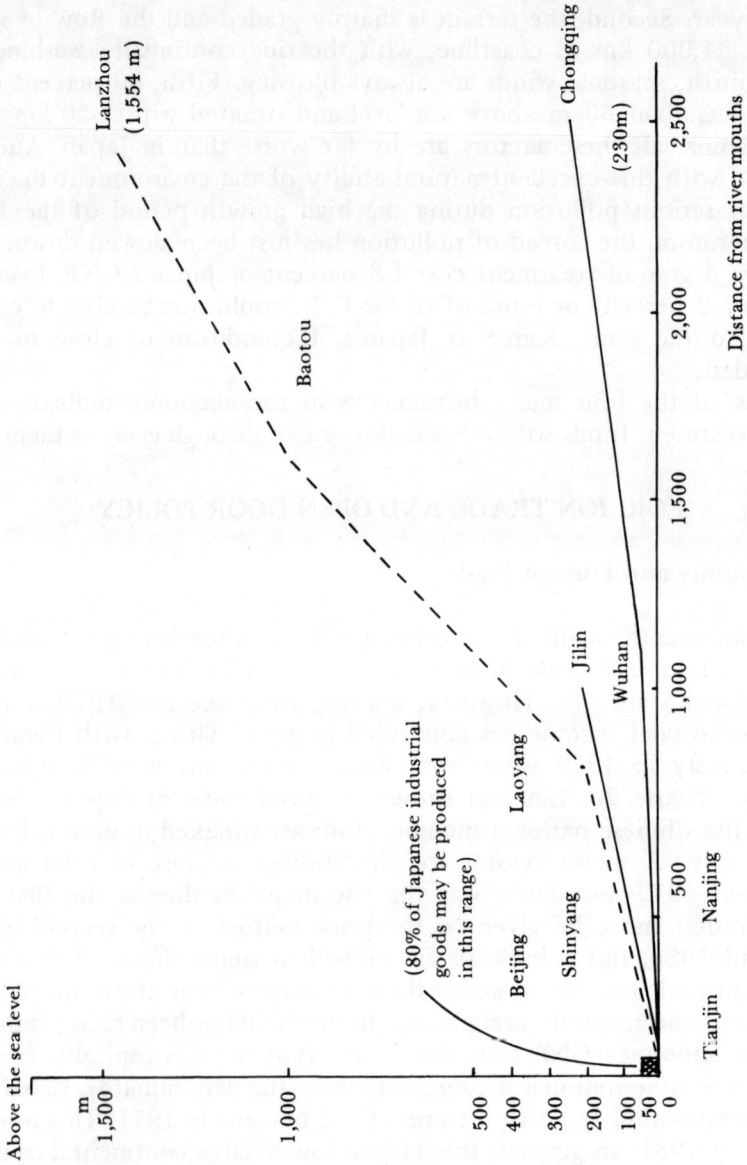

Figure 19. Industrial Location and Length of Rivers and Slope

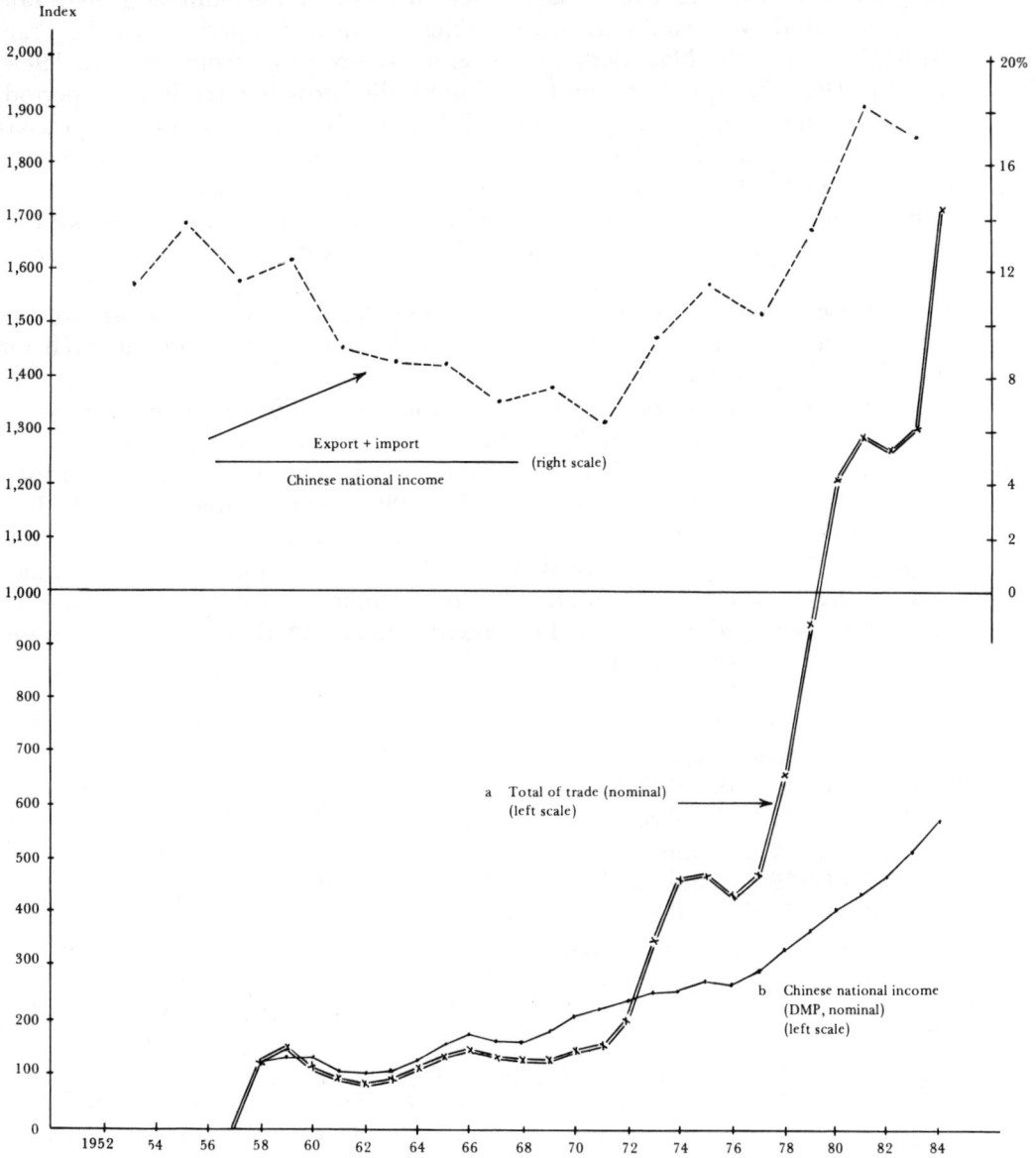

Source: *China's Statistical Yearbook, 1984*, pp. 29, 395.

Figure 20. Development of Trade and Chinese National Income

the ratio of China's total trade in global trade has been rising. It was a low 0.72 percent in 1970, but rose to 1.23 percent by 1983.[26]

2. The growth rate (nominal) of foreign trade has been faster than that of China's national income. The average annual growth rate of national income in the 32 years from 1953 to 1984 was 7.1 percent. The average annual growth rate of foreign trade was 10.9 percent. Dividing this into two periods, the 26 years until 1978, i.e., the Mao Zedong era, and the six years from 1979 to 1984, i.e., the Deng Xiaoping era, and looking at the growth rates in each period, we see that national income grew an average annual 5.7 percent and 9.7 percent and foreign trade 9.5 percent and 17.3 percent. Chinese statistics on the real growth rates for the two are unavailable. The difference between the inflation rate of the international economy and the inflation rate of China should be taken into consideration, but proper adjustments cannot be made because of a lack of data.

From these growth rates, the coefficient of growth of foreign trade against the growth rate of national income is 1.67 for the Mao Zedong era and 1.78 for the Deng Xiaoping era.

3. Projecting the foreign trade of China in the seventh five-year plan (1986 to 1990) using the above elasticities, the following results are obtained. In the September 1985 National Congress of the CCP, it was decided to double total industrial and agricultural output over the 1980 level as a target for 1990. This would mean an average annual increase of 7.2 percent. This corresponds roughly to 6.12 percent growth in terms of national income. If one multiplies this by the coefficient of growth of foreign trade with respect to growth of income between 1979-1985, an 11 percent annual growth rate of foreign trade is projected. The projections on the dollar amounts of foreign trade are as follows:

    1984: US$53.63 billion (Real, *China Economic News,* February 18, 1985)
    1985: US$59.53 billion
    1986: US$66.08 billion
    1987: US$73.35 billion
    1988: US$81.4 billion
    1989: US$90.37 billion
    1990: US$100.3 billion

Imports rose sharply in 1984, prompting the government to institute import restrictions in 1985, so the base of 1984 may be too large. Therefore, a more appropriate figure for total foreign trade in 1990 might be about US$95.0 billion.

4. The growth of foreign trade has fluctuated far more than that of the national income. This is shown in Figure 21. Up until 1971, it may be seen that the fluctuations in the growth rate of foreign trade were basically linked with those in the growth rate of the social material product. However, the correlation between the two has become weaker since 1972. It is likely that this was the result of strong government intervention.

However, it is impossible for government intervention to continue with no regard to economic realities for more than a few years, as can be seen from Figure 22. Figure 22 illustrates the trade balance. The large deficits in the three years from

---

[26] *China's International Economic Annual, 1984,* p. iv-5.

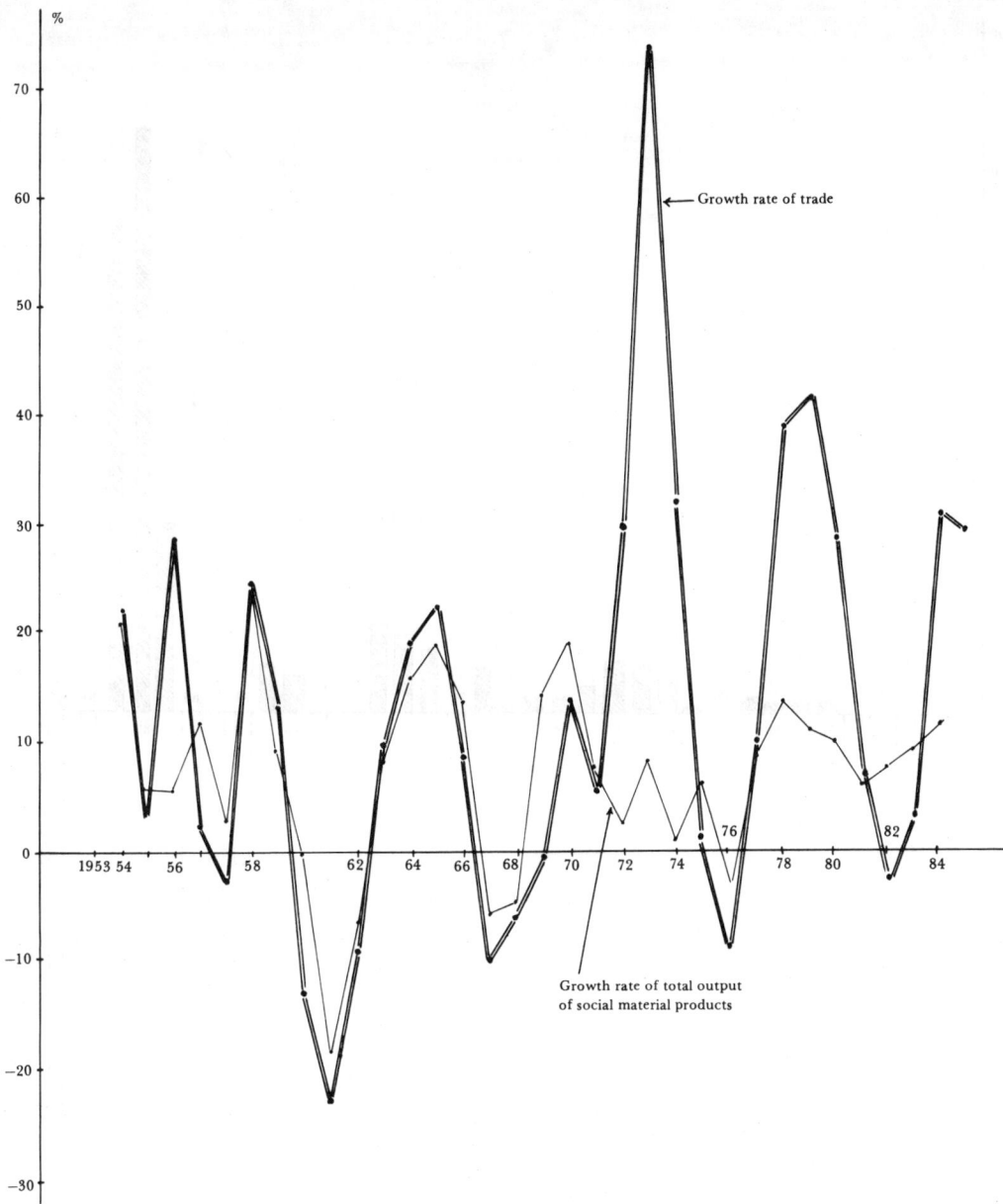

Sources: *Ibid.*
    1985: Feb. 29, 1986, *People's Daily.*

Figure 21. Comparison of Growth Rate Between Total Output of
Social Material Products and Trade

million $

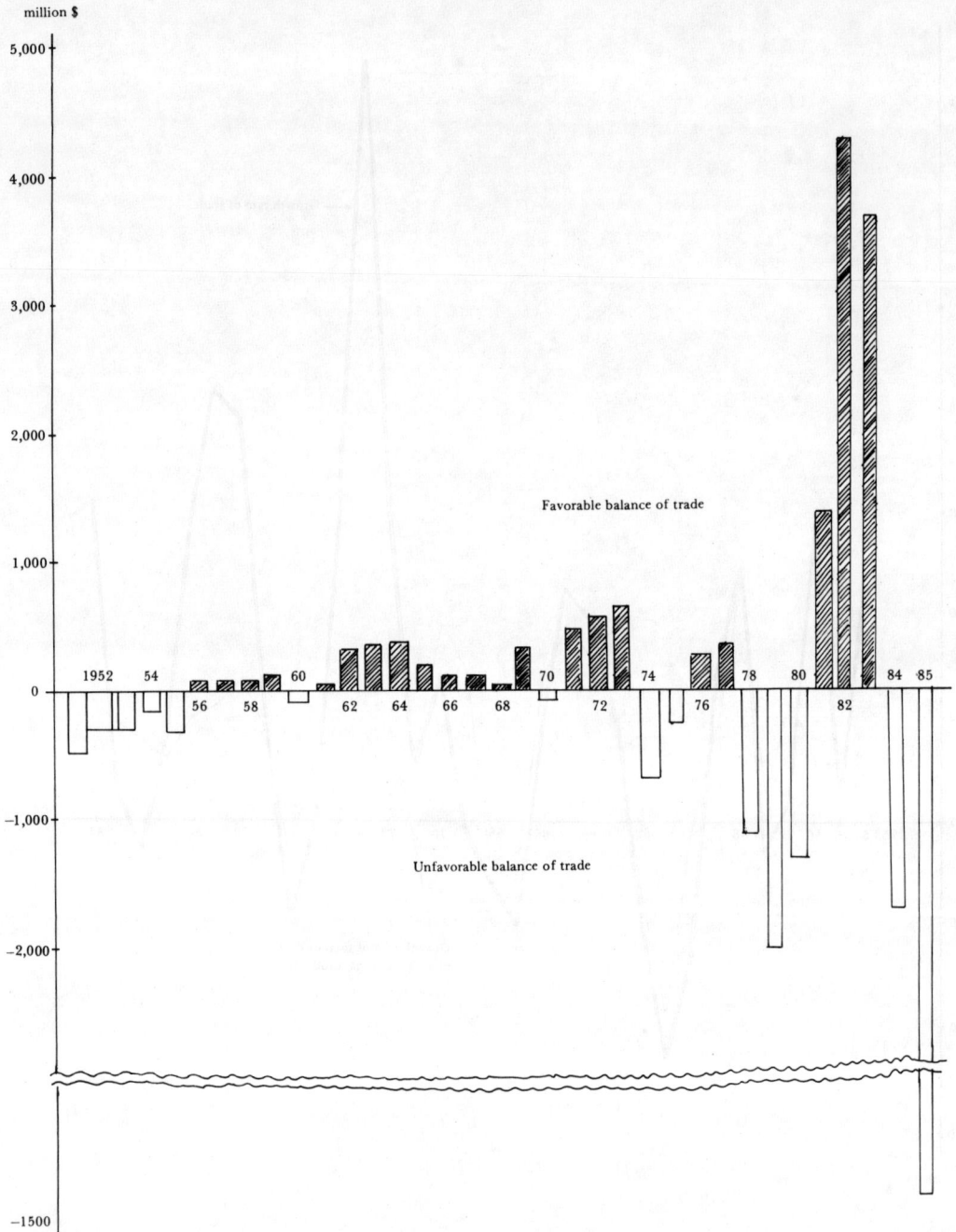

5,000

4,000

3,000

2,000

Favorable balance of trade

1,000

0   1952   54   56   58   60   62   64   66   68   70   72   74   76   78   80   82   84   85

Unfavorable balance of trade

−1,000

−2,000

−1500

Source: *Ibid*, p. 395.

Figure 22. Balance of Payments.

1978 were due to the so-called "Foreign Leap Forward" period of the days of Hua Guofeng when large amounts of industrial plant and equipment were imported. This lasted only for three years, however. Starting in 1981, the government instituted emergency belt-tightening measures for imports and restored the trade balance. From 1981 to 1983, China recorded large trade surpluses. Soon forces went to work to change the surplus to balanced trade and then a trade deficit in 1984.

Projections on Trade Volume and Commodities Structure

In this section, the likely future changes in the commodity composition of China's exports and imports are analyzed.

Exports

The nominal growth rate of exports was an annual average 10.8 percent for the 26 years from 1958 to 1984 and 17.7 percent for the six years from 1979 to 1984. These figures show just how much the rate of growth has changed since the new reformist trade policies began to be introduced.

Figure 23 shows the changes in the structure of commodity exports. From the 1950s up until the middle of the 1960s, the most important exports of China were raw and processed agricultural goods and textile products. From the end of the 1960s, exports of oil grew by leaps and bounds until they occupied a leading position among China's primary exports. In the late 1970s, however, oil exports began to stagnate. The major change since the inception of the Deng Xiaoping era has been the beginning of a rapid increase in exports of machinery. In 1980, machinery accounted for just 4.7 percent of China's exports, but by 1983 it rose to close to 15 percent.

The export commodities consistently important since the establishment of the PRC are textile products, accounting for 26.3 percent of all exports in 1957, 31 percent in 1965, 31.1 percent in 1975, and 31.8 percent in 1983.[27] Textile exports should remain important in the future. Their share in the commodity structure of China's exports will not increase much. Instead, the ratio of these goods to total exports will probably decline. In the next 10 years, it is projected that textile goods will account for 25 to 30 percent of all merchandize exports.

Neither can much of an increase in oil exports be expected. This is because domestic production has been stagnating in volume and domestic demand has been increasing. Domestic production passed the 100 million ton mark in 1978, but since then has stagnated. There was a slight increase, however, in 1985, bringing production to 120 million tons. The falling international price of oil has also sharply reduced the value of oil exports. It is unlikely oil prices will rebound much until after 1990.

Because of this, it is believed that the major changes in the composition of exports will be related to the prospects for exporting machinery and agricultural products.

---

[27] Concrete figures in this section are quoted or calculated either from *China's International Economic Annual, 1984* or *China's Statistical Yearbook*.

Industrial Goods

Textile and clothes 31.8%

14.9%

Primary goods

Machinery & transportation equiments

1952 54 56 58 60 62 64 66 68 70 72 74 76 78 80 82 83 84

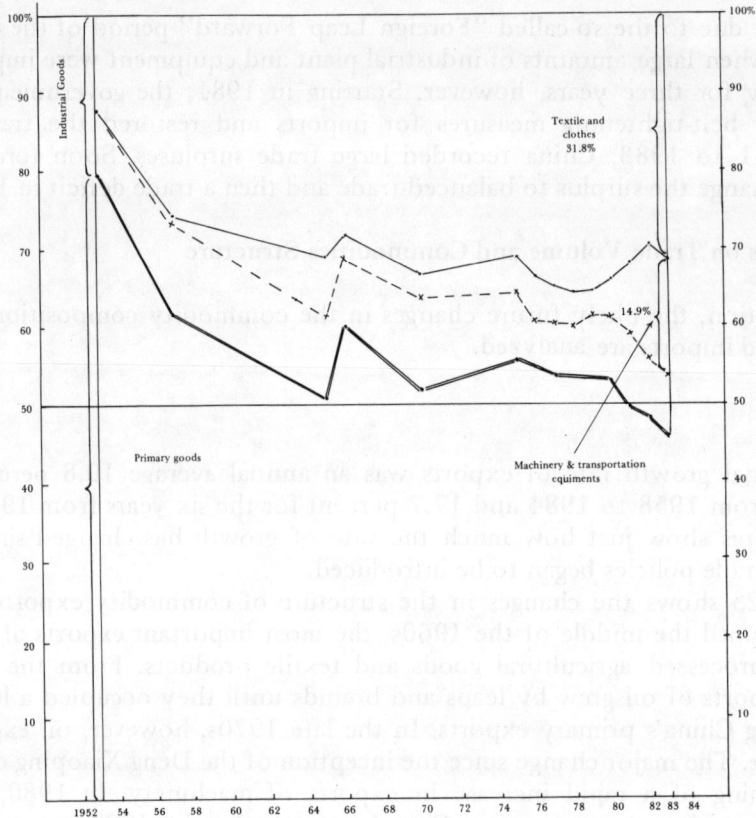

Source: *Zhong-guo duiwaijingji Nianjian* (China's International Economic Annual) 1984, p. IV-9.

Figure 23. Export Commodities Structure

Exports of Machinery

As seen from Figure 24, the ratio of exports of machinery in all exports up until 1980 was significantly lower in China than Japan and the Asian nations. The share of machinery exports in total was approximately equal to that of Thailand. This ratio, as mentioned earlier, began to rise rapidly after 1980. How much machinery exports will grow in the future basically depends on export competitiveness and trends in domestic demand. Therefore, export projections will be made through analysis of the domestic machinery production system. The most important of the exports of machinery are bicycles, televisions, and other mass production type consumer durables, so these will be examined.

For this analysis, the method developed by the Economic Institute of the Japan Machinery Promotion Association is borrowed. The institute published the results of its research in 1967 under the title *Ryosan Suijun to Kokusai Kyosoryoku* (Mass Production Scale and International Competitive Power). In the study, the institute analyzed the export competitiveness of Japan in motorcycles, sewing machines, cameras, radios, television sets, and other mass production type durable consumer goods from the end of the 1950s to the early 1960s. The Cobb Douglas type production function and Solow-type technical progress coefficient model are used to focus on the relationship between inputs of capital and labor and productivity. The institute revised the function as follows:

$$Y/L = K/L \times Y/K \text{ was modified to}$$
$$Y/L = K/L \times M/K \times 1/(M/Y)$$

where K is the input of capital, L labor, and M materials. Therefore, M/K is the ratio of materials over machinery and equipment, and 1/(M/Y) is the inverse of the basic materials input per unit of output. By determining the actual figures for M/K and 1/(M/Y) it was found that Japan succeeded in rapidly reducing materials usage compared with the more developed countries (MDCs) during the period in question. As a result, it was shown that Japan rapidly raised its labor productivity and succeeded in building up international competitiveness. Seen from the technical side, Japan's having moved ahead with innovations in materials and innovations in processes ahead of the MDCs was also a reason for Japan's success. In conclusion, it was found that, after the mass production scale reached 1 million units a year, Japan became more competitive than the other MDCs and rapidly increased its exports. This is shown in Figures 25, 26 and 27.

This method of analysis cannot be directly applied to China because of data limitations. However, consideration was given to Japan's exercise and an attempt made to obtain rough predictions for China from the available data.

Figure 28 shows the trends in production in the mass production machinery industries of China. The following can be read from this diagram: Bicycles, radios, sewing machines, wrist-watches, and other products of a first group had already reached the 1 million unit mass production scale something between the end of the 1950s and the early 1960s. China established a giant mass production system of between 10 to 30 million units a year by 1980. Television sets, tape recorders,

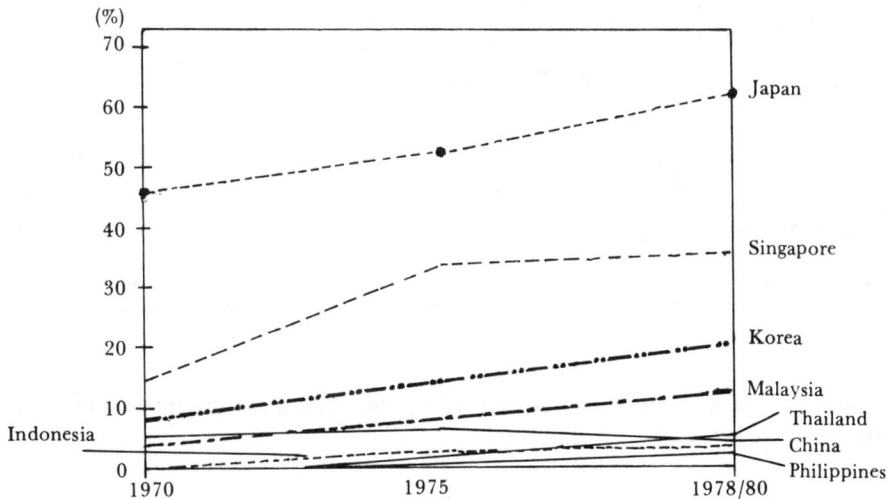

Source: Sueo Kojima's article in *Chugokukeizai no Chuchokitembo* [Long- and Middle-Term Projection of China's Economy], edited by S. Ishikawa, R. Kojima & S. Sekiguchi, p. 258.

Figure 24. Machinery Exports over Total Exports

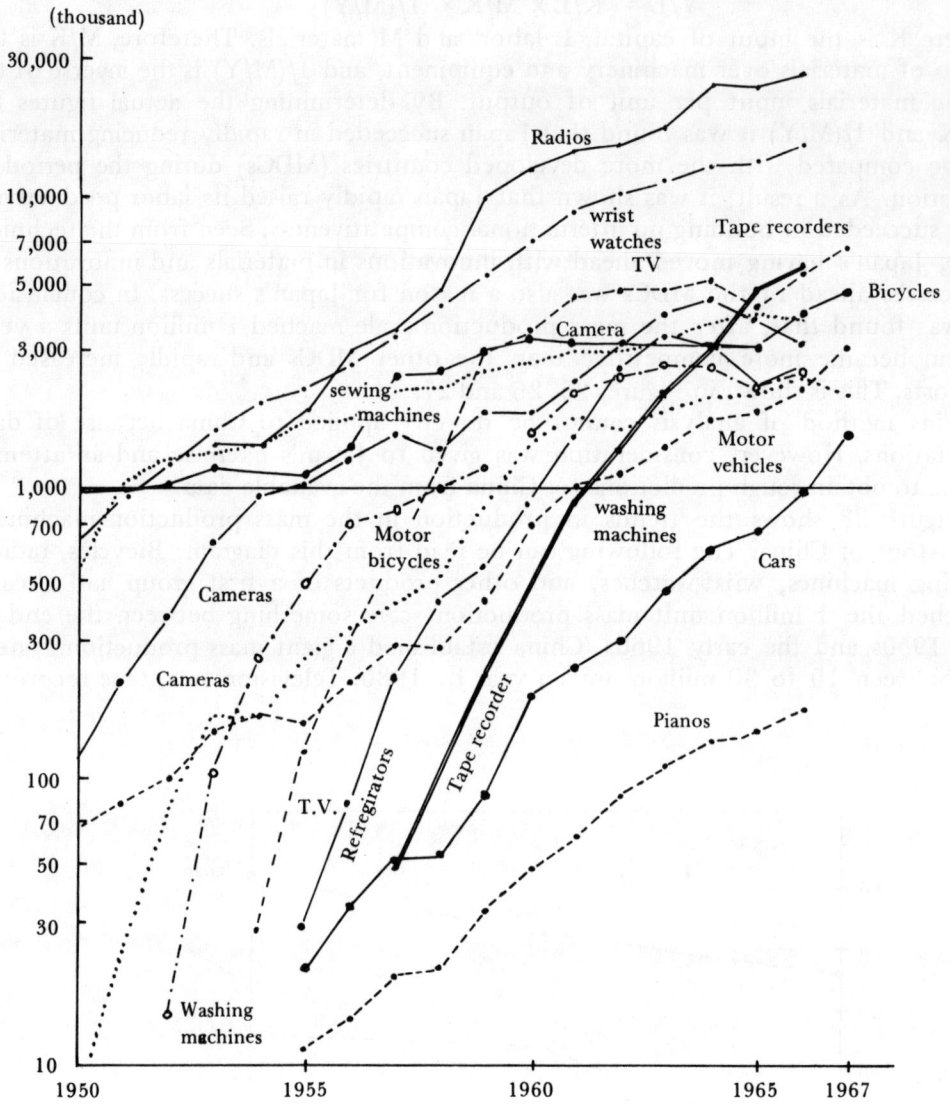

(thousand)

30,000

Radios

10,000

7,000

wrist
watches
TV   Tape recorders

5,000

Camera   Bicycles

3,000

sewing
machines

Motor
vehicles

1,000

700   Motor   washing
                   bicycles   machines   Cars

500   Cameras

300

        Cameras

        T.V.   Tape recorder   Pianos

100

                    Refregirators

70

50

30

        Washing
        machines

10
1950   1955   1960   1965   1967

Source: *Ryosan Suijun to Kokosai Kyosoryoku* [Mass production scale and international competitive power], 1968, pp. 20 & 21.

Figure 25. Mass Production Type of Machinery of Japan

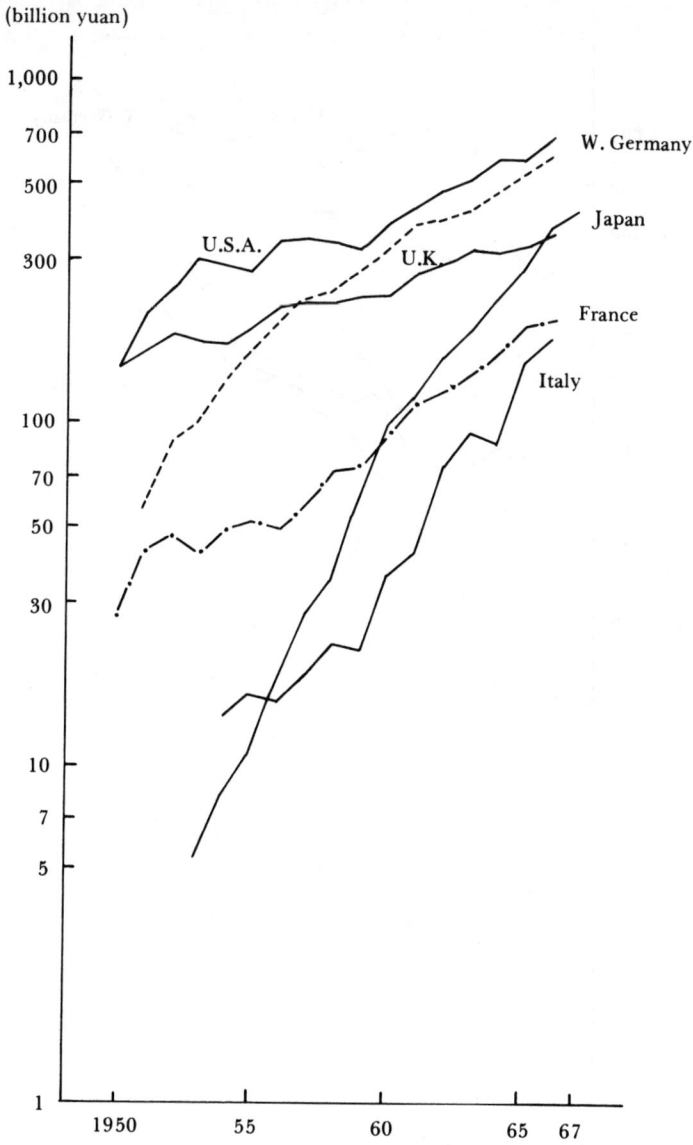

(billion yuan)

Source: *Ibid.*

Figure 26. Export Scale Comparison of Electrical Machines

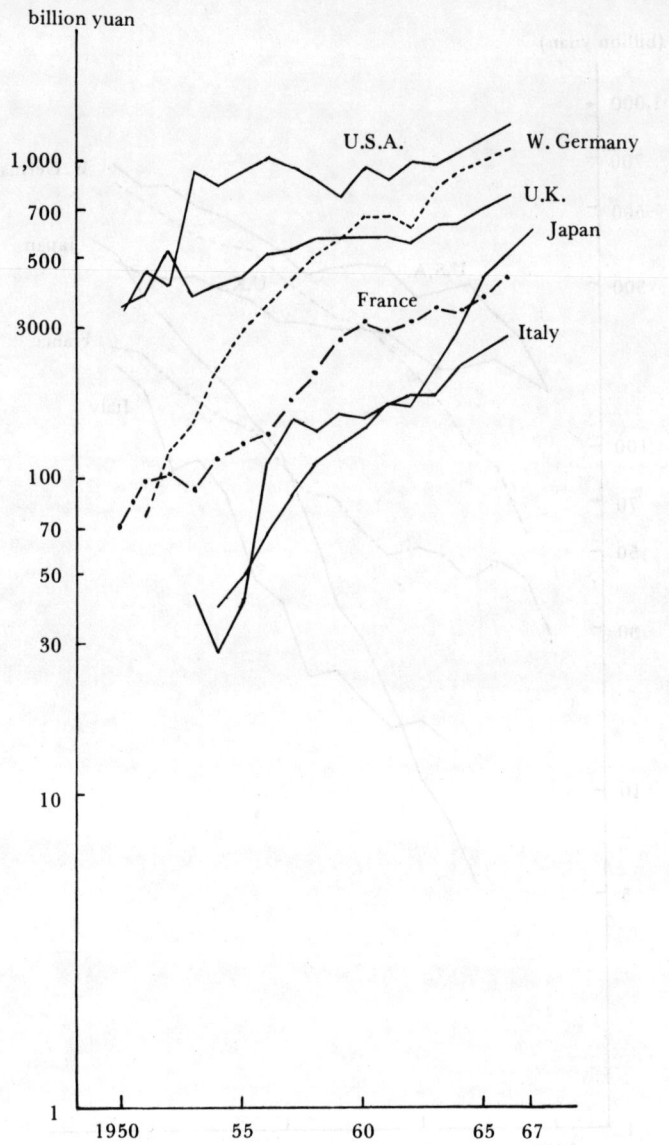

billion yuan

Source: *Ibid.*

Figure 27. Export Scale Comparison of Transportation Machines

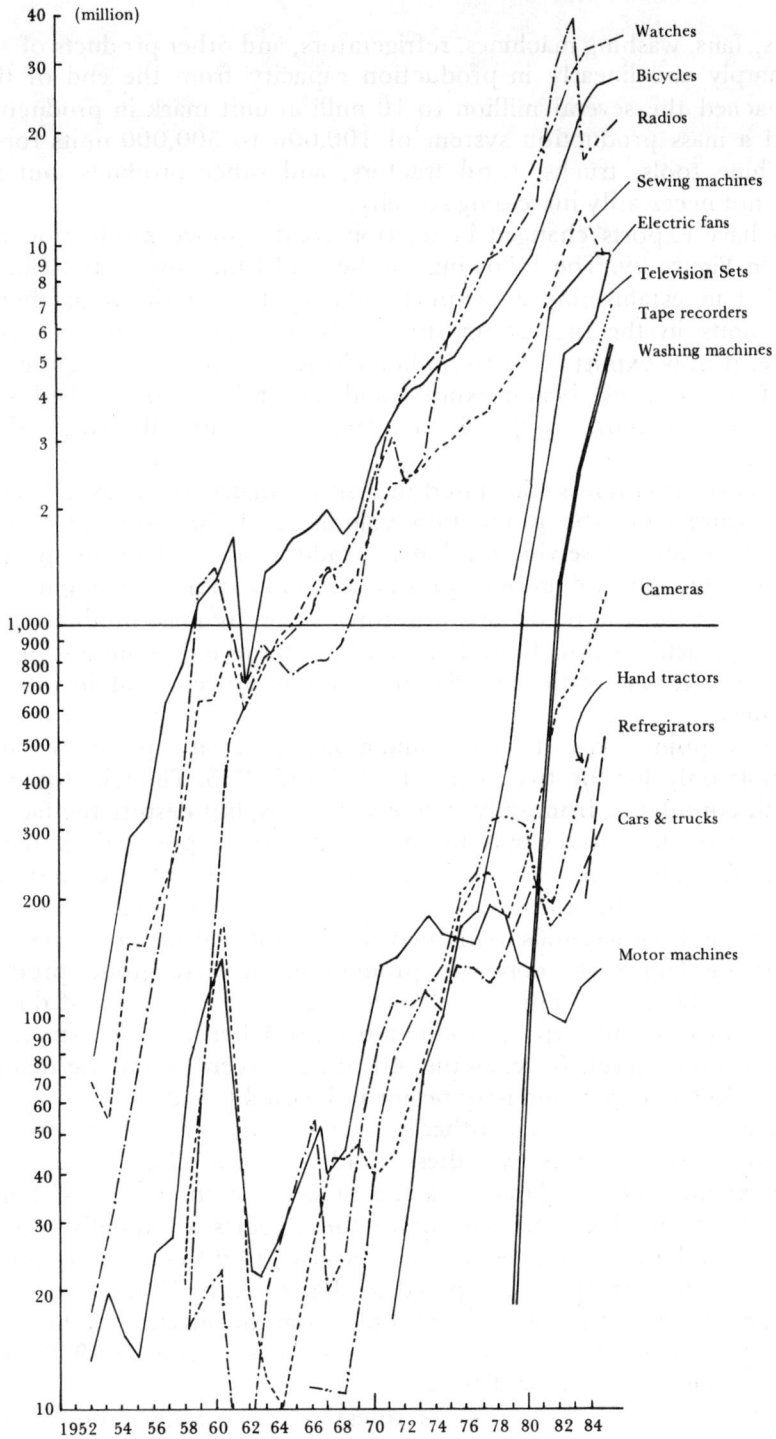

Sources: Op. cit. *China's International Economic Annual 1984; China's Statistical Yearbook* (See Footnote 27)

Figure 28. China's Mass Production Type — Machinery Production Volume

cameras, fans, washing machines, refrigerators, and other products of a second group rose sharply and linearly in production capacity from the end of the 1970s and have reached the several million to 10 million unit mark in production. China has reached a mass production system of 100,000 to 500,000 units for a third group of machine tools, trucks, hand tractors, and other products, but production of these is not necessarily increasing steadily.

How have exports changed in relation to the above production trends? This is shown in Figure 29. The following can be read from this figure: China has already succeeded in establishing an export industry for hundreds of thousands to 1.5 million units in the first group and has been steadily increasing its exports. For example, it now exports 6 to 10 million clocks, one item in the group. In the second group, China has just begun exports and has still not established a strong export industry. In the third group, China is exporting, but only irregularly and in small amounts.

The above situation is illustrated in a single figure in Figure 30. The vertical axis of the figure gives the production volume, and the horizontal axis the export volume. Bicycles and sewing machines, products of the first group, it may be seen, moved steadily upward in both production and exports starting in the 1980s. The trend for bicycles can be divided into three stages by mass production scale and that for sewing machines into four. This can be interpreted as suggesting some stepwise development in innovation in the production process and in international competitiveness.

The next point relates to the second group. Data on exports for the second group is available only for the two years of 1982 and 1983. Though nothing much can be said with confidence from only two observations, but despite the fact that domestic production of these items only began recently, the export ratio in the second group is relatively high compared with production. However, the trend is for exports to decline relative to production. This phenomenon also applied to the first group in the 1950s and early 1960s. This may be interpreted in the following way. In the stage before large-scale domestic production of first group products is firmly established, the export ratio is relatively high, but expansion of domestic demand leads to a drop in the export-production ratio. When the domestic rate of diffusion reaches a certain level, for example, 40 to 50 percent, domestic demand continues to be met and an export industry begins to be established.

Without analysis of some other related elements, no firm conclusions can be drawn as to whether this hypothesis holds true for China's mass production-type machinery industries. In Japan's case, a mass production scale of 1 million units is used as a benchmark in determining whether exports will rapidly increase. However, no easy conclusions may be drawn because of differences in the international economy of the mid-1980s compared to that of early 1960s. The conditions of the 1980s include strong competition not only from the advanced industrialized nations, but also the Asian NICs. A further difference from Japan in 1960s is the existence of a giant domestic market in China.

Despite these differences in order to estimate the possibilities for future exports of products of the second group, the temptation to use the hypothesis that when the domestic diffusion rate reaches 40 to 50 percent, an export industry is established was given in to. Based on this hypothesis, we try to predict the future of television exports — one industry for which necessary data is available. As seen in Figure 6, the diffusion rate of television sets among households was 30 percent in

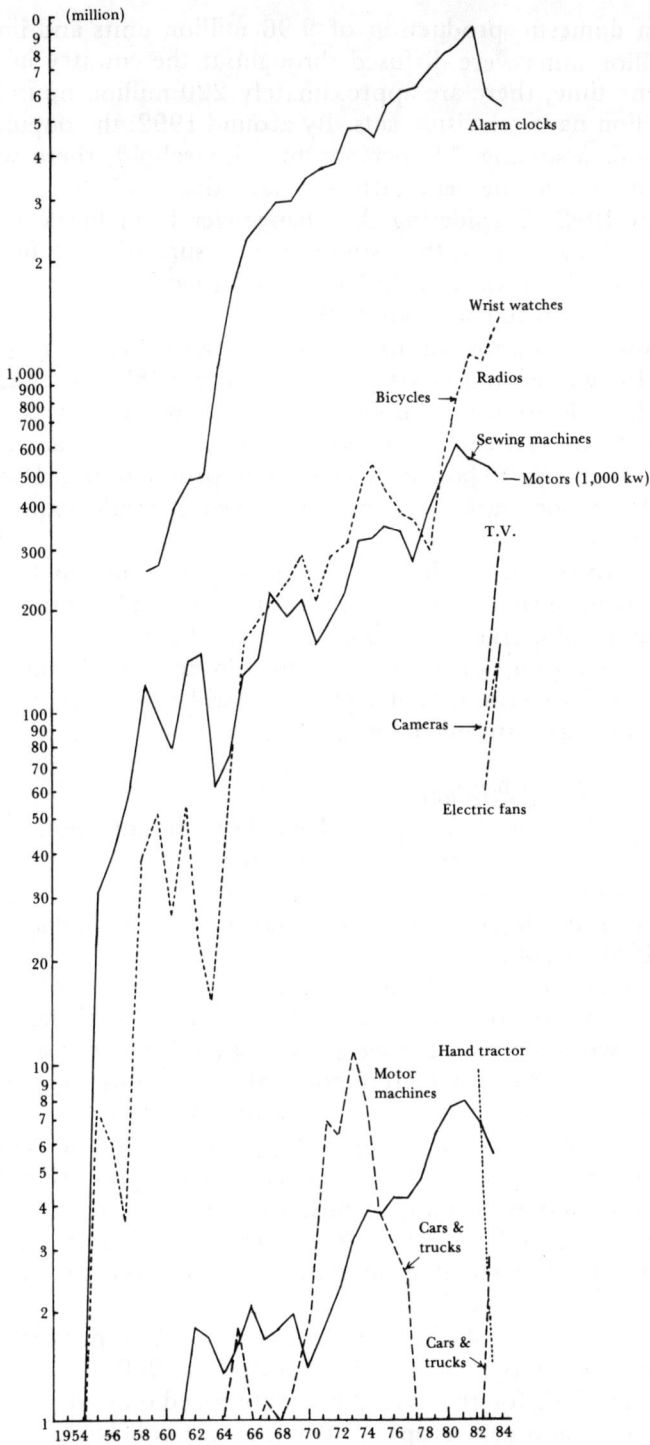

Figure 29. China's Mass Production Type of Machinery — Export Volume

Sources: *Ibid.*

1984. With a domestic production of 9.96 million units and imports of 4 million units, 14 million units were diffused throughout the country in a one-year period. At the present time, there are approximately 220 million households in China. Of these, 66 million have television sets. By around 1992, the population will be about 1.1 billion and, assuming 3.9 persons to a household, there will be 282 million households. With a 50 percent diffusion rate there will be 141 million television sets owned in 1992. Considering the changeover from black and white television sets to color television sets, this would mean a spread of 15 million sets a year to get a 50 percent diffusion rate in five years' time. It may be concluded that the export ratio will begin to rise around 1990.

Table 3 shows the export ratios of various mass production type machinery. The export ratio for television sets was 4.3 percent in 1983. Up until around 1990, the export ratio for television sets should move around the 4 percent level. After that, it should rise little by little. Assuming China achieves a giant production scale of 20 million units in 1990 (Japan's television set production in 1984 was 14.4 million units) and the export ratio is 5 percent, then it could export approximately 1 million sets a year.

Estimating exports of machinery of the second group in the same way as television sets, it is projected that exports of this group will begin to account for a large portion of the world market sometime in the 1990's.

As for the third group of products, which are technically more complicated than those of the second group, China probably will not enter into the international market on a full scale until much later.

Exports of Agricultural Products
Agricultural production and exports have been bright spots among the Chinese economic reforms. There has been an extremely large increase in production since 1979. Agricultural production is now basically able to meet domestic demand. Figure 31 shows the targets for agricultural output and the actual results up until 1985, using 1980 as 100.

From the figure one can see the increase in production of key agricultural products in the six years from 1979 to 1985 has been much faster than in the past. A comparison with the real annual growth rates for the years 1953 to 1978 and the years 1979 to 1985 shows production of grain crops went up from 2.4 percent to 3.4 percent, production of cotton was up from 2 percent to 15.2 percent, and of oil bearing crops the rise was from 0.8 percent to 14.6 percent. Meat production growth rose from 3.6 percent to 9.6 percent. This shows that the one percentage point rise in production of grain crops allowed production of cash crops and meat to advance by leaps and bounds. After reaching food grain self sufficiency, China has been shifting emphasis of production in agriculture to cash crops and animal husbandry.

A specutacular result of the new emphasis is that production of cotton has already exceeded the targets set in 1982 for the year 2000.

Targets set in 1982 for the year 2000 were based on policy considerations stressing animal protein and cash crops. Under the new policies, production targets have been realized at a much faster pace than the government anticipated.

How has China's foreign trade in agricultural produce changed due to these changes in the structure of its agricultural output?

Since 1983 China has changed from being a net importer to a net exporter of

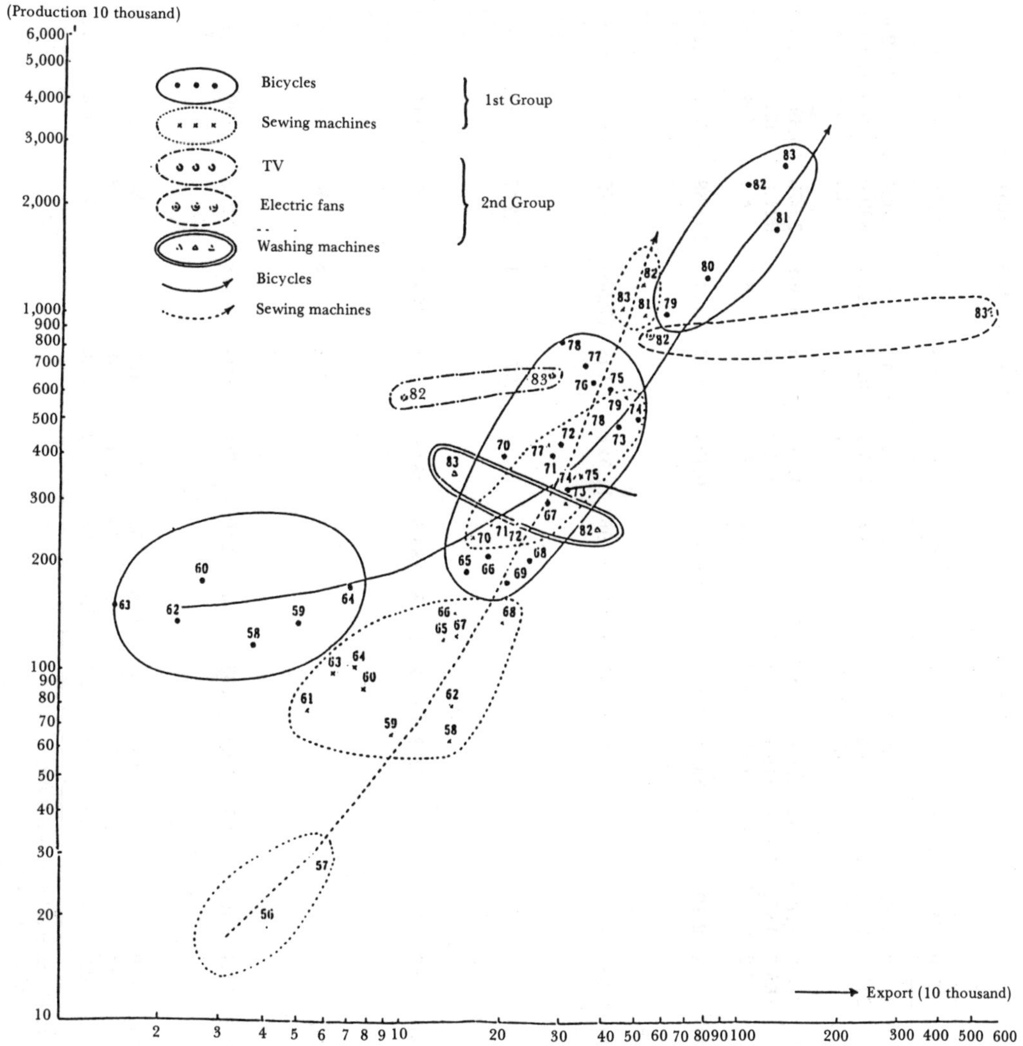

Source: *Ibid.*

Figure 30. Production and Export of Mass Production Type of Machines

Table 3. Ratio of Exports over Production (in number)

		1970	1971	1972	1973	1974	1975	1976	1977	1978	1979	1980	1981	1982	1983	1984
Bicycle	Production (1,000)	3,688	4,126	4,404	4,968	5,196	6,232	6,681	7,427	8,540	10,095	13,024	17,543	24,200	27,582	28,570
	Export (1,000)	215.1	290.5	312.0	463.8	531.3	441.7	393.8	375.9	302.8	642.1	839.0	1,119.4	1,091.3	1,392.0	
	Ratio (%)	5.8	7	7.1	9.3	10.2	7.1	5.9	5.1	3.5	6.4	6.4	6.4	4.5	5	
Sewing machines	Production (1,000)	2,352	2,499	2,632	2,936	3,189	3,567	3,638	4,242	4,865	5,868	7,678	10,391	12,860	10,872	9,320
	Export (1,000)	163.5	187.8	237.1	319.1	324.3	355.1	336.0	284.0	386.3	496.7	621.0	562.3	546.2	495.1	
	Ratio (%)	7.2	7.5	9	10.9	10.2	10	9.2	6.7	7.9	8.5	8.1	5.4	4.2	4.6	
Radios	Production (1,000)	3,231	2,403	2,739	5,028	7,230	9,356	9,691	10,494	11,677	13,807	30,038	40,572	17,239	19,989	21,860
	Export (1,000)													1,062	1,477	
	Ratio (%)													6.2	7.4	
Wrist watches	Production (1,000)	3,581	4,292	4,917	5,732	6,735	8,090	9,496	11,528	14,108	17,504	22,675	29,066	33,132	34,781	36,440
	Export (1,000)													1,293	1,575	
	Ratio (%)													3.9	4.5	
Electric fans	Production (1,000)									1,378	2,331	7,237	10,499	9,186	10,457	
	Export (1,000)													766	1,569	
	Ratio (%)													8.3	15	
TV sets	Production (1,000)	10.5	17.8	32.3	75.8	101.8	177.8	184.5	284.6	577.3	1,328.5	2,492	5,394	5,920	6,840	9,960
	Export (1,000)													105	297	
	Ratio (%)													1.8	4.3	
Washing machines	Production (1,000)									0.4	18	245	1,281	2,583	3,659	5,780
	Export (1,000)													40	129	
	Ratio (%)													1.5	3.5	
Hand tractors	Production (1,000)	51.4	80.9	89.5	119.3	138	209.4	240	321	324	318	218	199	298	498	670
	Export (1,000)													9.7	1.5	
	Ratio (%)													3.3	0.3	
Motor machine	Production (1,000)	139	146	162	183	165	175	157	199	183	140	134	103	100	121	131
	Export (1,000)	14	18	23	33	39	39	44	43	48	65	78	80	72	57	
	Ratio (%)	0.9	1.2	1.4	1.8	2.4	2.2	2.8	2.2	2.6	4.7	5.8	7.8	7.2	4.7	

Sources: Production 1970-83: *China's Statistical Yearbook, 1984.*
Production 1984: *People's Daily, 1985, 3.26.*
Export: *China's Trade Annual 1984.*

(1980 = 100)

Index

(2200) Milk

500 ─────────────────────────────────────── (500)
Fruit

450

400

350

300

(260)
250 ⊙Oil bearing crops

(225)
Cotton
(216)
200 ─────────────────────────────── (200)
Meat

(154)
Oil bearing (200) Meat
crops (135) (160) Cotton
150 (150) Food

(127)
Food (125) Population
Cotton (120)
100 ───────────────────────────────

Food
50
Meat Deng Xiaoping Period

1950 52 54 56 58 60 62 64 66 68/70 72 74 76 78 80 82 84 86 88 90   2000

Cultural Revolution Period

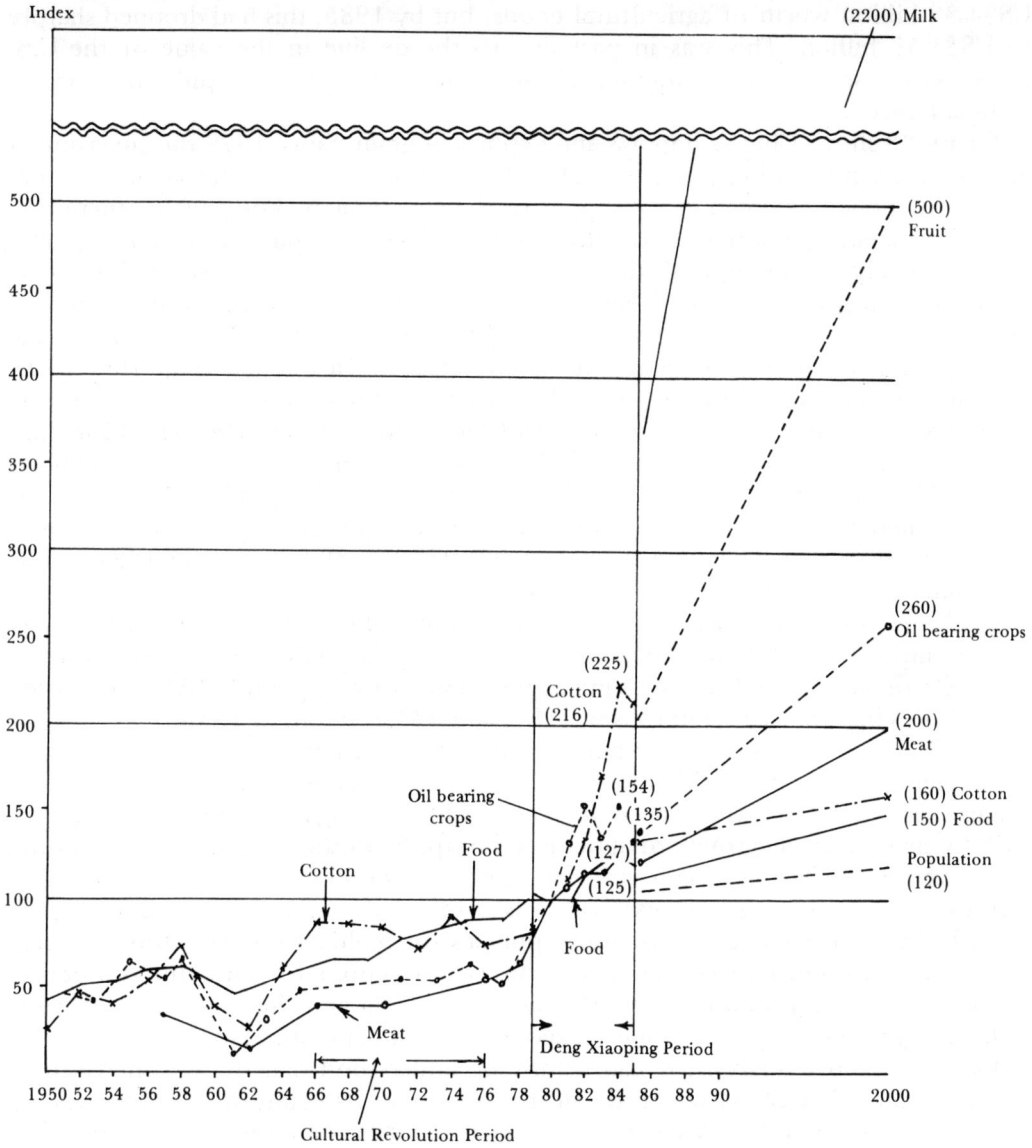

Sources: (1) *China's Statistical Yearbook,* 1984, 1985.
(2) 1985; *People's Daily,* Feb.
(3) 2000: T. Tajima's article, *Chugokukeizai no Chuchokitenbo* [Long & Middle Term Projections of Chinese Economy], Japan-China Association for Economy and Trade, 1984, p. 129.

Figure 31. Chinese Agricultural Production and Targets in 2000

agricultural produce (Figure 32). No data are available on the total value of China's imports of agricultural goods before 1981, but China is known to have been a net importer of agricultural produce over the years since 1961. In 1982, it imported US$4.32 billion worth of agricultural goods, but by 1985, this had dropped sharply to US$1.57 billion. This was in part due to the decline in the value of the U.S. dollar with respect to the renminbi. However, imports had also rapidly dropped in volume terms.

Figure 33 shows China's imports and exports of grain. Since 1979 the government has raised its purchasing price for agricultural produce and, at the same time, has relaxed its policy of compulsory supply to the government. For a while, therefore, the government did not increase the amount of grain it purchased domestically. Approximately 20 million of the young people who had been sent off into the rural areas during the Cultural Revolution returned to the cities of their birth in 1978 and 1979. To provide grain to feed the rapidly swelling urban populations, the government sharply increased its grain imports. In 1982, it imported 16.12 million tons of grain. However, with the growth in domestic grain production, the government was able to reduce imports to 13.44 million tons in 1983, 10.45 million tons in 1984, and 5.43 million tons in 1985. At the same time, it increased exports from 1.15 million tons in 1983 to 3.19 million tons in 1984, and 9.05 million tons in 1985, making China a net exporter. The most important of its grain exports is corn, exports of which shot up from zero in 1983 to 950,000 tons in 1984 and to 6.15 million tons in 1985.

Trade in cotton has also been changing remarkably. The past record high in cotton imports was 900,000 tons in 1980, but this had fallen to 220,000 tons by 1983. On the other hand, while China exported no cotton up until 1982, it exported 68,000 tons in 1983, 190,000 tons in 1984, and 335,000 tons in 1985.

This increase in agricultural exports, it must be noted, is not merely a temporary phenomenon. Since 1978, Chinese agriculture has been undergoing various structural changes. The domestic structure of demand has been changing at the same time.

With changes in the growth of agricultural output and the structure of agriculture, the government has launched policies aimed at developing certain agricultural regions of China with greater exports to international markets as a long-term goal. Specifically, China has begun to adopt policies for building up agriculture in three regions, i.e., the Pearl River Delta, to form export centers for agricultural produce. It has just started promoting the Shandong peninsula and the Liaodong peninsula of Liaoning province as similar specialized regions for agricultural exports.

From the above analysis, it can readily be understood that there is increasingly greater chance that China will in the near future make its debut on the international agricultural commodities market as a major exporter of farm produce. In 1972 (average value for 1971 to 1973) and 1982 (average value for 1981 to 1983), China exported US$1.37 billion and US$3.48 billion worth of agricultural produce. The nominal growth rate in those 10 years was thus 9.8 percent. If the above two points are considered, then it may be assumed that, so long as there are no great price changes, the nominal growth rate until 1990 will be 10 to 12 percent. Assuming a middle level of 11 percent growth is attained, China will be exporting around US$8.0 billion worth of agricultural goods in 1990.

Exports of Textile Products
Among China's overall exports, textile products have been most important. The

US$ (million)

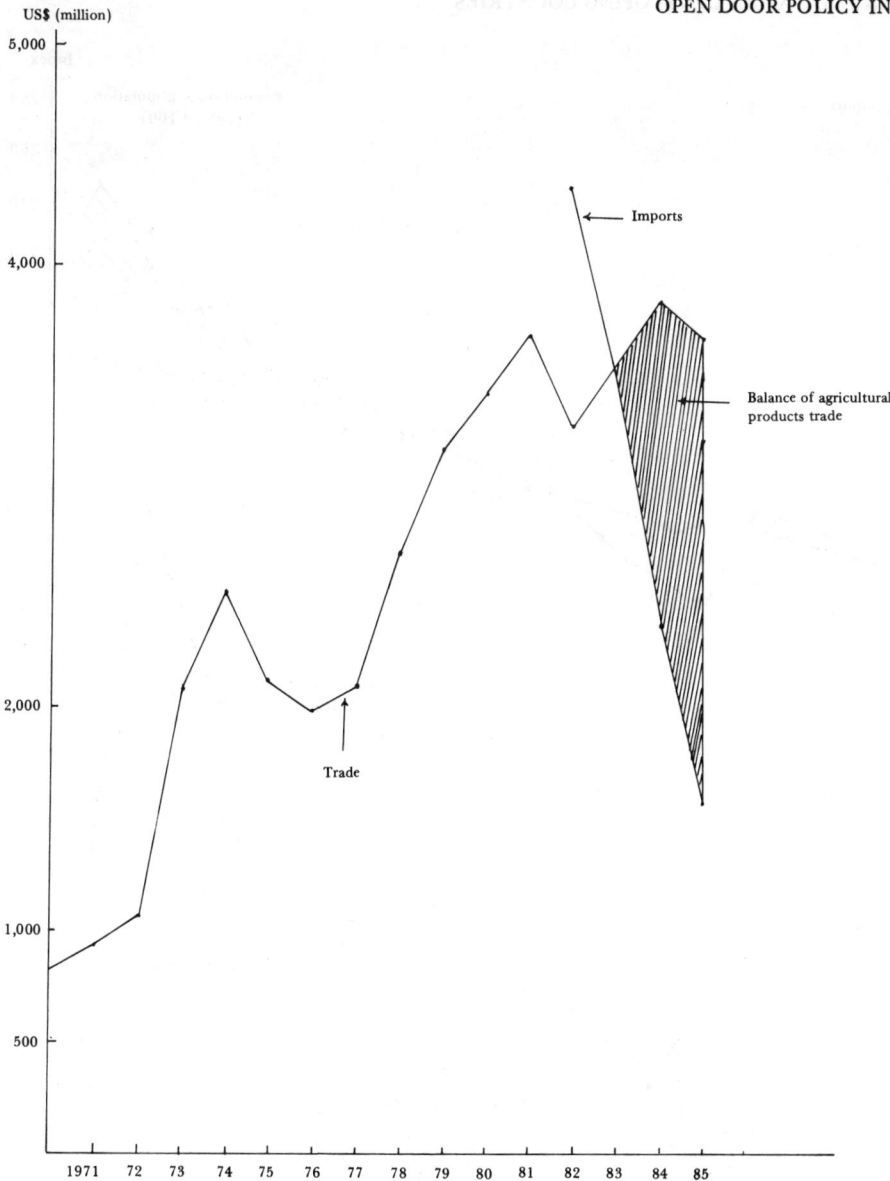

Sources: Exports 1970-83. *Zhongguo Duiwai Jingjimaoyi Nianian 1984* [Chinese Trade Annual
1984], China's Foreign Trade Publishing Company, 1984, p. IV-7.
1982: *Haiguan Tongji* [Custom Statistics] 1984, No. 3.
Imports 1982: *Haiguan Tongji*, Ibid.
1983-85: *Haiguan Tongji* 1985 No. 4-January to September figures are converted into
annual ones.

Note: Total figures until 1981 of agricultural products imports are not published. Figures after
1982 are published in the custom statistics in Chinese yuan. Figures after 1982 are
converted into US dollars by year-end official conversion rates between US dollar and
Chinese yuan. The coverage of agricultural products before 1981 and after 1982 seems
different. China has adopted the SITC classification since 1982. The Chinese yuan's
conversion rates have devalued since 1984.

Figure 32. China's Exports & Imports of Agricultural Products in Nominal Terms

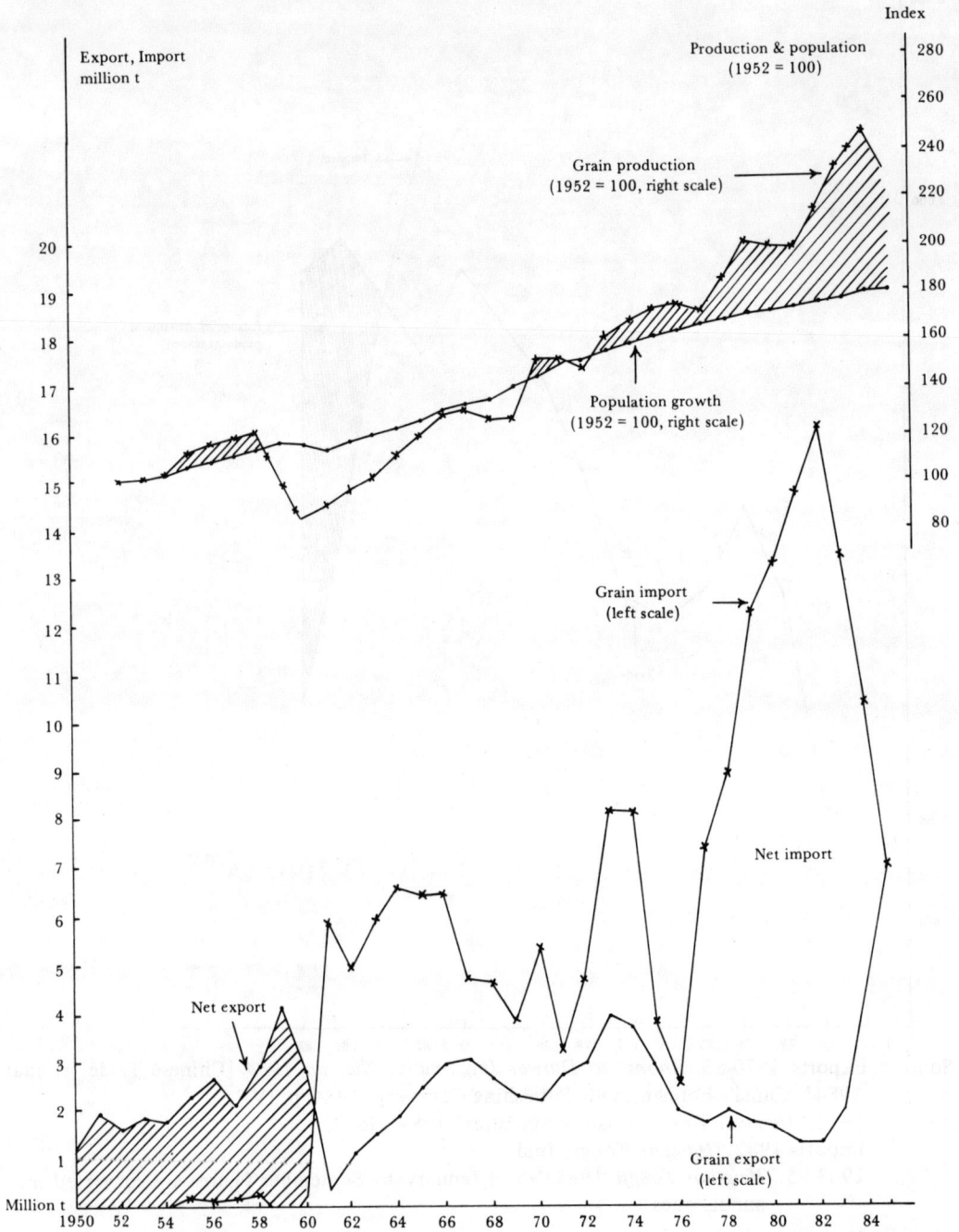

Sources: Grain production and population growth, calculated from *China's Statistical Yearbook,* 1984, 1985.

Grain import and export, *Zhongguo Duiwai Jingjimaoyi Nianjian* 1984, pp. IV-88, 118. Figures of 1985, *Peking shubo* [Peking Review, Japanese edition], Jan. 17, 1986, p. 46.

Figure 33. Production & Population and Grain Exports & Imports

maximum share held was in 1961, when textile product exports accounted for 35.2 percent of total exports, but this declined to 21.4 percent by 1970 and 18 percent by 1980. While the relative importance of these exports has declined, it is likely that exports of textile products will remain important in the future.

Table 4 lists the nominal annual growth rates in the 10 year period from 1972 (average value for 1971 to 1973) to 1982 (average value for 1981 to 1983). The growth rate for textile products as a whole was 15.6 percent. The items with above average rates of increase were knits, at 15.84 percent, woolens, at 17.9 percent, silk fabrics, at 20.83 percent, apparel, at 24.6 percent, and mixed cotton-synthetic fabrics, at 28.7 percent. Those with growth rates lower than the average were yarn and cotton cloth. Thus, in the 10 years from 1972, exports of products with higher value added have enjoyed high growth rates. This reflects a greater degree of sophistication in the domestic production structure for textiles and, at the same time, a gradual increase in the international competitiveness of products of high value and high degrees of processing. China will probably increasingly assume a greater role as an exporter of everything from primary processed goods to highly processed goods on the international textile products market in the future.

The nominal annual growth rate in exports of textile products should be higher than 15.6 percent. Here, future dollar values of textile exports were estimated assuming a growth rate of 16 percent.

The average for the three years spanning 1972 was US$8.86 billion, that for 1982 US$3.78 billion, and that for 1990, it is estimated to be around US$12.4 billion.

Trends in Imports

The value of imports reached US$42.26 billion in 1985, a 54.2 percent jump from the previous year. This was because of the massive importation of durable consumer goods, like television sets, home appliances and automobiles. For this reason, when

Table 4. Export Growth Rates of Textile Products in 1972 to 1982

	Growth Rate
Silk yarn (net weight)	2.63%
Cotton cloth (same)	3.26
Synthetic cloth (same)	5.1
Wool (same)	7.4
Cotton yarn (same)	9.48
Textile goods as a whole (price)	15.6
Cotton knits (same)	15.84
Wool knits (same)	17.9
Silk goods (net weight)	20.83
Clothing (value)	24.6
Cotton tetoron cloth (net weight)	28.7

Source: *Zhongguo Duiwai Jingjimaoyi Nianjian 1984* [Chinese Trade Annual 1984], China's Foreign Trade Publishing Company, 1984, pp. IV 92-93.

calculating the average annual growth rate of imports, it is better not to use the 1985 values for imports. Here, the value of imports in the benchmark years of 1952, 1978, and 1984 were used, taking the average for the surrounding three years, to calculate the likely future growth rate of imports (nominal). Calculation of the nominal average annual growth rates for the 26 years from 1953 to 1978 and the six years from 1979 to 1984 gives a figure of 8.9 percent for the former period and 18 percent for the latter. The average annual growth rate for the 32 years as a whole was 10.6 percent.

If we use the figure of 10.6 percent to forecast imports for the period of the seventh five-year plan (1986 to 1990), then we would get the following:

    1985: US$33.57 billion (compared to the actual figure of US$42.36 billion
       reported by the *People's Daily,* February 29, 1986)
    1986: US$37.13 billion
    1987: US$41.06 billion
    1988: US$45.51 billion
    1989: US$50.23 billion
    1990: US$55.55 billion

By commodity, the most important imports are agricultural produce, intermediate goods, and plant and equipment.

1. Imports of agricultural produce, as already mentioned, should not increase that much in the future.
2. The imports which will almost certainly increase steadily in the future are those of intermediate goods. This was already made clear with relation to iron and steel, plastics, and lumber (see Figure 18). Calculation of the rate of increase for imports of industrial raw materials for the 10 years from 1973 to 1982 using official statistics gives a figure of 17 percent (on a nominal value basis). The average rate of increase for total imports during the same period (by nominal value) was 18.5 percent, fairly close to that of imports of intermediate goods. This result arose due to the sharp increase in imports of consumption goods, principally grain, during the period. It is projected that imports of agricultural produce will decline on a relative basis, so the rate of increase of imports of intermediate goods should rise. They are expected to increase roughly parallel to the increase in imports forecast earlier.
3. Imports of plant and equipment (*Chengdaoshebei* in Chinese) display considerable ups and downs. In the past 35 years, there have been four great waves of plant and equipment imports. In the 1950s about 55 percent of all imports was accounted for by plant and equipment. During the economic turmoil of the years 1959 to 1961, these imports plummeted, but there was a second wave in 1965 to 1967 for the third five-year plan of 1966 to 1970, a third wave in the early 1970s, and a fourth wave in 1979 to 1981. The fourth wave was related to the investment needs for the sixth five-year plan of 1981 to 1985. Of the total US$14.44 billion in imports of plant and equipment during that period, the value of imports of industrial plant reached no less than US$6.9 billion. This import policy of the Hua Guofeng administration came under criticism later by the rightists as a "Foreign Leap Forward" policy.

These four great waves of imports were characterized by being concentrated in the last year of a prior five-year plan to the first half of a current five-year plan. This has been because of the need to purchase plants required for key projects of the current five-year plan in the first half of the plan. After progress was made in the key projects, foreign currency reserves were often drained necessitating a subsequent clampdown on imports in the third and fourth year of the plan. This cycle has been continuously repeated.

In 1984 and 1985, however, this old cycle was considerably changed. In those two years, the general economic policy of expanding consumption and the economic reforms delegating some import powers to local level authorities resulted in massive imports of television sets, passenger cars, and other durable consumer goods, resulting in a drain on foreign currency. No import contracts for valuable large scale plants were made in 1985 or 1986 up to March. The Deng Xiaoping administration, which had grasped the reigns of power through criticism of the imports of large-scale plants during the days of the Hua Guofeng administration as a "Foreign Leap Forward", adopted a policy of emphasis on technical renovation of existing facilities rather than construction of new large-scale projects. Only limited growth can be expected in productive capacity with just the improvement of the operational efficiency of existing plants. This is one of the reasons for the rapid rise in imports of intermediate goods these past two to three years. For example, imports of finished steel reached 9.78 million tons in 1983 and 13.32 million tons in 1984 — with massive amounts of steel being imported.

In consideration of the above, if China does not resort again soon to imports of large-scale plant in the middle to later period of its seventh five-year plan (1986 to 1990) for the next stage of growth, it is projected that it will run up against obstacles in raising its productive capacity in the early 1990s. Therefore, a fifth wave of plant imports is expected to arrive around 1988 to 1989.

Regional Structure of Trade

China's trade partners may be classified into OECD member countries, socialist countries, and developing countries. With respect to these three groupings, China enjoyed almost balanced trade in the 1960s and 1970s with the socialist countries, suffered a large deficit in trade with the OECD member countries, and paid for that deficit with a large surplus in its trade with the third world. China began to open up its economy in 1978. In the years since then to 1985, how has the regional structure of its trade changed?

The above-mentioned basic trade structure has remained the same, but trade has been expanding. This is shown in Figure 34. In the latter stage of the Cultural Revolution, from 1973 to 1977, the deficit in trade with the OECD member countries and the surplus in trade with the third world gradually increased. This trend became more apparent from 1978. The deficit in trade with the OECD member countries reached US$6.56 billion in 1981. This was due to the excess plant import contracts signed in the Hua Guofeng days. In 1981 and 1982, strong belt-tightening measures were taken and the trade deficit shrank in 1982, but it rose again in 1983. In 1984 and 1985, China again recorded a massive deficit due both to imports of capital goods from Japan and also to massive imports of television sets, automobiles, and the like. This resulted in adoption of new belt-tightening measures since the first half of 1985. The economic open door policy has been strengthening the trend toward increased imports from the OECD member countries even more than in the past.

On the other hand, China has launched an export drive to the third world and recorded large surpluses proportional to the increased deficit with the OECD

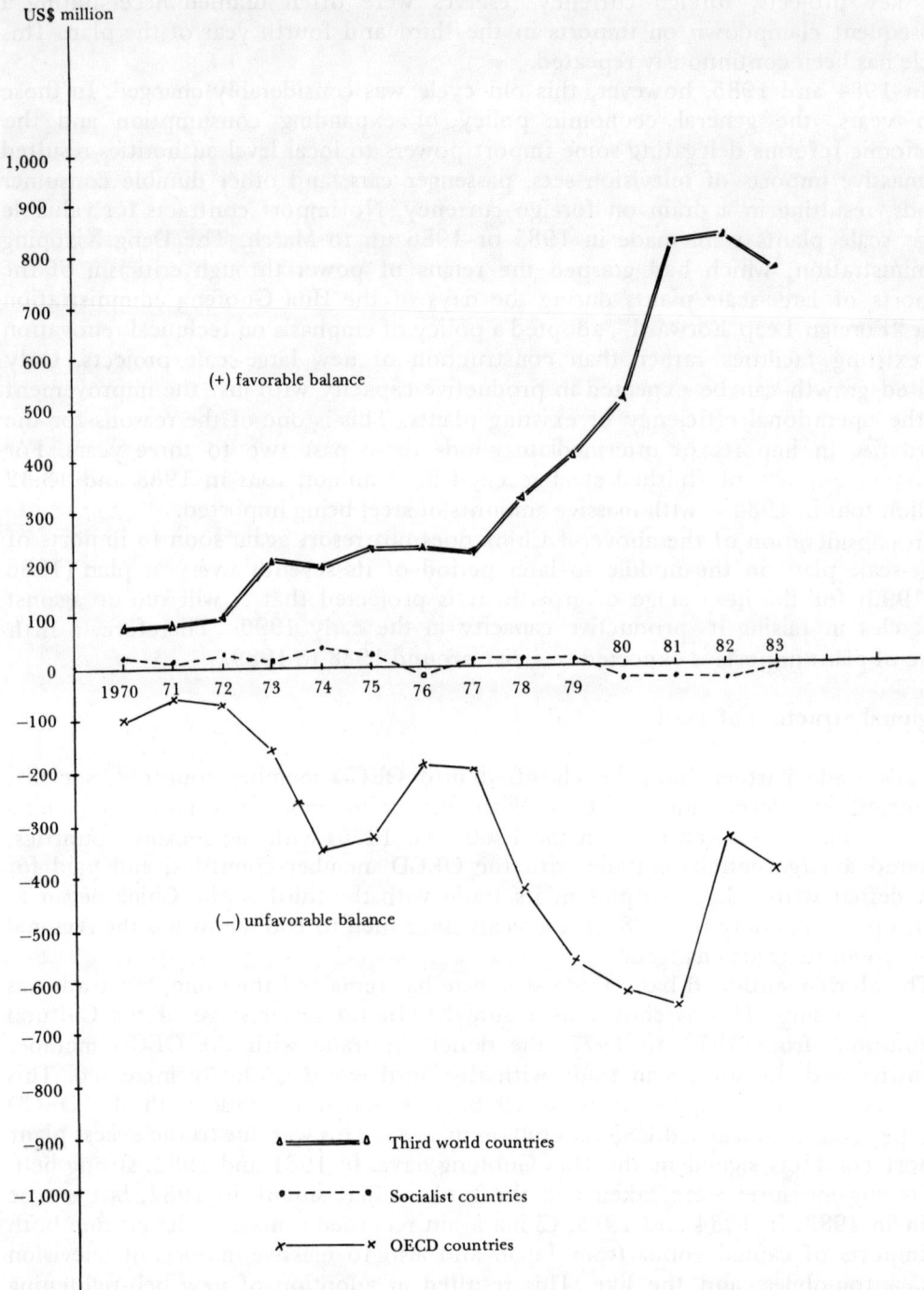

Source: *Zhongguo Duiwai Jingjimaoyi Nianjian 1984,* [Chinese Trade Annual 1984], ed. Chinese Trade Annual Editing Committee, Beijing: China's Foreign Trade Publishing Company, 1984.

Figure 34. China's Trade Balance According to Three Areas

countries. In 1981 and 1982, it recorded surpluses of US$8.2 billion and US$8.36 billion with the developing world. China is exporting more to the third world as it increases its imports from the OECD countries.

China adopted a basic policy of "paying for imports with exports" in the 1960s and 1970s. What this policy means is that China would limit its imports to within the range of foreign currency earned from exports. In Figure 22, it is seen that China recorded deficits for two consecutive years (1974 and 1975) suggesting some change in this policy. Those two years, however, were at the time of the most violent policy struggle between the leftists and the rightists. The leftists' deficit-increasing trade policies were criticized as "foreign servitude". When Hua Guofeng took power, imports from advanced capitalist countries rapidly increased, but this was only after 1977. In the three years 1978 to 1980, China recorded consecutive massive trade deficits. This was the first time this had happened since 1956. This deficit-producing policy was one of the reasons for the fall of the Hua Guofeng administration. After this, the basic policy of paying imports with exports was restored.

The basic policy became more flexible, however, as it was changed from one of maintaining a surplus for every year of deficit to one allowing two or three consecutive years' of deficits. Looking at the belt-tightening measures taken in the first half of 1985, however, one may conclude that things have not yet changed enough to allow four to five consecutive years of deficits.

The surge in imports from the OECD countries has led China to apply more effort in its export drive to the third world. In addition to this, however, it should be noted that exports to the OECD countries have also been increasing. Table 5 shows how much imports and exports have grown; by trade partner, in the 10 years from 1972 to 1982. Exports to the OECD nations have increased by an annual average of 21.3 percent (nominal). This is higher than the annual rate of increase of exports to the third world. Strongly contributing to this growth have been increased

Table 5. China's Trade Developments — 1972 and 1982

Trade partners	Growth rates (Nominal: %)
Total exports	18.5
to OECD countries	21.3
to socialist countries	4.6
to third world countries	20
of which Hong Kong and Macao	18
Total imports	18.3
from OECD countries	19.8
from socialist countries	9.4
from third world countries	19.5
of which from Hong Kong and Macao	37.2

Source: Same as Fig. 34.

Notes: 1972's figure is an average of 3 years of 1971-73.
1982's figure is that of 1981-83.

exports of textile products and oil to Japan.

A while ago, it was mentioned that China earned large amounts of foreign currency through its trade with the third world. Table 6 analyzes this. For the third world, we focus on three groups: Hong Kong and Macao, Singapore, and the oil exporting countries. The oil exporting countries have been focused on to determine whether or not they have increased their imports from China to any particular degree due to their increased income after the first and second oil crises.

Several interesting points can be read from Table 6. First, 80 to 95 percent of China's trade surplus with the third world derives from trade with these three groups. Among the three, most of the export surplus comes from trade with Hong Kong and Macao. Since 1981, however, the relative importance of the export surplus with these three regions has fallen rapidly. The major reason for this has been the relative decline in the surplus due to exports to Hong Kong and Macao. As seen from the bottom rows of Table 6, China's imports from Hong Kong and Macao have risen sharply by a nominal 37.2 percent a year in the 10 years from 1972 to 1982. The rise has been particularly great since 1981. 1981 was the year in which construction began in earnest on the Shenzhen Special Economic Zone (SEZ) though the decision for the establishment of the SEZs had been made back in 1978. The construction of the SEZs created increased demand for imports from Hong Kong and Macao and, as a result, meant a relative decline in the foreign currency surplus of China in trade with those territories.

A related point is that the trade surpluses with Singapore and the oil exporting countries have remained stable, each totaling several percent.

From the above, it may be concluded that of China's total trade surplus with the third world, the share from the above three regions has declined on a relative basis since 1981 and that from trade with other regions has increased. The construction of the SEZs is reducing the surplus of foreign currency acquired from Hong Kong and Macao. It will be interesting to watch that once the SEZs are fully operated whether together with Hong Kong and Macao they will be able to provide China with a large trade surplus.

Under the Deng Xiaoping administration, the Chinese Communist Party has launched a program to improve relations with the Soviet Union and Eastern Europe. The program has started with more active exchanges on the cultural and economic fronts. Heilongjiang Province, in the Northeast of China, has already begun active trade with the Soviet Union. So far as foreign trade as a whole goes, however, trade with the Soviet Union and Eastern Europe declined in relative importance, at least until 1983. This is shown in Figure 35. In terms of export shares, trade with the socialist nations had accounted for one-fifth of exports in 1972, but this had fallen to 5.8 percent by 1983. Imports similarly fell from 17.7 percent to 5.8 percent of the total.

Since the Sino-Soviet break, China has held to a strict policy of balanced trade with the Soviet Union and Eastern Europe. This basic policy did not change even in 1982 and 1983. It is not likely that any major change will occur in this basic stance in the near future.

Based upon the above trends, the regional structure of China's trade should be characterized by the following up until 1990.

1. China will continue to import from the same partners as in the past without any fundamental changes. The only change will be in increased imports from Hong Kong and Macao due to the SEZs.

Table 6. China's Earnings from the Third World Countries

	Hong Kong, Macao, Singapore and oil producing countries (million US$)	Ratio of three areas			
		Over total earnings from the Third World countries (%)	Hong Kong & Macao (%)	Singapore (%)	Oil producing countries (%)
1970	784.3	84	72	7.2	4.8
1971	846.6	86.4	73	9.1	4.3
1972	959.4	97.9	86.6	7.3	4.1
1973	2,043.5	72.7	67	2.9	2.8
1974	1,923.8	82.2	73.8	3.1	5.2
1975	2,299.7	81.5	70.2	8.8	2.5
1976	2,286.9	88	74.7	6.3	7
1977	2,207.0	94	80.5	5.7	8
1978	3,037.2	94.6	80.9	6.6	7.1
1979	4,107.1	86.4	75.8	4.7	5.9
1980	5,251.3	82.6	72.1	4.4	6.2
1981	8,223.5	63.1	50.5	5.5	7.1
1982	8,359.8	57	46.3	5.6	5.2
1983	7,730.4	64	52.6	5.6	6

Source: Calculated from *Zhongguo Duiwai Jingjimaoyi Nianjian*, 1984 [Chinese Trade Annual 1984], edited by Chinese Trade Annual Editing Committee, 1984.

China's Imports from Three Areas
1971-73 and 1981-83

Third World Countries 18.3%

Socialist Countries 8%

Third World Countries 21.7%

Socialist Countries 17.7%

1971–73

1981–83

OECD Countries 60.6%

OECD Countries 73.7%

China's Exports to Three Areas
– 1971-73 and 1981-83

53.1% Third World Countries

Third World Countries 46.8%

Socialist Countries 20.2%

1971–73

1981–83

OECD Countries 33%

5.8%

41.6% OECD Countries

Figure 35. China's Trade Partners

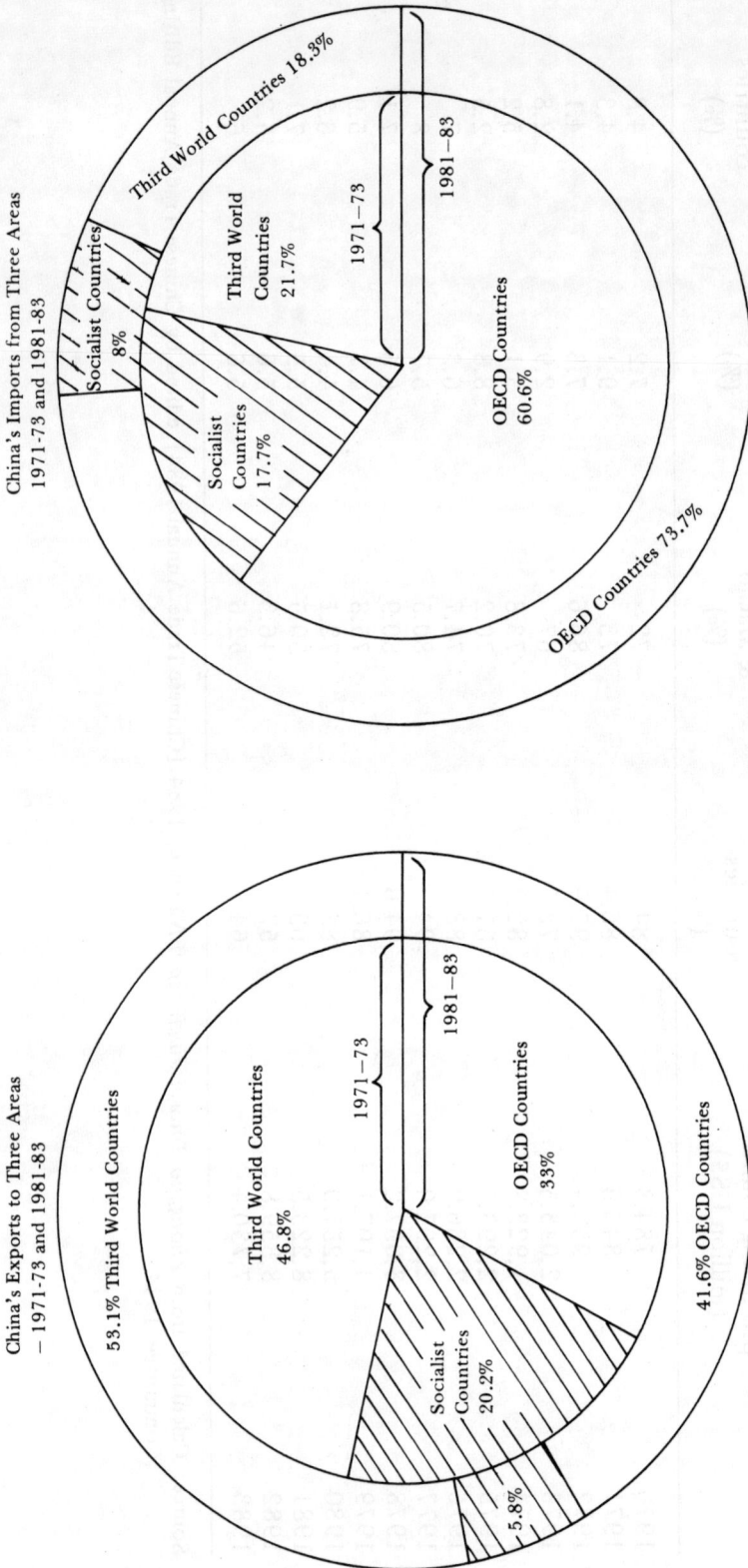

Note: Calculated from *Zhongguo Duiwai Jingjimaoyi Nianjian 1984* [Chinese Trade Annual 1984], edited by Chinese Trade Annual Editing Committee, 1984.

2. As to the partners to which China exports, the OECD member nations and the third world will continue to be important. Among these countries, the share of exports to those of the third world (besides Hong Kong and Macao, Singapore, and the oil exporting countries) will continue to rise.

The Chinese Communist Party made the decision for the establishment of four SEZs in 1978. In April 1984, it further designated Hainan Island and 14 coastal cities as open economic cities. The main objectives were, first, the attraction of foreign capital, second, the introduction of advanced technology, third, the fostering of centres for the acquisition of foreign currency, fourth, the transfer of the introduced technology into domestic industry, and, fifth, the acquisition of foreign economic information. Here, just the third objective, the fostering of the SEZs as zones for acquisition of foreign currency will be examined. The focus will be on Shenzhen, for which there is relatively complete data. Even with Shenzhen, however, most of the data only goes as far as 1983. Almost no relevant material is available for the years 1984 and 1985. Therefore, there are limits to the analysis.

Imports of the country as a whole skyrocketed in the second half of 1984, resulting in a drain on foreign currency holdings. While China held US$14.4 billion in foreign currency at the end of September 1984, this had fallen to US$10.85 billion by the end of the second quarter of 1985. Due to this situation, the authorities began reevaluating the Shenzhen SEZ to see if it were really growing into a center for acquisition of foreign currency. At the start of 1985, China's highest authorities viewed Shenzhen disfavorably.[28] For example, Yao Yilin stated, in April 1985, that "The growth of the SEZs cannot be maintained through just "transfusions" from the country over the long-term. We should, in consideration of the circumstances, decisively and quickly pull out the needle". In June, Deng Xiaoping, speaking before a delegation from Algeria, said "The SEZs represent one experiment. We will have to wait a while before we know whether it works or not. This is something new for socialism. We hope that it will succeed, but even if it doesn't succeed, it will be a useful experience to us".

These negative pronouncements made it seem that Shenzhen was not working up to expectations as a centre for acquisition of foreign currency. Table 7 shows a breakdown of investment in Shenzhen after the start of construction. Of the investment in Shenzhen in the five years from 1978 to 1983, 70 percent came from various government organizations of China and only 30 percent from foreigners. A market breakdown of the products of the SEZ and the products flowing into the SEZ shows 70 percent going to the domestic Chinese market, including the SEZ, and 30 percent going to overseas markets.[29] This market breakdown corresponds almost exactly to the investment breakdown. For the SEZ to develop as an export center, the share of products going to overseas markets has to be increased. However, fragmentary reports from Hong Kong in 1985 seem to indicate that the rate of foreign sales has even been dropping below 30 percent.

This seems primarily to be due to the rapid rise in imports of the Shenzhen region. Table 8 shows the breakdown of the supply of intermediate goods. In 1983 imports of intermediate goods soared. The more construction in the Shenzhen region progressed and the greater the degree of industrialization, the more imports of construction materials and intermediate materials became necessary. In 1984

---

[28] *Mingbao*, 1985, No. 8, p. 52.

[29] Gu, Shutang, ed. *Shenzhenjingjiteju Tiaocha be Jingjikaifaju Yanjiu* [The survey on Shenzhen special zone and study on economic development districts], Nankai University Press, 1984, p. 78.

Table 7. Breakdown of Investments in Shenzhen SEZ

(Unit: %)

	1979	1980	1981	1982	1983
1. Government organizations	72.3	36.9	17.4	16.6	12.7
2. Shenzhen city	16.7	19.9	31.4	50.4	58.1
3. Domestic enterprises			1.1	3.0	4.3
4. Foreign investment	11.0	43.2	50.2	30.0	24.9

Source: *Shenzhen Jingji techu Diaocha he Jingjikaifachu Yanjiu,* Gu Shudang ed., Nankai University, 1984, p. 38.

Table 8. Breakdown of Supply of Intermediate Materials in Shenzhen SEZ

	1979	1980	1981	1982	1984
1. Finished steel	100	100	100	100	100
Domestic	87.3	90.6	88.7	85.5	33.4
Shenzhen	0	0	0	0	0
Imports	12.7	9.4	11.3	14.5	66.6
2. Cement	100	100	100	100	100
Domestic	44.4	80.2	94.1	69.5	48.6
Shenzhen	55.6	19.8	2.3	4.4	4.3
Imports	—	—	3.6	26.1	47.1
3. Lumber	100	100	100	100	100
Domestic	100	100	89.9	73.6	11
Shenzhen	0	0	0	0	0
Imports	—	—	10.1	26.4	89

Source: Same as Table 7, p. 41.

and 1985 a new situation arose. This was the import of durable consumer goods. Exports from Hong Kong to China skyrocketed in 1983 and 1984, as already mentioned. This is thought to have been due in large part to the increase in exports to Shenzhen.

The domestic enterprise companies in the SEZ seem to have promoted the outflow of foreign currency. "Domestic enterprise" companies refer to investments made in the Shenzhen region by Chinese domestic enterprises. There are two major reasons for the establishment of such companies. One is to absorb the technical know-how introduced into the Shenzhen region from abroad for retransmittal to the inland areas. Another is to act as an outpost for the acquisition of foreign currency by the domestic enterprises. The latter objective has direct bearing on the problem being discussed.

"Domestic enterprise" companies, it must be emphasized, have not been performing their originally intended functions of acquiring foreign currency through export, but instead have been promoting the outflow of foreign currency. This has been happening through the following mechanism. The companies in the Shenzhen region are allowed a higher rate of retention of foreign currency obtained from exports than are regular domestic enterprises. Therefore, domestic enterprises find they can acquire more foreign currency for themselves by export through Shenzhen rather than exporting through usual routes. In other words, while there may be no change in the value of exports of the country as a whole, the share of foreign currency retained by the enterprises increases while that taken by the state decreases.

Using this retained foreign currency, the Shenzhen branches of domestic enterprises have been importing foreign consumer goods for resale on the domestic market to make further profits. Enterprises in the Shenzhen region have greater ability to import using foreign currency than regular domestic enterprises. The Hainan incident of 1984, in which island authorities imported automobiles for resale on the domestic market, was made possible by this mechanism. The island authorities considered this a natural action on the part of an enterprise.

From the viewpoint of the foreign currency of the country as a whole, however, such domestic enterprise companies are aggravating the outflow of foreign currency.

Another factor behind the outflow of foreign currency of Shenzhen is the increasingly stronger tendency of domestic consumers to go to Shenzhen for the purchase of imported foreign goods. Shenzhen has a black market for foreign currency coupons. Foreign currency coupons were originally meant to separate the international economy and domestic economy in China. The open existence of a black market, however, means that the domestic economy and international economy are no longer separated from each other in Shenzhen. With this in view, Chinese are traveling from around Guangzhou city to Shenzhen to purchase consumer goods imported from abroad. This is due to the severe controls on imported goods in the regular domestic market, where such goods can only be purchased with foreign currency coupons. These purchases by domestic consumers in Shenzhen have been another factor promoting imports of the Shenzhen region from abroad.

The above analysis is not backed up by import and export statistics of Shenzhen: such information has not been released. However, if one rationally analyzes the situation, it should be stressed that the possibility of the Shenzhen region becoming an import centre is greater than that of it becoming an export center. At the very least, we can understand that there are no guarantees that the SEZs and open cities will become export centers in the future.

International Balance of Payments

In terms of analysis of China's international balance of payments up until 1983 based on external data of China and projections on the balance for 1985 to 1990 and up to the year 2000, no one is better than Masahiro Hirano.[30] Of course, the projections can only be based on bold assumptions. The two years of 1984 and 1985 were characterized by great fluctuations in the trade balance. There were large increases in imports, principally for consumer goods, and, starting from the

---

[30] Hirano, Masahiro. "Kokusaishushi to gaishi riyo" [Chinese international balance of payments and introduction of foreign loans], in *Chugoku no chuchoki tenbo*, . . . , p. 307.

second half of 1985, sudden belt-tightening measures. In 1986, trade has been stagnating. Hirano's projections using data available up until 1983 are significant. Explanation of the methodology behind Hirano's analysis, however, will be omitted due to its complexity.

Hirano's projections are shown in Table 9. The main points are as follows: First, that the projected total of imports and exports for 1990 is US$83.4 billion, smaller than the US$95.0 billion estimated by Kojima in earlier section. It is also smaller than the US$97.5 to 100.44 billion pronounced by the Party National Congress in September 1985. About US$95.0 to 100 billion is probably appropriate. What

Table 9. International Balance of Payments Projections

(Unit: US$ billion)

		1986	1987	1988	1989	1990	1989-1990
Trade	Exports (FOB)	26.3	28.2	31.9	36	40.7	163.1
	Imports (FOB)	26.5	28.1	32.3	37.1	42.7	166.7
	Balance of trade	−0.2	1	−0.4	−1.1	−2	−3.6
Non-trade	Receipts	4.6	4.9	5.5	6.2	6.8	28
	Payments	4.3	5	5.8	6.8	7.9	29.8
	Interest payments	1.2	1.5	1.9	2.4	3	10
	Others	3.1	3.5	3.9	4.4	4.9	19.8
	Balance	0.3	−0.1	−0.3	−0.6	−1.1	−1.8
Transfered money balance		0.5	0.5	0.5	0.5	0.5	2.5
Current balance		0.6	0.5	−0.2	−1.2	−2.6	−2.9
Long-term trade	Inflow	4.5	5.8	7.7	8.6	10.2	36.8
	Outflow	0.9	1.2	1.6	2.1	2.8	8.6
	Balance	3.6	4.6	6.1	6.5	7.4	28.2
Short-term borrowings (net)		0	0	0	0	0	0
Total balance including others		0.5	0.6	1.4	1.6	1.8	5.9
Foreign exchange reserve		8.8	9.4	10.8	12.4	14.2	
Borrowing outstanding of large & middle term		15	19.6	25.7	32.2	39.6	
Borrowing outstanding of short-term		1.1	1.1	1.1	1.1	1.1	
Total		16.1	20.7	26.8	33.3	40.7	
Debt service amounts		2.1	2.7	3.5	4.5	5.8	18.6
Debt service ratio (%)		6.8	8.2	9.4	10.7	12.2	9.7

Source: Masahiro Hirano 'International Balance of Payments and Introduction of Foreign Loans', in *Chugokukeizai no Chuchokitembo* [Long- and Middle-Term Projections of Chinese Economy], edited by S. Ishikawa, R. Kojima & S. Sekiguchi, Nichukeizai Kyokai [Japan-China Association for Economy and Trade] 1984, p. 307.

is important about Hirano's projections is that it suggests a deficit trend in China's foreign trade. The plummeting price of oil will probably further contribute to this.

Second, Hirano projects that China's accumulated foreign debt will reach over US$40 billion in 1990. The debt service ratio in that case will be about 12 percent, still not high enough to make China a heavily indebted nation. Hirano incidentally estimates that China's debt balance in the year 2000 will be about US$100 billion. The current leadership in China considers the years up until 1990 a time for completing economic reforms and laying a proper foundation for the economy and envisions high economic growth in the 1990s (in other words, the eighth five-year plan). The author believes that achievement of a 7 percent growth rate in the 1990s will be difficult.

Whether or not the rising social costs result in a slow down in the growth of the economy as a whole will be largely governed by the foreign economic policies taken by the Party. In other words, everything depends on securing sufficient foreign funds and the efficiency with which these funds are used for investment in social capital. The ability to acquire foreign currency depends on China's ability to pay it back, i.e., its export capacity. Therefore, in the next five to 10 years, China may be expected to continue in its strong export drive.

By commodity, the main exports will probably be agricultural produce, textile goods, and durable consumer goods. Not much can be expected from oil exports. The regions most affected by China's export drive will be those with exporters of the above three items.

In the international economy, however, China will probably not have that much influence in trade. Rather, its importance will grow on the international money markets in the 1990s as a large borrower nation.

REFERENCES

Almanac of China's Economy 1981, ed., Editing Team of Almanac of China's Economy, Beijing: Jingjiguanli Zazhishe, 1981.

China's International Economic Annual 1984, ed. Editing Committee of China's International Economic Annual. Beijing: Chinese Ministry of Foreign Trade, 1984.

China's Statistical Yearbook, 1981, 1983, 1984, 1985, ed. State Statistical Bureau, Beijing: Zhongguotongji Chubanshe, 1981, 83, 84, 85.

Gongyuan Liangqiannian [China in 2000], ed. Study Group on China in 2000, Beijing: Kexue Zhishu Wenjian Chubanshe, 1948.

Hirano, Masahiro. "Kokusaishushi to Gaishi Riyo" [Chinese international balance of payments and introduction of foreign loans], *Chugokukeizai no Chuchoki Tembo* [long- and middle-term projection of Chinese economy], ed. S. Ishikawa, R. Kojima and S. Sekiguchi. Tokyo: Japan-China Association on Economy and Trade, 1984, pp. 297-314.

Inagaki, Kiyoshi, *Chugokushijo no Honto no Yomikata* [How to recognize real Chinese markets], Tokyo; PHP Institute, 1986, (in Japanese).

Kojima, Reiitsu. "Kogyo" [Industry], *Chugoku Keizai no Chuchoki Tembo* pp. 53-104 (in Japanese).

Kojima, Sueo. "Taigai Boeki" [Foreign trade], *Chugokukeizai no Chuchoki Tembo,* pp. 245-278 (in Japanese).

Koshizawa, Akira "Kotsu" [Transportation], *Chugoku Keizai no Chuchoki Tembo*, pp. 159-195 (in Japanese).

Lin, Zhiqun. "Lun Zhuzhai de Jianshe Shiyong yu zhufang xiaofei", [On housing construction, usage and consumption], *Chengshi Guihua* (Urban Planning), 1986, No. 1, 2, 4.

"Woguo Zhuzhai Jianshe Cunzai de Zhuyao Wenti ji Qigaige de Jianyi" [Main issues in our housing construction and some proposal to reform], *Jianzhu Xuebao* [Journal of Construction], 1982, No. 1.

Ryosan Suijun to Kokusai Kyosoryoku [Mass production scale and international competitive power], ed. published *The Institute of the Machinery Production Association*, Tokyo: 1967 (in Japanese).

Yonezawa, Yoshio. "Chugoku no Shohi Patan" [Consumption pattern in China] *Chugokukeizai no Chuchoki Tembo*, pp. 355-377 (in Japanese).

Yu Fanping "Chengshi Jiaotong Zhengce de Yige Zhongyao Wenti" [One of the serious problems in urban transportation policy], *Chengxiang jianshe* [Urban and Rural Construction], 1984, No. 6.

Zhongguo Jingji Jiegou Wenti Yanjiu [Studies on structural problems of Chinese economy], ed. Ma Hong and Sun Shangqing, Beijing: Renmin Chubanshe, 1981.

Zhongguo Shehui Tongji Ziliao [Materials on Chinese social statistics], ed. Department of Social Statistics, State Statistical Bureau, Beijing: Zhongguo Tongji Chubanshe, 1985.

12. Special Economic Zones in China

Tien-tung Hsueh and Tun-oy Woo

INTRODUCTION

Under Deng Xiaoping, since 1979 China has pursued far-reaching reforms in her development strategies and economic system. The new development strategies are the outcome of the decision to rank improving economic achievement before class struggle as the most important task for socialist construction. In contrast to the previous strategies, more emphasis is now placed on current consumption, balanced intensive growth rather than unbalanced extensive growth, rational economic calculation rather than mass movements, promoting inter-sectoral, inter-regional and rural-urban commodity trade rather than local autarky, and strengthening economic ties with foreign economies rather than keeping the economy closed. The old system of economic administration permitted little autonomy, provided little incentive, exerted practically no pressure on the basic economic units, and restrained inter-sectoral, inter-regional and rural-urban commodity circulation. The new strategies could not be implemented without administrative reforms. Institutional reforms on economic administration have thus been introduced. They are formulated based on the core spirit — internally, to activate the domestic economy, externally, to open up the economy to the outside world.

Theoretically, strengthening economic ties with foreign economies fosters economic development via relaxing both the demand and supply constraints the economy faces. Exports of commodities, services and capital give rise to additional demand apart from the domestic market, thus sustaining more rapid economic growth. Through imports of commodities, capital, technical knowhow and inflow of foreign direct investment, productivity can be improved, thus relaxing the supply constraint. Furthermore, by stabilizing and improving supply conditions of inputs, learning from managerial practice of foreign corporations as well as competition from imports and other competitors in overseas markets, opening up of the economy to the outside world also contributes to activating the domestic economy. Measures to strengthen foreign economic relations include institutional reforms on trade

481

administration and diversification of activities in addition to merchandise trade. The former includes granting of greater autonomy of trade to the local authorities especially the government of the coastal cities, merging of trade corporations with industrial, commercial and even research institutions, and adoption of normal business practice of the capitalist world. The latter refers to more flexible and lenient foreign loan policies, measures to attract foreign direct investment, exports of services and capital, and finally, establishment of Special Economic Zones (SEZs) within which all the above measures together with the policies for activating the domestic economy have been practised. Establishment and operation of the SEZs at Shenzhen, Zhuhai, Shantou in Guangdong Province and Xiamen in Fujian Province are, of course, the most spectacular, and may be most influential practice. This research aims at showing the underlying rationale, identifying special features, evaluating the contributions and opportunity costs of establishing the SEZ. In addition, problems and prospects of the Zones as well as their possible impact on other parts of China and countries of the Asian-Pacific area will be analyzed.

IDEOLOGICAL, ECONOMICAL AND POLITICAL JUSTIFICATION

Ideologically, the present legitimate justification of setting up the Zones rests with the belief that the Zones are conducive to economic progress and that economic construction should be the most important task for a socialist country because retreat to capitalism is unlikely after public property ownership has become pre-dominant. Even if the dominant ownership system within the SEZs is and will be state capitalism which definitely implies exploitation, and there are significant capitalist elements concerning economic administration, as long as ownership of productive means of the national economy is still predominantly public, and the joint-ventures and foreign corporations within the Zones behave in accordance with the law legislated and enforced by the Chinese government for the interest of the Chinese people, the Zones do contribute to consolidation and development of socialism.[1] Although extension of foreign economic relations may import some evils from the capitalist world, they can be contained at safety level by law and education.

Economically, the SEZs have been established to promote China's economic development via generating favorable direct, linkage, demonstration, and transfer effects. In theory, if the special policies practised in the Zones succeed to attract foreign investment resulting in establishment of foreign-involved enterprises, acce-lerate inflow of technical knowhow, technology and management skill, the Zones should achieve directly a higher level of productivity, national income, employment, living standard as well as more favorable trade balance situation. Provided that the momentum generated by the special policies is large enough to produce sufficient fiscal revenues, savings, and foreign exchange earnings for reinvestment, self-sustain-ed growth will finally be attained within the Zones transforming the Zones from predominantly agricultural to industrial, commercial and financial.

As economic activities in the Zones are related with other areas in China, through the immediate linkage effects — forward, backward and lateral, other areas will also

---

[1] See for instance Xu Dixin, "On Some Theoretical Problems of the Special Economic Zone", *Hong Kong and Macao Economic Digest*, Guangzhou, No. 9, 1982, pp. 2-7.

be benefited by the above-stated effects. The Zones may supply more inputs of better quality and at lower prices (via the forward linkages) and demand for more output from other areas in China (via the backward linkages). In addition, areas adjacent to the Zones may also enjoy the facilities which are originally supplied to the Zones (and would not be offered if without the Zones) — the lateral linkage effect.

Apart from the linkage effects, the Zones through their direct contact with the outside world and experiments in institutional reforms of economic administration may generate enormous demonstration and transfer effects onto other regions. As emphasized by the Chinese officials, the Zones act as the 'four windows' not only for themselves but for other regions as well — the window for technology, management, and information as well as the show window for China's foreign policies. They serve first to facilitate the imports of technology, information and managerial skill from the outside world and then transmit them (may be after modifications) to other regions. The transfer may be conducted directly by the Zones which are entrusted by the non-Zone areas as their import/export agencies, or indirectly via the demonstration effects i.e. learning from the experiences of the enterprises in the Zones which apply imported technology and management system. Of course, the most effective way is to allow enterprises from other areas to operate within the Zones enjoying all privileges granted to the indigenous firms in the Zones. Through actual practice and on-the-job training, they will be able to master and even modify the imported technology and managerial skill to be transferred back to their home regions. In addition, the Zones may act as regional financial center and investment consultant for foreign investors (who plan to invest within or outside the Zones) assembling funds and channeling them into different uses. Similarly, subject to the constraints imposed by the law, the foreign-involved enterprises in the Zones are free to adopt whatever management system they prefer. Even the state enterprises are granted much greater autonomy compared with the non-Zone areas. The state can make use of the Zones to experiment different types of management institutions and policies. After careful investigation and analysis, based on the outcome, the experimental reforms will be modified, consolidated and afterwards extended for practice in other regions. Limiting experimental reforms within the Zones first avoids the danger of the widespread of premature new institutions and policies throughout the whole economy. As a matter of fact, owing to the small size of the Zones relative to the national economy, China stresses on their linkage, demonstration, and transfer effects especially the demonstration effect whose scale can be independent of that of the Zones.

Apart from the economic rationale, the Zone experiment may serve political functions. Externally, the experiment is used to convince the foreign countries that keeping her doors open and maintaining good economic relations with foreign economies are, in fact, her long-term development strategy. As economics and politics can never be separated, maintenance of good economic relations will definitely lead to good political relations, the Zones may thus indirectly improve China's political relations with the outside world. Under a more peaceful political climate, it will be easier for China to transfer resources from the military sector to consumer goods industries and the rural sector in order to rectify the defects due to over-expansion of heavy industries but relatively snail-paced growth of light industry and agriculture. At the same time, China may be able to purchase some modern sophisticated weapons from the West for strengthening her defense power against USSR. In fact, keeping close relations with the West may help to check USSR's ambition over China because USSR dares not create two enemies at the same time. Internally, as mass political support always comes from successful economic performances, if the Zones can foster more rapid economic development, political power of the Dengists will thus be consolidated and strengthened.

Finally, apart from facilitating a way to urge the Chinese overseas to participate in China's Four Modernizations Drive, the Chinese government purposely demonstrates flexibility in economic management for the neighbouring Chinese communities. The Shenzhen SEZ pattern is mainly for Hong Kong, the Zhuhai SEZ pattern for Macao, and the Xiamen SEZ pattern for the ROC (Taiwan). The policy rationale for doing so is to pave a possible road to attain a unified and prosperous nation, the supreme long run goal of the Chinese politics. The special policies practised in the Shenzhen SEZ together with economic reforms in other areas which resemble some capitalist elements have been cited by Chinese officials to convince Hong Kong citizens that the Chinese government will fully adhere to the principle of 'One Country, Two Systems' and implement the Sino-British Agreement on the Future of Hong Kong.

HOW SPECIAL ARE THE SPECIAL ECONOMIC ZONES?

As mentioned in the earlier section, the direct and indirect effects generated by the SEZs will be realized if the Zones succeed in attracting foreign direct investment accompanied with inflow of technology, technical knowhow and managerial skill. To encourage foreign direct investment, the Chinese government has had to grant special privileges to the authorities of the Zones to reform the economic administration system, and to grant special concessions and autonomy for operation of foreign-involved enterprises within the Zones. The practice of all these concessions and special policies render the SEZs distinguished themselves from the non-Zone areas in China[2] and other free trade or product processing areas outside China. The following shows preferential treatments for foreign-involved enterprises i.e. Sino-foreign contractual joint-ventures, Sino-foreign joint-ventures, and fully foreign-owned enterprises in Shenzhen SEZ, which are basically implemented in other SEZs as well.

Special Treatment for Foreign-involved Enterprises

Employment and Remuneration Policies
The foreign-involved enterprises are free to decide the form of investment and employ personnel for technical and administrative works from abroad. For Chinese staff and workers, the enterprises may recruit them directly through interviews and tests arranged by themselves, or based on the recommendation of the SEZ's Labour Services Company. Once an employee has been recruited, he has to sign an employment contract with his employer — the enterprise. Employees are thus bound by factory discipline as listed in the contract. In breaking the contract they may be punished or even dismissed. Furthermore, enterprises are free to decide

---

[2]   Economic administration measures govering the SEZ in Guangdong Province is basically guided by *The Regulations on Special Economic Zones in Guangdong Province* promulgated in August 1980.

their own remuneration system disregarding the prevailing practice in other areas. As a rule, the average monthly wages for ordinary workers of an enterprise shall be higher than those for workers working in the same kind of enterprise in non-Zone areas, but lower than those in the same kind of enterprise in Hong Kong. On the other hand, for non-Zone areas, even at present, the direct job assignment system and iron-rice-bowl policies are still predominant.

Tax Concessions

Recently, the State Council promulgated some provisional regulations on tax reduction and exemption policies for foreign-involved enterprises operating within the SEZs, Hainan Island, and the fourteen newly opened port cities. According to the regulations, the corporation profit tax rate in the Zones is 15 percent, the same as listed in the Regulations on Special Economic Zones in Guangdong Province. In addition, those which participate in production activities such as industry, agriculture, forestry and husbandry with contracted period of practice longer than ten years, after getting approval, may be exempt from profit taxes for the first two years immediately after they start making profits, and enjoy 50 percent tax rate reduction for the 3rd, 4th and 5th year. Those which offer services but with an investment of US$5 million upwards and period of contracted practice longer than ten years may, after obtaining approval, get exemption for the first year immediately after making profits, and 50 percent reduction for the 2nd and 3rd year. Subject to the approval and at discretion of the local authorities of the SEZs, enterprises may also enjoy exemption from or reduction of local taxes. Furthermore, the after-tax profits obtained by the foreign investors from the joint ventures in the SEZs can be remitted back to their home countries with no additional taxes. Foreign investors who have income generated in China (excluding those which have been exempt from income taxes) but who haven't established offices in China are subject to 10 percent income tax charge. To reduce production costs, imports of machinery and equipment, spare parts and accessories, raw materials, means of transport, and other productive assets badly needed for production are exempt from import duties. Imported daily necessities are also exempt.[3] To encourage exports, all exported commodities are exempt from duties except those subject to export control or other state restrictions. Products to be sold within the SEZs are exempt from consolidated industry-commerce taxes. However, if these products are to be 'exported' to the interior regions outside the SEZs, the taxes which have been exempt must be paid. On the other hand, enterprises offering commercial, transportation and other services are required to pay consolidated industry-commerce taxes. The tax rate for banking and insurance industries is 3 percent. However, the People's Governments of the Zones may grant exemption or reduction during the early stage of operation of the above-mentioned enterprises at their discretion. Finally, according to the Regulations on The Special Economic Zones in Guangdong Province, foreign investors whose profits are reinvested in the Zones for not less than five years can apply for a tax reduction or an exemption for the reinvested profits.

Evidently, compared with non foreign-involved enterprises or even foreign-involved enterprises in non-Zone areas, foreign-involved enterprises operating in the SEZs do enjoy great concessions. Apart from paying local taxes, industry-

---

[3] As a matter of fact, the annual fees of land use for industry charged by Shenzhen SEZ have been changed three times so far (up to early 1985), from 10-30 Renminbi yuan to 5-15 yuan and then 1.2-1.6 yuan, per sq. m.

commerce taxes, import duties for imported material and others, non foreign-involved enterprises have to pay a 55 percent corporation profit tax. The foreign-involved enterprises outside the SEZs do enjoy some tax concessions, but the income tax rates (tax payments as a percentage of gross profits) are still higher than those in the SEZs, 33 percent – 39.7 percent (including 30 percent corporation profit tax, 10 percent local tax, and 10 percent charge on profits remitted out of China) for joint-ventures, or a progressive rate of 20 percent – 40 percent plus 10 percent local taxes for contractual joint-ventures which prefer the PRC Foreign Enterprises Income Tax Law. Surely, the foreign-involved enterprises in the non-Zone areas within Shenzhen, Xiamen, Zhuhai and Shantou as well as the 14 newly-opened coastal cities enjoy relatively more privilege but still not as much as the SEZs'. For instance, only those enterprises engaging in technology-intensive projects or projects related with transportation, energy development, and port construction, or with investment not less than US$30 million and a long retrieval term may pay a 15 percent income tax rate subject to the approval of the Ministry of Finance. Those which are not included in these categories but engage in projects preferred by the state may enjoy tax discount with 33 percent as the base. Others still have to pay the 33 percent tax rate. However, foreign-involved enterprises in Hainan Island enjoy exactly the same privilege as those in the SEZs. Besides, the Economic and Technological Development Zones within the 14 coastal cities have been granted the same special treatments except one – products to be sold within the Development Zones are subject to consolidated industry-commerce taxes charge. In short, other things being equal, establishing and running an enterprise in the SEZs yields higher profits due to lower costs (as a result of lower or exemption from customs duties and consolidated industry-commerce taxes) as well as lower income taxes compared with other areas. Actually the 15 percent income tax rate is among the lowest in the world even lower than that of Hong Kong, 18.5 percent.

Land Use
The maximum utilization periods of land within the SEZs for foreign investors depend on the types of activities. For example, in Shenzhen SEZ, they are: 30 years for industrial use, 20 years for commercial use (including restaurants), 50 years for commercial and residential use; and also for educational, scientific and technological, medical and hygienic use, 30 years for tourism, 20 years for truck gardening and cash crops, poultry farming, acqua-culture, and breeding use. Upon expiry of the lease, it can be renewed subject to the approval of appropriate authorities. The land utilization fees vary with the locality, type of business, and period of utilization. Nevertheless, they are fixed based on the preference of the government and level of the fees abroad. The rule is keeping the fees lower than potential overseas competitors especially by reference to Hong Kong's, as foreign direct investment in the SEZs has been mainly originated from Hong Kong. Furthermore, rate reduction is always possible.[4] Projects that are technology-intensive or non-profit making can be exempt. Starting from 1st January 1981, the fees have been readjusted every three years, but the range of (upward) adjustment does not exceed 30 percent. Compared with Shenzhen, the land-utilization fees charged by other SEZs are even lower and the terms more lenient. However, compared with other developing economies the land-utilization fees charged by the SEZs are not necessarily lower. As for land-utilization fees for foreign-involved enterprises in

---

[4] Except mineral oils, tobacco and alcoholic beverages which are taxed at ½ of the lowest rate.

non-Zone areas of China, they are negotiated between the authorities concerned and the foreign investors, and vary according to locality and use. Thus, under certain circumstances they can be lower than those charged by the SEZs.

Foreign Exchange Control

Foreign investors can open account at the Bank of China or foreign banks approved by China in the Zones to deal with matters relating to foreign exchange. Investors' post-tax profits and salaries and other legitimate earnings of employees in the Zones from Hong Kong, Macao and other economies can be remitted out of China through the Bank of China and the approved foreign banks in line with the Zone's foreign exchange control regulations. Enterprises that suspend operation, after going through all required procedures and clearing their debts can transfer their assets and remit their funds out of China. Furthermore, if necessary, foreign investors may also obtain loans and credits in foreign currencies from the Bank of China.

Marketing and Distribution

The SEZs authorities encourage sales of products of foreign-involved enterprises in overseas markets, but domestic sales may be allowed as well. The porportion of foreign to domestic sales has to be agreed by the authorities concerned and the enterprises. Normally, the proportion of domestic sales can be larger if the enterprise consumes more Chinese raw materials and equipment for production; the products are technology-intensive by China's standard, and badly needed in the domestic market. Exports manufactured at high cost are subject to exemption from or reduction of the consolidated industry-commerce taxes. Products of the enterprise allocated for domestic sales according to the agreement between the authorities and the enterprise and included in the category of distribution under the state plan should be listed as an item for distribution by the materials administration departments and sold by contract to the end users. If they are allocated for distribution by the materials administration and commerce departments, they should be sold to these departments first. The remainder and those which are not included in the above two categories may be sold by the enterprise itself or through its agencies.

Settlement of Disputes and Visas

In case a dispute occurs in the course of implementation of the contract and cannot be solved through negotiation between the two parties, usually the foreign investor and the concerned indigenous enterprise or authority of the Zone, request can be made to China's arbitration organization or even an international arbitration organization arranged and accepted by both parties.

The SEZ authorities have adopted a much simpler procedure to administer entry and exit visas so as to facilitate business travel. For instance, the Shenzhen SEZ Development Company furnishes necessary identification papers for foreign investors and foreigners who require regular travel. Entry into and exit from the Zone have become more convenient after the Administration Line started functioning.

Privileges Granted to the SEZ Authorities

Despite direct concessions and privileges enjoyed, foreign investors still won't invest in the SEZs if they find the institutional setting in the Zones is so alien and non-conducive to profitable operation. Thus, the SEZ authorities have been granted autonomy to reform economic administration and pursue various policies similar to those commonly practised in market economies for attracting foreign investment. The following shows the privileges bestowed on the Zones and the resultant special institutional arrangements and policies.

Ownership System

In contrast to the non-Zone areas where public ownership of means of production predominates, it is expected that foreign-involved state capitalist ownership will ultimately become predominant in the Zones. This is obvious, because no foreign investors want their investment and thus private property to become public property of China. So if the Zones really succeed to attract more and more foreign direct investment, foreign-involved state capitalist ownership should become more important. In 1985, all foreign-involved enterprises in Shenzhen SEZ already contributed to 67.8 percent of total industrial output. According to Marxism, capitalist mode of production implies exploitation, and if capitalist private ownership predominates, the pertinent economic system should be nothing but capitalism. Thus, as long as the Chinese government still sticks to Marxism (even in the loose sense) such a practice cannot be extended throughout China so that the SEZs need remain special. Besides, as collectives and even individuals have greater autonomy to start their own business in the Zones, on average, ownership by the people is not as significant as the non-Zone areas. For example, in 1984, state enterprises contributed to 73.6 percent of national industrial output but 33.5 percent in Shenzhen SEZ. Similarly in 1983, for the entire national economy, state enterprises accounted for 72.1 percent of commodity retail sales while they contributed to 69.5 percent in Shenzhen SEZ. As for incomes from transportation services, the former was 78 percent, while the latter was only 44.27 percent.

Fiscal Concessions

Since the formal establishment of the SEZs, within five years, Shenzhen and Zhuhai could retain all of their fiscal revenues for development purposes. For Xiamen and Shantou, their fiscal obligations are to be determined by the provincial governments without intervention from the central government. In practice, after fulfilling the obligations, they are free to dispose of whatever left. Furthermore, apart from the taxes and tax policies which have to be decided by the central authority, the SEZ's authorities have been empowered to adjust the rates or even to grant exemption for selected enterprises especially the foreign-involved within their jurisdiction. Their autonomy over local taxes and industry-commerce taxes are good examples.

Investment Concessions

The Zones have been given greater autonomy for approving foreign direct investment and utilizing bank credit to finance investment projects of investment level up to US$30 million each, whereas in other areas, in general, the level is much lower. Even for the 14 newly opened coastal cities only Shanghai and Tianjin have the same privileges. The limit for Dalian is US$10 million and for others US$5 million. Areas within Shenzhen, Zhuhai, Xiamen and Shantou but outside the SEZs can also approve productive investment projects up to US$5 million each.

Concerning the finance of investment projects, for the non-Zone areas, especially before 1980, fixed investment has been mainly financed by state budgetary grant, and bank credit for financing working capital only. However, credit finance has played a much more significant role in Shenzhen SEZ. For instance, in 1984, bank credit and foreign direct investment contributed to 44.10 percent and 16.19 percent respectively of Shenzhen's basic construction investment, but only 15.4 percnt and 2.2 percent respectively for all state enterprises in China. For a more detailed breakdown of the sources of Shenzhen's basic construction investment see Table 1.

Economic Administration System

As mentioned above, the SEZs have been assigned a very important task — experimenting with economic reforms especially institutional reforms. They have thus introduced some economic administrative institutions and policies very much different from the non-Zone areas'. These new arrangements are geared to remedying defects of the existing administration system as mentioned in the earlier section. Generally speaking, they involve the following: replacing imperative planning (partially) with the market mechanism, separating political and economic administration apart, relaxing administrative control on economic activities and prices, and replacing the 'iron rice-bowl' and 'eating from the same big pot' with the contract employment and floating wages system.

1. Increasing the Use of Market Mechanism

The SEZs have been given the right to determine their own socio-economic development plan to be approved by the State Council.[5] Based on the approved socio-economic plan, all investment projects within the Zones of scale smaller than certain level and which can be balanced by the Zones themselves are to be arranged by the Zone authorities. To implement these projects, the Zones prepare their own material supplies plan. The state and provincial governments will attempt to meet their needs. In contrast to the non-Zone areas, however, the Zones are given much more channels and leeways to acquire needed materials. The channels include imports, transfer of part of planned exports at prices similar to those supplied for Hong Kong, cooperation with other areas for increasing supplies via expanding production and exchange (e.g. by forming joint-ventures) of the needed materials, and finally increasing production within the Zones.

The Zones have developed very rapidly, and in order to produce for overseas markets, they find demand inputs not adequately supplied via the state or provincial plan. Thus, subject to the greater autonomy granted, they resort more and more to other supply channels. Accordingly, an increasing amount of materials acquired by the Zones are subject to negotiated prices (rather than fixed prices) which are largely affected by market conditions. This simply implies that market forces have played an increasingly important role in resource allocation within the Zones. For instance, the percentage of rolled steel, cement and timber supplied to Shenzhen according to the state and provincial materials supplies plan (under fixed prices) dropped from 29.5 percent, 24.8 percent and 77.6 percent respectively in 1979 to 2.4 percent, 14.3 percent and 8.5 percent in 1983, while those supplied from other parts of China and local producers (outside the plan) and imports jumped from 70.5 percent, 19.6 percent and 22.4 percent to 97.6 percent, 81.4 percent and 91.5 percent (See Table 2). Similarly in 1983, Shenzhen acquired on average 10.87 percent of her rolled steel, timber, cement, coal and electrical machinery and equip-

---

5   The state still prepares plans for Shenzhen SEZ (e.g. fiscal plan, population plan, foreign exchange plan) but only a few remain imperative. Others are indicative for enterprises' reference only. For instance, in 1984, the plans for 36 industrial products which are classified as imperative in non-zone areas are only indicative in Shenzhen SEZ. See *Economic Reporter*, Economic Information and Agency, No. 1907, Feb. 1985, p. 22.

Table 1. Distribution of Shenzhen's Basic Construction Investment by Sources, 1979-1984

(Unit: %)

Source	1979	1980	1983	1984	1979-1984
State	47.8 ⎫	26.4 ⎫	4.9 ⎫	1.29 ⎫	5.33 ⎫
Ministry, Province	24.5 ⎭ 72.3	10.5 ⎭ 36.9	7.93 ⎭ 12.83	9.16 ⎭ 10.45	9.11 ⎭ 14.44
Municipal government	⎱ 16.7	⎱ 14.25	⎱ 20.57	13.01 ⎫	11.23 ⎫
Local enterprise	⎰	⎰	⎰	5.27 ⎭ 18.28	10.96 ⎭ 22.19
Inward-linked enterprise		0	4.3	8.02	0
Bank credit		5.65	36.9	44.10	36.03
Foreign investment	11.0	43.2	25.07	16.19	24.25
Others	0	0	0.33	2.76	3.09

Sources: Zhao Yuanhao and Chen Zhaobin (eds.), *The Economy of the Chinese Special Economic Zones,* Science Popularization Publishing House, Guangzhou Branch, 1984, pp. 110, 173, *Shenzhen Special Economic Zone Yearbook 1985,* p. 593 and information provided by the Shenzhen SEZ authorities.

Note: Values for 1979-1984: arithmetic mean of the values of all items included.
          ⎱⎰ : the sum of the values of all items included.

ment from state allocation, but 50.1 percent from imports, and the remainder from the non-Zone areas and local production based on negotiated prices. At the same time, the price bureau of the Zones have started to decontrol some commodity prices so that prices better reflect market conditions, and can be used as rational reference for guiding economic activities. The authorities (such as that in Shenzhen) have even tried to link Zone prices to international prices. In fact, before the price reform, Shenzhen city price bureau used to control the prices of 72 vegetables, but now it only controls 4. In 1984, about 80 percent of retail sales were under free prices, a sharp increase compared with 15 percent in 1979. At present, the suppliers can decide the prices for mechanical and electrical equipment, timber, glass and other capital goods. Vegetable sellers can fix their prices according to changes in

Table 2. Relative Importance of Supply Sources of Five Major Commodities
for Shenzhen, 1979-1983

(Unit: %)

Distribution	Year 1979	1981	1983
Rolled Steel			
Under fixed prices	29.5	5.3	2.4
From other parts of China	57.8	83.5	31.6
Local goods	—	—	—
Imports	12.7	11.3	66.0
Cement			
Under fixed prices	24.8	3.6	14.3
From other parts of China	19.6	90.5	34.3
Local goods	55.6	2.3	4.3
Imports	—	3.6	47.1
Timber			
Under fixed prices	77.6	25.7	8.5
From other parts of China	22.4	64.25	4.5
Local goods	—	—	—
Imports	—	10.05	87
Coal			
Under fixed prices	NA	NA	46
Under flexible prices	NA	NA	54
Gas			
Under flexible prices	NA	NA	100

Sources: Zhao and Chen, *op. cit.*, p. 172; *Beijing Review*, Vol. 28, No. 1, January 7, 1985, p. 36; and Liang Wensen "Englightment from Bringing the Effects of Price Lever into Play in Shenzhen SEZ" in Qian Jiaju and Lu Zufa (eds.), *Essays on Theoretical Economic Problems of Special Economic Zones*, Beijing: People's Publishing House, 1984, p. 123.

Notes: — : nil.
         NA: not available.

market conditions. Prices for cereals, edible oils, pork and bottled gas are allowed to fluctuate under a ceiling rate, and the government has abolished price subsidies by pay raises so as to maintain inhabitants' living standard.

2. *Separation of Government Functions from Economic Administration*

To ensure that the basic economic units do enjoy the autonomy granted and that economic activities be determined according to economic law rather than arbitrarily by administrative bureaucrats who may know very little about economics and business and whose interests may not be directly linked with economic success, the SEZ such as Shenzhen has established specialized companies (which have to bear their own loss and profits) to administer economic activities within the Zones. For instance, in Shekou Industrial District, there are 13 specialized companies, each of which is responsible for administering the activities it specializes. They are in turn managed by a streamlined management committee which consists of only seven persons (one chairperson, three deputy chairpersons and three members). The whole administrative apparatus has been reduced in size, and procedures for getting approval for pursuing economic activities have been simplified. Usually, unlike the non-Zone areas, it takes just a few days to negotiate projects, complete with a land agreement, water and electricity supplies, installation of telecommunications equipment, the hiring of labor force, and the purchase of housing for the workers and staff. Even though the tasks, personnel, costs, and profits of the specialized companies are fixed by the management committee, the section managers are empowered to take charge of the day to day management of the personnel, finance and administration, and assume full responsibility of their sections. To ensure that only competent personnel lead the management committee, members of the committee are elected for a term of two years, and a vote of confidence is held after the first year. If a member receives less than 50 percent approval, he will be immediately dismissed and replaced. As for Shenzhen city, the economic administration machinery has also been reformed drastically since 1981. The basic principles are streamlining administration and separating government functions from enterprise management. Administrative bureaus under the leadership of the city have been reduced from 65 to 33. The original economic administrative bureaus such as commercial bureau, foreign trade bureau, industrial bureau and other 15 bureaus were abandoned to be replaced by specialized companies which act as economic entities pursuing economic activities independently. At the same time, duplication of administration has been avoided by eliminating duplicated machinery. Besides, autonomy of the enterprises over adjustment of production plans, financial control, commodity sales, materials purchase, and staff recruitment has been enhanced as well. Similarly, the SEZs in Zhuhai, Shantou and Xiamen have followed suit, establishing specialized companies especially development companies to take charge of economic activities replacing previous bureaucratic administrative apparatus.

3. *Contract Employment and Floating Wages System*

The state, in meeting the SEZs' needs for competent administrative and technical personnel, has, on one hand, directly transferred high-calibre engineers, administrators and cadres from other areas throughout China to the Zones, and on the other hand, permitted the Zones to recruit personnel freely from other areas via interviews and examinations. By the end of 1983, 28,400 cadres, 8,500 technical and administrative personnel, and 50,000 ordinary workers have been transferred from the interior regions to Shenzhen SEZ. However, cadres transferred have been assigned to new posts according to competence disregarding their former posts. Simultaneously, a system of inviting applications for jobs accompanied by contract employment has replaced the old system of direct appointment still widely practised in non-Zone areas. Furthermore, in Shekou Industrial District, workers have a direct voice in choosing the manager or factory director. The worker's congress of the enterprise votes on the nominees, and a contract is offered to the voted winner. However, after holding the post for six months, a vote of confidence is held by the workers. Those who cannot get more than 50 percent of the votes must leave their posts. Thus, the 'iron-rice bowl' has gone in the Zones.

In order to abolish 'everybody eating from the same big pot' the SEZs have adopted some sort of floating wages system. For example, in Shekou, total wages are divided into four parts — the basic wages, subsidies, wages corresponding to jobs and specific posts, and floating wages. The basic wages which form the base of total wages, are the wage grades earned by workers and staff members all over China, and is expected to be enough to support subsistence of a typical household. Wages corresponding to jobs and specific posts are determined by the nature of the jobs or posts, in particular, labor intensity, technical level, working conditions and import-ance. Subsidies refer to those payments helping workers pay higher commodity prices. Finally, the floating wages and bonuses are determined by the performance of the enterprise as well as the contribution of the pertinent worker or staff. No ceiling or lower limit is imposed on such bonuses which are instead subject to progressive tax charges. In 1984, the first two components account for 30.5 percent and 10.3 percent respectively (adding up to 40.8 percent) while the latter two 37.2 percent and 22 percent (adding up to 59.2 percent) of the total wages. Thus, the fixed part of wages accounts only for 40.8 percent of the total. In contrast, fixed wages still account for a dominant proportion in non-Zone areas.

Geographical Advantages

All the four SEZs are within coastal cities not far away from Hong Kong and Macao. Ocean transport can be very convenient, linking the Zones with overseas markets at lower costs compared with the interior regions. In addition, most inhabitants of these Zones have relatives and friends in Hong Kong, Macao and Southeast Asia. In fact, the Zones are the hometowns of many renown businessmen in Asia. Thus, other things being equal, they always prefer investing in the Zones rather than elsewhere. Furthermore, as inhabitants of the Zones have more opportunities to keep in touch with overseas Chinese and foreigners, they are more outward-looking and open-minded and so more willing and able to accept new ideas, and experiment with new policies. These are most essential to successful functioning of the SEZs. Surely, to a certain extent, these advantages can be shared by other coastal cities such as Shanghai, however, Shenzhen and Zhuhai enjoy an irreplace-able advantage: their geographical proximity to Hong Kong, the largest and most wealthy Chinese community outside the Mainland, which remains non-hostile to the Mainland. Hong Kong has maintained excellent relations with the western world and possesses some of the most energetic and able businessmen in the world.

In sum, the Chinese government has granted special direct support both financial and manpower for the SEZs, and allowed them to experiment with administrative institutions and policies significantly different from non-Zone areas for promoting production and attracting foreign direct investment. As a result, the SEZs turn out to be very special compared with the non-Zone areas, in particular, the interior regions. However, most recently, with the establishment of the Economic and Technological Development Zones within the 14 newly opened coastal cities, and granting of special preferential treatment for Hainan Island which enjoys nearly all privileges as the SEZs', the SEZs are no longer so special as before. As compared with foreign economies, in particular, the industrial processing areas or free trade areas in developing economies, the concessions on taxes, rent and wages are not particularly attractive, because they have been determined mainly by reference to conditions in Hong Kong. Surely, wages, rent and even charges for the use of water in Shenzhen are lower than Hong Kong's but not for all costs.[6] However, as Hong Kong is much more well-developed than typical developing economies, and her wages and rent are much higher, so the wages and rent fixed for the SEZs can be higher than some developing economies. Yet, the SEZs do enjoy two distinguished advantages compared with other developing economies. First of all, in general, China has a broader and stronger industrial base, and so provided the government desires, she can offer infrastructure and other supporting services for enterprises in the Zones, while in some developing economies even the infrastructure has to be established and run by foreign corporations. Secondly, and which from the viewpoint of many foreign investors is the most important, investing in the SEZs may function as the stepping-stone for opening up the China market!

EVALUATION OF THE SPECIAL ECONOMIC ZONES

Performance[7]

As among the four SEZs, we can only obtain more detailed time series of numerical data on economic performance from Shenzhen which started earlier than others, we have to rely mainly on Shenzhen's experience to evaluate economic performance of the SEZs.

Absorption of Foreign Direct Investment

During 1979-85, total utilized foreign direct investment in the four SEZs contributed to around 21 percent of that of the entire national economy. Shenzhen and Zhuhai are the most important, absorbing over US$700-790 million and US$350 million respectively, or 13 percent — 14 percent and 6 percent of the national total. For agreed (contract) foreign direct investment during 1979-1984, the SEZs altogether accounted for 38.7 percent of the national total. Shenzhen and Zhuhai contributed to US$2.12-2.68 billion and US$1.38 billion, 20.5 percent — 26 percent and 13.3 percent respectively of the national total. In 1984, Shenzhen alone utilized and contracted respectively HK$1.7 billion and HK$5 billion of foreign direct investment. During 1979-84, the number of agreed joint-ventures, contractual joint-ventures, and fully foreign-owned enterprises in Shenzhen SEZ amounted to 308, 423 and 51, accounting for 33.1 percent, 19.1 percent and 68.9 percent respectively

---

[6] See Paul Sham. "Soaring Business Costs Hit China Investment Drive," *South China Morning Post*, July 4, 1986.

[7] Special appreciation goes to the Shenzhen SEZ authorities, in particular, the Economic Research Centre, and Policy Research Office of Shenzhen Municipality Committee for providing us the information requested.

of the national total. Even though Shantou SEZ started later, China's largest fully foreign-owned enterprise, a petro-chemical complex with total investment over US$5 billion will be established there. Surely, the total area and population of the four SEZs account for less than 0.01 percent and 0.1 percent respectively of the national total. The SEZs have absorbed far more foreign direct investment in proportion to their size than the other part of the country, which implies they have at least succeeded in functioning as the window of foreign capital for China. In fact, in terms of the size of foreign direct investment contracted and utilized, Shenzhen has performed better than the export-processing areas in Singapore, Korea, and the ROC (Taiwan).

Concerning the structure of utilized foreign direct investments by organization of enterprises involved, we find, during 1979-84, fully foreign-owned enterprises, joint and contractual ventures, and enterprises engaging in processing imported raw materials and semi-finished products supplied by foreign investors, compensation trade and others accounted for 21.2 percent, 67.4 percent and 11.4 percent of total utilized foreign direct investment in Shenzhen SEZ respectively. In recent years, as a result of rapid improvement of economic conditions and investment climate in the Zone, the first two have become increasingly important, while the last contracted rapidly. The most spectacular, however, has been the rapid growth of fully foreign-owned enterprises. Their cumulative utilized investment in 1984 was 41.5 times that of 1980. Similar trend has appeared in non-Zone areas. Yet fully foreign-owned enterprises are still not so important (See Table 3). In 1984, approval and establishment of joint and contractual ventures as well as fully foreign-owned enterprises have been speeded up. Over 700 joint-ventures (of which more than 200 were in the four SEZs) absorbing US$1.1 billion, and 26 fully foreign-owned enterprises were approved. The former was 6.6 times that of 1983, more than the cumulative total during 1979-83. It is expected that with the permission to extend internal sales, more fully foreign-owned enterprises will be established.

A predominant proportion of foreign direct investment in the SEZs originated from Hong Kong, but recently Hong Kong's relative importance has declined moderately. For instance, before 1983, investors from Hong Kong provided 94.6 percent of total foreign direct investment in Shenzhen, but in 1984, the share dropped to 85 percent — 90 percent.[8] Even quantitatively, foreign direct investment has played quite a significant role in fostering investment in SEZs. During 1979-October 1984, foreign direct investment accounted for 26.4 percent, 21.1 percent, 30.2 percent, and 26.4 percent of Shenzhen SEZ's overall basic construction investment; basic construction investment in industries, property and construction; in commerce and services, communication and telecommunications; and in education and health respectively. During 1979-84, foreign direct investment in Shenzhen was concentrated in industries, real estate, commerce and services, and tourism and amusement, accounting respectively for 44.3 percent, 29.8 percent, 17.1 percent and 4.5 percent of total (See Table 4). Since 1984, as a result of improvement in investment climate of industrial sector, foreign industrial investment has increased rapidly, resulting in more rapid industrialization. At the same time, investment in communication and telecommunications has risen rapidly as well. The percentage share of the former rose from 43.9 percent in 1983 to 48.2 percent in 1984, while the latter rose from 2.3 percent to 4.3 percent. Owing to the rapid increase in foreign

---

[8]   Nevertheless, during 1981-84 industrial investment from Hong Kong still accounted for 60 percent of foreign direct investment in China's industrial sector. See *Ta Kung Pao,* Hong Kong 7/2/85, p. 16.

Table 3. Percentage Share of Utilized Foreign Investment by Type, 1979-84

(Unit: %)

	Fully Foreign-owned Enterprises	Joint & Contractual Ventures				Compensation Trade and Others
			Joint-ventures	Joint Exploration	Contractual Joint-ventures	
Shenzhen up to 1984	21.2	67.4				11.4
China 1979-1984	2.4	72.1	10.4	31.9	29.8	25.5
1983	4.7	64.4	8.0	31.8	24.8	30.7
1984	1.1	87.7	18.0	36.9	32.8	11.2

Sources: Zhao and Chen, *op. cit.*, p. 111; and *Almanac of China's Foreign Economic Relations and Trade 1984*, Hong Kong: China Resources Trade Consultancy Co. 1984, pp. 1094-1095; *1985*, p. 1066.

direct investment, foreign-involved enterprises have contributed to an increasing share of industrial output. In 1983, industrial output of joint-ventures, contractual joint-ventures and fully foreign-owned enterprises produced 38.1 percent of Shenzhen SEZ's total industrial output. The share rose to 55.9 percent in 1984. Together with the output contributed by local enterprises, processing raw materials and semi-finished products supplied by foreign economic units according to contract, the percentage share was 52 percent in 1983 and 57.7 percent for January — October 1984.

Output, Employment, Income, and Efficiency
Based on statistical data it appears that since 1979 Shenzhen has achieved brilliant economic performance in various aspects. During 1979-84, total fixed assets increased by 1.76 billion yuan, 37.45 times the size of total fixed assets for the whole 30 years before 1979. Compared with 1978, in 1984, industrial output, agricultural output, fiscal revenues, foreign exchange earnings rose by 27.3 fold, —28 percent, 18.6 fold and 2.6 fold. In fact, economic activities level during 1980-84 surpassed the cumulative total during the whole 30 years prior to 1979. For example, basic construction investment during 1980-83 exceeded the sum total taken place before 1979 by nearly 20 fold. Industrial output was larger by 66 percent; fiscal revenues by 1.2 fold; foreign exchange earnings by 57 percent, commodity retail sales by 69 percent. In addition, since its establishment the Shenzhen SEZ has arranged more than 80 thousand additional workers to work. The average labor productivity of state industrial enterprises grew at an average annual rate of 14.3 percent during 1979-83. Rapid improvement in labor productivity of Shenzhen can be attributed, among other factors, to the rapid increase in the size of the stock of fixed assets as well as the inflow of equipment, technology, technical knowhow, and managerial skill accompanied with foreign direct investment. In fact, during 1979-83, Shenzhen made use of foreign investment to import about 25,000 units (sets) of tools, machinery and equipment, of which 10 percent could be counted as advanced by international standard and 30 percent by China's standard. Similarly, Zhuhai has imported more than 3,300 units (sets) of production equipment, Shantou more than 1,000, and Xiamen more than 1,200 units (sets) up to 1983.

Rapid improvement in labor productivity has led to more rapid increase in income for inhabitants in Shenzhen SEZ. In 1984, average annual wage of state enterprise workers and staff was 2,365 yuan, higher than 1978's by 2.6 fold, while peasants' per capita net income in 1983 was 840 yuan, 3.5 times that of 1978. In 1984, economic performance of Shenzhen improved further. Value of industrial and agricultural output, commodity retail sales, national income, fiscal revenues, and average labor productivity was 8.2, 17, 6.3, 17, and 1.2 times that of 1978's respectively. Compared with the national economy as a whole, in general, Shenzhen achieved better performance especially in growth aspect during 1979-83 (See Table 5). However, both the marginal efficiency of fixed construction investment and that of fixed assets of Shenzhen were lower compared with the national average: 0.3051 and 0.593 against 0.622 and 0.781 respectively. In addition, Shenzhen also suffered much more serious inflation, with an average annual inflation rate of 9.4 percent much higher than the national average — 2.7 percent during the period.[9] As for

---

[9] The price indexes of commodity retail sales appear to be as follows:

1978	1979	1980	1981	1982	1983
100.0	117.1	133.1	142.2	153.3	156.5

Obviously the price level has been stabilizing since 1982 in Shenzhen SEZ.

Table 4. Utilized Foreign Investment in Shenzhen SEZ, 1979-1984

(Unit: HK$ million)

	1979-1984		1983		1984	
	Amount	% share	Amount	% share	Amount	% share
Industry	1,834.0	44.3	409.4	43.9	784.5	48.2
Real estate	1,230.9	29.8	386.5	41.5	216.3	13.3
Commerce and services	708	17.1	90.5	9.7	412.8	25.4
Tourism and amusement	185.1	4.5	17.0	1.8	131.1	8.1
Communication and telecommunications	127.8	3.1	21.5	2.3	69.3	4.3
Agriculture	8.6	0.2	0	0	3.0	0.2
Others	43.1	1.0	7.5	0.8	9.8	0.6
Total	4,137.3		932.4		1,626.9	

Source: *Shenzhen Special Economic Zone Yearbook 1985*, p. 600.

Table 5. Economic Performance of Shenzhen SEZ Compared with
the Chinese National Economy, 1979-1983

	Shenzhen	National Economy
Industrial Output (Growth Rate)[1]	63.6%	8.4
Agricultural Output (Growth Rate)	5.2%	14.8
Industrial and Agricultural Output (Growth Rate)	29.8%	9.2
National Income (Growth Rate)	37.2%	10.3
Wages, Workers and Staff (Growth Rate)	22.7%	6.1
Peasant's per capita Net Income (Growth Rate)	28.5%	18.3
Commodity Retail Sales (Growth Rate)	63.6%	12.8
Retail Prices (Inflation Rate)	9.4%	2.7
Foreign Exchange Earnings (Growth Rate)	24.6%	NA
Fiscal Revenues (Growth Rate)	63.3%	2.7
Employment, Worker and Staff (Growth Rate)	22.4%	3.9
Average Labour Productivity of Industry (Growth Rate)	14.3%	3.7
Basic Construction Investment ('00 million yuan)	19.64	2,674.94
Fixed Assets (Proportionate Growth)[2]	2,149.79%	46.82
Incremental National Income — Basic Construction Investment Ratio[3]	0.305	0.622
Incremental National Income — Fixed Asset Ratio[4]	0.593	0.781
Technicians & Administrators/Worker and Staff	22.4%	11.6
Gross Fixed Assets/Worker and Staff (yuan)	8,412	7,792
Net Fixed Asset/Worker and Staff (yuan)	6,730	5,195
Profit Rate of State Industrial Enterprise[5]	14.1%	14.6

Sources: For data concerning the National Economy: The Statistical Bureau of People's Republic
of China, *Statistical Yearbook of China 1984*, Overseas edition, Hong Kong Economic
Information & Agency, 1984.
Data concerning Shenzhen are supplied by the Shenzhen SEZ authorities.

Notes: 1. Growth rate: Average annual compound growth rate

2. Fixed assets (Proportionate Growth)

$$= \frac{\text{Increase in Fixed Assets during 1979-1983}}{\text{Stock of Fixed Assets up to the end of 1978}} \times 100\%$$

3. Incremental National Income — Basic Construction Investment Ratio

$$= \frac{\text{Increase in national income during 1979-1983}}{\text{Increase in fixed construction investment during 1979-1983}}$$

4. Incremental National Income — Fixed Asset Ratio

$$= \frac{\text{Increase in national income during 1979-1983}}{\text{Increase in fixed asset during 1979-1983}}$$

5. Profit rate $= \dfrac{\text{Profits after taxes}}{\text{Total sales level}} \times 100\%$

Zhuhai city, in 1984, its total output value of industry and agriculture increased by 88 percnet over 1978, of which industrial output rose by more than 2 times. Besides, foreign exchange earnings increased by 1.2 times, of which export earnings rose by 2.4 fold. Fiscal revenues also increased by 8.8 times.

Not only the level of economic activities of Shenzhen has changed drastically, its structure has also undergone rapid changes. The share of industrial output in total value of industry and agriculture rose from 34.3 percent in 1978 to 98.2 percent in 1984. As for composition of national income in 1978, the percentage contribution by primary, secondary and tertiary industries was 33 percent, 8 percent and 59 percent respectively, while in 1984 it became 2.8 percent, 53 percent and 44.2 percent, indicating sharp decrease in importance of agriculture, but rising importance of manufacturing and construction. In fact, in 1984, industry for the first time contributed to a larger share of the local product compared with construction and commerce. In 1983, industry, construction, and commerce contributed respectively to 15 percent, 25 percent, and 21 percent of Shenzhen's local product, while the respective share changed to 23 percent, 22 percent, and 21 percent in 1984. In short, all evidences show that establishment and operation of the SEZ have led to rapid industrialization of Shenzhen, in particular, in 1981 and then since 1983. In fact, the value of industrial output in 1985 was 2.67 billion yuan, much larger than the planned output target of 1.2 billion yuan for 1985. Of total industrial production, light industries accounted for 80 percent in 1983. The largest single industry, electronics is the most important. It alone contributed to 57.1 percent of total industrial output in 1984. Furthermore, some new industries which did not exist before 1979 have been established and developed, e.g. textile and leather.

Linkage, Demonstration, and Transfer Effects
Owing to the small size of the Zones and the reluctance (until recently) of the Chinese government to open up her domestic market, direct forward linkage effects generated by the Zones have been insignificant. In fact, at present, about 70 percent of electronic product inside Shenzhen SEZ are exported. In general, only a small portion of industrial products from the SEZs have been supplied for non-Zone areas. However, the indirect forward linkage effects due to transfer of technology, equipment, technical knowhow and managerial skill cannot be ignored.

In 1983, Shenzhen SEZ supplied more than 100 sets of scientific instrument and equipment, 575 sets of technical data, 72 samples, and translated various types of technical data for the non-Zone areas. In addition, only several months after operation, the Science and Technology Sales Division of the Import-Export Services Corporation, has received more than 1,000 orders for purchasing equipment worth more than five million yuan for the interior regions. Various study tours from the non-Zone areas have been organized to visit Shenzhen to investigate the new techniques and products imported. Besides, information has been sent to enterprises in other areas on request, and training courses on new techniques and managerial skill have been offered for personnel outside Shenzhen SEZ. As a result, some techniques and products employed first in Shenzhen SEZ have already been imitated by other areas in China. Of course, the inward-linked enterprises which operate in the Zones and may cooperate with foreign investors, have played a more important role in transferring production technique, equipment, and managerial skill back to their home areas. In fact, recently, they have become increasingly important. They were first established in 1979. By the end of 1984, Shenzhen SEZ altogether signed 497 contracts with 14 ministries, 20 provinces, cities, autonomous regions, and more than 80 Xians to establish joint cooperatives, of which 457 items have been implemented. During 1982-83, total agreed investment reached 700 million yuan and implemented investment amounting to 200 million yuan. Up to June 1984, they contributed to an industrial output of 222.85 million yuan, accounting for 20 percent of total industrial output. They have played the most significant role in laying down a firm base for electronic industry in Shenzhen by supplying equipment and skilled personnel, in particular, technicians and administrators. At present, the relatively well-developed electronic enterprises in Shenzhen are mainly inward-linked. At the same time, these electronic enterprises through Shenzhen have imported some advanced equipment and production technique thus narrowing the technology gap between China's and overseas' electronic industries. For instance, the Aiwa Electronic Company has made use of such imports to experiment production of some electronic products urgently needed by China, e.g. large-scale integrated circuit. In fact, through Shenzhen's Science and Technology Exchange Unit of Science and Technology Development Centre, they may invite experts from outside to teach new techniques and import the urgently needed technology offering favorable terms to the supply sources. Most recently, there are indications that some enterprises of the interior regions have decided to establish branches or form joint-ventures with foreign investors in the Zones, utilizing the Zones' special conditions to produce inputs or final products for themselves. For example, a joint-venture — the North-West Electronic Company has been established incorporating the Bank of China, Chengtu Branch, the Computing Machine Technology Production Services Company of Sichuan, one Japanese, one USA and a Hong Kong applied Computer Company. It will not only assemble electronic products for Hong Kong, USA and Japan participants, but also produce computer products designed by the Sichuan Company to be sold in Sichuan. This, in addition to the recent decision by the Chinese government to open up a larger part of her domestic market to foreign-involved enterprises in exchange for more advanced technology, permitting foreign-involved enterprises in the Zones (subject to approval) to supply a large share of their output for the interior regions, will promote the direct forward linkage effects generated by the Zones. Apart from forward linkage and transfer effects, the Zones have generated some backward linkage effects fostering economic development in some non-Zone areas. For instance, rapid expansion of construction works and other investment projects in the Zones has given rise to additional demand for construction workers, and engineers from other areas. This was especially important during 1980-82 when, under readjustment policies, many regions did not have enough basic construction investment tasks. In 1984, there were over 100 construction enterprises and 0.2 million construction workers from various areas participating in construction of investment projects in Shenzhen. At the end of 1983, the average monthly wage of construction workers in Shenzhen was 200 yuan, twice that of the national average. Furthermore, a significant proportion of construction materials (e.g. 2/3 in Shekou) has been supplied by the non-Zone areas. Thus, the construction boom in the SEZs alone has directly created hundreds of thousand jobs and hundreds of million income for other areas. Besides, establishment of new industries and activities in the Zones due to foreign direct investment, has created new demand, mobilizing and utilizing resources hitherto lying idle in other areas. It is estimated that foreign-involved enterprises in Shenzhen SEZ purchased 30 percent of their raw materials from non-Zone areas worth around 15.8

million yuan. In fact, according to the present practice, it is beneficial for foreign investors to purchase raw materials from non-Zone areas because they just pay the export prices charged by the Chinese government in foreign currencies which are usually lower than those paid for imports from overseas supply sources. Thus, disregarding the illegal practice to inflate import prices so as to understate real profits, with improvement in supply conditions of raw materials, semi-finished products and final products in the non-Zone areas, the direct backward linkage effects will definitely become much more significant.

Besides the forward and backward linkage effects, the Zones have also generated lateral linkage effects. Improvement in tourist services have attracted more tourists from Hong Kong, Macao, and overseas countries to visit the Zones, who may, afterwards, visit other areas nearby. Another example is the formation of the Guangdong and Hong Kong Nuclear Power Joint-venture Company which serves mainly to provide electricity to Hong Kong and Shenzhen. However, it may serve other regions and more importantly, serve as a standard model for other provinces to build their own nuclear plants in the future.

Finally and which may be the most important, institutional reforms in economic and business administration in the SEZs especially in Shekou Industrial District has created tremendous demonstration effect, some of which have been affirmed by China's top decision makers and propagated to other areas of China rapidly. For instance, the slogan: "Time is Money and Efficiency is Life" has been adopted throughout Guangdong Province and even in other provinces. The public bidding practice for alloting construction projects has been affirmed by the state and pursued in other areas. It is believed, as a result of practising public bidding, efficiency of building and construction in Shenzhen measured by the time required to complete a flat has been at par with Hong Kong. In addition, the contract employment and floating wages system have been imitated by some non-Zone areas. Similarly, many other reforms have been pursued to a certain extent in some non-Zone areas as well. In fact Shenzhen has already become well-known as the school or training center for administrators from other areas. In view of the success, many non-Zone areas have asked the state for similar autonomy and special preferential treatment enjoyed by the SEZs so as to experiment with similar reforms. Convinced by the good performance of the Zones especially that of Shenzhen, the Chinese government has opened up 14 coastal cities inside which some Economic and Technological Development Zones are established.

Costs

Many people especially the Chinese officials support the SEZ experiment by reference to the 'brilliant' economic performance achieved by Shenzhen in the past. Some even assert that the tremendous progress has been due to rapid improvement of productivity which, in turn, results from the special policies practised in the Zones. However, such arguments are not convincing based on empirical evidences because they neglect the opportunity costs incurred by the national economy in supporting the SEZ. In fact, defence supporting the Zones should be focused on their demonstration and transfer effects rather than the direct effects. As shown in Table 5 and discussed above, the Zones especially Shenzhen have enjoyed special privileges and deliberate strong supports from both the central and provincial governments such that the general supply conditions in the Zones have been much more favorable compared with the national average. In 1984, Shenzhen's average net fixed assets per worker was about 40 percent higher than that of the national average, not to mention differences in quality. Furthermore, as Shenzhen has been empowered to recruit competent administrators and engineers from every part of China, and the central government has directly transferred quite a large number of cadres of higher calibre to Shenzhen, average quality of the labor force should generally be superior than other areas. As shown in Table 5, the percentage of engineers, technicians and administrators to total workers in Shenzhen was twice as high as the national average in 1979-1984. Similarly, in Shekou Industrial District, over 60 percent of cadres have received university education or equivalent, while the national average is only slightly over 20 percent. Finally, due to reforms on commercial and import system, Shenzhen SEZ has been able to acquire whatever material inputs required via domestic and overseas' supply sources much more easily and with lower costs (due to tax concessions enjoyed). Accordingly, productivity in Shenzhen SEZ should have been higher compared with the national average. However, as shown in Table 5, based on empirical evidences, except average annual improvement of labor productivity in industry, we can't reach this conclusion without any further qualifications. In fact, the incremental national income to basic construction investment, and the incremental national income to fixed asset ratios of Shenzhen SEZ during 1979-83 were lower than the national average, which implies lower marginal efficiency of investment and fixed asset. Furthermore, in 1982, only 77 percent of the foreign-involved enterprises operating in Shenzhen SEZ got profits. Although the percentage rose to over 80 percent in 1984, the average profit rate (defined as profits to sales) attained by these profitable enterprises was 13.8 percent, of which industrial enterprises' was 13.9 percent, lower than the average profit rate of 14.6 percent for all state industrial enterprises in China. If profit rate best reflects efficiency, then it seems that, on average, foreign-involved industrial enterprises in Shenzhen were at best only as efficient as the national average so far. It should be noted, however, as most foreign-involved enterprises in Shenzhen are still during the early stage of operation, many construction works and investment projects have not yet been completed and put into use. Therefore, it is still too early to make any conclusive judgement on efficiency implication of the SEZs at the present moment. Nevertheless, from static point of view, disregarding all indirect effects, foreign investible funds have not necessarily been utilized most efficiently in Shenzhen. For instance, in Shanghai, it is estimated that on average, utilization of one additional US dollar of foreign funds generated 8.6 yuan, 3.2 yuan, and US\$1.9 of industrial output value, fiscal revenues, and foreign exchange earnings respectively.[10] During 1979-83, Shenzhen SEZ absorbed more than US\$400 million and thus should have created at least 3.44 billion yuan of industrial output, 1.28 billion fiscal revenues, and US\$0.76 billion of foreign exchange earnings, if her efficiency of utilizing foreign funds was as high as Shanghai's. However, Shenzhen's actual performance — 0.659 billion yuan of industrial output, 0.268 billion yuan of fiscal revenues, and HK\$0.48 billion of foreign exchange earnings, was much poorer, indicating malallocation of funds from static point of view.[11] Besides, even

---

[10] Wang Z. *Summaries on Economic Policies and Law Since the Third Plenary Session of the Eleventh Central Committee of the Chinese Communist Party,* 1984, p. 120.

[11] However, attention should be paid to the fact that a significant portion of the funds were put for construction purposes which usually yielded little returns in the short-run.

within the SEZs, non foreign-involved enterprises have been discriminated against. They receive lower tax concessions compared with foreign-involved enterprises. In short, they can't enjoy similar exemption from the reduction of income taxes during the first five years of operation immediately after profits have been made, and have to pay the higher industry-commerce taxes rather than the lower consolidated industry-commerce taxes.[12] Such prejudice inhibits expansion of inward-linked enterprises which do not have contractual cooperation with foreign investors, and may displace non foreign-involved local enterprises especially those run by collectives in the SEZs. Finally, as the Zones rely more and more heavily on foreign investment which, in turn, depends on overseas economic conditions, they may suffer more serious fluctuations, if economic fluctuations abroad are frequent. In fact, some foreign-involved enterprises such as those manufacturing containers had suffered sharp decrease in sales due to economic recession in the world market and the strong competition from Korea. They had to be supported by additional domestic demand arranged by the government. The container factory in Shekou was finally shut down simply because of insufficient demand and enormous loss.

IMPACT ON HONG KONG AND OTHER ECONOMIES

Apart from affecting their own economic activities as well as performance of other areas within China, operation of the SEZs may also influence economic achievements of other economies especially those which are close to and have good relations with China. Theoretically, the Zones can generate both positive and negative impacts on foreign economies. Positively, the Zones may directly open up new opportunities for foreign economies via their rapid increase in demand for imports of inputs and consumer goods, upsurge of investment abroad, provision of more investment opportunities in China as well as opening up of the large potential China market. Besides, they may indirectly provide demonstration effect showing the likely outcome of operating free trade and (or) export processing areas. Negatively, the SEZ experiment may ultimately succeed to enhance competitiveness of China's exports in overseas markets thus intensifying international competition and displacing products of less competitive exporting economies in the world market.

As discussed above, the core spirit of economic institutional reforms in the SEZs is greater autonomy, incentive, and pressure for the basic economic units to decide their own activities. Keeping in line with it, import restrictions have been lessened to a large extent and this will definitely continue in future. At the same time, current consumption has been encouraged. Thus, with rapid expansion of productive activities and the subsequent increase of income, there will be significant increase in demand for imports of inputs and consumer goods as long as supply conditions in China cannot improve fast enough to meet new demands. In fact, Shenzhen has relied more heavily on imports as the major supply source of commodities. She still suffered huge trade deficits in 1983 and 1984. The trade gap

---

[12] The tax laws also indicate the case that if the consolidated industry-commerce tax rate is higher than the industry-commerce one, the foreign-involved enterprises are allowed to adopt the latter instead of the former.

was correspondingly −91.6 percent and −66.9 percent.[13] In 1983, the commercial department in Shenzhen purchased 41.2 percent (of which 16.5 percent was through the Guangzhou Trade Fair) of total commodities from imports, and only 23.7 percent from local production. Thus, if the Shenzhen experience can be effectively transferred to other areas, and China can achieve sustained steady growth so as to quadruple her national income by 2000 compared with 1980, there will be a drastic upsurge of China's demand for imports. Accordingly, the exporting economies which used to supply the China market and are mainly within the Asian-Pacific area will gain. It is expected that those newly industrialized or mid-level developing economies will gain most, since under import liberalization and subject to the average level of living standard, China will demand for consumer durables which are less sophisticated but cheaper and less advanced producer goods. Exports from the newly industrailized economies which have comparative advantage in this respect should rise even faster.[14] In addition, foreign economies can make use of China to diversify economic activities and practise more delicate international division of labor. Through direct investment, they can participate in some economic activities which they can't pursue profitably in their home-countries, and shift part of the production process which the home-country has no advantage to China so as to lower production cost.

Economic Relations with Hong Kong

Owing to Hong Kong's geographical proximity to and historical ties with the SEZs (especially Shenzhen) the economic relations between Hong Kong and China, particularly Shenzhen provide the most vivid example demonstrating the impact of the SEZs on other economies.

Ever since mid fifties up to 1978, Sino-Hong Kong trade was uni-directional dominated by Hong Kong's importing from China. However, since 1979, as a result of China's open-door policies, and in particular, starting from the formal establishment of the SEZs, Hong Kong's exports to China has risen very rapidly. In 1978, imports from Hong Kong and Macao accounted only for 0.69 percent of China's total imports, ranking 17th among all import sources, but in 1983, Hong Kong alone accounted for 8.04 percent of China's total imports, ranking the third. In 1984, the share improved further to 12.46, (See Tables 6A and 6B). Most of Hong Kong's

---

[13] Imports and exports of the Shenzhen SEZ in US million dollars in 1983 and 1984 are as follows:

	Imports*			Exports*			Trade gap† (%)		
		State enterprise	Foreign-involved enterprise						
	(M)	(A)	(B)	(E)	(A)	(B)	Total	(A)	(B)
'83	708.40	568.35 (80.2%)	140.05 (19.8%)	60.94	32.15 (52.8%)	28.79 (47.2%)	−91.4	−94.3	−79.4
'84	802.65	600.58 (74.8%)	202.07 (25.2%)	265.40	42.58 (16.0%)	222.82 (84.0%)	−66.9	−92.0	10.3

Source: *Shenzhen Special Economic Zone Yearbook 1985*, pp. 439-443.
Note: * excluding the business acted as agent.

$$† \left(\frac{E - M}{M} \right) \times 100\%$$

[14] These goods are mainly demanded by small scale enterprises run by collectives or even individuals. Starting from 1st March 1985 the self-employed entrepreneur will be permitted to import means of production at price below 5,000 yuan without getting approval from the Xian government.

exports (including re-exports) to China are consumer goods especially consumer durables as expected. In 1984, China already replaced Britain as the second largest market for Hong Kong exports. In fact, in 1985 Hong Kong would have suffered negative economic growth (similar to Singapore) if her exports to China had not grown so rapidly.

Non-trade business relations between Hong Kong and Shenzhen have also been strengthened. Some Hong Kong industrialists have made use of investment opportunities in Shenzhen and then other industrial cities in China to practise cost-reducing regional division of labor. For instance, some textile, electronic and toy factories etc. in Hong Kong have shifted the labor, land and resource-intensive production processes to Shenzhen where rent and wages are lower, but specialized in those processes in which Hong Kong still enjoys comparative advantage. Furthermore, in view of the increasing demand and technical support from enterprises in China, it has become more likely for Hong Kong to develop some specialized branches and production process of heavy industries such as machine-building industry. Concerning China's investment in Hong Kong, during 1979-84, it outweighed Hong Kong's investment in China.[15] In fact, all of the SEZs have opened offices and run business undertakings in Hong Kong. The increase in investment from China has created more jobs. In recent years, quite a significant proportion of college leavers studying economics and business have been absorbed by China-related enterprises. Besides, China's willingness to export labor may offer another cost-reducing device for Hong Kong businessmen. In fact, some businessmen in Hong Kong have asked the Hong Kong government to open up some areas along the border as industrial centers employing workers from Mainland China on condition that the workers must go back to the Mainland after office hour.

Operation of the SEZs have definitely generated some displacement effects on Hong Kong. For instance, the shift of some industries or production process and investment from Hong Kong to the SEZs *per se* should have reduced employment in Hong Kong. Parallel trade between the SEZs and Hong Kong should have lowered the profits of some China trade agencies in Hong Kong (but benefited the consumers at least in the short-run). However, compared with the favorable impact it generates, particularly, consolidating the confidence of foreign investors in China's dedication to pragmatic policies, and so upholding the 'One Country Two Systems' model for Hong Kong which implies confidence in the future of Hong Kong, as well as the opening up of ample opportunities for Hong Kong investors and the gain from Hong Kong's serving as the bridge between foreign investors and the Mainland,[16] the displacement effects should be insignificant. Nevertheless, due cooperation and practice of regional division of labor between Hong Kong and the SEZs as well as pursuance of appropriate manpower training and re-training in Hong Kong will reduce them. On the whole, we expect in future economic activities of Hong Kong and the SEZs, especially, Shenzhen will be further integrated vertically.

---

[15] According to the Deputy Commissioner of Industry, Hong Kong, during 1981-84 China invested HK\$31 billion in Hong Kong much larger than what Hong Kong has invested in China during 1979-June 1984, HK\$4.5 billion, *Ta Kung Pao,* 7/2/85, p. 16.

[16] For discussion of the impact of the China factor on the Hong Kong economy, especially, on Hong Kong's investment activities and foreign direct investment in Hong Kong, see Hsueh Tien-tung and Tun-oy Woo "US Direct Investment in Hong Kong: Present Situation and Prospect", *The Columbia Journal of World Business,* Vol. XXI, No. 1, Spring 1986.

Table 6A. Imports from Hong Kong[†] as a % of China's Total Imports, 1979-1984

Year	% share	Ranking**
1978	0.69*	17
1979	1.37*	12
1980	2.92*	6
1981	5.23*	4
1982	6.34	3
1983	7.15	3
1984	12.46	3

Sources: The Statistical Bureau of People's Republic of China, *Statistical Yearbook of China 1981, 1983, 1984*; *Almanac of China's Foreign Economic Relations and Trade 1984*, *Ta Kung Pao*, 23/1/1985, p. 1.

Notes: † Computed in US dollar, including re-exports.
   * including imports from Macao.
   ** order of importance: 1, 2, 3, ...
     dependent on turnover value

Table 6B. Exports to China as a % of Hong Kong's Domestic Exports[†], 1979-1985

Year	% share	Ranking
1979	1.08	*
1980	2.35	*
1981	3.64	*
1982	4.58	4
1983	5.96	4
1984	8.18	2
1985	11.69	2

Sources: Hong Kong Government, *1983 Economic Background*, Feb. 1984, p. 12; Census and Statistics Department, *Hong Kong Monthly Digest of Statistics*, March 1986, Hong Kong, pp. 19-21.

Notes: * ranking 'over 10'.
     † computed in Hong Kong dollar.

Economic Relations with the Rest of the World

As a matter of fact, relative to western economies, China is still fairly immune from economic fluctuation in the capitalist world. Thus, investing in China can stabilize profit earnings to a certain extent, if the products supply mainly for the China market. Of course, China's recent decision to enlarge domestic sales proportion for foreign-involved enterprises in China so as to acquire more advanced production technique will offer ample opportunities for foreign investors, especially, those from technologically advanced economies such as Japan and USA. On the other hand, learning from foreign investors, China has also increased her investment abroad and exported labor as well as other services. Such practice will continue and be strengthened.[17] The recipients of Chinese investment normally will gain, and import of Chinese labor services help lessen excess demand pressure in the labor market, thus lowering local wages and production cost.

Consumers in those economies which rely heavily on China's exports have benefited due to drastic increase in supply sources in China and breakdown of the monopolized sole wholesale agency supply system. Shenzhen has been empowered to conduct trade directly with other economies. Thus, local authorities and enterprises in other areas have made use of Shenzhen, by-passing the trade corporations to export directly to overseas markets. The rapid increase in supply level and supply sources have led to keen competition in the importing economies and so lower prices for their consumers.

In a negative aspect, it is possible that with spread of the Shenzhen experience, China will improve her competitive power in the world market such that she may out-compete other economies especially the less-developed. Certainly, in recent years, China has placed more emphasis on export trade. She has pursued institutional reforms on trade administration and established specialized export bases to promote export. Not only have SEZs been assigned to function as the spear-head for export promotion, but the production structures of some areas have been altered and geared to serving the world market rather than the domestic market. As a result of all above measures, since 1979 China's exports have expanded tremendously. During 1978-1983, China attained an average annual real growth rate of 15.4 percent of exports much higher than that of world total, 2 percent. In 1978, China supplied 0.75 percent of world exports, and ranked 32nd among all exporting economies. However, in 1983 she contributed to 1.23 percent of world export ranking 16th.[18] We expect that China's exports will continue to rise. Nevertheless, due to her large population, the domestic market should still remain the most important one. Whether China's expected rapid export expansion will create disastrous displacement effects depends significantly on the shift of comparative advantage of China and other exporting economies as well as cooperation among the parties concerned. Owing to her size and widely diversified resource endowment, China need not have the same comparative advantage as other economies. The foreign economies may avoid displacement effects if they assist China to identify and then invest in these industries (within the SEZs and other open-up regions) in which the SEZs and other open-up regions have comparative advantage but which are non-existent or insignificant in their homeland. To reap such cost-reduction opportunity they may need to alter their spatial allocation of overseas investments and develop new industries. Furthermore, through negotiation among governments

---

[17] Since 1980, China has established and operated 113 contractual joint-ventures with investors of host countries abroad, of which 47 were established in 1984. In addition, in 1984, China signed contracts concerning foreign contracted projects and labor service cooperation with a turnover of US$1.68 billion, 82.6 percent higher than that of 1983. Realized turnover amounted to US$0.55 billion, 22 percent higher than the previous year. By the end of 1984, 47,000 Chinese participated in these projects working abroad. See *Ta Kung Pao*, 23/1/85, p. 2.

[18] According to *Almanac of China's Foreign Economic Relations and Trade 1984*, p. 825, China's export share and ranking in world total exports in selected years are as follows:

	1950	1960	1965	1970	1976	1980	1981	1982	1983
% share	0.91	1.44	1.19	0.72	0.69	0.92	1.06	1.18	1.23
ranking	28	17	18	30	34	28	21	18	16

or formation of some sort of international cooperation organization within the Asian-Pacific region, more rational international division of labor can be practised, thus avoiding unnecessary duplication of activities and harmful direct competition in the world market. However, as China emphasizes on acquiring foreign exchange, advanced technology, and efficient management skill, it is the developed and newly industrialized economies not the developing economies, which will gain most. In fact, there will be unavoidable displacement effects on those economies less developed than China, such as India. Nevertheless, it is expected that through the 'window effects' of the SEZs, international economic relations between China and other economies within the Asian-Pacific region will be strengthened, and if appropriately handled, should be beneficial to all.

PROBLEMS AND PROSPECTS OF THE SPECIAL ECONOMIC ZONES

Problems confronting the SEZs include those which hinder inflow of foreign direct investment and steady improvement in productivity within the Zones as well as those which inhibit the spread of beneficial linkage, demonstration, and transfer effects to other areas. We will depict the major problems which are followed by prospects.

Lack of Coordination

Although great strides have been made to accelerate establishment and improvement of infrastructures as well as removing obstacles under the existing administrative system or even reforming the system fundamentally, reforms introduced have always been piecemeal. They haven't been integrated into a well-coordinated setting. Thus, many projects cannot function effectively and efficiently, wasting resources and detering further inflow of foreign direct investment. At present, inadequate supplies of electricity, competent administrative personnel as well as lack of clearly-defined laws governing the obligations and rights of enterprises, especially those specifying the relations between the enterprise and various levels of government authorities, still remain the most severe bottleneck to further economic progress in the Zones. Furthermore, administrative procedures for foreign investors to apply for establishing and operating an enterprise in the Zones need to be further simplified. By early 1984, a foreign investor still had to go through 32 different administrative stages and pay 19 types of fees from the time he applied for establishing the enterprise to the time when the first lot of products has been transferred out of the enterprise. Recently, the most serious problem confronting the foreign investors in Shenzhen has been the tremendous upsurge of business cost especially the so-called hidden costs which are not included in the contract. It has been the consequence of general inflation in China as well as pursuance of maximum short-run profits by the Shenzhen authority.

There has been little coordination among the four SEZs so as to avoid duplication of activities. At present, the pattern of foreign direct investment in all SEZs are quite similar, thus reducing the scope of demonstration and transfer effects. Even Hainan Island is going to establish an electronic industry with scale not smaller than Shenzhen's. Worse still, there has been undue competition among the SEZs for the same type of foreign direct investment. For example, Shenzhen and Zhuhai in order to enhance their competitiveness have kept on revising the land rent several times downward. The same holds between the Zones and non-Zone areas. The Zones authorities have made use of their privilege to foster economic growth within their own boundary. Thus, with their subsidies and deliberate supports, some economic activities could be practised to their own advantage but at the expense of other areas, and, on balance, even against the interest of the whole nation. It is not unusual to find economic activities in the Zones not in accord with their comparative advantage, and which cannot survive without special privilege granted by the authorities, resulting in irrational resource allocation. As mentioned above, recently, some enterprises of the interior regions have made use of Shenzhen's authority to export their products directly to Hong Kong and Macao without going through Hong Kong's wholesale agency. As a result, the existing wholesale system in Hong Kong has been disrupted, and prices of some Chinese exportables in Hong Kong have dropped rapidly, reducing the state's total export earnings. The state's reputation within the business circle in Hong Kong has also been injured. The problem of malallocation of resources between the special and non-special areas will become even more serious, as more Economic and Technological Development Zones enjoying similar privileges as the Special Zones are to be established. Since many of these Development Zones have a sound and relatively more efficient industrial base, especially those in Shanghai[19] Tianjin and Dailin, and so greater real competitive power (neglecting subsidies and other concessions) compared with the SEZs, in order to maintain their competitiveness, the SEZs may again press the state for more privileges, and extend more concessions to foreign investors. Although with additional grant of concessions they can maintain prosperity, malallocation of resources may thus become more serious. As a matter of fact, activities of the SEZs should be arranged for the benefit of the whole nation, not for maximizing welfare of the SEZs *per se.* Thus, not only all required infrastructures, economic and non economic, within the Zone be well integrated and coordinated so as to improve the investment climate attracting more foreign direct investment, activities of various special zones as well as those between the Zones and non-Zone areas must also be coordinated and managed according to their comparative advantage.

The Currency Problem

As China has practised very restrictive foreign exchange control, and Renminbi is not convertible, it is extremely difficult for the common people to acquire foreign currencies. However, some industrial products can only be purchased with foreign currencies or foreign exchange certificate, and some may also be paid in Renminbi but at much higher prices, compared with paying in foreign currencies at official exchange rate. In addition, since the liberalization of state's control on imports, the local authorities and even enterprises have been permitted to import needed commodities, provided that they have foreign exchanges. And as selling imported commodities is most profitable, so foreign currencies have been in great demand. Acting as the window to the outside world, tourists and businessmen frequently visit Shenzhen and other SEZs, so there are supplies of Hong Kong dollar, other

---

[19] For instance, during January-November 1984, Shanghai approved establishment of 20 Sino-foreign joint-ventures, 17 contractual joint-ventures with total contracted investment US$519 million more than 5 times the cumulative sum during 1979-1983. See *Economic Reporter,* No. 1903, Jan. 1985, p. 22.

foreign currencies, and foreign exchange certificates in the Zones in addition to those from official sources. In fact, businessmen also prefer to use Hong Kong dollar directly for transaction because then there is no need for them to convert foreign currencies in Renminbi first and then from Renminbi back to foreign currencies. Thus, three types of currencies, Renminbi, Foreign Exchange Certificate, and Hong Kong dollars circulate simultaneously in Shenzhen and to a lesser extent in other SEZs. Most goods are then quoted in three currencies, rendering transaction more complicated. Of course, transactions in foreign currencies have grown in importance at the expense of Renminbi. In the first quarter 1984, sales level of commodities quoted in Renminbi accounted only for 28.8 percent of total sales. Such a multi-currency circulation system (biased against Renminbi but in favor of foreign currencies and to a lesser extent foreign exchange certificate) not only enhances transaction costs, but has led to very undesirable outcomes. First, it has given rise to a black market of foreign currencies in which the value of Renminbi is much lower than the official rate. In 1984, the black market exchange rate of the Hong Kong dollar was very close to one. As a result, businessmen and residents in Shenzhen purchased Renminbi in the black market rather than through the bank at official rate, leading to a loss of foreign exchange earnings for the state. Besides, as Shenzhen has become the center for illegal transaction of foreign exchanges, huge quantities of money, Renminbi and even foreign exchange certificate from other areas flow to Shenzhen. It was estimated that over 10 percent of foreign exchange certificates issued had flowed into Shenzhen. Under such circumstances, the Shenzhen authority cannot control the money supply and accordingly the general price level. As more and more money flows to Shenzhen, inflationary pressure has become very intense, thus reducing her price competitiveness. Last but not least, existence of the black market has widened income disparity and created ideological problems. Thus, if the currency problem can't be tackled successfully, China will continue to lose foreign exchange and the SEZs will become less attractive to foreign investors. In view of this, the decision makers have held discussions on reforming the currency system of the SEZs especially in Shenzhen. Many proposals have been raised, and the most likely concerns introduction of a new, freely convertible currency, the SEZ currency. The currency will be backed up by foreign exchange, can be freely bought and sold, and its value is subject to supply-demand conditions in the foreign exchange market. However, there are still two problems to be solved. First, what should be the relation between this new currency and Renminbi, and foreign exchange certificate? Will it become the only currency circulated in the Zones, and if not, what should be the conversion rate between Renminbi and SEZ currency, and that between SEZ currency and foreign exchange certificate? If the official exchange rate cannot accurately reflect relative purchasing power, a black market will still exist. If it becomes the only currency in circulation, with what currency be trade conducted between the special and non-special zones? Secondly, what authority will be responsible for issuing and backing up the new currency; on what base will the supply level be determined? Surely, these problems must be very carefully considered and tackled. Nevertheless, two basic criteria should be observed for final decision. The new system should not hinder the linkage, demonstration, and transfer effects, because these are the most important functions of the SEZs, and it should be geared to serving the interest of the whole national economy but not confined only to the SEZs. Thus, the danger of loss of valuable foreign exchanges by the national economy due to speculation in the foreign exchange market on the new currency as well as the import of overseas financial disturbances must be taken seriously into account.[20]

The Inward-Linkage Problems

As rightly asserted by some Chinese officials, the most important and fruitful function of the SEZs is to provide inward-linkage effects, transferring technical and administrative knowhow to the interior regions. However, so far, the policies pursued by the SEZs such as Shenzhen are the other way round. The special Zones authorities want to make use of the inward-linked enterprises to foster economic progress in their Zones. Thus, in general, only those which are relatively well-developed and efficient and trade-oriented have been allowed or invited to establish branches or joint-ventures in the Zones. Ironically, these are usually the last needing assistance. Certainly, if such policy is pursued temporarily as the means to lay down essential conditions for rapid economic growth so as to attract foreign investment, it can be accepted. However, the fact is, as economic conditions in Shenzhen have improved, the authority has imposed harsher rules for approving establishment of inward-linked enterprises. It implies those less efficient and are in urgend need of receiving training in the Zones are deprived of the chance. Consequently, it demonstrates the conflict between private interests (maximization of welfare for the Zones) and public interests (maximization of welfare for the national economy) which of course should be jointly settled by the central government and the Zones. The state may grant subsidies to the Zones for accepting less efficient inward-linked enterprises. In fact, as the Shenzhen authority has to bear its financial responsibility, in order to maximize short-run profits, most 'inward-linkage' services offered by Shenzhen have been entreport trade selling imports mainly consumer durables and as the center for single assembly of imported components and parts for resale in the interior regions. Nevertheless, the most serious obstacle to the spread of beneficial linkage and transfer effects may be establishment of the Administration Line (or Second Line) and the likely decision to use SEZ currency exclusively in the SEZs.[21] Establishment of the Administration Line is to simplify administration of imports and entry into Shenzhen from Hong Kong and other economies. After operation of the Administration Line, nearly all duties on imports into Shenzhen will be exempt. However, to ensure that these imported goods will not be resold to the interior regions without paying taxes, the Administration Line is the only possible way to keep a close watch on the flow of goods, and check whether there are illegal entry of people from non-Zone areas. Such practice will inhibit transaction between the Zones and non-Zone areas to a certain extent. It may, on one hand, reduce commercial earnings of the Zones, which at present constitute a significant income source, and, on the other, hinder unorganized informal transfer of information, technique, and managerial skills from the Zones to the other areas. Similarly, if under the new SEZ currency system, only the new currency is allowed for circulation in the Zones, but Renminbi is still used outside, and the Zones authorities place special emphasis on preventing non-Zone economic units from acquiring the freely convertible new currency illegally via transaction with Shenzhen SEZ, economic transaction between the SEZs and non-Zone areas will be restricted.

---

[20] Recently, the Chinese authority announced to suspend the decision to issue SEZ currency.

[21] The Administration Line was formally opened for use on 1 April, 1986.

Under very close supervision, transfer of technical knowhow and managerial skill from the SEZs to non-Zone areas will be inhibited to a certain extent.

Gradually as more and more defects of the SEZs have been exposed which indicate that the performance of the SEZs have not been as successful as expected and may have even done harm to the national economy, the Chinese government has to reconsider the role of the SEZs. The most controversial issues concern the inward-linkage effects which have been conducted against the original desire of the government resulting in huge loss of foreign exchange. Most recently, the central government has decided to turn the SEZs into export bases encouraging foreign investors and industries of the interior regions (in China) to establish and operate enterprises in the SEZs for producing exports. On the other hand, the inward-linkage effects are to be under tight control to ensure that the SEZs will no longer serve as the 'off-shore' center for illegal transactions in foreign exchange and trade for the interior regions. The formal operation of the Administration Line serves this purpose. In addition, the size of basic construction investment in the SEZs have to be curtailed so that economic efficiency can be enhanced for attracting foreign investment. Resources will be allocated between the SEZs and other regions by reference to comparative advantage. Investment within the SEZs is to be determined on the basis of more careful economic calculation. The core spirit is that national interest rather than regional interest should be observed first. The SEZs cannot prosper by injuring the national economy. Concessions and subsidies will be extended on a more selective basis to ensure that the resultant pattern of economic activities within the SEZs conforms with the new role assigned by the government.

In fact, the Chinese government learns a very valuable lesson from the SEZ experiment. Pursuance of nearly unrestricted economic liberalization plus unconditional self-financial responsibility policy within small areas (SEZs) in a country with a heavily regulated and controlled economy can be harmful to the national economy although these small areas may achieve very rapid growth. It is because in the face of the need to bear their own financial responsibilities, the SEZs will make use of their greatest advantage (preferential policies) to maximize their benefit. If the preferential policies are not well designed as to ensure that their implementation will definitely benefit the national economy, there can be conflict between the SEZs and the national economy. The SEZs may become the loophole for the non-Zone regions to violate the national plan. Theoretically, there are two ways to tackle the problem. One is to pursue all policies practised within the SEZs throughout the national economy which will, however, generate unpredictable huge shocks both economically and ideo-politically, and which cannot be coped with by the economy given its very rigid structure. Another way is to keep the SEZs special but to exert more guidance and control via granting financial concession (on selective basis) and enforcement of law to ensure conformity between national and regional interests. Certainly, the Chinese government has adopted the second alternative. As a matter of fact, in theory, there can be the third alternative — abandoning the SEZ experiment. However, it is politically infeasible. The SEZs serve as the window for China's open policy which is the core of Deng Xiaoping's development strategy. Abandonment of the SEZ experiment implies failure of Deng's strategy which is politically intolerable from the viewpoint of the Dengist. Furthermore, as discussed above, the Shenzhen experiment has been used to demonstrate China's endurance and flexibility in order to convince the Hong Kong citizens that the 'one country, two systems' model will be strictly adhered to since 1979. Its abandonment will create and worsen the confidence problem in Hong Kong. Future prospects of the SEZs depend on China's top decision makers' basic line of social and economic construction, performance of the SEZs, and the role (assigned by the decision makers) which the Zones are going to play for the national economy. Based on evidences, the prevailing basic line of social and economic construction for China, which emphasizes on economic achievements and improvement of consumption welfare has been welcome by most Chinese people, so we won't expect any major and fundamental change of this line. It goes without saying, the policy guideline "activating the domestic economy and opening the door to the outside world" will persist in the foreseeable future. In this respect, it is likely for the SEZs practice to continue. Concerning performance of the Zones, if the aforementioned problems can be successfully handled, and even more important, the state continues to extend support by granting additional privileges and concessions, through learning by doing, the SEZs will continue to achieve good economic performance, and may be even better than before. Based on current situation, there are no grounds to believe that the government will stop granting special preferential treatment for the SEZs. Actually, the fate of the SEZs, to a large extent, depends on the rise of and the possible role played by the Economic and Technological Development Zones as well as the decision makers' interpretation of basic features of socialism. Certainly, whether the SEZs will remain special compared with other areas in China, rests with the role assigned by the decision makers to them. To conclude, the SEZ experiment will be extended, yet we believe, compared with other areas (except the Economic and Technological Development Zones) they will remain special for quite a long time.

CONCLUSION

Establishment of the SEZs has been the boldest attempt among all reforms pursued by the Chinese government since 1979. The Zones have achieved quite brilliant economic performance during 1979-83, however the achievements have been attained at large opportunity cost from the static point of view. Yet, the Zones have generated some demonstration and transfer effects that may be greater than the direct linkage effects on non-Zone areas. Many new administrative practices have been transplanted to the non-Zone areas, and some proved to be quite successful. In addition, the Zones experiment has also opened up new opportunities for other region's economies such as Hong Kong's. Even though displacement effects may be generated, due cooperation between China and other economies within the Asian-Pacific area will render them insignificant. However, the Zones still have a lot of problems to be tackled, in particular, the inter-Zone coordination, currency, and inward-linkage issues, if they really want to function as the spear-head, generating growth momentum for the national economy rather than maximizing welfare for themselves. In view of current situation, we believe the SEZs will continue to get support from the government, and remain special. Nevertheless, their unique role will be shared by Economic and Technological Development Zones in the open cities.

REFERENCES

Almanac of China's Foreign Economic Relations and Trade, 1984. Hong Kong: China Resources Trade Consultancy Co., 1984.

Economic Reporter. Hong Kong: Economic Information & Agency, various issues.

Fang Siyuan, Wu Yuwen and He Guixi. "Development Strategies for Shantou's Economy", *Journal of South China Normal University,* 1984, pp. 34-37.

Hanson, Philip. *Trade and Technology in Soviet-Western Relation.* The Macmillan Press Ltd., 1981.

Hong Kong & Macao Economic Digest, Guangzhou, various issues.

Hsueh T.T. and T.O. Woo. "US Direct Investment in Hong Kong: Present Situation and Prospects", *The Columbia Journal of World Business,* Vol. XXI, No. 1, Spring, 1986, pp. 75-85.

Huang Yi and Liang Shisen. "Accelerating the Import of Advanced Technology to the Special Economic Zones", *Journal of South China Normal University,* 1984, pp. 33, 38-42.

The New Evening News & External Propaganda Center, Shenzhen. *Handbook of Special Economic Zones,* Hong Kong, 1984.

Office of The Administration of Zhuhai Special Economic Zone. *An Open Coastal City — Zhuhai.* 1984.

Qian Jiaju and Lu Zufa, eds. *Essays on Theoretical Economic Problems of Special Economic Zones.* Beijing: People's Publishing House, 1984.

Sham Paul. "Soaring business costs hit China investment drive". *South China Morning Post,* July 4, 1986.

Shenzhen Special Economic Zone Development Company. *Introduction to Shenzhen Special Economic Zone Investment Environment and Shenzhen SEZ Development Co.,* 1984.

Shenzhen Special Economic Zone Yearbook 1985. Hong Kong, Economic Information & Agency, 1985.

Shi Zupei & Ye Quiwen. "The Industrial Development in the Shenzhen Special Economic Zone Entering a New Stage". *Journal of Sun Yat Sen University,* Social Science Edition, 1984.

Statistical Yearbook of China. 1981, 1983, 1984, overseas edition, Hong Kong: Economic Information and Agency.

Ta Kung Pao, Hong Kong, various issues.

Wang Zhengming. *Summaries on Economic Policies and Law Since The Third Plenary Session of The Eleventh Central Committee of the Chinese Communist Party,* Beijing: The Law Publisher, 1984.

Wei Yuming. "Speech at the Opening Ceremony of the Investment Symposium for China's Open Cities", Nov. 1984, Hong Kong.

Yearbook of China's Special Economic Zones, 1983, Hong Kong: Yearbook of China's Special Economic Zones Publishing Co.

Zhao Yuanhao and Chen Zhaobin. eds., *The Economy of the Chinese Special Economic Zones,* Science Popularization Publishing House, Guangzhou Branch, 1984.

13. Productivity Issues and Development Strategies in India

V.R. Panchamukhi and K.M. Raipuria

INTRODUCTION

The problem of productivity or efficiency in resource use has been well recognized in the theory of economic growth and development. The role of productivity assumes special significance in developing economies where resources such as capital, skilled labor, foreign exchange, and energy are scarce.

Changes in productivity and sharing of the benefits of increased productivity are central themes of the long standing debate in international economic relations. The late Raul Prebisch propounded the thesis that the benefits of productivity changes in the developed countries have not been duly transferred to the importers in the developing countries, whereas benefits of increased productivity in the developing countries have been significantly transferred to the developed countries. In long-term studies of international development relations such as the OECD's *Interfutures,* 1979, convergence of productivity of the developed world has indeed been the basis for working out alternative policies. In recent analysis of the recession in the developed world, it has been contended that a falling rate of increase in productivity in a number of countries has been a major factor explaining the recessionary tendencies. The oil price hikes in 1973 and 1979 and the consequent global energy crisis have led to interpretation of the role of higher productivity in growth and development in terms of efficient use of energy per unit of GDP.

Productivity is a highly capsuled indicator of development. The concept and meaning of productivity is changing.[1] In fact, it is related not only to technology and scale adopted at the sector/industry level but also to overall development

---

* The authors are grateful to Shri G.A. Tadas for his competent research assistance.

[1] Productivity, according to Alvin Toffler, the author of *Third Wave* (William Morrow, New York, 1980), is "one of the spongiest, most trecherous of economic concepts . . . . . designed for a world of material production, when you could count how many workers and how many hours it took to turn out how many skirts or copper bars". He observes that in the present age (the Third Wave), more and more output consists of information, services, experiences, and "economic" productivity is frequently more an artifact of accounting and of permissible externalities than of anything else. (see *Previews and Premises,* 1984.)

516

strategies adopted by a country. There have been few studies to look into the relationship between dynamics of productivity changes and choice of development strategies in developing economies. The purpose of this chapter is to raise some issues on this relationship and analyze trends in the case of the Indian economy.

This chapter provides first an overview of the major dimensions and issues of development strategy in India which have to do with productivity, highlighting some of the recent significant developments, and then it reviews the problems of productivity measurement and presents an empirical assessment of the trends in productivity at the macro and sector/industry levels, covering the period 1965-66 to 1982-83.[2] Next, it gives an analysis of the relationship between productivity changes and selected economic variables, for example, industry size and capital-intensity. Finally, it briefly brings out the recent emphasis on productivity in India and some contours of the development plan perspectives through 1990, i.e., in the Seventh Plan (1985-90). A summary of conclusions has also been added at the end of the chapter.

DIMENSIONS AND ISSUES OF DEVELOPMENT STRATEGY
AND PRODUCTIVITY

Understanding of development strategy as indicated by the investment pattern and priorities in practice requires study of several details. As shown by the sectoral pattern of plan outlays (Table 1), Indian strategy has been oriented to infrastructure development with balanced emphasis on agriculture and industry. However, in a broader sense, development strategy in India has multiple dimensions. Some of these dimensions and their alternatives could be discussed under the following headings:
1. Import-substitution strategy and export promotion strategy;
2. Agriculture and industrial development;
3. Fiscal policies and physical intervention;
4. Structuralist and monetarist approach to the problems of control of inflation and growth;
5. Public sector and private sector;
6. Others: Rural-urban, small-large scale, balanced-unbalanced growth, etc.

Each of these seemingly dichotomous dimensions has some relevance to development of the Indian economy during the last three decades of planning. Indeed, the level and structure of productivity, and efficiency in resource allocation are influenced by the emphasis placed on individual alternatives in each of the dimensions listed above as well as by the overall blend in the strategy adopted. In this section, each of the six dimensions is reviewed in the context of the evolution of India's development strategy over time.

Import-substitution and Export Promotion

In India, most often these alternative strategies have been viewed in an "either — or"

---

[2] The beginning year of the reference period, i.e. 1965-66, is significant in many respects. Aside from being the last year of the Third Plan, it was perhaps the beginning of a period when export promotion was explicitly adopted as part of the plan strategy along with import-substitution orientation. It also coincides with the beginning of Green Revolution in agriculture.

Table 1. Pattern of Sectoral Outlays in Public Sector Under India's Five-Year Plans

(Unit: %)

Sector	First Plan	Second Plan	Third Plan	Annual Plans	Fourth Plan	Fifth Plan	Sixth Plan Projections
Agriculture, etc.	14.8	11.7	12.7	16.7	14.7	13.0	13.2
Industry							
Village and Small Scale Industries	4.9	24.1	22.9	24.7	19.7	24.3	22.7
Organized Industries and Mining	2.1	4.0	2.6	1.9	1.5	1.5	1.8
	2.8	20.1	20.1	22.8	18.2	22.8	20.9
Infrastructure	80.3	64.2	64.4	58.6	65.6	62.7	64.1
Irrigation	29.7	9.2	7.8	7.1	8.6	9.8	10.6
Power		9.7	14.6	18.3	18.6	18.7	19.9
Transport and Communications	26.4	27.0	24.6	18.5	19.5	17.0	15.9
Social Services, etc.	24.2	18.3	17.4	14.7	18.9	17.2	17.7
Total	100.0	100.0	100.0	100.0	100.0	100.0	100.0

Source: Based on various plan documents and issues of *Economic Survey*.

framework rather than as part of a suitable integrated approach to development. When India began the process of planned development in 1951 the strategy adopted was one of import-substitution toward 'self-reliance'. This strategy recieved particular emphasis after the launching of the second Five-year Plan in 1956. A serious foreign exchange crisis in 1956-57 was caused by heavy investment in the capital goods sector and this further induced policy makers to adopt rigorous import-substitution measures. The results may be seen in substantial reduction in the share of imports in total supplies of major items like food, iron and steel, fertilizers, petroleum, and machinery (Table 2). The strategy also reduced dependence on aid (Table 3).

Further, the approach toward import-substitution was to adopt physical controls and licensing methods rather than tariffs and other fiscal measures. The import licensing system implied evolution of a variety of institutions, aimed at implementation of controls. Institutions for issuing essentiality certificates, indigenous clearance certificates and import licences increased. They are today a rigid component of the institutional framework of the country. Tariffs played a secondary role in providing protection to the domestic industry. Studies decomposing the levels of effective protection into the tariff component and non-tariff component have clearly brought out this point.[3] The period of 1956 to 1961 could thus be characterized as a period of rigid import substitution strategies. Growth of exports as an objective of planning was recognized only from 1961 onwards. The Third Plan (1961-66) and more explicitly, the Fourth Plan (1969-74) mentioned a variety of measures aimed at export promotion. The period of 1961 to 1966 is the period when both import-substitution and export orientation became the basic elements of the strategy. The period of 1966 to 1968 is a period when efforts were made to rationalize the import licensing system and exchange rate policy was used as an instrument for external balance. The devaluation of 1966 could not be credited with success as current account deficits were large (Table 4). A number of unfavorable circumstances, drought conditions, a poor follow-up package of policies contributed to the failure and a reversal of policies emerged after 1968 leading to reduced external account imbalances. The period of 1968 to 1975 could be characterized as a period of intensive export-orientation and observed higher growth of exports (Table 5) while rigid import-substitution licensing system continued to characterize the trade policies. In the field of export promotion, this period saw emergence of a number of institutions, notably Export Promotion Councils and the Trade Development Authority, with a view to providing export services to the business community. During the period from 1975 to 1978, the government adopted a number of measures toward rationalizing the import licensing system including introduction of the Open General Licence (OGL). The year 1978 stands out as a landmark when as a result of the recommendations of a high powered committee (generally known as Alexander Committee) on import-export policies and procedures, the import licensing system was streamlined a great deal and the developmental role was intensified from 1978 onwards and still continues to guide government policies. This is clearly shown by various indicators (Table 6). At the same time, export promotion has also received considerable emphasis. Attempts by the government to link policies to provide exports and liberalize imports in recent years have been widely commended in and outside India, though this has meant that the balance of payments deficit has been as high as around US$3,000

---

[3] Bhagwati and Srinivasan, *Foreign Trade Regimes and Economic Development.* India, N-H, 1975.

Table 2. Import Substitution in India in Major Products

(% share of imports in total supplies)

Product	Pre-Plan 1950-51	First Plan '55-56	Second Plan '60-61	End of Third Plan '65-66	Annual Plans '68-69	Fourth Plan '73-74	Variation Col. 7/ Col. 2	End of Fifth Plan '78-79	Sixth Plan Period '80-81	'81-82	'82-83	Variation Col. 12/ Col. 2
Foodgrains	5.9	1.7	4.7	9.5	5.6	4.3	-1.6	(-)	(-)	0.6	1.4	-4.5
Iron & Steel	25.2	39.9	35.7	16.7	9.3	18.5	-6.7	14.8	16.7	14.2	14.7	-10.5
Machinery*	68.9	41.0	40.7	27.8	24.6	17.0	-51.9	10.2	16.4	N.A.	...	-52.5++
Petroleum	92.5	93.8	94.6	76.6	66.2	70.8	-21.7	56.4	63.0	48.0**	38.0**	-54.5
Nitrogenous fertilizers	72.5+	39.8	80.3	58.3	60.9	38.3	-34.2	36.0	41.1	24.4	11.1	-61.4

Sources: 1. Planning Commission, *Sixth Five-Year Plan (1980-85)*, p. 15.
2. Ministry of Finance *Economic Survey*, various volumes.

(−) means net exports
* Imports as a percentage of machinery component of gross investment on calendar year basis, at constant prices.
** Net imports as a percentage of machinery component (financial year).
*** Net imports in throughout (financial year).
+ For 1951-52.
++ Col. 9/Col. 2.

Table 3. Net Foreign Aid Received by India — Share in Aggregate (Gross) Plan Investment/Expenditure in the Five-Year Plans of India

(Rs. crore at current prices: crore = 10 millions)

Period	Net aid	Aggregate Plan Investment/ Expenditure	% share
First Plan 1951-52 to 1955-56	178	5,408 (1,960)	3.3 (9.1)
Second Plan 1956-57 to 1960-61	1,311	10,127 (4,600)	12.9 (28.5)
Third Plan 1961-62 to 1965-66	2,325	16,745 (8,577)	13.9 (27.1)
Annual Plans 1966-67 to 1968-69	2,247	15,884 (6,625)	14.1 (33.9)
Fourth Plan 1969-70 to 1973-74	1,739	41,288 (15,579)	4.2 (11.2)
Fifth Plan 1974-75 to 1978-79	3,539	85,634 (40,097)	4.1 (8.8)
Sixth Plan 1980-81 to 1984-85 (Projections)	5,889	158,710 (97,500)	3.7 (6.0)

Sources: 1. Central Statistical Organisation, *National Accounts Statistics.*
2. Ministry of Finance, *Economic Survey,* Various issues.
3. Planning Commission, *Five-Year Plans,* esp. *Sixth Five-Year Plan, 1980-85,* p. 14.

Parentheses refer to Public Sector Plan Investment/Expenditure.

million during 1980-81 to 1981-82 and a little less than US$2,500 million during 1982-83 (Table 4).

We find that India's development process that started with heavy import-substitution has now been moving toward a happy blend of import substitution and export-orientation with due emphasis on the latter. However, there have been periods of uncertainty and lack of clarity with regard to the relative emphasis to be placed on one or the other alternative strategies.

The following issue has yet to be resolved. How far has the strategy of import-substitution orientation in the early stages of development with its excessive protection of domestic products been responsible for the generation of a high cost economy, and, in turn, relatively inefficient allocation of resources and also inefficiency in individual industries? The converse of this issue is also worth raising. Does export-orientation imply an automatic increase in the efficiency of resource allocation and also higher productivity at the level of individual industries? Any linkage between export-orientation and higher efficiency has to be established through elaboration of the various intermediate factors responsible. Which is the

Table 4. India's Payments Gap (Current Account Deficit), 1965-66 to 1983-84

Year	Rs. Crore	US$ in millions
1965-66	−639.3	−1,342.5
1966-67	−958.5	−1,373.4
1967-68	−948.3	−1,204.4
1968-69	−507.5	−676.6
1969-70	−327.5	−436.7
1970-71	−473.8	−631.7
1971-72	−575.6	−772.4
1972-73	−389.1	−510.8
1973-74	−455.0	−371.1
1974-75	−760.6	−962.5
1975-76	−56.3	−92.9
1976-77	1,145.5	1,270.9
1977-78	1,319.9	1,538.3
1978-79	−244.8	−297.5
1979-80	−765.9	−945.6
1980-81	−2,218.6	−2,805.6
1981-82	−2,817.9	−3,142.1
1982-83 (P)	−2,746.1	−2,841.0
1983-84 (P)	−2,694.1	−2,605.5

Source: Ministry of Finance, *Economic Survey*, Various issues.

P = Provisional

cause and which is the effect? Should the strategy begin with improving the efficiency of production in various sectors and then searching for these with potential; or does the strategy of export orientation automatically lead to increases in efficiency?

Related to the above questions is the wider issue of protectionism in the importing developed countries and its impact on productivity, resource allocation, and efficiency in the production of exporting developing countries. The strategies of import-substitution and protection adopted in the developed countries may also influence the investment decisions and efficiency of production activities in a developing country like India.

Agricultural and Industrial Development

Another important dichotomy of development strategy that has pervaded the Indian policy framework is that of agricultural versus industrial development. The growth of the agricultural sector with its share of about 40 percent in GDP (1981-82) and about 67 percent in the total number of workers (1981 census), remains crucial to the pattern and direction of development in the rest of the economy. Productivity at the individual industry level and also overall efficiency in resource allocation depend significantly on the performance of the agricultural sector.

Table 5. Gap in India's Foreign Trade Growth (Real Value)* and
Terms of Trade Movements, 1965-66 to 1982-83

(Unit: %)

Year	Exports	Imports	Terms of Trade Movement
	— at constant prices* —		
1965-66	(−) 7.0	(−) 0.6	—
1966-67	(−) 4.2	2.3	3.7
1967-68	3.0	6.5	9.7
1968-69	15.3	(−) 9.0	4.8
1969-70	Nil	(−) 17.1	4.0
1970-71	6.6	3.3	1.9
1971-72	2.8	20.1	9.4
1972-73	10.3	(−) 1.9	6.9
1973-74	5.2	11.2	(−) 14.5
1974-75	5.3	(−) 11.7	(−) 27.4
1975-76	12.8	(−) 0.6	(−) 9.1
1976-77	19.3	(−) 3.5	8.6
1977-78	(−) 6.4	33.2	25.0
1978-79	6.8	8.4	(−) 5.3
1979-80	11.8	(−) 4.8	(−) 26.7
1980-81	18.5	41.7	(−) 12.1
1981-82	16.4 (−43.0)	—	31.0
1982-83	6.1 (−4.3)	3.4	4.0

Source: Ministry of Commerce — DGCI & S Data.

* 1958 base until 1968-69 and 1968-69 base thereafter.
Figures in parentheses refer to growth of exports (real value) excluding crude oil.

Sluggishness in the agricultural sector either due to weather conditions or wrong combination of policies could lead to distortions in the relative price structure and underutilization of capacities in the industrial sector, thereby adversely affecting efficiency both at the aggregate and at the micro levels. Many studies on the Indian economy have shown that overall inflation is largely due to the effect of inflation in the agricultural sector especially in the food sector. Additional effects on prices, income and employment result from wide fluctuations in the level of farm production both at the sectoral level and at the level of individual agricultural products.

Industrialization has been the major plank of development strategy in India in the last three decades. In this context, the changing pattern of industrial production, linkages with the agricultural and tertiary sectors, and also the strategies and the policy mixes adopted to bring about desired structure of industrialization assume special significance. The question, therefore, is how far the pattern of industrial production is responsible for low level of efficiency in resource use? To put it differently, was it possible that an alternative production pattern would have implied greater efficiency in the overall resource use and also the level of productivity

Table 6. Some Indicators of India's Liberalization and Openness,
1970-71, 1980-81 and 1984-85

Indicators	1970-71	1980-81	1984-85
1. Level of Foreign Investment (Rs. million)	25	89	1,130
2. Foreign Collaborations of which:	183	526	752
— Financial Collaborations	32	73	161
— Technical Collaborations	151	453	591
3. Import of Capital Goods[1]			
i) Rs. million	3,947	18,208	26,175
ii) As % of Total Imports (non-oil)	26.3	25.0	22.3
4. Economic "Openness"			
1) Share of Trade GDP[2]			
i) Merchandise Exports[3]	6.7	10.6	12.3
ii) Merchandise Imports	7.1	19.8	18.2
iii) Merchandise Foreign Trade (i) + (iii)	13.8	30.4	30.5
2) Share of Aggregate GDP[4]			
i) Merchandise Exports	4.2	6.9	6.1
	(3.8)	(5.2)	(5.4)
ii) Merchandise Imports	4.5	12.8	9.0
	(4.1)	(9.8)	(8.0)
iii) Merchandise Foreign Trade	8.7	19.7	15.1
	(7.9)	(15.0)	(13.4)
iv) Invisibles Receipts	0.9	4.7	4.0
	(0.8)	(4.2)	(3.6)
v) Invisibles Payments	1.4	1.4	2.3
	(1.2)	(1.2)	(2.0)
vi) Total External Trade Transactions (iii) + (iv) + (v)	11.0	25.8	21.4
	(9.9)	(20.4)	(19.0)

Sources: 1. Indian Investment Centre.
2. Ministry of Commerce-Directorate General of Commercial Intelligence and Statistics (DGCI & S).

[1] Covering non-electrical and electrical machinery, apparatus and appliances; and transport equipment.
[2] Comprised of primary and manufacturing sectors, both at factor cost; market price figures not available.
[3] Including exports of crude oil during 1981-82 onward which marginally increased 'openness' during 1982-83 to 1984-85.
[4] At factor cost; figures in parentheses relate to GDP at market prices.

in the individual industries?

The important element in industrialization strategy is that of technology development. While the debate surrounding technology and development is compounded with a wide variety of analytical and policy issues, the role that technology could play in increasing productivity and influencing allocational efficiency is non-controversial. For a long period, technology policy in India had not taken any clear shape. The government came out with a comprehensive technology policy in 1983 stating the objectives as development of indigenous technology and efficient absorption and adaptation of imported technology appropriate to national priorities and resources. Its aims *inter alia* are making maximum use of indigenous resources, providing the maximum of gainful and satisfying employment, minimizing capital outlay, encouraging modernization, fuller capacity utilization, and energy efficiency. The policy statement notes that the implementation of technology policy will depend on a system for efficient monitoring, review and guidance, and a scheme of incentives and disincentives. However, there arise several basic questions. How modern should the technology be in individual industries for a more efficient use of resources? What is the extent of trade-offs between technological efficiency and other objectives of development? What is the extent of capital-intensity that could be considered optimal in a labor abundant and employment-deficient economy?

Fiscal Policies and Physical Intervention

The available literature on development economics and growth theory does recognize the possibility of using a variety of instruments to achieve given objectives. For example, for regulating the pattern of industrial investment and production one would either use the tax-cum-subsidy policy or the approach of industrial licensing and similar regulatory measures, such as direct price and credit controls. A production activity is an aggregation of various sub-activities in each of which decision-making by the entrepreneurs is involved. The following sub-activities for choice may be recognized: (1) product mix for the activity; (2) scale of operation; (3) location of the industry; (4) type of technology; (5) nature of management and collaboration such as joint-ventures between the public and private sector and between domestic and foreign investors; (6) purchase of inputs through imports or domestic production; (7) the structure of employment; (8) phasing of investment and production activity; (9) expansion of the existing plant and equipment; (10) finding domestic and/or export markets; (11) alternative infrastructural facilities such as railways, roads, communication, information services, etc.; (12) the overall integration either vertical or horizontal and linkage with other industrial or agricultural activities.

Efficiency of resource use at the activity level is directly related to the efficiency at the various sub-activity levels. That is, productivity or efficiency at the macro-level is a direct function of efficiency at these various micro-levels and we must recognize that inefficiencies at these sub-activity levels add up to a colossal level of inefficiency at the national level rather than having a tendency of mutually cancelling each other out.

India has a mixed experience of using combination of fiscal policies and physical intervention as part of its economic policy framework. A detailed analysis of the government policies and the institutions which influence the decision-making process at the various sub-activity levels in the case of Indian economy could bring out how the activity is subjected to a variety of extraneous influences. The result could often be mutually contradictory and self-defeating, so as to make the whole system complex and relatively inefficient. Insofar as the sub-activities are inter-related and they have a definite time sequence, any disturbance in the time sequence and the mutual linkages caused by either policies or institutional constraints would also contribute to the inefficiencies at the sectoral and the national levels. While it would be interesting to work out a policy sector for each activity, and a policy matrix for the economy as a whole, it is worth noting at this stage that the Indian economy is characterized by excessive use of physical interventions by the government at the various sub-activity levels. The role of the import licensing system as against the tariff system has already been discussed. The use of industrial investment licensing system, reservation of a large number of products for small-scale industries, restraints through Monopoly and Restrictive Trade Practices (MRTP) laws, various regulations in regard to foreign collaboration, financial controls and related measures describe the nature of interventionist policies adopted in India. However, there has been growing awareness of the adverse implications of the physical intervention policies on efficiency and the structure of production. The Alexander Committee on import-export policies recommended in 1978 that the import licensing system should be gradually replaced by a rational tariff policy system. Further, a Committee on Controls and Subsidies (known as Dagli Committee) in 1979 which went into the questions of fiscal and physical interventions also made a number of recommendations for rationalizing the system. In recent years, a Committee has been constituted (known as Narasimham Committee) to examine the possibility of replacing the fiscal and the physical interventions of the government with the approach of financial controls by financial intermediaries.

The existence of physical interventions at the sub-activity levels means that the individual decision maker has to interact with the various agencies of the government. This has two obvious implications; (1) there is a cost of getting things done from the government agencies (so called corruption or goodwill money), and (2) there is a cost escalation caused by the delays and the consequent increase in prices of inputs. These effects have direct or indirect bearing on the efficiency of resource use at the level of industry and at the national level. The issue, therefore, that needs to be examined is to what extent the inefficiency in production activity is caused by the interventions of the government and how much inefficiency is due to the inherent problems of management and technology, endogenous to the activity. We could also pose the question as to whether the Indian economy could move to higher level of efficiency in resource use if physical interventions by the government were to be reduced to the minimum and wherever regulations are necessary, they are effected by fiscal and financial control measures. Debate on these options has become intense in recent years.

Structuralist and Monetarist Approach

The distinction between structuralist and the monetarist approaches, particularly in the context of control of inflation, has come to assume special significance in recent years with the experience of hyper-inflationary tendencies all over the world. The monetarist approach of controlling the money supply and credit expansion aims at containing inflation and its adverse effects. Monetarist measures tend to operate on the side of aggregate demand management rather than aggregate supply.

Structuralists recommend policy measures aimed at bringing about changes in production and consumption that, in turn, influence supply-demand imbalances, and thereby influence the level of prices as well as relative prices.

India has been credited with significant success in controlling inflation (Table 7) and also the ill-effects of the oil price shocks. The experience of the immediate post-1979 period is not a success story to the same extent as that of the post-1974 period as the inflation rate decelerated more rapidly after 1974 than after 1979. It has been documented sufficiently that the process of adjustment to external inflationary impulses was effected in the Indian economy through the adoption of monetarist approach rather than a structuralist approach. In this context arise the issues of whether productivity at the micro level and efficiency in resource allocation at the macro level have been effected and in what direction by use of the

Table 7. Percentage Variation in Implicit Price Deflator of GDP, Consumer Price and Whole Price Index, 1965-66 to 1982-85

Year	Percentage Variation (1970-71 Base)			
	GDP Implicit price deflator		Consumer price* index	Wholesale price index
	At Factor cost	At Market prices		
1965-66	9.3	9.1	7.6	7.7
1966-67	14.5	14.9	13.0	13.9
1967-68	7.8	7.7	11.5	11.6
1968-69	(−) 0.4	(−) 0.4	(−) 0.6	(−) 1.2
1969-70	4.0	4.1	1.8	3.8
1970-71	3.0	3.2	5.0	5.5
1971-72	5.2	5.2	3.2	5.6
1972-73	11.3	11.2	7.9	10.0
1973-74	18.8	18.9	20.8	20.2
1974-75	16.6	17.9	26.8	25.2
1975-76	(−) 4.1	7.9	(−) 1.2	(−) 1.1
1976-77	6.9	12.4	(−) 3.9	2.1
1977-78	3.7	3.4	7.7	5.2
1978-79	2.0	2.1	2.3	—
1979-80	15.2	15.8	8.6	17.1
1980-81	10.9	11.4	11.4	18.2
1981-82	9.3	9.4	12.5	9.3
1982-83	10.3	7.2	7.8	2.6
1983-84	9.7	9.3	12.6	9.2
1984-85	6.2	6.2	7.8	7.1

Sources: 1. The first col.: CSO, *National Accounts Statistics,* January 1984, and Quick Estimates, January 1986.

2. The second and third col.: Government of India, Ministry of Finance, *Economic Survey,* various issues.

* Industrial Workers.

monetarist approach in controlling inflation? What are the short-term and the long-term implications of such an approach on efficiency and resource allocations? In other words, would the structuralist approach of supply management, rather than demand management, be superior with regard to the overall efficiency of resource allocation? While inflation in itself is detrimental to efficient utilization of resources, control of inflation through strict monetary control could also be detrimental to the interests of efficiency and growth, by slowing down and misdirecting structural changes.

Public and Private Sector

Another major dichotomy of development strategy at the macro level is that of the public versus the private sector which has become a prominent issue in India for the last several years. Under the socialist pattern of development adopted by India the "Commanding heights" of the economy were to be occupied by the public sect-or. It was evisaged during the early stages of development that the public sector and central planning would be better instruments for bringing about social objectives of greater equity and employment benefits than the private sector and free markets. It followed that the public sector should not be confined only to the utilities but should also move into various large-scale production activities. The share of the public sector in national production of fuel, certain non-ferrous materials, telephones and teleprinters rose to 100 percent and is as high as 78 percent in steel (Table 8). In the area of foreign trade also, the role of the public sector has been significant. Public enterprises accounted for over 40 percent of merchandise exports in 1983-84 (Table 9).

The philosophy of socialism was based upon the assumption that the public sector would be more congenial to social welfare than the private sector. While, in theory, this approach seemed appropriate, the experience of the Indian economy in the last several years has not fully justified it. In recent years, the inefficiency of the public sector has received considerable attention. A variety of factors, including poor management, political interventions, irrational pricing policies, and inappro-priate product mix explain the poor performance of the public sector. While it can-not be categorically stated that the private sector is always efficient and the public sector always inefficient in resource use, one could point out that the inefficiencies of the public sector have been more obvious than those in the private sector. It is worth noting that the share of the private sector in gross domestic capital formation has remained near 50 percent or more since the mid 1960s. (Table 10) The share of the public sector has not significantly increased over the period despite the declared objective of leaving to the public sector the "commanding heights" of the economy. In recent years, the private sector has also been allowed into areas which were the monopoly of the public sector. Conversely, the public sector has also entered in some areas previously reserved for the private sector. In this context, the following issues need to be raised: whether commitment to a public sector-oriented framework of investment and production has always been conducive to better efficiency in resource use? What should be the optimum blend of the public sector and the private sector for the purpose of ensuring more efficient utilization of resources? In fact, the concept of the joint sector (with a mix of public and private enterprises) is an outcome of consideration of such issues. There is need to examine the experience of the joint sector industries in regard to their effects on improving

Table 8. Share of Public Sector in India's National Production 1968-69 and 1982-83

Item	Unit	National Production		Public Sector's Production		Share (%) of Public Sector in National Production	
		1968-69	1982-83	1968-69	1982-83	1968-69	1982-83
Fuel							
Coal	Min. tons	71.4	130.5	12.6	127.8*	17.7	97.9
Lignite	"	3.98	6.40	3.98	6.40	100.0	100.0
Petroleum Crude	"	6.05	21.06	3.09	21.06	51.1	100.0
Basic Metal Industries							
Steel Ingot	"	6.5	8.6	3.7	6.7	57.8	77.5
Saleable Steel	"	4.7	7.3	2.6	5.7	55.8	77.8
Non-Ferrous Metals							
Aluminium	Thousand tons	125.3	208.2	Nil	43.5	–	20.9
Copper	"	9.5	34.6	–	34.6	–	100.0
Lead	"	1.9	14.8	1.9	14.8	100.0	100.0
Zinc	"	17.0	52.0	13.7	43.7	80.0	84.1
Fertilizers							
Nitrogenous	"	563	3,424	391	1,586	60.5	46.3
Phosphatic	"	213	980	N.A.	288	N.A.	29.3
Electric Equipment							
Telephones	Lakhs	N.A.	5.22	N.A.	5.22	N.A.	100.0
Teleprinters	(10 thousand)	5,012	8,896	5,012	8,896	100.0	100.0

Source: Bureau of Public Enterprises, Ministry of Finance, *Public Enterprises Survey, 1982-83, Vol. I.*

* Includes Singareni Collieries Limited.

Table 9. India's Exports: Public Sector and Total

Year	Public Enterprises Exports of Goods			Total Exports of Goods	%
	Production Under-takings	Trading and Marketing Agencies	Total* (2) + (3)		
1970-71	963	1,798	2,761	15,352	18.0
1971-72	655	1,907	2,462	16,082	15.3
1972-73	788	2,869	3,657	19,708	18.5
1973-74	935	4,337	5,272	25,234	20.9
1974-75	1,442	7,785	9,227	33,306	27.7
1975-76	2,212	11,102	13,314	40,424	32.9
1976-77	4,216	14,159	18,375	51,423	35.7
1977-78	4,061	6,575	10,636	54,079	19.7
1978-79	4,657	7,231	11,888	57,263	20.7
1979-80	3,853	7,538	11,391	64,184	17.7
1980-81	7,270	6,607	13,877	67,107	20.7
1981-82	11,024	6,119	17,221	78,059	22.0
			(15,261)	(76,099)	(20.1)
1982-83	...	...	34,044	88,033	38.7
			(23,414)	(77,400)	(30.3)
1983-84	...	...	39,870	98,721	40.4
			(27,559)	(86,410)	(31.9)

Sources: Cols. 2-4: Bureau of Public Enterprises, *Annual Report on the Working of Industrial and Commercial Undertakings of the Central Government*, New Delhi, Vol. 1, various issues and Ministry of Commerce, *Annual Reports*.
Col. 5: Ministry of Commerce, DGCI & S.
Parentheses show non-oil exports.

*Note: Includes canalized goods, i.e., those goods under state trading monopoly. These include for example cotton, tobacco, jute, and other farm goods that are privately produced.

the overall efficiency in the economy. The percentage share of the joint sector in investment in mining and manufacturing is estimated to be more than 10 percent.

Related to these issues is also the question of sick units and the approach toward dealing with them. The number of sick units[4] of large and small scale has been rapidly growing, and the approach of taking them over in the name of social interest deserves critical evaluation. We should distinguish between sick units due to endogenous factors such as inefficient management, wrong choice of products and technology, and sick units due to exogenous factors such as sluggishness in demand, emergence of more efficient competing units, liberalized import policies of the government, etc. The policy approach to sick units has been one of excessive care and nourishing. A more pragmatic approach focused on improving efficiency in resource use is called for. Oversensitivity to the prospects of mortality in the Indian

---

[4] Defined (vide RBI guidelines) in terms of clear cash loss for one year, other financial indicators showing imbalance, and a worsening debt − equity ratio (i.e. net liabilities).

Table 10. Rate of Gross Savings and Gross Domestic Capital Formation (GDCF)
and Share of Private Sector in GDCF, 1965-66 to 1984-85

| Year | Rates | | | Share of Private Sector in GDCF |
	Gross Savings	Gross Domestic Capital Formation (GDCF)	Gap	
1965-66	15.7	18.2	2.5	50.0
1966-67	16.3	19.7	3.4	59.8
1967-68	13.9	16.5	2.6	59.2
1968-69	14.1	15.4	1.3	60.9
1969-70	16.4	17.1	0.7	65.1
1970-71	16.8	17.8	1.0	62.2
1971-72	17.3	18.4	1.1	62.4
1972-73	16.2	16.9	0.7	57.7
1973-74	19.3	20.0	0.7	57.6
1974-75	18.2	19.1	0.9	60.9
1975-76	20.0	19.9	(−) 0.1	51.6
1976-77	22.4	20.7	(−) 1.7	51.8
1977-78	22.1	20.4	(−) 1.7	59.8
1978-79	24.7	24.8	0.1	57.9
1979-80	23.2	23.7	0.5	55.0
1980-81	22.9	24.7	1.8	54.9
1981-82	22.1	23.9	1.8	51.7
1982-83 (P)	22.6	24.2	1.6	49.8
1983-84 (P)	22.1	23.4	1.3	53.3
1984-85 (P)	22.1	23.4	1.3	48.7

Source: Central Statistical Organisation, *National Accounts Statistics,* various volumes, and Quick
Estimates for 1984-85.

P = Provisional.

corporate sector — caused by sickness — seems to be unwarranted in the context of
overall productivity and growth.

Other Dimensions

The multiplicity of perspectives and objectives in the framework of Indian planning
and policy making has been contributing to the complexity of instruments, thereby
generating the possibility of inconsistencies and inefficiencies. The instances of
concurrent existence of diverse perspectives and objectives are many: rural development along with development of the urban centers; encouraging and sustaining the
small-scale sector while the medium- and the large-scale sectors also flourish
simultaneously; balanced growth, both in the regional and sectoral sense against
imbalances of various kinds, are some of the issues which deserve careful attention.

Duality or multiplicity in the system of development was debated extensively in the Indian literature on planning and development in the early sixties. In particular, the co-existence of the modern sector with the traditional sector drew the attention of analysts and policy makers alike. The conflicts and the inconsistencies which dualistic structures induce must be properly sorted out over time. The framework for integrating the dual or the multiple components of the system has not yet clearly emerged.

For example, the strategy of encouraging the small-scale industries[5] with the objective of encouraging growth of employment and small entrepreneurship to contribute to the development process is not always based upon sound empirical and analytical premises. It is not clearly proven that small-scale industries are necessarily less capital-intensive than the large-scale types of activities. On the other hand, adverse effects of restricting the scale of operation, such as loss of potential scale economies, have not been duly recognized in the Indian policy framework. Some analysts argued that if the constraints on the scale of operation were removed, then much of the subsidy doled out to industry and the export sector could be easily dispensed with. Even now, as many as 872 products spread over a number of industries[6] are reserved for the small-scale firms. A variety of restrictions are placed by the MRTP provisions on the expansion schemes of individual companies. The restrictions on the scale of operations affect the cost of production per unit and, as a result, the overall efficiency of resource use. Further, the system has not developed a large number of small units which are integrated with large scale enterprises either through demand linkages or through product sharing systems, as is observed in the case of the Japanese industrial structure. We should, therefore, question whether the scale of operation that has bothered policy makers for the last several years has been dealt with properly in the context of efficiency in resource use.

As for regional imbalances, notably in industrial development, it was expected that large investment in central sector projects would have a 'trickle-down effect' through stimulating growth of small and ancillary industries and employment. As noted in the Sixth Plan, this has not been realized in many states. The approach has not been successful as most investments have been captured, in fact, by the more developed states. The wealthier states seem to have always had an upper hand even with the incentive schemes in favor of the poorer states.

The issue is whether location of industries should be guided by purely economic cost considerations or by social considerations. A related issue is whether the problem of regional imbalances needs to be resolved by evolving integrated development schemes in place of policies affecting the location of some industries.

Recently, the government has adopted the mechanism of area planning integrated with national planning. A number of new approaches such as the Special Tribal Component Plan, Hill Area Schemes, and specific area plans/programmes as handled by the North East Council have been taken. The Central government incentive schemes for private enterprises include concessional finance, the seed/margin money scheme, the central investment subsidy, tax relief, and specific interest subsidies for engineer entrepreneurs choosing to locate in less developed states.

---

[5] Defined initially in terms of the original value of fixed capital (plant and machinery), at Rs 2 million and less, in the case of ancillaries at Rs 2.5 million, both irrespective of number of employees. It was revised in the beginning of 1985 to Rs 3.5 million and Rs 4.5 million respectively.

[6] Ministry of Industrial Development, *Annual Report 1983-84*.

TRENDS IN PRODUCTIVITY

Macro-Level Trend, 1965-66 to 1982-83

India's per capita GNP grew by about 1.5 percent during the review period. On an annual basis (Table 11) there were six years of negative growth and eleven years of positive growth in per capita GNP. Instability apart, the growth performance lagged far behind plan targets, except for the First and the Fifth Plans, as is shown in Table 12.[7]

The long-term annual compound growth rate since 1951-52, when planning began, through 1978-79 at 3.5 percent, compares favorably with only 1.2 percent rate during 1900-01 to 1945-46.[8]

Table 11. Growth of India's Per Capita GNP*, 1965-66 to 1984-85

Year	Per Capita GNP* (Rs at 1970-71 Prices)	Annual Growth (%)
1965-66	593.6	—
1966-67	587.6	(−) 1.02
1967-68	624.3	6.26
1968-69	626.6	0.37
1969-70	652.5	4.13
1970-71	673.8	3.26
1971-72	667.9	(−) 0.88
1972-73	645.5	(−) 3.35
1973-74	662.2	2.59
1974-75	655.3	(−) 1.04
1975-76	701.3	7.02
1976-77	692.0	(−) 1.33
1977-78	736.3	6.40
1978-79	761.2	3.38
1979-80	706.3	(−) 7.40
1980-81	745.3	5.52
1981-82	766.0	2.78
1982-83	773.4	1.0
1983-84 (P)	815.5	5.4
1984-85 (Q)	828.2	1.6

Sources: Central Statistical Organisation (CSO), *National Accounts Statistics 1970-71 to 1981-82,* and Quick Estimates of National Income for 1984-85.

* At factor cost
P = Provisional
Q Quick Estimates.

[7] Planning Commission, *Sixth Five-Year Plan, 1980-85.*
[8] *Ibid.*

Table 12. Growth Performance: 1951 to 1980

Five-Year Plan	Target	Actual
First 1951-52 to 1955-56	2.1*	3.6*
Second 1956-57 to 1960-61	4.5*	4.0*
Third 1961-62 to 1965-66	5.6*	2.2*
Fourth 1968-69 to 1973-74	5.7*	3.3*
Fifth 1974-75 to 1979-80	4.4**	5.2**

Source: Planning Commission, *Sixth Five-Year, 1980-85.*
        * National Income.
      ** Gross Domestic Product (GDP).

The growth rate of GDP from the non-traded sectors (excluding primary sector and manufacturing, but covering construction, electricity, gas, water supply, transport and communications, banking, personal and community services, etc.) has been higher and more stable than the rest of the economy in most of the years, reflecting aspects of India's development strategy. It indicates that emphasis was given to these sectors and expanded infrastructure under the plans (Table 13).

The planners have observed recently that compared to previous plans, the Sixth Plan growth performance has broken new ground in meeting the target of 5.2 percent.[9] The performance shows (Table 14), however, that industrial growth has not reached the target. The growth of population, as estimated by 1981 census, has exceeded the planned assumption of less than 2 percent, so that the overall growth of per capita income has been much slower than planned.

Macro-level productivity of an economy can be analyzed by a single indicator like GDP per worker. Productivity or efficiency in resource use, however, should be judged in the light of the totality of the national objective function, major socio-economic parameters and constraints, and a composite of indicators. In a wider sense, improvement in physical quality of life index (PQLI) may be considered as a measure of national productivity. In a more limited sense, productivity can also be measured by growth of per capita availability of essential goods and services.

Efficiency in resource use at the macro level can be gauged by a variety of measures. In addition to per capita GNP or GDP, we have chosen to include in this study the following commonly used measures: GDP per worker and its relation with investment per worker; GDP per unit of energy consumed; and incremental capital-output ratio (ICOR).

We find that GDP per worker increased from an average of Rs 1,863 during 1965-66 to 1967-68 to Rs 2,272 during 1980-81 to 1982-83 (Table 15). The long-term annual compound growth rate (Table 16) was 1.24 percent. The growth rate of GDP per worker was higher during 1973-74 to 1982-83 (1.6 percent) compared to 1965-66 to 1973-74 (1.2 percent).

The effects of policy changes on productivity can be considered for three separate time periods as follows: first, 1968-69 to 1972-73: the pre-oil shock period and also a period of rigid import controls and mild export-orientation; second: 1973-74

---

[9] Planning Commission, *Sixth Five-Year Plan, 1980-85: Mid Term Appraisal,* August 1983.

Table 13. Growth Analysis of India's Sectoral and Aggregate GDP,
1965-66 to 1982-83

Period	GDP Variable/Sector	Growth Rate*%
1965-66 to 1973-74	Primary	3.70
	Agriculture	3.80
	Secondary	3.67
	Manufacturing	3.89
	Tertiary	4.20
	Traded	3.45
	Non-traded	4.48
	Aggregate	3.85
1973-74 to 1982-83	Primary	1.92
	Agriculture	2.27
	Secondary	4.39
	Manufacturing	4.34
	Tertiary	8.76
	Traded	2.80
	Non-traded	5.53
	Aggregate	3.96

* Annual average geometric growth rate.

to 1977-78: the period of the first oil shock and intensive export-orientation and the beginning of a more liberal outlook toward imports; and third, 1978-79 to 1982-83, the period of liberal import policies, intensive export-orientation and the second oil shock. The average productivities in these periods work out respectively at Rs 1,998, 2,073 and 2,241. Thus, productivity at the macro-level shows a rising trend. Whether this could be attributed to the emergence of more liberal outlook on the trade policy front, success in control of inflation or a combination of other structural changes is a matter for further detailed analysis.

The macro-level capital-intensity of the economy measured by investment per worker has shown fluctuations from year to year but broadly shows a rising trend. The level increased from an average of Rs 391 for 1965-66 to 1967-68 to Rs 530 for 1980-81 to 1982-83. The growth rate (Table 16A) works out at 1.27 percent for the review period but goes up significantly during the years 1973-74 to 1982-83. A relationship between GDP per worker and capital-intensity and the scale of the economy measured by the level of GDP (Table 16B) brings out that the effect of increased investment per worker on productivity is positive only for the latter part of the sample period: 1970-71 to 1982-83, and that the effect of scale of the economy on productivity is positive and statistically significant.

The weak relationship between investment per worker and labor productivity call in question whether increases in productivity can be achieved only through the provision of more and more investment per unit of labor as is often contended on the basis of the experience of the developed economies. This weak relationship is possibly a reflection of constraints in various other factors, such as management,

Table 14. Growth (Annual Compound) of National Income, Agriculture and
Industrial Production, Plan-wise Since 1965-66

Variable	Annual Plans, 1965-66 to 1968-69	Fourth Plan, 1968-69 to 1973-74	Fifth Plan, 1973-74 to 1978-79	1979-80, Base Year of Sixth Plan	Sixth Plan, 1980-85						
					Target	Progress					
						1980-81	1981-82	1982-83	1983-84	1984-85	
National Income	4.0	3.3	5.4	(−) −5.5	5.2	7.9	4.9	1.6	7.8	3.5
Agriculture Production	6.2	2.9	9.2	(−) 15.5	3.8	15.3	5.5	(−) 4.1	13.8	—
Industrial Production	2.0	4.7	5.9	(−) 1.4	8.0	4.0	8.6	3.9	5.4	6.7

Sources: 1. Planning Commission, *Sixth Five-Year Plan, 1980-85.*
2. Ministry of Finance, *Economic Survey*, various issues.
3. Central Statistical Organisation, *National Accounts Statistics*, various volumes, and Quick Estimates for 1984-85.
4. Ministry of Industry, Office of Economic Adviser.

Table 15. Indicators of India's Macro-Level Productivity and
Capital Intensity, 1965-66 to 1984-85

(Rs at 1970-71 Prices)

Year	Macro-Level Productivity GDP* Per Worker	Capital-Intensity Investment** per Worker
1965-66	1,837	391
1966-67	1,820	415
1967-68	1,931	372
1968-69	1,936	341
1969-70	2,012	386
1970-71	2,052	401
1971-72	2,039	412
1972-73	1,953	374
1973-74	2,002	470
1974-75	1,979	416
1975-76	2,102	419
1976-77	2,077	447
1977-78	2,206	470
1978-79	2,279	566
1979-80	2,111	502
1980-81	2,186	535
1981-82	2,292	515
1982-83 (P)	2,332	534
1983-84 (P)	2,451	557
1984-85 (P)	2,488	551

Sources: CSO, *National Accounts Statistics 1970-71 to 1981-82* and Quick Estimates for 1984-85,
and Government of India Census for workers participation rate applied to population
estimates.

*At Factor Cost
**Gross Domestic Capital Formation (GDCF).
P = Provisional

infrastructure, institutional facilities, and government policies. The positive scale
effect on productivity is revealing. This is partly due to the shift in the structure
of production toward higher productivity areas as well as the productivity increases
in individual sectors through the economies of scale. The decomposition of growth
into productivity effects, scale effects and sectoral composition effects could throw
more light on this but is a subject for separate study.

Our analysis (Table 17 and 18) shows that the share of capital goods industries
increased significantly over the review period (1965-1980). They included (annual
percentage increase in parentheses) chemical products (2.93 percent), electricity,
light and power (2.75 percent), aside from electrical machinery (3.66 percent),
other machinery (1.19 percent), and shipbuilding (3.66 percent). The industries
which recorded positive growth in shares at less than 1 percent included motor
vehicles and repair and paper industries. Most of the intermediate goods and con-

Table 16A. Growth Analysis of Macro Level Productivity Indicators
and Capital Intensity 1965-66 to 1982-83

Period	Variable	Coefficient	Growth Rate (%)	R^2	Standard Error of Estimate
1965-66 to 1973-74	GDPfc/W	0.012* (0.004)	1.21	0.59	0.03
	I/W	0.013 (0.011)	1.33	0.16	0.09
1973-74 to 1982-83	GDPfc/W	0.016* (0.003)	1.59	0.75	0.03
	I/W	0.026** (0.008)	2.61	0.55	0.07
1965-66 to 1982-83	GDPfc/W	0.012 (0.001)	1.24	0.84	0.03
	I/W	0.013* (0.001)	1.27	0.85	0.03

Based on semi-log model with respect to time. Figures in parentheses are t-values.

GDPfc = Gross Domestic Product (1970-71 prices) at factor cost.
   I = Gross Domestic Capital Formation (at 1970-71 prices).
   W = Work Force.
  * Significant at 1% level.
** Significant at 5% level.

Table 16B. Analysis of Macro Level Productivity Indicator 1965-66 to 1982-83

Period	Dependent Variable	Constant	Independent Variables Coefficients		R^2
			Investment per worker	GDP	
1965-66 to 1982-83	GDPfc/ Worker	3.92	−0.01 (−0.19)	0.36* (7.30)	0.93
1970-71 to 1982-83	GDPfc Worker	3.75	0.04 (0.44)	0.34* (3.73)	0.88

Figures in parentheses are t-values.

  * Significant at 1% level.

Table 17. Share of Selected Industries in Their Total* Value Added, 1965 to 1980

	Basic Industries						Capital Goods Industries							
Year	Chemical & chemical products	Cement	Iron & steel	Non-ferrous basic metals	Electric light & power	All	Machinery except electric	Electric machinery, etc.	Ship-building & repairing	Railroad equipment	Motor vehicles	Repair of motor vehicles	Metal products except mach. & equip.	All
1965	10.35	1.70	12.13	1.49	8.78	34.45	6.54	4.99	.51	3.22	4.27	1.24	3.52	24.29
1970	13.15	1.70	9.54	1.22	12.72	38.33	6.95	6.73	.45	2.33	3.49	1.34	3.04	24.33
1975	13.94	1.34	10.00	.88	13.23	39.39	7.40	7.69	.60	1.63	4.37	1.45	2.57	25.73
1980	14.54	1.15	9.92	.51	14.24	40.45	7.89	8.95	.69	2.12	3.81	1.27	2.69	27.43

	Intermediate Goods Industries				Consumer Goods Industries					
Year	Rubber products	Petroleum	Structural clay products	All	Spinning, weaving & finishing of textiles	Manufacture of pulp paper & paper products	Misc. food products	Tobacco products	Sugar factories	All
1965	2.11	.94	.74	3.79	25.05	2.50	4.52	1.84	3.56	37.47
1970	2.44	1.72	.76	4.92	20.17	3.69	2.96	1.66	3.94	32.42
1975	2.32	1.09	.55	3.96	20.22	3.57	3.06	1.35	2.72	30.92
1980	1.72	1.06	.71	3.49	20.93	2.84	2.08	.99	1.78	28.62

Source: CSO, *Principal Characteristics of Selected Industries in Organized Manufactured Sector, 1960 to 1980*, December 1984 (mimeo.)

* Total of all selected industries.

Table 18. Growth Analysis of Share of Selected Industries
in Total Value Added, 1965 to 1980

Variable	Growth Rate
All Basic Industries	1.21
Chemical Products	2.93
Cement	−3.07
Iron & Steel	−1.26
Non-Ferrous Metals	−6.06
Electric Light & Power	2.75
All Capital Goods	.71
Machinery, except Electric	1.19
Elec. Machinery	3.66
Shipbuilding & Repair	3.66
Railroad Equipment	−5.22
Motor Vehicles	.11
Repair of Motor Vehicles	.53
Metal Products	−1.58
All Intermediate Goods	−1.83
Rubber Products	−1.22
Petroleum	−2.63
Structural Clay Products	−1.98
All Consumer Goods	−1.57
Spinning, Weaving & Finishing of Textiles	−1.30
Pulp, Paper and Paper Products	.59
Misc. Food Products	−3.84
Tobacco Products	−4.01
Sugar	1.94

Source: same as Table 17.

sumer industries, except for sugar, recorded declines in shares. The growth trends were complicated by the wide variations in the shares of various industries during the review period. Over the period 1965-66 to 1982-83, macro-level productivity change has been rather slow, while capital-intensity has been rising at a somewhat faster rate, notably from 1973-74 to 1982-83.

The estimates of ICOR for the plan periods are available for the economy as a whole and the major sectors (Table 19). ICOR for the economy has increased from 3.5 in the First Plan period to 6.00 in the Third Plan and 6.3 during the Fourth Plan period. The ICOR was 4.2 during the Fifth Plan period and was assumed to remain at that level in the Sixth Plan. The Seventh Plan assumes an ICOR of 5 (at 1984-85 period). As for sectoral ICORs, that in agriculture increased, that in construction declined and it fluctuated widely in other sectors.

An important theme of recent discussions on development strategy in India has been precisely the rise in the ICOR. This has come to the fore in the particular

Table 19. Incremental Capital*-Output** Ratio (ICOR), Overall and Sectoral Since First Plan

(1979-80 Prices)

Plan and Period	Overall ICOR	Sectoral ICOR				
		Agriculture and allied Services	Mining and Manu-facturing	Con-struction	Electricity & Water Supply	Transport, Storage & Communi-cations
First Plan, 1951-52 to 1955-56	3.5	2.5	5.5	3.4	17.5	10.5
Second Plan, 1956-57 to 1960-61	4.6	2.5	7.5	2.0	14.3	12.4
Third Plan, 1961-62 to 1965-66	6.0	(2.3+)@	6.7	2.2	19.6	13.1
Annual Plans, 1966-67 to 1968-69	5.4	2.0	29.8	1.6	14.7	11.1
Fourth Plan, 1969-70 to 1973-74	6.3	3.6	11.5	@	24.5	12.9
Fifth Plan, 1974-75 to 1978-79	4.2	3.4	8.7	1.5	18.3	7.6
Sixth Plan (projected) 1979-80 to 1983-84	4.2	4.8	6.9	1.3	34.3	11.1@@

Source: Planning Commission (Perspective Planning Division) *A Technical Note on the Sixth Plan of India (1980-85)*, 1981, p. 232.

  * Gross Domestic Capital Formation (GDCF) at market prices.

  ** Overall at market price, sectoral at factor cost.

  @ Very high because of low harvest caused by draught.

  @@ Excluding storage.

  + Refers to period, 1961-62 to 1964-66.

Parentheses refer to ratio with respect to GDP at market prices.
All figures rounded to one digit.

context of the relatively steady growth rate of GDP around 3.5 percent over the review period, when the saving and investment rates (Table 10) rose from 15.3 and 18.1 percent (Average of 1965-66 to 1967-68) to 22.6 and 24.3 percent (average of 1980-81 to 1982-83) respectively. Among the various observations the Working Group on Savings, popularly known as K.N. Raj Group[10] inferred that productivity of investment has been declining. The Group opined that "some noticeable shifts in patterns of investment" have taken place within the large-scale industrial sector in favor of sectors with relatively high ICORs for technological reasons; notably chemical fertilizers and electricity from the middle of the sixties, and petroleum, coal, steel and non-ferrous metals in more recent years. The Raj Group observed that "this is not to deny the possibility of the marginal capital-output ratios getting raised through mistaken choices or inefficient use of investment in fixed capital, under-utilization of capacity in some industries, and needless additions to inventory holdings." It is difficult to estimate the relative contribution of these different factors, apart from socio-political factors, vis-á-vis technological changes and consequent rise in ICOR due to shift in the pattern of investment.

It is note-worthy that estimates of fixed capital formation are made on the basis of the reported increase in the output of machinery, equipment and construction materials plus other evidence of increased household investment. The Raj Group observed that, "unincorporated enterprises in the non-farm sector must have a significant share in capital formation." In fact, this household sector exhibited the most sustained increase in the savings rate and constituted 70 percent of aggregate savings (Table 20). This ratio increased at the rate of about 3 percent annually, just about the rate of growth of the aggregate savings ratio, while the private corporate savings ratio recorded less than 2 percent change over the review period.

Table 20. Composition of Gross Domestic Savings

Years	Aggregate % of GDP	Composition					
		Public Sector		Private Corporate Sector		Household Sector	
		% of aggregate savings	% of GDP*	% of aggregate savings	% of GDP*	% of aggregate savings	% of GDP*
1965-70	15.3	17.3	2.7	9.3	1.4	73.4	1.2
1970-75	17.6	18.0	3.1	10.1	1.8	71.9	12.7
1975-80	22.5	21.4	4.8	7.2	1.6	57.4	16.1
1980-85	22.4	18.1	4.0	8.0	1.8	73.9	16.5

Source: C.S.O. *National Accounts Statistics, 1970-71 to 1982-83,* 1984 and Quick Estimates for 1984-85.
  * At Market Prices.

[10] Department of Statistics, *Capital Formation and Savings in India, 1950-51 to 1979-80,* Report of the Working Group on Savings, 1982.

According to the Raj Group, "the increase in household savings, particularly in its higher ratio of capital formation can be attributed to higher rate of profit in small-scale manufacturing enterprises." To the extent the output or value added of these enterprises go under-reported in the national data, these inadequate data may partly explain the high values of the estimated ICOR and low productivity of investment in India.

SECTORAL/INDUSTRIAL PRODUCTIVITY MEASUREMENT

Measurement of sectoral/industrial productivity in developing countries has not received much attention in the past. Recently, however, rising capital-output ratio and emergence of problems of scarce resources have compelled policy-makers to focus on detailed study of growth of sectoral productivity.

The first well-known approach is the measurement of total factor productivity (TFP). It is full of hazards due to the methodologies and data. The estimated growth rates of TFP based on indexes by using Kendrick's and Solow's methodologies[11] show wide differentials (Table 21) for some of the same industries. In the case of India, attempts have been made to study productivity,[12] and industrial data have been made available recently by the Central Statistical Organisation, covering a long period.[13] But, measurement of TFP is difficult due mainly to the book value basis of the data. Serious problems arise in respect to valuation of fixed capital which is defined as "the depreciated value of capital stock accumulated over the years," that is, "the summation of historical cost of the components of capital goods."[14] Thus, the present estimates[15] by definition, are not easily amendable to price adjustments for a particular base year. What the series at constant prices available in the CSO publications represent are the values deflated by the wholesale price index of machinery and transport equipment only. The estimates are not representative of true current price values. They assume that the depletion of the stock due to consumption of fixed capital was more or less balanced by the rise in the wholesale price index of machinery and transport equipment. It has been argued that existing estimates of depreciation are overestimates.

Ideally, what is required is to estimate economically appropriate depreciation, as

---

[11] The Kendrick's method of measuring TFP is based on a liner production function i.e. TFP being the sum of the partial productivities of labor and capital, and is defined as the ratio of the observed value added in a year to the value that would have been added with the given combination of capital and labor operating at their base year coefficients. In this analysis, the TFP index reflects the residual or technical progress which cannot be attributed to either labor or capital. See Kendrick, *Productivity Trends in the United States*.

In Solow's framework, the growth of TFP, in the case of a homogeneous output, is measured as a difference between the rate of growth of value added and the weighted sum of growth of total factor inputs i.e. labor and capital, the weights being the shares of each factor in the value of total output. The percentage change in output is taken as the end result of the percentage change in technology, the proportionate change in the labor input, and the proportionate change in the capital input. The problem of weighing the growth of total factor inputs is indeed tricky, and generally is solved by using the Divisia index number. See Solow in *Review of Economics and Statistics*.

For recent discussion and analysis, see Banerjee (1975), Nishimizu (1979), Kruegerand Tuncer (1980), Cowing and Stevenson (1981), Nishimizu and Robinson (1982), and Ahluwalia (1984).

[12] See Sandesara in *A Survey of Research in Economics*.

[13] CSO-Bulletin No. 158/9, Dec. 1984.

[14] *Ibid.*

[15] We learn that the CSO is attempting to revise the estimates to bring them upto the standard concept of capital, at appropriate prices.

Table 21. Differentials in Estimated Growth of Total Factor Productivity
of Selected Comparable Industry Groups Based on Different Methods

Industry Group	Growth Rate* of Total Factor Productivity, 1960-80	
	Kendrick Method	Solow Method
Basic Industries	−0.81	−1.13
Chemical Products	−0.57	−0.85
Cement	0.05	−0.70
Iron & Steel	0.77	−2.11
Non-Ferrous Metals	−7.46	−7.04
Electric Light & Power	−0.69	−1.67
Capital Goods Industries	2.15	1.89
Machinery Except Electrical	2.93	2.45
Electrical Machinery	3.23	2.52
Shipbuilding & Repair	1.14	−2.16
Railroad Equipment	−0.35	**
Motor Vehicles	1.38	0.71
Repair of Motor Vehicles	3.02	2.82
Metal Products Except M/C Equipment	1.10	0.73
Intermediate Goods Industries	0.38	−0.34
Rubber Products	−1.87	−3.07
Petroleum	0.74	−0.62
Structural Clay Products	1.26	1.22
Consumer Goods Industries	−0.52	0.56
Spinning, Weaving and Finishing of Textiles	1.93	1.91
Pulp, Paper and Paper Products	2.93	2.69
Misc. Food Products	−0.81	−1.45
Tobacco Products	−2.03	−2.42
Sugar	−3.44	−4.21
All Selected Industries	−0.40	−0.44

* Based on semi-log model. T values of the estimates not significant and R^2 poor in most of the cases. Data from CSO (1984).
** Data for the full sample period not available.

against the present estimates based on rules of thumb or tax-based accounting, and estimate net investment levels to arrive at capital stock estimates. Some attempts have been made to derive gross fixed capital stock by the replacement cost in a base year. Since the details of such adjustments are not made available by the authors, it is difficult to judge their accuracy, nor possible to get hold of the appropriate series of estimates of fixed capital in different industries at constant prices. In fact, several refinements would have to be made on the available estimates with respect to the changing composition, quality, vintage of equipment, the prices of the imported and domestic parts, the norm of net present value, the changing share and nature of construction, etc.

How much difference the adjustments in estimates of fixed capital can make is shown by the divergence in the percentage growth rate of TFP in certain comparable industry groups (Table 22) between the work of the CSO[16] and the one by Ahluwalia,[17] using the same Solow method.

This is not to argue against the use of TFP measures in studying growth of industrial efficiency, but to say that the present data can easily mislead analysis. This study, therefore, depends on more manageable and acceptable partial productivity: gross value added per worker, in line with the macro level measure of GDP per worker. Both are comparable internationally, too. The measure of capital productivity: gross value added per unit of fixed capital has also not been employed due to the evaluation problems of capital stock mentioned earlier.

Table 22. Differentials in Estimated Growth of Total Factor Productivity (Solow Method) Based on Adjusted (A) and Unadjusted Capital Values in Selected Comparable Industry Groups

Industry Group	A 1959-60 to 1979-80	B 1960-1979
— Chemicals	−1.3	−0.8
— Machinery, except electrical	−1.6	2.4
— Electrical machinery	−0.5	2.3
— Metal products	−2.5	0.7
— Rubber products	−6.7	−2.8
— Petroleum products	−5.4	−0.7
— Pulp, paper and paper products	0.5	3.4
— Tobacco manufactures	−1.4	−2.2
Manufacturing, total	−0.6	−0.5

* Growth rates worked out on the basis of indices (converted at 1970 prices), using semi-log model.

A — Ahluwalia, Ibid.
B — CSO, op. cit.

---

[16] *Ibid.*
[17] Ahluwalia, *Industrial Growth in India: Stagnation since the Mid-Sixties,* 1984.

We are aware that the labor productivity measure cannot distinguish between the contribution made to growth of productivity by increase in various inputs on the one hand and increased efficiency or technical progress on the other hand.

Sectoral/Industrial Trends, 1965 to 1980

The growth rates in labor productivity for different sectors and industry groups (Table 23) have been estimated for the period 1965 to 1980. They ranged from a negative level of over (−)7 percent (statistically not significant though) for sugar and tobacco products to a positive level of over 4 percent for electrical machinery. Productivity growth in the industries of the capital goods sector has been much higher (except motor vehicles) than that in the basic goods industries, intermediate goods and consumer goods sectors. Divergence in growth rates of labor productivity among different industries is shown below.

Growth	1965-73	1973-80	1965-80
1. Decline	—	Intermediate Ind. (−0.32) Consumer Ind. (−0.64)	Consumer Ind. (−0.16)
2. Little change	—	Basic Ind. (0.74)	Intermediate Ind. (0.45)
3. Rise	Consumer Goods Ind. (1.56) Basic Ind. (3.58) Capital Goods Ind. (4.28)	Capital Goods Ind. (2.32)	Basic Ind. (1.25) Capital Goods Ind. (3.51)

Energy Efficiency

Efficiency in use of energy per unit of GDP is an important criterion of change in productivity at the macro level. In India, the share of oil in total energy used (Tables 24 and 25) was 44 percent in 1965-66 and increased to 51 percent by 1972-73. It declined in the wake of hike in oil price in 1973-74 but rose again marginally by 1979-80 (49 percent). It declined thereafter, *albeit* marginally. Among two other major sources of energy, i.e. electricity and coal, the share of the former increased from 20 to 30 percent over the review period. The relative growth of use of three different sources of energy over the period (Table 25) shows that coal gained importance during subperiod 1973-74 to 1982-83 while oil declined somewhat. The growth analysis (Table 26) reveals that, the growth rate of electricity use works out at 7.32 percent compared to about 5 percent for total energy or 2.56 and 5.38 percent for coal and oil respectively. An attempt has also been made to estimate the elasticity of use of different sources of energy with respect to GDP (Table 27). We find that elasticity of oil use works out to be much lower during the subperiod since the first oil crisis. The elasticity of electricity use was expected to be higher in the subperiod; the regression results, however, show that the elasticity declined from a little over 2 during 1965-66 to 1973-74 to 1.72 during 1973-74 to 1982-83,

Table 23. Growth Analysis of Labor Productivity in India's Selected Industries

Industry	Labor Productivity Growth Analysis (%)		
	1965-73	1973-80	1965-80
Basic Industries	2.26	.74	1.25
Chemical & Chemical prod.	5.20	−.39	2.00
Cement	−3.72	3.37	−1.85
Iron & Steel	−.40	.59	.32
Non-Ferrous Basic Metals	−5.70	−2.64	−3.49
Electric Light & Power	3.19	1.38	1.58
Capital Goods Industries	4.28	2.32	3.51
Machinery, except Electric	4.52	2.62	3.74
Electric M/C, APP. & Supplies	6.04	3.16	4.24
Shipbuilding & Repairing	4.71	1.00	3.71
Railroad Equipment	.04	5.84	2.15
Motor Vehicles	2.18	−2.17	.99
Repair of Motor Vehicles	4.53	1.67	3.39
Metal Prod. except M/C equipment	1.70	2.93	1.38
Intermediate Industries	3.58	−.32	.45
Rubber Products	2.44	−1.23	.93
Petroleum	5.63	−3.48	.51
Structural Clay Products	3.97	4.06	.30
Consumer Industries	1.56	−.64	−.16
Spinning Weav. & Fing. of Text.	2.63	2.68	2.43
Pulp, Paper & Paper Prod.	5.67	−3.75	1.87
Misc. Good Products	−4.37	−.15	−1.71
Tobacco Products	−4.14	−4.51	−7.19
Sugar	−1.17	−7.13	−7.73
All Selected Industries	3.05	.80	1.49

Table 24. Consumption of Different Sources of Energy, 1965-66 to 1982-83

(Unit: million tons of coal replacement)

Year	Electricity	Coal-Direct Used	Oil-Direct Used	Total Energy-Direct Used
1965-66	30.09	51.80	64.61	146.50
1970-71	48.47	51.35	97.19	197.01
1975-76	66.06	70.96	115.64	252.66
1980-81	89.70	70.57	151.25	311.52
1982-83	103.80	74.80	161.30	339.90

Source: Advisory Board on Energy, Government of India.

Using the following conversion factors: One million ton oil = 6.5 mt coal replacement
10^9 Kilo watt. Hrs. electricity = 1 mt coal replacement.

Table 25. Share of Different Sources in Total Energy Consumption,
1965-66 to 1982-83

(Unit: %)

Year	Sources		
	Electricity	Coal	Oil
1965-66	20.54	35.36	44.10
1970-71	24.60	26.06	49.34
1975-76	26.14	28.08	45.78
1980-81	28.79	22.65	48.56
1982-83	30.54	22.01	47.55

Source: As in Table 24.

Table 26. Growth Analysis of Different Sources of Energy,
for Selected Periods, 1965-66 to 1982-83

Period	Dependent Variable	Independent Variable (t)
		Growth Rate
1965-66 to 1973-74	Electricity	8.42
	Coal, Direct use	0.98
	Oil, Direct use	7.88
	Total Energy, Direct Use	5.90
1973-74 to 1982-83	Electricity	7.13
	Coal, Direct use	1.49
	Oil, Direct use	4.61
	Total Energy, Direct Use	4.50
1965-66 to 1982-83	Electricity	7.32
	Coal, Direct use	2.56
	Oil, Direct use	5.38
	Total Energy, Direct Use	5.08

though it remained higher than the elasticity of total energy use. It should be borne in mind that the supply of electricity in India is constrained by several factors.

Macro-level efficiency in energy use has been examined in terms of total energy used (i.e. ton of coal replacement) per Rs 1,000 of GDP (Table 28 also shows this relationship in Rs per billion GDP per ton of coal replacement). It is found that the energy-GDP ratio increased from 0.52 (average) during 1965-66 to 1967-68 to 0.62 (average) during 1980-81 to 1982-83 implying increased energy-intensity of GDP in India over the review period.

Table 27. Energy Consumption in India: Elasticity with Respect to GDP[@]

Period	Dependent Variable	Coefficient of Independent Variable (GDP)
1956-66 to 1973-74	Coal, Direct use	0.23
	Electricity	2.08*
	Oil, Direct use	1.92*
	Total Energy	1.45*
1973-74 to 1982-83	Coal, Direct use	0.40**
	Electricity	1.72*
	Oil, Direct use	1.10*
	Total Energy	1.09*
1965-66 to 1982-83	Coal, Direct use	0.67*
	Electricity	1.91*
	Oil, Direct use	1.41*
	Total Energy	1.33*

[@] At factor cost.
 * Significant at 1% level.
** Significant at 5% level.

When we compare India's ratio of oil GDP/GNP with other countries (Table 29), two inferences emerge:
1. India's ratio is lower compared to other developing countries like China, Brazil and Mexico; and
2. India's oil-intensity of GNP increased over the period 1965-1979; it declined in 1980 from 0.83 to 0.78. In the case of China, the ratio increased until 1977 but declined in the following years. In the USA the ratio is shown to be highest; it increased until 1973 but declined thereafter. The ratio declined since 1973 in the U.K., France, Japan, West Germany, and other countries except the Soviet Union, China, and Mexico.

But, considering India's very low oil-intensity ratio (< 1), it is difficult to infer that efficiency in use declined, though the oil-GDP ratio increased over the review period. The ratio did show a decline after the second oil price hike in 1979. It fell from 0.83 in 1979 to 0.78 in the following year.

PRODUCTIVITY AND ECONOMIC VARIABLES

It is useful to link the productivity behavior with the various aspects of development strategy discussed earlier. In order to examine the relationship between productivity on the one hand and the industry size (measured by the number of employees), level of fixed capital, level of value added, and capital intensity (capital-labor or employee ratio) on the other, suitable models were formulated. In model I, size of

Table 28. Gross Domestic Product* per MTCR** of Energy Consumption in India 1965-66 to 1982-83

Year	Gross Domestic Product* (Rs Crore at 1970-71 Prices)	Total Energy Consumption (MTCR**)	Energy in TCR*** used per Rs.000 of GDP	GDP in Rs. Per MTCR of Energy Consumption
1	2	3	4	5
1965-66	29,023	146.50 (64.61)	0.50 (0.22)	198.11
1966-67	29,307	154.06 (69.07)	0.53 (0.24)	190.23
1967-68	31,868	164.19 (73.35)	0.52 (0.23)	194.09
1968-69	32,725	176.32 (82.27)	0.54 (0.25)	185.60
1969-70	34,802	191.74 (90.06)	0.55 (0.26)	181.51
1970-71	36,736	197.01 (97.19)	0.54 (0.26)	186.47
1971-72	37,313	209.42 (103.48)	0.56 (0.26)	178.17
1972-73	36,910	218.24 (110.89)	0.59 (0.30)	169.13
1973-74	38,646	229.64 (114.14)	0.59 (0.37)	168.29
1974-75	38,979	237.80 (112.45)	0.61 (0.29)	163.92
1975-76	42,662	252.66 (115.64)	0.59 (0.27)	168.85
1976-77	42,986	266.82 (122.40)	0.62 (0.28)	161.10
1977-78	46,773	282.19 (130.39)	0.60 (0.28)	165.75
1978-79	49,463	293.78 (140.92)	0.59 (0.28)	168.37
1979-80	46,854	301.41 (147.13)	0.64 (0.31)	155.45
1980-81	50,526	311.52 (151.25)	0.62 (0.30)	162.19
1981-82	53,168	329.44 (157.44)	0.62 (0.30)	161.39
1982-83	54,280	339.90 (161.30)	0.63 (0.30)	159.69

Sources: Col. (2): CSO, *National Accounts Statistics 1970/71 to 1981/82* and Quick Estimates for 1983-84.
Col. (3): Advisory Board on Energy, Government of India.

Parentheses show the corresponding figures in respect to coal replacement of oil (direct use).

    * At Factor Cost.
    ** Million tons of coal replacement. Refers to calender year.
    *** Ton of coal replacement.

Table 29. Oil Intensity of Gross National Product in Major Countries, 1965 and 1970-1980

(Unit: Barrels of oil used per $1,000 of GNP)

Year	United States	United Kingdom	France	West Germany	Japan	Soviet Union	China	India	Brazil	Mexico
1965	4.60	2.47	1.45	1.50	1.82	1.81	0.38	0.50	1.24	1.67
1970	5.03	3.06	1.93	1.82	2.36	2.05	0.73	0.58	1.33	1.76
1971	5.03	2.98	1.99	1.90	2.45	2.49	0.86	0.66	1.28	1.77
1972	5.11	3.12	2.04	1.93	2.35	2.24	0.95	0.67	1.34	1.77
1973	5.11	2.97	2.10	1.95	2.51	2.25	1.04	0.69	1.39	1.80
1974	4.94	2.80	1.91	1.73	2.48	2.31	1.23	0.69	1.36	1.87
1975	4.90	2.47	1.80	1.70	2.20	2.42	1.32	0.69	1.35	1.98
1976	4.98	2.37	1.83	1.74	2.22	2.38	1.41	0.70	1.38	2.09
1977	4.98	2.36	1.74	1.78	2.31	2.46	1.42	0.70	1.38	2.13
1978	4.88	2.25	1.64	1.84	2.16	2.47	1.26	0.75	1.35	2.18
1979	4.69	2.32	1.75	1.78	2.18	2.48	1.20	0.83	1.42	1.98
1980	4.36	2.12	1.63	1.54	1.89	2.54	1.13	0.78	1.29	2.48

Source: *State of the World, 1984*. A Worldwatch Institute Report on Progress Towards a Sustainable Society, Project Director, Lester R. Brown, W.W. Norton & Co. 1984, p. 48, Table 3-8.

industry measured by the number of employees and level of fixed capital (in real terms) were considered as independent variables. In model II, fixed capital per employee and level of value added were tried. The salient features of the results (Table 30) are presented below.

For a number of industries, viz., iron and steel, motor vehicles, metal products and paper, the effect of size, measured by the level of fixed capital, on growth of labor productivity seems to be negative. The implication is that an increase in fixed capital investment alone does not ensure any increase in labor productivity. Model II's results, show that productivity has declined in a few industries while total investment per unit of labor increased. Again this seems to indicate that expansion of investment alone may not be a strategic variable for expansion of productivity. But, the results relating to machinery industries show that productivity is positively related to scale and total investment per unit of labor. The coefficients of growth of productivity with respect to the level of value added are positive, except in case of railroad equipment. Whether the growth in productivity in different sectors had something to do with the protective regime in the country calls for a detailed analysis of the relationship between the productivity measure and the estimated Effective Rate of Protection (ERP) for a number of years. In view of the absence of reliable ERP estimates, we have not attempted to do this.[18]

PRODUCTIVITY AND FUTURE PERSPECTIVES

A brainstorming series of studies in the seventies provided wide-range reviews of development strategies for faster growth with efficient resource allocation. Some of these brought out, not without dissenting views, the misallocation of resources and low productivity levels all over the world. The productivity concerns were reinforced by the energy crisis, and countries tried to improve productivity of energy use. Productivity gains were also sought for by using the opportunities to reduce unit costs of production with new technology, new materials, new products and wider communication networks for faster knowledge and information flows.

The need to increase productivity in India has recently been emphasized by many economists.[19] Government has also emphasized this and declared 1982 'Productivity Year' in which several measures were taken to increase productivity.

"Improved efficiency and productivity" has been mentioned as one of the guiding principles of the Seventh Plan (1985-90) by the Planning Commission in its *Approach* paper, others being growth, equity and social justice, and self-reliance. Productivity is also mentioned as one of the basic priorities along with food and work in the Seventh Plan. The *Approach* paper states:

"This will require a strategy built around higher agricultural growth and creation of employment, improvement in efficiency and in quality of production and

---

[18] The estimates of ERP available in the literature on the Indian economy at different points of time made by different authors and organizations vary in methodology and data base so much that they are not only incomparable but many of them are unacceptable. Thus, they cannot be used as an independent variable in the required regression analysis, also because of the difficulty of incomparable sectoral classification of the studies and that of the CSO data. Such analysis is, therefore, likely to be misleading and has not been attempted in the present study.

[19] See many works by Ghosh, Brahmananda, Singh and Jha included in the Reference at the end of the chapter.

Table 30. India's Major Industries: Relationship Between Labor Productivity (Value Added Per Worker) and Selected Variables Using Different Models (Sample Period: 1965 to 1980)

Industries	Coefficients of Model I — Variables				Coefficients of Model II — Variables			
	Constant	No. of Employees	Level of Fixed Capital	R^2	Constant	Fixed Capital/ No. of Employees	Level of Value Added	R^2
Basic Industries	-6.087 (-8.295)	0.184 (1.171)	0.063 (.419)	0.66	-5.061 (-13.031)	0.051 (0.428)	0.214* (6.640)	0.79
Chemical & Chemical Products	-5.142 (-3.628)	-0.030 (-0.115)	0.286 (1.464)	0.62	-4.777 (-6.238)	0.137 (0.866)	0.257* (4.493)	0.78
Cement	1.747 (0.714)	-0.557 (-1.997)	0.179 (0.833)	0.52	-5.480 (-2.959)	0.241 (1.182)	0.409 (1.928)	0.29
Iron and Steel	-3.426 (-2.900)	0.136 (1.396)	-0.107 (-1.362)	0.16	-4.172 (-5.449)	-0.065 (-0.859)	0.118 (1.452)	0.30
Non-Ferrous Basic Metals	12.804 (2.787)	-1.459 (-2.613)	-0.018 (-0.862)	0.62	-12.629 (-9.209)	-0.254 (-2.244)	1.208* (6.667)	0.64
Electric, Light and Power	-6.377 (-10.349)	-0.085 (-0.521)	0.376 (2.189)	0.74	-5.069 (-17.562)	0.304** (2.369)	0.238* (8.227)	0.85

Table 30 (continued)

Industries	Coefficients of Model I – Variables				Coefficients of Model II – Variables			
	Constant	No. of Employees	Level of Fixed Capital	R^2	Constant	Fixed Capital/ No. of Employees	Level of Value Added	R^2
Capital Goods Industries	-22.757 (-7.605)	1.603* (5.017)	-0.238 (-1.175)	0.80	-10.026 (-22.122)	-0.113 (-1.410)	0.611* (18.560)	0.97
Machinery (except electrical)	-18.309 (6.664)	1.251* (4.972)	.058 (-0.223)	0.74	-8.712 (-23.006)	0.042 (0.380)	0.600* (13.890)	0.95
Elec. Machinery	-13.911 (-19.680)	0.906* (11.467)	0.003 (0.028)	0.96	-7.332 (-51.002)	0.014 (0.275)	0.484* (26.981)	0.99
Shipbuilding & Repairing	-4.931 (-3.586)	0.006 (0.036)	0.206* (3.547)	0.83	-4.837 (-7.325)	0.114 (2.041)	0.261* (3.601)	0.90
Railroad Equipments	1.035 (0.993)	-0.537 (-5.841)	0.214* (7.873)	0.86	-0.668 (-0.458)	0.260* (4.999)	-0.242 (-1.550)	0.73
Motor Vehicles	-1.366 (-0.882)	0.384* (3.309)	-0.606 (-3.252)	0.54	-4.370 (-3.990)	-0.208 (-0.799)	0.149 (0.848)	0.50
Repair of Motor Vehicles	-18.106 (-7.128)	1.287* (4.318)	-0.063 (-0.294)	0.75	-8.477 (-18.532)	-0.028 (-0.307)	0.593* (15.762)	0.95
Metal Products except Mach. & Trans. Equipment	-10.299 (-3.316)	0.628** (2.236)	-0.057 (-0.277)	0.32	-7.791 (-11.397)	0.039 (0.346)	0.531* (6.575)	0.80

Industries	Coefficients of Model I — Variables				Coefficients of Model II — Variables			
	Constant	No. of Employees	Level of Fixed Capital	R²	Constant	Fixed Capital/ No. of Employees	Level of Value Added	R²
Intermediate Goods Ind.	-7.503 (-2.826)	-0.009 (-0.049)	0.490 (1.962)	0.28	-6.445 (-8.877)	0.417* (3.567)	0.496* (5.844)	0.75
Rubber Products	-3.078 (-1.177)	-0.099 (-0.288)	0.178 (1.040)	0.22	-5.816 (-4.360)	-0.057 (-0.417)	0.353** (2.869)	0.53
Petro. Refinery Products	0.026 (0.006)	-0.403 (-1.092)	0.278 (0.764)	0.12	-7.311 (-6.829)	0.457* (3.267)	0.768* (5.784)	0.77
Structural Clay Prod.	-6.072 (-1.620)	-0.049 (-0.138)	0.345 (1.088)	0.10	-7.215 (-7.550)	0.326 (2.059)	0.602* (5.409)	0.72
Consumer Goods Industries	-3.333 (-2.111)	-0.217 (-1.824)	0.272 (1.544)	0.23	-4.493 (-4.772)	0.373 (2.915)	0.206 (2.039)	0.42
Spinning, Weav. & Finising	-25.332 (-6.574)	1.221* (-4.440)	0.456** (2.217)	0.73	-9.902 (-24.192)	0.187* (2.803)	0.673* (18.744)	0.97
Pulp, Paper & Paper Products	-8.434 (-4.522)	1.206* (3.845)	-0.841 (-2.754)	0.57	-6.850 (-11.220)	-0.462 (-2.025)	0.378* (4.998)	0.80
Miscellaneous Food Prod.	3.947 (0.664)	-0.505 (-1.811)	-0.159 (-0.399)	0.22	-9.822 (-9.751)	0.595* (5.611)	0.915* (6.386)	0.80
Tobacco Manufactures	4.878 (2.003)	-1.010 (-4.280)	0.469 (0.824)	0.76	-3.936 (-2.561)	1.293* (9.478)	0.788 (4.232)	0.89
Sugar Factories & Refineries	1.978 (0.633)	-0.969 (-3.797)	0.669 (1.191)	0.71	-5.725 (-4.058)	1.310* (8.721)	0.672* (3.877)	0.87
All Selected Industries	-8.009 (-6.663)	0.145 (0.910)	0.204 (1.575)	0.71	-6.284 (-11.140)	0.135 (1.404)	0.284* (7.340)	0.85

Parentheses show t-values.

* Significant at 1% level.
** Significant at 5% level.

technological upgradation in industry and infrastructure, the use of less capital-intensive techniques and shift in investment priorities towards items of mass consumption and measures to improve the quality of life."

The plan expects to lower the capital-output ratio in the whole economy and the industrial sectors. While more details will be available in the plan document, the *Approach* paper has brought out clearly "efficiency, modernization, and competition in industry" as one of twelve important features of the strategy during the Seventh Plan period.

Productivity was emphasized primarily "to generate adequate resources for investment," and efficiency was seen as a question of management and allocation of resources with emphasis on the public enterprises because in India, the public sector occupies a large share in total investment, production, and employment.

The *Approach* paper also mentioned the need to lay down productivity targets in disaggregated sectors, and to set appropriate norms for economizing material and energy used in all key sectors within a specific time-frame. It identified specific measures to realize these norms including monitoring. Five-Year Plans in India generally include a fifteen year perspective. According to the *Approach* paper,[20] the projected overall growth rate is a little over 5 percent. This rate was, also the estimate for the Sixth Plan period, 1980-85, and was higher than achieved during 1971-79; i.e. 3.8 percent. The *Approach* paper mentions the growth rates of agricultural and industrial production around 4 and 7 percent respectively in the medium term. The projected growth rates for the period of the Seventh Plan, compared with those of the Sixth Plan (1980-85) and long-term past, reveal that a higher growth rate is expected in industry (covering mining and quarrying, manufacturing, electricity, gas and water supply) and transport (other than railways) and communications. Although the value added in construction is projected to grow faster, the overall pattern of industrial growth is projected to be more balanced among different sectors.

The domestic savings rate is assumed at 26 percent which is the actual rate[21] for 1984-85, the final year of the Sixth Plan. The investment requirements have been estimated by assuming the growth rate objective of a little over 5 percent and an incremental capital-output ratio (ICOR) of 5. The aggregate requirements indicated in the *Approach* paper are Rs 320 thousand crores at 1984-85 prices. Out of this, a little over 53 percent is expected to be in the private sector. The observed share for 1982-83, for which the latest national accounts data are available, is about 51 percent. The assumed ICOR of 5 for the Seventh Plan period is lower than the 5.65 ICOR[22] estimated for the previous plan period, both at 1984-85 prices, despite the fact that the prices of capital goods are rising faster than the overall inflation rate. This is because of the thrust to increase productivity in the Seventh Plan.

CONCLUSIONS

This chapter discussed several dimensions of India's development strategies related to different sectors, economic policies, trade-orientation, and public and private ownership. All these dimensions and alternatives affect the pace of productivity

---

[20] Planning Commission, *The Approach to the Seventh Five-Year Plan, 1985-90.*

[21] *Ibid.*

[22] *Ibid.*

growth in the country.

The study of trends in productivity in India at the macro-level shows lags compared to the planned targets. The long-term trend (1965-66 to 1982-83) is of a rise with wide fluctuations. The growth rate works out to be significantly higher in the more recent years.

The trend in capital-intensity and the scale of the economy shows that the effect of increases in investment per worker on productivity are negative over the long term. However, the result turns out to be different in more recent years. The scale effect of the economy is positive. The negative relation with capital-intensity points to the different constraints caused by non-investment factors in India.

An analysis of the composition of industrial value added shows that the Indian economy has become more complex and has matured over the review period insofar as the shares of basic and capital goods industries have increased significantly.

Industry-level productivity in terms of labor productivity was analyzed, as against total factor productivity. The growth in labor productivity ranged from a significantly negative to substantially positive among the selected industries. What is striking is that labor productivity growth in the capital goods industries has been much higher than that in the other industries.

Energy efficiency has also been analyzed. The oil-intensity in India is very low, so that, it is difficult to infer any decline in energy efficiency, even though the oil-GDP ratio has been increasing over the review period.

The chapter analyzed the relationship of productivity with industry-size and capital intensity. In a few industries, productivity has declined with rising capital-intensity. The effect scale of industry (indicated by number of employees) is also found to be negative in the selected industries.

REFERENCES

Ahluwalia, Isher. *Industrial Growth in India: Stagnation Since the Mid-Sixties*, 1984.

Bhagwati J. and T.N. Srinivisan, *Foreign Trade Regimes and Economic Development: India*, N-H, 1975.

Banerjee, Asit. *Capital Intensity and Productivity in Indian Industry*, Mac. 1975.

Brahmananda, P.R., *Productivity in Indian Economy*, 1982.

Cowing, Thomas, G. and Rodney E. Stevenson, eds., *Productivity Measurement in Regulated Industries*, 1981.

Ghosh, A.K. "Inflation and Industrial Costs," *Commerce*, April 3, 1982 a.

Ghosh, A.K. "Planning for Greater Labor Utilization, *Commerce*, November 20, 1982 b.

Jha, L.K. "Productivity in the Seventh Plan," Foundation Lecture, National Productivity Council, New Delhi, April 1984.

Kendrick, J.W., *Productivity Trends in the United States*, New York, Princeton University Press, 1961.

Krueger Anne O., and Tuncer Baran, "Estimating Total Factor Productivity Growth and a Developing Country," World Bank Staff Working Paper No. 422, October, 1980.

Nishimizu, M., "On the Methodology and the Importance of the Measurement of Total Factor Productivity Change: The State of the Art," mimeo., World Bank, December 1979.

Nishimizu M. and S. Robinson, "Sectoral Productivity Growth in Semi-Industrial Countries: A Comparative Analysis," Division Working Paper No. 82-6, The World Bank, December 1982.

Panchamukhi, V.R., "Capital Formation and Output: A Quantitative Analysis of Lag-Structure" (mimeo), 1984.

Sandesara, J.C., "Industrial Economics: A Trend Report" (esp. "Technique, Size and Productivity", ch. 1), *A Survey of Research in Economics,* Vol. V, ICSSR, 1975, pp. 22-30.

Singh Manmohan, "Productivity and Social Change," *Reserve Bank of India Bulletin,* March 1983.

Solow, Robert M., "Technical Change and the Aggregate Production Function," *Review of Economics and Statistics,* August 1957.

A. Toffler, *Previews and Premises,* 1984.

Worldwatch Institute, *State of the World,* 1984, A Worldwatch Institute Report on Progress Towards a Sustainable Society, Project Director, Lester Brown, 1984.

Government of India Publications

Bureau of Public Enterprises, Ministry of Finance, *Annual Report on the Working of Industrial and Commercial Undertakings of the Central Government,* various reports.

Bureau of Public Enterprises, Ministry of Finance, *Public Enterprises Survey,* various volumes.

CSO, *Principal Characteristics of Selected Industries in Organized Manufacturing Sector,* 1960 to 1980, December, 1984, Bulletin No. ISD/9.

Department of Statistics, *Capital Formation and Savings in India, 1950-51 to 1979-80,* Report of the Working (K.N. Raj) Group on Savings, pub. by RBI, Feb. 1982.

Development Commissioner, Small-Scale Industries, Ministry of Industry, *Report of Census of Small-Scale Industrial Units,* Vols. I & II.

Ministry of Finance, *Economic Survey,* various issues.

Planning Commission, *Sixth Five-Year Plan,* 1980-85, 1981 a.

Planning Commission (Perspective Planning Division): *A Technical Note on the Sixth Plan of India,* (1980-85), July 1981 b.

Planning Commission, *Sixth Five-Year Plan, 1980-85: Mid-Term Appraisal,* August 1983.

Planning Commission, *The Approach to the Seventh Five-Year Plan 1985-90.* New Delhi, 1984. Also, "The Seventh Plan Formulation: A Broad Quantitative Framework," Meeting of Panel of Economists, pub. in *The Economic Times,* October 19, 1984. pp. 5-6.

14. Growth and Resource Mobilization in Four South Asian Countries

Godfrey Gunatilleke

INTRODUCTION

This chapter attempts to provide an overview of the trends in productivity and growth and the future economic prospects of four countries in the South Asian region — Pakistan, Bangladesh, Sri Lanka and Nepal. They are considered together as they form part of the region which has become identified as South Asia.

These countries are very diverse in their demographic and socio-economic characteristics. All four countries fall into the low-income group as defined by the World Bank, and two of them are among the poorest. The per capita incomes of Bangladesh and Nepal are less than half those of Sri Lanka and Pakistan. The relative income differences might be reduced if these figures were adjusted for purchasing power parity, as is attempted in the United Nations International Comparison project.

The four countries are also very different in their population size. While Bangladesh and Pakistan both have populations close to 100 million, Nepal and Sri Lanka are comparatively small countries with populations in the region of 16 million. In terms of social indicators, such as life expectancy and mortality, Sri Lanka stands out strikingly from the other three countries, having achieved a life expectancy of approximately 70 years, while the other three countries average approximately 50 years. The structures of their economies are also significantly different. Nepal and Bangladesh are much more heavily dependent on the agricultural sector than Sri Lanka and Pakistan. In the analysis that follows, the problems of each economy are considered separately and the prospects for their future growth are related to the specific constraints encountered by each.

---

* This chapter has drawn extensively on the data and analytical materials in the country studies prepared for the project by the following consultants:

Pakistan: Reza H. Syed, Investment Advisory Centre of Pakistan
Sri Lanka: Maurice Wanigaratne, Nimal Gunatilleke and Godfrey Gunatilleke, Marga Institute
Bangladesh: Atiqur Rahman, Bangladesh Institute of Development Studies
Nepal: Durgeshman Singh, National Planning Commission

There are, however, some common constraints to economic growth in all of them: heavy dependence on external resources, the low rate of domestic savings, and no dynamic growth sectors. Some of the basic socio-economic and demographic characteristics are summarized in tables 1 to 4. The data given in the tables provide a synoptic view of the economic situation in each country. Per capita income growth in both Bangladesh and Nepal has been close to zero. The domestic savings ratios of all but Sri Lanka were below 10 percent in 1983. With the exception of Sri Lanka, the capacity for mobilizing government revenues remains low. The trade deficits for the entire group are exceptionally large and the debt service ratios have been mounting except for Nepal which receives the major component of its external resources as outright grants.

The growth prospects in these countries are closely linked to the social infrastructure and the human capital that are available. Table 4 summarizes some of the main social and demographic characteristics. Bangladesh, Nepal, and Pakistan are at a stage of demographic growth where high birth rates are accompanied by high mortality rates. Sri Lanka is strikingly different in this respect with low birth and death rates. The demographic projections for the three countries which combine high fertility with high mortality indicate that expanding populations are likely to exert serious pressure on the growth of per capita income and the available resources as a whole, unless interventions of a very effective kind bring about a major reduction in birth rates.

In terms of human capital, once again, Sri Lanka is the exception with a high level of literacy and educational attainment. In Bangladesh and Nepal, the increase in the participation of children in the primary stage of education has been quite rapid. They have overtaken Pakistan in primary school enrollment. Nevertheless, female participation remains low, particularly in Nepal where the differential between male and female enrollment is quite marked. Infant mortality remains inordinately high for all of these countries except Sri Lanka. It does not significantly differ among the three despite the large gaps in per capita income.

Each country has to start the development effort from the present low level of income. With moderately high growth rates over the medium term, Bangladesh and Nepal will remain among the poorest countries in the world. Pakistan and Sri Lanka will move into the ranks of the lower-middle income countries if they are able to sustain real growth of 5 percent into the 1990s. The concluding section presents some alternative projections of their future incomes. These income levels reflect the broad parameters and growth strategies of these countries. An important issue is how such economic growth can be translated into an improvement of the quality of life. The growth effort must be directed not only to engineer the necessary structural changes in the economy but also to promote social transformations so as to satisfy the basic human needs of the population. In carrying out these tasks within the resource constraints, the four countries face formidable challenges. Some of them are examined in greater detail in the following sections. The development experiences of Sri Lanka are of special interest in providing lessons to the countries which seek to improve the well-being of the population at a low level of per capita income. Their positive and negative implications are also discussed in the following sections.

Table 1. Selected Economic Indicators

Country	Per Capita Income (1984)	Average Annual Growth Rate (1965-84)	Share of Agriculture in GDP (1984) (of per capita % income)	Gross Domestic Investment as % of GDP 1965	Gross Domestic Investment as % of GDP 1984	Gross Domestic Savings as % of GDP 1965	Gross Domestic Savings as % of GDP 1983
Bangladesh	130	0.6	48	11	16	8	2
Nepal	160	0.2	56	6	19	–	9
Sri Lanka	360	2.9	28	12	26	13	14
Pakistan	380	2.5	24	21	17	13	7

Sources: IBRD *World Development Report (WDR) 1986 — World Development Indicators*, Tables 1, 3, 5.

Table 2. Government Finance

Country	Central Government Expenditure as % of GNP 1983	Surplus and Deficit in Budget as % of GNP 1983	Total Current Revenue as % of GNP 1983
Bangladesh	14.7	−8.4	8.6
Nepal	17.2	−5.2	8.7 (1982)
Sri Lanka	33.6	−11.0	20.2
Pakistan	17.8	−6.2	14.5

Sources: IBRD WDR Tables 22 and 23.
   Bangladesh Bureau of Statistics.

Table 3. External Resources

Country	Net flow of Official Development Assistant as % of GDP (1984)	Total Exports as % of Total Imports (1984)	Debt Service Ratio (1984)	Annual Exports as % of Total long-term debt (a) (1984)
Bangladesh	9.3	48	16.6	18
Nepal	7.9	24	3.4	26
Sri Lanka	8.0	60	22.0 (1985)	59
Pakistan	2.1	41	26.7	26

Sources: − IBRD WDR 1986 Tables 9, 18, 21.
   − World Bank data from country reports.
   (a) Calculated from Table 17 and Table 9 of IBRD WDR 1986.

PAKISTAN

Growth and Productivity

The Pakistan economy has been able to sustain relatively high rates of growth during the last 25 years. The average annual rate of growth during this period was a healthy 5.6 percent. The interruptions in this sustained performance over the two and a half decades have been few and brief. In the first two years of the seventies, the economy virtually stagnated with an average rate of growth of less than 1 percent. After a brief spurt of growth in 1972-74, the growth rate fell below 4 percent in the three years that followed. With these exceptions, the Gross Domestic Product maintained an average growth of over 6 percent. During the more recent period 1977-83, the

Table 4. Selected Social Indicators

Country	Average Annual Growth Rate of Population (1973-84)	Crude Birth Rate (1984)	Crude Death Rate (1984)	Daily Calorie Supply per capita as % of minimum requirements (1983)	Primary School Enrollment as % of age group (1983)	% 1 Labor Force in Agriculture (1980)	% of Urban Population in Total Population (1984)
Bangladesh	2.5%	41	15	81	62	58.7 (a) (1983-84)	18
Nepal	2.6%	43	18	93	73	91	7
Sri Lanka	1.8%	25	06	106	100	45.8 (b)	21
Pakistan	2.9%	42	15	95	49	52 (c)	29

Sources: – IBRD WDR 1986, Tables 25, 26, 29, 30, 31.
– World Bank Data from country reports 1985 of 58.6%.

(a) Labor Force Survey 1983/84.
(b) Socio-Economic Survey 1980/81.

Note: The crude birth rates and death rates given in the *World Development Report* for 1986 are higher than those available in national documents, such as those of the Bangladesh Bureau of Statistics or the Sixth Five-Year Plan of Pakistan.

average annual growth rate of GDP has been 6.5 percent, reaching a high 8.4 percent in 1984-85. These high rates of economic growth were accompanied by fairly significant changes in the structure of Pakistan's economy. The share of agriculture in GDP was approximately 53 percent in 1950 but declined to 26 percent in 1984-85. The share of manufacturing increased from 8 percent to approximately 20 percent during the same period. The services sector share rose from 37 percent to 45 percent. These changes occurred along with vigorous growth, both in agriculture and manufacturing. The agricultural sector grew at approximately 3.8 percent per year, during the period 1960-85. The industrial sector, including manufacturing, mining and quarrying, and construction, grew at nearly 8 percent during this period.

The topography in Pakistan has enabled the country to provide a reliable irrigation system and a regular supply of water to maintain a fairly steady growth in agriculture. The country possesses a resource endowment of modest proportions to support the industrialization process. This includes large reserves of natural gas, deposits of coal and iron, industrial clays of various types, copper and substantial potentials for hydro-electric energy. While the aggregate output in the agricultural sector has grown rapidly there have been no major changes in the product mix. Food crops contribute approximately 68 percent of value added in agriculture, with wheat providing the predominant share of approximately 43 percent. Rice, sugarcane, and cotton are the other three major crops, contributing approximately 45 percent.

In the industrial sector, the rapid rate of growth was accompanied by fairly significant changes in the product-mix. The textile industry has dominated the manufacturing sector, but its share fell from 39 percent in the beginning of the sixties to 23 percent in 1980-81. The share of chemicals and chemical products increased from 8.3 percent to 13.5 percent during this period. Manufacture of chemical fertilizers made an important contribution to these increases. The share of the basic metal industry increased from 3 percent to 7 percent. The capacity in this sub-sector was greatly increased with the introduction of an integrated steel mill. The food processing industry's share increased from 7.6 percent to nearly 26 percent. Major increases were recorded in the shares of the sugar refining and edible oil processing industries. Despite the potential for greater industrial diversification, manufacturing output is still heavily concentrated in consumer goods.

The data for 1965-84 indicate that the average growth rate of the labor force was approximately 2.9 percent. With a GDP growth rate of 5.5 percent, the overall productivity growth rate was 2.6 percent. Per capita income growth approximated to this figure — about 2.5 percent. The rate of open unemployment is relatively low in Pakistan and estimated at approximately 4 percent. Around 10 percent of the labor force is estimated to be working abroad.

The employment situation in Pakistan draws attention to two features which are relevant for an analysis of productivity in countries in similar development stages. First, the low level of open unemployment is related to the low participation. According to the data of the 1981 Census, the participation of the male population over ten years of age is approximately 50.6 percent and female participation is only 2.1 percent. The labor force participation rate in Pakistan is low compared to the other three countries and this is primarily attributable to the low female participation. At present, the current rate of economic growth is sustaining a growing workforce without producing serious unemployment, as it happened in the case of Sri Lanka. But social changes like higher female education and other forces of

Table 5. Annual Growth Rates at 1959-60 Factor Cost

(Unit: %)

Year	Agriculture	Manufacturing	Total Commodity Sector	All Services	GDP	GNP
1950-51 to 1954-55	1.05	10.30	2.67	3.90	3.14	3.16
1955-56 to 1959-60 (1st Plan)	2.11	5.16	3.02	3.14	3.07	3.04
1960-61 to 1964-65 (2nd Plan)	3.75	11.73	6.47	7.28	6.78	6.76
1965-66 to 1969-70 (3rd Plan)	6.29	8.10	7.14	6.07	6.72	6.78
1970-71 to 1976-77 (Non-Plan)	1.55	2.93	2.57	5.52	3.76	4.21
1977-78 to 1981-82 (5th Plan)	3.97	10.53	6.39	7.19	6.74	7.11
1982-83 to 1984-85	2.2	8.62	5.00	7.14	6.00	6.03

Sources: Government of Pakistan, Federal Bureau of Statistics; *Pakistan Economic Survey*, 1984-85, Table 2.3, p. 22.

Table 6. Structural Changes in GDP (at Constant Factor Cost of 1959-60)

| Year | Share in GDP (%) | | | | |
	Agriculture	Manufacturing	Total Commodity Sector	All Services	GDP
1949-50	53.19	7.75	62.82	37.18	100.00
1954-55	48.02	10.84	61.43	38.57	100.00
1959-60	45.83	12.00	61.29	38.71	100.00
1964-65	39.68	15.04	60.39	39.61	100.00
1969-70	38.88	16.04	61.58	38.42	100.00
1974-75	39.19	15.58	56.09	43.91	100.00
1979-80	31.02	16.32	56.01	43.99	100.00
1980-81	30.19	16.94	55.83	44.17	100.00
1981-82	29.32	18.06	55.87	44.13	100.00
1982-83	28.59	18.58	55.44	44.56	100.00
1983-84	25.94	19.41	54.24	45.76	100.00
1984-85 P	26.28	19.43	54.44	45.56	100.00

Sources: Government of Pakistan, Federal Bureau of Statistics; *Pakistan Economic Review*, 1984-85, Table 2.4, p. 23.

P = Provisional.

modernization are likely to increase female participation in the workforce. The prevailing employment situation can, therefore, rapidly alter with these changes.

The second feature is the high share of the labor force in agriculture. The percentage of the labor force in agriculture has declined from approximately 60 percent in 1965 to 52 percent in 1984, although the share of agriculture in GDP had declined sharply during this period from 40 percent to 26 percent. Both the technological changes as well as the tenurial structures have not taken the agricultural sector in the direction of large-scale, capital intensive agriculture. Increases in productivity have depended primarily on inputs which have not significantly displaced labor: high-yielding varieties, new agricultural practices, irrigation and use of agro-chemicals. The process of structural transformation does not seem to be based on a rapid transfer of the workforce from agriculture to manufacturing and services, as was the experience of the industrialized countries. If the statistics are accurate, during the period 1965-85 a little less than half the increase in the labor force was employed by the agricultural sector. There is evidence that off-farm, non-agricultural employment is increasing in importance in rural South Asia including Pakistan.[1] Still the agricultural sector is likely to continue to absorb a large proportion of the new entrants to the workforce, and will increase in absolute numbers for a long period ahead, only at a declining rate. For example, if we assume that the 1985 workforce will grow at an annual rate of approximately 2.9 percent over the next 15 years and that the share of the agricultural workforce will decline from its

[1]   Islam, Non-Farm Employment in Rural Employment: Issues and Evidence in *Off Farm Employment in the Development of Rural Asia*, 1986.

present 52 percent to 40 percent by 2000 A.D., the agricultural workforce would still have increased from about 11.7 million to 13.8 million during this period.

The estimates of overall productivity growth and growth of sectoral productivity are set out in Table 8. With value added increasing in the agricultural sector at 3.5 percent per annum and the agricultural workforce growing at 2.1 percent, the annual increase in labor productivity in the agricultural sector was about 1.4 percent.

Table 7. Shares of the Different Manufacturing Industries in
Value Added in Manufacturing Sector

Industry	1954	1959-60	1969-70	1980-81
1. Food Manufacturing	8.5	7.6	10.0	25.9
2. Manufacturing of Beverages	0.4	0.3	0.1	0.8
3. Tobacco Manufacturing	5.5	5.3	6.1	3.4
4. Manufacturing of Textiles	46.7	39.1	28.5	23.3
5. Manufacturing of Footwear and other Wearing Apparel	3.5	2.4	3.8	3.0
6. Manufacturing of Paper and Paperboard	–	1.6	1.2	1.6
7. Printing and Publishing Industries	2.7	2.4	5.4	2.3
8. Manufacturing of Leather and Leather Products except Footwear	2.4	0.7	2.2	1.7
9. Rubber and Rubber Products	0.9	0.5	0.7	1.6
10. Chemicals and Chemical Products	9.5	8.3	7.9	13.5
11. Non-metallic Products	4.0	6.1	2.5	2.0
12. Basic Metal Industries	2.1	3.1	2.0	7.0
13. Manufacturing of Metal Products	2.1	3.9	3.7	1.3
14. Non-electrical Machinery	0.9	2.1	3.9	2.3
15. Electrical Machinery	0.8	2.7	2.6	4.5
16. Transport Equipment	1.1	3.4	1.6	2.3
17. Other Industries	8.9	10.5	18.1	6.2

Sources: Government of Pakistan, Finance Division; *Pakistan Economic Survey*, 1984-85, Table 4, p. 129.

Table 8. Total and Sectoral Rates of Growth of Productivity — 1965-84
(Annual Average Percentage Change)

	Agriculture	Industries	Services	Total
Growth of Labor Force	2.1	3.4	4.1	2.9
Growth of Value Added	3.5	7.2	6.0	5.5
Growth of Productivity	1.4	3.8	1.9	2.6

Source: Calculated from data available in *World Development Report* 1986, and country data obtained from *Pakistan Economic Review*, 1984-85.

The improvement in the yields per hectare in the main crops — wheat, rice, cotton and sugarcane — were in the order of 117, 101, 68 and 46 percent respectively during his period.

As stated earlier, the impressive performance of the agricultural sector has been the outcome of the interaction of a variety of factors. An irrigation system which assured a regular supply of water to nearly 70 percent of the country's agricultural land played a crucial part. This created conditions which were conducive to the quick application and absorption of the new technology.

The irrigation system has to be carefully protected against long-term deterioration. The Sixth Five-Year Plan document pinpoints several features which are causing concern. Owing to lack of adequate maintenance the canal system has deteriorated resulting in siltation, frequent breaches in distributories and other deficiencies that have seriously reduced its efficiency. The salination of soils is increasing. Some studies estimate that nearly 16 million tons of salt are added to the soil and ground-water annually. Protection against flooding is inadequate. Nearly ten million acres of canal irrigated land is subject to inundation. The sustained productivity of the agricultural sector therefore depends heavily on the careful maintenance of a system which is becoming vulnerable to a variety of hazards.

Pakistan's agriculture was primarily based on smallholders. Approximately 75 percent of these holdings were less than five hectares. The complex system of subsidies, support prices, concessional credit and state investments and services through provision of irrigation facilities as well as extension services support this smallholder agriculture. These subsidies, however, operate within an overall price structure, where, with the exception of the price of sugar, the domestic prices of agricultural products are significantly below the international market prices. It was estimated that the domestic price of wheat was about 73 percent of the international market price in 1984-85. The domestic prices of basmati rice and seed cotton were only 57 percent and 80 percent of the respective international prices in 1984-85. A recent estimate prepared by the government places the net subsidy in the agricultural sector at approximately Rs. 1.1 billion.[2] This estimate, however, does not take into account concessional credit on the one hand and the disparities between domestic and international prices on the other.

These policies in the agricultural sector have been a part of the framework of overall economic management in Pakistan. The complex system of price controls and subsidies in both the agricultural and manufacturing sector, have been operated avowedly for the purpose of controlling price inflation, promoting exports and increasing production. The adverse effects of some of these policies through distortion of relative prices and the consequent misallocation of resources have been recognized by the government. Subsequently, there has been an increasing effort at activating the market mechanisms by reducing the scope for regulations, administered prices and subsidies.

The growth of productivity was highest in the industrial sector. This sector maintained an annual rate of productivity growth of 3.8 percent during the period 1965-84. The productivity performance in the manufacturing sector has been mixed. Textile manufacturing, the most important private sector industry in Pakistan, has encountered serious problems of obsolescence and inefficiency. Cotton textiles account for about 25 percent of manufacturing value added and 40 percent of total

---

[2] *Pakistan Economic Survey*, 1985.

manufactured exports. The production of cloth has, however, been declining at an average rate of approximately 5 percent over the last eight years. While this is due largely to the restrictions imposed by the industrialized countries, the deteriorating conditions within the textile industry have also contributed to a decline in productivity and diminished its competitiveness in international markets. It is estimated (1986) that over 40 percent of the spinning and 85 percent of the weaving equipment is over twenty to twenty-five years old. In 1983-84, 28.5 percent of spinning capacity and 50 percent of weaving capacity were idle. The reasons were power shortages, obsolescence, and improper maintenance and subsequent equipment failure. The spindles and looms that were in working order were used very intensively and this could result in further problems (see Table 9).

Although manufactured exports now account for 65 percent of total exports, the main driving force in industrialization has been import substitution. Pakistan's industry suffers from many shortcomings associated with the inward looking industrial strategies. In an overall appraisal of the performance of the manufacturing sector, the Sixth Five-Year Plan[3] states that "the degree of protection has always been high and has resulted in the creation of excess capacity, some of which may not be regarded as suitable for utilization even in the long-run. Some industries remain uncompetitive even after long periods of operation. Studies carried out at different stages of development indicate that the value added in a number of cases may be negative if international prices are used for analysis. This implies that in cold reality a part of the industrial sector is using more of the national resources than its contribution to the national pool."

In the 1950s, the private sector was the main instrument of industrialization but the public sector assumed a pioneering role especially through its Pakistan Industrial Development Corporation. When the technology and the financial resources required were beyond the capacity of the private sector, it first established industries in the public sector and then transferred these industries to the private sector. By the late 1960s, the private sector had acquired a dominant position in manufacturing industries such as cement, chemicals and fertilizers. Private industrial investment had risen to about 3.5 percent of GNP. The entire industrial effort during this period was supported by incentives and protection of such a high order that they raised serious questions regarding the efficiency of this sector and its net contribution to national output.

The response to this situation in the 1970s was the major program of nationalization. As a result, the public sector acquired approximately one-third of the manufacturing capacity and controlled most of the major industrial enterprises, such as cement, fertilizers, edible oils, and steel. These drastic changes of policy resulted in a steep decline in private investment. This is partly the result of uncertainty regarding the relative roles of the public and private sector and future government policies on nationalization. In the late 1970s several measures were taken to restore the private sector's confidence. These included the denationalization of agro-based industries and a few engineering units and a declaration that no further nationalization would take place. This has been followed by a clear demarcation of the respective roles of the public and private sectors.

In an attempt to increase the efficiency of the manufacturing sector and improve its international competitiveness, the government has moved cautiously in the

---

[3] *Sixth Five-Year Plan*, pp. 117-118.

Table 9. Cotton Textiles Statistics

| Year | No. of reporting Mills | Installed Capacity | | Working at the end of the Periods | | Yarn produced (000 kg) | Surplus yarn (000 kg) | Total production of cloth (000 S.M.) |
		No. of spindles (000)	No. of looms (000)	No. of spindles (000)	No. of looms (000)			
1970-71	113	2,605	30	2,491	27	669,745	452,958	787,313
1971-72	131	2,848	30	2,650	26	335,702	236,917	628,189
1972-73	150	3,226	29	3,057	27	376,122	286,242	588,606
1973-74	155	3,308	29	3,034	26	379,460	283,404	592,172
1974-75	143	3,410	29	2,823	25	351,200	263,079	555,855
1975-76	127	3,478	29	2,579	23	349,653	265,710	520,338
1976-77	135	3,544	29	2,650	19	282,640	217,188	408,287
1977-78	140	3,560	26	2,680	15	297,894	242,730	391,347
1978-79	152	3,704	27	2,772	14	327,798	320,952	339,442
1979-80	149	3,731	26	2,841	16	362,862	..	342,335
1980-81	158	3,983	25	3,176	13	374,947	331,670	307,882
1981-82	155	4,180	25	2,944	13	430,154	387,530	325,021
1982-83	158	4,265	24	3,062	14	448,430	397,867	335,537
1983-84	162	4,224	24	3,020	12	431,581	..	296,596
1984-85	160	4,282	23	3,031	12	343,997	..	203,070

(July-March)

Source: *Pakistan Economic Survey* 1984-85, Table 4.5, p. 79 & 80.

direction of de-regulation and reform of the incentive structure. An industrial incentive reform cell in the Ministry of Finance has been entrusted with the task of rationalizing the structure of industrial incentives. For a large number of products price controls have been removed and more liberal import policies have been follow-ed in order to contain domestic prices. These measures, however, do not constitute as yet the adoption of a comprehensive system of market incentives as in the case of Sri Lanka where the dismantling of controls and the removal of administered prices have been undertaken on a much broader front.

As in the case of any developing country undergoing a relatively rapid pace of economic growth, Pakistan has experienced the problems caused by the failure of infrastructure development to keep pace with the overall growth of the economy. The Sixth Five-Year Plan assigns priority to the problems of energy, transport, and communication. Pakistan is relatively well placed to deal with these problems. The growth of value added in these sub-sectors has been quite high during the period 1960-85. In the case of electricity and gas, the increase in value added was more than twenty-fold. The value added in the transport, storage, and communication sub-sectors increased more than five-fold. The main problems highlighted in the Sixth Five-Year Plan were the shortage of energy and the imbalance between road and rail transportation. In terms of resource endowment in energy as well as the nature of the topography for transportation, Pakistan is far more fortunate than Nepal and, to a lesser extent, than Bangladesh or Sri Lanka.

Table 8 shows that the growth of productivity in the services sector has been the lowest. Though the commodity-producing sectors in Pakistan's economy have a larger share of GDP than in the other three countries, its service sector has taken up some of the slack in employment creation. It is also related to another aspect of Pakistan's development. Various appraisals of the Pakistan economy repeatedly pointed out that Pakistan ranks high in terms of economic indicators, but quite low in terms of social indicators. In life expectancy, infant mortality and fertility, it is not significantly different from Nepal or Bangladesh, where per capita incomes less than half of Pakistan's. Primary school enrollment in both Bangladesh and Nepal are considerably higher than in Pakistan. The development of human resources has, therefore, lagged far behind Pakistan's economic growth.

Pakistan's population increased at an annual rate of 3 percent during the period 1961-1981, substantially above the 2.4 percent in the preceding 10 years. The crude birth rate fell very slowly from 48 in 1965 to 42 in 1984. Mortality declined much faster, pushing up the rate of natural increase. Thus, current population trends can produce a per capita income growth of only about 3 percent per annum out of a high 6 percent growth rate of GDP. Per capita income growth for Sri Lanka was nearly 0.4 percent higher than that of Pakistan over the same period although GDP growth rate was lower.

Policies aimed at reducing population growth will play a critical role in Pakistan's future development. The success of these policies will, however, depend on rapid improvements in health and education, particularly improvements in the educational level of women. The current trends do not indicate the shifts in development effort to cause these changes at the desired pace. The structure of public expenditure has reflected a different set of priorities. Defense absorbs approximately 35 percent of total government expenditure. The share of education has risen from 1.2 percent in the early 1970s to 3.1 percent in 1983, which is still far below that of Sri Lanka or Nepal. Health receives a meagre 1 percent.

The Sixth Five-Year Plan points out that expenditure on education has declined from 1.8 percent of GNP in 1977-78 to 1.5 percent in 1982-83, and that it has been spending only one-fifth as much as other low income countries on national health care. These low shares in public expenditure must be seen in the context of a government budget which is relatively small as a share of GNP. These low shares in public expenditure must be seen in the context of a budget which is relatively small as a share of GNP.

Resource Mobilization, Savings and Investment

There are several features which distinguish the pattern of resource mobilization, investment and growth in Pakistan from that in the other three countries. Gross Domestic Investment in the first half of the 1960s was about 20 percent of GDP and declined to 16 percent in the second half of the 1960s, further declining to 12 and 13 percent in 1973 and 1974. From 1975 to 1984, the same ratio ranged between 18.4 in 1976-77 and 15.6 percent in 1983-84. The share of private investment was larger than that of the public sector during the 1960s and the first two years of the 1970s, ranging between 50 and 60 percent. The situation was dramatically reversed after 1973-74, when public investment had absorbed more than two-thirds of the total investment. This shift is due to the decline in private investment in manufacturing and the rapid increase of investments by public enterprises. After 1980-81, however, private sector investment has increased again reaching 40 percent in 1984-85.

Despite these changes in the composition of investment, the overall Incremental Capital Output Ratio has been relatively low, averaging about 3.1. This is partly due to the fact that growth came largely from the increases in productivity in agriculture, although the preponderant shares of investment went into manufacturing and infrastructure. Thus, Pakistan appears to be able to sustain a growth rate of around 6 percent with an investment rate around 16 percent. The Sixth Five-Year Plan investment outlays at 16.8 percent of GNP for the period 1985-88. The relatively low capital-output ratio in Pakistan is not easy to explain when the high capital intensity and the excess capacity in the industrial sector are taken into account. In agriculture, growth came out of increase in productivity with the existing capital stock. However, Pakistan's economy still appears to have several areas with underutilized capacities so that the overall capital-output ratios can be maintained at the present level.

The external dependence of Pakistan's economy, measured in terms of the ratio of the total value of imports and exports to GDP, is 32 percent, of which imports represents 21 percent of GDP. The trade deficit is about 11 percent of GDP. In the case of developing countries like Pakistan, Sri Lanka, and Bangladesh, merchandise trade is no longer a satisfactory indicator of external dependence. The current account on invisibles includes both the large influx of workers' remittances and the major liabilities on the servicing and repayment of debts. In 1983-84, the trade deficit stood at approximately 3.7 billion dollars, while the surplus on net private transfers derived mainly from workers' remittances was 2.7 billion dollars. The net balance of 1 billion dollars was financed by foreign capital inflows in the form of direct investments and long-term development assistance.

The rate of savings in Pakistan has been relatively low throughout the entire period. It has risen from about 9 percent of GDP in the early 1970s to around 12 percent in recent years. Workers' remittances appear to be contributing a significant share of national savings. Domestic savings alone appear to account for only 50 percent of national savings. The World Development Report 1984 shows gross domestic savings as 6 percent of GDP in 1984.[4]

The resource gap of approximately 4 percent of GDP has come out of foreign savings. These figures indicate the extent to which Pakistan's economy is dependent on the continuing flow of private transfers, foreign investments and development assistance. The Sixth Five-Year Plan, assumes that the flow of external resources will grow at approximately 10 percent per annum, and that real net aid inflows grows at about 6.6 percent per annum. In contrast to these expectations, net aid transfers continued to decline in the 1970s. The gross aid flows have barely kept pace with the increase in payments due on amortization and interest of the external public debt. The net aid inflow dropped from 5.8 percent of GDP in 1974-75 to a bare 0.2 percent in 1981-82. Amortization payments will increase during the next five years by around 7.5 percent per annum. Unless gross aid inflows increase at a higher rate, Pakistan will find it difficult to maintain the level of foreign savings required to finance gross domestic investment at a level of around 16 to 17 percent of GDP.

During the period 1980-84, the merchandise export experienced rapid growth and diversified its composition. The terms of trade declined sharply and there was a drop in workers' remittances. Real net factor income from abroad declined by 11.5 percent and national savings fell to 10.9 percent of GDP in 1985. The growth of exports witnessed a set back in 1984-85, falling 7.3 percent. Thus, the external resource situation of Pakistan remains highly vulnerable and can exert retarding effects on its development.

Government expenditure was 24 percent of GNP, whereas government revenue was only 14 percent in 1983. Nevertheless, current revenues have, by and large, been sufficient to finance current expenditures, and borrowing from the banking system seems to have been contained not to produce any major inflation. The rate of inflation has been below 10 percent during the last three years, 1983-85. The composition of the government's current expenditures is determined by certain large expenditure items. 58 percent goes to defense and interest payments on accumulated debts. Subsidies claim 5 percent; only 25 percent is allocated to economic and social services. Pakistani policy-makers have emphasized that since reduction in expenditure on defense and debt servicing has restricted scope, the improvement of social and economic services depend on the success in domestic resource mobilization. Such an effort would require wholesale reappraisals of existing subsidies and tax exemptions, including a direct tax on agricultural incomes which are exempted now.

Future Prospects

Despite the consistent high rates of growth in the agricultural sector, the gap between current and potential yields is large for almost all crops. The yields for wheat are only about one-fourth of the potential. Rehabilitation, improvement and proper maintenance of the irrigation system, together with reclamation, can clearly improve efficiency. However, from the point of view of demand, the scope for

---

[4]   World Bank, *World Development Report* 1984.

Table 10. Investment and Savings (Current Prices)

(Unit: Rs. million)

	1977-78	1978-79	1979-80	1980-81	1981-82	1982-83	1983-84 (Revised)	1984-85 (Provisional)
As % of GNP								
Investment	16.5	16.5	16.9	15.5	16.1	16.1	15.6	16.2
Foreign Saving	3.1	5.2	3.8	3.3	4.6	1.7	3.0	4.5
National Saving	13.4	11.3	10.7	12.2	11.6	14.4	12.6	11.6
Public Saving	1.7	1.0	1.7	3.8	3.1	1.1	1.9	:
Private Saving	11.7	10.3	9.0	8.4	8.5	13.2	10.7	:
Corporate	1.1	1.1	1.2	1.3	1.5	1.5	1.5	:
Household	10.6	9.2	7.8	7.0	7.0	11.7	9.2	:

Summary of Public Finances (as percent of GDP at Market Prices)

	1979-80	1980-81	1981-82	1982-83	1983-84 (Revised)	1984-85 (Budget)
Tax Revenue	13.7	13.9	13.3	13.4	13.9	13.3
Total Revenue	16.3	16.8	16.1	16.2	17.5	16.7
Expenditure	23.1	22.8	22.0	23.8	24.1	23.0
Overall deficit	6.2	5.2	5.3	7.0	6.0	5.6
Domestic Bank Financing	3.1	2.3	2.0	2.6	1.6	1.1
Of Which Budgetary Support	2.7	0.8	1.7	1.7	1.9	1.2

Source: *Pakistan Economic Survey* 1984-85, Table 2.9, p. 33 & Table 8.1, p. 123.

import substitution is limited only to edible oils as was identified in the Sixth Five-Year Plan. In the case of the other crops, production must move from self-sufficiency to export. They will then be subject to all the weaknesses and fluctuations of world primary commodity export markets. Therefore, the agricultural sector will have to contend with the inelasticities of demand and the program of diversification has to take this into account. These conditions indicate the limits within which the agricultural development strategy operates.

While its dynamic agriculture can still contribute to strengthening the export sector, the Pakistan economy will have to rely increasingly on the manufacturing and services sectors to sustain high growth over a long period. The manufacturing sector was able to maintain an overall rate of growth of 6 to 8 percent during the period 1977-83. The industrial sector as a whole experienced an annual growth of 9 percent, with large-scale manufacturing growing at 10 percent.

These trends broadly indicate the potential for the future growth in the industrial sector. The Sixth Five-Year Plan identifies several subsectors in manufacturing; including petro-chemicals, engineering goods and agro-industries. The first two will cater mainly to the internal market and to a lesser extent the export market. Agro-industries will be an important component which is directed at the Middle East market. Industrial growth will be further promoted by import substitution in basic consumer and intermediate goods, such as cement, paper, fertilizer and edible oils. With the potential in the energy sector and its resource endowments, the industrial sector in Pakistan can sustain higher trends or even accelerate them.

A major problem area, however, is in the textile industry which contributes nearly a quarter of the value added in the manufacturing sector and approximately 40 percent of manufactured exports at present. Declining productivity and constraints on the international market have led to its serious deterioration in efficiency and productivity. The efforts to revive the industry during the Fifth Five-Year Plan period, however, have not been successful. The yarn sector responded to the efforts, while the mill sector continued to deteriorate. The performance of the textile industry will continue to be critical until the share of the textile sector in manufacturing significantly declines with greater diversification.

The second problem facing Pakistan is in the flow of workers' remittances and the absorption of labor in the Arab countries. Workers' remittances have declined in the recent past. With the marked deceleration of growth in the Arab countries, it can decline further. Stagnation and decline in this area can have an adverse impact of considerable magnitude. Adjustments to the changes in external resource flow as well as labor adbsorption, must, therefore, form an important part of the development strategy in the medium term.

The third major problem is in the social and demographic field. The rapid improvement of social indicators would require considerable change in the structure of public expenditure and increased allocation for health, education, and basic infrastructure. This would require a more efficient and greater mobilization of resources for the government budget. As has been mentioned already, there is considerable scope for restructuring the present taxation system.

The social changes that occur as a result of significant improvements in health, education and the satisfaction of basic needs can lead to greater participation in the workforce but may also raise peoples' expectations and result in social unrest. Social instability has been witnessed in neighboring countries like Sri Lanka, that have gone through this process. Instability is likely unless the growth of the economy and the generation of employment keep pace with rising expectations. In the case of Pakistan, high rates of economic growth by themselves may not lead to the desired rate of growth in per capita incomes and household incomes if current trends in population growth continue. Improvement of the social conditions, including increasing female literacy will be vital to the management of the demographic situation. In time this can improve resource mobilization and accelerate growth. However, improvement of social conditions may lead to a decline in mortality, and initially result in an even higher spurt of population growth. In this context, the crucial importance of an effective population policy that leads to lowering of fertility and limitation of family size in the short- and medium-term cannot be over-emphasized. The demographic factor will be decisive in the development scenario of Pakistan in the next decade or two. Some of the relevant issues are discussed further in the section on Bangladesh.

Needless to say, this scenario of development will eventually depend on the political framework, both internal and external. In the past, despite changes of government and alternations between military and democratic rule, the economy was able to sustain relatively high rates of growth. The experience of the 1970's shows, however, that conditions of instability can seriously affect the framework of incentives and the performance of the economy. The way in which Pakistan will carry out its transition to democratic rule and resolve its internal conflicts will have far-reaching implications for its economic performance. Pakistan's relations with her neighbors will play an important part in the allocation of resources for defence and security on the one hand, and social improvement on the other. A lowering of political tension in the region and resolution of some of the ongoing conflicts can, therefore, have a dramatic impact on the prospects for Pakistan's development.

SRI LANKA

Aggregate Growth, Structural Change and Performance

The performance of the Sri Lankan economy, recorded an annual average growth of 3.7 percent, but has been quite uneven during the three decades 1950-81. During the period 1950-64, there were two distinct sub-periods. The average annual rate fell from 4.2 percent for 1950-55 to 2.5 percent during the 1956-1964 period. The 1965-1981 time-span contained three widely varying periods of growth. During 1965-1970, the average annual growth rate increased to 4.6 percent. However, the average fell to 2.5 percent for 1971-76, primarily due to very slow growth in 1971 and 1972. In fact, real GDP declined by 0.8 percent in 1971. The 1977-81 period observed the highest rates of growth in the nation's modern history: a growth rate of 6.2 percent.

Within this overall performance, the structural transformation in the sectoral share of GDP or the workforce has not been very significant. As Table 12 shows, the share of agriculture in real GDP fell from 41 percent to 24 percent during the 1950-1981 period. However, when the series is adjusted for consistent definitions and methods of valuation, the decline of the agricultural sector is much smaller: from 29 percent to 24 percent. The present discussion will use this new series. The share of manufacturing rose from 9 to 11 percent during the same period. The share of services was consistently high, although it declined from 58 percent in 1950 to

Table 11. Real GDP Growth Rates for Sri Lanka 1950-1981

Time Period	Annual Growth Rate	
	Least Squares Fit	Average of Computed Value
1950-1955	—	4.24
1956-1964	—	2.50
1965-1969	—	4.63
1970-1976	—	2.54
1977-1981	—	6.16
1950-1964	2.75	3.12
1965-1981	3.82	4.22
1950-1981	3.37	3.73

Source: Computed from data in Savundranayagam, T. "Estimates of Gross National Product from 1950-1981". Staff Studies, Central Bank of Ceylon, Vol. 13, Nos. 1 and 2, April/ September 1985.

Table 12. Structure of Real GDP: Percentage of GDP by Sector

Year	Central Bank Series				New Series			
	A	I	M	S	A	I	M	S
1950	41	18	14	41	29	13	9	58
1960	38	17	11	45	27	14	8	59
1970	28	24	17	48	26	19	12	55
1980	24	24	14	52	24	21	11	55

Source: Savundranayagam, T. "Estimates of Gross National Product from 1950 to 1981 – A Technical Note", Central Bank of Ceylon.

Notes: 1. A = Agriculture, Forestry and Fishery.
   B = Industry, includes mining and quarrying, manufacturing, construction, electricity, gas, water and sanitary services.
   M = Manufacturing.
   S = Services. Transport and communication, trade, banking, insurance and real estate, ownership of dwellings, public administration, defence, services not elsewhere stated.
   2. GDP from 1950 to 1969 at constant 1959 prices, and GDP from 1970 to 1981 at constant 1970 prices, for the Central Bank series.
   The new series is at 1970 prices throughout.

55 percent in 1980.

The annual growth rate of the agricultural sector was 2.78 percent for 1950 to 1981. During this period, the share of the agricultural workforce had declined from 53.0 percent to 45.8 percent. The corresponding growth rate for the manufacturing sector was 4.83 percent. Its share of the workforce increased from 10.1 percent to 12.0 percent. Both agriculture and manufacturing contributed almost equally to the rate of increase of total output during 1963-1970. This pattern changed during the 1971-81 period when agriculture led manufacturing in growth and had a greater impact. (See Table 13).

Calculations of labor productivity are rendered difficult and unreliable owing to wide discrepancies in the data derived from different sources. The census data for 1981 show rates of growth for the workforce over the period 1971 to 1981 which seem to be seriously understated and, therefore, unacceptable. Data derived from the socio-economic surveys of 1969-70 and 1980-81 provide a more reliable set of data as these are derived from four quarterly rounds of data gathered over a year which can capture seasonal variations and economic activity during a representative period. Comparable socio-economic surveys are available only after 1969-70. Even for those available the methodology and definitions are not identical. Therefore, these surveys should not be treated as firm estimates, but as broad indications of the trends. Tables 14 and 15 present the contrasting set of data obtained from both the census and the socio-economic surveys.

According to census data, between the year 1963 and 1971, the total employed workforce grew at an annual average rate of 1.67 percent. The rate declined to 1.22 percent during the 1971-81 period. The data from the socio-economic surveys however, suggest a growth rate of 2.8 percent for the period 1970-81. As against an annual rate of growth of aggregate labor productivity of 3.30 percent in the 1971-81 period, according to the census data, the socio-economic surveys reveal a more modest growth of 1.6 percent.

The productivity of labor was different across the sectors. In 1963, the transport and communication sector had the highest labor productivity, Rs. 9.4 thousand in 1970 prices. This was nearly six times larger than the sector with the lowest labor productivity, agriculture. However, during the period 1963-71, the productivity of

Table 13. Sectoral Growth Rates 1963-1981;
Computed Averages for Selected Sub-Periods

Time period	Annual Average Growth Rate %		
	Agriculture	Manufacturing	Total Output (GDP)
1963-1970	4.03 (0.98)	8.65 (1.30)	4.18 (0.57)
1971-1976	0.91 (1.51)	1.89 (1.45)	2.31 (0.68)
1977-1981	6.18 (1.74)	4.90 (1.16)	6.16 (0.59)
1971-1981	3.71 (1.37)	3.25 (1.02)	4.06 (0.75)
1963-1981	3.61 (0.87)	5.53 (1.00)	4.11 (0.48)

Source: See Table 1.

Note: Standard errors in parentheses.

the transport and communication sectors grew much more slowly than in the other sectors. By 1971, the utilities, trade, mining, and the banking and insurance sectors still maintained significant productivity advantages over the other sectors. Agriculture continued to provide the largest number of earning opportunities, nearly 28 percent of the new employment created between 1970 and 1981. Manufacturing contributed 16 percent.

The growth rate of employment was fastest in mining, construction, banking, trade and commerce, and manufacturing in that order, and ranged from 6.5 percent to 3.7 percent for 1970-81. The growth rate of agricultural employment was lower at 1.5 percent. The agricultural workforce has grown steadily over the period 1963-81. The extension of the land frontier and new settlements have contributed significantly to this growth. The employment creation in agriculture is likely to diminish in the future with the completion of the major irrigation schemes. The employment of the new entrants to the workforce will increasingly depend on the manufacturing and other sectors.

The treatment of unemployment is important in assessing the changes in productivity. Between 1963 and 1971, the rate of unemployment increased rapidly to about 13 percent of the workforce. The levels of unemployment were highest in the period 1970-77, rising to above 20 percent. According to available data, the higher economic growth after 1977 reduced unemployment substantially. According to some estimates, the unemployment rate still remains around 16 percent. Increased productivity, therefore, will have to be viewed together with high levels of unemployment. Once again the comparison of unemployment at different times is complicated by changes in definitions and measurement.

The share of GDCF in GDP (both in nominal and real terms) remained relatively stable at around 15 percent during the period 1963-1971. It rapidly increased to well over 25 percent by 1981. For 1963-1971, the incremental capital output ratio (ICOR) was 3.7. It increased to 4.5 for 1971-81. During the eary 1970's productivity in both domestic and export agriculture declined, pushing up the ICORs derived from overall estimates of capital formation and growth. In the post-1977 period, large outlays for capital intensive projects with relatively long gestation periods or low net value added as in the case of housing, contributed to this increase.

The Transformation of Agriculture

Although the structural change in terms of the sectoral composition of GDP has been marginal, there have been important changes and shifts in output within sectors. The most important changes occurred in agriculture. The value added from the smallholder sector producing for the domestic market rapidly outgrew that of the commercially organized plantation sector producing for export.

The paddy and other import substituting food crop subsectors played a dominant role in this transition. The most important feature of this change was the decline in the import dependency for the staple food item, rice. In 1963, the food import bill was equivalent to 40 percent of total export earnings. In 1975, food imports reached a peak level of 64 percent of export earnings, then declined sharply to only 16.5 percent in 1982. The paddy sector thus became vital for the economy.

Between 1952 and 1976, the total annual production of paddy increased from 28.9 million bushels to 60.3 million bushels.[5] Although this implies an annual rate

---

[5] Hussain, S.M. "Sectoral Analysis of Paddy Production, Marketing and Processing in Sri Lanka", Ministry of Planning & Economic Affairs, Development Planning Unit, June 1977.

Table 14. Estimates of Total Labor Productivity and Growth 1963-1981

	1963	1970[a]	1971	1981	1981[a]	1963-1971	1971-1981	1970-1981[a]
						Annual Growth Rate		
Real Output								
GDP at 1970 prices (Rs. million)	9,470	12,947	12,844	20,072	4.737	3.9	4.6	4.1
Workforce (millions)	3.195	3.595	3.649	4.119	5.575[1]	1.7	1.2	2.6
Labor force (millions)	3.451	4.146	4.488	4.882	4.237	3.3	0.8	2.7
Real Labor Productivity (Rs)	2,964	3,601	3,520	4,873		2.2	3.3	1.5

Sources: GDP Data, see Table 1.
1960, 1971, 1981 Labor force data — Department of Census & Statistics, 1971, "Census of Population, Sri Lanka 1971, General Report", Colombo, and Department of Census and Statistics 1981, Preliminary Release No. 4.

Notes: (a) 1970 and 1981 figures from Socio-Economic Survey of the Census Department 1969-70 and 1980-81.
(1) Labor force estimated at an annual increase of 120,000 in 1970, growing to 135,000 in 1981.
GDP does not contain value of dwellings.
Growth rates are average annual values based on uniform growth over the period.

Table 15. Sectoral Productivity and Growth 1963-1971

| Sector | Productivity in Rs. '000s | | | | | Average Annual Growth % | | |
	1963	1970	1971	1981	1981[a]	1963-1971	1971-1981	1970-1981[a]
1. Agriculture, Forestry & Fishery	1.57	1.91	1.89	2.69	2.30	2.3	3.6	1.7
2. Mining & quarring	5.21	2.47	8.56	18.45	11.31	6.4	8.0	12.2
3. Manufacturing	3.06	4.17	4.76	5.38	3.94	5.7	1.2	-0.5
4. Construction	4.72	6.12	6.84	8.69	4.73	4.7	2.4	-2.2
5. Electricity, water, gas & sanitation	7.69		9.41	15.43		2.5	5.1	
6. Transport & communication	9.40	8.37	8.23	10.82	10.9	-1.6	2.8	2.5
7. Wholesale & retail trade	7.29	9.67	8.88	10.23		2.5	1.4	
8. Banking, insurance & real estate	5.58		6.66	10.16	9.007	2.2	4.3	-0.6
9. Public Administration & other services	3.40	4.93[1]	4.38	6.26	6.90[1]	3.2	3.6	4.1

Source: See Table 4.

Notes: Productivity is in 1970 constant Rs.
The productivity growth rates are the compound average over the period.
In 1963, 175,000 persons, in 1971, 313,000, and in 1981, 386,000 persons were not classified according to their sectoral employment.

[1] Includes Electricity, water, gas and sanitation.

of growth of less than 3 percent, the growth rate up to 1970 was a very healthy average of over 5 percent. Recurrent drought and steep increases in fertilizer price after 1973, caused a nearly 4 percent decline during the 1970-76 period. After 1976, however, paddy production began a rapid increase again. By the end of 1983, paddy output had doubled the 1976 level, a nearly 10 percent annual rate of growth. Land productivity in the paddy sector shows a significant positive time trend for the 1952-76 period. It had increased at a rate of about 2.0 percent during the period 1952-53 to 1965-66.[6] The rate increased to 2.7 percent during the 1966-67 to 1975-76 period. Fertilizer use and rainfall have been identified as critical variables affecting the land productivity across locations.[7] Paddy yields have increased from approximately 2,400 kilograms per hectare in the early 1970s to about 3,500 kg in 1985. Well irrigated lands are estimated to have a potential of 10,000 kg per hectare.

The policies for agriculture, especially for paddy, seem to have had conflicting objectives. Both production and consumption were supported. Demand for consumption was supported, by price ceilings and consumption subsidies. Supply was stimulated by guaranteed price schemes. The package of these policies and the infusion of new technology and inputs led to notable productivity increases in agriculture.

Around 1967, in response to the worsening external payments, Sri Lanka embarked upon a further import substitution program in agriculture which included chillies, onions, potatoes and pulses. Except for a diversified market-oriented smallholding agriculture in the North, domestic agriculture was dominated by the paddy sector. Importation of a wide range of food items strained an over-burdened external payments situation. Developing an incentive system to promote local production through import substitution was an unavoidable step. Under these arrangements, the country was able to attain self-sufficiency in many food items. It must be acknowledged that the pursuit of self-sufficiency has been costly. World Bank estimates (1986) paddy production costs in the expensive Mahaweli Irrigation Scheme are a multiple of the production cost in nearby rice exporting countries, like Burma and Thailand.

In contrast to the performance of the domestically oriented smallholders sector, that of the export-oriented plantation sector has been disappointing. In 1960, the three plantation crops, tea rubber and coconut accounted for about 45 percent of value added in agriculture. By 1984, the faster growth of the smallholder agriculture and the relatively inelastic international demand for plantation output, resulted in halving the plantation sector's contribution to agricultural value added. The plantation sector has always been vitally important for the country's foreign earnings. It contributed more than 90 percent of total merchandise exports during the 1960s. Tea alone was responsible for about 60 percent of the total. During the 1970s, the relative importance of tea declined. By the end of the 1970s, the share of the plantation sector fell to 58 percent with tea contributing only 35 percent. The trend has continued during the early 1980s.

The plantation sector has also been an important source of revenue for the government. For the fiscal year 1962-63, export duties from plantation crops amounted to about 17 percent of total government revenue. By 1970-71, the

---

[6] Computed from Hussain, S.M., *Ibid*. p. 24.
[7] *Ibid.*, p. 66.

proportion had fallen to 8 percent, partly due to the dual exchange rate system. Plantation sector exports are defined as "traditional" and were valued at the low exchange rate. However, plantation exports became an important source of revenue once again with the unification of the exchange rate and with the high commodity prices in the late 1970s and the early 1980s. In 1980, export duties on plantation crops provided one-quarter of total government revenue with tea continuing as the largest single source.

Tea production reached a maximum level of 503 million lbs. in 1965 and then experienced a gradual decline to an average of 437 million lbs. for the 1975-84 period. Land productivity increased by about 8 percent during 1961-70. During the 1971-81 period, land productivity declined by about 5 percent from 803 lbs. per acre to 765 lbs. per acre, which is only approximately 60 percent of the yield obtained in other countries such as Kenya and India.

The situation for rubber was somewhat different. The rubber tree stock was rapidly replaced with new high yielding varieties. The total acreage was reduced significantly and productivity increased substantially, yet current average yields are 140 kg per hectare, compared with the average yields of 1,000 kg in Malaysia and with the potential of 2,000 kg for newly available clones.

The situation of coconut production is again different. Smallholders dominated this sub-sector. During the period 1960-71, the annual coconut output averaged 2,600 million nuts (S.E. 62). However, a combination of factors, including weather, reduced fertilizer application and plant disease, reduced the average output to 2,184 million nuts (S.E. 63) from 1973 to 1984. The potential yield per hectare is 6,600 nuts as against the current yields of 4,400.

Industrial growth

During the three decades from 1950 to 1980, the manufacturing sector contributed an almost constant share of GDP, but its composition changed significantly. (See Table 17).

In 1960, one-thord of the manufacturing output was the processing of tea, rubber and coconut. Value added in the processing industries in real terms increased upto 1960 and then, slowly declined.[8] In 1981, it accounted for only 12 percent of real value added in manufacturing. During the 1960-1981 period, output of the organized factory sector rose from less than one half to over two-thirds of real value added in manufacturing. Meanwhile, cottage industry, which accounted for only 7 percent in 1960, grew to 11 percent by 1981, comparable in size to that of the plantation processing sector.

Consumer goods accounted for the major share of industrial production. However, the proportion of such goods in total industrial production in nominal terms declined from nearly two-thirds in 1960 to less than one half in 1973. Various food items and cigarettes, soaps, cosmetics and finished textiles accounted for the major share of consumer goods, especially after the petroleum refinery came into operation. Products such as animal feed and coconut products, which dominated the intermediate industrial goods sector in the 1960s, quickly relinquished that position to petroleum products. The investment goods components of industry was dominated

---

[8] Based on data from Savundranayagam. T. *op. cit.*

Table 16. Relative Importance of the Plantation Sector in Total Exports, 1960-1982

	1960	1961	1965	1970	1971	1975	1980	1982
1. Export volume index	92	95	111	107	104	107	99	112
2. Proportion of Tea in total export value (%)	61	66	62	55	59	49	35	30
3. Proportion of plantation crops in export value (%)	96	96	92	89	99	76	58	56

Sources: Kurukulasuriya, G.I.O.M. "Macro-Economic Stabilisation Income Distribution and Poverty – Sri Lanka, Part II". Marga Institute, 1985, p. 21; and Central Bank of Ceylon, "Review of the Economy," 1977, 1979, and Annual Reports 1964, 1967, 1974, 1977, 1979.

Note: Proportions based on current f.o.b. export values.

Table 17. Value Added in Industrial Production Proportion
of Each Category in Selected Years

Category	1961	1970	1975	1978	1984[a]
1. Manufacture of food, beverages and tobacco	50.7	45.8	30.0	43.9	43.2
2. Textiles wearing apparel and leather industries	15.3	13.7	16.9	6.9	12.0
3. Manufacture of wood and wood products	1.1	1.1	2.0	2.0	3.2
4. Manufacture of paper and paper products	2.3	2.0	4.9	6.1	3.6
5. Manufacture of chemicals, petroleum, rubber and plastics	14.3	21.3	31.5	16.9	19.2
6. Manufacture of metallic mineral products (except petroleum and coal)	7.2	6.8	5.8	12.5	9.6
7. Basic metal products	0.5	0.7	2.4	1.8	0.2
8. Manufacture of fabricated metal products	8.5	8.1	5.9	9.4	8.5
9. Manufactured products (not elsewhere stated)	0.1	0.5	0.6	0.3	0.5
Total	100.0	100.0	100.0	100.0	100.0
Nominal value added (Rs. million)	962.0	1,134.9	3,320.	3,109.	11,158.

Sources: Central Bank of Ceylon *Annual Report* 1973, and *Review of the Economy* 1975, 1984.

Note: (a) Provisional.

by cement and cement-based products like asbestos cement sheets and building materials.

Up to the early 1970s, the main thrust of the industrial effort was import substitution. The State enterprises played the dominant role in industrial enterprises including cement, paper, plywood, ceramics, textiles, petroleum products and fertilizer. In the early 1960s, the private sector was encouraged to move into manufacturing through a wide range of incentives which included protection of markets from imports together with tax holidays and other fiscal concessions. Industrialization based on import substitution, however, soon ran into serious problems. Most of the new industries, particularly those in the private sector, had a high import content, and with growing foreign exchange shortages, it became increasingly difficult to maintain an adequate supply of imported raw materials. For many types of industries, the efficient plant sizes meant production capacity much in excess of local demand, One way out of the predicament would have been to use surplus capacity for exports. However, within the prevailing trade and industrial policy regime, industries had neither the incentives nor the ability to generate the efficiencies which would have made them internationally competitive. Foreign resource constraints prevented technological improvements. Competitiveness was hampered by restricted entry, and product quality suffered severely under the protectionist policies.

It is only in the 1970s that a coordinated effort was made to promote export-oriented industries. The government has had some initial success in increasing the flow of foreign investment into the export sector. A package of incentives has been offered to both local and foreign enterprises and an export processing zone has been established. Exports in manufactured goods have increased from US$67 million in 1975 to US$496 million in 1985. Nearly 60 percent of this increase came from textiles and apparels. The export sector in manufacturing, however, remains quite vulnerable. It is heavily dependent on textiles and garments, which are subject to protectionist barriers in the developed countries. Government has not yet developed a comprehensive industrial policy which can overcome the problems of the highly protected industrial structure that has grown out of past strategies and which could appropriately balance import substitution with export promotion.

The rapid expansion of public enterprises outpaced the development of managerial and technical capacity. Nationalization of private industry during 1970-77 imposed added strains on this capacity. By 1975, some public enterprises had reached disappointing levels of performance. Most operated well below capacity. Problems with raw material supply, poor product quality, turnover of staff, weak growth in domestic demands and subordination of professional management to political decision-making, all contributed to this situation. With growing unemployment, pressures to use the investment already made as a base to provide jobs to the growing labor force were strong. Pricing policies in the public sector were consumer-oriented and combined with inefficiencies of operation, which left little room for the generation of surpluses. As a result, the public sector relied heavily on the government subsidies to offset its losses and became a serious burden on the government budget.

Resource Mobilization and Development Policies

From Independence to the Mid-Seventies

Sri Lanka (then Ceylon) emerged as an independent nation with an economy highly dependent on external trade. Imports and exports amounted to approximately 65 percent of GDP in 1950. It was almost exclusively dependent on tea, rubber, and coconuts for foreign exchange earings. Food imports amounted to about 50 percent of merchandise imports. Sri Lanka imported approximately two-thirds of her domestic requirements for the main staple, rice, and was entirely dependent on imported supplies in the case of several other major food items, such as sugar, wheat, wheat flour, and processed milk. However, during this period Sri Lanka enjoyed a favorable balance of payments. Her current account was in surplus and external reserves amounted to the equivalent of about one year's imports. Public expenditures were also managed within the revenues available and the government had no need to resort to deficit financing of the budget.

By the end of the 1950s, however, the balance of payments ran into heavy deficits. This dramatic reversal can be attributed to two factors. Externally, the terms of trade began to deteriorate steadily despite significant improvements in growth and productivity in the export sector. The Central Bank of Ceylon has calculated that the increment to GDP measured in constant prices during the period 1959-65 had to be reduced by approximately 19 percent in order to adjust for the adverse effects of the terms of trade. The decline continued in the two decades that followed with a brief upturn during the period 1976-78, and again during the years 1983 and 1984. Sri Lanka was not able to make the necessary diversification of its export sector. Internally, government revenue depended critically on the export sector. Although, the balance of payments deteriorated and began imposing severe constraints on the government budget the government continued to keep public expenditure at the same levels. Government had to resort to heavy deficit financing through borrowings from the Central Bank. During most of this period, the government was able to contain the inflationary impact of these borrowings by running down external reserves and maintaining supplies to match the demand created by the government budget. At the beginning of the 1960s, however, the country moved into a prolonged economic crisis.

Within these overriding constraints, Sri Lanka was able to mobilize domestic resources at a level which was somewhat higher than that of the other three countries. Gross domestic savings were about 12 percent of GDP in the period 1950-60, and rose to approximately 16 percent by the end of the 1960s. The rate of domestic savings declined in the 1970s, particularly in the mid-70s, when the economy suffered under the adverse impact of higher oil prices. National savings inclusive of private remittances from abroad have once again risen to a level of 16 to 18 percent in the 80s. Gross domestic investment was not much above the level of domestic savings during the period prior to 1965, because external capital flows were relatively insignificant. As a proportion of GDP, gross domestic capital formation was 14 to 15 percent. In the period 1965-70, with the large inflow of external aid, gross domestic investment rose to about 20 percent of GDP.

In the post-1977 period, the rate of gross domestic investment averaged around 27 percent. The investment ratio reached a record level of 33 percent in 1980. The post-1977 investment performance was largely due to the massive increase in the flow of external capital, mainly concessional aid. A significant share of the capital formation was in the public sector. It was about 50 percent in the 1950s, and this declined to 40 percent in 1965 and to 30 percent in 1970. The share once again rose to more than 50 percent in the late 70s.

Government revenue as a percentage share of GDP was relatively high even in the early 1950s. It rose from 14.6 percent in 1950 to 21 percent in 1960 and continued to hover around the same figure with minor fluctuations. In the post-1977 period, it reached 26 percent in 1978, then declined to about 17 percent in 1982, and again rose to about 21 percent in 1985. Government expenditure, however, rapidly expanded. By the end of the 1950s, government revenue was barely sufficient to finance the recurrent expenditure in the budget. The increasing budgetary deficit was financed by expanded domestic and foreign borrowing.

As a low-income country, Sri Lanka was able to mobilize a fairly high level of government revenues because the country had a sizeable plantation sector which was commercially developed and organized in formal enterprises within easy reach of taxation and fiscal measures. It gave the government the necessary resources to make substantial investments in the economic and social infrastructure. This was a key factor which contributed to the unique mix of social and economic development in Sri Lanka.

The response to the deteriorating balance of payments during the 1960s was essentially a withdrawal from the open market economy into a system of exchange controls, regulations, and import licensing. During the period 1965-70, some efforts were made to move out of a strictly regulated system by introducing a dual exchange rate and enabling market forces to operate more freely in the economy.

Table 18. Industrial Exports 1975-85

(Unit: US$ million)

	1975	1980	1985[a]
Food, Beverages and Tobacco of which:	5.64	18.98	19.66
Fish and Fish Products	(3.13)	(14.95)	(17.25)
Textiles and Wearing Apparel of which:	3.49	110.45	290.81
Garments	(3.30)	(109.38)	(283.50)
Essential Oils	0.96	—	—
Chemical Products	1.58	4.25	12.44
Petroleum Products of which:	50.03	188.86	138.70
Naphtha	(8.09)	(38.71)	(27.40)
Bunkers and Aviation Fuel	(41.74)	(119.79)	(83.20)
Fuel Oil	(0.20)	(30.36)	(28.10)
Leather, Rubber, Wood and Ceramics	3.10	15.00	26.49
Other	2.12	4.56	7.96
Total Manufacturing	66.92	342.10	496.06

Source: The Central Bank of Sri Lanka.

[a] Provisional.

Table 19. Domestic and National Savings 1960-1985

(Unit: Rs. million)

	1960	1970	1980	1984	1985
1. G.D.P. at market prices	6,651	13,664	66,527	153,746	159,787
2. Investment	997	2,589	22,465	39,718	41,331
3. Investment as % of GDP	18.6	17.9	33.7	25.8	25.8
4. Domestic savings (2 − 3)	799	2,159	7,443	30,576	21,915
5. Domestic savings ratio (4 as % of 1)	12.0	15.8	11.2	19.9	13.7
6. Net private transfers	−31	−5	2,260	7,031	7,298
7. Net factor income from abroad			−482	−3,401	−3,410
8. National savings (4 + 6)	768	2,154	9,271	24,206	25,803
9. National savings ratio (8 as % of 1)	11.5	15.8	14.0	20.2	16.1

Source: Central Bank *Annual Reports.*

These trends were, however, halted when a leftist government assumed office in 1970 and the emphasis shifted towards policies in which the government played a dominant role in regulating the economy. During the mid 1960s and the first half of the 1970s, with the increasing pressure on the balance of payments, governments of the right and the left began to seek external assistance. Concessional external aid became an increasingly important factor for the management of the balance of payments as well as for the government investment program.

Despite its economic problems, Sri Lanka made far-reaching social advancements that were exceptional for a low income country. All governments accorded high priority to social welfare. The three major programs which formed the bases of the social welfare system were the distribution of a subsidized food ration, a public system of free medical care, and free universal education from the primary to the tertiary stages. These services covered the entire population with the exception of the resident labor of Indian descent in the plantations. The social policies resulted in dramatic improvements in the physical quality of life. Infant mortality fell, and the crude death rate declined (Table 20). Adult literacy rose to approximately 85 percent by the end of the 1970s. Following an increase in population growth during the 1950s when mortality declined, birth rates began to decline steadily from 34.1 in 1963 to 24.8 in 1984, and population growth rate dropped. Thus, social policies promoted significant demographic changes favorable for development.

Table 20. Social Indicators for Sri Lanka

Social Indicators	1953	1963	1971	1981	1984
Population (in thousands)	8,098.6	10,582.0	12,689	14,850	15,599
Crude Birth rate (per 1,000 population)	39.4	34.1	30.0	28.0	24.8
Crude Death rate (per 1,000 population)	10.9	8.5	7.7	6.0	6.5
Infant mortality (aged 0-1 years per 1,000 live births)	71	56	45	37.0 (1980)	25
Rate of growth of population	3.0	2.4	1.8	1.4	
Life expectancy at birth (year)	58	63.5	65.25	69.0	
Literacy (percentage)	69.0	76.9	78.5	86.3	87

Sources: Dept. of Census and Statistics — *Statistical Abstract of Ceylon*, 1955, 1965, 1977.
   Central Bank of Ceylon — *Sri Lanka Socio-Economic Data*, 1983.
   Central Bank of Ceylon — *Report on Consumer Finances and Socio-Economic Survey*, 1953, 1963 and 1978-79.
   World Bank — *World Development Report*, 1983.

The Post-1977 Orientation

Decisive changes in development policy came with the change of government in 1977. The new right of center government initiated major economic reforms. Large parts of the system of controls and regulations were dismantled, subsidies were reduced or removed, and administered prices were replaced by the market prices.

The liberalization was accompanied by a review of some of the components of the subsidy schemes. The food subsidy was replaced by a more discriminatory food rationing scheme, followed by a food stamp program. In many other areas such as in transport, petroleum, and food items such as flour and milk, the subsidy which had been maintained by previous governments was removed and market prices allowed to prevail. This step was to have important budgetary implications. With these changes, incentives through the price system began to take effect.

The new policies enhanced the role of the private sector. The public enterprises were brought under a regime requiring them to operate as profitable ventures, and a combination of measures were implemented, such as the removal of subsidies, breakup of large enterprises into several competing units, participation of the private sector through management contracts and consultancy arrangements, and privatization of the capital structure.

The new government and its policies were acceptable to prospective donors, and the country was able to mobilize unprecedented levels of concessional finance. Two important upswings in the price of commodity exports, and the large and growing volumes of foreign earnings of Sri Lankans working abroad, especially in the Middle East, resulted in a favorable external resource situation. But the bulk of the increase in external resources came from the development assistance given by the consortium of aid-giving countries. This was supplemented by a small flow of foreign investment and commercial borrowing. Foreign aid and borrowing provided financing for approximately 35 to 40 percent of imports and for 38 percent of national investment during the period 1978-84.

Under the new policies, the country experienced the highest rate of growth in the post-independence period. There was a rapid increase in capital formation which rose from 16 percent of GDP in the 1970-77 period to 28 percent for the period 1978-84. The liberalization was accompanied, however, by large deficits in the current balance of payments and by an unprecedented rate of inflation over 30 percent in certain years. The inflation was partly due to heavy budget deficits financed through Central Bank borrowings. The government was, however, able to bring these adverse developments under control by reducing the level of expansionary expenditure. The overall health and viability of the economy seems to have improved in recent years.

The economic performance during the 1978-84 period demonstrates that the mixture of domestic adjustments and international support enabled the economy to shift from growth retardation to rapid growth. Her capacity to undertake adjustments was largely due to the substantial balance of payments support from abroad. Sri Lanka avoided cutting back on consumption, and protected the major social gains. The resource flows from outside enabled the country to retain the core of the welfare system, while reducing subsidies and shifting to market-oriented regime.

The expansion of the economy in the post-1977 period was, however, accompanied by a widening trade gap and a large current account deficit. During the late 1970s, and early 1980s, Sri Lanka became heavily dependent on aid. The debt service ratio rose from 15 percent in 1977 to 26 percent in 1985. The debt service ratios in 1986 and 1987 are estimated to rise to nearly 30 percent. Despite the high rates of economic growth, the economy has not made any significant progress in diversifying the export sector.

Meanwhile, the ongoing ethnic violence has had serious consequences for implementation of development programs like the Mahaweli Diversion Scheme. Tourism has suffered a serious set back. The flow of foreign investment has shown a marked decline. Above all, there has been an unprecedented increase in defense expenditures from less than 1 percent of GDP in the mid-70s to nearly 6 percent in 1985.

Another unsatisfactory feature is the productivity of capital. With an average gross domestic investment of 27.7 percent for the period 1978-84, the average annual rate of growth has been approximately 6.1 percent, yielding a capital-output ratio of 4.5. The investment mix during this period contained costly outlays on social infrastructure like housing or projects with long gestation periods like the Mahaweli Diversion Scheme. These contributed to the high ICOR. Efficiency in the management and implementation of investment has also been a critical variable limiting the performance of the economy.

Potential and Prospects for Future Growth

The potential for economic growth in Sri Lanka can first be examined in terms of the macro-economic aggregates relating to investment and output. During the period 1978-84, the economy was able to maintain the rate of investment around 28 percent of GDP, achieving an annual rate of GDP growth about 6 percent. Assuming that domestic savings will average around 18 percent of GDP and that it would be possible to mobilize external resources including private remittances up to about 7 percnt of GDP, the economy could still sustain a rate of investment of 25 percent. With greater efficiency in the use of resources, growth rates could reach 6 to 7 percent. Such a growth scenario is not beyond the realm of feasibility. It would be prudent, however, to plan for a phased decline in the flow of external aid to about 4 percent of GDP, and to allow for some decrease or at least leveling of private remittances. To maintain the growth rate unchanged, this requires a corresponding increase in the export earnings.

The current account deficit in the balance of payments, excluding official transfers has ranged from 15 percent of GDP in 1982 to 3 percent in 1984, which was an exceptionally favorable year for exports of tea. If we take 1983 as a normal year, the external resource gap was about 11 percent. If the growth scenario is to be realized, export earnings would have to grow from about 22 percent of GDP (the level achieved in 1985) to about 26 percent of GDP. If this higher level is to be reached in five years, there has to be an overall increase of about 50 percent in export income between 1983 and 1989. This would enable the country to maintain the projected rates of growth while avoiding excessive foreign commercial borrowing. The import substitution program in sugar and milk foods can make a contribution, but the trade gap can hardly be reduced by such means. The maintenance of growth rates of 5 to 6 percent, therefore, depend on export earnings from other industrial sectors.

Agriculture is still the largest commodity producing sector, and the growth of the economy will depend heavily on the performance of this sector. The possibilities of extending the frontier of cultivated land are limited to approximately to 400,000 acres of irrigated land. The increase in agricultural output has to come from increased productivity of which the potential is substantial.

Given the improved irrigation system and better educated farmers, smallholder agriculture has the capacity for steady growth. Present paddy yields average about 3,000 kilograms per hectare. A modest estimate is that yields can increase by 50 percent. If this target is to be achieved by 2000, the estimated annual rate of increase in rice output is about 2.8 percent. This would be considerably more than the increase needed to keep pace with the increase in population of 1.5 percent. This may leave room for several options, including substitution of rice for flour, shifting paddy land into alterntive uses or cultivation of special rice varieties for export.

Meanwhile, improvements in the irrigation system could lead to the release of land for purposes other than paddy culture. Multiple cropping going beyond the double-cropping could lead to substantial gains in total agricultural output. Perennial crops could also be introduced into the dry zone and raise the productivity of a large area of agricultural land where the present irrigation system cannot be extended.

The plantation sector offers many possibilities for substitution and diverting land from its present use. Better management and new technology like high yielding varieties can lead to substantial increase in land productivity. It has been estimated that the present amount of tea could be obtained from one-third of the area under cultivation. If the present stock is replaced progressively by high yielding, vegetatively propagated tea, a large block of land could be released for other crops. Unless substantial increases in demand arise from new processing needs or export markets, it is inevitable that land will have to be released from the present uses to alternative crops. Owing to the inelasticity of demand in the international market, productivity gains do not always lead to a significant increase in total earnings. Inflexibility in land use will impose increasing opportunity costs, especially in mid-elevation tea, where alternative cash crops are emerging. However, a long-term strategy for tea will require some measures of coordination with other tea growing countries, particularly India and China. The domestic markets as well as the productive capacities of these two giants could be a critical factor in determining the international prices for tea. Reducing acreage for tea in Sri Lanka will lead to the diversification of the estate sector. New and various opportunities for income and employment are necessary for this sector. In the rubber subsector, higher yields do not necessarily have the same implications as in tea. The demand for rubber is more elastic, and several stages of processing could be undertaken within the domestic economy.

Another issue in plantation is the unused capacity in rubber and coconut land. Animal husbandry or intensive agriculture like floriculture have been adopted only on a small scale. They can be expanded to a larger scale to increase productivity of the plantation tree crops, particularly coconut.

Thus, it is clear that the agricultural sector can make a major contribution to GDP growth in the next two decades. There are, however, two constraints. First is the limited size of the domestic market for crops like sugar, pulses, cotton and lentils. The internal market is not likely to generate demand at the growth rate of 4 to 5 percent for non-plantation agriculture. This means that the agricultural growth will produce an exportable surplus. Second, the contribution that existing agricultural exports can make to additional export earnings is likely to be small. The international market for these products cannot increase with stable or rising prices. Furthermore, the scope for employment generation in agriculture is limited. Though the potential for productivity growth is high, the potential for additional employment is rather poor. If agricultural employment grows at 1 percent, it will create only 16 percent of the new employment required in the next ten years.

In order to maintain the projected rate of growth as well as the creation of employment at an adequate rate, the manufacturing sector, excluding the processing of the three traditional export crops, needs to grow at an annual rate of about 10 percent. This is considerably higher than 7 percent achieved during the period 1978-84.

No consistent industrial strategy has yet emerged which balances production for the domestic market with export promotion. The potential for industrial growth lies in several areas. First, the scope for the internal demand is considerable as per capita incomes increase. Second, the export of manufactures can be expanded, based on specialization appropriate to the factor mix and comparative advantages available to Sri Lanka. This would apply also to all export products — tea, rubber, coconut, food, fibre, gems, spices and minerals like ilmenite and graphite. Processing agricultural products for both the internal market as well as for export will be a very important area of activity. Tree crops and fruits could become a more important component of agriculture if a wider processing base is developed. Third, a larger regional and international market will become accessible as the pattern of comparative advantage changes. This will provide new opportunities also for Sri Lanka's export.

Export-oriented foreign investment and free trade zones will no doubt be an important industrial strategy. This will remain a special area in manufactures like the plantation sector in agriculture. The difficult task will be to ensure that this component promotes linkages and technology transfers in the industrial sector as a whole.

Future prospects for growth depends also on new possibilities for the physical and human resources. One area of such possibilities is the exploration of the coastal and contiguous ocean resources. The present level of production based on this resource is not very large. The exploitation of the resources of this zone would require new technical inputs as well as cooperation with neighboring nations.

As for energy resources, Sri Lanka has virtually exhausted its potential for hydro-electric energy and must move to thermal energy in the 1990s. Efforts to maximize domestic supply of energy from alternative sources, such as biomass, mini-hydro schemes, solar wind could also play a significant role.

The services sector contributes more than half of GDP, so that its efficiency and productivity will be important for the performance of the Sri Lankan economy. Some activities in this sector can strengthen the country's export sector. Examples are regional and international services in banking, insurance, professional and secretarial services. Human resource development could become an important export service in the future. Sri Lanka has been an exporter of manpower covering the entire spectrum ranging from professional skills to unskilled labor and domestic service. The availability of low cost services in health, education and a variety of fields may also offer scope for location of these services within the country to serve an international clientele. Regional cooperation may be essential in this area. The experience and skill gained will be of great value to the domestic economy as well.

Finally, the realization of the growth potential which has been sketched here will depend on the policy framework and the socio-political structure which can effectively release this potential. Past growth has been hamstrung by the policy equivocations of governments that have oscillated between policies predominantly relying on State enterprises and intervention and those relying on the market and private enterprise. The right mix of state and market and the appropriate partnership between the public and private sectors has yet to be evolved. The decisive departure from the regulated welfare-oriented economy in 1977 to a liberal market-oriented economy has produced its own contradictions. One of them is the negative trends in some social indicators such as income distribution. A major part of the past welfare system has, however, been retained and continues to be an important determinant of policy. The appropriate balance between growth and equity will be another major challenge to policy-makers. Above all, the liberalized regime has had little impact in stimulating industrial growth or increasing productivity in the plantation sector. These two factors are crucial for future growth — one for the essential structural changes in the economy; the other for stabilizing and improving the existing resource base. Prevailing policies have tended to favor enterprise in trade rather than in industry. Therefore, a reappraisal of current policies is essential to determine the right mix in several key areas.

BANGLADESH

Growth and Productivity

Bangladesh is poorer than Nepal with an income per capita of US$130, and ranks second from the bottom among the poorest countries in the world. The GDP growth rate was 5.6 percent during the period 1972 to 1984. This relatively high growth, however, reflected a period of recovery during the first few years after Independence, which took advantage of the idle productive capacity during the war. Its recovery began from a level of income significantly lower than that in 1969-70. The high rates of growth in the early years, therefore, reflect this phase of recovery rather than new growth. If the period 1975-76 to 1984-85 is taken separately, the growth rate drops to an annual average of approximately 3.6 percent. Growth of GDP since the mid-70s has fluctuated and dropped to as low as 0.8 and 1.3 percent in certain years. However, the average annual rate of growth of GNP which includes net factor income from abroad, during 1980-81 to 1984-85 was 4.6 percent. The higher rate of growth for GNP in this period was primarily due to the workers' remittances (Table 21).

There were some shifts in the sectoral composition of GDP during the period 1961-83 (Table 22), but the change was not significant. The economy still remains overwhelmingly agricultural. Agriculture contributes nearly half of GDP. The share of the manufacturing sector is only around 10 percent, inclusive of small-scale and cottage industries. The moderate rate of growth of the Bangladesh economy in the recent past was achieved in service sectors, such as trade and catering. It grew at 9.9 percent during this period and had a share of 15.9 percent of GDP in 1983.

Agriculture

Agriculture grew at approximately 2.8 percent per annum during the period 1973-84. The growth rate, however, would be lower if 1969-70 was taken as the base year, because the output of almost all crops was higher in 1969-70 than in 1973. The decline in production between 1969-70 and 1973-74 was approximately 0.74 percent for cereals, 14.5 percent for sugar, 10 percent for tea, and 17.3 percent for

Table 21. Growth Rates of GDP and its Components

Sectors	1960-61 1969-70[1]	1973-74 1983-84[2]
1 Gross Domestic Product	4.0	4.1
2 Population growth rate	2.5[3]	2.3[4]
3 Component sectors		
1 Agriculture, forestry, fishery	2.7	2.8
2 Manufacturing	6.8	5.9
i) Large-scale	5.6	5.4
ii) Small-scale	7.8	6.7
5 Electricity, gas and water	27.5	13.7
4 Construction	25.4	5.9
5 Transport and communication	4.2	4.5
6 Banking and insurance	13.6	4.8
7 Trade and catering	3.3	8.9
8 Other services	5.9	5.5

Source: Country study prepared by the Consultant from Bangladesh, Atiqur Rehman.

[1] At 1959-60 constant factor cost. Computed from Alamgir and Berlage (1974).
[2] At 1972-73 constant factor cost. Computed from World Bank (1984).
[3] 1961-1974.
[4] 1974-1983-84.

Table 22. Composition of GDP and Some Selected Indicators
on Bangladesh Economy

	1961[a]	1974[b]	1982-83
Composition of GDP			
Agriculture	59.9	56.4	48.3
Manufacturing	6.4	11.6	9.8
(Large-scale)	(3.3)	(4.8)	(5.4)
(Small-scale)	(3.1)	(6.8)	(4.4)
Construction	1.8	3.4	3.7
Transport and communication	6.3	7.1	6.9
Trade and catering	11.1	10.0	15.9
Housing	6.3	4.9	4.4
Services	8.2	6.6	7.0
GDP (in Taka million)	14,866[c]	49,321[d]	76,287[d]
Population (million)	50.8	75.4	89.0
Per capita income (US $)	80	100	135

Source: *Ibid.*

[a] Average of 1959-60, 1960-61 and 1961-62 figures.
[b] Average of 1972-73, 1973-74 and 1974-75 figures.
[c] 1960-61 estimated at 1959-60 factor cost.
    Estimates at constant 1972-73 market prices.

Table 23.   Sectoral Share of GDP at Constant (1972-73) Prices

(Unit: %)

Sector	1980-81	1981-82	1982-83	1983-84	1984-85 (P)
1 Agriculture	48.7	48.8	49.3	48.0	47.0
i) Crops	38.6	38.0	38.5	37.3	36.3
ii) Forestry	2.4	2.6	2.6	2.7	2.8
iii) Livestock	4.8	5.1	5.0	4.9	4.9
iv) Fisheries	2.9	3.1	3.2	3.1	3.0
2 Mining and quarrying	0.001	0.002	0.001	0.001	0.001
3 Industry	10.6	10.7	10.1	10.1	10.1
i) Large-scale	6.1	6.1	5.6	5.6	5.6
ii) Small-scale	4.5	4.6	4.5	4.5	4.5
4 Construction	4.0	4.2	4.1	4.7	4.8
5 Power, gas, water and sanitary services	0.3	0.4	0.6	0.6	0.7
6 Transport, storage and communication	6.8	6.7	7.0	6.8	6.8
7 Trade services	9.6	8.7	8.6	8.7	8.8
8 Housing services	7.4	7.5	7.4	7.3	7.2
9 Public administration and defence	3.8	4.0	3.9	4.5	5.0
10 Banking and insurance	1.9	1.8	1.6	1.7	1.7
11 Professional and Miscellaneous services	6.9	7.2	7.4	7.6	7.9
12 GDP at market prices	100.0	100.0	100.0	100.0	100.0

Source: Bangladesh Bureau of Statistics.
Reproduced from *Statistical Pocket Book of Bangladesh* 1984-85.

jute. As for cereal production, the total increase in output on the 1969-70 base for the period 1973 to 1984 was approximately 30 percent, of which one-third was contributed by wheat. Wheat output increased by more than ten-fold from 103,000 tons in 1969-70 to 1,192,000 tons in 1983-84. The remaining two-thirds of the incremental output came from rice. The preponderant part of the increase in rice output resulted from higher yields, while yields and extension of acreage accounted almost in equal measure for the increase in the output of wheat.

Rice contributes nearly three-fourths of the total value added in agriculture. Of the total crop area of 32 million acres, rice accounts for nearly 26 million. The annual rate of growth in productivity has been quite low in the rice subsector. It has risen from 1.11 tons per hectare in the late sixties to 1.32 tons in 1982-83, an annual rate of growth of 1.4 percent. The rate of growth of output was around 2.2 percent for the period 1970-71 to 1983-84, (Table 24). There is evidence that during the second Five-Year Plan 1981-85, grain production has achieved a higher level of productivity. During this period, the average annual rate of growth in agricultural and food grain production increased to 3.5 percent from 2.9 percent during the previous five years mainly due to more intensive cultivation and high yielding varieties. This was supported by the improved infrastructure in irrigation. Drainage and flood control facilities now cover nearly 25 percent of the cultivated area. This is still far from what is needed to provide a stable base for agriculture to cope with unfavorable natural conditions and weather. The situation, however, is now much better than it was in the early 1970s, when less than 10 percent of the cultivated acreage was covered by irrigation, drainage, and flood control.

The potential for growth in the rice subsector can be gauged by the wide gap between the actual and potential yields. The output per hectare in Sri Lanka is approximately two and a half times that of Bangladesh, but in Sri Lanka it is estimated that the optimum yield could be as much as 10 metric tons per hectare, giving a potential of a further three-fold increase. In 1984, food grain imports, largely wheat, accounted for nearly one-fifth of total merchandise imports, or about 3.3 percent of GDP. This figure indicates the scope currently available for import substitution in the food grains sector. In addition, there is the need to increase food production for the increase of population which is growing at the annual rate of 2.6 percent.

Jute is the most important agricultural export item in Bangladesh. In terms of cultivated acreage as well as its contribution to the value added in agriculture, the share of jute is relatively small, but it provides more than half of Bangladesh's merchandise exports. The performance of the jute sub-sector,however,is closely linked to cereals and other crops, because substitution takes place amongst these crops depending on relative prices. During the period 1970-84, the area under jute had dropped from 2.4 to 1.4 million acres and output had fallen by nearly 28 percent. Land productivity, however, had risen by nearly 20 percent. The output of sugarcane, the other major crop also dropped by 8 percent but with no change in land productivity.

Manufacturing

The manufacturing sector contributed approximately 10.1 percent of GDP in 1984-85 (See Table 25). About half of the value added in manufacturing is contributed by large-scale units, while the balance comes from small and cottage industries

Table 24. Trend Rates of Growth in Production of Some Major Crops
(1949-50 to 1983-84)

	1949-50 — 1957-58	1957-58 — 1970-71	1970-71 — 1983-84	1949-50 — 1983-84
Cereals	0.31	3.17	2.90	2.45
Rice	0.34	3.21	2.26	2.32
Aus	4.32	3.58	0.87	2.35
Aman	−0.09	1.48	2.08	1.26
Boro	−1.09	13.90	4.34	8.83
Wheat	0.38	11.50	25.70	13.42
Non-Cereal Food	nil	5.08	0.96	1.48
Pulses	−2.62	2.64	−0.56	−0.51
Oilseeds	3.97	5.04	1.12	1.82
Cash Crops	nil	3.48	nil	1.08
Jute	−2.22	1.45	−0.70	−0.36
Sugarcane	1.83	7.00	0.41	2.71
Tobacco	−2.49	1.45	2.02	0.50
All Crops	0.25	3.34	2.49	2.23

Source: Atiqur Rahman, *op. cit.*

located mostly in rural areas. Although the growth rate from 1973-74 to 1983-84 was estimated as 5.9 percent, this was partly due to the high growth rates during the phase of recovery. The growth rate for the period 1976-77 to 1981-82 appears to have been lower — approximately 4.8 percent. The growth rate for 1981-85 declined to 1.8 percent, with negative rates of growth in some years.[9]

The structure of manufacturing in the modern subsector remains heavily biased toward the production of consumer goods. Textiles, jute and, cotton accounted for nearly two-fifths of the total value added in manufacturing. Food processing comprises 12.5 percent, and chemical and chemical products 21 percent. The performance within the industrial sector has been very uneven. According to output data available, the production of many of the larger subsectors has fluctuated quite widely (Table 26). The performance of many of these industries, such as textiles, paper, sugar, will be largely dependent on the performance of the agricultural sector and would reflect the variations in output in the relative crops. In chemical fertilizers, based on natural gas available in abundance in Bangladesh, there has been a rapid expansion with production increasing from 100,000 tons in 1969-70 to 750,000 tons in 1984-85.

After independence, the industrial sector went through a major program of nationalization and, until recently, the preponderant share of the modern sector in manufacturing has been government owned. Most of the large industrial entities

---

[9] A more recent study by the World Bank has, however, concluded that on a revised production index, the manufacturing sector has grown faster than reflected in the official index — a rate of 5.1 percent for the period 1979-84 as against the official 1.5 percent.

Table 25. Growth of Value Added in Industry (Manufacturing, Mining and Quarrying) at constant 1972-73 prices, for 1976-77, 1981-82 and 1984-85

	Value Added (Taka in Crores)	Rate of Growth (percent)
1. 1976-77	611.8	4.8
1981-82	772.4	
2. 1984-85	816.9	1.8

Source: Bangladesh Bank — *Economic Trends* 1985, Table X1.

in textiles, jute, sugar, cement, fertilizer, paper, steel and energy, were in the public sector. An analysis of the ownership and structure of the industrial sector estimates that in 1978-79, approximately 80 percent of the value added in manufacturing came from the public enterprises. With the new industrial policy announced in 1982, the pace of denationalization has been accelerated. Approximately 31 textile mills, 33 jute mills and more than four hundred other industrial enterprises together with two commercial banks have been divested to the private sector. It is estimated that currently the public sector owns only about 40 percent of the fixed assets and employs not more than 20 percent of the labor force in manufacturing. With the implementation of these measures, the public sector now contains only about 160 industrial entities.[10]

The policy of denationalization has been a response to the low productivity and serious managerial inefficiencies of public enterprises. There have been however, conflicting views regarding the comparative performance of the public and private enterprises after independence. Some analysts have argued that the problems encountered during this period were not necessarily related to the forms of ownership and management but arose from the shortage of managerial skills, as well as the lack of clear directives and policies that could have helped to increase productivity and efficiency in the public enterprises.

The recent privatization of public enterprises and package of market-oriented policies have tried to promote export diversification. The exclusive reliance on jute-based products for exports has created difficulties. Jute is encountering problems, first on the demand side, through competition with synthetic fibres; and second, on the supply side, through competition with rice cultivation. The new policies aimed at maintaining a realistic exchange rate and improving export policy and administration caused a rapid growth of non-traditional exports for the last five years. The share of new exports in total merchandise exports increased from 5 percent in 1973-74 to 33 percent in 1984-85. The increase has been shared almost equally by primary products such as frog-legs, prawns, and shrimps, and manufactures such as leather and leather goods, and, more recently products such as ready-made garments. Each of these categories accounted for about 10 percent of the exports in 1983-84.

With its population of 100 million, the country has a potentially large internal

---

[10] Data obtained from Atiqur Rahman and country reports of World Bank.

Table 26. Production of Major Industrial Commodities Other Than Jute Goods (Public Sector)

Period	Cotton Cloth '000' Metres	Paper Metric Tons	News-print Metric Tons	Sugar Metric Tons	Fertilizers Metric Tons	Chemicals Metric Tons	Glass Sheets '000' Sq. Metres	Iron and Steel Metric Tons
1969-70	54,817	30,907	44,977	94,900	100,623	4,318	512	176,388
1972-73	53,452	20,313	28,806	19,604	216,563	1,565	673	203,939
1973-74	72,583	24,421	27,008	88,906	289,118	2,253	545	201,192
1974-75	77,417	29,485	29,144	100,044	74,053	2,136	532	184,820
1975-76	68,116	18,324	20,314	88,181	286,163	3,143	519	293,295
1976-77	62,292	24,286	14,821	142,258	295,116	3,600	540	328,853
1977-78	75,069	29,982	32,094	178,078	221,615	4,641	704	342,752
1978-79	77,735	31,880	37,820	132,817	300,816	3,807	796	447,656
1979-80	81,254	31,763	41,932	94,720	370,762	4,230	841	306,811
1980-81	78,609	31,819	34,164	145,210	350,976	6,492	623	400,175
1981-82	66,290	30,815	43,207	202,166	356,973	5,312	877	352,057
1982-83	44,262	25,777	30,836	181,495	383,291	5,351	962	127,469
1983-84	36,866	27,540	42,250	151,248	596,919	6,614	1,197	207,318

Source: Nationalised Industries Corporation.

market. This will enable Bangladesh to pursue a strategy which combines industrialization for export with production to meet domestic demand. This, however, requires the adjustment of current policies to increase the productivity of existing units in the public and private sectors. For this purpose, removal of the bottlenecks has high priority. Examples are regulations pertaining to approval of investments, rigidly designed investment schedules, the dual exchange rate system, and import regimes and tariff systems that are excessively protective of inefficient local industries.

In the energy sector, Bangladesh with its resources of natural gas, has the capacity to meet the major part of its commercial energy requirements at a relatively low cost. Gas output has increased by 300 percent between 1975-76 and 1983-84. Sufficient reserves are available to support the substantial development for electricity generation and other industrial use. At present, however, approximately 60 percent of the total energy use in Bangladesh is derived from firewood and other biomass fuels, including jute residues. The excessive dependence on these types of primary energy poses problems in view of the limited resources and the mounting pressure of population. A strategy to substitute natural gas for traditional energy such as biogas and solar energy, becomes critical for an ecologically sustainable process of development. This substitution is linked to a process of modernization of the rural sector which is appropriate for the Bangladesh economy.

Labor Productivity

Overall productivity in terms of GDP and workforce indicates that productivity has grown at an annual rate of approximately 1.4 percent (Table 27). The trends indicate higher productivity growth during the period 1960-70 at 2 percent. There has been a decline in the period 1973-84. This overall decline, however, conceals marked differences in the sectoral growth rates. Productivity in the agricultural sector has risen from a 1.5 percent growth rate during the decade of the sixties to 3.1 percent in the decade 1973-74 to 1983-84. In all other sectors, except in other services, the growth rates have been negative.

The agricultural workforce declined in absolute numbers from 16.8 million in 1974 to 16.3 million in 1983-84. The agricultural sector was unable to absorb new employment. The new workforce was absorbed in other sectors at a pace which outstripped the rate of growth of value added in these sectors. Consequently, there was a decline in productivity in most of these sectors. One factor that may have contributed to the ready absorption of labor in the other sectors like manufacturing, electricity, and water and gas, was the public ownership of large components of these sectors. Open unemployment, as revealed in the census of the labor force survey 1983-84, was low at approximately 2.5 percent for the workforce. The low level of unemployment taken together with the low growth of productivity of labor in the overall economy, as well as the decline in productivity in most sectors other than agriculture, suggests a process of labor absorption where there is a considerable degree of work sharing and underemployment. Another factor which contributes to the low level of open unemployment is the relatively low rate of participation in the workforce arising partly from the fact that, the participation of female population in the workforce is only 8 percent.

Table 27. Absolute Levels and Growth in Productivity

Sectors	Value added/worker (Taka)		Growth Rates	
	1961[1]	1983-84[2]	1960-61 – 1969-70	1973-74 – 1983-84
1 Agriculture, forestry & fishery	647	2,289	1.5	3.1
2 Manufacturing	1,268	3,735	5.0	−1.3
3 Electricity, gas and water	2,136	4,525	30.0	−12.3
4 Construction	3,098	11,370	32.9	−15.0
5 Transport and communication	4,746	4,420	−0.1	−7.7
6 Banking and Insurance	6,450	3,933	−1.1	−6.3
7 Trade services	2,803	3,922	0.9	−5.7
8 Other services	..	..	−2.6	1.7
All sectors	917	2,638	2.0	1.4

Sources: GDP estimates from Alamgir & Berlage (1976) and employment estimates from Preliminary Report on Labor Force Survey 1983/84, BBS (1984).
Reproduced from Atiqur Rahman, ibid, with revisions based on data from Bangladesh Bureau of Statistics for 1983/84.

Notes: Labor force growth rates are available for the years 1961 to 1974 whereas GDP growth rates are available only for the years 1960-61 to 1969-70. Labor force growth rates for the years 1961 to 1974 are assumed as those between the years 1960-61 to 1969-70 for all sectors. Although the sectoral classifications for employed labor force and GDP estimates do not exactly correspond to each other, for simplicity similarity in the classification has been assumed. For example, the 'community and personal services' sector, equated with 'other services' sector.

[1] At constant 1959-60 factor cost.
[2] At constant 1972-73 factor cost.

Mobilization of Resources

In recent years, Bangladesh has sustained the level of total investment at 15 to 16 percent of GDP. This compares with 11 percent in the late 1960s and mid-70s. Domestic savings have been quite low. In the last five years, these have fluctuated between 3.25 percent in 1980-81 and 0.34 percent in 1982-83. On the average it has been only 2 to 3 percent.

Domestic savings have been augmented by remittances from abroad to raise national savings to approximately 6 percent. Aid disbursements, about 9 to 10 percent of GDP, have therefore financed more than 60 percent of the total investment. The debt service ratio increased from 15 to 16 percent of export earnings plus workers' remittances in the early 1980s to 20 percent in the recent years and became as high as 25 percent in 1984-85.[11] This figure includes repayments of IMF

---

[11] Data obtained from publication of Bangladesh Bank, Bangladesh Bureau of Statistics, and country reports of World Bank.

Table 28. Savings/Investment Estimate at Current Prices

(Unit: Taka million)

	1979-80	1980-81	1981-82	1982-83	1983-84	1984-85(P)
1. Net Foreign Assistance[a]	15,713	16,995	22,320	28,733	28,480	31,328
2. Transfers by Bangladesh Nationals abroad[a]		6,190	7,720	14,220	13,760	
3. Domestic savings[a]	5.577	7,574	5,228	976	10,149	10,350
4. Domestic savings as % of GDP[a]	2.82	3.25	1.97	0.34	2.90	2.60
5. Net Foreign Assistance as % of GDP[a]	8.44	7.28	8.42	9.96	8.14	7.86
6. Transfers as % of GDP[a]		2.81	3.07	5.2	4.15	
7. Gross Domestic Investment as % of GDP	14[b] (1979)	17[b] (1980)	17[b] (1981)	14[b] (1982)	16.1[c]	16.2[c]

Sources: (a) Bangladesh Bureau of Statistics.
(b) *World Development Reports, 1982-1984.*
(c) Bangladesh Bank, *Annual Report, 1984-85.*

borrowings. If these are excluded, the debt service ratio drops to about 19 percent.

The foreign exchange earnings of Bangladesh from merchandise trade and private remittances amounted to only 60 per cent of its current external payments. Merchandise exports covered only a little more than one-third of its imports. In the late seventies, Bangladesh became heavily dependent on the remittances of workers in Middle East countries. In 1982-83, private remittances of US$628 million were nearly equal to the merchandise exports of US$687 million, and accounted for about 40 percent of the total earnings on the current account. Although non-traditional exports, excluding jute, tea, leather, and fish have more than doubled during the last five years, export income still depends heavily on jute products, which account for more than 50 percent.

If investment is sustained around the current level of 16 percent of GDP, the resource gap in the external account is unlikely to decrease unless exports are diversified and grow. The capacity to mobilize resources for the government budget has been low, total tax revenue remaining at about 7.8 percent of GDP. Including non-tax revenues, it goes up to 11 percent. The government budget has, however, left a current account surplus of 18 to 20 percent of total current revenues. The pattern of expenditures has permitted the government not to have recourse to deficit financing. This budget, however, corresponds to the low level of investment in the social and economic infrastructure. Any significant improvement in the quality and coverage of public services such as health and education would require higher levels of public expenditure and larger resources of government revenue.

Inflation has been managed with a moderate degree of success in recent years. The consumer price indices in major cities indicate increases of about 9 percent in 1983-84 and 11 percent in 1984-85.[12] The economic management in the period 1983-85 caused some concerns regarding the expansion of liquidity and its effects on prices and the balance of payments. Liquidity expanded much faster than GDP at current prices. But such policies have been reversed soon, and Bangladesh has succeeded in containing inflation and strengthening the balance of payments position.

External and internal factors continue to intensify the vulnerability and uncertainty of the Bangladesh economy. Externally, the main resource flows are subject to wide fluctuations and decisions outside the control of Bangladesh. They include the worker remittances, aid and export of jute products. Jute faces competition with synthetic products; worker remittances have begun to decline; and aid flows depend on policies of donor countries. These problems are compounded by unfavorable natural environment and ecological factors. Bangladesh, situated in the basin of two major rivers encompassing the delta extending into the Bay of Bengal, suffers from both serious flooding and tidal movements. These adversely affect its agriculture in different ways. One leads to inundation and loss of crops, and the other to salination. The full realization of the agricultural potential is crucial to Bangladesh in the medium-term. Success depends on flood control, irrigation, and water management. This, however, is not solely within the control of Bangladesh but requires regional cooperation with the other countries which contain parts of these major river systems: India and Nepal.

Finally, attention needs to be drawn to ICOR. Recent estimates by the World Bank indicate that GDP growth rates may have been higher than those estimated by Bangladesh planners and statisticians. If the growth is approximately 4 percent

---

[12] Bangladesh Bank, *Annual Report*, 1984-85.

for the period 1980-84, the ICOR seems to be about 4. This compares favorably with the ratios for Sri Lanka and Nepal, though the ratio for Pakistan is still lower. Underutilization of existing capacity and inefficiency in the implementation of investment projects may have contributed to the relatively high ICOR in Bangladesh. Even without substantial increases in investment, therefore, there appears to be considerable scope for pushing the rate of growth above prevailing levels.

Social and Demographic Factors

As in the case of Pakistan and Nepal, infant mortality and the crude death rate have remained exceptionally high. Infant mortality was approximately 124 and the crude birth rate was 41 in 1984. The crude death rate was around 15 per thousand.[13] The population has been increasing at approximately 2.5 percent per annum.

Although priority has been accorded to family planning there has been no reversal of rapid population growth. Recent reports indicate that family planning acceptance has declined. If the current rate of population growth is maintained, many problems related to resources are likely to intensify and impair seriously the long-term development effort. According to the population census, the literacy rate for the population aged five and above was 23.8 percent, and for the population aged 15 and above it was 22.7 percent. The adult literacy rate for males was 33 percent as against 11 for females.

The census figures for literacy are much lower than those which might be derived from figures relating to the enrollment in primary school education. The rate of participation in primary schooling was estimated at approximately 49 percent in 1965 and 62 percent in 1983. Female enrollment had risen during this period from 31 percent to 55 percent. If the literacy rate in 1981 is compared with the figure for primary school enrollment in 1965, it implies that a large proportion of children who participated in primary education have dropped out of the school system without acquiring literacy.

Future Prospects

It is unlikely that in the medium-term Bangladesh can mobilize additional resources that would step up the level of investment significantly above the prevailing levels of 16 percent GDP. The prospects for increase in aid are not very promising. With the sharp drop in oil revenues and the cut-back on development projects in the Middle-Eastern countries, private transfers from abroad are likely to stagnate. As for merchandise exports, the main export, jute, will have to continue to cope with the weak international market.

The low level of domestic savings suggests, however, that there is scope for mobilizing larger domestic savings and pushing investment to slightly higher levels. If the external resource flow can be maintained with larger domestic savings, it is possible to consider an optimistic scenario of around 6 percent growth. This would imply a level of total investment around 18 percent of GDP and an incremental capital output ratio around 3. Such an improvement in capital productivity would require a major effort in the efficient management of investments and the fuller use of existing capacities in various parts of the economy, particularly in the agri-

---

[13] The national data from the Bangladesh Demographic Survey give the birth rate for 1984 as 33.6 and the death rate as 11.9. The figures used in this chapter are from the *World Development Report.*

cultural sector which contributes nearly half of GDP. The appropriate model is a viable modern smallholder agriculture. The transformation of the present near-subsistence farming to this type would require infrastructure improvements in cooperation with neighboring countries. There is a need also for a flexible policy framework combining public investments in irrigation with credit and price support. The recent policies reducing fertilizer subsidies and offering rural credit appear to have contributed to a decline in fertilizer use and a reduction in the output of wheat.

Bangladesh agriculture faces the same basic problems as those of the three countries. The task of striking the right balance between the market-oriented incentives and the state interventions is not easy. The land holdings also pose some problems about viability of the minimum units. About 28.5 percent of the holdings are below 1.5 acres, and another 21 percent are between 1.5 acres and 2.5 acres. The present ownership, however, does not give much hope for a significant tenurial reform that would improve the viability of smallholders on a large scale. The Bangladesh smallholding agriculture is preponderantly owner-cultivated and is not subject to major problems of landlordism and tenancy. The rented acreage amounts to approximately 16 percent of the total.[14] However, with the improvement of the irrigation infrastructure and better control of flooding, the stability of the entire agricultural system should lower the land ceiling which is at present considered desirable for efficient production.

Agricultural growth faces the limits of import substitution. Domestic output of cereals met nearly 90 percent of internal demand in 1982-83. Therefore, the scope for increases in output is limited to a small margin of import substitution, raising the levels of people's nutrition and supply of food to the increase in population. This would imply a growth of about 3.5 percent for the next five to ten years, but thereafter such growth would lead to exportable surpluses. Substitution with jute is not an attractive prospect due to the weak international demand for jute. Long-term strategies for agricultural diversification will, therefore, have to form an essential part of the development effort. The development of fisheries, both coastal and marine, as well as livestock will be an important area of agricultural growth for internal demand as well as for export. It should be noted that the daily calorie supply was estimated at only 81 percent of the required minimum in 1983 (*World Development Report*). This indicates that there remains considerable room for improvement in living standards and increasing the domestic consumption of food grains to sustain a high rate of growth in the food grains sector.

The manufacturing sector now contributes only about 10 to 12 percent of GDP but will play a critical role in the growth of the economy. The preceding analysis indicated the importance of export diversification and the contribution that the manufacturing sector could make. At the same time, the domestic market provides considerable scope for import substitution. With a growth rate of 5 to 6 percent and the consequent increases in per capita income, domestic demand will grow for a wide range of consumers' and intermediate goods as well as certain types of capital goods. The latter particularly in the agricultural sector, are irrigation equipment and agricultural machinery. On a narrow base, the industrial sector in Bangladesh includes a few major industries such as paper and newsprint, fertilizer, cement, textiles and sugar. Bangladesh with large reserves of natural gas enjoys a source of relatively low cost energy. Recent trends also indicate that the industrial

[14] Data obtained from Bangladesh Bureau of Statistics; *Statistical Pocket Book of Bangladesh*, 1984-85.

sector has been able to sustain fairly high rates of growth. A recent analysis by the World Bank indicates that these growth rates were higher than what has been reported in the national accounts. In the external sectors, efforts have been made to diversify exports primarily with garments and textiles and reduce the dependence on jute products.

The industrial sector grew around 9 percent in 1984 and 1985. If this is sustained, it appears to be realizable for industry to contribute approximately 20 percent of the annual increment of GDP at about 5 percent. With agriculture growing at around 3.5 percent, other sectors would have to grow at a rate of a little above 5 percent. It would not be difficult for the Bangladesh economy to improve on this scenario. What is needed is a consistent effort to increase productivity of the existing capacities and improve the social infrastructure that has to underpin development.

The reversal of present population trends will be critical for development. This will depend on more durable social improvements in the fields of health and education. Female literacy will play a critical role in creating the conditions for a rapid demographic transition. The participation of females in education has, however, increased steadily and appears to be higher than that of Pakistan. The progressive increase in literacy of the younger generation, particularly the females, will have a positive long-term impact. This would have to be supplemented with effective programs of non-formal education and functional literacy directed at target groups if population policies are to take effect in the short-term. Improvement of the social infrastructure is essential for economic growth and would depend on the country's capacity to mobilize government revenues on an adequate scale.

The scenario of 5 percent growth with a population growth of 2.4 percent, as projected in the *World Development Report,* will result in a per capita income growth of 2.6 percent. This would yield a per capita income of approximately US$200 per head at the turn of the century calculated in 1984 dollar prices. Even after a substantial development effort, therefore, Bangladesh would remain a poor country. Given certain inextricable constraints, there would have to be further efforts in two directions. First, at the international and domestic fronts additional resources are needed to help Bangladesh move along a more rapid path of growth. Second, within the limits of incomes that are realizable, development should be directed to ensure a reasonable quality of life for the population as a whole giving due emphasis to the eradication of absolute poverty and the levels of education, health, nutrition, and housing.

NEPAL

Growth, Productivity, and Resource Mobilization

The annual growth rate of GDP in Nepal is approximately 1.7 percent for the period 1965-73 and 3.1 percent for the period 1973-83. With the population growing at 2 percent during the period 1965-73, per capita income growth was negative during this period. In the 1973-83 period, per capita income appears to have grown at a marginal 0.5 percent rate. As might be expected, the slow growth also implied the absence of any significant structural change. The economy has remained predominantly agricultural. The share of agriculture in GDP fell from approximately 65 percent in 1965 to 56 percent in 1984. The share of the workforce in agriculture was 94 percent in 1965 and 93 percent in 1980. The dependence on the primary sector is among the heaviest for developing countries in terms of total output and employment. Its share of agriculture in GDP was second highest in the world in 1980 and at 93 percent the agricultural workforce as proportion of the total was highest with that of two other countries. Marginal increases were recorded in the GDP shares in industry and the manufacturing component within it. Manufacturing, however, comprised only 4 percent of GDP in 1984. The services sector which was the second largest, increased its share from 23 percent in 1965 to 32 percent in 1984.

The rate of growth of agriculture, which was the dominant sector, was quite low during the entire period, hovering between 1 to 1.5 percent. The sector which grew fastest during the entire period was the services sector which recorded a rate of growth of about 7 percent.

The output of the food grains which occupied approximately 90 percent of the total crop area accounts for 80 percent of agricultural output. The growth of the food grains sector, therefore, largely determines agricultural growth and the overall rate of growth of the economy. Therefore, in Nepal's current phase of development, increased productivity in the agricultural sector is of the utmost importance in

Table 29. GDP Growth (Percent Per Annum in 1974-75 Prices)

	Average Annual Growth					
	1979-80	1980-81	1981-82	1982-83	1983-84	1984-85
Agriculture	−4.76	10.3	3.5	−2.5	8.7	2.5
Non-Agriculture	1.38	5.4	3.0	0.4	5.5	3.4
GDP	−2.3	8.3	3.8	−1.4	7.4	2.8
	Per cent Per Annum					
Population Growth Estimates				2.6	2.6	2.6

Source: Ministry of Finance, *Economic Surveys.*

Table 30. Change in the Composition of Gross Domestic Product
and Sectoral Rates of Growth

Sector	Percentage Share of Gross Domestic Product		Average Annual Growth Rate	
	1965	1984	1965-73	1973-83
Agriculture	65	56	1.5	1
Industry	11	12	n.a.	n.a.
Manufacturing	3	4	n.a.	n.a.
Services	23	32	2.1	6.9

Source: IBRD *World Development Report,* 1986: Tables 2 and 3.

laying the foundation for sustained development. The performance of the food grains sector is set out in Table 31. While the total areas under food grains increased by approximately 13 percent from 1976-77 to 1984-85, production increased only by 12 percent. Thus, yields declined. The performance during the ten year period from 1974-75 to 1984-85 fluctuated sharply both in terms of output as well as yields.

On the other hand, the performance of the principal cash crops — sugarcane, oil seeds, jute and tobacco — was more satisfactory. Yields increased by 1.8 percent and output by 7.4 percent. Cash crops form, however, a small component of total agricultural output.

The Nepalese economy plunged into negative growth of 2.3 percent and 1.4 percent in 1979-80 and 1982-83, and then in the following two years achieved high rates of 8.3 percent and 7.4 percent respectively. These fluctuations were largely determined by the output in the food grain sector, which declined by 16 percent in 1982-83 and then recovered with 28 percent increase in 1983-84.

Food grains accounted for the major portion of Nepal's exports in 1974-75, approximately 55 percent. The share in exports continued to fall over the next ten years to less than one-third. Domestic consumption of edible food grains rose from approximately 900,000 metric tons in 1974-75 to 1,260,000 metric tons in 1984-85, leaving a diminishing surplus for exports. In 1982-83, the output was not adequate to meet domestic demand. By 1984-85, the total surplus had been halved. These developments were the combined results of population increases on the one hand and stagnation in the food grains sector on the other. (See Tables 31-34)

The manufacturing sector grew at a comparatively high rate during the period 1974-75 to 1983-84. The industrial output for selected industries grew at 7 percent. But it was on an extremely small base of production: not more than about 3 percent of GDP. The main products were jute, sguar, tobacco and textiles but included leather goods, cement and plywood. Public enterprises constituted an important component of the medium and large-scale manufacturing industries. There were 53 public enterprises by the end of 1983-84, producing mainly cement, sugar, cigarettes, leather, agricultural tools and public utilities. Their performance has been poor. The returns on investment have been very low or negative, and many enterprises have had to rely on government loans and subsidies.

The fast growth in the services sector was evidently promoted by tourism growing over 10 percent. This is also reflected in the receipts from travel which increased from Rs. 636 million in 1979 to Rs. 844 million in 1983.[15]

Available estimates indicate that overall productivity of the economy increased at a rate of approximately 0.1 percent during the period 1965-73 and by 0.8 during the period 1973-83. These are derived from the estimates of GDP growth and the labor force. Calculations made for sectoral rates of productivity indicate that productivity may have declined in agriculture, particularly in the food grains. (Table 35).

Macroeconomic Trends and Mobilization of Resources

The macroeconomic indicators on recent trends in Nepal's development reflect an intensification of some of the basic structural problems but with a few elements

---

[15] Nepal Rashtra Bank, Research Department Statistical Tables 1985, Table 35.

Table 31. Area, Production and Yield of Principal Food Grains

Area: Hectare
Production: Metric Ton
Yield: Metric Ton per Hectare

Food Grains		1974-75	1979-80	1980-81	1981-82	1982-83	1983-84	1984-85	Percentage change in 1984-85 over 1983-84
Paddy:	Area	1,239,853	1,254,240	1,275,520	1,296,530	1,264,840	1,334,200	1,376,860	3.2
	Production	2,452,268	2,059,930	2,464,310	2,560,080	1,832,620	2,756,980	2,709,430	−1.7
	Yield	1.98	1.64	1.93	1.97	1.45	2.07	1.96	−5.3
Maize:	Area	458,027	432,340	457,450	475,490	510,770	503,770	578,720	14.9
	Production	826,651	553,760	742,940	751,520	718,240	761,110	819,150	7.6
	Yield	1.8	1.28	1.62	1.58	1.41	1.51	1.42	−6.0
Wheat:	Area	290,823	366,860	391,790	388,890	483,820	471,750	449,960*	−4.6
	Production	330,815	439,990	477,190	525,930	656,630	633,700	519,960*	−17.0
	Yield	1.14	1.2	1.22	1.32	1.36	1.36	1.16*	−13.4

Table 32. Index of Foodgrains

(1976-77 = 100)

	1974-75	1979-80	1980-81	1981-82	1982-83	1983-84	1984-85	Percentage change in 1984-85 over 1983-84
Area	98.08	99.50	102.00	104.00	104.60	108.50	113.20	4.3
Production	102.50	85.30	102.80	106.70	82.20	104.60	112.90	−1.5
Yield	1.05	0.86	1.00	1.02	0.83	1.04	0.97	−6.7

Source: Department of Food and Agricultural Marketing Services.
* Preliminary.

Table 33. Index of Cash Crops

(1976-77 = 100)

	1974-75	1979-80	1980-81	1981-82	1982-83	1983-84	1984-85	Percentage change in 1984-85 over 1983-84
Area	98.94	112.18	108.62	128.87	107.03	104.27	113.56	8.91
Production	108	107.81	113.29	128.66	141.98	139.34	149.69	7.43
Yield	105.53	100.28	107.91	117.63	117.48	117.3	119.51	1.88

Sources: Department of Food and Agriculture Marketing Services, and Jute Development Corporation.

Table 34. Edible Food Grains Production

(Unit: thousand metric tons)

	1974/75	1979/80	1980/81	1981/82	1982/83	1983/84	1984/85
1. Total Edible Food Grains Production*	2,420	2,000	2,409	2,509	2,197	2,742	2,678
2. Rice*							
a. Consumable Rice Production	1,288	1,059	1,273	1,324	938	1,475	1,448
b. Need for internal consumption	889	963	989	1,096	1,124	1,173	1,260
Surplus or Deficit (—)	339	96	284	228	-186	302	188

Source: Department of Food and Agriculture Marketing Service.
* Excluded seeds, losses and husk etc.

Table 35. Overall Growth of Productivity

	1965-1973	1975-1984
Growth of GDP	1.7	3.1
Average annual growth of workforce	1.6	2.3
Growth of overall productivity	0.1	0.8

Source: IBRD, *World Development Report,* 1986.

which show potential for changes in a positive direction.

Landlocked Nepal has a fairly low ratio of exports and imports in GDP of around 25 percent in 1984. Nepal's external dependence has grown rapidly in recent years with a substantial increase in imports, mainly as a result of the inflow of foreign development aid. Merchandise exports have been able to finance only about 25 percent of imports.

A positive feature, however, has been the steady increase in the surplus in the invisibles account, rising from approximately US$8.2 million in 1970 to about US$100 million in 1983-84.[16] This has been largely due to the steady increase of private remittances, which have grown from approximately Rs. 84 million in 1970 to Rs. 280 million in 1983-84; and tourist expenditures which have increased from Rs. 16 million to Rs. 585 million during the same period.[17] The surplus in invisibles was equal to a little less than 25 percent of imports in 1984. The net resource flows in the invisibles account has contained the current account deficit between 4 and 5 percent of GDP. The deficit in Nepal's current account, excluding official transfers such as aid grants, has risen from US$100 million in 1979 to US$175 million in 1984.[18] This has been financed by the flow of aid in the form of grants and concessional long-term loans. The large trade deficit as well as the deficit in the current account also reflect the fairly rapid increase in the volume of gross domestic investment. The large flow of external resources has been able to finance a significantly high level of investment in Nepal. Gross domestic investment has risen from around 9 percent of GDP in 1976 to 19 percent in 1984. Domestic savings have also risen from below 5 percent of GDP in the mid 1970s to approximately 10 percent in 1984. The proportion of the gross national investment financed by domestic savings is currently about 52 percent. Foreign savings, primarily external aid, have financed the balance.

The rate of growth of GDP still remains about 3 percent, yielding a very high capital output ratio. A considerable proportion of investment goes into infrastructure and similar investments whose initial capital outlays are high but have their impact over a long period.

Another encouraging development is the growing diversification of Nepal's exports. With the contraction in the share of food grain exports, there has been a significant expansion in the export of manufactured goods from Rs. 28 million in

---

[16] *Ibid.*

[17] and [18] *Ibid.* Research Department Statistical Tables, 1985; Tables 35 and 36.

Table 36. External Trade and Balance of Payments

Year	Balance of Payments Current Account	Trade Balance		Deficit
		Imports	Exports	
1979	−7	254	109	−145
1980	−53	345	97	−248
1981	−19	195	63	−132
1982	−86	252	46	−206
1983	−143	464	94	−370
1984	−102	437	111	−326

Source: IBRD, *World Development Report,* 1981 to 1986.

Table 37. Savings and Investment in Gross Domestic Products

Year	Gross Domestic Savings as % of GDP	Gross Domestic Investment as % of GDP
1976	3	9
1980	9	14
1981	8	14
1982	9	15
1983	9	20
1984	10	19

Source: IBRD, *World Development Report,* (1978-1984).

1974-75 to Rs. 581 million in 1983-84, in current prices.[19]

The effort to promote exports has included a number of policy measures. The rupee against the US$ has steadily depreciated from Rs. 10.50 in 1975, to Rs. 18.20 in January 1985. A nine-point export promotion policy has been recently implemented. It offered concessional interest rates for pre-export credit among other incentives. Nepal has also been able to diversify her trading partners. The share of India declined from 82 percent in 1974-75 to about 50 percent in 1981-82.

Central government revenues and expenditure have also increased during this period. Total government expenditure was about 8.5 percent of GNP in the early 1970s. This has now risen to 17.2 percent. Total revenues increased from 5.2 percent in 1972 to 8.7 percent in 1983. The overall budget deficit has grown from 1.2 percent to 5.2 percent during the same period. These changes were largely determined by the inflow of external resources. On the whole, the budget in recent years has kept the expansionary financing within reasonable limits. Treasury bills and overdrafts, however, have had an increasing role in financing the deficit between

---

[19] *Ibid.* Table 29.

1982 and 1984.[20] The overall index for national consumer prices rose from 177 in 1979-80 to 280 in 1984-85 an average rate of increase of 10 percent. The increases have fluctuated from 16 percent in 1982-83, to 6.2 percent in 1983-84.[21]

Thus, the Nepal economy has become increasingly dependent on aid. External aid has financed nearly 50 percent of imports, and 48 percent of gross domestic investment in 1984. It increased government revenues by increasing imports and thereby enlarging the base for indirect taxation. The increase in import capacity as a result of aid reduced the bottlenecks caused by the scarcity of the import component essential for investments, and thereby contributed to the recent improvement in domestic savings.

Table 38. Percentage Share of Merchandise Exports

	1978	1983
Primary commodities other than fuels and minerals	87	43
Textiles and clothing	6	28
Other manufactures	7	23
Machinery and transport equipment	—	1
Fuels, minerals and metals	—	5

Source: IBRD, *World Development Report*, 1981, Table 9; 1986, Table 10.

Socio-Economic Infrastructure and Human Resources

The health of status of the population in Nepal is among the lowest in the world when judged by the main relevant indicators. The life expectancy in 1984 stood at 47, infant mortality was 135, and the birth rate was 43. The percentage of population below minimum consumption levels has been estimated at about 32 percent.[22] The per capita availability of calories was estimated at 93 percent of requirement. The deficiency in daily calorie intake for the 32 percent of poor, mainly rural, households has been estimated at 38 percent. Based on the figures available for physicians and nursing personnel for the population as a whole it would seem that the health infrastructure is as yet grossly inadequate. The total health system is able to provide only one physician for 30,000 of the population and one nursing person for 33,000.

There has been fairly rapid progress in education during the last two decades. Enrollment in primary education has risen from 20 percent in 1965 to 73 percent in 1983 with near full participation of male children at the primary stage. The female participation has gone up from 4 percent to 43 percent during the same period.[23] While central government expenditures reflect an increasing share of the

[20] IBRD Tables 20 and 21.
[21] Research Department, Nepal Rastra Bank.
[22] Pilot Study on socio-economic indicators for monitoring and evaluation of agrarian reform and rural development in Nepal — FAO and the Department of Food & Agricultural Marketing — H.M.G. Nepal, 1983.
[23] IBRD — *World Development Report*, 1986, Table 29.

budget devoted for education, health expenditures have not increased in the same manner. A major problem is the limited volume of central government resources.

Economic Infrastructure

The infrastructure in Nepal is still at an early stage of development. The road transport network consists of the East-West highway that tranverses the terrai (the plains) in its entire length, but this is not completed yet in the western part. The road network extends to only 31 of the 75 districts. A network of 21 air-strips has been built in the hills. The districts, however, are all connected by radio communication.

The country has a total installed capacity of 149 MW of electricity with energy consumption per head which is perhaps the lowest in the world. The World Development Report gives it at 16 kg of oil equivalent per head for 1984 — lower than that for Ethiopia which uses 17. Nepal is, however, a country with enormous potential for hydro-electric power. These features highlight the major constraints which the country faces in regard to its prospects for future development.

Ecological and Demographic Constraints

The overriding factors that determine the growth and development of Nepal are ecological and demographic. The country has an area of 141,000 sq. km. Within its north-south width of 130 to 140 km, there is a wide range of topography and climate from the sub-tropical to the alpine. It extends from the terrai in the south, which forms a part of the Gangetic plains, to the highest mountain ranges in the world. The country can be broadly divided into three parallel geographic regions, extending from east to west, the terrai — i.e. the plains — the middle hills and the high mountains. These three areas cover respectively 23, 24 and 34 percent of the land area. The climate is monsoonal with 80 percent of the average annual rainfall occuring during the monsoon from June to September. The country has four main perennial rivers originating in the Himalayas and flowing into the greater Ganges.

Recent data available on land use indicate that about 22 percent of the area or 3.1 million hectares are under cultivation and 29 percent, or 4.1 million, are under forest. The remaining 49 percent, approximately 6.9 million hectares, includes a large proportion of poor pasture land, mountains and wasteland. Comparative data for 1975 and 1980, indicate that there has been a rapid expansion of the area under cultivation during this period and a decline in the area under forest by approximately 15 percent.

The population has been growing at the rapid rate of almost 2.6 percent during the last ten years. Nepal is in the stage in which both fertility and mortality are high. It is entering the phase in which mortality will decline faster than birth rates. As a result the rate of increase in population could rise even above the prevailing rates in the short-term unless effective family planning interventions are implemented. In the twenty-year period 1965-1984, the birth rate fell from 46 to 43, while the death rate dropped from 24 to 18. The natural increase of population rose from 2.2 percent to 2.6 percent.

While the average density of population in the country is 106 sq. km, the highest density of 299 per sq. km is recorded in the terrai and the lowest density of 39 per sq. km is in the far western hills. The quality of arable land and accessibility

varies widely between the hills and the terrai. The population per sq. km of cultivated land average 422 for the country as a whole, but ranges from 658 persons per
sq. km in the hills to 364 in the terrai. The deteriorating environment in the hills
and the declining food availability has led to a large flow of migration from the
hills to the terrai. This has resulted in an annual rate of population growth of 4.2
percent in the terrai compared to 1.6 percent in the hills during the last decade.

Despite these shifts in population, the environment both in the mountain region
and in the plains has been steadily deteriorating. A wide variety of interrelated
factors have contributed to this situation. In the hills, the mounting pressure of
population has led to much more intensive use of the scarce resources available in
the fragile micro-environments. In the plains, the natural increase and the large
migration led to the rapid expansion of cultivated land. This has been environmental-
ly damaging. The depletion of forests and the erosion of hill-slopes have posed a
serious threat to the ecological base of the Nepal economy. The erosion of the top
soil has increased in alarming proportions and caused a decline of natural fertility
and land productivity. Nepal's development strategy has therefore to be underpinned
by a massive effort to protect the environment and the ecological viability of the
country's natural resource base.

Nepal's location in mountain terrain has hampered access to markets, the delivery
of essential services by the State and the free movement of people and goods. In
this context, the urban sector is extremely small and the process of urbanization
has been painfully slow. Nepal had only 7 percent of its total population in the
urban sector and is one of the five least developed countries with urban sectors
below 10 percent of total population. The development of a good transportation
network connecting urban centres with different parts of the country therefore
assumes very high priority in the development strategy of Nepal.

One of the prerequisites for growth in Nepal is to preserve the ecosystem while
developing the infrastructure. The two objectives can be conflicting, unless the
ecological impacts are constantly monitored and environments are protected.

At first glance the investment program for these objectives may be thought of as
capital-intensive with long gestation periods. It could, however, adopt the technology
which could make better use of the large, underemployed rural workforce. The
Nepali situation appears to be ideally suited for imaginative ways of undertaking
public works in both ecological stabilization and infrastructure improvement. Such
programs could readily absorb aid flows including food aid, and could be carefully
designed not to conflict with production objectives.

Potential for Future Growth

From the information available, Nepal does not appear to have any major mineral
resources. Agricultural yields are quite low. Paddy yields are around 2 tons per acre
compared to 3.5 tons in Sri Lanka. The decline in natural fertility of the soil, the
slow absorption of new technologies and practices, the lack of adequate irrigation
facilities, the deficiencies in the land tenure system have all contributed to this
poor performance. At the end of 1980, only 7 percent of the total cultivated area
benefited from irrigation facilities. The Sixth Five-Year Plan had a target of substantial increase in irrigation facilities to 17 percent of the cultivated area.

Water is one of the abundant resources in Nepal, but in irrigation and energy,
it remains one of the least developed countries. The potential exists to support an

irrigation system which is fed by both lift and gravity.

The modest target of the Sixth Five-year Plan places the GDP growth rate at 4.3 percent. To achieve this target agriculture has to grow at 3.2 percent. Past performance has fallen well below this target, as was shown by the index of Food Grains Production in Table 32. It rose from 100 in 1976-77 to 112 in 1984-85, a bare 1.5 percent per annum.

Industry and manufacturing is still a small component of GDP but made a considerable contribution to diversify the exports. This contribution appears to have come largely from the small-scale and handicrafts sector. The high transportation costs associated with the landlocked situation of Nepal requires a special industrialization strategy. It includes the emphasis on small-scale firms geared to the internal market, where demand grows with the agricultural development and the satisfaction of basic needs. At the same time, however, the diversification of exports that has taken place indicates the scope for certain products of small-scale and handicraft manufactures. This output also caters to tourist demand.

The Sixth Five-Year Plan for the 1980-85 period gave a new emphasis to social development, aimed at ameliorating rural poverty and satisfying basic needs. It plans to get Nepal out of the vicious circle of low savings, low investment, and low growth. There has been a slow but steady increase in the rate of domestic savings. Domestic investment has risen to about 19 percent of the GDP in 1984. Nearly 45 percent came, however, from foreign resources in outright grants. As one of the least developed countries, Nepal enjoys very favorable terms of development assistance. The country's debt service ratio in 1984 stood at only 3.4 percent. Current trends indicate that Nepal can sustain a slow increase in domestic savings and, together with external aid, mobilize adequate resources to support gross domestic investment around 20 percent of GDP. With this level of investment and proper balance between quick yielding investments and those which require long periods of gestation such as the infrastructure projects, Nepal would be able to maintain a rate of economic growth of 5 percent. There is scope for reducing the capital output ratio further and achieving even higher growth rates.

Central government revenues have expanded to 8.7 percent in 1985. This would enable the government to raise the level of public expenditure on human development such as health and education.

Population projections indicate an annual rate of approximately 2.6 percent. Social changes in Nepal during the last two decades seem to be conducive to a reduction of the fertility rate. Primary school enrollment has risen from 20 to 73 percent during this period. Female enrollment has increased from 4 to 43 percent. With growing female literacy, family planning is likely to be more effective than in the past. It is pertinent to observe here that India was able to reduce birth rates from 45 to 33 during the 20 year period from 1965 to 1984. Primary school enrollment in India in 1965 was 74 percent, with female enrollment at 57 percent. The demographic changes will depend on the rapid expansion of primary education to include the female population and on the efficient delivery of primary health care.

The development of human resources in the broadest sense has to be given a central place in Nepal's strategy. The daily calorie intake of the rural population appears to be well below norms. This undoubtedly lowers the productivity of the rural workforce. This level of undernutrition in a country with an exportable surplus of food grain reflects grave inequality of income. It requires major changes in the distribution and access to resources. Improvements in the tenurial system, primary education, primary health care, and programs and policies related to food production and distribution, therefore, need high priority.

The economic development in Nepal depends on the rapid increase of productivity and output in agriculture, but it will come up against the limitations of the export market, particularly in food grains. Nepal's main market for food grains has been India. But with India achieving self-sufficiency in food, the prospects in that market have seriously diminished. Growth strategies will, therefore, have to give priority to the diversification of agriculture. This could include perennial crops like horticultural crops which are also ecologically more beneficial. Nepal will also have to rely on the growth of its tourism. Its industrial sector will have to exploit the potential of small-scale enterprise for both the domestic market as well as for export.

The State inevitably plays a major role in Nepal's development. The major part of the investable resources, consisting of external assistance, is in the hands of the State. The development of infrastructure, the satisfaction of basic needs, the delivery of primary health care, the expansion of education facilities, and the distribution of food would require considerable effort on the part of public agencies. The state may also have to provide the initiative in certain types of industry and commerce.

One of the major problems for Nepal as well as for the other three countries is the utilization of aid. Some of the processes of mobilizing aid, such as the formulation and presentation of projects as well as the subsequent use of aid funds, contribute to a certain degree of waste, extravagance, and inefficiency. The improvement of the entire system of project formulation, implementation, and accountability will therefore be a decisive factor in realizing the best returns and achieving a capital output ratio that will enable the country to realize desired rates of growth with the levels of investment that are possible. For all these tasks, the efficiency of public administration and the state apparatus commands very high priority.

The dominant role of the state does not diminish the crucial importance of the policies and incentives for the private sector. In Nepal, the bulk of private producers are the small-scale agricultural producers and the small-scale entrepreneurs in the industrial and service sectors. For them it is crucial that the market functions effectively. Hence, the whole framework of macroeconomic policies from budget, the exchange rate, and credit, to pricing policies would have to be so orchestrated as to provide the right signals and incentives. In its external transactions, Nepal has functioned largely as a regulated economy with foreign exchange control and licensing of imports. The operation of market forces has, therefore, been seriously restricted. There has recently been a liberalization of trade that has resulted in a rapid expansion of imports and a widening of the trade gap. Production incentives have suffered from the lack of appropriate adjustments of the exchange rate. This was particularly evident in the depletion of Indian rupee reserves as a result of maintaining a constant rate of exchange between the Indian and Nepali currency. Low and stable consumer prices for domestically produced food grains have been a disincentive to producers.

In coping with these problems, Nepal cannot afford to resort to policies that severely curtail demand and have a contractionary impact on the economy. One overriding objective is the satisfaction of the basic needs of the population. The task of realizing this objective while containing import demand within manageable limits is fraught with problems. In a package of policies which stimulate growth through a better functioning of the market system and a fairly liberal trade regime, further action may be possible in regard to the exchange rate and the shift of price incentives to promote exports. But these efforts need to be underpinned by an adequate flow of external resources that will provide Nepal sufficient long-term support to enable the growth-oriented policies to take effect.

CONCLUSION

This final section provides a brief summary of some of the salient issues which have emerged in the analysis of development trends of the four South Asian countries that have been surveyed. In the introductory section, attention was drawn to some of the basic socio-economic characteristics that these countries have in common, and also significant demographic and structural features which distinguish them from each other. All four countries fall into the low income category that contains the 36 poorest countries in the world. But within these narrow limits there are significant differences in per capita incomes. Comparisons of per capita income among countries, however, present various problems. The World Bank Project on inter-country comparisons of income and purchasing power parity has estimated per capita incomes for a number of developing and developed countries.

The adjustments that are suggested in these exercises result in considerable revisions of existing computations of the growth rates of gross domestic product as well as per capita income. For example, the ranking of the four South Asian countries is different from that in Table 1. Nepal emerges as the poorest country with a per capita income of US$402, Bangladesh next with 432 US$, Pakistan third with 629 US$ and Sri Lanka above Pakistan with 778 US$. The growth rates are also very different. Sri Lanka records a negative growth rate of −1.2 percent over the period 1960-78. [24] These estimates have not been taken into account in the present analysis, because they raise serious technical difficulties and are not easily reconcilable with the national series where GDP has been computed at constant prices over a long period. Even so, among the four countries surveyed, the revised estimates continue to show a significant gap between the two poorest countries, Nepal and Bangladesh and Pakistan and Sri Lanka.

On the assumption that the per capita incomes grow at 5 percent per annum for all four with population growth continuing at their respective present rates, Sri Lanka and Pakistan are likely to enjoy per capita incomes of 529 US dollars and 623 US dollars by 2000 A.D. In the case of Nepal and Bangladesh, with a population growth at 2.5 to 2.6 percent, per capita incomes are likely to be 230 US dollars and 190 US dollars at the turn of the century. All four countries would have to pursue development strategies which can achieve a satisfactory quality of life within the modest per capita income levels expected over the next 15 years. The challenge is greatest in the case of Nepal and Bangladesh. Development strategies which are consciously directed at such an outcome have to be continuously attentive to the appropriate balance between welfare and growth. They must aim simultaneously at the expansion of productive capacity and the development of the social infrastructure and human resources. They must be flexible and imaginative in the selection and use of policy instruments to provide the right combination of market

---

[24] These incomes are at the prices as reflected in the per capita incomes for 1984 given in the *World Development Report* 1986.

mechanisms and state interventions.

There are possibilities for further improvement on the per capita incomes. Population growth rates can be reduced, incremental output ratios can be lowered, and higher growth rates for GDP can be achieved, even without substantial increase in investment. Table 39 presents a set of alternative projections based on varying assumptions of growth for the economy and the population. Rates of growth of 6 to 7 percent are feasible for Sri Lanka and Pakistan. While in the case of Pakistan there is further scope for raising the levels of investment through greater resource mobilization, Sri Lanka could increase significantly the efficiency of its investment, whose level is already high and make greater gains in productivity. The need for higher rates of growth is, however, most urgent in Nepal and Bangladesh. While the growth rate of 7 percent is well above the average achieved by these two countries, it is not entirely beyond feasibility. Recent trends indicate significant improvement in the levels of investment. The additional 2 percent growth above the 5 percent adopted for most of the development plans can come through a small increase in the level of investment, matched by much greater efficiency in the use of resources and increases in productivity. A high growth scenario of this kind will require greater international support to underpin the domestic effort.

In all four countries, agriculture will remain the major commodity producing sector for sometime to come. With the exception of the plantation sector in Sri Lanka, the agricultural sector in all the countries relies on small and medium size farms. This is likely to remain the principal mode of production, and any rapid process of growth will depend heavily on the extent to which smallholder agriculture achieves rapid gains in productivity and income. Smallholder agriculture will also have its special combination of factors of production. Labor intensity will be relatively high and the economy will not be required to create capacities for the supply of large-scale machinery and other capital goods to the agricultural sector, as in the case of the capital intensive agriculture of the industrial countries. This would mean that despite the structural change in the economy, and the decline in the share of agriculture in GDP the agricultural workforce and its share in the total workforce will not decline at the same rapid rate. Such a pattern of development seems to correspond to the pattern that has emerged in the highly efficient smallholder agriculture of Korea or ROC (Taiwan). For example, Korea with an agricultural sector which contributed 16 percent of gross domestic production in 1980 had as much as 30 percent of its workforce in agriculture. (*World Development Report* 1982 and 1986).

An efficient smallholder agriculture, can become a dynamic element in economic growth. But this requires far-reaching changes that improve the human capital in this sector and increase the capacity for rapid absorption and use of technology.

Unemployment has not emerged as a major problem in these countries except in the case of Sri Lanka. But the case of Sri Lanka, with the changing character of its workforce and the emergence of large scale, open unemployment, prefigures the changes that can take place in the other countries if employment creation is not given adequate priority in their development strategies. At present, unemployment is masked through the absorptive capacity of the informal sector. With improvement in social conditions, higher educational levels, greater female participation in the workforce and new expectations, the character of the workforce will undergo far-reaching changes. Open unemployment is bound to rise if development strategies are not adequately employment-oriented and employment creation lags behind.

Table 39. Alternative Projections of Per Capita Income in 2000 A.D.

(1984 US Dollars)

	Per Capita Income (1984 US Dollars)	Rate of GNP Growth (Percent)		Rate of Population Growth (Percent)		Per Capita Income Growth (Percent)				Per Capita 2000 A.D.			
		(1)	(2)	(1)	(2)	(1)	(2)	(3)	(4)	(1)	(2)	(3)	(4)
Pakistan	380	5	6.5	2.9	2.6	2.1	2.4	3.6	3.9	529	555	668	700
Sri Lanka	360	5	6	1.5	1.3	3.5	3.7	4.5	4.7	623	643	727	750
Nepal	160	5	7	2.6	2.4	2.4	2.6	4.4	4.6	233	241	318	328
Bangladesh	130	5	7	2.5	2.2	2.5	2.8	4.5	4.8	192	202	262	275

The preceding sections discuss some of the basic problems relating to industrialization and the relative roles of the state and the market. In all four countries, the initiatives for large-scale industrialization came from the public sector. The market mechanisms alone do not appear to have been adequate to direct private capital to the industrial sector. All countries appear to have had recourse to a mix of high protective barriers and state enterprise in order to establish the base for the manufacturing sector. In some of the countries, industrial policy has undergone sharp alternations which veered between policies which favored private sector enterprise and those which promoted nationalization and state ownership. These policy changes were mainly due to changes in government and different political and economic ideologies which were advocated by the elites of the political parties which came into power. This is demonstrated clearly in the case of Pakistan, Sri Lanka and Bangladesh. This conflict of objectives and changes of policy covered several areas and created an environment and structures in which industrial growth was often hampered and even retarded. First, industrial policies seldom clearly demarcated the relative roles of the public and private sectors. Second, the policies for import substitution on the one hand, and export promotion on the other, came into conflict. The industrial structrue developed serious inefficiencies in highly protected domestic markets, creating conditions under which the development of an internationally competitive, export-oriented sector was made very difficult. Third, export-oriented strategies, on the other hand, often neglected the links between production for the domestic market and production for the export sector. Some of the liberalization policies in the post-1977 period in Sri Lanka had adverse effects on small industries which could have developed into competitive units such as in the light engineering sector. In the recent past, all four countries have been engaged in a reappraisal of industrial policy which included greater reliance on market mechanisms, dimunition of the role of public sector enterprise and an attempt to reconcile the objectives of import substitution and export promotion through a wide range of measures relating to exchange rates, tariffs, and financial policy. Liberalization policies by themselves, however, have not been able as yet to provide the stimulus for sustained industrial growth. In all these countries, therefore, comprehensive industrial strategies have yet to be evolved.

As already mentioned, Pakistan and Bangladesh have a different set of conditions, in that the potential internal market offers scope for a balanced industrial structure. In the case of Nepal and Sri Lanka with their smaller economies and limited internal markets, industrial growth relies heavily on external markets. Being small economies, both Sir Lanka and Nepal should be able to sustain export-oriented growth if they can build up the competitive capacity to secure small shares of the international market in a variety of products. Most likely, these niches will be based on labor costs and certain types of skills. In all the countries, however, achieving rates of economic growth from 5 to 6 percent depends on the industrial sector being able to maintain steady growth at rates between 8 and 10 percent. This is critically important for the diversification of the export sector and for ensuring an adequate flow of foreign exchange. None of the four countries have what can be considered a rich resource endowment in minerals and energy that could become a readily available base for industrialization. Only Pakistan, out of the four countries can claim to have more than a modest endowment of mineral and energy resources. The other countries depend largely on the further processing of their primary products and on comparative advantages in labor costs and skills. The discussion of the future prospects of the industrial sector in Sri Lanka indicated the selected combination of various elements that can provide for a viable industrial structure. These include the further processing of export products, production for the internal market, and allowing foreign investments that, in turn, provide access to external markets.

For all these economies, the international framework for trade and external assistance will eventually determine their performance. These countries, particularly Sri Lanka and Bangladesh, have been able to build up a signfiicant component of non-traditional exports in the recent past, largely because of quotas for textile exports. The fast growth of these components have, however, been prevented by the restrictions imposed by the importing countries. The successful diversification of exports in manufactures would, therefore, depend on the international trading regime. The uncertainties of external trade have to be considered together with the high dependence on external aid. A drastic decline in aid flows would lead to a severe contraction of imports on the one hand, and heavy cut-backs in public investment on the other, and would effectively cripple the development efforts.

The post-1977 experience of Sri Lanka illustrates how a large-scale injection of aid combined with appropriate domestic policy reforms, can release market forces and produce a fairly rapid process of growth. Sri Lanka was able to carry out a program of adjustment with growth, for reasons that are relevant to other countries undertaking such adjustments. First, the scale of external assistance was such that adjustments could be undertaken without any contraction of the economy or cut-backs in investment. On the contrary, Sri Lanka was able to embark on a large investment program and did not have to impose the normal austerities associated with adjustment. Second, Sri Lanka had already put in place a welfare system which to a large extent assured minimum levels of well-being for the population as a whole. During the process of adjustment Sri Lanka was therefore able to make modifications in this system, keeping intact the core of the welfare program which included public health, free education, and a free entitlement to food that could provide security to the poorer segments of society.

With the exception of Sri Lanka, population growth and the way in which demographic changes are managed, will be decisive factors in the performance of these countries. The management of these variables depends on two sets of policies — first, on population policies and family planning programs which are effective in lowering birth rates in the short-term, and second, on the improvement of social well-being on a wider front, resulting in the higher educational levels, particularly for the female population, primary health care which lowers mortality, and changes in attitudes regarding family size. These two sets of policies are closely linked and have to be pursued together to produce the desired changes in the demographic situation.

There are larger issues concerning the social sector, particularly in Nepal, Bangladesh, and Pakistan. The scenario of economic development, which has been described in the country surveys is not sustainable unless there is a much larger investment in human capital in these countries. The term "human capital" connotes an instrumentality of development that detracts from the importance of good health and educational attainments as states of well-being in their own right, and as goals of development that must be pursued for their own sake. Nevertheless, it is important to recognize the organic character of development in these poorest countries in which the social infrastructure is as important as the economic infrastructure. The low levels of productivity, underutilization of capacity, the failures and inefficiencies of management both in investment programs and large enterprises are all part of the deficiencies of human capital. As pointed out earlier, the growth and productivity of the rural sector based on small-scale farming units and the large informal sectors in these countries depend largely on the capacity of the farmers and small producers, to absorb technology and manage efficiently the new inputs and resources. Human resource development leads to changes in their patterns of consumption, changes in expectations for their children, changes in their life-styles, and sustained increases in their purchasing power and effective demand.

It will be possible for these countries to extract much more growth out of existing capacities and the resources that are currently invested through improvement of public administration and enhancement of managerial capacity. Much greater effort directed at implementation is therefore as important as the effort directed at the mobilization of resources and sustaining investment at the desired levels. With perhaps the exception of Pakistan, the incremental capital output ratio in all these countries is high and there is considerable scope for improving the efficiency of investment. In this task, the management of aid in order to improve cost effectiveness must be given high priority. While donor countries usually seek to ensure that assistance yields the maximum benefit and therefore seek to impose disciplines in the grant as well as the use of aid, it would appear that aid and the availability of resources that comes with it can lead to some relaxation in the process of accountability and result in some measure of waste and extravagance. This would particularly apply to aid programs that are tied to procurement from given sources. A reappraisal of the management of aid and its improvement are therefore important elements in the development strategies of these countries.

In all these countries, the mobilization of resources for development and maintaining a steady process of economic and social growth over a long time is critically dependent on a stable political infrastructure. But internal conflicts and political instability have seriously hampered the development efforts of these countries. They have prevented the evolution of a political framework within which there is a broad social consensus on the main development goals. In all these countries, the political system appears to be in a process of transition. New institutions and structures are evolving and democratic processes are being introduced or being restored. Maturation of the political process and development of an institutional framework that would provide for greater participation by the people as well as more orderly resolution of conflicts would, therefore, be one of the essential conditions for a sustained development process. These brief comments covering the social and political dimensions of development in these four countries highlight the vital links between these variables and indicate why the development processes related to all these must move closely together.

Finally, it is important to place the future of these four economies in the context of the new initiatives that have been taken in the South Asian region for regional cooperation. It is not possible to discuss the implications of these initiatives for the four countries without taking into account the main partner in such a program of regional cooperation — India. Therefore, the potential regional cooperation in South Asia and its likely impact on the growth of the economies of the region cannot be considered in any depth in this chapter. Nevertheless, there are certain broad generalizations that can be made on the basis of the country surveys. All four countries have in the past pursued trade policies based on elaborate systems of regulation and import control leaving little room for the expansion of trade among themselves. The changing structure of import demand with development resulted in a contraction of some of the trade flows based on primary products, textiles, and a few consumer goods, that had existed in the past. Within this regulated system, however, Nepal, Sri Lanka, and Bangladesh had India as an important trade partner. In the case of Nepal, India accounted for the preponderant share.

In the recent past all these countries have attempted to move toward a more liberal trade policy. This has been most pronounced in the case of Sri Lanka. Given the pattern of demand, however, these initiatives have resulted in an opening of the economy and a diversification of trade partners away from the region. Existing bilateral agreements as well as the participation in the Bangkok Agreement have not resulted in any major trade expansion among these countries. In the prevailing trade pattern, India would have a wide range of goods to offer to the other countries of the region, but in turn these countries would not have much to offer in exchange with India or for trade among themselves. The promotion of trade, therefore, has to be geared to future development.

The program of regional cooperation of the South Asian Association for Regional Cooperation (SAARC) has so far not entered the hard areas of economic cooperation, such as trade, monetary cooperation, development finance and joint investment. There has been some consideration given to collaboration in development planning so that countries could develop complementarities which would be of mutual benefit and would promote economic linkages among themselves. But a regime of cooperation which gives some preferential access to each other's markets provides for cooperation in the monetary field and promotes complementarities in development has yet to be evolved. Given the political environment and the tensions that prevail between some of the countries in the region, it is unlikely that such a regime would evolve in the near future to have an impact on the medium-term prospects of the development of these countries. Nevertheless, there are strong compulsions in certain selected areas which call for well-designed programs of regional cooperation. The country surveys of Nepal and Bangladesh highlighted some of the overriding ecological constraints of the mountain terrain and the major river systems which link the development prospects of these countries and demand their cooperation in the management and better utilization of these resources. Similarly, the management and exploitation of the ocean resources of the countries in the South Asian region can benefit significantly from regional cooperation. A beginning can also be made for collaboration in development planning that can chart the inter-country complementarities in development.

REFERENCES

General

I.B.R.D. *World Development Reports.*
UNCTAD — *Trade and Development Reports.*

Pakistan

Government of Pakistan — *Sixth Five-Year Plan* 1983.
Government of Pakistan — Finance Division (Economic Advisor's Wing) — *Pakistan Economic Survey,* 1984-85.

State Bank of Pakistan — *Annual Report* 1984-85.
R Islam, "Non-Farm Employment in Rural Asia: Issues and Evidence," in R.T. Strand, editor, *Off-Farm Employment in the Development of Rural Asia,* Vol. 1, Canberra, The Australian National University National Centre for Development Studies, 1986, pp. 153-174.

Sri Lanka

Central Bank of Ceylon, *Annual Reports.*
Ministry of Finance and Planning — *Public Investment 1984-88 and 1985-89.*
Department of Census and Statistics — *Census of Population in Sri Lanka,* 1971 and 1981.

Bangladesh

Bangladesh Bank, *Annual Report* 1984-85.
Bangladesh Bank, *Statistical Abstracts on Import & Export Payments.*
Bangladesh Bank, *Economic Trends* 1984-85.
Bangladesh Bureau of Statistics, *Statistical Pocket Book of Bangladesh,* 1984-85.
Syed Ahmed — *Implementation of Second Five-Year Plan and an Outline of Third Plan of Bangladesh.*

Nepal

Nepal Rashtra Bank, *Annual Report,* 1983-84.
Nepal Rashtra Bank Research Department, *Statistical Tables* 1984-85.
Govind Ram Agrawal, "Economic Management in Napal", Paper prepared for the Committee on South Asian Cooperation for Development — 1984.
Remeshwar Bahadur Singh, "A review of Nepal's efforts in Poverty Alleviation."
National Planning Commission, *The Sixth Five-Year Plan.*

15. Economic Development and Issues in Burma

Kazushi Hashimoto

INTRODUCTION

Burma's Development Strategy

As is well known, Burma's development strategy has been quite different from those of most of the Asian developing countries since the present government took over power in 1962. The development strategy is characterized by: (1) nationalization of the economy (excluding agriculture) in order to eliminate the dominance of non-Burmese capital; (2) the establishment of State Economic Enterprises with Burmese nationals in charge to manage the national economy; (3) agrarian reform (the establishment of landed farmers) in order to eliminate non-Burmese land ownership; (4) the strong regulation and control of the economy by the government, and (5) the overall control of the Burma Socialist Program Party in order to avoid the type of confusion which prevailed under parliamentary democracy in the 1950s.

It is notable that, while most Asian developing countries have been pursuing their development strategies characterized by (1) the introduction of the free economic system, (2) the open-window policy to direct foreign investment, (3) the introduction of the Official Development Assistance (ODA) as well as other financial inflows on a large scale in order to achieve a high level of investment, and (4) the export oriented industrialization policy, Burma has been proceeding on a different path.

The nationalization of the economy was conducted swiftly in the 1960s, and almost all of the major economic enterprises except agriculture, small-scale retail

---

* The author wrote this paper based on the data given in the very useful report to the PYITHU HLUTTAW on the Financial, Economic and Social Conditions of the Socialist Republic of the Union of Burma issued by the Ministry of Planning and Finance of Burma, and his experience and observation during his 29 months stay in Burma (Feb. '84 – June '86). No reference has been made to other books or documents except some official reports (World Bank's country report, IMF Report, etc.) which were not published publicly.

trading and small-scale service industry were nationalized by the early 1970s. At present Burma has established about fifty (50) State Economic Enterprises (SEEs) which cover such activities as banking, insurance, extension services for agriculture, forestry, fishery, livestock, mining, manufacturing (textile, food, metal, pharmaceutical, ceramic, vehicles, electric appliance, chemicals and others), energy, construction, transportation and communication, domestic trading and export as well as hotel and tourism, printing and cinema industries. Private business, even in the case of pure Burmese capital, has been deeply discouraged due to the fear of nationalization and the lack of governmental support. At present, according to statistics, the share of State-run activities in GDP is 38.9 percent. As the share of state-run activities in agricultural production, which comprises the largest share in GDP, remains negligible (only 0.4 percent), this figure shows the intensiveness of nationalization in the industry and service sectors (the shares of state-run activities in the output of mining, manufacturing, power, construction and service sector are 90.0 percent, 56.7 percent, 99.9 percent, 81.1 percent and 67.4 percent respectively).

In the process of nationalization and agrarian reform, not only non-Burmese merchants and non-Burmese landlords but also Western and Japanese capital was expelled from Burma. All joint ventures with Western and Japanese capitals were closed or nationalized, and until very recently, the Burmese Government has not accepted direct foreign investment of any kind in any field.

Regarding the introduction of foreign finance, Burma stopped borrowing from the World Bank Group for more than ten (10) years from 1962 up to 1973 due to political reasons. Burma started to introduce the ODA loans on a large scale only after the first Consultative Group Meeting for Burma was held in Tokyo in 1976.

Burma is still reluctant to introduce official finance other than ODA loans (like Exim Bank loans) or commercial loans. Burma's industrialization policy has been import substitution oriented rather than export oriented.

Burmese Way to Socialism

How about the achievements of the Burmese Way to Socialism in the 1960s and 1970s?

The main purpose of nationalization and the agrarian reform — 'The Burmanization of the economy' — seems to have been attained almost satisfactorily. As mentioned above, almost all of the main economic activities, except agriculture, are conducted by SEEs run by the Burmese nationals and there is no room for non-Burmese to participate in these activities. In this sense, the 'Burmese Way to Socialism' has been successful at least from the politcal viewpoint.

However, the data concerning the performance of Burma's economy in the 1960s and early 1970s show that the economic and productivity development has not been so successful as the political achievement.

During the period from 1961 to 1975, when the nationalization policy was implemented at a quick pace, the average GDP growth rate was only 2.7 percent per annum, which was slightly higher than the population growth (2.2 percent per annum), and the growth of the per capita GDP was marginal (0.5 percent per annum). Burma's foreign trade declined more sharply. The volume of Burma's export and import in 1975 was less than one-third of their levels in 1960.

After a period of long stagnation, the Burmese economy started to expand again

Table 1. Burma's Macro Economic Development

	1961-65	66-70	71-75	76-80	81	82	83
Annual GDP Growth (%)	1.7	3.4	4.1	6.2	6.4	5.7	4.8
(Agriculture)	(1.6)	(3.4)	(3.8)	(7.9)	(8.7)	(6.8)	(4.9)
(Manufacturing)	(3.4)	(1.8)	(4.8)	(5.5)	(7.6)	(5.3)	(3.4)
(Service)	(1.9)	(5.5)	(4.9)	(6.6)	(7.2)	(6.1)	(5.0)
(Trade)	(−0.1)	(2.7)	(3.5)	(3.5)	(2.4)	(3.5)	(4.2)
Annual GDP per Capita Growth (%)	−0.5	1.2	1.9	4.0	4.2	3.5	2.8
Annual Population Growth	(2.2)	(2.2)	(2.2)	(2.0)	(2.0)	(2.0)	(2.0)

Source: Report to the PYITHU HLUTTAW on the Financial, Economic and Social Conditions of the Socialist Republic of the Union of Burma.

in the mid 1970s. In the mid 1970s some modifications were made in the development stragegies of Burma within the framework of the 'Burmese Way to Socialism'.

1. The management reform of SEEs (called 'Commercialization') started in 1975. SEEs were required to run on a self paying basis and the Bonus system was introduced.
2. Incentive was given to the farmers from the input side, by the implementation of the 'Whole Township High Yielding Production Development Program' initiated in 1977.
3. Introduction of foreign financial assistance on a large scale after the first Consultative Group Meeting in 1976. This implied that the 'anti-foreign' policy of the 1960's and early 1970s had been partly removed.

As a result of these policy reforms, the GDP growth rate in the latter half of the 1970s (1976-1980) recovered to 6.2 percent per annum and the Burmese people could enjoy some improvement in their lives (the per capita GDP growth rate of this period was 4.0 percent per annum). The volume of export and import grew by 10.9 percent and 14.6 percent per annum respectively.

The other factor which enabled the recovery of Burma's economy in the late 1970s was the introduction of economic development planning. The 'Twenty (20) Year Long-Term Plan (1974/75 — 1993/94)' was drawn up as a basic plan in 1973, under which three (3) four-year plans have been drawn and implemented by now (the 'Second Four-Year Plan [1974/75 — 1977/78]', the 'Third Four-Year Plan [1978/79 — 1981/82]', and the 'Fourth Four-Year Plan [1982/83 — 1985/86]').

The economic planning has facilitated the introduction of the ODA into Burma. The Burmese government submits the list of projects to be implemented under the current economic plan to the C/G meeting which is held every 18 months under the sponsorship of the World Bank. The donor countries and international agencies pledge the ODA loans or grants to the projects included in the above list at the C/G meeting.

The ODA thus introduced, led to the expansion of public investment, and the increase of national investment (national investment grew by 21.6 percent per annum and the share of investment in GDP increased from 7.0 percent to 13.7 percent from 1976 to 1980, while the increase of national saving was slower than that of national investment, the gap between saving and investment was financed from the inflow of the ODA); this, combined with the expansion of agricultural production and the improvement of the performance of SEEs, stimulated the GDP growth. This was the mechanism of the recovery of Burma's economy which occured in the late 1970s.

Table 2. Burma's Foreign Trade (1969 = 100)

	1960	1965	1970	1975	1980	1981	1982	1983
Export (volume)	264.1	161.4	118.5	79.5	133.3	128.0	128.2	152.7
Import (volume)	157.9	123.8	77.5	53.7	106.0	113.3	110.5	96.9

Source: Same as Table 1.

NEW ECONOMIC PROBLEMS

Three Recent Critical Changes in Burmese Economy

The Burmese Government, which thus recovered from the long stagnation, is now facing new problems in the 1980s. The performance of the Burmese economy in the early 1980s are characterized by the following phenomena:

1. GDP continues to grow. However, its growth is slower than in the late 1970s (the average annual GDP growth rate and the per capital GDP growth rate during 1981-1983 were 5.5 percent and 3.4 percent, respectively).
2. Foreign trade stagnates again. The volume of export is increasing, but the growth rate is lower than in the late 1970s (the average annual growth rate during 1981-83 was 4.7 percent). Due to the drop of prices of exported goods from Burma (for example, the recent international price of rice, Burma's main export item, has become less than half of that in early 1980s), the nominal amount of Burmese export receipts is decreasing, rather than increasing. The balance of payment has been suffering from the pressure of the expanding trade deficit, and the volume of imports has apparently started to decrease due to lack of foreign exchange. Since 1983, the Burmese Government has tightened her control on import (Burmese import is under government monopoly).
3. The debt burden is affecting Burmese economy. Burma's external debt has increased since 1976 when the Burmese Government changed its foreign borrowing policy. The total debt in 1984 is estimated to be about SDRs 2.3 billion. Its share in the GDP has increased sharply from 7.6 percent in 1976 to 36.5 percent in 1984. The debt service in 1984 is estimated to be about SDRs 199 million, and the debt service ratio has increased from 15.7 percent in 1976 to 38.9 percent in 1984.

As mentioned above, the Burmese economy in the 1980s is encountering the problems of slower GDP growth, stagnation of export and a heavy debt burden. In the past, 1960s and early 1970s, Burmese economy was highly isolated, so it was insulated from the external shocks. However, since late 1970s, as Burmese economy

Table 3. GDP National Investment and National Saving (1975-83)

(Unit: Kyat million at 1969 constant price)

	1975	1976	1977	1978	1979	1980	1981	1982	1983
GDP	11,561	12,265	12,995	13,843	14,562	15,717	16,717	17,661	18,509
National investment	808	965	1,430	1,851	2,205	2,157	2,454	2,787	2,502
National investment/ GDP (%)	7.0	7.9	11.0	13.4	15.1	13.7	14.7	15.8	13.5
National saving	1,152	1,245	1,474	1,805	2,098	2,256	2,441	2,032	2,228
National saving/ GDP (%)	10.0	10.2	11.3	13.0	14.4	14.4	14.6	11.5	12.0

Source: Same as Table 1.

Table 4. Burma's Balance of Trade

(Unit: Kyat million)

	1975	1980	1981	1982	1983
Export	1,322	3,225	3,452	3,036	3,419
Import	1,443	4,635	5,611	6,313	5,197
Balance	−121	−1,410	−2,159	−3,277	−1,778

Source: Same as Table 1.
Note: The exchange rate in 1986: Kyat 8.5 per US Dollar.

Table 5. Burma's External Debt

(Unit: SDR$_s$ million)

	1979	1980	1981	1982	1983	1984
Medium and long term debt	941	1,183	1,472	1,816	2,086	2,287
Use of Fund credit	68	42	55	65	83	75
Total debt	1,009	1,225	1,527	1,881	2,169	2,362
(In percent of GDP)	(24.3)	(27.0)	(30.2)	(34.5)	(37.1)	(36.5)
Debt service	93	115	135	129	159	199
(In percent of current receipts, including private remittances)	(26.1)	(26.2)	(28.2)	(31.3)	(34.1)	(38.9)

Source: IMF Report.

has been partly involved in the world economy, the external factors such as the worldwide recession and external debt problem started to exert influence on Burmese economy.

Future Issues of the Burmese Economy

The following is an analysis of the causes and effects on the future development of the Burmese economy.

The Slower GDP Growth
There seem to be two main causes for the slower GDP growth in the 1980s. Firstly, the production of paddy, which is Burma's main crop, has reached its limit due to the completion of the Whole Township High Yielding Production Development Program at the beginning of 1980s and due to the insufficiency of adequate irrigation facilities. Secondly, the national investment has stopped expanding mainly due to lack of foreign exchange.

The Whole Township High Yielding Production Development Program started in 1977 and was almost completed in 1980. The paddy production of Burma expanded from 9.3 million tons in 1977 to 13.9 million tons in 1981 (average annual growth rate was 10.6 percent) due to the implementation of the Program. This expansion of paddy production was one of the major factors contributing to the high GDP growth of Burma in the late 1970s. After the completion of the Program, the increase of paddy production has been marginal (average annual growth rate of rice production during 1981-83 was only 0.5 percent), and in 1983 Burma experienced a decline of paddy production due to unfavorable rainfall.

Table 6. Production of Paddy in Burma

(Unit: million Ton)

	1961	1975	1977	1978	1979	1980	1981	1982	1983
Paddy	6.72	9.06	9.31	10.36	10.28	13.10	13.92	14.14	14.06
Pulses	0.25	0.24	0.36	0.36	0.37	0.40	0.51	0.48	0.59
Oil Seeds	0.46	0.54	0.58	0.60	0.45	0.62	0.81	0.81	0.84
Sugarcane	1.07	1.61	1.76	1.81	1.44	2.00	2.69	3.66	3.61

Source: Same as Table 1.

To expand agricultural production, besides high yielding varieties, Burma has been expanding the utilization of other inputs like quality seeds, chemical fertilizers, pesticides and agricultural loans, etc. (in the case of chemical fertilizers, the utilization was more than doubled during 1978-1983 from 192 to 400 thousand metric tons). However, although irrigation facilities are absolutely necessary for the extensive and efficient utilization of these inputs, the irrigation rate (irrigated area per net sown area) of Burma remains very low (12.87 percent in 1983), and there has been no major development in the past.

The other contributing factor for the GDP growth in the late 1970s was the rapid expansion of national investment (mainly public investment). In the early 1980s, the national investment had stopped expanding, and its share in GDP had decreased from 14.7 percent in 1981 to 13.5 percent in 1983. This stagnation of investment is apparently due to the tightening of government control on foreign exchange which was necessitated by the recent stagnation of exports and the increasing debt burden.

The Stagnation of Export
The Burmese Government explains that the recent stagnation of exports is caused by the decline of prices of export commodities from Burma due to the worldwide recession after the second oil crisis in 1979. Burmese exports, however, are decreasing in nominal terms even after the recovery of worldwide economy led by the recovery of the USA in 1983.

The characteristics of Burmese exports may be annalyzed as follows:
1. Composition of exports
    The composition of exports has not changed in the past 10 years. The shares of two major traditional items, rice (41.1 percent) and teak (25.5 percent) remain the same. The export of manufactured products remain negligible.

Table 7. Composition of Burmese Exports

(Unit: %)

	1972	1983
Agricultural Products	48.9	52.7
Fishery and Livestock Products	0.6	2.8
Forestry Products	30.8	27.3
Mining Products	18.2	14.9
Others	1.5	2.3

Source: Same as Table 1.

2. Destination of exports

The shares of industrialized countries (Japan, Western Europe, USA, etc.) in Burmese export have declined sharply, and the shares of South East Asia and South Asia have increased.

The present large shares of South East Asia and South Asia (Sri Lanka, India, Bangladesh) are apparently due to the exportation of rice to these regions. The decline of the share of industrialized countries would be explained partly by the increase of indirect export through Singapore or Hong Kong instead of direct export to industrialized countries, and partly by the decline of mineral exports.

Table 8. Destination of Burmese Exports

(Unit: %)

	1972	1983
Japan	22.3	6.7
USA and Canada	0.4	0.4
Australia and New Zealand	0.1	—
Western Europe	29.7	12.4
South East Asia	15.3	33.7
South Asia	13.4	20.3
Other parts of Asia	10.4	9.6
Others	8.4	16.9

Source: Same as Table 1.

The Heavy Debt Burden

Burma has not yet proposed rescheduling of its debt payments to the Paris Club, and she seems unlikely to do so for political reasons. However, it is undeniable that Burma is facing a debt problem. The heavy debt burden restricts the Burmese Government from expanding its foreign borrowing. In 1984, Burma did not sign any loan agreements with the World Bank or the Asian Development Bank. Although the total debt is still increasing, the increase in 1983-84 is much lower (12 percent per annum in nominal terms) than in 1980-82 (23 percent per annum).

Such a restriction of foreign borrowing has inevitably slowed down public investment. The investment of the Union government and SEEs has been decreasing since 1982, even in nominal terms (from 7,770 to 6,577 million Kyats). And this decrease of public investment is one of the major factors for the recent slow down of GDP growth as already mentioned.

The Burmese Government tends to prefer restriction of borrowing from abroad than going to the Paris Club for rescheduling arrangement because it would satisfy its feeling of self-dependence. However, as the further reduction of public investment seems to make the present economic stagnation of Burma more serious, the re-expansion of foreign borrowing would be needed to improve such facilities as irrigation, road, bridges and power.

How to avoid the increasing pressure of the debt burden out of the Burmese economy depends on whether or not Burma can sufficiently expand its exports.

ISSUES OF DEVELOPMENT AND PRODUCTIVITY

Agricultural Development

The share of the agriculture sector (including livestock, fishery and forestry) in the Burmese economy is quite large. It comprises 66 percent of the labor force, 48 percent of the GDP and 83 percent of exports. Its share in the GDP has even been increasing recently due to the slow industrial development.

Table 9. Distribution of Labor Force by Sector in 1984

(Unit: %)

Agriculture	66.1
Industry	10.6
Service	9.3
Trade	9.8
Worker n.e.s.	4.2

Source: Same as Table 1.

Table 10. Distribution of GDP by Sector

(Unit: %, at current prices)

	1961	1975	1980	1981	1982	1983
Agriculture	34.0	47.1	46.5	47.4	47.7	48.0
Industry	12.9	10.8	12.7	12.5	12.6	12.4
Service	25.1	13.0	14.6	15.1	15.1	15.1
Trade	28.0	29.1	26.2	25.0	24.6	24.5

Source: Same as Table 1.

In this context, it seems that the development of the Burmese economy will depend on the success of agricultural development in the foreseeable future.

It is generally said that Burmese agriculture is facing the following difficulties.

1. Although agriculture is not nationalized, the prices of agricultural products are controlled strictly by the government and are kept low. For example, in the case of rice, the farmer must sell all crops to the government except for family consumption and the selling price has not been raised for more than 10 years since 1974.
2. The loss of agricultural products in the process of production and distribution is very high due to the poor and inefficient condition of infrastructure like roads. There is a dearth of vehicles to transport agricultural products and insufficient grain storage capacity.
3. The level of utilization of inputs like quality seeds, chemical fertilizer, pesticide, etc. is still very low.
4. Under-developed irrigation.
5. Burmese agriculture has concentrated on rice production and diversification into other crops has not occurred.

Burma has to overcome these problems for further agricultural development. Among them, irrigation development is most urgently needed, as the effective utilization of agricultural inputs like chemical fertilizer and the diversification of agricultural production would be possible only after multi-cropping becomes possible by introduction of modern irrigation.

As is well known, ASEAN countries like Indonesia, have been developing irrigation energetically by introducing ODA to the irrigation sector from international agencies like the World Bank and the Asian Development Bank, and on a bilateral basis as well. However, Burma could not do so because Burma has had to allocate a large part of ODA for the industrial investment which would ordinarily be implemented with direct foreign investment and other related commercial finance. This was not possible in Burma, where they were not allowed. For example, 56 percent of the Yen Credit which had been extended to Burma by the end of December, 1984 by the Japanese Government, the largest donor (her contribution is more than double that of the World Bank and ADB), has been allocated to the industrial sector. (In the case of Yen credit to other developing countries, the share of the industrial sector is about 12 to 13 percent.)

Therefore, it is apparently necessary for Burma and donors to make a special effort to increase the share of irrigation assistance in total ODA.

Industrialization and Export Promotion

It is a fact that the industrialization of Burma has been greatly delayed. The experiences of Asian NICs and ASEAN countries show that direct foreign investment plays a vital role in the industrialization and export promotion of the developing countries. Firstly, the necessary foreign exchange for industrial investment can be gained by equity participation and related financing from the investor. Secondly, technology and management know-how can be transferred. Thirdly, access to the market in industrialized countries is facilitated by the help of partner companies.

Burma, not having allowed any type of direct foreign investment until very recently, announced recently the establishment of a new company with a West German machinery manufacturing company, based on the principle of the 'Mutual

Beneficiary Economic Cooperation'. Although Burmese officials stated that the new company is not a 'Joint-Venture', it is definitely a kind of direct foreign investment. Burmese officials, however, stated that Burma will approve a similar scheme only in the case where the size of the project is very large and where advanced technology is needed. As far as one can tell from the above explanation, Burma seems to have no intention of approving similar schemes in sectors like textile, food processing, forestry and fishery, where the size of each project is small, and advanced technology is not so much required, although direct foreign investment in these sectors would definitely contribute to the promotion of exports.

In this respect, an interesting fact is that top Burmese leaders have consecutively visited China recently, and have seen the actual consequences of China's Open Economy Policy and the dynamic presence of Western capital investment in the special economic zones in China like Shenzhen.

Burmese external trade is suffering from the stagnation of exports. The Burmese Government is aware of this problem and Burmese officials mention the necessity of diversification of export in their speeches and government publications. However, their endeavors have not been systematic. A classic example is the case where Burma exported fabrics, cement, paper pulp, crude oil, etc. on a spot basis in the last few years, even though these items were unavailable in sufficient quantities in Burma itself, and were not therefore continuously exportable items. The Burmese Government must first establish a systematic policy for export promotion to overcome the present crisis in the Burmese economy.

Burma has a plentiful supply of national resources, and many of them are exportable items. In addition to the traditional mineral resources, an offshore gas field was recently discovered, and the Burmese Government is trying to develop it. However, attention should be given to the fact that the experiences of Asian NICs and ASEAN countries show that industrialization which depends too much on natural resources is risky and is not entirely successful. The East Asian countries which could not depend on natural resources and so promoted labor-intensive manufacturing have been developing more smoothly. If the Burmese Government made efforts in the development of labor-intensive light industries like textile, and food processing, equal to or more than those made in natural resource development, it would have a greater chance of success.

As promotion of exports is the greatest issue facing the Burmese economy, the establishment of an administrative organization for exports is required. Burma's export activities are monopolized by the government, and private people cannot participate in the export business. SEEs under the Ministry of Trade are handling the export of rice and other agricultural products. Other products are being exported independently by various SEEs under different Ministries. Burma opened trade representative offices in Tokyo and London in 1960, but closed them soon due to some reason or other and has not reopened them yet. Several times we have heard complaints from Western trading firms that, even when they do find some products which may be easily imported from Burma, they are soon discouraged because the Burmese side requires tendering to decide on the buyer.

Therefore in order to promote Burma's export, the establishment of unified administration for export activities, establishment of trade representative offices in the developed countries, as well as active marketing activities are urgently needed.

Administrative Problem

Government administration in Burma is characterized by its decision making system highly centralized to the top people. Transfer of decision making downwards has not been implemented at all. Not only matters such as the price of government control-led goods or decision on new investment, but also such trivial matters as decision on procurement of machineries and goods for the implementation of the investment project already approved by the cabinet or selection of trainees abroad under the Colombo Plan, must be approved by the cabinet. This extremely centralized decision making system hampers the inter-ministry or inter-SEEs coordination, because middle class officials in ministries or SEEs are not given enough authorization to deal with the people in other ministries/SEEs.

Although the management reform of SEEs, started in 1975, introduced the principle of financial self-sufficiency in the accounting manner of SEEs, this reform did not go as far as permitting them to make their own independent decisions. SEE's cannot decide even the price of their own products, their investment plan or procurement matters of their own projects (these matters must be decided by the cabinet). Such a character of Burmese administration seems to derive from two factors: (1) Burmese people's traditional obedience to the higher authority as its national character, (2) monopoly of high government posts (Minister, Deputy Minister, Director-General, SEE's Managing Director) by military personnels, difficulty for middle class government officials (who are civilians) to oppose to those high rank officials (who are military personnels) under the present political environment. In effect, the status of technocrats in Burmese Government (even in case of the ministries concerned with the economy) is extremely low, reflective of the distrust of the armed force on civilians. Accordingly, all minister posts are occupied by military personnels and there is no technocrate in the cabinet. Under such circumstances, political and dogmatic viewpoints are enforced even in the economic policy and economic nationalism is sometimes sacrificed.

Under such environment, it would be very difficult for Burma to adapt to the rapid transformation of the worldwide economic situation. Burma will have to face it when she opens her economy to the outside world in the future. Accordingly, the transfer of decision making downwards and the active enrollment of technocrats is essential for the further development of Burmese economy.

Social Development

Education
Burmese people are very eager in educating their children. Monks and priests were teachers of reading and writing for village people in the traditional Burmese village life. Accordingly, people's literacy rate in Burma is relatively high (66 percent), compared with those in other developing countries. Many of Burmese government officials can use English very well. However, the number of young people who can use English is decreasing due to the long isolation of Burmese society from the outside world since 1962 revolution. This would hamper the modernization of Burma in future, because the translation of Western literature has not been conducted enough due to the strict government control on publication.

Population and Health

Although Burmese Government has no particular population policy, the population growth rate in Burma is relatively low and stable (present annual growth rate is roughly 2 percent). This is because of the high rate of infancy death due to the bad health condition prevailing in Burma. It is apparent that the bad health condition derives from the absolute poverty in Burma. In this context, economic development is essential for social development of Burma.

16. Indo-China Economy

Tetsusaburo Kimura

THE VIETNAMESE ECONOMY IN PERSPECTIVE

Before analyzing the Vietnamese economy, let us first look at the major economic trends since reunification in 1976. This writer will show economic trends using four indices as follows: (1) National income, (2) Gross industrial production, (3) Gross agriculture production and (4) Rice production.

Vietnam has not been generous in supplying economic data. Normally, it gives only the rate of increase compared with the previous years. In some cases, it publishes no statistical figures. Hence these indices were calculated from fragmented information from official statements or from Vietnam periodicals (*Party Daily* or *Economic Studies*). One often finds inconsistencies in this information.

Vietnam's statistical system has followed the Soviet Union's system. Normally, national income does not include the pure income of persons who do not work within the material sector. But in 1979 and 1980, Vietnam's General Statistical Office published national income data for the period 1975-79 calculated by U.N. methodology. These are used herein.

Table 1 and the graph show that production fell to the lowest level at the end of the second five-year plan period (1976-80) and began to recover in 1981 (Graph). Agricultural production declined from 1977 and began to recover in 1980. In 1975, national income was 4.682 billion dollars (exchange rate US$1 = 4 VN Dong),[1] thus 98.2 dollars per capita (calculated according to UN methods).[2] Because of the final stages of the war, Vietnam's economy was at its lowest level in 1975. In 1976,

---

[1] Though the official rate is US$ = 2.04 dong and SDR = 2.66 dong, we follow here the Vietnam Statistical Office (exchange rate US$ = 4 dong).

[2] National income of 1975 was 18,258 million dong, in U.S. currency 4,682 million dollars. We assume here that national income is calculated at the constant prices of 1975 and converted into U.S. dollars with the constant U.S. dollar of 1975.

the first year of the second five-year plan, national income was 4.975 billion dollars with per capita 101.2 dollars. After five years, per capita national income fell to 98.7 dollars, the same level as 1975.[3] In the second five-year plan, it was planned to expand national income by 13-14 percent, gross agricultural production by 8-10 percent, and gross industrial production by 16-18 percent each year. And Vietnam planned to produce 21 million tons of grain in 1980, but grain production in 1980 was 14.40 million tons. The second five-year plan (1976-80) was a complete failure.

Officials have cited such causes for failure as natural calamities and foreign aggression. Cold spells, drought, typhoons and widespread flooding succeeded one after another from 1976 to 1979, both North and South. The cutoff of Chinese aid and departure of Chinese experts in 1976 led to the closure of many enterprises and construction projects in the North. Conflict with the Khmer Rouge on the southwestern border with Kampuchea during the years 1976-78 devastated Tay Ninh and An Giang provinces. The direct attack by 600,000 Chinese troops in February 1979 against the six northern border provinces along a 1600-km front caused vast destruction estimated at one billion U.S. dollars, and put an end to a period of relative peace.[4]

These are objective factors contributing to the fiasco. There are subjective factors as well.

The officials have realized that they were not realistic. Their plan was too ambitious. They overestimated the potential growth of agricultural production. And they preferred to invest in industry. Of the roughly 30 billion dong to be invested during the period of the second plan (1976-80), they intended to allocate nearly 30 percent for agriculture and 35 percent for industry.[5] But in the third plan (1981-85), priorities of investment are concentrated on production of grain, the processing of agricultural products and on exports. The second factor is haste in collectivization. In his report to the Fourth Party Congress in 1976. Le Duan set forth the basic goal of achieving socialist transformation in the South, and consolidating and perfecting socialist production relations in the North.

Forcing the southern peasants into agricultural collectivization, the officials encountered peasant resistance. Peasants in the Mekong delta reduced their rice production to the lowest level and sold what remained not to the government but to Chinese merchants in Cholon who could supply consumer goods and tools of production to the peasants. The government could not procure grain for consumption by soldiers, civil servants and workers.

So the government attacked the Chinese in Cholon. On March 23, 1978 the industrial and commercial activities of private enterprises were suddenly banned. In May 1978 the government changed the currency and froze bank deposits. The

---

[3] There are many estimates of national income. A U.S. Senate report of April 1982 estimated per capita income of 1978 at 400 dong, about 180 dollars by the exchange rate SDR = 2.66358 dong. Ton That Thien (*Pacific Affairs*, Winter-Spring 1984, p. 711) estimates 198.5 dollars in 1976 and 191.9 dollars in 1979 by the official rate of US$1 = 2.04 dong. A World Bank estimate put the figure for 1979 at 175 dollars. *Asia Yearbook 1982* (published by the Far Eastern Economic Review) estimated GNP at market prices of 1980 at 16.0 billion dollars, per capita income of 1980 at 290 dollars. But *Asia Yearbook 1984* estimates GNP at market prices of 1982 at 9.0 billion dollars, per capita income 1982 at 160 dollars. That is reasonable. Some writers assume that national income equals Gross Domestic Product. See *U.N. Yearbook National Accounts Statistics*, 1981, Vol. 1, Part 2, p. 1968 and Ton That Thien, ibid., p. 711.

[4] Nguyen Xuan Lai, "Economic Development 1976-85", *Vietnamese Studies* #1 (new series began after VN Studies #70), 1984, pp. 32-33.

[5] Pham Van Dong's report to the 4th Party Congress (Dec. 1976).

Chinese were hit hard and became boat people. The destruction of the distribution machinery in the South discouraged the peasants' agricultural production.

The third factor was consolidation of socialist production relations in the North. During the war, the socialist division of labor in agricultural cooperatives was relaxed. The managing committee in cooperatives assigns working the land not to the teams, but to peasant families. But after the war, the Government began to enlarge the size of cooperatives, from village to commune.

At the same time it introduced the factory system in agricultural labor. The commune cooperative no longer allocates to groups of workers or families the complete production cycle on a given area of land. Rather it divides the entire labor force into teams, each specializing in given activities. This system is accompanied by a complicated work norms arrangement. Peasants lost incentives for increasing production. Labor force and other resources remained idle.[6]

The fourth factor is Vietnam's isolation. China cut off its aid in 1978 and destroyed the northern frontier region of Vietnam in the spring of 1979. Because of Vietnam's invasion of Cambodia, most Western countries suspended their economic programs. Being unable to import raw materials, spare parts and machinery from the Western countries, factories in Vietnam could not operate.

Faced with the deteriorating economy, the Sixth Plenum of the Central Committee of the Party (fall of 1979) announced the decision to change policy with a view to developing the national economy and urgently increasing the amount of agricultural produce, consumer goods and export items.

Peasants were permitted to go freely to the city to sell their surplus production. The campaign to collectivize agriculture in the South slowed. Small merchants and craftsmen were encouraged to continue their activities without fear of collectivization. The free market was allowed to coexist with the State sector.

Following much debate between ideologists and pragmatists, the resolutions of the Sixth Plenum were put into concrete form in 1980. The application of the contractual system in agriculture led to permitting cultivation of land and raising of pigs by peasant families. After delivering their quota, peasants can dispose of their surplus in the free market. Compulsory deliveries of grain to the State have been stabilized for five years. In 1981 the State's purchasing prices for agricultural produce was raised an average of 800 percent. The directors of the state-run enterprises have gained more power and more responsibility over enterprise management. The minimum wages and salaries of workers, employees and cadres were increased by 100 percent.

These new policies have become incentives to increase production among all strata of society. Table 1 shows that production increased. On the basis of these achievements, Vietnam published the direction of the third five-year plan (1981-85) in the Fifth Congress of the Party (March 1982).

It is expected that during the 1981-85 five-year plan there will be an average annual increase in agricultural production of about 6 percent to 7 percent, industrial production 4 percent to 5 percent and national income 4.5 percent to 5 percent. By 1985 the total increase in grain production will be 32 percent over 1980 and

---

[6] Nguyen Duc Nhuan, "The contradictions of the Rationalization of Agricultural Space and Work in Vietnam", *International Journal of Urban and Regional Research*, Vol. 7, No. 3, 1983 and Nguyen Duc Nhuan, "The Damage of Socialist Witch Doctors and Bureaucrats in Vietnam", *Politique Aujourd'hui*, March 1982 (translated in JPRS VN 2365, 5/18/82).

Table 1. Growth Index

	Population	National Income	Gross Production of Industry	Gross Production of Agriculture	Rice Production
1975	100	100	100	100	100
1976	103.2	114.6	112.6	110.2	112.6
1977	105.8	116.9	123.9	104.8	103.3
1978	107.9	119.6	130.6	104.9	95.3
1979	110.1	119.1	124.7	112.0	102.1
1980	112.8	113.4	112.8	119.0	111.0
1981	115.3	122.3	129.8	122.3	119.3
1982	117.9	132.2	141.8	132.4	134.4
1983	120.4	136.1	163.3	137.3	139.8
1984	123.4	143.6	175.1	145.8	148.1

Sources: 1. General Statistical Office, *Statistical Data of the Socialist Republic of Vietnam 1979*, Hanoi 1980.
2. Tong Cuc Thong Ke, *So Lien Thong Ke 1930-1984*, Hanoi 1985.
3. VNA, "Economic Achievements since Last Congress Noted," *FBIS*, March 24, 1982.
4. Vu Quoc Tuan, "Xay Dung Tung Buoc Mot Co Can Kinh Te Moi," *Nghien Cuu Kinh Te*, No. 1 (137), 1984.

Note: According to Vu Quoc Tuan, national income in 1983 increased by 20% compared to 1980 and gross production of industry in 1983 increased by 25% over 1978.

rice production in 1985 will be 16-16.5 million tons of paddy.[7]

This is a more modest plan than the second five-year plan. And during the three-years from 1981 to 1983, industrial and agricultural production increased and national income increased by 20 percent in 1983 compared to 1980.

The question, however, is whether the Vietnamese economy can continue the trend of economic growth that has taken place since 1981.

Development Performance and Issues

We will now analyze the development of the Vietnamese economy and view the third five-year plan (1981-85). Vietnam had expected most of investment capital for the second five-year plan (1976-80) to be financed from foreign countries including the Soviet Union, China and Western countries. The Soviet Union and China seemed to have committed respectively US$2.6 billion[8] and US$1.5 billion.[9]

Citibank estimated the economic aid to Vietnam from socialist countries as nearly US$5.0 billion (see Table 2).

But foreign aid fell short of Vietnam's expectations. China, which had already

---

[7] Pham Van Dong's report to the 5th Party Congress.
[8] Congressional Research Service, *Vietnam's Future Policies and Role in Southeast Asia,* April 1982, p. 16.
[9] Ton That Thien, "Vietnam's New Economic Policy", *Pacific Affairs,* Winter 1983-84, p. 696.

Table 2. Estimate of Economic Aid of Vietnam

(Unit: US$ million)

	1965-75	1976-80
China	1,491	1,500
Russia	1,778	2,666
East Germany	253	233
Poland	184	107
Hungary	167	167
Czechoslovakia	102	133
Bulgaria	98	127
Rumania	40	33
Cuba	3	996
Total	4,116	4,978
Annual Average	374	996

Source: Citibank Hong Kong, *An Economic Survey of Vietnam,* Sept. 1976, p. 26.

stopped all military aid to Vietnam in 1975 and interest-free loans in 1977, cut off all assistance and recalled its aid personnel in July 1978.[10] And most assistance from the socialist countries were not grants but long-term loans with low interest rates.

We do not know how much assistance Vietnam expected to receive from Western countries. Vietnam has not yet succeeded in normalizing relations with the United States. Among Western countries, France (US$366 million) and Sweden (US$ 100 million) showed their willingness to aid Vietnam, but because of the Cambodian invasion by Vietnam at the end of 1978, most Western countries suspended assistance. The Vietnamese attempt to induce foreign capital in joint-ventures has not succeeded.

The foregoing has presented a look at the foreign aid. Now we will try to examine domestic savings and capital formation. The ability to accrue investment money in each collective was extremely low. In 1975, it was estimated that investment from its own saving was sufficient to expand the cultivated area of each collective by only one hectare (cultivated area per cooperative in 1975 was 130 ha). The amount saved was insufficient to pay for small basic machinery.[11]

Most Vietnamese capitalists left after the fall of Saigon. Those who remained lost their accumulated capital due to the order of abolishing private enterprises in the South and freezing bank deposits in the spring of 1978.

Saving by handicraft cooperatives and local industries in the North appears very small, but we cannot calculate it.

Therefore, we can assume that most funds for investment come through the

---

[10] Ton That Thien, ibid., p. 696.

[11] Nguyen Gia Ngo's "On the Direction and Structure of Agricultural Production in the North", *Nghien Cuu Kinh Te,* No. 83, Feb. 1975 quoted in the Congressional Research Service's report (April 1982, See Footnote no. 3).

government budget. Vietnam has not published a breakdown of its budget. But we will try to construct the budget structure of Vietnam. Vo Nhan Tri showed the budget structure of North Vietnam in the period 1961-63 (Table 3).

During the period of the second five-year plan (1976-80), domestically produced national income constituted an average of 61.4 percent of total budget revenues and only provided for 94 percent of the expenditure related to the consumption through the budget and the repayment of state debts. All expenditures related to the accumulation of capital and 6 percent of the expenditure for consumption made through the budget were based on sources of revenue outside the country. Despite these rather large revenues in aid and loans (38.6 percent of total revenues), Vietnam was still unable to balance its budget and its annual deficit increased until 1982.[12]

The revenues of the state economic sector account for 80 percent of the domestic revenues of the state budget.[13] The amount of the agricultural tax during the second five-year period (1976-80) accounts for only 5 percent of the state budget.[14] Between 1976 and 1980, the commercial and industrial taxes amounted to about 7 or 8 percent of the total domestic budget revenues.[15]

Between 1976 and 1980, the amount of budget expenditure was a little over 10 billion dong. But in 1981 the application of the new economic policy and an

Table 3. Vietnam's Budget

(Unit: %)

	1961	1962	1963	1976-80[a]
I. Total Revenue	100	100	100	100
a) Domestic Revenue	82.6	79.7	79.5	61.4
1. Taxes	23.9	23.3	22.1	9.6
2. Contribution from the State Sector	56.9	54.3	56.0	49.1
3. Other Revenue	1.8	1.5	1.4	2.7
b) Revenue from Foreign Aid	17.4	20.3	20.5	38.6
II. Total Expenditures	100	100	100	100
a) Economic Development	60.4	60.9	61.0	39.2
b) Social and Cultural Expenses	14.6	13.8	13.8	17.8
c) Administration	5.6	5.5	5.4	
d) Defense	19.4	19.8	19.8	43.6[b]
III. Deficit	—	—	—	10% of GDP

Sources: 1. Vo Nhan Tri, *Croissance Economique de la Republique Democratique du Viet Nam,* Hanoi, 1967, p. 466.
2. Chu Tam Thuc, "Tich Luy va Tieu Dung", *Tap Chi Cong San,* Jan. 1984. pp. 28-29.

Notes: — (a) 1970-1980 estimate. Aid in this period includes grants and loans.
— (b) Defense calculated by this writer. Since Vo Nhan Tri did not show the percent of defense expenditure, this writer assumes the rest of the expenses are for defense.

[12] Chu Tam Thuc, *ibid,* pp. 28-29. See Table 3.
[13] *Nhan Dan,* May 18, 1982.
[14] *Nhan Dan,* March 2, 1983.
[15] *Nghien Cuu Kinh Te,* No. 5, Oct. 1983, p. 14.

increase of 100 percent in the nominal wages and salaries led to an inflation rate above 100 percent. Vietnamese currency was devaluated by 320 percent from 2.828 dong to the dollar (then official rate) to 9.09 dong in July 1981.

The amount of expenditure in 1983 was 50 billion dong.[16] The deficit reported was 5 billion dong in 1981,[17] 4 billion dong (US$440 million) in 1982 and 3 billion dong in 1983.[18] IMF's estimate of the deficit as a percent of GDP is as follows: 10 percent in 1981, 20 percent in 1982 and 10 percent in 1983.[19]

According to Radio Beijing, the military expenses out of the total financial expenditures were as follows: 41.4 percent in 1977, 40.4 percent in 1978, 47 percent in 1979.[20] After 1980, over 50 percent of the budget went to the military establishment. Another 18 percent is earmarked for the government-cum-political bureaucracy.[21]

Table 4 shows state investment outlays in the period of the second five-year plan (1976-80). The rate of accumulation is low compared to the Soviet Union and China with over 35 percent. The government was able to put together 18.44 billion dong for capital construction, of which 16.1 billion (87.3 percent) was to production sectors, with 7.5 billion (40.7 percent) to industry and construction, and 4.4 billion to agriculture and forestry (23.9 percent). Non-productive sectors got another 2.3 billion.[22]

Table 4. Investment

	National Income (million dong) (A)	Budget Expenditure (million dong) (B)	Investment (million dong) (C)	C A (%)	C B (%)
1976	19.901	10.400	2,474.4	15.0	28.7
1977	20.305	8.950	3,627.3	17.9	40.6
1978	20.742	10.770	3,850.0	18.6	35.8
1979	20.638	10.500	3,648.0	17.7	34.8
1980	20.705*	—	(4,340)	20.9	—

Source: — General Statistical Office, *Statistical Data of the Socialist Republic of Vietnam*, Hanoi, 1980.

Notes: — — means not available.
   — Vietnam did not announce the total investment for 1980, but we can arrive at an estimate by subtracting the cumulative total from 1976 to 1979 of 14.10 billion dong from the announced total of 18.44 billion dong during the 1976-80 period (see footnote No. 22).
   — *: 1.134 (index national income in 1980. 1975 = 1.0) multiplied by 18.258 (national income of 1975).

---

[16] Van Regemorter, Henri, "Reflection on 1970-80 Economic Policy", *Doan Ket*, Paris; Nov. 1983, pp. 15-16.
[17] *Asia Yearbook 1983*. This figure contradicts IMF estimate.
[18] *Far Eastern Economic Review*, July 14, 1983, p. 70.
[19] *The Nation Review*, Bangkok, July 30, 1984.
[20] Beijing Broadcast in Vietnamese, Nov. 28, 1980.
[21] *The Statesman*, Calcutta, Feb. 16, 1982.
[22] VNA, *Economic Achievements since Last Congress*, March 20, 1982.

Over this period fixed capital in productive sectors increased by 91 percent. The amount of capital accumulated has been small. Furthermore, the use of this capital has been poorly managed and inefficient. Capital was invested in a decentralized, evenly distributed manner lacking focus and coordination, lacking investigation and full preparation. Management of construction has not been good. Construction costs are high, usually 15 to 30 percent higher than estimated; construction time is long, an average of 1.9 times longer than planned; and the volume of unfinished work on projects is very large. Due to shortcomings in the structure of investments, newly created production capacity cannot be fully or continuously utilized. Taken together, the coefficient of the fixed assets and new production capacity put into operation during the five years from 1976-1980 amounted to 51.1 percent total investments, much less than during the period from 1960 to 1965 (70.4 percent).

Returns from investments are small: 1 dong in fixed assets within the state-operated sector produced 0.245 dong in national income in 1976 and 0.197 dong in 1980. One dong of production capital (fixed and liquid assets) only produced 0.111 dong in net income in 1976: this figure rose to 0.13 dong in 1977 and 1978, gradually declined to 0.108 dong in 1979 and 0.095 dong in 1980 and stood at roughly 0.09 dong in 1981 and 1982.[23]

From the above, we can calculate tentatively the capital output (k/o) ratio as follows:

Year	1976	1977	1978	1979	1980	1981	1982
k/o ratio	9.01	7.69	7.69	9.26	10.53	11.11	11.11

This means that if the rate of accumulation (saving rate) is 20 percent, Vietnam can have a growth rate of only 2 percent, which does not even match the 2.4 percent growth rate of the population.

In the third five-year plan (1981-85), the total capital invested by the State in capital construction for five years is estimated at approximately 16 to 18 billion dong, based on old money value.[24] The government is striving to reduce k/o ratio. If they can reduce k/o ratio to 8, the growth rate will be 3 percent at the most with the rate of accumulation 25 percent.[25]

As mentioned above, Vietnam's national income could meet only 94 percent of the needs of social consumption. All expenditures related to the accumulation of capital and 6 percent of the expenditures for consumption made through the budget, were based on foreign sources. Hence, Vietnam's trade gap is very large.

Table 5 shows Vietnam trade 1976-1983. Exports cover only 25-30 percent of the import. Since 1981, imports from Western countries decreased and these from Soviet Union increased. We cannot know the value of aid commitment for 1981-85 from the COMECON countries. They were irritated at Vietnam's request for more aid and the inefficient manner it was being used. Because of the delay in the Soviet Union's reply for aid, the Fifth Congress of the Vietnam Communist Party was postponed until March 1982, when the Party published the tasks and direction of the third five-year plan (1981-85). When Le Duan visited the Soviet Union in September 1981, he agreed that in five-year period the two countries would launch 40 joint construction projects of major economic significance.[26] Le Duan promised

---

[23] Chu Tam Chuc, ibid.

[24] Pham Van Dong's report to the 5th Party Congress, *Nhan Dan*, March 30, 1982.

[25] Average of the second plan (18%) plus 7% (saving in cooperatives and industries not made through the budget).

[26] Ton That Thien. "Vietnam's New Economic Policy", *Pacific Affairs*, Winter-Spring 1984, p. 703.

Table 5. Vietnam Trade

(Unit: US$ million)

	Import			Export			Deficit
	Total	USSR	IMF Total	Total	USSR	IMF Total	
1976	822.6	308.4	514.2	215.0	84.4	130.6	607.6
1977	1,044.1	372.0	672.1	309.3	176.1	132.9	735.1
1978	1,465.8	446.4	1,019.4	406.7	222.5	184.2	1,059.1
1979	1,653.0	680.3	972.7	383.1	225.0	158.1	1,269.9
1980	1,576.7	700.1	876.6	398.6	242.2	156.2	1,178.1
1981	1,697.3	1,006.4	690.9	388.3	232.2	156.1	1,309.0
1982	1,599.6	1,107.4	492.2	479.7	284.4	195.3	1,119.9
1983	1,689.2	1,213.9	475.3	534.5	315.3	219.2	1,154.7
1984	1,802.5	1,230.1	572.4	570.5	316.0	254.5	1,232.0

Sources: 1. IMF, *IMF Direction of Trade Statistics* (Yearbook), 1977-86.
2. USSR Ministry of Foreign Trade, *Foreign Trade*, 1975-85.
3. USSR-East Europe Trade Association (Tokyo), *Research Monthly*, Sept. 1982.

Notes: — IMF total includes the trade with non-socialist countries plus Hungary Rumania and Yugoslavia, but not with the USSR nor the other socialist countries.
— Based on exchange rate; US$100 = 74.48 rubles (in 1983), 81.62 rubles in 1984.

a significant increase in delivery of Vietnam goods to the USSR, particularly of vegetables and fruits to the Soviet Far East and Siberia.

In 1983, exports increased by 11.4 percent from 1982. In 1984, Vietnam's export increased only 6.7 percent over 1983 target of 22 percent. Despite efforts to increase exports, the trade deficit will continue to be large. The Soviet Union will be expected to maintain its credit grant ratio at 90 : 10.[27]

In 1982, Vietnam's exchange reserves were down to 30 million dollars and Vietnam stopped payment of its external debts which totalled 3.5 billion dollars. At the end of 1983, the foreign debt was estimated at 5.3 billion dollars (70 percent owned to the USSR). It is expected to reach 6 billion dollars at the end of 1984.[28] The debt and debt service that will have to be paid in 1984 is 186 million dollars. The external debt problem is fatal to the Vietnamese economy.

Future Prospects

To permit an overview of Vietnam's economy in the five year plan, it is necessary to review the performance of the productive sector.

Agriculture has provided 41.3 percent of the national income and utilized 70.2 percent of social labor in 1979. In the second five-year plan Vietnam did not become self-sufficient in food production, hence it had to use precious foreign exchange to import food. However, food production has increased since the new economic

[27] Ton That Thien, ibid., p. 705.
[28] *Nihon Keizai Shinbun*, Sep. 4, 1984.

policies were adopted. Rice production has risen remarkably. Food production per capita has risen from 268 kg in 1980 to nearly 300 kg in 1983.[29] Vietnam no longer needs to import food. The production increase of rice was primarily due to yield increases, from 19.80 quintals per hectare in 1979 to 26.6 quintal per hectare in 1983.

Rice acreage expanded from 5.2 million ha in 1976 to 5.6 million ha in 1980. In the third plan, rice acreage is to expand to 5.76 million ha in 1984 and 5.8 million ha in 1985. But Vietnam must increase its yield per hectare more than expand planting area if it is to continue to increase food production markedly. Rice yields per hectare are expected to average 27.3 quintals for 1984 and 29.8 quintals 1985.[30]

But high yield agriculture requires many inputs: fertilizer, oil, pesticides and machines. These Vietnam cannot supply in sufficient volume. It will be difficult to maintain the level of 26.6 quintals per hectare during the next five years. During 1981-83, deserving attention is the increase of production in industrial crops. Crop area expanded by 16 percent in 1982,[31] compared to 1980 and 8 percent in 1980 compared to 1983.[32] Exports increased because of expansion in production of rubber, tobacco and coffee. Despite the progress made, industrial crops still do not supply enough raw materials for local processing industries and for export. The economic recovery also was accompanied by a decrease in subsidiary food production. Because of the high price paid for rice under the contract system, the peasants concentrated on rice production. The new economic policies also led to an increase in family livestock and a decrease in livestock in the cooperatives and above all in the stage sectors. Though the numbers of swine increased from 10.493 million in 1981 to 10.784 million in 1982 (those in the family sector increased from 9.831 million to 10.073 million), swine in the state and cooperative sectors recorded a respective decrease of 88.1 percent and 5.9 percent compared to 1981. This was due to a shortage of feed and the inefficient use of land reserved for swine breeding.[33]

The new economic policy has improved the farm household economy which provides 50 to 60 percent of the income of the agricultural cooperative members.[34] But in some aspects the new economic policy is damaging the socialist sectors of agriculture, which cannot accumulate sufficient investment funds to construct the material and technical base for development.

Industry accounted for 27.6 percent of national income and 9.4 percent of the labor force in 1979. During the second five-year plan Vietnam's industry suffered from lack of raw materials, spare parts and machinery; also from poor management. Table 7 shows that while fixed assets increased, the gross production and productivity decreased.

Under the third five-year plan, the purchase prices of raw materials which are domestically produced were raised. Salaries and wages were also raised. And the enterprises gained independence in decision making and financial autonomy.

But because the Soviet Union prefers to aid big projects which take a long time

[29] Vu Quoc Tuan, "Xay Dung Tung Buoc Mot Co Cau Kinh Te Moi", *Nghien Cuu Kinh Te*, So 137, Feb. 1984, p. 2. Food production per capita in 1976 was 274 kilograms.

[30] *Vietnam Courrier*, No. 2, 1984.

[31] Vo Van Kiet's report to the National Assembly, Dec. 23, 1982.

[32] Vu Quoc Tuan, ibid., p. 3.

[33] Nguyen Xuan Lai, ibid., p. 56.

[34] Truong Son, "The Household Economy", *Tap Chi Cong San*, No. 7, 1983, translated into English by JPRS, No. 84288, p. 65.

Table 6. Agricultural Production

	Food Production (mill. tons)	Rice (mill. tons)	Rice Yield (q./ha.)	Other Food (mill. tons)	Buffalos (1,000 h.)	Cattle (1,000 h.)	Pig (1,000 h.)
1975	11.6	10.54	21.33	1.05	2,194	1,486	8,801
1976	13.5	11.87	22.33	1.64	2,244	1,582	9,224
1977	12.9	10.89	20.12	2.00	2,287	1,647	9,058
1978	12.9	10.04	18.45	2.86	2,324	1,648	8,823
1979	13.7	10.76	19.80	2.97	2,293	1,628	9,354
1980	14.38	11.7	–	2.70	2,300	1,600	10,000
1981	15.1	12.60	22.00	2.50	2,379	1,755	10,493
1982	16.59	14.17	25.60	2.42	2,445	1,943	10,784
1983	17.00	14.74	26.60	2.26	2,500	2,173	11,202
1984	17.90	15.61	27.70	2.29	2,546	2,105	11,765

Sources: 1. General Statistical Office, *Statistical Data of the Socialist Republic of Vietnam 1979*, Hanoi, 1980 and *So Lien Thong Ke 1930-1984*, Hanoi, 1985.
2. VNA, "Economic Achievements since Last Congress Noted", *FBIS*, March 24, 1982.
3. Nguyen Xuan Lai, "Economic Development 1976-85", *Vietnamese Studies 71*, Hanoi, 1984.
4. Food production and rice production were announced as 16.26 and 13.78 million tons, but revised to 16.59 and 14.17 million tons in *Nhan Dan* of March 6, 1983.
5. Vu Quoc Tuan, "Xay Dung Tung Buoc Co Cau Kinh Te Moi", *Nghien Cuu Kinh Te Moi*, Feb. 1984, pp. 2-3.

Note: – means figures not available.

to mature, and because of foreign exchange shortages, Vietnam suffers from lack of spare parts and machinery. Table 8 shows the major products of industry. In 1981-83, heavy industry had slower growth than light industry and handicrafts.

Between 1978 and 1983, production of state-operated industry declined by 6 percent and central state-operated industry declined by 12 percent; meanwhile, small industry and the handicraft trades increased by 76 percent and self-employed, private industry more than doubled (207 percent). As a result, the percentage which each segment constitutes of total industrial output value has changed in abnormal manner; state-operated industry declined from 66 percent in 1978 to only 51 percent in 1983, with central state-operated industry declining from 45.4 percent to 32.8 percent; small industry and the handicraft trades rose from 34 percent in 1978 to 49 percent in 1983, with self-employed and private industry increasing from

Table 7. Productivity of Industry

(Index 1975 = 100)

	1976	1977	1978	1979	1980
Value of Fixed Assets	114	140	176	177	181
Gross Production	115	129	140	128	105
Productivity of Labor	105	112	113	102	82

Source: Vu Cao Dan, "Vai Tro Quan Ly Trong Chinh Sach Dao Tu Chieu Sao (The Role of Management in the Policy of Intensive Investment)", *Nghien Cuu Kinh Te,* No. 2(132), April 1983, p. 41.

Note: – The index of gross production contradicts those of in Table 1 which include handicrafts and small industries.

Table 8. Output of Industrial Production

	1975	1980	1981	1982	1983	1984
Electricity (million kwh.)	2,428	3,680	3,844	4,045	4,184	4,853
Coal (million tons)	5.2	5.3	6.0	6.1	6.2	4.9
Cement (1,000 tons)	537	641	538	710	907	1,297
Timber (1,000 cube m.)	1,252	1,626	1,320	1,256	1,437	1,425
Paper (1,000 tons)	41.7	46.8	42.0	52.6	60.0	69.5
Salt (1,000 tons)	376.5	436.8	430.0	516.0	793.9	819.0
Sugar (1,000 tons)	46.5	174.9	246.0	222.0	305.8	383.2
Textiles (million m.)	146.4	175.3	158.0	223.0	287.3	364.3
Cigarettes (million packs)	544.0	351.6	522.0	640.0	911.3	1,041.1
Tea (1,000 tons)	15.9	15.5	17.5	15.9	17.0	18.0

Sources: 1. General Statistical Office, *Statistical Data of the Socialist Republic of Vietnam 1979,* Hanoi, 1980.

2. Tong Cuu Thong Ke, *So Lien Thong Ke 1930-1984,* Hanoi, 1985.

3. *Tap Chi Ke Hoach Hoa,* 4-1985 (144).

12.5 percent to 21.3 percent.[35]

In industry as in agriculture, the recovery is attributed to the retreat of the socialist sector.

Conclusion

To match the growth of population, Vietnam's agriculture requires high-yield rice. In turn this means much more fertilizer, pesticides, electricity, infrastructure, and support services. Vietnam's agriculture needs industrial support for its growth.

But the production of central state-operated industry (heavy industry) declined by 12 percent between 1978 and 1983. This is attributed to the shortage of investment and hard currencies.

In the middle of recovery, the government raised agricultural and other taxes,[36] and even issued bonds to raise funds for development. But military expenditure reduced money available for economic development. Lacking the raw material, spare parts and energy, factories operate at only 50 percent capacity. The Soviet Union prefers to aid big projects. Vietnam needs hard currencies to import raw materials and spare parts from the Western countries. Why should Vietnam not wish to end its isolation?

KAMPUCHEA AND LAOS

Kampuchea

Above all it is necessary to determine the exact population of Kampuchea. There have been two estimates on the population of Kampuchea which depended on whether one accepted the government's claim that only 4.5 million Khmers had survived Pol Pot, or Ministry of Agriculture's assessment that there were now 6 million Khmers alive.[37] FAO shows the population as follows:

Table 9. Population

(Unit: in thousands)

Year	1970	1975	1980	1981	1982	1983	1984
Population	6,938	7,098	6,400	6,828	6,921	6,888	7,149
Economically-active Population	2,800	2,802	2,460	2,612	2,657	2,610	2,696
in Agriculture (%)	78.2	76.1	74.0	73.5	72.9	72.4	71.9

Sources: FAO, *Production Yearbook*, 1982 & 1984.
The *World Development Report*, 1984 fixes 7.0 million at mid-1982, and projects 10 million in 2000.[38]

[35] Vu Quoc Tuan, ibid.
[36] The total amount of taxes collected in 1983 equals 225.3% of that in 1982. *Nhan Dan,* Feb. 13, 1984.
[37] Showcross, William, *The Quality of Mercy*, p. 109.
[38] The World Bank, *World Development Report*, 1984, p. 192.

To all Khmers rice production will be the most important matter in the next five or ten years. Rice production has not yet reached the self-sufficiency level of 1.7 million tons of paddy. Yields per hectare average between 8 and 10 quintals of paddy. The government announced that yields averaged 10 quintals in 1982. But the FAO yearbook shows the planted area and production of rice as follows:

Table 10. Rice Production

	1979	1980	1981	1982	1983	1984
Planted Area (1,000 ha.)	682.2	1,356	1,350	1,680	1,755	1,390
Paddy Production (1,000 tons)	637	1,470	1,160	1,400	1,700	1,300
Yields per hectare (kg.)	—	1,084	859	833	969	935

Sources: — IDE, *Ajia Choutoh Dohkoh Nenpoh* (in Japanese), 1982 & 1983.
　　　　 — Hanoi Domestic Service, Feb. 1984.
　　　　 — *FAO Production Yearbook*, 1984.

The planted area of other food crops increased by 300,000 ha to 404,444 ha in 1982. The areas of industrial crops increased from 24,700 ha in 1981 to 42,700 ha in 1982.[39]

Concerning livestock raising, as of 1983 the cattle population totalled 1.7 million head,[40] up from 1.4 million head in 1982.[41] Paddy production has only recovered to 40 percent of the prewar level of 3.8 million tons.[42] The shortage of food in 1984 was estimated to be 294,000 tons.

To survive Kampuchea needs to import everything from food and consumer goods to machine. Kampuchea's trade is as follows:

Table 11. Kampuchea's Trade

(Unit: US$ million)

	1976	1977	1978	1979	1980	1981	1982	1983	1984
Export (FOB)	29	83	3	6	7	4	6	3	
Import (CIF)	14	34	21	29	155	79	55	172	

Source: IMF, *Direction of Trade Statistics*, 1984.

[39] IDE, *Ajia Chutoh Dohkoh* Nenpoh (in Japanese), 1982 & 1983.
[40] Hanoi Domestic Service, Feb. 18, 1984.
[41] In 1979 there were said to be only 850,000 draft animals compared with 2.5 million before the war. Showcross, W., *ibid.*, p. 284.
[42] In 1969-70, 3.8 million tons of paddy had been harvested off 2.4 million hectares of land. Showcross, W., *ibid.*, p. 283.

The above data omit trade with the USSR and other socialist countries. The USSR's exports are 69 million dollars in 1982 and 88 million dollars in 1983.[43]

Therefore, Kampuchea's average imports are around 200 million dollars. We do not know how this trade deficit is financed. Kampuchea depends much on gratis international aid. During 1979-82, the USSR's aid amounted to 329 million dollars in grants plus 150 million dollars in credit.[44]

Laos

Laos had a population of 3.6 million in mid-1982. Its annual population growth rate projected for 1980-2000 is 2.6 percent.[45] A World Bank report estimates the Laos GNP per capita at 80 US dollars in 1981.[46] Labor force breakdown in 1980 was 75 percent in agriculture, 6 percent in industry, and 19 percent in services. The GNP in 1978 was produced as follows: 60 percent by agriculture, 14 percent by industry, and 26 percent by services.

The structure of demand in 1978 was as follows: public consumption 21 percent, private consumption 58 percent, gross domestic investment 40 percent and gross domestic savings 21 percent. The overall resource balance is minus 19 percent.[47] According to the International Institute of Strategic Studies, GNP in 1980 is estimated at 300 million US dollars, defence expenditure is estimated at 21 million US dollars. This is a big burden to Laos.[48]

The party and government in Laos have followed the Vietnamese model in managing the economy. Before 1979, they tried to force the peasants into collectives and to restrict the activities of private traders. The economy deteriorated and many Laotians fled to Thailand.

At the 7th Plenum of the Party Central Committee (Nov., 1979), the policy was changed to offer incentives to the people and to slow the tempo of collectivization. The purchase price of paddy was raised by 100 percent; wages and salaries were increased by 170 percent. Peasants were allowed to go freely to the city to sell their surplus product.

In 1981, the first five-year plan (1981-85) started. The first priority goes to agriculture, and second to industry, in particular consumer goods industries and handicrafts. This follows Vietnam's third plan. The plan's target was 1.6 million tons of food grain by 1985 (paddy output of 1.4 million tons), an increase of 246,000 tons (21 percent) compared to 1981.

The investment structure will be shaped so that 30 percent of the capital goes

---

[43] USSR's trade (in millions of rubles):

	1980	1981	1982	1983	1984
Export	2.5	82.9	73.5	91.0	93.4
Import	2.5	2.6	3.2	5.4	6.4

Sources: — USSR Ministry of Foreign Trade, *Foreign Trade*, 1984.
— USSR-East Europe Trade Association (Tokyo), *Research Monthly*, Feb. 1986.

[44] USSR's grants: US$85 million in 1979, US$134 million in 1980, US$95 million in 1981, and US$15 million in 1982. Source: IDE, *Ajia Chutoh Dokoh Nenpoh* (in Japanese), 1983.

[45] World Bank, *World Development Report*, 1984.

[46] World Bank, *World Development Report*, 1983.

[47] Takeuchi, I., "National Democratic Revolution and Nation Building in Laos", in *Nation Building in Indochina*, edited by Kimura, T. (Institute of Developing Economies, Tokyo, 1984), p. 195. Takeuchi quoted from World Development Report, 1980, which is controversial.

[48] *Asia Yearbook 1984*.

to production establishments; 20 percent to agriculture, forestry and water con-
servancy; 41 percent to communication and transportation; and 19 percent to
industry.[49]

At the Party Congress in 1982, the government announced that since paddy
production in 1981 reached 1,155,000 tons, Laos would not need to import rice.
It seemed that self-sufficient level of rice production is around 1.2 million tons.

When the rice harvest is good, it is very difficult for the government to collect
rice, the main cause of procurement problem seems to be the ridiculously low price
offered by the government for paddy.

Table 12. Food Production

	1976	1978	1980	1981	1982	1983	1984
Index of Food Production (1974-75 = 100)	99.16	100.76	136.26	148.67	149.03	150.42	175.52
Rice Production (1,000 tons)	858	796	1,053	1,155	1,184	1,002	1,322
Area (1,000 ha.)	680	665	732	745	737	670	610
Yield (kg/ha.)	1,262	1,197	1,439	1,550	1,477	1,494	2,167

Source: FAO, *Production Yearbook,* 1980, 1982 and 1984.

Table 13 shows the external trade of Laos. Exports in 1983 covered only 15
percent of the imports. We do not know how the deficit is financed. The 6th Anni-
versary of the Vietnam-Laos Treaty (July 18, 1983) provided an occasion for
publishing a detailed description of Vietnamese aid to Laos. Between 1976 and
1985, Vietnam would be giving Laos 1.33 billion dong in aid. Nearly half of this
figure is grant aid.[50]

---

[49] Economic report to the 3rd Congress of the Party, *FBIS,* May 6, 1982.

[50] *Asia Yearbook 1984*, p. 206.

Table 13. Laos Trade

(Unit: US$ million)

| | Imports | | IMF | Exports | | IMF | |
	Total	USSR	Total	Total	USSR	Total	Deficit
1976	58.7	14.1	44.6	11.7	—	11.7	47.0
1977	90.9	30.7	60.2	16.5	—	16.5	74.4
1978	88.3	17.2	71.1	12.3	0.3	11.9	76.0
1979	122.8	38.4	84.0	17.6	0.3	17.3	105.2
1980	180.7	57.4	123.3	23.8	0.5	23.3	156.9
1981	135.2	50.3	84.9	18.2	1.3	16.9	117.0
1982	176.0	88.4	87.6	28.5	2.8	25.7	147.5
1983	194.6	101.4	93.2	28.7	3.1	25.6	165.9
1984	129.1	79.6	49.5	25.2	2.6	12.6	103.9

Sources: — IMF, *Direction of Trade Statistics (Yearbook)*, 1977-1983.
— USSR Ministry of Foreign Trade, *Foreign Trade*, 1975-1984.
— USSR-East Europe Trade Association (Tokyo), *Research Monthly*, Sept. 1982 and Feb. 1986.

Notes: — The IMF total includes the trade with non-socialist countries plus Hungary, Romania, and Yugoslavia, but not with the USSR nor Vietnam and other socialist countries.
— Based on exchange rate: US$100 = 74.42 rubles (in 1983), 82.62 rubles (in 1984).

Graph — Growth Index

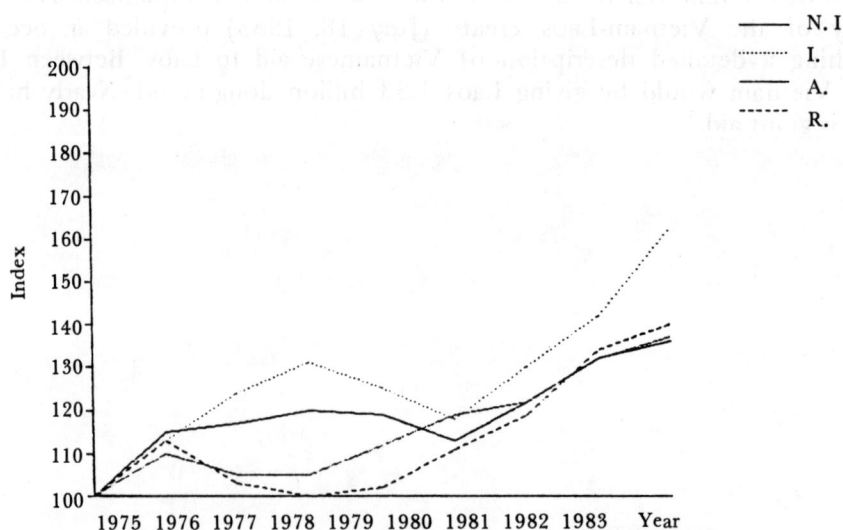

Notes: — N.I.; National Income, I; Industry, A; Agriculture, R; Rice Production.

Figure 1. Growth Index

17. Economic Development and Issues in Iran

A.A. Zaker-Shahrak

INTRODUCTION

The pace of change and development of Iranian economy over the last ten years has been, by all standards, very dramatic. This chapter purports to survey some of the most important economic happenings of the period.* This chapter falls under four distinct parts. In the first part entitled Islamic Revolution, subjects which have greatly affected the course of Iranian economic development have been discussed: the Islamic Revolution, and the role of oil and gas in the Iranian economic scene.

The second part entitled Economic Development and Issues, reviews the way the economy has changed and developed over the last six years or so. In this part, after a brief discussion of the national product and expenditure statistics, review will be offered on the performance of various sectors like agriculture, oil, industry, etc., foreign trade, government budget, monetary sector and inflation.

The third part entitled New Aspirations, reports the objectives and the priorities that the new Government has set for itself, and the aspirations that are expressed for the future of the country. This knowledge could be of great help to speculate about the future course of the economy.

---

* To get a more detailed picture of the topics discussed in this chapter, the following publications should be consulted:

1. Annual Government Budget Bills, submitted by the Cabinet to Islamic Consultative Assembly (Parliament) in autumn or winter of each year for approval. (In Persian)
2. Annual Government Budget Laws approved each year before the end of the winter by Majlis (Islamic Consultative Assembly). (In Persian)
3. Draft Bill of the First Five-Year Cultural-Social-Economic Development Plan, released by the Plan and Budget Organization in the year 1983. (In Persian)
4. Annual Economic Report and Balance Sheet of Bank Markazi Jomhouri Islami Iran (The Central Bank of Islamic Republic of Iran), released each year by the Central Bank. (In Persian and in English)
5. Iran Statistical Yearbook, published each year by the Iran Statistical Centre. (In Persian)
6. Various monthly and quarterly consumer price indexes, wholesale price indexes, indexes of production, employment of large manufacturing establishments, etc., that are compiled and published regularly by Economic Statistics Department of the Bank Markazi Jomhouri Islami Iran. (All in Persian)

The last part, New Economic System surveys some of the salient features of the new Islamic economic system. With the overthrow of the old regime, the old economic system and order was also set aside. Over the last six years a new economic order based on Islamic precepts has been gradually built up, and the process of construction is by no means at an end. Some topics to be touched upon in the last part will be: interest-free banking, the role of markets and prices, the shares of the government and private sectors, and the way of managing foreign trade.

THE ISLAMIC REVOLUTION

Iran has been undergoing change on an unprecedented scale in political, social and cultural events since 1978, which have changed the structure of Iranian society beyond recognition. Most of the economic changes since 1978 make sense only in the light of these political, social and cultural occurrences. Without any doubt the most important event in the recent political history of Iran has been the advent of the Islamic Revolution in 1978. The Revolution and its aftermath have had far-reaching consequences both internally and externally.

Small-scale protests and demonstrations against the old regime at the beginning of 1978 were transformed gradually into a country-wide protest, demonstration, and finally, general strike toward the end of the year. From the beginning of September of that year, literally the whole country, private as well as public sectors, went on strike, and as a result, economic activity was greatly reduced. The following figures should give some indication of the extent of disruption in economic activity. According to the official estimates of the national product compiled by the Central Bank of Islamic Republic of Iran, in the year 1357 (21 March 1978 to 20 March 1979)*, Gross Domestic Product at market prices and in constant prices showed 17.9 percent annual decline, Gross National Product showed 20.1 percent annual reduction, and per capita income recorded almost 24 percent annual decrease.

With the advent of the Islamic Revolution, many of the laws and institutions associated with the old regime were set aside. The most important was the old Constitution. Preparation of the new Constitution and establishment of the new government institutions: the Presidency, the Parliament (Islamic Consultative Assembly), the new Courts of Justice, required three years. During this period, uncertainty prevailed and economic activity was very badly affected.

The Revolution changed the political map of the region over-night. Many old political and economic alliances in the region and beyond were dissolved, and many new ones formed. Most of the foreign technicians, experts and 'advisors' left, or were asked to leave the country. Foreign investment in Iran was greatly reduced, and many of the Iranian investments abroad were sold out or liquidated. Foreign borrowing also decreased. Moreover, due to ample reserves which were accumulating as a result of second-round of the oil price rise in 1978-79, the new authorities decided to pay off most of the old loans as well.

Export of crude oil which had averaged almost five million barrels per day in 1977 (the exact figures being 4,986.3 thousand b.p.d.) averaged almost half that figure (2,579 thousand b.p.d.) in 1979. The level of export of crude oil further decreased in the following two years, averaging a mere 950 thousand and 315

---

* For a detailed correspondence of Iranian and Gregorian (Christian) calendars, see Table 1 on Page 660. Hereafter 1357 will be referred as 1978 and so on.

thousand b.p.d. in 1980 and 1981 respectively. In 1982 and 1983, the export level of crude oil recovered somewhat to 2,051 thousand b.p.d. and 2,078 thousand b.p.d. respectively. It may be that the sudden reduction in output and export of Iranian crude oil in 1978-79 was one of the factors which caused the second oil price shock to take place.

The export of natural gas to the Soviet Union which had throughout the years 1972-77 averaged 9 billion cubic meters, ceased altogether by 1980. Trading with some countries also ceased altogether, or greatly decreased. Examples of the first group are U.S.A., South Africa, Israel and Iraq, and that of the second group is France. On the other hand, trading with third world countries has gradually expanded. Imports from the socialist countries, mostly conducted in the form of bilateral agreements, have been encouraged. Imports from these countries which in the years 1976-78 was about 5 percent of the country's total imports, by the year 1982 had risen to 10 percent of the country's imports.

Barely two and half years had passed when the War broke out with Iraq, which in Iran has come to be known as the Imposed War. It has continued unabated ever since. Over this period, one third to one half of the total government expenditure has been earmarked to war efforts. For the last four years, the whole country and its economy has been on a war footing with the usual manifestations of a war-affected economy like rationing, price control, inflation, shortages of materials, etc.

The Contribution of Oil and Natural Gas

Oil and natural gas affect the course of development of Iranian economy in many ways. In recent years, due to the steep rise in their world prices, their importance has greatly increased.

It is currently estimated that Iran has about 55 thousand million barrels of extractable oil reserve underground. At current rates of production of about two million barrels per day that should last about 75 years.

Iranian extractable amount of natural gas is estimated around 492 trillion cubic feet, which is about 17 percent of the whole world's proven natural gas reserves. Only its small fraction is currently produced, and quite a large percentage of the produced amount is flared at the point of production and never consumed (Table 2). For example, in the year 1361 (1982-83) production of natural gas was reported to be about 30.4 thousand cubic meters (1,074 thousand cubic feet). At that rate of production, natural gas deposits would last for more than 450 years! Thus, Iran is very rich in oil and gas. To realize this potential, however, investments would be required to build oil refineries, especially after the destruction of Abadan Oil Refinery, and to distribute the refined products inside the country, or to export them. Also, huge amounts of investment would be needed to extract, refine and then to distribute the natural gas to domestic consumers.

Needless to say, Iranian economy has been highly dependent on the revenue from the export of crude oil. In recent years, a high percentage of government revenue — at times as high as 70 percent — has come directly from the export of oil. Even to the remaining 30 to 35 percent, oil export has contributed greatly in an indirect way.

Over the last ten years, the ratio of the value of non-oil exports to the value of imports of the country has never been above 10 percent, and in some years it has fallen to as low as 3 percent. The ratio of foreign exchange earnings from the export

thousand b.p.d. in 1980 and 1981 respectively. In 1982 and 1983, the export level of crude oil recovered somewhat to 2,081 thousand b.p.d. and 2,078 thousand b.p.d. respectively. It may be that the sudden reduction in output and export of Iranian crude oil in 1978/79 was one of the factors which caused the second oil price shock to take place.

The export of natural gas to the Soviet Union which had throughout the years 1972–77 averaged 9 billion cubic meters, ceased altogether by 1980. Trading with some countries ceased altogether [...]

Table 1. Correspondence of Iranian (1) and Grecorian Calendars

Month	1354	1355	1356	1357	1358	1359	1360	1361	1362
Farvardin	21 March / 20 April	21 March / 20 April	21 March / 20 April	21 March / 20 April	21 March / 20 April	21 March / 20 April	21 March / 20 April	21 March / 20 April	21 March / 20 April
Ordibehesht	21 April / 21 May	21 April / 21 May	21 April / 21 May	21 April / 21 May	21 April / 21 May	21 April / 21 May	21 April / 21 May	21 April / 21 May	21 April / 21 May
Khordad	22 May / 21 June	22 May / 21 June	22 May / 21 June	22 May / 21 June	22 May / 21 June	22 May / 21 June	22 May / 21 June	22 May / 21 June	22 May / 21 June
Tir	22 June / 22 July	22 June / 22 July	22 June / 22 July	22 June / 22 July	22 June / 22 July	22 June / 22 July	22 June / 22 July	22 June / 22 July	22 June / 22 July
Mordad	23 July / 22 August	23 July / 22 August	23 July / 22 August	23 July / 22 August	23 July / 22 August	23 July / 22 August	23 July / 22 August	23 July / 22 August	23 July / 22 August
Shahrivar	23 August / 22 September	23 August / 22 September	23 August / 22 September	23 August / 22 September	23 August / 22 September	23 August / 22 September	23 August / 22 September	23 August / 22 September	23 August / 22 September
Mehr	23 September / 22 October	23 September / 22 October	23 September / 22 October	23 September / 22 October	23 September / 22 October	23 September / 22 October	23 September / 22 October	23 September / 22 October	23 September / 22 October
Aban	23 October / 21 November	23 October / 21 November	23 October / 21 November	23 October / 21 November	23 October / 21 November	23 October / 21 November	23 October / 21 November	23 October / 21 November	23 October / 21 November
Azar	22 November / 21 December	22 November / 21 December	22 November / 21 December	22 November / 21 December	22 November / 21 December	22 November / 21 December	22 November / 21 December	22 November / 21 December	22 November / 21 December
Dey	22 December 1976 / 20 January	22 December 1977 / 20 January	22 December 1978 / 20 January	22 December 1979 / 20 January	22 December 1980 / 20 January	22 December 1981 / 20 January	22 December 1982 / 20 January	22 December 1983 / 20 January	22 December 1984 / 20 January
Bahman	21 January / 19 February	21 January / 19 February	21 January / 19 February	21 January / 19 February	21 January / 19 February	21 January / 19 February	21 January / 19 February	21 January / 19 February	21 January / 19 February
Esfand	20 February / 29/30 March	20 February / 20 March	20 February / 20 March	20 February / 20 March	20 February / 20 March	20 February / 20 March	20 February / 20 March	20 February / 20 March	20 February / 20 March

Note: There are 31 days in each of the first six months of the Iranian calendar, 30 days in each of the next 3 months and 29 days in the last 3 months, except in leap years when it has 30 days.

Table 2. Production, Export, Domestic Consumption and Flared Gas

(Unit: Billion cubic meters)

	1356*	1357	1358	1359	1360	1361	Percent Change				Share (%)				
							1356-61	1361	1360	1359	1357	1358	1359	1360	1361
Export	9.2	5.3	3.5	0	9.7	18.0	14.4	85.6		-100.0	11.9	8.4	0	61.8	59.2
Domestic Consumption	23.9	16.6	21.4	9.4	0	0	-100.0	0	-100.0	-56.1	37.4	51.3	56.6	0	0
Flared	26.4	22.5	16.8	7.2	6.0	12.4	-14.0	106.7	-16.7	-57.1	50.7	40.3	43.4	38.2	40.8
Production	59.5	44.4	41.7	16.6	15.7	30.4	-12.6	93.6	-5.4	-60.2	100.0	100.0	100.0	100.0	100.0

Source: Iranian Oil Ministry and National Gas Company.
* 1977.

of oil to foreign exchange receipts resulting from the export of oil and non-oil goods has never been less than 90 percent, usually being as high as 97 percent. The same of the total goods and services receipts which have made up more than 80 percent. As is well known, the world price of crude oil has been undergoing changes in an unprecedented scale in recent years. Table 3 below gives details of these changes. In 1985, it stood almost 30 percent below the height that it once attained in 1981, and the future outlook for the movement of this important parameter remains uncertain in many instances destabilizing.

ECONOMIC DEVELOPMENT AND ISSUES

National Product and Expenditure

The latest available national accounts statistics refer to the year 1361 (1982). National account statistics compiled by most third world countries suffer from

Table 3. Average Export Price of Iranian Crude Oil

(Unit: $ per barrel)

Year	Light 34°	Heavy 31°
1971	2.218	2.172
1972	2.491	2.441
1973	5.318	5.167
1974	11.574	11.338
1975	11.115	10.931
1976	11.894	11.614
1977	12.7	
1978	13.34	
1979		
1st April 1979	16.57	16.04
1st May 1979	17.17	16.64
1st June 1979	18.47	17.74
1st July 1979	22.00	19.90
1st Oct. 1979	23.50	22.77
1st Dec. 1979	28.50	27.77
1st Jan. 1980	30.00	29.27
1st Feb. 1980	32.50	31.77
1980		
21st March 1980	35.37	
21st Dec. 1980	37.00	
1981		
April 1981	37.00	
Oct. 1981	34.20	
Jan. 1982	34.20	
1982		
14 March 1982	29.00	

various shortcomings. Iranian statistics has not proved to be an exception to this general rule.

The basic framework employed in Iranian national accounts is the SNA framework by the United Nations. This framework, however, is appropriate for the economies where markets play a predominant role in the allocation of resources. However, when the ruling prices are not equilibrium prices, or when shortages and queues are rules rather than exceptions, there is no logical basis for using the arbitrarily set prices as weights in aggregation. This is exactly the sort of the problem with Iranian national account statistics in recent years. Since the start of the war, the Iranian economy has not been a market economy. The officially set prices of most goods and services are far from their equilibrium values. They are used in national product and expenditure, so that they are imprecise indicators of national economic well-being.

Moreover, the estimates of depreciation of fixed capital do not include the material loss inflicted by the Imposed War. Nor does it include the damages to the property and capital during the revolutionary years 1978-80. Therefore, the net national product and per capita figures given below are over-estimates, and the extent of over-estimation is very large.

Tables 4 and 5 give details of National Income and Product by Economic Sectors at current and constant prices for the years 1356-61 (1977-82). Tables 6 and 7 give details of Gross National Expenditure for the same period at constant and current prices. Over the six-year period reported in the tables, all the indexes of total output of the country at constant prices show a sizeable reduction: GDP showing 22.5 percent fall, GNP showing 22.3 percent reduction, national income showing 19 percent decline, per capita GNP showing 33.3 percent reduction, and per capita income showing 30.5 percent fall.

All the major indexes of total output declined until 1359 (1980); in 1360 (1981) there was a halt in the decline, with the GNP showing a modest 2.2 percent recovery in that year, then in the following year, a major rise in all the indexes of total output. The main cause of fluctuations in GNP over the period under review has been the fluctuations in the output and, hence, the export of oil.

Agriculture

Contrary to the trends in the general economic activity, the agricultural sector has been growing. Value added in this sector grew at a moderate rate until 1359 (1980), but in the following two years, recorded very high rates of growth, 11.3 percent and 7.9 percent respectively. These high rates of growth were realized because, according to official statistics, the output of such major crops as wheat, barley, sugar beet, sugar cane and potatoes increased considerably over the two-year period 1360-61 (1981-82). Table 8 gives details of production of the major farming crops. Preliminary reports indicate that in 1983 no dramatic rise is expected.

Table 9 reports the imports of some agricultural commodities for the years 1356-61 (1977-82). Import of wheat increased over the last few years but imports of other agricultural commodities fluctuated, and over the whole period, remained more or less constant. In Table 10, the level of production and the export of crude oil are given for the 12-year period 1351-62 (1972-83). Prior to the Revolution, the policy that was followed in this connection seems to have been to maximize the amount of extraction and export of crude oil. Moreover, by keeping down the

Table 4. Gross National Income and Product by Economic Sectors in Constant Prices (1974 = 100)

	Amount (Billion Rials)						Percent Change			Share in GDP (%)					
	1977	1978	1979	1980	1981	1982	1981	1982	77-82	77	78	79	80	81	82
Agriculture, hunting, forestry and fishery	340.9	352.6	356.3	362.9	404.0	436.0	11.3	7.9	5.0	8.7	10.8	11.6	14.1	14.3	14.3
Oil and gas	1,363.4	927.8	767.6	330.9	273.6	526.8	-17.2	92.5	-17.3	34.8	28.4	29.0	2.9	10.4	17.3
Industries and mining	645.6	553.9	511.9	526.2	534.9	598.7	2.7	10.5	-1.8	16.4	17.0	15.7	20.2	20.2	19.4
mining	(35.5)	(33.2)	(25.3)	(26.4)	(25.5)	(27.9)	-3.4	7.8	-5.0	(0.9)	(1.0)	(0.3)	(1.0)	(1.0)	(0.9)
manufacturing	(378.2)	(317.1)	(318.8)	(324.8)	(346.4)	(387.8)	6.6	12.2	-0.5	(9.6)	(9.7)	(10.4)	(12.1)	(12.1)	(12.8)
electricity, gas and water	(52.9)	(47.9)	(55.0)	(48.3)	(56.6)	(64.7)	17.2	14.3	4.1	(1.3)	(1.9)	(1.2)	(1.9)	(2.1)	(2.1)
construction	(179.0)	(155.7)	(112.9)	(120.7)	(105.2)	(110.7)	-12.2	4.4	-9.2	(4.6)	(2.8)	(3.7)	(4.7)	(4.0)	(0.6)
Services	1,753.8	1,620.4	1,560.7	1,475.5	1,504.1	1,546.2	1.9	2.3	-2.5	44.7	49.6	50.8	57.5	57.0	60.9
wholesale & retail trade, restaurant & hotels	(486.3)	(420.1)	(345.0)	(310.5)	(436.5)	(487.3)	40.6	11.6	0.04	(12.4)	(12.9)	(11.2)	12.1	(16.9)	(16.0)
transport, storage and communications	(180.6)	(169.9)	(196.7)	(174.3)	(158.3)	(168.1)	-9.2	6.2	-1.4	(4.6)	(5.2)	(6.4)	(6.8)	(6.0)	(5.5)
finance & insurance	(234.4)	(190.8)	(142.8)	(166.1)	(102.1)	(89.9)	-38.5	-15.9	-18.2	(5.0)	(5.8)	(4.7)	(6.5)	(3.9)	(2.8)
real estate & business services	(350.4)	(308.4)	(341.8)	(287.5)	(310.0)	(339.0)	7.8	8.1	-6.9	(8.9)	(9.9)	(7.9)	(11.8)	(11.8)	(1.0)
public services	(313.0)	(354.1)	(463.8)	(309.8)	(279.9)	(252.9)	-9.7	4.6	-1.3	(8.0)	(10.8)	(15.1)	(12.1)	(10.4)	(0.7)
community, social and personal services	(188.6)	(177.1)	(170.4)	(287.4)	(217.3)	(177.0)	-4.4	-18.5	-1.3	(4.8)	(5.4)	(5.5)	(8.8)	(9.2)	(5.8)
Less: Imputed Bank Service Charge	181.4	189.8	126.0	121.2	76.8	59.4	-36.6	-22.7	-20.0	4.6	5.8	4.1	4.7	2.9	1.9
Gross domestic product (at factor cost)	3,922.3	3,266.9	3,070.5	2,568.6	2,639.4	3,040.3	2.8	15.2	-5.0	100.0	100.0	100.0	100.0	100.0	100.0
Non-oil gross domestic product (at factor cost)	2,558.9	2,337.1	2,302.9	3,237.5	2,365.8	2,513.5	5.7	6.2	-0.4						
Net factor income received from abroad	-37.7	-71.9	58.6	32.7	51.6	31.1									
Net indirect taxes	121.0	92.8	-1.3	68.9	37.3	43.8									
Gross national product (at market prices)	4,005.6	3,287.8	3,127.8	2,669.6	2,728.3	3,119.2	2.2	14.2	-4.9						
Terms of trade adjustment	107.7	-0.7	255.1	256.7	269.5	335.2									
Gross national income (at market price)	4,113.3	3,287.1	3,382.9	2,926.3	2,997.8	3,450.4	2.4	15.1	-3.5						
Less: Consumption of fixed capital	171.8	182.8	181.0	183.9	209.4	232.1	13.3	11.4	6.2						
net indirect taxes	121.0	92.8	-1.3	68.9	37.3	43.8									
National income	3,820.9	3,011.5	3,203.2	2,673.5	2,752.1	3,174.9	2.9	15.3	-3.6						
Population (in million persons)	34.7	35.6	36.7	37.7	38.8	39.9	2.9	15.3	2.8						
Per capita income	110.1	84.6	87.3	70.9	70.9	79.6	—	12.3	-6.9						
GNP per capita (in thousand rials)	115.4	92.4	89.2	70.8	10.3	78.1	-0.7	11.1	-7.9						
GDP per capita (in thousand rails)	113.0	91.8	83.7	68.1	68.0	76.2	-0.1	12.1	-7.6						

Source: The Central Bank of the Islamic Republic of Iran.

Table 5. Gross National Income and Product by Economic Sectors in Current Prices

	Amount (Billion Rials)						Percent change				Share in GDP (%)					
	1977	1978	1979	1980	1981	1982	1980	1981	1982	1977-82	1977	1978	1979	1980	1981	1982
Agriculture, hunting, forestry and fishery	474.5	561.7	702.4	1,083.3	1,525.6	1,912.1	54.2	40.8	25.3	32.1	8.2	10.5	11.1	16.0	18.6	18.0
Oil and gas	1,740.8	1,185.5	1,660.2	950.4	930.8	1,763.9	-40.9	-5.1	20.1	0.3	30.2	22.1	26.2	14.5	11.3	16.7
Industries and mining	1,082.5	1,049.3	1,060.5	1,293.0	1,499.6	1,836.9	21.9	16.0	22.5	11.2	18.8	19.5	16.7	19.2	18.3	47.3
mining	(77.5)	(73.7)	(67.7)	(99.7)	(143.8)	(158.3)	47.3	44.2	10.1	15.4	(1.3)	(1.4)	(1.0)	(1.5)	(1.8)	(1.5)
manufacturing	(469.4)	(416.7)	(488.7)	(602.2)	(731.6)	(894.4)	23.2	21.5	22.3	13.8	(8.1)	(7.8)	(7.7)	(8.9)	(8.9)	(9.4)
electricity, gas and water	(58.3)	(54.0)	(62.6)	(61.3)	(77.8)	(98.6)	-2.1	26.9	26.7	10.9	(1.0)	(1.0)	(1.0)	(0.9)	(0.9)	(0.9)
construction	(476.8)	(501.4)	(441.5)	(529.8)	(546.5)	(685.6)	20.1	3.2	25.5	7.5	(8.3)	(9.3)	(7.0)	(7.8)	(6.7)	(6.5)
Services	2,755.1	2,895.8	3,162.0	3,696.0	4,491.2	5,313.9	16.9	21.5	18.3	14.0	47.8	54.1	49.9	54.7	54.6	50.0
wholesale & retail trade, restaurants & hotels	(676.6)	(652.9)	(640.4)	(753.5)	(1,245.0)	(1,702.8)	17.7	71.9	31.5	20.3	(11.7)	(12.2)	(10.1)	(11.1)	(15.8)	(16.0)
transport, storage and communications	(326.0)	(361.6)	(452.4)	(553.8)	(620.7)	(706.8)	72.4	12.1	14.4	16.8	(5.7)	(6.8)	(7.1)	(8.2)	(7.5)	(6.7)
finance & insurance	(375.5)	(336.1)	(280.4)	(402.9)	(304.2)	(305.0)	43.7	-24.5	0.3	4.1	(6.5)	(6.3)	(4.4)	(6.0)	(3.7)	(2.9)
real estate & business services	(583.0)	(610.4)	(538.0)	(680.5)	(795.6)	(948.0)	26.5	16.9	19.2	10.2	(10.1)	(11.4)	(8.5)	(10.1)	(9.7)	(8.9)
public services	(501.5)	(624.0)	(910.4)	(751.2)	(833.0)	(1,040.5)	-17.5	11.0	24.8	15.7	(8.7)	(11.8)	(14.4)	(11.1)	(10.1)	(0.8)
community, social and personal services	(292.5)	(310.8)	(340.3)	(554.1)	(641.8)	(607.8)	62.8	15.8	-5.3	15.8	(5.1)	(5.8)	(5.4)	(8.2)	(7.8)	(5.7)
Less: Imputed bank service charge	290.5	334.4	247.3	293.8	228.8	210.3	18.8	-22.1	-7.8	-6.2	15.0	6.2	3.9	4.3	2.8	2.0
Gross domestic product (at factor cost)	5,762.4	5,354.4	6,357.8	6,758.9	8,218.5	10,621.5	6.6	21.6	29.2	13.0	100.0	100.0	100.0	100.0	100.0	100.0
Non-oil gross domestic product (at factor cost)	4,021.6	4,168.9	4,677.6	5,778.9	7,287.7	8,852.0	23.5	26.1	21.5	17.1						
Net factor income received from abroad	-98.0	-189.8	55.5	5.4	32.9	-0.2										
Net indirect taxes	185.1	175.2	-2.5	167.1	104.4	134.8										
Gross national product (at market prices)	5,349.5	5,343.8	5,380.6	6,932.4	8,359.8	10,255.1	8.5	20.5	28.7	13.0						
Less: Consumption of real capital	283.1	333.3	374.4	462.2	583.4	408.1	23.5	26.2	21.4	20.1						
Net indirect taxes	185.1	175.2	-2.5	167.1	104.4	134.8										
National income	5,981.3	4,834.7	6,618.7	6,303.1	7,668.0	9,918.2	4.7	21.7	29.3	13.0						
Population (in million persons)	34.7	35.6	36.7	37.7	38.8	39.9	2.7	2.9	2.8	2.8						
GNP per capita (per capita income)	168.6	150.1	173.9	183.9	215.4	269.6	5.8	17.1	25.2	9.8						
GDP per capita (in thousand rials)	166.1	150.4	172.7	179.3	211.8	266.2	3.9	18.1	25.7	9.9						

Source: Ibid.

Table 6. Gross National Expenditure in Constant Prices (1974 = 100)

	Amount (Billion rials)						Percent Change				Share in GNP (%)					
	1977	1978	1979	1980	1981	1982	1980	1981	1982	1977-82	1977	1978	1979	1980	1981	1982
Private final consumption expenditure	1,839.1	1,745.0	1,525.9	1,459.7	1,548.3	1,642.9	-4.3	6.1	6.1	-2.2	45.5	51.9	49.0	55.4	57.9	53.3
General government final consumption expenditure	799.2	797.3	636.7	580.4	606.9	583.6	-8.8	4.6	-3.5	-6.1	19.8	23.7	20.7	22.0	22.7	18.9
Gross fixed capital formation	1,074.7	928.3	575.8	553.8	562.8	618.5	-3.8	1.6	9.9	-10.5	26.6	27.7	18.8	21.0	21.0	20.1
machinery & equipment	367.1	281.1	165.3	128.0	194.4	215.2	-22.6	51.9	11.0	-10.1	9.1	8.4	5.0	4.9	7.2	7.0
private sector	(161.7)	(62.6)	(41.2)	(33.0)	(78.2)	(53.1)	(-19.9)	(137.0)	(-32.1)	(-20.0)	(4.0)	(1.9)	(1.3)	(1.3)	(2.9)	(1.7)
public sector	(205.4)	(218.5)	(124.1)	(95.0)	(116.2)	(162.6)	(-23.4)	(22.3)	(39.9)	(-4.6)	(5.1)	(6.5)	(4.1)	(3.6)	(9.3)	(5.3)
construction	707.6	647.2	410.5	425.8	368.4	402.8	3.7	-13.5	9.3	-10.7	17.5	19.0	13.4	16.1	13.8	13.1
private sector	(250.5)	(218.0)	(217.0)	(230.6)	(175.1)	(186.8)	(6.3)	(-24.1)	(6.6)	(-5.7)	(6.2)	(6.0)	(7.1)	(8.7)	(6.6)	(6.1)
public sector	(457.1)	(429.2)	(193.5)	(195.2)	(193.3)	(216.1)	(0.9)	(-1.0)	(11.8)	(-13.9)	(11.3)	(12.8)	(6.3)	(7.4)	(7.2)	(7.0)
Increase in stocks	-122.0	-308.7	53.6	306.6	432.9	364.2					-3.0	-9.2	1.6	11.6	17.4	11.2
Net exports of goods & services	94.7	67.0	182.6	-342.9	-497.1	-100.7					2.3	2.0	5.9	-13.0	-16.8	-6.6
Statistical discrepancies	357.6	130.8	94.6	79.3	-32.1	-24.4					8.8	3.9	3.1	3.0	-0.7	3.1
Gross domestic expenditure	4,043.3	3,359.7	3,069.2	2,636.9	2,676.7	3,084.1	-14.1	1.5	15.2	-5.3	100.0	100.0	100.0	100.0	100.0	100.0
Net factor income received from abroad	-37.7	-71.9	58.6	32.7	51.6	31.1										
Gross national expenditure	4,005.6	3,287.8	3,127.8	2,669.6	2,728.3	3,115.2	-14.6	2.2	14.2	-4.9						
Terms of trade adjustment	107.7	-0.7	255.1	256.7	269.5	335.2										
Gross national income	4,113.3	3,287.1	3,382.9	2,926.3	2,992.8	3,450.4	-13.5	2.4	15.1	-3.4						

Source: *Ibid.*

Table 7. Gross National Expenditure in Current Prices

	Amount (Billion Rials)						Percent Change				Share in GNP (%)					
	1977	1978	1979	1980	1981	1982	1980	1981	1982	1977-82	1977	1978	1979	1980	1981	1982
Private final consumption expenditure	2,696.5	2,902.4	2,963.9	3,505.6	4,735.4	5,713.0	18.3	35.1	20.6	16.2	45.3	52.5	46.8	50.6	56.9	53.1
General government final consumption expenditure	1,133.7	1,255.0	1,223.0	1,377.1	1,676.6	1,844.2	12.6	21.7	10.0	10.2	19.1	22.7	19.3	19.9	20.1	17.2
Gross fixed capital formation	1,790.4	1,696.0	1,190.8	1,392.4	1,575.3	1,887.0	16.9	13.1	19.8	1.1	30.1	30.8	13.8	20.1	18.9	17.5
machinery & equipment	516.1	430.9	280.8	258.3	428.4	530.8	-8.0	65.4	23.9	0.6	8.7	7.8	4.4	3.7	5.1	4.9
private sector	(227.3)	(96.0)	(69.9)	(66.8)	(172.3)	(130.6)	(-4.4)	(157.9)	(-24.2)	(-10.5)	(3.8)	(1.7)	(1.1)	(1.0)	(2.0)	(1.2)
public sector	(288.8)	(334.9)	(210.9)	(191.5)	(256.1)	(400.2)	(-9.2)	(33.7)	(56.3)	(6.7)	(4.9)	(6.1)	(3.3)	(2.7)	(3.1)	(3.1)
construction	1,274.3	1,265.1	910.0	1,134.1	1,146.9	1,356.2	24.6	1.1	18.2	1.2	21.4	22.9	14.0	16.4	13.8	12.6
private sector	(469.0)	(448.5)	(507.7)	(647.0)	(547.5)	(671.0)	(26.9)	(-7.7)	(12.4)	(7.4)	(7.9)	(9.1)	(8.1)	(9.4)	(7.2)	(6.2)
public sector	(805.3)	(815.6)	(400.1)	(486.8)	(547.4)	(684.7)	(21.7)	(12.9)	(24.6)	(-3.2)	(13.5)	(14.8)	(6.3)	(7.0)	(6.6)	(6.4)
Increase in stocks	-168.8	-479.1	99.4	743.1	1,297.9	1,270.7					-2.8	-6.7	1.6	10.7	1.6	11.2
Net exports of goods & services	259.4	85.8	839.7	208.8	-423.8	613.1					4.3	1.5	13.2	-3.0	6.0	1.6
Statistical discrepancies	236.3	69.5	18.7	116.6	-538.5	-571.7					4.0	1.3	0.3	1.7	-6.5	-0.6
Gross domestic expenditure	5,947.5	5,524.6	6,335.3	6,926.0	8,322.9	10,756.3	9.3	20.2	29.2	12.6	100.0	100.0	100.0	100.0	100.0	100.0
Net factor income received from abroad	-98.0	-185.8	55.5	6.4	32.9	-0.2										
GNE = GNI[1]	5,849.5	5,343.8	6,390.8	6,932.4	8,355.8	10,756.1	8.5	20.5	28.7	13.0						

Source: *Ibid.*

[1] Gross national expenditure = Gross national income.

Table 8. Estimated Major Farming Crops

(Unit: Thousand tons)

	1977	1978	1979	1980	1981	1982	Percent change (%)					
							1978	1979	1980	1981	1982	1977-82
Wheat	5,500	5,526	5,946	5,744	6,610	6,660	0.5	7.6	-3.4	15.1	0.8	3.9
Barley	1,230	1,276	1,262	1,265	1,700	1,903	3.7	-1.1	0.2	34.4	11.9	9.1
Rice (Paddy)	1,400	1,531	1,271	1,181	1,624	1,605	9.4	-17.0	-7.1	31.5	-1.2	2.8
Cotton (raw)	535	427	322	219	275	358	-20.2	-24.6	-32.0	25.6	30.2	-7.7
Sugar beet	4,150	3,652	3,814	3,917	3,231	4,321	-12.0	4.4	2.7	-17.5	33.7	0.8
Sugar cane[1]	1,000	898	1,399	1,307	1,677	1,810	-10.2	55.8	-6.6	28.3	7.9	12.6
Tea (green)	116	120	136	143	147	157	3.4	13.3	5.1	2.8	6.8	6.2
Oil seeds[2]	105	126	99	69	81	123	20.0	-21.4	-30.3	17.4	51.9	3.2
Tobacco	15	14	20	24	27	25	-6.7	42.9	20.0	12.5	-7.4	10.8
Pulses	187	203	227	225	290	296	8.6	11.8	-0.9	28.9	2.1	9.6
Potatoes	697	932	997	1,270	1,540	1,214	33.7	7.0	27.4	21.3	17.8	21.1
Onions	392	506	515	631	675	965	29.1	1.8	22.5	7.0	43.0	19.7
Pistachios	27	69	9	23	122	95	155.6	-87.0	155.6	430.4	-22.1	28.6

Source: Ministry of Agriculture and Rural Affairs.

1 Statistics of caroon's sugar cane for 1980 and 1981 are received from the caroon Agri-business Complex.

2 Oil seeds consist of sunflower seeds and soybeans only.

Table 9. Imports of Major Agricultural Products

(Unit: thousand tons)

Year	Wheat	Barley	Rice	Corn	Oil seeds	Tea
1971	993	192	60	62	2	7
1972	771	23	92	70	22	9
1973	785	108	12	131	1	9
1974	1,433	178	191	223	2	13
1975	1,339	209	286	78	6	12
1976	406	220	260	341	4	17
1977	1,159	334	590	458	5	18
1978	730	337	301	380	3	13
1979	400	123	371	789	5	22
1980	862	388	402	690	9	7
1981	1,599	472	587	869	23	17
1982	2,029	527	432	708	9	13
1983	3,214	531		993		

Sources: 1. *Ibid.*
    2. Foreign Trade Statistics of Iran, different years.

price of various refined oil products at home, the domestic consumption of such products was encouraged. During the Revolution, this policy came under severe criticism. After the Revolution, the authorities reduced considerably the level of output and export of crude oil. With the outbreak of the Imposed War the production and export of crude oil was dramatically reduced — much more than the authorities desired or thought reasonable. Soon, however, output was increased to its pre-war level, and it has remained there up till now.

Over the years, the domestic refineries have produced refined oil products for home consumption and export. Table 11 describes the quantity of crude oil delivered to domestic refineries over the last few years, and Table 12 gives domestic consumption of refined petroleum products. Before the outbreak of the war, Iran was more than self-sufficient in the field of refined petroleum products. In fact, quite a substantial amount of the output of the Abadan Refinery was exported. With the outbreak of the war, and the destruction of the Abadan and Bakhtaran (previously known as Kermanshah) refineries, the capacity of domestic refineries was dramatically reduced. As a result, the consumption of oil products had to be rationed, and small quantities of such products had to be imported for some time. Over the last four years, however, the output of domestic refineries has steadily increased. As a result, rationing has been discontinued in most cases.

Manufacturing

Manufacturing has been the (sub)sector most affected by the recent political and

Table 10. Production, Exports and Domestic Consumption of Crude Oil

(Unit: thousand barrels per day)

| | 1972 | 1973 | 1974 | 1975 | 1976 | 1977 | 1978 | 1979 | 1980 | 1981 | 1982 | 1983 | Percent Change | | | | | |
													1978	1979	1980	1981	1982	1983
Production	5,369	5,926	5,888	5,249	6,019	5,586	4,252	3,433	1,476	1,441	2,679	2,696	-23.7	-19.3	-57.0	-2.4	85.9	0.6
Exports	4,424	5,306	5,230	4,607	5,280	4,816	3,455	2,632	770	791	2,051	2,078	-28.3	-23.8	-70.8	2.7	159.3	1.3
Domestic Consumption	645	620	658	642	739	770	797	801	706	650	628	618	3.5	0.5	-11.9	-7.9	-3.4	-1.6

Source: *Ibid.*

Table 11. Crude Oil Delivered to Domestic Refineries

(Unit: thousand barrels per day)

| | 1977 | 1978 | 1979 | 1980 | 1981 | 1982 | Percent Change | | Share % | |
							1981	1982	1981	1982
Abadan Refinery	488.5	451.5	509.0	278.0	0	0	-100.0	0	0	0
Tehran Refinery	207.1	179.3	181.7	188.8	188.7	204.8	—	8.5	36.2	36.4
Tabriz Refinery	0	62.0	58.1	60.4	73.8	71.5	22.2	-3.1	14.2	12.7
Shiraz Refinery	41.9	25.7	45.4	40.7	36.2	43.8	-11.1	21.0	6.9	7.8
Bakhtaran Refinery	17.3	13.4	12.0	4.4	0	0	-100.0	0	0	0
Esfahan Refinery	0	0	0	134.8	210.1	227.6	55.9	8.3	40.3	40.5
Lavan Topping Plant	11.8	0	0	9.1	12.5	14.7	37.4	17.6	2.4	2.6
Total	766.6	731.9	806.2	716.2	521.3	562.4	-27.2	7.9	100.0	100.0

Source: Iranian Oil Ministry.

social developments. Value added of this sector which for 1356 (1977) had totalled 378.2 thousand million Rials at constant prices, a year later decreased by more than 60 thousand million Rials to reach 317 thousand million Rials. It stayed almost at that level for another year. Gradually over the next three years it recovered and in 1361 (1982), the value added of manufacturing sector surpassed the 1356 (1977) figure for the first time since 1356 (1977).

The same conclusion holds for the index of production of large manufacturing establishments with more than fifty employees. Table 13 shows that the index of the output of such firms which in 1977 stood at 150.6, decreased significantly the next year, and only in 1982 surpassed the 1977 figure by reaching 157.6.

Housing and Construction

Value added in this sector declined sharply over the 1356-58 (1977-79) period, and for the next three years it has not increased. In 1362 (1983) a big rise in the value added of the construction sector may be expected. A similar picture can be observed with the private sector's investment in housing for the same period. Tables 14 and 15 indicate the number and the total floor-space estimate of the newly-started and completed structures by private sector in all urban areas over the years 1356-61 (1977-82).

Total floor-space area of the newly-started structures increased over the years 1357-59 (1978-80), but then decreased. In 1361 (1982) it has reached its bottom. Total floor-space of newly-started structures in 1362 (1983) has reached 32,799 thousand square meters which shows a 91 percent increase over the previous year. It also increased over the period 1357-59 (1978-80) and then started to decline. But it continued to decline in 1362 (1983), reaching the very low figure of 15,954 thousand square meters.

Consumption

Private consumption at constant prices decreased from 1977 to 1980, and increased for the next two years. Government final consumption expenditure has followed a similar pattern until 1980, but for the next two years it remained unchanged from the level of 1980 due to more than 3 percent growth rate of population, per capita private and public consumption declined.

Gross Investment

Gross fixed capital formation, as Table 7 shows, declined from 1977 to 1979, then remained unchanged for the next three years and showed a big increase — almost 10 percent — only in 1980.

Population Trends

According to census figures, average rate of growth of population over the decade 1966-76 was 2.68 percent. Since 1976 no new census has been carried out. The next census is to be conducted in 1986. On the basis of available indirect sources of information, the growth rate accelerated after the Revolution, and the population increased by more than eight million from 1977 to 83 period, and it is 42 millions

Table 12. Domestic Consumption of Oil Products

(Unit: thousand barrels per day)

	1977	1978	1979	1980	1981	1982	Percent Change				Share (%)					
							1980	1981	1982	77-82	1977	1978	1979	1980	1981	1982
Gasoline	79.7	87.7	98.0	82.6	76.3	78.3	−15.7	−7.6	2.6	−0.3	15.7	17.0	18.1	15.9	14.3	13.6
Kerosene	102.2	103.8	126.0	98.1	88.3	106.4	−22.1	−10.0	20.5	0.8	20.1	20.1	23.2	18.9	16.4	18.3
Gas oil	155.9	165.6	161.6	159.5	173.0	196.3	−1.3	8.5	13.5	4.7	30.6	32.1	29.8	30.8	32.2	34.3
Fuel oil	109.3	106.5	111.9	132.3	133.6	147.4	18.2	16.1	−4.0	6.2	21.5	20.3	20.6	25.5	28.8	25.6
Liquid petroleum gas	13.2	9.8	11.5	10.9	11.0	12.0	−5.2	0.9	9.1	−1.9	2.6	2.0	2.1	2.1	2.0	2.2
Other products[1]	48.5	44.0	33.9	34.7	34.6	34.6[2]	2.3	−0.3	0	−6.5	9.5	8.5	6.2	6.8	6.5	6.0
Total consumption	508.8	517.4	542.9	518.1	536.8	575.0	−4.6	3.1	7.1	2.5	100.0	100.0	100.0	100.0	100.0	100.0

Source: Iranian Oil Ministry, Distribution Department.

1 includes aviation fuel, tar, motor oil, etc.

2 data for other products for 1982 is not available, therefore data for 1981 has been considered for 1982.

Table 13. Production Index of Large Manufacturing Establishments

(1974 = 100)

	Relative weight	1977	1978	1979	1980	1981	1982	Percent Change				
								1978	1979	1980	1981	1982
Food, beverages and tobacco	21.55	123.4	111.9	117.2	105.4	105.7	111.8	−9.2	4.7	−9.9	0.3	5.8
Textiles, clothing and leather	15.84	149.8	143.7	162.8	172.5	211.1	226.5	−4.7	13.3	6.0	22.4	7.3
Wood and wooden products	0.54	191.5	201.0	219.9	210.2	249.1	335.0	−4.4	9.4	−4.4	18.5	34.5
Paper, cardboard and their products	1.67	148.9	134.7	135.2	96.0	110.9	149.3	−9.5	0.4	−29.0	15.5	34.6
Chemicals	15.32	148.1	119.2	118.8	98.3	104.4	122.1	−20.7	−0.3	−17.3	6.2	17.0
Non-metal mining products (except oil and coal)	9.10	162.8	151.3	177.7	181.7	203.7	233.6	−7.3	17.4	2.3	12.1	14.7
Basic metal	10.51	143.1	113.7	104.8	83.4	73.8	119.6	−20.5	−7.8	−20.4	−11.5	62.1
Metal machinery & equipments	24.81	175.6	138.8	118.8	113.4	143.5	163.6	−21.2	−14.4	−4.5	26.5	14.0
Other manufacturing industries	0.66	98.6	70.6	58.7	29.4	30.1	38.4	−28.3	−16.9	−49.9	2.4	27.6
General index	100.0	150.6	129.1	129.7	121.5	137.5	157.6	−14.7	0.5	−6.3	13.2	14.6

Source: The Central Bank of the Islamic Republic of Iran.

Table 14. Newly-started Structures in all Urban Areas by the Private Sector

| | 1977 | 1978 | 1979 | 1980 | 1981 | 1982 | 1983 | Percent change | | | | | |
								1978	1979	1980	1981	1982	1983
Number of structures	124,119	115,760	162,563	175,073	137,524	104,725	205,833	−6.7	40.4	7.7	−21.4	−23.8	96.5
Total floor-space estimate (thousand square meters)	26,451	22,268	28,182	29,967	22,584	17,169	32,799	−15.8	26.6	6.3	−24.6	−24.0	91.0

Source: *Ibid.*

Table 15. Newly Completed Structures in all Urban Areas by the Private Sector

| | 1977 | 1978 | 1979 | 1980 | 1981 | 1982 | 1983 | Percent Change | | | | | |
								1978	1979	1980	1981	1982	1983
Number of structures	94,231	112,589	141,631	163,242	122,325	101,646	93,865	19.5	25.8	15.3	−25.1	−16.9	−7.7
Total floor-space (thousand square meters)	18,852	20,984	24,686	29,659	22,414	18,808	15,954	11.3	17.8	20.1	−24.4	−16.1	−15.2

Source: *Ibid.*

in 1983. Over the last seven years the population has been increasing at 3.1 percent per year, and it will grow at this high rate according to the best projection at present for ten to twenty years to come.

Foreign Trade

Tables 16 to 23 describe some aspects of the country's foreign trade over the last twelve years 1971-82. The changes in direction of trade was already discussed in section 2. Table 16 shows foreign exchange receipts and payments. Foreign exchange earnings from the export of oil in 1971 amounted to a mere 2,114 million dollars, but in 1982 reached 20,050 million dollars. Table 17 tells a similar story on the balance of payments. Non-oil exports fluctuated narrowly around 523 — 635 million dollars over the period 1973-78. In 1979, it climbed to the historically unprecedented figure of 812 million dollars, but then it declined at a very fast rate. In 1982, it reached the figure as low as 284 million dollars. In view of the high rate of inflation in the world in 1973-82, the decline in non-oil exports in real terms was very serious.

Table 19 compares the value and the volume of non-oil exports of the country with those of the total imports for 1973-81, and demonstrates that non-oil exports made up a decreasing percentage of the total imports both in value and volume terms. Table 20 gives the geographic destination of Iranian exports. Table 21 reports on the value of imports for 1971-82. In 1971, the total value of imports of commodities was only a little above 2 billion dollars, but in 1977 it jumped up to the staggering figure of 14.6 billion dollars, more than seven times as much as 1971 figure. After 1977, however, the value of imports fluctuated. It decreased for 1978 and 79; in the following two years it increased. In 1982 it recovered to 11,845 million dollars but it was well below the height reached in 1977.

Table 22 gives the geographical distribution of the country's imports, and Table 23 lists the main importing partner countries. From these two tables, it is seen that imports from socialist countries, third world and Islamic countries increased, whereas imports from some countries like U.S.A., Iraq, Israel and South Africa ceased altogether. Japan and West Germany continued to be main importing partners. In recent years, imports from Turkey became very substantial, which was more than 774 million dollars in 1982. The average of annual imports from Turkey for 1978-79 was merely 23 million dollars.

Government Budget

Table 24 summarizes the annual budgets of the government for 1977-83. On the revenue side more than 60 percent comes from the production and export of crude oil. But that is not all. Other sources of Government revenue like import taxes and duties indirectly benefit from the oil sector, because without the oil export the country could not import such substantial amounts of goods and hence the import taxes and duties could not be so high.

The contribution of taxes to the total government revenue, however, is not very large. As Table 25 shows, tax proceeds accounted for about a quarter of total government revenue. Table 26 is more revealing to show that for 1970-77 tax proceeds have never been more than 9.4 percent of GDP. The comparable figures for other countries for 1970-80 is much higher, sometimes as high as 40 percent.

Table 16. Foreign Exchange Receipts and Payments

(Unit: US$ million)

	1971	1972	1973	1974	1975	1976	1977	1978	1979	1980	1981	1982	Percent change 82/81%
Current Account (Net)	-281.3	-165	345	8,483	2,914	3,590.9	1,094.1	1,499.0	6,109.7	-4,599.4	-2,736.9	6,591.8	
Current Receipt	2,733.5	3,337	6,732	20,972	21,922	24,618.0	26,690.1	22,737.4	22,669.4	14,814.0	14,320.3	21,406.8	49.9
Goods	2,478.4	2,863	5,493	19,217	19,621	21,142.7	21,428.5	18,532.8	19,629.1	12,478.6	12,865.7	20,334.9	59.0
exports of oil	(2,114.1)	(2,399)	(4,858)	(18,523)	(18,971)	(20,488.0)	(20,713.5)	(17,367.2)	(19,315.7)	(11,607.2)	(12,455.5)	(20,050.8)	61.0
other	(364.3)	(464)	(635)	(694)	(650)	(654.7)	(715.0)	(665.6)	(513.4)	(871.4)	(235.1)	(110.9)	-31.0
Services	255.1	474	739	1,705	2,451	3,475.6	4,161.6	4,204.8	2,829.3	1,735.4	1,450.6	1,071.9	-22.7
Current payments	-3,014.8	-3,502	-5,887	-12,439	-19,058	-21,087.1	-24,496.0	-21,238.6	-16,948.7	-18,813.4	-17,057.2	-17,904.0	-12.6
Goods	-2,567.6	-2,993	-4,969	-10,644	-16,046	-15,390.0	-16,593.3	-13,551.4	-11,545.1	-15,743.4	-15,344.8	-16,408.6	-12.6
Services	-444.4	-509	-918	-1,795	-3,012	-5,697.1	-7,942.9	-7,687.2	-5,003.6	-3,070.0	-1,713.0	-1,495.4	-12.7
Capital Account (Net)	667.8	592	925	-3,220	-3,607	-1,155.4	1,505.2	-1,683.5	-110.2	-306.6	283.9	-6,134.0	
Capital Receipts	1,013.8	1,064	1,505	702	961	1,430.0	3,617.6	2,273.5	1,224.9	647.8	1,040.7	304.0	-71.7
government utilization of foreign loans and credits	(958.2)	(978)	(1,296)	(257)	(300)	(561.1)	(1,744.6)	(619.0)	(3.0)	(4.0)	(440.9)	(129.7)	-70.6
other	(55.6)	(86)	(209)	(445)	(661)	(918.9)	(1,873.0)	(1,654.5)	(1,221.5)	(643.3)	(643.8)	(179.3)	-72.4
Capital payments	-346.0	-472	-580	-3,922	-4,568	-2,635.4	-2,112.4	-3,957.0	-1,334.7	-954.4	-802.2	-5,493.0	
repayment of principal of foreign loans and credits	(-326.5)	(-455)	(-541)	(-1,313)	(-729)	(-710.6)	(-680.2)	(-604.1)	(-937.6)	(-932.4)	(-634.8)	(-5,397.2)	
other	(-19.5)	(-17)	(-39)	(-2,609)	(-3,839)	(-1,924.8)	(-1,432.2)	(-3,352.9)	(-397.1)	(-22.0)	(-167.4)	(-55.5)	
Discrepencies, currency rate adjustments & registered transactions	-24.4	4	117	-187	-391	-87.1	-584.8	-394.5	-348.5	855.0	87.3	-63.2	
Total Balance	478.8	493	1,151	5,076	-1,084	2,288.4	2,014.9	-579.0	5,651.0	-4,051.0	-2,361.1	1,304.6	-42.8

Source: *Ibid.*

Table 17. The Balance of Payments

(Unit: US$ million)

	1973		1974		1975		1976		1977		1978		1979		1980		1981		1982	
	Credit	Debit	Credit	Debit	Credit	Debit	Credit	Debit	Credit	Debit	Credit	Debit	Credit	Debit	Credit	Debit	Credit	Debit	Credit	Debit
Current Account (Net)	3,555	—	11,793	—	4,360	—	7,233	—	3,037	—	—	1,353	12,784	—	—	2,747	—	5,819	7,368	—
Goods and services	9,698	6,141	23,310	11,483	23,092	18,714	27,998	20,748	28,460	25,298	20,422	21,760	27,809	15,010	13,756	16,564	18,113	17,223	23,209	15,341
Goods	8,953	4,785	21,596	9,285	20,626	15,240	24,719	16,086	23,974	18,197	16,203	13,872	24,970	10,020	12,343	13,441	10,939	15,515	22,084	14,365
oil and gas	(8,318)	(000)	(21,014)	(000)	(20,034)	(000)	(24,179)	(000)	(23,451)	(000)	(15,660)	(000)	(24,158)	(000)	(11,498)	(000)	(10,619)	(000)	(21,778)	(000)
other	(635)	(4,785)	(582)	(9,285)	(592)	(15,240)	(540)	(16,086)	(523)	(18,197)	(543)	(13,872)	(812)	(10,020)	(845)	(13,441)	(340)	(15,915)	(284)	(13,000)
Services	745	1,356	1,714	2,198	2,466	3,474	3,279	4,662	4,486	7,101	4,219	7,888	2,839	4,990	1,411	3,068	1,454	1,713	1,127	1,474
travel	147	240	253	550	350	802	457	1,253	581	1,897	(365)	1,649	(32)	(2,934)	(29)	(1,700)	(18)	(631)	(10)	(400)
other	598	1,116	1,461	1,648	2,116	2,672	2,812	3,409	3,905	5,204	(3,854)	(6,239)	(2,807)	(2,056)	(1,442)	(1,368)	(1,436)	(1,082)	(1,117)	(1,896)
Grant in-aid	4	—	—	6	—	34	—	17	—	125	—	15	—	15	—	2	—	—	—	—
Capital Account (Net)	—	2,180	—	4,699	—	3,471	—	4,007	—	1,274	1,760	—	—	6,974	—	906	2,099	—	7,100	—
Real sector	1,505	3,500	702	5,459	961	4,750	1,709	6,056	3,881	4,666	6,797	5,356	2,624	7,505	6,818	6,922	7,059	4,933	4,441	11,971
private	209	30	445	210	661	898	617	978	1,574	1,265	547	2,440	172	292	5	20	32	167	408	83
public	1,296	3,470	257	5,249	300	3,852	1,092	5,076	2,307	3,401	6,250	2,916	2,452	7,213	6,813	6,902	7,027	4,766	4,033	11,888
Monetary sector	83	268	123	65	318	—	376	38	7	496	510	191	113	2,206	867	1,059	537	664	986	700
Special Drawing Rights	—	—	—	—	—	—	—	—	68	—	91	—	85	—	93	—	245	—	—	—
Time Adjustment	—	379	—	1,910	—	1,578	—	442	—	—	—	195	—	1,894	5,909	2,819	—	—	—	—
Total Balance	—	996	—	5,184	689	—	—	2,784	—	1,831	—	303	—	4,001	—	—	2,501	—	—	574

Source: *Ibid.*

(000) statistical data unavailable.

Table 18. Major Groups of Exports (Excluding Oil and Gas)

(Unit: US$ thousand)

	1977	1978	1979	1980	1981	1982*	Percent Change 1980	1981	1982	77-82	Share (%) 1977	1978	1979	1980	1981	1982
Raw and intermediate goods	273,203	297,277	216,764	122,360	111,054	99,996	-43.6	-9.2	-10.0	-18.2	43.7	54.8	26.7	19.0	32.7	35.2
Capital goods	48,821	27,582	23,170	1,675	831	567	-92.8	-50.4	-31.8	-59.0	7.8	5.1	2.9	0.2	0.2	0.2
Consumer goods	303,196	217,945	571,849	521,122	227,641	183,175	-8.9	-56.3	-19.5	-9.6	48.5	40.1	70.4	80.8	67.1	64.6
Total	625,220	542,804	811,783	645,157	339,526	283,738	-20.5	-47.4	-16.4	-14.6	100.0	100.0	100.0	100.0	100.0	100.0

Source: Foreign Trade Statistics of Iran.
* Figures are provisional.

Table 19. Value and Quantity of Imports and Non-oil Exports

	Imports (1) Quantity (thousand tons)	Value (million rials)	Percent Change Qua.	Val.	Export (2) Quantity (thousand tons)	Value (million rials)	Percent Change Qua.	Val.	(2)/(1) % Qua.	Val.
1971	4,830	157,658	57.1	22.9	2,149	26,270	23.4	24.0	44.5	16.7
1972	5,137	193,651	6.4	22.8	2,349	33,862	9.3	28.9	45.7	17.5
1973	6,720	253,190	30.8	30.7	1,885	42,841	-19.8	26.5	28.1	16.9
1974	9,354	448,075	39.2	77.0	1,531	39,248	-18.8	-8.4	16.4	8.8
1975	13,328	800,819	42.5	78.7	1,189	40,723	-22.3	3.8	8.9	5.1
1976	13,835	901,761	3.8	12.6	793	38,001	-33.3	-6.7	5.7	4.2
1977	17,139	1,034,211	23.9	14.7	1,138	44,052	43.5	15.9	6.6	4.3
1978	12,438	732,293	-27.4	-29.2	1,336	38,186	17.4	-13.3	10.7	5.2
1979	10,370	684,491	-16.6	-6.5	579	57,109	-56.7	49.6	5.6	8.3
1980	9,734	776,841	-6.1	13.5	129	45,950	-77.7	-19.5	1.3	5.9
1981	13,952	1,081,951	43.3	39.3	154	27,029	19.4	-41.2	1.1	2.5
1982	15,009	1,002,326	7.5	-7.4	162	23,838	5.2	-11.7	1.1	2.4

Source: *Ibid.*

Table 20. Geographic Distribution of Exports (Excluding Oil and Gas)

(Unit: US$ million)

	1971	1972	1973	1974	1975	1976	1977	1978	1979	1980	1981	1982*	Percent Change 1981	Percent Change 1982	Share % 1981	Share % 1982
European Economic Community (EEC)	89.8	106.5	24.5	175.2	154.2	163.5	155.2	141.0	417.1	404.8	178.7	116.6	−55.9	−34.5	52.6	41.1
Socialist Countries (Party to Bilateral Agreements)	112.2	182.6	162.6	147.5	190.5	150.6	177.7	111.5	45.8	95.9	49.5	69.7	−48.4	40.8	14.6	24.6
Economic & Social Commission for Asia & Pacific (ESCAP)	155.3	210.7	299.9	251.7	248.1	179.4	281.0	207.4	251.4	143.4	63.9	104.1	−55.4	62.9	18.8	36.7
Regional Co-operation for Development (RCD)	0.8	0.8	1.7	3.6	1.9	0.1	1.1	3.5	3.1	1.0	2.1	1.2	110.0	−42.9	0.6	0.4
Organization of the Petroleum Exporting Countries (OPEC)	19.6	22.3	38.6	69.7	56.8	68.4	73.4	70.1	56.5	36.3	39.0	43.9	4.9	10.6	11.5	15.5
Americas	31.7	43.5	57.3	49.9	47.7	36.4	73.0	34.8	87.7	6.4	14.6	17.0	128.1	16.4	0.5	6.0
Europe	206.9	272.6	401.6	341.0	348.7	331.5	355.4	292.0	574.6	575.5	240.1	204.5	−53.1	−24.3	79.6	42.1
Asia	87.4	114.2	155.5	168.7	170.1	150.5	163.4	204.6	143.8	58.7	53.1	6.4	−9.3	15.6	15.6	21.6
Africa	8.0	8.2	17.7	19.1	23.1	18.3	31.7	10.6	2.6	1.5	0.9	0.5	−40.0	44.4	0.3	0.2
Australia	0.6	1.3	2.6	2.8	2.6	3.2	1.7	0.8	3.1	3.1	0.8	0.8	−74.2	62.5	0.2	0.1
Value of Exports	334.6	439.8	634.7	581.5	592.2	539.9	625.2	542.6	811.8	645.2	339.5	263.7	−47.4	−16.4	100.0	100.0

Source: *Ibid.*
* Figures are provisional.

Table 21. Composition of Imports

(Unit: US$ million)

	1971	1972	1973	1974	1975	1976	1977	1978	1979	1980	1981	1982	Percent Change 1980	Percent Change 1981	Percent Change 1982	Percent Change 77-82	Share % 1977	Share % 1978	Share % 1979	Share % 1980	Share % 1981	Share % 1982
Primary Products & intermediate goods	1,336.3	1,596	2,274	4,266	6,212	6,713	7,910	5,350	5,301	6,207	8,225	6,861	17.1	32.5	−1.6	−2.8	54.1	51.6	54.7	57.3	60.9	57.9
industries & mines	1,110.3	1,166	1,912	3,324	4,337	4,773	5,679	3,919	3,872	4,580	6,189	5,321	18.3	35.1	−14.0	−1.3	38.8	37.3	3.9	42.3	45.5	44.9
construction	138.5	204	238	376	917	987	1,186	650	465	517	489	436	11.2	−5.4	−10.8	−18.1	8.1	6.3	4.8	4.8	3.1	3.7
services	57.8	49	76	444	718	805	788	617	667	770	1,047	679	15.4	36.0	−35.0	−2.9	5.4	9.7	6.9	7.1	7.5	5.7
agriculture & animal husbandries	29.1	29	48	122	240	148	257	164	297	240	500	425	14.5	108.3	−15.0	10.6	1.8	1.6	3.1	3.1	3.7	3.0
Capital Goods	482.9	672	906	1,331	3,489	3,803	7,019	2,908	1,835	1,438	2,149	2,308	−5.3	23.6	9.4	−10.5	27.5	28.0	18.9	16.0	15.9	19.5
industries & mines	316.6	912	560	770	1,760	2,244	2,588	1,858	1,035	882	1,127	1,183	−14.8	27.8	5.0	−14.5	17.7	17.9	10.7	8.1	8.4	10.0
services	132.7	168	273	465	1,439	1,325	1,227	942	690	708	787	922	2.6	11.2	17.2	−5.6	8.4	9.1	7.1	6.5	5.3	7.8
agriculture	33.6	62	73	96	290	234	204	108	110	148	235	203	34.5	58.8	−13.6	−0.1	1.4	1.0	1.1	1.4	1.7	1.7
Consumer Goods	241.7	312	557	1,017	1,995	2,250	2,677	244	2,559	2,899	3,141	2,676	13.3	3.3	−14.8	−0.2	18.4	20.4	26.4	26.7	23.2	22.6
Total	2,060.9	2,570	3,737	8,614	11,695	12,766	14,626	10,372	9,545	10,844	13,515	11,845	11.9	24.6	−12.4	−4.1	100.0	100.0	100.0	100.0	100.0	100.0

Source: *Ibid.*
* Figures are provisional.

Table 22. Distribution of Imports by Countries

(Unit: US$ million)

| | 1971 | 1972 | 1973 | 1974 | 1975 | 1976 | 1977 | 1978 | 1979 | 1980 | 1981 | 1982* | Percent change | | | Share % | |
													1980	1981	1982	1981	1982
West Germany	389.7	474	732	1,186	2,024	2,273	2,804	2,142	1,750	1,639	2,252	1,936	-0.5	37.0	-14.0	16.7	16.3
Japan	275.7	360	548	999	1,853	2,201	2,319	1,757	1,343	1,061	1,619	1,250	-21.0	52.3	-22.8	12.0	10.5
Turkey	5.3	15	16	39	75	46	41	23	23	111	292	774	382.6	-63.1	169.1	2.2	6.5
United Kingdom	228.0	297	351	530	1,033	904	1,031	843	666	791	852	709	18.9	77.7	-16.8	6.3	0.5
Italy	94.6	113	141	199	497	735	809	596	547	601	715	552	9.9	-19.0	-22.8	5.3	4.7
Romania	39.8	34	47	58	167	147	191	142	164	207	301	463	26.2	45.4	53.8	2.3	5.9
South Korea	5.0	10	15	37	88	168	139	77	160	424	614	400	168.0	44.8	-31.8	4.5	6.8
France	94.1	120	180	242	516	716	661	508	556	526	456	382	-5.4	-13.3	-16.0	3.4	3.2
Spain	20.2	22	31	35	100	124	147	172	110	234	412	359	42.7	46.1	-32.0	3.0	2.0
Belgium	43.8	58	108	170	295	279	347	257	256	275	518	558	7.4	15.6	6.3	6.6	2.8
Netherlands	49.4	64	90	153	330	443	488	215	299	334	444	312	11.7	32.9	-29.0	3.3	2.6
Switzerland	29.9	55	73	124	271	473	444	275	273	450	530	296	64.8	17.8	44.3	3.9	2.5
Australia	55.2	44	52	68	192	172	228	151	184	139	193	295	-24.9	38.8	50.9	1.4	2.5
New Zealand	1.5	6	16	27	30	42	91	38	40	80	206	290	100.0	157.5	40.5	1.5	2.5
Soviet Union	141.4	72	214	270	168	117	273	195	182	819	194	270	35.0	-76.3	39.2	1.4	2.3
United States of America	293.0	428	487	1,322	2,287	1,972	2,344	1,508	1,311				-100.0				
Canada	11.9	10	24	56	84	103	107	57	48	47	83	173	-2.0	76.6	108.5	0.6	1.5
Brazil	0.6	13	53	24	59	66	69	68	72	43	84	222	-40.0	99.4	164.3	0.6	1.9
Other																	
Total	2,060.9	2,570	3,737	6,614	11,696	12,766	14,626	10,372	9,695	10,844	13,515	11,845	11.9	24.6	-12.4	100.0	100.0

Source: *Ibid.*
* Figures are provisional.

Table 23. Geographic Distribution of Imports

(Unit: US$ million)

	1971	1972	1973	1974	1975	1976	1977	1978	1979	1980	1981	1982*	Percent change 1981	Percent change 1982	Share % 1981	Share % 1982
European Economic Community (EEC)	920.0	1,144.1	1,627.1	2,511.9	4,667	5,437	6,254	4,649	3,729	4,308	5,197	4,357	20.1	−16.2	38.5	36.8
Socialist Countries (Party to Bilateral agreements)	237.6	171.2	354.5	542.8	564	594	765	499	589	1,643	902	1,293	−37.5	43.4	6.7	10.9
Economic & Social Commission for Asia & Pacific (ESCAP)	1,194.1	1,455.7	2,037.7	3,864.2	7,016	4,876	8,126	5,551	5,201	4,879	5,478	449	12.3	−19.4	40.5	37.3
Regional Co-operation for Development (RCD)	11.2	19.1	33.3	78.7	109	105	112	39	51	179	376	399	110.1	34.6	0.8	7.5
Organization of the Petroleum Exporting Countries (OPEC)	8.6	11.3	31.0	44.9	110	122	95	39	158	573	595	259	3.8	−57.1	4.8	2.0
Americas	313.8	462.6	598.2	1,461.4	2,517	2,207	2,608	1,674	1,484	356	644	858	80.9	23.3	4.8	4.0
Europe	1,282.1	1,495.2	2,218.8	3,363.7	5,674	6,715	8,137	5,998	5,591	7,404	8,100	7,141	9.4	−11.8	59.9	60.3
Asia	391.3	539.4	803.4	1,613.4	3,007	3,304	3,344	2,311	2,316	2,772	4,211	3,252	51.9	−22.5	31.2	29.5
Africa	17.3	23.1	48.0	80.1	198.1	126	213	199	76	89	162	40	82.0	−75.3	1.2	0.0
Australia	56.4	50.1	68.7	95.1	222	214	324	190	228	223	398	584	78.5	46.7	2.9	4.7
Value of Import	2,060.9	2,570.4	3,737.1	6,613.7	11,696	12,766	14,626	10,372	9,695	10,844	13,515	11,845	24.6	−12.4	100.0	100.0

Source: *Ibid.*

  * Figures are provisional.

On the expenditure side, the figures of Table 24 at current prices were deflated and converted to the amount of public goods and services in real terms. The deflators are the implicit deflators that are used in national expenditure calculations at constant prices shown in Table 7. They are given in Table 27. Total government expenditure, current expenditure and public fixed capital formation in real terms decreased from 1977 to 1980 and increased for 1981-82. However, total government expenditure as well as its constituent parts in 1982 were still below their respective levels in 1977. Table 28 clearly shows that government budgets in recent years always suffered from serious fiscal deficits. In 1980 when the war started, the budget deficit greatly increased and in the following year it reached the historically unprecedented figure of 1,055.5 billion Rials. As the war continues, the military expenditure amounts to more than a third of total government expenditure. This budget deficit caused the increase in money supply and inflation.

Money and Prices

There are at least three ways in which budget deficits can be financed: borrowing from abroad, borrowing from the private sector in the country, and borrowing from the banking system. Iranian budget deficits in recent years have been financed mainly by borrowing from the banking system, that is, primarily the Central Bank. Hence the net government borrowing from the banking system has increased tremendously over the last six years. Table 28 shows that the net government borrowing at the end of 1976 stood at 120 billion Rials but rose to 3,471.7 billion Rials by the end of 1982, an almost 29-fold increase. Increased government borrowing from the Central Bank resulted in rapid expansion of the money base. At the end of the year 1976, it was only 573.2 billion Rials but climbed to 3,415 billion Rials by the end of 1982, recording an annual rate of increase 34.6 percent for six years. Expansion of money base, in turn, rapidly increased the supply of money and liquidity. Table 29 shows that M_1 increased more than five times, quasi-money rose more than three times, and hence, liquidity of the private sector M_2 increased more than four times. Rapid expansion of money supply, coupled with the decline in real GDP, have resulted in the inflation of commodities prices. Table 30 reports three measures of inflation for twenty-one years from 1963 to 83. On the rate of inflation during this period, the following observations can be made.

First, in the 1960's price increase was very moderate, remaining within five percent per year. Inflation became acute only after the first oil price hike. Second, inflation is not exclusively a post-Revolutionary phenomenon; in 1977 CPI rose 25.1 percent. Third, the highest rate of inflation occurred in 1980, when the war broke out and the basic commodities, in particular refined oil products, had to be rationed. In that year, CPI recorded a 23.5 percent, and WPI an unprecedented 30.5 percent increased. Since then the rate of inflation has been declining. Lately, around 1984, the annual rate of inflation remains around 10 percent.

NEW ASPIRATIONS

Economic Independence

The future development of the Iranian economy will be conditioned, not only by

Table 24. Government Expenditures

	Amount (Billion Rials)							Percent Change (%)	
	1977	1978	1979	1980	1981	1982	1983	1982	1983
Current Expenditures[1]	1,248.1	1,387.1	1,494.9	1,683.7	2,032.4	2,252.6	2,564.5	10.8	13.9
Development Expenditures	926.8	657.1	523.3	568.1	674.7	914.8	1,163.6	35.6	27.2
Current Expenditures[2]	921.4	946.6	869.6	709.6	735.7	712.8	708.8	−0.1	−0.1
Development Expenditures	684.2	448.4	304.4	239.4	244.2	289.5	321.6	18.6	+11.1

Source: Plan and Budget Organization of Iran – The Ministry of Economic Affairs and Finance.

[1] At current prices.
[2] At constant price.

Table 25. Summary of General Government Revenues

	Amount (Billion Rials)							Share in Total (%)						
	1977	1978	1979	1980	1981	1982	1983	1977	1978	1979	1980	1981	1982	1983
General Government Revenues	2,126.7	1,699.3	1,791.8	1,348.7	1,702.9	2,391.7	2,787.3	100.0	100.0	100.0	100.0	100.0	100.0	100.0
Tax Revenues	443.6	465.9	368.3	340.4	554.1	613.9	789.6	20.9	27.4	20.6	25.2	32.5	25.7	28.3
Oil and Gas Revenues	1,590.3	1,013.2	1,219.7	888.8	937.9	1,563.5	1,779.4	74.8	59.6	68.0	65.9	55.1	65.4	63.8
Others	92.8	220.2	203.8	119.5	201.9	214.3	218.3	4.3	13.0	11.4	8.9	12.4	8.9	7.9

Source: *Ibid.*

Table 26. Share of Total Taxes in the G.D.P. of Some Countries

(Unit: %)

Country	1970	1971	1972	1973	1974	1975	1976	1977	1978	1979	1980
Iran	9.40	8.75	8.73	7.95	5.78	8.55	7.90	9.09	*	*	*
France	*	*	32.03	31.52	33.53	33.34	35.03	35.06	35.15	36.66	38.15
Sweden	*	29.32	30.56	28.89	28.59	29.45	34.64	36.59	39.74	34.35	*
United Kingdom	*	31.26	29.82	27.89	31.09	31.39	31.03	30.77	29.48	28.88	31.41
Italy	*	*	*	24.92	26.88	27.56	28.97	29.92	30.95	30.40	*
New Zealand	25.76	24.87	24.41	26.21	28.57	27.73	27.87	30.40	28.50	28.79	*
West Germany	23.45	23.60	24.23	25.19	27.85	25.18	25.88	26.25	26.17	25.93	*
United States of America	*	*	17.16	17.15	18.07	17.86	17.04	18.23	18.30	19.02	*
Switzerland	13.74	13.43	13.77	14.98	15.76	16.67	18.33	18.38	18.69	18.19	*
Indonesia	*	*	12.45	13.81	15.99	16.63	17.92	17.75	18.14	21.27	*
Brazil	15.55	16.04	16.71	17.63	17.56	17.81	18.84	19.57	18.75	18.28	*
Turkey	14.03	16.79	16.89	17.59	15.91	18.30	20.31	20.46	20.52	18.58	*
Canada	*	16.71	*	17.28	18.80	18.40	16.61	15.61	15.24	15.62	*
Mexico	*	*	10.49	10.37	11.16	12.88	12.95	13.70	14.52	25.83	*
Argentina	10.63	9.92	9.09	9.97	11.82	8.76	10.63	12.59	12.75	*	*
Pakistan	*	*	*	10.39	11.95	10.95	10.29	11.04	11.71	12.22	*
Japan	10.32	10.16	10.96	10.20	11.46	9.51	9.98	9.70	11.17	*	*
Marocco	16.42	15.01	16.41	17.27	16.50	20.95	18.34	22.32	21.58	22.65	*

Source: IMF.

* Statistical data not available.

Table 27. Expenditure Side of The Government Budget
(at constant 1974 prices)

(Unit: Rial billion)

	1977	1978	1979	1980	1981	1982
Current Payment	879.87	881.20	808.00	728.20	735.68	725.92
Fixed Capital Formation	561.19	369.61	422.35	243.05	259.24	328.73
Other Payments	223.69	103.93	22.28	1.05	0.00	11.55
Total Expenditures	1,664.75	1,354.74	1,252.63	972.30	994.92	1,066.20

Source: The Central Bank of the Islamic Republic of Iran.

Table 28. Budget Deficits, Net Gov't Borrowing & Money Base

(Unit: Rial billion)

	1976	1977	1978	1979	1980	1981	1982
Budget Deficit	169.8	458.0	608.9	528.3	972.5	1,055.5	898.0
Net Government Borrowing from The Banking System	120.1	337.9	654.0	987.3	1,865.9	2,696.6	3,471.7
Money Base	573.2	746.6	1,221.8	1,551.0	2,012.0	2,674.6	3,415.0

Source: *Ibid.*

the past events like the revolution and the war but also depends greatly on at least two more factors: first, the new objectives and priorities that the new Republic sets for itself; and second, the way in which the new economic system works under the new government. This section takes up the first point and the next section reviews some salient features of the new economic system.

The top priorities and the main economic objectives of the new Republic were seriously discussed and then answered, *albeit* in broad and general terms, by the new Constitution approved toward the end of 1979. In the process of preparing a draft for the first five year cultural-social-economic development plan, this question was investigated further. Toward the end of 1981 as special committee, known as Committee No. 10, was set up at the Plan and Budget Organization[1] to consider exactly this question. It prepared a report to submit to the Economic Council,[2] which suggested some alterations. On the basis of the guidance, the Plan and Budget

---

[1] Since February 1985, the Plan and Budget Organization has become a ministry. It is now called the Ministry of Plan and Budget.

[2] Economic Council is a permanent committee of the Cabinet with a number of ministers and the governor of the Central Bank as its members. Its meetings are chaired by the Prime Minister.

Table 29. Liquidity of The Private Sector

(Unit: Rial billion)

	Outstanding at the end of the year							Percent Change					
	1976	1977	1978	1979	1980	1981	1982	1978	1979	1980	1981	1982	77-82
1. Money (M_1)	677.2	790.5	1,236.5	1,665.8	2,203.3	2,707.5	3,483.9	56.4	34.7	32.3	22.9	28.7	34.5
Notes and coins in circulation	(249.2)	(325.5)	(802.7)	(927.9)	(1,231.2)	(1,407.2)	(1,642.6)	146.6	15.6	32.7	14.3	16.7	38.2
Sight deposits of the private sector	(362.0)	(465.0)	(433.8)	(737.9)	(972.1)	(1,300.3)	(1,841.3)	-6.7	70.1	31.7	33.8	41.6	31.7
2. Quasi-money [1]	982.3	1,306.5	1,342.1	1,884.2	2,134.5	2,404.2	2,866.8	2.7	40.4	13.3	12.6	19.2	17.0
Savings deposits of the private sector	(482.7)	(645.6)	(679.6)	(1,293.3)	(1,513.6)	(1,875.8)	(2,185.8)	5.3	90.3	17.0	23.9	16.5	27.6
Time deposits of private sector [2]	(499.6)	(660.9)	(662.5)	(590.4)	(620.9)	(528.4)	(681.0)	0.2	-10.8	5.1	-14.9	28.9	0.6
3. Liquidity of the private sector (1 + 2) (M_2)	(1,593.5)	2,077.0	2,578.6	3,550.0	4,337.8	5,111.7	6,350.7	23.0	37.7	22.2	17.8	24.2	24.8

Source: Ibid.

1. includes time & saving deposits of the private sector with saving and housing loans associations.
2. includes insurance premiums and personnel retirement funds of banks.

Table 30. Annual Rates of Increase of Various Prices Indexes

(Unit: %)

Year	Consumer Price Index (1974 = 100) Growth		Wholesale Price Index (1974 = 100) Growth		GNP Deflator (Growth %)	
1963	61.2	(1.0)	58.2	(0.5)	38.6	—
1964	63.9	(4.4)	61.9	(6.4)	39.2	(1.6)
1965	64.0	(0.2)	62.5	(1.0)	38.6	(−1.5)
1966	64.6	(0.9)	62.1	(−0.6)	38.3	(−0.8)
1967	65.1	(0.8)	62.2	(0.2)	38.2	(−0.8)
1968	66.1	(1.5)	62.7	(0.8)	38.0	(−0.5)
1969	68.4	(3.5)	65.1	(3.8)	39.3	(0.08)
1970	69.4	(1.5)	66.8	(2.6)	37.4	(−4.8)
1971	73.3	(5.6)	71.7	(7.3)	42.0	(12.3)
1972	77.9	(6.3)	75.3	(5.0)	45.6	(8.6)
1973	86.6	(11.2)	85.5	(13.5)	61.7	(35.3)
1974	100.0	(15.5)	100.0	(17.0)	100.0	(62.1)
1975	109.9	(9.9)	105.3	(5.3)	110.6	(10.6)
1976	128.1	(16.6)	119.5	(13.5)	124.8	(12.8)
1977	160.2	(25.1)	136.9	(14.6)	146.0	(17.0)
1978	176.2	(10.0)	149.9	(9.5)	162.5	(11.3)
1979	196.3	(11.4)	179.6	(19.8)	204.3	(25.7)
1980	242.5	(23.5)	234.3	(30.5)	259.7	(27.1)
1981	297.9	(22.8)	279.7	(19.4)	306.3	(17.9)
1982	355.2	(19.2)	318.1	(13.7)	345.3	(12.7)
1983	418.1	(17.7)	358.0	(12.5)	—	—

Source: *Ibid.*

Plan and Budget Organization prepared another report in September 1982.[3]

Iran has never been colonized, but the influence of foreign powers have been keenly felt. At least for a century and half prior to the Second World War, England and Russia interfered greatly in the internal politics and economic affairs of Iran. At one time, they had divided the country into two halves, each half being one country's zone of influence. After the Second World War it was felt that the United States reigned supreme and interfered in the internal affairs of Iran. Thus, Iranians have been very suspicious of foreign super powers. During the Revolution year 1978, the most popular slogan of the demonstrating crowds was "Independence, Freedom, Islamic Republic". In the same context the new popular slogan is "Neither East, nor West, Islamic Republic".

Some consequences of the pursuit of economic independence are to attain self-sufficiency in the production of 'vital' goods, particularly agricultural commodities like wheat, barley and rice, and restructuring of the present and old industrial structure.

---

[3] The report was entitled, "The quantitative objectives of the first cultural-social-economic development plan."

Self-Sufficiency

Nobody has advocated "autarky" after the Revolution. Policy of self-sufficiency should not be construed to mean a closed-door policy. But there is an important, though subtle, difference between reasonable interdependence and domination of one country by another through unfair trading relations. Many people advocate self-sufficiency in such basic commodities as steel, machine-tools, electric motors, because unless they are produced in Iran, it cannot be free from foreign domination to build up a truly independent and home-based industrial society.

There is another aspect of self-sufficiency in industrialization. Prior to the Revolution, many key industries like electric power-generating stations, e.g. Isfahan Steel Mill, were built and run by foreign experts. Existence of a large number of foreign experts, at the time of political domination by foreign powers, has instilled in the minds of many (if not all) Iranians the idea that the country will not achieve political independence, until most, if not all, of the industries in Iran are assembled and run by Iranians themselves.

Emphasis on Agriculture

Prior to the revolution, the low growth rate of agricultural sector was considered to be a necessity, but after the revolution, this sector has been accorded the highest priority. It is now considered to be the pivotal sector around which the country's economic development should revolve. That is how this sector was described in the draft proposal of the new five-year development plan prepared by the old Plan and Budget Organization in 1982. Thus, attainment of self-sufficiency in production of basic agricultural commodities like wheat, barley, rice, red and white meat within a period of ten years is a national goal.

This ideal is in sharp contrast with the prevailing situation. Presently, Iran has been importing large quantities of wheat, barley, rice and red and white meat for some time now. But as late as early 1950s, Iran was more than self-sufficient in the production of basic agricultural goods. Although the population almost doubled since then, it wants to regain its self-sufficiency.

Restructuring the Industry

For a quarter of a century prior to the revolution, import-substitution was the main strategy of industrial development in Iran. Firms were set up under the license and supervision of foreign companies to assemble mainly consumer goods using parts imported from those same companies or their subsidiaries. They heavily depended on foreign companies for license, know-how, expertise, experts and parts were engaged in the production of luxurious consumer goods. Nowadays, production of unnecessary or luxurious consumer goods and durables get very low priority in industrial planning. The main aim is to produce capital goods needed in various industrial sectors of the country.

Support for the "Mostaz:afin"

The next objective to discuss is called "support for the Mostaz:afin". "Mostaz:afin" is a plural of Mostaz:af. It means a person who has been wronged by the "system", a person who has not been able to obtain his 'rightful' share of national product. Roughly speaking, Mostaz:af is a synonym for the oppressed, for the under-privileged, for the poor, and for the needy people in the society. The phrase, "support for the Mostaz:afin" implies, depending on the particular context, one or more of the following: Redistribution of income and/or wealth, help for the needy, expropriation of the wealth and riches wrongfully amassed, help for the poor, help for the underprivileged and help for the oppressed people in the society.

Next to Economic Independence, another national objective has been the policy of 'support for the Mostaz:afin'. Thus, the government is committed to undertaking policies aimed at redistribution of income and wealth in the society and those which result in a more just and humane society.

NEW ECONOMIC SYSTEM

Prior to the Revolution, Iran was supposed to be developing along capitalistic lines, but in fact it was one of many underdeveloped countries. After the Revolution, the economic system of the country started a process of change; a new economic system based on Islamic principles and precepts was to be gradually created in the place of the old economic system. Nobody has a clear idea how long it would take for such an economic system to become fully installed and functional. The concrete evidence is only the experiences for the last six years.

The important characteristics of the new economic system may be observed on those bases.

1. *Private Ownership:* Although in the first few months following the Revolution the wealth and properties of some people who were believed to have earned them unlawfully were expropriated, it has become clear over the years that private ownership of property and wealth is allowed and legal. There are no limits to the amount of wealth and property that a person can hold as long as he or she earns it lawfully, and he or she pays all the necessary dues like government taxes and religious taxes like 'zakat' and 'khoms'.

2. *The Role of Government, Cooperative and Private Sector:* The new Constitution recognizes three economic sectors: public, private and cooperative sectors. Article 44 of the new Constitution states that the public sector will include all large and key (mother) manufacturing establishments and industries, foreign trade, large mining establishments, banking, insurance, supply of energy, dams and water distribution networks, public broadcasting, telecommunications, air, sea and rail transport.

In the early days of the new Republic, most large-, and in some cases even medium-scale manufacturing establishments were either nationalized, or, at least, run by managers chosen by the public authorities. So in the early days, it looked as if the public sector will become the all-important sector of the economy in the years to come. But of late the policy of whole-scale national-ization and collectivation have come under severe attack, and in recent months the government has sold off to private sector some manufacturing establish-ments not considered to be vital or strategic.

The Constitution is not clear as to what should exactly constitute the co-operative sector; specifically, what differentiates this sector from the private sector. Discussions about the nature of the cooperative sector which have been going on over the last six years seem to be convergoing to the conclusion that the cooperative sector is in fact a special form of the private sector. In the new economic system both private and public sectors will have an important role to play. Neither, it seems, will become the dominant sector.

3. *Banking and Credit Policy:* One of the most important differences between the new economic system and the old is in the area of banking and credit policy. In the old days, banking in Iran was in many ways similar to the banking system of capitalist countries. Payment and receipt of interest was the basic principle upon which the banking system operated. Some banks were owned by public authorities, and other banks privately owned. Moreover, private banks had in some instances very close ties with foreign banks; in fact, some banks in Iran were jointly owned by private Iranian and foreign nationals.

After the Revolution all the banks were nationalized, and hence, among other things, joint ownership of the banks came to an end. Secondly, as payment of interest (usury) is not allowed in Islam, a new law was passed through the Majlis (the parliament) in August 1983, entitled, "The Law For Usury-Free Banking". This law describes in detail the way the banks in Iran should operate in future. Of course, payment and receipt of interest is not allowed. However, the law describes other ways and means in which the banks can remunerate their depositors, and, also, the way they might charge their customers. Only time will show how the new banking system based on Islamic principles, will operate and work in practice.

As all the banks are now nationalized, the maximization of profit is not the motive behind credit and loan policy, the allocation of credit, however, has to be made on some principles. Credit will have to be rationed in one way or another. Over the years, some rough methods of credit rationing have been devised, but much more experiences need to be obtained.

4. *Pricing Policy:* So far the majority of goods and some services have dual prices: an official price and a free (black) market price. The supply of goods which are sold at official prices is far from enough. You might not get them when you need them most. Of course, prior to the Revolution, most goods had one single equilibrium price. The pre-revolution prices have formed the first basis of the official prices of goods and services after the Revolution. Then, the official prices of goods changed over time.

By and by, goods have become less available at official prices. As a result, black markets have developed for many goods and services. For the time being, it seems that most goods have dual prices, even for the foreseeable future. Price mechanism and competitive markets in Iran are unlikely to play a dominant role in the resolution of resource allocation problem.

5. *Production and Distribution Policy:* Since competitive markets lost their dominant role in the allocation of resources, other guidelines or methods for production and distribution of goods and services had to be devised. Various methods of rationing, formal and informal, were introduced with varying degrees of success. At the moment, black markets of various forms and appearances have come into existence to fill the gaps as the most powerful mechanism.

6. *Foreign Exchange:* After the Revolution, the official rate of foreign exchange remained, for all practical purposes, at its pre-revolution level. However, gradually more and more restrictions have been imposed, as a result of which the purchase of foreign currencies at official rates has become increasingly

difficult. The result has been a gradual appearance of a parallel free, black, market for foreign currencies. At present the free, black, market price of foreign currencies is more than six times the official rate.

With the increasingly wide divergence of free and official price of foreign currencies, various and elaborate methods of rationing of foreign currencies have been introduced, but mostly in vain. Due to the enormous gains involved, people go to incredible and bizarre length to obtain their share of foreign exchange 'ration' at official rate. This wide divergence affects in harmful ways the allocation of resources in the economy.

7. *Foreign Trade:* The new Constitution (in Article 44) had foreseen the nationalization of foreign trade. When the relevant bill was passed through the Majlis, the Council of Guardians (which have final say on the bills passed by the Majlis), raised some objections and returned it to Majlis for some amendments. So far Majlis has not passed a new law which incorporates the above amendments. As a matter of fact at present, both private and public sectors are engaged in the business of foreign trade. The signs are, therefore, that in future both private and public sectors will have an important share of foreign trade, and that foreign trade will not be in the hands of public sector as it was once envisaged.

The Uncertain Outlook

It is clear that over the last ten years, Iran has been going through a most critical period in her long history, a period which has by no means come to an end. The key word about its future is 'uncertainty'. Nobody knows when the war will end and how it will end. The political situations in the neighboring countries like Iraq, Afghanistan and Pakistan are precarious. Whatever happens in these countries can have a most profound effect on the future course of Iranian economic development. Much uncertainty also surrounds the exact nature and workings of the new economic system.

Appendix: Members of Advisory Group and Consultants

MEMBERS

Mr. Taroichi Yoshida (Chairman)
Advisor
The Industrial Bank of Japan
Tokyo

Prof. Shinichi Ichimura*   (Vice-Chairman and Research Coordinator)
Vice Chancellor
Osaka International University, Osaka
   and Professor Emeritus of Kyoto University

Mr. A.T. Bambawale
Former Vice-President of the Asian Development Bank

Dr. Mohamad Shahari Ahmad Jabar
Director
Asian and Pacific Development Center
Kuala Lumpur

Prof. Kiyoshi Kojima*
Department of Social Science
International Christian University
   and Professor Emeritus of Hitotsubashi University
Tokyo

Dr. Seiji Naya*
Director
Resource Systems Institute
East-West Center
Honolulu

Prof. Jun Nishikawa*
Faculty of Economics and Political Science
Waseda University
Tokyo

* Also worked as Consultant.

Prof. Sadako Ogata
Institute of International Relations
Sophia University
Tokyo

CONSULTANTS

Prof. George Cheng
Department of Economics
The University of the Philippines
Quezon City

Dr. Evelyn M. Go
Economist
Asian Development Bank
Manila

Dr. Godfrey Gunatilleke
Director
Marga Institute (Sri Lanka Center for Development Studies)
Colombo

Prof. Tien-tung Hsueh
Department of Economics
United College
The Chinese University of Hong Kong
Hong Kong

Mr. Kazushi Hashimoto
Deputy Director
Project Coordination Division, Coordination Department
Overseas Economic Cooperation Foundation
Tokyo

Dr. William E. James
Research Associate
Resource Systems Institute
East-West Center
Honolulu

Prof. Hojin Kang
Korea University
Seoul

Mr. Tetsusaburo Kimura
Counselor
Institute of Developing Economies
Tokyo

Prof. Wan-Soon Kim
School of Business Administration
Korea University
Seoul

Prof. Reiitsu Kojima
Department of International Relations
Daito-Bunka University
Ootsuki-shi, Japan

Dr. Jung-Soo Lee
Senior Economist
Asian Development Bank
Manila

Dr. Paul K.C. Liu
Director
The Institute of Economics
Academic Sinica
Taipei

Prof. Tsuneo Nakauchi
Department of Social Science
International Christian University
Tokyo

Prof. Harry T. Oshima
School of Economics
University of the Philippines
Quezon City

Dr. V.R. Panchamukhi
Director, Research & Information Center
    for Non-Aligned & Other Developing Countries
New Delhi

Dr. Ernesto Petnia
University of the Philippines
Quezon City

Dr. Wisarn Pupphavesa
School of Development Economies
National Institute of Development Administration
Bangkok

Dr. Atiqur Rahman
Senior Research Fellow
Bangladesh Institute of Development Studies
Dhaka

Dr. Mohan Man Sainju
Vice Chairman
National Planning Commission
Kathmandu

Dr. Durgeshman Singh
National Planning Commission
Kathmandu

Dr. Ali A. Zaker-Shahrak
Visiting Scholar
University of California — Los Angeles and
    Assistant Professor
Isfahan University of Technology
Isfahan

Dr. Yung-Wing Sung
Department of Economics
The Chinese University of Hong Kong
Hong Kong

Dr. Raza H. Syed
Managing Director
Investment Advisory Center of Pakistan
Karachi

Dr. Vijay Shankar Vyas
Senior Adviser
Agriculture and Rural Development Department
The World Bank
Washington

Prof. Toshio Watanabe
Faculty of Engineering,
Tokyo Institute of Technology
Tokyo

Prof. Ippei Yamazawa
Department of Economics
Hitotsubashi University
Tokyo